Probabilistic Machine Learning

Adaptive Computation and Machine Learning

Thomas Dietterich, Editor

Christopher Bishop, David Heckerman, Michael Jordan, and Michael Kearns, Associate Editors

Bioinformatics: The Machine Learning Approach, Pierre Baldi and Søren Brunak

Reinforcement Learning: An Introduction, Richard S. Sutton and Andrew G. Barto

Graphical Models for Machine Learning and Digital Communication, Brendan J. Frey

Learning in Graphical Models, Michael I. Jordan

Causation, Prediction, and Search, second edition, Peter Spirtes, Clark Glymour, and Richard Scheines

Principles of Data Mining, David Hand, Heikki Mannila, and Padhraic Smyth

Bioinformatics: The Machine Learning Approach, second edition, Pierre Baldi and Søren Brunak

Learning Kernel Classifiers: Theory and Algorithms, Ralf Herbrich

Learning with Kernels: Support Vector Machines, Regularization, Optimization, and Beyond, Bernhard Schölkopf and Alexander J. Smola

Introduction to Machine Learning, Ethem Alpaydin

Gaussian Processes for Machine Learning, Carl Edward Rasmussen and Christopher K.I. Williams

Semi-Supervised Learning, Olivier Chapelle, Bernhard Schölkopf, and Alexander Zien, Eds.

The Minimum Description Length Principle, Peter D. Grünwald

Introduction to Statistical Relational Learning, Lise Getoor and Ben Taskar, Eds.

Probabilistic Graphical Models: Principles and Techniques, Daphne Koller and Nir Friedman

Introduction to Machine Learning, second edition, Ethem Alpaydin

Boosting: Foundations and Algorithms, Robert E. Schapire and Yoav Freund

Machine Learning: A Probabilistic Perspective, Kevin P. Murphy

Foundations of Machine Learning, Mehryar Mohri, Afshin Rostami, and Ameet Talwalker

Probabilistic Machine Learning: An Introduction, Kevin P. Murphy

Probabilistic Machine Learning
An Introduction

Kevin P. Murphy

The MIT Press
Cambridge, Massachusetts
London, England

The MIT Press would like to thank the anonymous peer reviewers who provided comments on drafts of this book. The generous work of academic experts is essential for establishing the authority and quality of our publications. We acknowledge with gratitude the contributions of these otherwise uncredited readers.

Printed and bound in China.

Library of Congress Cataloging-in-Publication Data

    Names: Murphy, Kevin P., author.
    Title: Probabilistic machine learning : an introduction / Kevin P. Murphy.
    Description: Cambridge, Massachusetts : The MIT Press, [2022]
    Series: Adaptive computation and machine learning series
    Includes bibliographical references and index.
    Identifiers: LCCN 2021027430 | ISBN 9780262046824 (hardcover)
    Subjects: LCSH: Machine learning. | Probabilities.
    Classification: LCC Q325.5 .M872 2022 | DDC 006.3/1–dc23
    LC record available at https://lccn.loc.gov/2021027430

10 9 8 7 6 5 4 3 2

This book is dedicated to my mother, Brigid Murphy,
who introduced me to the joy of learning and teaching.

Brief Contents

Contents

IV   Nonparametric Models   541

16 Exemplar-based Methods   543

Preface

In 2012, I published a 1200-page book called *Machine Learning: A Probabilistic Perspective*, which provided a fairly comprehensive coverage of the field of machine learning (ML) at that time, under the unifying lens of probabilistic modeling. The book was well received, and won the De Groot prize in 2013.

The year 2012 is also generally considered the start of the "deep learning revolution". The term "deep learning" refers to a branch of ML that is based on neural networks (DNNs), which are nonlinear functions with many layers of processing (hence the term "deep"). Although this basic technology had been around for many years, it was in 2012 when [KSH12] used DNNs to win the ImageNet image classification challenge by such a large margin that it caught the attention of the wider community. Related advances on other hard problems, such as speech recognition, appeared around the same time (see e.g., [Cir+10; Cir+11; Hin+12]). These breakthroughs were enabled by advances in hardware technology (in particular, the repurposing of fast graphics processing units (GPUs) from video games to ML), data collection technology (in particular, the use of crowd sourcing tools, such as Amazon's Mechanical Turk platform, to collect large labeled datasets, such as ImageNet), as well as various new algorithmic ideas, some of which we cover in this book.

Since 2012, the field of deep learning has exploded, with new advances coming at an increasing pace. Interest in the field has also grown rapidly, fueled by the commercial success of the technology, and the breadth of applications to which it can be applied. Therefore, in 2018, I decided to write a second edition of my book, to attempt to summarize some of this progress.

By March 2020, my draft of the second edition had swollen to about 1600 pages, and I still had many topics left to cover. As a result, MIT Press told me I would need to split the book into two volumes. Then the COVID-19 pandemic struck. I decided to pivot away from book writing, and to help develop the risk score algorithm for Google's exposure notification app [MKS21] as well as to assist with various forecasting projects [Wah+22]. However, by the Fall of 2020, I decided to return to working on the book.

To make up for lost time, I asked several colleagues to help me finish by writing various sections (see acknowledgements below). The result of all this is two new books, "Probabilistic Machine Learning: An Introduction", which you are currently reading, and "Probabilistic Machine Learning: Advanced Topics", which is the sequel to this book [Mur23]. Together these two books attempt to present a fairly broad coverage of the field of ML c. 2021, using the same unifying lens of probabilistic modeling and Bayesian decision theory that I used in the 2012 book.

Nearly all of the content from the 2012 book has been retained, but it is now split fairly evenly between the two new books. In addition, each new book has lots of fresh material, covering topics from deep learning, as well as advances in other parts of the field, such as generative models, variational inference and reinforcement learning.

To make this introductory book more self-contained and useful for students, I have added some background material, on topics such as optimization and linear algebra, that was omitted from the 2012 book due to lack of space. Advanced material, that can be skipped during an introductory level course, is denoted by an asterisk * in the section or chapter title. Exercises can be found at the end of some chapters. Solutions to exercises marked with an asterisk * are available to qualified instructors by contacting MIT Press; solutions to all other exercises can be found online at `probml.github.io/book1`, along with additional teaching material (e.g., figures and slides).

Another major change is that all of the software now uses Python instead of Matlab. (In the future, we may create a Julia version of the code.) The new code leverages standard Python libraries, such as NumPy, Scikit-learn, JAX, PyTorch, TensorFlow, PyMC, etc.

If a figure caption says "Generated by `iris_plot.ipynb`", then you can find the corresponding Jupyter notebook at probml.github.io/notebooks#iris_plot.ipynb. Clicking on the figure link in the pdf version of the book will take you to this list of notebooks. Clicking on the notebook link will open it inside Google Colab, which will let you easily reproduce the figure for yourself, and modify the underlying source code to gain a deeper understanding of the methods. (Colab gives you access to a free GPU, which is useful for some of the more computationally heavy demos.)

Acknowledgements

I would like to thank the following people for helping me with the book:

- Zico Kolter (CMU), who helped write parts of Chapter 7 (Linear Algebra).
- Frederik Kunstner, Si Yi Meng, Aaron Mishkin, Sharan Vaswani, and Mark Schmidt who helped write parts of Chapter 8 (Optimization).
- Mathieu Blondel (Google), who helped write Section 13.3 (Backpropagation).
- Krzysztof Choromanski (Google), who wrote Section 15.6 (Efficient transformers *).
- Colin Raffel (UNC), who helped write Section 19.2 (Transfer learning) and Section 19.3 (Semi-supervised learning).
- Bryan Perozzi (Google), Sami Abu-El-Haija (USC) and Ines Chami, who helped write Chapter 23 (Graph Embeddings *).
- John Fearns and Peter Cerno for carefully proofreading the book.
- Many members of the github community for finding typos, etc (see `https://github.com/probml/pml-book/issues?q=is:issue` for a list of issues).
- The 4 anonymous reviewers solicited by MIT Press.
- Mahmoud Soliman for writing all the magic plumbing code that connects latex, colab, github, etc, and for teaching me about GCP and TPUs.
- The 2021 cohort of Google Summer of Code students who worked on code for the book: Aleyna Kara, Srikar Jilugu, Drishti Patel, Ming Liang Ang, Gerardo Durán-Martín. (See `https://probml.github.io/pml-book/gsoc/gsoc2021.html` for a summary of their contributions.)
- Zeel B Patel, Karm Patel, Nitish Sharma, Ankita Kumari Jain and Nipun Batra for help improving the figures and code after the book first came out.
- Many members of the github community for their code contributions (see `https://github.com/`

`probml/pyprobml#acknowledgements`).

- The authors of [Zha+20], [Gér17] and [Mar18] for letting me reuse or modify some of their open source code from their own excellent books.
- My manager at Google, Doug Eck, for letting me spend company time on this book.
- My wife Margaret for letting me spend family time on this book.

About the cover

The cover illustrates a neural network (Chapter 13) being used to classify a hand-written digit x into one of 10 class labels $y \in \{0, 1, \ldots, 9\}$. The histogram on the right is the output of the model, and corresponds to the conditional probability distribution $p(y|x)$.[1]

Kevin Patrick Murphy
Palo Alto, California
April 2023.

Changelog

- 2022-08-08. First printing.

- 2023-04-22. Second printing. Changes listed at `https://github.com/probml/pml-book/issues?page=2&q=is%3Aissue+created%3A2022-08-08..2023-04-22`.

---

1. There is an error in the illustration; it accidently has 11 bins.

1 Introduction

1.1 What is machine learning?

A popular definition of **machine learning** or **ML**, due to Tom Mitchell [Mit97], is as follows:

> A computer program is said to learn from experience E with respect to some class of tasks T, and performance measure P, if its performance at tasks in T, as measured by P, improves with experience E.

Thus there are many different kinds of machine learning, depending on the nature of the tasks T we wish the system to learn, the nature of the performance measure P we use to evaluate the system, and the nature of the training signal or experience E we give it.

In this book, we will cover the most common types of ML, but from a **probabilistic perspective**. Roughly speaking, this means that we treat all unknown quantities (e.g., predictions about the future value of some quantity of interest, such as tomorrow's temperature, or the parameters of some model) as **random variables**, that are endowed with **probability distributions** which describe a weighted set of possible values the variable may have. (See Chapter 2 for a quick refresher on the basics of probability, if necessary.)

There are two main reasons we adopt a probabilistic approach. First, it is the optimal approach to **decision making under uncertainty**, as we explain in Section 5.1. Second, probabilistic modeling is the language used by most other areas of science and engineering, and thus provides a unifying framework between these fields. As Shakir Mohamed, a researcher at DeepMind, put it:[1]

> Almost all of machine learning can be viewed in probabilistic terms, making probabilistic thinking fundamental. It is, of course, not the only view. But it is through this view that we can connect what we do in machine learning to every other computational science, whether that be in stochastic optimisation, control theory, operations research, econometrics, information theory, statistical physics or bio-statistics. For this reason alone, mastery of probabilistic thinking is essential.

1.2 Supervised learning

The most common form of ML is **supervised learning**. In this problem, the task T is to learn a mapping f from inputs $x \in \mathcal{X}$ to outputs $y \in \mathcal{Y}$. The inputs x are also called the **features**,

---

1. Source: Slide 2 of https://bit.ly/3pyHyPn

(a)   (b)   (c)

Figure 1.1: Three types of Iris flowers: Setosa, Versicolor and Virginica. Used with kind permission of Dennis Kramb and SIGNA.

index	sl	sw	pl	pw	label
0	5.1	3.5	1.4	0.2	Setosa
1	4.9	3.0	1.4	0.2	Setosa
	. . .				
50	7.0	3.2	4.7	1.4	Versicolor
	. . .				
149	5.9	3.0	5.1	1.8	Virginica

Table 1.1: A subset of the Iris design matrix. The features are: sepal length, sepal width, petal length, petal width. There are 50 examples of each class.

covariates, or **predictors**; this is often a fixed-dimensional vector of numbers, such as the height and weight of a person, or the pixels in an image. In this case, $\mathcal{X} = \mathbb{R}^D$, where D is the dimensionality of the vector (i.e., the number of input features). The output $\boldsymbol{y}$ is also known as the **label**, **target**, or **response**.[2] The experience E is given in the form of a set of N input-output pairs $\mathcal{D} = \{(\boldsymbol{x}_n, \boldsymbol{y}_n)\}_{n=1}^{N}$, known as the **training set**. (N is called the **sample size**.) The performance measure P depends on the type of output we are predicting, as we discuss below.

1.2.1   Classification

In **classification** problems, the output space is a set of C unordered and mutually exclusive labels known as **classes**, $\mathcal{Y} = \{1, 2, \ldots, C\}$. The problem of predicting the class label given an input is also called **pattern recognition**. (If there are just two classes, often denoted by $y \in \{0, 1\}$ or $y \in \{-1, +1\}$, it is called **binary classification**.)

1.2.1.1   Example: classifying Iris flowers

As an example, consider the problem of classifying Iris flowers into their 3 subspecies, Setosa, Versicolor and Virginica. Figure 1.1 shows one example of each of these classes.

---

2. Sometimes (e.g., in the statsmodels Python package) $\boldsymbol{x}$ are called the **exogenous variables** and $\boldsymbol{y}$ are called the **endogenous variables**.

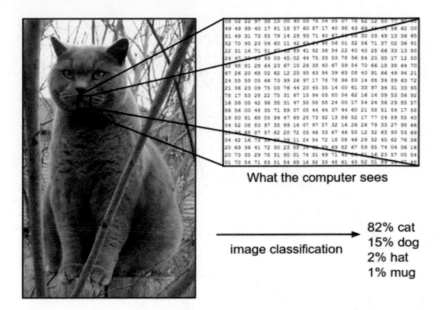

What the computer sees

image classification $\longrightarrow$ 82% cat
15% dog
2% hat
1% mug

Figure 1.2: Illustration of the image classification problem. From `https://cs231n.github.io/`. *Used with kind permission of Andrej Karpathy.*

In **image classification**, the input space $\mathcal{X}$ is the set of images, which is a very high-dimensional space: for a color image with $C = 3$ channels (e.g., RGB) and $D_1 \times D_2$ pixels, we have $\mathcal{X} = \mathbb{R}^D$, where $D = C \times D_1 \times D_2$. (In practice we represent each pixel intensity with an integer, typically from the range $\{0, 1, \ldots, 255\}$, but we assume real valued inputs for notational simplicity.) Learning a mapping $f : \mathcal{X} \to \mathcal{Y}$ from images to labels is quite challenging, as illustrated in Figure 1.2. However, it can be tackled using certain kinds of functions, such as a **convolutional neural network** or **CNN**, which we discuss in Section 14.1.

Fortunately for us, some botanists have already identified 4 simple, but highly informative, numeric features — sepal length, sepal width, petal length, petal width — which can be used to distinguish the three kinds of Iris flowers. In this section, we will use this much lower-dimensional input space, $\mathcal{X} = \mathbb{R}^4$, for simplicity. The **Iris dataset** is a collection of 150 labeled examples of Iris flowers, 50 of each type, described by these 4 features. It is widely used as an example, because it is small and simple to understand. (We will discuss larger and more complex datasets later in the book.)

When we have small datasets of features, it is common to store them in an $N \times D$ matrix, in which each row represents an example, and each column represents a feature. This is known as a **design matrix**; see Table 1.1 for an example.[3]

The Iris dataset is an example of **tabular data**. When the inputs are of variable size (e.g., sequences of words, or social networks), rather than fixed-length vectors, the data is usually stored

---

3. This particular design matrix has $N = 150$ rows and $D = 4$ columns, and hence has a **tall and skinny** shape, since $N \gg D$. By contrast, some datasets (e.g., genomics) have more features than examples, $D \gg N$; their design matrices are **short and fat**. The term "**big data**" usually means that N is large, whereas the term "**wide data**" means that D is large (relative to N).

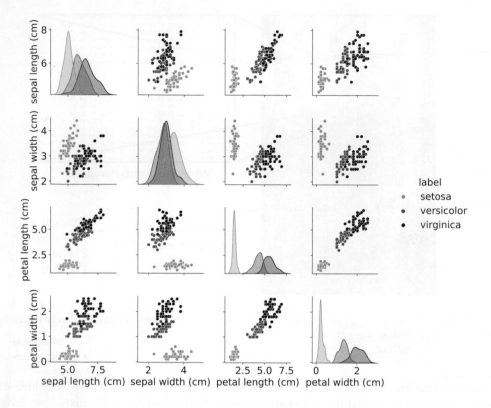

Figure 1.3: Visualization of the Iris data as a pairwise scatter plot. On the diagonal we plot the marginal distribution of each feature for each class. The off-diagonals contain scatterplots of all possible pairs of features. Generated by iris_plot.ipynb

in some other format rather than in a design matrix. However, such data is often converted to a fixed-sized feature representation (a process known as **featurization**), thus implicitly creating a design matrix for further processing. We give an example of this in Section 1.5.4.1, where we discuss the "bag of words" representation for sequence data.

1.2.1.2 Exploratory data analysis

Before tackling a problem with ML, it is usually a good idea to perform **exploratory data analysis**, to see if there are any obvious patterns (which might give hints on what method to choose), or any obvious problems with the data (e.g., label noise or outliers).

For tabular data with a small number of features, it is common to make a **pair plot**, in which panel (i, j) shows a scatter plot of variables i and j, and the diagonal entries (i, i) show the marginal density of variable i; all plots are optionally color coded by class label — see Figure 1.3 for an example.

For higher-dimensional data, it is common to first perform **dimensionality reduction**, and then

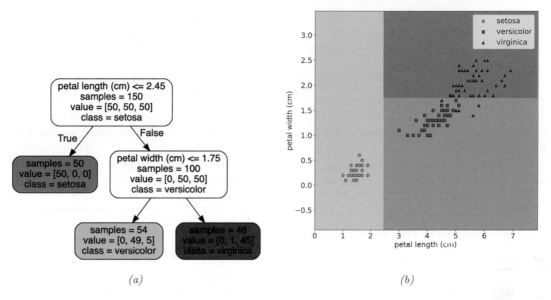

(a) *(b)*

Figure 1.4: Example of a decision tree of depth 2 applied to the Iris data, using just the petal length and petal width features. Leaf nodes are color coded according to the predicted class. The number of training samples that pass from the root to a node is shown inside each box; we show how many values of each class fall into this node. This vector of counts can be normalized to get a distribution over class labels for each node. We can then pick the majority class. Adapted from Figures 6.1 and 6.2 of [Gér19]. Generated by iris_dtree.ipynb.

to visualize the data in 2d or 3d. We discuss methods for dimensionality reduction in Chapter 20.

1.2.1.3 Learning a classifier

From Figure 1.3, we can see that the Setosa class is easy to distinguish from the other two classes. For example, suppose we create the following **decision rule**:

$$f(\boldsymbol{x}; \boldsymbol{\theta}) = \begin{cases} \text{Setosa if petal length} < 2.45 \\ \text{Versicolor or Virginica otherwise} \end{cases} \tag{1.1}$$

This is a very simple example of a classifier, in which we have partitioned the input space into two regions, defined by the one-dimensional (1d) **decision boundary** at $x_{\text{petal length}} = 2.45$. Points lying to the left of this boundary are classified as Setosa; points to the right are either Versicolor or Virginica.

We see that this rule perfectly classifies the Setosa examples, but not the Virginica and Versicolor ones. To improve performance, we can recursively partition the space, by splitting regions in which the classifier makes errors. For example, we can add another decision rule, to be applied to inputs that fail the first test, to check if the petal width is below 1.75cm (in which case we predict Versicolor) or above (in which case we predict Virginica). We can arrange these nested rules into a tree structure,

		Estimate		
		Setosa	Versicolor	Virginica
	Setosa	0	1	1
Truth	Versicolor	1	0	1
	Virginica	10	10	0

Table 1.2: Hypothetical asymmetric loss matrix for Iris classification.

called a **decision tree**, as shown in Figure 1.4a This induces the 2d **decision surface** shown in Figure 1.4b.

We can represent the tree by storing, for each internal node, the feature index that is used, as well as the corresponding threshold value. We denote all these **parameters** by $\boldsymbol{\theta}$. We discuss how to learn these parameters in Section 18.1.

1.2.1.4 Empirical risk minimization

The goal of supervised learning is to automatically come up with classification models such as the one shown in Figure 1.4a, so as to reliably predict the labels for any given input. A common way to measure performance on this task is in terms of the **misclassification rate** on the training set:

$$\mathcal{L}(\boldsymbol{\theta}) \triangleq \frac{1}{N} \sum_{n=1}^{N} \mathbb{I}\left(y_n \neq f(\boldsymbol{x}_n; \boldsymbol{\theta})\right) \tag{1.2}$$

where $\mathbb{I}(e)$ is the binary **indicator function**, which returns 1 iff (if and only if) the condition e is true, and returns 0 otherwise, i.e.,

$$\mathbb{I}(e) = \begin{cases} 1 & \text{if } e \text{ is true} \\ 0 & \text{if } e \text{ is false} \end{cases} \tag{1.3}$$

This assumes all errors are equal. However it may be the case that some errors are more costly than others. For example, suppose we are foraging in the wilderness and we find some Iris flowers. Furthermore, suppose that Setosa and Versicolor are tasty, but Virginica is poisonous. In this case, we might use the asymmetric **loss function** $\ell(y, \hat{y})$ shown in Table 1.2.

We can then define **empirical risk** to be the average loss of the predictor on the training set:

$$\mathcal{L}(\boldsymbol{\theta}) \triangleq \frac{1}{N} \sum_{n=1}^{N} \ell(y_n, f(\boldsymbol{x}_n; \boldsymbol{\theta})) \tag{1.4}$$

We see that the misclassification rate Equation (1.2) is equal to the empirical risk when we use **zero-one loss** for comparing the true label with the prediction:

$$\ell_{01}(y, \hat{y}) = \mathbb{I}(y \neq \hat{y}) \tag{1.5}$$

See Section 5.1 for more details.

One way to define the problem of **model fitting** or **training** is to find a setting of the parameters that minimizes the empirical risk on the training set:

$$\hat{\boldsymbol{\theta}} = \underset{\boldsymbol{\theta}}{\operatorname{argmin}}\, \mathcal{L}(\boldsymbol{\theta}) = \underset{\boldsymbol{\theta}}{\operatorname{argmin}}\, \frac{1}{N} \sum_{n=1}^{N} \ell(y_n, f(\boldsymbol{x}_n; \boldsymbol{\theta})) \tag{1.6}$$

This is called **empirical risk minimization**.

However, our true goal is to minimize the expected loss on *future data* that we have not yet seen. That is, we want to **generalize**, rather than just do well on the training set. We discuss this important point in Section 1.2.3.

1.2.1.5   Uncertainty

[We must avoid] false confidence bred from an ignorance of the probabilistic nature of the world, from a desire to see black and white where we should rightly see gray. — Immanuel Kant, as paraphrased by Maria Konnikova [Kon20].

In many cases, we will not be able to perfectly predict the exact output given the input, due to lack of knowledge of the input-output mapping (this is called **epistemic uncertainty** or **model uncertainty**), and/or due to intrinsic (irreducible) stochasticity in the mapping (this is called **aleatoric uncertainty** or **data uncertainty**).

Representing uncertainty in our prediction can be important for various applications. For example, let us return to our poisonous flower example, whose loss matrix is shown in Table 1.2. If we predict the flower is Virginica with high probability, then we should not eat the flower. Alternatively, we may be able to perform an **information gathering action**, such as performing a diagnostic test, to reduce our uncertainty. For more information about how to make optimal decisions in the presence of uncertainty, see Section 5.1.

We can capture our uncertainty using the following **conditional probability distribution**:

$$p(y = c|\boldsymbol{x}; \boldsymbol{\theta}) = f_c(\boldsymbol{x}; \boldsymbol{\theta}) \tag{1.7}$$

where $f : \mathcal{X} \to [0, 1]^C$ maps inputs to a probability distribution over the C possible output labels. Since $f_c(\boldsymbol{x}; \boldsymbol{\theta})$ returns the probability of class label c, we require $0 \le f_c \le 1$ for each c, and $\sum_{c=1}^{C} f_c = 1$. To avoid this restriction, it is common to instead require the model to return unnormalized log-probabilities. We can then convert these to probabilities using the **softmax function**, which is defined as follows

$$\operatorname{softmax}(\boldsymbol{a}) \triangleq \left[\frac{e^{a_1}}{\sum_{c'=1}^{C} e^{a_{c'}}}, \dots, \frac{e^{a_C}}{\sum_{c'=1}^{C} e^{a_{c'}}} \right] \tag{1.8}$$

This maps $\mathbb{R}^C$ to $[0, 1]^C$, and satisfies the constraints that $0 \le \operatorname{softmax}(\boldsymbol{a})_c \le 1$ and $\sum_{c=1}^{C} \operatorname{softmax}(\boldsymbol{a})_c = 1$. The inputs to the softmax, $\boldsymbol{a} = f(\boldsymbol{x}; \boldsymbol{\theta})$, are called **logits**. See Section 2.5.2 for details. We thus define the overall model as follows:

$$p(y = c|\boldsymbol{x}; \boldsymbol{\theta}) = \operatorname{softmax}_c(f(\boldsymbol{x}; \boldsymbol{\theta})) \tag{1.9}$$

A common special case of this arises when f is an **affine function** of the form

$$f(\boldsymbol{x};\boldsymbol{\theta}) = b + \boldsymbol{w}^\mathsf{T}\boldsymbol{x} = b + w_1 x_1 + w_2 x_2 + \cdots + w_D x_D \tag{1.10}$$

where $\boldsymbol{\theta} = (b, \boldsymbol{w})$ are the parameters of the model. This model is called **logistic regression**, and will be discussed in more detail in Chapter 10.

In statistics, the $\boldsymbol{w}$ parameters are usually called **regression coefficients** (and are typically denoted by $\boldsymbol{\beta}$) and b is called the **intercept**. In ML, the parameters $\boldsymbol{w}$ are called the **weights** and b is called the **bias**. This terminology arises from electrical engineering, where we view the function f as a circuit which takes in $\boldsymbol{x}$ and returns $f(\boldsymbol{x})$. Each input is fed to the circuit on "wires", which have weights $\boldsymbol{w}$. The circuit computes the weighted sum of its inputs, and adds a constant bias or offset term b. (This use of the term "bias" should not be confused with the statistical concept of bias discussed in Section 4.7.6.1.)

To reduce notational clutter, it is common to absorb the bias term b into the weights $\boldsymbol{w}$ by defining $\tilde{\boldsymbol{w}} = [b, w_1, \ldots, w_D]$ and defining $\tilde{\boldsymbol{x}} = [1, x_1, \ldots, x_D]$, so that

$$\tilde{\boldsymbol{w}}^\mathsf{T}\tilde{\boldsymbol{x}} = b + \boldsymbol{w}^\mathsf{T}\boldsymbol{x} \tag{1.11}$$

This converts the affine function into a **linear function**. We will usually assume that this has been done, so we can just write the prediction function as follows:

$$f(\boldsymbol{x};\boldsymbol{w}) = \boldsymbol{w}^\mathsf{T}\boldsymbol{x} \tag{1.12}$$

1.2.1.6   Maximum likelihood estimation

When fitting probabilistic models, it is common to use the negative log probability as our loss function:

$$\ell(y, f(\boldsymbol{x};\boldsymbol{\theta})) = -\log p(y|f(\boldsymbol{x};\boldsymbol{\theta})) \tag{1.13}$$

The reasons for this are explained in Section 5.1.6.1, but the intuition is that a good model (with low loss) is one that assigns a high probability to the true output y for each corresponding input $\boldsymbol{x}$. The average negative log probability of the training set is given by

$$\text{NLL}(\boldsymbol{\theta}) = -\frac{1}{N} \sum_{n=1}^{N} \log p(y_n|f(\boldsymbol{x}_n;\boldsymbol{\theta})) \tag{1.14}$$

This is called the **negative log likelihood**. If we minimize this, we can compute the **maximum likelihood estimate** or **MLE**:

$$\hat{\boldsymbol{\theta}}_{\text{mle}} = \underset{\boldsymbol{\theta}}{\arg\min}\, \text{NLL}(\boldsymbol{\theta}) \tag{1.15}$$

This is a very common way to fit models to data, as we will see.

1.2.2   Regression

Now suppose that we want to predict a real-valued quantity $y \in \mathbb{R}$ instead of a class label $y \in \{1, \ldots, C\}$; this is known as **regression**. For example, in the case of Iris flowers, y might be the degree of toxicity if the flower is eaten, or the average height of the plant.

Regression is very similar to classification. However, since the output is real-valued, we need to use a different loss function. For regression, the most common choice is to use **quadratic loss**, or ℓ_2 **loss**:

$$\ell_2(y, \hat{y}) = (y - \hat{y})^2 \tag{1.16}$$

This penalizes large **residuals** $y - \hat{y}$ more than small ones.[4] The empirical risk when using quadratic loss is equal to the **mean squared error** or **MSE**:

$$\text{MSE}(\boldsymbol{\theta}) = \frac{1}{N} \sum_{n=1}^{N} (y_n - f(\boldsymbol{x}_n; \boldsymbol{\theta}))^2 \tag{1.17}$$

Based on the discussion in Section 1.2.1.5, we should also model the uncertainty in our prediction. In regression problems, it is common to assume the output distribution is a **Gaussian** or **normal**. As we explain in Section 2.6, this distribution is defined by

$$\mathcal{N}(y|\mu, \sigma^2) \triangleq \frac{1}{\sqrt{2\pi\sigma^2}} e^{-\frac{1}{2\sigma^2}(y-\mu)^2} \tag{1.18}$$

where μ is the mean, σ^2 is the variance, and $\sqrt{2\pi\sigma^2}$ is the normalization constant needed to ensure the density integrates to 1. In the context of regression, we can make the mean depend on the inputs by defining $\mu = f(\boldsymbol{x}_n; \boldsymbol{\theta})$. We therefore get the following conditional probability distribution:

$$p(y|\boldsymbol{x}; \boldsymbol{\theta}) = \mathcal{N}(y|f(\boldsymbol{x}; \boldsymbol{\theta}), \sigma^2) \tag{1.19}$$

If we assume that the variance σ^2 is fixed (for simplicity), the corresponding average (per-sample) negative log likelihood becomes

$$\text{NLL}(\boldsymbol{\theta}) = -\frac{1}{N} \sum_{n=1}^{N} \log \left[\left(\frac{1}{2\pi\sigma^2} \right)^{\frac{1}{2}} \exp \left(-\frac{1}{2\sigma^2} (y_n - f(\boldsymbol{x}_n; \boldsymbol{\theta}))^2 \right) \right] \tag{1.20}$$

$$= \frac{1}{2\sigma^2} \text{MSE}(\boldsymbol{\theta}) + \text{const} \tag{1.21}$$

We see that the NLL is proportional to the MSE. Hence computing the maximum likelihood estimate of the parameters will result in minimizing the squared error, which seems like a sensible approach to model fitting.

1.2.2.1 Linear regression

As an example of a regression model, consider the 1d data in Figure 1.5a. We can fit this data using a **simple linear regression** model of the form

$$f(x; \boldsymbol{\theta}) = b + wx \tag{1.22}$$

---

4. If the data has outliers, the quadratic penalty can be too severe. In such cases, it can be better to use ℓ_1 loss instead, which is more **robust**. See Section 11.6 for details.

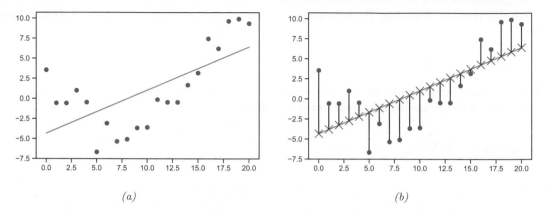

Figure 1.5: (a) Linear regression on some 1d data. (b) The vertical lines denote the residuals between the observed output value for each input (blue circle) and its predicted value (red cross). The goal of least squares regression is to pick a line that minimizes the sum of squared residuals. Generated by lin-reg_residuals_plot.ipynb.

where w is the **slope**, b is the **offset**, and $\boldsymbol{\theta} = (w, b)$ are all the parameters of the model. By adjusting $\boldsymbol{\theta}$, we can minimize the sum of squared errors, shown by the vertical lines in Figure 1.5b. until we find the **least squares solution**

$$\hat{\boldsymbol{\theta}} = \underset{\boldsymbol{\theta}}{\operatorname{argmin}} \operatorname{MSE}(\boldsymbol{\theta}) \tag{1.23}$$

See Section 11.2.2.1 for details.

If we have multiple input features, we can write

$$f(\boldsymbol{x}; \boldsymbol{\theta}) = b + w_1 x_1 + \cdots + w_D x_D = b + \boldsymbol{w}^\mathsf{T} \boldsymbol{x} \tag{1.24}$$

where $\boldsymbol{\theta} = (\boldsymbol{w}, b)$. This is called **multiple linear regression**.

For example, consider the task of predicting temperature as a function of 2d location in a room. Figure 1.6(a) plots the results of a linear model of the following form:

$$f(\boldsymbol{x}; \boldsymbol{\theta}) = b + w_1 x_1 + w_2 x_2 \tag{1.25}$$

We can extend this model to use $D > 2$ input features (such as time of day), but then it becomes harder to visualize.

1.2.2.2   Polynomial regression

The linear model in Figure 1.5a is obviously not a very good fit to the data. We can improve the fit by using a **polynomial regression** model of degree D. This has the form $f(x; \boldsymbol{w}) = \boldsymbol{w}^\mathsf{T} \boldsymbol{\phi}(x)$, where $\boldsymbol{\phi}(x)$ is a feature vector derived from the input, which has the following form:

$$\boldsymbol{\phi}(x) = [1, x, x^2, \ldots, x^D] \tag{1.26}$$

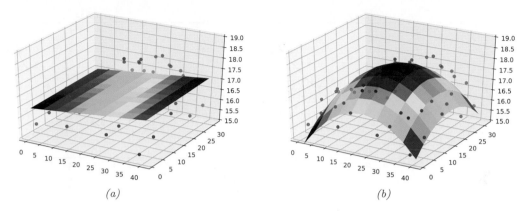

Figure 1.6: *Linear and polynomial regression applied to 2d data. Vertical axis is temperature, horizontal axes are location within a room. Data was collected by some remote sensing motes at Intel's lab in Berkeley, CA (data courtesy of Romain Thibaux). (a) The fitted plane has the form $\hat{f}(\boldsymbol{x}) = w_0 + w_1 x_1 + w_2 x_2$. (b) Temperature data is fitted with a quadratic of the form $\hat{f}(\boldsymbol{x}) = w_0 + w_1 x_1 + w_2 x_2 + w_3 x_1^2 + w_4 x_2^2$. Generated by* linreg_2d_surface_demo.ipynb.

This is a simple example of **feature preprocessing**, also called **feature engineering**.

In Figure 1.7a, we see that using $D = 2$ results in a much better fit. We can keep increasing D, and hence the number of parameters in the model, until $D = N - 1$; in this case, we have one parameter per data point, so we can perfectly **interpolate** the data. The resulting model will have 0 MSE, as shown in Figure 1.7c. However, intuitively the resulting function will not be a good predictor for future inputs, since it is too "wiggly". We discuss this in more detail in Section 1.2.3.

We can also apply polynomial regression to multi-dimensional inputs. For example, Figure 1.6(b) plots the predictions for the temperature model after performing a quadratic expansion of the inputs

$$f(\boldsymbol{x}; \boldsymbol{w}) = w_0 + w_1 x_1 + w_2 x_2 + w_3 x_1^2 + w_4 x_2^2 \tag{1.27}$$

The quadratic shape is a better fit to the data than the linear model in Figure 1.6(a), since it captures the fact that the middle of the room is hotter. We can also add cross terms, such as $x_1 x_2$, to capture interaction effects. See Section 1.5.3.2 for details.

Note that the above models still use a prediction function that is a linear function of the parameters $\boldsymbol{w}$, even though it is a nonlinear function of the original input $\boldsymbol{x}$. The reason this is important is that a linear model induces an MSE loss function $\mathrm{MSE}(\boldsymbol{\theta})$ that has a unique global optimum, as we explain in Section 11.2.2.1.

1.2.2.3 Deep neural networks

In Section 1.2.2.2, we manually specified the transformation of the input features, namely polynomial expansion, $\boldsymbol{\phi}(\boldsymbol{x}) = [1, x_1, x_2, x_1^2, x_2^2, \ldots]$. We can create much more powerful models by learning to do such nonlinear **feature extraction** automatically. If we let $\boldsymbol{\phi}(\boldsymbol{x})$ have its own set of parameters, say $\mathbf{V}$, then the overall model has the form

$$f(\boldsymbol{x}; \boldsymbol{w}, \mathbf{V}) = \boldsymbol{w}^{\mathsf{T}} \boldsymbol{\phi}(\boldsymbol{x}; \mathbf{V}) \tag{1.28}$$

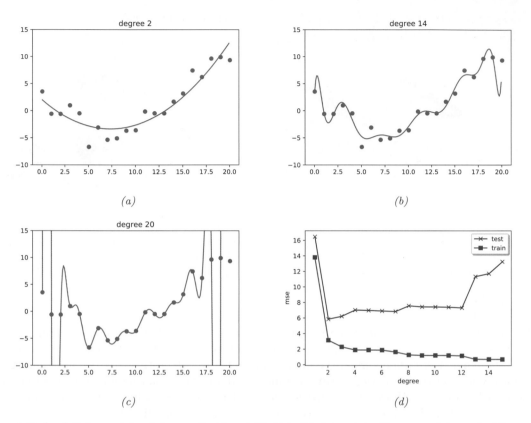

Figure 1.7: (a-c) Polynomials of degrees 2, 14 and 20 fit to 21 datapoints (the same data as in Figure 1.5). (d) MSE vs degree. Generated by linreg_poly_vs_degree.ipynb.

We can recursively decompose the feature extractor $\phi(\boldsymbol{x}; \mathbf{V})$ into a composition of simpler functions. The resulting model then becomes a stack of L nested functions:

$$f(\boldsymbol{x}; \boldsymbol{\theta}) = f_L(f_{L-1}(\cdots(f_1(\boldsymbol{x}))\cdots)) \tag{1.29}$$

where $f_\ell(\boldsymbol{x}) = f(\boldsymbol{x}; \boldsymbol{\theta}_\ell)$ is the function at layer ℓ. The final layer is linear and has the form $f_L(\boldsymbol{x}) = \boldsymbol{w}^\mathsf{T} f_{1:L-1}(\boldsymbol{x})$, where $f_{1:L-1}(\boldsymbol{x})$ is the learned feature extractor. This is the key idea behind **deep neural networks** or **DNNs**, which includes common variants such as **convolutional neural networks** (CNNs) for images, and **recurrent neural networks** (RNNs) for sequences. See Part III for details.

1.2.3   Overfitting and generalization

We can rewrite the empirical risk in Equation (1.4) in the following equivalent way:

$$\mathcal{L}(\boldsymbol{\theta}; \mathcal{D}_{\text{train}}) = \frac{1}{|\mathcal{D}_{\text{train}}|} \sum_{(\boldsymbol{x}, \boldsymbol{y}) \in \mathcal{D}_{\text{train}}} \ell(\boldsymbol{y}, f(\boldsymbol{x}; \boldsymbol{\theta})) \tag{1.30}$$

where $|\mathcal{D}_{\text{train}}|$ is the size of the training set $\mathcal{D}_{\text{train}}$. This formulation is useful because it makes explicit which dataset the loss is being evaluated on.

With a suitably flexible model, we can drive the training loss to zero (assuming no label noise), by simply memorizing the correct output for each input. For example, Figure 1.7(c) perfectly interpolates the training data (modulo the last point on the right). But what we care about is prediction accuracy on new data, which may not be part of the training set. A model that perfectly fits the training data, but which is too complex, is said to suffer from **overfitting**.

To detect if a model is overfitting, let us assume (for now) that we have access to the true (but unknown) distribution $p^*(\boldsymbol{x}, \boldsymbol{y})$ used to generate the training set. Then, instead of computing the empirical risk we compute the theoretical expected loss or **population risk**

$$\mathcal{L}(\boldsymbol{\theta}; p^*) \triangleq \mathbb{E}_{p^*(\boldsymbol{x}, \boldsymbol{y})} \left[\ell(\boldsymbol{y}, f(\boldsymbol{x}; \boldsymbol{\theta})) \right] \tag{1.31}$$

The difference $\mathcal{L}(\boldsymbol{\theta}; p^*) - \mathcal{L}(\boldsymbol{\theta}; \mathcal{D}_{\text{train}})$ is called the **generalization gap**. If a model has a large generalization gap (i.e., low empirical risk but high population risk), it is a sign that it is overfitting.

In practice we don't know p^*. However, we can partition the data we do have into two subsets, known as the training set and the **test set**. Then we can approximate the population risk using the **test risk**:

$$\mathcal{L}(\boldsymbol{\theta}; \mathcal{D}_{\text{test}}) \triangleq \frac{1}{|\mathcal{D}_{\text{test}}|} \sum_{(\boldsymbol{x}, \boldsymbol{y}) \in \mathcal{D}_{\text{test}}} \ell(y, f(\boldsymbol{x}; \boldsymbol{\theta})) \tag{1.32}$$

As an example, in Figure 1.7d, we plot the training error and test error for polynomial regression as a function of degree D. We see that the training error goes to 0 as the model becomes more complex. However, the test error has a characteristic **U-shaped curve**: on the left, where $D = 1$, the model is **underfitting**; on the right, where $D \gg 1$, the model is **overfitting**; and when $D = 2$, the model complexity is "just right".

How can we pick a model of the right complexity? If we use the training set to evaluate different models, we will always pick the most complex model, since that will have the most **degrees of freedom**, and hence will have minimum loss. So instead we should pick the model with minimum test loss.

In practice, we need to partition the data into three sets, namely the training set, the test set and a **validation set**; the latter is used for model selection, and we just use the test set to estimate future performance (the population risk), i.e., the test set is not used for model fitting or model selection. See Section 4.5.4 for further details.

1.2.4 No free lunch theorem

All models are wrong, but some models are useful. — George Box [BD87, p424].[5]

Given the large variety of models in the literature, it is natural to wonder which one is best. Unfortunately, there is no single best model that works optimally for all kinds of problems — this is sometimes called the **no free lunch theorem** [Wol96]. The reason is that a set of assumptions (also called **inductive bias**) that works well in one domain may work poorly in another. The best

---

5. George Box is a retired statistics professor at the University of Wisconsin.

way to pick a suitable model is based on domain knowledge, and/or trial and error (i.e., using model selection techniques such as cross validation (Section 4.5.4) or Bayesian methods (Section 5.2.2 and Section 5.2.6). For this reason, it is important to have many models and algorithmic techniques in one's toolbox to choose from.

1.3 Unsupervised learning

In supervised learning, we assume that each input example $\boldsymbol{x}$ in the training set has an associated set of output targets $\boldsymbol{y}$, and our goal is to learn the input-output mapping. Although this is useful, and can be difficult, supervised learning is essentially just "glorified curve fitting" [Pea18].

An arguably much more interesting task is to try to "make sense of" data, as opposed to just learning a mapping. That is, we just get observed "inputs" $\mathcal{D} = \{\boldsymbol{x}_n : n = 1 : N\}$ without any corresponding "outputs" $\boldsymbol{y}_n$. This is called **unsupervised learning**.

From a probabilistic perspective, we can view the task of unsupervised learning as fitting an unconditional model of the form $p(\boldsymbol{x})$, which can generate new data $\boldsymbol{x}$, whereas supervised learning involves fitting a conditional model, $p(\boldsymbol{y}|\boldsymbol{x})$, which specifies (a distribution over) outputs given inputs.[6]

Unsupervised learning avoids the need to collect large labeled datasets for training, which can often be time consuming and expensive (think of asking doctors to label medical images).

Unsupervised learning also avoids the need to learn how to partition the world into often arbitrary categories. For example, consider the task of labeling when an action, such as "drinking" or "sipping", occurs in a video. Is it when the person picks up the glass, or when the glass first touches the mouth, or when the liquid pours out? What if they pour out some liquid, then pause, then pour again — is that two actions or one? Humans will often disagree on such issues [Idr+17], which means the task is not well defined. It is therefore not reasonable to expect machines to learn such mappings.[7]

Finally, unsupervised learning forces the model to "explain" the high-dimensional inputs, rather than just the low-dimensional outputs. This allows us to learn richer models of "how the world works". As Geoff Hinton, who is a famous professor of ML at the University of Toronto, has said:

> When we're learning to see, nobody's telling us what the right answers are — we just look. Every so often, your mother says "that's a dog", but that's very little information. You'd be lucky if you got a few bits of information — even one bit per second — that way. The brain's visual system has $O(10^{14})$ neural connections. And you only live for $O(10^9)$ seconds. So it's no use learning one bit per second. You need more like $O(10^5)$ bits per second. And there's only one place you can get that much information: from the input itself. — Geoffrey Hinton, 1996 (quoted in [Gor06]).

1.3.1 Clustering

A simple example of unsupervised learning is the problem of finding **clusters** in data. The goal is to partition the input into regions that contain "similar" points. As an example, consider a 2d version

---

6. In the statistics community, it is common to use $\boldsymbol{x}$ to denote exogenous variables that are not modeled, but are simply given as inputs. Therefore an unconditional model would be denoted $p(\boldsymbol{y})$ rather than $p(\boldsymbol{x})$.
7. A more reasonable approach is to try to capture the probability distribution over labels produced by a "crowd" of annotators (see e.g., [Dum+18; Aro+19]). This embraces the fact that there can be multiple "correct" labels for a given input due to the ambiguity of the task itself.

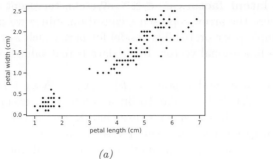
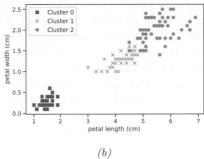

(a) (b)

Figure 1.8: (a) A scatterplot of the petal features from the iris dataset. (b) The result of unsupervised clustering using $K = 3$. Generated by iris_kmeans.ipynb.

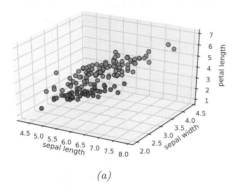
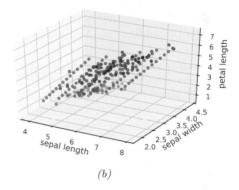

(a) (b)

Figure 1.9: (a) Scatterplot of iris data (first 3 features). Points are color coded by class. (b) We fit a 2d linear subspace to the 3d data using PCA. The class labels are ignored. Red dots are the original data, black dots are points generated from the model using $\hat{\boldsymbol{x}} = \mathbf{W}\boldsymbol{z} + \boldsymbol{\mu}$, where $\boldsymbol{z}$ are latent points on the underlying inferred 2d linear manifold. Generated by iris_pca.ipynb.

of the Iris dataset. In Figure 1.8a, we show the points without any class labels. Intuitively there are at least two clusters in the data, one in the bottom left and one in the top right. Furthermore, if we assume that a "good" set of clusters should be fairly compact, then we might want to split the top right into (at least) two subclusters. The resulting partition into three clusters is shown in Figure 1.8b. (Note that there is no correct number of clusters; instead, we need to consider the tradeoff between model complexity and fit to the data. We discuss ways to make this tradeoff in Section 21.3.7.)

1.3.2 Discovering latent "factors of variation"

When dealing with high-dimensional data, it is often useful to reduce the dimensionality by projecting it to a lower dimensional subspace which captures the "essence" of the data. One approach to this problem is to assume that each observed high-dimensional output $\boldsymbol{x}_n \in \mathbb{R}^D$ was generated by a set of hidden or unobserved low-dimensional **latent factors** $z_n \in \mathbb{R}^K$. We can represent the model diagrammatically as follows: $z_n \to x_n$, where the arrow represents causation. Since we don't know the latent factors z_n, we often assume a simple prior probability model for $p(z_n)$ such as a Gaussian, which says that each factor is a random K-dimensional vector. If the data is real-valued, we can use a Gaussian likelihood as well.

The simplest example is when we use a linear model, $p(x_n|z_n; \theta) = \mathcal{N}(x_n|\mathbf{W}z_n + \mu, \Sigma)$. The resulting model is called **factor analysis** (FA). It is similar to linear regression, except we only observe the outputs x_n, and not the inputs z_n. In the special case that $\Sigma = \sigma^2 \mathbf{I}$, this reduces to a model called probabilistic **principal components analysis** (**PCA**), which we will explain in Section 20.1. In Figure 1.9, we give an illustration of how this method can find a 2d linear subspace when applied to some simple 3d data.

Of course, assuming a linear mapping from z_n to x_n is very restrictive. However, we can create nonlinear extensions by defining $p(x_n|z_n; \theta) = \mathcal{N}(x_n|f(z_n; \theta), \sigma^2 \mathbf{I})$, where $f(z; \theta)$ is a nonlinear model, such as a deep neural network. It becomes much harder to fit such a model (i.e., to estimate the parameters θ), because the inputs to the neural net have to be inferred, as well as the parameters of the model. However, there are various approximate methods, such as the **variational autoencoder** which can be applied (see Section 20.3.5).

1.3.3   Self-supervised learning

A recently popular approach to unsupervised learning is known as **self-supervised learning**. In this approach, we create proxy supervised tasks from unlabeled data. For example, we might try to learn to predict a color image from a grayscale image, or to mask out words in a sentence and then try to predict them given the surrounding context. The hope is that the resulting predictor $\hat{x}_1 = f(x_2; \theta)$, where x_2 is the observed input and $\hat{x}_1$ is the predicted output, will learn useful features from the data, that can then be used in standard, downstream supervised tasks. This avoids the hard problem of trying to infer the "true latent factors" z behind the observed data, and instead relies on standard supervised learning methods. We discuss this approach in more detail in Section 19.2.

1.3.4   Evaluating unsupervised learning

Although unsupervised learning is appealing, it is very hard to evaluate the quality of the output of an unsupervised learning method, because there is no ground truth to compare to [TOB16].

A common method for evaluating unsupervised models is to measure the probability assigned by the model to unseen test examples. We can do this by computing the (unconditional) negative log likelihood of the data:

$$\mathcal{L}(\theta; \mathcal{D}) = -\frac{1}{|\mathcal{D}|} \sum_{x \in \mathcal{D}} \log p(x|\theta) \tag{1.33}$$

This treats the problem of unsupervised learning as one of **density estimation**. The idea is that a good model will not be "surprised" by actual data samples (i.e., will assign them high probability). Furthermore, since probabilities must sum to 1.0, if the model assigns high probability to regions of data space where the data samples come from, it implicitly assigns low probability to the regions where the data does not come from. Thus the model has learned to capture the **typical patterns** in the data. This can be used inside of a **data compression** algorithm.

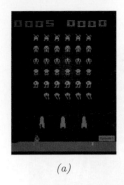

(a)   *(b)*

Figure 1.10: *Examples of some control problems. (a) Space Invaders Atari game. From* `https://gymnasium.` `farama.org/environments/atari/space_invaders/`*. (b) Controlling a humanoid robot in the MuJuCo* *simulator so it walks as fast as possible without falling over. From* `https://gymnasium.farama.org/` `environments/mujoco/humanoid/`*.*

Unfortunately, density estimation is difficult, especially in high dimensions. Furthermore, a model that assigns high probability to the data may not have learned useful high-level patterns (after all, the model could just memorize all the training examples).

An alternative evaluation metric is to use the learned unsupervised representation as features or input to a downstream supervised learning method. If the unsupervised method has discovered useful patterns, then it should be possible to use these patterns to perform supervised learning using much less labeled data than when working with the original features. For example, in Section 1.2.1.1, we saw how the 4 manually defined features of iris flowers contained most of the information needed to perform classification. We were thus able to train a classifier with nearly perfect performance using just 150 examples. If the input was raw pixels, we would need many more examples to achieve comparable performance (see Section 14.1). That is, we can increase the **sample efficiency** of learning (i.e., reduce the number of labeled examples needed to get good performance) by first learning a good representation.

Increased sample efficiency is a useful evaluation metric, but in many applications, especially in science, the goal of unsupervised learning is to *gain understanding*, not to improve performance on some prediction task. This requires the use of models that are **interpretable**, but which can also generate or "explain" most of the observed patterns in the data. To paraphrase Plato, the goal is to discover how to "carve nature at its joints". Of course, evaluating whether we have successfully discovered the true underlying structure behind some dataset often requires performing experiments and thus interacting with the world. We discuss this topic further in Section 1.4.

1.4   Reinforcement learning

In addition to supervised and unsupervised learning, there is a third kind of ML known as **reinforcement learning** (**RL**). In this class of problems, the system or **agent** has to learn how to interact with its environment. This can be encoded by means of a **policy** $a = \pi(x)$, which specifies which action to take in response to each possible input x (derived from the environment state).

For example, consider an agent that learns to play a video game, such as Atari Space Invaders (see

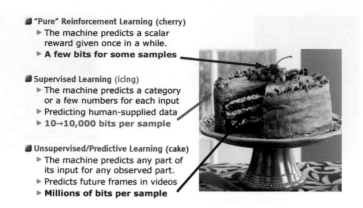

Figure 1.11: The three types of machine learning visualized as layers of a chocolate cake. This figure (originally from https://bit.ly/2m65Vs1) was used in a talk by Yann LeCun at NIPS'16, and is used with his kind permission.

Figure 1.10a). In this case, the input x is the image (or sequence of past images), and the output a is the direction to move in (left or right) and whether to fire a missile or not. As a more complex example, consider the problem of a robot learning to walk (see Figure 1.10b). In this case, the input x is the set of joint positions and angles for all the limbs, and the output a is a set of actuation or motor control signals.

The difference from supervised learning (SL) is that the system is not told which action is the best one to take (i.e., which output to produce for a given input). Instead, the system just receives an occasional **reward** (or punishment) signal in response to the actions that it takes. This is like **learning with a critic**, who gives an occasional thumbs up or thumbs down, as opposed to **learning with a teacher**, who tells you what to do at each step.

RL has grown in popularity recently, due to its broad applicability (since the reward signal that the agent is trying to optimize can be any metric of interest). However, it can be harder to make RL work than it is for supervised or unsupervised learning, for a variety of reasons. A key difficulty is that the reward signal may only be given occasionally (e.g., if the agent eventually reaches a desired state), and even then it may be unclear to the agent which of its many actions were responsible for getting the reward. (Think of playing a game like chess, where there is a single win or lose signal at the end of the game.)

To compensate for the minimal amount of information coming from the reward signal, it is common to use other information sources, such as expert demonstrations, which can be used in a supervised way, or unlabeled data, which can be used by an unsupervised learning system to discover the underlying structure of the environment. This can make it feasible to learn from a limited number of trials (interactions with the environment). As Yann LeCun put it, in an invited talk at the NIPS[8] conference in 2016: "If intelligence was a cake, unsupervised learning would be the chocolate sponge, supervised learning would be the icing, and reinforcement learning would be the cherry." This is illustrated in Figure 1.11.

8. NIPS stands for "Neural Information Processing Systems". It is one of the premier ML conferences. It has recently been renamed to NeurIPS.

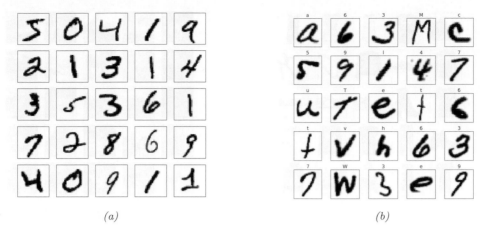

(a)

(b)

Figure 1.12: (a) Visualization of the MNIST dataset. Each image is 28×28. There are 60k training examples and 10k test examples. We show the first 25 images from the training set. Generated by *mnist_viz_tf.ipynb*. (b) Visualization of the EMNIST dataset. There are 697,932 training examples, and 116,323 test examples, each of size 28×28. There are 62 classes (a-z, A-Z, 0-9). We show the first 25 images from the training set. Generated by *emnist_viz_jax.ipynb*.

More information on RL can be found in the sequel to this book, [Mur23].

1.5 Data

Machine learning is concerned with fitting models to data using various algorithms. Although we focus on the modeling and algorithm aspects, it is important to mention that the nature and quality of the training data also plays a vital role in the success of any learned model.

In this section, we briefly describe some common image and text datasets that we will use in this book. We also briefly discuss the topic of data preprocessing.

1.5.1 Some common image datasets

In this section, we briefly discuss some image datasets that we will use in this book.

1.5.1.1 Small image datasets

One of the simplest and most widely used is known as **MNIST** [LeC+98; YB19].[9] This is a dataset of 60k training images and 10k test images, each of size 28×28 (grayscale), illustrating handwritten digits from 10 categories. Each pixel is an integer in the range $\{0, 1, \ldots, 255\}$; these are usually rescaled to $[0, 1]$, to represent pixel intensity. We can optionally convert this to a binary image by thresholding. See Figure 1.12a for an illustration.

9. The term "MNIST" stands for "Modified National Institute of Standards"; The term "modified" is used because the images have been preprocessed to ensure the digits are mostly in the center of the image.

(a)   (b)

Figure 1.13: (a) Visualization of the Fashion-MNIST dataset [XRV17]. The dataset has the same size as MNIST, but is harder to classify. There are 10 classes: T-shirt/top, Trouser, Pullover, Dress, Coat, Sandal, Shirt, Sneaker, Bag, Ankle-boot. We show the first 25 images from the training set. Generated by fashion_viz_tf.ipynb. (b) Some images from the CIFAR-10 dataset [KH09]. Each image is $32 \times 32 \times 3$, where the final dimension of size 3 refers to RGB. There are 50k training examples and 10k test examples. There are 10 classes: plane, car, bird, cat, deer, dog, frog, horse, ship, and truck. We show the first 25 images from the training set. Generated by cifar_viz_tf.ipynb.

MNIST is so widely used in the ML community that Geoff Hinton, a famous ML researcher, has called it the "drosophila of machine learning", since if we cannot make a method work well on MNIST, it will likely not work well on harder datasets. However, nowadays MNIST classification is considered "too easy", since it is possible to distinguish most pairs of digits by looking at just a single pixel. Various extensions have been proposed.

In [Coh+17], they proposed **EMNIST** (extended MNIST), that also includes lower and upper case letters. See Figure 1.12b for a visualization. This dataset is much harder than MNIST, since there are 62 classes, several of which are quite ambiguous (e.g., the digit 1 vs the lower case letter l).

In [XRV17], they proposed **Fashion-MNIST**, which has exactly the same size and shape as MNIST, but where each image is the picture of a piece of clothing instead of a handwritten digit. See Figure 1.13a for a visualization.

For small color images, the most common dataset is **CIFAR** [KH09].[10] This is a dataset of 60k images, each of size $32 \times 32 \times 3$, representing everyday objects from 10 or 100 classes; see Figure 1.13b for an illustration.[11]

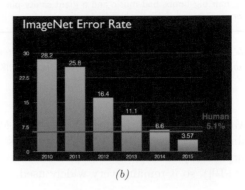

(a)   (b)

Figure 1.14: (a) Sample images from the **ImageNet** *dataset [Rus+15]. This subset consists of 1.3M color training images, each of which is* 256×256 *pixels in size. There are 1000 possible labels, one per image, and the task is to minimize the top-5 error rate, i.e., to ensure the correct label is within the 5 most probable predictions. Below each image we show the true label, and a distribution over the top 5 predicted labels. If the true label is in the top 5, its probability bar is colored red. Predictions are generated by a convolutional neural network (CNN) called "AlexNet" (Section 14.3.2). From Figure 4 of [KSH12]. Used with kind permission of Alex Krizhevsky. (b) Misclassification rate (top 5) on the ImageNet competition over time. Used with kind permission of Andrej Karpathy.*

1.5.1.2   ImageNet

Small datasets are useful for prototyping ideas, but it is also important to test methods on larger datasets, both in terms of image size and number of labeled examples. The most widely used dataset of this type is called **ImageNet** [Rus+15]. This is a dataset of $\sim 14M$ images of size $256 \times 256 \times 3$ illustrating various objects from 20,000 classes; see Figure 1.14a for some examples.

The ImageNet dataset was used as the basis of the ImageNet Large Scale Visual Recognition Challenge (**ILSVRC**), which ran from 2010 to 2018. This used a subset of 1.3M images from 1000 classes. During the course of the competition, significant progress was made by the community, as shown in Figure 1.14b. In particular, 2015 marked the first year in which CNNs could outperform humans (or at least one human, namely Andrej Karpathy) at the task of classifying images from ImageNet. Note that this does not mean that CNNs are better at vision than humans (see e.g., [YL21] for some common failure modes). Instead, it mostly likely reflects the fact that the dataset makes many **fine-grained classification** distinctions — such as between a "tiger" and a "tiger cat" — that humans find difficult to understand; by contrast, sufficiently flexible CNNs can learn arbitrary patterns, including random labels [Zha+17a].

---

10. CIFAR stands for "Canadian Institute For Advanced Research". This is the agency that funded labeling of the dataset, which was derived from the TinyImages dataset at http://groups.csail.mit.edu/vision/TinyImages/ created by Antonio Torralba. See [KH09] for details.

11. Despite its popularity, the CIFAR dataset has some issues. For example, the base error on CIFAR-100 is 5.85% due to mislabeling [NAM21]. This makes any results with accuracy above 94.15% acc suspicious. Also, 10% of CIFAR-100 training set images are duplicated in the test set [BD20].

---

1. this film was just brilliant casting location scenery story direction everyone's really suited the part they played robert <UNK> is an amazing actor ...

2. big hair big boobs bad music and a giant safety pin these are the words to best describe this terrible movie i love cheesy horror movies and i've seen hundreds...

Table 1.3: *We show snippets of the first two sentences from the IMDB movie review dataset. The first example is labeled positive and the second negative. (<UNK> refers to an unknown token.)*

Although ImageNet is much harder than MNIST and CIFAR as a classification benchmark, it too is almost "saturated" [Bey+20]. Nevertheless, relative performance of methods on ImageNet is often a surprisingly good predictor of performance on other, unrelated image classification tasks (see e.g., [Rec+19]), so it remains very widely used.

1.5.2   Some common text datasets

Machine learning is often applied to text to solve a variety of tasks. This is known as **natural language processing** or **NLP** (see e.g., [JM20] for details). Below we briefly mention a few text datasets that we will use in this book.

1.5.2.1   Text classification

A simple NLP task is text classification, which can be used for **email spam classification**, **sentiment analysis** (e.g., is a movie or product review positive or negative), etc. A common dataset for evaluating such methods is the **IMDB movie review dataset** from [Maa+11]. (IMDB stands for "Internet Movie Database".) This contains 25k labeled examples for training, and 25k for testing. Each example has a binary label, representing a positive or negative rating. See Table 1.3 for some example sentences.

1.5.2.2   Machine translation

A more difficult NLP task is to learn to map a sentence x in one language to a "semantically equivalent" sentence y in another language; this is called **machine translation**. Training such models requires aligned (x, y) pairs. Fortunately, several such datasets exist, e.g., from the Canadian parliament (English-French pairs), and the European Union (Europarl). A subset of the latter, known as the **WMT dataset** (Workshop on Machine Translation), consists of English-German pairs, and is widely used as a benchmark dataset.

1.5.2.3   Other seq2seq tasks

A generalization of machine translation is to learn a mapping from one sequence x to any other sequence y. This is called a **seq2seq model**, and can be viewed as a form of high-dimensional classification (see Section 15.2.3 for details). This framing of the problem is very general, and includes many tasks, such as **document summarization**, **question answering**, etc. For example, Table 1.4 shows how to formulate question answering as a seq2seq problem: the input is the text T

T: In meteorology, precipitation is any product of the condensation of atmospheric water vapor that falls under **gravity**. The main forms of precipitation include drizzle, rain, sleet, snow, **graupel** and hail... Precipitation forms as smaller droplets coalesce via collision with other rain drops or ice crystals within a cloud. Short, intense periods of rain in scattered locations are called "showers".

Q1: What causes precipitation to fall? A1: **gravity**
Q2: What is another main form of precipitation besides drizzle, rain, snow, sleet and hail? A2: **graupel**
Q3: Where do water droplets collide with ice crystals to form precipitation? A3: within a cloud

---

Table 1.4: Question-answer pairs for a sample passage in the SQuAD dataset. Each of the answers is a segment of text from the passage. This can be solved using sentence pair tagging. The input is the paragraph text T and the question Q. The output is a tagging of the relevant words in T that answer the question in Q. From Figure 1 of [Raj+16]. Used with kind permission of Percy Liang.

and question Q, and the output is the answer A, which is a set of words, possibly extracted from the input.

1.5.2.4 Language modeling

The rather grandiose term "**language modeling**" refers to the task of creating unconditional generative models of text sequences, $p(x_1, \ldots, x_T)$. This only requires input sentences $\boldsymbol{x}$, without any corresponding "labels" $\boldsymbol{y}$. We can therefore think of this as a form of unsupervised learning, which we discuss in Section 1.3. If the language model generates output in response to an input, as in scq2seq, we can regard it as a conditional generative model.

1.5.3 Preprocessing discrete input data

Many ML models assume that the data consists of real-valued feature vectors, $\boldsymbol{x} \in \mathbb{R}^D$. However, sometimes the input may have discrete input features, such as categorical variables like race and gender, or words from some vocabulary. In the sections below, we discuss some ways to preprocess such data to convert it to vector form. This is a common operation that is used for many different kinds of models.

1.5.3.1 One-hot encoding

When we have categorical features, we need to convert them to a numerical scale, so that computing weighted combinations of the inputs makes sense. The standard way to preprocess such categorical variables is to use a **one-hot encoding**, also called a **dummy encoding**. If a variable x has K values, we will denote its dummy encoding as follows: one-hot$(x) = [\mathbb{I}(x = 1), \ldots, \mathbb{I}(x = K)]$. For example, if there are 3 colors (say red, green and blue), the corresponding one-hot vectors will be one-hot(red) $= [1, 0, 0]$, one-hot(green) $= [0, 1, 0]$, and one-hot(blue) $= [0, 0, 1]$.

1.5.3.2 Feature crosses

A linear model using a dummy encoding for each categorical variable can capture the **main effects** of each variable, but cannot capture **interaction effects** between them. For example, suppose we want to predict the fuel efficiency of a vehicle given two categorical input variables: the type (say SUV, Truck, or Family car), and the country of origin (say USA or Japan). If we concatenate the one-hot encodings for the ternary and binary features, we get the following input encoding:

$$\boldsymbol{\phi}(\boldsymbol{x}) = [1, \mathbb{I}\,(x_1 = S)\,, \mathbb{I}\,(x_1 = T)\,, \mathbb{I}\,(x_1 = F)\,, \mathbb{I}\,(x_2 = U)\,, \mathbb{I}\,(x_2 = J)] \qquad (1.34)$$

where x_1 is the type and x_2 is the country of origin.

This model cannot capture dependencies between the features. For example, we expect trucks to be less fuel efficient, but perhaps trucks from the USA are even less efficient than trucks from Japan. This cannot be captured using the linear model in Equation (1.34) since the contribution from the country of origin is independent of the car type.

We can fix this by computing explicit **feature crosses**. For example, we can define a new composite feature with 3×2 possible values, to capture the interaction of type and country of origin. The new model becomes

$$
\begin{aligned}
f(\boldsymbol{x}; \boldsymbol{w}) &= \boldsymbol{w}^{\mathsf{T}} \boldsymbol{\phi}(\boldsymbol{x}) && (1.35)\\
&= w_0 + w_1 \mathbb{I}\,(x_1 = S) + w_2 \mathbb{I}\,(x_1 = T) + w_3 \mathbb{I}\,(x_1 = F) \\
&\quad + w_4 \mathbb{I}\,(x_2 = U) + w_5 \mathbb{I}\,(x_2 = J) \\
&\quad + w_6 \mathbb{I}\,(x_1 = S, x_2 = U) + w_7 \mathbb{I}\,(x_1 = T, x_2 = U) + w_8 \mathbb{I}\,(x_1 = F, x_2 = U) \\
&\quad + w_9 \mathbb{I}\,(x_1 = S, x_2 = J) + w_{10} \mathbb{I}\,(x_1 = T, x_2 = J) + w_{11} \mathbb{I}\,(x_1 = F, x_2 = J) && (1.36)
\end{aligned}
$$

We can see that the use of feature crosses converts the original dataset into a **wide format**, with many more columns.

1.5.4   Preprocessing text data

In Section 1.5.2, we briefly discussed text classification and other NLP tasks. To feed text data into a classifier, we need to tackle various issues. First, documents have a variable length, and are thus not fixed-length feature vectors, as assumed by many kinds of models. Second, words are categorical variables with many possible values (equal to the size of the vocabulary), so the corresponding one-hot encodings will be very high-dimensional, with no natural notion of similarity. Third, we may encounter words at test time that have not been seen during training (so-called **out-of-vocabulary** or **OOV** words). We discuss some solutions to these problems below. More details can be found in e.g., [BKL10; MRS08; JM20].

1.5.4.1   Bag of words model

A simple approach to dealing with variable-length text documents is to interpret them as a **bag of words**, in which we ignore word order. To convert this to a vector from a fixed input space, we first map each word to a **token** from some vocabulary.

To reduce the number of tokens, we often use various pre-processing techniques such as the following: dropping punctuation, converting all words to lower case; dropping common but uninformative words, such as "and" and "the" (this is called **stop word removal**); replacing words with their base form, such as replacing "running" and "runs" with "run" (this is called **word stemming**); etc. For details, see e.g., [BL12], and for some sample code, see text_preproc_jax.ipynb.

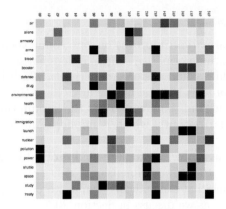

Figure 1.15: Example of a term-document matrix, where raw counts have been replaced by their TF-IDF values (see Section 1.5.4.2). Darker cells are larger values. From `https://bit.ly/2kByLQI`. Used with kind permission of Christoph Carl Kling.

Let x_{nt} be the token at location t in the n'th document. If there are D unique tokens in the vocabulary, then we can represent the n'th document as a D-dimensional vector $\tilde{x}_n$, where $\tilde{x}_{nv}$ is the number of times that word v occurs in document n:

$$\tilde{x}_{nv} = \sum_{t=1}^{T} \mathbb{I}(x_{nt} = v) \tag{1.37}$$

where T is the length of document n. We can now interpret documents as vectors in $\mathbb{R}^D$. This is called the **vector space model** of text [SWY75; TP10].

We traditionally store input data in an $N \times D$ design matrix denoted by $\mathbf{X}$, where D is the number of features. In the context of vector space models, it is more common to represent the input data as a $D \times N$ **term frequency matrix**, where TF_{ij} is the frequency of term i in document j. See Figure 1.15 for an illustration.

1.5.4.2 TF-IDF

One problem with representing documents as word count vectors is that frequent words may have undue influence, just because the magnitude of their word count is higher, even if they do not carry much semantic content. A common solution to this is to transform the counts by taking logs, which reduces the impact of words that occur many times within a single document.

To reduce the impact of words that occur many times in general (across all documents), we compute a quantity called the **inverse document frequency**, defined as follows: $\text{IDF}_i \triangleq \log \frac{N}{1+\text{DF}_i}$, where DF_i is the number of documents with term i. We can combine these transformations to compute the **TF-IDF** matrix as follows:

$$\text{TFIDF}_{ij} = \log(\text{TF}_{ij} + 1) \times \text{IDF}_i \tag{1.38}$$

(We often normalize each row as well.) This provides a more meaningful representation of documents, and can be used as input to many ML algorithms. See tfidf_demo.ipynb for an example.

1.5.4.3   Word embeddings

Although the TF-IDF transformation improves on raw count vectors by placing more weight on "informative" words and less on "uninformative" words, it does not solve the fundamental problem with the one-hot encoding (from which count vectors are derived), which is that that semantically similar words, such as "man" and "woman", may be not be any closer (in vector space) than semantically dissimilar words, such as "man" and "banana". Thus the assumption that points that are close in input space should have similar outputs, which is implicitly made by most prediction models, is invalid.

The standard way to solve this problem is to use **word embeddings**, in which we map each sparse one-hot vector, $\boldsymbol{x}_{nt} \in \{0,1\}^V$, to a lower-dimensional dense vector, $\boldsymbol{e}_{nt} \in \mathbb{R}^K$ using $\boldsymbol{e}_{nt} = \mathbf{E}\boldsymbol{x}_{nt}$, where $\mathbf{E} \in \mathbb{R}^{K \times V}$ is learned such that semantically similar words are placed close by. There are many ways to learn such embeddings, as we discuss in Section 20.5.

Once we have an embedding matrix, we can represent a variable-length text document as a **bag of word embeddings**. We can then convert this to a fixed length vector by summing (or averaging) the embeddings:

$$\overline{\boldsymbol{e}}_n = \sum_{t=1}^T \boldsymbol{e}_{nt} = \mathbf{E}\tilde{\boldsymbol{x}}_n \tag{1.39}$$

where $\tilde{\boldsymbol{x}}_n$ is the bag of words representation from Equation (1.37). We can then use this inside of a logistic regression classifier, which we briefly introduced in Section 1.2.1.5. The overall model has the form

$$p(y = c|\boldsymbol{x}_n, \boldsymbol{\theta}) = \text{softmax}_c(\mathbf{W}\mathbf{E}\tilde{\boldsymbol{x}}_n) \tag{1.40}$$

We often use a **pre-trained word embedding** matrix $\mathbf{E}$, in which case the model is linear in $\mathbf{W}$, which simplifies parameter estimation (see Chapter 10). See also Section 15.7 for a discussion of contextual word embeddings.

1.5.4.4   Dealing with novel words

At test time, the model may encounter a completely novel word that it has not seen before. This is known as the **out of vocabulary** or **OOV** problem. Such novel words are bound to occur, because the set of words is an **open class**. For example, the set of proper nouns (names of people and places) is unbounded.

A standard heuristic to solve this problem is to replace all novel words with the special symbol **UNK**, which stands for "unknown". However, this loses information. For example, if we encounter the word "athazagoraphobia", we may guess it means "fear of something", since phobia is a common suffix in English (derived from Greek) to mean "fear of". (It turns out that athazagoraphobia means "fear of being forgotten about or ignored".)

We could work at the character level, but this would require the model to learn how to group common letter combinations together into words. It is better to leverage the fact that words have substructure, and then to take as input **subword units** or **wordpieces** [SHB16; Wu+16]; these are often created using a method called **byte-pair encoding** [Gag94], which is a form of data compression that creates new symbols to represent common substrings.

1.5.5 Handling missing data

Sometimes we may have **missing data**, in which parts of the input x or output y may be unknown. If the output is unknown during training, the example is unlabeled; we consider such semi-supervised learning scenarios in Section 19.3. We therefore focus on the case where some of the input features may be missing, either at training or testing time, or both.

To model this, let $\mathbf{M}$ be an $N \times D$ matrix of binary variables, where $M_{nd} = 1$ if feature d in example n is missing, and $M_{nd} = 0$ otherwise. Let $\mathbf{X}_v$ be the visible parts of the input feature matrix, corresponding to $M_{nd} = 0$, and $\mathbf{X}_h$ be the missing parts, corresponding to $M_{nd} = 1$. Let $\mathbf{Y}$ be the output label matrix, which we assume is fully observed. If we assume $p(\mathbf{M}|\mathbf{X}_v, \mathbf{X}_h, \mathbf{Y}) = p(\mathbf{M})$, we say the data is **missing completely at random** or **MCAR**, since the missingness does not depend on the hidden or observed features. If we assume $p(\mathbf{M}|\mathbf{X}_v, \mathbf{X}_h, \mathbf{Y}) = p(\mathbf{M}|\mathbf{X}_v, \mathbf{Y})$, we say the data is **missing at random** or **MAR**, since the missingness does not depend on the hidden features, but may depend on the visible features. If neither of these assumptions hold, we say the data is **not missing at random** or **NMAR**.

In the MCAR and MAR cases, we can ignore the missingness mechanism, since it tells us nothing about the hidden features. However, in the NMAR case, we need to model the **missing data mechanism**, since the lack of information may be informative. For example, the fact that someone did not fill out an answer to a sensitive question on a survey (e.g., "Do you have COVID?") could be informative about the underlying value. See e.g., [LR87; Mar08] for more information on missing data models.

In this book, we will always make the MAR assumption. However, even with this assumption, we cannot directly use a discriminative model, such as a DNN, when we have missing input features, since the input x will have some unknown values.

A common heuristic is called **mean value imputation**, in which missing values are replaced by their empirical mean. More generally, we can fit a generative model to the input, and use that to **fill in** the missing values. We briefly discuss some suitable generative models for this task in Chapter 20, and in more detail in the sequel to this book, [Mur23].

1.6 Discussion

In this section, we situate ML and this book into a larger context.

1.6.1 The relationship between ML and other fields

There are several subcommunities that work on ML-related topics, each of which have different names. The field of **predictive analytics** is similar to supervised learning (in particular, classification and regression), but focuses more on business applications. **Data mining** covers both supervised and unsupervised machine learning, but focuses more on structured data, usually stored in large commercial databases. **Data science** uses techniques from machine learning and statistics, but also emphasizes other topics, such as data integration, data visualization, and working with domain experts, often in an iterative feedback loop (see e.g., [BS17]). The difference between these areas is often just one of terminology.[12]

---

12. See https://developers.google.com/machine-learning/glossary/ for a useful "ML glossary".

ML is also very closely related to the field of **statistics**. Indeed, Jerry Friedman, a famous statistics professor at Stanford, said[13]

> [If the statistics field had] incorporated computing methodology from its inception as a fundamental tool, as opposed to simply a convenient way to apply our existing tools, many of the other data related fields [such as ML] would not have needed to exist — they would have been part of statistics. — Jerry Friedman [Fri97b]

Machine learning is also related to **artificial intelligence** (**AI**). Historically, the field of AI assumed that we could program "intelligence" by hand (see e.g., [RN10; PM17]), but this approach has largely failed to live up to expectations, mostly because it proved to be too hard to explicitly encode all the knowledge such systems need. Consequently, there is renewed interest in using ML to help an AI system acquire its own knowledge. (Indeed the connections are so close that sometimes the terms "ML" and "AI" are used interchangeably, although this is arguably misleading [Pre21].)

1.6.2 Structure of the book

We have seen that ML is closely related to many other subjects in mathematics, statistics, computer science, etc. It can be hard to know where to start.

In this book, we take one particular path through this interconnected landscape, using probability theory as our unifying lens. We cover statistical foundations in Part I, supervised learning in Part II–Part IV, and unsupervised learning in Part V. For more information on these (and other) topics, please see the sequel to this book, [Mur23],

In addition to the book, you may find the online Python notebooks that accompany this book helpful. See `probml.github.io/book1` for details.

1.6.3 Caveats

In this book, we will see how machine learning can be used to create systems that can (attempt to) predict outputs given inputs. These predictions can then be used to choose actions so as to minimize expected loss. When designing such systems, it can be hard to design a loss function that correctly specifies all of our preferences; this can result in "**reward hacking**" in which the machine optimizes the reward function we give it, but then we realize that the function did not capture various constraints or preferences that we forgot to specify [Wei76; Amo+16; D'A+20]. (This is particularly important when tradeoffs need to be made between multiple objectives.)

Reward hacking is an example of a larger problem known as the "**alignment problem**" [Chr20], which refers to the potential discrepancy between what we ask our algorithms to optimize and what we actually want them to do for us; this has raised various concerns in the context of **AI ethics** and **AI safety** (see e.g., [KR19; Lia20; Spe+22]). Russell [Rus19] proposes to solve this problem by not explicitly specifying a reward function, but instead forcing the machine to infer the reward by observing human behavior, an approach known as **inverse reinforcement learning**. However, emulating current or past human behavior too closely may be undesirable, and can be biased by the data that is available for training (see e.g., [Pau+20]).

The above view of AI, in which an "intelligent" system makes decisions on its own, without a human in the loop, is believed by many to be the path towards "**artificial general intelligence**"

---

13. Quoted in `https://brenocon.com/blog/2008/12/statistics-vs-machine-learning-fight/`

or **AGI**. An alternative approach is to view AI as "**augmented intelligence**" (sometimes called **intelligence augmentation** or **IA**). In this paradigm, AI is a process for creating "smart tools", like adaptive cruise control or auto-complete in search engines; such tools maintain a human in the decision-making loop. In this framing, systems which have AI/ML components in them are not that different from other complex, semi-autonomous human artefacts, such as aeroplanes with autopilot, online trading platforms or medical diagnostic systems (c.f. [Jor19; Ace]). Of course, as the AI tools becomes more powerful, they can end up doing more and more on their own, making this approach similar to AGI. However, in augmented intelligence, the goal is not to emulate or exceed human behavior at certain tasks, but instead to help humans get stuff done more easily; this is how we treat most other technologies [Kap16].

PART I

Foundations

2 Probability: Univariate Models

2.1 Introduction

In this chapter, we give a brief introduction to the basics of probability theory. There are many good books that go into more detail, e.g., [GS97; BT08; Cha21].

2.1.1 What is probability?

> Probability theory is nothing but common sense reduced to calculation. — Pierre Laplace, 1812

We are all comfortable saying that the probability that a (fair) coin will land heads is 50%. But what does this mean? There are actually two different interpretations of probability. One is called the **frequentist** interpretation. In this view, probabilities represent long run frequencies of **events** that can happen multiple times. For example, the above statement means that, if we flip the coin many times, we expect it to land heads about half the time.[1]

The other interpretation is called the **Bayesian** interpretation of probability. In this view, probability is used to quantify our **uncertainty** or ignorance about something; hence it is fundamentally related to information rather than repeated trials [Jay03; Lin06]. In the Bayesian view, the above statement means we believe the coin is equally likely to land heads or tails on the next toss.

One big advantage of the Bayesian interpretation is that it can be used to model our uncertainty about one-off events that do not have long term frequencies. For example, we might want to compute the probability that the polar ice cap will melt by 2030 CE. This event will happen zero or one times, but cannot happen repeatedly. Nevertheless, we ought to be able to quantify our uncertainty about this event; based on how probable we think this event is, we can decide how to take the optimal action, as discussed in Chapter 5. We shall therefore adopt the Bayesian interpretation in this book. Fortunately, the basic rules of probability theory are the same, no matter which interpretation is adopted.

2.1.2 Types of uncertainty

The uncertainty in our predictions can arise for two fundamentally different reasons. The first is due to our ignorance of the underlying hidden causes or mechanism generating our data. This is

---

1. Actually, the Stanford statistician (and former professional magician) Persi Diaconis has shown that a coin is about 51% likely to land facing the same way up as it started, due to the physics of the problem [DHM07].

called **epistemic uncertainty**, since epistemology is the philosophical term used to describe the study of knowledge. However, a simpler term for this is **model uncertainty**. The second kind of uncertainty arises from intrinsic variability, which cannot be reduced even if we collect more data. This is sometimes called **aleatoric uncertainty** [Hac75; KD09], derived from the Latin word for "dice", although a simpler term would be **data uncertainty**. As a concrete example, consider tossing a fair coin. We might know for sure that the probability of heads is $p = 0.5$, so there is no epistemic uncertainty, but we still cannot perfectly predict the outcome.

This distinction can be important for applications such as active learning. A typical strategy is to query examples for which $\mathbb{H}(p(y|\boldsymbol{x}, \mathcal{D}))$ is large (where $\mathbb{H}(p)$ is the entropy, discussed in Section 6.1). However, this could be due to uncertainty about the parameters, i.e., large $\mathbb{H}(p(\boldsymbol{\theta}|\mathcal{D}))$, or just due to inherent variability of the outcome, corresponding to large entropy of $p(y|\boldsymbol{x}, \boldsymbol{\theta})$. In the latter case, there would not be much use collecting more samples, since our uncertainty would not be reduced. See [Osb16] for further discussion of this point.

2.1.3   Probability as an extension of logic

In this section, we review the basic rules of probability, following the presentation of [Jay03], in which we view probability as an extension of **Boolean logic**.

2.1.3.1   Probability of an event

We define an **event**, denoted by the binary variable A, as some state of the world that either holds or does not hold. For example, A might be event "it will rain tomorrow", or "it rained yesterday", or "the label is $y = 1$", or "the parameter θ is between 1.5 and 2.0", etc. The expression $\Pr(A)$ denotes the probability with which you believe event A is true (or the long run fraction of times that A will occur). We require that $0 \le \Pr(A) \le 1$, where $\Pr(A) = 0$ means the event definitely will not happen, and $\Pr(A) = 1$ means the event definitely will happen. We write $\Pr(\overline{A})$ to denote the probability of event A not happening; this is defined to be $\Pr(\overline{A}) = 1 - \Pr(A)$.

2.1.3.2   Probability of a conjunction of two events

We denote the **joint probability** of events A and B both happening as follows:

$$\Pr(A \wedge B) = \Pr(A, B) \tag{2.1}$$

If A and B are independent events, we have

$$\Pr(A, B) = \Pr(A)\Pr(B) \tag{2.2}$$

For example, suppose X and Y are chosen uniformly at random from the set $\mathcal{X} = \{1, 2, 3, 4\}$. Let A be the event that $X \in \{1, 2\}$, and B be the event that $Y \in \{3\}$. Then we have $\Pr(A, B) = \Pr(A)\Pr(B) = \frac{1}{2} \cdot \frac{1}{4}$.

2.1.3.3   Probability of a union of two events

The probability of event A or B happening is given by

$$\Pr(A \vee B) = \Pr(A) + \Pr(B) - \Pr(A \wedge B) \tag{2.3}$$

If the events are mutually exclusive (so they cannot happen at the same time), we get

$$\Pr(A \vee B) = \Pr(A) + \Pr(B) \tag{2.4}$$

For example, suppose X is chosen uniformly at random from the set $\mathcal{X} = \{1, 2, 3, 4\}$. Let A be the event that $X \in \{1, 2\}$ and B be the event that $X \in \{3\}$. Then we have $\Pr(A \vee B) = \frac{2}{4} + \frac{1}{4}$.

2.1.3.4 Conditional probability of one event given another

We define the **conditional probability** of event B happening given that A has occurred as follows:

$$\Pr(B|A) \triangleq \frac{\Pr(A, B)}{\Pr(A)} \tag{2.5}$$

This is not defined if $\Pr(A) = 0$, since we cannot condition on an impossible event.

2.1.3.5 Independence of events

We say that event A is **independent** of event B if

$$\Pr(A, B) = \Pr(A)\Pr(B) \tag{2.6}$$

2.1.3.6 Conditional independence of events

We say that events A and B are **conditionally independent** given event C if

$$\Pr(A, B|C) = \Pr(A|C)\Pr(B|C) \tag{2.7}$$

This is written as $A \perp B|C$. Events are often dependent on each other, but may be rendered independent if we condition on the relevant intermediate variables, as we discuss in more detail later in this chapter.

2.2 Random variables

Suppose X represents some unknown quantity of interest, such as which way a dice will land when we roll it, or the temperature outside your house at the current time. If the value of X is unknown and/or could change, we call it a **random variable** or **rv**. The set of possible values, denoted $\mathcal{X}$, is known as the **sample space** or **state space**. An **event** is a set of outcomes from a given sample space. For example, if X represents the face of a dice that is rolled, so $\mathcal{X} = \{1, 2, \ldots, 6\}$, the event of "seeing a 1" is denoted $X = 1$, the event of "seeing an odd number" is denoted $X \in \{1, 3, 5\}$, the event of "seeing a number between 1 and 3" is denoted $1 \leq X \leq 3$, etc.

2.2.1 Discrete random variables

If the sample space $\mathcal{X}$ is finite or countably infinite, then X is called a **discrete random variable**. In this case, we denote the probability of the event that X has value x by $\Pr(X = x)$. We define the

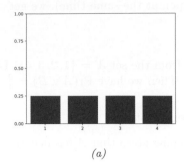
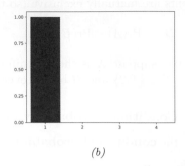

(a)   *(b)*

Figure 2.1: Some discrete distributions on the state space $\mathcal{X} = \{1, 2, 3, 4\}$. (a) A uniform distribution with $p(x = k) = 1/4$. (b) A degenerate distribution (delta function) that puts all its mass on $x = 1$. Generated by discrete_prob_dist_plot.ipynb.

probability mass function or **pmf** as a function which computes the probability of events which correspond to setting the rv to each possible value:

$$p(x) \triangleq \Pr(X = x) \tag{2.8}$$

The pmf satisfies the properties $0 \leq p(x) \leq 1$ and $\sum_{x \in \mathcal{X}} p(x) = 1$.

If X has a finite number of values, say K, the pmf can be represented as a list of K numbers, which we can plot as a histogram. For example, Figure 2.1 shows two pmf's defined on $\mathcal{X} = \{1, 2, 3, 4\}$. On the left we have a uniform distribution, $p(x) = 1/4$, and on the right, we have a degenerate distribution, $p(x) = \mathbb{I}(x = 1)$, where $\mathbb{I}()$ is the binary indicator function. Thus the distribution in Figure 2.1(b) represents the fact that X is always equal to the value 1. (Thus we see that random variables can also be constant.)

2.2.2   Continuous random variables

If $X \in \mathbb{R}$ is a real-valued quantity, it is called a **continuous random variable**. In this case, we can no longer create a finite (or countable) set of distinct possible values it can take on. However, there are a countable number of *intervals* which we can partition the real line into. If we associate events with X being in each one of these intervals, we can use the methods discussed above for discrete random variables. Informally speaking, we can represent the probability of X taking on a specific real value by allowing the size of the intervals to shrink to zero, as we show below.

2.2.2.1   Cumulative distribution function (cdf)

Define the events $A = (X \leq a)$, $B = (X \leq b)$ and $C = (a < X \leq b)$, where $a < b$. We have that $B = A \vee C$, and since A and C are mutually exclusive, the sum rules gives

$$\Pr(B) = \Pr(A) + \Pr(C) \tag{2.9}$$

and hence the probability of being in interval C is given by

$$\Pr(C) = \Pr(B) - \Pr(A) \tag{2.10}$$

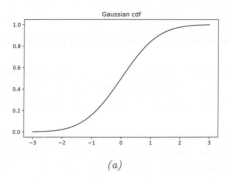

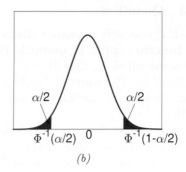

(a)   (b)

Figure 2.2: (a) Plot of the cdf for the standard normal, $\mathcal{N}(0,1)$. Generated by gauss_plot.ipynb. (b) Corresponding pdf. The shaded regions each contain $\alpha/2$ of the probability mass. Therefore the nonshaded region contains $1 - \alpha$ of the probability mass. The leftmost cutoff point is $\Phi^{-1}(\alpha/2)$, where Φ is the cdf of the Gaussian. By symmetry, the rightmost cutoff point is $\Phi^{-1}(1 - \alpha/2) = -\Phi^{-1}(\alpha/2)$. Generated by quantile_plot.ipynb.

In general, we define the **cumulative distribution function** or **cdf** of the rv X as follows:

$$P(x) \triangleq \Pr(X \le x) \tag{2.11}$$

(Note that we use a capital P to represent the cdf.) Using this, we can compute the probability of being in any interval as follows:

$$\Pr(a < X \le b) = P(b) - P(a) \tag{2.12}$$

Cdf's are monotonically non-decreasing functions. See Figure 2.2a for an example, where we illustrate the cdf of a standard normal distribution, $\mathcal{N}(x|0,1)$; see Section 2.6 for details.

2.2.2.2   Probability density function (pdf)

We define the **probability density function** or **pdf** as the derivative of the cdf:

$$p(x) \triangleq \frac{d}{dx}P(x) \tag{2.13}$$

(Note that this derivative does not always exist, in which case the pdf is not defined.) See Figure 2.2b for an example, where we illustrate the pdf of a univariate Gaussian (see Section 2.6 for details).

Given a pdf, we can compute the probability of a continuous variable being in a finite interval as follows:

$$\Pr(a < X \le b) = \int_a^b p(x)dx = P(b) - P(a) \tag{2.14}$$

As the size of the interval gets smaller, we can write

$$\Pr(x < X \le x + dx) \approx p(x)dx \tag{2.15}$$

Intuitively, this says the probability of X being in a small interval around x is the density at x times the width of the interval.

2.2.2.3   Quantiles

If the cdf P is strictly monotonically increasing, it has an inverse, called the **inverse cdf**, or **percent point function (ppf)**, or **quantile function**.

If P is the cdf of X, then $P^{-1}(q)$ is the value x_q such that $\Pr(X \le x_q) = q$; this is called the q'th **quantile** of P. The value $P^{-1}(0.5)$ is the **median** of the distribution, with half of the probability mass on the left, and half on the right. The values $P^{-1}(0.25)$ and $P^{-1}(0.75)$ are the lower and upper **quartiles**.

For example, let Φ be the cdf of the Gaussian distribution $\mathcal{N}(0, 1)$, and Φ^{-1} be the inverse cdf. Then points to the left of $\Phi^{-1}(\alpha/2)$ contain $\alpha/2$ of the probability mass, as illustrated in Figure 2.2b. By symmetry, points to the right of $\Phi^{-1}(1 - \alpha/2)$ also contain $\alpha/2$ of the mass. Hence the central interval $(\Phi^{-1}(\alpha/2), \Phi^{-1}(1 - \alpha/2))$ contains $1 - \alpha$ of the mass. If we set $\alpha = 0.05$, the central 95% interval is covered by the range

$$(\Phi^{-1}(0.025), \Phi^{-1}(0.975)) = (-1.96, 1.96) \tag{2.16}$$

If the distribution is $\mathcal{N}(\mu, \sigma^2)$, then the 95% interval becomes $(\mu - 1.96\sigma, \mu + 1.96\sigma)$. This is often approximated by writing $\mu \pm 2\sigma$.

2.2.3   Sets of related random variables

In this section, we discuss distributions over sets of related random variables.

Suppose, to start, that we have two random variables, X and Y. We can define the **joint distribution** of two random variables using $p(x, y) = p(X = x, Y = y)$ for all possible values of X and Y. If both variables have finite cardinality, we can represent the joint distribution as a 2d table, all of whose entries sum to one. For example, consider the following example with two binary variables:

$p(X, Y)$	$Y = 0$	$Y = 1$
$X = 0$	0.2	0.3
$X = 1$	0.3	0.2

If two variables are independent, we can represent the joint as the product of the two marginals. If both variables have finite cardinality, we can factorize the 2d joint table into a product of two 1d vectors, as shown in Figure 2.3.

Given a joint distribution, we define the **marginal distribution** of an rv as follows:

$$p(X = x) = \sum_y p(X = x, Y = y) \tag{2.17}$$

where we are summing over all possible states of Y. This is sometimes called the **sum rule** or the **rule of total probability**. We define $p(Y = y)$ similarly. For example, from the above 2d table, we see $p(X = 0) = 0.2 + 0.3 = 0.5$ and $p(Y = 0) = 0.2 + 0.3 = 0.5$. (The term "marginal" comes from the accounting practice of writing the sums of rows and columns on the side, or margin, of a table.)

We define the **conditional distribution** of an rv using

$$p(Y = y | X = x) = \frac{p(X = x, Y = y)}{p(X = x)} \tag{2.18}$$

We can rearrange this equation to get

$$p(x, y) = p(x)p(y|x) \tag{2.19}$$

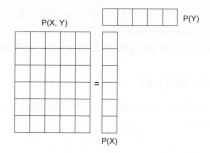

Figure 2.3: Computing $p(x, y) = p(x)p(y)$, where $X \perp Y$. Here X and Y are discrete random variables; X has 6 possible states (values) and Y has 5 possible states. A general joint distribution on two such variables would require $(6 \times 5) - 1 = 29$ parameters to define it (we subtract 1 because of the sum-to-one constraint). By assuming (unconditional) independence, we only need $(6 - 1) + (5 - 1) = 9$ parameters to define $p(x, y)$.

This is called the **product rule**.

By extending the product rule to D variables, we get the **chain rule of probability**:

$$p(\boldsymbol{x}_{1:D}) = p(x_1)p(x_2|x_1)p(x_3|x_1, x_2)p(x_4|x_1, x_2, x_3) \ldots p(x_D|\boldsymbol{x}_{1:D-1}) \tag{2.20}$$

This provides a way to create a high dimensional joint distribution from a set of conditional distributions. We discuss this in more detail in Section 3.6.

2.2.4 Independence and conditional independence

We say X and Y are **unconditionally independent** or **marginally independent**, denoted $X \perp Y$, if we can represent the joint as the product of the two marginals (see Figure 2.3), i.e.,

$$X \perp Y \iff p(X, Y) = p(X)p(Y) \tag{2.21}$$

In general, we say a set of variables $X_1, \ldots, X_n$ is (mutually) **independent** if the joint can be written as a product of marginals for all subsets $\{X_1, \ldots, X_m\} \subseteq \{X_1, \ldots, X_n\}$: i.e.,

$$p(X_1, \ldots, X_m) = \prod_{i=1}^{m} p(X_i) \tag{2.22}$$

For example, we say X_1, X_2, X_3 are mutually independent if the following conditions hold: $p(X_1, X_2, X_3) = p(X_1)p(X_2)p(X_3)$, $p(X_1, X_2) = p(X_1)p(X_2)$, $p(X_2, X_3) = p(X_2)p(X_3)$, and $p(X_1, X_3) = p(X_1)p(X_3)$.[2]

Unfortunately, unconditional independence is rare, because most variables can influence most other variables. However, usually this influence is mediated via other variables rather than being direct. We therefore say X and Y are **conditionally independent** (CI) given Z iff the conditional joint can be written as a product of conditional marginals:

$$X \perp Y \mid Z \iff p(X, Y|Z) = p(X|Z)p(Y|Z) \tag{2.23}$$

---

2. For further discussion, see https://github.com/probml/pml-book/issues/353#issuecomment-1120327442.

We can write this assumption as a graph $X - Z - Y$, which captures the intuition that all the dependencies between X and Y are mediated via Z. By using larger graphs, we can define complex joint distributions; these are known as **graphical models**, and are discussed in Section 3.6.

2.2.5 Moments of a distribution

In this section, we describe various summary statistics that can be derived from a probability distribution (either a pdf or pmf).

2.2.5.1 Mean of a distribution

The most familiar property of a distribution is its **mean**, or **expected value**, often denoted by μ. For continuous rv's, the mean is defined as follows:

$$\mathbb{E}[X] \triangleq \int_{\mathcal{X}} x \, p(x) dx \tag{2.24}$$

If the integral is not finite, the mean is not defined; we will see some examples of this later.

For discrete rv's, the mean is defined as follows:

$$\mathbb{E}[X] \triangleq \sum_{x \in \mathcal{X}} x \, p(x) \tag{2.25}$$

However, this is only meaningful if the values of x are ordered in some way (e.g., if they represent integer counts).

Since the mean is a linear operator, we have

$$\mathbb{E}[aX + b] = a\mathbb{E}[X] + b \tag{2.26}$$

This is called the **linearity of expectation**.

For a set of n random variables, one can show that the expectation of their sum is as follows:

$$\mathbb{E}\left[\sum_{i=1}^{n} X_i\right] = \sum_{i=1}^{n} \mathbb{E}[X_i] \tag{2.27}$$

If they are independent, the expectation of their product is given by

$$\mathbb{E}\left[\prod_{i=1}^{n} X_i\right] = \prod_{i=1}^{n} \mathbb{E}[X_i] \tag{2.28}$$

2.2.5.2 Variance of a distribution

The **variance** is a measure of the "spread" of a distribution, often denoted by σ^2. This is defined as follows:

$$\mathbb{V}[X] \triangleq \mathbb{E}\left[(X - \mu)^2\right] = \int (x - \mu)^2 p(x) dx \tag{2.29}$$

$$= \int x^2 p(x) dx + \mu^2 \int p(x) dx - 2\mu \int x p(x) dx = \mathbb{E}\left[X^2\right] - \mu^2 \tag{2.30}$$

from which we derive the useful result

$$\mathbb{E}\left[X^2\right] = \sigma^2 + \mu^2 \tag{2.31}$$

The **standard deviation** is defined as

$$\text{std}\left[X\right] \triangleq \sqrt{\mathbb{V}\left[X\right]} = \sigma \tag{2.32}$$

This is useful since it has the same units as X itself.

The variance of a shifted and scaled version of a random variable is given by

$$\mathbb{V}\left[aX + b\right] = a^2 \mathbb{V}\left[X\right] \tag{2.33}$$

If we have a set of n independent random variables, the variance of their sum is given by the sum of their variances:

$$\mathbb{V}\left[\sum_{i=1}^n X_i\right] = \sum_{i=1}^n \mathbb{V}\left[X_i\right] \tag{2.34}$$

The variance of their product can also be derived, as follows:

$$\mathbb{V}\left[\prod_{i=1}^n X_i\right] = \mathbb{E}\left[(\prod_i X_i)^2\right] - (\mathbb{E}\left[\prod_i X_i\right])^2 \tag{2.35}$$

$$= \mathbb{E}\left[\prod_i X_i^2\right] - (\prod_i \mathbb{E}\left[X_i\right])^2 \tag{2.36}$$

$$= \prod_i \mathbb{E}\left[X_i^2\right] - \prod_i (\mathbb{E}\left[X_i\right])^2 \tag{2.37}$$

$$= \prod_i (\mathbb{V}\left[X_i\right] + (\mathbb{E}\left[X_i\right])^2) - \prod_i (\mathbb{E}\left[X_i\right])^2 \tag{2.38}$$

$$= \prod_i (\sigma_i^2 + \mu_i^2) - \prod_i \mu_i^2 \tag{2.39}$$

2.2.5.3 Mode of a distribution

The **mode** of a distribution is the value with the highest probability mass or probability density:

$$\boldsymbol{x}^* = \operatorname*{argmax}_{\boldsymbol{x}} p(\boldsymbol{x}) \tag{2.40}$$

If the distribution is **multimodal**, this may not be unique, as illustrated in Figure 2.4. Furthermore, even if there is a unique mode, this point may not be a good summary of the distribution.

2.2.5.4 Conditional moments

When we have two or more dependent random variables, we can compute the moments of one given knowledge of the other. For example, the **law of iterated expectations**, also called the **law of total expectation**, tells us that

$$\mathbb{E}\left[X\right] = \mathbb{E}_Y\left[\mathbb{E}\left[X|Y\right]\right] \tag{2.41}$$

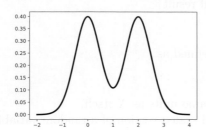

Figure 2.4: Illustration of a mixture of two 1d Gaussians, $p(x) = 0.5\mathcal{N}(x|0, 0.5) + 0.5\mathcal{N}(x|2, 0.5)$. Generated by bimodal_dist_plot.ipynb.

To prove this, let us suppose, for simplicity, that X and Y are both discrete rv's. Then we have

$$\mathbb{E}_Y\left[\mathbb{E}\left[X|Y\right]\right] = \mathbb{E}_Y\left[\sum_x x\, p(X = x|Y)\right] \tag{2.42}$$

$$= \sum_y\left[\sum_x x\, p(X = x|Y = y)\right]p(Y = y) = \sum_{x,y} x p(X = x, Y = y) = \mathbb{E}\left[X\right] \tag{2.43}$$

To give a more intuitive explanation, consider the following simple example.[3] Let X be the lifetime duration of a lightbulb, and let Y be the factory the lightbulb was produced in. Suppose $\mathbb{E}\left[X|Y = 1\right] = 5000$ and $\mathbb{E}\left[X|Y = 2\right] = 4000$, indicating that factory 1 produces longer lasting bulbs. Suppose factory 1 supplies 60% of the lightbulbs, so $p(Y = 1) = 0.6$ and $p(Y = 2) = 0.4$. Then the expected duration of a random lightbulb is given by

$$\mathbb{E}\left[X\right] = \mathbb{E}\left[X|Y = 1\right]p(Y = 1) + \mathbb{E}\left[X|Y = 2\right]p(Y = 2) = 5000 \times 0.6 + 4000 \times 0.4 = 4600 \tag{2.44}$$

There is a similar formula for the variance. In particular, the **law of total variance**, also called the **conditional variance formula**, tells us that

$$\mathbb{V}\left[X\right] = \mathbb{E}_Y\left[\mathbb{V}\left[X|Y\right]\right] + \mathbb{V}_Y\left[\mathbb{E}\left[X|Y\right]\right] \tag{2.45}$$

To see this, let us define the conditional moments, $\mu_{X|Y} = \mathbb{E}\left[X|Y\right]$, $s_{X|Y} = \mathbb{E}\left[X^2|Y\right]$, and $\sigma^2_{X|Y} = \mathbb{V}\left[X|Y\right] = s_{X|Y} - \mu^2_{X|Y}$, which are functions of Y (and therefore are random quantities). Then we have

$$\mathbb{V}\left[X\right] = \mathbb{E}\left[X^2\right] - (\mathbb{E}\left[X\right])^2 = \mathbb{E}_Y\left[s_{X|Y}\right] - \left(\mathbb{E}_Y\left[\mu_{X|Y}\right]\right)^2 \tag{2.46}$$

$$= \mathbb{E}_Y\left[\sigma^2_{X|Y}\right] + \mathbb{E}_Y\left[\mu^2_{X|Y}\right] - \left(\mathbb{E}_Y\left[\mu_{X|Y}\right]\right)^2 \tag{2.47}$$

$$= \mathbb{E}_Y\left[\mathbb{V}\left[X|Y\right]\right] + \mathbb{V}_Y\left[\mu_{X|Y}\right] \tag{2.48}$$

To get some intuition for these formulas, consider a mixture of K univariate Gaussians. Let Y be the hidden indicator variable that specifies which mixture component we are using, and let

---

3. This example is from `https://en.wikipedia.org/wiki/Law_of_total_expectation`, but with modified notation.

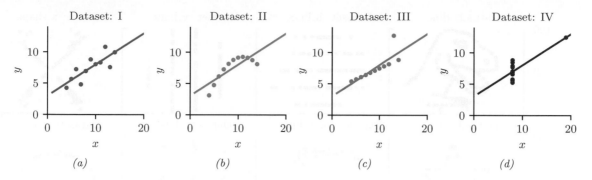

Figure 2.5: Illustration of Anscombe's quartet. All of these datasets have the same low order summary statistics. Generated by anscombes_quartet.ipynb.

$X = \sum_{y=1}^{K} \pi_y \mathcal{N}(X|\mu_y, \sigma_y)$. In Figure 2.4, we have $\pi_1 = \pi_2 = 0.5$, $\mu_1 = 0$, $\mu_2 = 2$, $\sigma_1 = \sigma_2 = 0.5$. Thus

$$\mathbb{E}\left[\mathbb{V}\left[X|Y\right]\right] = \pi_1 \sigma_1^2 + \pi_2 \sigma_2^2 = 0.25 \tag{2.49}$$

$$\mathbb{V}\left[\mathbb{E}\left[X|Y\right]\right] = \pi_1(\mu_1 - \overline{\mu})^2 + \pi_2(\mu_2 - \overline{\mu})^2 = 0.5(0-1)^2 + 0.5(2-1)^2 = 0.5 + 0.5 = 1 \tag{2.50}$$

So we get the intuitive result that the variance of X is dominated by which centroid it is drawn from (i.e., difference in the means), rather than the local variance around each centroid.

2.2.6 Limitations of summary statistics *

Although it is common to summarize a probability distribution (or points sampled from a distribution) using simple statistics such as the mean and variance, this can lose a lot of information. A striking example of this is known as **Anscombe's quartet** [Ans73], which is illustrated in Figure 2.5. This shows 4 different datasets of (x, y) pairs, all of which have identical mean, variance and correlation coefficient ρ (defined in Section 3.1.2): $\mathbb{E}[x] = 9$, $\mathbb{V}[x] = 11$, $\mathbb{E}[y] = 7.50$, $\mathbb{V}[y] = 4.12$, and $\rho = 0.816$.[4] However, the joint distributions $p(x, y)$ from which these points were sampled are clearly very different. Anscombe invented these datasets, each consisting of 10 data points, to counter the impression among statisticians that numerical summaries are superior to data visualization [Ans73].

An even more striking example of this phenomenon is shown in Figure 2.6. This consists of a dataset that looks like a dinosaur[5], plus 11 other datasets, all of which have identical low order statistics. This collection of datasets is called the **Datasaurus Dozen** [MF17]. The exact values of the (x, y) points are available online.[6] They were computed using simulated annealing, a derivative free optimization method which we discuss in the sequel to this book, [Mur23]. (The objective

---

4. The maximum likelihood estimate for the variance in Equation (4.36) differs from the unbiased estimate in Equation (4.38). For the former, we have $\mathbb{V}[x] = 10.00$, $\mathbb{V}[y] = 3.75$, for the latter, we have $\mathbb{V}[x] = 11.00$, $\mathbb{V}[y] = 4.12$.
5. This dataset was created by Alberto Cairo, and is available at http://www.thefunctionalart.com/2016/08/download-datasaurus-never-trust-summary.html
6. https://www.autodesk.com/research/publications/same-stats-different-graphs. There are actually 13 datasets in total, including the dinosaur. We omitted the "away" dataset for visual clarity.

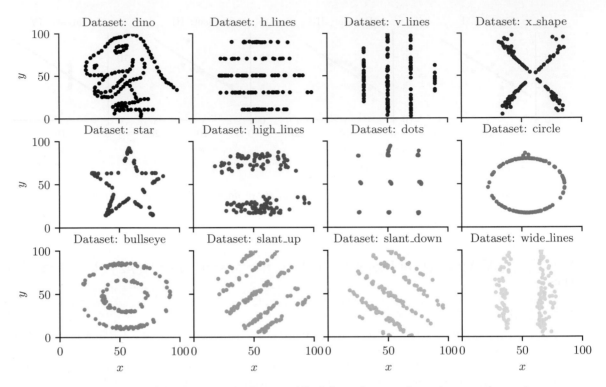

Figure 2.6: Illustration of the Datasaurus Dozen. All of these datasets have the same low order summary statistics. Adapted from Figure 1 of [MF17]. Generated by datasaurus_dozen.ipynb.

function being optimized measures deviation from the target summary statistics of the original dinosaur, plus distance from a particular target shape.)

The same simulated annealing approach can be applied to 1d datasets, as shown in Figure 2.7. We see that all the datasets are quite different, but they all have the same median and **inter-quartile range** as shown by the central shaded part of the **box plots** in the middle. A better visualization is known as a **violin plot**, shown on the right. This shows (two copies of) the 1d kernel density estimate (Section 16.3) of the distribution on the vertical axis, in addition to the median and IQR markers. This visualization is better able to distinguish differences in the distributions. However, the technique is limited to 1d data.

2.3   Bayes' rule

Bayes's theorem is to the theory of probability what Pythagoras's theorem is to geometry.
— Sir Harold Jeffreys, 1973 [Jef73].

In this section, we discuss the basics of **Bayesian inference**. According to the Merriam-Webster dictionary, the term "inference" means "the act of passing from sample data to generalizations, usually with calculated degrees of certainty". The term "Bayesian" is used to refer to inference methods

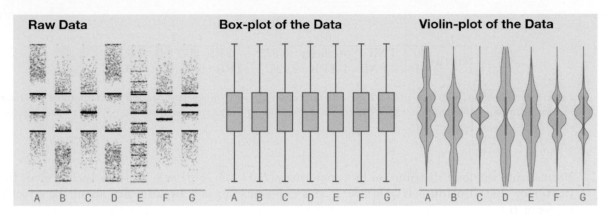

Figure 2.7: Illustration of 7 different datasets (left), the corresponding box plots (middle) and violin box plots (right). From Figure 8 of https://www.autodesk.com/research/publications/same-stats-different-graphs. Used with kind permission of Justin Matejka.

that represent "degrees of certainty" using probability theory, and which leverage **Bayes' rule**[7], to update the degree of certainty given data.

Bayes' rule itself is very simple: it is just a formula for computing the probability distribution over possible values of an unknown (or **hidden**) quantity H given some observed data $Y = y$:

$$p(H = h|Y = y) = \frac{p(H = h)p(Y = y|H = h)}{p(Y = y)} \tag{2.51}$$

This follows automatically from the identity

$$p(h|y)p(y) = p(h)p(y|h) = p(h, y) \tag{2.52}$$

which itself follows from the **product rule of probability**.

In Equation (2.51), the term $p(H)$ represents what we know about possible values of H before we see any data; this is called the **prior distribution**. (If H has K possible values, then $p(H)$ is a vector of K probabilities, that sum to 1.) The term $p(Y|H = h)$ represents the distribution over the possible outcomes Y we expect to see if $H = h$; this is called the **observation distribution**. When we evaluate this at a point corresponding to the actual observations, y, we get the function $p(Y = y|H = h)$, which is called the **likelihood**. (Note that this is a function of h, since y is fixed, but it is not a probability distribution, since it does not sum to one.) Multiplying the prior distribution $p(H = h)$ by the likelihood function $p(Y = y|H = h)$ for each h gives the unnormalized joint distribution $p(H = h, Y = y)$. We can convert this into a normalized distribution by dividing by $p(Y = y)$, which is known as the **marginal likelihood**, since it is computed by marginalizing over the unknown H:

$$p(Y = y) = \sum_{h' \in \mathcal{H}} p(H = h')p(Y = y|H = h') = \sum_{h' \in \mathcal{H}} p(H = h', Y = y) \tag{2.53}$$

---

7. Thomas Bayes (1702–1761) was an English mathematician and Presbyterian minister. For a discussion of whether to spell this as Bayes rule, Bayes' rule or Bayes's rule, see https://bit.ly/2kDtLuK.

		Observation	
		0	1
Truth	0	TNR=Specificity=0.975	FPR=1-TNR=0.025
	1	FNR=1-TPR=0.125	TPR=Sensitivity=0.875

Table 2.1: *Likelihood function $p(Y|H)$ for a binary observation Y given two possible hidden states H. Each row sums to one. Abbreviations: TNR is true negative rate, TPR is true positive rate, FNR is false negative rate, FPR is false positive rate.*

Normalizing the joint distribution by computing $p(H = h, Y = y)/p(Y = y)$ for each h gives the **posterior distribution** $p(H = h|Y = y)$; this represents our new **belief state** about the possible values of H.

We can summarize Bayes rule in words as follows:

$$\text{posterior} \propto \text{prior} \times \text{likelihood} \tag{2.54}$$

Here we use the symbol $\propto$ to denote "proportional to", since we are ignoring the denominator, which is just a constant, independent of H. Using Bayes rule to update a distribution over unknown values of some quantity of interest, given relevant observed data, is called **Bayesian inference**, or **posterior inference**. It can also just be called **probabilistic inference**.

Below we give some simple examples of Bayesian inference in action. We will see many more interesting examples later in this book.

2.3.1   Example: Testing for COVID-19

Suppose you think you may have contracted **COVID-19**, which is an infectious disease caused by the **SARS-CoV-2** virus. You decide to take a diagnostic test, and you want to use its result to determine if you are infected or not.

Let $H = 1$ be the event that you are infected, and $H = 0$ be the event you are not infected. Let $Y = 1$ if the test is positive, and $Y = 0$ if the test is negative. We want to compute $p(H = h|Y = y)$, for $h \in \{0, 1\}$, where y is the observed test outcome. (We will write the distribution of values, $[p(H = 0|Y = y), p(H = 1|Y = y)]$ as $p(H|y)$, for brevity.) We can think of this as a form of **binary classification**, where H is the unknown class label, and y is the feature vector.

First we must specify the likelihood. This quantity obviously depends on how reliable the test is. There are two key parameters. The **sensitivity** (aka **true positive rate**) is defined as $p(Y = 1|H = 1)$, i.e., the probability of a positive test given that the truth is positive. The **false negative rate** is defined as one minus the sensitivity. The **specificity** (aka **true negative rate**) is defined as $p(Y = 0|H = 0)$, i.e., the probability of a negative test given that the truth is negative. The **false positive rate** is defined as one minus the specificity. We summarize all these quantities in Table 2.1. (See Section 5.1.3.1 for more details.) Following https://nyti.ms/31MTZgV, we set the sensitivity to 87.5% and the specificity to 97.5%.

Next we must specify the prior. The quantity $p(H = 1)$ represents the **prevalence** of the disease in the area in which you live. We set this to $p(H = 1) = 0.1$ (i.e., 10%), which was the prevalence in New York City in Spring 2020. (This example was chosen to match the numbers in https://nyti.ms/31MTZgV.)

Now suppose you test positive. We have

$$p(H = 1|Y = 1) = \frac{p(Y = 1|H = 1)p(H = 1)}{p(Y = 1|H = 1)p(H = 1) + p(Y = 1|H = 0)p(H = 0)} \tag{2.55}$$

$$= \frac{\text{TPR} \times \text{prior}}{\text{TPR} \times \text{prior} + \text{FPR} \times (1 - \text{prior})} \tag{2.56}$$

$$= \frac{0.875 \times 0.1}{0.875 \times 0.1 + 0.025 \times 0.9} = 0.795 \tag{2.57}$$

So there is a 79.5% chance you are infected.

Now suppose you test negative. The probability you are infected is given by

$$p(H = 1|Y = 0) = \frac{p(Y = 0|H = 1)p(H = 1)}{p(Y = 0|H = 1)p(H = 1) + p(Y = 0|H = 0)p(H = 0)} \tag{2.58}$$

$$= \frac{\text{FNR} \times \text{prior}}{\text{FNR} \times \text{prior} + \text{TNR} \times (1 - \text{prior})} \tag{2.59}$$

$$= \frac{0.125 \times 0.1}{0.125 \times 0.1 + 0.975 \times 0.9} = 0.014 \tag{2.60}$$

So there is just a 1.4% chance you are infected.

Nowadays COVID-19 prevalence is much lower. Suppose we repeat these calculations using a base rate of 1%; now the posteriors reduce to 26% and 0.13% respectively.

The fact that you only have a 26% chance of being infected with COVID-19, even after a positive test, is very counter-intuitive. The reason is that a single positive test is more likely to be a false positive than due to the disease, since the disease is rare. To see this, suppose we have a population of 100,000 people, of whom 1000 are infected. Of those who are infected, $875 = 0.875 \times 1000$ test positive, and of those who are uninfected, $2475 = 0.025 \times 99,000$ test positive. Thus the total number of positives is $3350 = 875 + 2475$, so the posterior probability of being infected given a positive test is $875/3350 = 0.26$.

Of course, the above calculations assume we know the sensitivity and specificity of the test. See [GC20] for how to apply Bayes rule for diagnostic testing when there is uncertainty about these parameters.

2.3.2 Example: The Monty Hall problem

In this section, we consider a more "frivolous" application of Bayes rule. In particular, we apply it to the famous **Monty Hall problem**.

Imagine a game show with the following rules: There are three doors, labeled 1, 2, 3. A single prize (e.g., a car) has been hidden behind one of them. You get to select one door. Then the gameshow host opens one of the other two doors (not the one you picked), in such a way as to not reveal the prize location. At this point, you will be given a fresh choice of door: you can either stick with your first choice, or you can switch to the other closed door. All the doors will then be opened and you will receive whatever is behind your final choice of door.

For example, suppose you choose door 1, and the gameshow host opens door 3, revealing nothing behind the door, as promised. Should you (a) stick with door 1, or (b) switch to door 2, or (c) does it make no difference?

Door 1	Door 2	Door 3	Switch	Stay
Car	-	-	Lose	Win
-	Car	-	Win	Lose
-	-	Car	Win	Lose

Table 2.2: *3 possible states for the Monty Hall game, showing that switching doors is two times better (on average) than staying with your original choice. Adapted from Table 6.1 of [PM18].*

Intuitively, it seems it should make no difference, since your initial choice of door cannot influence the location of the prize. However, the fact that the host opened door 3 tells us something about the location of the prize, since he made his choice conditioned on the knowledge of the true location and on your choice. As we show below, you are in fact twice as likely to win the prize if you switch to door 2.

To show this, we will use Bayes' rule. Let H_i denote the hypothesis that the prize is behind door i. We make the following assumptions: the three hypotheses H_1, H_2 and H_3 are equiprobable *a priori*, i.e.,

$$P(H_1) = P(H_2) = P(H_3) = \frac{1}{3}. \tag{2.61}$$

The datum we receive, after choosing door 1, is either $Y = 3$ and $Y = 2$ (meaning door 3 or 2 is opened, respectively). We assume that these two possible outcomes have the following probabilities. If the prize is behind door 1, then the host selects at random between $Y = 2$ and $Y = 3$. Otherwise the choice of the host is forced and the probabilities are 0 and 1.

$$\left| \begin{array}{c|c|c} P(Y=2|H_1)=\frac{1}{2} & P(Y=2|H_2)=0 & P(Y=2|H_3)=1 \\ P(Y=3|H_1)=\frac{1}{2} & P(Y=3|H_2)=1 & P(Y=3|H_3)=0 \end{array} \right| \tag{2.62}$$

Now, using Bayes' theorem, we evaluate the posterior probabilities of the hypotheses:

$$P(H_i|Y=3) = \frac{P(Y=3|H_i)P(H_i)}{P(Y=3)} \tag{2.63}$$

$$\left| P(H_1|Y=3)=\frac{(1/2)(1/3)}{P(Y=3)} \right| P(H_2|Y=3)=\frac{(1)(1/3)}{P(Y=3)} \left| P(H_3|Y=3)=\frac{(0)(1/3)}{P(Y=3)} \right| \tag{2.64}$$

The denominator $P(Y=3)$ is $P(Y=3) = \frac{1}{6} + \frac{1}{3} = \frac{1}{2}$. So

$$\left| P(H_1|Y=3) \quad = \quad \frac{1}{3} \right| P(H_2|Y=3) \quad = \quad \frac{2}{3} \left| P(H_3|Y=3) \quad = \quad 0. \right| \tag{2.65}$$

So the contestant should switch to door 2 in order to have the biggest chance of getting the prize. See Table 2.2 for a worked example.

Many people find this outcome surprising. One way to make it more intuitive is to perform a thought experiment in which the game is played with a million doors. The rules are now that the contestant chooses one door, then the game show host opens 999,998 doors in such a way as not to reveal the prize, leaving the *contestant's* selected door and *one other door* closed. The contestant may now stick or switch. Imagine the contestant confronted by a million doors, of which doors 1 and 234,598 have not been opened, door 1 having been the contestant's initial guess. Where do you think the prize is?

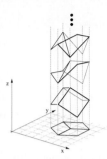

Figure 2.8: Any planar line-drawing is geometrically consistent with infinitely many 3-D structures. From Figure 11 of [SA93]. Used with kind permission of Pawan Sinha.

2.3.3 Inverse problems *

Probability theory is concerned with predicting a distribution over outcomes y given knowledge (or assumptions) about the state of the world, h. By contrast, **inverse probability** is concerned with inferring the state of the world from observations of outcomes. We can think of this as inverting the $h \rightarrow y$ mapping.

For example, consider trying to infer a 3d shape h from a 2d image y, which is a classic problem in **visual scene understanding**. Unfortunately, this is a fundamentally **ill-posed** problem, as illustrated in Figure 2.8, since there are multiple possible hidden h's consistent with the same observed y (see e.g., [Piz01]). Similarly, we can view **natural language understanding** as an ill-posed problem, in which the listener must infer the intention h from the (often ambiguous) words spoken by the speaker (see e.g., [Sab21]).

To tackle such **inverse problems**, we can use Bayes' rule to compute the posterior, $p(h|y)$, which gives a distribution over possible states of the world. This requires specifying the **forwards model**, $p(y|h)$, as well as a prior $p(h)$, which can be used to rule out (or downweight) implausible world states. We discuss this topic in more detail in the sequel to this book, [Mur23].

2.4 Bernoulli and binomial distributions

Perhaps the simplest probability distribution is the **Bernoulli distribution**, which can be used to model binary events, as we discuss below.

2.4.1 Definition

Consider tossing a coin, where the probability of event that it lands heads is given by $0 \le \theta \le 1$. Let $Y = 1$ denote this event, and let $Y = 0$ denote the event that the coin lands tails. Thus we are assuming that $p(Y = 1) = \theta$ and $p(Y = 0) = 1 - \theta$. This is called the **Bernoulli distribution**, and can be written as follows

$$Y \sim \text{Ber}(\theta) \tag{2.66}$$

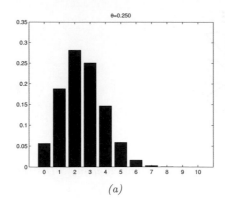
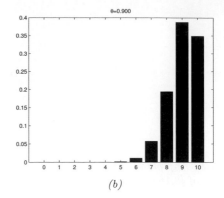

Figure 2.9: Illustration of the binomial distribution with $N = 10$ and (a) $\theta = 0.25$ and (b) $\theta = 0.9$. Generated by binom_ dist_ plot.ipynb.

where the symbol $\sim$ means "is sampled from" or "is distributed as", and Ber refers to Bernoulli. The probability mass function (pmf) of this distribution is defined as follows:

$$\text{Ber}(y|\theta) = \begin{cases} 1 - \theta & \text{if } y = 0 \\ \theta & \text{if } y = 1 \end{cases} \tag{2.67}$$

(See Section 2.2.1 for details on pmf's.) We can write this in a more concise manner as follows:

$$\text{Ber}(y|\theta) \triangleq \theta^y (1 - \theta)^{1-y} \tag{2.68}$$

The Bernoulli distribution is a special case of the **binomial distribution**. To explain this, suppose we observe a set of N Bernoulli trials, denoted $y_n \sim \text{Ber}(\cdot|\theta)$, for $n = 1 : N$. Concretely, think of tossing a coin N times. Let us define s to be the total number of heads, $s \triangleq \sum_{n=1}^{N} \mathbb{I}(y_n = 1)$. The distribution of s is given by the binomial distribution:

$$\text{Bin}(s|N, \theta) \triangleq \binom{N}{s} \theta^s (1 - \theta)^{N-s} \tag{2.69}$$

where

$$\binom{N}{k} \triangleq \frac{N!}{(N - k)!k!} \tag{2.70}$$

is the number of ways to choose k items from N (this is known as the **binomial coefficient**, and is pronounced "N choose k"). See Figure 2.9 for some examples of the binomial distribution. If $N = 1$, the binomial distribution reduces to the Bernoulli distribution.

2.4.2 Sigmoid (logistic) function

When we want to predict a binary variable $y \in \{0, 1\}$ given some inputs $\boldsymbol{x} \in \mathcal{X}$, we need to use a **conditional probability distribution** of the form

$$p(y|\boldsymbol{x}, \boldsymbol{\theta}) = \text{Ber}(y|f(\boldsymbol{x}; \boldsymbol{\theta})) \tag{2.71}$$

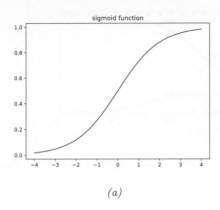
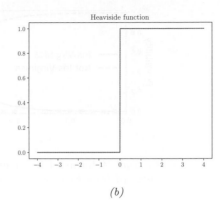

(a)   (b)

Figure 2.10: (a) The sigmoid (logistic) function $\sigma(a) = (1 + e^{-a})^{-1}$. (b) The Heaviside function $\mathbb{I}(a > 0)$. Generated by activation_fun_plot.ipynb.

$$\sigma(x) \triangleq \frac{1}{1 + e^{-x}} = \frac{e^x}{1 + e^x} \tag{2.72}$$

$$\frac{d}{dx}\sigma(x) = \sigma(x)(1 - \sigma(x)) \tag{2.73}$$

$$1 - \sigma(x) = \sigma(-x) \tag{2.74}$$

$$\sigma^{-1}(p) = \log\left(\frac{p}{1 - p}\right) \triangleq \text{logit}(p) \tag{2.75}$$

$$\sigma_+(x) \triangleq \log(1 + e^x) \triangleq \text{softplus}(x) \tag{2.76}$$

$$\frac{d}{dx}\sigma_+(x) = \sigma(x) \tag{2.77}$$

Table 2.3: Some useful properties of the sigmoid (logistic) and related functions. Note that the **logit** *function is the inverse of the sigmoid function, and has a domain of $[0, 1]$.*

where $f(\boldsymbol{x}; \boldsymbol{\theta})$ is some function that predicts the mean parameter of the output distribution. We will consider many different kinds of function f in Part II–Part IV.

To avoid the requirement that $0 \le f(\boldsymbol{x}; \boldsymbol{\theta}) \le 1$, we can let f be an unconstrained function, and use the following model:

$$p(y|\boldsymbol{x}, \boldsymbol{\theta}) = \text{Ber}(y|\sigma(f(\boldsymbol{x}; \boldsymbol{\theta}))) \tag{2.78}$$

Here $\sigma()$ is the **sigmoid** or **logistic** function, defined as follows:

$$\sigma(a) \triangleq \frac{1}{1 + e^{-a}} \tag{2.79}$$

where $a = f(\boldsymbol{x}; \boldsymbol{\theta})$. The term "sigmoid" means S-shaped: see Figure 2.10a for a plot. We see that it

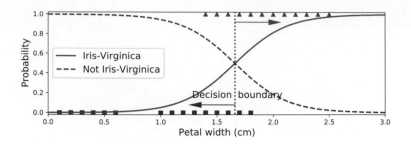

Figure 2.11: Logistic regression applied to a 1-dimensional, 2-class version of the Iris dataset. Generated by iris_logreg.ipynb. Adapted from Figure 4.23 of [Gér19].

maps the whole real line to $[0, 1]$, which is necessary for the output to be interpreted as a probability (and hence a valid value for the Bernoulli parameter θ). The sigmoid function can be thought of as a "soft" version of the **heaviside step function**, defined by

$$H(a) \triangleq \mathbb{I}(a > 0) \tag{2.80}$$

as shown in Figure 2.10b.

Plugging the definition of the sigmoid function into Equation (2.78) we get

$$p(y = 1|\boldsymbol{x}, \boldsymbol{\theta}) = \frac{1}{1 + e^{-a}} = \frac{e^a}{1 + e^a} = \sigma(a) \tag{2.81}$$

$$p(y = 0|\boldsymbol{x}, \boldsymbol{\theta}) = 1 - \frac{1}{1 + e^{-a}} = \frac{e^{-a}}{1 + e^{-a}} = \frac{1}{1 + e^a} = \sigma(-a) \tag{2.82}$$

The quantity a is equal to the **log odds**, $\log(\frac{p}{1-p})$, where $p = p(y = 1|\boldsymbol{x}; \boldsymbol{\theta})$. To see this, note that

$$\log\left(\frac{p}{1-p}\right) = \log\left(\frac{e^a}{1 + e^a} \frac{1 + e^a}{1}\right) = \log(e^a) = a \tag{2.83}$$

The **logistic function** or **sigmoid** function maps the log-odds a to p:

$$p = \text{logistic}(a) = \sigma(a) \triangleq \frac{1}{1 + e^{-a}} = \frac{e^a}{1 + e^a} \tag{2.84}$$

The inverse of this is called the **logit function**, and maps p to the log-odds a:

$$a = \text{logit}(p) = \sigma^{-1}(p) \triangleq \log\left(\frac{p}{1-p}\right) \tag{2.85}$$

See Table 2.3 for some useful properties of these functions.

2.4.3 Binary logistic regression

In this section, we use a conditional Bernoulli model, where we use a linear predictor of the form $f(\boldsymbol{x}; \boldsymbol{\theta}) = \boldsymbol{w}^\mathsf{T}\boldsymbol{x} + b$. Thus the model has the form

$$p(y|\boldsymbol{x}; \boldsymbol{\theta}) = \text{Ber}(y|\sigma(\boldsymbol{w}^\mathsf{T}\boldsymbol{x} + b)) \tag{2.86}$$

In other words,

$$p(y = 1|\boldsymbol{x}; \boldsymbol{\theta}) = \sigma(\boldsymbol{w}^\mathsf{T}\boldsymbol{x} + b) = \frac{1}{1 + e^{-(\boldsymbol{w}^\mathsf{T}\boldsymbol{x} + b)}} \tag{2.87}$$

This is called **logistic regression**.

For example consider a 1-dimensional, 2-class version of the iris dataset, where the positive class is "Virginica" and the negative class is "not Virginica", and the feature x we use is the petal width. We fit a logistic regression model to this and show the results in Figure 2.11. The **decision boundary** corresponds to the value x^* where $p(y = 1|x = x^*, \boldsymbol{\theta}) = 0.5$. We see that, in this example, $x^* \approx 1.7$. As x moves away from this boundary, the classifier becomes more confident in its prediction about the class label.

It should be clear from this example why it would be inappropriate to use linear regression for a (binary) classification problem. In such a model, the probabilities would increase above 1 as we move far enough to the right, and below 0 as we move far enough to the left.

For more detail on logistic regression, see Chapter 10.

2.5 Categorical and multinomial distributions

To represent a distribution over a finite set of labels, $y \in \{1, \dots, C\}$, we can use the **categorical** distribution, which generalizes the Bernoulli to $C > 2$ values.

2.5.1 Definition

The categorical distribution is a discrete probability distribution with one parameter per class:

$$\text{Cat}(y|\boldsymbol{\theta}) \triangleq \prod_{c=1}^{C} \theta_c^{\mathbb{I}(y=c)} \tag{2.88}$$

In other words, $p(y = c|\boldsymbol{\theta}) = \theta_c$. Note that the parameters are constrained so that $0 \le \theta_c \le 1$ and $\sum_{c=1}^{C} \theta_c = 1$; thus there are only $C - 1$ independent parameters.

We can write the categorical distribution in another way by converting the discrete variable y into a **one-hot vector** with C elements, all of which are 0 except for the entry corresponding to the class label. (The term "one-hot" arises from electrical engineering, where binary vectors are encoded as electrical current on a set of wires, which can be active ("hot") or not ("cold").) For example, if $C = 3$, we encode the classes 1, 2 and 3 as $(1, 0, 0)$, $(0, 1, 0)$, and $(0, 0, 1)$. More generally, we can encode the classes using **unit vectors**, where $\boldsymbol{e}_c$ is all 0s except for dimension c. (This is also called a **dummy encoding**.) Using one-hot encodings, we can write the categorical distribution as follows:

$$\text{Cat}(\boldsymbol{y}|\boldsymbol{\theta}) \triangleq \prod_{c=1}^{C} \theta_c^{y_c} \tag{2.89}$$

The categorical distribution is a special case of the **multinomial distribution**. To explain this, suppose we observe N categorical trials, $y_n \sim \text{Cat}(\cdot|\boldsymbol{\theta})$, for $n = 1 : N$. Concretely, think of rolling a C-sided dice N times. Let us define $\boldsymbol{y}$ to be a vector that counts the number of times each face

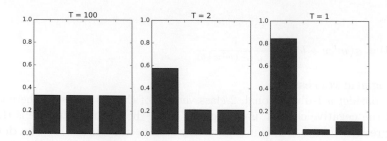

Figure 2.12: Softmax distribution $\mathrm{softmax}(\boldsymbol{a}/T)$, *where* $\boldsymbol{a} = (3, 0, 1)$, *at temperatures of* $T = 100$, $T = 2$ *and* $T = 1$. *When the temperature is high (left), the distribution is uniform, whereas when the temperature is low (right), the distribution is "spiky", with most of its mass on the largest element. Generated by* softmax_plot.ipynb.

shows up, i.e., $y_c = N_c \triangleq \sum_{n=1}^{N} \mathbb{I}(y_n = c)$. Now $\boldsymbol{y}$ is no longer one-hot, but is "multi-hot", since it has a non-zero entry for every value of c that was observed across all N trials. The distribution of $\boldsymbol{y}$ is given by the **multinomial distribution**:

$$\mathcal{M}(\boldsymbol{y}|N, \boldsymbol{\theta}) \triangleq \binom{N}{y_1 \ldots y_C} \prod_{c=1}^{C} \theta_c^{y_c} = \binom{N}{N_1 \ldots N_C} \prod_{c=1}^{C} \theta_c^{N_c} \tag{2.90}$$

where θ_c is the probability that side c shows up, and

$$\binom{N}{N_1 \ldots N_C} \triangleq \frac{N!}{N_1! N_2! \cdots N_C!} \tag{2.91}$$

is the **multinomial coefficient**, which is the number of ways to divide a set of size $N = \sum_{c=1}^{C} N_c$ into subsets with sizes N_1 up to N_C. If $N = 1$, the multinomial distribution becomes the categorical distribution.

2.5.2   Softmax function

In the conditional case, we can define

$$p(y|\boldsymbol{x}, \boldsymbol{\theta}) = \mathrm{Cat}(y|f(\boldsymbol{x}; \boldsymbol{\theta})) \tag{2.92}$$

which we can also write as

$$p(y|\boldsymbol{x}, \boldsymbol{\theta}) = \mathcal{M}(\boldsymbol{y}|1, f(\boldsymbol{x}; \boldsymbol{\theta})) \tag{2.93}$$

We require that $0 \le f_c(\boldsymbol{x}; \boldsymbol{\theta}) \le 1$ and $\sum_{c=1}^{C} f_c(\boldsymbol{x}; \boldsymbol{\theta}) = 1$.

To avoid the requirement that f directly predict a probability vector, it is common to pass the output from f into the **softmax** function [Bri90], also called the **multinomial logit**. This is defined as follows:

$$\mathrm{softmax}(\boldsymbol{a}) \triangleq \left[\frac{e^{a_1}}{\sum_{c'=1}^{C} e^{a_{c'}}}, \ldots, \frac{e^{a_C}}{\sum_{c'=1}^{C} e^{a_{c'}}} \right] \tag{2.94}$$

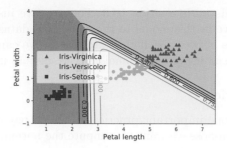

Figure 2.13: Logistic regression on the 3-class, 2-feature version of the Iris dataset. Adapted from Figure of 4.25 [Gér19]. Generated by iris_logreg.ipynb.

This maps $\mathbb{R}^C$ to $[0,1]^C$, and satisfies the constraints that $0 \leq \text{softmax}(\boldsymbol{a})_c \leq 1$ and $\sum_{c=1}^{C} \text{softmax}(\boldsymbol{a})_c = 1$. The inputs to the softmax, $\boldsymbol{a} = f(\boldsymbol{x}; \boldsymbol{\theta})$, are called **logits**, and are a generalization of the log odds.

The softmax function is so-called since it acts a bit like the argmax function. To see this, let us divide each a_c by a constant T called the **temperature**.[8] Then as $T \to 0$, we find

$$\text{softmax}(\boldsymbol{a}/T)_c = \begin{cases} 1.0 & \text{if } c = \text{argmax}_{c'} \, a_{c'} \\ 0.0 & \text{otherwise} \end{cases} \tag{2.95}$$

In other words, at low temperatures, the distribution puts most of its probability mass in the most probable state (this is called **winner takes all**), whereas at high temperatures, it spreads the mass uniformly. See Figure 2.12 for an illustration.

2.5.3 Multiclass logistic regression

If we use a linear predictor of the form $f(\boldsymbol{x}; \boldsymbol{\theta}) = \mathbf{W}\boldsymbol{x} + \boldsymbol{b}$, where $\mathbf{W}$ is a $C \times D$ matrix, and $\boldsymbol{b}$ is a C-dimensional bias vector, the final model becomes

$$p(y|\boldsymbol{x}; \boldsymbol{\theta}) = \text{Cat}(y|\text{softmax}(\mathbf{W}\boldsymbol{x} + \boldsymbol{b})) \tag{2.96}$$

Let $\boldsymbol{a} = \mathbf{W}\boldsymbol{x} + \boldsymbol{b}$ be the C-dimensional vector of **logits**. Then we can rewrite the above as follows:

$$p(y = c|\boldsymbol{x}; \boldsymbol{\theta}) = \frac{e^{a_c}}{\sum_{c'=1}^{C} e^{a_{c'}}} \tag{2.97}$$

This is known as **multinomial logistic regression**.

If we have just two classes, this reduces to binary logistic regression. To see this, note that

$$\text{softmax}(\boldsymbol{a})_0 = \frac{e^{a_0}}{e^{a_0} + e^{a_1}} = \frac{1}{1 + e^{a_1 - a_0}} = \sigma(a_0 - a_1) \tag{2.98}$$

so we can just train the model to predict $a = a_1 - a_0$. This can be done with a single weight vector $\boldsymbol{w}$; if we use the multi-class formulation, we will have two weight vectors, $\boldsymbol{w}_0$ and $\boldsymbol{w}_1$. Such a model is **over-parameterized**, which can hurt interpretability, but the predictions will be the same.

---

8. This terminology comes from the area of statistical physics. The **Boltzmann distribution** is a distribution over states which has the same form as the softmax function.

We discuss this in more detail in Section 10.3. For now, we just give an example. Figure 2.13 shows what happens when we fit this model to the 3-class iris dataset, using just 2 features. We see that the decision boundaries between each class are linear. We can create nonlinear boundaries by transforming the features (e.g., using polynomials), as we discuss in Section 10.3.1.

2.5.4 Log-sum-exp trick

In this section, we discuss one important practical detail to pay attention to when working with the softmax distribution. Suppose we want to compute the normalized probability $p_c = p(y = c|\boldsymbol{x})$, which is given by

$$p_c = \frac{e^{a_c}}{Z(\boldsymbol{a})} = \frac{e^{a_c}}{\sum_{c'=1}^{C} e^{a_{c'}}} \tag{2.99}$$

where $\boldsymbol{a} = f(\boldsymbol{x}; \boldsymbol{\theta})$ are the logits. We might encounter numerical problems when computing the **partition function** Z. For example, suppose we have 3 classes, with logits $\boldsymbol{a} = (0, 1, 0)$. Then we find $Z = e^0 + e^1 + e^0 = 4.71$. But now suppose $\boldsymbol{a} = (1000, 1001, 1000)$; we find $Z = \infty$, since on a computer, even using 64 bit precision, `np.exp(1000)=inf`. Similarly, suppose $\boldsymbol{a} = (-1000, -999, -1000)$; now we find $Z = 0$, since `np.exp(-1000)=0`. To avoid numerical problems, we can use the following identity:

$$\log \sum_{c=1}^{C} \exp(a_c) = m + \log \sum_{c=1}^{C} \exp(a_c - m) \tag{2.100}$$

This holds for any m. It is common to use $m = \max_c a_c$ which ensures that the largest value you exponentiate will be zero, so you will definitely not overflow, and even if you underflow, the answer will be sensible. This is known as the **log-sum-exp trick**. We use this trick when implementing the **lse** function:

$$\text{lse}(\boldsymbol{a}) \triangleq \log \sum_{c=1}^{C} \exp(a_c) \tag{2.101}$$

We can use this to compute the probabilities from the logits:

$$p(y = c|\boldsymbol{x}) = \exp(a_c - \text{lse}(\boldsymbol{a})) \tag{2.102}$$

We can then pass this to the cross-entropy loss, defined in Equation (5.41).

However, to save computational effort, and for numerical stability, it is quite common to modify the cross-entropy loss so that it takes the logits $\boldsymbol{a}$ as inputs, instead of the probability vector $\boldsymbol{p}$. For example, consider the binary case. The CE loss for one example is

$$\mathcal{L} = -\left[\mathbb{I}(y = 0) \log p_0 + \mathbb{I}(y = 1) \log p_1 \right] \tag{2.103}$$

where

$$\log p_1 = \log \left(\frac{1}{1 + \exp(-a)} \right) = \log(1) - \log(1 + \exp(-a)) = 0 - \text{lse}([0, -a]) \tag{2.104}$$

$$\log p_0 = 0 - \text{lse}([0, +a]) \tag{2.105}$$

2.6 Univariate Gaussian (normal) distribution

The most widely used distribution of real-valued random variables $y \in \mathbb{R}$ is the **Gaussian distribution**, also called the **normal distribution** (see Section 2.6.4 for a discussion of these names).

2.6.1 Cumulative distribution function

We define the **cumulative distribution function** or **cdf** of a continuous random variable Y as follows:

$$P(y) \triangleq \Pr(Y \leq y) \tag{2.106}$$

(Note that we use a capital P to represent the cdf.) Using this, we can compute the probability of being in any interval as follows:

$$\Pr(a < Y \leq b) = P(b) - P(a) \tag{2.107}$$

Cdf's are monotonically non-decreasing functions.

The cdf of the Gaussian is defined by

$$\Phi(y; \mu, \sigma^2) \triangleq \int_{-\infty}^{y} \mathcal{N}(z|\mu, \sigma^2) dz \tag{2.108}$$

See Figure 2.2a for a plot. Note that the cdf of the Gaussian is often implemented using $\Phi(y; \mu, \sigma^2) = \frac{1}{2}[1 + \text{erf}(z/\sqrt{2})]$, where $z = (y - \mu)/\sigma$ and $\text{erf}(u)$ is the **error function**, defined as

$$\text{erf}(u) \triangleq \frac{2}{\sqrt{\pi}} \int_{0}^{u} e^{-t^2} dt \tag{2.109}$$

The parameter μ encodes the mean of the distribution; in the case of a Gaussian, this is also the same as the mode. The parameter σ^2 encodes the variance. (Sometimes we talk about the **precision** of a Gaussian, which is the inverse variance, denoted $\lambda = 1/\sigma^2$.) When $\mu = 0$ and $\sigma = 1$, the Gaussian is called the **standard normal** distribution.

If P is the cdf of Y, then $P^{-1}(q)$ is the value y_q such that $p(Y \leq y_q) = q$; this is called the q'th **quantile** of P. The value $P^{-1}(0.5)$ is the **median** of the distribution, with half of the probability mass on the left, and half on the right. The values $P^{-1}(0.25)$ and $P^{-1}(0.75)$ are the lower and upper **quartiles**.

For example, let Φ be the cdf of the Gaussian distribution $\mathcal{N}(0, 1)$, and Φ^{-1} be the inverse cdf (also known as the **probit function**). Then points to the left of $\Phi^{-1}(\alpha/2)$ contain $\alpha/2$ of the probability mass, as illustrated in Figure 2.2b. By symmetry, points to the right of $\Phi^{-1}(1 - \alpha/2)$ also contain $\alpha/2$ of the mass. Hence the central interval $(\Phi^{-1}(\alpha/2), \Phi^{-1}(1 - \alpha/2))$ contains $1 - \alpha$ of the mass. If we set $\alpha = 0.05$, the central 95% interval is covered by the range

$$(\Phi^{-1}(0.025), \Phi^{-1}(0.975)) = (-1.96, 1.96) \tag{2.110}$$

If the distribution is $\mathcal{N}(\mu, \sigma^2)$, then the 95% interval becomes $(\mu - 1.96\sigma, \mu + 1.96\sigma)$. This is often approximated by writing $\mu \pm 2\sigma$.

2.6.2 Probability density function

We define the **probability density function** or **pdf** as the derivative of the cdf:

$$p(y) \triangleq \frac{d}{dy} P(y) \tag{2.111}$$

The pdf of the Gaussian is given by

$$\mathcal{N}(y|\mu, \sigma^2) \triangleq \frac{1}{\sqrt{2\pi\sigma^2}} e^{-\frac{1}{2\sigma^2}(y-\mu)^2} \tag{2.112}$$

where $\sqrt{2\pi\sigma^2}$ is the normalization constant needed to ensure the density integrates to 1 (see Exercise 2.12). See Figure 2.2b for a plot.

Given a pdf, we can compute the probability of a continuous variable being in a finite interval as follows:

$$\Pr(a < Y \le b) = \int_a^b p(y) dy = P(b) - P(a) \tag{2.113}$$

As the size of the interval gets smaller, we can write

$$\Pr(y \le Y \le y + dy) \approx p(y) dy \tag{2.114}$$

Intuitively, this says the probability of Y being in a small interval around y is the density at y times the width of the interval. One important consequence of the above result is that the pdf at a point can be larger than 1. For example, $\mathcal{N}(0|0, 0.1) = 3.99$.

We can use the pdf to compute the **mean**, or **expected value**, of the distribution:

$$\mathbb{E}[Y] \triangleq \int_{\mathcal{Y}} y \, p(y) dy \tag{2.115}$$

For a Gaussian, we have the familiar result that $\mathbb{E}\left[\mathcal{N}(\cdot|\mu, \sigma^2)\right] = \mu$. (Note, however, that for some distributions, this integral is not finite, so the mean is not defined.)

We can also use the pdf to compute the **variance** of a distribution. This is a measure of the "spread", and is often denoted by σ^2. The variance is defined as follows:

$$\mathbb{V}[Y] \triangleq \mathbb{E}\left[(Y - \mu)^2\right] = \int (y - \mu)^2 p(y) dy \tag{2.116}$$

$$= \int y^2 p(y) dy + \mu^2 \int p(y) dy - 2\mu \int y p(y) dy = \mathbb{E}\left[Y^2\right] - \mu^2 \tag{2.117}$$

from which we derive the useful result

$$\mathbb{E}\left[Y^2\right] = \sigma^2 + \mu^2 \tag{2.118}$$

The **standard deviation** is defined as

$$\operatorname{std}[Y] \triangleq \sqrt{\mathbb{V}[Y]} = \sigma \tag{2.119}$$

(The standard deviation can be more intepretable than the variance since it has the same units as Y itself.) For a Gaussian, we have the familiar result that $\operatorname{std}\left[\mathcal{N}(\cdot|\mu, \sigma^2)\right] = \sigma$.

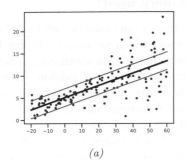
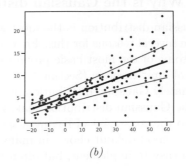

(a)   (b)

Figure 2.14: Linear regression using Gaussian output with mean $\mu(x) = b + wx$ and (a) fixed variance σ^2 (homoskedastic) or (b) input-dependent variance $\sigma(x)^2$ (heteroscedastic). Generated by linreg_1d_hetero_tfp.ipynb.

2.6.3 Regression

So far we have been considering the unconditional Gaussian distribution. In some cases, it is helpful to make the parameters of the Gaussian be functions of some input variables, i.e., we want to create a conditional density model of the form

$$p(y|\boldsymbol{x};\boldsymbol{\theta}) = \mathcal{N}(y|f_\mu(\boldsymbol{x};\boldsymbol{\theta}), f_\sigma(\boldsymbol{x};\boldsymbol{\theta})^2) \tag{2.120}$$

where $f_\mu(\boldsymbol{x};\boldsymbol{\theta}) \in \mathbb{R}$ predicts the mean, and $f_\sigma(\boldsymbol{x};\boldsymbol{\theta})^2 \in \mathbb{R}_+$ predicts the variance.

It is common to assume that the variance is fixed, and is independent of the input. This is called **homoscedastic regression**. Furthermore it is common to assume the mean is a linear function of the input. The resulting model is called **linear regression**:

$$p(y|\boldsymbol{x};\boldsymbol{\theta}) = \mathcal{N}(y|\boldsymbol{w}^{\mathsf{T}}\boldsymbol{x} + b, \sigma^2) \tag{2.121}$$

where $\boldsymbol{\theta} = (\boldsymbol{w}, b, \sigma^2)$. See Figure 2.14(a) for an illustration of this model in 1d. and Section 11.2 for more details on this model.

However, we can also make the variance depend on the input; this is called **heteroskedastic regression**. In the linear regression setting, we have

$$p(y|\boldsymbol{x};\boldsymbol{\theta}) = \mathcal{N}(y|\boldsymbol{w}_\mu^{\mathsf{T}}\boldsymbol{x} + b, \sigma_+(\boldsymbol{w}_\sigma^{\mathsf{T}}\boldsymbol{x})) \tag{2.122}$$

where $\boldsymbol{\theta} = (\boldsymbol{w}_\mu, \boldsymbol{w}_\sigma)$ are the two forms of regression weights, and

$$\sigma_+(a) = \log(1 + e^a) \tag{2.123}$$

is the **softplus** function, that maps from $\mathbb{R}$ to $\mathbb{R}_+$, to ensure the predicted standard deviation is non-negative. See Figure 2.14(b) for an illustration of this model in 1d.

Note that Figure 2.14 plots the 95% predictive interval, $[\mu(x) - 2\sigma(x), \mu(x) + 2\sigma(x)]$. This is the uncertainty in the predicted *observation* y given $\boldsymbol{x}$, and captures the variability in the blue dots. By contrast, the uncertainty in the underlying (noise-free) function is represented by $\sqrt{\mathbb{V}\left[f_\mu(\boldsymbol{x};\boldsymbol{\theta})\right]}$, which does not involve the σ term; now the uncertainty is over the parameters $\boldsymbol{\theta}$, rather than the output y. See Section 11.7 for details on how to model parameter uncertainty.

2.6.4   Why is the Gaussian distribution so widely used?

The Gaussian distribution is the most widely used distribution in statistics and machine learning. There are several reasons for this. First, it has two parameters which are easy to interpret, and which capture some of the most basic properties of a distribution, namely its mean and variance. Second, the central limit theorem (Section 2.8.6) tells us that sums of independent random variables have an approximately Gaussian distribution, making it a good choice for modeling residual errors or "noise". Third, the Gaussian distribution makes the least number of assumptions (has maximum entropy), subject to the constraint of having a specified mean and variance, as we show in Section 3.4.4; this makes it a good default choice in many cases. Finally, it has a simple mathematical form, which results in easy to implement, but often highly effective, methods, as we will see in Section 3.2.

From a historical perspective, it's worth remarking that the term "Gaussian distribution" is a bit misleading, since, as Jaynes [Jay03, p241] notes: "The fundamental nature of this distribution and its main properties were noted by Laplace when Gauss was six years old; and the distribution itself had been found by de Moivre before Laplace was born". However, Gauss popularized the use of the distribution in the 1800s, and the term "Gaussian" is now widely used in science and engineering.

The name "normal distribution" seems to have arisen in connection with the normal equations in linear regression (see Section 11.2.2.2). However, we prefer to avoid the term "normal", since it suggests other distributions are "abnormal", whereas, as Jaynes [Jay03] points out, it is the Gaussian that is abnormal in the sense that it has many special properties that are untypical of general distributions.

2.6.5   Dirac delta function as a limiting case

As the variance of a Gaussian goes to 0, the distribution approaches an infinitely narrow, but infinitely tall, "spike" at the mean. We can write this as follows:

$$\lim_{\sigma \to 0} \mathcal{N}(y|\mu, \sigma^2) \to \delta(y - \mu) \tag{2.124}$$

where δ is the **Dirac delta function**, defined by

$$\delta(x) = \begin{cases} +\infty & \text{if } x = 0 \\ 0 & \text{if } x \neq 0 \end{cases} \tag{2.125}$$

where

$$\int_{-\infty}^{\infty} \delta(x)dx = 1 \tag{2.126}$$

A slight variant of this is to define

$$\delta_y(x) = \begin{cases} +\infty & \text{if } x = y \\ 0 & \text{if } x \neq y \end{cases} \tag{2.127}$$

Note that we have

$$\delta_y(x) = \delta(x - y) \tag{2.128}$$

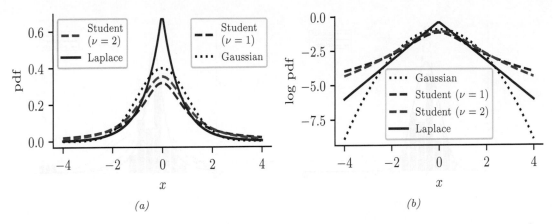

Figure 2.15: (a) The pdf's for a $\mathcal{N}(0,1)$, $\mathcal{T}(\mu = 0, \sigma = 1, \nu = 1)$, $\mathcal{T}(\mu = 0, \sigma = 1, \nu = 2)$, and Laplace$(0, 1/\sqrt{2})$. The mean is 0 and the variance is 1 for both the Gaussian and Laplace. When $\nu = 1$, the Student is the same as the Cauchy, which does not have a well-defined mean and variance. (b) Log of these pdf's. Note that the Student distribution is not log-concave for any parameter value, unlike the Laplace distribution. Nevertheless, both are unimodal. Generated by student_laplace_pdf_plot.ipynb.

The delta function distribution satisfies the following **sifting property**, which we will use later on:

$$\int_{-\infty}^{\infty} f(y)\delta(x - y)dy = f(x) \tag{2.129}$$

2.7 Some other common univariate distributions *

In this section, we briefly introduce some other univariate distributions that we will use in this book.

2.7.1 Student t distribution

The Gaussian distribution is quite sensitive to **outliers**. A **robust** alternative to the Gaussian is the **Student t-distribution**, which we shall call the **Student distribution** for short.[9] Its pdf is as follows:

$$\mathcal{T}(y|\mu, \sigma^2, \nu) \propto \left[1 + \frac{1}{\nu}\left(\frac{y - \mu}{\sigma}\right)^2 \right]^{-\left(\frac{\nu+1}{2}\right)} \tag{2.130}$$

where μ is the mean, $\sigma > 0$ is the scale parameter (not the standard deviation), and $\nu > 0$ is called the **degrees of freedom** (although a better term would be the **degree of normality** [Kru13], since large values of ν make the distribution act like a Gaussian).

---

9. This distribution has a colorful etymology. It was first published in 1908 by William Sealy Gosset, who worked at the Guinness brewery in Dublin, Ireland. Since his employer would not allow him to use his own name, he called it the "Student" distribution. The origin of the term t seems to have arisen in the context of tables of the Student distribution, used by Fisher when developing the basis of classical statistical inference. See http://jeff560.tripod.com/s.html for more historical details.

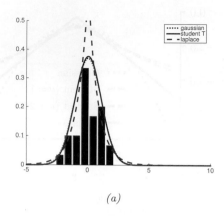 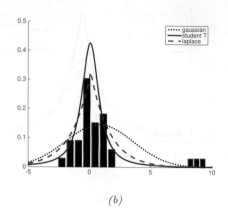

(a)   (b)

Figure 2.16: Illustration of the effect of outliers on fitting Gaussian, Student and Laplace distributions. (a) No outliers (the Gaussian and Student curves are on top of each other). (b) With outliers. We see that the Gaussian is more affected by outliers than the Student and Laplace distributions. Adapted from Figure 2.16 of [Bis06]. Generated by robust_pdf_plot.ipynb.

We see that the probability density decays as a polynomial function of the squared distance from the center, as opposed to an exponential function, so there is more probability mass in the tail than with a Gaussian distribution, as shown in Figure 2.15. We say that the Student distribution has **heavy tails**, which makes it robust to outliers.

To illustrate the robustness of the Student distribution, consider Figure 2.16. On the left, we show a Gaussian and a Student distribution fit to some data with no outliers. On the right, we add some outliers. We see that the Gaussian is affected a lot, whereas the Student hardly changes. We discuss how to use the Student distribution for robust linear regression in Section 11.6.2.

For later reference, we note that the Student distribution has the following properties:

$$\text{mean} = \mu, \ \text{mode} = \mu, \ \text{var} = \frac{\nu \sigma^2}{(\nu - 2)} \tag{2.131}$$

The mean is only defined if $\nu > 1$. The variance is only defined if $\nu > 2$. For $\nu \gg 5$, the Student distribution rapidly approaches a Gaussian distribution and loses its robustness properties. It is common to use $\nu = 4$, which gives good performance in a range of problems [LLT89].

2.7.2 Cauchy distribution

If $\nu = 1$, the Student distribution is known as the **Cauchy** or **Lorentz** distribution. Its pdf is defined by

$$\mathcal{C}(x|\mu, \gamma) = \frac{1}{\gamma \pi} \left[1 + \left(\frac{x - \mu}{\gamma} \right)^2 \right]^{-1} \tag{2.132}$$

This distribution has very heavy tails compared to a Gaussian. For example, 95% of the values from a standard normal are between -1.96 and 1.96, but for a standard Cauchy they are between -12.7 and 12.7. In fact the tails are so heavy that the integral that defines the mean does not converge.

The **half Cauchy** distribution is a version of the Cauchy (with $\mu = 0$) that is "folded over" on itself, so all its probability density is on the positive reals. Thus it has the form

$$\mathcal{C}_+(x|\gamma) \triangleq \frac{2}{\pi\gamma}\left[1 + \left(\frac{x}{\gamma}\right)^2\right]^{-1} \tag{2.133}$$

This is useful in Bayesian modeling, where we want to use a distribution over positive reals with heavy tails, but finite density at the origin.

2.7.3 Laplace distribution

Another distribution with heavy tails is the **Laplace distribution**[10], also known as the **double sided exponential** distribution. This has the following pdf:

$$\text{Laplace}(y|\mu, b) \triangleq \frac{1}{2b} \exp\left(-\frac{|y - \mu|}{b}\right) \tag{2.134}$$

See Figure 2.15 for a plot. Here μ is a location parameter and $b > 0$ is a scale parameter. This distribution has the following properties:

$$\text{mean} = \mu, \text{ mode} = \mu, \text{ var} = 2b^2 \tag{2.135}$$

In Section 11.6.1, we discuss how to use the Laplace distribution for robust linear regression, and in Section 11.4, we discuss how to use the Laplace distribution for sparse linear regression.

2.7.4 Beta distribution

The **beta distribution** has support over the interval $[0, 1]$ and is defined as follows:

$$\text{Beta}(x|a, b) = \frac{1}{B(a, b)} x^{a-1}(1 - x)^{b-1} \tag{2.136}$$

where $B(a, b)$ is the **beta function**, defined by

$$B(a, b) \triangleq \frac{\Gamma(a)\Gamma(b)}{\Gamma(a + b)} \tag{2.137}$$

where $\Gamma(a)$ is the Gamma function defined by

$$\Gamma(a) \triangleq \int_0^\infty x^{a-1} e^{-x} dx \tag{2.138}$$

See Figure 2.17a for plots of some beta distributions.

We require $a, b > 0$ to ensure the distribution is integrable (i.e., to ensure $B(a, b)$ exists). If $a = b = 1$, we get the uniform distribution. If a and b are both less than 1, we get a bimodal distribution with "spikes" at 0 and 1; if a and b are both greater than 1, the distribution is unimodal.

For later reference, we note that the distribution has the following properties (Exercise 2.8):

$$\text{mean} = \frac{a}{a + b}, \text{ mode} = \frac{a - 1}{a + b - 2}, \text{ var} = \frac{ab}{(a + b)^2(a + b + 1)} \tag{2.139}$$

---

10. Pierre-Simon Laplace (1749–1827) was a French mathematician, who played a key role in creating the field of Bayesian statistics.

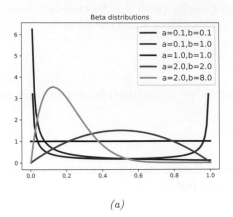
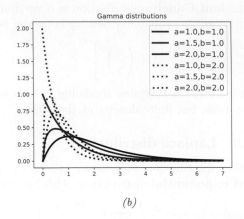

(a)   (b)

Figure 2.17: (a) Some beta distributions. If $a < 1$, we get a "spike" on the left, and if $b < 1$, we get a "spike" on the right. if $a = b = 1$, the distribution is uniform. If $a > 1$ and $b > 1$, the distribution is unimodal. Generated by beta_dist_plot.ipynb. (b) Some gamma distributions. If $a \leq 1$, the mode is at 0, otherwise the mode is away from 0. As we increase the rate b, we reduce the horizontal scale, thus squeezing everything leftwards and upwards. Generated by gamma_dist_plot.ipynb.

2.7.5   Gamma distribution

The **gamma distribution** is a flexible distribution for positive real valued rv's, $x > 0$. It is defined in terms of two parameters, called the shape $a > 0$ and the rate $b > 0$:

$$\text{Ga}(x|\text{shape} = a, \text{rate} = b) \triangleq \frac{b^a}{\Gamma(a)} x^{a-1} e^{-xb} \tag{2.140}$$

Sometimes the distribution is parameterized in terms of the shape a and the **scale** $s = 1/b$:

$$\text{Ga}(x|\text{shape} = a, \text{scale} = s) \triangleq \frac{1}{s^a \Gamma(a)} x^{a-1} e^{-x/s} \tag{2.141}$$

See Figure 2.17b for some plots of the gamma pdf.

For reference, we note that the distribution has the following properties:

$$\text{mean} = \frac{a}{b}, \ \text{mode} = \frac{a-1}{b}, \ \text{var} = \frac{a}{b^2} \tag{2.142}$$

There are several distributions which are just special cases of the Gamma, which we discuss below.

- **Exponential distribution**. This is defined by

$$\text{Expon}(x|\lambda) \triangleq \text{Ga}(x|\text{shape} = 1, \text{rate} = \lambda) \tag{2.143}$$

This distribution describes the times between events in a Poisson process, i.e. a process in which events occur continuously and independently at a constant average rate λ.

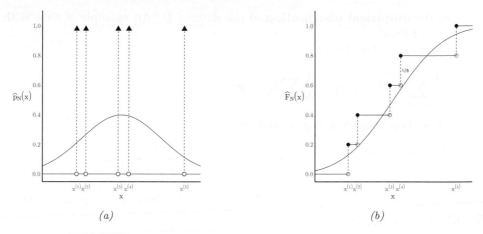

Figure 2.18: Illustration of the (a) empirical pdf and (b) empirical cdf derived from a set of $N = 5$ samples. From `https://bit.ly/3hFgi0e`. Used with kind permission of Mauro Escudero.

- **Chi-squared distribution**. This is defined by

$$\chi_\nu^2(x) \triangleq \text{Ga}(x|\text{shape} = \frac{\nu}{2}, \text{rate} = \frac{1}{2}) \tag{2.144}$$

where ν is called the degrees of freedom. This is the distribution of the sum of squared Gaussian random variables. More precisely, if $Z_i \sim \mathcal{N}(0,1)$, and $S = \sum_{i=1}^{\nu} Z_i^2$, then $S \sim \chi_\nu^2$.

- The **inverse Gamma distribution** is defined as follows:

$$\text{IG}(x|\text{shape} = a, \text{scale} = b) \triangleq \frac{b^a}{\Gamma(a)} x^{-(a+1)} e^{-b/x} \tag{2.145}$$

The distribution has these properties

$$\text{mean} = \frac{b}{a-1}, \text{mode} = \frac{b}{a+1}, \text{var} = \frac{b^2}{(a-1)^2(a-2)} \tag{2.146}$$

The mean only exists if $a > 1$. The variance only exists if $a > 2$. Note: if $X \sim \text{Ga}(\text{shape} = a, \text{rate} = b)$, then $1/X \sim \text{IG}(\text{shape} = a, \text{scale} = b)$. (Note that b plays two different roles in this case.)

2.7.6 Empirical distribution

Suppose we have a set of N samples $\mathcal{D} = \{x^{(1)}, \ldots, x^{(N)}\}$, derived from a distribution $p(X)$, where $X \in \mathbb{R}$. We can approximate the pdf using a set of delta functions (Section 2.6.5) or "spikes", centered on these samples:

$$\hat{p}_N(x) = \frac{1}{N} \sum_{n=1}^{N} \delta_{x^{(n)}}(x) \tag{2.147}$$

This is called the **empirical distribution** of the dataset $\mathcal{D}$. An example of this, with $N = 5$, is shown in Figure 2.18(a).

The corresponding cdf is given by

$$\hat{P}_N(x) = \frac{1}{N} \sum_{n=1}^{N} \mathbb{I}\left(x^{(n)} \leq x\right) = \frac{1}{N} \sum_{n=1}^{N} u_{x^{(n)}}(x) \tag{2.148}$$

where $u_y(x)$ is a **step function** at y defined by

$$u_y(x) = \begin{cases} 1 & \text{if } x \geq y \\ 0 & \text{if } x < y \end{cases} \tag{2.149}$$

This can be visualized as a "stair case", as in Figure 2.18(b), where the jumps of height $1/N$ occur at every sample.

2.8   Transformations of random variables *

Suppose $\boldsymbol{x} \sim p()$ is some random variable, and $\boldsymbol{y} = f(\boldsymbol{x})$ is some deterministic transformation of it. In this section, we discuss how to compute $p(\boldsymbol{y})$.

2.8.1   Discrete case

If X is a discrete rv, we can derive the pmf for Y by simply summing up the probability mass for all the x's such that $f(x) = y$:

$$p_y(y) = \sum_{x : f(x) = y} p_x(x) \tag{2.150}$$

For example, if $f(X) = 1$ if X is even and $f(X) = 0$ otherwise, and $p_x(X)$ is uniform on the set $\{1, \ldots, 10\}$, then $p_y(1) = \sum_{x \in \{2,4,6,8,10\}} p_x(x) = 0.5$, and hence $p_y(0) = 0.5$ also. Note that in this example, f is a many-to-one function.

2.8.2   Continuous case

If X is continuous, we cannot use Equation (2.150) since $p_x(x)$ is a density, not a pmf, and we cannot sum up densities. Instead, we work with cdf's, as follows:

$$P_y(y) \triangleq \Pr(Y \leq y) = \Pr(f(X) \leq y) = \Pr(X \in \{x | f(x) \leq y\}) \tag{2.151}$$

If f is invertible, we can derive the pdf of y by differentiating the cdf, as we show below. If f is not invertible, we can use numerical integration, or a Monte Carlo approximation.

2.8.3   Invertible transformations (bijections)

In this section, we consider the case of monotonic and hence invertible functions. (Note a function is invertible iff it is a **bijector**). With this assumption, there is a simple formula for the pdf of y, as we will see. (This can be generalized to invertible, but non-monotonic, functions, but we ignore this case.)

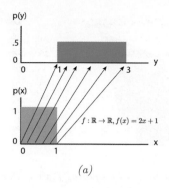

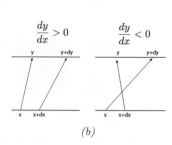

(a)   (b)

Figure 2.19: (a) Mapping a uniform pdf through the function $f(x) = 2x + 1$. (b) Illustration of how two nearby points, x and $x + dx$, get mapped under f. If $\frac{dy}{dx} > 0$, the function is locally increasing, but if $\frac{dy}{dx} < 0$, the function is locally decreasing. (In the latter case, if $f(x) = y + dy$, then $f(x + dx) = y$, since increasing x by dx should decrease the output by dy.) $x + dx > x$. From [Jan18]. Used with kind permission of Eric Jang.

2.8.3.1   Change of variables: scalar case

We start with an example. Suppose $x \sim \mathrm{Unif}(0, 1)$, and $y = f(x) = 2x + 1$. This function stretches and shifts the probability distribution, as shown in Figure 2.19(a). Now let us zoom in on a point x and another point that is infinitesimally close, namely $x + dx$. We see this interval gets mapped to $(y, y + dy)$. The probability mass in these intervals must be the same, hence $p(x)dx = p(y)dy$, and so $p(y) = p(x)dx/dy$. However, since it does not matter (in terms of probability preservation) whether $dx/dy > 0$ or $dx/dy < 0$, we get

$$p_y(y) = p_x(x)|\frac{dx}{dy}| \tag{2.152}$$

Now consider the general case for any $p_x(x)$ and any monotonic function $f : \mathbb{R} \to \mathbb{R}$. Let $g = f^{-1}$, so $y = f(x)$ and $x = g(y)$. If we assume that $f : \mathbb{R} \to \mathbb{R}$ is monotonically increasing we get

$$P_y(y) = \Pr(f(X) \le y) = \Pr(X \le f^{-1}(y)) = P_x(f^{-1}(y)) = P_x(g(y)) \tag{2.153}$$

Taking derivatives we get

$$p_y(y) \triangleq \frac{d}{dy}P_y(y) = \frac{d}{dy}P_x(x) = \frac{dx}{dy}\frac{d}{dx}P_x(x) = \frac{dx}{dy}p_x(x) \tag{2.154}$$

We can derive a similar expression (but with opposite signs) for the case where f is monotonically decreasing. To handle the general case we take the absolute value to get

$$p_y(y) = p_x\left(g(y)\right)\left|\frac{d}{dy}g(y)\right| \tag{2.155}$$

This is called **change of variables** formula.

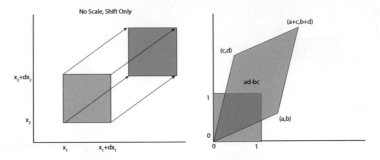

Figure 2.20: Illustration of an affine transformation applied to a unit square, $f(x) = \mathbf{A}x + b$. (a) Here $\mathbf{A} = \mathbf{I}$. (b) Here $b = 0$. From [Jan18]. Used with kind permission of Eric Jang.

2.8.3.2   Change of variables: multivariate case

We can extend the previous results to multivariate distributions as follows. Let f be an invertible function that maps $\mathbb{R}^n$ to $\mathbb{R}^n$, with inverse g. Suppose we want to compute the pdf of $y = f(x)$. By analogy with the scalar case, we have

$$p_y(y) = p_x\left(g(y)\right) \left| \det\left[\mathbf{J}_g(y)\right] \right| \tag{2.156}$$

where $\mathbf{J}_g = \frac{dg(y)}{dy^\mathsf{T}}$ is the Jacobian of g, and $|\det \mathbf{J}(y)|$ is the absolute value of the determinant of $\mathbf{J}$ evaluated at y. (See Section 7.8.5 for a discussion of Jacobians.) In Exercise 3.6 you will use this formula to derive the normalization constant for a multivariate Gaussian.

Figure 2.20 illustrates this result in 2d, for the case where $f(x) = \mathbf{A}x + b$, where $\mathbf{A} = \begin{pmatrix} a & c \\ b & d \end{pmatrix}$. We see that the area of the unit square changes by a factor of $\det(\mathbf{A}) = ad - bc$, which is the area of the parallelogram.

As another example, consider transforming a density from Cartesian coordinates $x = (x_1, x_2)$ to polar coordinates $y = f(x_1, x_2)$, so $g(r, \theta) = (r\cos\theta, r\sin\theta)$. Then

$$\mathbf{J}_g = \begin{pmatrix} \frac{\partial x_1}{\partial r} & \frac{\partial x_1}{\partial \theta} \\ \frac{\partial x_2}{\partial r} & \frac{\partial x_2}{\partial \theta} \end{pmatrix} = \begin{pmatrix} \cos\theta & -r\sin\theta \\ \sin\theta & r\cos\theta \end{pmatrix} \tag{2.157}$$

$$|\det(\mathbf{J}_g)| = |r\cos^2\theta + r\sin^2\theta| = |r| \tag{2.158}$$

Hence

$$p_{r,\theta}(r, \theta) = p_{x_1,x_2}(r\cos\theta, r\sin\theta)\, r \tag{2.159}$$

To see this geometrically, notice that the area of the shaded patch in Figure 2.21 is given by

$$\Pr(r \le R \le r + dr, \theta \le \Theta \le \theta + d\theta) = p_{r,\theta}(r, \theta)drd\theta \tag{2.160}$$

In the limit, this is equal to the density at the center of the patch times the size of the patch, which is given by $r\, dr\, d\theta$. Hence

$$p_{r,\theta}(r, \theta)\, dr\, d\theta = p_{x_1,x_2}(r\cos\theta, r\sin\theta)\, r\, dr\, d\theta \tag{2.161}$$

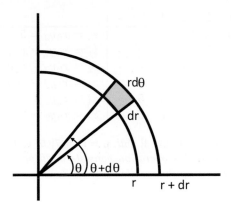

Figure 2.21: *Change of variables from polar to Cartesian. The area of the shaded patch is r dr dθ. Adapted from Figure 3.16 of [Ric95].*

2.8.4 Moments of a linear transformation

Suppose f is an affine function, so $\boldsymbol{y} = \mathbf{A}\boldsymbol{x} + \boldsymbol{b}$. In this case, we can easily derive the mean and covariance of $\boldsymbol{y}$ as follows. First, for the mean, we have

$$\mathbb{E}[\boldsymbol{y}] = \mathbb{E}[\mathbf{A}\boldsymbol{x} + \boldsymbol{b}] = \mathbf{A}\boldsymbol{\mu} + \boldsymbol{b} \tag{2.162}$$

where $\boldsymbol{\mu} = \mathbb{E}[\boldsymbol{x}]$. If f is a scalar-valued function, $f(\boldsymbol{x}) = \boldsymbol{a}^\mathsf{T}\boldsymbol{x} + b$, the corresponding result is

$$\mathbb{E}[\boldsymbol{a}^\mathsf{T}\boldsymbol{x} + b] = \boldsymbol{a}^\mathsf{T}\boldsymbol{\mu} + b \tag{2.163}$$

For the covariance, we have

$$\mathrm{Cov}[\boldsymbol{y}] = \mathrm{Cov}[\mathbf{A}\boldsymbol{x} + \boldsymbol{b}] = \mathbf{A}\boldsymbol{\Sigma}\mathbf{A}^\mathsf{T} \tag{2.164}$$

where $\boldsymbol{\Sigma} = \mathrm{Cov}[\boldsymbol{x}]$. We leave the proof of this as an exercise.

As a special case, if $y = \boldsymbol{a}^\mathsf{T}\boldsymbol{x} + b$, we get

$$\mathbb{V}[y] = \mathbb{V}[\boldsymbol{a}^\mathsf{T}\boldsymbol{x} + b] = \boldsymbol{a}^\mathsf{T}\boldsymbol{\Sigma}\boldsymbol{a} \tag{2.165}$$

For example, to compute the variance of the sum of two scalar random variables, we can set $\boldsymbol{a} = [1, 1]$ to get

$$\mathbb{V}[x_1 + x_2] = \begin{pmatrix} 1 & 1 \end{pmatrix} \begin{pmatrix} \Sigma_{11} & \Sigma_{12} \\ \Sigma_{21} & \Sigma_{22} \end{pmatrix} \begin{pmatrix} 1 \\ 1 \end{pmatrix} \tag{2.166}$$

$$= \Sigma_{11} + \Sigma_{22} + 2\Sigma_{12} = \mathbb{V}[x_1] + \mathbb{V}[x_2] + 2\mathrm{Cov}[x_1, x_2] \tag{2.167}$$

Note, however, that although some distributions (such as the Gaussian) are completely characterized by their mean and covariance, in general we must use the techniques described above to derive the full distribution of $\boldsymbol{y}$.

-	-	1	2	3	4	-	-
7	6	5	-	-	-	-	-
-	7	6	5	-	-	-	-
-	-	7	6	5	-	-	-
-	-	-	7	6	5	-	-
-	-	-	-	7	6	5	-
-	-	-	-	-	7	6	5

$z_0 = x_0 y_0 = 5$
$z_1 = x_0 y_1 + x_1 y_0 = 16$
$z_2 = x_0 y_2 + x_1 y_1 + x_2 y_0 = 34$
$z_3 = x_1 y_2 + x_2 y_1 + x_3 y_0 = 52$
$z_4 = x_2 y_2 + x_3 y_1 = 45$
$z_5 = x_3 y_2 = 28$

Table 2.4: Discrete convolution of $\boldsymbol{x} = [1, 2, 3, 4]$ with $\boldsymbol{y} = [5, 6, 7]$ to yield $\boldsymbol{z} = [5, 16, 34, 52, 45, 28]$. In general, $z_n = \sum_{k=-\infty}^{\infty} x_k y_{n-k}$. We see that this operation consists of "flipping" $\boldsymbol{y}$ and then "dragging" it over $\boldsymbol{x}$, multiplying elementwise, and adding up the results.

2.8.5 The convolution theorem

Let $y = x_1 + x_2$, where x_1 and x_2 are independent rv's. If these are discrete random variables, we can compute the pmf for the sum as follows:

$$p(y = j) = \sum_k p(x_1 = k)p(x_2 = j - k) \tag{2.168}$$

for $j = \ldots, -2, -1, 0, 1, 2, \ldots$.

If x_1 and x_2 have pdf's $p_1(x_1)$ and $p_2(x_2)$, what is the distribution of y? The cdf for y is given by

$$P_y(y^*) = \Pr(y \le y^*) = \int_{-\infty}^{\infty} p_1(x_1) \left[\int_{-\infty}^{y^* - x_1} p_2(x_2)dx_2 \right] dx_1 \tag{2.169}$$

where we integrate over the region R defined by $x_1 + x_2 < y^*$. Thus the pdf for y is

$$p(y) = \left[\frac{d}{dy^*} P_y(y^*) \right]_{y^* = y} = \int p_1(x_1)p_2(y - x_1)dx_1 \tag{2.170}$$

where we used the rule of **differentiating under the integral sign**:

$$\frac{d}{dx} \int_{a(x)}^{b(x)} f(t)dt = f(b(x))\frac{db(x)}{dx} - f(a(x))\frac{da(x)}{dx} \tag{2.171}$$

We can write Equation (2.170) as follows:

$$p = p_1 \circledast p_2 \tag{2.172}$$

where $\circledast$ represents the **convolution** operator. For finite length vectors, the integrals become sums, and convolution can be thought of as a "flip and drag" operation, as illustrated in Table 2.4. Consequently, Equation (2.170) is called the **convolution theorem**.

For example, suppose we roll two dice, so p_1 and p_2 are both the discrete uniform distributions

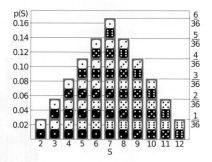

Figure 2.22: *Distribution of the sum of two dice rolls, i.e., $p(y)$ where $y = x_1 + x_2$ and $x_i \sim \mathrm{Unif}(\{1, 2, \ldots, 6\})$. From* `https://en.wikipedia.org/wiki/Probability_distribution`. *Used with kind permission of Wikipedia author Tim Stellmach.*

over $\{1, 2, \ldots, 6\}$. Let $y = x_1 + x_2$ be the sum of the dice. We have

$$p(y = 2) = p(x_1 = 1)p(x_2 = 1) = \frac{1}{6}\frac{1}{6} = \frac{1}{36} \tag{2.173}$$

$$p(y = 3) = p(x_1 = 1)p(x_2 = 2) + p(x_1 = 2)p(x_2 = 1) = \frac{1}{6}\frac{1}{6} + \frac{1}{6}\frac{1}{6} = \frac{2}{36} \tag{2.174}$$

$$\cdots \tag{2.175}$$

Continuing in this way, we find $p(y = 4) = 3/36$, $p(y = 5) = 4/36$, $p(y = 6) = 5/36$, $p(y = 7) = 6/36$, $p(y = 8) = 5/36$, $p(y = 9) = 4/36$, $p(y = 10) = 3/36$, $p(y = 11) = 2/36$ and $p(y = 12) = 1/36$. See Figure 2.22 for a plot. We see that the distribution looks like a Gaussian; we explain the reasons for this in Section 2.8.6.

We can also compute the pdf of the sum of two continuous rv's. For example, in the case of Gaussians, where $x_1 \sim \mathcal{N}(\boldsymbol{\mu}_1, \sigma_1^2)$ and $x_2 \sim \mathcal{N}(\boldsymbol{\mu}_2, \sigma_2^2)$, one can show (Exercise 2.4) that if $y = x_1 + x_2$ then

$$p(y) = \mathcal{N}(x_1 | \boldsymbol{\mu}_1, \sigma_1^2) \otimes \mathcal{N}(x_2 | \boldsymbol{\mu}_2, \sigma_2^2) = \mathcal{N}(y | \boldsymbol{\mu}_1 + \boldsymbol{\mu}_2, \sigma_1^2 + \sigma_2^2) \tag{2.176}$$

Hence the convolution of two Gaussians is a Gaussian.

2.8.6 Central limit theorem

Now consider N random variables with pdf's (not necessarily Gaussian) $p_n(x)$, each with mean μ and variance σ^2. We assume each variable is **independent and identically distributed** or **iid** for short, which means $X_n \sim p(X)$ are independent samples from the same distribution. Let $S_N = \sum_{n=1}^{N} X_n$ be the sum of the rv's. One can show that, as N increases, the distribution of this sum approaches

$$p(S_N = u) = \frac{1}{\sqrt{2\pi N \sigma^2}} \exp\left(-\frac{(u - N\mu)^2}{2N\sigma^2}\right) \tag{2.177}$$

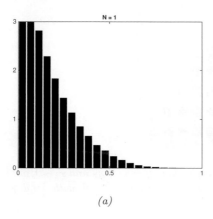
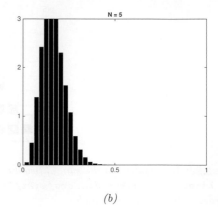

(a)   (b)

Figure 2.23: The central limit theorem in pictures. We plot a histogram of $\hat{\mu}_N^s = \frac{1}{N}\sum_{n=1}^{N} x_{ns}$, where $x_{ns} \sim \text{Beta}(1,5)$, for $s = 1 : 10000$. As $N \to \infty$, the distribution tends towards a Gaussian. (a) $N = 1$. (b) $N = 5$. Adapted from Figure 2.6 of [Bis06]. Generated by centralLimitDemo.ipynb.

Hence the distribution of the quantity

$$Z_N \triangleq \frac{S_N - N\mu}{\sigma\sqrt{N}} = \frac{\overline{X} - \mu}{\sigma/\sqrt{N}} \tag{2.178}$$

converges to the standard normal, where $\overline{X} = S_N/N$ is the sample mean. This is called the **central limit theorem**. See e.g., [Jay03, p222] or [Ric95, p169] for a proof.

In Figure 2.23 we give an example in which we compute the sample mean of rv's drawn from a beta distribution. We see that the sampling distribution of this mean rapidly converges to a Gaussian distribution.

2.8.7   Monte Carlo approximation

Suppose x is a random variable, and $y = f(x)$ is some function of x. It is often difficult to compute the induced distribution $p(y)$ analytically. One simple but powerful alternative is to draw a large number of samples from the x's distribution, and then to use these samples (instead of the distribution) to approximate $p(y)$.

For example, suppose $x \sim \text{Unif}(-1,1)$ and $y = f(x) = x^2$. We can approximate $p(y)$ by drawing many samples from $p(x)$ (using a uniform **random number generator**), squaring them, and computing the resulting empirical distribution, which is given by

$$p_S(y) \triangleq \frac{1}{N_s}\sum_{s=1}^{N_s} \delta(y - y_s) \tag{2.179}$$

This is just an equally weighted "sum of spikes", each centered on one of the samples (see Section 2.7.6). By using enough samples, we can approximate $p(y)$ rather well. See Figure 2.24 for an illustration.

This approach is called a **Monte Carlo approximation** to the distribution. (The term "Monte Carlo" comes from the name of a famous gambling casino in Monaco.) Monte Carlo techniques were

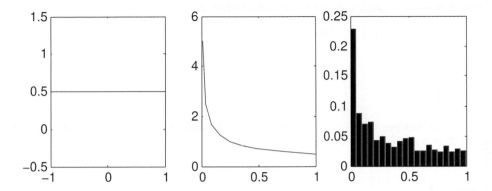

Figure 2.24: Computing the distribution of $y = x^2$, where $p(x)$ is uniform (left). The analytic result is shown in the middle, and the Monte Carlo approximation is shown on the right. Generated by change_of_vars_demo1d.ipynb.

first developed in the area of statistical physics — in particular, during development of the atomic bomb — but are now widely used in statistics and machine learning as well. More details can be found in the sequel to this book, [Mur23], as well as specialized books on the topic, such as [Liu01; RC04; KTB11; BZ20].

2.9 Exercises

Exercise 2.1 [Conditional independence *]

(Source: Koller.)

a. Let $H \in \{1, \ldots, K\}$ be a discrete random variable, and let e_1 and e_2 be the observed values of two other random variables E_1 and E_2. Suppose we wish to calculate the vector

$$\vec{P}(H|e_1, e_2) = (P(H = 1|e_1, e_2), \ldots, P(H = K|e_1, e_2))$$

Which of the following sets of numbers are sufficient for the calculation?

   i. $P(e_1, e_2)$, $P(H)$, $P(e_1|H)$, $P(e_2|H)$
  ii. $P(e_1, e_2)$, $P(H)$, $P(e_1, e_2|H)$
 iii. $P(e_1|H)$, $P(e_2|H)$, $P(H)$

b. Now suppose we now assume $E_1 \perp E_2|H$ (i.e., E_1 and E_2 are conditionally independent given H). Which of the above 3 sets are sufficient now?

Show your calculations as well as giving the final result. Hint: use Bayes rule.

Exercise 2.2 [Pairwise independence does not imply mutual independence]

We say that two random variables are pairwise independent if

$$p(X_2|X_1) = p(X_2) \tag{2.180}$$

and hence

$$p(X_2, X_1) = p(X_1)p(X_2|X_1) = p(X_1)p(X_2) \tag{2.181}$$

We say that n random variables are mutually independent if

$$p(X_i | X_S) = p(X_i) \quad \forall S \subseteq \{1, \ldots, n\} \setminus \{i\} \tag{2.182}$$

and hence

$$p(X_{1:n}) = \prod_{i=1}^{n} p(X_i) \tag{2.183}$$

Show that pairwise independence between all pairs of variables does not necessarily imply mutual independence. It suffices to give a counter example.

Exercise 2.3 [Conditional independence iff joint factorizes *]

In the text we said $X \perp Y | Z$ iff

$$p(x, y | z) = p(x | z) p(y | z) \tag{2.184}$$

for all x, y, z such that $p(z) > 0$. Now prove the following alternative definition: $X \perp Y | Z$ iff there exist functions g and h such that

$$p(x, y | z) = g(x, z) h(y, z) \tag{2.185}$$

for all x, y, z such that $p(z) > 0$.

Exercise 2.4 [Convolution of two Gaussians is a Gaussian]

Show that the convolution of two Gaussians is a Gaussian, i.e.,

$$p(y) = \mathcal{N}(x_1 | \mu_1, \sigma_1^2) \otimes \mathcal{N}(x_2 | \mu_2, \sigma_2^2) = \mathcal{N}(y | \mu_1 + \mu_2, \sigma_1^2 + \sigma_2^2) \tag{2.186}$$

where $y = x_1 + x_2$, $x_1 \sim \mathcal{N}(\mu_1, \sigma_1^2)$ and $x_2 \sim \mathcal{N}(\mu_2, \sigma_2^2)$ are independent rv's.

Exercise 2.5 [Expected value of the minimum of two rv's *]

Suppose X, Y are two points sampled independently and uniformly at random from the interval $[0, 1]$. What is the expected location of the leftmost point?

Exercise 2.6 [Variance of a sum]

Show that the variance of a sum is

$$\mathbb{V}[X + Y] = \mathbb{V}[X] + \mathbb{V}[Y] + 2\text{Cov}[X, Y], \tag{2.187}$$

where $\text{Cov}[X, Y]$ is the covariance between X and Y.

Exercise 2.7 [Deriving the inverse gamma density *]

Let $X \sim \text{Ga}(a, b)$, and $Y = 1/X$. Derive the distribution of Y.

Exercise 2.8 [Mean, mode, variance for the beta distribution]

Suppose $\theta \sim \text{Beta}(a, b)$. Show that the mean, mode and variance are given by

$$\mathbb{E}[\theta] = \frac{a}{a + b} \tag{2.188}$$

$$\mathbb{V}[\boldsymbol{\theta}] = \frac{ab}{(a + b)^2 (a + b + 1)} \tag{2.189}$$

$$\text{mode}[\boldsymbol{\theta}] = \frac{a - 1}{a + b - 2} \tag{2.190}$$

Exercise 2.9 [Bayes rule for medical diagnosis *]

After your yearly checkup, the doctor has bad news and good news. The bad news is that you tested positive for a serious disease, and that the test is 99% accurate (i.e., the probability of testing positive given that you have the disease is 0.99, as is the probability of testing negative given that you don't have the disease). The good news is that this is a rare disease, striking only one in 10,000 people. What are the chances that you actually have the disease? (Show your calculations as well as giving the final result.)

Exercise 2.10 [Legal reasoning]

(Source: Peter Lee.) Suppose a crime has been committed. Blood is found at the scene for which there is no innocent explanation. It is of a type which is present in 1% of the population.

a. The prosecutor claims: "There is a 1% chance that the defendant would have the crime blood type if he were innocent. Thus there is a 99% chance that he is guilty". This is known as the **prosecutor's fallacy**. What is wrong with this argument?

b. The defender claims: "The crime occurred in a city of 800,000 people. The blood type would be found in approximately 8000 people. The evidence has provided a probability of just 1 in 8000 that the defendant is guilty, and thus has no relevance." This is known as the **defender's fallacy**. What is wrong with this argument?

Exercise 2.11 [Probabilities are sensitive to the form of the question that was used to generate the answer *]

(Source: Minka.) My neighbor has two children. Assuming that the gender of a child is like a coin flip, it is most likely, a priori, that my neighbor has one boy and one girl, with probability 1/2. The other possibilities—two boys or two girls—have probabilities 1/4 and 1/4.

a. Suppose I ask him whether he has any boys, and he says yes. What is the probability that one child is a girl?

b. Suppose instead that I happen to see one of his children run by, and it is a boy. What is the probability that the other child is a girl?

Exercise 2.12 [Normalization constant for a 1D Gaussian]

The normalization constant for a zero-mean Gaussian is given by

$$Z = \int_a^b \exp\left(-\frac{x^2}{2\sigma^2}\right) dx \tag{2.191}$$

where $a = -\infty$ and $b = \infty$. To compute this, consider its square

$$Z^2 = \int_a^b \int_a^b \exp\left(-\frac{x^2 + y^2}{2\sigma^2}\right) dxdy \tag{2.192}$$

Let us change variables from cartesian (x, y) to polar (r, θ) using $x = r\cos\theta$ and $y = r\sin\theta$. Since $dxdy = rdrd\theta$, and $\cos^2\theta + \sin^2\theta = 1$, we have

$$Z^2 = \int_0^{2\pi} \int_0^\infty r\exp\left(-\frac{r^2}{2\sigma^2}\right) drd\theta \tag{2.193}$$

Evaluate this integral and hence show $Z = \sqrt{\sigma^2 2\pi}$. Hint 1: separate the integral into a product of two terms, the first of which (involving $d\theta$) is constant, so is easy. Hint 2: if $u = e^{-r^2/2\sigma^2}$ then $du/dr = -\frac{1}{\sigma^2}re^{-r^2/2\sigma^2}$, so the second integral is also easy (since $\int u'(r)dr = u(r)$).

3 Probability: Multivariate Models

3.1 Joint distributions for multiple random variables

In this section, we discuss various ways to measure the dependence of one or more variables on each other.

3.1.1 Covariance

The **covariance** between two rv's X and Y measures the degree to which X and Y are (linearly) related. Covariance is defined as

$$\text{Cov}\left[X, Y\right] \triangleq \mathbb{E}\left[(X - \mathbb{E}\left[X\right])(Y - \mathbb{E}\left[Y\right])\right] = \mathbb{E}\left[XY\right] - \mathbb{E}\left[X\right]\mathbb{E}\left[Y\right] \tag{3.1}$$

If $\boldsymbol{x}$ is a D-dimensional random vector, its **covariance matrix** is defined to be the following symmetric, positive semi definite matrix:

$$\text{Cov}\left[\boldsymbol{x}\right] \triangleq \mathbb{E}\left[(\boldsymbol{x} - \mathbb{E}\left[\boldsymbol{x}\right])(\boldsymbol{x} - \mathbb{E}\left[\boldsymbol{x}\right])^{\mathsf{T}}\right] \triangleq \boldsymbol{\Sigma} \tag{3.2}$$

$$= \begin{pmatrix} \mathbb{V}\left[X_1\right] & \text{Cov}\left[X_1, X_2\right] & \cdots & \text{Cov}\left[X_1, X_D\right] \\ \text{Cov}\left[X_2, X_1\right] & \mathbb{V}\left[X_2\right] & \cdots & \text{Cov}\left[X_2, X_D\right] \\ \vdots & \vdots & \ddots & \vdots \\ \text{Cov}\left[X_D, X_1\right] & \text{Cov}\left[X_D, X_2\right] & \cdots & \mathbb{V}\left[X_D\right] \end{pmatrix} \tag{3.3}$$

from which we get the important result

$$\mathbb{E}\left[\boldsymbol{x}\boldsymbol{x}^{\mathsf{T}}\right] = \boldsymbol{\Sigma} + \boldsymbol{\mu}\boldsymbol{\mu}^{\mathsf{T}} \tag{3.4}$$

Another useful result is that the covariance of a linear transformation is given by

$$\text{Cov}\left[\mathbf{A}\boldsymbol{x} + \boldsymbol{b}\right] = \mathbf{A}\text{Cov}\left[\boldsymbol{x}\right]\mathbf{A}^{\mathsf{T}} \tag{3.5}$$

as shown in Exercise 3.4.

The **cross-covariance** between two random vectors is defined as

$$\text{Cov}\left[\boldsymbol{x}, \boldsymbol{y}\right] = \mathbb{E}\left[(\boldsymbol{x} - \mathbb{E}\left[\boldsymbol{x}\right])(\boldsymbol{y} - \mathbb{E}\left[\boldsymbol{y}\right])^{\mathsf{T}}\right] \tag{3.6}$$

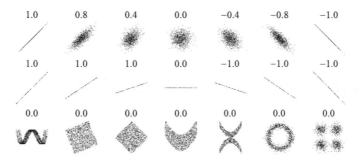

Figure 3.1: *Several sets of (x, y) points, with the correlation coefficient of x and y for each set. Note that the correlation reflects the noisiness and direction of a linear relationship (top row), but not the slope of that relationship (middle), nor many aspects of nonlinear relationships (bottom). (Note: the figure in the center has a slope of 0 but in that case the correlation coefficient is undefined because the variance of Y is zero.) From* `https://en.wikipedia.org/wiki/Pearson_correlation_coefficient`. *Used with kind permission of Wikipedia author Imagecreator.*

3.1.2   Correlation

Covariances can be between negative and positive infinity. Sometimes it is more convenient to work with a normalized measure, with a finite lower and upper bound. The (Pearson) **correlation coefficient** between X and Y is defined as

$$\rho \triangleq \mathrm{corr}\left[X, Y\right] \triangleq \frac{\mathrm{Cov}\left[X, Y\right]}{\sqrt{\mathbb{V}\left[X\right]\mathbb{V}\left[Y\right]}} \tag{3.7}$$

One can show (Exercise 3.2) that $-1 \le \rho \le 1$.

One can also show that $\mathrm{corr}\left[X, Y\right] = 1$ if and only if $Y = aX + b$ (and $a > 0$) for some parameters a and b, i.e., if there is a *linear* relationship between X and Y (see Exercise 3.3). Intuitively one might expect the correlation coefficient to be related to the slope of the regression line, i.e., the coefficient a in the expression $Y = aX + b$. However, as we show in Equation (11.27), the regression coefficient is in fact given by $a = \mathrm{Cov}\left[X, Y\right]/\mathbb{V}\left[X\right]$. In Figure 3.1, we show that the correlation coefficient can be 0 for strong, but nonlinear, relationships. (Compare to Figure 6.6.) Thus a better way to think of the correlation coefficient is as *a degree of linearity*. (See correlation2d.ipynb for a demo to illustrate this idea.)

In the case of a vector $\boldsymbol{x}$ of related random variables, the **correlation matrix** is given by

$$\mathrm{corr}(\boldsymbol{x}) = \begin{pmatrix} 1 & \frac{\mathbb{E}[(X_1-\mu_1)(X_2-\mu_2)]}{\sigma_1\sigma_2} & \cdots & \frac{\mathbb{E}[(X_1-\mu_1)(X_D-\mu_D)]}{\sigma_1\sigma_D} \\ \frac{\mathbb{E}[(X_2-\mu_2)(X_1-\mu_1)]}{\sigma_2\sigma_1} & 1 & \cdots & \frac{\mathbb{E}[(X_2-\mu_2)(X_D-\mu_D)]}{\sigma_2\sigma_D} \\ \vdots & \vdots & \ddots & \vdots \\ \frac{\mathbb{E}[(X_D-\mu_D)(X_1-\mu_1)]}{\sigma_D\sigma_1} & \frac{\mathbb{E}[(X_D-\mu_D)(X_2-\mu_2)]}{\sigma_D\sigma_2} & \cdots & 1 \end{pmatrix} \tag{3.8}$$

This can be written more compactly as

$$\mathrm{corr}(\boldsymbol{x}) = (\mathrm{diag}(\mathbf{K}_{xx}))^{-\frac{1}{2}}\mathbf{K}_{xx}(\mathrm{diag}(\mathbf{K}_{xx}))^{-\frac{1}{2}} \tag{3.9}$$

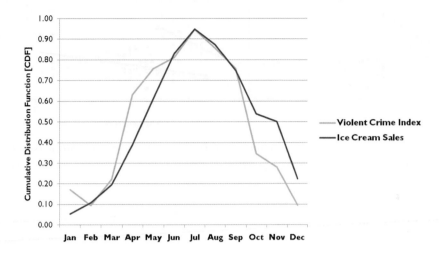

Figure 3.2: *Examples of spurious correlation between causally unrelated time series. Consumption of ice cream (red) and violent crime rate (yellow). over time. From* http://icbseverywhere.com/blog/2014/10/the-logic-of-causal-conclusions/. *Used with kind permission of Barbara Drescher.*

where $\mathbf{K}_{xx}$ is the **auto-covariance matrix**

$$\mathbf{K}_{xx} = \mathbf{\Sigma} = \mathbb{E}\left[(\mathbf{x} - \mathbb{E}\left[\mathbf{x}\right])(\mathbf{x} - \mathbb{E}\left[\mathbf{x}\right])^{\mathsf{T}}\right] = \mathbf{R}_{xx} - \boldsymbol{\mu}\boldsymbol{\mu}^{\mathsf{T}} \tag{3.10}$$

and $\mathbf{R}_{xx} = \mathbb{E}\left[\mathbf{x}\mathbf{x}^{\mathsf{T}}\right]$ is the **autocorrelation matrix**.

3.1.3 Uncorrelated does not imply independent

If X and Y are independent, meaning $p(X,Y) = p(X)p(Y)$, then $\text{Cov}\left[X,Y\right] = 0$, and hence $\text{corr}\left[X,Y\right] = 0$. So independent implies uncorrelated. However, the converse is not true: *uncorrelated does not imply independent*. For example, let $X \sim U(-1,1)$ and $Y = X^2$. Clearly Y is dependent on X (in fact, Y is uniquely determined by X), yet one can show (Exercise 3.1) that $\text{corr}\left[X,Y\right] = 0$. Some striking examples of this fact are shown in Figure 3.1. This shows several data sets where there is clear dependence between X and Y, and yet the correlation coefficient is 0. A more general measure of dependence between random variables is mutual information, discussed in Section 6.3. This is zero only if the variables truly are independent.

3.1.4 Correlation does not imply causation

It is well known that "**correlation does not imply causation**". For example, consider Figure 3.2. In red, we plot $x_{1:T}$, where x_t is the amount of ice cream sold in month t. In yellow, we plot $y_{1:T}$, where y_t is the violent crime rate in month t. (Quantities have been rescaled to make the plots overlap.) We see a strong correlation between these signals. Indeed, it is sometimes claimed that "eating ice cream causes murder" [Pet13]. Of course, this is just a **spurious correlation**, due to a **hidden common cause**, namely the weather. Hot weather increases ice cream sales, for obvious

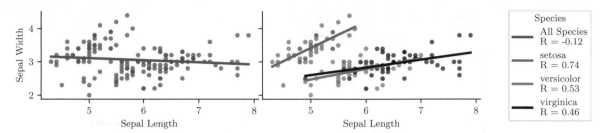

Figure 3.3: *Illustration of Simpson's paradox on the Iris dataset. (Left) Overall, y (sepal width) decreases with x (sepal length). (Right) Within each group, y increases with x. Generated by simpsons_paradox.ipynb.*

reasons. Hot weather also increases violent crime; the reason for this is hotly (ahem) debated; some claim it is due to an increase in anger [And01], but other claim it is merely due to more people being outside [Ash18], where most murders occur.

Another famous example concerns the positive correlation between birth rates and the presence of storks (a kind of bird). This has given rise to the urban legend that storks deliver babies [Mat00]. Of course, the true reason for the correlation is more likely due to hidden factors, such as increased living standards and hence more food. Many more amusing examples of such spurious correlations can be found in [Vig15].

These examples serve as a "warning sign", that we should not treat the ability for x to predict y as an indicator that x causes y.

3.1.5 Simpson's paradox

Simpson's paradox says that a statistical trend or relationship that appears in several different groups of data can disappear or reverse sign when these groups are combined. This results in counterintuitive behavior if we misinterpret claims of statistical dependence in a causal way.

A visualization of the paradox is given in Figure 3.3. Overall, we see that y decreases with x, but within each subpopulation, y increases with x.

For a recent real-world example of Simpson's paradox in the context of COVID-19, consider Figure 3.4(a). This shows that the case fatality rate (CFR) of COVID-19 in Italy is less than in China in each age group, but is higher overall. The reason for this is that there are more older people in Italy, as shown in Figure 3.4(b). In other words, Figure 3.4(a) shows $p(F = 1|A, C)$, where A is age, C is country, and $F = 1$ is the event that someone dies from COVID-19, and Figure 3.4(b) shows $p(A|C)$, which is the probability someone is in age bucket A for country C. Combining these, we find $p(F = 1|C = \text{Italy}) > p(F = 1|C = \text{China})$. See [KGS20] for more details.

3.2 The multivariate Gaussian (normal) distribution

The most widely used joint probability distribution for continuous random variables is the **multivariate Gaussian** or **multivariate normal** (**MVN**). This is mostly because it is mathematically convenient, but also because the Gaussian assumption is fairly reasonable in many cases (see the discussion in Section 2.6.4).

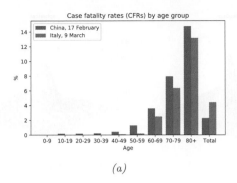
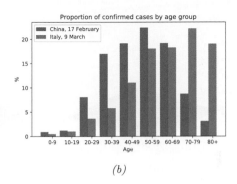

(a)   (b)

Figure 3.4: Illustration of Simpson's paradox using COVID-19, (a) Case fatality rates (CFRs) in Italy and China by age group, and in aggregated form ("Total", last pair of bars), up to the time of reporting (see legend). (b) Proportion of all confirmed cases included in (a) within each age group by country. From Figure 1 of [KGS20]. Used with kind permission of Julius von Kügelgen.

3.2.1 Definition

The MVN density is defined by the following:

$$\mathcal{N}(\boldsymbol{y}|\boldsymbol{\mu}, \boldsymbol{\Sigma}) \triangleq \frac{1}{(2\pi)^{D/2}|\boldsymbol{\Sigma}|^{1/2}} \exp\left[-\frac{1}{2}(\boldsymbol{y}-\boldsymbol{\mu})^{\mathsf{T}}\boldsymbol{\Sigma}^{-1}(\boldsymbol{y}-\boldsymbol{\mu})\right] \tag{3.11}$$

where $\boldsymbol{\mu} = \mathbb{E}[\boldsymbol{y}] \in \mathbb{R}^D$ is the mean vector, and $\boldsymbol{\Sigma} = \text{Cov}[\boldsymbol{y}]$ is the $D \times D$ **covariance matrix**, defined as follows:

$$\text{Cov}[\boldsymbol{y}] \triangleq \mathbb{E}\left[(\boldsymbol{y}-\mathbb{E}[\boldsymbol{y}])(\boldsymbol{y}-\mathbb{E}[\boldsymbol{y}])^{\mathsf{T}}\right] \tag{3.12}$$

$$= \begin{pmatrix} \mathbb{V}[Y_1] & \text{Cov}[Y_1, Y_2] & \cdots & \text{Cov}[Y_1, Y_D] \\ \text{Cov}[Y_2, Y_1] & \mathbb{V}[Y_2] & \cdots & \text{Cov}[Y_2, Y_D] \\ \vdots & \vdots & \ddots & \vdots \\ \text{Cov}[Y_D, Y_1] & \text{Cov}[Y_D, Y_2] & \cdots & \mathbb{V}[Y_D] \end{pmatrix} \tag{3.13}$$

where

$$\text{Cov}[Y_i, Y_j] \triangleq \mathbb{E}[(Y_i - \mathbb{E}[Y_i])(Y_j - \mathbb{E}[Y_j])] = \mathbb{E}[Y_i Y_j] - \mathbb{E}[Y_i]\mathbb{E}[Y_j] \tag{3.14}$$

and $\mathbb{V}[Y_i] = \text{Cov}[Y_i, Y_i]$. From Equation (3.12), we get the important result

$$\mathbb{E}\left[\boldsymbol{y}\boldsymbol{y}^{\mathsf{T}}\right] = \boldsymbol{\Sigma} + \boldsymbol{\mu}\boldsymbol{\mu}^{\mathsf{T}} \tag{3.15}$$

The normalization constant in Equation (3.11) $Z = (2\pi)^{D/2}|\boldsymbol{\Sigma}|^{1/2}$ just ensures that the pdf integrates to 1 (see Exercise 3.6).

In 2d, the MVN is known as the **bivariate Gaussian** distribution. Its pdf can be represented as $\boldsymbol{y} \sim \mathcal{N}(\boldsymbol{\mu}, \boldsymbol{\Sigma})$, where $\boldsymbol{y} \in \mathbb{R}^2$, $\boldsymbol{\mu} \in \mathbb{R}^2$ and

$$\boldsymbol{\Sigma} = \begin{pmatrix} \sigma_1^2 & \sigma_{12}^2 \\ \sigma_{21}^2 & \sigma_2^2 \end{pmatrix} = \begin{pmatrix} \sigma_1^2 & \rho\sigma_1\sigma_2 \\ \rho\sigma_1\sigma_2 & \sigma_2^2 \end{pmatrix} \tag{3.16}$$

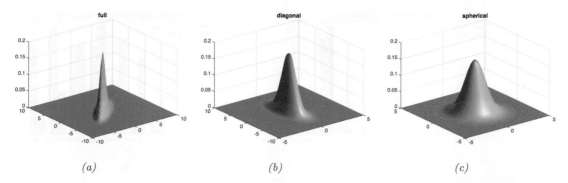

(a)   *(b)*   *(c)*

Figure 3.5: *Visualization of a 2d Gaussian density as a surface plot. (a) Distribution using a full covariance matrix can be oriented at any angle. (b) Distribution using a diagonal covariance matrix must be parallel to the axis. (c) Distribution using a spherical covariance matrix must have a symmetric shape. Generated by* gauss_plot_2d.ipynb.

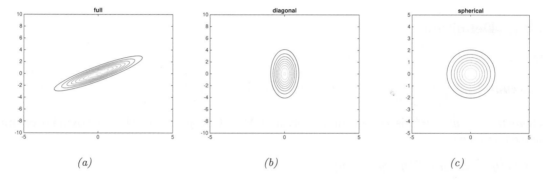

(a)   *(b)*   *(c)*

Figure 3.6: *Visualization of a 2d Gaussian density in terms of level sets of constant probability density. (a) A full covariance matrix has elliptical contours. (b) A diagonal covariance matrix is an* **axis aligned** *ellipse. (c) A spherical covariance matrix has a circular shape. Generated by* gauss_plot_2d.ipynb.

where ρ is the **correlation coefficient**, defined by

$$\text{corr}\left[Y_1, Y_2\right] \triangleq \frac{\text{Cov}\left[Y_1, Y_2\right]}{\sqrt{\mathbb{V}\left[Y_1\right]\mathbb{V}\left[Y_2\right]}} = \frac{\sigma_{12}^2}{\sigma_1 \sigma_2} \tag{3.17}$$

One can show (Exercise 3.2) that $-1 \leq \text{corr}\left[Y_1, Y_2\right] \leq 1$. Expanding out the pdf in the 2d case gives the following rather intimidating-looking result:

$$p(y_1, y_2) = \frac{1}{2\pi \sigma_1 \sigma_2 \sqrt{1-\rho^2}} \exp\left(-\frac{1}{2(1-\rho^2)} \times \right.$$
$$\left.\left[\frac{(y_1 - \mu_1)^2}{\sigma_1^2} + \frac{(y_2 - \mu_2)^2}{\sigma_2^2} - 2\rho\frac{(y_1 - \mu_1)}{\sigma_1}\frac{(y_2 - \mu_2)}{\sigma_2}\right]\right) \tag{3.18}$$

Figure 3.5 and Figure 3.6 plot some MVN densities in 2d for three different kinds of covariance matrices. A **full covariance matrix** has $D(D+1)/2$ parameters, where we divide by 2 since $\mathbf{\Sigma}$ is symmetric. (The reason for the elliptical shape is explained in Section 7.4.4, where we discuss the geometry of quadratic forms.) A **diagonal covariance matrix** has D parameters, and has 0s in the off-diagonal terms. A **spherical covariance matrix**, also called **isotropic covariance matrix**, has the form $\boldsymbol{\Sigma} = \sigma^2 \mathbf{I}_D$, so it only has one free parameter, namely σ^2.

3.2.2 Mahalanobis distance

In this section, we attempt to gain some insights into the geometric shape of the Gaussian pdf in multiple dimensions. To do this, we will consider the shape of the **level sets** of constant (log) probability.

The log probability at a specific point $\boldsymbol{y}$ is given by

$$\log p(\boldsymbol{y}|\boldsymbol{\mu}, \boldsymbol{\Sigma}) = -\frac{1}{2}(\boldsymbol{y} - \boldsymbol{\mu})^{\mathsf{T}} \boldsymbol{\Sigma}^{-1}(\boldsymbol{y} - \boldsymbol{\mu}) + \text{const} \tag{3.19}$$

The dependence on $\boldsymbol{y}$ can be expressed in terms of the **Mahalanobis distance** Δ between $\boldsymbol{y}$ and $\boldsymbol{\mu}$, whose square is defined as follows:

$$\Delta^2 \triangleq (\boldsymbol{y} - \boldsymbol{\mu})^{\mathsf{T}} \boldsymbol{\Sigma}^{-1}(\boldsymbol{y} - \boldsymbol{\mu}) \tag{3.20}$$

Thus contours of constant (log) probability are equivalent to contours of constant Mahalanobis distance.

To gain insight into the contours of constant Mahalanobis distance, we exploit the fact that $\boldsymbol{\Sigma}$, and hence $\boldsymbol{\Lambda} = \boldsymbol{\Sigma}^{-1}$, are both positive definite matrices (by assumption). Consider the following eigendecomposition (Section 7.4) of $\boldsymbol{\Sigma}$:

$$\boldsymbol{\Sigma} = \sum_{d=1}^{D} \lambda_d \boldsymbol{u}_d \boldsymbol{u}_d^{\mathsf{T}} \tag{3.21}$$

We can similarly write

$$\boldsymbol{\Sigma}^{-1} = \sum_{d=1}^{D} \frac{1}{\lambda_d} \boldsymbol{u}_d \boldsymbol{u}_d^{\mathsf{T}} \tag{3.22}$$

Let us define $z_d \triangleq \boldsymbol{u}_d^{\mathsf{T}}(\boldsymbol{y} - \boldsymbol{\mu})$, so $\boldsymbol{z} = \mathbf{U}(\boldsymbol{y} - \boldsymbol{\mu})$. Then we can rewrite the Mahalanobis distance as follows:

$$(\boldsymbol{y} - \boldsymbol{\mu})^{\mathsf{T}} \boldsymbol{\Sigma}^{-1}(\boldsymbol{y} - \boldsymbol{\mu}) = (\boldsymbol{y} - \boldsymbol{\mu})^{\mathsf{T}} \left(\sum_{d=1}^{D} \frac{1}{\lambda_d} \boldsymbol{u}_d \boldsymbol{u}_d^{\mathsf{T}} \right) (\boldsymbol{y} - \boldsymbol{\mu}) \tag{3.23}$$

$$= \sum_{d=1}^{D} \frac{1}{\lambda_d} (\boldsymbol{y} - \boldsymbol{\mu})^{\mathsf{T}} \boldsymbol{u}_d \boldsymbol{u}_d^{\mathsf{T}}(\boldsymbol{y} - \boldsymbol{\mu}) = \sum_{d=1}^{D} \frac{z_d^2}{\lambda_d} \tag{3.24}$$

As we discuss in Section 7.4.4, this means we can interpret the Mahalanobis distance as Euclidean distance in a new coordinate frame $\boldsymbol{z}$ in which we rotate $\boldsymbol{y}$ by $\mathbf{U}$ and scale by $\boldsymbol{\Lambda}$.

For example, in 2d, let us consider the set of points (z_1, z_2) that satisfy this equation:

$$\frac{z_1^2}{\lambda_1} + \frac{z_2^2}{\lambda_2} = r \tag{3.25}$$

Since these points have the same Mahalanobis distance, they correspond to points of equal probability. Hence we see that the contours of equal probability density of a 2d Gaussian lie along ellipses. This is illustrated in Figure 7.6. The eigenvectors determine the orientation of the ellipse, and the eigenvalues determine how elongated it is.

3.2.3   Marginals and conditionals of an MVN *

Suppose $\boldsymbol{y} = (\boldsymbol{y}_1, \boldsymbol{y}_2)$ is jointly Gaussian with parameters

$$\boldsymbol{\mu} = \begin{pmatrix} \boldsymbol{\mu}_1 \\ \boldsymbol{\mu}_2 \end{pmatrix}, \quad \boldsymbol{\Sigma} = \begin{pmatrix} \boldsymbol{\Sigma}_{11} & \boldsymbol{\Sigma}_{12} \\ \boldsymbol{\Sigma}_{21} & \boldsymbol{\Sigma}_{22} \end{pmatrix}, \quad \boldsymbol{\Lambda} = \boldsymbol{\Sigma}^{-1} = \begin{pmatrix} \boldsymbol{\Lambda}_{11} & \boldsymbol{\Lambda}_{12} \\ \boldsymbol{\Lambda}_{21} & \boldsymbol{\Lambda}_{22} \end{pmatrix} \tag{3.26}$$

where $\boldsymbol{\Lambda}$ is the **precision matrix**. Then the marginals are given by

$$\begin{aligned} p(\boldsymbol{y}_1) &= \mathcal{N}(\boldsymbol{y}_1 | \boldsymbol{\mu}_1, \boldsymbol{\Sigma}_{11}) \\ p(\boldsymbol{y}_2) &= \mathcal{N}(\boldsymbol{y}_2 | \boldsymbol{\mu}_2, \boldsymbol{\Sigma}_{22}) \end{aligned} \tag{3.27}$$

and the posterior conditional is given by

$$\begin{aligned} p(\boldsymbol{y}_1 | \boldsymbol{y}_2) &= \mathcal{N}(\boldsymbol{y}_1 | \boldsymbol{\mu}_{1|2}, \boldsymbol{\Sigma}_{1|2}) \\ \boldsymbol{\mu}_{1|2} &= \boldsymbol{\mu}_1 + \boldsymbol{\Sigma}_{12} \boldsymbol{\Sigma}_{22}^{-1} (\boldsymbol{y}_2 - \boldsymbol{\mu}_2) \\ &= \boldsymbol{\mu}_1 - \boldsymbol{\Lambda}_{11}^{-1} \boldsymbol{\Lambda}_{12} (\boldsymbol{y}_2 - \boldsymbol{\mu}_2) \\ &= \boldsymbol{\Sigma}_{1|2} \left(\boldsymbol{\Lambda}_{11} \boldsymbol{\mu}_1 - \boldsymbol{\Lambda}_{12} (\boldsymbol{y}_2 - \boldsymbol{\mu}_2) \right) \\ \boldsymbol{\Sigma}_{1|2} &= \boldsymbol{\Sigma}_{11} - \boldsymbol{\Sigma}_{12} \boldsymbol{\Sigma}_{22}^{-1} \boldsymbol{\Sigma}_{21} = \boldsymbol{\Lambda}_{11}^{-1} \end{aligned} \tag{3.28}$$

These equations are of such crucial importance in this book that we have put a box around them, so you can easily find them later. For the derivation of these results (which relies on computing the Schur complement $\boldsymbol{\Sigma}/\boldsymbol{\Sigma}_{22} = \boldsymbol{\Sigma}_{11} - \boldsymbol{\Sigma}_{12} \boldsymbol{\Sigma}_{22}^{-1} \boldsymbol{\Sigma}_{21}$), see Section 7.3.5.

We see that both the marginal and conditional distributions are themselves Gaussian. For the marginals, we just extract the rows and columns corresponding to $\boldsymbol{y}_1$ or $\boldsymbol{y}_2$. For the conditional, we have to do a bit more work. However, it is not that complicated: the conditional mean is just a linear function of $\boldsymbol{y}_2$, and the conditional covariance is just a constant matrix that is independent of $\boldsymbol{y}_2$. We give three different (but equivalent) expressions for the posterior mean, and two different (but equivalent) expressions for the posterior covariance; each one is useful in different circumstances.

3.2.4 Example: conditioning a 2d Gaussian

Let us consider a 2d example. The covariance matrix is

$$\mathbf{\Sigma} = \begin{pmatrix} \sigma_1^2 & \rho\sigma_1\sigma_2 \\ \rho\sigma_1\sigma_2 & \sigma_2^2 \end{pmatrix} \tag{3.29}$$

The marginal $p(y_1)$ is a 1D Gaussian, obtained by projecting the joint distribution onto the y_1 line:

$$p(y_1) = \mathcal{N}(y_1|\mu_1, \sigma_1^2) \tag{3.30}$$

Suppose we observe $Y_2 = y_2$; the conditional $p(y_1|y_2)$ is obtained by "slicing" the joint distribution through the $Y_2 = y_2$ line:

$$p(y_1|y_2) = \mathcal{N}\left(y_1|\mu_1 + \frac{\rho\sigma_1\sigma_2}{\sigma_2^2}(y_2 - \mu_2),\ \sigma_1^2 - \frac{(\rho\sigma_1\sigma_2)^2}{\sigma_2^2}\right) \tag{3.31}$$

If $\sigma_1 = \sigma_2 = \sigma$, we get

$$p(y_1|y_2) = \mathcal{N}\left(y_1|\mu_1 + \rho(y_2 - \mu_2),\ \sigma^2(1 - \rho^2)\right) \tag{3.32}$$

For example, suppose $\rho = 0.8$, $\sigma_1 = \sigma_2 = 1$, $\mu_1 = \mu_2 = 0$, and $y_2 = 1$. We see that $\mathbb{E}[y_1|y_2 = 1] = 0.8$, which makes sense, since $\rho = 0.8$ means that we believe that if y_2 increases by 1 (beyond its mean), then y_1 increases by 0.8. We also see $\mathbb{V}[y_1|y_2 = 1] = 1 - 0.8^2 = 0.36$. This also makes sense: our uncertainty about y_1 has gone down, since we have learned something about y_1 (indirectly) by observing y_2. If $\rho = 0$, we get $p(y_1|y_2) = \mathcal{N}\left(y_1|\mu_1,\ \sigma_1^2\right)$, since y_2 conveys no information about y_1 if they are uncorrelated (and hence independent).

3.2.5 Example: Imputing missing values *

As an example application of the above results, suppose we observe some parts (dimensions) of $\boldsymbol{y}$, with the remaining parts being missing or unobserved. We can exploit the correlation amongst the dimensions (encoded by the covariance matrix) to infer the missing entries; this is called **missing value imputation**.

Figure 3.7 shows a simple example. We sampled N vectors from a $D = 10$-dimensional Gaussian, and then deliberately "hid" 50% of the data in each sample (row). We then inferred the missing entries given the observed entries and the true model parameters.[1] More precisely, for each row n of the data matrix, we compute $p(\boldsymbol{y}_{n,h}|\boldsymbol{y}_{n,v}, \boldsymbol{\theta})$, where $\boldsymbol{v}$ are the indices of the visible entries in that row, $\boldsymbol{h}$ are the remaining indices of the hidden entries, and $\boldsymbol{\theta} = (\boldsymbol{\mu}, \boldsymbol{\Sigma})$. From this, we compute the marginal distribution of each missing variable $i \in \boldsymbol{h}$, $p(y_{n,i}|\boldsymbol{y}_{n,v}, \boldsymbol{\theta})$. From the marginal, we compute the posterior mean, $\bar{y}_{n,i} = \mathbb{E}[y_{n,i}|\boldsymbol{y}_{n,v}, \boldsymbol{\theta}]$.

The posterior mean represents our "best guess" about the true value of that entry, in the sense that it minimizes our expected squared error, as explained in Chapter 5. We can use $\mathbb{V}[y_{n,i}|\boldsymbol{y}_{n,v}, \boldsymbol{\theta}]$ as a measure of confidence in this guess, although this is not shown. Alternatively, we could draw multiple posterior samples from $p(\boldsymbol{y}_{n,h}|\boldsymbol{y}_{n,v}, \boldsymbol{\theta})$; this is called **multiple imputation**, and provides a more robust estimate to downstream algorithms that consume the "filled in" data.

---

1. In practice, we would need to estimate the parameters from the partially observed data. Unfortunately the MLE results in Section 4.2.6 no longer apply, but we can use the EM algorithm to derive an approximate MLE in the presence of missing data. See the sequel to this book for details.

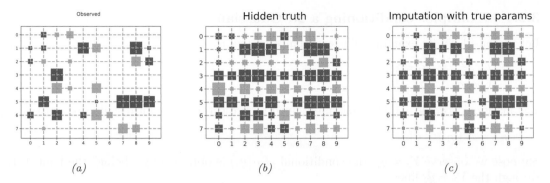

*Figure 3.7: Illustration of data imputation using an MVN. (a) Visualization of the data matrix. Blank entries are missing (not observed). Blue are positive, green are negative. Area of the square is proportional to the value. (This is known as a **Hinton diagram**, named after Geoff Hinton, a famous ML researcher.) (b) True data matrix (hidden). (c) Mean of the posterior predictive distribution, based on partially observed data in that row, using the true model parameters. Generated by gauss_imputation_known_params_demo.ipynb.*

3.3   Linear Gaussian systems *

In Section 3.2.3, we conditioned on noise-free observations to infer the posterior over the hidden parts of a Gaussian random vector. In this section, we extend this approach to handle noisy observations.

Let $z \in \mathbb{R}^L$ be an unknown vector of values, and $y \in \mathbb{R}^D$ be some noisy measurement of z. We assume these variables are related by the following joint distribution:

$$p(z) = \mathcal{N}(z|\boldsymbol{\mu}_z, \boldsymbol{\Sigma}_z) \tag{3.33}$$
$$p(y|z) = \mathcal{N}(y|\mathbf{W}z + b, \boldsymbol{\Sigma}_y) \tag{3.34}$$

where $\mathbf{W}$ is a matrix of size $D \times L$. This is an example of a **linear Gaussian system**.

The corresponding joint distribution, $p(z, y) = p(z)p(y|z)$, is a $L + D$ dimensional Gaussian, with mean and covariance given by

$$\boldsymbol{\mu} = \begin{pmatrix} \boldsymbol{\mu}_z \\ \mathbf{W}\boldsymbol{\mu}_z + b \end{pmatrix} \tag{3.35}$$

$$\boldsymbol{\Sigma} = \begin{pmatrix} \boldsymbol{\Sigma}_z & \boldsymbol{\Sigma}_z \mathbf{W}^\mathsf{T} \\ \mathbf{W}\boldsymbol{\Sigma}_z & \boldsymbol{\Sigma}_y + \mathbf{W}\boldsymbol{\Sigma}_z \mathbf{W}^\mathsf{T} \end{pmatrix} \tag{3.36}$$

By applying the Gaussian conditioning formula in Equation (3.28) to the joint $p(y, z)$ we can compute the posterior $p(z|y)$, as we explain below. This can be interpreted as inverting the $z \to y$ arrow in the generative model from latents to observations.

3.3.1   Bayes rule for Gaussians

The posterior over the latent is given by

$$
\begin{aligned}
p(\boldsymbol{z}|\boldsymbol{y}) &= \mathcal{N}(\boldsymbol{z}|\boldsymbol{\mu}_{z|y}, \boldsymbol{\Sigma}_{z|y}) \\
\boldsymbol{\Sigma}_{z|y}^{-1} &= \boldsymbol{\Sigma}_z^{-1} + \mathbf{W}^\mathsf{T}\boldsymbol{\Sigma}_y^{-1}\mathbf{W} \\
\boldsymbol{\mu}_{z|y} &= \boldsymbol{\Sigma}_{z|y}[\mathbf{W}^\mathsf{T}\boldsymbol{\Sigma}_y^{-1}\,(\boldsymbol{y}-\boldsymbol{b}) + \boldsymbol{\Sigma}_z^{-1}\boldsymbol{\mu}_z]
\end{aligned}
\tag{3.37}
$$

This is known as **Bayes rule for Gaussians**. Furthermore, the normalization constant of the posterior is given by

$$
p(\boldsymbol{y}) = \int \mathcal{N}(\boldsymbol{z}|\boldsymbol{\mu}_z, \boldsymbol{\Sigma}_z)\mathcal{N}(\boldsymbol{y}|\mathbf{W}\boldsymbol{z}+\boldsymbol{b}, \boldsymbol{\Sigma}_y)d\boldsymbol{z} = \mathcal{N}(\boldsymbol{y}|\mathbf{W}\boldsymbol{\mu}_z+\boldsymbol{b}, \boldsymbol{\Sigma}_y + \mathbf{W}\boldsymbol{\Sigma}_z\mathbf{W}^\mathsf{T})
\tag{3.38}
$$

We see that the Gaussian prior $p(\boldsymbol{z})$, combined with the Gaussian likelihood $p(\boldsymbol{y}|\boldsymbol{z})$, results in a Gaussian posterior $p(\boldsymbol{z}|\boldsymbol{y})$. Thus Gaussians are closed under Bayesian conditioning. To describe this more generally, we say that the Gaussian prior is a **conjugate prior** for the Gaussian likelihood, since the posterior distribution has the same type as the prior. We discuss the notion of conjugate priors in more detail in Section 4.6.1.

In the sections below, we give various applications of this result. But first, we give the derivation.

3.3.2   Derivation *

We now derive Equation 3.37. The basic idea is to derive the joint distribution, $p(\boldsymbol{z}, \boldsymbol{y}) = p(\boldsymbol{z})p(\boldsymbol{y}|\boldsymbol{z})$, and then to use the results from Section 3.2.3 for computing $p(\boldsymbol{z}|\boldsymbol{y})$.

In more detail, we proceed as follows. The log of the joint distribution is as follows (dropping irrelevant constants):

$$
\log p(\boldsymbol{z}, \boldsymbol{y}) = -\frac{1}{2}(\boldsymbol{z}-\boldsymbol{\mu}_z)^T\boldsymbol{\Sigma}_z^{-1}(\boldsymbol{z}-\boldsymbol{\mu}_z) - \frac{1}{2}(\boldsymbol{y}-\mathbf{W}\boldsymbol{z}-\boldsymbol{b})^T\boldsymbol{\Sigma}_y^{-1}(\boldsymbol{y}-\mathbf{W}\boldsymbol{z}-\boldsymbol{b})
\tag{3.39}
$$

This is clearly a joint Gaussian distribution, since it is the exponential of a quadratic form.

Expanding out the quadratic terms involving $\boldsymbol{z}$ and $\boldsymbol{y}$, and ignoring linear and constant terms, we have

$$
Q = -\frac{1}{2}\boldsymbol{z}^T\boldsymbol{\Sigma}_z^{-1}\boldsymbol{z} - \frac{1}{2}\boldsymbol{y}^T\boldsymbol{\Sigma}_y^{-1}\boldsymbol{y} - \frac{1}{2}(\mathbf{W}\boldsymbol{z})^T\boldsymbol{\Sigma}_y^{-1}(\mathbf{W}\boldsymbol{z}) + \boldsymbol{y}^T\boldsymbol{\Sigma}_y^{-1}\mathbf{W}\boldsymbol{z}
\tag{3.40}
$$

$$
= -\frac{1}{2}\begin{pmatrix}\boldsymbol{z} \\ \boldsymbol{y}\end{pmatrix}^T\begin{pmatrix}\boldsymbol{\Sigma}_z^{-1} + \mathbf{W}^T\boldsymbol{\Sigma}_y^{-1}\mathbf{W} & -\mathbf{W}^T\boldsymbol{\Sigma}_y^{-1} \\ -\boldsymbol{\Sigma}_y^{-1}\mathbf{W} & \boldsymbol{\Sigma}_y^{-1}\end{pmatrix}\begin{pmatrix}\boldsymbol{z} \\ \boldsymbol{y}\end{pmatrix}
\tag{3.41}
$$

$$
= -\frac{1}{2}\begin{pmatrix}\boldsymbol{z} \\ \boldsymbol{y}\end{pmatrix}^T\boldsymbol{\Sigma}^{-1}\begin{pmatrix}\boldsymbol{z} \\ \boldsymbol{y}\end{pmatrix}
\tag{3.42}
$$

where the precision matrix of the joint is defined as

$$
\boldsymbol{\Sigma}^{-1} = \begin{pmatrix}\boldsymbol{\Sigma}_z^{-1} + \mathbf{W}^T\boldsymbol{\Sigma}_y^{-1}\mathbf{W} & -\mathbf{W}^T\boldsymbol{\Sigma}_y^{-1} \\ -\boldsymbol{\Sigma}_y^{-1}\mathbf{W} & \boldsymbol{\Sigma}_y^{-1}\end{pmatrix} \triangleq \boldsymbol{\Lambda} = \begin{pmatrix}\boldsymbol{\Lambda}_{zz} & \boldsymbol{\Lambda}_{zy} \\ \boldsymbol{\Lambda}_{yz} & \boldsymbol{\Lambda}_{yy}\end{pmatrix}
\tag{3.43}
$$

From Equation 3.28, and using the fact that $\boldsymbol{\mu}_y = \mathbf{W}\boldsymbol{\mu}_z + \boldsymbol{b}$, we have

$$p(\boldsymbol{z}|\boldsymbol{y}) = \mathcal{N}(\boldsymbol{\mu}_{z|y}, \boldsymbol{\Sigma}_{z|y}) \tag{3.44}$$

$$\boldsymbol{\Sigma}_{z|y} = \boldsymbol{\Lambda}_{zz}^{-1} = (\boldsymbol{\Sigma}_z^{-1} + \mathbf{W}^T\boldsymbol{\Sigma}_y^{-1}\mathbf{W})^{-1} \tag{3.45}$$

$$\boldsymbol{\mu}_{z|y} = \boldsymbol{\Sigma}_{z|y}\left(\boldsymbol{\Lambda}_{zz}\boldsymbol{\mu}_z - \boldsymbol{\Lambda}_{zy}(\boldsymbol{y} - \boldsymbol{\mu}_y)\right) \tag{3.46}$$

$$= \boldsymbol{\Sigma}_{z|y}\left(\boldsymbol{\Sigma}_z^{-1}\boldsymbol{\mu}_z + \mathbf{W}^\mathsf{T}\boldsymbol{\Sigma}_y^{-1}\mathbf{W}\boldsymbol{\mu}_z + \mathbf{W}^\mathsf{T}\boldsymbol{\Sigma}_y^{-1}(\boldsymbol{y} - \boldsymbol{\mu}_y)\right) \tag{3.47}$$

$$= \boldsymbol{\Sigma}_{z|y}\left(\boldsymbol{\Sigma}_z^{-1}\boldsymbol{\mu}_z + \mathbf{W}^\mathsf{T}\boldsymbol{\Sigma}_y^{-1}(\mathbf{W}\boldsymbol{\mu}_z + \boldsymbol{y} - \boldsymbol{\mu}_y)\right) \tag{3.48}$$

$$= \boldsymbol{\Sigma}_{z|y}\left(\boldsymbol{\Sigma}_z^{-1}\boldsymbol{\mu}_z + \mathbf{W}^T\boldsymbol{\Sigma}_y^{-1}(\boldsymbol{y} - \boldsymbol{b})\right) \tag{3.49}$$

3.3.3   Example: Inferring an unknown scalar

Suppose we make N noisy measurements y_i of some underlying quantity z; let us assume the measurement noise has fixed precision $\lambda_y = 1/\sigma^2$, so the likelihood is

$$p(y_i|z) = \mathcal{N}(y_i|z, \lambda_y^{-1}) \tag{3.50}$$

Now let us use a Gaussian prior for the value of the unknown source:

$$p(z) = \mathcal{N}(z|\mu_0, \lambda_0^{-1}) \tag{3.51}$$

We want to compute $p(z|y_1, \ldots, y_N, \sigma^2)$. We can convert this to a form that lets us apply Bayes rule for Gaussians by defining $\boldsymbol{y} = (y_1, \ldots, y_N)$, $\mathbf{W} = \mathbf{1}_N$ (an $N \times 1$ column vector of 1's), and $\boldsymbol{\Sigma}_y^{-1} = \mathrm{diag}(\lambda_y \mathbf{I})$. Then we get

$$p(z|\boldsymbol{y}) = \mathcal{N}(z|\mu_N, \lambda_N^{-1}) \tag{3.52}$$

$$\lambda_N = \lambda_0 + N\lambda_y \tag{3.53}$$

$$\mu_N = \frac{N\lambda_y\overline{y} + \lambda_0\mu_0}{\lambda_N} = \frac{N\lambda_y}{N\lambda_y + \lambda_0}\overline{y} + \frac{\lambda_0}{N\lambda_y + \lambda_0}\mu_0 \tag{3.54}$$

These equations are quite intuitive: the posterior precision λ_N is the prior precision λ_0 plus N units of measurement precision λ_y. Also, the posterior mean μ_N is a convex combination of the MLE $\overline{y}$ and the prior mean μ_0. This makes it clear that the posterior mean is a compromise between the MLE and the prior. If the prior is weak relative to the signal strength (λ_0 is small relative to λ_y), we put more weight on the MLE. If the prior is strong relative to the signal strength (λ_0 is large relative to λ_y), we put more weight on the prior. This is illustrated in Figure 3.8.

Note that the posterior mean is written in terms of $N\lambda_y\overline{y}$, so having N measurements each of precision λ_y is like having one measurement with value $\overline{y}$ and precision $N\lambda_y$.

We can rewrite the results in terms of the posterior variance, rather than posterior precision, as follows:

$$p(z|\mathcal{D}, \sigma^2) = \mathcal{N}(z|\mu_N, \tau_N^2) \tag{3.55}$$

$$\tau_N^2 = \frac{1}{\frac{N}{\sigma^2} + \frac{1}{\tau_0^2}} = \frac{\sigma^2\tau_0^2}{N\tau_0^2 + \sigma^2} \tag{3.56}$$

$$\mu_N = \tau_N^2\left(\frac{\mu_0}{\tau_0^2} + \frac{N\overline{y}}{\sigma^2}\right) = \frac{\sigma^2}{N\tau_0^2 + \sigma^2}\mu_0 + \frac{N\tau_0^2}{N\tau_0^2 + \sigma^2}\overline{y} \tag{3.57}$$

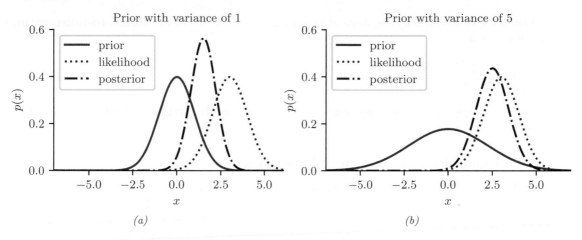

Figure 3.8: Inference about z given a noisy observation $y = 3$. (a) Strong prior $\mathcal{N}(0, 1)$. The posterior mean is "shrunk" towards the prior mean, which is 0. (b) Weak prior $\mathcal{N}(0, 5)$. The posterior mean is similar to the MLE. Generated by gauss_infer_1d.ipynb.

where $\tau_0^2 = 1/\lambda_0$ is the prior variance and $\tau_N^2 = 1/\lambda_N$ is the posterior variance.

We can also compute the posterior sequentially, by updating after each observation. If $N = 1$, we can rewrite the posterior after seeing a single observation as follows (where we define $\Sigma_y = \sigma^2$, $\Sigma_0 = \tau_0^2$ and $\Sigma_1 = \tau_1^2$ to be the variances of the likelihood, prior and posterior):

$$p(z|y) = \mathcal{N}(z|\mu_1, \Sigma_1) \tag{3.58}$$

$$\Sigma_1 = \left(\frac{1}{\Sigma_0} + \frac{1}{\Sigma_y} \right)^{-1} = \frac{\Sigma_y \Sigma_0}{\Sigma_0 + \Sigma_y} \tag{3.59}$$

$$\mu_1 = \Sigma_1 \left(\frac{\mu_0}{\Sigma_0} + \frac{y}{\Sigma_y} \right) \tag{3.60}$$

We can rewrite the posterior mean in 3 different ways:

$$\mu_1 = \frac{\Sigma_y}{\Sigma_y + \Sigma_0} \mu_0 + \frac{\Sigma_0}{\Sigma_y + \Sigma_0} y \tag{3.61}$$

$$= \mu_0 + (y - \mu_0) \frac{\Sigma_0}{\Sigma_y + \Sigma_0} \tag{3.62}$$

$$= y - (y - \mu_0) \frac{\Sigma_y}{\Sigma_y + \Sigma_0} \tag{3.63}$$

The first equation is a convex combination of the prior and the data. The second equation is the prior mean adjusted towards the data. The third equation is the data adjusted towards the prior mean; this is called **shrinkage**. These are all equivalent ways of expressing the tradeoff between likelihood and prior. If Σ_0 is small relative to Σ_y, corresponding to a strong prior, the amount of shrinkage is large (see Figure 3.8(a)), whereas if Σ_0 is large relative to Σ_y, corresponding to a weak prior, the amount of shrinkage is small (see Figure 3.8(b)).

Another way to quantify the amount of shrinkage is in terms of the **signal-to-noise ratio**, which is defined as follows:

$$\text{SNR} \triangleq \frac{\mathbb{E}\left[Z^2\right]}{\mathbb{E}\left[\epsilon^2\right]} = \frac{\Sigma_0 + \mu_0^2}{\Sigma_y} \tag{3.64}$$

where $z \sim \mathcal{N}(\mu_0, \Sigma_0)$ is the true signal, $y = z + \epsilon$ is the observed signal, and $\epsilon \sim \mathcal{N}(0, \Sigma_y)$ is the noise term.

3.3.4   Example: inferring an unknown vector

Suppose we have an unknown quantity of interest, $\boldsymbol{z} \in \mathbb{R}^D$, which we endow with a Gaussian prior, $p(\boldsymbol{z}) = \mathcal{N}(\boldsymbol{\mu}_z, \boldsymbol{\Sigma}_z)$. If we "know nothing" about $\boldsymbol{z}$ a priori, we can set $\boldsymbol{\Sigma}_z = \infty \mathbf{I}$, which means we are completely uncertain about what the value of $\boldsymbol{z}$ should be. (In practice, we can use a large but finite value for the covariance.) By symmetry, it seems reasonable to set $\boldsymbol{\mu}_z = \mathbf{0}$.

Now suppose we make N noisy but independent measurements of $\boldsymbol{z}$, $\boldsymbol{y}_n \sim \mathcal{N}(\boldsymbol{z}, \boldsymbol{\Sigma}_y)$, each of size D. One can show that the likelihood of N observations can be represented by a single Gaussian evaluated at their average, $\overline{\boldsymbol{y}}$, provided we scale down the covariance by $1/N$ to compensate for the increased measurement precision, i.e.,

$$p(\mathcal{D}|\boldsymbol{z}) = \prod_{n=1}^{N} \mathcal{N}(\boldsymbol{y}_n|\boldsymbol{z}, \boldsymbol{\Sigma}_y) \propto \mathcal{N}(\overline{\boldsymbol{y}}|\boldsymbol{z}, \tfrac{1}{N}\boldsymbol{\Sigma}_y) \tag{3.65}$$

To see why this is true, consider the case of two measurements. The log likelihood can then be written using canonical parameters as follows:[2]

$$
\begin{aligned}
\log(p(\boldsymbol{y}_1|\boldsymbol{z})p(\boldsymbol{y}_2|\boldsymbol{z})) &= K_1 - \frac{1}{2}\left(\boldsymbol{z}^\mathsf{T}\boldsymbol{\Sigma}_y^{-1}\boldsymbol{z} - 2\boldsymbol{z}^\mathsf{T}\boldsymbol{\Sigma}_y^{-1}\boldsymbol{y}_1\right) - \frac{1}{2}\left(\boldsymbol{z}^\mathsf{T}\boldsymbol{\Sigma}_y^{-1}\boldsymbol{z} - 2\boldsymbol{z}^\mathsf{T}\boldsymbol{\Sigma}_y^{-1}\boldsymbol{y}_1\right) \\
&= K_1 - \frac{1}{2}\left(\boldsymbol{z}^\mathsf{T}2\boldsymbol{\Sigma}_y^{-1}\boldsymbol{z} - 2\boldsymbol{z}^\mathsf{T}\boldsymbol{\Sigma}_y^{-1}\left(\boldsymbol{y}_1 + \boldsymbol{y}_2\right)\right) \\
&= K_1 - \frac{1}{2}\left(\boldsymbol{z}^\mathsf{T}2\boldsymbol{\Sigma}_y^{-1}\boldsymbol{z} - 2\boldsymbol{z}^\mathsf{T}2\boldsymbol{\Sigma}_y^{-1}\bar{\boldsymbol{y}}\right) \\
&= K_2 + \log\mathcal{N}(\boldsymbol{z}|\bar{\boldsymbol{y}}, \tfrac{\Sigma_y}{2}) = K_2 + \log\mathcal{N}(\bar{\boldsymbol{y}}|\boldsymbol{z}, \tfrac{\Sigma_y}{2})
\end{aligned}
$$

where K_1 and K_2 are constants independent of $\boldsymbol{z}$.

Using this, and setting $\mathbf{W} = \mathbf{I}$, $\boldsymbol{b} = \mathbf{0}$, we can then use Bayes rule for Gaussian to compute the posterior over $\boldsymbol{z}$:

$$p(\boldsymbol{z}|\boldsymbol{y}_1, \ldots, \boldsymbol{y}_N) = \mathcal{N}(\boldsymbol{z}|\,\widehat{\boldsymbol{\mu}}, \widehat{\boldsymbol{\Sigma}}) \tag{3.66}$$

$$\widehat{\boldsymbol{\Sigma}}^{-1} = \boldsymbol{\Sigma}_z^{-1} + N\boldsymbol{\Sigma}_y^{-1} \tag{3.67}$$

$$\widehat{\boldsymbol{\mu}} = \widehat{\boldsymbol{\Sigma}}\left(\boldsymbol{\Sigma}_y^{-1}(N\overline{\boldsymbol{y}}) + \boldsymbol{\Sigma}_z^{-1}\boldsymbol{\mu}_z\right) \tag{3.68}$$

where $\widehat{\boldsymbol{\mu}}$ and $\widehat{\boldsymbol{\Sigma}}$ are the parameters of the posterior.

---

2. This derivation is due to Joaquin Rapela. See https://github.com/probml/pml-book/issues/512.

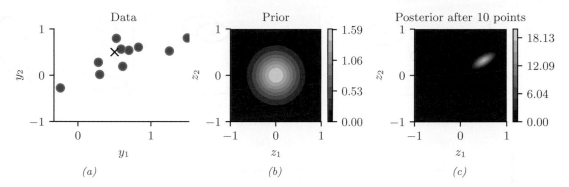

Figure 3.9: Illustration of Bayesian inference for a 2d Gaussian random vector $\boldsymbol{z}$. (a) The data is generated from $\boldsymbol{y}_n \sim \mathcal{N}(\boldsymbol{z}, \boldsymbol{\Sigma}_y)$, where $\boldsymbol{z} = [0.5, 0.5]^\mathsf{T}$ and $\boldsymbol{\Sigma}_y = 0.1[2, 1; 1, 1])$. We assume the sensor noise covariance $\boldsymbol{\Sigma}_y$ is known but $\boldsymbol{z}$ is unknown. The black cross represents $\boldsymbol{z}$. (b) The prior is $p(\boldsymbol{z}) = \mathcal{N}(\boldsymbol{z}|\boldsymbol{0}, 0.1\mathbf{I}_2)$. (c) We show the posterior after 10 data points have been observed. Generated by gauss_infer_2d.ipynb.

Figure 3.9 gives a 2d example. We can think of $\boldsymbol{z}$ as representing the true, but unknown, location of an object in 2d space, such as a missile or airplane, and the $\boldsymbol{y}_n$ as being noisy observations, such as radar "blips". As we receive more blips, we are better able to localize the source. (In the sequel to this book, [Mur23], we discuss the **Kalman filter** algorithm, which extends this idea to a temporal sequence of observations.)

The posterior uncertainty about each component of $\boldsymbol{z}$ location vector depends on how reliable the sensor is in each of these dimensions. In the above example, the measurement noise in dimension 1 is higher than in dimension 2, so we have more posterior uncertainty about z_1 (horizontal axis) than about z_2 (vertical axis).

3.3.5 Example: sensor fusion

In this section, we extend Section 3.3.4, to the case where we have multiple measurements, coming from different sensors, each with different reliabilities. That is, the model has the form

$$p(\boldsymbol{z}, \boldsymbol{y}) = p(\boldsymbol{z}) \prod_{m=1}^{M} \prod_{n=1}^{N_m} \mathcal{N}(\boldsymbol{y}_{n,m}|\boldsymbol{z}, \boldsymbol{\Sigma}_m) \tag{3.69}$$

where M is the number of sensors (measurement devices), and N_m is the number of observations from sensor m, and $\boldsymbol{y} = \boldsymbol{y}_{1:N,1:M} \in \mathbb{R}^K$. Our goal is to combine the evidence together, to compute $p(\boldsymbol{z}|\boldsymbol{y})$. This is known as **sensor fusion**.

We now give a simple example, where there are just two sensors, so $\boldsymbol{y}_1 \sim \mathcal{N}(\boldsymbol{z}, \boldsymbol{\Sigma}_1)$ and $\boldsymbol{y}_2 \sim \mathcal{N}(\boldsymbol{z}, \boldsymbol{\Sigma}_2)$. Pictorially, we can represent this example as $\boldsymbol{y}_1 \leftarrow \boldsymbol{z} \rightarrow \boldsymbol{y}_2$. We can combine $\boldsymbol{y}_1$ and $\boldsymbol{y}_2$ into a single vector $\boldsymbol{y}$, so the model can be represented as $\boldsymbol{z} \rightarrow [\boldsymbol{y}_1, \boldsymbol{y}_2]$, where $p(\boldsymbol{y}|\boldsymbol{z}) = \mathcal{N}(\boldsymbol{y}|\mathbf{W}\boldsymbol{z}, \boldsymbol{\Sigma}_y)$, where $\mathbf{W} = [\mathbf{I}; \mathbf{I}]$ and $\boldsymbol{\Sigma}_y = [\boldsymbol{\Sigma}_1, \boldsymbol{0}; \boldsymbol{0}, \boldsymbol{\Sigma}_2]$ are block-structured matrices. We can then apply Bayes' rule for Gaussians to compute $p(\boldsymbol{z}|\boldsymbol{y})$.

Figure 3.10(a) gives a 2d example, where we set $\boldsymbol{\Sigma}_1 = \boldsymbol{\Sigma}_2 = 0.01\mathbf{I}_2$, so both sensors are equally reliable. In this case, the posterior mean is halfway between the two observations, $\boldsymbol{y}_1$ and $\boldsymbol{y}_2$. In

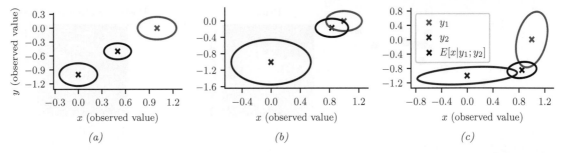

Figure 3.10: We observe $\boldsymbol{y}_1 = (0, -1)$ (red cross) and $\boldsymbol{y}_2 = (1, 0)$ (green cross) and estimate $\mathbb{E}\left[\boldsymbol{z}|\boldsymbol{y}_1, \boldsymbol{y}_2\right]$ (black cross). (a) Equally reliable sensors, so the posterior mean estimate is in between the two circles. (b) Sensor 2 is more reliable, so the estimate shifts more towards the green circle. (c) Sensor 1 is more reliable in the vertical direction, Sensor 2 is more reliable in the horizontal direction. The estimate is an appropriate combination of the two measurements. Generated by sensor_fusion_2d.ipynb.

Figure 3.10(b), we set $\boldsymbol{\Sigma}_1 = 0.05\mathbf{I}_2$ and $\boldsymbol{\Sigma}_2 = 0.01\mathbf{I}_2$, so sensor 2 is more reliable than sensor 1. In this case, the posterior mean is closer to $\boldsymbol{y}_2$. In Figure 3.10(c), we set

$$\boldsymbol{\Sigma}_1 = 0.01 \begin{pmatrix} 10 & 1 \\ 1 & 1 \end{pmatrix}, \quad \boldsymbol{\Sigma}_2 = 0.01 \begin{pmatrix} 1 & 1 \\ 1 & 10 \end{pmatrix} \tag{3.70}$$

so sensor 1 is more reliable in the second component (vertical direction), and sensor 2 is more reliable in the first component (horizontal direction). In this case, the posterior mean uses $\boldsymbol{y}_1$'s vertical component and $\boldsymbol{y}_2$'s horizontal component.

3.4   The exponential family *

In this section, we define the **exponential family**, which includes many common probability distributions. The exponential family plays a crucial role in statistics and machine learning. In this book, we mainly use it in the context of generalized linear models, which we discuss in Chapter 12. We will see more applications of the exponential family in the sequel to this book, [Mur23].

3.4.1   Definition

Consider a family of probability distributions parameterized by $\boldsymbol{\eta} \in \mathbb{R}^K$ with fixed support over $\mathcal{Y}^D \subseteq \mathbb{R}^D$. We say that the distribution $p(\boldsymbol{y}|\boldsymbol{\eta})$ is in the **exponential family** if its density can be written in the following way:

$$p(\boldsymbol{y}|\boldsymbol{\eta}) \triangleq \frac{1}{Z(\boldsymbol{\eta})} h(\boldsymbol{y}) \exp[\boldsymbol{\eta}^\mathsf{T} \mathcal{T}(\boldsymbol{y})] = h(\boldsymbol{y}) \exp[\boldsymbol{\eta}^\mathsf{T} \mathcal{T}(\boldsymbol{y}) - A(\boldsymbol{\eta})] \tag{3.71}$$

where $h(\boldsymbol{y})$ is a scaling constant (also known as the **base measure**, often 1), $\mathcal{T}(\boldsymbol{y}) \in \mathbb{R}^K$ are the **sufficient statistics**, $\boldsymbol{\eta}$ are the **natural parameters** or **canonical parameters**, $Z(\boldsymbol{\eta})$ is a normalization constant known as the **partition function**, and $A(\boldsymbol{\eta}) = \log Z(\boldsymbol{\eta})$ is the **log partition function**. One can show that A is a convex function over the convex set $\Omega \triangleq \{\boldsymbol{\eta} \in \mathbb{R}^K : A(\boldsymbol{\eta}) < \infty\}$.

It is convenient if the natural parameters are independent of each other. Formally, we say that an exponential family is **minimal** if there is no $\boldsymbol{\eta} \in \mathbb{R}^K \setminus \{0\}$ such that $\boldsymbol{\eta}^\mathsf{T} \mathcal{T}(\boldsymbol{y}) = 0$. This last condition can be violated in the case of multinomial distributions, because of the sum to one constraint on the parameters; however, it is easy to reparameterize the distribution using $K - 1$ independent parameters, as we show below.

Equation (3.71) can be generalized by defining $\boldsymbol{\eta} = f(\boldsymbol{\phi})$, where $\boldsymbol{\phi}$ is some other, possibly smaller, set of parameters. In this case, the distribution has the form

$$p(\boldsymbol{y}|\boldsymbol{\phi}) = h(\boldsymbol{y}) \exp[f(\boldsymbol{\phi})^\mathsf{T} \mathcal{T}(\boldsymbol{y}) - A(f(\boldsymbol{\phi}))] \tag{3.72}$$

If the mapping from $\boldsymbol{\phi}$ to $\boldsymbol{\eta}$ is nonlinear, we call this a **curved exponential family**. If $\boldsymbol{\eta} = f(\boldsymbol{\phi}) = \boldsymbol{\phi}$, the model is said to be in **canonical form**. If, in addition, $\mathcal{T}(\boldsymbol{y}) = \boldsymbol{y}$, we say this is a **natural exponential family** or **NEF**. In this case, it can be written as

$$p(\boldsymbol{y}|\boldsymbol{\eta}) = h(\boldsymbol{y}) \exp[\boldsymbol{\eta}^\mathsf{T} \boldsymbol{y} - A(\boldsymbol{\eta})] \tag{3.73}$$

3.4.2 Example

As a simple example, let us consider the Bernoulli distribution. We can write this in exponential family form as follows:

$$\mathrm{Ber}(y|\mu) = \mu^y (1 - \mu)^{1-y} \tag{3.74}$$
$$= \exp[y \log(\mu) + (1 - y) \log(1 - \mu)] \tag{3.75}$$
$$= \exp[\mathcal{T}(y)^\mathsf{T} \boldsymbol{\eta}] \tag{3.76}$$

where $\mathcal{T}(y) = [\mathbb{I}(y = 1), \mathbb{I}(y = 0)]$, $\boldsymbol{\eta} = [\log(\mu), \log(1 - \mu)]$, and μ is the mean parameter. However, this is an **over-complete representation** since there is a linear dependence between the features. We can see this as follows:

$$\mathbf{1}^\mathsf{T} \mathcal{T}(y) = \mathbb{I}(y = 0) + \mathbb{I}(y = 1) = 1 \tag{3.77}$$

If the representation is overcomplete, $\boldsymbol{\eta}$ is not uniquely identifiable. It is common to use a **minimal representation**, which means there is a unique $\boldsymbol{\eta}$ associated with the distribution. In this case, we can just define

$$\mathrm{Ber}(y|\mu) = \exp\left[y \log\left(\frac{\mu}{1 - \mu} \right) + \log(1 - \mu) \right] \tag{3.78}$$

We can put this into exponential family form by defining

$$\eta = \log\left(\frac{\mu}{1 - \mu} \right) \tag{3.79}$$
$$\mathcal{T}(y) = y \tag{3.80}$$
$$A(\eta) = -\log(1 - \mu) = \log(1 + e^\eta) \tag{3.81}$$
$$h(y) = 1 \tag{3.82}$$

We can recover the mean parameter μ from the canonical parameter η using

$$\mu = \sigma(\eta) = \frac{1}{1 + e^{-\eta}} \tag{3.83}$$

which we recognize as the logistic (sigmoid) function.

See the sequel to this book, [Mur23], for more examples.

3.4.3   Log partition function is cumulant generating function

The first and second **cumulants** of a distribution are its mean $\mathbb{E}[Y]$ and variance $\mathbb{V}[Y]$, whereas the first and second moments are $\mathbb{E}[Y]$ and $\mathbb{E}[Y^2]$. We can also compute higher order cumulants (and moments). An important property of the exponential family is that derivatives of the log partition function can be used to generate all the **cumulants** of the sufficient statistics. In particular, the first and second cumulants are given by

$$\nabla A(\boldsymbol{\eta}) = \mathbb{E}[\mathcal{T}(\boldsymbol{y})] \tag{3.84}$$
$$\nabla^2 A(\boldsymbol{\eta}) = \mathrm{Cov}[\mathcal{T}(\boldsymbol{y})] \tag{3.85}$$

From the above result, we see that the Hessian is positive definite, and hence $A(\boldsymbol{\eta})$ is convex in $\boldsymbol{\eta}$. Since the log likelihood has the form $\log p(\boldsymbol{y}|\boldsymbol{\eta}) = \boldsymbol{\eta}^\mathsf{T} \mathcal{T}(\boldsymbol{y}) - A(\boldsymbol{\eta}) + \text{const}$, we see that this is concave, and hence the MLE has a unique global maximum.

3.4.4   Maximum entropy derivation of the exponential family

Suppose we want to find a distribution $p(\boldsymbol{x})$ to describe some data, where all we know are the expected values (F_k) of certain features or functions $f_k(\boldsymbol{x})$:

$$\int d\boldsymbol{x}\, p(\boldsymbol{x}) f_k(\boldsymbol{x}) = F_k \tag{3.86}$$

For example, f_1 might compute x, f_2 might compute x^2, making F_1 the empirical mean and F_2 the empirical second moment. Our prior belief in the distribution is $q(x)$.

To formalize what we mean by "least number of assumptions", we will search for the distribution that is as close as possible to our prior $q(\boldsymbol{x})$, in the sense of KL divergence (Section 6.2), while satisfying our constraints:

$$p = \operatorname*{argmin}_p D_{\mathbb{KL}}(p \parallel q) \text{ subject to constraints} \tag{3.87}$$

If we use a uniform prior, $q(\boldsymbol{x}) \propto 1$, minimizing the KL divergence is equivalent to maximizing the entropy (Section 6.1):

$$p = \operatorname*{argmax}_p \mathbb{H}(p) \text{ subject to constraints} \tag{3.88}$$

The result is called a **maximum entropy model**.

To minimize the KL subject to the constraints in Equation (3.86), and the constraint that $p(\boldsymbol{x}) \geq 0$ and $\sum_{\boldsymbol{x}} p(\boldsymbol{x}) = 1$, we will use Lagrange multipliers (see Section 8.5.1). The Lagrangian is given by

$$J(p, \boldsymbol{\lambda}) = -\sum_{\boldsymbol{x}} p(\boldsymbol{x}) \log \frac{p(\boldsymbol{x})}{q(\boldsymbol{x})} + \lambda_0 \left(1 - \sum_{\boldsymbol{x}} p(\boldsymbol{x})\right) + \sum_k \lambda_k \left(F_k - \sum_{\boldsymbol{x}} p(\boldsymbol{x}) f_k(\boldsymbol{x})\right) \tag{3.89}$$

We can use the calculus of variations to take derivatives wrt the function p, but we will adopt a simpler approach and treat $\boldsymbol{p}$ as a fixed length vector (since we are assuming that $\boldsymbol{x}$ is discrete). Then we have

$$\frac{\partial J}{\partial p_c} = -1 - \log \frac{p(x = c)}{q(x = c)} - \lambda_0 - \sum_k \lambda_k f_k(x = c) \tag{3.90}$$

Setting $\frac{\partial J}{\partial p_c} = 0$ for each c yields

$$p(\boldsymbol{x}) = \frac{q(\boldsymbol{x})}{Z} \exp\left(-\sum_k \lambda_k f_k(\boldsymbol{x})\right) \tag{3.91}$$

where we have defined $Z \triangleq e^{1 + \lambda_0}$. Using the sum-to-one constraint, we have

$$1 = \sum_{\boldsymbol{x}} p(\boldsymbol{x}) = \frac{1}{Z} \sum_{\boldsymbol{x}} q(\boldsymbol{x}) \exp\left(-\sum_k \lambda_k f_k(\boldsymbol{x})\right) \tag{3.92}$$

Hence the normalization constant is given by

$$Z = \sum_{\boldsymbol{x}} q(\boldsymbol{x}) \exp\left(-\sum_k \lambda_k f_k(\boldsymbol{x})\right) \tag{3.93}$$

This has exactly the form of the exponential family, where $\boldsymbol{f}(\boldsymbol{x})$ is the vector of sufficient statistics, $-\boldsymbol{\lambda}$ are the natural parameters, and $q(\boldsymbol{x})$ is our base measure.

For example, if the features are $f_1(x) = x$ and $f_2(x) = x^2$, and we want to match the first and second moments, we get the Gaussian disribution.

3.5 Mixture models

One way to create more complex probability models is to take a convex combination of simple distributions. This is called a **mixture model**. This has the form

$$p(\boldsymbol{y}|\boldsymbol{\theta}) = \sum_{k=1}^K \pi_k p_k(\boldsymbol{y}) \tag{3.94}$$

where p_k is the k'th mixture component, and π_k are the mixture weights which satisfy $0 \leq \pi_k \leq 1$ and $\sum_{k=1}^K \pi_k = 1$.

We can re-express this model as a hierarchical model, in which we introduce the discrete **latent variable** $z \in \{1, \dots, K\}$, which specifies which distribution to use for generating the output $\boldsymbol{y}$. The

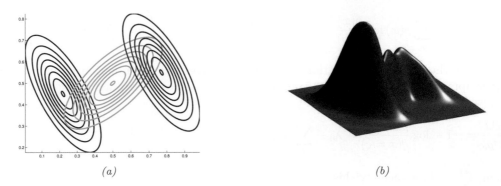

Figure 3.11: A mixture of 3 Gaussians in 2d. (a) We show the contours of constant probability for each component in the mixture. (b) A surface plot of the overall density. Adapted from Figure 2.23 of [Bis06]. Generated by gmm_plot_demo.ipynb

prior on this latent variable is $p(z = k|\boldsymbol{\theta}) = \pi_k$, and the conditional is $p(\boldsymbol{y}|z = k, \boldsymbol{\theta}) = p_k(\boldsymbol{y}) = p(\boldsymbol{y}|\boldsymbol{\theta}_k)$. That is, we define the following joint model:

$$p(z|\boldsymbol{\theta}) = \mathrm{Cat}(z|\boldsymbol{\pi}) \tag{3.95}$$

$$p(\boldsymbol{y}|z = k, \boldsymbol{\theta}) = p(\boldsymbol{y}|\boldsymbol{\theta}_k) \tag{3.96}$$

where $\boldsymbol{\theta} = (\pi_1, \dots, \pi_K, \boldsymbol{\theta}_1, \dots, \boldsymbol{\theta}_K)$ are all the model parameters. The "generative story" for the data is that we first sample a specific component z, and then we generate the observations $\boldsymbol{y}$ using the parameters chosen according to the value of z. By marginalizing out z, we recover Equation (3.94):

$$p(\boldsymbol{y}|\boldsymbol{\theta}) = \sum_{k=1}^{K} p(z = k|\boldsymbol{\theta})p(\boldsymbol{y}|z = k, \boldsymbol{\theta}) = \sum_{k=1}^{K} \pi_k p(\boldsymbol{y}|\boldsymbol{\theta}_k) \tag{3.97}$$

We can create different kinds of mixture model by varying the base distribution p_k, as we illustrate below.

3.5.1   Gaussian mixture models

A **Gaussian mixture model** or **GMM**, also called a **mixture of Gaussians (MoG)**, is defined as follows:

$$p(\boldsymbol{y}|\boldsymbol{\theta}) = \sum_{k=1}^{K} \pi_k \mathcal{N}(\boldsymbol{y}|\boldsymbol{\mu}_k, \boldsymbol{\Sigma}_k) \tag{3.98}$$

In Figure 3.11 we show the density defined by a mixture of 3 Gaussians in 2d. Each mixture component is represented by a different set of elliptical contours. If we let the number of mixture components grow sufficiently large, a GMM can approximate any smooth distribution over $\mathbb{R}^D$.

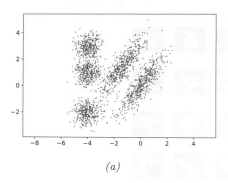
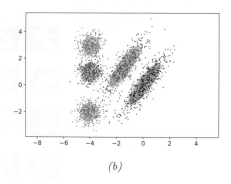

(a)   (b)

Figure 3.12: (a) Some data in 2d. (b) A possible clustering using $K = 5$ clusters computed using a GMM. Generated by gmm_2d.ipynb.

GMMs are often used for unsupervised **clustering** of real-valued data samples $\boldsymbol{y}_n \in \mathbb{R}^D$. This works in two stages. First we fit the model e.g., by computing the MLE $\hat{\boldsymbol{\theta}} = \text{argmax} \log p(\mathcal{D}|\boldsymbol{\theta})$, where $\mathcal{D} = \{\boldsymbol{y}_n : n = 1 : N\}$. (We discuss how to compute this MLE in Section 8.7.3.) Then we associate each data point $\boldsymbol{y}_n$ with a discrete latent or hidden variable $z_n \in \{1, \ldots, K\}$ which specifies the identity of the mixture component or cluster which was used to generate $\boldsymbol{y}_n$. These latent identities are unknown, but we can compute a posterior over them using Bayes rule:

$$r_{nk} \triangleq p(z_n = k | \boldsymbol{y}_n, \boldsymbol{\theta}) = \frac{p(z_n = k | \boldsymbol{\theta}) p(\boldsymbol{y}_n | z_n = k, \boldsymbol{\theta})}{\sum_{k'=1}^{K} p(z_n = k' | \boldsymbol{\theta}) p(\boldsymbol{y}_n | z_n = k', \boldsymbol{\theta})} \tag{3.99}$$

The quantity r_{nk} is called the **responsibility** of cluster k for data point n. Given the responsibilities, we can compute the most probable cluster assignment as follows:

$$\hat{z}_n = \arg\max_k r_{nk} = \arg\max_k \left[\log p(\boldsymbol{y}_n | z_n = k, \boldsymbol{\theta}) + \log p(z_n = k | \boldsymbol{\theta}) \right] \tag{3.100}$$

This is known as **hard clustering**. (If we use the responsibilities to fractionally assign each data point to different clusters, it is called **soft clustering**.) See Figure 3.12 for an example.

If we have a uniform prior over z_n, and we use spherical Gaussians with $\boldsymbol{\Sigma}_k = \mathbf{I}$, the hard clustering problem reduces to

$$z_n = \underset{k}{\text{argmin}} \, ||\boldsymbol{y}_n - \hat{\boldsymbol{\mu}}_k||_2^2 \tag{3.101}$$

In other words, we assign each data point to its closest centroid, as measured by Euclidean distance. This is the basis of the **K-means clustering** algorithm, which we discuss in Section 21.3.

3.5.2 Bernoulli mixture models

If the data is binary valued, we can use a **Bernoulli mixture model** or **BMM** (also called a **mixture of Bernoullis**), where each mixture component has the following form:

$$p(\boldsymbol{y} | z = k, \boldsymbol{\theta}) = \prod_{d=1}^{D} \text{Ber}(y_d | \mu_{dk}) = \prod_{d=1}^{D} \mu_{dk}^{y_d} (1 - \mu_{dk})^{1 - y_d} \tag{3.102}$$

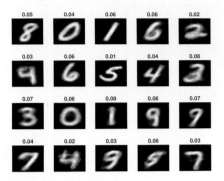

Figure 3.13: We fit a mixture of 20 Bernoullis to the binarized MNIST digit data. We visualize the estimated cluster means $\hat{\boldsymbol{\mu}}_k$. The numbers on top of each image represent the estimated mixing weights $\hat{\pi}_k$. No labels were used when training the model. Generated by mix_bernoulli_em_mnist.ipynb.

Here μ_{dk} is the probability that bit d turns on in cluster k.

As an example, we fit a BMM using $K = 20$ components to the MNIST dataset (Section 3.5.2). (We use the EM algorithm to do this fitting, which is similar to EM for GMMs discussed in Section 8.7.3; however we can also use SGD to fit the model, which is more efficient for large datasets.[3]) The resulting parameters for each mixture component (i.e., $\boldsymbol{\mu}_k$ and π_k) are shown in Figure 3.13. We see that the model has "discovered" a representation of each type of digit. (Some digits are represented multiple times, since the model does not know the "true" number of classes. See Section 21.3.7 for more information on how to choose the number K of mixture components.)

3.6   Probabilistic graphical models *

I basically know of two principles for treating complicated systems in simple ways: the first is the principle of modularity and the second is the principle of abstraction. I am an apologist for computational probability in machine learning because I believe that probability theory implements these two principles in deep and intriguing ways — namely through factorization and through averaging. Exploiting these two mechanisms as fully as possible seems to me to be the way forward in machine learning. — Michael Jordan, 1997 (quoted in [Fre98]).

We have now introduced a few simple probabilistic building blocks. In Section 3.3, we showed one way to combine some Gaussian building blocks to build a high dimensional distribution $p(\boldsymbol{y})$ from simpler parts, namely the marginal $p(\boldsymbol{y}_1)$ and the conditional $p(\boldsymbol{y}_2|\boldsymbol{y}_1)$. This idea can be extended to define joint distributions over sets of many random variables. The key assumption we will make is that some variables are **conditionally independent** of others. We will represent our CI assumptions using graphs, as we briefly explain below. (See the sequel to this book, [Mur23], for more information.)

---

3. For the SGD code, see mix_bernoulli_sgd_mnist.ipynb.

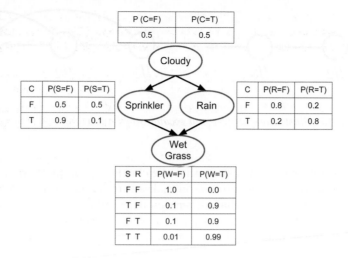

Figure 3.14: Water sprinkler PGM with corresponding binary CPTs. T and F stand for true and false.

3.6.1 Representation

A **probabilistic graphical model** or **PGM** is a joint probability distribution that uses a graph structure to encode conditional independence assumptions. When the graph is a **directed acyclic graph** or **DAG**, the model is sometimes called a **Bayesian network**, although there is nothing inherently Bayesian about such models.

The basic idea in PGMs is that each node in the graph represents a random variable, and each edge represents a direct dependency. More precisely, each lack of edge represents a conditional independency. In the DAG case, we can number the nodes in **topological order** (parents before children), and then we connect them such that each node is conditionally independent of all its predecessors given its parents:

$$Y_i \perp \mathbf{Y}_{\text{pred}(i)\backslash\text{pa}(i)} | \mathbf{Y}_{\text{pa}(i)} \tag{3.103}$$

where $\text{pa}(i)$ are the parents of node i, and $\text{pred}(i)$ are the predecessors of node i in the ordering. (This is called the **ordered Markov property**.) Consequently, we can represent the joint distribution as follows:

$$p(\mathbf{Y}_{1:N_G}) = \prod_{i=1}^{N_G} p(Y_i | \mathbf{Y}_{\text{pa}(i)}) \tag{3.104}$$

where N_G is the number of nodes in the graph.

3.6.1.1 Example: water sprinkler network

Suppose we want to model the dependencies between 4 random variables: C (whether it is cloudy season or not), R (whether it is raining or not), S (whether the water sprinkler is on or not), and W

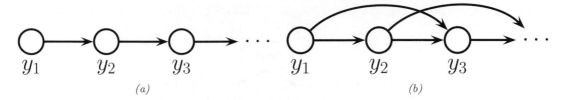

Figure 3.15: Illustration of first and second order autoregressive (Markov) models.

(whether the grass is wet or not). We know that the cloudy season makes rain more likely, so we add a $C \to R$ arc. We know that the cloudy season makes turning on a water sprinkler less likely, so we add a $C \to S$ arc. Finally, we know that either rain or sprinklers can cause the grass to get wet, so we add $S \to W$ and $R \to W$ edges.

Formally, this defines the following joint distribution:

$$p(C, S, R, W) = p(C)p(S|C)p(R|C, \cancel{S})p(W|S, R, \cancel{C}) \tag{3.105}$$

where we strike through terms that are not needed due to the conditional independence properties of the model.

Each term $p(Y_i|\mathbf{Y}_{\text{pa}(i)})$ is a called the **conditional probability distribution** or **CPD** for node i. This can be any kind of distribution we like. In Figure 3.14, we assume each CPD is a conditional categorical distribution, which can be represented as a **conditional probability table** or **CPT**. We can represent the i'th CPT as follows:

$$\theta_{ijk} \triangleq p(Y_i = k|\mathbf{Y}_{\text{pa}(i)} = j) \tag{3.106}$$

This satisfies the properties $0 \le \theta_{ijk} \le 1$ and $\sum_{k=1}^{K_i} \theta_{ijk} = 1$ for each row j. Here i indexes nodes, $i \in [N_G]$; k indexes node states, $k \in [K_i]$, where K_i is the number of states for node i; and j indexes joint parent states, $j \in [J_i]$, where $J_i = \prod_{p \in \text{pa}(i)} K_p$. For example, the wet grass node has 2 binary parents, so there are 4 parent states.

3.6.1.2   Example: Markov chain

Suppose we want to create a joint probability distribution over variable-length sequences, $p(y_{1:T})$. If each variable y_t represents a word from a vocabulary with K possible values, so $y_t \in \{1, \ldots, K\}$, the resulting model represents a distribution over possible sentences of length T; this is often called a **language model**.

By the chain rule of probability, we can represent any joint distribution over T variables as follows:

$$p(\boldsymbol{y}_{1:T}) = p(y_1)p(y_2|y_1)p(y_3|y_2, y_1)p(y_4|y_3, y_2, y_1) \ldots = \prod_{t=1}^{T} p(y_t|\boldsymbol{y}_{1:t-1}) \tag{3.107}$$

Unfortunately, the number of parameters needed to represent each conditional distribution $p(y_t|\boldsymbol{y}_{1:t-1})$ grows exponentially with t. However, suppose we make the conditional independence assumption that the future, $\boldsymbol{y}_{t+1:T}$, is independent of the past, $\boldsymbol{y}_{1:t-1}$, given the present, y_t. This is called the **first**

order Markov condition, and is repesented by the PGM in Figure 3.15(a). With this assumption, we can write the joint distribution as follows:

$$p(\boldsymbol{y}_{1:T}) = p(y_1)p(y_2|y_1)p(y_3|y_2)p(y_4|y_3)\ldots = p(y_1)\prod_{t=2}^{T} p(y_t|y_{t-1}) \tag{3.108}$$

This is called a **Markov chain**, **Markov model** or **autoregressive model** of order 1.

The function $p(y_t|y_{t-1})$ is called the **transition function**, **transition kernel** or **Markov kernel**. This is just a conditional distribution over the states at time t given the state at time $t-1$, and hence it satisfies the conditions $p(y_t|y_{t-1}) \geq 0$ and $\sum_{k=1}^{K} p(y_t = k|y_{t-1} = j) = 1$. We can represent this CPT as a **stochastic matrix**, $A_{jk} = p(y_t = k|y_{t-1} = j)$, where each row sums to 1. This is known as the **state transition matrix**. We assume this matrix is the same for all time steps, so the model is said to be **homogeneous**, **stationary**, or **time-invariant**. This is an example of **parameter tying**, since the same parameter is shared by multiple variables. This assumption allows us to model an arbitrary number of variables using a fixed number of parameters.

The first-order Markov assumption is rather strong. Fortunately, we can easily generalize first-order models to depend on the last M observations, thus creating a model of order (memory length) M:

$$p(\boldsymbol{y}_{1:T}) = p(\boldsymbol{y}_{1:M})\prod_{t=M+1}^{T} p(y_t|\boldsymbol{y}_{t-M:t-1}) \tag{3.109}$$

This is called an M'**th order Markov model**. For example, if $M = 2$, y_t depends on y_{t-1} and y_{t-2}, as shown in Figure 3.15(b). This is called a **trigram model**, since it models the distribution over word triples. If we use $M = 1$, we get a **bigram model**, which models the distribution over word pairs.

For large vocabulary sizes, the number of parameters needed to estimate the conditional distributions for M-gram models for large M can become prohibitive. In this case, we need to make additional assumptions beyond conditional independence. For example, we can assume that $p(y_t|\boldsymbol{y}_{t-M:t-1})$ can be represented as a low-rank matrix, or in terms of some kind of neural network. This is called a **neural language model**. See Chapter 15 for details.

3.6.2 Inference

A PGM defines a joint probability distribution. We can therefore use the rules of marginalization and conditioning to compute $p(\mathbf{Y}_i|\mathbf{Y}_j = \boldsymbol{y}_j)$ for any sets of variables i and j. Efficient algorithms to perform this computation are discussed in the sequel to this book, [Mur23].

For example, consider the water sprinkler example in Figure 3.14. Our prior belief that it has rained is given by $p(R = 1) = 0.5$. If we see that the grass is wet, then our posterior belief that it has rained changes to $p(R = 1|W = 1) = 0.7079$. Now suppose we also notice the water sprinkler was turned on: our belief that it rained goes down to $p(R = 1|W = 1, S = 1) = 0.3204$. This negative mutual interaction between multiple causes of some observations is called the **explaining away** effect, also known as **Berkson's paradox**. (See sprinkler_pgm.ipynb for some code that reproduces these calculations.)

3.6.3 Learning

If the parameters of the CPDs are unknown, we can view them as additional random variables, add them as nodes to the graph, and then treat them as **hidden variables** to be inferred. Figure 3.16(a) shows a simple example, in which we have N iid random variables, $\boldsymbol{y}_n$, all drawn from the same distribution with common parameter $\boldsymbol{\theta}$. (The **shaded nodes** represent observed values, whereas the unshaded (hollow) nodes represent latent variables or parameters.)

More precisely, the model encodes the following "generative story" about the data:

$$\boldsymbol{\theta} \sim p(\boldsymbol{\theta}) \tag{3.110}$$

$$\boldsymbol{y}_n \sim p(\boldsymbol{y}|\boldsymbol{\theta}) \tag{3.111}$$

where $p(\boldsymbol{\theta})$ is some (unspecified) prior over the parameters, and $p(\boldsymbol{y}|\boldsymbol{\theta})$ is some specified likelihood function. The corresponding joint distribution has the form

$$p(\mathcal{D}, \boldsymbol{\theta}) = p(\boldsymbol{\theta})p(\mathcal{D}|\boldsymbol{\theta}) \tag{3.112}$$

where $\mathcal{D} = (\boldsymbol{y}_1, \ldots, \boldsymbol{y}_N)$. By virtue of the iid assumption, the likelihood can be rewritten as follows:

$$p(\mathcal{D}|\boldsymbol{\theta}) = \prod_{n=1}^{N} p(\boldsymbol{y}_n|\boldsymbol{\theta}) \tag{3.113}$$

Notice that the order of the data vectors is not important for defining this model, i.e., we can permute the numbering of the leaf nodes in the PGM. When this property holds, we say that the data is **exchangeable**.

3.6.3.1 Plate notation

In Figure 3.16(a), we see that the $\boldsymbol{y}$ nodes are repeated N times. To avoid visual clutter, it is common to use a form of **syntactic sugar** called **plates**. This is a notational convention in which we draw a little box around the repeated variables, with the understanding that nodes within the box will get repeated when the model is **unrolled**. We often write the number of copies or repetitions in the bottom right corner of the box. This is illustrated in Figure 3.16(b). This notation is widely used to represent certain kinds of Bayesian model.

Figure 3.17 shows a more interesting example, in which we represent a GMM (Section 3.5.1) as a graphical model. We see that this encodes the joint distribution

$$p(\boldsymbol{y}_{1:N}, \boldsymbol{z}_{1:N}, \boldsymbol{\theta}) = p(\boldsymbol{\pi}) \left[\prod_{k=1}^{K} p(\boldsymbol{\mu}_k)p(\boldsymbol{\Sigma}_k) \right] \left[\prod_{n=1}^{N} p(z_n|\boldsymbol{\pi})p(\boldsymbol{y}_n|z_n, \boldsymbol{\mu}_{1:K}, \boldsymbol{\Sigma}_{1:K}) \right] \tag{3.114}$$

We see that the latent variables z_n as well as the unknown paramters, $\boldsymbol{\theta} = (\boldsymbol{\pi}, \boldsymbol{\mu}_{1:K}, \boldsymbol{\Sigma}_{1:K})$, are all shown as unshaded nodes.

3.7 Exercises

Exercise 3.1 [Uncorrelated does not imply independent *]

Let $X \sim U(-1, 1)$ and $Y = X^2$. Clearly Y is dependent on X (in fact, Y is uniquely determined by X). However, show that $\rho(X, Y) = 0$. Hint: if $X \sim U(a, b)$ then $E[X] = (a + b)/2$ and $\mathbb{V}[X] = (b - a)^2/12$.

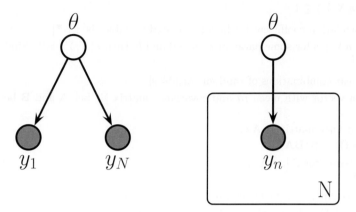

Figure 3.16: Left: data points $\boldsymbol{y}_n$ are conditionally independent given $\boldsymbol{\theta}$. Right: Same model, using plate notation. This represents the same model as the one on the left, except the repeated $\boldsymbol{y}_n$ nodes are inside a box, known as a plate; the number in the lower right hand corner, N, specifies the number of repetitions of the $\boldsymbol{y}_n$ node.

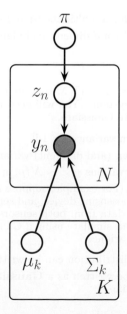

Figure 3.17: A Gaussian mixture model represented as a graphical model.

Exercise 3.2 [Correlation coefficient is between -1 and +1]

Prove that $-1 \leq \rho(X, Y) \leq 1$

Exercise 3.3 [Correlation coefficient for linearly related variables is ± 1 *]

Show that, if $Y = aX + b$ for some parameters $a > 0$ and b, then $\rho(X, Y) = 1$. Similarly show that if $a < 0$, then $\rho(X, Y) = -1$.

Exercise 3.4 [Linear combinations of random variables]

Let $\boldsymbol{x}$ be a random vector with mean $\boldsymbol{m}$ and covariance matrix Σ. Let $\mathbf{A}$ and $\mathbf{B}$ be matrices.

a. Derive the covariance matrix of $\mathbf{A}\boldsymbol{x}$.
b. Show that $\operatorname{tr}(\mathbf{AB}) = \operatorname{tr}(\mathbf{BA})$.
c. Derive an expression for $\mathbb{E}\left[\boldsymbol{x}^T \mathbf{A} \boldsymbol{x}\right]$.

Exercise 3.5 [Gaussian vs *jointly* Gaussian]

Let $X \sim \mathcal{N}(0, 1)$ and $Y = WX$, where $p(W = -1) = p(W = 1) = 0.5$. It is clear that X and Y are not independent, since Y is a function of X.

a. Show $Y \sim \mathcal{N}(0, 1)$.
b. Show $\operatorname{Cov}[X, Y] = 0$. Thus X and Y are uncorrelated but dependent, even though they are Gaussian. Hint: use the definition of covariance

$$\operatorname{Cov}[X, Y] = \mathbb{E}[XY] - \mathbb{E}[X]\mathbb{E}[Y] \tag{3.115}$$

   and the **rule of iterated expectation**

$$\mathbb{E}[XY] = \mathbb{E}[\mathbb{E}[XY|W]] \tag{3.116}$$

Exercise 3.6 [Normalization constant for a multidimensional Gaussian]

Prove that the normalization constant for a d-dimensional Gaussian is given by

$$(2\pi)^{d/2}|\boldsymbol{\Sigma}|^{\frac{1}{2}} = \int \exp(-\frac{1}{2}(\boldsymbol{x} - \mu)^T \boldsymbol{\Sigma}^{-1}(\boldsymbol{x} - \boldsymbol{\mu}))d\boldsymbol{x} \tag{3.117}$$

Hint: diagonalize $\boldsymbol{\Sigma}$ and use the fact that $|\boldsymbol{\Sigma}| = \prod_i \lambda_i$ to write the joint pdf as a product of d one-dimensional Gaussians in a transformed coordinate system. (You will need the change of variables formula.) Finally, use the normalization constant for univariate Gaussians.

Exercise 3.7 [Sensor fusion with known variances in 1d]

Suppose we have two sensors with known (and different) variances v_1 and v_2, but unknown (and the same) mean μ. Suppose we observe n_1 observations $y_i^{(1)} \sim \mathcal{N}(\mu, v_1)$ from the first sensor and n_2 observations $y_i^{(2)} \sim \mathcal{N}(\mu, v_2)$ from the second sensor. (For example, suppose μ is the true temperature outside, and sensor 1 is a precise (low variance) digital thermosensing device, and sensor 2 is an imprecise (high variance) mercury thermometer.) Let $\mathcal{D}$ represent all the data from both sensors. What is the posterior $p(\mu|\mathcal{D})$, assuming a non-informative prior for μ (which we can simulate using a Gaussian with a precision of 0)? Give an explicit expression for the posterior mean and variance.

Exercise 3.8 [Show that the Student distribution can be written as a Gaussian scale mixture]

Show that a Student distribution can be written as a **Gaussian scale mixture**, where we use a Gamma mixing distribution on the precision α, i.e.

$$p(x|\mu, a, b) = \int_0^\infty \mathcal{N}(x|\mu, \alpha^{-1})\operatorname{Ga}(\alpha|a, b)d\alpha \tag{3.118}$$

This can be viewed as an infinite mixture of Gaussians, with different precisions.

4 Statistics

4.1 Introduction

In Chapter 2–Chapter 3, we assumed all the parameters $\boldsymbol{\theta}$ of our probability models were known. In this chapter, we discuss how to learn these parameters from data.

The process of estimating $\boldsymbol{\theta}$ from $\mathcal{D}$ is called **model fitting**, or **training**, and is at the heart of machine learning. There are many methods for producing such estimates, but most boil down to an optimization problem of the form

$$\hat{\boldsymbol{\theta}} = \operatorname*{argmin}_{\boldsymbol{\theta}} \mathcal{L}(\boldsymbol{\theta}) \tag{4.1}$$

where $\mathcal{L}(\boldsymbol{\theta})$ is some kind of loss function or objective function. We discuss several different loss functions in this chapter. In some cases, we also discuss how to solve the optimization problem in closed form. In general, however, we will need to use some kind of generic optimization algorithm, which we discuss in Chapter 8.

In addition to computing a **point estimate**, $\hat{\boldsymbol{\theta}}$, we discuss how to model our uncertainty or confidence in this estimate. In statistics, the process of quantifying uncertainty about an unknown quantity estimated from a finite sample of data is called **inference**. We will discuss both Bayesian and frequentist approaches to inference.[1]

4.2 Maximum likelihood estimation (MLE)

The most common approach to parameter estimation is to pick the parameters that assign the highest probability to the training data; this is called **maximum likelihood estimation** or **MLE**. We give more details below, and then give a series of worked examples.

4.2.1 Definition

We define the MLE as follows:

$$\hat{\boldsymbol{\theta}}_{\text{mle}} \triangleq \operatorname*{argmax}_{\boldsymbol{\theta}} p(\mathcal{D}|\boldsymbol{\theta}) \tag{4.2}$$

---

1. In the deep learning community, the term "inference" refers to what we will call "prediction", namely computing $p(y|\boldsymbol{x}, \hat{\boldsymbol{\theta}})$.

We usually assume the training examples are independently sampled from the same distribution, so the (conditional) likelihood becomes

$$p(\mathcal{D}|\boldsymbol{\theta}) = \prod_{n=1}^{N} p(\boldsymbol{y}_n|\boldsymbol{x}_n, \boldsymbol{\theta}) \tag{4.3}$$

This is known as the **iid** assumption, which stands for "independent and identically distributed". We usually work with the **log likelihood**, which is given by

$$\ell(\boldsymbol{\theta}) \triangleq \log p(\mathcal{D}|\boldsymbol{\theta}) = \sum_{n=1}^{N} \log p(\boldsymbol{y}_n|\boldsymbol{x}_n, \boldsymbol{\theta}) \tag{4.4}$$

This decomposes into a sum of terms, one per example. Thus the MLE is given by

$$\hat{\boldsymbol{\theta}}_{\text{mle}} = \underset{\boldsymbol{\theta}}{\text{argmax}} \sum_{n=1}^{N} \log p(\boldsymbol{y}_n|\boldsymbol{x}_n, \boldsymbol{\theta}) \tag{4.5}$$

Since most optimization algorithms (such as those discussed in Chapter 8) are designed to *minimize* cost functions, we can redefine the **objective function** to be the (conditional) **negative log likelihood** or **NLL**:

$$\text{NLL}(\boldsymbol{\theta}) \triangleq -\log p(\mathcal{D}|\boldsymbol{\theta}) = -\sum_{n=1}^{N} \log p(\boldsymbol{y}_n|\boldsymbol{x}_n, \boldsymbol{\theta}) \tag{4.6}$$

Minimizing this will give the MLE. If the model is unconditional (unsupervised), the MLE becomes

$$\hat{\boldsymbol{\theta}}_{\text{mle}} = \underset{\boldsymbol{\theta}}{\text{argmin}} -\sum_{n=1}^{N} \log p(\boldsymbol{y}_n|\boldsymbol{\theta}) \tag{4.7}$$

since we have outputs $\boldsymbol{y}_n$ but no inputs $\boldsymbol{x}_n$.[2]

Alternatively we may want to maximize the *joint* likelihood of inputs and outputs. The MLE in this case becomes

$$\hat{\boldsymbol{\theta}}_{\text{mle}} = \underset{\boldsymbol{\theta}}{\text{argmin}} -\sum_{n=1}^{N} \log p(\boldsymbol{y}_n, \boldsymbol{x}_n|\boldsymbol{\theta}) \tag{4.8}$$

4.2.2   Justification for MLE

There are several ways to justify the method of MLE. One way is to view it as simple point approximation to the Bayesian posterior $p(\boldsymbol{\theta}|\mathcal{D})$ using a uniform prior, as explained in Section 4.6.7.1.

---

2. In statistics, it is standard to use $\boldsymbol{y}$ to represent variables whose generative distribution we choose to model, and to use $\boldsymbol{x}$ to represent exogenous inputs which are given but not generated. Thus supervised learning concerns fitting conditional models of the form $p(\boldsymbol{y}|\boldsymbol{x})$, and unsupervised learning is the special case where $\boldsymbol{x} = \emptyset$, so we are just fitting the unconditional distribution $p(\boldsymbol{y})$. In the ML literature, supervised learning treats $\boldsymbol{y}$ as generated and $\boldsymbol{x}$ as given, but in the unsupervised case, it often switches to using $\boldsymbol{x}$ to represent generated variables.

In particular, suppose we approximate the posterior by a delta function, $p(\boldsymbol{\theta}|\mathcal{D}) = \delta(\boldsymbol{\theta} - \hat{\boldsymbol{\theta}}_{\text{map}})$, where $\hat{\boldsymbol{\theta}}_{\text{map}}$ is the posterior mode, given by

$$\hat{\boldsymbol{\theta}}_{\text{map}} = \underset{\boldsymbol{\theta}}{\text{argmax}} \log p(\boldsymbol{\theta}|\mathcal{D}) = \underset{\boldsymbol{\theta}}{\text{argmax}} \log p(\mathcal{D}|\boldsymbol{\theta}) + \log p(\boldsymbol{\theta}) \tag{4.9}$$

If we use a uniform prior, $p(\boldsymbol{\theta}) \propto 1$, the MAP estimate becomes equal to the MLE, $\hat{\boldsymbol{\theta}}_{\text{map}} = \hat{\boldsymbol{\theta}}_{\text{mle}}$.

Another way to justify the use of the MLE is that the resulting predictive distribution $p(\boldsymbol{y}|\hat{\boldsymbol{\theta}}_{\text{mle}})$ is as close as possible (in a sense to be defined below) to the **empirical distribution** of the data. In the unconditional case, the empirical distribution is defined by

$$p_{\mathcal{D}}(\boldsymbol{y}) \triangleq \frac{1}{N} \sum_{n=1}^{N} \delta(\boldsymbol{y} - \boldsymbol{y}_n) \tag{4.10}$$

We see that the empirical distribution is a series of delta functions or "spikes" at the observed training points. We want to create a model whose distribution $q(\boldsymbol{y}) = p(\boldsymbol{y}|\boldsymbol{\theta})$ is similar to $p_{\mathcal{D}}(\boldsymbol{y})$.

A standard way to measure the (dis)similarity between probability distributions p and q is the **Kullback Leibler divergence**, or **KL divergence**. We give the details in Section 6.2, but in brief this is defined as

$$D_{\mathbb{KL}}(p \,\|\, q) = \sum_{\boldsymbol{y}} p(\boldsymbol{y}) \log \frac{p(\boldsymbol{y})}{q(\boldsymbol{y})} \tag{4.11}$$

$$= \underbrace{\sum_{\boldsymbol{y}} p(\boldsymbol{y}) \log p(\boldsymbol{y})}_{-\mathbb{H}(p)} - \underbrace{\sum_{\boldsymbol{y}} p(\boldsymbol{y}) \log q(\boldsymbol{y})}_{\mathbb{H}_{ce}(p,q)} \tag{4.12}$$

where $\mathbb{H}(p)$ is the entropy of p (see Section 6.1), and $\mathbb{H}_{ce}(p,q)$ is the cross-entropy of p and q (see Section 6.1.2). One can show that $D_{\mathbb{KL}}(p \,\|\, q) \geq 0$, with equality iff $p = q$.

If we define $q(\boldsymbol{y}) = p(\boldsymbol{y}|\boldsymbol{\theta})$, and set $p(\boldsymbol{y}) = p_{\mathcal{D}}(\boldsymbol{y})$, then the KL divergence becomes

$$D_{\mathbb{KL}}(p \,\|\, q) = \sum_{\boldsymbol{y}} [p_{\mathcal{D}}(\boldsymbol{y}) \log p_{\mathcal{D}}(\boldsymbol{y}) - p_{\mathcal{D}}(\boldsymbol{y}) \log q(\boldsymbol{y})] \tag{4.13}$$

$$= -\mathbb{H}(p_{\mathcal{D}}) - \frac{1}{N} \sum_{n=1}^{N} \log p(\boldsymbol{y}_n|\boldsymbol{\theta}) \tag{4.14}$$

$$= \text{const} + \text{NLL}(\boldsymbol{\theta}) \tag{4.15}$$

The first term is a constant which we can ignore, leaving just the NLL. Thus minimizing the KL is equivalent to minimizing the NLL which is equivalent to computing the MLE, as in Equation (4.7).

We can generalize the above results to the supervised (conditional) setting by using the following empirical distribution:

$$p_{\mathcal{D}}(\boldsymbol{x}, \boldsymbol{y}) = p_{\mathcal{D}}(\boldsymbol{y}|\boldsymbol{x}) p_{\mathcal{D}}(\boldsymbol{x}) = \frac{1}{N} \sum_{n=1}^{N} \delta(\boldsymbol{x} - \boldsymbol{x}_n) \delta(\boldsymbol{y} - \boldsymbol{y}_n) \tag{4.16}$$

The expected KL then becomes

$$\mathbb{E}_{p_{\mathcal{D}}(\boldsymbol{x})}\left[D_{\mathrm{KL}}\left(p_{\mathcal{D}}(Y|\boldsymbol{x}) \parallel q(Y|\boldsymbol{x})\right)\right] = \sum_{\boldsymbol{x}} p_{\mathcal{D}}(\boldsymbol{x})\left[\sum_{\boldsymbol{y}} p_{\mathcal{D}}(\boldsymbol{y}|\boldsymbol{x}) \log \frac{p_{\mathcal{D}}(\boldsymbol{y}|\boldsymbol{x})}{q(\boldsymbol{y}|\boldsymbol{x})}\right] \tag{4.17}$$

$$= \mathrm{const} - \sum_{\boldsymbol{x},\boldsymbol{y}} p_{\mathcal{D}}(\boldsymbol{x},\boldsymbol{y}) \log q(\boldsymbol{y}|\boldsymbol{x}) \tag{4.18}$$

$$= \mathrm{const} - \frac{1}{N}\sum_{n=1}^{N} \log p(\boldsymbol{y}_n|\boldsymbol{x}_n,\boldsymbol{\theta}) \tag{4.19}$$

Minimizing this is equivalent to minimizing the conditional NLL in Equation (4.6).

4.2.3   Example: MLE for the Bernoulli distribution

Suppose Y is a random variable representing a coin toss, where the event $Y = 1$ corresponds to heads and $Y = 0$ corresponds to tails. Let $\theta = p(Y = 1)$ be the probability of heads. The probability distribution for this rv is the Bernoulli, which we introduced in Section 2.4.

The NLL for the Bernoulli distribution is given by

$$\mathrm{NLL}(\theta) = -\log \prod_{n=1}^{N} p(y_n|\theta) \tag{4.20}$$

$$= -\log \prod_{n=1}^{N} \theta^{\mathbb{I}(y_n=1)}(1-\theta)^{\mathbb{I}(y_n=0)} \tag{4.21}$$

$$= -\sum_{n=1}^{N}\left[\mathbb{I}\left(y_n = 1\right)\log\theta + \mathbb{I}\left(y_n = 0\right)\log(1-\theta)\right] \tag{4.22}$$

$$= -[N_1 \log\theta + N_0 \log(1-\theta)] \tag{4.23}$$

where we have defined $N_1 = \sum_{n=1}^{N}\mathbb{I}\left(y_n = 1\right)$ and $N_0 = \sum_{n=1}^{N}\mathbb{I}\left(y_n = 0\right)$, representing the number of heads and tails. (The NLL for the binomial is the same as for the Bernoulli, modulo an irrelevant $\binom{N}{c}$ term, which is a constant independent of θ.) These two numbers are called the **sufficient statistics** of the data, since they summarize everything we need to know about $\mathcal{D}$. The total count, $N = N_0 + N_1$, is called the **sample size**.

The MLE can be found by solving $\frac{d}{d\theta}\mathrm{NLL}(\theta) = 0$. The derivative of the NLL is

$$\frac{d}{d\theta}\mathrm{NLL}(\theta) = \frac{-N_1}{\theta} + \frac{N_0}{1-\theta} \tag{4.24}$$

and hence the MLE is given by

$$\hat{\theta}_{\mathrm{mle}} = \frac{N_1}{N_0 + N_1} \tag{4.25}$$

We see that this is just the empirical fraction of heads, which is an intuitive result.

4.2.4   Example: MLE for the categorical distribution

Suppose we roll a K-sided dice N times. Let $Y_n \in \{1, \ldots, K\}$ be the n'th outcome, where $Y_n \sim \text{Cat}(\boldsymbol{\theta})$. We want to estimate the probabilities $\boldsymbol{\theta}$ from the dataset $\mathcal{D} = \{y_n : n = 1 : N\}$. The NLL is given by

$$\text{NLL}(\boldsymbol{\theta}) = -\sum_k N_k \log \theta_k \tag{4.26}$$

where N_k is the number of times the event $Y = k$ is observed. (The NLL for the multinomial is the same, up to irrelevant scale factors.)

To compute the MLE, we have to minimize the NLL subject to the constraint that $\sum_{k=1}^{K} \theta_k = 1$. To do this, we will use the method of Lagrange multipliers (see Section 8.5.1).[3]

The Lagrangian is as follows:

$$\mathcal{L}(\boldsymbol{\theta}, \lambda) \triangleq -\sum_k N_k \log \theta_k - \lambda \left(1 - \sum_k \theta_k\right) \tag{4.27}$$

Taking derivatives with respect to λ yields the original constraint:

$$\frac{\partial \mathcal{L}}{\partial \lambda} = 1 - \sum_k \theta_k = 0 \tag{4.28}$$

Taking derivatives with respect to θ_k yields

$$\frac{\partial \mathcal{L}}{\partial \theta_k} = -\frac{N_k}{\theta_k} + \lambda = 0 \implies N_k = \lambda \theta_k \tag{4.29}$$

We can solve for λ using the sum-to-one constraint:

$$\sum_k N_k = N = \lambda \sum_k \theta_k = \lambda \tag{4.30}$$

Thus the MLE is given by

$$\hat{\theta}_k = \frac{N_k}{\lambda} = \frac{N_k}{N} \tag{4.31}$$

which is just the empirical fraction of times event k occurs.

4.2.5   Example: MLE for the univariate Gaussian

Suppose $Y \sim \mathcal{N}(\mu, \sigma^2)$ and let $\mathcal{D} = \{y_n : n = 1 : N\}$ be an iid sample of size N. We can estimate the parameters $\boldsymbol{\theta} = (\mu, \sigma^2)$ using MLE as follows. First, we derive the NLL, which is given by

$$\text{NLL}(\mu, \sigma^2) = -\sum_{n=1}^{N} \log \left[\left(\frac{1}{2\pi\sigma^2}\right)^{\frac{1}{2}} \exp\left(-\frac{1}{2\sigma^2}(y_n - \mu)^2\right) \right] \tag{4.32}$$

$$= \frac{1}{2\sigma^2} \sum_{n=1}^{N} (y_n - \mu)^2 + \frac{N}{2} \log(2\pi\sigma^2) \tag{4.33}$$

---

3. We do not need to explicitly enforce the constraint that $\theta_k \geq 0$ since the gradient of the Lagrangian has the form $-N_k/\theta_k - \lambda$; so negative values of θ_k would increase the objective, rather than minimize it. (Of course, this does not preclude setting $\theta_k = 0$, and indeed this is the optimal solution if $N_k = 0$.)

The minimum of this function must satisfy the following conditions, which we explain in Section 8.1.1.1:

$$\frac{\partial}{\partial \mu} \text{NLL}(\mu, \sigma^2) = 0, \;\; \frac{\partial}{\partial \sigma^2} \text{NLL}(\mu, \sigma^2) = 0 \tag{4.34}$$

So all we have to do is to find this stationary point. Some simple calculus (Exercise 4.1) shows that the solution is given by the following:

$$\hat{\mu}_{\text{mle}} = \frac{1}{N} \sum_{n=1}^{N} y_n = \overline{y} \tag{4.35}$$

$$\hat{\sigma}^2_{\text{mle}} = \frac{1}{N} \sum_{n=1}^{N} (y_n - \hat{\mu}_{\text{mle}})^2 = \frac{1}{N} \sum_{n=1}^{N} \left[y_n^2 + \hat{\mu}_{\text{mle}}^2 - 2 y_n \hat{\mu}_{\text{mle}} \right] = s^2 - \overline{y}^2 \tag{4.36}$$

$$s^2 \triangleq \frac{1}{N} \sum_{n=1}^{N} y_n^2 \tag{4.37}$$

The quantities $\overline{y}$ and s^2 are called the **sufficient statistics** of the data, since they are sufficient to compute the MLE, without loss of information relative to using the raw data itself.

Note that you might be used to seeing the estimate for the variance written as

$$\hat{\sigma}^2_{\text{unb}} = \frac{1}{N-1} \sum_{n=1}^{N} (y_n - \hat{\mu}_{\text{mle}})^2 \tag{4.38}$$

where we divide by $N - 1$. This is not the MLE, but is a different kind of estimate, which happens to be unbiased (unlike the MLE); see Section 4.7.6.1 for details.[4]

4.2.6   Example: MLE for the multivariate Gaussian

In this section, we derive the maximum likelihood estimate for the parameters of a multivariate Gaussian.

First, let us write the log-likelihood, dropping irrelevant constants:

$$\ell(\boldsymbol{\mu}, \boldsymbol{\Sigma}) = \log p(\mathcal{D}|\boldsymbol{\mu}, \boldsymbol{\Sigma}) = \frac{N}{2} \log |\boldsymbol{\Lambda}| - \frac{1}{2} \sum_{n=1}^{N} (\boldsymbol{y}_n - \boldsymbol{\mu})^\mathsf{T} \boldsymbol{\Lambda} (\boldsymbol{y}_n - \boldsymbol{\mu}) \tag{4.39}$$

where $\boldsymbol{\Lambda} = \boldsymbol{\Sigma}^{-1}$ is the **precision matrix** (inverse covariance matrix).

---

4. Note that, in Python, numpy defaults to the MLE, but Pandas defaults to the unbiased estimate, as explained in
https://stackoverflow.com/questions/24984178/different-std-in-pandas-vs-numpy/.

4.2.6.1 MLE for the mean

Using the substitution $\boldsymbol{z}_n = \boldsymbol{y}_n - \boldsymbol{\mu}$, the derivative of a quadratic form (Equation (7.264)) and the chain rule of calculus, we have

$$\frac{\partial}{\partial \boldsymbol{\mu}}(\boldsymbol{y}_n - \boldsymbol{\mu})^\mathsf{T}\boldsymbol{\Sigma}^{-1}(\boldsymbol{y}_n - \boldsymbol{\mu}) = \frac{\partial}{\partial \boldsymbol{z}_n}\boldsymbol{z}_n^\mathsf{T}\boldsymbol{\Sigma}^{-1}\boldsymbol{z}_n\frac{\partial \boldsymbol{z}_n}{\partial \boldsymbol{\mu}^\mathsf{T}} \tag{4.40}$$

$$= -1(\boldsymbol{\Sigma}^{-1} + \boldsymbol{\Sigma}^{-T})\boldsymbol{z}_n \tag{4.41}$$

since $\frac{\partial \boldsymbol{z}_n}{\partial \boldsymbol{\mu}^\mathsf{T}} = -\mathbf{I}$. Hence

$$\frac{\partial}{\partial \boldsymbol{\mu}}\ell(\boldsymbol{\mu}, \boldsymbol{\Sigma}) = -\frac{1}{2}\sum_{n=1}^{N}-2\boldsymbol{\Sigma}^{-1}(\boldsymbol{y}_n - \boldsymbol{\mu}) = \boldsymbol{\Sigma}^{-1}\sum_{n=1}^{N}(\boldsymbol{y}_n - \boldsymbol{\mu}) = 0 \tag{4.42}$$

$$\hat{\boldsymbol{\mu}} = \frac{1}{N}\sum_{n=1}^{N}\boldsymbol{y}_n = \overline{\boldsymbol{y}} \tag{4.43}$$

So the MLE of $\boldsymbol{\mu}$ is just the empirical mean.

4.2.6.2 MLE for the covariance matrix

We can use the trace trick (Equation (7.36)) to rewrite the log-likelihood in terms of the precision matrix $\boldsymbol{\Lambda} = \boldsymbol{\Sigma}^{-1}$ as follows:

$$\ell(\hat{\boldsymbol{\mu}}, \boldsymbol{\Lambda}) = \frac{N}{2}\log|\boldsymbol{\Lambda}| - \frac{1}{2}\sum_n \mathrm{tr}[(\boldsymbol{y}_n - \hat{\boldsymbol{\mu}})(\boldsymbol{y}_n - \hat{\boldsymbol{\mu}})^\mathsf{T}\boldsymbol{\Lambda}] \tag{4.44}$$

$$= \frac{N}{2}\log|\boldsymbol{\Lambda}| - \frac{1}{2}\mathrm{tr}\,[\mathbf{S}_{\overline{\boldsymbol{y}}}\boldsymbol{\Lambda}] \tag{4.45}$$

$$\mathbf{S}_{\overline{\boldsymbol{y}}} \triangleq \sum_{n=1}^{N}(\boldsymbol{y}_n - \overline{\boldsymbol{y}})(\boldsymbol{y}_n - \overline{\boldsymbol{y}})^\mathsf{T} = \left(\sum_n \boldsymbol{y}_n\boldsymbol{y}_n^\mathsf{T}\right) - N\overline{\boldsymbol{y}}\overline{\boldsymbol{y}}^\mathsf{T} \tag{4.46}$$

where $\mathbf{S}_{\overline{\boldsymbol{y}}}$ is the **scatter matrix** centered on $\overline{\boldsymbol{y}}$.

We can rewrite the scatter matrix in a more compact form as follows:

$$\mathbf{S}_{\overline{\boldsymbol{y}}} = \tilde{\mathbf{Y}}^\mathsf{T}\tilde{\mathbf{Y}} = \mathbf{Y}^\mathsf{T}\mathbf{C}_N^\mathsf{T}\mathbf{C}_N\mathbf{Y} = \mathbf{Y}^\mathsf{T}\mathbf{C}_N\mathbf{Y} \tag{4.47}$$

where

$$\mathbf{C}_N \triangleq \mathbf{I}_N - \frac{1}{N}\mathbf{1}_N\mathbf{1}_N^\mathsf{T} \tag{4.48}$$

is the **centering matrix**, which converts $\mathbf{Y}$ to $\tilde{\mathbf{Y}}$ by subtracting the mean $\overline{\boldsymbol{y}} = \frac{1}{N}\mathbf{Y}^\mathsf{T}\mathbf{1}_N$ off every row.

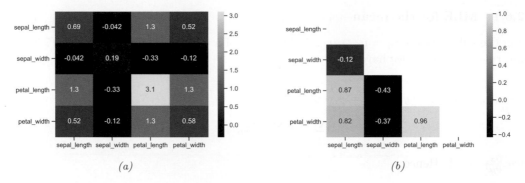

Figure 4.1: (a) Covariance matrix for the features in the iris dataset from Section 1.2.1.1. (b) Correlation matrix. We only show the lower triangle, since the matrix is symmetric and has a unit diagonal. Compare this to Figure 1.3. Generated by iris_cov_mat.ipynb.

Using results from Section 7.8, we can compute derivatives of the loss with respect to $\mathbf{\Lambda}$ to get

$$\frac{\partial \ell(\hat{\boldsymbol{\mu}}, \mathbf{\Lambda})}{\partial \mathbf{\Lambda}} = \frac{N}{2} \mathbf{\Lambda}^{-T} - \frac{1}{2} \mathbf{S}_{\overline{\boldsymbol{y}}}^{\mathsf{T}} = \mathbf{0} \tag{4.49}$$

$$\mathbf{\Lambda}^{-\mathsf{T}} = \mathbf{\Lambda}^{-1} = \mathbf{\Sigma} = \frac{1}{N} \mathbf{S}_{\overline{\boldsymbol{y}}} \tag{4.50}$$

$$\hat{\mathbf{\Sigma}} = \frac{1}{N} \sum_{n=1}^{N} (\boldsymbol{y}_n - \overline{\boldsymbol{y}})(\boldsymbol{y}_n - \overline{\boldsymbol{y}})^{\mathsf{T}} = \frac{1}{N} \mathbf{Y}^{\mathsf{T}} \mathbf{C}_N \mathbf{Y} \tag{4.51}$$

Thus the MLE for the covariance matrix is the empirical covariance matrix. See Figure 4.1a for an example.

Sometimes it is more convenient to work with the correlation matrix defined in Equation (3.8). This can be computed using

$$\mathrm{corr}(\mathbf{Y}) = (\mathrm{diag}(\mathbf{\Sigma}))^{-\frac{1}{2}} \, \mathbf{\Sigma} \, (\mathrm{diag}(\mathbf{\Sigma}))^{-\frac{1}{2}} \tag{4.52}$$

where $\mathrm{diag}(\mathbf{\Sigma})^{-\frac{1}{2}}$ is a diagonal matrix containing the entries $1/\sigma_i$. See Figure 4.1b for an example.

Note, however, that the MLE may overfit or be numerically unstable, especially when the number of samples N is small compared to the number of dimensions D. The main problem is that $\mathbf{\Sigma}$ has $O(D^2)$ parameters, so we may need a lot of data to reliably estimate it. In particular, as we see from Equation (4.51), the MLE for a full covariance matrix is singular if $N < D$. And even when $N > D$, the MLE can be ill-conditioned, meaning it is close to singular. We discuss solutions to this problem in Section 4.5.2.

4.2.7 Example: MLE for linear regression

We briefly mentioned linear regression in Section 2.6.3. Recall that it corresponds to the following model:

$$p(y|\boldsymbol{x}; \boldsymbol{\theta}) = \mathcal{N}(y|\boldsymbol{w}^{\mathsf{T}} \boldsymbol{x}, \sigma^2) \tag{4.53}$$

where $\boldsymbol{\theta} = (\boldsymbol{w}, \sigma^2)$. Let us assume for now that σ^2 is fixed, and focus on estimating the weights $\boldsymbol{w}$. The negative log likelihood or NLL is given by

$$\text{NLL}(\boldsymbol{w}) = -\sum_{n=1}^{N} \log \left[\left(\frac{1}{2\pi\sigma^2} \right)^{\frac{1}{2}} \exp \left(-\frac{1}{2\sigma^2} (y_n - \boldsymbol{w}^\mathsf{T} \boldsymbol{x}_n)^2 \right) \right] \tag{4.54}$$

Dropping the irrelevant additive constants gives the following simplified objective, known as the **residual sum of squares** or **RSS**:

$$\text{RSS}(\boldsymbol{w}) \triangleq \sum_{n=1}^{N} (y_n - \boldsymbol{w}^\mathsf{T} \boldsymbol{x}_n)^2 = \sum_{n=1}^{N} r_n^2 \tag{4.55}$$

where r_n the n'th **residual error**. Scaling by the number of examples N gives the **mean squared error** or **MSE**:

$$\text{MSE}(\boldsymbol{w}) = \frac{1}{N} \text{RSS}(\boldsymbol{w}) = \frac{1}{N} \sum_{n=1}^{N} (y_n - \boldsymbol{w}^\mathsf{T} \boldsymbol{x}_n)^2 \tag{4.56}$$

Finally, taking the square root gives the **root mean squared error** or **RMSE**:

$$\text{RMSE}(\boldsymbol{w}) = \sqrt{\text{MSE}(\boldsymbol{w})} = \sqrt{\frac{1}{N} \sum_{n=1}^{N} (y_n - \boldsymbol{w}^\mathsf{T} \boldsymbol{x}_n)^2} \tag{4.57}$$

We can compute the MLE by minimizing the NLL, RSS, MSE or RMSE. All will give the same results, since these objective functions are all the same, up to irrelevant constants

Let us focus on the RSS objective. It can be written in matrix notation as follows:

$$\text{RSS}(\boldsymbol{w}) = \sum_{n=1}^{N} (y_n - \boldsymbol{w}^\mathsf{T} \boldsymbol{x}_n)^2 = ||\mathbf{X}\boldsymbol{w} - \boldsymbol{y}||_2^2 = (\mathbf{X}\boldsymbol{w} - \boldsymbol{y})^\mathsf{T} (\mathbf{X}\boldsymbol{w} - \boldsymbol{y}) \tag{4.58}$$

In Section 11.2.2.1, we prove that the optimum, which occurs where $\nabla_{\boldsymbol{w}} \text{RSS}(\boldsymbol{w}) = \boldsymbol{0}$, satisfies the following equation:

$$\hat{\boldsymbol{w}}_{\text{mle}} \triangleq \underset{\boldsymbol{w}}{\text{argmin}} \, \text{RSS}(\boldsymbol{w}) = (\mathbf{X}^\mathsf{T}\mathbf{X})^{-1}\mathbf{X}^\mathsf{T}\boldsymbol{y} \tag{4.59}$$

This is called the **ordinary least squares** or **OLS** estimate, and is equivalent to the MLE.

4.3 Empirical risk minimization (ERM)

We can generalize MLE by replacing the (conditional) log loss term in Equation (4.6), $\ell(\boldsymbol{y}_n, \boldsymbol{\theta}; \boldsymbol{x}_n) = -\log p(\boldsymbol{y}_n | \boldsymbol{x}_n, \boldsymbol{\theta})$, with any other loss function, to get

$$\mathcal{L}(\boldsymbol{\theta}) = \frac{1}{N} \sum_{n=1}^{N} \ell(\boldsymbol{y}_n, \boldsymbol{\theta}; \boldsymbol{x}_n) \tag{4.60}$$

This is known as **empirical risk minimization** or **ERM**, since it is the expected loss where the expectation is taken wrt the empirical distribution. See Section 5.4 for more details.

4.3.1   Example: minimizing the misclassification rate

If we are solving a classification problem, we might want to use 0-1 loss:

$$\ell_{01}(\boldsymbol{y}_n, \boldsymbol{\theta}; \boldsymbol{x}_n) = \begin{cases} 0 & \text{if } \boldsymbol{y}_n = f(\boldsymbol{x}_n; \boldsymbol{\theta}) \\ 1 & \text{if } \boldsymbol{y}_n \neq f(\boldsymbol{x}_n; \boldsymbol{\theta}) \end{cases} \tag{4.61}$$

where $f(\boldsymbol{x}; \boldsymbol{\theta})$ is some kind of predictor. The empirical risk becomes

$$\mathcal{L}(\boldsymbol{\theta}) = \frac{1}{N} \sum_{n=1}^{N} \ell_{01}(\boldsymbol{y}_n, \boldsymbol{\theta}; \boldsymbol{x}_n) \tag{4.62}$$

This is just the empirical **misclassification rate** on the training set.

Note that for binary problems, we can rewrite the misclassifcation rate in the following notation. Let $\tilde{y} \in \{-1, +1\}$ be the true label, and $\hat{y} \in \{-1, +1\} = f(\boldsymbol{x}; \boldsymbol{\theta})$ be our prediction. We define the 0-1 loss as follows:

$$\ell_{01}(\tilde{y}, \hat{y}) = \mathbb{I}\left(\tilde{y} \neq \hat{y}\right) = \mathbb{I}\left(\tilde{y}\,\hat{y} < 0\right) \tag{4.63}$$

The corresponding empirical risk becomes

$$\mathcal{L}(\boldsymbol{\theta}) = \frac{1}{N} \sum_{n=1}^{N} \ell_{01}(y_n, \hat{y}_n) = \frac{1}{N} \sum_{n=1}^{N} \mathbb{I}\left(\tilde{y}_n\,\hat{y}_n < 0\right) \tag{4.64}$$

where the dependence on $\boldsymbol{x}_n$ and $\boldsymbol{\theta}$ is implicit.

4.3.2   Surrogate loss

Unfortunately, the 0-1 loss used in Section 4.3.1 is a non-smooth step function, as shown in Figure 4.2, making it difficult to optimize. (In fact, it is NP-hard [BDEL03].) In this section we consider the use of a **surrogate loss function** [BJM06]. The surrogate is usually chosen to be a maximally tight convex upper bound, which is then easy to minimize.

For example, consider a probabilistic binary classifier, which produces the following distribution over labels:

$$p(\tilde{y}|\boldsymbol{x}, \boldsymbol{\theta}) = \sigma(\tilde{y}\eta) = \frac{1}{1 + e^{-\tilde{y}\eta}} \tag{4.65}$$

where $\eta = f(\boldsymbol{x}; \boldsymbol{\theta})$ is the log odds. Hence the log loss is given by

$$\ell_{ll}(\tilde{y}, \eta) = -\log p(\tilde{y}|\eta) = \log(1 + e^{-\tilde{y}\eta}) \tag{4.66}$$

Figure 4.2 shows that this is a smooth upper bound to the 0-1 loss, where we plot the loss vs the quantity $\tilde{y}\eta$, known as the **margin**, since it defines a "margin of safety" away from the threshold value of 0. Thus we see that minimizing the negative log likelihood is equivalent to minimizing a (fairly tight) upper bound on the empirical 0-1 loss.

Another convex upper bound to 0-1 loss is the **hinge loss**, which is defined as follows:

$$\ell_{\text{hinge}}(\tilde{y}, \eta) = \max(0, 1 - \tilde{y}\eta) \triangleq (1 - \tilde{y}\eta)_+ \tag{4.67}$$

This is plotted in Figure 4.2; we see that it has the shape of a partially open door hinge. This is convex upper bound to the 0-1 loss, although it is only piecewise differentiable, not everywhere differentiable.

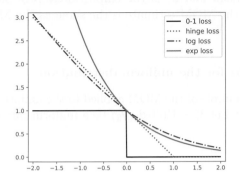

Figure 4.2: Illustration of various loss functions for binary classification. The horizontal axis is the margin $z = \tilde{y}\eta$, the vertical axis is the loss. 0-1 loss is $\mathbb{I}(z < 0)$. Hinge-loss is $\max(0, 1 - z)$. Log-loss is $\log_2(1 + e^{-z})$. Exp-loss is e^{-z}. Generated by hinge_loss_plot.ipynb.

4.4 Other estimation methods *

4.4.1 The method of moments

Computing the MLE requires solving the equation $\nabla_{\boldsymbol{\theta}}\mathrm{NLL}(\boldsymbol{\theta}) = \mathbf{0}$. Sometimes this is computationally difficult. In such cases, we may be able to use a simpler approach known as the **method of moments** (MOM). In this approach, we equate the theoretical moments of the distribution to the empirical moments, and solve the resulting set of K simultaneous equations, where K is the number of parameters. The theoretical moments are given by $\mu_k = \mathbb{E}\left[Y^k\right]$, for $k = 1 : K$, and the empirical moments are given by

$$\hat{\mu}_k = \frac{1}{N} \sum_{n=1}^{n} y_n^k \tag{4.68}$$

so we just need to solve $\mu_k = \hat{\mu}_k$ for each k. We give some examples below.

The method of moments is simple, but it is theoretically inferior to the MLE approach, since it may not use all the data as efficiently. (For details on these theoretical results, see e.g., [CB02].) Furthermore, it can sometimes produce inconsistent results (see Section 4.4.1.2). However, when it produces valid estimates, it can be used to initialize iterative algorithms that are used to optimize the NLL (see e.g., [AHK12]), thus combining the computational efficiency of MOM with the statistical accuracy of MLE.

4.4.1.1 Example: MOM for the univariate Gaussian

For example, consider the case of a univariate Gaussian distribution. From Section 4.2.5, we have

$$\mu_1 = \mu = \overline{y} \tag{4.69}$$

$$\mu_2 = \sigma^2 + \mu^2 = s^2 \tag{4.70}$$

where $\bar{y}$ is the empirical mean and s^2 is the empirical average sum of squares. so $\hat{\mu} = \bar{y}$ and $\hat{\sigma}^2 = s^2 - \bar{y}^2$. In this case, the MOM estimate is the same as the MLE, but this is not always the case.

4.4.1.2   Example: MOM for the uniform distribution

In this section, we give an example of the MOM applied to the uniform distribution. Our presentation follows the wikipedia page.[5] Let $Y \sim \text{Unif}(\theta_1, \theta_2)$ be a uniform random variable, so

$$p(y|\theta) = \frac{1}{\theta_2 - \theta_1} \mathbb{I}(\theta_1 \leq y \leq \theta_2) \tag{4.71}$$

The first two moments are

$$\mu_1 = \mathbb{E}[Y] = \frac{1}{2}(\theta_1 + \theta_2) \tag{4.72}$$

$$\mu_2 = \mathbb{E}[Y^2] = \frac{1}{3}(\theta_1^2 + \theta_1\theta_2 + \theta_2^2) \tag{4.73}$$

Inverting these equations gives

$$(\theta_1, \theta_2) = \left(\mu_1 - \sqrt{3(\mu_2 - \mu_1^2)}, 2\mu_1 - \theta_1\right) \tag{4.74}$$

Unfortunately this estimator can sometimes give invalid results. For example, suppose $\mathcal{D} = \{0, 0, 0, 0, 1\}$. The empirical moments are $\hat{\mu}_1 = \frac{1}{5}$ and $\hat{\mu}_2 = \frac{1}{5}$, so the estimated parameters are $\hat{\theta}_1 = \frac{1}{5} - \frac{2\sqrt{3}}{5} = -0.493$ and $\hat{\theta}_2 = \frac{1}{5} + \frac{2\sqrt{3}}{5} = 0.893$. However, these cannot possibly be the correct parameters, since if $\theta_2 = 0.893$, we cannot generate a sample as large as 1.

By contrast, consider the MLE. Let $y_{(1)} \leq y_{(2)} \leq \cdots \leq y_{(N)}$ be the **order statistics** of the data (i.e., the values sorted in increasing order). Let $\theta = \theta_2 - \theta_1$. Then the likelihood is given by

$$p(\mathcal{D}|\boldsymbol{\theta}) = (\theta)^{-N} \mathbb{I}(y_{(1)} \geq \theta_1) \mathbb{I}(y_{(N)} \leq \theta_2) \tag{4.75}$$

Within the permitted bounds for θ, the derivative of the log likelihood is given by

$$\frac{d}{d\theta} \log p(\mathcal{D}|\theta) = -\frac{N}{\theta} < 0 \tag{4.76}$$

Hence the likelihood is a decreasing function of θ, so we should pick

$$\hat{\theta}_1 = y_{(1)}, \hat{\theta}_2 = y_{(N)} \tag{4.77}$$

In the above example, we get $\hat{\theta}_1 = 0$ and $\hat{\theta}_2 = 1$, as one would expect.

---

5. https://en.wikipedia.org/wiki/Method_of_moments_(statistics).

4.4.2 Online (recursive) estimation

If the entire dataset $\mathcal{D}$ is available before training starts, we say that we are doing **batch learning**. However, in some cases, the data set arrives sequentially, so $\mathcal{D} = \{y_1, y_2, \ldots\}$ in an unbounded stream. In this case, we want to perform **online learning**.

Let $\hat{\boldsymbol{\theta}}_{t-1}$ be our estimate (e.g., MLE) given $\mathcal{D}_{1:t-1}$. To ensure our learning algorithm takes constant time per update, we need to find a learning rule of the form

$$\boldsymbol{\theta}_t = f(\hat{\boldsymbol{\theta}}_{t-1}, \boldsymbol{y}_t) \tag{4.78}$$

This is called a **recursive update**. Below we give some examples of such online learning methods.

4.4.2.1 Example: recursive MLE for the mean of a Gaussian

Let us reconsider the example from Section 4.2.5 where we computed the MLE for a univariate Gaussian. We know that the batch estimate for the mean is given by

$$\hat{\mu}_t = \frac{1}{t} \sum_{n=1}^{t} \boldsymbol{y}_n \tag{4.79}$$

This is just a **running sum** of the data, so we can easily convert this into a recursive estimate as follows:

$$\hat{\mu}_t = \frac{1}{t} \sum_{n=1}^{t} \boldsymbol{y}_n = \frac{1}{t} \left((t-1)\hat{\mu}_{t-1} + \boldsymbol{y}_t \right) \tag{4.80}$$

$$= \hat{\mu}_{t-1} + \frac{1}{t}(\boldsymbol{y}_t - \hat{\mu}_{t-1}) \tag{4.81}$$

This is known as a **moving average**.

We see from Equation (4.81) that the new estimate is the old estimate plus a correction term. The size of the correction diminishes over time (i.e., as we get more samples). However, if the distribution is changing, we want to give more weight to more recent data examples. We discuss how to do this in Section 4.4.2.2.

4.4.2.2 Exponentially-weighted moving average

Equation (4.81) shows how to compute the moving average of a signal. In this section, we show how to adjust this to give more weight to more recent examples. In particular, we will compute the following **exponentially weighted moving average** or **EWMA**, also called an **exponential moving average** or **EMA**:

$$\hat{\mu}_t = \beta\mu_{t-1} + (1-\beta)\boldsymbol{y}_t \tag{4.82}$$

where $0 < \beta < 1$. The contribution of a data point k steps in the past is weighted by $\beta^k(1-\beta)$. Thus the contribution from old data is exponentially decreasing. In particular, we have

$$\hat{\mu}_t = \beta\mu_{t-1} + (1-\beta)\boldsymbol{y}_t \tag{4.83}$$

$$= \beta^2\mu_{t-2} + \beta(1-\beta)\boldsymbol{y}_{t-1} + (1-\beta)\boldsymbol{y}_t \quad\vdots \tag{4.84}$$

$$= \beta^t\boldsymbol{y}_0 + (1-\beta)\beta^{t-1}\boldsymbol{y}_1 + \cdots + (1-\beta)\beta\boldsymbol{y}_{t-1} + (1-\beta)\boldsymbol{y}_t \tag{4.85}$$

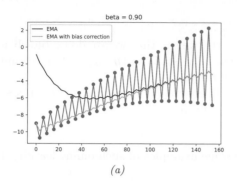
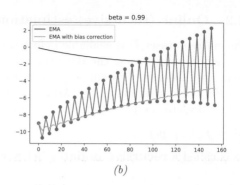

$$(a) \qquad\qquad\qquad\qquad\qquad (b)$$

Figure 4.3: Illustration of exponentially-weighted moving average with and without bias correction. (a) Short memory: $\beta = 0.9$. (a) Long memory: $\beta = 0.99$. Generated by ema_demo.ipynb.

The sum of a **geometric series** is given by

$$\beta^t + \beta^{t-1} + \cdots + \beta^1 + \beta^0 = \frac{1 - \beta^{t+1}}{1 - \beta} \tag{4.86}$$

Hence

$$(1 - \beta) \sum_{k=0}^{t} \beta^k = (1 - \beta)\frac{1 - \beta^{t+1}}{1 - \beta} = 1 - \beta^{t+1} \tag{4.87}$$

Since $0 < \beta < 1$, we have $\beta^{t+1} \to 0$ as $t \to \infty$, so smaller β forgets the past more quickly, and adapts to the more recent data more rapidly. This is illustrated in Figure 4.3.

Since the initial estimate starts from $\hat{\boldsymbol{\mu}}_0 = \mathbf{0}$, there is an initial bias. This can be corrected by scaling as follows [KB15]:

$$\tilde{\boldsymbol{\mu}}_t = \frac{\hat{\boldsymbol{\mu}}_t}{1 - \beta^t} \tag{4.88}$$

(Note that the update in Equation (4.82) is still applied to the uncorrected EMA, $\hat{\boldsymbol{\mu}}_{t-1}$, before being corrected for the current time step.) The benefit of this is illustrated in Figure 4.3.

4.5   Regularization

A fundamental problem with MLE, and ERM, is that it will try to pick parameters that minimize loss on the training set, but this may not result in a model that has low loss on future data. This is called **overfitting**.

As a simple example, suppose we want to predict the probability of heads when tossing a coin. We toss it $N = 3$ times and observe 3 heads. The MLE is $\hat{\theta}_{\text{mle}} = N_1/(N_0 + N_1) = 3/(3 + 0) = 1$ (see Section 4.2.3). However, if we use $\text{Ber}(y|\hat{\theta}_{\text{mle}})$ to make predictions, we will predict that all future coin tosses will also be heads, which seems rather unlikely.

The core of the problem is that the model has enough parameters to perfectly fit the observed training data, so it can perfectly match the empirical distribution. However, in most cases the empirical distribution is not the same as the true distribution, so putting all the probability mass on the observed set of N examples will not leave over any probability for novel data in the future. That is, the model may not **generalize**.

The main solution to overfitting is to use **regularization**, which means to add a penalty term to the NLL (or empirical risk). Thus we optimize an objective of the form

$$\mathcal{L}(\boldsymbol{\theta}; \lambda) = \left[\frac{1}{N} \sum_{n=1}^{N} \ell(\boldsymbol{y}_n, \boldsymbol{\theta}; \boldsymbol{x}_n) \right] + \lambda C(\boldsymbol{\theta}) \tag{4.89}$$

where $\lambda \geq 0$ is the **regularization parameter**, and $C(\boldsymbol{\theta})$ is some form of **complexity penalty**.

A common complexity penalty is to use $C(\boldsymbol{\theta}) = -\log p(\boldsymbol{\theta})$, where $p(\boldsymbol{\theta})$ is the **prior** for $\boldsymbol{\theta}$. If ℓ is the log loss, the regularized objective becomes

$$\mathcal{L}(\boldsymbol{\theta}; \lambda) = -\frac{1}{N} \sum_{n=1}^{N} \log p(\boldsymbol{y}_n | \boldsymbol{x}_n, \boldsymbol{\theta}) - \lambda \log p(\boldsymbol{\theta}) \tag{4.90}$$

By setting $\lambda = 1$ and rescaling $p(\boldsymbol{\theta})$ appropriately, we can equivalently minimize the following:

$$\mathcal{L}(\boldsymbol{\theta}; \lambda) = -\left[\sum_{n=1}^{N} \log p(\boldsymbol{y}_n | \boldsymbol{x}_n, \boldsymbol{\theta}) + \log p(\boldsymbol{\theta}) \right] = -\left[\log p(\mathcal{D}|\boldsymbol{\theta}) + \log p(\boldsymbol{\theta}) \right] \tag{4.91}$$

Minimizing this is equivalent to maximizing the log posterior:

$$\hat{\boldsymbol{\theta}} = \underset{\boldsymbol{\theta}}{\operatorname{argmax}} \log p(\boldsymbol{\theta}|\mathcal{D}) = \underset{\boldsymbol{\theta}}{\operatorname{argmax}} \left[\log p(\mathcal{D}|\boldsymbol{\theta}) + \log p(\boldsymbol{\theta}) - \operatorname{const} \right] \tag{4.92}$$

This is known as **MAP estimation**, which stands for **maximum a posterior estimation**.

4.5.1 Example: MAP estimation for the Bernoulli distribution

Consider again the coin tossing example. If we observe just one head, the MLE is $\theta_{\mathrm{mle}} = 1$, which predicts that all future coin tosses will also show up heads. To avoid such overfitting, we can add a penalty to θ to discourage "extreme" values, such as $\theta = 0$ or $\theta = 1$. We can do this by using a beta distribution as our prior, $p(\theta) = \operatorname{Beta}(\theta|a, b)$, where $a, b > 1$ encourages values of θ near to $a/(a+b)$ (see Section 2.7.4 for details). The log likelihood plus log prior becomes

$$\ell(\theta) = \log p(\mathcal{D}|\theta) + \log p(\theta) \tag{4.93}$$
$$= [N_1 \log \theta + N_0 \log(1-\theta)] + [(a-1)\log(\theta) + (b-1)\log(1-\theta)] \tag{4.94}$$

Using the method from Section 4.2.3 we find that the MAP estimate is

$$\theta_{\mathrm{map}} = \frac{N_1 + a - 1}{N_1 + N_0 + a + b - 2} \tag{4.95}$$

If we set $a = b = 2$ (which weakly favors a value of θ near 0.5), the estimate becomes

$$\theta_{\text{map}} = \frac{N_1 + 1}{N_1 + N_0 + 2} \tag{4.96}$$

This is called **add-one smoothing**, and is a simple but widely used technique to avoid the **zero count** problem. (See also Section 4.6.2.9.)

The zero-count problem, and overfitting more generally, is analogous to a problem in philosophy called the **black swan paradox**. This is based on the ancient Western conception that all swans were white. In that context, a black swan was a metaphor for something that could not exist. (Black swans were discovered in Australia by European explorers in the 17th Century.) The term "black swan paradox" was first coined by the famous philosopher of science Karl Popper; the term has also been used as the title of a recent popular book [Tal07]. This paradox was used to illustrate the problem of **induction**, which is the problem of how to draw general conclusions about the future from specific observations from the past. The solution to the paradox is to admit that induction is in general impossible, and that the best we can do is to make plausible guesses about what the future might hold, by combining the empirical data with prior knowledge.

4.5.2   Example: MAP estimation for the multivariate Gaussian *

In Section 4.2.6, we showed that the MLE for the mean of an MVN is the empirical mean, $\hat{\boldsymbol{\mu}}_{\text{mle}} = \overline{\boldsymbol{y}}$. We also showed that the MLE for the covariance is the empirical covariance, $\hat{\boldsymbol{\Sigma}} = \frac{1}{N}\mathbf{S}_{\overline{\boldsymbol{y}}}$.

In high dimensions the estimate for $\boldsymbol{\Sigma}$ can easily become singular. One solution to this is to perform MAP estimation, as we explain below.

4.5.2.1   Shrinkage estimate

A convenient prior to use for $\boldsymbol{\Sigma}$ is the inverse Wishart prior. This is a distribution over positive definite matrices, where the parameters are defined in terms of a prior scatter matrix, $\breve{\mathbf{S}}$, and a prior sample size or strength $\breve{N}$. One can show that the resulting MAP estimate is given by

$$\hat{\boldsymbol{\Sigma}}_{\text{map}} = \frac{\breve{\mathbf{S}} + \mathbf{S}_{\overline{\boldsymbol{y}}}}{\breve{N} + N} = \frac{\breve{N}}{\breve{N} + N}\frac{\breve{\mathbf{S}}}{\breve{N}} + \frac{N}{\breve{N} + N}\frac{\mathbf{S}_{\overline{\boldsymbol{y}}}}{N} = \lambda\boldsymbol{\Sigma}_0 + (1 - \lambda)\hat{\boldsymbol{\Sigma}}_{\text{mle}} \tag{4.97}$$

where $\lambda = \frac{\breve{N}}{\breve{N}+N}$ controls the amount of regularization.

A common choice (see e.g., [FR07, p6]) for the prior scatter matrix is to use $\breve{\mathbf{S}} = \breve{N}\,\text{diag}(\hat{\boldsymbol{\Sigma}}_{\text{mle}})$. With this choice, we find that the MAP estimate for $\boldsymbol{\Sigma}$ is given by

$$\hat{\boldsymbol{\Sigma}}_{\text{map}}(i,j) = \begin{cases} \hat{\boldsymbol{\Sigma}}_{\text{mle}}(i,j) & \text{if } i = j \\ (1-\lambda)\hat{\boldsymbol{\Sigma}}_{\text{mle}}(i,j) & \text{otherwise} \end{cases} \tag{4.98}$$

Thus we see that the diagonal entries are equal to their ML estimates, and the off-diagonal elements are "shrunk" somewhat towards 0. This technique is therefore called **shrinkage estimation**.

The other parameter we need to set is λ, which controls the amount of regularization (shrinkage towards the MLE). It is common to set λ by cross validation (Section 4.5.5). Alternatively, we can use the closed-form formula provided in [LW04a; LW04b; SS05], which is the optimal

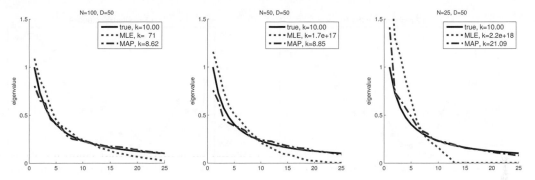

Figure 4.4: Estimating a covariance matrix in $D = 50$ dimensions using $N \in \{100, 50, 25\}$ samples. We plot the eigenvalues in descending order for the true covariance matrix (solid black), the MLE (dotted blue) and the MAP estimate (dashed red), using Equation (4.98) with $\lambda = 0.9$. We also list the condition number of each matrix in the legend. We see that the MLE is often poorly conditioned, but the MAP estimate is numerically well behaved. Adapted from Figure 1 of [SS05]. Generated by shrinkcov_plots.ipynb.

frequentist estimate if we use squared loss. This is implemented in the sklearn function https://scikit-learn.org/stable/modules/generated/sklearn.covariance.LedoitWolf.html.

The benefits of this approach are illustrated in Figure 4.4. We consider fitting a 50-dimensional Gaussian to $N = 100$, $N = 50$ and $N = 25$ data points. We see that the MAP estimate is always well-conditioned, unlike the MLE (see Section 7.1.4.4 for a discussion of condition numbers). In particular, we see that the eigenvalue spectrum of the MAP estimate is much closer to that of the true matrix than the MLE's spectrum. The eigenvectors, however, are unaffected.

4.5.3 Example: weight decay

In Figure 1.7, we saw how using polynomial regression with too high of a degree can result in overfitting. One solution is to reduce the degree of the polynomial. However, a more general solution is to penalize the magnitude of the weights (regression coefficients). We can do this by using a zero-mean Gaussian prior, $p(\boldsymbol{w})$. The resulting MAP estimate is given by

$$\hat{\boldsymbol{w}}_{\mathrm{map}} = \underset{\boldsymbol{w}}{\operatorname{argmin}} \operatorname{NLL}(\boldsymbol{w}) + \lambda ||\boldsymbol{w}||_2^2 \tag{4.99}$$

where $||\boldsymbol{w}||_2^2 = \sum_{d=1}^{D} w_d^2$. (We write $\boldsymbol{w}$ rather than $\boldsymbol{\theta}$, since it only really make sense to penalize the magnitude of weight vectors, rather than other parameters, such as bias terms or noise variances.)

Equation (4.99) is called ℓ_2 **regularization** or **weight decay**. The larger the value of λ, the more the parameters are penalized for being "large" (deviating from the zero-mean prior), and thus the less flexible the model.

In the case of linear regression, this kind of penalization scheme is called **ridge regression**. For example, consider the polynomial regression example from Section 1.2.2.2, where the predictor has the form

$$f(x; \boldsymbol{w}) = \sum_{d=0}^{D} w_d x^d = \boldsymbol{w}^\mathsf{T}[1, x, x^2, \dots, x^D] \tag{4.100}$$

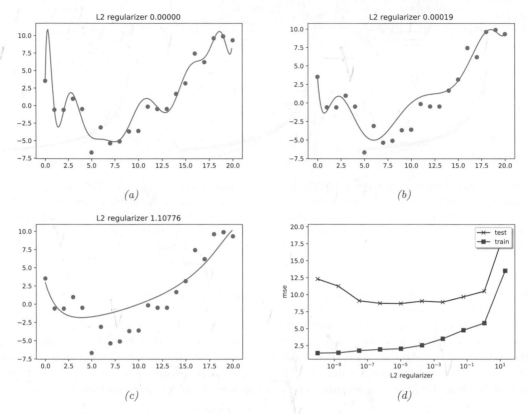

Figure 4.5: (a-c) Ridge regression applied to a degree 14 polynomial fit to 21 datapoints. (d) MSE vs strength of regularizer. The degree of regularization increases from left to right, so model complexity decreases from left to right. Generated by linreg_poly_ridge.ipynb.

Suppose we use a high degree polynomial, say $D = 14$, even though we have a small dataset with just $N = 21$ examples. MLE for the parameters will enable the model to fit the data very well, by carefully adjusting the weights, but the resulting function is very "wiggly", thus resulting in overfitting. Figure 4.5 illustrates how increasing λ can reduce overfitting. For more details on ridge regression, see Section 11.3.

4.5.4   Picking the regularizer using a validation set

A key question when using regularization is how to choose the strength of the regularizer λ: a small value means we will focus on minimizing empirical risk, which may result in overfitting, whereas a large value means we will focus on staying close to the prior, which may result in **underfitting**.

In this section, we describe a simple but very widely used method for choosing λ. The basic idea is to partition the data into two disjoint sets, the training set $\mathcal{D}_{\text{train}}$ and a **validation set** $\mathcal{D}_{\text{valid}}$ (also called a **development set**). (Often we use about 80% of the data for the training set, and

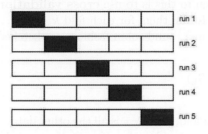

Figure 4.6: Schematic of 5-fold cross validation.

20% for the validation set.) We fit the model on $\mathcal{D}_{\text{train}}$ (for each setting of λ) and then evaluate its performance on $\mathcal{D}_{\text{valid}}$. We then pick the value of λ that results in the best validation performance. (This optimization method is a 1d example of grid search, discussed in Section 8.8.)

To explain the method in more detail, we need some notation. Let us define the regularized empirical risk on a dataset as follows:

$$R_\lambda(\boldsymbol{\theta}, \mathcal{D}) = \frac{1}{|\mathcal{D}|} \sum_{(\boldsymbol{x}, \boldsymbol{y}) \in \mathcal{D}} \ell(\boldsymbol{y}, f(\boldsymbol{x}; \boldsymbol{\theta})) + \lambda C(\boldsymbol{\theta}) \tag{4.101}$$

For each λ, we compute the parameter estimate

$$\hat{\boldsymbol{\theta}}_\lambda(\mathcal{D}_{\text{train}}) = \operatorname*{argmin}_{\boldsymbol{\theta}} R_\lambda(\boldsymbol{\theta}, \mathcal{D}_{\text{train}}) \tag{4.102}$$

We then compute the **validation risk**:

$$R_\lambda^{\text{val}} \triangleq R_0(\hat{\boldsymbol{\theta}}_\lambda(\mathcal{D}_{\text{train}}), \mathcal{D}_{\text{valid}}) \tag{4.103}$$

This is an estimate of the **population risk**, which is the expected loss under the true distribution $p^*(\boldsymbol{x}, \boldsymbol{y})$. Finally we pick

$$\lambda^* = \operatorname*{argmin}_{\lambda \in \mathcal{S}} R_\lambda^{\text{val}} \tag{4.104}$$

(This requires fitting the model once for each value of λ in $\mathcal{S}$, although in some cases, this can be done more efficiently.)

After picking λ^*, we can refit the model to the entire dataset, $\mathcal{D} = \mathcal{D}_{\text{train}} \cup \mathcal{D}_{\text{valid}}$, to get

$$\hat{\boldsymbol{\theta}}^* = \operatorname*{argmin}_{\boldsymbol{\theta}} R_{\lambda^*}(\boldsymbol{\theta}, \mathcal{D}) \tag{4.105}$$

4.5.5 Cross-validation

The above technique in Section 4.5.4 can work very well. However, if the size of the training set is small, leaving aside 20% for a validation set can result in an unreliable estimate of the model parameters.

A simple but popular solution to this is to use **cross validation** (**CV**). The idea is as follows: we split the training data into K **folds**; then, for each fold $k \in \{1, \ldots, K\}$, we train on all the folds but the k'th, and test on the k'th, in a round-robin fashion, as sketched in Figure 4.6. Formally, we have

$$R_\lambda^{\mathrm{cv}} \triangleq \frac{1}{K} \sum_{k=1}^{K} R_0(\hat{\boldsymbol{\theta}}_\lambda(\mathcal{D}_{-k}), \mathcal{D}_k) \tag{4.106}$$

where $\mathcal{D}_k$ is the data in the k'th fold, and $\mathcal{D}_{-k}$ is all the other data. This is called the **cross-validated risk**. Figure 4.6 illustrates this procedure for $K = 5$. If we set $K = N$, we get a method known as **leave-one-out cross-validation**, since we always train on $N - 1$ items and test on the remaining one.

We can use the CV estimate as an objective inside of an optimization routine to pick the optimal hyperparameter, $\hat{\lambda} = \mathrm{argmin}_\lambda R_\lambda^{\mathrm{cv}}$. Finally we combine all the available data (training and validation), and re-estimate the model parameters using $\hat{\boldsymbol{\theta}} = \mathrm{argmin}_{\boldsymbol{\theta}} R_{\hat{\lambda}}(\boldsymbol{\theta}, \mathcal{D})$. See Section 5.4.3 for more details.

4.5.5.1   The one standard error rule

CV gives an estimate of $\hat{R}_\lambda$, but does not give any measure of uncertainty. A standard frequentist measure of uncertainty of an estimate is the **standard error of the mean**, which is the mean of the sampling distribution of the estimate (see Section 4.7.1). We can compute this as follows. First let $L_n = \ell(\boldsymbol{y}_n, f(\boldsymbol{x}_n; \hat{\boldsymbol{\theta}}_\lambda(\mathcal{D}_{-n})))$ be the loss on the n'th example, where we use the parameters that were estimated using whichever training fold excludes n. (Note that L_n depends on λ, but we drop this from the notation.) Next let $\hat{\mu} = \frac{1}{N} \sum_{n=1}^{N} L_n$ be the empirical mean and $\hat{\sigma}^2 = \frac{1}{N} \sum_{n=1}^{N} (L_n - \hat{\mu})^2$ be the empirical variance. Given this, we define our estimate to be $\hat{\mu}$, and the standard error of this estimate to be $\mathrm{se}(\hat{\mu}) = \frac{\hat{\sigma}}{\sqrt{N}}$. Note that σ measures the intrinsic variability of L_n across samples, whereas $\mathrm{se}(\hat{\mu})$ measures our uncertainty about the mean $\hat{\mu}$.

Suppose we apply CV to a set of models and compute the mean and se of their estimated risks. A common heuristic for picking a model from these noisy estimates is to pick the value which corresponds to the simplest model whose risk is no more than one standard error above the risk of the best model; this is called the **one-standard error rule** [HTF01, p216].

4.5.5.2   Example: ridge regression

As an example, consider picking the strength of the ℓ_2 regularizer for the ridge regression problem in Section 4.5.3. In Figure 4.7a, we plot the error vs $\log(\lambda)$ on the train set (blue) and test set (red curve). We see that the test error has a U-shaped curve, where it decreases as we increase the regularizer, and then increases as we start to underfit. In Figure 4.7b, we plot the 5-fold CV estimate of the test MSE vs $\log(\lambda)$. We see that the minimum CV error is close the optimal value for the test set (although it does underestimate the spike in the test error for large lambda, due to the small sample size.)

4.5.6   Early stopping

A very simple form of regularization, which is often very effective in practice (especially for complex models), is known as **early stopping**. This leverages the fact that optimization algorithms are

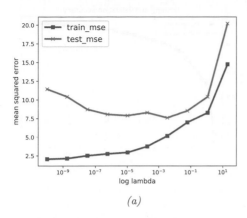
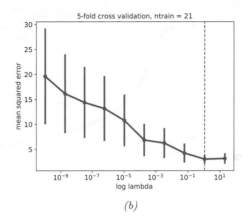

(a)   (b)

Figure 4.7: Ridge regression is applied to a degree 14 polynomial fit to 21 datapoints shown in Figure 4.5 for different values of the regularizer λ. The degree of regularization increases from left to right, so model complexity decreases from left to right. (a) MSE on train (blue) and test (red) vs $\log(\lambda)$. (b) 5-fold cross-validation estimate of test MSE; error bars are standard error of the mean. Vertical line is the point chosen by the one standard error rule. Generated by polyfitRidgeCV.ipynb.

iterative, and so they take many steps to move away from the initial parameter estimates. If we detect signs of overfitting (by monitoring performance on the validation set), we can stop the optimization process, to prevent the model memorizing too much information about the training set. See Figure 4.8 for an illustration.

4.5.7   Using more data

As the amount of data increases, the chance of overfitting (for a model of fixed complexity) decreases (assuming the data contains suitably informative examples, and is not too redundant). This is illustrated in Figure 4.9. We show the MSE on the training and test sets for four different models (polynomials of increasing degree) as a function of the training set size N. (A plot of error vs training set size is known as a **learning curve**.) The horizontal black line represents the **Bayes error**, which is the error of the optimal predictor (the true model) due to inherent noise. (In this example, the true model is a degree 2 polynomial, and the noise has a variance of $\sigma^2 = 4$; this is called the **noise floor**, since we cannot go below it.)

We notice several interesting things. First, the test error for degree 1 remains high, even as N increases, since the model is too simple to capture the truth; this is called underfitting. The test error for the other models decreases to the optimal level (the noise floor), but it decreases more rapidly for the simpler models, since they have fewer parameters to estimate. The gap between the test error and training error is larger for more complex models, but decreases as N grows.

Another interesting thing we can note is that the training error (blue line) initially *increases* with N, at least for the models that are sufficiently flexible. The reason for this is as follows: as the data set gets larger, we observe more distinct input-output pattern combinations, so the task of fitting the data becomes harder. However, eventually the training set will come to resemble the test set, and

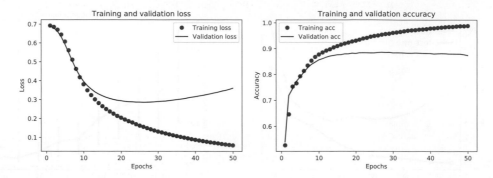

Figure 4.8: *Performance of a text classifier (a neural network applied to a bag of word embeddings using average pooling) vs number of training epochs on the IMDB movie sentiment dataset. Blue = train, red = validation. (a) Cross entropy loss. Early stopping is triggered at about epoch 25. (b) Classification accuracy. Generated by imdb_ mlp_ bow_ tf.ipynb.*

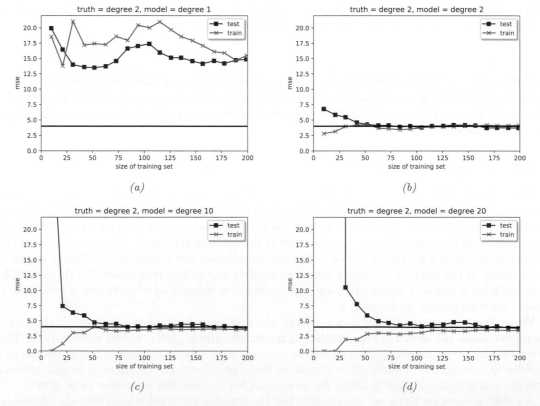

Figure 4.9: *MSE on training and test sets vs size of training set, for data generated from a degree 2 polynomial with Gaussian noise of variance $\sigma^2 = 4$. We fit polynomial models of varying degree to this data. Generated by linreg_ poly_ vs_ n.ipynb.*

the error rates will converge, and will reflect the optimal performance of that model.

4.6 Bayesian statistics *

So far, we have discussed several ways to estimate parameters from data. However, these approaches ignore any uncertainty in the estimates, which can be important for some applications, such as active learning, or avoiding overfitting, or just knowing how much to trust the estimate of some scientifically meaningful quantity. In statistics, modeling uncertainty about parameters using a probability distribution (as opposed to just computing a point estimate) is known as **inference**.

In this section, we use the **posterior distribution** to represent our uncertainty. This is the approach adopted in the field of **Bayesian statistics**. We give a brief introduction here, but more details can be found in the sequel to this book, [Mur23], as well as other good books, such as [Lam18; Kru15; McE20; Gel+14; MKL21; MFR20].

To compute the posterior, we start with a **prior** distribution $p(\boldsymbol{\theta})$, which reflects what we know before seeing the data. We then define a **likelihood function** $p(\mathcal{D}|\boldsymbol{\theta})$, which reflects the data we expect to see for each setting of the parameters. We then use Bayes rule to condition the prior on the observed data to compute the posterior $p(\boldsymbol{\theta}|\mathcal{D})$ as follows:

$$p(\boldsymbol{\theta}|\mathcal{D}) = \frac{p(\boldsymbol{\theta})p(\mathcal{D}|\boldsymbol{\theta})}{p(\mathcal{D})} = \frac{p(\boldsymbol{\theta})p(\mathcal{D}|\boldsymbol{\theta})}{\int p(\boldsymbol{\theta}')p(\mathcal{D}|\boldsymbol{\theta}')d\boldsymbol{\theta}'} \tag{4.107}$$

The denominator $p(\mathcal{D})$ is called the **marginal likelihood**, since it is computed by **marginalizing over** (or **integrating out**) the unknown $\boldsymbol{\theta}$. This can be interpreted as the average probability of the data, where the average is wrt the prior. Note, however, that $p(\mathcal{D})$ is a constant, independent of $\boldsymbol{\theta}$, so we will often ignore it when we just want to infer the relative probabilities of $\boldsymbol{\theta}$ values.

Equation (4.107) is analogous to the use of Bayes rule for COVID-19 testing in Section 2.3.1. The difference is that the unknowns correspond to parameters of a statistical model, rather than the unknown disease state of a patient. In addition, we usually condition on a set of observations $\mathcal{D}$, as opposed to a single observation (such as a single test outcome). In particular, for a supervised or conditional model, the observed data has the form $\mathcal{D} = \{(\boldsymbol{x}_n, \boldsymbol{y}_n) : n = 1 : N\}$. For an unsupervised or unconditional model, the observed data has the form $\mathcal{D} = \{(\boldsymbol{y}_n) : n = 1 : N\}$.

Once we have computed the posterior over the parameters, we can compute the **posterior predictive distribution** over outputs given inputs by **marginalizing out** the unknown parameters. In the supervised/ conditional case, this becomes

$$p(\boldsymbol{y}|\boldsymbol{x}, \mathcal{D}) = \int p(\boldsymbol{y}|\boldsymbol{x}, \boldsymbol{\theta})p(\boldsymbol{\theta}|\mathcal{D})d\boldsymbol{\theta} \tag{4.108}$$

This can be viewed as a form of **Bayes model averaging (BMA)**, since we are making predictions using an infinite set of models (parameter values), each one weighted by how likely it is. The use of BMA reduces the chance of overfitting (Section 1.2.3), since we are not just using the single best model.

4.6.1 Conjugate priors

In this section, we consider a set of (prior, likelihood) pairs for which we can compute the posterior in closed form. In particular, we will use priors that are "conjugate" to the likelihood. We say that a prior $p(\boldsymbol{\theta}) \in \mathcal{F}$ is a **conjugate prior** for a likelihood function $p(\mathcal{D}|\boldsymbol{\theta})$ if the posterior is in the same parameterized family as the prior, i.e., $p(\boldsymbol{\theta}|\mathcal{D}) \in \mathcal{F}$. In other words, $\mathcal{F}$ is closed under Bayesian updating. If the family $\mathcal{F}$ corresponds to the exponential family (defined in Section 3.4), then the computations can be performed in closed form.

In the sections below, we give some common examples of this framework, which we will use later in the book. For simplicity, we focus on unconditional models (i.e., there are only outcomes or targets y, and no inputs or features $\boldsymbol{x}$); we relax this assumption in Section 4.6.7.

4.6.2 The beta-binomial model

Suppose we toss a coin N times, and want to infer the probability of heads. Let $y_n = 1$ denote the event that the n'th trial was heads, $y_n = 0$ represent the event that the n'th trial was tails, and let $\mathcal{D} = \{y_n : n = 1 : N\}$ be all the data. We assume $y_n \sim \text{Ber}(\theta)$, where $\theta \in [0, 1]$ is the rate parameter (probability of heads). In this section, we discuss how to compute $p(\theta|\mathcal{D})$.

4.6.2.1 Bernoulli likelihood

We assume the data are **iid** or **independent and identically distributed**. Thus the likelihood has the form

$$p(\mathcal{D}|\theta) = \prod_{n=1}^{N} \theta^{y_n} (1-\theta)^{1-y_n} = \theta^{N_1} (1-\theta)^{N_0} \tag{4.109}$$

where we have defined $N_1 = \sum_{n=1}^{N} \mathbb{I}(y_n = 1)$ and $N_0 = \sum_{n=1}^{N} \mathbb{I}(y_n = 0)$, representing the number of heads and tails. These counts are called the **sufficient statistics** of the data, since this is all we need to know about $\mathcal{D}$ to infer θ. The total count, $N = N_0 + N_1$, is called the **sample size**.

4.6.2.2 Binomial likelihood

Note that we can also consider a Binomial likelihood model, in which we perform N trials and observe the number of heads, y, rather than observing a sequence of coin tosses. Now the likelihood has the following form:

$$p(\mathcal{D}|\theta) = \text{Bin}(y|N, \theta) = \binom{N}{y} \theta^y (1-\theta)^{N-y} \tag{4.110}$$

The scaling factor $\binom{N}{y}$ is independent of θ, so we can ignore it. Thus this likelihood is proportional to the Bernoulli likelihood in Equation (4.109), so our inferences about θ will be the same for both models.

4.6.2.3 Prior

To simplify the computations, we will assume that the prior $p(\boldsymbol{\theta}) \in \mathcal{F}$ is a conjugate prior for the likelihood function $p(\boldsymbol{y}|\boldsymbol{\theta})$. This means that the posterior is in the same parameterized family as the prior, i.e., $p(\boldsymbol{\theta}|\mathcal{D}) \in \mathcal{F}$.

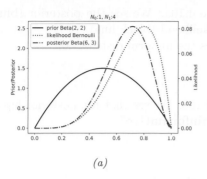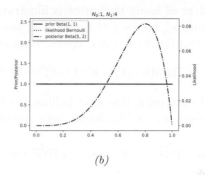

Figure 4.10: Updating a Beta prior with a Bernoulli likelihood with sufficient statistics $N_1 = 4, N_0 = 1$. (a) Beta(2,2) prior. (b) Uniform Beta(1,1) prior. Generated by beta_binom_post_plot.ipynb.

To ensure this property when using the Bernoulli (or Binomial) likelihood, we should use a prior of the following form:

$$p(\theta) \propto \theta^{\breve{\alpha}-1}(1-\theta)^{\breve{\beta}-1} \propto \text{Beta}(\theta|\, \breve{\alpha}, \breve{\beta}) \tag{4.111}$$

We recognize this as the pdf of a beta distribution (see Section 2.7.4).

4.6.2.4 Posterior

If we multiply the Bernoulli likelihood in Equation (4.109) with the beta prior in Equation (2.136) we get a beta posterior:

$$p(\theta|\mathcal{D}) \propto \theta^{N_1}(1-\theta)^{N_0}\, \theta^{\breve{\alpha}-1}(1-\theta)^{\breve{\beta}-1} \tag{4.112}$$

$$\propto \text{Beta}(\theta|\, \breve{\alpha}+N_1, \breve{\beta}+N_0) \tag{4.113}$$

$$= \text{Beta}(\theta|\, \widehat{\alpha}, \widehat{\beta}) \tag{4.114}$$

where $\widehat{\alpha} \triangleq \breve{\alpha}+N_1$ and $\widehat{\beta} \triangleq \breve{\beta}+N_0$ are the parameters of the posterior. Since the posterior has the same functional form as the prior, we say that the beta distribution is a conjugate prior for the Bernoulli likelihood.

The parameters of the prior are called **hyper-parameters**. It is clear that (in this example) the hyper-parameters play a role analogous to the sufficient statistics; they are therefore often called **pseudo counts**. We see that we can compute the posterior by simply adding the observed counts (from the likelihood) to the pseudo counts (from the prior).

The strength of the prior is controlled by $\breve{N} = \breve{\alpha} + \breve{\beta}$; this is called the **equivalent sample size**, since it plays a role analogous to the observed sample size, $N = N_0 + N_1$.

4.6.2.5 Example

For example, suppose we set $\breve{\alpha} = \breve{\beta} = 2$. This is like saying we believe we have already seen two heads and two tails before we see the actual data; this is a very weak preference for the value of $\theta = 0.5$.

The effect of using this prior is illustrated in Figure 4.10a. We see the posterior (blue line) is a "compromise" between the prior (red line) and the likelihood (black line).

If we set $\breve{\alpha}=\breve{\beta}=1$, the corresponding prior becomes the uniform distribution:

$$p(\theta) = \text{Beta}(\theta|1,1) \propto \theta^0 (1-\theta)^0 = \text{Unif}(\theta|0,1) \tag{4.115}$$

The effect of using this prior is illustrated in Figure 4.10b. We see that the posterior has exactly the same shape as the likelihood, since the prior was "**uninformative**".

4.6.2.6   Posterior mode (MAP estimate)

The most probable value of the parameter is given by the MAP estimate

$$\hat{\theta}_{\text{map}} = \arg\max_{\theta} p(\theta|\mathcal{D}) \tag{4.116}$$

$$= \arg\max_{\theta} \log p(\theta|\mathcal{D}) \tag{4.117}$$

$$= \arg\max_{\theta} \log p(\theta) + \log p(\mathcal{D}|\theta) \tag{4.118}$$

Using calculus, one can show that this is given by

$$\hat{\theta}_{\text{map}} = \frac{\breve{\alpha} + N_1 - 1}{\breve{\alpha} + N_1 - 1 + \breve{\beta} + N_0 - 1} \tag{4.119}$$

If we use a $\text{Beta}(\theta|2,2)$ prior, this amounts to **add-one smoothing**:

$$\hat{\theta}_{\text{map}} = \frac{N_1 + 1}{N_1 + 1 + N_0 + 1} = \frac{N_1 + 1}{N + 2} \tag{4.120}$$

If we use a uniform prior, $p(\theta) \propto 1$, the MAP estimate becomes the MLE, since $\log p(\theta) = 0$:

$$\hat{\theta}_{\text{mle}} = \arg\max_{\theta} \log p(\mathcal{D}|\theta) \tag{4.121}$$

When we use a Beta prior, the uniform distribution is $\breve{\alpha}=\breve{\beta}=1$. In this case, the MAP estimate reduces to the MLE:

$$\hat{\theta}_{\text{mle}} = \frac{N_1}{N_1 + N_0} = \frac{N_1}{N} \tag{4.122}$$

If $N_1 = 0$, we will estimate that $p(Y = 1) = 0.0$, which says that we do not predict any future observations to be 1. This is a very extreme estimate, that is likely due to insufficient data. We can solve this problem using a MAP estimate with a stronger prior, or using a fully Bayesian approach, in which we marginalize out θ instead of estimating it, as explained in Section 4.6.2.9.

4.6.2.7   Posterior mean

The posterior mode can be a poor summary of the posterior, since it corresponds to a single point. The posterior mean is a more robust estimate, since it integrates over the whole space.

If $p(\theta|\mathcal{D}) = \text{Beta}(\theta|\,\widehat{\alpha}, \widehat{\beta})$, then the posterior mean is given by

$$\overline{\theta} \triangleq \mathbb{E}\left[\theta|\mathcal{D}\right] = \frac{\widehat{\alpha}}{\widehat{\beta} + \widehat{\alpha}} = \frac{\widehat{\alpha}}{\widehat{N}} \tag{4.123}$$

where $\widehat{N} = \widehat{\beta} + \widehat{\alpha}$ is the strength (equivalent sample size) of the posterior.

We will now show that the posterior mean is a convex combination of the prior mean, $m = \breve{\alpha}\,/\,\breve{N}$ (where $\breve{N} \triangleq \breve{\alpha} + \breve{\beta}$ is the prior strength), and the MLE: $\hat{\theta}_{\text{mle}} = \frac{N_1}{N}$:

$$\mathbb{E}\left[\theta|\mathcal{D}\right] = \frac{\breve{\alpha} + N_1}{\breve{\alpha} + N_1 + \breve{\beta} + N_0} = \frac{\breve{N}\,m + N_1}{N + \breve{N}} = \frac{\breve{N}}{N + \breve{N}}m + \frac{N}{N + \breve{N}}\frac{N_1}{N} = \lambda m + (1-\lambda)\hat{\theta}_{\text{mle}} \tag{4.124}$$

where $\lambda = \frac{\breve{N}}{\widehat{N}}$ is the ratio of the prior to posterior equivalent sample size. So the weaker the prior, the smaller is λ, and hence the closer the posterior mean is to the MLE.

4.6.2.8 Posterior variance

To capture some notion of uncertainty in our estimate, a common approach is to compute the **standard error** of our estimate, which is just the posterior standard deviation:

$$\text{se}(\theta) = \sqrt{\mathbb{V}\left[\theta|\mathcal{D}\right]} \tag{4.125}$$

In the case of the Bernoulli model, we showed that the posterior is a beta distribution. The variance of the beta posterior is given by

$$\mathbb{V}\left[\theta|\mathcal{D}\right] = \frac{\widehat{\alpha}\widehat{\beta}}{(\widehat{\alpha} + \widehat{\beta})^2(\widehat{\alpha} + \widehat{\beta} + 1)} = \mathbb{E}\left[\theta|\mathcal{D}\right]^2 \frac{\widehat{\beta}}{\widehat{\alpha}\,(1 + \widehat{\alpha} + \widehat{\beta})} \tag{4.126}$$

where $\widehat{\alpha} = \breve{\alpha} + N_1$ and $\widehat{\beta} = \breve{\beta} + N_0$. If $N \gg \breve{\alpha} + \breve{\beta}$, this simplifies to

$$\mathbb{V}\left[\theta|\mathcal{D}\right] \approx \frac{N_1 N_0}{N^3} = \frac{\hat{\theta}(1-\hat{\theta})}{N} \tag{4.127}$$

where $\hat{\theta}$ is the MLE. Hence the standard error is given by

$$\sigma = \sqrt{\mathbb{V}\left[\theta|\mathcal{D}\right]} \approx \sqrt{\frac{\hat{\theta}(1-\hat{\theta})}{N}} \tag{4.128}$$

We see that the uncertainty goes down at a rate of $1/\sqrt{N}$. We also see that the uncertainty (variance) is maximized when $\hat{\theta} = 0.5$, and is minimized when $\hat{\theta}$ is close to 0 or 1. This makes sense, since it is easier to be sure that a coin is biased than to be sure that it is fair.

4.6.2.9 Posterior predictive

Suppose we want to predict future observations. A very common approach is to first compute an estimate of the parameters based on training data, $\hat{\boldsymbol{\theta}}(\mathcal{D})$, and then to plug that parameter back into the model and use $p(y|\hat{\boldsymbol{\theta}})$ to predict the future; this is called a **plug-in approximation**. However, this can result in overfitting. As an extreme example, suppose we have seen $N = 3$ heads in a row. The MLE is $\hat{\theta} = 3/3 = 1$. However, if we use this estimate, we would predict that tails are impossible.

One solution to this is to compute a MAP estimate, and plug that in, as we discussed in Section 4.5.1. Here we discuss a fully Bayesian solution, in which we marginalize out θ.

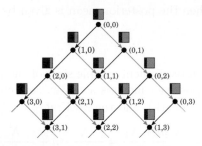

Figure 4.11: Illustration of sequential Bayesian updating for the beta-Bernoulli model. Each colored box represents the predicted distribution $p(x_t|\boldsymbol{h}_t)$, where $\boldsymbol{h}_t = (N_{1,t}, N_{0,t})$ is the sufficient statistic derived from history of observations up until time t, namely the total number of heads and tails. The probability of heads (blue bar) is given by $p(x_t = 1|\boldsymbol{h}_t) = (N_{t,1} + 1)/(t + 2)$, assuming we start with a uniform Beta($\theta|1, 1$) prior. From Figure 3 of [Ort+19]. Used with kind permission of Pedro Ortega.

Bernoulli model

For the Bernoulli model, the resulting **posterior predictive distribution** has the form

$$p(y = 1|\mathcal{D}) = \int_0^1 p(y = 1|\theta)p(\theta|\mathcal{D})d\theta \tag{4.129}$$

$$= \int_0^1 \theta \, \text{Beta}(\theta| \, \widehat{\alpha}, \widehat{\beta})d\theta = \mathbb{E}\left[\theta|\mathcal{D}\right] = \frac{\widehat{\alpha}}{\widehat{\alpha} + \widehat{\beta}} \tag{4.130}$$

In Section 4.5.1, we had to use the Beta(2,2) prior to recover add-one smoothing, which is a rather unnatural prior. In the Bayesian approach, we can get the same effect using a uniform prior, $p(\theta) = \text{Beta}(\theta|1, 1)$, since the predictive distribution becomes

$$p(y = 1|\mathcal{D}) = \frac{N_1 + 1}{N_1 + N_0 + 2} \tag{4.131}$$

This is known as **Laplace's rule of succession**. See Figure 4.11 for an illustration of this in the sequential setting.

Binomial model

Now suppose we were interested in predicting the number of heads in $M > 1$ future coin tossing trials, i.e., we are using the binomial model instead of the Bernoulli model. The posterior over θ is the same as before, but the posterior predictive distribution is different:

$$p(y|\mathcal{D}, M) = \int_0^1 \text{Bin}(y|M, \theta)\text{Beta}(\theta| \, \widehat{\alpha}, \widehat{\beta})d\theta \tag{4.132}$$

$$= \binom{M}{y} \frac{1}{B(\widehat{\alpha}, \widehat{\beta})} \int_0^1 \theta^y(1 - \theta)^{M-y}\theta^{\widehat{\alpha}-1}(1 - \theta)^{\widehat{\beta}-1}d\theta \tag{4.133}$$

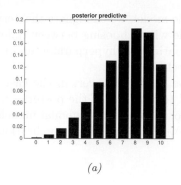
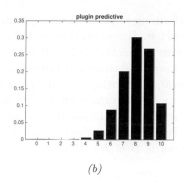

(a)   (b)

Figure 4.12: (a) Posterior predictive distributions for 10 future trials after seeing $N_1 = 4$ heads and $N_0 = 1$ tails. (b) Plug-in approximation based on the same data. In both cases, we use a uniform prior. Generated by beta_binom_post_pred_plot.ipynb.

We recognize the integral as the normalization constant for a Beta($\widehat{\alpha} + y, M - y + \widehat{\beta}$) distribution. Hence

$$\int_0^1 \theta^{y + \widehat{\alpha} - 1}(1 - \theta)^{M - y + \widehat{\beta} - 1}d\theta = B(y + \widehat{\alpha}, M - y + \widehat{\beta}) \tag{4.134}$$

Thus we find that the posterior predictive is given by the following, known as the (compound) **beta-binomial** distribution:

$$Bb(x|M, \widehat{\alpha}, \widehat{\beta}) \triangleq \binom{M}{x} \frac{B(x + \widehat{\alpha}, M - x + \widehat{\beta})}{B(\widehat{\alpha}, \widehat{\beta})} \tag{4.135}$$

In Figure 4.12(a), we plot the posterior predictive density for $M = 10$ after seeing $N_1 = 4$ heads and $N_0 = 1$ tails, when using a uniform Beta(1,1) prior. In Figure 4.12(b), we plot the plug-in approximation, given by

$$p(\theta|\mathcal{D}) \approx \delta(\theta - \hat{\theta}) \tag{4.136}$$

$$p(y|\mathcal{D}, M) = \int_0^1 \text{Bin}(y|M, \theta)p(\theta|\mathcal{D})d\theta = \text{Bin}(y|M, \hat{\theta}) \tag{4.137}$$

where $\hat{\theta}$ is the MAP estimate. Looking at Figure 4.12, we see that the Bayesian prediction has longer tails, spreading its probability mass more widely, and is therefore less prone to overfitting and black-swan type paradoxes. (Note that we use a uniform prior in both cases, so the difference is not arising due to the use of a prior; rather, it is due to the fact that the Bayesian approach integrates out the unknown parameters when making its predictions.)

4.6.2.10 Marginal likelihood

The **marginal likelihood** or **evidence** for a model $\mathcal{M}$ is defined as

$$p(\mathcal{D}|\mathcal{M}) = \int p(\boldsymbol{\theta}|\mathcal{M})p(\mathcal{D}|\boldsymbol{\theta}, \mathcal{M})d\boldsymbol{\theta} \tag{4.138}$$

When performing inference for the parameters of a specific model, we can ignore this term, since it is constant wrt $\boldsymbol{\theta}$. However, this quantity plays a vital role when choosing between different models, as we discuss in Section 5.2.2. It is also useful for estimating the hyperparameters from data (an approach known as empirical Bayes), as we discuss in Section 4.6.5.3.

In general, computing the marginal likelihood can be hard. However, in the case of the beta-Bernoulli model, the marginal likelihood is proportional to the ratio of the posterior normalizer to the prior normalizer. To see this, recall that the posterior for the beta-binomial models is given by $p(\theta|\mathcal{D}) = \text{Beta}(\theta|a', b')$, where $a' = a + N_1$ and $b' = b + N_0$. We know the normalization constant of the posterior is $B(a', b')$. Hence

$$p(\theta|\mathcal{D}) = \frac{p(\mathcal{D}|\theta)p(\theta)}{p(\mathcal{D})} \tag{4.139}$$

$$= \frac{1}{p(\mathcal{D})} \left[\frac{1}{B(a,b)} \theta^{a-1}(1-\theta)^{b-1} \right] \left[\binom{N}{N_1} \theta^{N_1}(1-\theta)^{N_0} \right] \tag{4.140}$$

$$= \binom{N}{N_1} \frac{1}{p(\mathcal{D})} \frac{1}{B(a,b)} \left[\theta^{a+N_1-1}(1-\theta)^{b+N_0-1} \right] \tag{4.141}$$

So

$$\frac{1}{B(a+N_1, b+N_0)} = \binom{N}{N_1} \frac{1}{p(\mathcal{D})} \frac{1}{B(a,b)} \tag{4.142}$$

$$p(\mathcal{D}) = \binom{N}{N_1} \frac{B(a+N_1, b+N_0)}{B(a,b)} \tag{4.143}$$

The marginal likelihood for the beta-Bernoulli model is the same as above, except it is missing the $\binom{N}{N_1}$ term.

4.6.2.11   Mixtures of conjugate priors

The beta distribution is a conjugate prior for the binomial likelihood, which enables us to easily compute the posterior in closed form, as we have seen. However, this prior is rather restrictive. For example, suppose we want to predict the outcome of a coin toss at a casino, and we believe that the coin may be fair, but may equally likely be biased towards heads. This prior cannot be represented by a beta distribution. Fortunately, it can be represented as a **mixture of beta distributions**. For example, we might use

$$p(\theta) = 0.5 \, \text{Beta}(\theta|20, 20) + 0.5 \, \text{Beta}(\theta|30, 10) \tag{4.144}$$

If θ comes from the first distribution, the coin is fair, but if it comes from the second, it is biased towards heads.

We can represent a mixture by introducing a latent indicator variable h, where $h = k$ means that θ comes from mixture component k. The prior has the form

$$p(\theta) = \sum_k p(h = k)p(\theta|h = k) \tag{4.145}$$

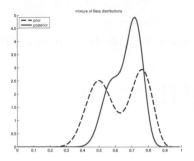

Figure 4.13: A mixture of two Beta distributions. Generated by mixbetademo.ipynb.

where each $p(\theta|h = k)$ is conjugate, and $p(h = k)$ are called the (prior) mixing weights. One can show (Exercise 4.6) that the posterior can also be written as a mixture of conjugate distributions as follows:

$$p(\theta|\mathcal{D}) = \sum_k p(h = k|\mathcal{D})p(\theta|\mathcal{D}, h = k) \tag{4.146}$$

where $p(h = k|\mathcal{D})$ are the posterior mixing weights given by

$$p(h = k|\mathcal{D}) = \frac{p(h = k)p(\mathcal{D}|h = k)}{\sum_{k'} p(h = k')p(\mathcal{D}|h = k')} \tag{4.147}$$

Here the quantity $p(\mathcal{D}|h = k)$ is the marginal likelihood for mixture component k (see Section 4.6.2.10).

Returning to our example above, if we have the prior in Equation (4.144), and we observe $N_1 = 20$ heads and $N_0 = 10$ tails, then, using Equation (4.143), the posterior becomes

$$p(\theta|\mathcal{D}) = 0.346\,\text{Beta}(\theta|40, 30) + 0.654\,\text{Beta}(\theta|50, 20) \tag{4.148}$$

See Figure 4.13 for an illustration.

We can compute the posterior probability that the coin is biased towards heads as follows:

$$\Pr(\theta > 0.5|\mathcal{D}) = \sum_k \Pr(\theta > 0.5|\mathcal{D}, h = k)p(h = k|\mathcal{D}) = 0.9604 \tag{4.149}$$

If we just used a single Beta(20,20) prior, we would get a slightly smaller value of $\Pr(\theta > 0.5|\mathcal{D}) = 0.8858$. So if we were "suspicious" initially that the casino might be using a biased coin, our fears would be confirmed more quickly than if we had to be convinced starting with an open mind.

4.6.3 The Dirichlet-multinomial model

In this section, we generalize the results from Section 4.6.2 from binary variables (e.g., coins) to K-ary variables (e.g., dice).

4.6.3.1   Likelihood

Let $Y \sim \mathrm{Cat}(\boldsymbol{\theta})$ be a discrete random variable drawn from a categorical distribution. The likelihood has the form

$$p(\mathcal{D}|\boldsymbol{\theta}) = \prod_{n=1}^{N} \mathrm{Cat}(y_n|\boldsymbol{\theta}) = \prod_{n=1}^{N}\prod_{c=1}^{C} \theta_c^{\mathbb{I}(y_n=c)} = \prod_{c=1}^{C} \theta_c^{N_c} \tag{4.150}$$

where $N_c = \sum_n \mathbb{I}(y_n = c)$.

4.6.3.2   Prior

The conjugate prior for a categorical distribution is the **Dirichlet distribution**, which is a multivariate generalization of the beta distribution. This has support over the **probability simplex**, defined by

$$S_K = \{\boldsymbol{\theta} : 0 \le \theta_k \le 1, \sum_{k=1}^{K} \theta_k = 1\} \tag{4.151}$$

The pdf of the Dirichlet is defined as follows:

$$\mathrm{Dir}(\boldsymbol{\theta}|\, \breve{\boldsymbol{\alpha}}) \triangleq \frac{1}{B(\breve{\boldsymbol{\alpha}})} \prod_{k=1}^{K} \theta_k^{\breve{\alpha}_k-1} \mathbb{I}(\boldsymbol{\theta} \in S_K) \tag{4.152}$$

where $B(\breve{\boldsymbol{\alpha}})$ is the multivariate beta function,

$$B(\breve{\boldsymbol{\alpha}}) \triangleq \frac{\prod_{k=1}^{K} \Gamma(\breve{\alpha}_k)}{\Gamma(\sum_{k=1}^{K} \breve{\alpha}_k)} \tag{4.153}$$

Figure 4.14 shows some plots of the Dirichlet when $K = 3$. We see that $\breve{\alpha}_0 = \sum_k \breve{\alpha}_k$ controls the strength of the distribution (how peaked it is), and the $\breve{\alpha}_k$ control where the peak occurs. For example, $\mathrm{Dir}(1,1,1)$ is a uniform distribution, $\mathrm{Dir}(2,2,2)$ is a broad distribution centered at $(1/3,1/3,1/3)$, and $\mathrm{Dir}(20,20,20)$ is a narrow distribution centered at $(1/3,1/3,1/3)$. $\mathrm{Dir}(3,3,20)$ is an asymmetric distribution that puts more density in one of the corners. If $\breve{\alpha}_k < 1$ for all k, we get "spikes" at the corners of the simplex. Samples from the distribution when $\breve{\alpha}_k < 1$ will be sparse, as shown in Figure 4.15.

4.6.3.3   Posterior

We can combine the multinomial likelihood and Dirichlet prior to compute the posterior, as follows:

$$p(\boldsymbol{\theta}|\mathcal{D}) \propto p(\mathcal{D}|\boldsymbol{\theta})\mathrm{Dir}(\boldsymbol{\theta}|\, \breve{\boldsymbol{\alpha}}) \tag{4.154}$$

$$= \left[\prod_k \theta_k^{N_k}\right]\left[\prod_k \theta_k^{\breve{\alpha}_k-1}\right] \tag{4.155}$$

$$= \mathrm{Dir}(\boldsymbol{\theta}|\, \breve{\alpha}_1 + N_1, \ldots, \breve{\alpha}_K + N_K) \tag{4.156}$$

$$= \mathrm{Dir}(\boldsymbol{\theta}|\, \widehat{\boldsymbol{\alpha}}) \tag{4.157}$$

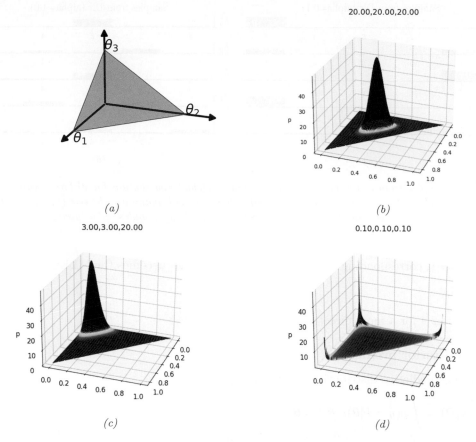

Figure 4.14: (a) The Dirichlet distribution when $K = 3$ defines a distribution over the simplex, which can be represented by the triangular surface. Points on this surface satisfy $0 \le \theta_k \le 1$ and $\sum_{k=1}^{3} \theta_k = 1$. Generated by dirichlet_3d_triangle_plot.ipynb. (b) Plot of the Dirichlet density for $\breve{\alpha} = (20, 20, 20)$. (c) Plot of the Dirichlet density for $\breve{\alpha} = (3, 3, 20)$. (d) Plot of the Dirichlet density for $\breve{\boldsymbol{\alpha}} = (0.1, 0.1, 0.1)$. Generated by dirichlet_3d_spiky_plot.ipynb.

where $\widehat{\alpha}_k = \breve{\alpha}_k + N_k$ are the parameters of the posterior. So we see that the posterior can be computed by adding the empirical counts to the prior counts.

The posterior mean is given by

$$\overline{\theta}_k = \frac{\widehat{\alpha}_k}{\sum_{k'=1}^{K} \widehat{\alpha}_{k'}} \tag{4.158}$$

The posterior mode, which corresponds to the MAP estimate, is given by

$$\hat{\theta}_k = \frac{\widehat{\alpha}_k - 1}{\sum_{k'=1}^{K} (\widehat{\alpha}_{k'} - 1)} \tag{4.159}$$

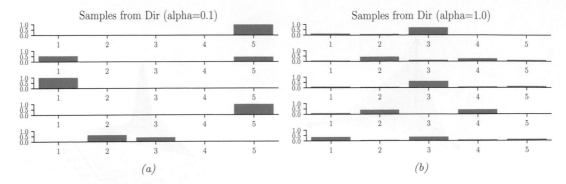

Figure 4.15: Samples from a 5-dimensional symmetric Dirichlet distribution for different parameter values. (a) $\breve{\boldsymbol{\alpha}} = (0.1, \ldots, 0.1)$. This results in very sparse distributions, with many 0s. (b) $\breve{\boldsymbol{\alpha}} = (1, \ldots, 1)$. This results in more uniform (and dense) distributions. Generated by dirichlet_samples_plot.ipynb.

If we use $\breve{\alpha}_k = 1$, corresponding to a uniform prior, the MAP becomes the MLE:

$$\hat{\theta}_k = N_k / N \tag{4.160}$$

(See Section 4.2.4 for a more direct derivation of this result.)

4.6.3.4   Posterior predictive

The posterior predictive distribution is given by

$$p(y = k | \mathcal{D}) = \int p(y = k | \boldsymbol{\theta}) p(\boldsymbol{\theta} | \mathcal{D}) d\boldsymbol{\theta} \tag{4.161}$$

$$= \int \theta_k p(\theta_k | \mathcal{D}) d\theta_k = \mathbb{E}\left[\theta_k | \mathcal{D}\right] = \frac{\widehat{\alpha}_k}{\sum_{k'} \widehat{\alpha}_{k'}} \tag{4.162}$$

In other words, the posterior predictive distribution is given by

$$p(y | \mathcal{D}) = \mathrm{Cat}(y | \overline{\boldsymbol{\theta}}) \tag{4.163}$$

where $\overline{\boldsymbol{\theta}} \triangleq \mathbb{E}\left[\boldsymbol{\theta} | \mathcal{D}\right]$ are the posterior mean parameters. If instead we plug-in the MAP estimate, we will suffer from the zero-count problem. The only way to get the same effect as add-one smoothing is to use a MAP estimate with $\breve{\alpha}_c = 2$.

Equation (4.162) gives the probability of a single future event, conditioned on past observations $\boldsymbol{y} = (y_1, \ldots, y_N)$. In some cases, we want to know the probability of observing a batch of future data, say $\tilde{\boldsymbol{y}} = (\tilde{y}_1, \ldots, \tilde{y}_M)$. We can compute this as follows:

$$p(\tilde{\boldsymbol{y}} | \boldsymbol{y}) = \frac{p(\tilde{\boldsymbol{y}}, \boldsymbol{y})}{p(\boldsymbol{y})} \tag{4.164}$$

The denominator is the marginal likelihood of the training data, and the numerator is the marginal likelihood of the training and future test data. We discuss how to compute such marginal likelihoods in Section 4.6.3.5.

4.6.3.5   Marginal likelihood

By the same reasoning as in Section 4.6.2.10, one can show that the marginal likelihood for the Dirichlet-categorical model is given by

$$p(\mathcal{D}) = \frac{B(\mathbf{N} + \boldsymbol{\alpha})}{B(\boldsymbol{\alpha})} \tag{4.165}$$

where

$$B(\boldsymbol{\alpha}) = \frac{\prod_{k=1}^{K} \Gamma(\alpha_k)}{\Gamma(\sum_k \alpha_k)} \tag{4.166}$$

Hence we can rewrite the above result in the following form, which is what is usually presented in the literature:

$$p(\mathcal{D}) = \frac{\Gamma(\sum_k \alpha_k)}{\Gamma(N + \sum_k \alpha_k)} \prod_k \frac{\Gamma(N_k + \alpha_k)}{\Gamma(\alpha_k)} \tag{4.167}$$

4.6.4   The Gaussian-Gaussian model

In this section, we derive the posterior for the parameters of a Gaussian distribution. For simplicity, we assume the variance is known. (The general case is discussed in the sequel to this book, [Mur23], as well as other standard references on Bayesian statistics.)

4.6.4.1   Univariate case

If σ^2 is a known constant, the likelihood for μ has the form

$$p(\mathcal{D}|\mu) \propto \exp\left(-\frac{1}{2\sigma^2} \sum_{n=1}^{N} (y_n - \mu)^2\right) \tag{4.168}$$

One can show that the conjugate prior is another Gaussian, $\mathcal{N}(\mu| \breve{m}, \breve{\tau}^2)$. Applying Bayes' rule for Gaussians, as in Section 4.6.4.1, we find that the corresponding posterior is given by

$$p(\mu|\mathcal{D}, \sigma^2) = \mathcal{N}(\mu| \hat{m}, \hat{\tau}^2) \tag{4.169}$$

$$\hat{\tau}^2 = \frac{1}{\frac{N}{\sigma^2} + \frac{1}{\breve{\tau}^2}} = \frac{\sigma^2 \, \breve{\tau}^2}{N \, \breve{\tau}^2 + \sigma^2} \tag{4.170}$$

$$\hat{m} = \hat{\tau}^2 \left(\frac{\breve{m}}{\breve{\tau}^2} + \frac{N\overline{y}}{\sigma^2}\right) = \frac{\sigma^2}{N \, \breve{\tau}^2 + \sigma^2} \, \breve{m} + \frac{N \, \breve{\tau}^2}{N \, \breve{\tau}^2 + \sigma^2} \overline{y} \tag{4.171}$$

where $\overline{y} \triangleq \frac{1}{N} \sum_{n=1}^{N} y_n$ is the empirical mean.

This result is easier to understand if we work in terms of the precision parameters, which are just inverse variances. Specifically, let $\kappa = 1/\sigma^2$ be the observation precision, and $\breve{\lambda} = 1/\breve{\tau}^2$ be the

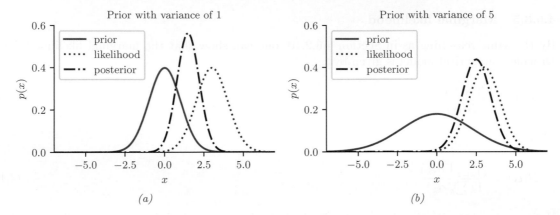

Figure 4.16: *Inferring the mean of a univariate Gaussian with known σ^2 given observation $y = 3$. (a) Using strong prior, $p(\mu) = \mathcal{N}(\mu|0,1)$. (b) Using weak prior, $p(\mu) = \mathcal{N}(\mu|0,5)$. Generated by gauss_infer_1d.ipynb.*

precision of the prior. We can then rewrite the posterior as follows:

$$p(\mu|\mathcal{D},\kappa) = \mathcal{N}(\mu|\,\widehat{m},\widehat{\lambda}^{-1}) \tag{4.172}$$

$$\widehat{\lambda} = \widecheck{\lambda} + N\kappa \tag{4.173}$$

$$\widehat{m} = \frac{N\kappa\overline{y} + \widecheck{\lambda}\widecheck{m}}{\widehat{\lambda}} = \frac{N\kappa}{N\kappa + \widecheck{\lambda}}\overline{y} + \frac{\widecheck{\lambda}}{N\kappa + \widecheck{\lambda}}\,\widecheck{m} \tag{4.174}$$

These equations are quite intuitive: the posterior precision $\widehat{\lambda}$ is the prior precision $\widecheck{\lambda}$ plus N units of measurement precision κ. Also, the posterior mean $\widehat{m}$ is a convex combination of the empirical mean $\overline{y}$ and the prior mean $\widecheck{m}$. This makes it clear that the posterior mean is a compromise between the empirical mean and the prior. If the prior is weak relative to the signal strength ($\widecheck{\lambda}$ is small relative to κ), we put more weight on the empirical mean. If the prior is strong relative to the signal strength ($\widecheck{\lambda}$ is large relative to κ), we put more weight on the prior. This is illustrated in Figure 4.16. Note also that the posterior mean is written in terms of $N\kappa\overline{y}$, so having N measurements each of precision κ is like having one measurement with value $\overline{y}$ and precision $N\kappa$.

Posterior after seeing $N = 1$ examples

To gain further insight into these equations, consider the posterior after seeing a single data point y (so $N = 1$). Then the posterior mean can be written in the following equivalent ways:

$$\widehat{m} = \frac{\widecheck{\lambda}}{\widehat{\lambda}}\,\widecheck{m} + \frac{\kappa}{\widehat{\lambda}}y \tag{4.175}$$

$$= \widecheck{m} + \frac{\kappa}{\widehat{\lambda}}(y - \widecheck{m}) \tag{4.176}$$

$$= y - \frac{\widecheck{\lambda}}{\widehat{\lambda}}(y - \widecheck{m}) \tag{4.177}$$

The first equation is a convex combination of the prior mean and the data. The second equation is the prior mean adjusted towards the data y. The third equation is the data adjusted towards the prior mean; this is called a **shrinkage** estimate. This is easier to see if we define the weight $w = \breve{\lambda}/\hat{\lambda}$, which is the ratio of the prior to posterior precision. Then we have

$$\hat{m} = y - w(y - \breve{m}) = (1 - w)y + w\,\breve{m} \tag{4.178}$$

Note that, for a Gaussian, the posterior mean and posterior mode are the same. Thus we can use the above equations to perform MAP estimation. See Exercise 4.2 for a simple example.

Posterior variance

In addition to the posterior mean or mode of μ, we might be interested in the posterior variance, which gives us a measure of confidence in our estimate. The square root of this is called the **standard error of the mean**:

$$\text{se}(\mu) \triangleq \sqrt{\mathbb{V}\left[\mu|\mathcal{D}\right]} \tag{4.179}$$

Suppose we use an uninformative prior for μ by setting $\breve{\lambda} = 0$ (see Section 4.6.5.1). In this case, the posterior mean is equal to the MLE, $\hat{m} = \overline{y}$. Suppose, in addition, that we approximate σ^2 by the **sample variance**

$$s^2 \triangleq \frac{1}{N} \sum_{n=1}^{N} (y_n - \overline{y})^2 \tag{4.180}$$

Hence $\hat{\lambda} = N\hat{\kappa} = N/s^2$, so the SEM becomes

$$\text{se}(\mu) = \sqrt{\mathbb{V}\left[\mu|\mathcal{D}\right]} = \frac{1}{\sqrt{\hat{\lambda}}} = \frac{s}{\sqrt{N}} \tag{4.181}$$

Thus we see that the uncertainty in μ is reduced at a rate of $1/\sqrt{N}$.

In addition, we can use the fact that 95% of a Gaussian distribution is contained within 2 standard deviations of the mean to approximate the 95% **credible interval** for μ using

$$I_{.95}(\mu|\mathcal{D}) = \overline{y} \pm 2\frac{s}{\sqrt{N}} \tag{4.182}$$

4.6.4.2 Multivariate case

For D-dimensional data, the likelihood has the following form (where we drop terms that are independent of $\boldsymbol{\mu}$):

$$p(\mathcal{D}|\boldsymbol{\mu}) = \prod_{n=1}^{N} \mathcal{N}(y_n|\boldsymbol{\mu}, \boldsymbol{\Sigma}) \tag{4.183}$$

$$= \left(\frac{1}{(2\pi)^{D/2}|\boldsymbol{\Sigma}|^{\frac{1}{2}}}\right)^N \exp\left[-\frac{1}{2}\sum_{n=1}^{N}(y_n - \boldsymbol{\mu})^\mathsf{T}\boldsymbol{\Sigma}^{-1}(y_n - \boldsymbol{\mu})\right] \tag{4.184}$$

$$\propto \mathcal{N}(\overline{y}|\boldsymbol{\mu}, \frac{1}{N}\boldsymbol{\Sigma}) \tag{4.185}$$

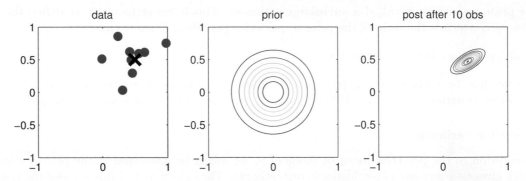

Figure 4.17: Illustration of Bayesian inference for the mean of a 2d Gaussian. (a) The data is generated from $y_n \sim \mathcal{N}(\mu, \Sigma)$, where $\mu = [0.5, 0.5]^{\mathsf{T}}$ and $\Sigma = 0.1[2, 1; 1, 1])$. (b) The prior is $p(\mu) = \mathcal{N}(\mu|0, 0.1\mathbf{I}_2)$. (c) We show the posterior after 10 data points have been observed. Generated by gauss_infer_2d.ipynb.

where $\overline{y} = \frac{1}{N} \sum_{n=1}^{N} y_n$. (The proof of the last equation is given right after Equation (3.65).) Thus we replace the set of observations with their mean, and scale down the covariance by a factor of N.

For simplicity, we will use a conjugate prior, which in this case is a Gaussian, namely

$$p(\mu) = \mathcal{N}(\mu| \; \breve{m}, \breve{\mathbf{V}}) \tag{4.186}$$

We can derive a Gaussian posterior for μ based on the results in Section 3.3.1. We get

$$p(\mu|\mathcal{D}, \Sigma) = \mathcal{N}(\mu| \; \widehat{m}, \widehat{\mathbf{V}}) \tag{4.187}$$

$$\widehat{\mathbf{V}}^{-1} = \breve{\mathbf{V}}^{-1} + N\Sigma^{-1} \tag{4.188}$$

$$\widehat{m} = \widehat{\mathbf{V}} \; (\Sigma^{-1}(N\overline{y}) + \breve{\mathbf{V}}^{-1} \breve{m}) \tag{4.189}$$

Figure 4.17 gives a 2d example of these results.

4.6.5 Beyond conjugate priors

We have seen various examples of conjugate priors, all of which have come from the exponential family (see Section 3.4). These priors have the advantage of being easy to interpret (in terms of sufficient statistics from a virtual prior dataset), and easy to compute with. However, for most models, there is no prior in the exponential family that is conjugate to the likelihood. Furthermore, even where there is a conjugate prior, the assumption of conjugacy may be too limiting. Therefore in the sections below, we briefly discuss various other kinds of priors.

4.6.5.1 Noninformative priors

When we have little or no domain specific knowledge, it is desirable to use an **uninformative**, **noninformative** or **objective** priors, to "let the data speak for itself". For example, if we want to infer a real valued quantity, such as a location parameter $\mu \in \mathbb{R}$, we can use a **flat prior** $p(\mu) \propto 1$. This can be viewed as an "infinitely wide" Gaussian.

Unfortunately, there is no unique way to define uninformative priors, and they all encode some kind of knowledge. It is therefore better to use the term **diffuse prior**, **minimally informative prior** or **default prior**. See the sequel to this book, [Mur23], for more details.

4.6.5.2 Hierarchical priors

Bayesian models require specifying a prior $p(\boldsymbol{\theta})$ for the parameters. The parameters of the prior are called **hyperparameters**, and will be denoted by $\boldsymbol{\xi}$. If these are unknown, we can put a prior on them; this defines a **hierarchical Bayesian model**, or **multi-level model**, which can visualize like this: $\boldsymbol{\xi} \rightarrow \boldsymbol{\theta} \rightarrow \mathcal{D}$. We assume the prior on the hyper-parameters is fixed (e.g., we may use some kind of minimally informative prior), so the joint distribution has the form

$$p(\boldsymbol{\xi}, \boldsymbol{\theta}, \mathcal{D}) = p(\boldsymbol{\xi})p(\boldsymbol{\theta}|\boldsymbol{\xi})p(\mathcal{D}|\boldsymbol{\theta}) \tag{4.190}$$

The hope is that we can learn the hyperparameters by treating the parameters themselves as datapoints. This is useful when we have multiple related parameters that need to be estimated (e.g., from different subpopulations, or muliple tasks); this provides a learning signal to the top level of the model. See the sequel to this book, [Mur23], for details.

4.6.5.3 Empirical priors

In Section 4.6.5.2, we discussed hierarchical Bayes as a way to infer parameters from data. Unfortunately, posterior inference in such models can be computationally challenging. In this section, we discuss a computationally convenient approximation, in which we first compute a point estimate of the hyperparameters, $\hat{\boldsymbol{\xi}}$, and then compute the conditional posterior, $p(\boldsymbol{\theta}|\hat{\boldsymbol{\xi}}, \mathcal{D})$, rather than the joint posterior, $p(\boldsymbol{\theta}, \boldsymbol{\xi}|\mathcal{D})$.

To estimate the hyper-parameters, we can maximize the marginal likelihood:

$$\hat{\boldsymbol{\xi}}_{\mathrm{mml}}(\mathcal{D}) = \underset{\boldsymbol{\xi}}{\mathrm{argmax}}\, p(\mathcal{D}|\boldsymbol{\xi}) = \underset{\boldsymbol{\xi}}{\mathrm{argmax}} \int p(\mathcal{D}|\boldsymbol{\theta})p(\boldsymbol{\theta}|\boldsymbol{\xi})d\boldsymbol{\theta} \tag{4.191}$$

This technique is known as **type II maximum likelihood**, since we are optimizing the hyperparameters, rather than the parameters. Once we have estimated $\hat{\boldsymbol{\xi}}$, we compute the posterior $p(\boldsymbol{\theta}|\hat{\boldsymbol{\xi}}, \mathcal{D})$ in the usual way.

Since we are estimating the prior parameters from data, this approach is **empirical Bayes** (**EB**) [CL96]. This violates the principle that the prior should be chosen independently of the data. However, we can view it as a computationally cheap approximation to inference in the full hierarchical Bayesian model, just as we viewed MAP estimation as an approximation to inference in the one level model $\boldsymbol{\theta} \rightarrow \mathcal{D}$. In fact, we can construct a hierarchy in which the more integrals one performs, the "more Bayesian" one becomes, as shown below.

Method	Definition
Maximum likelihood	$\hat{\boldsymbol{\theta}} = \mathrm{argmax}_{\boldsymbol{\theta}}\, p(\mathcal{D}|\boldsymbol{\theta})$
MAP estimation	$\hat{\boldsymbol{\theta}}(\boldsymbol{\xi}) = \mathrm{argmax}_{\boldsymbol{\theta}}\, p(\mathcal{D}|\boldsymbol{\theta})p(\boldsymbol{\theta}|\boldsymbol{\xi})$
ML-II (Empirical Bayes)	$\hat{\boldsymbol{\xi}} = \mathrm{argmax}_{\boldsymbol{\xi}} \int p(\mathcal{D}|\boldsymbol{\theta})p(\boldsymbol{\theta}|\boldsymbol{\xi})d\boldsymbol{\theta}$
MAP-II	$\hat{\boldsymbol{\xi}} = \mathrm{argmax}_{\boldsymbol{\xi}} \int p(\mathcal{D}|\boldsymbol{\theta})p(\boldsymbol{\theta}|\boldsymbol{\xi})p(\boldsymbol{\xi})d\boldsymbol{\theta}$
Full Bayes	$p(\boldsymbol{\theta}, \boldsymbol{\xi}|\mathcal{D}) \propto p(\mathcal{D}|\boldsymbol{\theta})p(\boldsymbol{\theta}|\boldsymbol{\xi})p(\boldsymbol{\xi})$

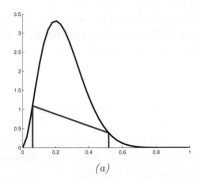
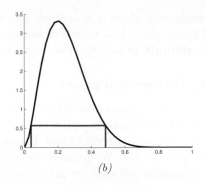

(a)   *(b)*

Figure 4.18: (a) Central interval and (b) HPD region for a Beta(3,9) posterior. The CI is (0.06, 0.52) and the HPD is (0.04, 0.48). Adapted from Figure 3.6 of [Hof09]. Generated by betaHPD.ipynb.

Note that ML-II is less likely to overfit than "regular" maximum likelihood, because there are typically fewer hyper-parameters $\boldsymbol{\xi}$ than there are parameters $\boldsymbol{\theta}$. See the sequel to this book, [Mur23], for details.

4.6.6   Credible intervals

A posterior distribution is (usually) a high dimensional object that is hard to visualize and work with. A common way to summarize such a distribution is to compute a point estimate, such as the posterior mean or mode, and then to compute a **credible interval**, which quantifies the uncertainty associated with that estimate. (A credible interval is not the same as a confidence interval, which is a concept from frequentist statistics which we discuss in Section 4.7.4.)

More precisely, we define a $100(1-\alpha)\%$ credible interval to be a (contiguous) region $C = (\ell, u)$ (standing for lower and upper) which contains $1-\alpha$ of the posterior probability mass, i.e.,

$$C_\alpha(\mathcal{D}) = (\ell, u) : P(\ell \le \theta \le u|\mathcal{D}) = 1 - \alpha \tag{4.192}$$

There may be many intervals that satisfy Equation (4.192), so we usually choose one such that there is $(1-\alpha)/2$ mass in each tail; this is called a **central interval**. If the posterior has a known functional form, we can compute the posterior central interval using $\ell = F^{-1}(\alpha/2)$ and $u = F^{-1}(1-\alpha/2)$, where F is the cdf of the posterior, and F^{-1} is the inverse cdf. For example, if the posterior is Gaussian, $p(\theta|\mathcal{D}) = \mathcal{N}(0, 1)$, and $\alpha = 0.05$, then we have $\ell = \Phi^{-1}(\alpha/2) = -1.96$, and $u = \Phi^{-1}(1-\alpha/2) = 1.96$, where Φ denotes the cdf of the Gaussian. This is illustrated in Figure 2.2b. This justifies the common practice of quoting a credible interval in the form of $\mu \pm 2\sigma$, where μ represents the posterior mean, σ represents the posterior standard deviation, and 2 is a good approximation to 1.96.

In general, it is often hard to compute the inverse cdf of the posterior. In this case, a simple alternative is to draw samples from the posterior, and then to use a Monte Carlo approximation to the posterior quantiles: we simply sort the S samples, and find the one that occurs at location α/S along the sorted list. As $S \to \infty$, this converges to the true quantile. See beta_credible_int_demo.ipynb for a demo of this.

A problem with central intervals is that there might be points outside the central interval which have higher probability than points that are inside, as illustrated in Figure 4.18(a). This motivates

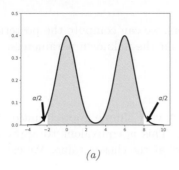
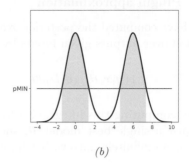

(a)   (b)

Figure 4.19: (a) Central interval and (b) HPD region for a hypothetical multimodal posterior. Adapted from Figure 2.2 of [Gel+04]. Generated by postDensityIntervals.ipynb.

an alternative quantity known as the **highest posterior density** or **HPD** region, which is the set of points which have a probability above some threshold. More precisely we find the threshold p^* on the pdf such that

$$1 - \alpha = \int_{\theta : p(\theta|\mathcal{D}) > p^*} p(\theta|\mathcal{D})d\theta \tag{4.193}$$

and then define the HPD as

$$C_\alpha(\mathcal{D}) = \{\theta : p(\theta|\mathcal{D}) \geq p^*\} \tag{4.194}$$

In 1d, the HPD region is sometimes called a **highest density interval** or **HDI**. For example, Figure 4.18(b) shows the 95% HDI of a Beta$(3, 9)$ distribution, which is $(0.04, 0.48)$. We see that this is narrower than the central interval, even though it still contains 95% of the mass; furthermore, every point inside of it has higher density than every point outside of it.

For a unimodal distribution, the HDI will be the narrowest interval around the mode containing 95% of the mass. To see this, imagine "water filling" in reverse, where we lower the level until 95% of the mass is revealed, and only 5% is submerged. This gives a simple algorithm for computing HDIs in the 1d case: simply search over points such that the interval contains 95% of the mass and has minimal width. This can be done by 1d numerical optimization if we know the inverse CDF of the distribution, or by search over the sorted data points if we have a bag of samples (see betaHPD.ipynb for some code).

If the posterior is multimodal, the HDI may not even be a connected region: see Figure 4.19(b) for an example. However, summarizing multimodal posteriors is always difficult.

4.6.7 Bayesian machine learning

So far, we have focused on unconditional models of the form $p(\boldsymbol{y}|\boldsymbol{\theta})$. In supervised machine learning, we use conditional models of the form $p(\boldsymbol{y}|\boldsymbol{x}, \boldsymbol{\theta})$. The posterior over the parameters is now $p(\boldsymbol{\theta}|\mathcal{D})$, where $\mathcal{D} = \{(\boldsymbol{x}_n, \boldsymbol{y}_n) : n = 1 : N\}$. Computing this posterior can be done using the principles we have already discussed. This approach is called **Bayesian machine learning**, since we are "being Bayesian" about the model parameters.

4.6.7.1   Plugin approximation

Once we have computed the posterior over the parameters, we can compute the posterior predictive distribution over outputs given inputs by marginalizing out the unknown parameters:

$$p(\boldsymbol{y}|\boldsymbol{x}, \mathcal{D}) = \int p(\boldsymbol{y}|\boldsymbol{x}, \boldsymbol{\theta}) p(\boldsymbol{\theta}|\mathcal{D}) d\boldsymbol{\theta} \tag{4.195}$$

Of course, computing this integral is often intractable. A very simple approximation is to assume there is just a single best model, $\hat{\boldsymbol{\theta}}$, such as the MLE. This is equivalent to approximating the posterior as an infinitely narrow, but infinitely tall, "spike" at the chosen value. We can write this as follows:

$$p(\boldsymbol{\theta}|\mathcal{D}) = \delta(\boldsymbol{\theta} - \hat{\boldsymbol{\theta}}) \tag{4.196}$$

where δ is the Dirac delta function (see Section 2.6.5). If we use this approximation, then the predictive distribution can be obtained by simply "plugging in" the point estimate into the likelihood:

$$p(\boldsymbol{y}|\boldsymbol{x}, \mathcal{D}) = \int p(\boldsymbol{y}|\boldsymbol{x}, \boldsymbol{\theta}) p(\boldsymbol{\theta}|\mathcal{D}) d\boldsymbol{\theta} \approx \int p(\boldsymbol{y}|\boldsymbol{x}, \boldsymbol{\theta}) \delta(\boldsymbol{\theta} - \hat{\boldsymbol{\theta}}) d\boldsymbol{\theta} = p(\boldsymbol{y}|\boldsymbol{x}, \hat{\boldsymbol{\theta}}) \tag{4.197}$$

This follows from the sifting property of delta functions (Equation (2.129)).

The approach in Equation (4.197) is called a **plug-in approximation**. This approach is equivalent to the standard approach used in most of machine learning, in which we first fit the model (i.e. compute a point estimate $\hat{\boldsymbol{\theta}}$) and then use it to make predicitons. However, the standard (plug-in) approach can suffer from overfitting and overconfidence, as we discussed in Section 1.2.3. The fully Bayesian approach avoids this by marginalizing out the parameters, but can be expensive. Fortunately, even simple approximations, in which we average over a few plausible parameter values, can improve performance. We give some examples of this below.

4.6.7.2   Example: scalar input, binary output

Suppose we want to perform binary classification, so $y \in \{0, 1\}$. We will use a model of the form

$$p(y|\boldsymbol{x}; \boldsymbol{\theta}) = \text{Ber}(y|\sigma(\boldsymbol{w}^\mathsf{T}\boldsymbol{x} + b)) \tag{4.198}$$

where

$$\sigma(a) \triangleq \frac{e^a}{1 + e^a} \tag{4.199}$$

is the **sigmoid** or **logistic function** which maps $\mathbb{R} \to [0, 1]$, and $\text{Ber}(y|\mu)$ is the Bernoulli distribution with mean μ (see Section 2.4 for details). In other words,

$$p(y = 1|\boldsymbol{x}; \boldsymbol{\theta}) = \sigma(\boldsymbol{w}^\mathsf{T}\boldsymbol{x} + b) = \frac{1}{1 + e^{-(\boldsymbol{w}^\mathsf{T}\boldsymbol{x} + b)}} \tag{4.200}$$

This model is called **logistic regression**. (We discuss this in more detail in Chapter 10.)

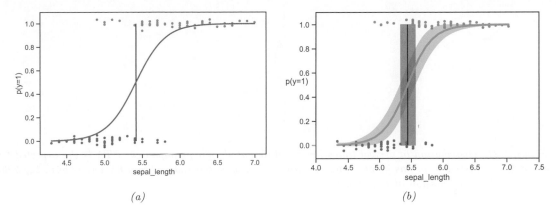

Figure 4.20: (a) Logistic regression for classifying if an Iris flower is Versicolor ($y = 1$) or setosa ($y = 0$) using a single input feature x corresponding to sepal length. Labeled points have been (vertically) jittered to avoid overlapping too much. Vertical line is the decision boundary. Generated by logreg_iris_1d.ipynb. (b) Same as (a) but showing posterior distribution. Adapted from Figure 4.4 of [Mar18]. Generated by logreg_iris_bayes_1d_pymc3.ipynb.

Let us apply this model to the task of determining if an iris flower is of type Setosa or Versicolor, $y_n \in \{0, 1\}$, given information about the sepal length, x_n. (See Section 1.2.1.1 for a description of the iris dataset.)

We first fit a 1d logistic regression model of the following form

$$p(y = 1 | x; \boldsymbol{\theta}) = \sigma(b + wx) \tag{4.201}$$

to the dataset $\mathcal{D} = \{(x_n, y_n)\}$ using maximum likelihood estimation. (See Section 10.2.3 for details on how to compute the MLE for this model.) Figure 4.20a shows the plugin approximation to the posterior predictive, $p(y = 1 | x, \hat{\boldsymbol{\theta}})$, where $\hat{\boldsymbol{\theta}}$ is the MLE of the parameters. We see that we become more confident that the flower is of type Versicolor as the sepal length gets larger, as represented by the sigmoidal (S-shaped) logistic function.

The **decision boundary** is defined to be the input value x^* where $p(y = 1 | x^*; \hat{\boldsymbol{\theta}}) = 0.5$. We can solve for this value as follows:

$$\sigma(b + wx^*) = \frac{1}{1 + e^{-(b + wx^*)}} = \frac{1}{2} \tag{4.202}$$

$$b + wx^* = 0 \tag{4.203}$$

$$x^* = -\frac{b}{w} \tag{4.204}$$

From Figure 4.20a, we see that $x^* \approx 5.5$ cm.

However, the above approach does not model the uncertainty in our estimate of the parameters, and therefore ignores the induced uncertainty in the output probabilities, and the location of the decision boundary. To capture this additional uncertainty, we can use a Bayesian approach to approximate

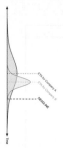

Figure 4.21: Distribution of arrival times for two different shipping companies. ETA is the expected time of arrival. A's distribution has greater uncertainty, and may be too risky. From `https://bit.ly/39bc4XL`. *Used with kind permission of Brendan Hasz.*

the posterior $p(\boldsymbol{\theta}|\mathcal{D})$. (See Section 10.5 for details.) Given this, we can approximate the posterior predictive distribution using a Monte Carlo approximation:

$$p(y = 1|x, \mathcal{D}) \approx \frac{1}{S} \sum_{s=1}^{S} p(y = 1|x, \boldsymbol{\theta}^s) \tag{4.205}$$

where $\boldsymbol{\theta}^s \sim p(\boldsymbol{\theta}|\mathcal{D})$ is a posterior sample. Figure 4.20b plots the mean and 95% credible interval of this function. We see that there is now a range of predicted probabilities for each input. We can also compute a distribution over the location of the decision boundary by using the Monte Carlo approximation

$$p(x^*|\mathcal{D}) \approx \frac{1}{S} \sum_{s=1}^{S} \delta\left(x^* - \left(-\frac{b^s}{w^s}\right)\right) \tag{4.206}$$

where $(b^s, w^s) = \boldsymbol{\theta}^s$. The 95% credible interval for this distribution is shown by the "fat" vertical line in Figure 4.20b.

Although carefully modeling our uncertainty may not matter for this application, it can be important in risk-sensitive applications, such as health care and finance, as we discuss in Chapter 5.

4.6.7.3   Example: binary input, scalar output

Now suppose we want to predict the delivery time for a package, $y \in \mathbb{R}$, if shipped by company A vs B. We can encode the company id using a binary feature $x \in \{0, 1\}$, where $x = 0$ means company A and $x = 1$ means company B. We will use the following discriminative model for this problem:

$$p(y|x, \boldsymbol{\theta}) = \mathcal{N}(y|\mu_x, \sigma_x^2) \tag{4.207}$$

where $\mathcal{N}(y|\mu, \sigma^2)$ is the Gaussian distribution

$$\mathcal{N}(y|\mu, \sigma^2) \triangleq \frac{1}{\sqrt{2\pi\sigma^2}} e^{-\frac{1}{2\sigma^2}(y-\mu)^2} \tag{4.208}$$

and $\boldsymbol{\theta} = (\mu_0, \mu_1, \sigma_0, \sigma_1)$ are the parameters of the model. We can fit this model using maximum likelihood estimation as we discuss in Section 4.2.5; alternatively, we can adopt a Bayesian approach, as we discuss in Section 4.6.4.

The advantage of the Bayesian approach is that by capturing uncertainty in the parameters $\boldsymbol{\theta}$, we also capture uncertainty in our forecasts $p(y|x, \mathcal{D})$, whereas using a plug-in approximation $p(y|x, \hat{\boldsymbol{\theta}})$ would underestimate this uncertainty. For example, suppose we have only used each company once, so our training set has the form $\mathcal{D} = \{(x_1 = 0, y_1 = 15), (x_2 = 1, y_2 = 20)\}$. As we show in Section 4.2.5, the MLE for the means will be the empirical means, $\hat{\mu}_0 = 15$ and $\hat{\mu}_1 = 20$, but the MLE for the standard deviations will be zero, $\hat{\sigma}_0 = \hat{\sigma}_1 = 0$, since we only have a single sample from each "class". The resulting plug-in prediction will therefore not capture any uncertainty.

To see why modeling the uncertainty is important, consider Figure 4.21. We see that the expected time of arrival (ETA) for company A is less than for company B; however, the variance of A's distribution is larger, which makes it a risky choice if you want to be confident the package will arrive by the specified deadline. (For more details on how to choose optimal actions in the presence of uncertainty, see Chapter 5.)

Of course, the above example is extreme, because we assumed we only had one example from each delivery company. However, this kind of problem occurs whenever we have few examples of a given kind of input, as can happen whenever the data has a long tail of novel patterns, such as a new combination of words or categorical features.

4.6.7.4   Scaling up

The above examples were both extremely simple, involving 1d input and 1d output, and just 2–4 parameters. Most practical problems involve high dimensional inputs, and sometimes high dimensional outputs, and therefore use models with lots of parameters. Unfortunately, computing the posterior, $p(\boldsymbol{\theta}|\mathcal{D})$, and the posterior predictive, $p(\boldsymbol{y}|\boldsymbol{x}, \mathcal{D})$, can be computationally challenging in such cases. We discuss this issue in Section 4.6.8.

4.6.8   Computational issues

Given a likelihood $p(\mathcal{D}|\boldsymbol{\theta})$ and a prior $p(\boldsymbol{\theta})$, we can compute the posterior $p(\boldsymbol{\theta}|\mathcal{D})$ using Bayes' rule. However, actually performing this computation is usually intractable, except for simple special cases, such as conjugate models (Section 4.6.1), or models where all the latent variables come from a small finite set of possible values. We therefore need to approximate the posterior. There are a large variety of methods for performing **approximate posterior inference**, which trade off accuracy, simplicity, and speed. We briefly discuss some of these algorithms below, but go into more detail in the sequel to this book, [Mur23]. (See also [MFR20] for a review of various approximate inference methods, starting with Bayes' original method in 1763.)

As a running example, we will use the problem of approximating the posterior of a beta-Bernoulli model. Specifically, the goal is to approximate

$$p(\theta|\mathcal{D}) \propto \left[\prod_{n=1}^{N} \mathrm{Bin}(y_n|\theta) \right] \mathrm{Beta}(\theta|1, 1) \tag{4.209}$$

where $\mathcal{D}$ consists of 10 heads and 1 tail (so the total number of observations is $N = 11$), and we use a uniform prior. Although we can compute this posterior exactly (see Figure 4.22), using the

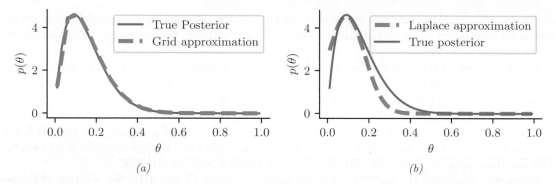

Figure 4.22: Approximating the posterior of a beta-Bernoulli model. (a) Grid approximation using 20 grid points. (b) Laplace approximation. Generated by laplace_ approx_ beta_ binom_ jax.ipynb.

method discussed in Section 4.6.2, this serves as a useful pedagogical example since we can compare the approximation to the exact answer. Also, since the target distribution is just 1d, it is easy to visualize the results. (Note, however, that the problem is not completely trivial, since the posterior is highly skewed, due to the use of an imbalanced sample of 10 heads and 1 tail.)

4.6.8.1   Grid approximation

The simplest approach to approximate posterior inference is to partition the space of possible values for the unknowns into a finite set of possibilities, call them $\boldsymbol{\theta}_1, \ldots, \boldsymbol{\theta}_K$, and then to approximate the posterior by brute-force enumeration, as follows:

$$p(\boldsymbol{\theta} = \boldsymbol{\theta}_k | \mathcal{D}) \approx \frac{p(\mathcal{D}|\boldsymbol{\theta}_k)p(\boldsymbol{\theta}_k)}{p(\mathcal{D})} = \frac{p(\mathcal{D}|\boldsymbol{\theta}_k)p(\boldsymbol{\theta}_k)}{\sum_{k'=1}^{K} p(\mathcal{D}, \boldsymbol{\theta}_{k'})} \tag{4.210}$$

This is called a **grid approximation**. In Figure 4.22a, we illustrate this method applied to our 1d problem. We see that it is easily able to capture the skewed posterior. Unfortunately, this approach does not scale to problems in more than 2 or 3 dimensions, because the number of grid points grows exponentially with the number of dimensions.

4.6.8.2   Quadratic (Laplace) approximation

In this section, we discuss a simple way to approximate the posterior using a multivariate Gaussian; this is known as a **Laplace approximation** or a **quadratic approximation** (see e.g., [TK86; RMC09]).

To derive this, suppose we write the posterior as follows:

$$p(\boldsymbol{\theta}|\mathcal{D}) = \frac{1}{Z} e^{-\mathcal{E}(\boldsymbol{\theta})} \tag{4.211}$$

where $\mathcal{E}(\boldsymbol{\theta}) = -\log p(\boldsymbol{\theta}, \mathcal{D})$ is called an energy function, and $Z = p(\mathcal{D})$ is the normalization constant. Performing a Taylor series expansion around the mode $\hat{\boldsymbol{\theta}}$ (i.e., the lowest energy state) we get

$$\mathcal{E}(\boldsymbol{\theta}) \approx \mathcal{E}(\hat{\boldsymbol{\theta}}) + (\boldsymbol{\theta} - \hat{\boldsymbol{\theta}})^{\mathsf{T}} \boldsymbol{g} + \frac{1}{2}(\boldsymbol{\theta} - \hat{\boldsymbol{\theta}})^{\mathsf{T}} \mathbf{H}(\boldsymbol{\theta} - \hat{\boldsymbol{\theta}}) \tag{4.212}$$

where $\boldsymbol{g}$ is the gradient at the mode, and $\mathbf{H}$ is the Hessian. Since $\hat{\boldsymbol{\theta}}$ is the mode, the gradient term is zero. Hence

$$\hat{p}(\boldsymbol{\theta}, \mathcal{D}) = e^{-\mathcal{E}(\hat{\boldsymbol{\theta}})} \exp\left[-\frac{1}{2}(\boldsymbol{\theta} - \hat{\boldsymbol{\theta}})^\mathsf{T}\mathbf{H}(\boldsymbol{\theta} - \hat{\boldsymbol{\theta}})\right] \tag{4.213}$$

$$\hat{p}(\boldsymbol{\theta}|\mathcal{D}) = \frac{1}{Z}\hat{p}(\boldsymbol{\theta}, \mathcal{D}) = \mathcal{N}(\boldsymbol{\theta}|\hat{\boldsymbol{\theta}}, \mathbf{H}^{-1}) \tag{4.214}$$

$$Z = e^{-\mathcal{E}(\hat{\boldsymbol{\theta}})}(2\pi)^{D/2}|\mathbf{H}|^{-\frac{1}{2}} \tag{4.215}$$

The last line follows from normalization constant of the multivariate Gaussian.

The Laplace approximation is easy to apply, since we can leverage existing optimization algorithms to compute the MAP estimate, and then we just have to compute the Hessian at the mode. (In high dimensional spaces, we can use a diagonal approximation.)

In Figure 4.22b, we illustrate this method applied to our 1d problem. Unfortunately we see that it is not a particularly good approximation. This is because the posterior is skewed, whereas a Gaussian is symmetric. In addition, the parameter of interest lies in the constrained interval $\theta \in [0, 1]$, whereas the Gaussian assumes an unconstrained space, $\boldsymbol{\theta} \in \mathbb{R}$. Fortunately, we can solve this latter problem by using a change of variable. For example, in this case we can apply the Laplace approximation to $\alpha = \text{logit}(\theta)$. This is a common trick to simplify the job of inference.

4.6.8.3 Variational approximation

In Section 4.6.8.2, we discussed the Laplace approximation, which uses an optimization procedure to find the MAP estimate, and then approximates the curvature of the posterior at that point based on the Hessian. In this section, we discuss **variational inference** (**VI**), which is another optimization-based approach to posterior inference, but which has much more modeling flexibility (and thus can give a much more accurate approximation).

VI attempts to approximate an intractable probability distribution, such as $p(\boldsymbol{\theta}|\mathcal{D})$, with one that is tractable, $q(\boldsymbol{\theta})$, so as to minimize some discrepancy D between the distributions:

$$q^* = \underset{q \in \mathcal{Q}}{\text{argmin}}\, D(q, p) \tag{4.216}$$

where $\mathcal{Q}$ is some tractable family of distributions (e.g., multivariate Gaussian). If we define D to be the KL divergence (see Section 6.2), then we can derive a lower bound to the log marginal likelihood; this quantity is known as the **evidence lower bound** or **ELBO**. By maximizing the ELBO, we can improve the quality of the posterior approximation. See the sequel to this book, [Mur23], for details.

4.6.8.4 Markov Chain Monte Carlo (MCMC) approximation

Although VI is a fast, optimization-based method, it can give a biased approximation to the posterior, since it is restricted to a specific function form $q \in \mathcal{Q}$. A more flexible approach is to use a non-parametric approximation in terms of a set of samples, $q(\boldsymbol{\theta}) \approx \frac{1}{S}\sum_{s=1}^{S}\delta(\boldsymbol{\theta} - \boldsymbol{\theta}^s)$. This is called a **Monte Carlo approximation** to the posterior. The key issue is how to create the posterior samples $\boldsymbol{\theta}^s \sim p(\boldsymbol{\theta}|\mathcal{D})$ efficiently, without having to evaluate the normalization constant $p(\mathcal{D}) = \int p(\boldsymbol{\theta}, \mathcal{D})d\boldsymbol{\theta}$. A common approach to this problem is known as **Markov chain Monte Carlo** or **MCMC**. If we augment this algorithm with gradient-based information, derived from $\nabla \log p(\boldsymbol{\theta}, \mathcal{D})$, we can significantly speed up the method; this is called **Hamiltonian Monte Carlo** or **HMC**. See the sequel to this book, [Mur23], for details.

4.7   Frequentist statistics *

The approach to statistical inference that we described in Section 4.6 is called Bayesian statistics. It treats parameters of models just like any other unknown random variable, and applies the rules of probability theory to infer them from data. Attempts have been made to devise approaches to statistical inference that avoid treating parameters like random variables, and which thus avoid the use of priors and Bayes rule. This alternative approach is known as **frequentist statistics**, **classical statistics** or **orthodox statistics**.

The basic idea (formalized in Section 4.7.1) is to represent uncertainty by calculating how a quantity estimated from data (such as a parameter or a predicted label) would change if the data were changed. It is this notion of variation across repeated trials that forms the basis for modeling uncertainty used by the frequentist approach. By contrast, the Bayesian approach views probability in terms of information rather than repeated trials. This allows the Bayesian to compute the probability of one-off events, as we discussed in Section 2.1.1. Perhaps more importantly, the Bayesian approach avoids certain paradoxes that plague the frequentist approach (see Section 4.7.5 and Section 5.5.4). These pathologies led the famous statistician George Box to say:

> I believe that it would be very difficult to persuade an intelligent person that current [frequentist] statistical practice was sensible, but that there would be much less difficulty with an approach via likelihood and Bayes' theorem. — George Box, 1962 (quoted in [Jay76]).

Nevertheless, it is useful to be familiar with frequentist statistics, since it is widely used, and has some key concepts that are useful even for Bayesians [Rub84].

4.7.1   Sampling distributions

In frequentist statistics, uncertainty is not represented by the posterior distribution of a random variable, but instead by the **sampling distribution** of an **estimator**. (We define these two terms below.)

As explained in the section on decision theory in Section 5.1, an estimator is a decision procedure that specifies what action to take given some observed data. In the context of parameter estimation, where the action space is to return a parameter vector, we will denote this by $\hat{\boldsymbol{\theta}} = \delta(\mathcal{D})$. For example, $\hat{\boldsymbol{\theta}}$ could be the maximum likelihood estimate, the MAP estimate, or the method of moments estimate.

The sampling distribution of an estimator is the distribution of results we would see if we applied the estimator multiple times to different datasets sampled from some distribution; in the context of parameter estimation, it is the distribution of $\hat{\boldsymbol{\theta}}$, viewed as a random variable that depends on the random sample $\mathcal{D}$. In more detail, imagine sampling S different data sets, each of size N, from some true model $p(\boldsymbol{x}|\boldsymbol{\theta}^*)$ to generate

$$\tilde{\mathcal{D}}^{(s)} = \{\boldsymbol{x}_n \sim p(\boldsymbol{x}_n|\boldsymbol{\theta}^*) : n = 1 : N\} \tag{4.217}$$

We denote this by $\mathcal{D}^{(s)} \sim \boldsymbol{\theta}^*$ for brevity. Now apply the estimator to each $\mathcal{D}^{(s)}$ to get a set of estimates, $\{\hat{\boldsymbol{\theta}}(\mathcal{D}^{(s)})\}$. As we let $S \to \infty$, the distribution induced by this set is the sampling distribution of the estimator. More precisely, we have

$$p(\delta(\tilde{\mathcal{D}}) = \boldsymbol{\theta}|\tilde{\mathcal{D}} \sim \boldsymbol{\theta}^*) \approx \frac{1}{S} \sum_{s=1}^{S} \delta(\boldsymbol{\theta} = \delta(\mathcal{D}^{(s)})) \tag{4.218}$$

In some cases, we can compute this analytically, as we discuss in Section 4.7.2, although typically we need to approximate it by Monte Carlo, as we discuss in Section 4.7.3.

4.7.2 Gaussian approximation of the sampling distribution of the MLE

The most common estimator is the MLE. When the sample size becomes large, the sampling distribution of the MLE for certain models becomes Gaussian. This is known as the **asymptotic normality** of the sampling distribution. More formally, we have the following result:

Theorem 4.7.1. *If the parameters are identifiable, then*

$$p(\delta(\tilde{\mathcal{D}}) = \hat{\boldsymbol{\theta}}|\tilde{\mathcal{D}} \sim \boldsymbol{\theta}^*) \to \mathcal{N}(\hat{\boldsymbol{\theta}}|\boldsymbol{\theta}^*, (N\mathbf{F}(\boldsymbol{\theta}^*))^{-1}) \tag{4.219}$$

where $\mathbf{F}(\boldsymbol{\theta}^*)$ is the **Fisher information matrix**, *defined in Equation* (4.220).

The Fisher information matrix measures the amount of curvature of the log-likelihood surface at its peak, as we show below.

More formally, the **Fisher information matrix (FIM)** is defined to be the covariance of the gradient of the log likelihood (also called the **score function**):

$$\mathbf{F} \triangleq \mathbb{E}_{\boldsymbol{x} \sim p(\boldsymbol{x}|\boldsymbol{\theta})} \left[\nabla \log p(\boldsymbol{x}|\boldsymbol{\theta}) \nabla \log p(\boldsymbol{x}|\boldsymbol{\theta})^{\mathsf{T}} \right] \tag{4.220}$$

Hence the (i, j)'th entry has the form

$$F_{ij} = \mathbb{E}_{\boldsymbol{x} \sim \boldsymbol{\theta}} \left[\left(\frac{\partial}{\partial \theta_i} \log p(\boldsymbol{x}|\boldsymbol{\theta}) \right) \left(\frac{\partial}{\partial \theta_j} \log p(\boldsymbol{x}|\boldsymbol{\theta}) \right) \right] \tag{4.221}$$

One can show the following result.

Theorem 4.7.2. *If $\log p(\boldsymbol{x}|\boldsymbol{\theta})$ is twice differentiable, and under certain regularity conditions, the FIM is equal to the expected Hessian of the NLL, i.e.,*

$$\mathbf{F}_{ij} = -\mathbb{E}_{\boldsymbol{x} \sim \boldsymbol{\theta}} \left[\frac{\partial^2}{\partial \theta_i \theta_j} \log p(\boldsymbol{x}|\boldsymbol{\theta}) \right] \tag{4.222}$$

Thus we can interpret the FIM as the Hessian of the NLL.

This helps us understand the result in Equation (4.219): a log-likelihood function with high curvature (large Hessian) will result in a low variance estimate, since the parameters are "well determined" by the data, and hence robust to repeated sampling.

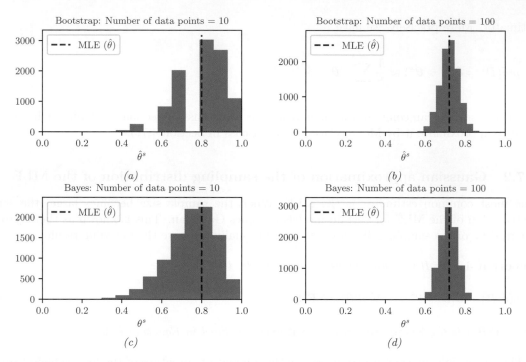

Figure 4.23: Bootstrap (top row) vs Bayes (bottom row). The N data cases were generated from $\mathrm{Ber}(\theta = 0.7)$. *Left column:* $N = 10$. *Right column:* $N = 100$. *(a-b) A bootstrap approximation to the sampling distribution of the MLE for a Bernoulli distribution. We show the histogram derived from* $B = 10,000$ *bootstrap samples. (c-d) Histogram of 10,000 samples from the posterior distribution using a uniform prior. Generated by bootstrap_demo_bernoulli.ipynb.*

4.7.3 Bootstrap approximation of the sampling distribution of any estimator

In cases where the estimator is a complex function of the data (e.g., not just an MLE), or when the sample size is small, we can approximate its sampling distribution using a Monte Carlo technique known as the **bootstrap**.

The idea is simple. If we knew the true parameters $\boldsymbol{\theta}^*$, we could generate many (say S) fake datasets, each of size N, from the true distribution, using $\tilde{\mathcal{D}}^{(s)} = \{\boldsymbol{x}_n \sim p(\boldsymbol{x}_n|\boldsymbol{\theta}^*) : n = 1 : N\}$. We could then compute our estimate from each sample, $\hat{\boldsymbol{\theta}}^s = \delta(\tilde{\mathcal{D}}^{(s)})$ and use the empirical distribution of the resulting $\hat{\boldsymbol{\theta}}^s$ as our estimate of the sampling distribution, as in Equation (4.218). Since $\boldsymbol{\theta}^*$ is unknown, the idea of the **parametric bootstrap** is to generate each sampled dataset using $\hat{\boldsymbol{\theta}} = \delta(\mathcal{D})$ instead of $\boldsymbol{\theta}^*$, i.e., we use $\tilde{\mathcal{D}}^{(s)} = \{\boldsymbol{x}_n \sim p(\boldsymbol{x}_n|\hat{\boldsymbol{\theta}}) : n = 1 : N\}$ in Equation (4.218). This is a plug-in approximation to the sampling distribution.

The above approach requires that we have a parametric generative model for the data, $p(\boldsymbol{x}|\boldsymbol{\theta})$. An alternative, called the **non-parametric bootstrap**, is to sample N data points from the original dataset with replacement. This creates a new distribution $\mathcal{D}^{(s)}$ which has the same size as the original. However, the number of unique data points in a bootstrap sample is just $0.632 \times N$, on average. (To see this, note that the probability an item is picked at least once is $(1 - (1 - 1/N)^N)$, which approaches $1 - e^{-1} \approx 0.632$ for large N.)

Figure 4.23(a-b) shows an example where we compute the sampling distribution of the MLE for a Bernoulli using the parametric bootstrap. (Results using the non-parametric bootstrap are essentially the same.) When $N = 10$, we see that the sampling distribution is asymmetric, and therefore quite far from Gaussian, but when $N = 100$, the distribution looks more Gaussian, as theory suggests (see Section 4.7.2).

4.7.3.1 Bootstrap is a "poor man's" posterior

A natural question is: what is the connection between the parameter estimates $\hat{\boldsymbol{\theta}}^s = \delta(\mathcal{D}^{(s)})$ computed by the bootstrap and parameter values sampled from the posterior, $\boldsymbol{\theta}^s \sim p(\cdot|\mathcal{D})$? Conceptually they are quite different. But in the common case that the estimator is MLE and the prior is not very strong, they can be quite similar. For example, Figure 4.23(c-d) shows an example where we compute the posterior using a uniform Beta(1,1) prior, and then sample from it. We see that the posterior and the sampling distribution are quite similar. So one can think of the bootstrap distribution as a "poor man's" posterior [HTF01, p235].

However, perhaps surprisingly, bootstrap can be slower than posterior sampling. The reason is that the bootstrap has to generate S sampled datasets, and then fit a model to each one. By contrast, in posterior sampling, we only have to "fit" a model once given a single dataset. (Some methods for speeding up the bootstrap when applied to massive data sets are discussed in [Kle+11].)

4.7.4 Confidence intervals

In frequentist statistics, we use the variability induced by the sampling distribution as a way to estimate uncertainty of a parameter estimate. More precisely, we define a $100(1 - \alpha)\%$ **confidence interval** for a parameter estimate θ as any interval $I(\tilde{\mathcal{D}}) = (\ell(\tilde{\mathcal{D}}), u(\tilde{\mathcal{D}}))$ derived from a hypothetical dataset $\tilde{\mathcal{D}}$ such that

$$\Pr(\theta \in I(\tilde{\mathcal{D}})|\tilde{\mathcal{D}} \sim \theta) = 1 - \alpha \tag{4.223}$$

It is common to set $\alpha = 0.05$, which yields a 95% CI. This means that, if we repeatedly sampled data, and compute $I(\tilde{\mathcal{D}})$ for each such dataset, then about 95% of such intervals will contain the true parameter θ.

Note, however, that Equation (4.223) does *not* mean that for any particular dataset that $\theta \in I(\mathcal{D})$ with 95% probability; this is what a Bayesian credible interval computes (Section 4.6.6), but is not what a frequentist confidence interval computes. For more details on this important distinction, see Section 4.7.5.

Let us put aside such "philosophical" concerns, and discuss how to compute a confidence interval. Suppose that $\hat{\theta}$ is an estimate of the parameter θ. Let θ^* be its true but unknown value. Also, suppose that the sampling distribution of $\Delta = \theta^* - \hat{\theta}$ is known. Let $\underline{\delta}$ and $\overline{\delta}$ denote its $\alpha/2$ and $1 - \alpha/2$ quantiles. Hence

$$\Pr(\underline{\delta} \leq \Delta \leq \overline{\delta}) = \Pr(\underline{\delta} \leq \theta^* - \hat{\theta} \leq \overline{\delta}) = 1 - \alpha \tag{4.224}$$

Rearranging we get

$$\Pr(\hat{\theta} + \underline{\delta}) \leq \theta^* \leq \hat{\theta} + \overline{\delta} = 1 - \alpha \tag{4.225}$$

And hence

$$I(\tilde{\mathcal{D}}) = (\hat{\theta}(\tilde{\mathcal{D}}) + \underline{\delta}(\tilde{\mathcal{D}}), \hat{\theta}(\tilde{\mathcal{D}}) + \overline{\delta}(\tilde{\mathcal{D}})) \tag{4.226}$$

is a $100(1 - \alpha)\%$ confidence interval.

In some cases, we can analytically compute the distribution of $\Delta = \hat{\theta} - \theta^*$. This can be used to derive exact confidence intervals. However, it is more common to assume a Gaussian approximation to the sampling distribution, as in Section 4.7.2. In this case, we have $\sqrt{NF(\hat{\theta})}(\hat{\theta} - \theta^*) \sim \mathcal{N}(0, 1)$. Hence we can compute an approximate CI using

$$\hat{\theta} \pm z_{\alpha/2}\hat{se} \tag{4.227}$$

where $z_{\alpha/2}$ is the $\alpha/2$ quantile of the Gaussian cdf, and $\hat{se} = 1/\sqrt{NF(\hat{\theta})}$ is the estimated standard error. If we set $\alpha = 0.05$, we have $z_{\alpha/2} = 1.96$, which justifies the common approximation $\hat{\theta} \pm 2\hat{se}$.

If the Gaussian approximation is not a good one, we can use a bootstrap approximation (see Section 4.7.3). In particular, we sample S datasets from $\hat{\theta}(\mathcal{D})$, and apply the estimator to each one to get $\hat{\theta}(\mathcal{D}^{(s)})$; we then use the empirical distribution of $\hat{\theta}(\mathcal{D}) - \hat{\theta}(\mathcal{D}^{(s)})$ as an approximation to the sampling distribution of Δ.

4.7.5   Caution: Confidence intervals are not credible

A 95% frequentist confidence interval for a parameter θ is defined as any interval $I(\tilde{\mathcal{D}})$ such that $\Pr(\theta \in I(\tilde{\mathcal{D}})|\tilde{\mathcal{D}} \sim \theta) = 0.95$, as we explain in Section 4.7.4. This does *not* mean that the parameter is 95% likely to live inside this interval given the observed data. That quantity — which is usually what we want to compute — is instead given by the Bayesian credible interval $p(\theta \in I|\mathcal{D})$, as we explain in Section 4.6.6. These concepts are quite different: In the frequentist approach, θ is treated as an unknown fixed constant, and the data is treated as random. In the Bayesian approach, we treat the data as fixed (since it is known) and the parameter as random (since it is unknown).

This counter-intuitive definition of confidence intervals can lead to bizarre results. Consider the following example from [Ber85, p11]. Suppose we draw two integers $\mathcal{D} = (y_1, y_2)$ from

$$p(y|\theta) = \begin{cases} 0.5 & \text{if } y = \theta \\ 0.5 & \text{if } y = \theta + 1 \\ 0 & \text{otherwise} \end{cases} \tag{4.228}$$

If $\theta = 39$, we would expect the following outcomes each with probability 0.25:

$$(39, 39), (39, 40), (40, 39), (40, 40) \tag{4.229}$$

Let $m = \min(y_1, y_2)$ and define the following interval:

$$[\ell(\mathcal{D}), u(\mathcal{D})] = [m, m] \tag{4.230}$$

For the above samples this yields

$$[39, 39], \quad [39, 39], \quad [39, 39], \quad [40, 40] \tag{4.231}$$

Hence Equation (4.230) is clearly a 75% CI, since 39 is contained in 3/4 of these intervals. However, if we observe $\mathcal{D} = (39, 40)$ then $p(\theta = 39|\mathcal{D}) = 1.0$, so we know that θ must be 39, yet we only have 75% "confidence" in this fact. We see that the CI will "cover" the true parameter 75% of the time, if we compute multiple CIs from different randomly sampled datasets, but if we just have a single observed dataset, and hence a single CI, then the frequentist "coverage" probability can be very misleading.

Another, less contrived, example is as follows. Suppose we want to estimate the parameter θ of a Bernoulli distribution. Let $\bar{y} = \frac{1}{N} \sum_{n=1}^{N} y_n$ be the sample mean. The MLE is $\hat{\theta} = \bar{y}$. An approximate 95% confidence interval for a Bernoulli parameter is $\bar{y} \pm 1.96 \sqrt{\bar{y}(1 - \bar{y})/N}$ (this is called a **Wald interval** and is based on a Gaussian approximation to the Binomial distribution; compare to Equation (4.128)). Now consider a single trial, where $N = 1$ and $y_1 = 0$. The MLE is 0, which overfits, as we saw in Section 4.5.1. But our 95% confidence interval is also $(0, 0)$, which seems even worse. It can be argued that the above flaw is because we approximated the true sampling distribution with a Gaussian, or because the sample size was too small, or the parameter "too extreme". However, the Wald interval can behave badly even for large N, and non-extreme parameters [BCD01]. By contrast, a Bayesian credible interval with a non-informative Jeffreys prior behaves in the way we would expect.

Several more interesting examples, along with Python code, can be found at [Van14]. See also [Hoe+14; Mor+16; Lyu+20; Cha+19b], who show that many people, including professional statisticians, misunderstand and misuse frequentist confidence intervals in practice, whereas Bayesian credible intervals do not suffer from these problems.

4.7.6 The bias-variance tradeoff

An estimator is a procedure applied to data which returns an estimand. Let $\hat{\theta}()$ be the estimator, and $\hat{\theta}(\mathcal{D})$ be the estimand. In frequentist statistics, we treat the data as a random variable, drawn from some true but unknown distribution, $p^*(\mathcal{D})$; this induces a distribution over the estimand, $p^*(\hat{\theta}(\mathcal{D}))$, known as the sampling distribution (see Section 4.7.1). In this section, we discuss two key properties of this distribution, its bias and its variance, which we define below.

4.7.6.1 Bias of an estimator

The **bias** of an estimator is defined as

$$\text{bias}(\hat{\theta}(\cdot)) \triangleq \mathbb{E}\left[\hat{\theta}(\mathcal{D})\right] - \theta^* \tag{4.232}$$

where θ^* is the true parameter value, and the expectation is wrt "nature's distribution" $p(\mathcal{D}|\theta^*)$. If the bias is zero, the estimator is called **unbiased**. For example, the MLE for a Gaussian mean is unbiased:

$$\text{bias}(\hat{\mu}) = \mathbb{E}[\bar{x}] - \mu = \mathbb{E}\left[\frac{1}{N} \sum_{n=1}^{N} x_n\right] - \mu = \frac{N\mu}{N} - \mu = 0 \tag{4.233}$$

where $\bar{x}$ is the sample mean.

However, the MLE for a Gaussian variance, $\sigma_{\text{mle}}^2 = \frac{1}{N}\sum_{n=1}^{N}(x_n - \overline{x})^2$, is not an unbiased estimator of σ^2. In fact, one can show (Exercise 4.7) that

$$\mathbb{E}\left[\sigma_{\text{mle}}^2\right] = \frac{N-1}{N}\sigma^2 \tag{4.234}$$

so the ML estimator slightly underestimates the variance. Intuitively, this is because we "use up" one of the data points to estimate the mean, so if we have a sample size of 1, we will estimate the variance to be 0. If, however, μ is known, the ML estimator is unbiased (see Exercise 4.8).

Now consider the following estimator

$$\sigma_{\text{unb}}^2 \triangleq \frac{1}{N-1}\sum_{n=1}^{N}(x_n - \overline{x})^2 = \frac{N}{N-1}\sigma_{\text{mle}}^2 \tag{4.235}$$

This is an unbiased estimator, which we can easily prove as follows:

$$\mathbb{E}\left[\sigma_{\text{unb}}^2\right] = \frac{N}{N-1}\mathbb{E}\left[\sigma_{\text{mle}}^2\right] = \frac{N}{N-1}\frac{N-1}{N}\sigma^2 = \sigma^2 \tag{4.236}$$

4.7.6.2 Variance of an estimator

It seems intuitively reasonable that we want our estimator to be unbiased. However, being unbiased is not enough. For example, suppose we want to estimate the mean of a Gaussian from $\mathcal{D} = \{x_1, \ldots, x_N\}$. The estimator that just looks at the first data point, $\hat{\theta}(\mathcal{D}) = x_1$, is an unbiased estimator, but will generally be further from θ^* than the empirical mean $\overline{x}$ (which is also unbiased). So the variance of an estimator is also important.

We define the variance of an estimator as follows:

$$\mathbb{V}\left[\hat{\theta}\right] \triangleq \mathbb{E}\left[\hat{\theta}^2\right] - \left(\mathbb{E}\left[\hat{\theta}\right]\right)^2 \tag{4.237}$$

where the expectation is taken wrt $p(\mathcal{D}|\theta^*)$. This measures how much our estimate will change as the data changes. We can extend this to a covariance matrix for vector valued estimators.

Intuitively we would like the variance of our estimator to be as small as possible. Therefore, a natural question is: how low can the variance go? A famous result, called the **Cramer-Rao lower bound**, provides a lower bound on the variance of any unbiased estimator. More precisely, let $X_1, \ldots, X_N \sim p(X|\theta^*)$ and $\hat{\theta} = \hat{\theta}(x_1, \ldots, x_N)$ be an unbiased estimator of θ^*. Then, under various smoothness assumptions on $p(X|\theta^*)$, we have $\mathbb{V}\left[\hat{\theta}\right] \geq \frac{1}{NF(\theta^*)}$, where $F(\theta^*)$ is the Fisher information matrix (Section 4.7.2). A proof can be found e.g., in [Ric95, p275].

It can be shown that the MLE achieves the Cramer Rao lower bound, and hence has the smallest asymptotic variance of any unbiased estimator. Thus MLE is said to be **asymptotically optimal**.

4.7.6.3 The bias-variance tradeoff

In this section, we discuss a fundamental tradeoff that needs to be made when picking a method for parameter estimation, assuming our goal is to minimize the mean squared error (MSE) of our estimate. Let $\hat{\theta} = \hat{\theta}(\mathcal{D})$ denote the estimate, and $\overline{\theta} = \mathbb{E}\left[\hat{\theta}\right]$ denote the expected value of the estimate

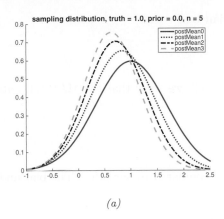
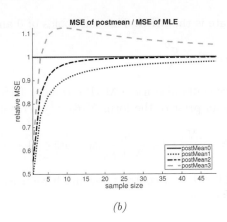

(a)   (b)

Figure 4.24: Left: Sampling distribution of the MAP estimate (equivalent to the posterior mean) under a $\mathcal{N}(\theta_0 = 0, \sigma^2/\kappa_0)$ prior with different prior strengths κ_0. (If we set $\kappa = 0$, the MAP estimate reduces to the MLE.) The data is $n = 5$ samples drawn from $\mathcal{N}(\theta^* = 1, \sigma^2 = 1)$. Right: MSE relative to that of the MLE versus sample size. Adapted from Figure 5.6 of [Hof09]. Generated by samplingDistributionGaussianShrinkage.ipynb.

(as we vary $\mathcal{D}$). (All expectations and variances are wrt $p(\mathcal{D}|\theta^*)$, but we drop the explicit conditioning for notational brevity.) Then we have

$$\mathbb{E}\left[(\hat{\theta} - \theta^*)^2\right] = \mathbb{E}\left[\left[(\hat{\theta} - \overline{\theta}) + (\overline{\theta} - \theta^*)\right]^2\right] \tag{4.238}$$

$$= \mathbb{E}\left[\left(\hat{\theta} - \overline{\theta}\right)^2\right] + 2(\overline{\theta} - \theta^*)\mathbb{E}\left[\hat{\theta} - \overline{\theta}\right] + (\overline{\theta} - \theta^*)^2 \tag{4.239}$$

$$= \mathbb{E}\left[\left(\hat{\theta} - \overline{\theta}\right)^2\right] + (\overline{\theta} - \theta^*)^2 \tag{4.240}$$

$$= \mathbb{V}\left[\hat{\theta}\right] + \text{bias}^2(\hat{\theta}) \tag{4.241}$$

In words,

$$\boxed{\text{MSE} = \text{variance} + \text{bias}^2} \tag{4.242}$$

This is called the **bias-variance tradeoff** (see e.g., [GBD92]). What it means is that it might be wise to use a biased estimator, so long as it reduces our variance by more than the square of the bias, assuming our goal is to minimize squared error.

4.7.6.4 Example: MAP estimator for a Gaussian mean

Let us give an example, based on [Hof09, p79]. Suppose we want to estimate the mean of a Gaussian from $\boldsymbol{x} = (x_1, \ldots, x_N)$. We assume the data is sampled from $x_n \sim \mathcal{N}(\theta^* = 1, \sigma^2)$. An obvious estimate is the MLE. This has a bias of 0 and a variance of

$$\mathbb{V}\left[\overline{x}|\theta^*\right] = \frac{\sigma^2}{N} \tag{4.243}$$

But we could also use a MAP estimate. In Section 4.6.4.2, we show that the MAP estimate under a Gaussian prior of the form $\mathcal{N}(\theta_0, \sigma^2/\kappa_0)$ is given by

$$\tilde{x} \triangleq \frac{N}{N + \kappa_0}\overline{x} + \frac{\kappa_0}{N + \kappa_0}\theta_0 = w\overline{x} + (1 - w)\theta_0 \tag{4.244}$$

where $0 \le w \le 1$ controls how much we trust the MLE compared to our prior. The bias and variance are given by

$$\mathbb{E}\left[\tilde{x}\right] - \theta^* = w\theta^* + (1 - w)\theta_0 - \theta^* = (1 - w)(\theta_0 - \theta^*) \tag{4.245}$$

$$\mathbb{V}\left[\tilde{x}\right] = w^2\frac{\sigma^2}{N} \tag{4.246}$$

So although the MAP estimate is biased (assuming $w < 1$), it has lower variance.

Let us assume that our prior is slightly misspecified, so we use $\theta_0 = 0$, whereas the truth is $\theta^* = 1$. In Figure 4.24(a), we see that the sampling distribution of the MAP estimate for $\kappa_0 > 0$ is biased away from the truth, but has lower variance (is narrower) than that of the MLE.

In Figure 4.24(b), we plot $\mathrm{mse}(\tilde{x})/\mathrm{mse}(\overline{x})$ vs N. We see that the MAP estimate has lower MSE than the MLE for $\kappa_0 \in \{1, 2\}$. The case $\kappa_0 = 0$ corresponds to the MLE, and the case $\kappa_0 = 3$ corresponds to a strong prior, which hurts performance because the prior mean is wrong. Thus we see that, provided the prior strength is properly "tuned", a MAP estimate can outperform an ML estimate in terms of minimizing MSE.

4.7.6.5 Example: MAP estimator for linear regression

Another important example of the bias-variance tradeoff arises in ridge regression, which we discuss in Section 11.3. In brief, this corresponds to MAP estimation for linear regression under a Gaussian prior, $p(\boldsymbol{w}) = \mathcal{N}(\boldsymbol{w}|\boldsymbol{0}, \lambda^{-1}\mathbf{I})$ The zero-mean prior encourages the weights to be small, which reduces overfitting; the precision term, λ, controls the strength of this prior. Setting $\lambda = 0$ results in the MLE; using $\lambda > 0$ results in a biased estimate. To illustrate the effect on the variance, consider a simple example where we fit a 1d ridge regression model using 2 different values of λ. Figure 4.25 on the left plots each individual fitted curve, and on the right plots the average fitted curve. We see that as we increase the strength of the regularizer, the variance decreases, but the bias increases.

See also Figure 4.26 where we give a cartoon sketch of the bias variance tradeoff in terms of model complexity.

4.7.6.6 Bias-variance tradeoff for classification

If we use 0-1 loss instead of squared error, the frequentist risk is no longer expressible as squared bias plus variance. In fact, one can show (Exercise 7.2 of [HTF09]) that the bias and variance combine multiplicatively. If the estimate is on the correct side of the decision boundary, then the bias is negative, and decreasing the variance will decrease the misclassification rate. But if the estimate

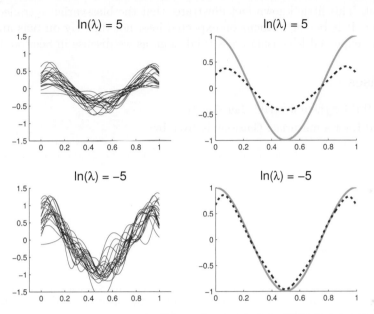

Figure 4.25: *Illustration of bias-variance tradeoff for ridge regression. We generate 100 data sets from the true function, shown in solid green. Left: we plot the regularized fit for 20 different data sets. We use linear regression with a Gaussian RBF expansion, with 25 centers evenly spread over the $[0, 1]$ interval. Right: we plot the average of the fits, averaged over all 100 datasets. Top row: strongly regularized: we see that the individual fits are similar to each other (low variance), but the average is far from the truth (high bias). Bottom row: lightly regularized: we see that the individual fits are quite different from each other (high variance), but the average is close to the truth (low bias). Adapted from [Bis06] Figure 3.5. Generated by biasVarModelComplexity3.ipynb.*

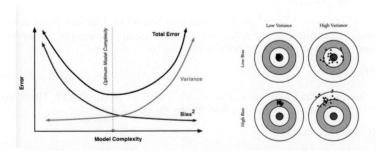

Figure 4.26: *Cartoon illustration of the bias variance tradeoff. From http://scott.fortmann-roe.com/docs/BiasVariance.html. Used with kind permission of Scott Fortmann-Roe.*

is on the wrong side of the decision boundary, then the bias is positive, so it pays to *increase* the variance [Fri97a]. This little known fact illustrates that the bias-variance tradeoff is not very useful for classification. It is better to focus on expected loss, not directly on bias and variance. We can approximate the expected loss using cross validation, as we discuss in Section 4.5.5.

4.8   Exercises

Exercise 4.1 [MLE for the univariate Gaussian *]

Show that the MLE for a univariate Gaussian is given by

$$\hat{\mu} = \frac{1}{N} \sum_{n=1}^{N} y_n \tag{4.247}$$

$$\hat{\sigma}^2 = \frac{1}{N} \sum_{n=1}^{N} (y_n - \hat{\mu})^2 \tag{4.248}$$

Exercise 4.2 [MAP estimation for 1D Gaussians *]

(Source: Jaakkola.)

Consider samples $x_1, \ldots, x_n$ from a Gaussian random variable with known variance σ^2 and unknown mean μ. We further assume a prior distribution (also Gaussian) over the mean, $\mu \sim \mathcal{N}(m, s^2)$, with fixed mean m and fixed variance s^2. Thus the only unknown is μ.

a. Calculate the MAP estimate $\hat{\mu}_{MAP}$. You can state the result without proof. Alternatively, with a lot more work, you can compute derivatives of the log posterior, set to zero and solve.

b. Show that as the number of samples n increase, the MAP estimate converges to the maximum likelihood estimate.

c. Suppose n is small and fixed. What does the MAP estimator converge to if we increase the prior variance s^2?

d. Suppose n is small and fixed. What does the MAP estimator converge to if we decrease the prior variance s^2?

Exercise 4.3 [Gaussian posterior credible interval]

(Source: DeGroot.) Let $X \sim \mathcal{N}(\mu, \sigma^2 = 4)$ where μ is unknown but has prior $\mu \sim \mathcal{N}(\mu_0, \sigma_0^2 = 9)$. The posterior after seeing n samples is $\mu \sim \mathcal{N}(\mu_n, \sigma_n^2)$. (This is called a credible interval, and is the Bayesian analog of a confidence interval.) How big does n have to be to ensure

$$p(\ell \leq \mu_n \leq u | D) \geq 0.95 \tag{4.249}$$

where (ℓ, u) is an interval (centered on μ_n) of width 1 and D is the data? Hint: recall that 95% of the probability mass of a Gaussian is within $\pm 1.96\sigma$ of the mean.

Exercise 4.4 [BIC for Gaussians *]

(Source: Jaakkola.)

The Bayesian information criterion (BIC) is a penalized log-likelihood function that can be used for model selection. It is defined as

$$BIC = \log p(\mathcal{D}|\hat{\boldsymbol{\theta}}_{ML}) - \frac{d}{2} \log(N) \tag{4.250}$$

where d is the number of free parameters in the model and N is the number of samples. In this question, we will see how to use this to choose between a full covariance Gaussian and a Gaussian with a diagonal covariance. Obviously a full covariance Gaussian has higher likelihood, but it may not be "worth" the extra parameters if the improvement over a diagonal covariance matrix is too small. So we use the BIC score to choose the model.

We can write

$$\log p(\mathcal{D}|\hat{\boldsymbol{\Sigma}}, \hat{\boldsymbol{\mu}}) = -\frac{N}{2}\text{tr}\left(\hat{\boldsymbol{\Sigma}}^{-1}\hat{\mathbf{S}}\right) - \frac{N}{2}\log(|\hat{\boldsymbol{\Sigma}}|) \tag{4.251}$$

$$\hat{\mathbf{S}} = \frac{1}{N}\sum_{i=1}^{N}(\boldsymbol{x}_i - \overline{\boldsymbol{x}})(\boldsymbol{x}_i - \overline{\boldsymbol{x}})^T \tag{4.252}$$

where $\hat{\mathbf{S}}$ is the scatter matrix (empirical covariance), the trace of a matrix is the sum of its diagonals, and we have used the trace trick.

a. Derive the BIC score for a Gaussian in D dimensions with full covariance matrix. Simplify your answer as much as possible, exploiting the form of the MLE. Be sure to specify the number of free parameters d.

b. Derive the BIC score for a Gaussian in D dimensions with a *diagonal* covariance matrix. Be sure to specify the number of free parameters d. Hint: for the digaonal case, the ML estimate of $\boldsymbol{\Sigma}$ is the same as $\hat{\boldsymbol{\Sigma}}_{ML}$ except the off-diagonal terms are zero:

$$\hat{\boldsymbol{\Sigma}}_{diag} = \text{diag}(\hat{\boldsymbol{\Sigma}}_{ML}(1,1), \ldots, \hat{\boldsymbol{\Sigma}}_{ML}(D,D)) \tag{4.253}$$

Exercise 4.5 [BIC for a 2d discrete distribution]

(Source: Jaakkola.)

Let $x \in \{0,1\}$ denote the result of a coin toss ($x = 0$ for tails, $x = 1$ for heads). The coin is potentially biased, so that heads occurs with probability θ_1. Suppose that someone else observes the coin flip and reports to you the outcome, y. But this person is unreliable and only reports the result correctly with probability θ_2; i.e., $p(y|x, \theta_2)$ is given by

	$y = 0$	$y = 1$
$x = 0$	θ_2	$1 - \theta_2$
$x = 1$	$1 - \theta_2$	θ_2

Assume that θ_2 is independent of x and θ_1.

a. Write down the joint probability distribution $p(x, y|\boldsymbol{\theta})$ as a 2×2 table, in terms of $\boldsymbol{\theta} = (\theta_1, \theta_2)$.

b. Suppose have the following dataset: $\boldsymbol{x} = (1, 1, 0, 1, 1, 0, 0)$, $\boldsymbol{y} = (1, 0, 0, 0, 1, 0, 1)$. What are the MLEs for θ_1 and θ_2? Justify your answer. Hint: note that the likelihood function factorizes,

$$p(x, y|\boldsymbol{\theta}) = p(y|x, \theta_2)p(x|\theta_1) \tag{4.254}$$

What is $p(\mathcal{D}|\hat{\boldsymbol{\theta}}, M_2)$ where M_2 denotes this 2-parameter model? (You may leave your answer in fractional form if you wish.)

c. Now consider a model with 4 parameters, $\boldsymbol{\theta} = (\theta_{0,0}, \theta_{0,1}, \theta_{1,0}, \theta_{1,1})$, representing $p(x, y|\boldsymbol{\theta}) = \theta_{x,y}$. (Only 3 of these parameters are free to vary, since they must sum to one.) What is the MLE of $\boldsymbol{\theta}$? What is $p(\mathcal{D}|\hat{\boldsymbol{\theta}}, M_4)$ where M_4 denotes this 4-parameter model?

d. Suppose we are not sure which model is correct. We compute the leave-one-out cross validated log likelihood of the 2-parameter model and the 4-parameter model as follows:

$$L(m) = \sum_{i=1}^{n} \log p(x_i, y_i|m, \hat{\theta}(\mathcal{D}_{-i})) \tag{4.255}$$

and $\hat{\theta}(\mathcal{D}_{-i})$) denotes the MLE computed on $\mathcal{D}$ excluding row i. Which model will CV pick and why? Hint: notice how the table of counts changes when you omit each training case one at a time.

e. Recall that an alternative to CV is to use the BIC score, defined as

$$\text{BIC}(M, \mathcal{D}) \triangleq \log p(\mathcal{D}|\hat{\boldsymbol{\theta}}_{MLE}) - \frac{\text{dof}(M)}{2} \log N \tag{4.256}$$

where $\text{dof}(M)$ is the number of free parameters in the model, Compute the BIC scores for both models (use log base e). Which model does BIC prefer?

Exercise 4.6 [A mixture of conjugate priors is conjugate *]

Consider a mixture prior

$$p(\theta) = \sum_k p(z = k)p(\theta|z = k) \tag{4.257}$$

where each $p(\theta|z = k)$ is conjugate to the likelihood. Prove that this is a conjugate prior.

Exercise 4.7 [ML estimator σ^2_{mle} is biased]

Show that $\hat{\sigma}^2_{MLE} = \frac{1}{N} \sum_{n=1}^{N} (x_n - \hat{\mu})^2$ is a biased estimator of σ^2, i.e., show

$$\mathbf{E}_{X_1,\dots,X_n \sim \mathcal{N}(\mu,\sigma)}[\hat{\sigma}^2(X_1, \dots, X_n)] \neq \sigma^2$$

Hint: note that $X_1, \dots, X_N$ are independent, and use the fact that the expectation of a product of independent random variables is the product of the expectations.

Exercise 4.8 [Estimation of σ^2 when μ is known *]

Suppose we sample $x_1, \dots, x_N \sim \mathcal{N}(\mu, \sigma^2)$ where μ is a *known* constant. Derive an expression for the MLE for σ^2 in this case. Is it unbiased?

Exercise 4.9 [Variance and MSE of estimators for Gaussian variance *]

Prove that the standard error for the MLE for a Gaussian variance is

$$\sqrt{\mathbb{V}[\sigma^2_{\text{mle}}]} = \sqrt{\frac{2(N-1)}{N^2}} \sigma^2 \tag{4.258}$$

Hint: use the fact that

$$\frac{N-1}{\sigma^2} \sigma^2_{\text{unb}} \sim \chi^2_{N-1}, \tag{4.259}$$

and that $\mathbb{V}[\chi^2_{N-1}] = 2(N-1)$. Finally, show that $\text{MSE}(\sigma^2_{\text{unb}}) = \frac{2N-1}{N^2}\sigma^4$ and $\text{MSE}(\sigma^2_{\text{mle}}) = \frac{2}{N-1}\sigma^4$.

5 Decision Theory

5.1 Bayesian decision theory

Bayesian inference provides the optimal way to update our beliefs about hidden quantities H given observed data $\mathbf{X} = \boldsymbol{x}$ by computing the posterior $p(H|\boldsymbol{x})$. However, at the end of the day, we need to turn our beliefs into **actions** that we can perform in the world. How can we decide which action is best? This is where **Bayesian decision theory** comes in. In this chapter, we give a brief introduction. For more details, see e.g., [DeG70; KWW22].

5.1.1 Basics

In decision theory, we assume the decision maker, or **agent**, has a set of possible actions, $\mathcal{A}$, to choose from. For example, consider the case of a hypothetical doctor treating someone who may have COVID-19. Suppose the actions are to do nothing, or to give the patient an expensive drug with bad side effects, but which can save their life.

Each of these actions has costs and benefits, which will depend on the underlying **state of nature** $H \in \mathcal{H}$. We can encode this information into a **loss function** $\ell(h, a)$, that specifies the loss we incur if we take action $a \in \mathcal{A}$ when the state of nature is $h \in \mathcal{H}$.

For example, suppose the state is defined by the age of the patient (young vs old), and whether they have COVID-19 or not. Note that the age can be observed directly, but the disease state must be inferred from noisy observations, as we discussed in Section 2.3. Thus the state is **partially observed**.

Let us assume that the cost of administering a drug is the same, no matter what the state of the patient is. However, the benefits will differ. If the patient is young, we expect them to live a long time, so the cost of not giving the drug if they have COVID-19 is high; but if the patient is old, they have fewer years to live, so the cost of not giving the drug if they have COVID-19 is arguably less (especially in view of the side effects). In medical circles, a common unit of cost is **quality-adjusted life years** or **QALY**. Suppose that the expected QALY for a young person is 60, and for an old person is 10. Let us assume the drug costs the equivalent of 8 QALY, due to induced pain and suffering from side effects. Then we get the loss matrix shown in Table 5.1.

These numbers reflect relative costs and benefits, and will depend on many factors. The numbers can be derived by asking the decision maker about their **preferences** about different possible outcomes. It is a theorem of decision theory that any consistent set of preferences can be converted into an ordinal cost scale (see e.g., https://en.wikipedia.org/wiki/Preference_(economics)).

Once we have specified the loss function, we can compute the **posterior expected loss** or **risk**

State	Nothing	Drugs
No COVID-19, young	0	8
COVID-19, young	60	8
No COVID-19, old	0	8
COVID-19, old	10	8

Table 5.1: Hypothetical loss matrix for a decision maker, where there are 4 states of nature, and 2 possible actions.

test	age	pr(covid)	cost-noop	cost-drugs	action
0	0	0.01	0.84	8.00	0
0	1	0.01	0.14	8.00	0
1	0	0.80	47.73	8.00	1
1	1	0.80	7.95	8.00	0

Table 5.2: Optimal policy for treating COVID-19 patients for each possible observation.

for each possible action a given all the relevant evidence, which may be a single datum $\boldsymbol{x}$ or an entire data set $\mathcal{D}$, depending on the problem:

$$\rho(a|\boldsymbol{x}) \triangleq \mathbb{E}_{p(h|\boldsymbol{x})}\left[\ell(h,a)\right] = \sum_{h \in \mathcal{H}} \ell(h,a)p(h|\boldsymbol{x}) \tag{5.1}$$

The **optimal policy** $\pi^*(\boldsymbol{x})$, also called the **Bayes estimator** or **Bayes decision rule** $\delta^*(\boldsymbol{x})$, specifies what action to take when presented with evidence $\boldsymbol{x}$ so as to minimize the risk:

$$\pi^*(\boldsymbol{x}) = \underset{a \in \mathcal{A}}{\operatorname{argmin}} \, \mathbb{E}_{p(h|\boldsymbol{x})}\left[\ell(h,a)\right] \tag{5.2}$$

An alternative, but equivalent, way of stating this result is as follows. Let us define a **utility function** $U(h,a)$ to be the desirability of each possible action in each possible state. If we set $U(h,a) = -\ell(h,a)$, then the optimal policy is as follows:

$$\pi^*(\boldsymbol{x}) = \underset{a \in \mathcal{A}}{\operatorname{argmax}} \, \mathbb{E}_h\left[U(h,a)\right] \tag{5.3}$$

This is called the **maximum expected utility principle**.

Let us return to our COVID-19 example. The observation $\boldsymbol{x}$ consists of the age (young or old) and the test result (positive or negative). Using the results from Section 2.3.1 on Bayes rule for COVID-19 diagnosis, we can convert the test result into a distribution over disease states (i.e., compute the probability the patient has COVID-19 or not). Given this belief state, and the loss matrix in Table 5.1, we can compute the optimal policy for each possible observation, as shown in Table 5.2.

We see from Table 5.2 that the drug should only be given to young people who test positive. If, however, we reduce the cost of the drug from 8 units to 5, then the optimal policy changes: in this case, we should give the drug to everyone who tests positive. The policy can also change depending on the reliability of the test. For example, if we increase the sensitivity from 0.875 to 0.975, then the probability that someone has COVID-19 if they test positive increases from 0.80 to 0.81, which changes the optimal policy to be one in which we should administer the drug to everyone who tests positive, even if the drug costs 8 QALY. (See dtheory.ipynb for the code to reproduce this example.)

So far, we have implicitly assumed that the agent is **risk neutral**. This means that their decision is not affected by the degree of certainty in a set of outcomes. For example, such an agent would be indifferent between getting $50 for sure, or a 50% chance of $100 or $0. By contrast, a **risk averse** agent would choose the first. We can generalize the framework of Bayesian decision theory to **risk sensitive** applications, but we do not pursue the matter here. (See e.g., [Cho+15] for details.)

5.1.2 Classification problems

In this section, we use Bayesian decision theory to decide the optimal class label to predict given an observed input $x \in \mathcal{X}$.

5.1.2.1 Zero-one loss

Suppose the states of nature correspond to class labels, so $\mathcal{H} = \mathcal{Y} = \{1, \ldots, C\}$. Furthermore, suppose the actions also correspond to class labels, so $\mathcal{A} = \mathcal{Y}$. In this setting, a very commonly used loss function is the **zero-one loss** $\ell_{01}(y^*, \hat{y})$, defined as follows:

$$
\begin{array}{c|cc}
 & \hat{y} = 0 & \hat{y} = 1 \\
\hline
y^* = 0 & 0 & 1 \\
y^* = 1 & 1 & 0
\end{array}
\tag{5.4}
$$

We can write this more concisely as follows:

$$
\ell_{01}(y^*, \hat{y}) = \mathbb{I}(y^* \neq \hat{y})
\tag{5.5}
$$

In this case, the posterior expected loss is

$$
\rho(\hat{y}|x) = p(\hat{y} \neq y^*|x) = 1 - p(y^* = \hat{y}|x)
\tag{5.6}
$$

Hence the action that minimizes the expected loss is to choose the most probable label:

$$
\pi(x) = \underset{y \in \mathcal{Y}}{\operatorname{argmax}} \, p(y|x)
\tag{5.7}
$$

This corresponds to the **mode** of the posterior distribution, also known as the **maximum a posteriori** or **MAP estimate**.

5.1.2.2 Cost-sensitive classification

Consider a binary classification problem where the loss function is $\ell(y^*, \hat{y})$ is as follows:

$$
\begin{pmatrix}
\ell_{00} & \ell_{01} \\
\ell_{10} & \ell_{11}
\end{pmatrix}
\tag{5.8}
$$

Let $p_0 = p(y^* = 0|x)$ and $p_1 = 1 - p_0$. Thus we should choose label $\hat{y} = 0$ iff

$$\ell_{00} p_0 + \ell_{10} p_1 < \ell_{01} p_0 + \ell_{11} p_1 \tag{5.9}$$

If $\ell_{00} = \ell_{11} = 0$, this simplifies to

$$p_1 < \frac{\ell_{01}}{\ell_{01} + \ell_{10}} \tag{5.10}$$

Now suppose $\ell_{10} = c\ell_{01}$, so a false negative costs c times more than a false positive. The decision rule further simplifies to the following: pick $a = 0$ iff $p_1 < 1/(1+c)$. For example, if a false negative costs twice as much as false positive, so $c = 2$, then we use a decision threshold of $1/3$ before declaring a positive.

5.1.2.3   Classification with the "reject" option

In some cases, we may able to say "I don't know" instead of returning an answer that we don't really trust; this is called picking the **reject option** (see e.g., [BW08]). This is particularly important in domains such as medicine and finance where we may be risk averse.

We can formalize the reject option as follows. Suppose the states of nature are $\mathcal{H} = \mathcal{Y} = \{1, \ldots, C\}$, and the actions are $\mathcal{A} = \mathcal{Y} \cup \{0\}$, where action 0 represents the reject action. Now define the following loss function:

$$\ell(y^*, a) = \begin{cases} 0 & \text{if } y^* = a \text{ and } a \in \{1, \ldots, C\} \\ \lambda_r & \text{if } a = 0 \\ \lambda_e & \text{otherwise} \end{cases} \tag{5.11}$$

where λ_r is the cost of the reject action, and λ_e is the cost of a classification error. Exercise 5.1 asks you to show that the optimal action is to pick the reject action if the most probable class has a probability below $\lambda^* = 1 - \frac{\lambda_r}{\lambda_e}$; otherwise you should just pick the most probable class. In other words, the optimal policy is as follows:

$$a^* = \begin{cases} y^* & \text{if } p^* > \lambda^* \\ \text{reject} & \text{otherwise} \end{cases} \tag{5.12}$$

where

$$y^* = \operatorname*{argmax}_{y \in \{1, \ldots, C\}} p(y|x) \tag{5.13}$$

$$p^* = p(y^*|x) = \max_{y \in \{1, \ldots, C\}} p(y|x) \tag{5.14}$$

$$\lambda^* = 1 - \frac{\lambda_r}{\lambda_e} \tag{5.15}$$

See Figure 5.1 for an illustration.

One interesting application of the reject option arises when playing the TV game show Jeopardy. In this game, contestants have to solve various word puzzles and answer a variety of trivia questions, but if they answer incorrectly, they lose money. In 2011, IBM unveiled a computer system called **Watson**

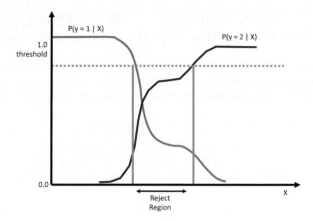

Figure 5.1: *For some regions of input space, where the class posteriors are uncertain, we may prefer not to choose class 1 or 2; instead we may prefer the reject option. Adapted from Figure 1.26 of [Bis06].*

		Estimate		Row sum
		0	1	
Truth	0	TN	FP	N
	1	FN	TP	P
Col. sum		$\hat{N}$	$\hat{P}$	

Table 5.3: *Class confusion matrix for a binary classification problem. TP is the number of true positives, FP is the number of false positives, TN is the number of true negatives, FN is the number of false negatives, P is the true number of positives, $\hat{P}$ is the predicted number of positives, N is the true number of negatives, $\hat{N}$ is the predicted number of negatives.*

which beat the top human Jeopardy champion. Watson uses a variety of interesting techniques [Fer+10], but the most pertinent one for our present discussion is that it contains a module that estimates how confident it is of its answer. The system only chooses to "buzz in" its answer if sufficiently confident it is correct.

For some other methods and applications, see e.g., [Cor+16; GEY19].

5.1.3   ROC curves

In Section 5.1.2.2, we showed that we can pick the optimal label in a binary classification problem by thresholding the probability using a value τ, derived from the relative cost of a false positive and false negative. Instead of picking a single threshold, we can consider using a set of different thresholds, and comparing the resulting performance, as we discuss below.

		Estimate	
		0	1
Truth	0	TN/N=TNR=Spec	FP/N =FPR=Type I = Fallout
	1	FN/P=FNR=Miss=Type II	TP/P=TPR=Sens=Recall

Table 5.4: Class confusion matrix for a binary classification problem normalized per row to get $p(\hat{y}|y)$. Abbreviations: TNR = true negative rate, Spec = specificity, FPR = false positive rate, FNR = false negative rate, Miss = miss rate, TPR = true positive rate, Sens = sensitivity. Note FNR=1-TPR and FPR=1-TNR.

		Estimate	
		0	1
Truth	0	TN/$\hat{N}$=NPV	FP/$\hat{P}$=FDR
	1	FN/$\hat{N}$=FOR	TP/$\hat{P}$=Prec=PPV

Table 5.5: Class confusion matrix for a binary classification problem normalized per column to get $p(y|\hat{y})$. Abbreviations: NPV = negative predictive value, FDR = false discovery rate, FOR = false omission rate, PPV = positive predictive value, Prec = precision. Note that FOR=1-NPV and FDR=1-PPV.

5.1.3.1   Class confusion matrices

For any fixed threshold τ, we consider the following decision rule:

$$\hat{y}_\tau(\boldsymbol{x}) = \mathbb{I}\left(p(y=1|\boldsymbol{x}) \geq 1-\tau\right) \tag{5.16}$$

We can compute the empirical number of false positives (FP) that arise from using this policy on a set of N labeled examples as follows:

$$FP_\tau = \sum_{n=1}^{N} \mathbb{I}\left(\hat{y}_\tau(\boldsymbol{x}_n) = 1, y_n = 0\right) \tag{5.17}$$

Similarly, we can compute the empirical number of false negatives (FN), true positives (TP), and true negatives (TN). We can store these results in a 2×2 **class confusion matrix** C, where C_{ij} is the number of times an item with true class label i was (mis)classified as having label j. In the case of binary classification problems, the resulting matrix will look like Table 5.3.

From this table, we can compute $p(\hat{y}|y)$ or $p(y|\hat{y})$, depending on whether we normalize across the rows or columns. We can derive various summary statistics from these distributions, as summarized in Table 5.4 and Table 5.5. For example, the **true positive rate** (TPR), also known as the **sensitivity**, **recall** or **hit rate**, is defined as

$$TPR_\tau = p(\hat{y} = 1|y = 1, \tau) = \frac{TP_\tau}{TP_\tau + FN_\tau} \tag{5.18}$$

and the **false positive rate** (FPR), also called the **false alarm rate**, or the **type I error rate**, is defined as

$$FPR_\tau = p(\hat{y} = 1|y = 0, \tau) = \frac{FP_\tau}{FP_\tau + TN_\tau} \tag{5.19}$$

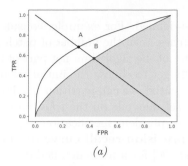
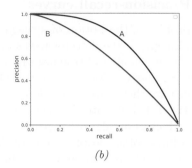

(a)   (b)

Figure 5.2: (a) ROC curves for two hypothetical classification systems. The red curve for system A is better than the blue curve for system B. We plot the true positive rate (TPR) vs the false positive rate (FPR) as we vary the threshold τ. We also indicate the equal error rate (EER) with the red and blue dots, and the area under the curve (AUC) for classifier B by the shaded area. Generated by roc_plot.ipynb. (b) A precision-recall curve for two hypothetical classification systems. The red curve for system A is better than the blue curve for system B. Generated by pr_plot.ipynb.

We can now plot the TPR vs FPR as an implicit function of τ. This is called a **receiver operating characteristic** or **ROC** curve. See Figure 5.2(a) for an example.

5.1.3.2 Summarizing ROC curves as a scalar

The quality of a ROC curve is often summarized as a single number using the **area under the curve** or **AUC**. Higher AUC scores are better; the maximum is obviously 1. Another summary statistic that is used is the **equal error rate** or **EER**, also called the **cross-over rate**, defined as the value which satisfies FPR = FNR. Since FNR=1-TPR, we can compute the EER by drawing a line from the top left to the bottom right and seeing where it intersects the ROC curve (see points A and B in Figure 5.2(a)). Lower EER scores are better; the minimum is obviously 0 (corresponding to the top left corner).

5.1.3.3 Class imbalance

In some problems, there is severe **class imbalance**. For example, in information retrieval, the set of negatives (irrelevant items) is usually much larger than the set of positives (relevant items). The ROC curve is unaffected by class imbalance, as the TPR and FPR are fractions within the positives and negatives, respectively. However, the usefulness of an ROC curve may be reduced in such cases, since a large change in the absolute number of false positives will not change the false positive *rate* very much, since FPR is divided by FP+TN (see e.g., [SR15] for discussion). Thus all the "action" happens in the extreme left part of the curve. In such cases, we may choose to use other ways of summarizing the class confusion matrix, such as precision-recall curves, which we discuss in Section 5.1.4.

5.1.4   Precision-recall curves

In some problems, the notion of a "negative" is not well-defined. For example, consider detecting objects in images: if the detector works by classifying patches, then the number of patches examined — and hence the number of true negatives — is a parameter of the algorithm, not part of the problem definition. Similarly, information retrieval systems usually get to choose the initial set of candidate items, which are then ranked for relevance; by specifying a cutoff, we can partition this into a positive and negative set, but note that the size of the negative set depends on the total number of items retrieved, which is an algorithm parameter, not part of the problem specification.

In these kinds of situations, we may choose to use a **precision-recall curve** to summarize the performance of our system, as we explain below. (See [DG06] for a more detailed discussion of the connection between ROC curves and PR curves.)

5.1.4.1   Computing precision and recall

The key idea is to replace the FPR with a quantity that is computed just from positives, namely the **precision**:

$$\mathcal{P}(\tau) \triangleq p(y = 1 | \hat{y} = 1, \tau) = \frac{TP_\tau}{TP_\tau + FP_\tau} \tag{5.20}$$

The precision measures what fraction of our detections are actually positive. We can compare this to the **recall** (which is the same as the TPR), which measures what fraction of the positives we actually detected:

$$\mathcal{R}(\tau) \triangleq p(\hat{y} = 1 | y = 1, \tau) = \frac{TP_\tau}{TP_\tau + FN_\tau} \tag{5.21}$$

If $\hat{y}_n \in \{0, 1\}$ is the predicted label, and $y_n \in \{0, 1\}$ is the true label, we can estimate precision and recall using

$$\mathcal{P}(\tau) = \frac{\sum_n y_n \hat{y}_n}{\sum_n \hat{y}_n} \tag{5.22}$$

$$\mathcal{R}(\tau) = \frac{\sum_n y_n \hat{y}_n}{\sum_n y_n} \tag{5.23}$$

We can now plot the precision vs recall as we vary the threshold τ. See Figure 5.2(b). Hugging the top right is the best one can do.

5.1.4.2   Summarizing PR curves as a scalar

The PR curve can be summarized as a single number in several ways. First, we can quote the precision for a fixed recall level, such as the precision of the first $K = 10$ entities recalled. This is called the **precision at K** score. Alternatively, we can compute the area under the PR curve. However, it is possible that the precision does not drop monotonically with recall. For example, suppose a classifier has 90% precision at 10% recall, and 96% precision at 20% recall. In this case, rather than measuring the precision *at* a recall of 10%, we should measure the maximum precision we can achieve with *at least* a recall of 10% (which would be 96%). This is called the **interpolated**

precision. The average of the interpolated precisions is called the **average precision**; it is equal to the area under the interpolated PR curve, but may not be equal to the area under the raw PR curve.[1] The **mean average precision** or **mAP** is the mean of the AP over a set of different PR curves.

5.1.4.3 F-scores

For a fixed threshold, corresponding to a single point on the PR curve, we can compute a single precision and recall value, which we will denote by $\mathcal{P}$ and $\mathcal{R}$. These are often combined into a single statistic called the F_β, defined as follows:[2]

$$\frac{1}{F_\beta} = \frac{1}{1+\beta^2}\frac{1}{\mathcal{P}} + \frac{\beta^2}{1+\beta^2}\frac{1}{\mathcal{R}} \tag{5.24}$$

or equivalently

$$F_\beta \triangleq (1+\beta^2)\frac{\mathcal{P}\cdot\mathcal{R}}{\beta^2\mathcal{P}+\mathcal{R}} = \frac{(1+\beta^2)TP}{(1+\beta^2)TP + \beta^2 FN + FP} \tag{5.25}$$

If we set $\beta = 1$, we get the harmonic mean of precision and recall:

$$\frac{1}{F_1} = \frac{1}{2}\left(\frac{1}{\mathcal{P}} + \frac{1}{\mathcal{R}}\right) \tag{5.26}$$

$$F_1 = \frac{2}{1/\mathcal{R} + 1/\mathcal{P}} = 2\frac{\mathcal{P}\cdot\mathcal{R}}{\mathcal{P}+\mathcal{R}} = \frac{TP}{TP + \frac{1}{2}(FP + FN)} \tag{5.27}$$

To understand why we use the harmonic mean instead of the arithmetic mean, $(\mathcal{P}+\mathcal{R})/2$, consider the following scenario. Suppose we recall all entries, so $\hat{y}_n = 1$ for all n, and $\mathcal{R} = 1$. In this case, the precision $\mathcal{P}$ will be given by the **prevalence**, $p(y=1) = \frac{\sum_n \mathbb{I}(y_n=1)}{N}$. Suppose the prevalence is low, say $p(y=1) = 10^{-4}$. The arithmetic mean of $\mathcal{P}$ and $\mathcal{R}$ is given by $(\mathcal{P}+\mathcal{R})/2 = (10^{-4}+1)/2 \approx 50\%$. By contrast, the harmonic mean of this strategy is only $\frac{2\times 10^{-4}\times 1}{1+10^{-4}} \approx 0.02\%$. In general, the harmonic mean is more conservative, and requires both precision and recall to be high.

Using F_1 score weights precision and recall equally. However, if recall is more important, we may use $\beta = 2$, and if precision is more important, we may use $\beta = 0.5$.

5.1.4.4 Class imbalance

ROC curves are insensitive to class imbalance, but PR curves are not, as noted in [Wil20]. To see this, let the fraction of positives in the dataset be $\pi = P/(P+N)$, and define the ratio $r = P/N = \pi/(1-\pi)$. Let $n = P + N$ be the population size. ROC curves are not affected by changes in r, since the TPR is defined as a ratio within the positive examples, and FPR is defined as a ratio within the negative examples. This means it does not matter which class we define as positive, and which we define as negative.

---

1. For details, see `https://sanchom.wordpress.com/tag/average-precision/`.
2. We follow the notation from `https://en.wikipedia.org/wiki/F-score#F%CE%B2`.

Now consider PR curves. The precision can be written as

$$\text{Prec} = \frac{TP}{TP + FP} = \frac{P \cdot TPR}{P \cdot TPR + N \cdot FPR} = \frac{TPR}{TPR + \frac{1}{r}FPR} \tag{5.28}$$

Thus $\text{Prec} \to 1$ as $\pi \to 1$ and $r \to \infty$, and $\text{Prec} \to 0$ as $\pi \to 0$ and $r \to 0$. For example, if we change from a balanced problem where $r = 0.5$ to an imbalanced problem where $r = 0.1$ (so positives are rarer), the precision at each threshold will drop, and the recall (aka TPR) will stay the same, so the overall PR curve will be lower. Thus if we have multiple binary problems with different prevalences (e.g., object detection of common or rare objects), we should be careful when averaging their precisions [HCD12].

The F-score is also affected by class imbalance. To see this, note that we can rewrite the F-score as follows:

$$\frac{1}{F_\beta} = \frac{1}{1 + \beta^2} \frac{1}{\mathcal{P}} + \frac{\beta^2}{1 + \beta^2} \frac{1}{\mathcal{R}} \tag{5.29}$$

$$= \frac{1}{1 + \beta^2} \frac{TPR + \frac{N}{P}FPR}{TPR} + \frac{\beta^2}{1 + \beta^2} \frac{1}{TPR} \tag{5.30}$$

$$F_\beta = \frac{(1 + \beta^2)TPR}{TPR + \frac{1}{r}FPR + \beta^2} \tag{5.31}$$

5.1.5   Regression problems

So far, we have considered the case where there are a finite number of actions $\mathcal{A}$ and states of nature $\mathcal{H}$. In this section, we consider the case where the set of actions and states are both equal to the real line, $\mathcal{A} = \mathcal{H} = \mathbb{R}$. We will specify various commonly used loss functions for this case (which can be extended to $\mathbb{R}^D$ by computing the loss elementwise.) The resulting decision rules can be used to compute the optimal parameters for an estimator to return, or the optimal action for a robot to take, etc.

5.1.5.1   L2 loss

The most common loss for continuous states and actions is the ℓ_2 **loss**, also called **squared error** or **quadratic loss**, which is defined as follows:

$$\ell_2(h, a) = (h - a)^2 \tag{5.32}$$

In this case, the risk is given by

$$\rho(a|\boldsymbol{x}) = \mathbb{E}\left[(h - a)^2 | \boldsymbol{x}\right] = \mathbb{E}\left[h^2 | \boldsymbol{x}\right] - 2a\mathbb{E}\left[h|\boldsymbol{x}\right] + a^2 \tag{5.33}$$

The optimal action must satisfy the condition that the derivative of the risk (at that point) is zero (as explained in Chapter 8). Hence the optimal action is to pick the posterior mean:

$$\frac{\partial}{\partial a}\rho(a|\boldsymbol{x}) = -2\mathbb{E}\left[h|\boldsymbol{x}\right] + 2a = 0 \;\Rightarrow\; \pi(\boldsymbol{x}) = \mathbb{E}\left[h|\boldsymbol{x}\right] = \int h \, p(h|\boldsymbol{x})dh \tag{5.34}$$

This is often called the **minimum mean squared error** estimate or **MMSE** estimate.

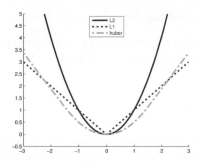

Figure 5.3: Illustration of ℓ_2, ℓ_1, and Huber loss functions with $\delta = 1.5$. Generated by huberLossPlot.ipynb.

5.1.5.2 L1 loss

The ℓ_2 loss penalizes deviations from the truth quadratically, and thus is sensitive to **outliers**. A more **robust** alternative is the absolute or ℓ_1 **loss**

$$\ell_1(h, a) = |h - a| \tag{5.35}$$

This is sketched in Figure 5.3. Exercise 5.4 asks you to show that the optimal estimate is the **posterior median**, i.e., a value a such that $\Pr(h < a|\boldsymbol{x}) = \Pr(h \geq a|\boldsymbol{x}) = 0.5$. We can use this for robust regression as discussed in Section 11.6.1.

5.1.5.3 Huber loss

Another robust loss function is the **Huber loss** [Hub64], defined as follows:

$$\ell_\delta(h, a) = \begin{cases} r^2/2 & \text{if } |r| \leq \delta \\ \delta|r| - \delta^2/2 & \text{if } |r| > \delta \end{cases} \tag{5.36}$$

where $r = h - a$. This is equivalent to ℓ_2 for errors that are smaller than δ, and is equivalent to ℓ_1 for larger errors. See Figure 5.3 for a plot. We can use this for robust regression as discussed in Section 11.6.3.

5.1.6 Probabilistic prediction problems

In Section 5.1.2, we assumed the set of possible actions was to pick a single class label (or possibly the "reject" or "do not know" action). In Section 5.1.5, we assumed the set of possible actions was to pick a real valued scalar. In this section, we assume the set of possible actions is to pick a **probability distribution** over some value of interest. That is, we want to perform **probabilistic prediction** or **probabilistic forecasting**, rather than predicting a specific value. More precisely, we assume the true "state of nature" is a *distribution*, $h = p(Y|x)$, the action is another distribution, $a = q(Y|x)$, and we want to pick q to minimize $\mathbb{E}[\ell(p, q)]$ for a given x. We discuss various possible loss functions below.

5.1.6.1   KL, cross-entropy and log-loss

A common form of loss functions for comparing two distributions is the **Kullback Leibler divergence**, or **KL divergence**, which is defined as follows:

$$D_{\mathrm{KL}}\left(p \parallel q\right) \triangleq \sum_{y \in \mathcal{Y}} p(y) \log \frac{p(y)}{q(y)} \tag{5.37}$$

(We have assumed the variable y is discrete, for notational simplicity, but this can be generalized to real-valued variables.) In Section 6.2, we show that the KL divergence satisfies the following properties: $D_{\mathrm{KL}}\left(p \parallel q\right) \geq 0$ with equality iff $p = q$. Note that it is an asymmetric function of its arguments.

We can expand the KL as follows:

$$D_{\mathrm{KL}}\left(p \parallel q\right) = \sum_{y \in \mathcal{Y}} p(y) \log p(y) - \sum_{y \in \mathcal{Y}} p(y) \log q(y) \tag{5.38}$$

$$= -\mathbb{H}(p) + \mathbb{H}_{ce}(p, q) \tag{5.39}$$

$$\mathbb{H}(p) \triangleq -\sum_{y} p(y) \log p(y) \tag{5.40}$$

$$\mathbb{H}_{ce}(p, q) \triangleq -\sum_{y} p(y) \log q(y) \tag{5.41}$$

The $\mathbb{H}(p)$ term is known as the **entropy**. This is a measure of uncertainty or variance of p; it is maximal if p is uniform, and is 0 if p is a degenerate or deterministic delta function. Entropy is often used in the field of **information theory**, which is concerned with optimal ways of compressing and communicating data (see Chapter 6). The optimal coding scheme will allocate fewer bits to more frequent symbols (i.e., values of Y for which $p(y)$ is large), and more bits to less frequent symbols. A key result states that the number of bits needed to compress a dataset generated by a distribution p is at least $\mathbb{H}(p)$; the entropy therefore provides a lower bound on the degree to which we can compress data without losing information. The $\mathbb{H}_{ce}(p, q)$ term is known as the **cross-entropy**. This measures the expected number of bits we need to use to compress a dataset coming from distribution p if we design our code using distribution q. Thus the KL is the extra number of bits we need to use to compress the data due to using the incorrect distribution q. If the KL is zero, it means that we can correctly predict the probabilities of all possible future events, and thus we have learned to predict the future as well as an "oracle" that has access to the true distribution p.

To find the optimal distribution to use when predicting future data, we can minimize $D_{\mathrm{KL}}\left(p \parallel q\right)$. Since $\mathbb{H}(p)$ is a constant wrt q, it can be ignored, and thus we can equivalently minimize the cross-entropy:

$$q^*(Y|x) = \underset{q}{\operatorname{argmin}} \, \mathbb{H}_{ce}(q(Y|x), p(Y|x)) \tag{5.42}$$

Now consider the special case in which the true state of nature is a degenerate distribution, which puts all its mass on a single outcome, say c, i.e., $h = p(Y|x) = \mathbb{I}\,(Y = c)$. This is often called a "**one-hot**" distribution, since it turns "on" the c'th element of the vector, and leaves the other elements "off", as shown in Figure 2.1. In this case, the cross entropy becomes

$$\mathbb{H}_{ce}(\delta(Y = c), q) = -\sum_{y \in \mathcal{Y}} \delta(y = c) \log q(y) = -\log q(c) \tag{5.43}$$

This is known as the **log loss** of the predictive distribution q when given target label c.

5.1.6.2   Proper scoring rules

Cross-entropy loss is a very common choice for probabilistic forecasting, but is not the only possible metric. The key property we desire is that the loss function is minimized iff the decision maker picks the distribution q that matches the true distribution p, i.e., $\ell(p, p) \leq \ell(p, q)$, with equality iff $p = q$. Such a loss function ℓ is called a **proper scoring rule** [GR07].

We can show that cross-entropy loss is a proper scoring rule by virtue of the fact that $D_{\mathrm{KL}}(p \parallel p) \leq D_{\mathrm{KL}}(p \parallel q)$. However, the $\log p(y)/q(y)$ term can be quite sensitive to errors for low probability events [QC+06]. A common alternative is to use the **Brier score** [Bri50], which is defined as follows (for a discrete distribution with C values):

$$\ell(p, q) \triangleq \frac{1}{C} \sum_{c=1}^{C} (q(y = c|x) - p(y = c|x))^2 \tag{5.44}$$

This is just the squared error of the predictive distribution compared to the true distribution, when viewed as vectors. Since it is based on squared error, the Brier score is less sensitive to extremely rare or extremely common classes. Fortunately, it is also a proper scoring rule.

5.2   Choosing the "right" model

In this section, we consider the setting in which we have several candidate (parametric) models (e.g., neural networks with different numbers of layers), and we want to choose the "right" one. This can be tackled using tools from Bayesian decision theory.

5.2.1   Bayesian hypothesis testing

Suppose we have two hypotheses or models, commonly called the **null hypothesis**, M_0, and the **alternative hypothesis**, M_1, and we want to know which one is more likely to be true. This is called **hypothesis testing**.

If we use 0-1 loss, the optimal decision is to pick the alternative hypothesis iff $p(M_1|\mathcal{D}) > p(M_0|\mathcal{D})$, or equivalently, if $p(M_1|\mathcal{D})/p(M_0|\mathcal{D}) > 1$. If we use a uniform prior, $p(M_0) = p(M_1) = 0.5$, the decision rule becomes: select M_1 iff $p(\mathcal{D}|M_1)/p(\mathcal{D}|M_0) > 1$. This quantity, which is the ratio of marginal likelihoods of the two models, is known as the **Bayes factor**:

$$B_{1,0} \triangleq \frac{p(\mathcal{D}|M_1)}{p(\mathcal{D}|M_0)} \tag{5.45}$$

This is like a **likelihood ratio**, except we integrate out the parameters, which allows us to compare models of different complexity, due to the Bayesian Occam's razor effect explained in Section 5.2.3.

Bayes factor $BF(1,0)$	Interpretation
$BF < \frac{1}{100}$	Decisive evidence for M_0
$BF < \frac{1}{10}$	Strong evidence for M_0
$\frac{1}{10} < BF < \frac{1}{3}$	Moderate evidence for M_0
$\frac{1}{3} < BF < 1$	Weak evidence for M_0
$1 < BF < 3$	Weak evidence for M_1
$3 < BF < 10$	Moderate evidence for M_1
$BF > 10$	Strong evidence for M_1
$BF > 100$	Decisive evidence for M_1

Table 5.6: *Jeffreys scale of evidence for interpreting Bayes factors.*

If $B_{1,0} > 1$ then we prefer model 1, otherwise we prefer model 0. Of course, it might be that $B_{1,0}$ is only slightly greater than 1. In that case, we are not very confident that model 1 is better. Jeffreys [Jef61] proposed a scale of evidence for interpreting the magnitude of a Bayes factor, which is shown in Table 5.6. This is a Bayesian alternative to the frequentist concept of a p-value (see Section 5.5.3).

We give a worked example of how to compute Bayes factors in Section 5.2.1.1.

5.2.1.1 Example: Testing if a coin is fair

As an example, suppose we observe some coin tosses, and want to decide if the data was generated by a fair coin, $\theta = 0.5$, or a potentially biased coin, where θ could be any value in $[0, 1]$. Let us denote the first model by M_0 and the second model by M_1. The marginal likelihood under M_0 is simply

$$p(\mathcal{D}|M_0) = \left(\frac{1}{2}\right)^N \tag{5.46}$$

where N is the number of coin tosses. From Equation (4.143), the marginal likelihood under M_1, using a Beta prior, is

$$p(\mathcal{D}|M_1) = \int p(\mathcal{D}|\theta)p(\theta)d\theta = \frac{B(\alpha_1 + N_1, \alpha_0 + N_0)}{B(\alpha_1, \alpha_0)} \tag{5.47}$$

We plot $\log p(\mathcal{D}|M_1)$ vs the number of heads N_1 in Figure 5.4(a), assuming $N = 5$ and a uniform prior, $\alpha_1 = \alpha_0 = 1$. (The shape of the curve is not very sensitive to α_1 and α_0, as long as the prior is symmetric, so $\alpha_0 = \alpha_1$.) If we observe 2 or 3 heads, the unbiased coin hypothesis M_0 is more likely than M_1, since M_0 is a simpler model (it has no free parameters) — it would be a suspicious coincidence if the coin were biased but happened to produce almost exactly 50/50 heads/tails. However, as the counts become more extreme, we favor the biased coin hypothesis. Note that, if we plot the log Bayes factor, $\log B_{1,0}$, it will have exactly the same shape, since $\log p(\mathcal{D}|M_0)$ is a constant.

5.2.2 Bayesian model selection

Now suppose we have a set $\mathcal{M}$ of more than 2 models, and we want to pick the most likely. This is called **model selection**. We can view this as a decision theory problem, where the action space

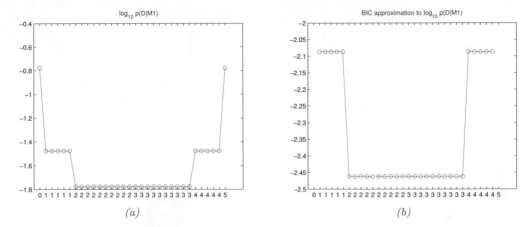

Figure 5.4: (a) Log marginal likelihood vs number of heads for the coin tossing example. (b) BIC approximation. (The vertical scale is arbitrary, since we are holding N fixed.) Generated by coins_model_sel_demo.ipynb.

requires choosing one model, $m \in \mathcal{M}$. If we have a 0-1 loss, the optimal action is to pick the most probable model:

$$\hat{m} = \operatorname*{argmax}_{m \in \mathcal{M}} p(m|\mathcal{D}) \tag{5.48}$$

where

$$p(m|\mathcal{D}) = \frac{p(\mathcal{D}|m)p(m)}{\sum_{m \in \mathcal{M}} p(\mathcal{D}|m)p(m)} \tag{5.49}$$

is the posterior over models. If the prior over models is uniform, $p(m) = 1/|\mathcal{M}|$, then the MAP model is given by

$$\hat{m} = \operatorname*{argmax}_{m \in \mathcal{M}} p(\mathcal{D}|m) \tag{5.50}$$

The quantity $p(\mathcal{D}|m)$ is given by

$$p(\mathcal{D}|m) = \int p(\mathcal{D}|\boldsymbol{\theta}, m)p(\boldsymbol{\theta}|m)d\boldsymbol{\theta} \tag{5.51}$$

This is known as the **marginal likelihood**, or the **evidence** for model m. Intuitively, it is the likelihood of the data averaged over all possible parameter values, weighted by the prior $p(\boldsymbol{\theta}|m)$. If all settings of $\boldsymbol{\theta}$ assign high probability to the data, then this is probably a good model.

5.2.2.1 Example: polynomial regression

As an example of Bayesian model selection, we will consider polynomial regression in 1d. Figure 5.5 shows the posterior over three different models, corresponding to polynomials of degrees 1, 2 and 3 fit

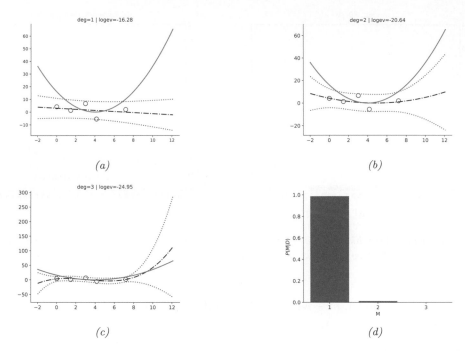

Figure 5.5: Ilustration of Bayesian model selection for polynomial regression. (a-c) We fit polynomials of degrees 1, 2 and 3 fit to $N = 5$ data points. The solid green curve is the true function, the dashed red curve is the prediction (dotted blue lines represent $\pm 2\sigma$ around the mean). (d) We plot the posterior over models, $p(m|\mathcal{D})$, assuming a uniform prior $p(m) \propto 1$. Generated by linreg_ eb_ modelsel_ vs_ n.ipynb.

to $N = 5$ data points. We use a uniform prior over models, and use empirical Bayes to estimate the prior over the regression weights (see Section 11.7.7). We then compute the evidence for each model (see Section 11.7 for details on how to do this). We see that there is not enough data to justify a complex model, so the MAP model is $m = 1$. Figure 5.6 shows the analogous plot for $N = 30$ data points. Now we see that the MAP model is $m = 2$; the larger sample size means we can safely pick a more complex model.

5.2.3 Occam's razor

Consider two models, a simple one, m_1, and a more complex one, m_2. Suppose that both can explain the data by suitably optimizing their parameters, i.e., for which $p(\mathcal{D}|\hat{\boldsymbol{\theta}}_1, m_1)$ and $p(\mathcal{D}|\hat{\boldsymbol{\theta}}_2, m_2)$ are both large. Intuitively we should prefer m_1, since it is simpler and just as good as m_2. This principle is known as **Occam's razor**.

Let us now see how ranking models based on their marginal likelihood, which involves averaging the likelihood wrt the prior, will give rise to this behavior. The complex model will put less prior probability on the "good" parameters that explain the data, $\hat{\boldsymbol{\theta}}_2$, since the prior must integrate to 1.0 over the entire parameter space. Thus it will take averages in parts of parameter space with low likelihood. By contrast, the simpler model has fewer parameters, so the prior is concentrated

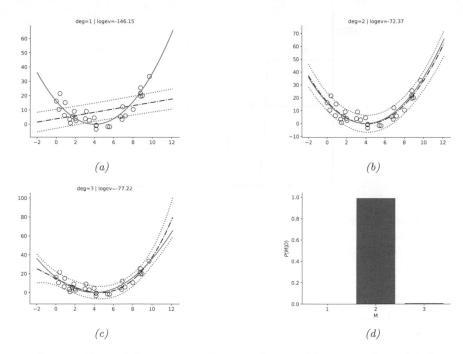

Figure 5.6: Same as Figure 5.5 except now $N = 30$. Generated by linreg_eb_modelsel_vs_n.ipynb.

over a smaller volume; thus its averages will mostly be in the good part of parameter space, near $\hat{\boldsymbol{\theta}}_1$. Hence we see that the marginal likelihood will prefer the simpler model. This is called the **Bayesian Occam's razor** effect [Mac95; MG05].

Another way to understand the Bayesian Occam's razor effect is to compare the relative predictive abilities of simple and complex models. Since probabilities must sum to one, we have $\sum_{\mathcal{D}'} p(\mathcal{D}'|m) = 1$, where the sum is over all possible datasets. Complex models, which can predict many things, must spread their predicted probability mass thinly, and hence will not obtain as large a probability for any given data set as simpler models. This is sometimes called the **conservation of probability mass** principle, and is illustrated in Figure 5.7. On the horizontal axis we plot all possible data sets in order of increasing complexity (measured in some abstract sense). On the vertical axis we plot the predictions of 3 possible models: a simple one, M_1; a medium one, M_2; and a complex one, M_3. We also indicate the actually observed data $\mathcal{D}_0$ by a vertical line. Model 1 is too simple and assigns low probability to $\mathcal{D}_0$. Model 3 also assigns $\mathcal{D}_0$ relatively low probability, because it can predict many data sets, and hence it spreads its probability quite widely and thinly. Model 2 is "just right": it predicts the observed data with a reasonable degree of confidence, but does not predict too many other things. Hence model 2 is the most probable model.

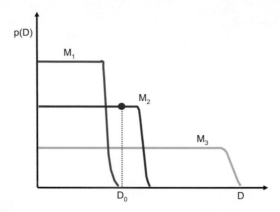

Figure 5.7: A schematic illustration of the Bayesian Occam's razor. The broad (green) curve corresponds to a complex model, the narrow (blue) curve to a simple model, and the middle (red) curve is just right. Adapted from Figure 3.13 of [Bis06]. See also [MG05, Figure 2] for a similar plot produced on real data.

5.2.4   Connection between cross validation and marginal likelihood

We have seen how the marginal likelihood helps us choose models of the "right" complexity. In non-Bayesian approaches to model selection, it is standard to use cross validation (Section 4.5.5) for this purpose.

It turns out that the marginal likelihood is closely related to the leave-one-out cross-validation (LOO-CV) estimate, as we now show. We start with the marginal likelihood for model m, which we write in sequential form as follows:

$$p(\mathcal{D}|m) = \prod_{n=1}^{N} p(y_n|y_{1:n-1}, \boldsymbol{x}_{1:N}, m) = \prod_{n=1}^{N} p(y_n|\boldsymbol{x}_n, \mathcal{D}_{1:n-1}, m) \tag{5.52}$$

where

$$p(y|\boldsymbol{x}, \mathcal{D}_{1:n-1}, m) = \int p(y|\boldsymbol{x}, \boldsymbol{\theta}) p(\boldsymbol{\theta}|\mathcal{D}_{1:n-1}, m) d\boldsymbol{\theta} \tag{5.53}$$

Suppose we use a plugin approximation to the above distribution to get

$$p(y|\boldsymbol{x}, \mathcal{D}_{1:n-1}, m) \approx \int p(y|\boldsymbol{x}, \boldsymbol{\theta}) \delta(\boldsymbol{\theta} - \hat{\boldsymbol{\theta}}_m(\mathcal{D}_{1:n-1})) d\boldsymbol{\theta} = p(y|\boldsymbol{x}, \hat{\boldsymbol{\theta}}_m(\mathcal{D}_{1:n-1})) \tag{5.54}$$

Then we get

$$\log p(\mathcal{D}|m) \approx \sum_{n=1}^{N} \log p(y_n|\boldsymbol{x}_n, \hat{\boldsymbol{\theta}}_m(\mathcal{D}_{1:n-1})) \tag{5.55}$$

This is similar to a leave-one-out cross-validation estimate of the likelihood, which has the form $\frac{1}{N}\sum_{n=1}^{N} \log p(y_n|\boldsymbol{x}_n, \hat{\boldsymbol{\theta}}_m(\mathcal{D}_{1:n-1,n+1:N}))$, except we ignore the $\mathcal{D}_{n+1:N}$ part. The intuition behind the connection is this: an overly complex model will overfit the "early" examples and will then predict the remaining ones poorly, and thus will also get a low cross-validation score. See [FH20] for a more detailed discussion of the connection between these performance metrics.

5.2.5   Information criteria

The marginal likelihood, $p(\mathcal{D}|m) = \int p(\mathcal{D}|\boldsymbol{\theta}, m)p(\boldsymbol{\theta})d\boldsymbol{\theta}$, which is needed for Bayesian model selection discussed in Section 5.2.2, can be difficult to compute, since it requires marginalizing over the entire parameter space. Furthermore, the result can be quite sensitive to the choice of prior. In this section, we discuss some other related metrics for model selection known as **information criteria**. We only give a brief discussion; see e.g., [GHV14] for further details.

5.2.5.1   The Bayesian information criterion (BIC)

The **Bayesian information criterion** or **BIC** [Sch78] can be thought of as a simple approximation to the log marginal likelihood. In particular, if we make a Gaussian approximation to the posterior, as discussed in Section 4.6.8.2, we get (from Equation (4.215)) the following:

$$\log p(\mathcal{D}|m) \approx \log p(\mathcal{D}|\hat{\boldsymbol{\theta}}_{\mathrm{map}}) + \log p(\hat{\boldsymbol{\theta}}_{\mathrm{map}}) - \frac{1}{2}\log|\mathbf{H}| \tag{5.56}$$

where $\mathbf{H}$ is the Hessian of the negative log joint, $-\log p(\mathcal{D}, \boldsymbol{\theta})$, evaluated at the MAP estimate $\hat{\boldsymbol{\theta}}_{\mathrm{map}}$. We see that Equation (5.56) is the log likelihood plus some penalty terms. If we have a uniform prior, $p(\boldsymbol{\theta}) \propto 1$, we can drop the prior term, and replace the MAP estimate with the MLE, $\hat{\boldsymbol{\theta}}$, yielding

$$\log p(\mathcal{D}|m) \approx \log p(\mathcal{D}|\hat{\boldsymbol{\theta}}) - \frac{1}{2}\log|\mathbf{H}| \tag{5.57}$$

We now focus on approximating the $\log|\mathbf{H}|$ term, which is sometimes called the **Occam factor**, since it is a measure of model complexity (volume of the posterior distribution). We have $\mathbf{H} = \sum_{i=1}^{N}\mathbf{H}_i$, where $\mathbf{H}_i = \nabla\nabla\log p(\mathcal{D}_i|\boldsymbol{\theta})$. Let us approximate each $\mathbf{H}_i$ by a fixed matrix $\hat{\mathbf{H}}$. Then we have

$$\log|\mathbf{H}| = \log|N\hat{\mathbf{H}}| = \log(N^D|\hat{\mathbf{H}}|) = D\log N + \log|\hat{\mathbf{H}}| \tag{5.58}$$

where $D = \dim(\boldsymbol{\theta})$ and we have assumed $\mathbf{H}$ is full rank. We can drop the $\log|\hat{\mathbf{H}}|$ term, since it is independent of N, and thus will get overwhelmed by the likelihood. Putting all the pieces together, we get the **BIC score** that we want to maximize:

$$J_{\mathrm{BIC}}(m) = \log p(\mathcal{D}|m) \approx \log p(\mathcal{D}|\hat{\boldsymbol{\theta}}, m) - \frac{D_m}{2}\log N \tag{5.59}$$

We can also define the **BIC loss**, that we want to minimize, by multiplying by -2:

$$\mathcal{L}_{\mathrm{BIC}}(m) = -2\log p(\mathcal{D}|\hat{\boldsymbol{\theta}}, m) + D_m\log N \tag{5.60}$$

(The use of 2 as a scale factor is chosen to simplify the expression when using a model with a Gaussian likelihood.)

5.2.5.2   Akaike information criterion

The **Akaike information criterion** [Aka74] is closely related to the BIC. It has the form

$$\mathcal{L}_{\mathrm{AIC}}(m) = -2\log p(\mathcal{D}|\hat{\boldsymbol{\theta}}, m) + 2D \tag{5.61}$$

This penalizes complex models less heavily than BIC, since the regularization term is independent of N. This estimator can be derived from a frequentist perspective.

5.2.5.3 Minimum description length (MDL)

We can think about the problem of scoring different models in terms of information theory (Chapter 6). The goal is for the sender to communicate the data to the receiver. First the sender needs to specify which model m to use; this takes $C(m) = -\log p(m)$ bits (see Section 6.1). Then the receiver can fit the model, by computing $\hat{\boldsymbol{\theta}}_m$, and can thus approximately reconstruct the data. To perfectly reconstruct the data, the sender needs to send the residual errors that cannot be explained by the model; this takes $-L(m) = -\log p(\mathcal{D}|\hat{\boldsymbol{\theta}}, m) = -\sum_n \log p(y_n|\hat{\boldsymbol{\theta}}, m)$ bits. The total cost is

$$\mathcal{L}_{\text{MDL}}(m) = -\log p(\mathcal{D}|\hat{\boldsymbol{\theta}}, m) + C(m) \tag{5.62}$$

We see that this has the same basic form as BIC/AIC. Choosing the model which minimizes this objective is known as the **minimum description length** or **MDL** principle. See e.g., [HY01] for details.

5.2.6 Posterior inference over effect sizes and Bayesian significance testing

The approach to hypothesis testing discussed in Section 5.2.1 relies on computing the Bayes factors for the null vs the alternative model, $p(\mathcal{D}|H_0)/p(\mathcal{D}|H_1)$. Unfortunately, computing the necessary marginal likelihoods can be computationally difficult, and the results can be sensitive to the choice of prior. Furthermore, we are often more interested in estimating an **effect size**, which is the difference in magnitude between two parameters, rather than in deciding if an effect size is 0 (null hypothesis) or not (alternative hypothesis) — the latter is called a **point null hypothesis**, and is often regarded as an irrelevant "straw man" (see e.g., [Mak+19] and references therein).

For example, suppose we have two classifiers, m_1 and m_2, and we want to know which one is better. That is, we want to perform a **comparison of classifiers**. Let μ_1 and μ_2 be their average accuracies, and let $\Delta = \mu_1 - \mu_2$ be the difference in their accuracies. The probability that model 1 is more accurate, on average, than model 2 is given by $p(\Delta > 0|\mathcal{D})$. However, even if this probability is large, the improvement may be not be practically significant. So it is better to compute a probability such as $p(\Delta > \epsilon|\mathcal{D})$ or $p(|\Delta| > \epsilon|\mathcal{D})$, where ϵ represents the minimal magnitude of effect size that is meaningful for the problem at hand. This is called a **one-sided test** or **two-sided test**.

More generally, let $R = [-\epsilon, \epsilon]$ represent a **region of practical equivalence** or **ROPE** [Kru15; KL17]. We can define 3 events of interest: the null hypothesis $H_0 : \Delta \in R$, which says both methods are practically the same (which is a more realistic assumption than $H_0 : \Delta = 0$); $H_A : \Delta > \epsilon$, which says m_1 is better than m_2; and $H_B : \Delta < -\epsilon$, which says m_2 is better than m_1. To choose amongst these 3 hypotheses, we just have to compute $p(\Delta|\mathcal{D})$, which avoids the need to compute Bayes factors. In the sections below, we discuss how to compute this quantity using two different kinds of model.

5.2.6.1 Bayesian t-test for difference in means

Suppose we have two classifiers, m_1 and m_2, which are evaluated on the same set of N test examples. Let e_i^m be the error of method m on test example i. (Or this could be the conditional log likelihood, $e_i^m = \log p^m(y_i|\boldsymbol{x}_i)$.) Since the classifiers are applied to the same data, we can use a **paired test** for comparing them, which is more sensitive than looking at average performance, since the factors that make one example easy or hard to classify (e.g., due to label noise) will be shared by both methods. Thus we will work with the differences, $d_i = e_i^1 - e_i^2$. We assume $d_i \sim \mathcal{N}(\Delta, \sigma^2)$. We are interested in $p(\Delta|\boldsymbol{d})$, where $\boldsymbol{d} = (d_1, \ldots, d_N)$.

If we use an uninformative prior for the unknown parameters (Δ, σ), one can show that the posterior marginal for the mean is given by a Student distribution:

$$p(\Delta|\boldsymbol{d}) = \mathcal{T}_{N-1}(\Delta|\mu, s^2/N)$$

where $\mu = \frac{1}{N}\sum_{i=1}^{N} d_i$ is the sample mean, and $s^2 = \frac{1}{N-1}\sum_{i=1}^{N}(d_i - \mu)^2$ is an unbiased estimate of the variance. Hence we can easily compute $p(|\Delta| > \epsilon|\boldsymbol{d})$, with a ROPE of $\epsilon = 0.01$ (say). This is known as a **Bayesian t-test** [Ben+17]. (See also [Rou+09] for Bayesian t-test based on Bayes factors, and [Die98] for a non-Bayesian approach to comparing classifiers.)

An alternative to a formal test is to just plot the posterior $p(\Delta|\boldsymbol{d})$. If this distribution is tightly centered on 0, we can conclude that there is no significant difference between the methods. (In fact, an even simpler approach is to just make a boxplot of the data, $\{d_i\}$, which avoids the need for any formal statistical analysis.)

Note that this kind of problem arises in many applications, not just evaluating classifiers. For example, suppose we have a set of N people, each of whom is exposed two drugs; let e_i^m be the outcome (e.g., sickness level) when person i is exposed to drug m, and let $d_i^m = e_i^1 - e_i^2$ be the difference in response. We can then analyse the effect of the drug by computing $p(\Delta|\boldsymbol{d})$ as we discussed above.

5.2.6.2 Bayesian χ^2-test for difference in rates

Now suppose we have two classifiers which are evaluated on different test sets. Let y_m be the number of correct examples from method $m \in \{1, 2\}$ out of N_m trials, so the accuracy rate is y_m/N_m. We assume $y_m \sim \text{Bin}(N_m, \theta_m)$, so we are interested in $p(\Delta|\mathcal{D})$, where $\Delta = \theta_1 - \theta_2$, and $\mathcal{D} = (y_1, N_1, y_2, N_2)$ is all the data.

If we use a uniform prior for θ_1 and θ_2 (i.e., $p(\theta_j) = \text{Beta}(\theta_j|1, 1)$), the posterior is given by

$$p(\theta_1, \theta_2|\mathcal{D}) = \text{Beta}(\theta_1|y_1 + 1, N_1 - y_1 + 1)\text{Beta}(\theta_2|y_2 + 1, N_2 - y_2 + 1)$$

The posterior for Δ is given by

$$p(\Delta|\mathcal{D}) = \int_0^1 \int_0^1 \mathbb{I}(\Delta = \theta_1 - \theta_2)\, p(\theta_1|\mathcal{D}_1)p(\theta_2|\mathcal{D}_2)$$

$$= \int_0^1 \text{Beta}(\theta_1|y_1 + 1, N_1 - y_1 + 1)\text{Beta}(\theta_1 - \Delta|y_2 + 1, N_2 - y_2 + 1)d\theta_1$$

We can then evaluate this for any value of Δ that we choose. For example, we can compute

$$p(\Delta > \epsilon|\mathcal{D}) = \int_\epsilon^\infty p(\Delta|\mathcal{D})d\Delta \tag{5.63}$$

(We can compute this using 1 dimensional numerical integration or analytically [Coo05].) This is called a **Bayesian χ^2-test**.

Note that this kind of problem arises in many applications, not just evaluating classifiers, For example, suppose the two groups are different companies selling the same product on Amazon, and y_m is the number of positive reviews for merchant m. Or suppose the two groups correspond to men and women, and y_m is the number of people in group m who are left handed, and $N_m - y_m$ to be

	LH	RH	
Male	9	43	$N_1 = 52$
Female	4	44	$N_2 = 48$
Totals	13	87	100

Table 5.7: A 2×2 contingency table from http://en.wikipedia.org/wiki/Contingency_table. The MLEs for the left handedness rate in males and females are $\hat{\theta}_1 = 9/52 = 0.1731$ and $\hat{\theta}_2 = 4/48 = 0.0417$.

the number who are right handed.[3] We can represent the data as a 2×2 **contingency table** of counts, as shown in Table 5.7.

The MLEs for the left handedness rate in males and females are $\hat{\theta}_1 = 9/52 = 0.1731$ and $\hat{\theta}_2 = 4/48 = 0.0417$. It seems that there is a difference, but the sample size is low, so we cannot be sure. Hence we will represent our uncertainty by computing $p(\Delta|\mathcal{D})$, where $\Delta = \theta_1 - \theta_2$ and $\mathcal{D}$ is the table of counts. We find $p(\theta_1 > \theta_2|\mathcal{D}) = \int_0^\infty p(\Delta|\mathcal{D}) = 0.901$, which suggests that left handedness is more common in males, consistent with other studies [PP+20].

5.3   Frequentist decision theory

In this section, we discuss **frequentist decision theory**. This is similar to Bayesian decision theory, discussed in Section 5.1, but differs in that there is no prior, and hence no posterior, over the unknown state of nature. Consequently we cannot define the risk as the posterior expected loss. We will consider other definitions in Section 5.3.1.

5.3.1   Computing the risk of an estimator

We define the frequentist **risk** of an estimator δ given an unknown state of nature $\boldsymbol{\theta}$ to be the expected loss when applying that estimator to data $\boldsymbol{x}$ sampled from the likelihood function $p(\boldsymbol{x}|\boldsymbol{\theta})$:

$$R(\boldsymbol{\theta}, \delta) \triangleq \mathbb{E}_{p(\boldsymbol{x}|\boldsymbol{\theta})} \left[\ell(\boldsymbol{\theta}, \delta(\boldsymbol{x})) \right] \tag{5.64}$$

We give an example of this in Section 5.3.1.1.

5.3.1.1   Example

Let us give an example, based on [BS94]. Consider the problem of estimating the mean of a Gaussian. We assume the data is sampled from $x_n \sim \mathcal{N}(\theta^*, \sigma^2 = 1)$, and we let $\boldsymbol{x} = (x_1, \ldots, x_N)$. If we use quadratic loss, $\ell_2(\theta, \hat{\theta}) = (\theta - \hat{\theta})^2$, the corresponding risk function is the MSE.

We now consider 5 different estimators for computing θ:

- $\delta_1(\boldsymbol{x}) = \overline{x}$, the sample mean.

- $\delta_2(\boldsymbol{x}) = \text{median}(\boldsymbol{x})$, the sample median.

- $\delta_3(\boldsymbol{x}) = \theta_0$, a fixed value

---

3. This example is based on the following blog post by Bob Carpenter: https://bit.ly/2FykD1C.

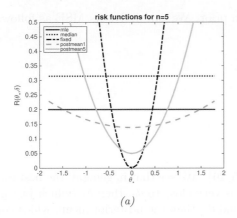 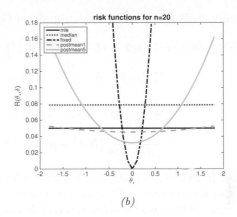

(a)   *(b)*

Figure 5.8: Risk functions for estimating the mean of a Gaussian. Each curve represents $R(\hat{\theta}_i(\cdot), \theta^*)$ plotted vs θ^*, where i indexes the estimator. Each estimator is applied to N samples from $\mathcal{N}(\theta^*, \sigma^2 = 1)$. The dark blue horizontal line is the sample mean (MLE); the red line horizontal line is the sample median; the black curved line is the estimator $\hat{\theta} = \theta_0 = 0$; the green curved line is the posterior mean when $\kappa = 1$; the light blue curved line is the posterior mean when $\kappa = 5$. (a) $N = 5$ samples. (b) $N = 20$ samples. Adapted from Figure B.1 of [BS94]. Generated by riskFnGauss.ipynb.

- $\delta_\kappa(\boldsymbol{x})$, the posterior mean under a $\mathcal{N}(\theta|\theta_0, \sigma^2/\kappa)$ prior:

$$\delta_\kappa(\boldsymbol{x}) = \frac{N}{N+\kappa}\overline{x} + \frac{\kappa}{N+\kappa}\theta_0 = w\overline{x} + (1-w)\theta_0 \tag{5.65}$$

For δ_κ, we use $\theta_0 = 0$, and consider a weak prior, $\kappa = 1$, and a stronger prior, $\kappa = 5$.

Let $\hat{\theta} = \hat{\theta}(\boldsymbol{x}) = \delta(\boldsymbol{x})$ be the estimated parameter. The risk of this estimator is given by the MSE. In Section 4.7.6.3, we show that the MSE can be decomposed into squared bias plus variance:

$$\mathrm{MSE}(\hat{\theta}|\theta^*) = \mathbb{V}\left[\hat{\theta}\right] + \mathrm{bias}^2(\hat{\theta}) \tag{5.66}$$

where the bias is defined as $\mathrm{bias}(\hat{\theta}) = \mathbb{E}\left[\hat{\theta} - \theta^*\right]$. We now use this expression to derive the risk for each estimator.

δ_1 is the sample mean. This is unbiased, so its risk is

$$\mathrm{MSE}(\delta_1|\theta^*) = \mathbb{V}\left[\overline{x}\right] = \frac{\sigma^2}{N} \tag{5.67}$$

δ_2 is the sample median. This is also unbiased. Furthermore, one can show that its variance is approximately $\pi/(2N)$ (where $\pi = 3.14$) so the risk is

$$\mathrm{MSE}(\delta_2|\theta^*) = \frac{\pi}{2N} \tag{5.68}$$

δ_3 returns the constant θ_0, so its bias is $(\theta^* - \theta_0)$ and its variance is zero. Hence the risk is

$$\mathrm{MSE}(\delta_3|\theta^*) = (\theta^* - \theta_0)^2 \tag{5.69}$$

Finally, δ_4 is the posterior mean under a Gaussian prior. We can derive its MSE as follows:

$$\text{MSE}(\delta_\kappa | \theta^*) = \mathbb{E}\left[(w\bar{x} + (1-w)\theta_0 - \theta^*)^2\right] \tag{5.70}$$

$$= \mathbb{E}\left[(w(\bar{x} - \theta^*) + (1-w)(\theta_0 - \theta^*))^2\right] \tag{5.71}$$

$$= w^2 \frac{\sigma^2}{N} + (1-w)^2(\theta_0 - \theta^*)^2 \tag{5.72}$$

$$= \frac{1}{(N+\kappa)^2}\left(N\sigma^2 + \kappa^2(\theta_0 - \theta^*)^2\right) \tag{5.73}$$

These functions are plotted in Figure 5.8 for $N \in \{5, 20\}$. We see that in general, the best estimator depends on the value of θ^*, which is unknown. If θ^* is very close to θ_0, then δ_3 (which just predicts θ_0) is best. If θ^* is within some reasonable range around θ_0, then the posterior mean, which combines the prior guess of θ_0 with the actual data, is best. If θ^* is far from θ_0, the MLE is best.

5.3.1.2 Bayes risk

In general, the true state of nature $\boldsymbol{\theta}$ that generates the data $\boldsymbol{x}$ is unknown, so we cannot compute the risk given in Equation (5.64). One solution to this is to assume a prior π_0 for $\boldsymbol{\theta}$, and then average it out. This gives us the **Bayes risk**, also called the **integrated risk**:

$$R_{\pi_0}(\delta) \triangleq \mathbb{E}_{\pi_0(\boldsymbol{\theta})}\left[R(\boldsymbol{\theta}, \delta)\right] = \int d\boldsymbol{\theta}\, d\boldsymbol{x}\, \pi_0(\boldsymbol{\theta})p(\boldsymbol{x}|\boldsymbol{\theta})\ell(\boldsymbol{\theta}, \delta(\boldsymbol{x})) \tag{5.74}$$

A decision rule that minimizes the Bayes risk is known as a **Bayes estimator**. This is equivalent to the optimal policy recommended by Bayesian decision theory in Equation (5.2) since

$$\delta(\boldsymbol{x}) = \underset{a}{\operatorname{argmin}} \int d\boldsymbol{\theta}\, \pi_0(\boldsymbol{\theta})p(\boldsymbol{x}|\boldsymbol{\theta})\ell(\boldsymbol{\theta}, a) = \underset{a}{\operatorname{argmin}} \int d\boldsymbol{\theta}\, p(\boldsymbol{\theta}|\boldsymbol{x})\ell(\boldsymbol{\theta}, a) \tag{5.75}$$

Hence we see that picking the optimal action on a case-by-case basis (as in the Bayesian approach) is optimal on average (as in the frequentist approach). In other words, the Bayesian approach provides a good way of achieving frequentist goals. See [BS94, p448] for further discussion of this point.

5.3.1.3 Maximum risk

Of course the use of a prior might seem undesirable in the context of frequentist statistics. We can therefore define the **maximum risk** as follows:

$$R_{\max}(\delta) \triangleq \sup_{\boldsymbol{\theta}} R(\boldsymbol{\theta}, \delta) \tag{5.76}$$

A decision rule that minimizes the maximum risk is called a **minimax estimator**, and is denoted δ_{MM}. For example, in Figure 5.9, we see that δ_1 has lower worst-case risk than δ_2, ranging over all possible values of $\boldsymbol{\theta}$, so it is the minimax estimator.

Minimax estimators have a certain appeal. However, computing them can be hard. And furthermore, they are very pessimistic. In fact, one can show that all minimax estimators are equivalent to Bayes estimators under a **least favorable prior**. In most statistical situations (excluding game theoretic ones), assuming nature is an adversary is not a reasonable assumption.

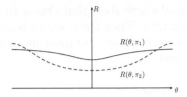

Figure 5.9: Risk functions for two decision procedures, δ_1 and δ_2. Since δ_1 has lower worst case risk, it is the minimax estimator, even though δ_2 has lower risk for most values of θ. Thus minimax estimators are overly conservative.

5.3.2 Consistent estimators

Suppose we have a dataset $\boldsymbol{x} = \{\boldsymbol{x}_n : n = 1 : N\}$ where the samples $\boldsymbol{x}_n \in \mathcal{X}$ are generated iid from a distribution $p(\mathbf{X}|\boldsymbol{\theta}^*)$, where $\boldsymbol{\theta}^* \in \Theta$ is the true parameter. Furthermore, suppose the parameters are **identifiable**, meaning that $p(\boldsymbol{x}|\boldsymbol{\theta}) = p(\boldsymbol{x}|\boldsymbol{\theta}')$ iff $\boldsymbol{\theta} = \boldsymbol{\theta}'$ for any dataset $\boldsymbol{x}$. Then we say that an estimator $\delta : \mathcal{X}^N \to \Theta$ is a **consistent estimator** if $\hat{\boldsymbol{\theta}}(\boldsymbol{x}) \to \boldsymbol{\theta}^*$ as $N \to \infty$ (where the arrow denotes convergence in probability). In other words, the procedure δ recovers the true parameter (or a subset of it) in the limit of infinite data. This is equivalent to minimizing the 0-1 loss, $\mathcal{L}(\boldsymbol{\theta}^*, \hat{\boldsymbol{\theta}}) = \mathbb{I}\left(\boldsymbol{\theta}^* \neq \hat{\boldsymbol{\theta}}\right)$. An example of a consistent estimator is the maximum likelihood estimator (MLE).

Note that an estimator can be unbiased but not consistent. For example, consider the estimator $\delta(\boldsymbol{x}) = \delta(\{\boldsymbol{x}_1, \ldots, \boldsymbol{x}_N\}) = \boldsymbol{x}_N$. This is an unbiased estimator of the true mean $\boldsymbol{\mu}$, since $\mathbb{E}\left[\delta(\boldsymbol{x})\right] = \mathbb{E}\left[\boldsymbol{x}_N\right] = \boldsymbol{\mu}$. But the sampling distribution of $\delta(\boldsymbol{x})$ does not converge to a fixed value, so it cannot converge to the point $\boldsymbol{\theta}^*$.

Although consistency is a desirable property, it is of somewhat limited usefulness in practice since most real datasets do not come from our chosen model family (i.e., there is no $\boldsymbol{\theta}^*$ such that $p(\cdot|\boldsymbol{\theta}^*)$ generates the observed data $\boldsymbol{x}$). In practice, it is more useful to find estimators that minimize some discrepancy measure between the empirical distribution and the estimated distribution. If we use KL divergence as our discrepancy measure, our estimate becomes the MLE.

5.3.3 Admissible estimators

We say that δ_1 **dominates** δ_2 if $R(\boldsymbol{\theta}, \delta_1) \leq R(\boldsymbol{\theta}, \delta_2)$ for all $\boldsymbol{\theta}$. The domination is said to be strict if the inequality is strict for some $\boldsymbol{\theta}^*$. An estimator is said to be **admissible** if it is not strictly dominated by any other estimator. Interestingly, [Wal47] proved that all admissible decision rules are equivalent to some kind of Bayesian decision rule, under some technical conditions. (See [DR21] for a more general version of this result.)

For example, in Figure 5.8, we see that the sample median (dotted red line) always has higher risk than the sample mean (solid blue line). Therefore the sample median is not an admissible estimator for the mean. More surprisingly, one can show that the sample mean is not always an admissible estimator either, even under a Gaussian likelihood model with squared error loss (this is known as **Stein's paradox** [Ste56]).

However, the concept of admissibility is of somewhat limited value. For example, let $X \sim \mathcal{N}(\theta, 1)$, and consider estimating θ under squared loss. Consider the estimator $\delta_1(x) = \theta_0$, where θ_0 is a constant *independent of the data*. We now show that this is an admissible estimator.

To see this, suppose it were not true. Then there would be some other estimator δ_2 with smaller risk, so $R(\theta^*, \delta_2) \leq R(\theta^*, \delta_1)$, where the inequality must be strict for some θ^*. Consider the risk at $\theta^* = \theta_0$. We have $R(\theta_0, \delta_1) = 0$, and

$$R(\theta_0, \delta_2) = \int (\delta_2(x) - \theta_0)^2 p(x|\theta_0) dx \tag{5.77}$$

Since $0 \leq R(\theta^*, \delta_2) \leq R(\theta^*, \delta_1)$ for all θ^*, and $R(\theta_0, \delta_1) = 0$, we have $R(\theta_0, \delta_2) = 0$ and hence $\delta_2(x) = \theta_0 = \delta_1(x)$. Thus the only way δ_2 can avoid having higher risk than δ_1 at θ_0 is by being equal to δ_1. Hence there is no other estimator δ_2 with strictly lower risk, so δ_2 is admissible.

Thus we see that the estimator $\delta_1(x) = \theta_0$ is admissible, even though it ignores the data, so is useless as an estimator. Conversely, it is possible to construct useful estimators that are not admissable (see e.g., [Jay03, Sec 13.7]).

5.4   Empirical risk minimization

In this section, we consider how to apply frequentist decision theory in the context of supervised learning.

5.4.1   Empirical risk

In standard accounts of frequentist decision theory used in statistics textbooks, there is a single unknown "state of nature", corresponding to the unknown parameters $\boldsymbol{\theta}^*$ of some model, and we define the risk as in Equation (5.64), namely $R(\delta, \boldsymbol{\theta}^*) = \mathbb{E}_{p(\mathcal{D}|\boldsymbol{\theta}^*)} [\ell(\boldsymbol{\theta}^*, \delta(\mathcal{D}))]$.

In supervised learning, we have a different unknown state of nature (namely the output y) for each input $\boldsymbol{x}$, and our estimator δ is a prediction function $\hat{\boldsymbol{y}} = f(\boldsymbol{x})$, and the state of nature is the true distribution $p^*(\boldsymbol{x}, \boldsymbol{y})$. Thus the risk of an estimator is as follows:

$$R(f, p^*) = R(f) \triangleq \mathbb{E}_{p^*(\boldsymbol{x}) p^*(\boldsymbol{y}|\boldsymbol{x})} [\ell(\boldsymbol{y}, f(\boldsymbol{x}))] \tag{5.78}$$

This is called the **population risk**, since the expectations are taken wrt the true joint distribution $p^*(\boldsymbol{x}, \boldsymbol{y})$. Of course, p^* is unknown, but we can approximate it using the empirical distribution with N samples:

$$p_{\mathcal{D}}(\boldsymbol{x}, \boldsymbol{y}|\mathcal{D}) \triangleq \frac{1}{|\mathcal{D}|} \sum_{(\boldsymbol{x}_n, \boldsymbol{y}_n) \in \mathcal{D}} \delta(\boldsymbol{x} - \boldsymbol{x}_n) \delta(\boldsymbol{y} - \boldsymbol{y}_n) \tag{5.79}$$

where $p_{\mathcal{D}}(\boldsymbol{x}, \boldsymbol{y}) = p_{\text{tr}}(\boldsymbol{x}, \boldsymbol{y})$. Plugging this in gives us the **empirical risk**:

$$R(f, \mathcal{D}) \triangleq \mathbb{E}_{p_{\mathcal{D}}(\boldsymbol{x}, \boldsymbol{y})} [\ell(\boldsymbol{y}, f(\boldsymbol{x}))] = \frac{1}{N} \sum_{n=1}^{N} \ell(\boldsymbol{y}_n, f(\boldsymbol{x}_n)) \tag{5.80}$$

Note that $R(f, \mathcal{D})$ is a random variable, since it depends on the training set.

A natural way to choose the predictor is to use

$$\hat{f}_{\text{ERM}} = \underset{f \in \mathcal{H}}{\operatorname{argmin}} R(f, \mathcal{D}) = \underset{f \in \mathcal{H}}{\operatorname{argmin}} \frac{1}{N} \sum_{n=1}^{N} \ell(\boldsymbol{y}_n, f(\boldsymbol{x}_n)) \tag{5.81}$$

where we optimize over a specific **hypothesis space** $\mathcal{H}$ of functions. This is called **empirical risk minimization (ERM)**.

5.4.1.1 Approximation error vs estimation error

In this section, we analyze the theoretical performance of functions that are fit using the ERM principle. Let $f^{**} = \mathrm{argmin}_f R(f)$ be the function that achieves the minimal possible population risk, where we optimize over all possible functions. Of course, we cannot consider all possible functions, so let us also define $f^* = \mathrm{argmin}_{f \in \mathcal{H}} R(f)$ to be the best function in our hypothesis space, $\mathcal{H}$. Unfortunately we cannot compute f^*, since we cannot compute the population risk, so let us finally define the prediction function that minimizes the empirical risk in our hypothesis space:

$$f_N^* = \underset{f \in \mathcal{H}}{\mathrm{argmin}}\, R(f, \mathcal{D}) = \underset{f \in \mathcal{H}}{\mathrm{argmin}}\, \mathbb{E}_{p_{\mathrm{tr}}}\left[\ell(\boldsymbol{y}, f(\boldsymbol{x}))\right] \tag{5.82}$$

One can show [BB08] that the risk of our chosen predictor compared to the best possible predictor can be decomposed into two terms, as follows:

$$\mathbb{E}_{p^*}\left[R(f_N^*) - R(f^{**})\right] = \underbrace{R(f^*) - R(f^{**})}_{\mathcal{E}_{\mathrm{app}}(\mathcal{H})} + \underbrace{\mathbb{E}_{p^*}\left[R(f_N^*) - R(f^*)\right]}_{\mathcal{E}_{\mathrm{est}}(\mathcal{H}, N)} \tag{5.83}$$

The first term, $\mathcal{E}_{\mathrm{app}}(\mathcal{H})$, is the **approximation error**, which measures how closely $\mathcal{H}$ can model the true optimal function f^{**}. The second term, $\mathcal{E}_{\mathrm{est}}(\mathcal{H}, N)$, is the **estimation error** or **generalization error**, which measures the difference in estimated risks due to having a finite training set. We can approximate this by the difference between the training set error and the test set error, using two empirical distributions drawn from p^*:

$$\mathbb{E}_{p^*}\left[R(f_N^*) - R(f^*)\right] \approx \mathbb{E}_{p_{\mathrm{tr}}}\left[\ell(\boldsymbol{y}, f_N^*(\boldsymbol{x}))\right] - \mathbb{E}_{p_{\mathrm{te}}}\left[\ell(\boldsymbol{y}, f_N^*(\boldsymbol{x}))\right] \tag{5.84}$$

This difference is often called the **generalization gap**.

We can decrease the approximation error by using a more expressive family of functions $\mathcal{H}$, but this usually increases the generalization error, due to overfitting. We discuss solutions to this tradeoff below.

5.4.1.2 Regularized risk

To avoid the chance of overfitting, it is common to add a complexity penalty to the objective function, giving us the **regularized empirical risk**:

$$R_\lambda(f, \mathcal{D}) = R(f, \mathcal{D}) + \lambda C(f) \tag{5.85}$$

where $C(f)$ measures the complexity of the prediction function $f(\boldsymbol{x}; \boldsymbol{\theta})$, and $\lambda \geq 0$, which is known as a **hyperparameter**, controls the strength of the complexity penalty. (We discuss how to pick λ in Section 5.4.2.)

In practice, we usually work with parametric functions, and apply the regularizer to the parameters themselves. This yields the following form of the objective:

$$R_\lambda(\boldsymbol{\theta}, \mathcal{D}) = R(\boldsymbol{\theta}, \mathcal{D}) + \lambda C(\boldsymbol{\theta}) \tag{5.86}$$

Note that, if the loss function is log loss, and the regularizer is a negative log prior, the regularized risk is given by

$$R_\lambda(\boldsymbol{\theta}, \mathcal{D}) = -\frac{1}{N} \sum_{n=1}^{N} \log p(\boldsymbol{y}_n | \boldsymbol{x}_n, \boldsymbol{\theta}) - \lambda \log p(\boldsymbol{\theta}) \tag{5.87}$$

Minimizing this is equivalent to MAP estimation.

5.4.2   Structural risk

A natural way to estimate the hyperparameters is to minimize for the lowest achievable empirical risk:

$$\hat{\lambda} = \operatorname*{argmin}_{\lambda} \min_{\boldsymbol{\theta}} R_\lambda(\boldsymbol{\theta}, \mathcal{D}) \tag{5.88}$$

(This is an example of **bilevel optimization**, also called **nested optimization**.) Unfortunately, this technique will not work, since it will always pick the least amount of regularization, i.e., $\hat{\lambda} = 0$. To see this, note that

$$\operatorname*{argmin}_{\lambda} \min_{\boldsymbol{\theta}} R_\lambda(\boldsymbol{\theta}, \mathcal{D}) = \operatorname*{argmin}_{\lambda} \min_{\boldsymbol{\theta}} R(\boldsymbol{\theta}, \mathcal{D}) + \lambda C(\boldsymbol{\theta}) \tag{5.89}$$

which is minimized by setting $\lambda = 0$. The problem is that the empirical risk underestimates the population risk, resulting in overfitting when we choose λ. This is called **optimism of the training error**.

If we knew the regularized population risk $R_\lambda(\boldsymbol{\theta})$, instead of the regularized empirical risk $R_\lambda(\boldsymbol{\theta}, \mathcal{D})$, we could use it to pick a model of the right complexity (e.g., value of λ). This is known as **structural risk minimization** [Vap98]. There are two main ways to estimate the population risk for a given model (value of λ), namely cross-validation (Section 5.4.3), and statistical learning theory (Section 5.4.4), which we discuss below.

5.4.3   Cross-validation

In this section, we discuss a simple way to estimate the population risk for a supervised learning setup. We simply partition the dataset into two, the part used for training the model, and a second part, called the **validation set** or **holdout set**, used for assessing the risk. We can fit the model on the training set, and use its performance on the validation set as an approximation to the population risk.

To explain the method in more detail, we need some notation. First we make the dependence of the empirical risk on the dataset more explicit as follows:

$$R_\lambda(\boldsymbol{\theta}, \mathcal{D}) = \frac{1}{|\mathcal{D}|} \sum_{(\boldsymbol{x}, \boldsymbol{y}) \in \mathcal{D}} \ell(\boldsymbol{y}, f(\boldsymbol{x}; \boldsymbol{\theta})) + \lambda C(\boldsymbol{\theta}) \tag{5.90}$$

Let us also define $\hat{\boldsymbol{\theta}}_\lambda(\mathcal{D}) = \operatorname{argmin}_{\boldsymbol{\theta}} R_\lambda(\mathcal{D}, \boldsymbol{\theta})$. Finally, let $\mathcal{D}_{\text{train}}$ and $\mathcal{D}_{\text{valid}}$ be a partition of $\mathcal{D}$. (Often we use about 80% of the data for the training set, and 20% for the validation set.)

For each model λ, we fit it to the training set to get $\hat{\boldsymbol{\theta}}_\lambda(\mathcal{D}_{\text{train}})$. We then use the unregularized empirical risk on the validation set as an estimate of the population risk. This is known as the **validation risk**:

$$R_\lambda^{\text{val}} \triangleq R_0(\hat{\boldsymbol{\theta}}_\lambda(\mathcal{D}_{\text{train}}), \mathcal{D}_{\text{valid}}) \tag{5.91}$$

Note that we use different data to train and evaluate the model.

The above technique can work very well. However, if the number of training cases is small, this technique runs into problems, because the model won't have enough data to train on, and we won't have enough data to make a reliable estimate of the future performance.

A simple but popular solution to this is to use **cross validation (CV)**. The idea is as follows: we split the training data into K **folds**; then, for each fold $k \in \{1, \ldots, K\}$, we train on all the folds but the k'th, and test on the k'th, in a round-robin fashion, as sketched in Figure 4.6. Formally, we have

$$R_\lambda^{\text{cv}} \triangleq \frac{1}{K} \sum_{k=1}^{K} R_0(\hat{\boldsymbol{\theta}}_\lambda(\mathcal{D}_{-k}), \mathcal{D}_k) \tag{5.92}$$

where $\mathcal{D}_k$ is the data in the k'th fold, and $\mathcal{D}_{-k}$ is all the other data. This is called the **cross-validated risk**. Figure 4.6 illustrates this procedure for $K = 5$. If we set $K = N$, we get a method known as **leave-one-out cross-validation**, since we always train on $N - 1$ items and test on the remaining one.

We can use the CV estimate as an objective inside of an optimization routine to pick the optimal hyperparameter, $\hat{\lambda} = \operatorname{argmin}_\lambda R_\lambda^{\text{cv}}$. Finally we combine all the available data (training and validation), and re-estimate the model parameters using $\hat{\boldsymbol{\theta}} = \operatorname{argmin}_{\boldsymbol{\theta}} R_{\hat{\lambda}}(\boldsymbol{\theta}, \mathcal{D})$.

5.4.4 Statistical learning theory *

The principal problem with cross validation is that it is slow, since we have to fit the model multiple times. This motivates the desire to compute analytic approximations or bounds on the population risk. This is studied in the field of **statistical learning theory** (SLT) (see e.g., [Vap98]).

More precisely, the goal of SLT is to upper bound the generalization error with a certain probability. If the bound is satisfied, then we can be confident that a hypothesis that is chosen by minimizing the empirical risk will have low population risk. In the case of binary classifiers, this means the hypothesis will make the correct predictions; in this case we say it is **probably approximately correct**, and that the hypothesis class is **PAC learnable** (see e.g., [KV94] for details).

5.4.4.1 Bounding the generalization error

In this section, we establish conditions under which we can prove that a hypothesis class is PAC learnable. Let us initially consider the case where the hypothesis space is finite, with size $\dim(\mathcal{H}) = |\mathcal{H}|$. In other words, we are selecting a hypothesis from a finite list, rather than optimizing real-valued parameters. In this case, we can prove the following.

Theorem 5.4.1. *For any data distribution p^*, and any dataset $\mathcal{D}$ of size N drawn from p^*, the probability that the generalization error of a binary classifier will be more than ϵ, in the worst case,* *is upper bounded as follows:*

$$P\left(\max_{h\in\mathcal{H}}|R(h)-R(h,\mathcal{D})|>\epsilon\right)\leq 2\dim(\mathcal{H})e^{-2N\epsilon^2} \tag{5.93}$$

where $R(h,\mathcal{D})=\frac{1}{N}\sum_{i=1}^{N}\mathbb{I}\left(f(\boldsymbol{x}_i)\neq y_i^*\right)$ is the empirical risk, and $R(h)=\mathbb{E}\left[\mathbb{I}\left(f(\boldsymbol{x})\neq y^*\right)\right]$ is the population risk.

Proof. Before we prove this, we introduce two useful results. First, **Hoeffding's inequality**, which states that if $E_1,\ldots,E_N\sim\mathrm{Ber}(\theta)$, then, for any $\epsilon>0$,

$$P(|\overline{E}-\theta|>\epsilon)\leq 2e^{-2N\epsilon^2} \tag{5.94}$$

where $\overline{E}=\frac{1}{N}\sum_{i=1}^{N}E_i$ is the empirical error rate, and θ is the true error rate. Second, the **union bound**, which says that if $A_1,\ldots,A_d$ are a set of events, then $P(\cup_{i=1}^{d}A_i)\leq\sum_{i=1}^{d}P(A_i)$. Using these results, we have

$$P\left(\max_{h\in\mathcal{H}}|R(h)-R(h,\mathcal{D})|>\epsilon\right)=P\left(\bigcup_{h\in\mathcal{H}}|R(h)-R(h,\mathcal{D})|>\epsilon\right) \tag{5.95}$$

$$\leq\sum_{h\in\mathcal{H}}P\left(|R(h)-R(h,\mathcal{D})|>\epsilon\right) \tag{5.96}$$

$$\leq\sum_{h\in\mathcal{H}}2e^{-2N\epsilon^2}=2\dim(\mathcal{H})e^{-2N\epsilon^2} \tag{5.97}$$

$\square$

This bound tells us that the optimism of the training error increases with $\dim(\mathcal{H})$ but decreases with $N=|\mathcal{D}|$, as is to be expected.

5.4.4.2   VC dimension

If the hypothesis space $\mathcal{H}$ is infinite (e.g., we have real-valued parameters), we cannot use $\dim(\mathcal{H})=|\mathcal{H}|$. Instead, we can use a quantity called the **VC dimension** of the hypothesis class, named after Vapnik and Chervonenkis; this measures the degrees of freedom (effective number of parameters) of the hypothesis class. See e.g., [Vap98] for the details.

Unfortunately, it is hard to compute the VC dimension for many interesting models, and the upper bounds are usually very loose, making this approach of limited practical value. However, various other, more practical, estimates of generalization error have recently been devised, especially for DNNs, such as [Jia+20].

5.5   Frequentist hypothesis testing *

Suppose we have two hypotheses, known as the **null hypothesis** H_0 and an **alternative hypothesis** H_1, and we want to choose the one we think is correct on the basis of a dataset $\mathcal{D}$. We could use a Bayesian approach and compute the Bayes factor $p(H_0|\mathcal{D})/p(H_1|\mathcal{D})$, as we discussed in Section 5.2.1. However, this requires integrating over all possible parameterizations of the models H_0 and H_1, which can be computationally difficult, and which can be sensitive to the choice of prior. In this section, we consider a frequentist approach to the problem.

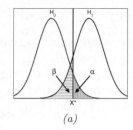
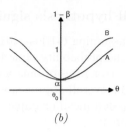

(a)   (b)

Figure 5.10: (a) Illustration of the Neyman-Pearson hypothesis testing paradigm. Generated by neyman-Pearson2.ipynb. (b) Two hypothetical two-sided power curves. B dominates A. Adapted from Figure 6.3.5 of [LM86]. Generated by twoPowerCurves.ipynb.

5.5.1 Likelihood ratio test

If we use 0-1 loss, and assume $p(H_0) = p(H_1)$, then the optimal decision rule is to accept H_0 iff $\frac{p(\mathcal{D}|H_0)}{p(\mathcal{D}|H_1)} > 1$. This is called the **likelihood ratio test**. We give some examples of this below.

5.5.1.1 Example: comparing Gaussian means

Suppose we are interested in testing whether some data comes from a Gaussian with mean μ_0 or from a Gaussian with mean μ_1. (We assume a known shared variance σ^2.) This is illustrated in Figure 5.10a, where we plot $p(x|H_0)$ and $p(x|H_1)$. We can derive the likelihood ratio as follows:

$$\frac{p(\mathcal{D}|H_0)}{p(\mathcal{D}|H_1)} = \frac{\exp\left(-\frac{1}{2\sigma^2}\sum_{n=1}^{N}(x_n - \mu_0)^2\right)}{\exp\left(-\frac{1}{2\sigma^2}\sum_{n=1}^{N}(x_n - \mu_1)^2\right)} \tag{5.98}$$

$$= \exp\left(\frac{1}{2\sigma^2}(2N\bar{x}(\mu_0 - \mu_1) + N\mu_1^2 - N\mu_0^2)\right) \tag{5.99}$$

We see that this ratio only depends on the observed data via its mean, $\bar{x}$. This is an example of a **test statistic** test($\mathcal{D}$), which is a scalar sufficient statistic for hypothesis testing. From Figure 5.10a, we can see that $\frac{p(\mathcal{D}|H_0)}{p(\mathcal{D}|H_1)} > 1$ iff $\bar{x} < x^*$, where x^* is the point where the two pdf's intersect (we are assuming this point is unique).

5.5.1.2 Simple vs compound hypotheses

In Section 5.5.1.1, the parameters for the null and alternative hypotheses were either fully specified (μ_0 and μ_1) or shared (σ^2). This is called a **simple hypothesis** test. In general, a hypothesis might not fully specify all the parameters; this is called a **compound hypothesis**. In this case, we should integrate out these unknown parameters, as in the Bayesian approach, since a hypothesis with more parameters will always have higher likelihood. As an approximation, we can "maximize them out", which gives us the maximum likelihood ratio test:

$$\frac{p(H_0|\mathcal{D})}{p(H_1|\mathcal{D})} = \frac{\int_{\boldsymbol{\theta} \in H_0} p(\boldsymbol{\theta})p_{\boldsymbol{\theta}}(\mathcal{D})}{\int_{\boldsymbol{\theta} \in H_1} p(\boldsymbol{\theta})p_{\boldsymbol{\theta}}(\mathcal{D})} \approx \frac{\max_{\boldsymbol{\theta} \in H_0} p_{\boldsymbol{\theta}}(\mathcal{D})}{\max_{\boldsymbol{\theta} \in H_1} p_{\boldsymbol{\theta}}(\mathcal{D})} \tag{5.100}$$

5.5.2   Null hypothesis significance testing (NHST)

Rather than assuming 0-1 loss, it is conventional to design the decision rule so that it has a **type I error rate** (the probability of accidentally rejecting the null hypothesis H_0) of α. (See Section 5.1.3 for details on error rates of binary decision rules.) The error rate α is called the **significance** of the test. Hence the overall approach is called **null hypothesis significance testing** or **NHST**.

In our Gaussian mean example, we see from Figure 5.10a that the type I error rate is the vertical shaded blue area:

$$\alpha(\mu_0) = p(\text{reject } H_0 | H_0 \text{ is true}) \tag{5.101}$$

$$= p(\overline{X}(\tilde{\mathcal{D}}) > x^* | \tilde{\mathcal{D}} \sim H_0) \tag{5.102}$$

$$= p\left(\frac{\overline{X} - \mu_0}{\sigma/\sqrt{N}} > \frac{x^* - \mu_0}{\sigma/\sqrt{N}} \right) \tag{5.103}$$

Hence $x^* = z_\alpha \sigma / \sqrt{N} + \mu_0$, where z_α is the upper α quantile of the standard Normal.

The type II error rate is the probability we accidentally accept the null when the alternative is true:

$$\beta(\mu_1) = p(\text{type II error}) = p(\text{accept } H_0 | H_1 \text{ is true}) = p(\text{test}(\tilde{\mathcal{D}}) < \text{test}^* | \tilde{\mathcal{D}} \sim H_1) \tag{5.104}$$

This is shown by the horizontal shaded red area in Figure 5.10a. We define the **power** of a test as $1 - \beta(\mu_1)$; this is the probability that we reject H_0 given that H_1 is true. In other words, it is the ability to correctly recognize that the null hypothesis is wrong. Clearly the least power occurs if $\mu_1 = \mu_0$ (so the curves overlap); in this case, we have $1 - \beta(\mu_1) = \alpha(\mu_0)$. As μ_1 and μ_0 become further apart, the power approaches 1 (because the shaded red area gets smaller, $\beta \to 0$). If we have two tests, A and B, where $\text{power}(B) \geq \text{power}(A)$ for the same type I error rate, we say B **dominates** A. See Figure 5.10b. A test with highest power under H_1 amongst all tests with significance level α is called a **most powerful test**. It turns out that the likelihood ratio test is a most powerful test, a result known as the **Neyman-Pearson lemma**.

5.5.3   p-values

When we reject H_0 we often say the result is **statistically significant** at level α. However, the result may be statistically significant but not practically significant, depending on how far from the decision boundary the test statistic is.

Rather than arbitrarily declaring a result as significant or not, it is preferable to quote the **p-value**. This is defined as the probability, under the null hypothesis, of observing a test statistic that is as large or larger than that actually observed:

$$\text{pval}(\text{test}(\mathcal{D})) \triangleq \Pr(\text{test}(\tilde{\mathcal{D}}) \geq \text{test}(\mathcal{D}) | \tilde{\mathcal{D}} \sim H_0) \tag{5.105}$$

In other words, $\text{pval}(\text{test}_{\text{obs}}) \triangleq \Pr(\text{test}_{\text{null}} \geq \text{test}_{\text{obs}})$, where $\text{test}_{\text{obs}} = \text{test}(\mathcal{D})$ and $\text{test}_{\text{null}} = \text{test}(\tilde{\mathcal{D}})$, where $\tilde{\mathcal{D}} \sim H_0$ is hypothetical future data. To see the connection with hypothesis testing, suppose we pick a decision threshold t^* such that $\Pr(\text{test}(\tilde{\mathcal{D}}) \geq t^* | H_0) = \alpha$. If we set $t^* = \text{test}(\mathcal{D})$, then $\alpha = \text{pval}(\text{test}(\mathcal{D}))$.

Thus if we only accept hypotheses where the p-value is less than $\alpha = 0.05$, then 95% of the time we will correctly reject the null hypothesis. However, this does *not* mean that the alternative hypothesis

H_1 is true with probability 0.95. Indeed, even most scientists misinterpret p-values.[4] The quantity that most people want to compute is the Bayesian posterior $p(H_1|\mathcal{D}) = 0.95$. For more on this important distinction, see Section 5.5.4.

5.5.4 p-values considered harmful

A p-value is often interpreted as the likelihood of the data under the null hypothesis, so small values are interpreted to mean that H_0 is unlikely, and therefore that H_1 is likely. The reasoning is roughly as follows:

> If H_0 is true, then this test statistic would probably not occur. This statistic did occur. Therefore H_0 is probably false.

However, this is invalid reasoning. To see why, consider the following example (from [Coh94]):

> If a person is an American, then he is probably not a member of Congress. This person is a member of Congress. Therefore he is probably not an American.

This is obviously fallacious reasoning. By contrast, the following logical argument is valid reasoning:

> If a person is a Martian, then he is not a member of Congress. This person is a member of Congress. Therefore he is not a Martian.

The difference between these two cases is that the Martian example is using **deduction**, that is, reasoning forward from logical definitions to their consequences. More precisely, this example uses a rule from logic called **modus tollens**, in which we start out with a definition of the form $P \Rightarrow Q$; when we observe $\neg Q$, we can conclude $\neg P$. By contrast, the American example concerns **induction**, that is, reasoning backwards from observed evidence to probable (but not necessarily true) causes using statistical regularities, not logical definitions.

To perform induction, we need to use probabilistic inference (as explained in detail in [Jay03]). In particular, to compute the probability of the null hypothesis, we should use Bayes rule, as follows:

$$p(H_0|\mathcal{D}) = \frac{p(\mathcal{D}|H_0)p(H_0)}{p(\mathcal{D}|H_0)p(H_0) + p(\mathcal{D}|H_1)p(H_1)} \tag{5.106}$$

If the prior is uniform, so $p(H_0) = p(H_1) = 0.5$, this can be rewritten in terms of the **likelihood ratio** $LR = p(\mathcal{D}|H_0)/p(\mathcal{D}|H_1)$ as follows:

$$p(H_0|\mathcal{D}) = \frac{LR}{LR+1} \tag{5.107}$$

In the American Congress example, $\mathcal{D}$ is the observation that the person is a member of Congress. The null hypothesis H_0 is that the person is American, and the alternative hypothesis H_1 is that the person is not American. We assume that $p(\mathcal{D}|H_0)$ is low, since most Americans are not members of Congress. However, $p(\mathcal{D}|H_1)$ is also low — in fact, in this example, it is 0, since only Americans can be members of Congress. Hence $LR = \infty$, so $p(H_0|\mathcal{D}) = 1.0$, as intuition suggests. Note, however, that NHST ignores $p(\mathcal{D}|H_1)$ as well as the prior $p(H_0)$, so it gives the wrong results — not just in this problem, but in many problems.

---

4. See e.g., `https://fivethirtyeight.com/features/not-even-scientists-can-easily-explain-p-values/`.

	Ineffective	Effective	
"Not significant"	171	4	175
"Significant"	9	16	25
	180	20	200

Table 5.8: Some statistics of a hypothetical clinical trial. Source: [SAM04, p74].

In general there can be huge differences between p-values and $p(H_0|\mathcal{D})$. In particular, [SBB01] show that even if the p-value is as low as 0.05, the posterior probability of H_0 can be as high as 30% or more, even with a uniform prior.

Consider this concrete example from [SAM04, p74]. Suppose 200 clinical trials are carried out for some drug, and we get the data in Table 5.8. Suppose we perform a statistical test of whether the drug has a significant effect or not. The test has a type I error rate of $\alpha = 9/180 = 0.05$ and a type II error rate of $\beta = 4/20 = 0.2$.

We can compute the probability that the drug is not effective, given that the result is supposedly "significant", as follows:

$$p(H_0|\text{'significant'}) = \frac{p(\text{'significant'}|H_0)p(H_0)}{p(\text{'significant'}|H_0)p(H_0) + p(\text{'significant'}|H_1)p(H_1)} \tag{5.108}$$

$$= \frac{p(\text{type I error})p(H_0)}{p(\text{type I error})p(H_0) + (1 - p(\text{type II error}))p(H_1)} \tag{5.109}$$

$$= \frac{\alpha p(H_0)}{\alpha p(H_0) + (1 - \beta)p(H_1)} \tag{5.110}$$

If we have prior knowledge, based on past experience, that most (say 90%) drugs are ineffective, then we find $p(H_0|\text{'significant'}) = 0.36$, which is much more than the 5% probability people usually associate with a p-value of $\alpha = 0.05$.

Thus we should distrust claims of statistical significance if they violate our prior knowledge.

5.5.5 Why isn't everyone a Bayesian?

In Section 4.7.5 and Section 5.5.4, we have seen that inference based on frequentist principles can exhibit various forms of counter-intuitive behavior that can sometimes contradict common sense reason, as has been pointed out in multiple articles (see e.g., [Mat98; MS11; Kru13; Gel16; Hoe+14; Lyu+20; Cha+19b; Cla21]).

The fundamental reason for these problems is that frequentist inference violates the **likelihood principle** [BW88], which says that inference should be based on the likelihood of the observed data, not on hypothetical future data that you have not observed. Bayes obviously satisfies the likelihood principle, and consequently does not suffer from these pathologies.

Given these fundamental flaws of frequentist statistics, and the fact that Bayesian methods do not have such flaws, an obvious question to ask is: "Why isn't everyone a Bayesian?" The (frequentist) statistician Bradley Efron wrote a paper with exactly this title [Efr86]. His short paper is well worth reading for anyone interested in this topic. Below we quote his opening section:

The title is a reasonable question to ask on at least two counts. First of all, everyone used to

Figure 5.11: Cartoon illustrating the difference between frequentists and Bayesians. (The $p < 0.05$ comment is explained in Section 5.5.4. The betting comment is a reference to the Dutch book theorem, which essentially proves that the Bayesian approach to gambling (and other decision theory problems) is optimal, as explained in e.g., [Háj08].) From `https://xkcd.com/1132/`. *Used with kind permission of Rundall Munroe (author of xkcd).*

be a Bayesian. Laplace wholeheartedly endorsed Bayes's formulation of the inference problem, and most 19th-century scientists followed suit. This included Gauss, whose statistical work is usually presented in frequentist terms.

A second and more important point is the cogency of the Bayesian argument. Modern statisticians, following the lead of Savage and de Finetti, have advanced powerful theoretical arguments for preferring Bayesian inference. A byproduct of this work is a disturbing catalogue of inconsistencies in the frequentist point of view.

Nevertheless, everyone is not a Bayesian. The current era (1986) is the first century in which statistics has been widely used for scientific reporting, and in fact, 20th-century statistics is mainly non-Bayesian. However, Lindley (1975) predicts a change for the 21st century.

Time will tell whether Lindley was right. However, the trends seem to be going in this direction. For example, some journals have banned p-values [TM15; AGM19], and the journal *The American Statistician* (produced by the American Statistical Association) published a whole special issue warning about the use of p-values and NHST [WSL19].

Traditionally, computation has been a barrier to using Bayesian methods, but this is less of an issue these days, due to faster computers and better algorithms (which we will discuss in the sequel to this book, [Mur23]). Another, more fundamental, concern is that the Bayesian approach is only as correct as its modeling assumptions. However, this criticism also applies to frequentist methods, since the sampling distribution of an estimator must be derived using assumptions about the data generating mechanism. (In fact [BT73] show that the sampling distributions for the MLE for common models are identical to the posterior distributions under a noninformative prior.) Fortunately, we can check modeling assumptions empirically using cross validation (Section 4.5.5), calibration, and Bayesian model checking. We discuss these topics in the sequel to this book, [Mur23].

To summarize, it is worth quoting Donald Rubin, who wrote a paper [Rub84] called "Bayesianly Justifiable and Relevant Frequency Calculations for the Applied Statistician". In it, he writes

> The applied statistician should be Bayesian in principle and calibrated to the real world in practice. [They] should attempt to use specifications that lead to approximately calibrated procedures under reasonable deviations from [their assumptions]. [They] should avoid models that are contradicted by observed data in relevant ways — frequency calculations for hypothetical replications can model a model's adequacy and help to suggest more appropriate models.

5.6   Exercises

Exercise 5.1 [Reject option in classifiers]

(Source: [DHS01, Q2.13].) In many classification problems one has the option either of assigning x to class j or, if you are too uncertain, of choosing the **reject option**. If the cost for rejects is less than the cost of falsely classifying the object, it may be the optimal action. Let α_i mean you choose action i, for $i = 1 : C+1$, where C is the number of classes and $C+1$ is the reject action. Let $Y = j$ be the true (but unknown) **state of nature**. Define the loss function as follows

$$\lambda(\alpha_i | Y = j) = \begin{cases} 0 & \text{if } i = j \text{ and } i, j \in \{1, \ldots, C\} \\ \lambda_r & \text{if } i = C+1 \\ \lambda_s & \text{otherwise} \end{cases} \tag{5.111}$$

In other words, you incur 0 loss if you correctly classify, you incur λ_r loss (cost) if you choose the reject option, and you incur λ_s loss (cost) if you make a substitution error (misclassification).

a. Show that the minimum risk is obtained if we decide $Y = j$ if $p(Y = j|x) \geq p(Y = k|x)$ for all k (i.e., j is the most probable class) *and* if $p(Y = j|x) \geq 1 - \frac{\lambda_r}{\lambda_s}$; otherwise we decide to reject.

b. Describe qualitatively what happens as λ_r / λ_s is increased from 0 to 1 (i.e., the relative cost of rejection increases).

Exercise 5.2 [Newsvendor problem *]

Consider the following classic problem in decision theory / economics. Suppose you are trying to decide how much quantity Q of some product (e.g., newspapers) to buy to maximize your profits. The optimal amount will depend on how much demand D you think there is for your product, as well as its cost to you C and its selling price P. Suppose D is unknown but has pdf $f(D)$ and cdf $F(D)$. We can evaluate the expected profit by considering two cases: if $D > Q$, then we sell all Q items, and make profit $\pi = (P - C)Q$; but if $D < Q$, we only sell D items, at profit $(P - C)D$, but have wasted $C(Q - D)$ on the unsold items. So the expected profit if we buy quantity Q is

$$E\pi(Q) = \int_Q^\infty (P - C)Q f(D) dD + \int_0^Q (P - C)D f(D) dD - \int_0^Q C(Q - D) f(D) dD \tag{5.112}$$

Simplify this expression, and then take derivatives wrt Q to show that the optimal quantity Q^* (which maximizes the expected profit) satisfies

$$F(Q^*) = \frac{P - C}{P} \tag{5.113}$$

Exercise 5.3 [Bayes factors and ROC curves *]

Let $B = p(D|H_1)/p(D|H_0)$ be the Bayes factor in favor of model 1. Suppose we plot two ROC curves, one computed by thresholding B, and the other computed by thresholding $p(H_1|D)$. Will they be the same or different? Explain why.

Exercise 5.4 [Posterior median is optimal estimate under L1 loss]

Prove that the posterior median is the optimal estimate under L1 loss.

6 Information Theory

In this chapter, we introduce a few basic concepts from the field of **information theory**. More details can be found in other books such as [Mac03; CT06], as well as the sequel to this book, [Mur23].

6.1 Entropy

The **entropy** of a probability distribution can be interpreted as a measure of uncertainty, or lack of predictability, associated with a random variable drawn from a given distribution, as we explain below.

We can also use entropy to define the **information content** of a data source. For example, suppose we observe a sequence of symbols $X_n \sim p$ generated from distribution p. If p has high entropy, it will be hard to predict the value of each observation X_n. Hence we say that the dataset $\mathcal{D} = (X_1, \ldots, X_n)$ has high information content. By contrast, if p is a degenerate distribution with 0 entropy (the minimal value), then every X_n will be the same, so $\mathcal{D}$ does not contain much information. (All of this can be formalized in terms of data compression, as we discuss in the sequel to this book.)

6.1.1 Entropy for discrete random variables

The entropy of a discrete random variable X with distribution p over K states is defined by

$$\mathbb{H}(X) \triangleq -\sum_{k=1}^{K} p(X = k) \log_2 p(X = k) = -\mathbb{E}_X [\log p(X)] \tag{6.1}$$

(Note that we use the notation $\mathbb{H}(X)$ to denote the entropy of the rv with distribution p, just as people write $\mathbb{V}[X]$ to mean the variance of the distribution associated with X; we could alternatively write $\mathbb{H}(p)$.) Usually we use log base 2, in which case the units are called **bits** (short for binary digits). For example, if $X \in \{1, \ldots, 5\}$ with histogram distribution $p = [0.25, 0.25, 0.2, 0.15, 0.15]$, we find $H = 2.29$ bits. If we use log base e, the units are called **nats**.

The discrete distribution with **maximum entropy** is the uniform distribution. Hence for a K-ary random variable, the entropy is maximized if $p(x = k) = 1/K$; in this case, $\mathbb{H}(X) = \log_2 K$. To see this, note that

$$\mathbb{H}(X) = -\sum_{k=1}^{K} \frac{1}{K} \log(1/K) = -\log(1/K) = \log(K) \tag{6.2}$$

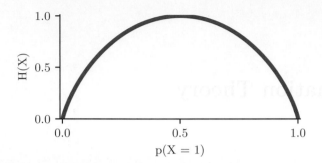

Figure 6.1: *Entropy of a Bernoulli random variable as a function of θ. The maximum entropy is $\log_2 2 = 1$. Generated by bernoulli_entropy_fig.ipynb.*

| (a) | (b) | (c) |

Figure 6.2: *(a) Some aligned DNA sequences. Each row is a sequence, each column is a location within the sequence. (b) The corresponding position weight matrix, visualized as a sequence of histograms. Each column represents a probability distribution over the alphabet $\{A, C, G, T\}$ for the corresponding location in the sequence. The size of the letter is proportional to the probability. (c) A sequence logo. See text for details. Generated by seq_logo_demo.ipynb.*

Conversely, the distribution with minimum entropy (which is zero) is any delta-function that puts all its mass on one state. Such a distribution has no uncertainty.

For the special case of binary random variables, $X \in \{0, 1\}$, we can write $p(X = 1) = \theta$ and $p(X = 0) = 1 - \theta$. Hence the entropy becomes

$$\mathbb{H}(X) = -[p(X = 1) \log_2 p(X = 1) + p(X = 0) \log_2 p(X = 0)] \tag{6.3}$$

$$= -[\theta \log_2 \theta + (1 - \theta) \log_2 (1 - \theta)] \tag{6.4}$$

This is called the **binary entropy function**, and is also written $\mathbb{H}(\theta)$. We plot this in Figure 6.1. We see that the maximum value of 1 bit occurs when the distribution is uniform, $\theta = 0.5$. A fair coin requires a single yes/no question to determine its state.

6.1.1.1   Application: DNA sequence logos

As an interesting application of entropy, consider the problem of representing **DNA sequence motifs**, which is a distribution over short DNA strings. We can estimate this distribution by aligning a set of DNA sequences (e.g., from different species), and then estimating the empirical distribution of each possible nucleotide from the 4 letter alphabet $X \sim \{A, C, G, T\}$ at each location t in the ith sequence as follows:

$$\mathbf{N}_t = \left(\sum_{i=1}^{N} \mathbb{I}(X_{it} = A), \sum_{i=1}^{N} \mathbb{I}(X_{it} = C), \sum_{i=1}^{N} \mathbb{I}(X_{it} = G), \sum_{i=1}^{N} \mathbb{I}(X_{it} = T) \right) \tag{6.5}$$

$$\hat{\boldsymbol{\theta}}_t = \mathbf{N}_t / N, \tag{6.6}$$

This $\mathbf{N}_t$ is a length four vector counting the number of times each letter appears at each location amongst the set of sequences. This $\hat{\boldsymbol{\theta}}_t$ distribution is known as a **position weight matrix** or a **sequence motif.** We can visualize this as shown in Figure 6.2b. Here we plot the letters A, C, G and T, where the size of letter k at location t is proportional to the empirical frequency θ_{tk}.

An alternative visualization, known as a **sequence logo**, is shown in Figure 6.2c. Each column is scaled by $R_t = 2 - H_t$, where H_t is the entropy of $\hat{\boldsymbol{\theta}}_t$, and $2 = \log_2(4)$ is the maximum possible entropy for a distribution over 4 letters. Thus a deterministic distribution, which has entropy 0 and thus maximal information content, has height 2. Such informative locations are highly conserved by evolution, often because they are part of a gene coding region. We can also just compute the most probable letter in each location, regardless of the uncertainty; this is called the **consensus sequence.**

6.1.1.2 Estimating entropy

Estimating the entropy of a random variable with many possible states requires estimating its distribution, which can require a lot of data. For example, imagine if X represents the identity of a word in an English document. Since there is a long tail of rare words, and since new words are invented all the time, it can be difficult to reliably estimate $p(X)$ and hence $\mathbb{H}(X)$. For one possible solution to this problem, see [VV13].

6.1.2 Cross entropy

The **cross entropy** between distribution p and q is defined by

$$\mathbb{H}_{ce}(p, q) \triangleq - \sum_{k=1}^{K} p_k \log q_k \tag{6.7}$$

One can show that the cross entropy is the expected number of bits needed to compress some data samples drawn from distribution p using a code based on distribution q. This can be minimized by setting $q = p$, in which case the expected number of bits of the optimal code is $\mathbb{H}_{ce}(p, p) = \mathbb{H}(p)$ — this is known as **Shannon's source coding theorem** (see e.g., [CT06]).

6.1.3 Joint entropy

The joint entropy of two random variables X and Y is defined as

$$\mathbb{H}(X, Y) = - \sum_{x,y} p(x, y) \log_2 p(x, y) \tag{6.8}$$

For example, consider choosing an integer from 1 to 8, $n \in \{1, \ldots, 8\}$. Let $X(n) = 1$ if n is even, and $Y(n) = 1$ if n is prime:

n	1	2	3	4	5	6	7	8
X	0	1	0	1	0	1	0	1
Y	0	1	1	0	1	0	1	0

The joint distribution is

$p(X, Y)$	$Y = 0$	$Y = 1$
$X = 0$	$\frac{1}{8}$	$\frac{3}{8}$
$X = 1$	$\frac{3}{8}$	$\frac{1}{8}$

so the joint entropy is given by

$$\mathbb{H}(X, Y) = - \left[\frac{1}{8} \log_2 \frac{1}{8} + \frac{3}{8} \log_2 \frac{3}{8} + \frac{3}{8} \log_2 \frac{3}{8} + \frac{1}{8} \log_2 \frac{1}{8} \right] = 1.81 \text{ bits} \tag{6.9}$$

Clearly the marginal probabilities are uniform: $p(X = 1) = p(X = 0) = p(Y = 0) = p(Y = 1) = 0.5$, so $\mathbb{H}(X) = \mathbb{H}(Y) = 1$. Hence $\mathbb{H}(X, Y) = 1.81$ bits $< \mathbb{H}(X) + \mathbb{H}(Y) = 2$ bits. In fact, this upper bound on the joint entropy holds in general. If X and Y are independent, then $\mathbb{H}(X, Y) = \mathbb{H}(X) + \mathbb{H}(Y)$, so the bound is tight. This makes intuitive sense: when the parts are correlated in some way, it reduces the "degrees of freedom" of the system, and hence reduces the overall entropy.

What is the lower bound on $\mathbb{H}(X, Y)$? If Y is a deterministic function of X, then $\mathbb{H}(X, Y) = \mathbb{H}(X)$. So

$$\mathbb{H}(X, Y) \geq \max\{\mathbb{H}(X), \mathbb{H}(Y)\} \geq 0 \tag{6.10}$$

Intuitively this says combining variables together does not make the entropy go down: you cannot reduce uncertainty merely by adding more unknowns to the problem, you need to observe some data, a topic we discuss in Section 6.1.4.

We can extend the definition of joint entropy from two variables to n in the obvious way.

6.1.4   Conditional entropy

The **conditional entropy** of Y given X is the uncertainty we have in Y after seeing X, averaged over possible values for X:

$$\mathbb{H}(Y|X) \triangleq \mathbb{E}_{p(X)} \left[\mathbb{H}(p(Y|X)) \right] \tag{6.11}$$

$$= \sum_x p(x) \, \mathbb{H}(p(Y|X = x)) = - \sum_x p(x) \sum_y p(y|x) \log p(y|x) \tag{6.12}$$

$$= - \sum_{x,y} p(x, y) \log p(y|x) = - \sum_{x,y} p(x, y) \log \frac{p(x, y)}{p(x)} \tag{6.13}$$

$$= - \sum_{x,y} p(x, y) \log p(x, y) + \sum_x p(x) \log p(x) \tag{6.14}$$

$$= \mathbb{H}(X, Y) - \mathbb{H}(X) \tag{6.15}$$

If Y is a deterministic function of X, then knowing X completely determines Y, so $\mathbb{H}(Y|X) = 0$. If X and Y are independent, knowing X tells us nothing about Y and $\mathbb{H}(Y|X) = \mathbb{H}(Y)$. Since

$\mathbb{H}(X, Y) \le \mathbb{H}(Y) + \mathbb{H}(X)$, we have

$$\mathbb{H}(Y|X) \le \mathbb{H}(Y) \tag{6.16}$$

with equality iff X and Y are independent. This shows that, on average, conditioning on data never increases one's uncertainty. The caveat "on average" is necessary because for any *particular* observation (value of X), one may get more "confused" (i.e., $\mathbb{H}(Y|x) > \mathbb{H}(Y)$). However, in expectation, looking at the data is a good thing to do. (See also Section 6.3.8.)

We can rewrite Equation (6.15) as follows:

$$\mathbb{H}(X_1, X_2) = \mathbb{H}(X_1) + \mathbb{H}(X_2|X_1) \tag{6.17}$$

This can be generalized to get the **chain rule for entropy**:

$$\mathbb{H}(X_1, X_2, \ldots, X_n) = \sum_{i=1}^{n} \mathbb{H}(X_i|X_1, \ldots, X_{i-1}) \tag{6.18}$$

6.1.5 Perplexity

The **perplexity** of a discrete probability distribution p is defined as

$$\text{perplexity}(p) \triangleq 2^{\mathbb{H}(p)} \tag{6.19}$$

This is often interpreted as a measure of predictability. For example, suppose p is a uniform distribution over K states. In this case, the perplexity is K. Obviously the lower bound on perplexity is $2^0 = 1$, which will be achieved if the distribution can perfectly predict outcomes.

Now suppose we have an empirical distribution based on data $\mathcal{D}$:

$$p_{\mathcal{D}}(x|\mathcal{D}) = \frac{1}{N} \sum_{n=1}^{N} \delta(x - x_n) \tag{6.20}$$

We can measure how well p predicts $\mathcal{D}$ by computing

$$\text{perplexity}(p_{\mathcal{D}}, p) \triangleq 2^{\mathbb{H}_{ce}(p_{\mathcal{D}}, p)} \tag{6.21}$$

Perplexity is often used to evaluate the quality of statistical language models, which is a generative model for sequences of tokens. Suppose the data is a single long document x of length N, and suppose p is a simple unigram model. In this case, the cross entropy term is given by

$$H = -\frac{1}{N} \sum_{n=1}^{N} \log p(x_n) \tag{6.22}$$

and hence the perplexity is given by

$$\text{perplexity}(p_{\mathcal{D}}, p) = 2^H = 2^{-\frac{1}{N} \log(\prod_{n=1}^{N} p(x_n))} = \sqrt[N]{\prod_{n=1}^{N} \frac{1}{p(x_n)}} \tag{6.23}$$

This is sometimes called the **exponentiated cross entropy**. We see that this is the geometric mean of the inverse predictive probabilities.

In the case of language models, we usually condition on previous words when predicting the next word. For example, in a bigram model, we use a first order Markov model of the form $p(x_i|x_{i-1})$. We define the **branching factor** of a language model as the number of possible words that can follow any given word. We can thus interpret the perplexity as the weighted average branching factor. For example, suppose the model predicts that each word is equally likely, regardless of context, so $p(x_i|x_{i-1}) = 1/K$. Then the perplexity is $((1/K)^N)^{-1/N} = K$. If some symbols are more likely than others, and the model correctly reflects this, its perplexity will be lower than K. However, as we show in Section 6.2, we have $\mathbb{H}(p^*) \leq \mathbb{H}_{ce}(p^*, p)$, so we can never reduce the perplexity below the entropy of the underlying stochastic process p^*.

See [JM08, p96] for further discussion of perplexity and its uses in language models.

6.1.6   Differential entropy for continuous random variables *

If X is a continuous random variable with pdf $p(x)$, we define the **differential entropy** as

$$h(X) \triangleq - \int_{\mathcal{X}} p(x) \log p(x)\, dx \tag{6.24}$$

assuming this integral exists. For example, suppose $X \sim U(0, a)$. Then

$$h(X) = - \int_0^a dx\, \frac{1}{a} \log \frac{1}{a} = \log a \tag{6.25}$$

Note that, unlike the discrete case, *differential entropy can be negative*. This is because pdf's can be bigger than 1. For example if $X \sim U(0, 1/8)$, we have $h(X) = \log_2(1/8) = -3$.

One way to understand differential entropy is to realize that all real-valued quantities can only be represented to finite precision. It can be shown [CT91, p228] that the entropy of an n-bit quantization of a continuous random variable X is approximately $h(X) + n$. For example, suppose $X \sim U(0, \frac{1}{8})$. Then in a binary representation of X, the first 3 bits to the right of the binary point must be 0 (since the number is $\leq 1/8$). So to describe X to n bits of accuracy only requires $n - 3$ bits, which agrees with $h(X) = -3$ calculated above.

6.1.6.1   Example: Entropy of a Gaussian

The entropy of a d-dimensional Gaussian is

$$h(\mathcal{N}(\boldsymbol{\mu}, \boldsymbol{\Sigma})) = \frac{1}{2} \ln |2\pi e \boldsymbol{\Sigma}| = \frac{1}{2} \ln[(2\pi e)^d |\boldsymbol{\Sigma}|] = \frac{d}{2} + \frac{d}{2} \ln(2\pi) + \frac{1}{2} \ln |\boldsymbol{\Sigma}| \tag{6.26}$$

In the 1d case, this becomes

$$h(\mathcal{N}(\mu, \sigma^2)) = \frac{1}{2} \ln \left[2\pi e \sigma^2\right] \tag{6.27}$$

6.1.6.2 Connection with variance

The entropy of a Gaussian increases monotonically as the variance increases. However, this is not always the case. For example, consider a mixture of two 1d Gaussians centered at -1 and +1. As we move the means further apart, say to -10 and +10, the variance increases (since the average distance from the overall mean gets larger). However, the entropy remains more or less the same, since we are still uncertain about where a sample might fall, even if we know that it will be near -10 or +10. (The exact entropy of a GMM is hard to compute, but a method to compute upper and lower bounds is presented in [Hub+08].)

6.1.6.3 Discretization

In general, computing the differential entropy for a continuous random variable can be difficult. A simple approximation is to **discretize** or **quantize** the variables. There are various methods for this (see e.g., [DKS95; KK06] for a summary), but a simple approach is to bin the distribution based on its empirical quantiles. The critical question is how many bins to use [LM04]. Scott [Sco79] suggested the following heuristic:

$$
B = N^{1/3} \frac{\max(\mathcal{D}) - \min(\mathcal{D})}{3.5 \sigma(\mathcal{D})} \tag{6.28}
$$

where $\sigma(\mathcal{D})$ is the empirical standard deviation of the data, and $N = |\mathcal{D}|$ is the number of datapoints in the empirical distribution. However, the technique of discretization does not scale well if X is a multi-dimensional random vector, due to the curse of dimensionality.

6.2 Relative entropy (KL divergence) *

Given two distributions p and q, it is often useful to define a **distance metric** to measure how "close" or "similar" they are. In fact, we will be more general and consider a **divergence measure** $D(p, q)$ which quantifies how far q is from p, without requiring that D be a metric. More precisely, we say that D is a divergence if $D(p, q) \geq 0$ with equality iff $p = q$, whereas a metric also requires that D be symmetric and satisfy the **triangle inequality**, $D(p, r) \leq D(p, q) + D(q, r)$. There are many possible divergence measures we can use. In this section, we focus on the **Kullback-Leibler divergence** or **KL divergence**, also known as the **information gain** or **relative entropy**, between two distributions p and q.

6.2.1 Definition

For discrete distributions, the KL divergence is defined as follows:

$$
D_{\mathbb{KL}}(p \parallel q) \triangleq \sum_{k=1}^{K} p_k \log \frac{p_k}{q_k} \tag{6.29}
$$

This naturally extends to continuous distributions as well:

$$
D_{\mathbb{KL}}(p \parallel q) \triangleq \int dx \, p(x) \log \frac{p(x)}{q(x)} \tag{6.30}
$$

6.2.2   Interpretation

We can rewrite the KL as follows:

$$D_{KL}(p \parallel q) = \underbrace{\sum_{k=1}^{K} p_k \log p_k}_{-\mathbb{H}(p)} - \underbrace{\sum_{k=1}^{K} p_k \log q_k}_{\mathbb{H}_{ce}(p,q)} \tag{6.31}$$

We recognize the first term as the negative entropy, and the second term as the cross entropy. It can be shown that the cross entropy $\mathbb{H}_{ce}(p,q)$ is a lower bound on the number of bits needed to compress data coming from distribution p if your code is designed based on distribution q; thus we can interpret the KL divergence as the "extra number of bits" you need to pay when compressing data samples if you use the incorrect distribution q as the basis of your coding scheme compared to the true distribution p.

There are various other interpretations of KL divergence. See the sequel to this book, [Mur23], for more information.

6.2.3   Example: KL divergence between two Gaussians

For example, one can show that the KL divergence between two multivariate Gaussian distributions is given by

$$D_{KL}\left(\mathcal{N}(\boldsymbol{x}|\boldsymbol{\mu}_1, \boldsymbol{\Sigma}_1) \parallel \mathcal{N}(\boldsymbol{x}|\boldsymbol{\mu}_2, \boldsymbol{\Sigma}_2)\right)$$
$$= \frac{1}{2}\left[\text{tr}(\boldsymbol{\Sigma}_2^{-1}\boldsymbol{\Sigma}_1) + (\boldsymbol{\mu}_2 - \boldsymbol{\mu}_1)^{\mathsf{T}}\boldsymbol{\Sigma}_2^{-1}(\boldsymbol{\mu}_2 - \boldsymbol{\mu}_1) - D + \log\left(\frac{\det(\boldsymbol{\Sigma}_2)}{\det(\boldsymbol{\Sigma}_1)}\right)\right] \tag{6.32}$$

In the scalar case, this becomes

$$D_{KL}\left(\mathcal{N}(x|\mu_1, \sigma_1) \parallel \mathcal{N}(x|\mu_2, \sigma_2)\right) = \log\frac{\sigma_2}{\sigma_1} + \frac{\sigma_1^2 + (\mu_1 - \mu_2)^2}{2\sigma_2^2} - \frac{1}{2} \tag{6.33}$$

6.2.4   Non-negativity of KL

In this section, we prove that the KL divergence is always non-negative.

To do this, we use **Jensen's inequality**. This states that, for any convex function f, we have that

$$f\left(\sum_{i=1}^{n} \lambda_i \boldsymbol{x}_i\right) \le \sum_{i=1}^{n} \lambda_i f(\boldsymbol{x}_i) \tag{6.34}$$

where $\lambda_i \ge 0$ and $\sum_{i=1}^{n} \lambda_i = 1$. In words, this result says that f of the average is less than the average of the f's. This is clearly true for $n = 2$, since a convex function curves up above a straight line connecting the two end points (see Section 8.1.3). To prove for general n, we can use induction.

For example, if $f(x) = \log(x)$, which is a concave function, we have

$$\log(\mathbb{E}_x g(x)) \ge \mathbb{E}_x \log(g(x)) \tag{6.35}$$

We use this result below.

Theorem 6.2.1. *(Information inequality)* $D_{\mathrm{KL}}(p \parallel q) \geq 0$ *with equality iff* $p = q$.

Proof. We now prove the theorem following [CT06, p28]. Let $A = \{x : p(x) > 0\}$ be the support of $p(x)$. Using the concavity of the log function and Jensen's inequality (Section 6.2.4), we have that

$$-D_{\mathrm{KL}}(p \parallel q) = -\sum_{x \in A} p(x) \log \frac{p(x)}{q(x)} = \sum_{x \in A} p(x) \log \frac{q(x)}{p(x)} \tag{6.36}$$

$$\leq \log \sum_{x \in A} p(x) \frac{q(x)}{p(x)} = \log \sum_{x \in A} q(x) \tag{6.37}$$

$$\leq \log \sum_{x \in \mathcal{X}} q(x) = \log 1 = 0 \tag{6.38}$$

Since $\log(x)$ is a strictly concave function ($-\log(x)$ is convex), we have equality in Equation (6.37) iff $p(x) = cq(x)$ for some c that tracks the fraction of the whole space $\mathcal{X}$ contained in A. We have equality in Equation (6.38) iff $\sum_{x \in A} q(x) = \sum_{x \in \mathcal{X}} q(x) = 1$, which implies $c = 1$. Hence $D_{\mathrm{KL}}(p \parallel q) = 0$ iff $p(x) = q(x)$ for all x. $\square$

This theorem has many important implications, as we will see throughout the book. For example, we can show that the uniform distribution is the one that maximizes the entropy:

Corollary 6.2.1. *(Uniform distribution maximizes the entropy)* $\mathbb{H}(X) \leq \log |\mathcal{X}|$, *where* $|\mathcal{X}|$ *is the number of states for* X, *with equality iff* $p(x)$ *is uniform.*

Proof. Let $u(x) = 1/|\mathcal{X}|$. Then

$$0 \leq D_{\mathrm{KL}}(p \parallel u) = \sum_x p(x) \log \frac{p(x)}{u(x)} = \log |\mathcal{X}| - \mathbb{H}(X) \tag{6.39}$$

$\square$

6.2.5 KL divergence and MLE

Suppose we want to find the distribution q that is as close as possible to p, as measured by KL divergence:

$$q^* = \arg\min_q D_{\mathrm{KL}}(p \parallel q) = \arg\min_q \int p(x) \log p(x) dx - \int p(x) \log q(x) dx \tag{6.40}$$

Now suppose p is the empirical distribution, which puts a probability atom on the observed training data and zero mass everywhere else:

$$p_{\mathcal{D}}(x) = \frac{1}{N} \sum_{n=1}^{N} \delta(x - x_n) \tag{6.41}$$

Using the sifting property of delta functions we get

$$D_{\mathrm{KL}}\left(p_{\mathcal{D}} \parallel q\right) = -\int p_{\mathcal{D}}(x) \log q(x) dx + C \tag{6.42}$$

$$= -\int \left[\frac{1}{N} \sum_n \delta(x - x_n)\right] \log q(x) dx + C \tag{6.43}$$

$$= -\frac{1}{N} \sum_n \log q(x_n) + C \tag{6.44}$$

where $C = \int p(x) \log p(x) dx$ is a constant independent of q. This is called the **cross entropy** objective, and is equal to the average negative log likelihood of q on the training set. Thus we see that minimizing KL divergence to the empirical distribution is equivalent to maximizing likelihood.

This perspective points out the flaw with likelihood-based training, namely that it puts too much weight on the training set. In most applications, we do not really believe that the empirical distribution is a good representation of the true distribution, since it just puts "spikes" on a finite set of points, and zero density everywhere else. Even if the dataset is large (say 1M images), the universe from which the data is sampled is usually even larger (e.g., the set of "all natural images" is much larger than 1M). We could smooth the empirical distribution using kernel density estimation (Section 16.3), but that would require a similar kernel on the space of images. An alternative, algorithmic approach is to use **data augmentation**, which is a way of perturbing the observed data samples in way that we believe reflects plausible "natural variation". Applying MLE on this augmented dataset often yields superior results, especially when fitting models with many parameters (see Section 19.1).

6.2.6   Forward vs reverse KL

Suppose we want to approximate a distribution p using a simpler distribution q. We can do this by minimizing $D_{\mathrm{KL}}\left(q \parallel p\right)$ or $D_{\mathrm{KL}}\left(p \parallel q\right)$. This gives rise to different behavior, as we discuss below.

First we consider the **forwards KL**, also called the **inclusive KL**, defined by

$$D_{\mathrm{KL}}\left(p \parallel q\right) = \int p(x) \log \frac{p(x)}{q(x)} dx \tag{6.45}$$

Minimizing this wrt q is known as an **M-projection** or **moment projection**.

We can gain an understanding of the optimal q by considering inputs x for which $p(x) > 0$ but $q(x) = 0$. In this case, the term $\log p(x)/q(x)$ will be infinite. Thus minimizing the KL will force q to include all the areas of space for which p has non-zero probability. Put another way, q will be **zero-avoiding** or **mode-covering**, and will typically over-estimate the support of p. Figure 6.3(a) illustrates mode covering where p is a bimodal distribution but q is unimodal.

Now consider the **reverse KL**, also called the **exclusive KL**:

$$D_{\mathrm{KL}}\left(q \parallel p\right) = \int q(x) \log \frac{q(x)}{p(x)} dx \tag{6.46}$$

Minimizing this wrt q is known as an **I-projection** or **information projection**.

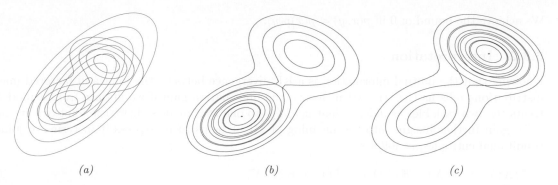

$$(a) \qquad\qquad\qquad (b) \qquad\qquad\qquad (c)$$

Figure 6.3: Illustrating forwards vs reverse KL on a bimodal distribution. The blue curves are the contours of the true distribution p. The red curves are the contours of the unimodal approximation q. (a) Minimizing forwards KL, $D_{\mathrm{KL}}(p \parallel q)$, wrt q causes q to "cover" p. (b-c) Minimizing reverse KL, $D_{\mathrm{KL}}(q \parallel p)$ wrt q causes q to "lock onto" one of the two modes of p. Adapted from Figure 10.3 of [Bis06]. Generated by KLfwdReverseMixGauss.ipynb.

We can gain an understanding of the optimal q by consider inputs x for which $p(x) = 0$ but $q(x) > 0$. In this case, the term $\log q(x)/p(x)$ will be infinite. Thus minimizing the exclusive KL will force q to exclude all the areas of space for which p has zero probability. One way to do this is for q to put probability mass in very few parts of space; this is called **zero-forcing** or **mode-seeking** behavior. In this case, q will typically under-estimate the support of p. We illustrate mode seeking when p is bimodal but q is unimodal in Figure 6.3(b-c).

6.3   Mutual information *

The KL divergence gave us a way to measure how similar two distributions were. How should we measure how dependant two random variables are? One thing we could do is turn the question of measuring the dependence of two random variables into a question about the similarity of their distributions. This gives rise to the notion of **mutual information** (MI) between two random variables, which we define below.

6.3.1   Definition

The mutual information between rv's X and Y is defined as follows:

$$\mathbb{I}(X;Y) \triangleq D_{\mathrm{KL}}(p(x,y) \parallel p(x)p(y)) = \sum_{y \in Y} \sum_{x \in X} p(x,y) \log \frac{p(x,y)}{p(x)\,p(y)} \tag{6.47}$$

(We write $\mathbb{I}(X;Y)$ instead of $\mathbb{I}(X,Y)$, in case X and/or Y represent sets of variables; for example, we can write $\mathbb{I}(X;Y,Z)$ to represent the MI between X and (Y,Z).) For continuous random variables, we just replace sums with integrals.

It is easy to see that MI is always non-negative, even for continuous random variables, since

$$\mathbb{I}(X;Y) = D_{\mathrm{KL}}(p(x,y) \parallel p(x)p(y)) \geq 0 \tag{6.48}$$

We achieve the bound of 0 iff $p(x, y) = p(x)p(y)$.

6.3.2 Interpretation

Knowing that the mutual information is a KL divergence between the joint and factored marginal distributions tells us that the MI measures the information gain if we update from a model that treats the two variables as independent $p(x)p(y)$ to one that models their true joint density $p(x, y)$.

To gain further insight into the meaning of MI, it helps to re-express it in terms of joint and conditional entropies, as follows:

$$\mathbb{I}(X; Y) = \mathbb{H}(X) - \mathbb{H}(X|Y) = \mathbb{H}(Y) - \mathbb{H}(Y|X) \tag{6.49}$$

Thus we can interpret the MI between X and Y as the reduction in uncertainty about X after observing Y, or, by symmetry, the reduction in uncertainty about Y after observing X. Incidentally, this result gives an alternative proof that conditioning, on average, reduces entropy. In particular, we have $0 \leq \mathbb{I}(X; Y) = \mathbb{H}(X) - \mathbb{H}(X|Y)$, and hence $\mathbb{H}(X|Y) \leq \mathbb{H}(X)$.

We can also obtain a different interpretation. One can show that

$$\mathbb{I}(X; Y) = \mathbb{H}(X, Y) - \mathbb{H}(X|Y) - \mathbb{H}(Y|X) \tag{6.50}$$

Finally, one can show that

$$\mathbb{I}(X; Y) = \mathbb{H}(X) + \mathbb{H}(Y) - \mathbb{H}(X, Y) \tag{6.51}$$

See Figure 6.4 for a summary of these equations in terms of an **information diagram**. (Formally, this is a signed measure mapping set expressions to their information-theoretic counterparts [Yeu91].)

6.3.3 Example

As an example, let us reconsider the example concerning prime and even numbers from Section 6.1.3. Recall that $\mathbb{H}(X) = \mathbb{H}(Y) = 1$. The conditional distribution $p(Y|X)$ is given by normalizing each row:

	Y=0	Y=1
X=0	$\frac{1}{4}$	$\frac{3}{4}$
X=1	$\frac{3}{4}$	$\frac{1}{4}$

Hence the conditional entropy is

$$\mathbb{H}(Y|X) = -\left[\frac{1}{8}\log_2\frac{1}{4} + \frac{3}{8}\log_2\frac{3}{4} + \frac{3}{8}\log_2\frac{3}{4} + \frac{1}{8}\log_2\frac{1}{4} \right] = 0.81 \text{ bits} \tag{6.52}$$

and the mutual information is

$$\mathbb{I}(X; Y) = \mathbb{H}(Y) - \mathbb{H}(Y|X) = (1 - 0.81) \text{ bits} = 0.19 \text{ bits} \tag{6.53}$$

You can easily verify that

$$\mathbb{H}(X, Y) = \mathbb{H}(X|Y) + \mathbb{I}(X; Y) + \mathbb{H}(Y|X) \tag{6.54}$$
$$= (0.81 + 0.19 + 0.81) \text{ bits} = 1.81 \text{ bits} \tag{6.55}$$

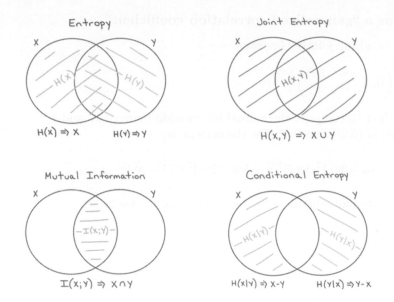

Figure 6.4: *The marginal entropy, joint entropy, conditional entropy and mutual information represented as information diagrams. Used with kind permission of Katie Everett.*

6.3.4 Conditional mutual information

We can define the **conditional mutual information** in the obvious way

$$\mathbb{I}(X;Y|Z) \triangleq \mathbb{E}_{p(Z)}\left[\mathbb{I}(X;Y)|Z\right] \tag{6.56}$$

$$= \mathbb{E}_{p(x,y,z)}\left[\log\frac{p(x,y|z)}{p(x|z)p(y|z)}\right] \tag{6.57}$$

$$= \mathbb{H}(X|Z) + \mathbb{H}(Y|Z) - \mathbb{H}(X,Y|Z) \tag{6.58}$$

$$= \mathbb{H}(X|Z) - \mathbb{H}(X|Y,Z) = \mathbb{H}(Y|Z) - \mathbb{H}(Y|X,Z) \tag{6.59}$$

$$= \mathbb{H}(X,Z) + \mathbb{H}(Y,Z) - \mathbb{H}(Z) - \mathbb{H}(X,Y,Z) \tag{6.60}$$

$$= \mathbb{I}(Y;X,Z) - \mathbb{I}(Y;Z) \tag{6.61}$$

The last equation tells us that the conditional MI is the extra (residual) information that X tells us about Y, excluding what we already knew about Y given Z alone.

We can rewrite Equation (6.61) as follows:

$$\mathbb{I}(Z,Y;X) = \mathbb{I}(Z;X) + \mathbb{I}(Y;X|Z) \tag{6.62}$$

Generalizing to N variables, we get the **chain rule for mutual information**:

$$\mathbb{I}(Z_1,\ldots,Z_N;X) = \sum_{n=1}^{N}\mathbb{I}(Z_n;X|Z_1,\ldots,Z_{n-1}) \tag{6.63}$$

6.3.5 MI as a "generalized correlation coefficient"

Suppose that (x, y) are jointly Gaussian:

$$\begin{pmatrix} x \\ y \end{pmatrix} \sim \mathcal{N}\left(\mathbf{0}, \begin{pmatrix} \sigma^2 & \rho\sigma^2 \\ \rho\sigma^2 & \sigma^2 \end{pmatrix}\right) \tag{6.64}$$

We now show how to compute the mutual information between X and Y.

Using Equation (6.26), we find that the entropy is

$$h(X, Y) = \frac{1}{2} \log\left[(2\pi e)^2 \det \Sigma\right] = \frac{1}{2} \log\left[(2\pi e)^2 \sigma^4 (1 - \rho^2)\right] \tag{6.65}$$

Since X and Y are individually normal with variance σ^2, we have

$$h(X) = h(Y) = \frac{1}{2} \log\left[2\pi e \sigma^2\right] \tag{6.66}$$

Hence

$$I(X, Y) = h(X) + h(Y) - h(X, Y) \tag{6.67}$$

$$= \log[2\pi e \sigma^2] - \frac{1}{2} \log[(2\pi e)^2 \sigma^4 (1 - \rho^2)] \tag{6.68}$$

$$= \frac{1}{2} \log[(2\pi e \sigma^2)^2] - \frac{1}{2} \log[(2\pi e \sigma^2)^2 (1 - \rho^2)] \tag{6.69}$$

$$= \frac{1}{2} \log \frac{1}{1 - \rho^2} = -\frac{1}{2} \log[1 - \rho^2] \tag{6.70}$$

We now discuss some interesting special cases.

1. $\rho = 1$. In this case, $X = Y$, and $I(X, Y) = \infty$, which makes sense. Observing Y tells us an infinite amount of information about X (as we know its real value exactly).

2. $\rho = 0$. In this case, X and Y are independent, and $I(X, Y) = 0$, which makes sense. Observing Y tells us nothing about X.

3. $\rho = -1$. In this case, $X = -Y$, and $I(X, Y) = \infty$, which again makes sense. Observing Y allows us to predict X to infinite precision.

Now consider the case where X and Y are scalar, but not jointly Gaussian. In general it can be difficult to compute the mutual information between continuous random variables, because we have to estimate the joint density $p(X, Y)$. For scalar variables, a simple approximation is to **discretize** or **quantize** them, by dividing the ranges of each variable into bins, and computing how many values fall in each histogram bin [Sco79]. We can then easily compute the MI using the empirical pmf.

Unfortunately, the number of bins used, and the location of the bin boundaries, can have a significant effect on the results. One way to avoid this is to use K-nearest neighbor distances to estimate densities in a non-parametric, adaptive way. This is the basis of the **KSG estimator** for MI proposed in [KSG04]. This is implemented in the sklearn.feature_selection.mutual_info_regression function. For papers related to this estimator, see [GOV18; HN19].

6.3.6 Normalized mutual information

For some applications, it is useful to have a normalized measure of dependence, between 0 and 1. We now discuss one way to construct such a measure.

First, note that

$$\mathbb{I}(X;Y) = \mathbb{H}(X) - \mathbb{H}(X|Y) \leq \mathbb{H}(X) \tag{6.71}$$
$$= \mathbb{H}(Y) - \mathbb{H}(Y|X) \leq \mathbb{H}(Y) \tag{6.72}$$

so

$$0 \leq \mathbb{I}(X;Y) \leq \min(\mathbb{H}(X), \mathbb{H}(Y)) \tag{6.73}$$

Therefore we can define the **normalized mutual information** as follows:

$$NMI(X,Y) = \frac{\mathbb{I}(X;Y)}{\min(\mathbb{H}(X), \mathbb{H}(Y))} \leq 1 \tag{6.74}$$

This normalized mutual information ranges from 0 to 1. When $NMI(X,Y) = 0$, we have $\mathbb{I}(X;Y) = 0$, so X and Y are independent. When $NMI(X,Y) = 1$, and $\mathbb{H}(X) < \mathbb{H}(Y)$, we have

$$\mathbb{I}(X;Y) = \mathbb{H}(X) - \mathbb{H}(X|Y) = \mathbb{H}(X) \implies \mathbb{H}(X|Y) = 0 \tag{6.75}$$

and so X is a deterministic function of Y. For example, suppose X is a discrete random variable with pmf $[0.5, 0.25, 0.25]$. We have $MI(X,X) = 1.5$ (using log base 2), and $H(X) = 1.5$, so the normalized MI is 1, as is to be expected.

For continuous random variables, it is harder to normalize the mutual information, because of the need to estimate the differential entropy, which is sensitive to the level of quantization. See Section 6.3.7 for further discussion.

6.3.7 Maximal information coefficient

As we discussed in Section 6.3.6, it is useful to have a normalized estimate of the mutual information, but this can be tricky to compute for real-valued data. One approach, known as the maximal information coefficient (MIC) [Res+11], is to define the following quantity:

$$\text{MIC}(X,Y) = \max_G \frac{\mathbb{I}((X,Y)|_G)}{\log||G||} \tag{6.76}$$

where G is the set of 2d grids, and $(X,Y)|_G$ represents a discretization of the variables onto this grid, and $||G||$ is $\min(G_x, G_y)$, where G_x is the number of grid cells in the x direction, and G_y is the number of grid cells in the y direction. (The maximum grid resolution depends on the sample size n; they suggest restricting grids so that $G_x G_y \leq B(n)$, where $B(n) = n^\alpha$, where $\alpha = 0.6$.) The denominator is the entropy of a uniform joint distribution; dividing by this ensures $0 \leq \text{MIC} \leq 1$.

The intuition behind this statistic is the following: if there is a relationship between X and Y, then there should be some discrete gridding of the 2d input space that captures this. Since we don't know the correct grid to use, MIC searches over different grid resolutions (e.g., 2x2, 2x3, etc), as well as over locations of the grid boundaries. Given a grid, it is easy to quantize the data and compute

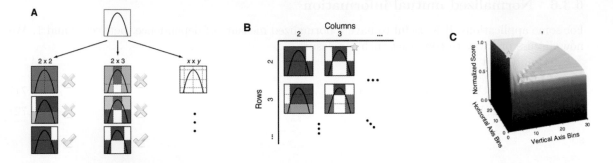

Figure 6.5: Illustration of how the maximal information coefficient (MIC) is computed. (a) We search over different grid resolutions, and grid cell locations, and compute the MI for each. (b) For each grid resolution (k, l), we define set $M(k, l)$ to be the maximum MI for any grid of that size, normalized by $\log(\min(k, l))$. (c) We visualize the matrix $\mathbf{M}$. The maximum entry (denoted by a star) is defined to be the MIC. From Figure 1 of [Res+11]. Used with kind permission of David Reshef.

MI. We define the **characteristic matrix** $M(k, l)$ to be the maximum MI achievable by any grid of size (k, l), normalized by $\log(\min(k, l))$. The MIC is then the maximum entry in this matrix, $\max_{kl \leq B(n)} M(k, l)$. See Figure 6.5 for a visualization of this process.

In [Res+11], they show that this quantity exhibits a property known as **equitability**, which means that it gives similar scores to equally noisy relationships, regardless of the type of relationship (e.g., linear, non-linear, non-functional).

In [Res+16], they present an improved estimator, called **MICe**, which is more efficient to compute, and only requires optimizing over 1d grids, which can be done in $O(n)$ time using dynamic programming. They also present another quantity, called **TICe** (total information content), that has higher power to detect relationships from small sample sizes, but lower equitability. This is defined to be $\sum_{kl \leq B(n)} M(k, l)$. They recommend using TICe to screen a large number of candidate relationships, and then using MICe to quantify the strength of the relationship. For an efficient implementation of both of these metrics, see [Alb+18].

We can interpret MIC of 0 to mean there is no relationship between the variables, and 1 to represent a noise-free relationship of any form. This is illustrated in Figure 6.6. Unlike correlation coefficients, MIC is not restricted to finding linear relationships. For this reason, the MIC has been called "a correlation for the 21st century" [Spe11].

In Figure 6.7, we give a more interesting example, from [Res+11]. The data consists of 357 variables measuring a variety of social, economic, health and political indicators, collected by the World Health Organization (WHO). On the left of the figure, we see the correlation coefficient (CC) plotted against the MIC for all 63,546 variable pairs. On the right of the figure, we see scatter plots for particular pairs of variables, which we now discuss:

- The point marked C (near 0,0 on the plot) has a low CC and a low MIC. The corresponding scatter plot makes it clear that there is no relationship between these two variables (percentage of lives lost to injury and density of dentists in the population).

- The points marked D and H have high CC (in absolute value) and high MIC, because they

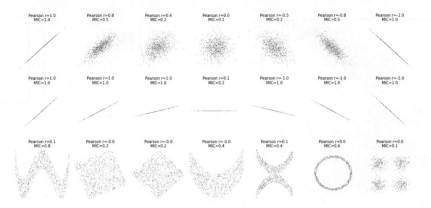

Figure 6.6: Plots of some 2d distributions and the corresponding estimate of correlation coefficient R^2 and the maximal information coefficient (MIC). Compare to Figure 3.1. Generated by MIC_correlation_2d.ipynb.

represent nearly linear relationships.

- The points marked E, F, and G have low CC but high MIC. This is because they correspond to non-linear (and sometimes, as in the case of E and F, non-functional, i.e., one-to-many) relationships between the variables.

6.3.8 Data processing inequality

Suppose we have an unknown variable X, and we observe a noisy function of it, call it Y. If we process the noisy observations in some way to create a new variable Z, it should be intuitively obvious that we cannot increase the amount of information we have about the unknown quantity, X. This is known as the **data processing inequality**. We now state this more formally, and then prove it.

Theorem 6.3.1. *Suppose $X \to Y \to Z$ forms a Markov chain, so that $X \perp Z | Y$. Then $\mathbb{I}(X; Y) \geq \mathbb{I}(X; Z)$.*

Proof. By the chain rule for mutual information (Equation (6.62)), we can expand the mutual information in two different ways:

$$\mathbb{I}(X; Y, Z) = \mathbb{I}(X; Z) + \mathbb{I}(X; Y | Z) \tag{6.77}$$
$$= \mathbb{I}(X; Y) + \mathbb{I}(X; Z | Y) \tag{6.78}$$

Since $X \perp Z | Y$, we have $\mathbb{I}(X; Z | Y) = 0$, so

$$\mathbb{I}(X; Z) + \mathbb{I}(X; Y | Z) = \mathbb{I}(X; Y) \tag{6.79}$$

Since $\mathbb{I}(X; Y | Z) \geq 0$, we have $\mathbb{I}(X; Y) \geq \mathbb{I}(X; Z)$. Similarly one can prove that $\mathbb{I}(Y; Z) \geq \mathbb{I}(X; Z)$. $\square$

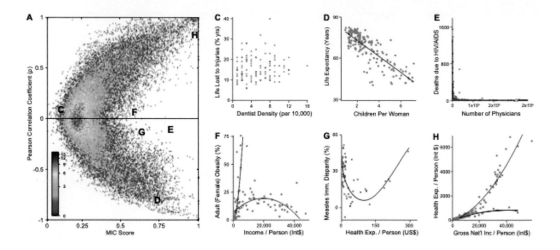

Figure 6.7: Left: Correlation coefficient vs maximal information criterion (MIC) for all pairwise relationships in the WHO data. Right: scatter plots of certain pairs of variables. The red lines are non-parametric smoothing regressions fit separately to each trend. From Figure 4 of [Res+11]. Used with kind permission of David Reshef.

6.3.9   Sufficient Statistics

An important consequence of the DPI is the following. Suppose we have the chain $\theta \to \mathcal{D} \to s(\mathcal{D})$. Then

$$\mathbb{I}\left(\theta; s(\mathcal{D})\right) \leq \mathbb{I}\left(\theta; \mathcal{D}\right) \tag{6.80}$$

If this holds with equality, then we say that $s(\mathcal{D})$ is a **sufficient statistic** of the data $\mathcal{D}$ for the purposes of inferring θ. In this case, we can equivalently write $\theta \to s(\mathcal{D}) \to \mathcal{D}$, since we can reconstruct the data from knowing $s(\mathcal{D})$ just as accurately as from knowing θ.

An example of a sufficient statistic is the data itself, $s(\mathcal{D}) = \mathcal{D}$, but this is not very useful, since it doesn't summarize the data at all. Hence we define a **minimal sufficient statistic** $s(\mathcal{D})$ as one which is sufficient, and which contains no extra information about θ; thus $s(\mathcal{D})$ maximally compresses the data $\mathcal{D}$ without losing information which is relevant to predicting θ. More formally, we say s is a *minimal* sufficient statistic for $\mathcal{D}$ if for all sufficient statistics $s'(\mathcal{D})$ there is some function f such that $s(\mathcal{D}) = f(s'(\mathcal{D}))$. We can summarize the situation as follows:

$$\theta \to s(\mathcal{D}) \to s'(\mathcal{D}) \to \mathcal{D} \tag{6.81}$$

Here $s'(\mathcal{D})$ takes $s(\mathcal{D})$ and adds redundant information to it, thus creating a one-to-many mapping.

For example, a minimal sufficient statistic for a set of N Bernoulli trials is simply N and $N_1 = \sum_n \mathbb{I}(X_n = 1)$, i.e., the number of successes. In other words, we don't need to keep track of the entire sequence of heads and tails and their ordering, we only need to keep track of the total number of heads and tails. Similarly, for inferring the mean of a Gaussian distribution with known variance we only need to know the empirical mean and number of samples.

6.3.10 Fano's inequality *

A common method for **feature selection** is to pick input features X_d which have high mutual information with the response variable Y. Below we justify why this is a reasonable thing to do. In particular, we state a result, known as **Fano's inequality**, which bounds the probability of misclassification (for any method) in terms of the mutual information between the features X and the class label Y.

Theorem 6.3.2. *(Fano's inequality) Consider an estimator $\hat{Y} = f(X)$ such that $Y \to X \to \hat{Y}$ forms a Markov chain. Let E be the event $\hat{Y} \neq Y$, indicating that an error occured, and let $P_e = P(Y \neq \hat{Y})$ be the probability of error. Then we have*

$$\mathbb{H}(Y|X) \leq \mathbb{H}\left(Y|\hat{Y}\right) \leq \mathbb{H}(E) + P_e \log |\mathcal{Y}| \tag{6.82}$$

Since $\mathbb{H}(E) \leq 1$, as we saw in Figure 6.1, we can weaken this result to get

$$1 + P_e \log |\mathcal{Y}| \geq \mathbb{H}(Y|X) \tag{6.83}$$

and hence

$$P_e \geq \frac{\mathbb{H}(Y|X) - 1}{\log |\mathcal{Y}|} \tag{6.84}$$

Thus minimizing $\mathbb{H}(Y|X)$ (which can be done by maximizing $\mathbb{I}(X;Y)$) will also minimize the lower bound on P_e.

Proof. (From [CT06, p38].) Using the chain rule for entropy, we have

$$\mathbb{H}\left(E, Y|\hat{Y}\right) = \mathbb{H}\left(Y|\hat{Y}\right) + \underbrace{\mathbb{H}\left(E|Y, \hat{Y}\right)}_{=0} \tag{6.85}$$

$$= \mathbb{H}\left(E|\hat{Y}\right) + \mathbb{H}\left(Y|E, \hat{Y}\right) \tag{6.86}$$

Since conditioning reduces entropy (see Section 6.2.4), we have $\mathbb{H}\left(E|\hat{Y}\right) \leq \mathbb{H}(E)$. The final term can be bounded as follows:

$$\mathbb{H}\left(Y|E, \hat{Y}\right) = P(E=0)\mathbb{H}\left(Y|\hat{Y}, E=0\right) + P(E=1)\mathbb{H}\left(Y|\hat{Y}, E=1\right) \tag{6.87}$$

$$\leq (1 - P_e)0 + P_e \log |\mathcal{Y}| \tag{6.88}$$

Hence

$$\mathbb{H}\left(Y|\hat{Y}\right) \leq \underbrace{\mathbb{H}\left(E|\hat{Y}\right)}_{\leq \mathbb{H}(E)} + \underbrace{\mathbb{H}\left(Y|E, \hat{Y}\right)}_{P_e \log |\mathcal{Y}|} \tag{6.89}$$

Finally, by the data processing inequality, we have $\mathbb{I}(Y; \hat{Y}) \leq \mathbb{I}(Y; X)$, so $\mathbb{H}(Y|X) \leq \mathbb{H}\left(Y|\hat{Y}\right)$, which establishes Equation (6.82). $\qquad \square$

6.4   Exercises

Exercise 6.1 [Expressing mutual information in terms of entropies *]
Prove the following identities:

$$I(X;Y) = H(X) - H(X|Y) = H(Y) - H(Y|X) \tag{6.90}$$

and

$$H(X,Y) = H(X|Y) + H(Y|X) + I(X;Y) \tag{6.91}$$

Exercise 6.2 [Relationship between $D(p||q)$ and χ^2 statistic]
(Source: [CT91, Q12.2].)
Show that, if $p(x) \approx q(x)$, then

$$D_{\mathrm{KL}}(p \parallel q) \approx \frac{1}{2}\chi^2 \tag{6.92}$$

where

$$\chi^2 = \sum_x \frac{(p(x)-q(x))^2}{q(x)} \tag{6.93}$$

Hint: write

$$p(x) = \Delta(x) + q(x) \tag{6.94}$$
$$\frac{p(x)}{q(x)} = 1 + \frac{\Delta(x)}{q(x)} \tag{6.95}$$

and use the Taylor series expansion for $\log(1+x)$.

$$\log(1+x) = x - \frac{x^2}{2} + \frac{x^3}{3} - \frac{x^4}{4} \cdots \tag{6.96}$$

for $-1 < x \le 1$.

Exercise 6.3 [Fun with entropies *]
(Source: Mackay.)
Consider the joint distribution $p(X,Y)$

		1	2	3	4
	1	1/8	1/16	1/32	1/32
y	2	1/16	1/8	1/32	1/32
	3	1/16	1/16	1/16	1/16
	4	1/4	0	0	0

a. What is the joint entropy $H(X,Y)$?
b. What are the marginal entropies $H(X)$ and $H(Y)$?
c. The entropy of X conditioned on a specific value of y is defined as

$$H(X|Y=y) = -\sum_x p(x|y)\log p(x|y) \tag{6.97}$$

Compute $H(X|y)$ for each value of y. Does the posterior entropy on X ever increase given an observation of Y?

d. The conditional entropy is defined as

$$H(X|Y) = \sum_y p(y)H(X|Y = y) \tag{6.98}$$

Compute this. Does the posterior entropy on X increase or decrease when averaged over the possible values of Y?

e. What is the mutual information between X and Y?

Exercise 6.4 [Forwards vs reverse KL divergence]

(Source: Exercise 33.7 of [Mac03].) Consider a factored approximation $q(x, y) = q(x)q(y)$ to a joint distribution $p(x, y)$. Show that to minimize the forwards KL $D_{\mathrm{KL}}(p \| q)$ we should set $q(x) = p(x)$ and $q(y) = p(y)$, i.e., the optimal approximation is a product of marginals.

Now consider the following joint distribution, where the rows represent y and the columns x.

	1	2	3	4
1	1/8	1/8	0	0
2	1/8	1/8	0	0
3	0	0	1/4	0
4	0	0	0	1/4

Show that the reverse KL $D_{\mathrm{KL}}(q \| p)$ for this p has three distinct minima. Identify those minima and evaluate $D_{\mathrm{KL}}(q \| p)$ at each of them. What is the value of $D_{\mathrm{KL}}(q \| p)$ if we set $q(x, y) = p(x)p(y)$?

7 Linear Algebra

This chapter is co-authored with Zico Kolter.

7.1 Introduction

Linear algebra is the study of matrices and vectors. In this chapter, we summarize the key material that we will need throughout the book. Much more information can be found in other sources, such as [Str09; Ips09; Kle13; Mol04; TB97; Axl15; Tho17; Agg20].

7.1.1 Notation

In this section, we define some notation.

7.1.1.1 Vectors

A **vector** $x \in \mathbb{R}^n$ is a list of n numbers, usually written as a **column vector**

$$
x = \begin{bmatrix} x_1 \\ x_2 \\ \vdots \\ x_n \end{bmatrix}. \tag{7.1}
$$

The vector of all ones is denoted $\mathbf{1}$. The vector of all zeros is denoted $\mathbf{0}$.

The **unit vector** e_i is a vector of all 0's, except entry i, which has value 1:

$$
e_i = (0, \dots, 0, 1, 0, \dots, 0) \tag{7.2}
$$

This is also called a **one-hot vector**.

7.1.1.2 Matrices

A **matrix** $\mathbf{A} \in \mathbb{R}^{m \times n}$ with m rows and n columns is a 2d array of numbers, arranged as follows:

$$
\mathbf{A} = \begin{bmatrix} a_{11} & a_{12} & \cdots & a_{1n} \\ a_{21} & a_{22} & \cdots & a_{2n} \\ \vdots & \vdots & \ddots & \vdots \\ a_{m1} & a_{m2} & \cdots & a_{mn} \end{bmatrix}. \tag{7.3}
$$

If $m = n$, the matrix is said to be **square**.

We use the notation A_{ij} or $A_{i,j}$ to denote the entry of $\mathbf{A}$ in the ith row and jth column. We use the notation $\mathbf{A}_{i,:}$ to denote the i'th row and $\mathbf{A}_{:,j}$ to denote the j'th column. We treat all vectors as column vectors by default (so $\mathbf{A}_{i,:}$ is viewed as a column vector with n entries). We use bold upper case letters to denote matrices, bold lower case letters to denote vectors, and non-bold letters to denote scalars.

We can view a matrix as a set of columns stacked along the horizontal axis:

$$\mathbf{A} = \left[\begin{array}{cccc} | & | & & | \\ \mathbf{A}_{:,1} & \mathbf{A}_{:,2} & \cdots & \mathbf{A}_{:,n} \\ | & | & & | \end{array} \right]. \tag{7.4}$$

For brevity, we will denote this by

$$\mathbf{A} = [\mathbf{A}_{:,1}, \mathbf{A}_{:,2}, \dots, \mathbf{A}_{:,n}] \tag{7.5}$$

We can also view a matrix as a set of rows stacked along the vertical axis:

$$\mathbf{A} = \left[\begin{array}{ccc} - & \mathbf{A}_{1,:}^{\mathsf{T}} & - \\ - & \mathbf{A}_{2,:}^{\mathsf{T}} & - \\ & \vdots & \\ - & \mathbf{A}_{m,:}^{\mathsf{T}} & - \end{array} \right]. \tag{7.6}$$

For brevity, we will denote this by

$$\mathbf{A} = [\mathbf{A}_{1,:}; \mathbf{A}_{2,:}; \dots; \mathbf{A}_{m,:}] \tag{7.7}$$

(Note the use of a semicolon.)

The **transpose** of a matrix results from "flipping" the rows and columns. Given a matrix $\mathbf{A} \in \mathbb{R}^{m \times n}$, its transpose, written $\mathbf{A}^{\mathsf{T}} \in \mathbb{R}^{n \times m}$, is defined as

$$(\mathbf{A}^{\mathsf{T}})_{ij} = A_{ji} \tag{7.8}$$

The following properties of transposes are easily verified:

$$(\mathbf{A}^{\mathsf{T}})^{\mathsf{T}} = \mathbf{A} \tag{7.9}$$

$$(\mathbf{A}\mathbf{B})^{\mathsf{T}} = \mathbf{B}^{\mathsf{T}}\mathbf{A}^{\mathsf{T}} \tag{7.10}$$

$$(\mathbf{A} + \mathbf{B})^{\mathsf{T}} = \mathbf{A}^{\mathsf{T}} + \mathbf{B}^{\mathsf{T}} \tag{7.11}$$

If a square matrix satisfies $\mathbf{A} = \mathbf{A}^{\mathsf{T}}$, it is called **symmetric**. We denote the set of all symmetric matrices of size n as $\mathbb{S}^n$.

7.1.1.3 Tensors

A **tensor** (in machine learning terminology) is just a generalization of a 2d array to more than 2 dimensions, as illustrated in Figure 7.1. For example, the entries of a 3d tensor are denoted by A_{ijk}.

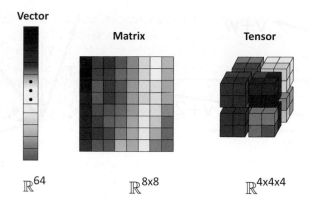

Figure 7.1: *Illustration of a 1d vector, 2d matrix, and 3d tensor. The colors are used to represent individual entries of the vector; this list of numbers can also be stored in a 2d matrix, as shown. (In this example, the matrix is layed out in column-major order, which is the opposite of that used by Python.) We can also reshape the vector into a 3d tensor, as shown.*

Figure 7.2: *Illustration of (a) row-major vs (b) column-major order. From* `https://commons.wikimedia.org/wiki/File:Row_and_column_major_order.svg`. *Used with kind permission of Wikipedia author Cmglee.*

The number of dimensions is known as the **order** or **rank** of the tensor.[1] In mathematics, tensors can be viewed as a way to define multilinear maps, just as matrices can be used to define linear functions, although we will not need to use this interpretation.

We can **reshape** a matrix into a vector by stacking its columns on top of each other, as shown in Figure 7.1. This is denoted by

$$\mathrm{vec}(\mathbf{A}) = [\mathbf{A}_{:,1}; \cdots; \mathbf{A}_{:,n}] \in \mathbb{R}^{mn \times 1} \tag{7.12}$$

Conversely, we can reshape a vector into a matrix. There are two choices for how to do this, known as **row-major order** (used by languages such as Python and C++) and **column-major order** (used by languages such as Julia, Matlab, R and Fortran). See Figure 7.2 for an illustration of the difference.

_____

1. Note, however, that the rank of a 2d matrix is a different concept, as discussed in Section 7.1.4.3.

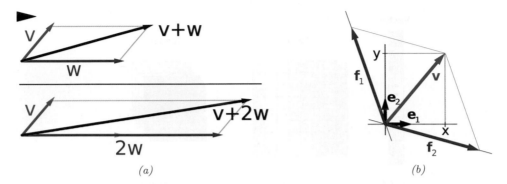

Figure 7.3: (a) Top: A vector $\boldsymbol{v}$ (blue) is added to another vector $\boldsymbol{w}$ (red). Bottom: $\boldsymbol{w}$ is stretched by a factor of 2, yielding the sum $\boldsymbol{v} + 2\boldsymbol{w}$. From https://en.wikipedia.org/wiki/Vector_space. *Used with kind permission of Wikipedia author IkamusumeFan (b) A vector $\boldsymbol{v}$ in $\mathbb{R}^2$ (blue) expressed in terms of different bases: using the standard basis of $\mathbb{R}^2$, $\boldsymbol{v} = x\boldsymbol{e}_1 + y\boldsymbol{e}_2$ (black), and using a different, non-orthogonal basis: $\boldsymbol{v} = \boldsymbol{f}_1 + \boldsymbol{f}_2$ (red). From* https://en.wikipedia.org/wiki/Vector_space. *Used with kind permission of Wikiepdia author Jakob.scholbach.*

7.1.2   Vector spaces

In this section, we discuss some fundamental concepts in linear algebra.

7.1.2.1   Vector addition and scaling

We can view a vector $\boldsymbol{x} \in \mathbb{R}^n$ as defining a point in n-dimensional Euclidean space. A **vector space** is a collection of such vectors, which can be added together, and scaled by **scalars** (1-dimensional numbers), in order to create new points. These operations are defined to operate elementwise, in the obvious way, namely $\boldsymbol{x} + \boldsymbol{y} = (x_1 + y_1, \ldots, x_n + y_n)$ and $c\boldsymbol{x} = (cx_1, \ldots, cx_n)$, where $c \in \mathbb{R}$. See Figure 7.3a for an illustration.

7.1.2.2   Linear independence, spans and basis sets

A set of vectors $\{\boldsymbol{x}_1, \boldsymbol{x}_2, \ldots \boldsymbol{x}_n\}$ is said to be **(linearly) independent** if no vector can be represented as a linear combination of the remaining vectors. Conversely, a vector which *can* be represented as a linear combination of the remaining vectors is said to be **(linearly) dependent**. For example, if

$$\boldsymbol{x}_n = \sum_{i=1}^{n-1} \alpha_i \boldsymbol{x}_i \tag{7.13}$$

for some $\{\alpha_1, \ldots, \alpha_{n-1}\}$ then $\boldsymbol{x}_n$ is dependent on $\{\boldsymbol{x}_1, \ldots, \boldsymbol{x}_{n-1}\}$; otherwise, it is independent of $\{\boldsymbol{x}_1, \ldots, \boldsymbol{x}_{n-1}\}$.

The **span** of a set of vectors $\{\boldsymbol{x}_1, \boldsymbol{x}_2, \ldots, \boldsymbol{x}_n\}$ is the set of all vectors that can be expressed as a linear combination of $\{\boldsymbol{x}_1, \ldots, \boldsymbol{x}_n\}$. That is,

$$\text{span}(\{\boldsymbol{x}_1, \ldots, \boldsymbol{x}_n\}) \triangleq \left\{ \boldsymbol{v} : \boldsymbol{v} = \sum_{i=1}^{n} \alpha_i \boldsymbol{x}_i, \ \alpha_i \in \mathbb{R} \right\}. \tag{7.14}$$

It can be shown that if $\{\boldsymbol{x}_1, \ldots, \boldsymbol{x}_n\}$ is a set of n linearly independent vectors, where each $\boldsymbol{x}_i \in \mathbb{R}^n$, then $\text{span}(\{\boldsymbol{x}_1, \ldots, \boldsymbol{x}_n\}) = \mathbb{R}^n$. In other words, *any* vector $\boldsymbol{v} \in \mathbb{R}^n$ can be written as a linear combination of $\boldsymbol{x}_1$ through $\boldsymbol{x}_n$.

A **basis** $\mathcal{B}$ is a set of linearly independent vectors that spans the whole space, meaning that $\text{span}(\mathcal{B}) = \mathbb{R}^n$. There are often multiple bases to choose from, as illustrated in Figure 7.3b. The **standard basis** uses the **coordinate vectors** $\boldsymbol{e}_1 = (1, 0, \ldots, 0)$, up to $\boldsymbol{e}_n = (0, 0, \ldots, 0, 1)$. This lets us translate back and forth between viewing a vector in $\mathbb{R}^2$ as an either an "arrow in the plane", rooted at the origin, or as an ordered list of numbers (corresponding to the coefficients for each basis vector).

7.1.2.3 Linear maps and matrices

A **linear map** or **linear transformation** is any function $f : \mathcal{V} \to \mathcal{W}$ such that $f(\boldsymbol{v} + \boldsymbol{w}) = f(\boldsymbol{v}) + f(\boldsymbol{w})$ and $f(a\,\boldsymbol{v}) = a\,f(\boldsymbol{v})$ for all $\boldsymbol{v}, \boldsymbol{w} \in \mathcal{V}$. Once the basis of $\mathcal{V}$ is chosen, a linear map $f : \mathcal{V} \to \mathcal{W}$ is completely determined by specifying the images of the basis vectors, because any element of $\mathcal{V}$ can be expressed uniquely as a linear combination of them.

Suppose $\mathcal{V} = \mathbb{R}^n$ and $\mathcal{W} = \mathbb{R}^m$. We can compute $f(\boldsymbol{v}_i) \in \mathbb{R}^m$ for each basis vector in $\mathcal{V}$, and store these along the columns of an $m \times n$ matrix $\mathbf{A}$. We can then compute $\boldsymbol{y} = f(\boldsymbol{x}) \in \mathbb{R}^m$ for any $\boldsymbol{x} \in \mathbb{R}^n$ as follows:

$$\boldsymbol{y} = \left(\sum_{j=1}^{n} a_{1j}x_j, \ldots, \sum_{j=1}^{n} a_{mj}x_j \right) \tag{7.15}$$

This corresponds to multiplying the vector $\boldsymbol{x}$ by the matrix $\mathbf{A}$:

$$\boldsymbol{y} = \mathbf{A}\boldsymbol{x} \tag{7.16}$$

See Section 7.2 for more details.

If the function is invertible, we can write

$$\boldsymbol{x} = \mathbf{A}^{-1}\boldsymbol{y} \tag{7.17}$$

See Section 7.3 for details.

7.1.2.4 Range and nullspace of a matrix

Suppose we view a matrix $\mathbf{A} \in \mathbb{R}^{m \times n}$ as a set of n vectors in $\mathbb{R}^m$. The **range** (sometimes also called the **column space**) of this matrix is the span of the columns of $\mathbf{A}$. In other words,

$$\text{range}(\mathbf{A}) \triangleq \{\boldsymbol{v} \in \mathbb{R}^m : \boldsymbol{v} = \mathbf{A}\boldsymbol{x}, \boldsymbol{x} \in \mathbb{R}^n\}. \tag{7.18}$$

This can be thought of as the set of vectors that can be "reached" or "generated" by $\mathbf{A}$; it is a subspace of $\mathbb{R}^m$ whose dimensionality is given by the rank of $\mathbf{A}$ (see Section 7.1.4.3). The **nullspace** of a matrix $\mathbf{A} \in \mathbb{R}^{m \times n}$ is the set of all vectors that get mapped to the null vector when multiplied by $\mathbf{A}$, i.e.,

$$\text{nullspace}(\mathbf{A}) \triangleq \{\boldsymbol{x} \in \mathbb{R}^n : \mathbf{A}\boldsymbol{x} = \mathbf{0}\}. \tag{7.19}$$

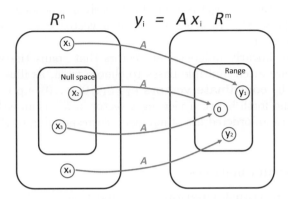

Figure 7.4: *Visualization of the nullspace and range of an $m \times n$ matrix $\mathbf{A}$. Here $\boldsymbol{y}_1 = \mathbf{A}\boldsymbol{x}_1$ and $\boldsymbol{y}_2 = \mathbf{A}\boldsymbol{x}_4$, so $\boldsymbol{y}_1$ and $\boldsymbol{y}_2$ are in the range of $\mathbf{A}$ (are reachable from some $\boldsymbol{x}$). Also $\mathbf{A}\boldsymbol{x}_2 = \mathbf{0}$ and $\mathbf{A}\boldsymbol{x}_3 = \mathbf{0}$, so $\boldsymbol{x}_2$ and $\boldsymbol{x}_3$ are in the nullspace of $\mathbf{A}$ (get mapped to 0). We see that the range is often a subset of the input domain of the mapping.*

The span of the rows of $\mathbf{A}$ is the complement to the nullspace of $\mathbf{A}$.

See Figure 7.4 for an illustration of the range and nullspace of a matrix. We shall discuss how to compute the range and nullspace of a matrix numerically in Section 7.5.4 below.

7.1.2.5   Linear projection

The **projection** of a vector $\boldsymbol{y} \in \mathbb{R}^m$ onto the span of $\{\boldsymbol{x}_1, \ldots, \boldsymbol{x}_n\}$ (here we assume $\boldsymbol{x}_i \in \mathbb{R}^m$) is the vector $\boldsymbol{v} \in \operatorname{span}(\{\boldsymbol{x}_1, \ldots, \boldsymbol{x}_n\})$, such that $\boldsymbol{v}$ is as close as possible to $\boldsymbol{y}$, as measured by the Euclidean norm $\|\boldsymbol{v} - \boldsymbol{y}\|_2$. We denote the projection as $\operatorname{Proj}(\boldsymbol{y}; \{\boldsymbol{x}_1, \ldots, \boldsymbol{x}_n\})$ and can define it formally as

$$\operatorname{Proj}(\boldsymbol{y}; \{\boldsymbol{x}_1, \ldots, \boldsymbol{x}_n\}) = \operatorname{argmin}_{\boldsymbol{v} \in \operatorname{span}(\{\boldsymbol{x}_1, \ldots, \boldsymbol{x}_n\})} \|\boldsymbol{y} - \boldsymbol{v}\|_2. \tag{7.20}$$

Given a (full rank) matrix $\mathbf{A} \in \mathbb{R}^{m \times n}$ with $m \geq n$, we can define the projection of a vector $\boldsymbol{y} \in \mathbb{R}^m$ onto the range of $\mathbf{A}$ as follows:

$$\operatorname{Proj}(\boldsymbol{y}; \mathbf{A}) = \operatorname{argmin}_{\boldsymbol{v} \in \mathcal{R}(\mathbf{A})} \|\boldsymbol{v} - \boldsymbol{y}\|_2 = \mathbf{A}(\mathbf{A}^\mathsf{T}\mathbf{A})^{-1}\mathbf{A}^\mathsf{T}\boldsymbol{y} . \tag{7.21}$$

These are the same as the normal equations from Section 11.2.2.2.

7.1.3   Norms of a vector and matrix

In this section, we discuss ways of measuring the "size" of a vector and matrix.

7.1.3.1   Vector norms

A **norm** of a vector $\|\boldsymbol{x}\|$ is, informally, a measure of the "length" of the vector. More formally, a norm is any function $f : \mathbb{R}^n \to \mathbb{R}$ that satisfies 4 properties:

- For all $\boldsymbol{x} \in \mathbb{R}^n$, $f(\boldsymbol{x}) \geq 0$ (non-negativity).

- $f(\boldsymbol{x}) = 0$ if and only if $\boldsymbol{x} = \boldsymbol{0}$ (definiteness).

- For all $\boldsymbol{x} \in \mathbb{R}^n$, $t \in \mathbb{R}$, $f(t\boldsymbol{x}) = |t| f(x)$ (absolute value homogeneity).

- For all $\boldsymbol{x}, \boldsymbol{y} \in \mathbb{R}^n$, $f(\boldsymbol{x} + \boldsymbol{y}) \le f(\boldsymbol{x}) + f(\boldsymbol{y})$ (triangle inequality).

Consider the following common examples:

p-norm $\|\boldsymbol{x}\|_p = \left(\sum_{i=1}^n |x_i|^p\right)^{1/p}$, for $p \ge 1$.

2-norm $\|\boldsymbol{x}\|_2 = \sqrt{\sum_{i=1}^n x_i^2}$, also called Euclidean norm. Note that $\|\boldsymbol{x}\|_2^2 = \boldsymbol{x}^\mathsf{T} \boldsymbol{x}$.

1-norm $\|\boldsymbol{x}\|_1 = \sum_{i=1}^n |x_i|$.

Max-norm $\|\boldsymbol{x}\|_\infty = \max_i |x_i|$.

0-norm $\|\boldsymbol{x}\|_0 = \sum_{i=1}^n \mathbb{I}(|x_i| > 0)$. This is a **pseudo norm**, since it does not satisfy homogeneity. It counts the number of non-zero elements in $\boldsymbol{x}$. If we define $0^0 = 0$, we can write this as $\|\boldsymbol{x}\|_0 = \sum_{i=1}^n x_i^0$.

7.1.3.2 Matrix norms

Suppose we think of a matrix $\mathbf{A} \in \mathbb{R}^{m \times n}$ as defining a linear function $f(\boldsymbol{x}) = \mathbf{A}\boldsymbol{x}$. We define the **induced norm** of $\mathbf{A}$ as the maximum amount by which f can lengthen any unit-norm input:

$$\|\mathbf{A}\|_p = \max_{\boldsymbol{x} \ne \boldsymbol{0}} \frac{\|\mathbf{A}\boldsymbol{x}\|_p}{\|\boldsymbol{x}\|_p} = \max_{\|\boldsymbol{x}\| = 1} \|\mathbf{A}\boldsymbol{x}\|_p \tag{7.22}$$

Typically $p = 2$, in which case

$$\|\mathbf{A}\|_2 = \sqrt{\lambda_{\max}(\mathbf{A}^\mathsf{T} \mathbf{A})} = \max_i \sigma_i \tag{7.23}$$

where $\lambda_{\max}(\mathbf{M})$ is the largest eigenvalue of $\mathbf{M}$, and σ_i is the i'th singular value.

The **nuclear norm**, also called the **trace norm**, is defined as

$$\|\mathbf{A}\|_* = \mathrm{tr}(\sqrt{\mathbf{A}^\mathsf{T} \mathbf{A}}) = \sum_i \sigma_i \tag{7.24}$$

where $\sqrt{\mathbf{A}^\mathsf{T} \mathbf{A}}$ is the matrix square root. Since the singular values are always non-negative, we have

$$\|\mathbf{A}\|_* = \sum_i |\sigma_i| = \|\boldsymbol{\sigma}\|_1 \tag{7.25}$$

Using this as a regularizer encourages many singular values to become zero, resulting in a low rank matrix. More generally, we can define the **Schatten p-norm** as

$$\|\mathbf{A}\|_p = \left(\sum_i \sigma_i^p(\mathbf{A})\right)^{1/p} \tag{7.26}$$

If we think of a matrix as a vector, we can define the matrix norm in terms of a vector norm, $||\mathbf{A}|| = ||\text{vec}(\mathbf{A})||$. If the vector norm is the 2-norm, the corresponding matrix norm is the **Frobenius norm**:

$$||\mathbf{A}||_F = \sqrt{\sum_{i=1}^{m}\sum_{j=1}^{n} a_{ij}^2} = \sqrt{\text{tr}(\mathbf{A}^{\mathsf{T}}\mathbf{A})} = ||\text{vec}(\mathbf{A})||_2 \tag{7.27}$$

If $\mathbf{A}$ is expensive to evaluate, but $\mathbf{A}\boldsymbol{v}$ is cheap (for a random vector $\boldsymbol{v}$), we can create a stochastic approximation to the Frobenius norm by using the Hutchinson trace estimator from Equation (7.37) as follows:

$$||\mathbf{A}||_F^2 = \text{tr}(\mathbf{A}^{\mathsf{T}}\mathbf{A}) = \mathbb{E}\left[\boldsymbol{v}^{\mathsf{T}}\mathbf{A}^{\mathsf{T}}\mathbf{A}\boldsymbol{v}\right] = \mathbb{E}\left[||\mathbf{A}\boldsymbol{v}||_2^2\right] \tag{7.28}$$

where $\boldsymbol{v} \sim \mathcal{N}(\mathbf{0}, \mathbf{I})$.

7.1.4   Properties of a matrix

In this section, we discuss various scalar properties of matrices.

7.1.4.1   Trace of a square matrix

The **trace** of a square matrix $\mathbf{A} \in \mathbb{R}^{n \times n}$, denoted $\text{tr}(\mathbf{A})$, is the sum of diagonal elements in the matrix:

$$\text{tr}(\mathbf{A}) \triangleq \sum_{i=1}^{n} A_{ii}. \tag{7.29}$$

The trace has the following properties, where $c \in \mathbb{R}$ is a scalar, and $\mathbf{A}, \mathbf{B} \in \mathbb{R}^{n \times n}$ are square matrices:

$$\text{tr}(\mathbf{A}) = \text{tr}(\mathbf{A}^{\mathsf{T}}) \tag{7.30}$$
$$\text{tr}(\mathbf{A} + \mathbf{B}) = \text{tr}(\mathbf{A}) + \text{tr}(\mathbf{B}) \tag{7.31}$$
$$\text{tr}(c\mathbf{A}) = c\,\text{tr}(\mathbf{A}) \tag{7.32}$$
$$\text{tr}(\mathbf{A}\mathbf{B}) = \text{tr}(\mathbf{B}\mathbf{A}) \tag{7.33}$$
$$\text{tr}(\mathbf{A}) = \sum_{i=1}^{n} \lambda_i \text{ where } \lambda_i \text{ are the eigenvalues of } \mathbf{A} \tag{7.34}$$

We also have the following important **cyclic permutation property**: For $\mathbf{A}, \mathbf{B}, \mathbf{C}$ such that $\mathbf{ABC}$ is square,

$$\text{tr}(\mathbf{ABC}) = \text{tr}(\mathbf{BCA}) = \text{tr}(\mathbf{CAB}) \tag{7.35}$$

From this, we can derive the **trace trick**, which rewrites the scalar inner product $\boldsymbol{x}^{\mathsf{T}}\mathbf{A}\boldsymbol{x}$ as follows

$$\boldsymbol{x}^{\mathsf{T}}\mathbf{A}\boldsymbol{x} = \text{tr}(\boldsymbol{x}^{\mathsf{T}}\mathbf{A}\boldsymbol{x}) = \text{tr}(\boldsymbol{x}\boldsymbol{x}^{\mathsf{T}}\mathbf{A}) \tag{7.36}$$

In some cases, it may be expensive to evaluate the matrix $\mathbf{A}$, but we may be able to cheaply evaluate matrix-vector products $\mathbf{A}\boldsymbol{v}$. Suppose $\boldsymbol{v}$ is a random vector such that $\mathbb{E}\left[\boldsymbol{v}\boldsymbol{v}^\mathsf{T}\right] = \mathbf{I}$. In this case, we can create a Monte Carlo approximation to $\operatorname{tr}(\mathbf{A})$ using the following identity:

$$\operatorname{tr}(\mathbf{A}) = \operatorname{tr}(\mathbf{A}\mathbb{E}\left[\boldsymbol{v}\boldsymbol{v}^\mathsf{T}\right]) = \mathbb{E}\left[\operatorname{tr}(\mathbf{A}\boldsymbol{v}\boldsymbol{v}^\mathsf{T})\right] = \mathbb{E}\left[\operatorname{tr}(\boldsymbol{v}^\mathsf{T}\mathbf{A}\boldsymbol{v})\right] = \mathbb{E}\left[\boldsymbol{v}^\mathsf{T}\mathbf{A}\boldsymbol{v}\right] \tag{7.37}$$

This is called the **Hutchinson trace estimator** [Hut90].

7.1.4.2 Determinant of a square matrix

The **determinant** of a square matrix, denoted $\det(\mathbf{A})$ or $|\mathbf{A}|$, is a measure of how much it changes a unit volume when viewed as a linear transformation. (The formal definition is rather complex and is not needed here.)

The determinant operator satisfies these properties, where $\mathbf{A}, \mathbf{B} \in \mathbb{R}^{n \times n}$

$$|\mathbf{A}| = |\mathbf{A}^\mathsf{T}| \tag{7.38}$$
$$|c\mathbf{A}| = c^n|\mathbf{A}| \tag{7.39}$$
$$|\mathbf{A}\mathbf{B}| = |\mathbf{A}||\mathbf{B}| \tag{7.40}$$
$$|\mathbf{A}| = 0 \text{ iff } \mathbf{A} \text{ is singular} \tag{7.41}$$
$$|\mathbf{A}^{-1}| = 1/|\mathbf{A}| \text{ if } \mathbf{A} \text{ is not singular} \tag{7.42}$$
$$|\mathbf{A}| = \prod_{i=1}^{n} \lambda_i \text{ where } \lambda_i \text{ are the eigenvalues of } \mathbf{A} \tag{7.43}$$

For a positive definite matrix $\mathbf{A}$, we can write $\mathbf{A} = \mathbf{L}\mathbf{L}^\mathsf{T}$, where $\mathbf{L}$ is the lower triangular Cholesky decomposition. In this case, we have

$$\det(\mathbf{A}) = \det(\mathbf{L})\det(\mathbf{L}^\mathsf{T}) = \det(\mathbf{L})^2 \tag{7.44}$$

so

$$\log\det(\mathbf{A}) = 2\log\det(\mathbf{L}) = 2\log\prod_i L_{ii} = 2\operatorname{tr}(\log(\operatorname{diag}(\mathbf{L}))) \tag{7.45}$$

7.1.4.3 Rank of a matrix

The **column rank** of a matrix $\mathbf{A}$ is the dimension of the space spanned by its columns, and the **row rank** is the dimension of the space spanned by its rows. It is a basic fact of linear algebra (that can be shown using the SVD, discussed in Section 7.5) that for any matrix $\mathbf{A}$, $\operatorname{columnrank}(\mathbf{A}) = \operatorname{rowrank}(\mathbf{A})$, and so this quantity is simply referred to as the **rank** of $\mathbf{A}$, denoted as $\operatorname{rank}(\mathbf{A})$. The following are some basic properties of the rank:

- For $\mathbf{A} \in \mathbb{R}^{m \times n}$, $\operatorname{rank}(\mathbf{A}) \leq \min(m, n)$. If $\operatorname{rank}(\mathbf{A}) = \min(m, n)$, then $\mathbf{A}$ is said to be **full rank**, otherwise it is called **rank deficient**.

- For $\mathbf{A} \in \mathbb{R}^{m \times n}$, $\operatorname{rank}(\mathbf{A}) = \operatorname{rank}(\mathbf{A}^\mathsf{T}) = \operatorname{rank}(\mathbf{A}^\mathsf{T}\mathbf{A}) = \operatorname{rank}(\mathbf{A}\mathbf{A}^\mathsf{T})$.

- For $\mathbf{A} \in \mathbb{R}^{m \times n}$, $\mathbf{B} \in \mathbb{R}^{n \times p}$, $\operatorname{rank}(\mathbf{A}\mathbf{B}) \leq \min(\operatorname{rank}(\mathbf{A}), \operatorname{rank}(\mathbf{B}))$.

- For $\mathbf{A}, \mathbf{B} \in \mathbb{R}^{m \times n}$, $\mathrm{rank}(\mathbf{A} + \mathbf{B}) \leq \mathrm{rank}(\mathbf{A}) + \mathrm{rank}(\mathbf{B})$.

One can show that a square matrix is invertible iff it is full rank.

7.1.4.4   Condition numbers

The **condition number** of a matrix $\mathbf{A}$ is a measure of how numerically stable any computations involving $\mathbf{A}$ will be. It is defined as follows:

$$\kappa(\mathbf{A}) \triangleq ||\mathbf{A}|| \cdot ||\mathbf{A}^{-1}|| \tag{7.46}$$

where $||\mathbf{A}||$ is the norm of the matrix. We can show that $\kappa(\mathbf{A}) \geq 1$. (The condition number depends on which norm we use; we will assume the ℓ_2-norm unless stated otherwise.)

We say $\mathbf{A}$ is **well-conditioned** if $\kappa(\mathbf{A})$ is small (close to 1), and **ill-conditioned** if $\kappa(\mathbf{A})$ is large. A large condition number means $\mathbf{A}$ is nearly singular. This is a better measure of nearness to singularity than the size of the determinant. For example, suppose $\mathbf{A} = 0.1 \mathbf{I}_{100 \times 100}$. Then $\det(\mathbf{A}) = 10^{-100}$, which suggests $\mathbf{A}$ is nearly singular, but $\kappa(\mathbf{A}) = 1$, which means $\mathbf{A}$ is well-conditioned, reflecting the fact that $\mathbf{A}\boldsymbol{x}$ simply scales the entries of $\boldsymbol{x}$ by 0.1.

To get a better understanding of condition numbers, consider the linear system of equations $\mathbf{A}\boldsymbol{x} = \boldsymbol{b}$. If $\mathbf{A}$ is non-singular, the unique solution is $\boldsymbol{x} = \mathbf{A}^{-1}\boldsymbol{b}$. Suppose we change $\boldsymbol{b}$ to $\boldsymbol{b} + \Delta\boldsymbol{b}$; what effect will that have on $\boldsymbol{x}$? The new solution must satisify

$$\mathbf{A}(\boldsymbol{x} + \Delta\boldsymbol{x}) = \boldsymbol{b} + \Delta\boldsymbol{b} \tag{7.47}$$

where

$$\Delta\boldsymbol{x} = \mathbf{A}^{-1}\Delta\boldsymbol{b} \tag{7.48}$$

We say that $\mathbf{A}$ is well-conditioned if a small $\Delta\boldsymbol{b}$ results in a small $\Delta\boldsymbol{x}$; otherwise we say that $\mathbf{A}$ is ill-conditioned.

For example, suppose

$$\mathbf{A} = \frac{1}{2}\begin{pmatrix} 1 & 1 \\ 1 + 10^{-10} & 1 - 10^{-10} \end{pmatrix}, \quad \mathbf{A}^{-1} = \begin{pmatrix} 1 - 10^{10} & 10^{10} \\ 1 + 10^{10} & -10^{10} \end{pmatrix} \tag{7.49}$$

The solution for $\boldsymbol{b} = (1, 1)$ is $\boldsymbol{x} = (1, 1)$. If we change $\boldsymbol{b}$ by $\Delta\boldsymbol{b}$, the solution changes to

$$\Delta\boldsymbol{x} = \mathbf{A}^{-1}\Delta\boldsymbol{b} = \begin{pmatrix} \Delta b_1 - 10^{10}(\Delta b_1 - \Delta b_2) \\ \Delta b_1 + 10^{10}(\Delta b_1 - \Delta b_2) \end{pmatrix} \tag{7.50}$$

So a small change in $\boldsymbol{b}$ can lead to an extremely large change in $\boldsymbol{x}$, because $\mathbf{A}$ is ill-conditioned ($\kappa(\mathbf{A}) = 2 \times 10^{10}$).

In the case of the ℓ_2-norm, the condition number is equal to the ratio of the largest to smallest singular values (defined in Section 7.5); furthermore, the singular values of $\mathbf{A}$ are the square roots of the eigenvalues of $\mathbf{A}^\mathsf{T}\mathbf{A}$, and so

$$\kappa(\mathbf{A}) = \sigma_{max}/\sigma_{min} = \sqrt{\frac{\lambda_{\max}}{\lambda_{\min}}} \tag{7.51}$$

We can gain further insight into condition numbers by considering a quadratic objective function $f(\boldsymbol{x}) = \boldsymbol{x}^{\mathsf{T}} \mathbf{A} \boldsymbol{x}$. If we plot the level set of this function, it will be elliptical, as shown in Section 7.4.4. As we increase the condition number of $\mathbf{A}$, the ellipses become more and more elongated along certain directions, corresponding to a very narrow valley in function space. If $\kappa = 1$ (the minimum possible value), the level set will be circular.

7.1.5   Special types of matrices

In this section, we will list some common kinds of matrices with various forms of structure.

7.1.5.1   Diagonal matrix

A **diagonal matrix** is a matrix where all non-diagonal elements are 0. This is typically denoted $\mathbf{D} = \mathrm{diag}(d_1, d_2, \ldots, d_n)$, with

$$\mathbf{D} = \begin{pmatrix} d_1 & & & \\ & d_2 & & \\ & & \ddots & \\ & & & d_n \end{pmatrix} \tag{7.52}$$

The **identity matrix**, denoted $\mathbf{I} \in \mathbb{R}^{n \times n}$, is a square matrix with ones on the diagonal and zeros everywhere else, $\mathbf{I} = \mathrm{diag}(1, 1, \ldots, 1)$. It has the property that for all $\mathbf{A} \in \mathbb{R}^{n \times n}$,

$$\mathbf{A}\mathbf{I} = \mathbf{A} = \mathbf{I}\mathbf{A} \tag{7.53}$$

where the size of $\mathbf{I}$ is determined by the dimensions of $\mathbf{A}$ so that matrix multiplication is possible.

We can extract the diagonal vector from a matrix using $\boldsymbol{d} = \mathrm{diag}(\mathbf{D})$. We can convert a vector into a diagonal matrix by writing $\mathbf{D} = \mathrm{diag}(\boldsymbol{d})$.

A **block diagonal** matrix is one which contains matrices on its main diagonal, and is 0 everywhere else, e.g.,

$$\begin{pmatrix} \mathbf{A} & \mathbf{0} \\ \mathbf{0} & \mathbf{B} \end{pmatrix} \tag{7.54}$$

A **band-diagonal matrix** only has non-zero entries along the diagonal, and on k sides of the diagonal, where k is the bandwidth. For example, a **tridiagonal** 6×6 matrix looks like this:

$$\begin{bmatrix} A_{11} & A_{12} & 0 & \cdots & \cdots & 0 \\ A_{21} & A_{22} & A_{23} & \ddots & \ddots & \vdots \\ 0 & A_{32} & A_{33} & A_{34} & \ddots & \vdots \\ \vdots & \ddots & A_{43} & A_{44} & A_{45} & 0 \\ \vdots & \ddots & \ddots & A_{54} & A_{55} & A_{56} \\ 0 & \cdots & \cdots & 0 & A_{65} & A_{66} \end{bmatrix} \tag{7.55}$$

7.1.5.2   Triangular matrices

An **upper triangular matrix** only has non-zero entries on and above the diagonal. A **lower triangular matrix** only has non-zero entries on and below the diagonal.

Triangular matrices have the useful property that the diagonal entries of $\mathbf{A}$ are the eigenvalues of $\mathbf{A}$, and hence the determinant is the product of diagonal entries: $\det(\mathbf{A}) = \prod_i A_{ii}$.

7.1.5.3   Positive definite matrices

Given a square matrix $\mathbf{A} \in \mathbb{R}^{n \times n}$ and a vector $\boldsymbol{x} \in \mathbb{R}^n$, the scalar value $\boldsymbol{x}^\mathsf{T} \mathbf{A} \boldsymbol{x}$ is called a **quadratic form**. Written explicitly, we see that

$$\boldsymbol{x}^\mathsf{T} \mathbf{A} \boldsymbol{x} = \sum_{i=1}^n \sum_{j=1}^n A_{ij} x_i x_j \ . \tag{7.56}$$

Note that,

$$\boldsymbol{x}^\mathsf{T} \mathbf{A} \boldsymbol{x} = (\boldsymbol{x}^\mathsf{T} \mathbf{A} \boldsymbol{x})^\mathsf{T} = \boldsymbol{x}^\mathsf{T} \mathbf{A}^\mathsf{T} \boldsymbol{x} = \boldsymbol{x}^\mathsf{T} (\tfrac{1}{2} \mathbf{A} + \tfrac{1}{2} \mathbf{A}^\mathsf{T}) \boldsymbol{x} \tag{7.57}$$

For this reason, we often implicitly assume that the matrices appearing in a quadratic form are symmetric.

We give the following definitions:

- A symmetric matrix $\mathbf{A} \in \mathbb{S}^n$ is **positive definite** iff for all non-zero vectors $\boldsymbol{x} \in \mathbb{R}^n$, $\boldsymbol{x}^\mathsf{T} \mathbf{A} \boldsymbol{x} > 0$. This is usually denoted $\mathbf{A} \succ 0$ (or just $\mathbf{A} > 0$). If it is possible that $\boldsymbol{x}^\mathsf{T} \mathbf{A} \boldsymbol{x} = 0$, we say the matrix is **positive semidefinite** or **psd**. We denote the set of all positive definite matrices by $\mathbb{S}^n_{++}$.

- A symmetric matrix $\mathbf{A} \in \mathbb{S}^n$ is **negative definite**, denoted $\mathbf{A} \prec 0$ (or just $\mathbf{A} < 0$) iff for all non-zero $\boldsymbol{x} \in \mathbb{R}^n$, $\boldsymbol{x}^\mathsf{T} \mathbf{A} \boldsymbol{x} < 0$. If it is possible that $\boldsymbol{x}^\mathsf{T} \mathbf{A} \boldsymbol{x} = 0$, we say the matrix is **negative semidefinite**.

- A symmetric matrix $\mathbf{A} \in \mathbb{S}^n$ is **indefinite**, if it is neither positive semidefinite nor negative semidefinite — i.e., if there exists $\boldsymbol{x}_1, \boldsymbol{x}_2 \in \mathbb{R}^n$ such that $\boldsymbol{x}_1^\mathsf{T} \mathbf{A} \boldsymbol{x}_1 > 0$ and $\boldsymbol{x}_2^\mathsf{T} \mathbf{A} \boldsymbol{x}_2 < 0$.

It should be obvious that if $\mathbf{A}$ is positive definite, then $-\mathbf{A}$ is negative definite and vice versa. Likewise, if $\mathbf{A}$ is positive semidefinite then $-\mathbf{A}$ is negative semidefinite and vice versa. If $\mathbf{A}$ is indefinite, then so is $-\mathbf{A}$. It can also be shown that positive definite and negative definite matrices are always invertible.

In Section 7.4.3.1, we show that a symmetric matrix is positive definite iff its eigenvalues are positive. Note that if all elements of $\mathbf{A}$ are positive, it does not mean $\mathbf{A}$ is necessarily positive definite. For example, $\mathbf{A} = \begin{pmatrix} 4 & 3 \\ 3 & 2 \end{pmatrix}$ is not positive definite. Conversely, a positive definite matrix can have negative entries e.g., $\mathbf{A} = \begin{pmatrix} 2 & -1 \\ -1 & 2 \end{pmatrix}$.

A sufficient condition for a (real, symmetric) matrix to be positive definite is that it is **diagonally dominant**, i.e., if in every row of the matrix, the magnitude of the diagonal entry in that row is larger than the sum of the magnitudes of all the other (non-diagonal) entries in that row. More precisely,

$$|a_{ii}| > \sum_{j \neq i} |a_{ij}| \quad \text{for all } i \tag{7.58}$$

In 2d, any real, symmetric 2×2 matrix $\begin{pmatrix} a & b \\ b & d \end{pmatrix}$ is positive definite iff $a > 0$, $d > 0$ and $ad > b^2$.

Finally, there is one type of positive definite matrix that comes up frequently, and so deserves some special mention. Given any matrix $\mathbf{A} \in \mathbb{R}^{m \times n}$ (not necessarily symmetric or even square), the **Gram matrix** $\mathbf{G} = \mathbf{A}^\mathsf{T} \mathbf{A}$ is always positive semidefinite. Further, if $m \geq n$ (and we assume for convenience that $\mathbf{A}$ is full rank), then $\mathbf{G} = \mathbf{A}^\mathsf{T} \mathbf{A}$ is positive definite.

7.1.5.4   Orthogonal matrices

Two vectors $x, y \in \mathbb{R}^n$ are **orthogonal** if $x^\mathsf{T} y = 0$. A vector $x \in \mathbb{R}^n$ is **normalized** if $\|x\|_2 = 1$. A set of vectors that is pairwise orthogonal and normalized is called **orthonormal**. A square matrix $\mathbf{U} \in \mathbb{R}^{n \times n}$ is **orthogonal** if all its columns are orthonormal. (Note the different meaning of the term orthogonal when talking about vectors versus matrices.) If the entries of $\mathbf{U}$ are complex valued, we use the term **unitary** instead of orthogonal.

It follows immediately from the definition of orthogonality and normality that $\mathbf{U}$ is orthogonal iff

$$\mathbf{U}^\mathsf{T} \mathbf{U} = \mathbf{I} = \mathbf{U} \mathbf{U}^\mathsf{T}. \tag{7.59}$$

In other words, the inverse of an orthogonal matrix is its transpose. Note that if $\mathbf{U}$ is not square — i.e., $\mathbf{U} \in \mathbb{R}^{m \times n}$, $n < m$ — but its columns are still orthonormal, then $\mathbf{U}^\mathsf{T} \mathbf{U} = \mathbf{I}$, but $\mathbf{U} \mathbf{U}^\mathsf{T} \neq I$. We generally only use the term orthogonal to describe the previous case, where $\mathbf{U}$ is square.

An example of an orthogonal matrix is a **rotation matrix** (see Exercise 7.1). For example, a rotation in 3d by angle α about the z axis is given by

$$\mathbf{R}(\alpha) = \begin{pmatrix} \cos(\alpha) & -\sin(\alpha) & 0 \\ \sin(\alpha) & \cos(\alpha) & 0 \\ 0 & 0 & 1 \end{pmatrix} \tag{7.60}$$

If $\alpha = 45°$, this becomes

$$\mathbf{R}(45) = \begin{pmatrix} \frac{1}{\sqrt{2}} & -\frac{1}{\sqrt{2}} & 0 \\ \frac{1}{\sqrt{2}} & \frac{1}{\sqrt{2}} & 0 \\ 0 & 0 & 1 \end{pmatrix} \tag{7.61}$$

where $\frac{1}{\sqrt{2}} = 0.7071$. We see that $\mathbf{R}(-\alpha) = \mathbf{R}(\alpha)^{-1} = \mathbf{R}(\alpha)^\mathsf{T}$, so this is an orthogonal matrix.

One nice property of orthogonal matrices is that operating on a vector with an orthogonal matrix will not change its Euclidean norm, i.e.,

$$\|\mathbf{U}x\|_2 = \|x\|_2 \tag{7.62}$$

for any nonzero $x \in \mathbb{R}^n$, and orthogonal $\mathbf{U} \in \mathbb{R}^{n \times n}$.

Similarly, one can show that the angle between two vectors is preserved after they are transformed by an orthogonal matrix. The cosine of the angle between $\boldsymbol{x}$ and $\boldsymbol{y}$ is given by

$$\cos(\alpha(\boldsymbol{x}, \boldsymbol{y})) = \frac{\boldsymbol{x}^\mathsf{T}\boldsymbol{y}}{||\boldsymbol{x}||\,||\boldsymbol{y}||} \tag{7.63}$$

so

$$\cos(\alpha(\mathbf{U}\boldsymbol{x}, \mathbf{U}\boldsymbol{y})) = \frac{(\mathbf{U}\boldsymbol{x})^\mathsf{T}(\mathbf{U}\boldsymbol{y})}{||\mathbf{U}\boldsymbol{x}||\,||\mathbf{U}\boldsymbol{y}||} = \frac{\boldsymbol{x}^\mathsf{T}\boldsymbol{y}}{||\boldsymbol{x}||\,||\boldsymbol{y}||} = \cos(\alpha(\boldsymbol{x}, \boldsymbol{y})) \tag{7.64}$$

In summary, transformations by orthogonal matrices are generalizations of rotations (if $\det(\mathbf{U}) = 1$) and reflections (if $\det(\mathbf{U}) = -1$), since they preserve lengths and angles.

Note that there is a technique called Gram Schmidt orthogonalization which is a way to make any square matrix orthogonal, but we will not cover it here.

7.2   Matrix multiplication

The product of two matrices $\mathbf{A} \in \mathbb{R}^{m \times n}$ and $\mathbf{B} \in \mathbb{R}^{n \times p}$ is the matrix

$$\mathbf{C} = \mathbf{A}\mathbf{B} \in \mathbb{R}^{m \times p}, \tag{7.65}$$

where

$$C_{ij} = \sum_{k=1}^{n} A_{ik} B_{kj}. \tag{7.66}$$

Note that in order for the matrix product to exist, the number of columns in $\mathbf{A}$ must equal the number of rows in $\mathbf{B}$.

Matrix multiplication generally takes $O(mnp)$ time, although faster methods exist. In addition, specialized hardware, such as GPUs and TPUs, can be leveraged to speed up matrix multiplication significantly, by performing operations across the rows (or columns) in parallel.

It is useful to know a few basic properties of matrix multiplication:

- Matrix multiplication is **associative**: $(\mathbf{A}\mathbf{B})\mathbf{C} = \mathbf{A}(\mathbf{B}\mathbf{C})$.

- Matrix multiplication is **distributive**: $\mathbf{A}(\mathbf{B} + \mathbf{C}) = \mathbf{A}\mathbf{B} + \mathbf{A}\mathbf{C}$.

- Matrix multiplication is, in general, *not* **commutative**; that is, it can be the case that $\mathbf{A}\mathbf{B} \neq \mathbf{B}\mathbf{A}$.

(In each of the above cases, we are assuming that the dimensions match.)

There are many important special cases of matrix multiplication, as we discuss below.

7.2.1   Vector–vector products

Given two vectors $\boldsymbol{x}, \boldsymbol{y} \in \mathbb{R}^n$, the quantity $\boldsymbol{x}^\mathsf{T}\boldsymbol{y}$, called the **inner product**, **dot product** or **scalar product** of the vectors, is a real number given by

$$\langle \boldsymbol{x}, \boldsymbol{y} \rangle \triangleq \boldsymbol{x}^\mathsf{T}\boldsymbol{y} = \sum_{i=1}^{n} x_i y_i. \tag{7.67}$$

Note that it is always the case that $\boldsymbol{x}^\mathsf{T}\boldsymbol{y} = \boldsymbol{y}^\mathsf{T}\boldsymbol{x}$.

Given vectors $\boldsymbol{x} \in \mathbb{R}^m$, $\boldsymbol{y} \in \mathbb{R}^n$ (they no longer have to be the same size), $\boldsymbol{x}\boldsymbol{y}^\mathsf{T}$ is called the **outer product** of the vectors. It is a matrix whose entries are given by $(\boldsymbol{x}\boldsymbol{y}^\mathsf{T})_{ij} = x_i y_j$, i.e.,

$$\boldsymbol{x}\boldsymbol{y}^\mathsf{T} \in \mathbb{R}^{m \times n} = \begin{bmatrix} x_1 y_1 & x_1 y_2 & \cdots & x_1 y_n \\ x_2 y_1 & x_2 y_2 & \cdots & x_2 y_n \\ \vdots & \vdots & \ddots & \vdots \\ x_m y_1 & x_m y_2 & \cdots & x_m y_n \end{bmatrix}. \tag{7.68}$$

7.2.2 Matrix–vector products

Given a matrix $\mathbf{A} \in \mathbb{R}^{m \times n}$ and a vector $\boldsymbol{x} \in \mathbb{R}^n$, their product is a vector $\boldsymbol{y} = \mathbf{A}\boldsymbol{x} \in \mathbb{R}^m$. There are a couple of ways of looking at matrix-vector multiplication, and we will look at them both.

If we write $\mathbf{A}$ by rows, then we can express $\boldsymbol{y} = \mathbf{A}\boldsymbol{x}$ as follows:

$$\boldsymbol{y} = \mathbf{A}\boldsymbol{x} = \begin{bmatrix} - & \boldsymbol{a}_1^\mathsf{T} & - \\ - & \boldsymbol{a}_2^\mathsf{T} & - \\ & \vdots & \\ - & \boldsymbol{a}_m^\mathsf{T} & - \end{bmatrix} \boldsymbol{x} = \begin{bmatrix} \boldsymbol{a}_1^\mathsf{T}\boldsymbol{x} \\ \boldsymbol{a}_2^\mathsf{T}\boldsymbol{x} \\ \vdots \\ \boldsymbol{a}_m^\mathsf{T}\boldsymbol{x} \end{bmatrix}. \tag{7.69}$$

In other words, the ith entry of $\boldsymbol{y}$ is equal to the inner product of the ith *row* of $\mathbf{A}$ and $\boldsymbol{x}$, $y_i = \boldsymbol{a}_i^\mathsf{T}\boldsymbol{x}$.

Alternatively, let's write $\mathbf{A}$ in column form. In this case we see that

$$\boldsymbol{y} = \mathbf{A}\boldsymbol{x} = \begin{bmatrix} | & | & & | \\ \boldsymbol{a}_1 & \boldsymbol{a}_2 & \cdots & \boldsymbol{a}_n \\ | & | & & | \end{bmatrix} \begin{bmatrix} x_1 \\ x_2 \\ \vdots \\ x_n \end{bmatrix} = \begin{bmatrix} | \\ \boldsymbol{a}_1 \\ | \end{bmatrix} x_1 + \begin{bmatrix} | \\ \boldsymbol{a}_2 \\ | \end{bmatrix} x_2 + \ldots + \begin{bmatrix} | \\ \boldsymbol{a}_n \\ | \end{bmatrix} x_n. \tag{7.70}$$

In other words, $\boldsymbol{y}$ is a **linear combination** of the *columns* of $\mathbf{A}$, where the coefficients of the linear combination are given by the entries of $\boldsymbol{x}$. We can view the columns of $\mathbf{A}$ as a set of **basis vectors** defining a **linear subspace**. We can construct vectors in this subspace by taking linear combinations of the basis vectors. See Section 7.1.2 for details.

7.2.3 Matrix–matrix products

Below we look at four different (but, of course, equivalent) ways of viewing the matrix-matrix multiplication $\mathbf{C} = \mathbf{A}\mathbf{B}$.

First we can view matrix-matrix multiplication as a set of vector-vector products. The most obvious viewpoint, which follows immediately from the definition, is that the i, j entry of $\mathbf{C}$ is equal to the inner product of the ith row of $\mathbf{A}$ and the jth column of $\mathbf{B}$. Symbolically, this looks like the following,

$$\mathbf{C} = \mathbf{A}\mathbf{B} = \begin{bmatrix} - & \boldsymbol{a}_1^\mathsf{T} & - \\ - & \boldsymbol{a}_2^\mathsf{T} & - \\ & \vdots & \\ - & \boldsymbol{a}_m^\mathsf{T} & - \end{bmatrix} \begin{bmatrix} | & | & & | \\ \boldsymbol{b}_1 & \boldsymbol{b}_2 & \cdots & \boldsymbol{b}_p \\ | & | & & | \end{bmatrix} = \begin{bmatrix} \boldsymbol{a}_1^\mathsf{T}\boldsymbol{b}_1 & \boldsymbol{a}_1^\mathsf{T}\boldsymbol{b}_2 & \cdots & \boldsymbol{a}_1^\mathsf{T}\boldsymbol{b}_p \\ \boldsymbol{a}_2^\mathsf{T}\boldsymbol{b}_1 & \boldsymbol{a}_2^\mathsf{T}\boldsymbol{b}_2 & \cdots & \boldsymbol{a}_2^\mathsf{T}\boldsymbol{b}_p \\ \vdots & \vdots & \ddots & \vdots \\ \boldsymbol{a}_m^\mathsf{T}\boldsymbol{b}_1 & \boldsymbol{a}_m^\mathsf{T}\boldsymbol{b}_2 & \cdots & \boldsymbol{a}_m^\mathsf{T}\boldsymbol{b}_p \end{bmatrix}. \tag{7.71}$$

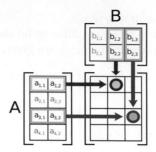

Figure 7.5: Illustration of matrix multiplication. From `https://en.wikipedia.org/wiki/Matrix_` `multiplication`*. Used with kind permission of Wikipedia author Bilou.*

Remember that since $\mathbf{A} \in \mathbb{R}^{m \times n}$ and $\mathbf{B} \in \mathbb{R}^{n \times p}$, $\boldsymbol{a}_i \in \mathbb{R}^n$ and $\boldsymbol{b}_j \in \mathbb{R}^n$, so these inner products all make sense. This is the most "natural" representation when we represent $\mathbf{A}$ by rows and $\mathbf{B}$ by columns. See Figure 7.5 for an illustration.

Alternatively, we can represent $\mathbf{A}$ by columns, and $\mathbf{B}$ by rows, which leads to the interpretation of $\mathbf{AB}$ as a sum of outer products. Symbolically,

$$\mathbf{C} = \mathbf{AB} = \begin{bmatrix} | & | & & | \\ \boldsymbol{a}_1 & \boldsymbol{a}_2 & \cdots & \boldsymbol{a}_n \\ | & | & & | \end{bmatrix} \begin{bmatrix} - & \boldsymbol{b}_1^\mathsf{T} & - \\ - & \boldsymbol{b}_2^\mathsf{T} & - \\ & \vdots & \\ - & \boldsymbol{b}_n^\mathsf{T} & - \end{bmatrix} = \sum_{i=1}^{n} \boldsymbol{a}_i \boldsymbol{b}_i^\mathsf{T} \ . \tag{7.72}$$

Put another way, $\mathbf{AB}$ is equal to the sum, over all i, of the outer product of the ith column of $\mathbf{A}$ and the ith row of $\mathbf{B}$. Since, in this case, $\boldsymbol{a}_i \in \mathbb{R}^m$ and $\boldsymbol{b}_i \in \mathbb{R}^p$, the dimension of the outer product $\boldsymbol{a}_i \boldsymbol{b}_i^\mathsf{T}$ is $m \times p$, which coincides with the dimension of $\mathbf{C}$.

We can also view matrix-matrix multiplication as a set of matrix-vector products. Specifically, if we represent $\mathbf{B}$ by columns, we can view the columns of $\mathbf{C}$ as matrix-vector products between $\mathbf{A}$ and the columns of $\mathbf{B}$. Symbolically,

$$\mathbf{C} = \mathbf{AB} = \mathbf{A} \begin{bmatrix} | & | & & | \\ \boldsymbol{b}_1 & \boldsymbol{b}_2 & \cdots & \boldsymbol{b}_p \\ | & | & & | \end{bmatrix} = \begin{bmatrix} | & | & & | \\ \mathbf{A}\boldsymbol{b}_1 & \mathbf{A}\boldsymbol{b}_2 & \cdots & \mathbf{A}\boldsymbol{b}_p \\ | & | & & | \end{bmatrix} . \tag{7.73}$$

Here the ith column of $\mathbf{C}$ is given by the matrix-vector product with the vector on the right, $\boldsymbol{c}_i = \mathbf{A}\boldsymbol{b}_i$. These matrix-vector products can in turn be interpreted using both viewpoints given in the previous subsection.

Finally, we have the analogous viewpoint, where we represent $\mathbf{A}$ by rows, and view the rows of $\mathbf{C}$ as the matrix-vector product between the rows of $\mathbf{A}$ and the matrix $\mathbf{B}$. Symbolically,

$$\mathbf{C} = \mathbf{AB} = \begin{bmatrix} - & \boldsymbol{a}_1^\mathsf{T} & - \\ - & \boldsymbol{a}_2^\mathsf{T} & - \\ & \vdots & \\ - & \boldsymbol{a}_m^\mathsf{T} & - \end{bmatrix} \mathbf{B} = \begin{bmatrix} - & \boldsymbol{a}_1^\mathsf{T}\mathbf{B} & - \\ - & \boldsymbol{a}_2^\mathsf{T}\mathbf{B} & - \\ & \vdots & \\ - & \boldsymbol{a}_m^\mathsf{T}\mathbf{B} & - \end{bmatrix} . \tag{7.74}$$

Here the ith row of $\mathbf{C}$ is given by the matrix-vector product with the vector on the left, $\boldsymbol{c}_i^{\mathsf{T}} = \boldsymbol{a}_i^{\mathsf{T}} \mathbf{B}$.

It may seem like overkill to dissect matrix multiplication to such a large degree, especially when all these viewpoints follow immediately from the initial definition we gave (in about a line of math) at the beginning of this section. However, virtually all of linear algebra deals with matrix multiplications of some kind, and it is worthwhile to spend some time trying to develop an intuitive understanding of the viewpoints presented here.

Finally, a word on notation. We write $\mathbf{A}^2$ as shorthand for $\mathbf{AA}$, which is the matrix product. To denote elementwise squaring of the elements of a matrix, we write $\mathbf{A}^{\odot 2} = [A_{ij}^2]$. (If $\mathbf{A}$ is diagonal, then $\mathbf{A}^2 = \mathbf{A}^{\odot 2}$.)

We can also define the inverse of $\mathbf{A}^2$ using the **matrix square root**: we say $\mathbf{A} = \sqrt{\mathbf{M}}$ if $\mathbf{A}^2 = \mathbf{M}$. To denote elementwise square root of the elements of a matrix, we write $[\sqrt{M_{ij}}]$.

7.2.4 Application: manipulating data matrices

As an application of the above results, consider the case where $\mathbf{X}$ is the $N \times D$ design matrix, whose rows are the data cases. There are various common preprocessing operations that we apply to this matrix, which we summarize below. (Writing these operations in matrix form is useful because it is notationally compact, and it allows us to implement the methods quickly using fast matrix code.)

7.2.4.1 Summing slices of the matrix

Suppose $\mathbf{X}$ is an $N \times D$ matrix. We can sum across the rows by premultiplying by a $1 \times N$ matrix of ones to create a $1 \times D$ matrix:

$$\mathbf{1}_N^{\mathsf{T}} \mathbf{X} = \left(\sum_n x_{n1} \quad \cdots \quad \sum_n x_{nD} \right) \tag{7.75}$$

Hence the mean of the data vectors is given by

$$\overline{\boldsymbol{x}}^{\mathsf{T}} = \frac{1}{N} \mathbf{1}_N^{\mathsf{T}} \mathbf{X} \tag{7.76}$$

We can sum across the columns by postmultiplying by a $D \times 1$ matrix of ones to create a $N \times 1$ matrix:

$$\mathbf{X} \mathbf{1}_D = \begin{pmatrix} \sum_d x_{1d} \\ \vdots \\ \sum_d x_{Nd} \end{pmatrix} \tag{7.77}$$

We can sum all entries in a matrix by pre and post multiplying by a vector of 1s:

$$\mathbf{1}_N^{\mathsf{T}} \mathbf{X} \mathbf{1}_D = \sum_{ij} X_{ij} \tag{7.78}$$

Hence the overall mean is given by

$$\overline{x} = \frac{1}{ND} \mathbf{1}_N^{\mathsf{T}} \mathbf{X} \mathbf{1}_D \tag{7.79}$$

7.2.4.2   Scaling rows and columns of a matrix

We often want to scale rows or columns of a data matrix (e.g., to standardize them). We now show how to write this in matrix notation.

If we pre-multiply $\mathbf{X}$ by a diagonal matrix $\mathbf{S} = \text{diag}(\boldsymbol{s})$, where $\boldsymbol{s}$ is an N-vector, then we just scale each row of $\mathbf{X}$ by the corresponding scale factor in $\boldsymbol{s}$:

$$\text{diag}(\boldsymbol{s})\mathbf{X} = \begin{pmatrix} s_1 & \cdots & 0 \\ & \ddots & \\ 0 & \cdots & s_N \end{pmatrix} \begin{pmatrix} x_{1,1} & \cdots & x_{1,D} \\ & \ddots & \\ x_{N,1} & \cdots & x_{N,D} \end{pmatrix} = \begin{pmatrix} s_1 x_{1,1} & \cdots & s_1 x_{1,D} \\ & \ddots & \\ s_N x_{N,1} & \cdots & s_N x_{N,D} \end{pmatrix} \tag{7.80}$$

If we post-multiply $\mathbf{X}$ by a diagonal matrix $\mathbf{S} = \text{diag}(\boldsymbol{s})$, where $\boldsymbol{s}$ is a D-vector, then we just scale each column of $\mathbf{X}$ by the corresponding element in $\boldsymbol{s}$.

$$\mathbf{X}\text{diag}(\boldsymbol{s}) = \begin{pmatrix} x_{1,1} & \cdots & x_{1,D} \\ & \ddots & \\ x_{N,1} & \cdots & x_{N,D} \end{pmatrix} \begin{pmatrix} s_1 & \cdots & 0 \\ & \ddots & \\ 0 & \cdots & s_D \end{pmatrix} = \begin{pmatrix} s_1 x_{1,1} & \cdots & s_D x_{1,D} \\ & \ddots & \\ s_1 x_{N,1} & \cdots & s_D x_{N,D} \end{pmatrix} \tag{7.81}$$

Thus we can rewrite the standardization operation from Section 10.2.8 in matrix form as follows:

$$\text{standardize}(\mathbf{X}) = (\mathbf{X} - \mathbf{1}_N \boldsymbol{\mu}^T)\text{diag}(\boldsymbol{\sigma})^{-1} \tag{7.82}$$

where $\boldsymbol{\mu} = \overline{\boldsymbol{x}}$ is the empirical mean, and $\boldsymbol{\sigma}$ is a vector of the empirical standard deviations.

7.2.4.3   Sum of squares and scatter matrix

The **sum of squares matrix** is $D \times D$ matrix defined by

$$\mathbf{S}_0 \triangleq \mathbf{X}^T\mathbf{X} = \sum_{n=1}^N \boldsymbol{x}_n \boldsymbol{x}_n^T = \sum_{n=1}^N \begin{pmatrix} x_{n,1}^2 & \cdots & x_{n,1}x_{n,D} \\ & \ddots & \\ x_{n,D}x_{n,1} & \cdots & x_{n,D}^2 \end{pmatrix} \tag{7.83}$$

The **scatter matrix** is a $D \times D$ matrix defined by

$$\mathbf{S}_{\overline{\boldsymbol{x}}} \triangleq \sum_{n=1}^N (\boldsymbol{x}_n - \overline{\boldsymbol{x}})(\boldsymbol{x}_n - \overline{\boldsymbol{x}})^T = \left(\sum_n \boldsymbol{x}_n \boldsymbol{x}_n^T\right) - N\overline{\boldsymbol{x}}\,\overline{\boldsymbol{x}}^T \tag{7.84}$$

We see that this is the sum of squares matrix applied to the mean-centered data. More precisely, define $\tilde{\mathbf{X}}$ to be a version of $\mathbf{X}$ where we subtract the mean $\overline{\boldsymbol{x}} = \frac{1}{N}\mathbf{X}^T\mathbf{1}_N$ off every row. Hence we can compute the centered data matrix using

$$\tilde{\mathbf{X}} = \mathbf{X} - \mathbf{1}_N\overline{\boldsymbol{x}}^T = \mathbf{X} - \frac{1}{N}\mathbf{1}_N\mathbf{1}_N^T\mathbf{X} = \mathbf{C}_N\mathbf{X} \tag{7.85}$$

where

$$\mathbf{C}_N \triangleq \mathbf{I}_N - \frac{1}{N}\mathbf{J}_N \tag{7.86}$$

is the **centering matrix**, and $\mathbf{J}_N = \mathbf{1}_N \mathbf{1}_N^\mathsf{T}$ is a matrix of all 1s. The scatter matrix can now be computed as follows:

$$\mathbf{S}_{\overline{x}} = \tilde{\mathbf{X}}^\mathsf{T}\tilde{\mathbf{X}} = \mathbf{X}^\mathsf{T}\mathbf{C}_N^\mathsf{T}\mathbf{C}_N\mathbf{X} = \mathbf{X}^\mathsf{T}\mathbf{C}_N\mathbf{X} \tag{7.87}$$

where we exploited the fact that $\mathbf{C}_N$ is symmetric and idempotent, i.e., $\mathbf{C}_N^k = \mathbf{C}_N$ for $k = 1, 2, \ldots$ (since once we subtract the mean, subtracting it again has no effect).

7.2.4.4 Gram matrix

The $N \times N$ matrix $\mathbf{X}\mathbf{X}^\mathsf{T}$ is a matrix of inner products called the **Gram matrix**:

$$\mathbf{K} \triangleq \mathbf{X}\mathbf{X}^\mathsf{T} = \begin{pmatrix} \boldsymbol{x}_1^\mathsf{T}\boldsymbol{x}_1 & \cdots & \boldsymbol{x}_1^\mathsf{T}\boldsymbol{x}_N \\ & \ddots & \\ \boldsymbol{x}_n^\mathsf{T}\boldsymbol{x}_1 & \cdots & \boldsymbol{x}_N^\mathsf{T}\boldsymbol{x}_N \end{pmatrix} \tag{7.88}$$

Sometimes we want to compute the inner products of the mean-centered data vectors, $\tilde{\mathbf{K}} = \tilde{\mathbf{X}}\tilde{\mathbf{X}}^\mathsf{T}$. However, if we are working with a feature similarity matrix instead of raw features, we will only have access to $\mathbf{K}$, not $\mathbf{X}$. (We will see examples of this in Section 20.4.4 and Section 20.4.6.) Fortunately, we can compute $\tilde{\mathbf{K}}$ from $\mathbf{K}$ using the **double centering trick**:

$$\tilde{\mathbf{K}} = \tilde{\mathbf{X}}\tilde{\mathbf{X}}^\mathsf{T} = \mathbf{C}_N\mathbf{K}\mathbf{C}_N = \mathbf{K} - \frac{1}{N}\mathbf{J}\mathbf{K} - \frac{1}{N}\mathbf{K}\mathbf{J} + \frac{1}{N^2}\mathbf{1}^\mathsf{T}\mathbf{K}\mathbf{1} \tag{7.89}$$

This subtracts the row means and column means from $\mathbf{K}$, and adds back the global mean that gets subtracted twice, so that both row means and column means of $\tilde{\mathbf{K}}$ are equal to zero.

To see why Equation (7.89) is true, consider the scalar form:

$$\tilde{K}_{ij} = \tilde{\boldsymbol{x}}_i^\mathsf{T}\tilde{\boldsymbol{x}}_j = (\boldsymbol{x}_i - \frac{1}{N}\sum_{k=1}^{N}\boldsymbol{x}_k)(\boldsymbol{x}_j - \frac{1}{N}\sum_{l=1}^{N}\boldsymbol{x}_l) \tag{7.90}$$

$$= \boldsymbol{x}_i^\mathsf{T}\boldsymbol{x}_j - \frac{1}{N}\sum_{k=1}^{N}\boldsymbol{x}_i^\mathsf{T}\boldsymbol{x}_k - \frac{1}{N}\sum_{k=1}^{N}\boldsymbol{x}_j^\mathsf{T}\boldsymbol{x}_k + \frac{1}{N^2}\sum_{k=1}^{N}\sum_{l=1}^{N}\boldsymbol{x}_k^\mathsf{T}\boldsymbol{x}_l \tag{7.91}$$

7.2.4.5 Distance matrix

Let $\mathbf{X}$ be $N_x \times D$ datamatrix, and $\mathbf{Y}$ be another $N_y \times D$ datamatrix. We can compute the squared pairwise distances between these using

$$\mathbf{D}_{ij} = (\boldsymbol{x}_i - \boldsymbol{y}_j)^\mathsf{T}(\boldsymbol{x}_i - \boldsymbol{y}_j) = ||\boldsymbol{x}_i||^2 - 2\boldsymbol{x}_i^\mathsf{T}\boldsymbol{y}_j + ||\boldsymbol{y}_j||^2 \tag{7.92}$$

Let us now write this in matrix form. Let $\hat{\boldsymbol{x}} = [||\boldsymbol{x}_1||^2; \cdots; ||\boldsymbol{x}_{N_x}||^2] = \text{diag}(\mathbf{X}\mathbf{X}^\mathsf{T})$ be a vector where each element is the squared norm of the examples in $\mathbf{X}$, and define $\hat{\boldsymbol{y}}$ similarly. Then we have

$$\mathbf{D} = \hat{\boldsymbol{x}}\mathbf{1}_{N_y}^\mathsf{T} - 2\mathbf{X}\mathbf{Y}^\mathsf{T} + \mathbf{1}_{N_x}\hat{\boldsymbol{y}}^\mathsf{T} \tag{7.93}$$

In the case that $\mathbf{X} = \mathbf{Y}$, we have

$$\mathbf{D} = \hat{\boldsymbol{x}}\mathbf{1}_N^\mathsf{T} - 2\mathbf{X}\mathbf{X}^\mathsf{T} + \mathbf{1}_N\hat{\boldsymbol{x}}^\mathsf{T} \tag{7.94}$$

This vectorized computation is often much faster than using for loops.

7.2.5 Kronecker products *

If $\mathbf{A}$ is an $m \times n$ matrix and $\mathbf{B}$ is a $p \times q$ matrix, then the **Kronecker product** $\mathbf{A} \otimes \mathbf{B}$ is the $mp \times nq$ block matrix

$$\mathbf{A} \otimes \mathbf{B} = \begin{bmatrix} a_{11}\mathbf{B} & \cdots & a_{1n}\mathbf{B} \\ \vdots & \ddots & \vdots \\ a_{m1}\mathbf{B} & \cdots & a_{mn}\mathbf{B} \end{bmatrix} \tag{7.95}$$

For example,

$$\begin{bmatrix} a_{11} & a_{12} \\ a_{21} & a_{22} \\ a_{31} & a_{32} \end{bmatrix} \otimes \begin{bmatrix} b_{11} & b_{12} & b_{13} \\ b_{21} & b_{22} & b_{23} \end{bmatrix} = \begin{bmatrix} a_{11}b_{11} & a_{11}b_{12} & a_{11}b_{13} & a_{12}b_{11} & a_{12}b_{12} & a_{12}b_{13} \\ a_{11}b_{21} & a_{11}b_{22} & a_{11}b_{23} & a_{12}b_{21} & a_{12}b_{22} & a_{12}b_{23} \\ a_{21}b_{11} & a_{21}b_{12} & a_{21}b_{13} & a_{22}b_{11} & a_{22}b_{12} & a_{22}b_{13} \\ a_{21}b_{21} & a_{21}b_{22} & a_{21}b_{23} & a_{22}b_{21} & a_{22}b_{22} & a_{22}b_{23} \\ a_{31}b_{11} & a_{31}b_{12} & a_{31}b_{13} & a_{32}b_{11} & a_{32}b_{12} & a_{32}b_{13} \\ a_{31}b_{21} & a_{31}b_{22} & a_{31}b_{23} & a_{32}b_{21} & a_{32}b_{22} & a_{32}b_{23} \end{bmatrix} \tag{7.96}$$

Here are some useful identities:

$$(\mathbf{A} \otimes \mathbf{B})^{-1} = \mathbf{A}^{-1} \otimes \mathbf{B}^{-1} \tag{7.97}$$

$$(\mathbf{A} \otimes \mathbf{B})\text{vec}(\mathbf{C}) = \text{vec}(\mathbf{B}\mathbf{C}\mathbf{A}^\mathsf{T}) \tag{7.98}$$

where $\text{vec}(\mathbf{M})$ stacks the *columns* of $\mathbf{M}$. (If we stack along the rows, we get $(\mathbf{A} \otimes \mathbf{B})\text{vec}(\mathbf{C}) = \text{vec}(\mathbf{A}\mathbf{C}\mathbf{B}^\mathsf{T})$.) See [Loa00] for a list of other useful properties.

7.2.6 Einstein summation *

Einstein summation, or **einsum** for short, is a notational shortcut for working with tensors. The convention was introduced by Einstein [Ein16, sec 5], who later joked to a friend, "I have made a great discovery in mathematics; I have suppressed the summation sign every time that the summation must be made over an index which occurs twice..." [Pai05, p.216]. For example, instead of writing matrix multiplication as $C_{ij} = \sum_k A_{ik}B_{kj}$, we can just write it as $C_{ij} = A_{ik}B_{kj}$, where we drop the $\sum_k$.

As a more complex example, suppose we have a 3d tensor S_{ntk} where n indexes examples in the batch, t indexes locations in the sequence, and k indexes words in a one-hot representation. Let W_{kd} be an embedding matrix that maps sparse one-hot vectors $\mathbb{R}^k$ to dense vectors in $\mathbb{R}^d$. We can convert the batch of sequences of one-hots to a batch of sequences of embeddings as follows:

$$E_{ntd} = \sum_k S_{ntk}W_{kd} \tag{7.99}$$

We can compute the sum of the embedding vectors for each sequence (to get a global representation of each bag of words) as follows:

$$E_{nd} = \sum_k \sum_t S_{ntk}W_{kd} \tag{7.100}$$

Finally we can pass each sequence's vector representation through another linear transform V_{dc} to map to the logits over a classifier with c labels:

$$L_{nc} = \sum_d E_{nd} V_{dc} = \sum_d \sum_k \sum_t S_{ntk} W_{kd} V_{dc} \qquad (7.101)$$

In einsum notation, we write $L_{nc} = S_{ntk} W_{kd} V_{dc}$. We sum over k and d because those indices occur twice on the RHS. We sum over t because that index does not occur on the LHS.

Einsum is implemented in NumPy, Tensorflow, PyTorch, etc. What makes it particularly useful is that it can perform the relevant tensor multiplications in complex expressions in an optimal order, so as to minimize time and intermediate memory allocation.[2] The library is best illustrated by the examples in einsum_demo.ipynb.

Note that the speed of einsum depends on the order in which the operations are performed, which depends on the shapes of the relevant arguments. The optimal ordering minimizes the treewidth of the resulting computation graph, as explained in [GASG18]. In general, the time to compute the optimal ordering is exponential in the number of arguments, so it is common to use a greedy approximation. However, if we expect to repeat the same calculation many times, using tensors of the same shape but potentially different content, we can compute the optimal ordering once and reuse it multiple times.

7.3 Matrix inversion

In this section, we discuss how to invert different kinds of matrices.

7.3.1 The inverse of a square matrix

The **inverse** of a square matrix $\mathbf{A} \in \mathbb{R}^{n \times n}$ is denoted $\mathbf{A}^{-1}$, and is the unique matrix such that

$$\mathbf{A}^{-1}\mathbf{A} = \mathbf{I} = \mathbf{A}\mathbf{A}^{-1}. \qquad (7.102)$$

Note that $\mathbf{A}^{-1}$ exists if and only if $\det(\mathbf{A}) \neq 0$. If $\det(\mathbf{A}) = 0$, it is called a **singular** matrix.

The following are properties of the inverse; all assume that $\mathbf{A}, \mathbf{B} \in \mathbb{R}^{n \times n}$ are non-singular:

$$(\mathbf{A}^{-1})^{-1} = \mathbf{A} \qquad (7.103)$$

$$(\mathbf{AB})^{-1} = \mathbf{B}^{-1}\mathbf{A}^{-1} \qquad (7.104)$$

$$(\mathbf{A}^{-1})^{\mathsf{T}} = (\mathbf{A}^{\mathsf{T}})^{-1} \triangleq \mathbf{A}^{-T} \qquad (7.105)$$

For the case of a 2×2 matrix, the expression for $\mathbf{A}^{-1}$ is simple enough to give explicitly. We have

$$\mathbf{A} = \begin{pmatrix} a & b \\ c & d \end{pmatrix}, \quad \mathbf{A}^{-1} = \frac{1}{|\mathbf{A}|} \begin{pmatrix} d & -b \\ -c & a \end{pmatrix} \qquad (7.106)$$

For a block diagonal matrix, the inverse is obtained by simply inverting each block separately, e.g.,

$$\begin{pmatrix} \mathbf{A} & \mathbf{0} \\ \mathbf{0} & \mathbf{B} \end{pmatrix}^{-1} = \begin{pmatrix} \mathbf{A}^{-1} & \mathbf{0} \\ \mathbf{0} & \mathbf{B}^{-1} \end{pmatrix} \qquad (7.107)$$

---

2. These optimizations are implemented in the **opt-einsum** library [GASG18]. Its core functionality is included in NumPy and JAX einsum functions, provided you set optimize=True parameter.

7.3.2 Schur complements *

In this section, we review some useful results concerning block structured matrices.

Theorem 7.3.1 (Inverse of a partitioned matrix). *Consider a general partitioned matrix*

$$\mathbf{M} = \begin{pmatrix} \mathbf{E} & \mathbf{F} \\ \mathbf{G} & \mathbf{H} \end{pmatrix} \tag{7.108}$$

where we assume $\mathbf{E}$ *and* $\mathbf{H}$ *are invertible. We have*

$$\mathbf{M}^{-1} = \begin{pmatrix} (\mathbf{M}/\mathbf{H})^{-1} & -(\mathbf{M}/\mathbf{H})^{-1}\mathbf{F}\mathbf{H}^{-1} \\ -\mathbf{H}^{-1}\mathbf{G}(\mathbf{M}/\mathbf{H})^{-1} & \mathbf{H}^{-1} + \mathbf{H}^{-1}\mathbf{G}(\mathbf{M}/\mathbf{H})^{-1}\mathbf{F}\mathbf{H}^{-1} \end{pmatrix} \tag{7.109}$$

$$= \begin{pmatrix} \mathbf{E}^{-1} + \mathbf{E}^{-1}\mathbf{F}(\mathbf{M}/\mathbf{E})^{-1}\mathbf{G}\mathbf{E}^{-1} & -\mathbf{E}^{-1}\mathbf{F}(\mathbf{M}/\mathbf{E})^{-1} \\ -(\mathbf{M}/\mathbf{E})^{-1}\mathbf{G}\mathbf{E}^{-1} & (\mathbf{M}/\mathbf{E})^{-1} \end{pmatrix} \tag{7.110}$$

where

$$\mathbf{M}/\mathbf{H} \triangleq \mathbf{E} - \mathbf{F}\mathbf{H}^{-1}\mathbf{G} \tag{7.111}$$

$$\mathbf{M}/\mathbf{E} \triangleq \mathbf{H} - \mathbf{G}\mathbf{E}^{-1}\mathbf{F} \tag{7.112}$$

We say that $\mathbf{M}/\mathbf{H}$ *is the* **Schur complement** *of* $\mathbf{M}$ *wrt* $\mathbf{H}$*, and* $\mathbf{M}/\mathbf{E}$ *is the Schur complement of* $\mathbf{M}$ *wrt* $\mathbf{E}$*.*

Equation (7.109) *and Equation* (7.110) *are called the* **partitioned inverse formulae**.

Proof. If we could block diagonalize $\mathbf{M}$, it would be easier to invert. To zero out the top right block of $\mathbf{M}$ we can pre-multiply as follows

$$\begin{pmatrix} \mathbf{I} & -\mathbf{F}\mathbf{H}^{-1} \\ 0 & \mathbf{I} \end{pmatrix} \begin{pmatrix} \mathbf{E} & \mathbf{F} \\ \mathbf{G} & \mathbf{H} \end{pmatrix} = \begin{pmatrix} \mathbf{E} - \mathbf{F}\mathbf{H}^{-1}\mathbf{G} & 0 \\ \mathbf{G} & \mathbf{H} \end{pmatrix} \tag{7.113}$$

Similarly, to zero out the bottom left we can post-multiply as follows

$$\begin{pmatrix} \mathbf{E} - \mathbf{F}\mathbf{H}^{-1}\mathbf{G} & 0 \\ \mathbf{G} & \mathbf{H} \end{pmatrix} \begin{pmatrix} \mathbf{I} & 0 \\ -\mathbf{H}^{-1}\mathbf{G} & \mathbf{I} \end{pmatrix} = \begin{pmatrix} \mathbf{E} - \mathbf{F}\mathbf{H}^{-1}\mathbf{G} & 0 \\ 0 & \mathbf{H} \end{pmatrix} \tag{7.114}$$

Putting it all together we get

$$\underbrace{\begin{pmatrix} \mathbf{I} & -\mathbf{F}\mathbf{H}^{-1} \\ 0 & \mathbf{I} \end{pmatrix}}_{\mathbf{X}} \underbrace{\begin{pmatrix} \mathbf{E} & \mathbf{F} \\ \mathbf{G} & \mathbf{H} \end{pmatrix}}_{\mathbf{M}} \underbrace{\begin{pmatrix} \mathbf{I} & 0 \\ -\mathbf{H}^{-1}\mathbf{G} & \mathbf{I} \end{pmatrix}}_{\mathbf{Z}} = \underbrace{\begin{pmatrix} \mathbf{E} - \mathbf{F}\mathbf{H}^{-1}\mathbf{G} & 0 \\ 0 & \mathbf{H} \end{pmatrix}}_{\mathbf{W}} \tag{7.115}$$

Taking the inverse of both sides yields

$$\mathbf{Z}^{-1}\mathbf{M}^{-1}\mathbf{X}^{-1} = \mathbf{W}^{-1} \tag{7.116}$$

$$\mathbf{M}^{-1} = \mathbf{Z}\mathbf{W}^{-1}\mathbf{X} \tag{7.117}$$

Substituting in the definitions we get

$$
\begin{pmatrix} \mathbf{E} & \mathbf{F} \\ \mathbf{G} & \mathbf{H} \end{pmatrix}^{-1} = \begin{pmatrix} \mathbf{I} & \mathbf{0} \\ -\mathbf{H}^{-1}\mathbf{G} & \mathbf{I} \end{pmatrix} \begin{pmatrix} (\mathbf{M}/\mathbf{H})^{-1} & \mathbf{0} \\ \mathbf{0} & \mathbf{H}^{-1} \end{pmatrix} \begin{pmatrix} \mathbf{I} & -\mathbf{F}\mathbf{H}^{-1} \\ \mathbf{0} & \mathbf{I} \end{pmatrix} \tag{7.118}
$$

$$
= \begin{pmatrix} (\mathbf{M}/\mathbf{H})^{-1} & \mathbf{0} \\ -\mathbf{H}^{-1}\mathbf{G}(\mathbf{M}/\mathbf{H})^{-1} & \mathbf{H}^{-1} \end{pmatrix} \begin{pmatrix} \mathbf{I} & -\mathbf{F}\mathbf{H}^{-1} \\ \mathbf{0} & \mathbf{I} \end{pmatrix} \tag{7.119}
$$

$$
= \begin{pmatrix} (\mathbf{M}/\mathbf{H})^{-1} & -(\mathbf{M}/\mathbf{H})^{-1}\mathbf{F}\mathbf{H}^{-1} \\ -\mathbf{H}^{-1}\mathbf{G}(\mathbf{M}/\mathbf{H})^{-1} & \mathbf{H}^{-1} + \mathbf{H}^{-1}\mathbf{G}(\mathbf{M}/\mathbf{H})^{-1}\mathbf{F}\mathbf{H}^{-1} \end{pmatrix} \tag{7.120}
$$

Alternatively, we could have decomposed the matrix $\mathbf{M}$ in terms of $\mathbf{E}$ and $\mathbf{M}/\mathbf{E} = (\mathbf{H} - \mathbf{G}\mathbf{E}^{-1}\mathbf{F})$, yielding

$$
\begin{pmatrix} \mathbf{E} & \mathbf{F} \\ \mathbf{G} & \mathbf{H} \end{pmatrix}^{-1} = \begin{pmatrix} \mathbf{E}^{-1} + \mathbf{E}^{-1}\mathbf{F}(\mathbf{M}/\mathbf{E})^{-1}\mathbf{G}\mathbf{E}^{-1} & -\mathbf{E}^{-1}\mathbf{F}(\mathbf{M}/\mathbf{E})^{-1} \\ -(\mathbf{M}/\mathbf{E})^{-1}\mathbf{G}\mathbf{E}^{-1} & (\mathbf{M}/\mathbf{E})^{-1} \end{pmatrix} \tag{7.121}
$$

$\square$

7.3.3 The matrix inversion lemma *

Equating the top left block of the first matrix in Equation (7.119) with the top left block of the matrix in Equation (7.121)

$$
(\mathbf{M}/\mathbf{H})^{-1} = (\mathbf{E} - \mathbf{F}\mathbf{H}^{-1}\mathbf{G})^{-1} = \mathbf{E}^{-1} + \mathbf{E}^{-1}\mathbf{F}(\mathbf{H} - \mathbf{G}\mathbf{E}^{-1}\mathbf{F})^{-1}\mathbf{G}\mathbf{E}^{-1} \tag{7.122}
$$

This is known as the **matrix inversion lemma** or the **Sherman-Morrison-Woodbury formula**.

A typical application in machine learning is the following. Let $\mathbf{X}$ be an $N \times D$ data matrix, and $\mathbf{\Sigma}$ be $N \times N$ diagonal matrix. Then we have (using the substitutions $\mathbf{E} = \mathbf{\Sigma}$, $\mathbf{F} = \mathbf{G}^{\mathsf{T}} = \mathbf{X}$, and $\mathbf{H}^{-1} = -\mathbf{I}$) the following result:

$$
(\mathbf{\Sigma} + \mathbf{X}\mathbf{X}^{\mathsf{T}})^{-1} = \mathbf{\Sigma}^{-1} - \mathbf{\Sigma}^{-1}\mathbf{X}(\mathbf{I} + \mathbf{X}^{\mathsf{T}}\mathbf{\Sigma}^{-1}\mathbf{X})^{-1}\mathbf{X}^{\mathsf{T}}\mathbf{\Sigma}^{-1} \tag{7.123}
$$

The LHS takes $O(N^3)$ time to compute, the RHS takes time $O(D^3)$ to compute.

Another application concerns computing a **rank one update** of an inverse matrix. Let $\mathbf{E} = \mathbf{A}$, $\mathbf{F} = \boldsymbol{u}$, $\mathbf{G} = \boldsymbol{v}^{\mathsf{T}}$, and $H = -1$. Then we have

$$
(\mathbf{A} + \boldsymbol{u}\boldsymbol{v}^{\mathsf{T}})^{-1} = \mathbf{A}^{-1} + \mathbf{A}^{-1}\boldsymbol{u}(-1 - \boldsymbol{v}^{\mathsf{T}}\mathbf{A}^{-1}\boldsymbol{u})^{-1}\boldsymbol{v}^{\mathsf{T}}\mathbf{A}^{-1} \tag{7.124}
$$

$$
= \mathbf{A}^{-1} - \frac{\mathbf{A}^{-1}\boldsymbol{u}\boldsymbol{v}^{\mathsf{T}}\mathbf{A}^{-1}}{1 + \boldsymbol{v}^{\mathsf{T}}\mathbf{A}^{-1}\boldsymbol{u}} \tag{7.125}
$$

This is known as the **Sherman-Morrison formula**.

7.3.4 Matrix determinant lemma *

We now use the above results to derive an efficient way to compute the determinant of a block-structured matrix.

From Equation (7.115), we have

$$|\mathbf{X}||\mathbf{M}||\mathbf{Z}| = |\mathbf{W}| = |\mathbf{E} - \mathbf{F}\mathbf{H}^{-1}\mathbf{G}||\mathbf{H}| \tag{7.126}$$

$$\left|\begin{pmatrix} \mathbf{E} & \mathbf{F} \\ \mathbf{G} & \mathbf{H} \end{pmatrix}\right| = |\mathbf{E} - \mathbf{F}\mathbf{H}^{-1}\mathbf{G}||\mathbf{H}| \tag{7.127}$$

$$|\mathbf{M}| = |\mathbf{M}/\mathbf{H}||\mathbf{H}| \tag{7.128}$$

$$|\mathbf{M}/\mathbf{H}| = \frac{|\mathbf{M}|}{|\mathbf{H}|} \tag{7.129}$$

So we can see that $\mathbf{M}/\mathbf{H}$ acts somewhat like a division operator (hence the notation). Furthermore, we have

$$|\mathbf{M}| = |\mathbf{M}/\mathbf{H}||\mathbf{H}| = |\mathbf{M}/\mathbf{E}||\mathbf{E}| \tag{7.130}$$

$$|\mathbf{M}/\mathbf{H}| = \frac{|\mathbf{M}/\mathbf{E}||\mathbf{E}|}{|\mathbf{H}|} \tag{7.131}$$

$$|\mathbf{E} - \mathbf{F}\mathbf{H}^{-1}\mathbf{G}| = |\mathbf{H} - \mathbf{G}\mathbf{E}^{-1}\mathbf{F}||\mathbf{H}^{-1}||\mathbf{E}| \tag{7.132}$$

Hence (setting $\mathbf{E} = \mathbf{A}$, $\mathbf{F} = -\boldsymbol{u}$, $\mathbf{G} = \boldsymbol{v}^\mathsf{T}$, $\mathbf{H} = 1$) we have

$$|\mathbf{A} + \boldsymbol{u}\boldsymbol{v}^\mathsf{T}| = (1 + \boldsymbol{v}^\mathsf{T}\mathbf{A}^{-1}\boldsymbol{u})|\mathbf{A}| \tag{7.133}$$

This is known as the **matrix determinant lemma**.

7.3.5   Application: deriving the conditionals of an MVN *

Consider a joint Gaussian of the form $p(\boldsymbol{x}_1, \boldsymbol{x}_2) = \mathcal{N}(\boldsymbol{x}|\boldsymbol{\mu}, \boldsymbol{\Sigma})$, where

$$\boldsymbol{\mu} = \begin{pmatrix} \boldsymbol{\mu}_1 \\ \boldsymbol{\mu}_2 \end{pmatrix}, \quad \boldsymbol{\Sigma} = \begin{pmatrix} \boldsymbol{\Sigma}_{11} & \boldsymbol{\Sigma}_{12} \\ \boldsymbol{\Sigma}_{21} & \boldsymbol{\Sigma}_{22} \end{pmatrix} \tag{7.134}$$

In Section 3.2.3, we claimed that

$$p(\boldsymbol{x}_1|\boldsymbol{x}_2) = \mathcal{N}(\boldsymbol{x}_1|\boldsymbol{\mu}_1 + \boldsymbol{\Sigma}_{12}\boldsymbol{\Sigma}_{22}^{-1}(\boldsymbol{x}_2 - \boldsymbol{\mu}_2), \ \boldsymbol{\Sigma}_{11} - \boldsymbol{\Sigma}_{12}\boldsymbol{\Sigma}_{22}^{-1}\boldsymbol{\Sigma}_{21}) \tag{7.135}$$

In this section, we derive this result using Schur complements.

Let us factor the joint $p(\boldsymbol{x}_1, \boldsymbol{x}_2)$ as $p(\boldsymbol{x}_2)p(\boldsymbol{x}_1|\boldsymbol{x}_2)$ as follows:

$$p(\boldsymbol{x}_1, \boldsymbol{x}_2) \propto \exp\left\{ -\frac{1}{2} \begin{pmatrix} \boldsymbol{x}_1 - \boldsymbol{\mu}_1 \\ \boldsymbol{x}_2 - \boldsymbol{\mu}_2 \end{pmatrix}^\mathsf{T} \begin{pmatrix} \boldsymbol{\Sigma}_{11} & \boldsymbol{\Sigma}_{12} \\ \boldsymbol{\Sigma}_{21} & \boldsymbol{\Sigma}_{22} \end{pmatrix}^{-1} \begin{pmatrix} \boldsymbol{x}_1 - \boldsymbol{\mu}_1 \\ \boldsymbol{x}_2 - \boldsymbol{\mu}_2 \end{pmatrix} \right\} \tag{7.136}$$

Using Equation (7.118) the above exponent becomes

$$p(\boldsymbol{x}_1, \boldsymbol{x}_2) \propto \exp\left\{-\frac{1}{2}\begin{pmatrix}\boldsymbol{x}_1 - \boldsymbol{\mu}_1\\\boldsymbol{x}_2 - \boldsymbol{\mu}_2\end{pmatrix}^{\mathsf{T}}\begin{pmatrix}\mathbf{I} & \mathbf{0}\\-\boldsymbol{\Sigma}_{22}^{-1}\boldsymbol{\Sigma}_{21} & \mathbf{I}\end{pmatrix}\begin{pmatrix}(\boldsymbol{\Sigma}/\boldsymbol{\Sigma}_{22})^{-1} & \mathbf{0}\\\mathbf{0} & \boldsymbol{\Sigma}_{22}^{-1}\end{pmatrix}\right. \tag{7.137}$$

$$\times\left.\begin{pmatrix}\mathbf{I} & -\boldsymbol{\Sigma}_{12}\boldsymbol{\Sigma}_{22}^{-1}\\\mathbf{0} & \mathbf{I}\end{pmatrix}\begin{pmatrix}\boldsymbol{x}_1 - \boldsymbol{\mu}_1\\\boldsymbol{x}_2 - \boldsymbol{\mu}_2\end{pmatrix}\right\} \tag{7.138}$$

$$= \exp\left\{-\frac{1}{2}(\boldsymbol{x}_1 - \boldsymbol{\mu}_1 - \boldsymbol{\Sigma}_{12}\boldsymbol{\Sigma}_{22}^{-1}(\boldsymbol{x}_2 - \boldsymbol{\mu}_2))^{\mathsf{T}}(\boldsymbol{\Sigma}/\boldsymbol{\Sigma}_{22})^{-1}\right. \tag{7.139}$$

$$\left.(\boldsymbol{x}_1 - \boldsymbol{\mu}_1 - \boldsymbol{\Sigma}_{12}\boldsymbol{\Sigma}_{22}^{-1}(\boldsymbol{x}_2 - \boldsymbol{\mu}_2))\right\} \times \exp\left\{-\frac{1}{2}(\boldsymbol{x}_2 - \boldsymbol{\mu}_2)^{\mathsf{T}}\boldsymbol{\Sigma}_{22}^{-1}(\boldsymbol{x}_2 - \boldsymbol{\mu}_2)\right\} \tag{7.140}$$

This is of the form

$$\exp(\text{quadratic form in } \boldsymbol{x}_1, \boldsymbol{x}_2) \times \exp(\text{quadratic form in } \boldsymbol{x}_2) \tag{7.141}$$

Hence we have successfully factorized the joint as

$$p(\boldsymbol{x}_1, \boldsymbol{x}_2) = p(\boldsymbol{x}_1|\boldsymbol{x}_2)p(\boldsymbol{x}_2) \tag{7.142}$$

$$= \mathcal{N}(\boldsymbol{x}_1|\boldsymbol{\mu}_{1|2}, \boldsymbol{\Sigma}_{1|2})\mathcal{N}(\boldsymbol{x}_2|\boldsymbol{\mu}_2, \boldsymbol{\Sigma}_{22}) \tag{7.143}$$

where the parameters of the conditional distribution can be read off from the above equations using

$$\boldsymbol{\mu}_{1|2} = \boldsymbol{\mu}_1 + \boldsymbol{\Sigma}_{12}\boldsymbol{\Sigma}_{22}^{-1}(\boldsymbol{x}_2 - \boldsymbol{\mu}_2) \tag{7.144}$$

$$\boldsymbol{\Sigma}_{1|2} = \boldsymbol{\Sigma}/\boldsymbol{\Sigma}_{22} = \boldsymbol{\Sigma}_{11} - \boldsymbol{\Sigma}_{12}\boldsymbol{\Sigma}_{22}^{-1}\boldsymbol{\Sigma}_{21} \tag{7.145}$$

We can also use the fact that $|\mathbf{M}| = |\mathbf{M}/\mathbf{H}||\mathbf{H}|$ to check the normalization constants are correct:

$$(2\pi)^{(d_1+d_2)/2}|\boldsymbol{\Sigma}|^{\frac{1}{2}} = (2\pi)^{(d_1+d_2)/2}(|\boldsymbol{\Sigma}/\boldsymbol{\Sigma}_{22}| \, |\boldsymbol{\Sigma}_{22}|)^{\frac{1}{2}} \tag{7.146}$$

$$= (2\pi)^{d_1/2}|\boldsymbol{\Sigma}/\boldsymbol{\Sigma}_{22}|^{\frac{1}{2}} \, (2\pi)^{d_2/2}|\boldsymbol{\Sigma}_{22}|^{\frac{1}{2}} \tag{7.147}$$

where $d_1 = \dim(\boldsymbol{x}_1)$ and $d_2 = \dim(\boldsymbol{x}_2)$.

7.4 Eigenvalue decomposition (EVD)

In this section, we review some standard material on the **eigenvalue decomposition** or **EVD** of square (real-valued) matrices.

7.4.1 Basics

Given a square matrix $\mathbf{A} \in \mathbb{R}^{n \times n}$, we say that $\lambda \in \mathbb{R}$ is an **eigenvalue** of $\mathbf{A}$ and $\boldsymbol{u} \in \mathbb{R}^n$ is the corresponding **eigenvector** if

$$\mathbf{A}\boldsymbol{u} = \lambda\boldsymbol{u}, \quad \boldsymbol{u} \neq 0 \ . \tag{7.148}$$

Intuitively, this definition means that multiplying $\mathbf{A}$ by the vector $\boldsymbol{u}$ results in a new vector that points in the same direction as $\boldsymbol{u}$, but is scaled by a factor λ. For example, if $\mathbf{A}$ is a rotation matrix, then $\boldsymbol{u}$ is the axis of rotation and $\lambda = 1$.

Note that for any eigenvector $\boldsymbol{u} \in \mathbb{R}^n$, and scalar $c \in \mathbb{R}$,

$$\mathbf{A}(c\boldsymbol{u}) = c\mathbf{A}\boldsymbol{u} = c\lambda\boldsymbol{u} = \lambda(c\boldsymbol{u}) \tag{7.149}$$

Hence $c\boldsymbol{u}$ is also an eigenvector. For this reason when we talk about "the" eigenvector associated with λ, we usually assume that the eigenvector is normalized to have length 1 (this still creates some ambiguity, since $\boldsymbol{u}$ and $-\boldsymbol{u}$ will both be eigenvectors, but we will have to live with this).

We can rewrite the equation above to state that $(\lambda, \boldsymbol{x})$ is an eigenvalue-eigenvector pair of $\mathbf{A}$ if

$$(\lambda\mathbf{I} - \mathbf{A})\boldsymbol{u} = \mathbf{0}, \quad \boldsymbol{u} \neq 0 \ . \tag{7.150}$$

Now $(\lambda\mathbf{I} - \mathbf{A})\boldsymbol{u} = \mathbf{0}$ has a non-zero solution to $\boldsymbol{u}$ if and only if $(\lambda\mathbf{I} - \mathbf{A})$ has a non-empty nullspace, which is only the case if $(\lambda\mathbf{I} - \mathbf{A})$ is singular, i.e.,

$$\det(\lambda\mathbf{I} - \mathbf{A}) = 0 \ . \tag{7.151}$$

This is called the **characteristic equation** of $\mathbf{A}$. (See Exercise 7.2.) The n solutions of this equation are the n (possibly complex-valued) eigenvalues λ_i, and $\boldsymbol{u}_i$ are the corresponding eigenvectors. It is standard to sort the eigenvectors in order of their eigenvalues, with the largest magnitude ones first.

The following are properties of eigenvalues and eigenvectors.

- The trace of a matrix is equal to the sum of its eigenvalues,

$$\text{tr}(\mathbf{A}) = \sum_{i=1}^{n} \lambda_i \ . \tag{7.152}$$

- The determinant of $\mathbf{A}$ is equal to the product of its eigenvalues,

$$\det(\mathbf{A}) = \prod_{i=1}^{n} \lambda_i \ . \tag{7.153}$$

- The rank of $\mathbf{A}$ is equal to the number of non-zero eigenvalues of $\mathbf{A}$.

- If $\mathbf{A}$ is non-singular then $1/\lambda_i$ is an eigenvalue of $\mathbf{A}^{-1}$ with associated eigenvector $\boldsymbol{u}_i$, i.e., $\mathbf{A}^{-1}\boldsymbol{u}_i = (1/\lambda_i)\boldsymbol{u}_i$.

- The eigenvalues of a diagonal or triangular matrix are just the diagonal entries.

7.4.2 Diagonalization

We can write all the eigenvector equations simultaneously as

$$\mathbf{A}\mathbf{U} = \mathbf{U}\mathbf{\Lambda} \tag{7.154}$$

where the columns of $\mathbf{U} \in \mathbb{R}^{n \times n}$ are the eigenvectors of $\mathbf{A}$ and $\mathbf{\Lambda}$ is a diagonal matrix whose entries are the eigenvalues of $\mathbf{A}$, i.e.,

$$\mathbf{U} \in \mathbb{R}^{n \times n} = \begin{bmatrix} | & | & & | \\ \boldsymbol{u}_1 & \boldsymbol{u}_2 & \cdots & \boldsymbol{u}_n \\ | & | & & | \end{bmatrix}, \quad \mathbf{\Lambda} = \mathrm{diag}(\lambda_1, \ldots, \lambda_n) \ . \tag{7.155}$$

If the eigenvectors of $\mathbf{A}$ are linearly independent, then the matrix $\mathbf{U}$ will be invertible, so

$$\mathbf{A} = \mathbf{U}\mathbf{\Lambda}\mathbf{U}^{-1}. \tag{7.156}$$

A matrix that can be written in this form is called **diagonalizable**.

7.4.3 Eigenvalues and eigenvectors of symmetric matrices

When $\mathbf{A}$ is real and symmetric, it can be shown that all the eigenvalues are real, and the eigenvectors are **orthonormal**, i.e., $\boldsymbol{u}_i^\mathsf{T} \boldsymbol{u}_j = 0$ if $i \neq j$, and $\boldsymbol{u}_i^\mathsf{T} \boldsymbol{u}_i = 1$, where $\boldsymbol{u}_i$ are the eigenvectors. In matrix form, this becomes $\mathbf{U}^\mathsf{T}\mathbf{U} = \mathbf{U}\mathbf{U}^\mathsf{T} = \mathbf{I}$; hence we see that $\mathbf{U}$ is an orthogonal matrix.

We can therefore represent $\mathbf{A}$ as

$$\mathbf{A} = \mathbf{U}\mathbf{\Lambda}\mathbf{U}^\mathsf{T} = \begin{pmatrix} | & | & & | \\ \boldsymbol{u}_1 & \boldsymbol{u}_2 & \cdots & \boldsymbol{u}_n \\ | & | & & | \end{pmatrix} \begin{pmatrix} \lambda_1 & & & \\ & \lambda_2 & & \\ & & \ddots & \\ & & & \lambda_n \end{pmatrix} \begin{pmatrix} - & \boldsymbol{u}_1^\mathsf{T} & - \\ - & \boldsymbol{u}_2^\mathsf{T} & - \\ & \vdots & \\ - & \boldsymbol{u}_n^\mathsf{T} & - \end{pmatrix} \tag{7.157}$$

$$= \lambda_1 \begin{pmatrix} | \\ \boldsymbol{u}_1 \\ | \end{pmatrix} \begin{pmatrix} - & \boldsymbol{u}_1^\mathsf{T} & - \end{pmatrix} + \cdots + \lambda_n \begin{pmatrix} | \\ \boldsymbol{u}_n \\ | \end{pmatrix} \begin{pmatrix} - & \boldsymbol{u}_n^\mathsf{T} & - \end{pmatrix} = \sum_{i=1}^{n} \lambda_i \boldsymbol{u}_i \boldsymbol{u}_i^\mathsf{T} \tag{7.158}$$

Thus multiplying by any symmetric matrix $\mathbf{A}$ can be interpreted as multiplying by a rotation matrix $\mathbf{U}^\mathsf{T}$, a scaling matrix $\mathbf{\Lambda}$, followed by an inverse rotation $\mathbf{U}$.

Once we have diagonalized a matrix, it is easy to invert. Since $\mathbf{A} = \mathbf{U}\mathbf{\Lambda}\mathbf{U}^\mathsf{T}$, where $\mathbf{U}^\mathsf{T} = \mathbf{U}^{-1}$, we have

$$\mathbf{A}^{-1} = \mathbf{U}\mathbf{\Lambda}^{-1}\mathbf{U}^\mathsf{T} = \sum_{i=1}^{d} \frac{1}{\lambda_i} \boldsymbol{u}_i \boldsymbol{u}_i^\mathsf{T} \tag{7.159}$$

This corresponds to rotating, unscaling, and then rotating back.

7.4.3.1 Checking for positive definiteness

We can also use the diagonalization property to show that a symmetric matrix is positive definite iff all its eigenvalues are positive. To see this, note that

$$\boldsymbol{x}^\mathsf{T}\mathbf{A}\boldsymbol{x} = \boldsymbol{x}^\mathsf{T}\mathbf{U}\mathbf{\Lambda}\mathbf{U}^\mathsf{T}\boldsymbol{x} = \boldsymbol{y}^\mathsf{T}\mathbf{\Lambda}\boldsymbol{y} = \sum_{i=1}^{n} \lambda_i y_i^2 \tag{7.160}$$

where $\boldsymbol{y} = \mathbf{U}^\mathsf{T}\boldsymbol{x}$. Because y_i^2 is always nonnegative, the sign of this expression depends entirely on the λ_i's. If all $\lambda_i > 0$, then the matrix is positive definite; if all $\lambda_i \geq 0$, it is positive semidefinite. Likewise, if all $\lambda_i < 0$ or $\lambda_i \leq 0$, then $\mathbf{A}$ is negative definite or negative semidefinite respectively. Finally, if $\mathbf{A}$ has both positive and negative eigenvalues, it is indefinite.

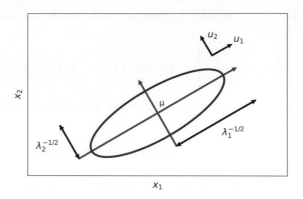

Figure 7.6: *Visualization of a level set of the quadratic form* $(\boldsymbol{x} - \boldsymbol{\mu})^{\mathsf{T}} \mathbf{A}(\boldsymbol{x} - \boldsymbol{\mu})$ *in 2d. The major and minor axes of the ellipse are defined by the first two eigenvectors of* $\mathbf{A}$, *namely* $\boldsymbol{u}_1$ *and* $\boldsymbol{u}_2$. *Adapted from Figure 2.7 of [Bis06]. Generated by* gaussEvec.ipynb.

7.4.4   Geometry of quadratic forms

A **quadratic form** is a function that can be written as

$$f(\boldsymbol{x}) = \boldsymbol{x}^{\mathsf{T}} \mathbf{A} \boldsymbol{x} \tag{7.161}$$

where $\boldsymbol{x} \in \mathbb{R}^n$ and $\mathbf{A}$ is a positive definite, symmetric n-by-n matrix. Let $\mathbf{A} = \mathbf{U}\boldsymbol{\Lambda}\mathbf{U}^{\mathsf{T}}$ be a diagonalization of $\mathbf{A}$ (see Section 7.4.3). Hence we can write

$$f(\boldsymbol{x}) = \boldsymbol{x}^{\mathsf{T}} \mathbf{A} \boldsymbol{x} = \boldsymbol{x}^{\mathsf{T}} \mathbf{U}\boldsymbol{\Lambda}\mathbf{U}^{\mathsf{T}} \boldsymbol{x} = \boldsymbol{y}^{\mathsf{T}} \boldsymbol{\Lambda} \boldsymbol{y} = \sum_{i=1}^{n} \lambda_i y_i^2 \tag{7.162}$$

where $y_i = \boldsymbol{x}^{\mathsf{T}} \boldsymbol{u}_i$ and $\lambda_i > 0$ (since $\mathbf{A}$ is positive definite). The level sets of $f(\boldsymbol{x})$ define hyper-ellipsoids. For example, in 2d, we have

$$\lambda_1 y_1^2 + \lambda_2 y_2^2 = r \tag{7.163}$$

which is the equation of a 2d ellipse. This is illustrated in Figure 7.6. The eigenvectors determine the orientation of the ellipse, and the eigenvalues determine how elongated it is. In particular, the major and minor semi-axes of the ellipse satisfy $a^{-2} = \lambda_1$ and $b^{-2} = \lambda_2$. In the case of a Gaussian distribution, we have $\mathbf{A} = \boldsymbol{\Sigma}^{-1}$, so small values of λ_i correspond to directions where the posterior has low precision and hence high variance.

7.4.5   Standardizing and whitening data

Suppose we have a dataset $\mathbf{X} \in \mathbb{R}^{N \times D}$. It is common to preprocess the data so that each column has zero mean and unit variance. This is called standardizing the data, as we discuss in Section 10.2.8. Although standardizing forces the variance to be 1, it does not remove correlation between the columns. To do that, we must **whiten** the data. To define this, let the empirical covariance matrix

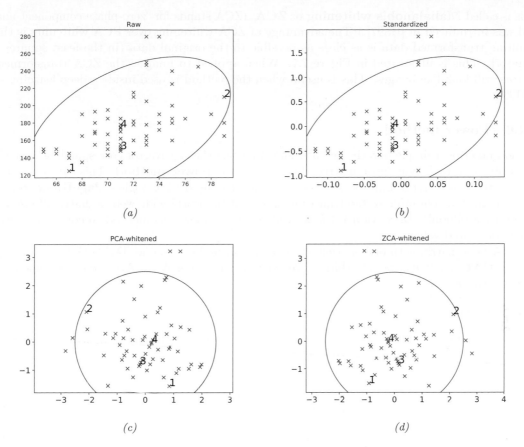

Figure 7.7: (a) Height/weight data. (b) Standardized. (c) PCA Whitening. (d) ZCA whitening. Numbers refer to the first 4 datapoints, but there are 73 datapoints in total. Generated by height_weight_whiten_plot.ipynb.

be $\boldsymbol{\Sigma} = \frac{1}{N}\mathbf{X}^\mathsf{T}\mathbf{X}$, and let $\boldsymbol{\Sigma} = \mathbf{E}\mathbf{D}\mathbf{E}^\mathsf{T}$ be its diagonalization. Equivalently, let $[\mathbf{U}, \mathbf{S}, \mathbf{V}]$ be the SVD of $\mathbf{X}$ (so $\mathbf{E} = \mathbf{V}$ and $\mathbf{D} = \mathbf{S}^2$, as we discuss in Section 20.1.3.3.) Now define

$$\mathbf{W}_{pca} = \mathbf{D}^{-\frac{1}{2}}\mathbf{E}^\mathsf{T} \tag{7.164}$$

This is called the **PCA whitening** matrix. (We discuss PCA in Section 20.1.) Let $\boldsymbol{y} = \mathbf{W}_{pca}\boldsymbol{x}$ be a transformed vector. We can check that its covariance is white as follows:

$$\mathrm{Cov}\left[\boldsymbol{y}\right] = \mathbf{W}\mathbb{E}\left[\boldsymbol{x}\boldsymbol{x}^\mathsf{T}\right]\mathbf{W}^\mathsf{T} = \mathbf{W}\boldsymbol{\Sigma}\mathbf{W}^\mathsf{T} = (\mathbf{D}^{-\frac{1}{2}}\mathbf{E}^\mathsf{T})(\mathbf{E}\mathbf{D}\mathbf{E}^\mathsf{T})(\mathbf{E}\mathbf{D}^{-\frac{1}{2}}) = \mathbf{I} \tag{7.165}$$

The whitening matrix is not unique, since any rotation of it, $\mathbf{W} = \mathbf{R}\mathbf{W}_{pca}$, will still maintain the whitening property, i.e., $\mathbf{W}^\mathsf{T}\mathbf{W} = \boldsymbol{\Sigma}^{-1}$. For example, if we take $\mathbf{R} = \mathbf{E}$, we get

$$\mathbf{W}_{zca} = \mathbf{E}\mathbf{D}^{-\frac{1}{2}}\mathbf{E}^\mathsf{T} = \boldsymbol{\Sigma}^{-\frac{1}{2}} = \mathbf{V}\mathbf{S}^{-1}\mathbf{V}^\mathsf{T} \tag{7.166}$$

This is called **Mahalanobis whitening** or **ZCA**. (ZCA stands for "zero-phase component analysis", and was introduced in [BS97].) The advantage of ZCA whitening over PCA whitening is that the resulting transformed data is as close as possible to the original data (in the least squares sense) [Amo17]. This is illustrated in Figure 7.7. When applied to images, the ZCA transformed data vectors still look like images. This is useful when the method is used inside a deep learning system [KH09].

7.4.6 Power method

We now describe a simple iterative method for computing the eigenvector corresponding to the largest eigenvalue of a real, symmetric matrix; this is called the **power method**. This can be useful when the matrix is very large but sparse. For example, it is used by Google's **PageRank** to compute the stationary distribution of the transition matrix of the world wide web (a matrix of size about 3 billion by 3 billion!). In Section 7.4.7, we will see how to use this method to compute subsequent eigenvectors and values.

Let $\mathbf{A}$ be a matrix with orthonormal eigenvectors $\boldsymbol{u}_i$ and eigenvalues $|\lambda_1| > |\lambda_2| \geq \cdots \geq |\lambda_m| \geq 0$, so $\mathbf{A} = \mathbf{U}\boldsymbol{\Lambda}\mathbf{U}^\mathsf{T}$. Let $\boldsymbol{v}_{(0)}$ be an arbitrary vector in the range of $\mathbf{A}$, so $\mathbf{A}\boldsymbol{x} = \boldsymbol{v}_{(0)}$ for some $\boldsymbol{x}$. Hence we can write $\boldsymbol{v}_{(0)}$ as

$$\boldsymbol{v}_0 = \mathbf{U}(\boldsymbol{\Lambda}\mathbf{U}^\mathsf{T}\boldsymbol{x}) = a_1\boldsymbol{u}_1 + \cdots + a_m\boldsymbol{u}_m \tag{7.167}$$

for some constants a_i. We can now repeatedly multiply $\boldsymbol{v}$ by $\mathbf{A}$ and renormalize:

$$\boldsymbol{v}_t \propto \mathbf{A}\boldsymbol{v}_{t-1} \tag{7.168}$$

(We normalize at each iteration for numerical stability.)

Since $\boldsymbol{v}_t$ is a multiple of $\mathbf{A}^t\boldsymbol{v}_0$, we have

$$\boldsymbol{v}_t \propto a_1\lambda_1^t\boldsymbol{u}_1 + a_2\lambda_2^t\boldsymbol{u}_2 + \cdots + a_m\lambda_m^t\boldsymbol{u}_m \tag{7.169}$$

$$= \lambda_1^t \left(a_1\boldsymbol{u}_1 + a_1(\lambda_2/\lambda_1)^t\boldsymbol{u}_2 + \cdots + a_m(\lambda_m/\lambda_1)^t\boldsymbol{u}_m \right) \tag{7.170}$$

$$\to \lambda_1^t a_1\boldsymbol{u}_1 \tag{7.171}$$

since $\frac{|\lambda_k|}{|\lambda_1|} < 1$ for $k > 1$ (assuming the eigenvalues are sorted in descending order). So we see that this converges to $\boldsymbol{u}_1$, although not very quickly (the error is reduced by approximately $|\lambda_2/\lambda_1|$ at each iteration). The only requirement is that the initial guess satisfy $\boldsymbol{v}_0^\mathsf{T}\boldsymbol{u}_1 \neq 0$, which will be true for a random $\boldsymbol{v}_0$ with high probability.

We now discuss how to compute the corresponding eigenvalue, λ_1. Define the **Rayleigh quotient** to be

$$R(\mathbf{A}, \boldsymbol{x}) \triangleq \frac{\boldsymbol{x}^\mathsf{T}\mathbf{A}\boldsymbol{x}}{\boldsymbol{x}^\mathsf{T}\boldsymbol{x}} \tag{7.172}$$

Hence

$$R(\mathbf{A}, \boldsymbol{u}_i) = \frac{\boldsymbol{u}_i^\mathsf{T}\mathbf{A}\boldsymbol{u}_i}{\boldsymbol{u}_i^\mathsf{T}\boldsymbol{u}_i} = \frac{\lambda_i\boldsymbol{u}_i^\mathsf{T}\boldsymbol{u}_i}{\boldsymbol{u}_i^\mathsf{T}\boldsymbol{u}_i} = \lambda_i \tag{7.173}$$

Thus we can easily compute λ_1 from $\boldsymbol{u}_1$ and $\mathbf{A}$. See power_method_demo.ipynb for a demo.

7.4.7 Deflation

Suppose we have computed the first eigenvector and value u_1, λ_1 by the power method. We now describe how to compute subsequent eigenvectors and values. Since the eigenvectors are orthonormal, and the eigenvalues are real, we can project out the u_1 component from the matrix as follows:

$$\mathbf{A}^{(2)} = (\mathbf{I} - u_1 u_1^\mathsf{T})\mathbf{A}^{(1)} = \mathbf{A}^{(1)} - u_1 u_1^\mathsf{T}\mathbf{A}^{(1)} = \mathbf{A}^{(1)} - \lambda_1 u_1 u_1^\mathsf{T} \tag{7.174}$$

This is called matrix **deflation**. We can then apply the power method to $\mathbf{A}^{(2)}$, which will find the largest eigenvector/value in the subspace orthogonal to u_1.

In Section 20.1.2, we show that the optimal estimate $\hat{\mathbf{W}}$ for the PCA model (described in Section 20.1) is given by the first K eigenvectors of the empirical covariance matrix. Hence deflation can be used to implement PCA. It can also be modified to implement sparse PCA [Mac09].

7.4.8 Eigenvectors optimize quadratic forms

We can use matrix calculus to solve an optimization problem in a way that leads directly to eigenvalue/eigenvector analysis. Consider the following, equality constrained optimization problem:

$$\max_{x \in \mathbb{R}^n} \ x^\mathsf{T}\mathbf{A}x \quad \text{subject to } \|x\|_2^2 = 1 \tag{7.175}$$

for a symmetric matrix $\mathbf{A} \in \mathbb{S}^n$. A standard way of solving optimization problems with equality constraints is by forming the Lagrangian, an objective function that includes the equality constraints (see Section 8.5.1). The Lagrangian in this case can be given by

$$\mathcal{L}(x, \lambda) = x^\mathsf{T}\mathbf{A}x + \lambda(1 - x^\mathsf{T}x) \tag{7.176}$$

where λ is called the Lagrange multiplier associated with the equality constraint. It can be established that for x^* to be a optimal point to the problem, the gradient of the Lagrangian has to be zero at x^* (this is not the only condition, but it is required). That is,

$$\nabla_x \mathcal{L}(x, \lambda) = 2\mathbf{A}^\mathsf{T}x - 2\lambda x = \mathbf{0}. \tag{7.177}$$

Notice that this is just the linear equation $\mathbf{A}x = \lambda x$. This shows that the only points which can possibly maximize (or minimize) $x^\mathsf{T}\mathbf{A}x$ assuming $x^\mathsf{T}x = 1$ are the eigenvectors of $\mathbf{A}$.

7.5 Singular value decomposition (SVD)

We now discuss the SVD, which generalizes EVD to rectangular matrices.

7.5.1 Basics

Any (real) $m \times n$ matrix $\mathbf{A}$ can be decomposed as

$$\mathbf{A} = \mathbf{U}\mathbf{S}\mathbf{V}^\mathsf{T} = \sigma_1 \begin{pmatrix} | \\ u_1 \\ | \end{pmatrix} \begin{pmatrix} - & v_1^\mathsf{T} & - \end{pmatrix} + \cdots + \sigma_r \begin{pmatrix} | \\ u_r \\ | \end{pmatrix} \begin{pmatrix} - & v_r^\mathsf{T} & - \end{pmatrix} \tag{7.178}$$

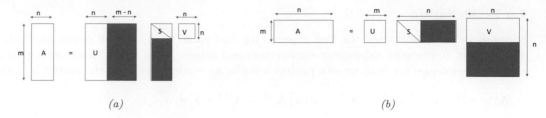

Figure 7.8: SVD decomposition of a matrix, $\mathbf{A} = \mathbf{USV}^\mathsf{T}$. The shaded parts of each matrix are not computed in the economy-sized version. (a) Tall skinny matrix. (b) Short wide matrix.

where $\mathbf{U}$ is an $m \times m$ whose columns are orthornormal (so $\mathbf{U}^\mathsf{T}\mathbf{U} = \mathbf{I}_m$), $\mathbf{V}$ is $n \times n$ matrix whose rows and columns are orthonormal (so $\mathbf{V}^\mathsf{T}\mathbf{V} = \mathbf{VV}^\mathsf{T} = \mathbf{I}_n$), and $\mathbf{S}$ is a $m \times n$ matrix containing the $r = \min(m, n)$ **singular values** $\sigma_i \geq 0$ on the main diagonal, with 0s filling the rest of the matrix. The columns of $\mathbf{U}$ are the left **singular vectors**, and the columns of $\mathbf{V}$ are the right singular vectors. This is called the **singular value decomposition** or **SVD** of the matrix. See Figure 7.8 for an example.

As is apparent from Figure 7.8a, if $m > n$, there are at most n singular values, so the last $m - n$ columns of $\mathbf{U}$ are irrelevant (since they will be multiplied by 0). The **economy sized SVD**, also called a **thin SVD**, avoids computing these unnecessary elements. In other words, if we write the $\mathbf{U}$ matrix as $\mathbf{U} = [\mathbf{U}_1, \mathbf{U}_2]$, we only compute $\mathbf{U}_1$. Figure 7.8b shows the opposite case, where $m < n$, where we represent $\mathbf{V} = [\mathbf{V}_1; \mathbf{V}_2]$, and only compute $\mathbf{V}_1$.

The cost of computing the SVD is $O(\min(mn^2, m^2n))$. Details on how it works can be found in standard linear algebra textbooks.

7.5.2   Connection between SVD and EVD

If $\mathbf{A}$ is real, symmetric and positive definite, then the singular values are equal to the eigenvalues, and the left and right singular vectors are equal to the eigenvectors (up to a sign change):

$$\mathbf{A} = \mathbf{USV}^\mathsf{T} = \mathbf{USU}^\mathsf{T} = \mathbf{USU}^{-1} \tag{7.179}$$

Note, however, that NumPy always returns the singular values in decreasing order, whereas the eigenvalues need not necessarily be sorted.

In general, for an arbitrary real matrix $\mathbf{A}$, if $\mathbf{A} = \mathbf{USV}^\mathsf{T}$, we have

$$\mathbf{A}^\mathsf{T}\mathbf{A} = \mathbf{VS}^\mathsf{T}\mathbf{U}^\mathsf{T}\,\mathbf{USV}^\mathsf{T} = \mathbf{V}(\mathbf{S}^\mathsf{T}\mathbf{S})\mathbf{V}^\mathsf{T} \tag{7.180}$$

Hence

$$(\mathbf{A}^\mathsf{T}\mathbf{A})\mathbf{V} = \mathbf{VD}_n \tag{7.181}$$

so the eigenvectors of $\mathbf{A}^\mathsf{T}\mathbf{A}$ are equal to $\mathbf{V}$, the right singular vectors of $\mathbf{A}$, and the eigenvalues of $\mathbf{A}^\mathsf{T}\mathbf{A}$ are equal to $\mathbf{D}_n = \mathbf{S}^\mathsf{T}\mathbf{S}$, which is an $n \times n$ diagonal matrix containing the squared singular values. Similarly

$$\mathbf{AA}^\mathsf{T} = \mathbf{USV}^\mathsf{T}\,\mathbf{VS}^\mathsf{T}\mathbf{U}^\mathsf{T} = \mathbf{U}(\mathbf{SS}^\mathsf{T})\mathbf{U}^\mathsf{T} \tag{7.182}$$

$$(\mathbf{AA}^\mathsf{T})\mathbf{U} = \mathbf{UD}_m \tag{7.183}$$

so the eigenvectors of $\mathbf{A}\mathbf{A}^\mathsf{T}$ are equal to $\mathbf{U}$, the left singular vectors of $\mathbf{A}$, and the eigenvalues of $\mathbf{A}\mathbf{A}^\mathsf{T}$ are equal to $\mathbf{D}_m = \mathbf{S}\mathbf{S}^\mathsf{T}$, which is an $m \times m$ diagonal matrix containing the squared singular values. In summary,

$$\mathbf{U} = \mathrm{evec}(\mathbf{A}\mathbf{A}^\mathsf{T}), \ \ \mathbf{V} = \mathrm{evec}(\mathbf{A}^\mathsf{T}\mathbf{A}), \ \mathbf{D}_m = \mathrm{eval}(\mathbf{A}\mathbf{A}^\mathsf{T}), \mathbf{D}_n = \mathrm{eval}(\mathbf{A}^\mathsf{T}\mathbf{A}) \tag{7.184}$$

If we just use the computed (non-zero) parts in the economy-sized SVD, then we can define

$$\mathbf{D} = \mathbf{S}^2 = \mathbf{S}^\mathsf{T}\mathbf{S} = \mathbf{S}\mathbf{S}^\mathsf{T} \tag{7.185}$$

Note also that an EVD does not always exist, even for square $\mathbf{A}$, whereas an SVD always exists.

7.5.3 Pseudo inverse

The **Moore-Penrose pseudo-inverse** of $\mathbf{A}$, pseudo inverse denoted $\mathbf{A}^\dagger$, is defined as the unique matrix that satisfies the following 4 properties:

$$\mathbf{A}\mathbf{A}^\dagger\mathbf{A} = \mathbf{A}, \ \mathbf{A}^\dagger\mathbf{A}\mathbf{A}^\dagger = \mathbf{A}^\dagger, \ (\mathbf{A}\mathbf{A}^\dagger)^\mathsf{T} = \mathbf{A}\mathbf{A}^\dagger, \ (\mathbf{A}^\dagger\mathbf{A})^\mathsf{T} = \mathbf{A}^\dagger\mathbf{A} \tag{7.186}$$

If $\mathbf{A}$ is square and non-singular, then $\mathbf{A}^\dagger = \mathbf{A}^{-1}$.

If $m > n$ (tall, skinny) and the columns of $\mathbf{A}$ are linearly independent (so $\mathbf{A}$ is full rank), then

$$\mathbf{A}^\dagger = (\mathbf{A}^\mathsf{T}\mathbf{A})^{-1}\mathbf{A}^\mathsf{T} \tag{7.187}$$

which is the same expression as arises in the normal equations (see Section 11.2.2.1). In this case, $\mathbf{A}^\dagger$ is a left inverse of $\mathbf{A}$ because

$$\mathbf{A}^\dagger\mathbf{A} = (\mathbf{A}^\mathsf{T}\mathbf{A})^{-1}\mathbf{A}^\mathsf{T}\mathbf{A} = \mathbf{I} \tag{7.188}$$

but is not a right inverse because

$$\mathbf{A}\mathbf{A}^\dagger = \mathbf{A}(\mathbf{A}^\mathsf{T}\mathbf{A})^{-1}\mathbf{A}^\mathsf{T} \tag{7.189}$$

only has rank n, and so cannot be the $m \times m$ identity matrix.

If $m < n$ (short, fat) and the rows of $\mathbf{A}$ are linearly independent (so $\mathbf{A}^\mathsf{T}$ is full rank), then the pseudo inverse is

$$\mathbf{A}^\dagger = \mathbf{A}^\mathsf{T}(\mathbf{A}\mathbf{A}^\mathsf{T})^{-1} \tag{7.190}$$

In this case, $\mathbf{A}^\dagger$ is a right inverse of $\mathbf{A}$.

We can compute the pseudo inverse using the SVD decomposition $\mathbf{A} = \mathbf{U}\mathbf{S}\mathbf{V}^\mathsf{T}$. In particular, one can show that

$$\mathbf{A}^\dagger = \mathbf{V}[\mathrm{diag}(1/\sigma_1, \cdots, 1/\sigma_r, 0, \cdots, 0)]\mathbf{U}^\mathsf{T} = \mathbf{V}\mathbf{S}^{-1}\mathbf{U}^\mathsf{T} \tag{7.191}$$

where r is the rank of the matrix, and where we define $\mathbf{S}^{-1} = \mathrm{diag}(\sigma_1^{-1}, \ldots, \sigma_r^{-1}, 0, \ldots, 0)$. Indeed if the matrices were square and full rank we would have

$$(\mathbf{U}\mathbf{S}\mathbf{V}^\mathsf{T})^{-1} = \mathbf{V}\mathbf{S}^{-1}\mathbf{U}^\mathsf{T} \tag{7.192}$$

7.5.4   SVD and the range and null space of a matrix *

In this section, we show that the left and right singular vectors form an orthonormal basis for the range and null space.

From Equation (7.178) we have

$$\mathbf{A}\boldsymbol{x} = \sum_{j:\sigma_j>0} \sigma_j(\boldsymbol{v}_j^\mathsf{T}\boldsymbol{x})\boldsymbol{u}_j = \sum_{j=1}^{r} \sigma_j(\boldsymbol{v}_j^\mathsf{T}\boldsymbol{x})\boldsymbol{u}_j \tag{7.193}$$

where r is the rank of $\mathbf{A}$. Thus any $\mathbf{A}\boldsymbol{x}$ can be written as a linear combination of the left singular vectors $\boldsymbol{u}_1, \ldots, \boldsymbol{u}_r$, so the range of $\mathbf{A}$ is given by

$$\text{range}(\mathbf{A}) = \text{span}\left(\{\boldsymbol{u}_j : \sigma_j > 0\}\right) \tag{7.194}$$

with dimension r.

To find a basis for the null space, let us now define a second vector $\boldsymbol{y} \in \mathbb{R}^n$ that is a linear combination solely of the right singular vectors for the zero singular values,

$$\boldsymbol{y} = \sum_{j:\sigma_j=0} c_j\boldsymbol{v}_j = \sum_{j=r+1}^{n} c_j\boldsymbol{v}_j \tag{7.195}$$

Since the $\boldsymbol{v}_j$'s are orthonormal, we have

$$\mathbf{A}\boldsymbol{y} = \mathbf{U}\begin{pmatrix} \sigma_1\boldsymbol{v}_1^\mathsf{T}\boldsymbol{y} \\ \vdots \\ \sigma_r\boldsymbol{v}_r^\mathsf{T}\boldsymbol{y} \\ \sigma_{r+1}\boldsymbol{v}_{r+1}^\mathsf{T}\boldsymbol{y} \\ \vdots \\ \sigma_n\boldsymbol{v}_n^\mathsf{T}\boldsymbol{y} \end{pmatrix} = \mathbf{U}\begin{pmatrix} \sigma_1 0 \\ \vdots \\ \sigma_r 0 \\ 0\boldsymbol{v}_{r+1}^\mathsf{T}\boldsymbol{y} \\ \vdots \\ 0\boldsymbol{v}_n^\mathsf{T}\boldsymbol{y} \end{pmatrix} = \mathbf{U}\mathbf{0} = \mathbf{0} \tag{7.196}$$

Hence the right singular vectors form an orthonormal basis for the null space:

$$\text{nullspace}(\mathbf{A}) = \text{span}\left(\{\boldsymbol{v}_j : \sigma_j = 0\}\right) \tag{7.197}$$

with dimension $n - r$. We see that

$$\dim(\text{range}(\mathbf{A})) + \dim(\text{nullspace}(\mathbf{A})) = r + (n - r) = n \tag{7.198}$$

In words, this is often written as

$$\text{rank} + \text{nullity} = n \tag{7.199}$$

This is called the **rank-nullity theorem**. It follows from this that the rank of a matrix is the number of nonzero singular values.

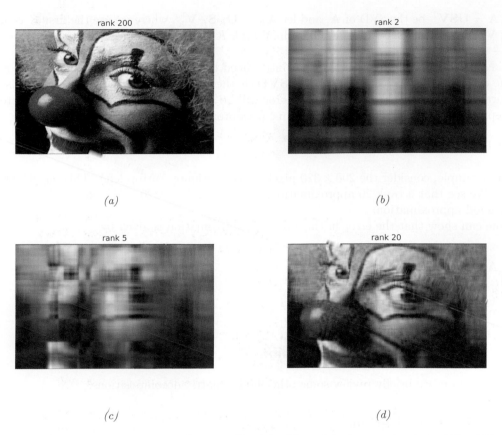

(a)

(b)

(c)

(d)

Figure 7.9: *Low rank approximations to an image. Top left: The original image is of size* 200×320, *so has rank 200. Subsequent images have ranks 2, 5, and 20 Generated by* svd_image_demo.ipynb.

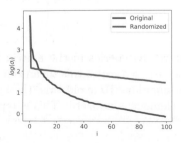

Figure 7.10: *First 100 log singular values for the clown image (red line), and for a data matrix obtained by randomly shuffling the pixels (blue line). Generated by* svd_image_demo.ipynb. *Adapted from Figure 14.24 of [HTF09].*

7.5.5   Truncated SVD

Let $\mathbf{A} = \mathbf{U}\mathbf{S}\mathbf{V}^T$ be the SVD of $\mathbf{A}$, and let $\hat{\mathbf{A}}_K = \mathbf{U}_K\mathbf{S}_K\mathbf{V}_K^\mathsf{T}$, where we use the first K columns of $\mathbf{U}$ and $\mathbf{V}$. This can be shown to be the optimal rank K approximation, in the sense that it minimizes $||\mathbf{A} - \hat{\mathbf{A}}_K||_F^2$.

If $K = r = \text{rank}(\mathbf{A})$, there is no error introduced by this decomposition. But if $K < r$, we incur some error. This is called a **truncated SVD**. If the singular values die off quickly, as is typical in natural data (see e.g., Figure 7.10), the error will be small. The total number of parameters needed to represent an $N \times D$ matrix using a rank K approximation is

$$NK + KD + K = K(N + D + 1) \tag{7.200}$$

As an example, consider the 200×320 pixel image in Figure 7.9(top left). This has 64,000 numbers in it. We see that a rank 20 approximation, with only $(200 + 320 + 1) \times 20 = 10,420$ numbers is a very good approximation.

One can show that the error in this rank-K approximation is given by

$$||\mathbf{A} - \hat{\mathbf{A}}||_F = \sum_{k=K+1}^{r} \sigma_k \tag{7.201}$$

where σ_k is the k'th singular value of $\mathbf{A}$.

7.6   Other matrix decompositions *

In this section, we briefly review some other useful matrix decompositions.

7.6.1   LU factorization

We can factorize any square matrix $\mathbf{A}$ into a product of a lower triangular matrix $\mathbf{L}$ and an upper triangular matrix $\mathbf{U}$. For example,

$$\begin{bmatrix} a_{11} & a_{12} & a_{13} \\ a_{21} & a_{22} & a_{23} \\ a_{31} & a_{32} & a_{33} \end{bmatrix} = \begin{bmatrix} l_{11} & 0 & 0 \\ l_{21} & l_{22} & 0 \\ l_{31} & l_{32} & l_{33} \end{bmatrix} \begin{bmatrix} u_{11} & u_{12} & u_{13} \\ 0 & u_{22} & u_{23} \\ 0 & 0 & u_{33} \end{bmatrix}. \tag{7.202}$$

In general we may need to permute the entries in the matrix before creating this decomposition. To see this, suppose $a_{11} = 0$. Since $a_{11} = l_{11}u_{11}$, this means either l_{11} or u_{11} or both must be zero, but that would imply $\mathbf{L}$ or $\mathbf{U}$ are singular. To avoid this, the first step of the algorithm can simply reorder the rows so that the first element is nonzero. This is repeated for subsequent steps. We can denote this process by

$$\mathbf{PA} = \mathbf{LU} \tag{7.203}$$

where $\mathbf{P}$ is a permutation matrix, i.e., a square binary matrix where $P_{ij} = 1$ if row j gets permuted to row i. This is called **partial pivoting**.

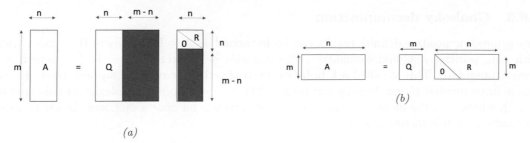

Figure 7.11: Illustration of QR decomposition, $\mathbf{A} = \mathbf{QR}$, where $\mathbf{Q}^\top \mathbf{Q} = \mathbf{I}$ and $\mathbf{R}$ is upper triangular. (a) Tall, skinny matrix. The shaded parts are not computed in the economy-sized version, since they are not needed. (b) Short, wide matrix.

7.6.2 QR decomposition

Suppose we have $\mathbf{A} \in \mathbb{R}^{m \times n}$ representing a set of linearly independent basis vectors (so $m \geq n$), and we want to find a series of orthonormal vectors $\boldsymbol{q}_1, \boldsymbol{q}_2, \ldots$ that span the successive subspaces of $\mathrm{span}(\boldsymbol{a}_1)$, $\mathrm{span}(\boldsymbol{a}_1, \boldsymbol{a}_2)$, etc. In other words, we want to find vectors $\boldsymbol{q}_j$ and coefficients r_{ij} such that

$$
\begin{pmatrix} | & | & & | \\ \boldsymbol{a}_1 & \boldsymbol{a}_2 & \cdots & \boldsymbol{a}_n \\ | & | & & | \end{pmatrix} = \begin{pmatrix} | & | & & | \\ \boldsymbol{q}_1 & \boldsymbol{q}_2 & \cdots & \boldsymbol{q}_n \\ | & | & & | \end{pmatrix} \begin{pmatrix} r_{11} & r_{12} & \cdots & r_{1n} \\ & r_{22} & \cdots & r_{2n} \\ & & \ddots & \\ & & & r_{nn} \end{pmatrix} \tag{7.204}
$$

We can write this

$$\boldsymbol{a}_1 = r_{11} \boldsymbol{q}_1 \tag{7.205}$$
$$\boldsymbol{a}_2 = r_{12} \boldsymbol{q}_1 + r_{22} \boldsymbol{q}_2 \tag{7.206}$$
$$\vdots$$
$$\boldsymbol{a}_n = r_{1n} \boldsymbol{q}_1 + \cdots + r_{nn} \boldsymbol{q}_n \tag{7.207}$$

so we see $\boldsymbol{q}_1$ spans the space of $\boldsymbol{a}_1$, and $\boldsymbol{q}_1$ and $\boldsymbol{q}_2$ span the space of $\{\boldsymbol{a}_1, \boldsymbol{a}_2\}$, etc.

In matrix notation, we have

$$\mathbf{A} = \hat{\mathbf{Q}} \hat{\mathbf{R}} \tag{7.208}$$

where $\hat{\mathbf{Q}}$ is $m \times n$ with orthonormal columns and $\hat{\mathbf{R}}$ is $n \times n$ and upper triangular. This is called a **reduced QR** or **economy sized QR** factorization of $\mathbf{A}$; see Figure 7.11.

A full QR factorization appends an additional $m - n$ orthonormal columns to $\hat{\mathbf{Q}}$ so it becomes a square, orthogonal matrix $\mathbf{Q}$, which satisfies $\mathbf{Q}\mathbf{Q}^\top = \mathbf{Q}^\top \mathbf{Q} = \mathbf{I}$. Also, we append rows made of zero to $\hat{\mathbf{R}}$ so it becomes an $m \times n$ matrix that is still upper triangular, called $\mathbf{R}$: see Figure 7.11. The zero entries in $\mathbf{R}$ "kill off" the new columns in $\mathbf{Q}$, so the result is the same as $\hat{\mathbf{Q}}\hat{\mathbf{R}}$.

QR decomposition is commonly used to solve systems of linear equations, as we discuss in Section 11.2.2.3.

7.6.3   Cholesky decomposition

Any symmetric positive definite matrix can be factorized as $\mathbf{A} = \mathbf{R}^\mathsf{T}\mathbf{R}$, where $\mathbf{R}$ is upper triangular with real, positive diagonal elements. (This can also be written as $\mathbf{A} = \mathbf{L}\mathbf{L}^\mathsf{T}$, where $\mathbf{L} = \mathbf{R}^\mathsf{T}$ is lower triangular.) This is called a **Cholesky factorization** or **matrix square root**. In NumPy, this is implemented by `np.linalg.cholesky`. The computational complexity of this operation is $O(V^3)$, where V is the number of variables, but can be less for sparse matrices. Below we give some applications of this factorization.

7.6.3.1   Application: Sampling from an MVN

The Cholesky decomposition of a covariance matrix can be used to sample from a multivariate Gaussian. Let $\boldsymbol{y} \sim \mathcal{N}(\boldsymbol{\mu}, \boldsymbol{\Sigma})$ and $\boldsymbol{\Sigma} = \mathbf{L}\mathbf{L}^\mathsf{T}$. We first sample $\boldsymbol{x} \sim \mathcal{N}(\mathbf{0}, \mathbf{I})$, which is easy because it just requires sampling from d separate 1d Gaussians. We then set $\boldsymbol{y} = \mathbf{L}\boldsymbol{x} + \boldsymbol{\mu}$. This is valid since

$$\text{Cov}\left[\boldsymbol{y}\right] = \mathbf{L}\text{Cov}\left[\boldsymbol{x}\right]\mathbf{L}^\mathsf{T} = \mathbf{L}\,\mathbf{I}\,\mathbf{L}^\mathsf{T} = \boldsymbol{\Sigma} \tag{7.209}$$

See cholesky_demo.ipynb for some code.

7.7   Solving systems of linear equations *

An important application of linear algebra is the study of systems of linear equations. For example, consider the following set of 3 equations:

$$3x_1 + 2x_2 - x_3 = 1 \tag{7.210}$$
$$2x_1 - 2x_2 + 4x_3 = -2 \tag{7.211}$$
$$-x_1 + \frac{1}{2}x_2 - x_3 = 0 \tag{7.212}$$

We can represent this in matrix-vector form as follows:

$$\mathbf{A}\boldsymbol{x} = \boldsymbol{b} \tag{7.213}$$

where

$$\mathbf{A} = \begin{pmatrix} 3 & 2 & -1 \\ 2 & -2 & 4 \\ -1 & \frac{1}{2} & -1 \end{pmatrix}, \; \boldsymbol{b} = \begin{pmatrix} 1 \\ -2 \\ 0 \end{pmatrix} \tag{7.214}$$

The solution is $\boldsymbol{x} = [1, -2, -2]$.

In general, if we have m equations and n unknowns, then $\mathbf{A}$ will be a $m \times n$ matrix, and $\boldsymbol{b}$ will be a $m \times 1$ vector. If $m = n$ (and $\mathbf{A}$ is full rank), there is a single unique solution. If $m < n$, the system is **underdetermined**, so there is not a unique solution. If $m > n$, the system is **overdetermined**, since there are more constraints than unknowns, and not all the lines intersect at the same point. See Figure 7.12 for an illustration. We discuss how to compute solutions in each of these cases below.

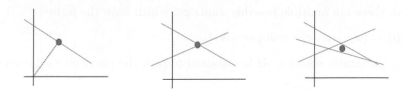

Figure 7.12: Solution of a set of m linear equations in $n = 2$ variables. (a) $m = 1 < n$ so the system is underdetermined. We show the minimal norm solution as a blue circle. (The dotted red line is orthogonal to the line, and its length is the distance to the origin.) (b) $m = n = 2$, so there is a unique solution. (c) $m = 3 > n$, so there is no unique solution. We show the least squares solution.

7.7.1 Solving square systems

In the case where $m = n$, we can solve for x by computing an LU decomposition, $\mathbf{A} = \mathbf{LU}$, and then proceeding as follows:

$$\mathbf{A}x = b \tag{7.215}$$
$$\mathbf{LU}x = b \tag{7.216}$$
$$\mathbf{U}x = \mathbf{L}^{-1}b \triangleq y \tag{7.217}$$
$$x = \mathbf{U}^{-1}y \tag{7.218}$$

The crucial point is that $\mathbf{L}$ and $\mathbf{U}$ are both triangular matrices, so we can avoid taking matrix inverses, and use a method known as **backsubstitution** instead.

In particular, we can solve $y = \mathbf{L}^{-1}b$ without taking inverses as follows. First we write

$$\begin{pmatrix} L_{11} & & & \\ L_{21} & L_{22} & & \\ & & \ddots & \\ L_{n1} & L_{n2} & \cdots & L_{nn} \end{pmatrix} \begin{pmatrix} y_1 \\ \vdots \\ y_n \end{pmatrix} = \begin{pmatrix} b_1 \\ \vdots \\ b_n \end{pmatrix} \tag{7.219}$$

We start by solving $L_{11}y_1 = b_1$ to find y_1 and then substitute this in to solve

$$L_{21}y_1 + L_{22}y_2 = b_2 \tag{7.220}$$

for y_2. We repeat this recursively. This process is often denoted by the **backslash operator**, $y = \mathbf{L} \setminus b$. Once we have y, we can solve $x = \mathbf{U}^{-1}y$ using backsubstitution in a similar manner.

7.7.2 Solving underconstrained systems (least norm estimation)

In this section, we consider the underconstrained setting, where $m < n$.[3] We assume the rows are linearly independent, so $\mathbf{A}$ is full rank.

---

3. Our presentation is based in part on lecture notes by Stephen Boyd at `http://ee263.stanford.edu/lectures/min-norm.pdf`.

When $m < n$, there are multiple possible solutions, which have the form

$$\{x : \mathbf{A}x = b\} = \{x_p + z : z \in \text{nullspace}(\mathbf{A})\} \tag{7.221}$$

where x_p is any particular solution. It is standard to pick the particular solution with minimal ℓ_2 norm, i.e.,

$$\hat{x} = \underset{x}{\text{argmin}} \, ||x||_2^2 \quad \text{s.t.} \quad \mathbf{A}x = b \tag{7.222}$$

We can compute the minimal norm solution using the **right pseudo inverse**:

$$x_{\text{pinv}} = \mathbf{A}^\mathsf{T}(\mathbf{A}\mathbf{A}^\mathsf{T})^{-1}b \tag{7.223}$$

(See Section 7.5.3 for more details.)

To see this, suppose x is some other solution, so $\mathbf{A}x = b$, and $\mathbf{A}(x - x_{\text{pinv}}) = 0$. Thus

$$(x - x_{\text{pinv}})^\mathsf{T}x_{\text{pinv}} = (x - x_{\text{pinv}})^\mathsf{T}\mathbf{A}^\mathsf{T}(\mathbf{A}\mathbf{A}^\mathsf{T})^{-1}b = (\mathbf{A}(x - x_{\text{pinv}}))^\mathsf{T}(\mathbf{A}\mathbf{A}^\mathsf{T})^{-1}b = 0 \tag{7.224}$$

and hence $(x - x_{\text{pinv}}) \perp x_{\text{pinv}}$. By **Pythagoras's theorem**, the norm of x is

$$||x||^2 = ||x_{\text{pinv}} + x - x_{\text{pinv}}||^2 = ||x_{\text{pinv}}||^2 + ||x - x_{\text{pinv}}||^2 \geq ||x_{\text{pinv}}||^2 \tag{7.225}$$

Thus any solution apart from x_{pinv} has larger norm.

We can also solve the constrained optimization problem in Equation (7.222) by minimizing the following unconstrained objective

$$\mathcal{L}(x, \lambda) = x^\mathsf{T}x + \lambda^\mathsf{T}(\mathbf{A}x - b) \tag{7.226}$$

From Section 8.5.1, the optimality conditions are

$$\nabla_x \mathcal{L} = 2x + \mathbf{A}^\mathsf{T}\lambda = 0, \quad \nabla_\lambda \mathcal{L} = \mathbf{A}x - b = 0 \tag{7.227}$$

From the first condition we have $x = -\mathbf{A}^\mathsf{T}\lambda/2$. Subsituting into the second we get

$$\mathbf{A}x = -\frac{1}{2}\mathbf{A}\mathbf{A}^\mathsf{T}\lambda = b \tag{7.228}$$

which implies $\lambda = -2(\mathbf{A}\mathbf{A}^\mathsf{T})^{-1}b$. Hence $x = \mathbf{A}^\mathsf{T}(\mathbf{A}\mathbf{A}^\mathsf{T})^{-1}b$, which is the right pseudo inverse solution.

7.7.3 Solving overconstrained systems (least squares estimation)

If $m > n$, we have an overdetermined solution, which typically does not have an exact solution, but we will try to find the solution that gets as close as possible to satisfying all of the constraints specified by $\mathbf{A}x = b$. We can do this by minimizing the following cost function, known as the **least squares objective**:[4]

$$f(x) = \frac{1}{2}||\mathbf{A}x - b||_2^2 \tag{7.233}$$

---

4. Note that some equation numbers have been skipped. This is intentional. The reason is that I have omitted some erroneous material from an earlier version (described in https://github.com/probml/pml-book/issues/266), but want to make sure the equation numbering is consistent across different versions of the book.

Using matrix calculus results from Section 7.8 we have that the gradient is given by

$$g(x) = \frac{\partial}{\partial x} f(x) = \mathbf{A}^\mathsf{T} \mathbf{A} x - \mathbf{A}^\mathsf{T} b \tag{7.234}$$

The optimum can be found by solving $g(x) = \mathbf{0}$. This gives

$$\mathbf{A}^\mathsf{T} \mathbf{A} x = \mathbf{A}^\mathsf{T} b \tag{7.235}$$

These are known as the **normal equations**, since, at the optimal solution, $b - \mathbf{A}x$ is normal (orthogonal) to the range of $\mathbf{A}$, as we explain in Section 11.2.2.2. The corresponding solution $\hat{x}$ is the **ordinary least squares** (**OLS**) solution, which is given by

$$\hat{x} = (\mathbf{A}^\mathsf{T} \mathbf{A})^{-1} \mathbf{A}^\mathsf{T} b \tag{7.236}$$

The quantity $\mathbf{A}^\dagger = (\mathbf{A}^\mathsf{T} \mathbf{A})^{-1} \mathbf{A}^\mathsf{T}$ is the **left pseudo inverse** of the (non-square) matrix $\mathbf{A}$ (see Section 7.5.3 for more details).

We can check that the solution is unique by showing that the Hessian is positive definite. In this case, the Hessian is given by

$$\mathbf{H}(x) = \frac{\partial^2}{\partial x^2} f(x) = \mathbf{A}^\mathsf{T} \mathbf{A} \tag{7.237}$$

If $\mathbf{A}$ is full rank (so the columns of $\mathbf{A}$ are linearly independent), then $\mathbf{H}$ is positive definite, since for any $v > \mathbf{0}$, we have

$$v^\mathsf{T} (\mathbf{A}^\mathsf{T} \mathbf{A}) v = (\mathbf{A}v)^\mathsf{T} (\mathbf{A}v) = ||\mathbf{A}v||^2 > 0 \tag{7.238}$$

Hence in the full rank case, the least squares objective has a unique global minimum.

7.8 Matrix calculus

The topic of **calculus** concerns computing "rates of change" of functions as we vary their inputs. It is of vital importance to machine learning, as well as almost every other numerical discipline. In this section, we review some standard results. In some cases, we use some concepts and notation from matrix algebra, which we cover in Chapter 7. For more details on these results from a deep learning perspective, see [PH18].

7.8.1 Derivatives

Consider a scalar-argument function $f : \mathbb{R} \to \mathbb{R}$. We define its **derivative** at a point x to be the quantity

$$f'(x) \triangleq \lim_{h \to 0} \frac{f(x+h) - f(x)}{h} \tag{7.239}$$

assuming the limit exists. This measures how quickly the output changes when we move a small distance in input space away from x (i.e., the "rate of change" of the function). We can interpret $f'(x)$ as the slope of the tangent line at $f(x)$, and hence

$$f(x+h) \approx f(x) + f'(x)h \tag{7.240}$$

for small h.

We can compute a **finite difference** approximation to the derivative by using a finite step size h, as follows:

$$f'(x) \equiv \underbrace{\lim_{h \to 0} \frac{f(x+h) - f(x)}{h}}_{\text{forward difference}} = \underbrace{\lim_{h \to 0} \frac{f(x+h/2) - f(x-h/2)}{h}}_{\text{central difference}} = \underbrace{\lim_{h \to 0} \frac{f(x) - f(x-h)}{h}}_{\text{backward difference}} \qquad (7.241)$$

The smaller the step size h, the better the estimate, although if h is too small, there can be errors due to numerical cancellation.

We can think of differentiation as an operator that maps functions to functions, $D(f) = f'$, where $f'(x)$ computes the derivative at x (assuming the derivative exists at that point). The use of the prime symbol f' to denote the derivative is called **Lagrange notation**. The second derivative function, which measures how quickly the gradient is changing, is denoted by f''. The n'th derivative function is denoted $f^{(n)}$.

Alternatively, we can use **Leibniz notation**, in which we denote the function by $y = f(x)$, and its derivative by $\frac{dy}{dx}$ or $\frac{d}{dx} f(x)$. To denote the evaluation of the derivative at a point a, we write $\frac{df}{dx}\Big|_{x=a}$.

7.8.2 Gradients

We can extend the notion of derivatives to handle vector-argument functions, $f : \mathbb{R}^n \to \mathbb{R}$, by defining the **partial derivative** of f with respect to x_i to be

$$\frac{\partial f}{\partial x_i} = \lim_{h \to 0} \frac{f(\boldsymbol{x} + h\boldsymbol{e}_i) - f(\boldsymbol{x})}{h} \qquad (7.242)$$

where $\boldsymbol{e}_i$ is the i'th unit vector.

The **gradient** of a function at a point $\boldsymbol{x}$ is the vector of its partial derivatives:

$$\boldsymbol{g} = \frac{\partial f}{\partial \boldsymbol{x}} = \nabla f = \begin{pmatrix} \frac{\partial f}{\partial x_1} \\ \vdots \\ \frac{\partial f}{\partial x_n} \end{pmatrix} \qquad (7.243)$$

To emphasize the point at which the gradient is evaluated, we can write

$$\boldsymbol{g}(\boldsymbol{x}^*) \triangleq \frac{\partial f}{\partial \boldsymbol{x}}\Big|_{\boldsymbol{x}^*} \qquad (7.244)$$

We see that the operator ∇ (pronounced "nabla") maps a function $f : \mathbb{R}^n \to \mathbb{R}$ to another function $\boldsymbol{g} : \mathbb{R}^n \to \mathbb{R}^n$. Since $\boldsymbol{g}()$ is a vector-valued function, it is known as a **vector field**. By contrast, the derivative function f' is a **scalar field**.

7.8.3 Directional derivative

The **directional derivative** measures how much the function $f : \mathbb{R}^n \to \mathbb{R}$ changes along a direction $\boldsymbol{v}$ in space. It is defined as follows

$$D_{\boldsymbol{v}} f(\boldsymbol{x}) = \lim_{h \to 0} \frac{f(\boldsymbol{x} + h\boldsymbol{v}) - f(\boldsymbol{x})}{h} \qquad (7.245)$$

We can approximate this numerically using 2 function calls to f, regardless of n. By contrast, a numerical approximation to the standard gradient vector takes $n + 1$ calls (or $2n$ if using central differences).

Note that the directional derivative along v is the scalar product of the gradient g and the vector v:

$$D_v f(x) = \nabla f(x) \cdot v \tag{7.246}$$

7.8.4 Total derivative *

Suppose that some of the arguments to the function depend on each other. Concretely, suppose the function has the form $f(t, x(t), y(t))$. We define the **total derivative** of f wrt t as follows:

$$\frac{df}{dt} = \frac{\partial f}{\partial t} + \frac{\partial f}{\partial x}\frac{dx}{dt} + \frac{\partial f}{\partial y}\frac{dy}{dt} \tag{7.247}$$

If we multiply both sides by the differential dt, we get the **total differential**

$$df = \frac{\partial f}{\partial t}dt + \frac{\partial f}{\partial x}dx + \frac{\partial f}{\partial y}dy \tag{7.248}$$

This measures how much f changes when we change t, both via the direct effect of t on f, but also indirectly, via the effects of t on x and y.

7.8.5 Jacobian

Consider a function that maps a vector to another vector, $f : \mathbb{R}^n \to \mathbb{R}^m$. The **Jacobian matrix** of this function is an $m \times n$ matrix of partial derivatives:

$$\mathbf{J}_f(x) = \frac{\partial f}{\partial x^\mathsf{T}} \triangleq \begin{pmatrix} \frac{\partial f_1}{\partial x_1} & \cdots & \frac{\partial f_1}{\partial x_n} \\ \vdots & \ddots & \vdots \\ \frac{\partial f_m}{\partial x_1} & \cdots & \frac{\partial f_m}{\partial x_n} \end{pmatrix} = \begin{pmatrix} \nabla f_1(x)^\mathsf{T} \\ \vdots \\ \nabla f_m(x)^\mathsf{T} \end{pmatrix} \tag{7.249}$$

Note that we lay out the results in the same orientation as the output f; this is sometimes called numerator layout or the Jacobian formulation.[5]

7.8.5.1 Multiplying Jacobians and vectors

The **Jacobian vector product** or **JVP** is defined to be the operation that corresponds to right-multiplying the Jacobian matrix $\mathbf{J} \in \mathbb{R}^{m \times n}$ by a vector $v \in \mathbb{R}^n$:

$$\mathbf{J}_f(x)v = \begin{pmatrix} \nabla f_1(x)^\mathsf{T} \\ \vdots \\ \nabla f_m(x)^\mathsf{T} \end{pmatrix} v = \begin{pmatrix} \nabla f_1(x)^\mathsf{T} v \\ \vdots \\ \nabla f_m(x)^\mathsf{T} v \end{pmatrix} \tag{7.250}$$

---

5. For a much more detailed discussion of notation, see https://en.wikipedia.org/wiki/Matrix_calculus.

So we can see that we can approximate this numerically using just 2 calls to $\boldsymbol{f}$.

The **vector Jacobian product** or **VJP** is defined to be the operation that corresponds to left-multiplying the Jacobian matrix $\mathbf{J} \in \mathbb{R}^{m \times n}$ by a vector $\boldsymbol{u} \in \mathbb{R}^m$:

$$\boldsymbol{u}^\mathsf{T}\mathbf{J}_{\boldsymbol{f}}(\boldsymbol{x}) = \boldsymbol{u}^\mathsf{T}\left(\frac{\partial \boldsymbol{f}}{\partial x_1}, \cdots, \frac{\partial \boldsymbol{f}}{\partial x_n}\right) = \left(\boldsymbol{u} \cdot \frac{\partial \boldsymbol{f}}{\partial x_1}, \cdots, \boldsymbol{u} \cdot \frac{\partial \boldsymbol{f}}{\partial x_n}\right) \tag{7.251}$$

The JVP is more efficient if $m \geq n$, and the VJP is more efficient if $m \leq n$. See Section 13.3 for details on how this can be used to perform automatic differentiation in a computation graph such as a DNN.

7.8.5.2 Jacobian of a composition

Sometimes it is useful to take the Jacobian of the composition of two functions. Let $h(\boldsymbol{x}) = g(f(\boldsymbol{x}))$. By the chain rule of calculus, we have

$$\mathbf{J}_h(\boldsymbol{x}) = \mathbf{J}_g(f(\boldsymbol{x}))\mathbf{J}_f(\boldsymbol{x}) \tag{7.252}$$

For example, suppose $f : \mathbb{R} \to \mathbb{R}^2$ and $g : \mathbb{R}^2 \to \mathbb{R}^2$. We have

$$\frac{\partial \boldsymbol{g}}{\partial x} = \begin{pmatrix} \frac{\partial}{\partial x}g_1(f_1(x), f_2(x)) \\ \frac{\partial}{\partial x}g_2(f_1(x), f_2(x)) \end{pmatrix} = \begin{pmatrix} \frac{\partial g_1}{\partial f_1}\frac{\partial f_1}{\partial x} + \frac{\partial g_1}{\partial f_2}\frac{\partial f_2}{\partial x} \\ \frac{\partial g_2}{\partial f_1}\frac{\partial f_1}{\partial x} + \frac{\partial g_2}{\partial f_2}\frac{\partial f_2}{\partial x} \end{pmatrix} \tag{7.253}$$

$$= \frac{\partial \boldsymbol{g}}{\partial \boldsymbol{f}^\mathsf{T}}\frac{\partial \boldsymbol{f}}{\partial x} = \begin{pmatrix} \frac{\partial g_1}{\partial f_1} & \frac{\partial g_1}{\partial f_2} \\ \frac{\partial g_2}{\partial f_1} & \frac{\partial g_2}{\partial f_2} \end{pmatrix}\begin{pmatrix} \frac{\partial f_1}{\partial x} \\ \frac{\partial f_2}{\partial x} \end{pmatrix} \tag{7.254}$$

7.8.6 Hessian

For a function $f : \mathbb{R}^n \to \mathbb{R}$ that is twice differentiable, we define the **Hessian matrix** as the (symmetric) $n \times n$ matrix of second partial derivatives:

$$\mathbf{H}_f = \frac{\partial^2 f}{\partial \boldsymbol{x}^2} = \nabla^2 f = \begin{pmatrix} \frac{\partial^2 f}{\partial x_1^2} & \cdots & \frac{\partial^2 f}{\partial x_1 \partial x_n} \\ & \vdots & \\ \frac{\partial^2 f}{\partial x_n \partial x_1} & \cdots & \frac{\partial^2 f}{\partial x_n^2} \end{pmatrix} \tag{7.255}$$

We see that the Hessian is the Jacobian of the gradient.

7.8.7 Gradients of commonly used functions

In this section, we list without proof the gradients of certain widely used functions.

7.8.7.1 Functions that map scalars to scalars

Consider a differentiable function $f : \mathbb{R} \to \mathbb{R}$. Here are some useful identities from scalar calculus, which you should already be familiar with.

$$\frac{d}{dx} cx^n = cn x^{n-1} \qquad (7.256)$$

$$\frac{d}{dx} \log(x) = 1/x \qquad (7.257)$$

$$\frac{d}{dx} \exp(x) = \exp(x) \qquad (7.258)$$

$$\frac{d}{dx}[f(x) + g(x)] = \frac{df(x)}{dx} + \frac{dg(x)}{dx} \qquad (7.259)$$

$$\frac{d}{dx}[f(x)g(x)] = f(x)\frac{dg(x)}{dx} + g(x)\frac{df(x)}{dx} \qquad (7.260)$$

$$\frac{d}{dx} f(u(x)) = \frac{du}{dx}\frac{df(u)}{du} \qquad (7.261)$$

Equation (7.261) is known as the **chain rule of calculus**.

7.8.7.2 Functions that map vectors to scalars

Consider a differentiable function $f : \mathbb{R}^n \to \mathbb{R}$. Here are some useful identities:[6]

$$\frac{\partial(\boldsymbol{a}^\mathsf{T}\boldsymbol{x})}{\partial \boldsymbol{x}} = \boldsymbol{a} \qquad (7.262)$$

$$\frac{\partial(\boldsymbol{b}^\mathsf{T}\mathbf{A}\boldsymbol{x})}{\partial \boldsymbol{x}} = \mathbf{A}^\mathsf{T}\boldsymbol{b} \qquad (7.263)$$

$$\frac{\partial(\boldsymbol{x}^\mathsf{T}\mathbf{A}\boldsymbol{x})}{\partial \boldsymbol{x}} = (\mathbf{A} + \mathbf{A}^\mathsf{T})\boldsymbol{x} \qquad (7.264)$$

It is fairly easy to prove these identities by expanding out the quadratic form, and applying scalar calculus.

7.8.7.3 Functions that map matrices to scalars

Consider a function $f : \mathbb{R}^{m \times n} \to \mathbb{R}$ which maps a matrix to a scalar. We are using the following natural layout for the derivative matrix:

$$\frac{\partial f}{\partial \mathbf{X}} = \begin{pmatrix} \frac{\partial f}{\partial x_{11}} & \cdots & \frac{\partial f}{\partial x_{1n}} \\ & \vdots & \\ \frac{\partial f}{\partial x_{m1}} & \cdots & \frac{\partial f}{\partial x_{mn}} \end{pmatrix} \qquad (7.265)$$

Below are some useful identities.

---

6. Some of the identities are taken from the list at http://www.cs.nyu.edu/~roweis/notes/matrixid.pdf.

Identities involving quadratic forms

One can show the following results.

$$\frac{\partial}{\partial \mathbf{X}}(a^\mathsf{T}\mathbf{X}b) = ab^\mathsf{T} \tag{7.266}$$

$$\frac{\partial}{\partial \mathbf{X}}(a^\mathsf{T}\mathbf{X}^\mathsf{T}b) = ba^\mathsf{T} \tag{7.267}$$

Identities involving matrix trace

One can show the following results.

$$\frac{\partial}{\partial \mathbf{X}}\operatorname{tr}(\mathbf{A}\mathbf{X}\mathbf{B}) = \mathbf{A}^\mathsf{T}\mathbf{B}^\mathsf{T} \tag{7.268}$$

$$\frac{\partial}{\partial \mathbf{X}}\operatorname{tr}(\mathbf{X}^\mathsf{T}\mathbf{A}) = \mathbf{A} \tag{7.269}$$

$$\frac{\partial}{\partial \mathbf{X}}\operatorname{tr}(\mathbf{X}^{-1}\mathbf{A}) = -\mathbf{X}^{-\mathsf{T}}\mathbf{A}^\mathsf{T}\mathbf{X}^{-\mathsf{T}} \tag{7.270}$$

$$\frac{\partial}{\partial \mathbf{X}}\operatorname{tr}(\mathbf{X}^\mathsf{T}\mathbf{A}\mathbf{X}) = (\mathbf{A} + \mathbf{A}^\mathsf{T})\mathbf{X} \tag{7.271}$$

Identities involving matrix determinant

One can show the following results.

$$\frac{\partial}{\partial \mathbf{X}}\det(\mathbf{A}\mathbf{X}\mathbf{B}) = \det(\mathbf{A}\mathbf{X}\mathbf{B})\mathbf{X}^{-\mathsf{T}} \tag{7.272}$$

$$\frac{\partial}{\partial \mathbf{X}}\log(\det(\mathbf{X})) = \mathbf{X}^{-\mathsf{T}} \tag{7.273}$$

7.9 Exercises

Exercise 7.1 [Orthogonal matrices]

a. A rotation in 3d by angle α about the z axis is given by the following matrix:

$$\mathbf{R}(\alpha) = \begin{pmatrix} \cos(\alpha) & -\sin(\alpha) & 0 \\ \sin(\alpha) & \cos(\alpha) & 0 \\ 0 & 0 & 1 \end{pmatrix} \tag{7.274}$$

Prove that $\mathbf{R}$ is an orthogonal matrix, i.e., $\mathbf{R}^T\mathbf{R} = \mathbf{I}$, for any α.

b. What is the only eigenvector v of $\mathbf{R}$ with an eigenvalue of 1.0 and of unit norm (i.e., $||v||^2 = 1$)? (Your answer should be the same for any α.) Hint: think about the geometrical interpretation of eigenvectors.

Exercise 7.2 [Eigenvectors by hand *]

Find the eigenvalues and eigenvectors of the following matrix

$$A = \begin{pmatrix} 2 & 0 \\ 0 & 3 \end{pmatrix} \tag{7.275}$$

Compute your result by hand and check it with Python.

8 Optimization

Parts of this chapter were written by Frederik Kunstner, Si Yi Meng, Aaron Mishkin, Sharan Vaswani, and Mark Schmidt.

8.1 Introduction

We saw in Chapter 4 that the core problem in machine learning is parameter estimation (aka model fitting). This requires solving an **optimization problem**, where we try to find the values for a set of variables $\boldsymbol{\theta} \in \Theta$, that minimize a scalar-valued **loss function** or **cost function** $\mathcal{L} : \Theta \to \mathbb{R}$:

$$\boldsymbol{\theta}^* \in \underset{\boldsymbol{\theta} \in \Theta}{\operatorname{argmin}} \, \mathcal{L}(\boldsymbol{\theta}) \tag{8.1}$$

We will assume that the **parameter space** is given by $\Theta \subseteq \mathbb{R}^D$, where D is the number of variables being optimized over. Thus we are focusing on **continuous optimization**, rather than **discrete optimization**.

If we want to *maximize* a **score function** or **reward function** $R(\boldsymbol{\theta})$, we can equivalently minimize $\mathcal{L}(\boldsymbol{\theta}) = -R(\boldsymbol{\theta})$. We will use the term **objective function** to refer generically to a function we want to maximize or minimize. An algorithm that can find an optimum of an objective function is often called a **solver**.

In the rest of this chapter, we discuss different kinds of solvers for different kinds of objective functions, with a focus on methods used in the machine learning community. For more details on optimization, please consult some of the many excellent textbooks, such as [KW19b; BV04; NW06; Ber15; Ber16] as well as various review articles, such as [BCN18; Sun+19b; PPS18; Pey20].

8.1.1 Local vs global optimization

A point that satisfies Equation (8.1) is called a **global optimum**. Finding such a point is called **global optimization**.

In general, finding global optima is computationally intractable [Neu04]. In such cases, we will just try to find a **local optimum**. For continuous problems, this is defined to be a point $\boldsymbol{\theta}^*$ which has lower (or equal) cost than "nearby" points. Formally, we say $\boldsymbol{\theta}^*$ is a **local minimum** if

$$\exists \delta > 0, \, \forall \boldsymbol{\theta} \in \Theta \ \text{ s.t. } \ ||\boldsymbol{\theta} - \boldsymbol{\theta}^*|| < \delta, \ \mathcal{L}(\boldsymbol{\theta}^*) \leq \mathcal{L}(\boldsymbol{\theta}) \tag{8.2}$$

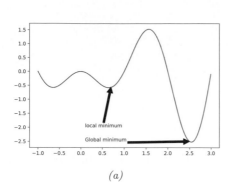
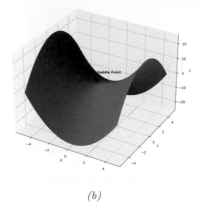

(a)   (b)

Figure 8.1: (a) Illustration of local and global minimum in 1d. Generated by extrema_ fig_ 1d.ipynb. (b) Illustration of a saddle point in 2d. Generated by saddle.ipynb.

A local minimum could be surrounded by other local minima with the same objective value; this is known as a **flat local minimum**. A point is said to be a **strict local minimum** if its cost is strictly lower than those of neighboring points:

$$\exists \delta > 0, \ \forall \boldsymbol{\theta} \in \Theta, \boldsymbol{\theta} \neq \boldsymbol{\theta}^* : ||\boldsymbol{\theta} - \boldsymbol{\theta}^*|| < \delta, \ \mathcal{L}(\boldsymbol{\theta}^*) < \mathcal{L}(\boldsymbol{\theta}) \tag{8.3}$$

We can define a (strict) **local maximum** analogously. See Figure 8.1a for an illustration.

A final note on terminology; if an algorithm is guaranteed to converge to a stationary point from any starting point, it is called **globally convergent**. However, this does not mean (rather confusingly) that it will converge to a global optimum; instead, it just means it will converge to some stationary point.

8.1.1.1   Optimality conditions for local vs global optima

For continuous, twice differentiable functions, we can precisely characterize the points which correspond to local minima. Let $\boldsymbol{g}(\boldsymbol{\theta}) = \nabla \mathcal{L}(\boldsymbol{\theta})$ be the gradient vector, and $\mathbf{H}(\boldsymbol{\theta}) = \nabla^2 \mathcal{L}(\boldsymbol{\theta})$ be the Hessian matrix. (See Section 7.8 for a refresher on these concepts, if necessary.) Consider a point $\boldsymbol{\theta}^* \in \mathbb{R}^D$, and let $\boldsymbol{g}^* = \boldsymbol{g}(\boldsymbol{\theta})|_{\boldsymbol{\theta}^*}$ be the gradient at that point, and $\mathbf{H}^* = \mathbf{H}(\boldsymbol{\theta})|_{\boldsymbol{\theta}^*}$ be the corresponding Hessian. One can show that the following conditions characterize every local minimum:

- Necessary condition: If $\boldsymbol{\theta}^*$ is a local minimum, then we must have $\boldsymbol{g}^* = \boldsymbol{0}$ (i.e., $\boldsymbol{\theta}^*$ must be a **stationary point**), and $\mathbf{H}^*$ must be positive semi-definite.

- Sufficient condition: If $\boldsymbol{g}^* = \boldsymbol{0}$ and $\mathbf{H}^*$ is positive definite, then $\boldsymbol{\theta}^*$ is a local optimum.

To see why the first condition is necessary, suppose we were at a point $\boldsymbol{\theta}^*$ at which the gradient is non-zero: at such a point, we could decrease the function by following the negative gradient a small distance, so this would not be optimal. So the gradient must be zero. (In the case of nonsmooth functions, the necessary condition is that the zero is a local subgradient at the minimum.) To see why a zero gradient is not sufficient, note that the stationary point could be a local minimum, maximum or **saddle point**, which is a point where some directions point downhill, and some uphill (see Figure 8.1b). More precisely, at a saddle point, the eigenvalues of the Hessian will be both positive and negative. However, if the Hessian at a point is positive semi-definite, then some directions may point uphill, while others are flat. Moreover, if the Hessian is strictly positive definite, then we are at the bottom of a "bowl", and all directions point uphill, which is sufficient for this to be a minimum.

8.1.2 Constrained vs unconstrained optimization

In **unconstrained optimization**, we define the optimization task as finding any value in the parameter space Θ that minimizes the loss. However, we often have a set of **constraints** on the allowable values. It is standard to partition the set of constraints $\mathcal{C}$ into **inequality constraints**, $g_j(\boldsymbol{\theta}) \leq 0$ for $j \in \mathcal{I}$ and **equality constraints**, $h_k(\boldsymbol{\theta}) = 0$ for $k \in \mathcal{E}$. For example, we can represent a sum-to-one constraint as an equality constraint $h(\boldsymbol{\theta}) = (1 - \sum_{i=1}^{D} \theta_i) = 0$, and we can represent a non-negativity constraint on the parameters by using D inequality constraints of the form $g_i(\boldsymbol{\theta}) = -\theta_i \leq 0$
.

We define the **feasible set** as the subset of the parameter space that satisfies the constraints:

$$\mathcal{C} = \{\boldsymbol{\theta} : g_j(\boldsymbol{\theta}) \leq 0 : j \in \mathcal{I}, h_k(\boldsymbol{\theta}) = 0 : k \in \mathcal{E}\} \subseteq \mathbb{R}^D \tag{8.4}$$

Our **constrained optimization** problem now becomes

$$\boldsymbol{\theta}^* \in \underset{\boldsymbol{\theta} \in \mathcal{C}}{\operatorname{argmin}} \mathcal{L}(\boldsymbol{\theta}) \tag{8.5}$$

If $\mathcal{C} = \mathbb{R}^D$, it is called **unconstrained optimization**.

The addition of constraints can change the number of optima of a function. For example, a function that was previously unbounded (and hence had no well-defined global maximum or minimum) can "acquire" multiple maxima or minima when we add constraints, as illustrated in Figure 8.2. However, if we add too many constraints, we may find that the feasible set becomes empty. The task of finding any point (regardless of its cost) in the feasible set is called a **feasibility problem**; this can be a hard subproblem in itself.

A common strategy for solving constrained problems is to create penalty terms that measure how much we violate each constraint. We then add these terms to the objective and solve an unconstrained optimization problem. The **Lagrangian** is a special case of such a combined objective (see Section 8.5 for details).

8.1.3 Convex vs nonconvex optimization

In **convex optimization**, we require the objective to be a convex function defined over a convex set (we define these terms below). In such problems, every local minimum is also a global minimum. Thus many models are designed so that their training objectives are convex.

8.1.3.1 Convex sets

We say $\mathcal{S}$ is a **convex set** if, for any $\boldsymbol{x}, \boldsymbol{x}' \in \mathcal{S}$, we have

$$\lambda \boldsymbol{x} + (1 - \lambda)\boldsymbol{x}' \in \mathcal{S}, \quad \forall \lambda \in [0, 1] \tag{8.6}$$

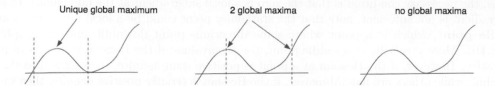

Figure 8.2: *Illustration of constrained maximization of a nonconvex 1d function. The area between the dotted vertical lines represents the feasible set. (a) There is a unique global maximum since the function is concave within the support of the feasible set. (b) There are two global maxima, both occuring at the boundary of the feasible set. (c) In the unconstrained case, this function has no global maximum, since it is unbounded.*

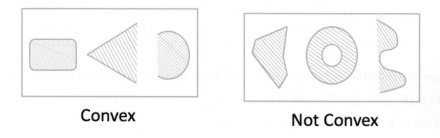

Figure 8.3: *Illustration of some convex and non-convex sets.*

That is, if we draw a line from $\boldsymbol{x}$ to $\boldsymbol{x}'$, all points on the line lie inside the set. See Figure 8.3 for some illustrations of convex and non-convex sets.

8.1.3.2 Convex functions

We say f is a **convex function** if its **epigraph** (the set of points above the function, illustrated in Figure 8.4a) defines a convex set. Equivalently, a function $f(\boldsymbol{x})$ is called convex if it is defined on a convex set and if, for any $\boldsymbol{x}, \boldsymbol{y} \in \mathcal{S}$, and for any $0 \le \lambda \le 1$, we have

$$f(\lambda \boldsymbol{x} + (1 - \lambda)\boldsymbol{y}) \le \lambda f(\boldsymbol{x}) + (1 - \lambda)f(\boldsymbol{y}) \tag{8.7}$$

See Figure 8.5(a) for a 1d example of a convex function. A function is called **strictly convex** if the inequality is strict. A function $f(\boldsymbol{x})$ is **concave** if $-f(\boldsymbol{x})$ is convex, and **strictly concave** if $-f(\boldsymbol{x})$ is strictly convex. See Figure 8.5(b) for a 1d example of a function that is neither convex nor concave.

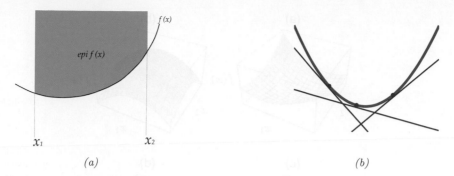

Figure 8.4: (a) Illustration of the epigraph of a function. (b) For a convex function $f(x)$, its epipgraph can be represented as the intersection of half-spaces defined by linear lower bounds derived from the **conjugate function** $f^*(\lambda) = \max_x \lambda x - f(x)$.

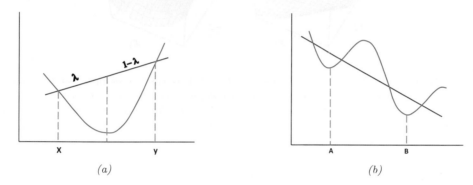

Figure 8.5: (a) Illustration of a convex function. We see that the chord joining $(x, f(x))$ to $(y, f(y))$ lies above the function. (b) A function that is neither convex nor concave. **A** is a local minimum, **B** is a global minimum.

Here are some examples of 1d convex functions:

$$x^2$$
$$e^{ax}$$
$$-\log x$$
$$x^a, \ a > 1, x > 0$$
$$|x|^a, \ a \geq 1$$
$$x \log x, \ x > 0$$

8.1.3.3 Characterization of convex functions

Intuitively, a convex function is shaped like a bowl. Formally, one can prove the following important result:

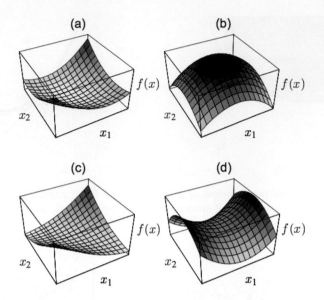

Figure 8.6: *The quadratic form $f(\boldsymbol{x}) = \boldsymbol{x}^\mathsf{T}\mathbf{A}\boldsymbol{x}$ in 2d. (a) $\mathbf{A}$ is positive definite, so f is convex. (b) $\mathbf{A}$ is negative definite, so f is concave. (c) $\mathbf{A}$ is positive semidefinite but singular, so f is convex, but not strictly. Notice the valley of constant height in the middle. (d) $\mathbf{A}$ is indefinite, so f is neither convex nor concave. The stationary point in the middle of the surface is a saddle point. From Figure 5 of [She94].*

Theorem 8.1.1. *Suppose $f : \mathbb{R}^n \to \mathbb{R}$ is twice differentiable over its domain. Then f is convex iff $\mathbf{H} = \nabla^2 f(\boldsymbol{x})$ is positive semi definite (Section 7.1.5.3) for all $\boldsymbol{x} \in \mathrm{dom}(f)$. Furthermore, f is strictly convex if $\mathbf{H}$ is positive definite.*

For example, consider the quadratic form

$$f(\boldsymbol{x}) = \boldsymbol{x}^\mathsf{T}\mathbf{A}\boldsymbol{x} \tag{8.8}$$

This is convex if $\mathbf{A}$ is positive semi definite, and is strictly convex if $\mathbf{A}$ is positive definite. It is neither convex nor concave if $\mathbf{A}$ has eigenvalues of mixed sign. See Figure 8.6.

8.1.3.4 Strongly convex functions

We say a function f is **strongly convex** with parameter $m > 0$ if the following holds for all $\boldsymbol{x}$, $\boldsymbol{y}$ in f's domain:

$$(\nabla f(\boldsymbol{x}) - \nabla f(\boldsymbol{y}))^\mathsf{T}(\boldsymbol{x} - \boldsymbol{y}) \geq m||\boldsymbol{x} - \boldsymbol{y}||_2^2 \tag{8.9}$$

A strongly convex function is also strictly convex, but not vice versa.

If the function f is twice continuously differentiable, then it is strongly convex with parameter m if and only if $\nabla^2 f(\boldsymbol{x}) \succeq m\mathbf{I}$ for all $\boldsymbol{x}$ in the domain, where $\mathbf{I}$ is the identity and $\nabla^2 f$ is the Hessian matrix, and the inequality $\succeq$ means that $\nabla^2 f(\boldsymbol{x}) - m\mathbf{I}$ is positive semi-definite. This is equivalent

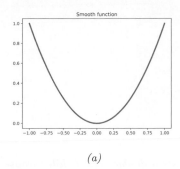

(a)

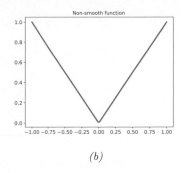

(b)

Figure 8.7: (a) Smooth 1d function. (b) Non-smooth 1d function. (There is a discontinuity at the origin.)
Generated by smooth-vs-nonsmooth-1d.ipynb.

to requiring that the minimum eigenvalue of $\nabla^2 f(\boldsymbol{x})$ be at least m for all $\boldsymbol{x}$. If the domain is just the real line, then $\nabla^2 f(x)$ is just the second derivative $f''(x)$, so the condition becomes $f''(x) \geq m$. If $m = 0$, then this means the Hessian is positive semidefinite (or if the domain is the real line, it means that $f''(x) \geq 0$), which implies the function is convex, and perhaps strictly convex, but not strongly convex.

The distinction between convex, strictly convex, and strongly convex is rather subtle. To better understand this, consider the case where f is twice continuously differentiable and the domain is the real line. Then we can characterize the differences as follows:

- f is convex if and only if $f''(x) \geq 0$ for all x.
- f is strictly convex if $f''(x) > 0$ for all x (note: this is sufficient, but not necessary).
- f is strongly convex if and only if $f''(x) \geq m > 0$ for all x.

Note that it can be shown that a function f is strongly convex with parameter m iff the function

$$J(\boldsymbol{x}) = f(\boldsymbol{x}) - \frac{m}{2}||\boldsymbol{x}||^2 \tag{8.10}$$

is convex.

8.1.4 Smooth vs nonsmooth optimization

In **smooth optimization**, the objective and constraints are continuously differentiable functions. For smooth functions, we can quantify the degree of smoothness using the **Lipschitz constant**. In the 1d case, this is defined as any constant $L \geq 0$ such that, for all real x_1 and x_2, we have

$$|f(x_1) - f(x_2)| \leq L|x_1 - x_2| \tag{8.11}$$

This is illustrated in Figure 8.8: for a given constant L, the function output cannot change by more than L if we change the function input by 1 unit. This can be generalized to vector inputs using a suitable norm.

In **nonsmooth optimization**, there are at least some points where the gradient of the objective function or the constraints is not well-defined. See Figure 8.7 for an example. In some optimization

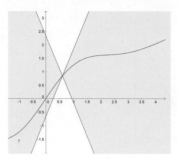

Figure 8.8: For a Lipschitz continuous function f, there exists a double cone (white) whose origin can be moved along the graph of f so that the whole graph always stays outside the double cone. From `https://en.` `wikipedia.org/wiki/Lipschitz_continuity`. *Used with kind permission of Wikipedia author Taschee.*

problems, we can partition the objective into a part that only contains smooth terms, and a part that contains the nonsmooth terms:

$$\mathcal{L}(\boldsymbol{\theta}) = \mathcal{L}_s(\boldsymbol{\theta}) + \mathcal{L}_r(\boldsymbol{\theta}) \tag{8.12}$$

where $\mathcal{L}_s$ is smooth (differentiable), and $\mathcal{L}_r$ is nonsmooth ("rough"). This is often referred to as a **composite objective**. In machine learning applications, $\mathcal{L}_s$ is usually the training set loss, and $\mathcal{L}_r$ is a regularizer, such as the ℓ_1 norm of $\boldsymbol{\theta}$. This composite structure can be exploited by various algorithms.

8.1.4.1   Subgradients

In this section, we generalize the notion of a derivative to work with functions which have local discontinuities. In particular, for a convex function of several variables, $f : \mathbb{R}^n \to \mathbb{R}$, we say that $\boldsymbol{g} \in \mathbb{R}^n$ is a **subgradient** of f at $\boldsymbol{x} \in \text{dom}(f)$ if for all $\boldsymbol{z} \in \text{dom}(f)$,

$$f(\boldsymbol{z}) \geq f(\boldsymbol{x}) + \boldsymbol{g}^{\mathsf{T}}(\boldsymbol{z} - \boldsymbol{x}) \tag{8.13}$$

Note that a subgradient can exist even when f is not differentiable at a point, as shown in Figure 8.9.

A function f is called **subdifferentiable** at $\boldsymbol{x}$ if there is at least one subgradient at $\boldsymbol{x}$. The set of such subgradients is called the **subdifferential** of f at $\boldsymbol{x}$, and is denoted $\partial f(\boldsymbol{x})$.

For example, consider the absolute value function $f(x) = |x|$. Its subdifferential is given by

$$\partial f(x) = \begin{cases} \{-1\} & \text{if } x < 0 \\ [-1, 1] & \text{if } x = 0 \\ \{+1\} & \text{if } x > 0 \end{cases} \tag{8.14}$$

where the notation $[-1, 1]$ means any value between -1 and 1 inclusive. See Figure 8.10 for an illustration.

8.2   First-order methods

In this section, we consider iterative optimization methods that leverage **first-order** derivatives of the objective function, i.e., they compute which directions point "downhill", but they ignore curvature

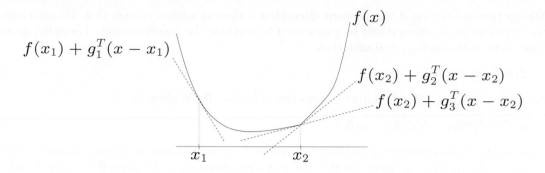

Figure 8.9: *Illustration of subgradients. At $\boldsymbol{x}_1$, the convex function f is differentiable, and $\boldsymbol{g}_1$ (which is the derivative of f at $\boldsymbol{x}_1$) is the unique subgradient at $\boldsymbol{x}_1$. At the point $\boldsymbol{x}_2$, f is not differentiable, because of the "kink". However, there are many subgradients at this point, of which two are shown. From* https://web.stanford.edu/class/ee364b/lectures/subgradients_slides.pdf. *Used with kind permission of Stephen Boyd.*

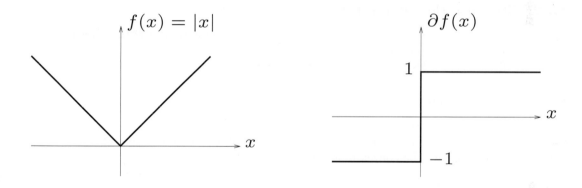

Figure 8.10: *The absolute value function (left) and its subdifferential (right). From* https://web.stanford.edu/class/ee364b/lectures/subgradients_slides.pdf. *Used with kind permission of Stephen Boyd.*

information. All of these algorithms require that the user specify a starting point $\boldsymbol{\theta}_0$. Then at each iteration t, they perform an update of the following form:

$$\boldsymbol{\theta}_{t+1} = \boldsymbol{\theta}_t + \eta_t \boldsymbol{d}_t \qquad (8.15)$$

where η_t is known as the **step size** or **learning rate**, and d_t is a **descent direction**, such as the negative of the **gradient**, given by $\boldsymbol{g}_t = \nabla_{\boldsymbol{\theta}} \mathcal{L}(\boldsymbol{\theta})|_{\boldsymbol{\theta}_t}$. These update steps are continued until the method reaches a stationary point, where the gradient is zero.

8.2.1   Descent direction

We say that a direction $\boldsymbol{d}$ is a **descent direction** if there is a small enough (but nonzero) amount η we can move in direction $\boldsymbol{d}$ and be guaranteed to decrease the function value. Formally, we require that there exists an $\eta_{\max} > 0$ such that

$$\mathcal{L}(\boldsymbol{\theta} + \eta\boldsymbol{d}) < \mathcal{L}(\boldsymbol{\theta}) \tag{8.16}$$

for all $0 < \eta < \eta_{\max}$. The gradient at the current iterate, $\boldsymbol{\theta}_t$, is given by

$$\boldsymbol{g}_t \triangleq \nabla\mathcal{L}(\boldsymbol{\theta})|_{\boldsymbol{\theta}_t} = \nabla\mathcal{L}(\boldsymbol{\theta}_t) = \boldsymbol{g}(\boldsymbol{\theta}_t) \tag{8.17}$$

This points in the direction of maximal increase in f, so the negative gradient is a descent direction. It can be shown that any direction $\boldsymbol{d}$ is also a descent direction if the angle θ between $\boldsymbol{d}$ and $-\boldsymbol{g}_t$ is less than 90 degrees and satisfies

$$\boldsymbol{d}^\mathsf{T}\boldsymbol{g}_t = ||\boldsymbol{d}||\,||\boldsymbol{g}_t||\,\cos(\theta) < 0 \tag{8.18}$$

It seems that the best choice would be to pick $\boldsymbol{d}_t = -\boldsymbol{g}_t$. This is known as the direction of **steepest descent**. However, this can be quite slow. We consider faster versions later.

8.2.2   Step size (learning rate)

In machine learning, the sequence of step sizes $\{\eta_t\}$ is called the **learning rate schedule**. There are several widely used methods for picking this, some of which we discuss below. (See also Section 8.4.3, where we discuss schedules for stochastic optimization.)

8.2.2.1   Constant step size

The simplest method is to use a constant step size, $\eta_t = \eta$. However, if it is too large, the method may fail to converge, and if it is too small, the method will converge but very slowly.

For example, consider the convex function

$$\mathcal{L}(\boldsymbol{\theta}) = 0.5(\theta_1^2 - \theta_2)^2 + 0.5(\theta_1 - 1)^2 \tag{8.19}$$

Let us pick as our descent direction $\boldsymbol{d}_t = -\boldsymbol{g}_t$. Figure 8.11 shows what happens if we use this descent direction with a fixed step size, starting from $(0,0)$. In Figure 8.11(a), we use a small step size of $\eta = 0.1$; we see that the iterates move slowly along the valley. In Figure 8.11(b), we use a larger step size $\eta = 0.6$; we see that the iterates start oscillating up and down the sides of the valley and never converge to the optimum, even though this is a convex problem.

In some cases, we can derive a theoretical upper bound on the maximum step size we can use. For example, consider a quadratic objective, $\mathcal{L}(\boldsymbol{\theta}) = \frac{1}{2}\boldsymbol{\theta}^\mathsf{T}\mathbf{A}\boldsymbol{\theta} + \boldsymbol{b}^\mathsf{T}\boldsymbol{\theta} + c$ with $\mathbf{A} \succeq \mathbf{0}$. One can show that steepest descent will have global convergence iff the step size satisfies

$$\eta < \frac{2}{\lambda_{\max}(\mathbf{A})} \tag{8.20}$$

where $\lambda_{\max}(\mathbf{A})$ is the largest eigenvalue of $\mathbf{A}$. The intuitive reason for this can be understood by thinking of a ball rolling down a valley. We want to make sure it doesn't take a step that is larger than the slope of the steepest direction, which is what the largest eigenvalue measures (see Section 3.2.2).

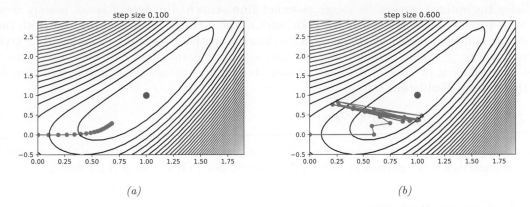

Figure 8.11: *Steepest descent on a simple convex function, starting from* $(0,0)$, *for 20 steps, using a fixed step size. The global minimum is at* $(1,1)$. *(a)* $\eta = 0.1$. *(b)* $\eta = 0.6$. *Generated by steepestDescentDemo.ipynb.*

More generally, setting $\eta < 2/L$, where L is the Lipschitz constant of the gradient (Section 8.1.4), ensures convergence. Since this constant is generally unknown, we usually need to adapt the step size, as we discuss below.

8.2.2.2 Line search

The optimal step size can be found by finding the value that maximally decreases the objective along the chosen direction by solving the 1d minimization problem

$$\eta_t = \underset{\eta > 0}{\operatorname{argmin}}\, \phi_t(\eta) = \underset{\eta > 0}{\operatorname{argmin}}\, \mathcal{L}(\boldsymbol{\theta}_t + \eta \boldsymbol{d}_t) \tag{8.21}$$

This is known as **line search**, since we are searching along the line defined by $\boldsymbol{d}_t$.

If the loss is convex, this subproblem is also convex, because $\phi_t(\eta) = \mathcal{L}(\boldsymbol{\theta}_t + \eta \boldsymbol{d}_t)$ is a convex function of an affine function of η, for fixed $\boldsymbol{\theta}_t$ and $\boldsymbol{d}_t$. For example, consider the quadratic loss

$$\mathcal{L}(\boldsymbol{\theta}) = \frac{1}{2}\boldsymbol{\theta}^\mathsf{T}\mathbf{A}\boldsymbol{\theta} + \boldsymbol{b}^\mathsf{T}\boldsymbol{\theta} + c \tag{8.22}$$

Computing the derivative of ϕ gives

$$\frac{d\phi(\eta)}{d\eta} = \frac{d}{d\eta}\left[\frac{1}{2}(\boldsymbol{\theta} + \eta \boldsymbol{d})^\mathsf{T}\mathbf{A}(\boldsymbol{\theta} + \eta \boldsymbol{d}) + \boldsymbol{b}^\mathsf{T}(\boldsymbol{\theta} + \eta \boldsymbol{d}) + c\right] \tag{8.23}$$

$$= \boldsymbol{d}^\mathsf{T}\mathbf{A}(\boldsymbol{\theta} + \eta \boldsymbol{d}) + \boldsymbol{d}^\mathsf{T}\boldsymbol{b} \tag{8.24}$$

$$= \boldsymbol{d}^\mathsf{T}(\mathbf{A}\boldsymbol{\theta} + \boldsymbol{b}) + \eta \boldsymbol{d}^\mathsf{T}\mathbf{A}\boldsymbol{d} \tag{8.25}$$

Solving for $\frac{d\phi(\eta)}{d\eta} = 0$ gives

$$\eta = -\frac{\boldsymbol{d}^\mathsf{T}(\mathbf{A}\boldsymbol{\theta} + \boldsymbol{b})}{\boldsymbol{d}^\mathsf{T}\mathbf{A}\boldsymbol{d}} \tag{8.26}$$

Using the optimal step size is known as **exact line search**. However, it is not usually necessary to be so precise. There are several methods, such as the **Armijo backtracking method**, that try to ensure sufficient reduction in the objective function without spending too much time trying to solve Equation (8.21). In particular, we can start with the current stepsize (or some maximum value), and then reduce it by a factor $0 < c < 1$ at each step until we satisfy the following condition, known as the **Armijo-Goldstein** test:

$$\mathcal{L}(\boldsymbol{\theta}_t + \eta \boldsymbol{d}_t) \leq \mathcal{L}(\boldsymbol{\theta}_t) + c\eta \boldsymbol{d}_t^{\mathsf{T}} \nabla \mathcal{L}(\boldsymbol{\theta}_t) \tag{8.27}$$

where $c \in [0, 1]$ is a constant, typically $c = 10^{-4}$. In practice, the initialization of the line-search and how to backtrack can significantly affect performance. See [NW06, Sec 3.1] for details.

8.2.3   Convergence rates

We want to find optimization algorithms that converge quickly to a (local) optimum. For certain convex problems, with a gradient with bounded Lipschitz constant, one can show that gradient descent converges at a **linear rate**. This means that there exists a number $0 < \mu < 1$ such that

$$|\mathcal{L}(\boldsymbol{\theta}_{t+1}) - \mathcal{L}(\boldsymbol{\theta}_*)| \leq \mu |\mathcal{L}(\boldsymbol{\theta}_t) - \mathcal{L}(\boldsymbol{\theta}_*)| \tag{8.28}$$

Here μ is called the **rate of convergence**.

For some simple problems, we can derive the convergence rate explicitly, For example, consider a quadratic objective $\mathcal{L}(\boldsymbol{\theta}) = \frac{1}{2}\boldsymbol{\theta}^{\mathsf{T}}\mathbf{A}\boldsymbol{\theta} + \boldsymbol{b}^{\mathsf{T}}\boldsymbol{\theta} + c$ with $\mathbf{A} \succ 0$. Suppose we use steepest descent with exact line search. One can show (see e.g., [Ber15]) that the convergence rate is given by

$$\mu = \left(\frac{\lambda_{\max} - \lambda_{\min}}{\lambda_{\max} + \lambda_{\min}}\right)^2 \tag{8.29}$$

where $\lambda_{\max}$ is the largest eigenvalue of $\mathbf{A}$ and $\lambda_{\min}$ is the smallest eigenvalue. We can rewrite this as $\mu = \left(\frac{\kappa-1}{\kappa+1}\right)^2$, where $\kappa = \frac{\lambda_{\max}}{\lambda_{\min}}$ is the condition number of $\mathbf{A}$. Intuitively, the condition number measures how "skewed" the space is, in the sense of being far from a symmetrical "bowl". (See Section 7.1.4.4 for more information on condition numbers.)

Figure 8.12 illustrates the effect of the condition number on the convergence rate. On the left we show an example where $\mathbf{A} = [20, 5; 5, 2]$, $\boldsymbol{b} = [-14; -6]$ and $c = 10$, so $\kappa(\mathbf{A}) = 30.234$. On the right we show an example where $\mathbf{A} = [20, 5; 5, 16]$, $\boldsymbol{b} = [-14; -6]$ and $c = 10$, so $\kappa(\mathbf{A}) = 1.8541$. We see that steepest descent converges much more quickly for the problem with the smaller condition number.

In the more general case of non-quadratic functions, the objective will often be locally quadratic around a local optimum. Hence the convergence rate depends on the condition number of the Hessian, $\kappa(\mathbf{H})$, at that point. We can often improve the convergence speed by optimizing a surrogate objective (or model) at each step which has a Hessian that is close to the Hessian of the objective function as we discuss in Section 8.3.

Although line search works well, we see from Figure 8.12 that the path of steepest descent with an exact line-search exhibits a characteristic **zig-zag** behavior, which is inefficient. This problem can be overcome using a method called **conjugate gradient** descent (see e.g., [She94]).

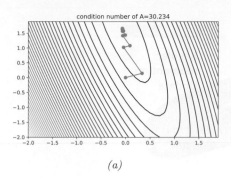
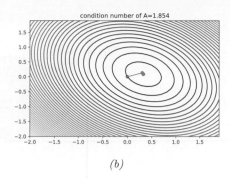

(a)   (b)

Figure 8.12: Illustration of the effect of condition number κ on the convergence speed of steepest descent with exact line searches. (a) Large κ. (b) Small κ. Generated by lineSearchConditionNum.ipynb.

8.2.4 Momentum methods

Gradient descent can move very slowly along flat regions of the loss landscape, as we illustrated in Figure 8.11. We discuss some solutions to this below.

8.2.4.1 Momentum

One simple heuristic, known as the **heavy ball** or **momentum** method [Ber99], is to move faster along directions that were previously good, and to slow down along directions where the gradient has suddenly changed, just like a ball rolling downhill. This can be implemented as follows:

$$\boldsymbol{m}_t = \beta \boldsymbol{m}_{t-1} + \boldsymbol{g}_{t-1} \tag{8.30}$$
$$\boldsymbol{\theta}_t = \boldsymbol{\theta}_{t-1} - \eta_t \boldsymbol{m}_t \tag{8.31}$$

where $\boldsymbol{m}_t$ is the momentum (mass times velocity) and $0 < \beta < 1$. A typical value of β is 0.9. For $\beta = 0$, the method reduces to gradient descent.

We see that $\boldsymbol{m}_t$ is like an exponentially weighted moving average of the past gradients (see Section 4.4.2.2):

$$\boldsymbol{m}_t = \beta \boldsymbol{m}_{t-1} + \boldsymbol{g}_{t-1} = \beta^2 \boldsymbol{m}_{t-2} + \beta \boldsymbol{g}_{t-2} + \boldsymbol{g}_{t-1} = \cdots = \sum_{\tau=0}^{t-1} \beta^\tau \boldsymbol{g}_{t-\tau-1} \tag{8.32}$$

If all the past gradients are a constant, say $\boldsymbol{g}$, this simplifies to

$$\boldsymbol{m}_t = \boldsymbol{g} \sum_{\tau=0}^{t-1} \beta^\tau \tag{8.33}$$

The scaling factor is a geometric series, whose infinite sum is given by

$$1 + \beta + \beta^2 + \cdots = \sum_{i=0}^{\infty} \beta^i = \frac{1}{1-\beta} \tag{8.34}$$

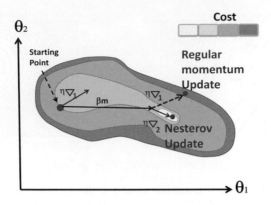

Figure 8.13: Illustration of the Nesterov update. Adapted from Figure 11.6 of [Gér19].

Thus in the limit, we multiply the gradient by $1/(1 - \beta)$. For example, if $\beta = 0.9$, we scale the gradient up by 10.

Since we update the parameters using the gradient average $\boldsymbol{m}_{t-1}$, rather than just the most recent gradient, $\boldsymbol{g}_{t-1}$, we see that past gradients can exhibit some influence on the present. Furthermore, when momentum is combined with SGD, discussed in Section 8.4, we will see that it can simulate the effects of a larger minibatch, without the computational cost.

8.2.4.2   Nesterov momentum

One problem with the standard momentum method is that it may not slow down enough at the bottom of a valley, causing oscillation. The **Nesterov accelerated gradient** method of [Nes04] instead modifies the gradient descent to include an extrapolation step, as follows:

$$\tilde{\boldsymbol{\theta}}_{t+1} = \boldsymbol{\theta}_t + \beta(\boldsymbol{\theta}_t - \boldsymbol{\theta}_{t-1}) \tag{8.35}$$

$$\boldsymbol{\theta}_{t+1} = \tilde{\boldsymbol{\theta}}_{t+1} - \eta_t \nabla \mathcal{L}(\tilde{\boldsymbol{\theta}}_{t+1}) \tag{8.36}$$

This is essentially a form of one-step "look ahead", that can reduce the amount of oscillation, as illustrated in Figure 8.13.

Nesterov accelerated gradient can also be rewritten in the same format as standard momentum. In this case, the momentum term is updated using the gradient at the predicted new location,

$$\boldsymbol{m}_{t+1} = \beta \boldsymbol{m}_t - \eta_t \nabla \mathcal{L}(\boldsymbol{\theta}_t + \beta \boldsymbol{m}_t) \tag{8.37}$$

$$\boldsymbol{\theta}_{t+1} = \boldsymbol{\theta}_t + \boldsymbol{m}_{t+1} \tag{8.38}$$

This explains why the Nesterov accelerated gradient method is sometimes called Nesterov momentum. It also shows how this method can be faster than standard momentum: the momentum vector is already roughly pointing in the right direction, so measuring the gradient at the new location, $\boldsymbol{\theta}_t + \beta \boldsymbol{m}_t$, rather than the current location, $\boldsymbol{\theta}_t$, can be more accurate.

The Nesterov accelerated gradient method is provably faster than steepest descent for convex functions when β and η_t are chosen appropriately. It is called "accelerated" because of this improved convergence rate, which is optimal for gradient-based methods using only first-order information when the objective function is convex and has Lipschitz-continuous gradients. In practice, however, using Nesterov momentum can be slower than steepest descent, and can even unstable if β or η_t are misspecified.

8.3 Second-order methods

Optimization algorithms that only use the gradient are called **first-order** methods. They have the advantage that the gradient is cheap to compute and to store, but they do not model the curvature of the space, and hence they can be slow to converge, as we have seen in Figure 8.12. **Second-order** optimization methods incorporate curvature in various ways (e.g., via the Hessian), which may yield faster convergence. We discuss some of these methods below.

8.3.1 Newton's method

The classic second-order method is **Newton's method**. This consists of updates of the form

$$\boldsymbol{\theta}_{t+1} = \boldsymbol{\theta}_t - \eta_t \mathbf{H}_t^{-1} \boldsymbol{g}_t \tag{8.39}$$

where

$$\mathbf{H}_t \triangleq \nabla^2 \mathcal{L}(\boldsymbol{\theta})|_{\boldsymbol{\theta}_t} = \nabla^2 \mathcal{L}(\boldsymbol{\theta}_t) = \mathbf{H}(\boldsymbol{\theta}_t) \tag{8.40}$$

is assumed to be positive-definite to ensure the update is well-defined. The pseudo-code for Newton's method is given in Algorithm 8.1. The intuition for why this is faster than gradient descent is that the matrix inverse $\mathbf{H}^{-1}$ "undoes" any skew in the local curvature, converting a topology like Figure 8.12a to one like Figure 8.12b.

Algorithm 8.1: Newton's method for minimizing a function

1 Initialize $\boldsymbol{\theta}_0$
2 **for** $t = 1, 2, \ldots$ *until convergence* **do**
3   Evaluate $\boldsymbol{g}_t = \nabla \mathcal{L}(\boldsymbol{\theta}_t)$
4   Evaluate $\mathbf{H}_t = \nabla^2 \mathcal{L}(\boldsymbol{\theta}_t)$
5   Solve $\mathbf{H}_t \boldsymbol{d}_t = -\boldsymbol{g}_t$ for $\boldsymbol{d}_t$
6   Use line search to find stepsize η_t along $\boldsymbol{d}_t$
7     $\boldsymbol{\theta}_{t+1} = \boldsymbol{\theta}_t + \eta_t \boldsymbol{d}_t$

This algorithm can be derived as follows. Consider making a second-order Taylor series approximation of $\mathcal{L}(\boldsymbol{\theta})$ around $\boldsymbol{\theta}_t$:

$$\mathcal{L}_{\text{quad}}(\boldsymbol{\theta}) = \mathcal{L}(\boldsymbol{\theta}_t) + \boldsymbol{g}_t^\mathsf{T}(\boldsymbol{\theta} - \boldsymbol{\theta}_t) + \frac{1}{2}(\boldsymbol{\theta} - \boldsymbol{\theta}_t)^\mathsf{T} \mathbf{H}_t (\boldsymbol{\theta} - \boldsymbol{\theta}_t) \tag{8.41}$$

The minimum of $\mathcal{L}_{\text{quad}}$ is at

$$\boldsymbol{\theta} = \boldsymbol{\theta}_t - \mathbf{H}_t^{-1} \boldsymbol{g}_t \tag{8.42}$$

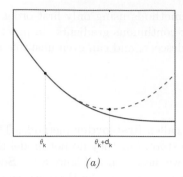 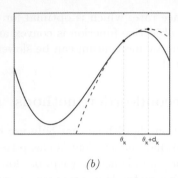

(a)   *(b)*

Figure 8.14: Illustration of Newton's method for minimizing a 1d function. (a) The solid curve is the function $\mathcal{L}(x)$. The dotted line $\mathcal{L}_{\text{quad}}(\theta)$ is its second order approximation at θ_t. The Newton step d_t is what must be added to θ_t to get to the minimum of $\mathcal{L}_{\text{quad}}(\theta)$. Adapted from Figure 13.4 of [Van06]. Generated by newtonsMethodMinQuad.ipynb. (b) Illustration of Newton's method applied to a nonconvex function. We fit a quadratic function around the current point θ_t and move to its stationary point, $\theta_{t+1} = \theta_t + d_t$. Unfortunately, this takes us near a local maximum of f, not minimum. This means we need to be careful about the extent of our quadratic approximation. Adapted from Figure 13.11 of [Van06]. Generated by newtonsMethodNonConvex.ipynb.

So if the quadratic approximation is a good one, we should pick $d_t = -\mathbf{H}_t^{-1} g_t$ as our descent direction. See Figure 8.14(a) for an illustration. Note that, in a "pure" Newton method, we use $\eta_t = 1$ as our stepsize. However, we can also use linesearch to find the best stepsize; this tends to be more robust as using $\eta_t = 1$ may not always converge globally.

If we apply this method to linear regression, we get to the optimum in one step, since (as we show in Section 11.2.2.1) we have $\mathbf{H} = \mathbf{X}^\mathsf{T}\mathbf{X}$ and $g = \mathbf{X}^\mathsf{T}\mathbf{X}w - \mathbf{X}^\mathsf{T}y$, so the Newton update becomes

$$w_1 = w_0 - \mathbf{H}^{-1}g = w_0 - (\mathbf{X}^\mathsf{T}\mathbf{X})^{-1}(\mathbf{X}^\mathsf{T}\mathbf{X}w_0 - \mathbf{X}^\mathsf{T}y) = w_0 - w_0 + (\mathbf{X}^\mathsf{T}\mathbf{X})^{-1}\mathbf{X}^\mathsf{T}y \tag{8.43}$$

which is the OLS estimate. However, when we apply this method to logistic regression, it may take multiple iterations to converge to the global optimum, as we discuss in Section 10.2.6.

8.3.2   BFGS and other quasi-Newton methods

Quasi-Newton methods, sometimes called **variable metric** methods, iteratively build up an approximation to the Hessian using information gleaned from the gradient vector at each step. The most common method is called **BFGS** (named after its simultaneous inventors, Broyden, Fletcher, Goldfarb and Shanno), which updates the approximation to the Hessian $\mathbf{B}_t \approx \mathbf{H}_t$ as follows:

$$\mathbf{B}_{t+1} = \mathbf{B}_t + \frac{y_t y_t^\mathsf{T}}{y_t^\mathsf{T} s_t} - \frac{(\mathbf{B}_t s_t)(\mathbf{B}_t s_t)^\mathsf{T}}{s_t^\mathsf{T} \mathbf{B}_t s_t} \tag{8.44}$$

$$s_t = \theta_t - \theta_{t-1} \tag{8.45}$$

$$y_t = g_t - g_{t-1} \tag{8.46}$$

This is a rank-two update to the matrix. If $\mathbf{B}_0$ is positive-definite, and the step size η is chosen via line search satisfying both the Armijo condition in Equation (8.27) and the following curvature

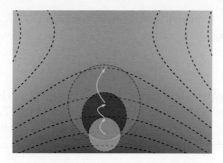

Figure 8.15: Illustration of the trust region approach. The dashed lines represents contours of the original nonconvex objective. The circles represent successive quadratic approximations. From Figure 4.2 of [Pas14]. Used with kind permission of Razvan Pascanu.

condition

$$\nabla \mathcal{L}(\boldsymbol{\theta}_t + \eta \boldsymbol{d}_t) \geq c_2 \eta \boldsymbol{d}_t^\mathsf{T} \nabla \mathcal{L}(\boldsymbol{\theta}_t) \tag{8.47}$$

then $\mathbf{B}_{t+1}$ will remain positive definite. The constant c_2 is chosen within $(c, 1)$ where c is the tunable parameter in Equation (8.27). The two step size conditions are together known as the **Wolfe conditions**. We typically start with a diagonal approximation, $\mathbf{B}_0 = \mathbf{I}$. Thus BFGS can be thought of as a "diagonal plus low-rank" approximation to the Hessian.

Alternatively, BFGS can iteratively update an approximation to the inverse Hessian, $\mathbf{C}_t \approx \mathbf{H}_t^{-1}$, as follows:

$$\mathbf{C}_{t+1} = \left(\mathbf{I} - \frac{\boldsymbol{s}_t \boldsymbol{y}_t^\mathsf{T}}{\boldsymbol{y}_t^\mathsf{T} \boldsymbol{s}_t} \right) \mathbf{C}_t \left(\mathbf{I} - \frac{\boldsymbol{y}_t \boldsymbol{s}_t^\mathsf{T}}{\boldsymbol{y}_t^\mathsf{T} \boldsymbol{s}_t} \right) + \frac{\boldsymbol{s}_t \boldsymbol{s}_t^\mathsf{T}}{\boldsymbol{y}_t^\mathsf{T} \boldsymbol{s}_t} \tag{8.48}$$

Since storing the Hessian approximation still takes $O(D^2)$ space, for very large problems, one can use **limited memory BFGS**, or **L-BFGS**, where we control the rank of the approximation by only using the M most recent $(\boldsymbol{s}_t, \boldsymbol{y}_t)$ pairs while ignoring older information. Rather than storing $\mathbf{B}_t$ explicitly, we just store these vectors in memory, and then approximate $\mathbf{H}_t^{-1} \boldsymbol{g}_t$ by performing a sequence of inner products with the stored $\boldsymbol{s}_t$ and $\boldsymbol{y}_t$ vectors. The storage requirements are therefore $O(MD)$. Typically choosing M to be between 5–20 suffices for good performance [NW06, p177].

Note that sklearn uses LBFGS as its default solver for logistic regression.[1]

8.3.3 Trust region methods

If the objective function is nonconvex, then the Hessian $\mathbf{H}_t$ may not be positive definite, so $\boldsymbol{d}_t = -\mathbf{H}_t^{-1} \boldsymbol{g}_t$ may not be a descent direction. This is illustrated in 1d in Figure 8.14(b), which shows that Newton's method can end up in a local maximum rather than a local minimum.

In general, any time the quadratic approximation made by Newton's method becomes invalid, we are in trouble. However, there is usually a local region around the current iterate where we can safely

---

1. See https://scikit-learn.org/stable/modules/generated/sklearn.linear_model.LogisticRegression.html.

approximate the objective by a quadratic. Let us call this region $\mathcal{R}_t$, and let us call $M(\boldsymbol{\delta})$ the model (or approximation) to the objective, where $\boldsymbol{\delta} = \boldsymbol{\theta} - \boldsymbol{\theta}_t$. Then at each step we can solve

$$\boldsymbol{\delta}^* = \operatorname*{argmin}_{\boldsymbol{\delta} \in \mathcal{R}_t} M_t(\boldsymbol{\delta}) \tag{8.49}$$

This is called **trust-region optimization**. (This can be seen as the "opposite" of line search, in the sense that we pick a distance we want to travel, determined by $\mathcal{R}_t$, and then solve for the optimal direction, rather than picking the direction and then solving for the optimal distance.)

We usually assume that $M_t(\boldsymbol{\delta})$ is a quadratic approximation:

$$M_t(\boldsymbol{\delta}) = \mathcal{L}(\boldsymbol{\theta}_t) + \boldsymbol{g}_t^\mathsf{T}\boldsymbol{\delta} + \frac{1}{2}\boldsymbol{\delta}^\mathsf{T}\mathbf{H}_t\boldsymbol{\delta} \tag{8.50}$$

where $\boldsymbol{g}_t = \nabla_{\boldsymbol{\theta}}\mathcal{L}(\boldsymbol{\theta})|_{\boldsymbol{\theta}_t}$ is the gradient, and $\mathbf{H}_t = \nabla_{\boldsymbol{\theta}}^2\mathcal{L}(\boldsymbol{\theta})|_{\boldsymbol{\theta}_t}$ is the Hessian. Furthermore, it is common to assume that $\mathcal{R}_t$ is a ball of radius r, i.e., $\mathcal{R}_t = \{\boldsymbol{\delta} : ||\boldsymbol{\delta}||_2 \leq r\}$. Using this, we can convert the constrained problem into an unconstrained one as follows:

$$\boldsymbol{\delta}^* = \operatorname*{argmin}_{\boldsymbol{\delta}} M(\boldsymbol{\delta}) + \lambda||\boldsymbol{\delta}||_2^2 = \operatorname*{argmin}_{\boldsymbol{\delta}} \boldsymbol{g}^\mathsf{T}\boldsymbol{\delta} + \frac{1}{2}\boldsymbol{\delta}^\mathsf{T}(\mathbf{H} + \lambda\mathbf{I})\boldsymbol{\delta} \tag{8.51}$$

for some Lagrange multiplier $\lambda > 0$ which depends on the radius r (see Section 8.5.1 for a discussion of Lagrange multipliers). We can solve this using

$$\boldsymbol{\delta} = -(\mathbf{H} + \lambda\mathbf{I})^{-1}\boldsymbol{g} \tag{8.52}$$

This is called **Tikhonov damping** or **Tikhonov regularization**. See Figure 8.15 for an illustration.

Note that adding a sufficiently large $\lambda\mathbf{I}$ to $\mathbf{H}$ ensures the resulting matrix is always positive definite. As $\lambda \to 0$, this trust method reduces to Newton's method, but for λ large enough, it will make all the negative eigenvalues positive (and all the 0 eigenvalues become equal to λ).

8.4 Stochastic gradient descent

In this section, we consider **stochastic optimization**, where the goal is to minimize the average value of a function:

$$\mathcal{L}(\boldsymbol{\theta}) = \mathbb{E}_{q(\boldsymbol{z})}\left[\mathcal{L}(\boldsymbol{\theta}, \boldsymbol{z})\right] \tag{8.53}$$

where $\boldsymbol{z}$ is a random input to the objective. This could be a "noise" term, coming from the environment, or it could be a training example drawn randomly from the training set, as we explain below.

At each iteration, we assume we observe $\mathcal{L}_t(\boldsymbol{\theta}) = \mathcal{L}(\boldsymbol{\theta}, \boldsymbol{z}_t)$, where $\boldsymbol{z}_t \sim q$. We also assume a way to compute an unbiased estimate of the gradient of $\mathcal{L}$. If the distribution $q(\boldsymbol{z})$ is independent of the parameters we are optimizing, we can use $\boldsymbol{g}_t = \nabla_{\boldsymbol{\theta}}\mathcal{L}_t(\boldsymbol{\theta}_t)$. In this case, the resulting algorithm can be written as follows:

$$\boldsymbol{\theta}_{t+1} = \boldsymbol{\theta}_t - \eta_t\nabla\mathcal{L}(\boldsymbol{\theta}_t, \boldsymbol{z}_t) = \boldsymbol{\theta}_t - \eta_t\boldsymbol{g}_t \tag{8.54}$$

This method is known as **stochastic gradient descent** or **SGD**. As long as the gradient estimate is unbiased, then this method will converge to a stationary point, providing we decay the step size η_t at a certain rate, as we discuss in Section 8.4.3.

8.4.1 Application to finite sum problems

SGD is very widely used in machine learning. To see why, recall from Section 4.3 that many model fitting procedures are based on empirical risk minimization, which involve minimizing the following loss:

$$\mathcal{L}(\boldsymbol{\theta}_t) = \frac{1}{N} \sum_{n=1}^{N} \ell(\boldsymbol{y}_n, f(\boldsymbol{x}_n; \boldsymbol{\theta}_t)) = \frac{1}{N} \sum_{n=1}^{N} \mathcal{L}_n(\boldsymbol{\theta}_t) \tag{8.55}$$

This is called a **finite sum problem**. The gradient of this objective has the form

$$\boldsymbol{g}_t = \frac{1}{N} \sum_{n=1}^{N} \nabla_{\boldsymbol{\theta}} \mathcal{L}_n(\boldsymbol{\theta}_t) = \frac{1}{N} \sum_{n=1}^{N} \nabla_{\boldsymbol{\theta}} \ell(\boldsymbol{y}_n, f(\boldsymbol{x}_n; \boldsymbol{\theta}_t)) \tag{8.56}$$

This requires summing over all N training examples, and thus can be slow if N is large. Fortunately we can approximate this by sampling a **minibatch** of $B \ll N$ samples to get

$$\boldsymbol{g}_t \approx \frac{1}{|\mathcal{B}_t|} \sum_{n \in \mathcal{B}_t} \nabla_{\boldsymbol{\theta}} \mathcal{L}_n(\boldsymbol{\theta}_t) = \frac{1}{|\mathcal{B}_t|} \sum_{n \in \mathcal{B}_t} \nabla_{\boldsymbol{\theta}} \ell(\boldsymbol{y}_n, f(\boldsymbol{x}_n; \boldsymbol{\theta}_t)) \tag{8.57}$$

where $\mathcal{B}_t$ is a set of randomly chosen examples to use at iteration t.[2] This is an unbiased approximation to the empirical average in Equation (8.56). Hence we can safely use this with SGD.

Although the theoretical rate of convergence of SGD is slower than batch GD (in particular, SGD has a sublinear convergence rate), in practice SGD is often faster, since the per-step time is much lower [BB08; BB11]. To see why SGD can make faster progress than full batch GD, suppose we have a dataset consisting of a single example duplicated K times. Batch training will be (at least) K times slower than SGD, since it will waste time computing the gradient for the repeated examples. Even if there are no duplicates, batch training can be wasteful, since early on in training the parameters are not well estimated, so it is not worth carefully evaluating the gradient.

8.4.2 Example: SGD for fitting linear regression

In this section, we show how to use SGD to fit a linear regression model. Recall from Section 4.2.7 that the objective has the form

$$\mathcal{L}(\boldsymbol{\theta}) = \frac{1}{2N} \sum_{n=1}^{N} (\boldsymbol{x}_n^\mathsf{T} \boldsymbol{\theta} - y_n)^2 = \frac{1}{2N} ||\mathbf{X}\boldsymbol{\theta} - \boldsymbol{y}||_2^2 \tag{8.58}$$

The gradient is

$$\boldsymbol{g}_t = \frac{1}{N} \sum_{n=1}^{N} (\boldsymbol{\theta}_t^\mathsf{T} \boldsymbol{x}_n - y_n) \boldsymbol{x}_n \tag{8.59}$$

---

2. In practice we usually sample $\mathcal{B}_t$ without replacement. However, once we reach the end of the dataset (i.e., after a single training **epoch**), we can perform a random shuffling of the examples, to ensure that each minibatch on the next epoch is different from the last. This version of SGD is analyzed in [HS19].

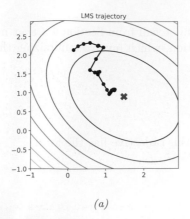
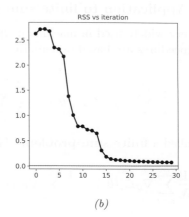

| (a) | (b) |

Figure 8.16: Illustration of the LMS algorithm. Left: we start from $\boldsymbol{\theta} = (-0.5, 2)$ and slowly converging to the least squares solution of $\hat{\boldsymbol{\theta}} = (1.45, 0.93)$ (red cross). Right: plot of objective function over time. Note that it does not decrease monotonically. Generated by lms_demo.ipynb.

Now consider using SGD with a minibatch size of $B = 1$. The update becomes

$$\boldsymbol{\theta}_{t+1} = \boldsymbol{\theta}_t - \eta_t(\boldsymbol{\theta}_t^\mathsf{T}\boldsymbol{x}_n - y_n)\boldsymbol{x}_n \tag{8.60}$$

where $n = n(t)$ is the index of the example chosen at iteration t. The overall algorithm is called the **least mean squares** (**LMS**) algorithm, and is also known as the **delta rule**, or the **Widrow-Hoff rule**.

Figure 8.16 shows the results of applying this algorithm to the data shown in Figure 11.2. We start at $\boldsymbol{\theta} = (-0.5, 2)$ and converge (in the sense that $||\boldsymbol{\theta}_t - \boldsymbol{\theta}_{t-1}||_2^2$ drops below a threshold of 10^{-2}) in about 26 iterations. Note that SGD (and hence LMS) may require multiple passes through the data to find the optimum.

8.4.3   Choosing the step size (learning rate)

When using SGD, we need to be careful in how we choose the learning rate in order to achieve convergence. For example, in Figure 8.17 we plot the loss vs the learning rate when we apply SGD to a deep neural network classifier (see Chapter 13 for details). We see a U-shaped curve, where an overly small learning rate results in underfitting, and overly large learning rate results in instability of the model (c.f., Figure 8.11(b)); in both cases, we fail to converge to a local optimum.

One heuristic for choosing a good learning rate, proposed in [Smi18], is to start with a small learning rate and gradually increase it, evaluating performance using a small number of minibatches. We then make a plot like the one in Figure 8.17, and pick the learning rate with the lowest loss. (In practice, it is better to pick a rate that is slightly smaller than (i.e., to the left of) the one with the lowest loss, to ensure stability.)

Rather than choosing a single constant learning rate, we can use a **learning rate schedule**, in which we adjust the step size over time. Theoretically, a sufficient condition for SGD to achieve

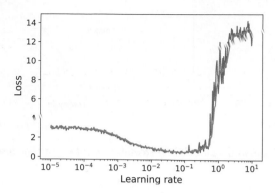

Figure 8.17: Loss vs learning rate (horizontal axis). Training loss vs learning rate for a small MLP fit to FashionMNIST using vanilla SGD. (Raw loss in blue, EWMA smoothed version in orange). Generated by lrschedule_tf.ipynb.

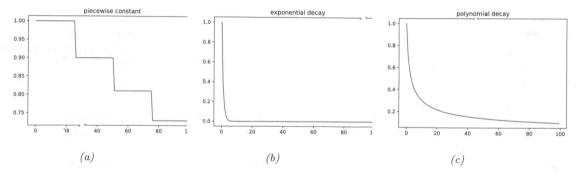

Figure 8.18: Illustration of some common learning rate schedules. (a) Piecewise constant. (b) Exponential decay. (c) Polynomial decay. Generated by learning_rate_plot.ipynb.

convergence is if the learning rate schedule satisfies the **Robbins-Monro conditions**:

$$\eta_t \to 0, \quad \frac{\sum_{t=1}^{\infty} \eta_t^2}{\sum_{t=1}^{\infty} \eta_t} \to 0 \tag{8.61}$$

Some common examples of learning rate schedules are listed below:

$$\eta_t = \eta_i \text{ if } t_i \leq t \leq t_{i+1} \quad \text{piecewise constant} \tag{8.62}$$

$$\eta_t = \eta_0 e^{-\lambda t} \quad \text{exponential decay} \tag{8.63}$$

$$\eta_t = \eta_0 (\beta t + 1)^{-\alpha} \quad \text{polynomial decay} \tag{8.64}$$

In the piecewise constant schedule, t_i are a set of time points at which we adjust the learning rate to a specified value. For example, we may set $\eta_i = \eta_0 \gamma^i$, which reduces the initial learning rate by a factor of γ for each threshold (or milestone) that we pass. Figure 8.18a illustrates this for $\eta_0 = 1$

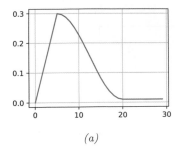

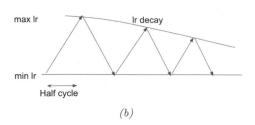

(a)   (b)

Figure 8.19: (a) Linear warm-up followed by cosine cool-down. (b) Cyclical learning rate schedule.

and $\gamma = 0.9$. This is called **step decay**. Sometimes the threshold times are computed adaptively, by estimating when the train or validation loss has plateaued; this is called **reduce-on-plateau**. Exponential decay is typically too fast, as illustrated in Figure 8.18b. A common choice is polynomial decay, with $\alpha = 0.5$ and $\beta = 1$, as illustrated in Figure 8.18c; this corresponds to a **square-root schedule**, $\eta_t = \eta_0 \frac{1}{\sqrt{t+1}}$.

In the deep learning community, another common schedule is to quickly increase the learning rate and then gradually decrease it again, as shown in Figure 8.19a. This is called **learning rate warmup**, or the **one-cycle learning rate schedule** [Smi18]. The motivation for this is the following: initially the parameters may be in a part of the loss landscape that is poorly conditioned, so a large step size will "bounce around" too much (c.f., Figure 8.11(b)) and fail to make progress downhill. However, with a slow learning rate, the algorithm can discover flatter regions of space, where a larger step size can be used. Once there, fast progress can be made. However, to ensure convergence to a point, we must reduce the learning rate to 0. See [Got+19; Gil+21] for more details.

It is also possible to increase and decrease the learning rate multiple times, in a cyclical fashion. This is called a **cyclical learning rate** [Smi18], and was popularized by the `fast.ai` course. See Figure 8.19b for an illustration using triangular shapes. The motivation behind this approach is to escape local minima. The minimum and maximum learning rates can be found based on the initial "dry run" described above, and the half-cycle can be chosen based on how many restarts you want to do with your training budget. A related approach, known as **stochastic gradient descent with warm restarts**, was proposed in [LH17]; they proposed storing all the checkpoints visited after each cool down, and using all of them as members of a model ensemble. (See Section 18.2 for a discussion of ensemble learning.)

An alternative to using heuristics for estimating the learning rate is to use line search (Section 8.2.2.2). This is tricky when using SGD, because the noisy gradients make the computation of the Armijo condition difficult [CS20]. However, [Vas+19] show that it can be made to work if the variance of the gradient noise goes to zero over time. This can happen if the model is sufficiently flexible that it can perfectly interpolate the training set.

8.4.4 Iterate averaging

The parameter estimates produced by SGD can be very unstable over time. To reduce the variance of the estimate, we can compute the average using

$$\overline{\boldsymbol{\theta}}_t = \frac{1}{t} \sum_{i=1}^{t} \boldsymbol{\theta}_i = \frac{1}{t} \boldsymbol{\theta}_t + \frac{t-1}{t} \overline{\boldsymbol{\theta}}_{t-1} \tag{8.65}$$

where $\boldsymbol{\theta}_t$ are the usual SGD iterates. This is called **iterate averaging** or **Polyak-Ruppert averaging** [Rup88].

In [PJ92], they prove that the estimate $\overline{\boldsymbol{\theta}}_t$ achieves the best possible asymptotic convergence rate among SGD algorithms, matching that of variants using second-order information, such as Hessians.

This averaging can also have statistical benefits. For example, in [NR18], they prove that, in the case of linear regression, this method is equivalent to ℓ_2 regularization (i.e., ridge regression).

Rather than an exponential moving average of SGD iterates, **Stochastic Weight Averaging** (SWA) [Izm+18] uses an *equal* average in conjunction with a modified learning rate schedule. In contrast to standard Polyak-Ruppert averaging, which was motivated for faster convergence rates, SWA exploits the flatness in objectives used to train deep neural networks, to find solutions which provide better generalization.

8.4.5 Variance reduction *

In this section, we discuss various ways to reduce the variance in SGD. In some cases, this can improve the theoretical convergence rate from sublinear to linear (i.e., the same as full-batch gradient descent) [SLRB17; JZ13; DBLJ14]. These methods reduce the variance of the gradients, rather than the parameters themselves and are designed to work for finite sum problems.

8.4.5.1 SVRG

The basic idea of **stochastic variance reduced gradient** (**SVRG**) [JZ13] is to use a control variate, in which we estimate a baseline value of the gradient based on the full batch, which we then use to compare the stochastic gradients to.

More precisely, ever so often (e.g., once per epoch), we compute the full gradient at a "snapshot" of the model parameters $\tilde{\boldsymbol{\theta}}$; the corresponding "exact" gradient is therefore $\nabla \mathcal{L}(\tilde{\boldsymbol{\theta}})$. At step t, we compute the usual stochastic gradient at the current parameters, $\nabla \mathcal{L}_t(\boldsymbol{\theta}_t)$, but also at the snapshot parameters, $\nabla \mathcal{L}_t(\tilde{\boldsymbol{\theta}})$, which we use as a baseline. We can then use the following improved gradient estimate

$$\boldsymbol{g}_t = \nabla \mathcal{L}_t(\boldsymbol{\theta}_t) - \nabla \mathcal{L}_t(\tilde{\boldsymbol{\theta}}) + \nabla \mathcal{L}(\tilde{\boldsymbol{\theta}}) \tag{8.66}$$

to compute $\boldsymbol{\theta}_{t+1}$. This is unbiased because $\mathbb{E}\left[\nabla \mathcal{L}_t(\tilde{\boldsymbol{\theta}})\right] = \nabla \mathcal{L}(\tilde{\boldsymbol{\theta}})$. Furthermore, the update only involves two gradient computations, since we can compute $\nabla \mathcal{L}(\tilde{\boldsymbol{\theta}})$ once per epoch. At the end of the epoch, we update the snapshot parameters, $\tilde{\boldsymbol{\theta}}$, based on the most recent value of $\boldsymbol{\theta}_t$, or a running average of the iterates, and update the expected baseline. (We can compute snapshots less often, but then the baseline will not be correlated with the objective and can hurt performance, as shown in [DB18].)

Iterations of SVRG are computationally faster than those of full-batch GD, but SVRG can still match the theoretical convergence rate of GD.

8.4.5.2   SAGA

In this section, we describe the **stochastic averaged gradient accelerated (SAGA)** algorithm of [DBLJ14]. Unlike SVRG, it only requires one full batch gradient computation, at the start of the algorithm. However, it "pays" for this saving in time by using more memory. In particular, it must store N gradient vectors. This enables the method to maintain an approximation of the global gradient by removing the old local gradient from the overall sum and replacing it with the new local gradient. This is called an **aggregated gradient** method.

More precisely, we first initialize by computing $\boldsymbol{g}_n^{\text{local}} = \nabla \mathcal{L}_n(\boldsymbol{\theta}_0)$ for all n, and the average, $\boldsymbol{g}^{\text{avg}} = \frac{1}{N} \sum_{n=1}^{N} \boldsymbol{g}_n^{\text{local}}$. Then, at iteration t, we use the gradient estimate

$$\boldsymbol{g}_t = \nabla \mathcal{L}_n(\boldsymbol{\theta}_t) - \boldsymbol{g}_n^{\text{local}} + \boldsymbol{g}^{\text{avg}} \tag{8.67}$$

where $n \sim \text{Unif}\{1, \dots, N\}$ is the example index sampled at iteration t. We then update $\boldsymbol{g}_n^{\text{local}} = \nabla \mathcal{L}_n(\boldsymbol{\theta}_t)$ and $\boldsymbol{g}^{\text{avg}}$ by replacing the old $\boldsymbol{g}_n^{\text{local}}$ by its new value.

This has an advantage over SVRG since it only has to do one full batch sweep at the start. (In fact, the initial sweep is not necessary, since we can compute $\boldsymbol{g}^{\text{avg}}$ "lazily", by only incorporating gradients we have seen so far.) The downside is the large extra memory cost. However, if the features (and hence gradients) are sparse, the memory cost can be reasonable. Indeed, the SAGA algorithm is recommended for use in the sklearn logistic regression code when N is large and $\boldsymbol{x}$ is sparse.[3]

8.4.5.3   Application to deep learning

Variance reduction methods are widely used for fitting ML models with convex objectives, such as linear models. However, there are various difficulties associated with using SVRG with conventional deep learning training practices. For example, the use of batch normalization (Section 14.2.4.1), data augmentation (Section 19.1) and dropout (Section 13.5.4) all break the assumptions of the method, since the loss will differ randomly in ways that depend not just on the parameters and the data index n. For more details, see e.g., [DB18; Arn+19].

8.4.6   Preconditioned SGD

In this section, we consider **preconditioned SGD**, which involves the following update:

$$\boldsymbol{\theta}_{t+1} = \boldsymbol{\theta}_t - \eta_t \mathbf{M}_t^{-1} \boldsymbol{g}_t, \tag{8.68}$$

where $\mathbf{M}_t$ is a **preconditioning matrix**, or simply the **preconditioner**, typically chosen to be positive-definite. Unfortunately the noise in the gradient estimates make it difficult to reliably estimate the Hessian, which makes it difficult to use the methods from Section 8.3. In addition, it is expensive to solve for the update direction with a full preconditioning matrix. Therefore most practitioners use a diagonal preconditioner $\mathbf{M}_t$. Such preconditioners do not necessarily use second-order information, but often result in speedups compared to vanilla SGD. See also [Roo+21]

---

3. See `https://scikit-learn.org/stable/modules/linear_model.html#logistic-regression`.

for a probabilitic interpretation of these heuristics, and sgd_comparison.ipynb for an empirical comparison on some simple datasets.

8.4.6.1 ADAGRAD

The **ADAGRAD** (short for "adaptive gradient") method of [DHS11] was originally designed for optimizing convex objectives where many elements of the gradient vector are zero; these might correspond to features that are rarely present in the input, such as rare words. The update has the following form

$$\theta_{t+1,d} = \theta_{t,d} - \eta_t \frac{1}{\sqrt{s_{t,d} + \epsilon}} g_{t,d} \tag{8.69}$$

where $d = 1 : D$ indexes the dimensions of the parameter vector, and

$$s_{t,d} = \sum_{i=1}^{t} g_{i,d}^2 \tag{8.70}$$

is the sum of the squared gradients and $\epsilon > 0$ is a small term to avoid dividing by zero. Equivalently we can write the update in vector form as follows:

$$\Delta \boldsymbol{\theta}_t = -\eta_t \frac{1}{\sqrt{\boldsymbol{s}_t + \epsilon}} \boldsymbol{g}_t \tag{8.71}$$

where the square root and division is performed elementwise. Viewed as preconditioned SGD, this is equivalent to taking $\mathbf{M}_t = \text{diag}(\boldsymbol{s}_t + \boldsymbol{\epsilon})^{1/2}$. This is an example of an **adaptive learning rate**; the overall stepsize η_t still needs to be chosen, but the results are less sensitive to it compared to vanilla GD. In particular, we usually fix $\eta_t = \eta_0$.

8.4.6.2 RMSPROP and ADADELTA

A defining feature of ADAGRAD is that the term in the denominator gets larger over time, so the effective learning rate drops. While it is necessary to ensure convergence, it might hurt performance as the denominator gets large too fast.

An alternative is to use an exponentially weighted moving average (EWMA, Section 4.4.2.2) of the past squared gradients, rather than their sum:

$$s_{t+1,d} = \beta s_{t,d} + (1 - \beta) g_{t,d}^2 \tag{8.72}$$

In practice we usually use $\beta \sim 0.9$, which puts more weight on recent examples. In this case,

$$\sqrt{s_{t,d}} \approx \text{RMS}(\boldsymbol{g}_{1:t,d}) = \sqrt{\frac{1}{t} \sum_{\tau=1}^{t} g_{\tau,d}^2} \tag{8.73}$$

where RMS stands for "root mean squared". Hence this method, (which is based on the earlier **RPROP** method of [RB93]) is known as **RMSPROP** [Hin14]. The overall update of RMSPROP is

$$\Delta \boldsymbol{\theta}_t = -\eta_t \frac{1}{\sqrt{\boldsymbol{s}_t + \epsilon}} \boldsymbol{g}_t. \tag{8.74}$$

The **AdaDelta** method was independently introduced in [Zei12], and is similar to RMSprop. However, in addition to accumulating an EWMA of the gradients in $\hat{s}$, it also keeps an EWMA of the updates δ_t to obtain an update of the form

$$\Delta\boldsymbol{\theta}_t = -\eta_t \frac{\sqrt{\boldsymbol{\delta}_{t-1} + \epsilon}}{\sqrt{\boldsymbol{s}_t + \epsilon}} \boldsymbol{g}_t \tag{8.75}$$

where

$$\boldsymbol{\delta}_t = \beta\boldsymbol{\delta}_{t-1} + (1-\beta)(\Delta\boldsymbol{\theta}_t)^2 \tag{8.76}$$

and $\boldsymbol{s}_t$ is the same as in RMSProp. This has the advantage that the "units" of the numerator and denominator cancel, so we are just elementwise-multiplying the gradient by a scalar. This eliminates the need to tune the learning rate η_t, which means one can simply set $\eta_t = 1$, although popular implementations of AdaDelta still keep η_t as a tunable hyperparameter. However, since these adaptive learning rates need not decrease with time (unless we choose η_t to explicitly do so), these methods are not guaranteed to converge to a solution.

8.4.6.3 Adam

It is possible to combine RMSProp with momentum. In particular, let us compute an EWMA of the gradients (as in momentum) and squared gradients (as in RMSProp)

$$\boldsymbol{m}_t = \beta_1\boldsymbol{m}_{t-1} + (1-\beta_1)\boldsymbol{g}_t \tag{8.77}$$
$$\boldsymbol{s}_t = \beta_2\boldsymbol{s}_{t-1} + (1-\beta_2)\boldsymbol{g}_t^2 \tag{8.78}$$

We then perform the following update:

$$\Delta\boldsymbol{\theta}_t = -\eta_t \frac{1}{\sqrt{\boldsymbol{s}_t + \epsilon}} \boldsymbol{m}_t \tag{8.79}$$

The resulting method is known as **Adam**, which stands for "adaptive moment estimation" [KB15].

The standard values for the various constants are $\beta_1 = 0.9$, $\beta_2 = 0.999$ and $\epsilon = 10^{-6}$. (If we set $\beta_1 = 0$ and no bias-correction, we recover RMSProp, which does not use momentum.) For the overall learning rate, it is common to use a fixed value such as $\eta_t = 0.001$. Again, as the adaptive learning rate may not decrease over time, convergence is not guaranteed (see Section 8.4.6.4).

If we initialize with $\boldsymbol{m}_0 = \boldsymbol{s}_0 = \boldsymbol{0}$, then initial estimates will be biased towards small values. The authors therefore recommend using the bias-corrected moments, which increase the values early in the optimization process. These estimates are given by

$$\hat{\boldsymbol{m}}_t = \boldsymbol{m}_t/(1-\beta_1^t) \tag{8.80}$$
$$\hat{\boldsymbol{s}}_t = \boldsymbol{s}_t/(1-\beta_2^t) \tag{8.81}$$

The advantage of bias-correction is shown in Figure 4.3.

8.4.6.4   Issues with adaptive learning rates

When using diagonal scaling methods, the overall learning rate is determined by $\eta_0 \mathbf{M}_t^{-1}$, which changes with time. Hence these methods are often called **adaptive learning rate** methods. However, they still require setting the base learning rate η_0.

Since the EWMA methods are typically used in the stochastic setting where the gradient estimates are noisy, their learning rate adaptation can result in non-convergence even on convex problems [RKK18]. Various solutions to this problem have been proposed, including AMSGRAD [RKK18], PADAM [CG18; Zho+18], and YOGI [Zah+18]. For example, the YOGI update modifies ADAM by replacing

$$\boldsymbol{s}_t = \beta_2 \boldsymbol{s}_{t-1} + (1 - \beta_2)\boldsymbol{g}_t^2 = \boldsymbol{s}_{t-1} + (1 - \beta_2)(\boldsymbol{g}_t^2 - \boldsymbol{s}_{t-1}) \qquad (8.82)$$

with

$$\boldsymbol{s}_t = \boldsymbol{s}_{t-1} + (1 - \beta_2)\boldsymbol{g}_t^2 \odot \operatorname{sgn}(\boldsymbol{g}_t^2 - \boldsymbol{s}_{t-1}) \qquad (8.83)$$

However, more recent work [Zha+22] has shown that vanilla Adam can be made to always converge provided the β_1 and β_2 parameters are tuned on a per-dataset basis. (In practice, it is common to fix $\beta_1 = 0.9$ and just tune β_2.)

8.4.6.5   Non-diagonal preconditioning matrices

Although the methods we have discussed above can adapt the learning rate of each parameter, they do not solve the more fundamental problem of ill-conditioning due to correlation of the parameters, and hence do not always provide as much of a speed boost over vanilla SGD as one may hope.

One way to get faster convergence is to use the following preconditioning matrix, known as **full-matrix Adagrad** [DHS11]:

$$\mathbf{M}_t = [(\mathbf{G}_t \mathbf{G}_t^\mathsf{T})^{\frac{1}{2}} + \epsilon \mathbf{I}_D]^{-1} \qquad (8.84)$$

where

$$\mathbf{G}_t = [\boldsymbol{g}_t, \ldots, \boldsymbol{g}_1] \qquad (8.85)$$

Here $\boldsymbol{g}_i = \nabla_\psi c(\boldsymbol{\psi}_i)$ is the D-dimensional gradient vector computed at step i. Unfortunately, $\mathbf{M}_t$ is a $D \times D$ matrix, which is expensive to store and invert.

The **Shampoo** algorithm [GKS18] makes a block diagonal approximation to $\mathbf{M}$, one per layer of the model, and then exploits Kronecker product structure to efficiently invert it. (It is called "shampoo" because it uses a conditioner.) Recently, [Ani+20] scaled this method up to fit very large deep models in record time.

8.5   Constrained optimization

In this section, we consider the following **constrained optimization problem**:

$$\boldsymbol{\theta}^* = \arg\min_{\boldsymbol{\theta} \in \mathcal{C}} \mathcal{L}(\boldsymbol{\theta}) \qquad (8.86)$$

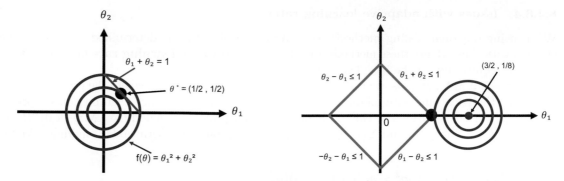

Figure 8.20: Illustration of some constrained optimization problems. Red contours are the level sets of the objective function $\mathcal{L}(\boldsymbol{\theta})$. Optimal constrained solution is the black dot, (a) Blue line is the equality constraint $h(\boldsymbol{\theta}) = 0$. (b) Blue lines denote the inequality constraints $|\theta_1| + |\theta_2| \leq 1$. (Compare to Figure 11.8 (left).)

where the feasible set, or constraint set, is

$$\mathcal{C} = \{\boldsymbol{\theta} \in \mathbb{R}^D : h_i(\boldsymbol{\theta}) = 0, i \in \mathcal{E}, \ g_j(\boldsymbol{\theta}) \leq 0, j \in \mathcal{I}\} \tag{8.87}$$

where $\mathcal{E}$ is the set of **equality constraints**, and $\mathcal{I}$ is the set of **inequality constraints**.

For example, suppose we have a quadratic objective, $\mathcal{L}(\boldsymbol{\theta}) = \theta_1^2 + \theta_2^2$, subject to a linear equality constraint, $h(\boldsymbol{\theta}) = 1 - \theta_1 - \theta_2 = 0$. Figure 8.20(a) plots the level sets of $\mathcal{L}$, as well as the constraint surface. What we are trying to do is find the point $\boldsymbol{\theta}^*$ that lives on the line, but which is closest to the origin. It is clear from the geometry that the optimal solution is $\boldsymbol{\theta} = (0.5, 0.5)$, indicated by the solid black dot.

In the following sections, we briefly describe some of the theory and algorithms underlying constrained optimization. More details can be found in other books, such as [BV04; NW06; Ber15; Ber16].

8.5.1   Lagrange multipliers

In this section, we discuss how to solve equality contrained optimization problems. We initially assume that we have just one equality constraint, $h(\boldsymbol{\theta}) = 0$.

First note that for any point on the constraint surface, $\nabla h(\boldsymbol{\theta})$ will be orthogonal to the constraint surface. To see why, consider another point nearby, $\boldsymbol{\theta} + \boldsymbol{\epsilon}$, that also lies on the surface. If we make a first-order Taylor expansion around $\boldsymbol{\theta}$ we have

$$h(\boldsymbol{\theta} + \boldsymbol{\epsilon}) \approx h(\boldsymbol{\theta}) + \boldsymbol{\epsilon}^\mathsf{T} \nabla h(\boldsymbol{\theta}) \tag{8.88}$$

Since both $\boldsymbol{\theta}$ and $\boldsymbol{\theta} + \boldsymbol{\epsilon}$ are on the constraint surface, we must have $h(\boldsymbol{\theta}) = h(\boldsymbol{\theta} + \boldsymbol{\epsilon})$ and hence $\boldsymbol{\epsilon}^\mathsf{T} \nabla h(\boldsymbol{\theta}) \approx 0$. Since $\boldsymbol{\epsilon}$ is parallel to the constraint surface, $\nabla h(\boldsymbol{\theta})$ must be perpendicular to it.

We seek a point $\boldsymbol{\theta}^*$ on the constraint surface such that $\mathcal{L}(\boldsymbol{\theta})$ is minimized. We just showed that it must satisfy the condition that $\nabla h(\boldsymbol{\theta}^*)$ is orthogonal to the constraint surface. In addition, such a point must have the property that $\nabla \mathcal{L}(\boldsymbol{\theta})$ is also orthogonal to the constraint surface, as otherwise we could decrease $\mathcal{L}(\boldsymbol{\theta})$ by moving a short distance along the constraint surface. Since both $\nabla h(\boldsymbol{\theta})$

and $\nabla\mathcal{L}(\boldsymbol{\theta})$ are orthogonal to the constraint surface at $\boldsymbol{\theta}^*$, they must be parallel (or anti-parallel) to each other. Hence there must exist a constant $\lambda^* \in \mathbb{R}$ such that

$$\nabla\mathcal{L}(\boldsymbol{\theta}^*) = \lambda^*\nabla h(\boldsymbol{\theta}^*) \tag{8.89}$$

(We cannot just equate the gradient vectors, since they may have different magnitudes.) The constant λ^* is called a **Lagrange multiplier**, and can be positive, negative, or zero. This latter case occurs when $\nabla\mathcal{L}(\boldsymbol{\theta}^*) = 0$.

We can convert Equation (8.89) into an objective, known as the **Lagrangian**, that we should find a stationary point of the following:

$$L(\boldsymbol{\theta}, \lambda) \triangleq \mathcal{L}(\boldsymbol{\theta}) + \lambda h(\boldsymbol{\theta}) \tag{8.90}$$

At a stationary point of the Lagrangian, we have

$$\nabla_{\boldsymbol{\theta},\lambda} L(\boldsymbol{\theta}, \lambda) = \mathbf{0} \iff \lambda\nabla_{\boldsymbol{\theta}} h(\boldsymbol{\theta}) = \nabla\mathcal{L}(\boldsymbol{\theta}),\ h(\boldsymbol{\theta}) = 0 \tag{8.91}$$

This is called a **critical point**, and satisfies the original constraint $h(\boldsymbol{\theta}) = 0$ and Equation (8.89).

If we have $m > 1$ constraints, we can form a new constraint function by addition, as follows:

$$L(\boldsymbol{\theta}, \boldsymbol{\lambda}) = \mathcal{L}(\boldsymbol{\theta}) + \sum_{j=1}^{m} \lambda_j h_j(\boldsymbol{\theta}) \tag{8.92}$$

We now have $D+m$ equations in $D+m$ unknowns and we can use standard unconstrained optimization methods to find a stationary point. We give some examples below.

8.5.1.1 Example: 2d Quadratic objective with one linear equality constraint

Consider minimizing $\mathcal{L}(\boldsymbol{\theta}) = \theta_1^2 + \theta_2^2$ subject to the constraint that $\theta_1 + \theta_2 = 1$.

(This is the problem illustrated in Figure 8.20(a).) The Lagrangian is

$$L(\theta_1, \theta_2, \lambda) = \theta_1^2 + \theta_2^2 + \lambda(\theta_1 + \theta_2 - 1) \tag{8.93}$$

We have the following conditions for a stationary point:

$$\frac{\partial}{\partial\theta_1} L(\theta_1, \theta_2, \lambda) = 2\theta_1 + \lambda = 0 \tag{8.94}$$

$$\frac{\partial}{\partial\theta_2} L(\theta_1, \theta_2, \lambda) = 2\theta_2 + \lambda = 0 \tag{8.95}$$

$$\frac{\partial}{\partial\lambda} L(\theta_1, \theta_2, \lambda) = \theta_1 + \theta_2 - 1 = 0 \tag{8.96}$$

From Equations 8.94 and 8.95 we find $2\theta_1 = -\lambda = 2\theta_2$, so $\theta_1 = \theta_2$. Also, from Equation (8.96), we find $2\theta_1 = 1$. So $\boldsymbol{\theta}^* = (0.5, 0.5)$, as we claimed earlier. Furthermore, this is the global minimum since the objective is convex and the constraint is affine.

8.5.2 The KKT conditions

In this section, we generalize the concept of Lagrange multipliers to additionally handle inequality constraints.

First consider the case where we have a single inequality constraint $g(\boldsymbol{\theta}) \leq 0$. To find the optimum, one approach would be to consider an unconstrained problem where we add the penalty as an infinite step function:

$$\hat{\mathcal{L}}(\boldsymbol{\theta}) = \mathcal{L}(\boldsymbol{\theta}) + \infty \, \mathbb{I}\,(g(\boldsymbol{\theta}) > 0) \tag{8.97}$$

However, this is a discontinuous function that is hard to optimize.

Instead, we create a lower bound of the form $\mu g(\boldsymbol{\theta})$, where $\mu \geq 0$. This gives us the following Lagrangian:

$$L(\boldsymbol{\theta}, \mu) = \mathcal{L}(\boldsymbol{\theta}) + \mu g(\boldsymbol{\theta}) \tag{8.98}$$

Note that the step function can be recovered using

$$\hat{\mathcal{L}}(\boldsymbol{\theta}) = \max_{\mu \geq 0} L(\boldsymbol{\theta}, \mu) = \begin{cases} \infty & \text{if } g(\boldsymbol{\theta}) > 0, \\ \mathcal{L}(\boldsymbol{\theta}) & \text{otherwise} \end{cases} \tag{8.99}$$

Thus our optimization problem becomes

$$\min_{\boldsymbol{\theta}} \max_{\mu \geq 0} L(\boldsymbol{\theta}, \mu) \tag{8.100}$$

Now consider the general case where we have multiple inequality constraints, $\boldsymbol{g}(\boldsymbol{\theta}) \leq \mathbf{0}$, and multiple equality constraints, $\boldsymbol{h}(\boldsymbol{\theta}) = \mathbf{0}$. The **generalized Lagrangian** becomes

$$L(\boldsymbol{\theta}, \boldsymbol{\mu}, \boldsymbol{\lambda}) = \mathcal{L}(\boldsymbol{\theta}) + \sum_i \mu_i g_i(\boldsymbol{\theta}) + \sum_j \lambda_j h_j(\boldsymbol{\theta}) \tag{8.101}$$

(We are free to change $-\lambda_j h_j$ to $+\lambda_j h_j$ since the sign is arbitrary.) Our optimization problem becomes

$$\min_{\boldsymbol{\theta}} \max_{\boldsymbol{\mu} \geq 0, \boldsymbol{\lambda}} L(\boldsymbol{\theta}, \boldsymbol{\mu}, \boldsymbol{\lambda}) \tag{8.102}$$

When $\mathcal{L}$ and g are convex, then all critical points of this problem must satisfy the following criteria (under some conditions [BV04, Sec.5.2.3]):

- All constraints are satisfied (this is called **feasibility**):

$$\boldsymbol{g}(\boldsymbol{\theta}) \leq \mathbf{0}, \; \boldsymbol{h}(\boldsymbol{\theta}) = \mathbf{0} \tag{8.103}$$

- The solution is a stationary point:

$$\nabla \mathcal{L}(\boldsymbol{\theta}^*) + \sum_i \mu_i \nabla g_i(\boldsymbol{\theta}^*) + \sum_j \lambda_j \nabla h_j(\boldsymbol{\theta}^*) = \mathbf{0} \tag{8.104}$$

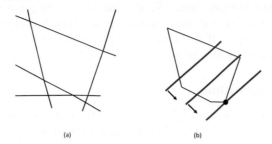

(a) (b)

Figure 8.21: (a) A convex polytope in 2d defined by the intersection of linear constraints. (b) Depiction of the feasible set as well as the linear objective function. The red line is a level set of the objective, and the arrow indicates the direction in which it is improving. We see that the optimal solution lies at a vertex of the polytope.

- The penalty for the inequality constraint points in the right direction (this is called **dual feasibility**):

$$\boldsymbol{\mu} \geq \mathbf{0} \tag{8.105}$$

- The Lagrange multipliers pick up any slack in the inactive constraints, i.e., either $\mu_i = 0$ or $g_i(\boldsymbol{\theta}^*) = 0$, so

$$\boldsymbol{\mu} \odot \boldsymbol{g} = \mathbf{0} \tag{8.106}$$

This is called **complementary slackness**.

To see why the last condition holds, consider (for simplicity) the case of a single inequality constraint, $g(\boldsymbol{\theta}) \leq 0$. Either it is **active**, meaning $g(\boldsymbol{\theta}) = 0$, or it is inactive, meaning $g(\boldsymbol{\theta}) < 0$. In the active case, the solution lies on the constraint boundary, and $g(\boldsymbol{\theta}) = 0$ becomes an equality constraint; then we have $\nabla \mathcal{L} = \mu \nabla g$ for some constant $\mu \neq 0$, because of Equation (8.89). In the inactive case, the solution is not on the constraint boundary; we still have $\nabla \mathcal{L} = \mu \nabla g$, but now $\mu = 0$.

These are called called the **Karush-Kuhn-Tucker (KKT)** conditions. If $\mathcal{L}$ is a convex function, and the constraints define a convex set, the KKT conditions are sufficient for (global) optimality, as well as necessary.

8.5.3 Linear programming

Consider optimizing a linear function subject to linear constraints. When written in **standard form**, this can be represented as

$$\min_{\boldsymbol{\theta}} \boldsymbol{c}^\mathsf{T} \boldsymbol{\theta} \quad \text{s.t.} \quad \mathbf{A}\boldsymbol{\theta} \leq \boldsymbol{b}, \ \boldsymbol{\theta} \geq \mathbf{0} \tag{8.107}$$

The feasible set defines a convex **polytope**, which is a convex set defined as the intersection of half spaces. See Figure 8.21(a) for a 2d example. Figure 8.21(b) shows a linear cost function that decreases as we move to the bottom right. We see that the lowest point that is in the feasible set is a vertex. In fact, it can be proved that the optimum point always occurs at a vertex of the polytope, assuming the solution is unique. If there are multiple solutions, the line will be parallel to a face. There may also be no optima inside the feasible set; in this case, the problem is said to be infeasible.

8.5.3.1   The simplex algorithm

It can be shown that the optima of an LP occur at vertices of the polytope defining the feasible set (see Figure 8.21(b) for an example). The **simplex algorithm** solves LPs by moving from vertex to vertex, each time seeking the edge which most improves the objective.

In the worst-case scenario, the simplex algorithm can take time exponential in D, although in practice it is usually very efficient. There are also various polynomial-time algorithms, such as the interior point method, although these are often slower in practice.

8.5.3.2   Applications

There are many applications of linear programming in science, engineering and business. It is also useful in some machine learning problems. For example, Section 11.6.1.1 shows how to use it to solve robust linear regression. It is also useful for state estimation in graphical models (see e.g., [SGJ11]).

8.5.4   Quadratic programming

Consider minimizing a quadratic objective subject to linear equality and inequality constraints. This kind of problem is known as a **quadratic program** or **QP**, and can be written as follows:

$$\min_{\boldsymbol{\theta}} \frac{1}{2}\boldsymbol{\theta}^\mathsf{T}\mathbf{H}\boldsymbol{\theta} + \boldsymbol{c}^\mathsf{T}\boldsymbol{\theta} \quad \text{s.t.} \quad \mathbf{A}\boldsymbol{\theta} \le \boldsymbol{b},\ \mathbf{C}\boldsymbol{\theta} = \boldsymbol{d} \tag{8.108}$$

If $\mathbf{H}$ is positive semidefinite, then this is a convex optimization problem.

8.5.4.1   Example: 2d quadratic objective with linear inequality constraints

As a concrete example, suppose we want to minimize

$$\mathcal{L}(\boldsymbol{\theta}) = (\theta_1 - \frac{3}{2})^2 + (\theta_2 - \frac{1}{8})^2 = \frac{1}{2}\boldsymbol{\theta}^\mathsf{T}\mathbf{H}\boldsymbol{\theta} + \boldsymbol{c}^\mathsf{T}\boldsymbol{\theta} + \text{const} \tag{8.109}$$

where $\mathbf{H} = 2\mathbf{I}$ and $\boldsymbol{c} = -(3, 1/4)$, subject to

$$|\theta_1| + |\theta_2| \le 1 \tag{8.110}$$

See Figure 8.20(b) for an illustration.

We can rewrite the constraints as

$$\theta_1 + \theta_2 \le 1, \quad \theta_1 - \theta_2 \le 1, \quad -\theta_1 + \theta_2 \le 1, \quad -\theta_1 - \theta_2 \le 1 \tag{8.111}$$

which we can write more compactly as

$$\mathbf{A}\boldsymbol{\theta} \le \boldsymbol{b} \tag{8.112}$$

where $\boldsymbol{b} = \mathbf{1}$ and

$$\mathbf{A} = \begin{pmatrix} 1 & 1 \\ 1 & -1 \\ -1 & 1 \\ -1 & -1 \end{pmatrix} \tag{8.113}$$

This is now in the standard QP form.

From the geometry of the problem, shown in Figure 8.20(b), we see that the constraints corresponding to the two left faces of the diamond) are inactive (since we are trying to get as close to the center of the circle as possible, which is outside of, and to the right of, the constrained feasible region). Denoting $g_i(\boldsymbol{\theta})$ as the inequality constraint corresponding to row i of $\mathbf{A}$, this means $g_3(\boldsymbol{\theta}^*) > 0$ and $g_4(\boldsymbol{\theta}^*) > 0$, and hence, by complementarity, $\mu_3^* = \mu_4^* = 0$. We can therefore remove these inactive constraints.

From the KKT conditions we know that

$$\mathbf{H}\boldsymbol{\theta} + \boldsymbol{c} + \mathbf{A}^\mathsf{T}\boldsymbol{\mu} = \mathbf{0} \tag{8.114}$$

Using these for the actively constrained subproblem, we get

$$\begin{pmatrix} 2 & 0 & 1 & 1 \\ 0 & 2 & 1 & -1 \\ 1 & 1 & 0 & 0 \\ 1 & -1 & 0 & 0 \end{pmatrix} \begin{pmatrix} \theta_1 \\ \theta_2 \\ \mu_1 \\ \mu_2 \end{pmatrix} = \begin{pmatrix} 3 \\ 1/4 \\ 1 \\ 1 \end{pmatrix} \tag{8.115}$$

Hence the solution is

$$\boldsymbol{\theta}_* = (1,0)^\mathsf{T}, \boldsymbol{\mu}_* = (0.625, 0.375, 0, 0)^\mathsf{T} \tag{8.116}$$

Notice that the optimal value of $\boldsymbol{\theta}$ occurs at one of the vertices of the ℓ_1 "ball" (the diamond shape).

8.5.4.2 Applications

There are several applications of quadratic programming in ML. For example, in Section 11.4, we discuss the lasso method for sparse linear regression, which amounts to optimizing $\mathcal{L}(\boldsymbol{w}) = ||\mathbf{X}\boldsymbol{w} - \boldsymbol{y}||_2^2 + \lambda ||\boldsymbol{w}||_1$, which can be reformulated into a QP. And in Section 17.3, we show how to use QP for SVMs (support vector machines).

8.5.5 Mixed integer linear programming *

Integer linear programming or **ILP** corresponds to minimizing a linear objective, subject to linear constraints, where the optimization variables are discrete integers instead of reals. In standard form, the problem is as follows:

$$\min_{\boldsymbol{\theta}} \boldsymbol{c}^\mathsf{T}\boldsymbol{\theta} \quad \text{s.t.} \quad \mathbf{A}\boldsymbol{\theta} \le \boldsymbol{b}, \boldsymbol{\theta} \ge 0, \boldsymbol{\theta} \in \mathbb{Z}^D \tag{8.117}$$

where $\mathbb{Z}$ is the set of integers. If some of the optimization variables are real-valued, it is called a **mixed ILP**, often called a **MIP** for short. (If all of the variables are real-valued, it becomes a standard LP.)

MIPs have a large number of applications, such as in vehicle routing, scheduling and packing. They are also useful for some ML applications, such as formally verifying the behavior of certain kinds of deep neural networks [And+18], and proving robustness properties of DNNs to adversarial (worst-case) perturbations [TXT19].

8.6 Proximal gradient method *

We are often interested in optimizing an objective of the form

$$\mathcal{L}(\boldsymbol{\theta}) = \mathcal{L}_s(\boldsymbol{\theta}) + \mathcal{L}_r(\boldsymbol{\theta}) \tag{8.118}$$

where $\mathcal{L}_s$ is differentiable (smooth), and $\mathcal{L}_r$ is convex but not necessarily differentiable (i.e., it may be non-smooth or "rough"). For example, $\mathcal{L}_s$ might be the negative log likelihood (NLL), and $\mathcal{L}_r$ might be an indicator function that is infinite if a constraint is violated (see Section 8.6.1), or $\mathcal{L}_r$ might be the ℓ_1 norm of some parameters (see Section 8.6.2), or $\mathcal{L}_r$ might measure how far the parameters are from a set of allowed quantized values (see Section 8.6.3).

One way to tackle such problems is to use the **proximal gradient method** (see e.g., [PB+14; PSW15]). Roughly speaking, this takes a step of size η in the direction of the gradient, and then projects the resulting parameter update into a space that respects $\mathcal{L}_r$. More precisely, the update is as follows

$$\boldsymbol{\theta}_{t+1} = \text{prox}_{\eta_t \mathcal{L}_r}(\boldsymbol{\theta}_t - \eta_t \nabla \mathcal{L}_s(\boldsymbol{\theta}_t)) \tag{8.119}$$

where $\text{prox}_{\eta \mathcal{L}_r}(\boldsymbol{\theta})$ is the **proximal operator** of $\mathcal{L}_r$ (scaled by η) evaluated at $\boldsymbol{\theta}$:

$$\text{prox}_{\eta \mathcal{L}_r}(\boldsymbol{\theta}) \triangleq \underset{\boldsymbol{z}}{\text{argmin}} \left(\mathcal{L}_r(\boldsymbol{z}) + \frac{1}{2\eta} ||\boldsymbol{z} - \boldsymbol{\theta}||_2^2 \right) \tag{8.120}$$

(The factor of $\frac{1}{2}$ is an arbitrary convention.) We can rewrite the proximal operator as solving a constrained optimization problem, as follows:

$$\text{prox}_{\eta \mathcal{L}_r}(\boldsymbol{\theta}) = \underset{\boldsymbol{z}}{\text{argmin}}\, \mathcal{L}_r(\boldsymbol{z}) \quad \text{s.t.} \quad ||\boldsymbol{z} - \boldsymbol{\theta}||_2 \leq \rho \tag{8.121}$$

where the bound ρ depends on the scaling factor η. Thus we see that the proximal projection minimizes the function while staying close to (i.e., proximal to) the current iterate. We give some examples below.

8.6.1 Projected gradient descent

Suppose we want to solve the problem

$$\underset{\boldsymbol{\theta}}{\text{argmin}}\, \mathcal{L}_s(\boldsymbol{\theta}) \quad \text{s.t.} \quad \boldsymbol{\theta} \in \mathcal{C} \tag{8.122}$$

where $\mathcal{C}$ is a convex set. For example, we may have the **box constraints** $\mathcal{C} = \{\boldsymbol{\theta} : \boldsymbol{l} \leq \boldsymbol{\theta} \leq \boldsymbol{u}\}$, where we specify lower and upper bounds on each element. These bounds can be infinite for certain

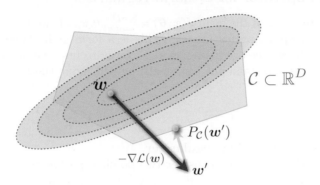

Figure 8.22: Illustration of projected gradient descent. $\boldsymbol{w}$ is the current parameter estimate, $\boldsymbol{w}'$ is the update after a gradient step, and $P_{\mathcal{C}}(\boldsymbol{w}')$ projects this onto the constraint set $\mathcal{C}$. From https: // bit. ly/ 3eJ3BhZ Used with kind permission of Martin Jaggi.

elements if we don't want to constrain values along that dimension. For example, if we just want to ensure the parameters are non-negative, we set $l_d = 0$ and $u_d = \infty$ for each dimension d.

We can convert the constrained optimization problem into an unconstrained one by adding a **penalty term** to the original objective:

$$\mathcal{L}(\boldsymbol{\theta}) = \mathcal{L}_s(\boldsymbol{\theta}) + \mathcal{L}_r(\boldsymbol{\theta}) \tag{8.123}$$

where $\mathcal{L}_r(\boldsymbol{\theta})$ is the indicator function for the convex set $\mathcal{C}$, i.e.,

$$\mathcal{L}_r(\boldsymbol{\theta}) = I_{\mathcal{C}}(\boldsymbol{\theta}) = \begin{cases} 0 & \text{if } \boldsymbol{\theta} \in \mathcal{C} \\ \infty & \text{if } \boldsymbol{\theta} \notin \mathcal{C} \end{cases} \tag{8.124}$$

We can use proximal gradient descent to solve Equation (8.123). The proximal operator for the indicator function is equivalent to projection onto the set $\mathcal{C}$:

$$\text{proj}_{\mathcal{C}}(\boldsymbol{\theta}) = \underset{\boldsymbol{\theta}' \in \mathcal{C}}{\text{argmin}} \, ||\boldsymbol{\theta}' - \boldsymbol{\theta}||_2 \tag{8.125}$$

This method is known as **projected gradient descent**. See Figure 8.22 for an illustration.

For example, consider the box constraints $\mathcal{C} = \{\boldsymbol{\theta} : \boldsymbol{l} \le \boldsymbol{\theta} \le \boldsymbol{u}\}$. The projection operator in this case can be computed elementwise by simply thresholding at the boundaries:

$$\text{proj}_{\mathcal{C}}(\boldsymbol{\theta})_d = \begin{cases} l_d & \text{if } \theta_d \le l_d \\ \theta_d & \text{if } l_d \le \theta_d \le u_d \\ u_d & \text{if } \theta_d \ge u_d \end{cases} \tag{8.126}$$

For example, if we want to ensure all elements are non-negative, we can use

$$\text{proj}_{\mathcal{C}}(\boldsymbol{\theta}) = \boldsymbol{\theta}_+ = [\max(\theta_1, 0), \dots, \max(\theta_D, 0)] \tag{8.127}$$

See Section 11.4.9.2 for an application of this method to sparse linear regression.

8.6.2   Proximal operator for ℓ_1-norm regularizer

Consider a linear predictor of the form $f(\boldsymbol{x}; \boldsymbol{\theta}) = \sum_{d=1}^{D} \theta_d x_d$. If we have $\theta_d = 0$ for any dimension d, we ignore the corresponding feature x_d. This is a form of **feature selection**, which can be useful both as a way to reduce overfitting as well as way to improve model interpretability. We can encourage weights to be zero (and not just small) by penalizing the ℓ_1 norm,

$$||\boldsymbol{\theta}||_1 = \sum_{d=1}^{D} |\theta_d| \tag{8.128}$$

This is called a **sparsity inducing regularizer**.

To see why this induces sparsity, consider two possible parameter vectors, one which is sparse, $\boldsymbol{\theta} = (1, 0)$, and one which is non-sparse, $\boldsymbol{\theta}' = (1/\sqrt{2}, 1/\sqrt{2})$. Both have the same ℓ_2 norm

$$||(1,0)||_2^2 = ||(1/\sqrt{2}, 1/\sqrt{2})||_2^2 = 1 \tag{8.129}$$

Hence ℓ_2 regularization (Section 4.5.3) will not favor the sparse solution over the dense solution. However, when using ℓ_1 regularization, the sparse solution is cheaper, since

$$||(1,0)||_1 = 1 < ||(1/\sqrt{2}, 1/\sqrt{2})||_1 = \sqrt{2} \tag{8.130}$$

See Section 11.4 for more details on sparse regression.

If we combine this regularizer with our smooth loss, we get

$$\mathcal{L}(\boldsymbol{\theta}) = \mathrm{NLL}(\boldsymbol{\theta}) + \lambda ||\boldsymbol{\theta}||_1 \tag{8.131}$$

We can optimize this objective using proximal gradient descent. The key question is how to compute the prox operator for the function $f(\boldsymbol{\theta}) = ||\boldsymbol{\theta}||_1$. Since this function decomposes over dimensions d, the proximal projection can be computed componentwise. From Equation (8.120), with $\eta = 1$, we have

$$\mathrm{prox}_{\lambda f}(\theta) = \underset{z}{\mathrm{argmin}} \, |z| + \frac{1}{2\lambda}(z - \theta)^2 = \underset{z}{\mathrm{argmin}} \, \lambda|z| + \frac{1}{2}(z - \theta)^2 \tag{8.132}$$

In Section 11.4.3, we show that the solution to this is given by

$$\mathrm{prox}_{\lambda f}(\theta) = \begin{cases} \theta - \lambda & \text{if } \theta \geq \lambda \\ 0 & \text{if } |\theta| \leq \lambda \\ \theta + \lambda & \text{if } \theta \leq -\lambda \end{cases} \tag{8.133}$$

This is known as the **soft thresholding operator**, since values less than λ in absolute value are set to 0 (thresholded), but in a continuous way. Note that soft thresholding can be written more compactly as

$$\mathrm{SoftThreshold}(\theta, \lambda) = \mathrm{sign}(\theta) \left(|\theta| - \lambda \right)_+ \tag{8.134}$$

where $\theta_+ = \max(\theta, 0)$ is the positive part of θ. In the vector case, we perform this elementwise:

$$\mathrm{SoftThreshold}(\boldsymbol{\theta}, \lambda) = \mathrm{sign}(\boldsymbol{\theta}) \odot \left(|\boldsymbol{\theta}| - \lambda \right)_+ \tag{8.135}$$

See Section 11.4.9.3 for an application of this method to sparse linear regression.

8.6.3 Proximal operator for quantization

In some applications (e.g., when training deep neural networks to run on memory-limited **edge devices**, such as mobile phones) we want to ensure that the parameters are **quantized**. For example, in the extreme case where each parameter can only be -1 or +1, the state space becomes $\mathcal{C} = \{-1, +1\}^D$.

Let us define a regularizer that measures distance to the nearest quantized version of the parameter vector:

$$\mathcal{L}_r(\boldsymbol{\theta}) = \inf_{\boldsymbol{\theta}_0 \in \mathcal{C}} ||\boldsymbol{\theta} - \boldsymbol{\theta}_0||_1 \tag{8.136}$$

(We could also use the ℓ_2 norm.) In the case of $\mathcal{C} = \{-1, +1\}^D$, this becomes

$$\mathcal{L}_r(\boldsymbol{\theta}) = \sum_{d=1}^{D} \inf_{[\theta_0]_d \in \{\pm 1\}} |\theta_d - [\theta_0]_d| = \sum_{d=1}^{D} \min\{|\theta_d - 1|, |\theta_d + 1|\} = ||\boldsymbol{\theta} - \text{sign}(\boldsymbol{\theta})||_1 \tag{8.137}$$

Let us define the corresponding quantization operator to be

$$q(\boldsymbol{\theta}) = \text{proj}_{\mathcal{C}}(\boldsymbol{\theta}) = \text{argmin}\, \mathcal{L}_r(\boldsymbol{\theta}) = \text{sign}(\boldsymbol{\theta}) \tag{8.138}$$

The core difficulty with quantized learning is that quantization is not a differentiable operation. A popular solution to this is to use the **straight-through estimator**, which uses the approximation $\frac{\partial \mathcal{L}}{\partial q(\boldsymbol{\theta})} \approx \frac{\partial \mathcal{L}}{\partial \boldsymbol{\theta}}$ (see e.g., [Yin+19]). The corresponding update can be done in two steps: first compute the gradient vector at the quantized version of the current parameters, and then update the unconstrained parameters using this approximate gradient:

$$\tilde{\boldsymbol{\theta}}_t = \text{proj}_{\mathcal{C}}(\boldsymbol{\theta}_t) = q(\boldsymbol{\theta}_t) \tag{8.139}$$

$$\boldsymbol{\theta}_{t+1} = \boldsymbol{\theta}_t - \eta_t \nabla \mathcal{L}_s(\tilde{\boldsymbol{\theta}}_t) \tag{8.140}$$

When applied to $\mathcal{C} = \{-1, +1\}^D$, this is known as the **binary connect** method [CBD15].

We can get better results using proximal gradient descent, in which we treat quantization as a regularizer, rather than a hard constraint; this is known as **ProxQuant** [BWL19]. The update becomes

$$\tilde{\boldsymbol{\theta}}_t = \text{prox}_{\lambda \mathcal{L}_r}(\boldsymbol{\theta}_t - \eta_t \nabla \mathcal{L}_s(\boldsymbol{\theta}_t)) \tag{8.141}$$

In the case that $\mathcal{C} = \{-1, +1\}^D$, one can show that the proximal operator is a generalization of the soft thresholding operator in Equation (8.135):

$$\text{prox}_{\lambda \mathcal{L}_r}(\boldsymbol{\theta}) = \text{SoftThreshold}(\boldsymbol{\theta}, \lambda, \text{sign}(\boldsymbol{\theta})) \tag{8.142}$$

$$= \text{sign}(\boldsymbol{\theta}) + \text{sign}(\boldsymbol{\theta} - \text{sign}(\boldsymbol{\theta})) \odot (|\boldsymbol{\theta} - \text{sign}(\boldsymbol{\theta})| - \lambda)_+ \tag{8.143}$$

This can be generalized to other forms of quantization; see [Yin+19] for details.

8.6.4 Incremental (online) proximal methods

Many ML problems have an objective function which is a sum of losses, one per example. Such problems can be solved incrementally; this is a special case of **online learning**. It is possible to extend proximal methods to this setting. For a probabilistic perspective on such methods (in terms of Kalman filtering), see [AEM18; Aky+19].

8.7   Bound optimization *

In this section, we consider a class of algorithms known as **bound optimization** or **MM** algorithms. In the context of minimization, MM stands for **majorize-minimize**. In the context of maximization, MM stands for **minorize-maximize**. We will discuss a special case of MM, known as **expectation maximization** or **EM**, in Section 8.7.2.

8.7.1   The general algorithm

In this section, we give a brief outline of MM methods. (More details can be found in e.g., [HL04; Mai15; SBP17; Nad+19].) To be consistent with the literature, we assume our goal is to *maximize* some function $\ell(\boldsymbol{\theta})$, such as the log likelihood, wrt its parameters $\boldsymbol{\theta}$. The basic approach in MM algorithms is to construct a **surrogate function** $Q(\boldsymbol{\theta}, \boldsymbol{\theta}^t)$ which is a tight lowerbound to $\ell(\boldsymbol{\theta})$ such that $Q(\boldsymbol{\theta}, \boldsymbol{\theta}^t) \leq \ell(\boldsymbol{\theta})$ and $Q(\boldsymbol{\theta}^t, \boldsymbol{\theta}^t) = \ell(\boldsymbol{\theta}^t)$. If these conditions are met, we say that Q minorizes ℓ. We then perform the following update at each step:

$$\boldsymbol{\theta}^{t+1} = \underset{\boldsymbol{\theta}}{\operatorname{argmax}} \, Q(\boldsymbol{\theta}, \boldsymbol{\theta}^t) \tag{8.144}$$

This guarantees us monotonic increases in the original objective:

$$\ell(\boldsymbol{\theta}^{t+1}) \geq Q(\boldsymbol{\theta}^{t+1}, \boldsymbol{\theta}^t) \geq Q(\boldsymbol{\theta}^t, \boldsymbol{\theta}^t) = \ell(\boldsymbol{\theta}^t) \tag{8.145}$$

where the first inequality follows since $Q(\boldsymbol{\theta}^{t+1}, \boldsymbol{\theta}')$ is a lower bound on $\ell(\boldsymbol{\theta}^{t+1})$ for any $\boldsymbol{\theta}'$; the second inequality follows from Equation (8.144); and the final equality follows the tightness property. As a consequence of this result, if you do not observe monotonic increase of the objective, you must have an error in your math and/or code. This is a surprisingly powerful debugging tool.

This process is sketched in Figure 8.23. The dashed red curve is the original function (e.g., the log-likelihood of the observed data). The solid blue curve is the lower bound, evaluated at $\boldsymbol{\theta}^t$; this touches the objective function at $\boldsymbol{\theta}^t$. We then set $\boldsymbol{\theta}^{t+1}$ to the maximum of the lower bound (blue curve), and fit a new bound at that point (dotted green curve). The maximum of this new bound becomes $\boldsymbol{\theta}^{t+2}$, etc.

If Q is a quadratic lower bound, the overall method is similar to Newton's method, which repeatedly fits and then optimizes a quadratic approximation, as shown in Figure 8.14(a). The difference is that optimizing Q is guaranteed to lead to an improvement in the objective, even if it is not convex, whereas Newton's method may overshoot or lead to a decrease in the objective, as shown in Figure 8.24, since it is a quadratic approximation and not a bound.

8.7.2   The EM algorithm

In this section, we discuss the **expectation maximization (EM)** algorithm [DLR77; MK97], which is a bound optimization algorithm designed to compute the MLE or MAP parameter estimate for probability models that have **missing data** and/or **hidden variables**. We let $\boldsymbol{y}_n$ be the visible data for example n, and $\boldsymbol{z}_n$ be the hidden data.

The basic idea behind EM is to alternate between estimating the hidden variables (or missing values) during the **E step** (expectation step), and then using the fully observed data to compute the MLE during the **M step** (maximization step). Of course, we need to iterate this process, since the expected values depend on the parameters, but the parameters depend on the expected values.

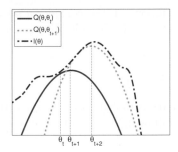

Figure 8.23: Illustration of a bound optimization algorithm. Adapted from Figure 9.14 of [Bis06]. Generated by emLogLikelihoodMax.ipynb.

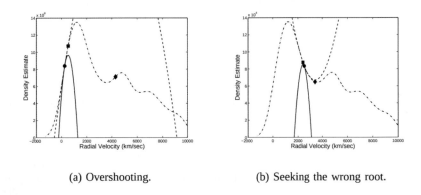

(a) Overshooting.   (b) Seeking the wrong root.

Figure 8.24: The quadratic lower bound of an MM algorithm (solid) and the quadratic approximation of Newton's method (dashed) superimposed on an empirical density esitmate (dotted). The starting point of both algorithms is the circle. The square denotes the outcome of one MM update. The diamond denotes the outcome of one Newton update. (a) Newton's method overshoots the global maximum. (b) Newton's method results in a reduction of the objective. From Figure 4 of [FT05]. Used with kind permission of Carlo Tomasi.

In Section 8.7.2.1, we show that EM is an MM algorithm, which implies that this iterative procedure will converge to a local maximum of the log likelihood. The speed of convergence depends on the amount of missing data, which affects the tightness of the bound [XJ96; MD97; SRG03; KKS20].

8.7.2.1   Lower bound

The goal of EM is to maximize the log likelihood of the observed data:

$$\ell(\boldsymbol{\theta}) = \sum_{n=1}^{N} \log p(\boldsymbol{y}_n|\boldsymbol{\theta}) = \sum_{n=1}^{N} \log \left[\sum_{\boldsymbol{z}_n} p(\boldsymbol{y}_n, \boldsymbol{z}_n|\boldsymbol{\theta}) \right] \tag{8.146}$$

where $\boldsymbol{y}_n$ are the visible variables and $\boldsymbol{z}_n$ are the hidden variables. Unfortunately this is hard to optimize, since the log cannot be pushed inside the sum.

EM gets around this problem as follows. First, consider a set of arbitrary distributions $q_n(\boldsymbol{z}_n)$ over each hidden variable $\boldsymbol{z}_n$. The observed data log likelihood can be written as follows:

$$\ell(\boldsymbol{\theta}) = \sum_{n=1}^{N} \log \left[\sum_{\boldsymbol{z}_n} q_n(\boldsymbol{z}_n) \frac{p(\boldsymbol{y}_n, \boldsymbol{z}_n | \boldsymbol{\theta})}{q_n(\boldsymbol{z}_n)} \right] \tag{8.147}$$

Using Jensen's inequality (Equation (6.34)), we can push the log (which is a concave function) inside the expectation to get the following lower bound on the log likelihood:

$$\ell(\boldsymbol{\theta}) \geq \sum_{n} \sum_{\boldsymbol{z}_n} q_n(\boldsymbol{z}_n) \log \frac{p(\boldsymbol{y}_n, \boldsymbol{z}_n | \boldsymbol{\theta})}{q_n(\boldsymbol{z}_n)} \tag{8.148}$$

$$= \sum_{n} \underbrace{\mathbb{E}_{q_n} \left[\log p(\boldsymbol{y}_n, \boldsymbol{z}_n | \boldsymbol{\theta}) \right] + \mathbb{H}(q_n)}_{\text{Ł}(\boldsymbol{\theta}, q_n)} \tag{8.149}$$

$$= \sum_{n} \text{Ł}(\boldsymbol{\theta}, q_n) \triangleq \text{Ł}(\boldsymbol{\theta}, \{q_n\}) = \text{Ł}(\boldsymbol{\theta}, q_{1:N}) \tag{8.150}$$

where $\mathbb{H}(q)$ is the entropy of probability distribution q, and $\text{Ł}(\boldsymbol{\theta}, \{q_n\})$ is called the **evidence lower bound** or **ELBO**, since it is a lower bound on the log marginal likelihood, $\log p(\boldsymbol{y}_{1:N} | \boldsymbol{\theta})$, also called the evidence. Optimizing this bound is the basis of variational inference, which we discuss in Section 4.6.8.3.

8.7.2.2 E step

We see that the lower bound is a sum of N terms, each of which has the following form:

$$\text{Ł}(\boldsymbol{\theta}, q_n) = \sum_{\boldsymbol{z}_n} q_n(\boldsymbol{z}_n) \log \frac{p(\boldsymbol{y}_n, \boldsymbol{z}_n | \boldsymbol{\theta})}{q_n(\boldsymbol{z}_n)} \tag{8.151}$$

$$= \sum_{\boldsymbol{z}_n} q_n(\boldsymbol{z}_n) \log \frac{p(\boldsymbol{z}_n | \boldsymbol{y}_n, \boldsymbol{\theta}) p(\boldsymbol{y}_n | \boldsymbol{\theta})}{q_n(\boldsymbol{z}_n)} \tag{8.152}$$

$$= \sum_{\boldsymbol{z}_n} q_n(\boldsymbol{z}_n) \log \frac{p(\boldsymbol{z}_n | \boldsymbol{y}_n, \boldsymbol{\theta})}{q_n(\boldsymbol{z}_n)} + \sum_{\boldsymbol{z}_n} q_n(\boldsymbol{z}_n) \log p(\boldsymbol{y}_n | \boldsymbol{\theta}) \tag{8.153}$$

$$= -D_{\mathbb{KL}}\left(q_n(\boldsymbol{z}_n) \| p(\boldsymbol{z}_n | \boldsymbol{y}_n, \boldsymbol{\theta}) \right) + \log p(\boldsymbol{y}_n | \boldsymbol{\theta}) \tag{8.154}$$

where $D_{\mathbb{KL}}\left(q \| p \right) \triangleq \sum_z q(z) \log \frac{q(z)}{p(z)}$ is the Kullback-Leibler divergence (or KL divergence for short) between probability distributions q and p. We discuss this in more detail in Section 6.2, but the key property we need here is that $D_{\mathbb{KL}}\left(q \| p \right) \geq 0$ and $D_{\mathbb{KL}}\left(q \| p \right) = 0$ iff $q = p$. Hence we can maximize the lower bound $\text{Ł}(\boldsymbol{\theta}, \{q_n\})$ wrt $\{q_n\}$ by setting each one to $q_n^* = p(\boldsymbol{z}_n | \boldsymbol{y}_n, \boldsymbol{\theta})$. This is called the **E step**. This ensures the ELBO is a tight lower bound:

$$\text{Ł}(\boldsymbol{\theta}, \{q_n^*\}) = \sum_{n} \log p(\boldsymbol{y}_n | \boldsymbol{\theta}) = \ell(\boldsymbol{\theta}) \tag{8.155}$$

To see how this connects to bound optimization, let us define

$$Q(\boldsymbol{\theta}, \boldsymbol{\theta}^t) = \text{Ł}(\boldsymbol{\theta}, \{p(\boldsymbol{z}_n | \boldsymbol{y}_n; \boldsymbol{\theta}^t)\}) \tag{8.156}$$

Then we have $Q(\boldsymbol{\theta}, \boldsymbol{\theta}^t) \leq \ell(\boldsymbol{\theta})$ and $Q(\boldsymbol{\theta}^t, \boldsymbol{\theta}^t) = \ell(\boldsymbol{\theta}^t)$, as required.

However, if we cannot compute the posteriors $p(\boldsymbol{z}_n|\boldsymbol{y}_n; \boldsymbol{\theta}^t)$ exactly, we can still use an approximate distribution $q(\boldsymbol{z}_n|\boldsymbol{y}_n; \boldsymbol{\theta}^t)$; this will yield a non-tight lower-bound on the log-likelihood. This generalized version of EM is known as **variational EM** [NH98]. See the sequel to this book, [Mur23], for details.

8.7.2.3   M step

In the M step, we need to maximize $Ł(\boldsymbol{\theta}, \{q_n^t\})$ wrt $\boldsymbol{\theta}$, where the q_n^t are the distributions computed in the E step at iteration t. Since the entropy terms $\mathbb{H}(q_n)$ are constant wrt $\boldsymbol{\theta}$, so we can drop them in the M step. We are left with

$$\ell^t(\boldsymbol{\theta}) = \sum_n \mathbb{E}_{q_n^t(\boldsymbol{z}_n)} \left[\log p(\boldsymbol{y}_n, \boldsymbol{z}_n | \boldsymbol{\theta}) \right] \tag{8.157}$$

This is called the **expected complete data log likelihood**. If the joint probability is in the exponential family (Section 3.4), we can rewrite this as

$$\ell^t(\boldsymbol{\theta}) = \sum_n \mathbb{E} \left[\mathcal{T}(\boldsymbol{y}_n, \boldsymbol{z}_n)^\mathsf{T} \boldsymbol{\theta} - A(\boldsymbol{\theta}) \right] = \sum_n (\mathbb{E} \left[\mathcal{T}(\boldsymbol{y}_n, \boldsymbol{z}_n) \right]^\mathsf{T} \boldsymbol{\theta} - A(\boldsymbol{\theta})) \tag{8.158}$$

where $\mathbb{E}\left[\mathcal{T}(\boldsymbol{y}_n, \boldsymbol{z}_n) \right]$ are called the **expected sufficient statistics**.

In the M step, we maximize the expected complete data log likelihood to get

$$\boldsymbol{\theta}^{t+1} = \arg\max_{\boldsymbol{\theta}} \sum_n \mathbb{E}_{q_n^t} \left[\log p(\boldsymbol{y}_n, \boldsymbol{z}_n | \boldsymbol{\theta}) \right] \tag{8.159}$$

In the case of the exponential family, the maximization can be solved in closed-form by matching the moments of the expected sufficient statistics.

We see from the above that the E step does not in fact need to return the full set of posterior distributions $\{q(\boldsymbol{z}_n)\}$, but can instead just return the sum of the expected sufficient statistics, $\sum_n \mathbb{E}_{q(\boldsymbol{z}_n)} \left[\mathcal{T}(\boldsymbol{y}_n, \boldsymbol{z}_n) \right]$. This will become clearer in the examples below.

8.7.3   Example: EM for a GMM

In this section, we show how to use the EM algorithm to compute MLE and MAP estimates of the parameters for a Gaussian mixture model (GMM).

8.7.3.1   E step

The E step simply computes the **responsibility** of cluster k for generating data point n, as estimated using the current parameter estimates $\boldsymbol{\theta}^{(t)}$:

$$r_{nk}^{(t)} = p^*(z_n = k | \boldsymbol{y}_n, \boldsymbol{\theta}^{(t)}) = \frac{\pi_k^{(t)} p(\boldsymbol{y}_n | \boldsymbol{\theta}_k^{(t)})}{\sum_{k'} \pi_{k'}^{(t)} p(\boldsymbol{y}_n | \boldsymbol{\theta}_{k'}^{(t)})} \tag{8.160}$$

8.7.3.2   M step

The M step maximizes the expected complete data log likelihood, given by

$$\ell^t(\boldsymbol{\theta}) = \mathbb{E}\left[\sum_n \log p(z_n|\boldsymbol{\pi}) + \sum_n \log p(\boldsymbol{y}_n|z_n, \boldsymbol{\theta})\right] \tag{8.161}$$

$$= \mathbb{E}\left[\sum_n \log\left(\prod_k \pi_k^{z_{nk}}\right) + \sum_n \log\left(\prod_k \mathcal{N}(\boldsymbol{y}_n|\boldsymbol{\mu}_k, \boldsymbol{\Sigma}_k)^{z_{nk}}\right)\right] \tag{8.162}$$

$$= \sum_n \sum_k \mathbb{E}[z_{nk}] \log \pi_k + \sum_n \sum_k \mathbb{E}[z_{nk}] \log \mathcal{N}(\boldsymbol{y}_n|\boldsymbol{\mu}_k, \boldsymbol{\Sigma}_k) \tag{8.163}$$

$$= \sum_n \sum_k r_{nk}^{(t)} \log(\pi_k) - \frac{1}{2}\sum_n \sum_k r_{nk}^{(t)}\left[\log|\boldsymbol{\Sigma}_k| + (\boldsymbol{y}_n - \boldsymbol{\mu}_k)^\mathsf{T}\boldsymbol{\Sigma}_k^{-1}(\boldsymbol{y}_n - \boldsymbol{\mu}_k)\right] + \text{const} \tag{8.164}$$

where $z_{nk} = \mathbb{I}(z_n = k)$ is a one-hot encoding of the categorical value z_n. This objective is just a weighted version of the standard problem of computing the MLEs of an MVN (see Section 4.2.6). One can show that the new parameter estimates are given by

$$\boldsymbol{\mu}_k^{(t+1)} = \frac{\sum_n r_{nk}^{(t)}\boldsymbol{y}_n}{r_k^{(t)}} \tag{8.165}$$

$$\boldsymbol{\Sigma}_k^{(t+1)} = \frac{\sum_n r_{nk}^{(t)}(\boldsymbol{y}_n - \boldsymbol{\mu}_k^{(t+1)})(\boldsymbol{y}_n - \boldsymbol{\mu}_k^{(t+1)})^\mathsf{T}}{r_k^{(t)}}$$

$$= \frac{\sum_n r_{nk}^{(t)}\boldsymbol{y}_n\boldsymbol{y}_n^\mathsf{T}}{r_k^{(t)}} - \boldsymbol{\mu}_k^{(t+1)}(\boldsymbol{\mu}_k^{(t+1)})^\mathsf{T} \tag{8.166}$$

where $r_k^{(t)} \triangleq \sum_n r_{nk}^{(t)}$ is the weighted number of points assigned to cluster k. The mean of cluster k is just the weighted average of all points assigned to cluster k, and the covariance is proportional to the weighted empirical scatter matrix.

The M step for the mixture weights is simply a weighted form of the usual MLE:

$$\pi_k^{(t+1)} = \frac{1}{N}\sum_n r_{nk}^{(t)} = \frac{r_k^{(t)}}{N} \tag{8.167}$$

8.7.3.3   Example

An example of the algorithm in action is shown in Figure 8.25 where we fit some 2d data with a 2 component GMM. The data set, from [Bis06], is derived from measurements of the Old Faithful geyser in Yellowstone National Park. In particular, we plot the time to next eruption in minutes versus the duration of the eruption in minutes. The data was standardized, by removing the mean and dividing by the standard deviation, before processing; this often helps convergence. We start with $\boldsymbol{\mu}_1 = (-1, 1)$, $\boldsymbol{\Sigma}_1 = \mathbf{I}$, $\boldsymbol{\mu}_2 = (1, -1)$, $\boldsymbol{\Sigma}_2 = \mathbf{I}$. We then show the cluster assignments, and corresponding mixture components, at various iterations.

For more details on applying GMMs for clustering, see Section 21.4.1.

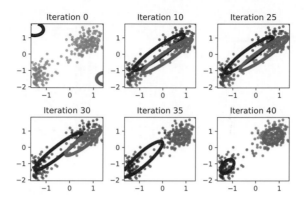

Figure 8.25: Illustration of the EM for a GMM applied to the Old Faithful data. The degree of redness indicates the degree to which the point belongs to the red cluster, and similarly for blue; thus purple points have a roughly 50/50 split in their responsibilities to the two clusters. Adapted from [Bis06] Figure 9.8. Generated by mix_gauss_demo_faithful.ipynb.

8.7.3.4 MAP estimation

Computing the MLE of a GMM often suffers from numerical problems and overfitting. To see why, suppose for simplicity that $\boldsymbol{\Sigma}_k = \sigma_k^2 \mathbf{I}$ for all k. It is possible to get an infinite likelihood by assigning one of the centers, say $\boldsymbol{\mu}_k$, to a single data point, say $\boldsymbol{y}_n$, since then the likelihood of that data point is given by

$$\mathcal{N}(\boldsymbol{y}_n | \boldsymbol{\mu}_k = \boldsymbol{y}_n, \sigma_k^2 \mathbf{I}) = \frac{1}{\sqrt{2\pi\sigma_k^2}} e^0 \tag{8.168}$$

Hence we can drive this term to infinity by letting $\sigma_k \to 0$, as shown in Figure 8.26(a). We call this the "collapsing variance problem".

An easy solution to this is to perform MAP estimation. Fortunately, we can still use EM to find this MAP estimate. Our goal is now to maximize the expected complete data log-likelihood plus the log prior:

$$\ell^t(\boldsymbol{\theta}) = \left[\sum_n \sum_k r_{nk}^{(t)} \log \pi_{nk} + \sum_n \sum_k r_{nk}^{(t)} \log p(\boldsymbol{y}_n | \boldsymbol{\theta}_k) \right] + \log p(\boldsymbol{\pi}) + \sum_k \log p(\boldsymbol{\theta}_k) \tag{8.169}$$

Note that the E step remains unchanged, but the M step needs to be modified, as we now explain.

For the prior on the mixture weights, it is natural to use a Dirichlet prior (Section 4.6.3.2), $\boldsymbol{\pi} \sim \text{Dir}(\boldsymbol{\alpha})$, since this is conjugate to the categorical distribution. The MAP estimate is given by

$$\tilde{\pi}_k^{(t+1)} = \frac{r_k^{(t)} + \alpha_k - 1}{N + \sum_k \alpha_k - K} \tag{8.170}$$

If we use a uniform prior, $\alpha_k = 1$, this reduces to the MLE.

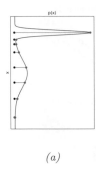

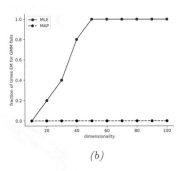

(a)   (b)

Figure 8.26: (a) Illustration of how singularities can arise in the likelihood function of GMMs. Here $K = 2$, but the first mixture component is a narrow spike (with $\sigma_1 \approx 0$) centered on a single data point x_1. Adapted from Figure 9.7 of [Bis06]. Generated by mix_gauss_singularity.ipynb. (b) Illustration of the benefit of MAP estimation vs ML estimation when fitting a Gaussian mixture model. We plot the fraction of times (out of 5 random trials) each method encounters numerical problems vs the dimensionality of the problem, for $N = 100$ samples. Solid red (upper curve): MLE. Dotted black (lower curve): MAP. Generated by mix_gauss_mle_vs_map.ipynb.

For the prior on the mixture components, let us consider a conjugate prior of the form

$$p(\boldsymbol{\mu}_k, \boldsymbol{\Sigma}_k) = \mathrm{NIW}(\boldsymbol{\mu}_k, \boldsymbol{\Sigma}_k \mid \breve{\boldsymbol{m}}, \breve{\kappa}, \breve{\nu}, \breve{\mathbf{S}}) \tag{8.171}$$

This is called the **Normal-Inverse-Wishart distribution** (see the sequel to this book, [Mur23], for details.) Suppose we set the hyper-parameters for $\boldsymbol{\mu}$ to be $\breve{\kappa} = 0$, so that the $\boldsymbol{\mu}_k$ are unregularized; thus the prior will only influence our estimate of $\boldsymbol{\Sigma}_k$. In this case, the MAP estimates are given by

$$\tilde{\boldsymbol{\mu}}_k^{(t+1)} = \hat{\boldsymbol{\mu}}_k^{(t+1)} \tag{8.172}$$

$$\tilde{\boldsymbol{\Sigma}}_k^{(t+1)} = \frac{\breve{\mathbf{S}} + \hat{\boldsymbol{\Sigma}}_k^{(t+1)}}{\breve{\nu} + r_k^{(t)} + D + 2} \tag{8.173}$$

where $\hat{\boldsymbol{\mu}}_k$ is the MLE for $\boldsymbol{\mu}_k$ from Equation (8.165), and $\hat{\boldsymbol{\Sigma}}_k$ is the MLE for $\boldsymbol{\Sigma}_k$ from Equation (8.166).

Now we discuss how to set the prior covariance, $\breve{\mathbf{S}}$. One possibility (suggested in [FR07, p163]) is to use

$$\breve{\mathbf{S}} = \frac{1}{K^{2/D}} \mathrm{diag}(s_1^2, \dots, s_D^2) \tag{8.174}$$

where $s_d^2 = (1/N) \sum_{n=1}^{N} (x_{nd} - \overline{x}_d)^2$ is the pooled variance for dimension d. The parameter $\breve{\nu}$ controls how strongly we believe this prior. The weakest prior we can use, while still being proper, is to set $\breve{\nu} = D + 2$, so this is a common choice.

We now illustrate the benefits of using MAP estimation instead of ML estimation in the context of GMMs. We apply EM to some synthetic data with $N = 100$ samples in D dimensions, using either ML or MAP estimation. We count the trial as a "failure" if there are numerical issues involving singular matrices. For each dimensionality, we conduct 5 random trials. The results are illustrated in Figure 8.26(b). We see that as soon as D becomes even moderately large, ML estimation crashes and burns, whereas MAP with an appropriate prior estimation rarely encounters numerical problems.

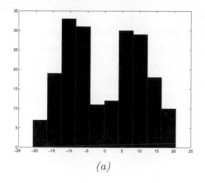
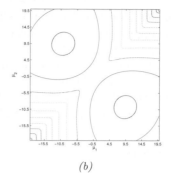

(a)   (b)

Figure 8.27: Left: $N = 200$ data points sampled from a mixture of 2 Gaussians in 1d, with $\pi_k = 0.5$, $\sigma_k = 5$, $\mu_1 = -10$ and $\mu_2 = 10$. Right: Likelihood surface $p(\mathcal{D}|\mu_1, \mu_2)$, with all other parameters set to their true values. We see the two symmetric modes, reflecting the unidentifiability of the parameters. Generated by gmm_lik_surface_plot.ipynb.

8.7.3.5   Nonconvexity of the NLL

The likelihood for a mixture model is given by

$$\ell(\boldsymbol{\theta}) = \sum_{n=1}^{N} \log \left[\sum_{z_n=1}^{K} p(\boldsymbol{y}_n, z_n | \boldsymbol{\theta}) \right] \tag{8.175}$$

In general, this will have multiple modes, and hence there will not be a unique global optimum.

Figure 8.27 illustrates this for a mixture of 2 Gaussians in 1d. We see that there are two equally good global optima, corresponding to two different labelings of the clusters, one in which the left peak corresponds to $z = 1$, and one in which the left peak corresponds to $z = 2$. This is called the **label switching problem**; see Section 21.4.1.2 for more details.

The question of how many modes there are in the likelihood function is hard to answer. There are $K!$ possible labelings, but some of the peaks might get merged, depending on how far apart the μ_k are. Nevertheless, there can be an exponential number of modes. Consequently, finding any global optimum is NP-hard [Alo+09; Dri+04]. We will therefore have to be satisfied with finding a local optimum. To find a good local optimum, we can use Kmeans++ (Section 21.3.4) to initialize EM.

8.8   Blackbox and derivative free optimization

In some optimization problems, the objective function is a **blackbox**, meaning that its functional form is unknown. This means we cannot use gradient-based methods to optimize it. Instead, solving such problems require **blackbox optimization** (**BBO**) methods, also called **derivative free optimization** (**DFO**).

In ML, this kind of problem often arises when performing model selection. For example, suppose we have some hyper-parameters, $\boldsymbol{\lambda} \in \boldsymbol{\Lambda}$, which control the type or complexity of a model. We often define the objective function $\mathcal{L}(\boldsymbol{\lambda})$ to be the loss on a validation set (see Section 4.5.4). Since the validation loss depends on the optimal model parameters, which are computed using a complex algorithm, this objective function is effectively a blackbox.[4]

A simple approach to such problems is to use **grid search**, where we evaluate each point in the parameter space, and pick the one with the lowest loss. Unfortunately, this does not scale to high dimensions, because of the curse of dimensionality. In addition, even in low dimensions this can be expensive if evaluating the blackbox objective is expensive (e.g., if it first requires training the model before computing the validation loss). Various solutions to this problem have been proposed. See the sequel to this book, [Mur23], for details.

8.9   Exercises

Exercise 8.1 [Subderivative of the hinge loss function *]

Let $f(x) = (1 - x)_+$ be the hinge loss function, where $(z)_+ = \max(0, z)$. What are $\partial f(0)$, $\partial f(1)$, and $\partial f(2)$?

Exercise 8.2 [EM for the Student distribution]

Derive the EM equations for computing the MLE for a multivariate Student distribution. Consider the case where the dof parameter is known and unknown separately. Hint: write the Student distribution as a scale mixture of Gaussians.

---

4. If the optimal parameters are computed using a gradient-based optimizer, we can "unroll" the gradient steps, to create a deep circuit that maps from the training data to the optimal parameters and hence to the validation loss. We can then optimize through the optimizer (see e.g., [Fra+17]). However, this technique can only be applied in limited settings.

PART II

Linear Models

9 Linear Discriminant Analysis

9.1 Introduction

In this chapter, we consider classification models of the following form:

$$p(y = c|\boldsymbol{x}, \boldsymbol{\theta}) = \frac{p(\boldsymbol{x}|y = c, \boldsymbol{\theta})p(y = c|\boldsymbol{\theta})}{\sum_{c'} p(\boldsymbol{x}|y = c', \boldsymbol{\theta})p(y = c'|\boldsymbol{\theta})} \tag{9.1}$$

The term $p(y = c|\boldsymbol{\theta})$ is the prior over class labels, and the term $p(\boldsymbol{x}|y = c, \boldsymbol{\theta})$ is called the **class conditional density** for class c.

The overall model is called a **generative classifier**, since it specifies a way to *generate* the features $\boldsymbol{x}$ for each class c, by sampling from $p(\boldsymbol{x}|y = c, \boldsymbol{\theta})$. By contrast, a **discriminative classifier** directly models the class posterior $p(y|\boldsymbol{x}, \boldsymbol{\theta})$. We discuss the pros and cons of these two approaches to classification in Section 9.4.

If we choose the class conditional densities in a special way, we will see that the resulting posterior over classes is a linear function of $\boldsymbol{x}$, i.e., $\log p(y = c|\boldsymbol{x}, \boldsymbol{\theta}) = \boldsymbol{w}^{\mathsf{T}}\boldsymbol{x} + \text{const}$, where $\boldsymbol{w}$ is derived from $\boldsymbol{\theta}$. Thus the overall method is called **linear discriminant analysis or LDA**.[1]

9.2 Gaussian discriminant analysis

In this section, we consider a generative classifier where the class conditional densities are multivariate Gaussians:

$$p(\boldsymbol{x}|y = c, \boldsymbol{\theta}) = \mathcal{N}(\boldsymbol{x}|\boldsymbol{\mu}_c, \boldsymbol{\Sigma}_c) \tag{9.2}$$

The corresponding class posterior therefore has the form

$$p(y = c|\boldsymbol{x}, \boldsymbol{\theta}) \propto \pi_c \mathcal{N}(\boldsymbol{x}|\boldsymbol{\mu}_c, \boldsymbol{\Sigma}_c) \tag{9.3}$$

where $\pi_c = p(y = c|\boldsymbol{\theta})$ is the prior probability of label c. (Note that we can ignore the normalization constant in the denominator of the posterior, since it is independent of c.) We call this model **Gaussian discriminant analysis or GDA**.

---

1. This term is rather confusing for two reasons. First, LDA is a generative, not discriminative, classifier. Second, LDA also stands for "latent Dirichlet allocation", which is a popular unsupervised generative model for bags of words [BNJ03].

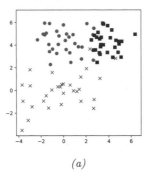
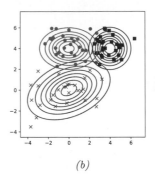

(a)   (b)

Figure 9.1: (a) Some 2d data from 3 different classes. (b) Fitting 2d Gaussians to each class. Generated by discrim_analysis_dboundaries_plot2.ipynb.

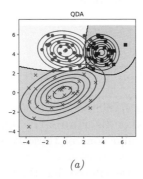
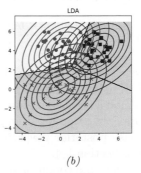

(a)   (b)

Figure 9.2: Gaussian discriminant analysis fit to data in Figure 9.1. (a) Unconstrained covariances induce quadratic decision boundaries. (b) Tied covariances induce linear decision boundaries. Generated by discrim_analysis_dboundaries_plot2.ipynb.

9.2.1   Quadratic decision boundaries

From Equation (9.3), we see that the log posterior over class labels is given by

$$\log p(y = c | \boldsymbol{x}, \boldsymbol{\theta}) = \log \pi_c - \frac{1}{2} \log |2\pi \boldsymbol{\Sigma}_c| - \frac{1}{2}(\boldsymbol{x} - \boldsymbol{\mu}_c)^\mathsf{T} \boldsymbol{\Sigma}_c^{-1}(\boldsymbol{x} - \boldsymbol{\mu}_c) + \text{const} \tag{9.4}$$

This is called the **discriminant function**. We see that the decision boundary between any two classes, say c and c', will be a quadratic function of $\boldsymbol{x}$. Hence this is known as **quadratic discriminant analysis** (QDA).

For example, consider the 2d data from 3 different classes in Figure 9.1a. We fit full covariance Gaussian class-conditionals (using the method explained in Section 9.2.4), and plot the results in Figure 9.1b. We see that the features for the blue class are somewhat correlated, whereas the features for the green class are independent, and the features for the red class are independent and isotropic (spherical covariance). In Figure 9.2a, we see that the resulting decision boundaries are quadratic functions of $\boldsymbol{x}$.

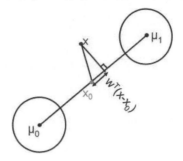

Figure 9.3: Geometry of LDA in the 2 class case where $\boldsymbol{\Sigma}_1 = \boldsymbol{\Sigma}_2 = \mathbf{I}$.

9.2.2 Linear decision boundaries

Now we consider a special case of Gaussian discriminant analysis in which the covariance matrices are **tied** or **shared** across classes, so $\boldsymbol{\Sigma}_c = \boldsymbol{\Sigma}$. If $\boldsymbol{\Sigma}$ is independent of c, we can simplify Equation (9.4) as follows:

$$\log p(y = c | \boldsymbol{x}, \boldsymbol{\theta}) = \log \pi_c - \frac{1}{2}(\boldsymbol{x} - \boldsymbol{\mu}_c)^{\mathsf{T}} \boldsymbol{\Sigma}^{-1}(\boldsymbol{x} - \boldsymbol{\mu}_c) + \text{const} \tag{9.5}$$

$$= \underbrace{\log \pi_c - \frac{1}{2}\boldsymbol{\mu}_c^{\mathsf{T}} \boldsymbol{\Sigma}^{-1} \boldsymbol{\mu}_c}_{\gamma_c} + \boldsymbol{x}^{\mathsf{T}} \underbrace{\boldsymbol{\Sigma}^{-1} \boldsymbol{\mu}_c}_{\boldsymbol{\beta}_c} + \underbrace{\text{const} - \frac{1}{2}\boldsymbol{x}^{\mathsf{T}} \boldsymbol{\Sigma}^{-1} \boldsymbol{x}}_{\kappa} \tag{9.6}$$

$$= \gamma_c + \boldsymbol{x}^{\mathsf{T}} \boldsymbol{\beta}_c + \kappa \tag{9.7}$$

The final term is independent of c, and hence is an irrelevant additive constant that can be dropped. Hence we see that the discriminant function is a linear function of $\boldsymbol{x}$, so the decision boundaries will be linear. Hence this method is called **linear discriminant analysis** or **LDA**. See Figure 9.2b for an example.

9.2.3 The connection between LDA and logistic regression

In this section, we derive an interesting connection between LDA and logistic regression, which we introduced in Section 2.5.3. From Equation (9.7) we can write

$$p(y = c | \boldsymbol{x}, \boldsymbol{\theta}) = \frac{e^{\boldsymbol{\beta}_c^{\mathsf{T}} \boldsymbol{x} + \gamma_c}}{\sum_{c'} e^{\boldsymbol{\beta}_{c'}^{\mathsf{T}} \boldsymbol{x} + \gamma_{c'}}} = \frac{e^{\boldsymbol{w}_c^{\mathsf{T}} [1, \boldsymbol{x}]}}{\sum_{c'} e^{\boldsymbol{w}_{c'}^{\mathsf{T}} [1, \boldsymbol{x}]}} \tag{9.8}$$

where $\boldsymbol{w}_c = [\gamma_c, \boldsymbol{\beta}_c]$. We see that Equation (9.8) has the same form as the multinomial logistic regression model. The key difference is that in LDA, we first fit the Gaussians (and class prior) to maximize the joint likelihood $p(\boldsymbol{x}, y | \boldsymbol{\theta})$, as discussed in Section 9.2.4, and then we derive $\boldsymbol{w}$ from $\boldsymbol{\theta}$. By contrast, in logistic regression, we estimate $\boldsymbol{w}$ directly to maximize the conditional likelihood $p(y | \boldsymbol{x}, \boldsymbol{w})$. In general, these can give different results (see Exercise 10.3).

To gain further insight into Equation (9.8), let us consider the binary case. In this case, the posterior is given by

$$p(y = 1|\boldsymbol{x}, \boldsymbol{\theta}) = \frac{e^{\boldsymbol{\beta}_1^\mathsf{T}\boldsymbol{x}+\gamma_1}}{e^{\boldsymbol{\beta}_1^\mathsf{T}\boldsymbol{x}+\gamma_1} + e^{\boldsymbol{\beta}_0^\mathsf{T}\boldsymbol{x}+\gamma_0}} = \frac{1}{1 + e^{(\boldsymbol{\beta}_0-\boldsymbol{\beta}_1)^\mathsf{T}\boldsymbol{x}+(\gamma_0-\gamma_1)}} \tag{9.9}$$

$$= \sigma\left((\boldsymbol{\beta}_1 - \boldsymbol{\beta}_0)^\mathsf{T}\boldsymbol{x} + (\gamma_1 - \gamma_0)\right) \tag{9.10}$$

where $\sigma(\eta)$ refers to the sigmoid function.

Now

$$\gamma_1 - \gamma_0 = -\frac{1}{2}\boldsymbol{\mu}_1^\mathsf{T}\boldsymbol{\Sigma}^{-1}\boldsymbol{\mu}_1 + \frac{1}{2}\boldsymbol{\mu}_0^\mathsf{T}\boldsymbol{\Sigma}^{-1}\boldsymbol{\mu}_0 + \log(\pi_1/\pi_0) \tag{9.11}$$

$$= -\frac{1}{2}(\boldsymbol{\mu}_1 - \boldsymbol{\mu}_0)^\mathsf{T}\boldsymbol{\Sigma}^{-1}(\boldsymbol{\mu}_1 + \boldsymbol{\mu}_0) + \log(\pi_1/\pi_0) \tag{9.12}$$

So if we define

$$\boldsymbol{w} = \boldsymbol{\beta}_1 - \boldsymbol{\beta}_0 = \boldsymbol{\Sigma}^{-1}(\boldsymbol{\mu}_1 - \boldsymbol{\mu}_0) \tag{9.13}$$

$$\boldsymbol{x}_0 = \frac{1}{2}(\boldsymbol{\mu}_1 + \boldsymbol{\mu}_0) - (\boldsymbol{\mu}_1 - \boldsymbol{\mu}_0)\frac{\log(\pi_1/\pi_0)}{(\boldsymbol{\mu}_1 - \boldsymbol{\mu}_0)^\mathsf{T}\boldsymbol{\Sigma}^{-1}(\boldsymbol{\mu}_1 - \boldsymbol{\mu}_0)} \tag{9.14}$$

then we have $\boldsymbol{w}^\mathsf{T}\boldsymbol{x}_0 = -(\gamma_1 - \gamma_0)$, and hence

$$p(y = 1|\boldsymbol{x}, \boldsymbol{\theta}) = \sigma(\boldsymbol{w}^\mathsf{T}(\boldsymbol{x} - \boldsymbol{x}_0)) \tag{9.15}$$

This has the same form as binary logistic regression. Hence the MAP decision rule is

$$\hat{y}(\boldsymbol{x}) = 1 \text{ iff } \boldsymbol{w}^\mathsf{T}\boldsymbol{x} > c \tag{9.16}$$

where $c = \boldsymbol{w}^\mathsf{T}\boldsymbol{x}_0$. If $\pi_0 = \pi_1 = 0.5$, then the threshold simplifies to $c = \frac{1}{2}\boldsymbol{w}^\mathsf{T}(\boldsymbol{\mu}_1 + \boldsymbol{\mu}_0)$.

To interpret this equation geometrically, suppose $\boldsymbol{\Sigma} = \sigma^2\mathbf{I}$. In this case, $\boldsymbol{w} = \sigma^{-2}(\boldsymbol{\mu}_1 - \boldsymbol{\mu}_0)$, which is parallel to a line joining the two centroids, $\boldsymbol{\mu}_0$ and $\boldsymbol{\mu}_1$. So we can classify a point by projecting it onto this line, and then checking if the projection is closer to $\boldsymbol{\mu}_0$ or $\boldsymbol{\mu}_1$, as illustrated in Figure 9.3. The question of how close it has to be depends on the prior over classes. If $\pi_1 = \pi_0$, then $\boldsymbol{x}_0 = \frac{1}{2}(\boldsymbol{\mu}_1 + \boldsymbol{\mu}_0)$, which is halfway between the means. If we make $\pi_1 > \pi_0$, we have to be closer to $\boldsymbol{\mu}_0$ than halfway in order to pick class 0. And vice versa if $\pi_0 > \pi_1$. Thus we see that the class prior just changes the decision threshold, but not the overall shape of the decision boundary. (A similar argument applies in the multi-class case.)

9.2.4 Model fitting

We now discuss how to fit a GDA model using maximum likelihood estimation. The likelihood function is as follows

$$p(\mathcal{D}|\boldsymbol{\theta}) = \prod_{n=1}^{N} \text{Cat}(y_n|\boldsymbol{\pi}) \prod_{c=1}^{C} \mathcal{N}(\boldsymbol{x}_n|\boldsymbol{\mu}_c, \boldsymbol{\Sigma}_c)^{\mathbb{I}(y_n=c)} \tag{9.17}$$

Hence the log-likelihood is given by

$$\log p(\mathcal{D}|\boldsymbol{\theta}) = \left[\sum_{n=1}^{N}\sum_{c=1}^{C}\mathbb{I}(y_n = c)\log \pi_c\right] + \sum_{c=1}^{C}\left[\sum_{n:y_n=c}\log \mathcal{N}(\boldsymbol{x}_n|\boldsymbol{\mu}_c, \boldsymbol{\Sigma}_c)\right] \tag{9.18}$$

Thus we see that we can optimize $\boldsymbol{\pi}$ and the $(\boldsymbol{\mu}_c, \boldsymbol{\Sigma}_c)$ terms separately.

From Section 4.2.4, we have that the MLE for the class prior is $\hat{\pi}_c = \frac{N_c}{N}$. Using the results from Section 4.2.6, we can derive the MLEs for the Gaussians as follows:

$$\hat{\boldsymbol{\mu}}_c = \frac{1}{N_c}\sum_{n:y_n=c}\boldsymbol{x}_n \tag{9.19}$$

$$\hat{\boldsymbol{\Sigma}}_c = \frac{1}{N_c}\sum_{n:y_n=c}(\boldsymbol{x}_n - \hat{\boldsymbol{\mu}}_c)(\boldsymbol{x}_n - \hat{\boldsymbol{\mu}}_c)^\mathsf{T} \tag{9.20}$$

Unfortunately the MLE for $\hat{\boldsymbol{\Sigma}}_c$ can easily overfit (i.e., the estimate may not be well-conditioned) if N_c is small compared to D, the dimensionality of the input features. We discuss some solutions to this below.

9.2.4.1 Tied covariances

If we force $\boldsymbol{\Sigma}_c = \boldsymbol{\Sigma}$ to be tied, we will get linear decision boundaries, as we have seen. This also usually results in a more reliable parameter estimate, since we can pool all the samples across classes:

$$\hat{\boldsymbol{\Sigma}} = \frac{1}{N}\sum_{c=1}^{C}\sum_{n:y_n=c}(\boldsymbol{x}_n - \hat{\boldsymbol{\mu}}_c)(\boldsymbol{x}_n - \hat{\boldsymbol{\mu}}_c)^\mathsf{T} \tag{9.21}$$

9.2.4.2 Diagonal covariances

If we force $\boldsymbol{\Sigma}_c$ to be diagonal, we reduce the number of parameters from $O(CD^2)$ to $O(CD)$, which avoids the overfitting problem. However, this loses the ability to capture correlations between the features. (This is known as the naive Bayes assumption, which we discuss further in Section 9.3.) Despite this approximation, this approach scales well to high dimensions.

We can further restrict the model capacity by using a shared (tied) diagonal covariace matrix. This is called "diagonal LDA" [BL04].

9.2.4.3 MAP estimation

Forcing the covariance matrix to be diagonal is a rather strong assumption. An alternative approach is to perform MAP estimation of a (shared) full covariance Gaussian, rather than using the MLE. Based on the results of Section 4.5.2, we find that the MAP estimate is

$$\hat{\boldsymbol{\Sigma}}_{\text{map}} = \lambda \text{diag}(\hat{\boldsymbol{\Sigma}}_{\text{mle}}) + (1 - \lambda)\hat{\boldsymbol{\Sigma}}_{\text{mle}} \tag{9.22}$$

where λ controls the amount of regularization. This technique is known as **regularized discriminant analysis** or RDA [HTF09, p656].

9.2.5   Nearest centroid classifier

If we assume a uniform prior over classes, we can compute the most probable class label as follows:

$$\hat{y}(\boldsymbol{x}) = \operatorname*{argmax}_c \log p(y = c|\boldsymbol{x}, \boldsymbol{\theta}) = \operatorname*{argmin}_c (\boldsymbol{x} - \boldsymbol{\mu}_c)^\mathsf{T} \boldsymbol{\Sigma}^{-1} (\boldsymbol{x} - \boldsymbol{\mu}_c) \tag{9.23}$$

This is called the **nearest centroid classifier**, or **nearest class mean classifier (NCM)**, since we are assigning $\boldsymbol{x}$ to the class with the closest $\boldsymbol{\mu}_c$, where distance is measured using (squared) Mahalanobis distance.

We can replace this with any other distance metric to get the decision rule

$$\hat{y}(\boldsymbol{x}) = \operatorname*{argmin}_c d^2(\boldsymbol{x}, \boldsymbol{\mu}_c) \tag{9.24}$$

We discuss how to learn distance metrics in Section 16.2, but one simple approach is to use

$$d^2(\boldsymbol{x}, \boldsymbol{\mu}_c) = ||\boldsymbol{x} - \boldsymbol{\mu}_c||_\mathbf{W}^2 = (\boldsymbol{x} - \boldsymbol{\mu}_c)^\mathsf{T} (\mathbf{W}\mathbf{W}^\mathsf{T})(\boldsymbol{x} - \boldsymbol{\mu}_c) = ||\mathbf{W}(\boldsymbol{x} - \boldsymbol{\mu}_c)||^2 \tag{9.25}$$

The corresponding class posterior becomes

$$p(y = c|\boldsymbol{x}, \boldsymbol{\mu}, \mathbf{W}) = \frac{\exp(-\frac{1}{2}||\mathbf{W}(\boldsymbol{x} - \boldsymbol{\mu}_c)||_2^2)}{\sum_{c'=1}^C \exp(-\frac{1}{2}||\mathbf{W}(\boldsymbol{x} - \boldsymbol{\mu}_{c'})||_2^2)} \tag{9.26}$$

We can optimize $\mathbf{W}$ using gradient descent applied to the discriminative loss. This is called **nearest class mean metric learning** [Men+12]. The advantage of this technique is that it can be used for **one-shot learning** of new classes, since we just need to see a single labeled prototype $\boldsymbol{\mu}_c$ per class (assuming we have learned a good $\mathbf{W}$ already).

9.2.6   Fisher's linear discriminant analysis *

Discriminant analysis is a generative approach to classification, which requires fitting an MVN to the features. As we have discussed, this can be problematic in high dimensions. An alternative approach is to reduce the dimensionality of the features $\boldsymbol{x} \in \mathbb{R}^D$ and then fit an MVN to the resulting low-dimensional features $\boldsymbol{z} \in \mathbb{R}^K$. The simplest approach is to use a linear projection matrix, $\boldsymbol{z} = \mathbf{W}\boldsymbol{x}$, where $\mathbf{W}$ is a $K \times D$ matrix. One approach to finding $\mathbf{W}$ would be to use principal components analysis or PCA (Section 20.1). However, PCA is an unsupervised technique that does not take class labels into account. Thus the resulting low dimensional features are not necessarily optimal for classification, as illustrated in Figure 9.4.

An alternative approach is to use gradient based methods to optimize the log likelihood, derived from the class posterior in the low dimensional space, as we discussed in Section 9.2.5.

A third approach (which relies on an eigendecomposition, rather than a gradient-based optimizer) is to find the matrix $\mathbf{W}$ such that the low-dimensional data can be classified as well as possible using a Gaussian class-conditional density model. The assumption of Gaussianity is reasonable since we are computing linear combinations of (potentially non-Gaussian) features. This approach is called **Fisher's linear discriminant analysis**, or **FLDA**.

FLDA is an interesting hybrid of discriminative and generative techniques. The drawback of this technique is that it is restricted to using $K \leq C - 1$ dimensions, regardless of D, for reasons that we will explain below. In the two-class case, this means we are seeking a single vector $\boldsymbol{w}$ onto which we can project the data. Below we derive the optimal $\boldsymbol{w}$ in the two-class case. We then generalize to the multi-class case, and finally we give a probabilistic interpretation of this technique.

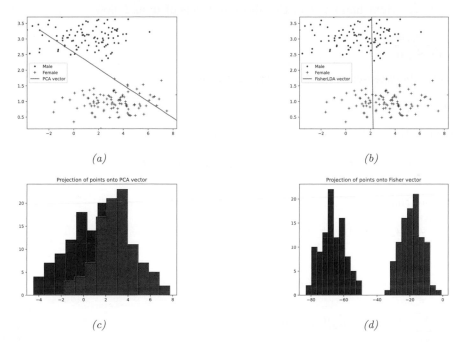

Figure 9.4: Linear discriminant analysis applied to two class dataset in 2d, representing (standardized) height and weight for male and female adults (a) PCA direction. (b) FLDA direction. (c) Projection onto PCA direction shows poor class separation. (d) Projection onto FLDA direction shows good class separation. Generated by fisher_lda_demo.ipynb.

9.2.6.1 Derivation of the optimal 1d projection

We now derive this optimal direction $\boldsymbol{w}$, for the two-class case, following the presentation of [Bis06, Sec 4.1.4]. Define the class-conditional means as

$$\boldsymbol{\mu}_1 = \frac{1}{N_1} \sum_{n:y_n=1} \boldsymbol{x}_n, \ \boldsymbol{\mu}_2 = \frac{1}{N_2} \sum_{n:y_n=2} \boldsymbol{x}_n \tag{9.27}$$

Let $m_k = \boldsymbol{w}^\mathsf{T} \boldsymbol{\mu}_k$ be the projection of each mean onto the line $\boldsymbol{w}$. Also, let $z_n = \boldsymbol{w}^\mathsf{T} \boldsymbol{x}_n$ be the projection of the data onto the line. The variance of the projected points is proportional to

$$s_k^2 = \sum_{n:y_n=k} (z_n - m_k)^2 \tag{9.28}$$

The goal is to find $\boldsymbol{w}$ such that we maximize the distance between the means, $m_2 - m_1$, while also ensuring the projected clusters are "tight", which we can do by minimizing their variance. This suggests the following objective:

$$J(\boldsymbol{w}) = \frac{(m_2 - m_1)^2}{s_1^2 + s_2^2} \tag{9.29}$$

We can rewrite the right hand side of the above in terms of $\boldsymbol{w}$ as follows

$$J(\boldsymbol{w}) = \frac{\boldsymbol{w}^\mathsf{T}\mathbf{S}_B\boldsymbol{w}}{\boldsymbol{w}^\mathsf{T}\mathbf{S}_W\boldsymbol{w}} \tag{9.30}$$

where $\mathbf{S}_B$ is the between-class scatter matrix given by

$$\mathbf{S}_B = (\boldsymbol{\mu}_2 - \boldsymbol{\mu}_1)(\boldsymbol{\mu}_2 - \boldsymbol{\mu}_1)^\mathsf{T} \tag{9.31}$$

and $\mathbf{S}_W$ is the within-class scatter matrix, given by

$$\mathbf{S}_W = \sum_{n:y_n=1}(\boldsymbol{x}_n - \boldsymbol{\mu}_1)(\boldsymbol{x}_n - \boldsymbol{\mu}_1)^\mathsf{T} + \sum_{n:y_n=2}(\boldsymbol{x}_n - \boldsymbol{\mu}_2)(\boldsymbol{x}_n - \boldsymbol{\mu}_2)^\mathsf{T} \tag{9.32}$$

To see this, note that

$$\boldsymbol{w}^\mathsf{T}\mathbf{S}_B\boldsymbol{w} = \boldsymbol{w}^\mathsf{T}(\boldsymbol{\mu}_2 - \boldsymbol{\mu}_1)(\boldsymbol{\mu}_2 - \boldsymbol{\mu}_1)^\mathsf{T}\boldsymbol{w} = (m_2 - m_1)(m_2 - m_1) \tag{9.33}$$

and

$$\boldsymbol{w}^\mathsf{T}\mathbf{S}_W\boldsymbol{w} = \sum_{n:y_n=1}\boldsymbol{w}^\mathsf{T}(\boldsymbol{x}_n - \boldsymbol{\mu}_1)(\boldsymbol{x}_n - \boldsymbol{\mu}_1)^\mathsf{T}\boldsymbol{w}+$$

$$\sum_{n:y_n=2}\boldsymbol{w}^\mathsf{T}(\boldsymbol{x}_n - \boldsymbol{\mu}_2)(\boldsymbol{x}_n - \boldsymbol{\mu}_2)^\mathsf{T}\boldsymbol{w} \tag{9.34}$$

$$= \sum_{n:y_n=1}(z_n - m_1)^2 + \sum_{n:y_n=2}(z_n - m_2)^2 \tag{9.35}$$

Equation (9.30) is a ratio of two scalars; we can take its derivative with respect to $\boldsymbol{w}$ and equate to zero. One can show (Exercise 9.1) that $J(\boldsymbol{w})$ is maximized when

$$\mathbf{S}_B\boldsymbol{w} = \lambda\mathbf{S}_W\boldsymbol{w} \tag{9.36}$$

where

$$\lambda = \frac{\boldsymbol{w}^\mathsf{T}\mathbf{S}_B\boldsymbol{w}}{\boldsymbol{w}^\mathsf{T}\mathbf{S}_W\boldsymbol{w}} \tag{9.37}$$

Equation (9.36) is called a **generalized eigenvalue** problem. If $\mathbf{S}_W$ is invertible, we can convert it to a regular eigenvalue problem:

$$\mathbf{S}_W^{-1}\mathbf{S}_B\boldsymbol{w} = \lambda\boldsymbol{w} \tag{9.38}$$

However, in the two class case, there is a simpler solution. In particular, since

$$\mathbf{S}_B\boldsymbol{w} = (\boldsymbol{\mu}_2 - \boldsymbol{\mu}_1)(\boldsymbol{\mu}_2 - \boldsymbol{\mu}_1)^\mathsf{T}\boldsymbol{w} = (\boldsymbol{\mu}_2 - \boldsymbol{\mu}_1)(m_2 - m_1) \tag{9.39}$$

then, from Equation (9.38) we have

$$\lambda\,\boldsymbol{w} = \mathbf{S}_W^{-1}(\boldsymbol{\mu}_2 - \boldsymbol{\mu}_1)(m_2 - m_1) \tag{9.40}$$

$$\boldsymbol{w} \propto \mathbf{S}_W^{-1}(\boldsymbol{\mu}_2 - \boldsymbol{\mu}_1) \tag{9.41}$$

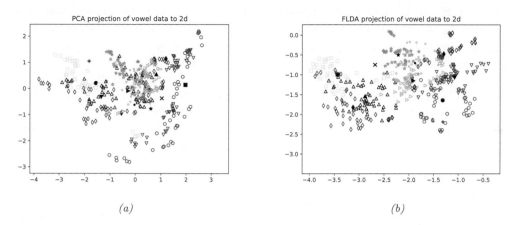

Figure 9.5: (a) PCA projection of vowel data to 2d. (b) FLDA projection of vowel data to 2d. We see there is better class separation in the FLDA case. Adapted from Figure 4.11 of [HTF09]. Generated by fisher_discrim_vowel.ipynb.

Since we only care about the directionality, and not the scale factor, we can just set

$$\boldsymbol{w} = \mathbf{S}_W^{-1}(\boldsymbol{\mu}_2 - \boldsymbol{\mu}_1) \tag{9.42}$$

This is the optimal solution in the two-class case. If $\mathbf{S}_W \propto \mathbf{I}$, meaning the pooled covariance matrix is isotropic, then $\boldsymbol{w}$ is proportional to the vector that joins the class means. This is an intuitively reasonable direction to project onto, as shown in Figure 9.3.

9.2.6.2 Extension to higher dimensions and multiple classes

We can extend the above idea to multiple classes, and to higher dimensional subspaces, by finding a projection *matrix* $\mathbf{W}$ which maps from D to K. Let $\boldsymbol{z}_n = \mathbf{W}\boldsymbol{x}_n$ be the low dimensional projection of the n'th data point. Let $\boldsymbol{m}_c = \frac{1}{N_c} \sum_{n:y_n=c} \boldsymbol{z}_n$ be the corresponding mean for the c'th class and $\boldsymbol{m} = \frac{1}{N} \sum_{c=1}^C N_c \boldsymbol{m}_c$ be the overall mean, both in the low dimensional space. We define the following scatter matrices:

$$\tilde{\mathbf{S}}_W = \sum_{c=1}^C \sum_{n:y_n=c} (\boldsymbol{z}_n - \boldsymbol{m}_c)(\boldsymbol{z}_n - \boldsymbol{m}_c)^\mathsf{T} \tag{9.43}$$

$$\tilde{\mathbf{S}}_B = \sum_{c=1}^C N_c (\boldsymbol{m}_c - \boldsymbol{m})(\boldsymbol{m}_c - \boldsymbol{m})^\mathsf{T} \tag{9.44}$$

Finally, we define the objective function as maximizing the following:[2]

$$J(\mathbf{W}) = \frac{|\tilde{\mathbf{S}}_B|}{|\tilde{\mathbf{S}}_W|} = \frac{|\mathbf{W}^\mathsf{T} \mathbf{S}_B \mathbf{W}|}{|\mathbf{W}^\mathsf{T} \mathbf{S}_W \mathbf{W}|} \tag{9.45}$$

---

2. An alternative criterion that is sometimes used [Fuk90] is $J(\mathbf{W}) = \mathrm{tr}\left\{ \tilde{\mathbf{S}}_W^{-1} \tilde{\mathbf{S}}_B \right\} = \mathrm{tr}\left\{ (\mathbf{W}\mathbf{S}_W \mathbf{W}^\mathsf{T})^{-1}(\mathbf{W}\mathbf{S}_B \mathbf{W}^\mathsf{T}) \right\}$.

where $\mathbf{S}_W$ and $\mathbf{S}_B$ are defined in the original high dimensional space in the obvious way (namely using $\boldsymbol{x}_n$ instead of $\boldsymbol{z}_n$, $\boldsymbol{\mu}_c$ instead of $\boldsymbol{m}_c$, and $\boldsymbol{\mu}$ instead of $\boldsymbol{m}$). The solution can be shown [DHS01] to be $\mathbf{W} = \mathbf{S}_W^{-\frac{1}{2}}\mathbf{U}$, where $\mathbf{U}$ are the K leading eigenvectors of $\mathbf{S}_W^{-\frac{1}{2}}\mathbf{S}_B\mathbf{S}_W^{-\frac{1}{2}}$, assuming $\mathbf{S}_W$ is non-singular. (If it is singular, we can first perform PCA on all the data.)

Figure 9.5 gives an example of this method applied to some $D = 10$ dimensional speech data, representing $C = 11$ different vowel sounds. We project to $K = 2$ dimensions in order to visualize the data. We see that FLDA gives better class separation than PCA.

Note that FLDA is restricted to finding at most a $K \leq C - 1$ dimensional linear subspace, no matter how large D, because the rank of the between class scatter matrix $\mathbf{S}_B$ is $C - 1$. (The -1 term arises because of the $\boldsymbol{\mu}$ term, which is a linear function of the $\boldsymbol{\mu}_c$.) This is a rather severe restriction which limits the usefulness of FLDA.

9.3   Naive Bayes classifiers

In this section, we discuss a simple generative approach to classification in which we assume the features are conditionally independent given the class label. This is called the **naive Bayes assumption**. The model is called "naive" since we do not expect the features to be independent, even conditional on the class label. However, even if the naive Bayes assumption is not true, it often results in classifiers that work well [DP97]. One reason for this is that the model is quite simple (it only has $O(CD)$ parameters, for C classes and D features), and hence it is relatively immune to overfitting.

More precisely, the naive Bayes assumption corresponds to using a class conditional density of the following form:

$$p(\boldsymbol{x}|y = c, \boldsymbol{\theta}) = \prod_{d=1}^{D} p(x_d|y = c, \boldsymbol{\theta}_{dc}) \tag{9.46}$$

where $\boldsymbol{\theta}_{dc}$ are the parameters for the class conditional density for class c and feature d. Hence the posterior over class labels is given by

$$p(y = c|\boldsymbol{x}, \boldsymbol{\theta}) = \frac{p(y = c|\boldsymbol{\pi}) \prod_{d=1}^{D} p(x_d|y = c, \boldsymbol{\theta}_{dc})}{\sum_{c'} p(y = c'|\boldsymbol{\pi}) \prod_{d=1}^{D} p(x_d|y = c', \boldsymbol{\theta}_{dc'})} \tag{9.47}$$

where π_c is the prior probability of class c, and $\boldsymbol{\theta} = (\boldsymbol{\pi}, \{\boldsymbol{\theta}_{dc}\})$ are all the parameters. This is known as a **naive Bayes classifier** or **NBC**.

9.3.1   Example models

We still need to specify the form of the probability distributions in Equation (9.46). This depends on what type of feature x_d is. We give some examples below:

- In the case of binary features, $x_d \in \{0, 1\}$, we can use the Bernoulli distribution: $p(\boldsymbol{x}|y = c, \boldsymbol{\theta}) = \prod_{d=1}^{D} \mathrm{Ber}(x_d|\theta_{dc})$, where θ_{dc} is the probability that $x_d = 1$ in class c. This is sometimes called the **multivariate Bernoulli naive Bayes** model. For example, Figure 9.6 shows the estimated parameters for each class when we fit this model to a binarized version of MNIST. This approach does surprisingly well, and has a test set accuracy of 84.3%. (See Figure 9.7 for some sample predictions.)

Figure 9.6: *Visualization of the Bernoulli class conditional densities for a naive Bayes classifier fit to a binarized version of the MNIST dataset. Generated by* naive_bayes_mnist_jax.ipynb.

Figure 9.7: *Visualization of the predictions made by the model in Figure 9.6 when applied to some binarized MNIST test images. The title shows the most probable predicted class. Generated by* naive_bayes_mnist_jax.ipynb.

- In the case of categorical features, $x_d \in \{1, \ldots, K\}$, we can use the categorical distribution: $p(\boldsymbol{x}|y = c, \boldsymbol{\theta}) = \prod_{d=1}^{D} \text{Cat}(x_d|\boldsymbol{\theta}_{dc})$, where θ_{dck} is the probability that $x_d = k$ given that $y = c$.

- In the case of real-valued features, $x_d \in \mathbb{R}$, we can use the univariate Gaussian distribution: $p(\boldsymbol{x}|y = c, \boldsymbol{\theta}) = \prod_{d=1}^{D} \mathcal{N}(x_d|\mu_{dc}, \sigma_{dc}^2)$, where μ_{dc} is the mean of feature d when the class label is c, and σ_{dc}^2 is its variance. (This is equivalent to Gaussian discriminant analysis using diagonal covariance matrices.)

9.3.2 Model fitting

In this section, we discuss how to fit a naive Bayes classifier using maximum likelihood estimation. We can write the likelihood as follows:

$$p(\mathcal{D}|\boldsymbol{\theta}) = \prod_{n=1}^{N} \left[\text{Cat}(y_n|\boldsymbol{\pi}) \prod_{d=1}^{D} p(x_{nd}|y_n, \boldsymbol{\theta}_d) \right] \tag{9.48}$$

$$= \prod_{n=1}^{N} \left[\text{Cat}(y_n|\boldsymbol{\pi}) \prod_{d=1}^{D} \prod_{c=1}^{C} p(x_{nd}|\boldsymbol{\theta}_{dc})^{\mathbb{I}(y_n=c)} \right] \tag{9.49}$$

so the log-likelihood is given by

$$\log p(\mathcal{D}|\boldsymbol{\theta}) = \left[\sum_{n=1}^{N} \sum_{c=1}^{C} \mathbb{I}(y_n = c) \log \pi_c \right] + \sum_{c=1}^{C} \sum_{d=1}^{D} \left[\sum_{n:y_n=c} \log p(x_{nd}|\boldsymbol{\theta}_{dc}) \right] \tag{9.50}$$

We see that this decomposes into a term for $\boldsymbol{\pi}$, and CD terms for each $\boldsymbol{\theta}_{dc}$:

$$\log p(\mathcal{D}|\boldsymbol{\theta}) = \log p(\mathcal{D}_y|\boldsymbol{\pi}) + \sum_{c} \sum_{d} \log p(\mathcal{D}_{dc}|\boldsymbol{\theta}_{dc}) \tag{9.51}$$

where $\mathcal{D}_y = \{y_n : n = 1 : N\}$ are all the labels, and $\mathcal{D}_{dc} = \{x_{nd} : y_n = c\}$ are all the values of feature d for examples from class c. Hence we can estimate these parameters separately.

In Section 4.2.4, we show that the MLE for $\boldsymbol{\pi}$ is the vector of empirical counts, $\hat{\pi}_c = \frac{N_c}{N}$. The MLEs for $\boldsymbol{\theta}_{dc}$ depend on the choice of the class conditional density for feature d. We discuss some common choices below.

- In the case of discrete features, we can use a categorical distribution. A straightforward extension of the results in Section 4.2.4 gives the following expression for the MLE:

$$\hat{\theta}_{dck} = \frac{N_{dck}}{\sum_{k'=1}^{K} N_{dck'}} = \frac{N_{dck}}{N_c} \tag{9.52}$$

where $N_{dck} = \sum_{n=1}^{N} \mathbb{I}\left(x_{nd} = k, y_n = c\right)$ is the number of times that feature d had value k in examples of class c.

- In the case of binary features, the categorical distribution becomes the Bernoulli, and the MLE becomes

$$\hat{\theta}_{dc} = \frac{N_{dc}}{N_c} \tag{9.53}$$

which is the empirical fraction of times that feature d is on in examples of class c.

- In the case of real-valued features, we can use a Gaussian distribution. A straightforward extension of the results in Section 4.2.5 gives the following expression for the MLE:

$$\hat{\mu}_{dc} = \frac{1}{N_c} \sum_{n:y_n=c} x_{nd} \tag{9.54}$$

$$\hat{\sigma}^2_{dc} = \frac{1}{N_c} \sum_{n:y_n=c} (x_{nd} - \hat{\mu}_{dc})^2 \tag{9.55}$$

Thus we see that fitting a naive Bayes classifier is extremely simple and efficient.

9.3.3 Bayesian naive Bayes

In this section, we extend our discussion of MLE estimation for naive Bayes classifiers from Section 9.3.2 to compute the posterior distribution over the parameters. For simplicity, let us assume we have categorical features, so $p(x_d|\boldsymbol{\theta}_{dc}) = \mathrm{Cat}(x_d|\boldsymbol{\theta}_{dc})$, where $\theta_{dck} = p(x_d = k|y = c)$. In Section 4.6.3.2, we show that the conjugate prior for the categorical likelihood is the Dirichlet distribution, $p(\boldsymbol{\theta}_{dc}) = \mathrm{Dir}(\boldsymbol{\theta}_{dc}|\boldsymbol{\beta}_{dc})$, where β_{dck} can be intereperted as a set of "**pseudo counts**", corresponding to counts N_{dck} that come from prior data. Similarly we use a Dirichlet prior for the label frequencies, $p(\boldsymbol{\pi}) = \mathrm{Dir}(\boldsymbol{\pi}|\boldsymbol{\alpha})$. By using a conjugate prior, we can compute the posterior in closed form, as we explain in Section 4.6.3. In particular, we have

$$p(\boldsymbol{\theta}|\mathcal{D}) = \mathrm{Dir}(\boldsymbol{\pi}|\,\widehat{\boldsymbol{\alpha}}) \prod_{d=1}^{D} \prod_{c=1}^{C} \mathrm{Dir}(\boldsymbol{\theta}_{dc}|\,\widehat{\boldsymbol{\beta}}_{dc}) \tag{9.56}$$

where $\widehat{\alpha}_c = \breve{\alpha}_c + N_c$ and $\widehat{\beta}_{dck} = \breve{\beta}_{dck} + N_{dck}$.

Using the results from Section 4.6.3.4, we can derive the posterior predictive distribution as follows. For the label prior (before seeing $\boldsymbol{x}$, but after seeing $\mathcal{D}$), we have $p(y|\mathcal{D}) = \text{Cat}(y|\overline{\boldsymbol{\pi}})$, where $\overline{\pi}_c = \widehat{\alpha}_c / \sum_{c'} \widehat{\alpha}_{c'}$. For the feature likelihood of $\boldsymbol{x}$ (given y and $\mathcal{D}$), we have $p(x_d = k|y = c, \mathcal{D}) = \overline{\theta}_{dck}$, where

$$\overline{\theta}_{dck} = \frac{\widehat{\beta}_{dck}}{\sum_{k'=1}^{K} \widehat{\beta}_{dck'}} = \frac{\widecheck{\beta}_{dck} + N_{dck}}{\sum_{k'=1}^{K} \widecheck{\beta}_{dck'} + N_{dck'}} \tag{9.57}$$

is the posterior mean of the parameters. (Note that $\sum_{k'=1}^{K} N_{dck'} = N_{dc} = N_c$ is the number of examples for class c.)

If $\widecheck{\beta}_{dck} = 0$, this reduces to the MLE in Equation (9.52). By contrast, if we set $\widecheck{\beta}_{dck} = 1$, we add 1 to all the empirical counts before normalizing. This is called **add-one smoothing** or **Laplace smoothing**. For example, in the binary case, this gives

$$\overline{\theta}_{dc} = \frac{\widecheck{\beta}_{dc1} + N_{dc1}}{\widecheck{\beta}_{dc0} + N_{dc0} + \widecheck{\beta}_{dc1} + N_{dc1}} = \frac{1 + N_{dc1}}{2 + N_{dc}} \tag{9.58}$$

We can finally compute the posterior predictive distribution over the label as follows:

$$p(y = c|\boldsymbol{x}, \mathcal{D}) \propto p(y = c|\mathcal{D}) \prod_d p(x_d|y = c, \mathcal{D}) = \overline{\pi}_c \prod_d \prod_k \overline{\theta}_{dck}^{\mathbb{I}(x_d=k)} \tag{9.59}$$

This gives us a fully Bayesian form of naive Bayes, in which we have integrated out all the parameters. (In this case, the predictive distribution can be obtained merely by plugging in the posterior mean parameters.)

9.3.4 The connection between naive Bayes and logistic regression

In this section, we show that the class posterior $p(y|\boldsymbol{x}, \boldsymbol{\theta})$ for a NBC model has the same form as multinomial logistic regression. For simplicity, we assume that the features are all discrete, and each has K states, although the result holds for arbitrary feature distributions in the exponential family.

Let $x_{dk} = \mathbb{I}(x_d = k)$, so $\boldsymbol{x}_d$ is a one-hot encoding of feature d. Then the class conditional density can be written as follows:

$$p(\boldsymbol{x}|y = c, \boldsymbol{\theta}) = \prod_{d=1}^{D} \text{Cat}(x_d|y = c, \boldsymbol{\theta}) = \prod_{d=1}^{D} \prod_{k=1}^{K} \theta_{dck}^{x_{dk}} \tag{9.60}$$

Hence the posterior over classes is given by

$$p(y = c|\boldsymbol{x}, \boldsymbol{\theta}) = \frac{\pi_c \prod_d \prod_k \theta_{dck}^{x_{dk}}}{\sum_{c'} \pi_{c'} \prod_d \prod_k \theta_{dc'k}^{x_{dk}}} = \frac{\exp[\log \pi_c + \sum_d \sum_k x_{dk} \log \theta_{dck}]}{\sum_{c'} \exp[\log \pi_{c'} + \sum_d \sum_k x_{dk} \log \theta_{dc'k}]} \tag{9.61}$$

This can be written as a softmax

$$p(y = c|\boldsymbol{x}, \boldsymbol{\theta}) = \frac{e^{\boldsymbol{\beta}_c^{\mathsf{T}} \boldsymbol{x} + \gamma_c}}{\sum_{c'=1}^{C} e^{\boldsymbol{\beta}_{c'}^{\mathsf{T}} \boldsymbol{x} + \gamma_{c'}}} \tag{9.62}$$

by suitably defining $\boldsymbol{\beta}_c$ and γ_c. This has exactly the same form as multinomial logistic regression in Section 2.5.3. The difference is that with naive Bayes we optimize the joint likelihood $\prod_n p(y_n, \boldsymbol{x}_n|\boldsymbol{\theta})$, whereas with logistic regression, we optimize the conditional likelihood $\prod_n p(y_n|\boldsymbol{x}_n, \boldsymbol{\theta})$. In general, these can give different results (see Exercise 10.3).

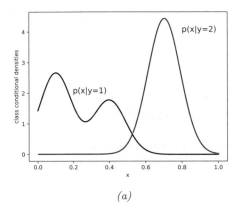
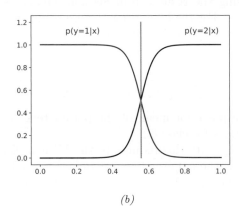

(a)   (b)

Figure 9.8: The class-conditional densities $p(x|y = c)$ (left) may be more complex than the class posteriors $p(y = c|x)$ (right). Adapted from Figure 1.27 of [Bis06]. Generated by generativeVsDiscrim.ipynb.

9.4   Generative vs discriminative classifiers

A model of the form $p(\boldsymbol{x}, y) = p(y)p(\boldsymbol{x}|y)$ is called a **generative classifier**, since it can be used to generate examples $\boldsymbol{x}$ from each class y. By contrast, a model of the form $p(y|\boldsymbol{x})$ is called a **discriminative classifier**, since it can only be used to discriminate between different classes. Below we discuss various pros and cons of the generative and discriminative approaches to classification. (See also [BT04; UB05; LBM06; BL07a; Rot+18].)

9.4.1   Advantages of discriminative classifiers

The main advantages of discriminative classifiers are as follows:

- **Better predictive accuracy**. Discriminative classifiers are often much more accurate than generative classifiers [NJ02]. The reason is that the conditional distribution $p(y|\boldsymbol{x})$ is often much simpler (and therefore easier to learn) than the joint distribution $p(y, \boldsymbol{x})$, as illustrated in Figure 9.8. In particular, discriminative models do not need to "waste effort" modeling the distribution of the input features.

- **Can handle feature preprocessing**. A big advantage of discriminative methods is that they allow us to preprocess the input in arbitrary ways. For example, we can perform a polynomial expansion of the input features, and we can replace a string of words with embedding vectors (see Section 20.5). It is often hard to define a generative model on such pre-processed data, since the new features can be correlated in complex ways which are hard to model.

- **Well-calibrated probabilities**. Some generative classifiers, such as naive Bayes (described in Section 9.3), make strong independence assumptions which are often not valid. This can result in very extreme posterior class probabilities (very near 0 or 1). Discriminative models, such as logistic regression, are often better calibrated in terms of their probability estimates, although they also sometimes need adjustment (see e.g., [NMC05]).

9.4.2 Advantages of generative classifiers

The main advantages of generative classifiers are as follows:

- **Easy to fit.** Generative classifiers are often very easy to fit. For example, in Section 9.3.2, we show how to fit a naive Bayes classifier by simple counting and averaging. By contrast, logistic regression requires solving a convex optimization problem (see Section 10.2.3 for the details), and neural nets require solving a non-convex optimization problem, both of which are much slower.

- **Can easily handle missing input features.** Sometimes some of the inputs (components of x) are not observed. In a generative classifier, there is a simple method for dealing with this, as we show in Section 1.5.5. However, in a discriminative classifier, there is no principled solution to this problem, since the model assumes that x is always available to be conditioned on.

- **Can fit classes separately.** In a generative classifier, we estimate the parameters of each class conditional density independently (as we show in Section 9.3.2), so we do not have to retrain the model when we add more classes. In contrast, in discriminative models, all the parameters interact, so the whole model must be retrained if we add a new class.

- **Can handle unlabeled training data.** It is easy to use generative models for semi-supervised learning, in which we combine labeled data $\mathcal{D}_{xy} = \{(x_n, y_n)\}$ and unlabeled data, $\mathcal{D}_x = \{x_n\}$. However, this is harder to do with discriminative models, since there is no uniquely optimal way to exploit $\mathcal{D}_x$.

- **May be more robust to spurious features**. A discriminative model $p(y|x)$ may pick up on features of the input x that can discriminate different values of y in the training set, but which are not robust and do not generalize beyond the training set. These are called **spurious features** (see e.g., [Arj21; Zho+21]). By contrast, a generative model $p(x|y)$ may be better able to capture the causal mechanisms of the underlying data generating process; such causal models can be more robust to distribution shift (see e.g., [Sch19; LBS19; LN81]).

9.4.3 Handling missing features

Sometimes we are missing parts of the input x during training and/or testing. In a generative classifier, we can handle this situation by marginalizing out the missing values. (We assume that the missingness of a feature is not informative about its potential value.) By contrast, when using a discriminative model, there is no unique best way to handle missing inputs, as we discuss in Section 1.5.5.

For example, suppose we are missing the value of x_1. We just have to compute

$$p(y = c|x_{2:D}, \theta) \propto p(y = c|\pi)p(x_{2:D}|y = c, \theta) \tag{9.63}$$

$$= p(y = c|\pi) \sum_{x_1} p(x_1, x_{2:D}|y = c, \theta) \tag{9.64}$$

In Gaussian discriminant analysis, we can marginalize out x_1 using the equations from Section 3.2.3.

If we make the naive Bayes assumption, things are even easier, since we can just ignore the likelihood term for x_1. This follows because

$$\sum_{x_1} p(x_1, x_{2:D}|y = c, \boldsymbol{\theta}) = \left[\sum_{x_1} p(x_1|\boldsymbol{\theta}_{1c})\right] \prod_{d=2}^{D} p(x_d|\boldsymbol{\theta}_{dc}) = \prod_{d=2}^{D} p(x_d|\boldsymbol{\theta}_{dc}) \qquad (9.65)$$

where we exploited the fact that $p(x_d|y = c, \boldsymbol{\theta}) = p(x_d|\boldsymbol{\theta}_{dc})$ and $\sum_{x_1} p(x_1|\boldsymbol{\theta}_{1c}) = 1$.

9.5   Exercises

Exercise 9.1 [Derivation of Fisher's linear discriminant]

Show that the maximum of $J(\boldsymbol{w}) = \frac{\boldsymbol{w}^T \mathbf{S}_B \boldsymbol{w}}{\boldsymbol{w}^T \mathbf{S}_W \boldsymbol{w}}$ is given by $\mathbf{S}_B \boldsymbol{w} = \lambda \mathbf{S}_W \boldsymbol{w}$

where $\lambda = \frac{\boldsymbol{w}^T \mathbf{S}_B \boldsymbol{w}}{\boldsymbol{w}^T \mathbf{S}_W \boldsymbol{w}}$. Hint: recall that the derivative of a ratio of two scalars is given by $\frac{d}{dx} \frac{f(x)}{g(x)} = \frac{f'g - fg'}{g^2}$, where $f' = \frac{d}{dx} f(x)$ and $g' = \frac{d}{dx} g(x)$. Also, recall that $\frac{d}{d\boldsymbol{x}} \boldsymbol{x}^T \mathbf{A} \boldsymbol{x} = (\mathbf{A} + \mathbf{A}^T)\boldsymbol{x}$.

10 Logistic Regression

10.1 Introduction

Logistic regression is a widely used discriminative classification model $p(y|\boldsymbol{x}; \boldsymbol{\theta})$, where $\boldsymbol{x} \in \mathbb{R}^D$ is a fixed-dimensional input vector, $y \in \{1, \ldots, C\}$ is the class label, and $\boldsymbol{\theta}$ are the parameters. If $C = 2$, this is known as **binary logistic regression**, and if $C > 2$, it is known as **multinomial logistic regression**, or alternatively, **multiclass logistic regression**. We give the details below.

10.2 Binary logistic regression

Binary logistic regression corresponds to the following model

$$p(y|\boldsymbol{x}, \boldsymbol{\theta}) = \text{Ber}(y|\sigma(\boldsymbol{w}^{\mathsf{T}}\boldsymbol{x} + b)) \tag{10.1}$$

where σ is the sigmoid function defined in Section 2.4.2, $\boldsymbol{w}$ are the weights, b is the bias, and $\boldsymbol{\theta} = (\boldsymbol{w}, b)$ are all the parameters. In other words,

$$p(y = 1|\boldsymbol{x}, \boldsymbol{\theta}) = \sigma(a) = \frac{1}{1 + e^{-a}} \tag{10.2}$$

where $a = \boldsymbol{w}^{\mathsf{T}}\boldsymbol{x} + b = \log(\frac{p}{1-p})$, is the log-odds, and $p = p(y = 1|\boldsymbol{x}, \boldsymbol{\theta})$. (In ML, the quantity a is usually called the **logit** or the **pre-activation**.)

Sometimes we choose to use the labels $\tilde{y} \in \{-1, +1\}$ instead of $y \in \{0, 1\}$. We can compute the probability of these alternative labels using

$$p(\tilde{y}|\boldsymbol{x}, \boldsymbol{\theta}) = \sigma(\tilde{y}a) \tag{10.3}$$

since $\sigma(-a) = 1 - \sigma(a)$. This slightly more compact notation is widely used in the ML literature.

10.2.1 Linear classifiers

The sigmoid gives the probability that the class label is $y = 1$. If the loss for misclassifying each class is the same, then the optimal decision rule is to predict $y = 1$ iff class 1 is more likely than class 0, as we explained in Section 5.1.2.2. Thus

$$f(\boldsymbol{x}) = \mathbb{I}\left(p(y = 1|\boldsymbol{x}) > p(y = 0|\boldsymbol{x})\right) = \mathbb{I}\left(\log\frac{p(y = 1|\boldsymbol{x})}{p(y = 0|\boldsymbol{x})} > 0\right) = \mathbb{I}(a > 0) \tag{10.4}$$

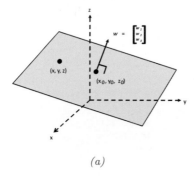
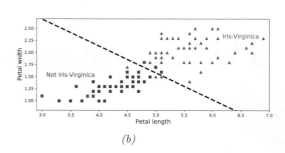

(a)   (b)

Figure 10.1: (a) Visualization of a 2d plane in a 3d space with surface normal $\boldsymbol{w}$ going through point $\boldsymbol{x}_0 = (x_0, y_0, z_0)$. See text for details. (b) Visualization of optimal linear decision boundary induced by logistic regression on a 2-class, 2-feature version of the iris dataset. Generated by iris_logreg.ipynb. Adapted from Figure 4.24 of [Gér19].

where $a = \boldsymbol{w}^\mathsf{T} \boldsymbol{x} + b$.

Thus we can write the prediction function as follows:

$$f(\boldsymbol{x}; \boldsymbol{\theta}) = b + \boldsymbol{w}^\mathsf{T} \boldsymbol{x} = b + \sum_{d=1}^{D} w_d x_d \tag{10.5}$$

where $\boldsymbol{w}^\mathsf{T} \boldsymbol{x} = \langle \boldsymbol{w}, \boldsymbol{x} \rangle$ is the inner product between the weight vector $\boldsymbol{w}$ and the feature vector $\boldsymbol{x}$. This function defines a linear **hyperplane**, with normal vector $\boldsymbol{w} \in \mathbb{R}^D$ and an offset $b \in \mathbb{R}$ from the origin.

Equation (10.5) can be understood by looking at Figure 10.1a. Here we show a plane in a 3d feature space going through the point $\boldsymbol{x}_0$ with surface normal $\boldsymbol{w}$. Points on the surface satisfy $\boldsymbol{w}^\mathsf{T} (\boldsymbol{x} - \boldsymbol{x}_0) = 0$. If we define $b = -\boldsymbol{w}^\mathsf{T} \boldsymbol{x}_0$, we can rewrite this as $\boldsymbol{w}^\mathsf{T} \boldsymbol{x} + b = 0$. This plane separates 3d space into two **half spaces**. This linear plane is known as a **decision boundary**. If we can perfectly separate the training examples by such a linear boundary (without making any classification errors on the training set), we say the data is **linearly separable**. From Figure 10.1b, we see that the two-class, two-feature version of the iris dataset is not linearly separable.

In general, there will be uncertainty about the correct class label, so we need to predict a probability distribution over labels, and not just decide which side of the decision boundary we are on. In Figure 10.2, we plot $p(y = 1|(x_1, x_2), \boldsymbol{w}) = \sigma(w_1 x_1 + w_2 x_2)$ for different weight vectors $\boldsymbol{w}$. The vector $\boldsymbol{w}$ defines the orientation of the decision boundary, and its magnitude, $||\boldsymbol{w}|| = \sqrt{\sum_{d=1}^{D} w_d^2}$, controls the steepness of the sigmoid, and hence the confidence of the predictions.

10.2.2   Nonlinear classifiers

We can often make a problem linearly separable by preprocessing the inputs in a suitable way. In particular, let $\boldsymbol{\phi}(\boldsymbol{x})$ be a transformed version of the input feature vector. For example, suppose we use $\boldsymbol{\phi}(x_1, x_2) = [1, x_1^2, x_2^2]$, and we let $\boldsymbol{w} = [-R^2, 1, 1]$. Then $\boldsymbol{w}^\mathsf{T} \boldsymbol{\phi}(\boldsymbol{x}) = x_1^2 + x_2^2 - R^2$, so the decision boundary (where $f(\boldsymbol{x}) = 0$) defines a circle with radius R, as shown in Figure 10.3. The resulting

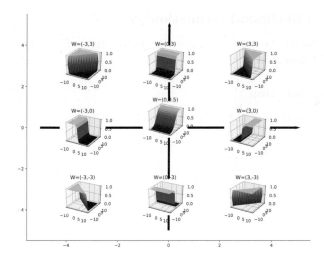

Figure 10.2: Plots of $\sigma(w_1 x_1 + w_2 x_2)$. Here $\boldsymbol{w} = (w_1, w_2)$ defines the normal to the decision boundary. Points to the right of this have $\sigma(\boldsymbol{w}^\mathsf{T} \boldsymbol{x}) > 0.5$, and points to the left have $\sigma(\boldsymbol{w}^\mathsf{T} \boldsymbol{x}) < 0.5$. Adapted from Figure 39.3 of [Mac03]. Generated by sigmoid_2d_plot.ipynb.

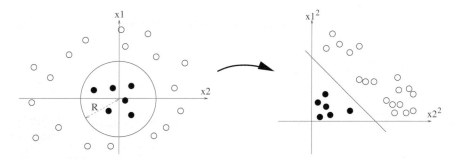

Figure 10.3: Illustration of how we can transform a quadratic decision boundary into a linear one by transforming the features from $\boldsymbol{x} = (x_1, x_2)$ to $\boldsymbol{\phi}(\boldsymbol{x}) = (x_1^2, x_2^2)$. Used with kind permission of Jean-Philippe Vert.

function f is still linear in the parameters $\boldsymbol{w}$, which is important for simplifying the learning problem, as we will see in Section 10.2.3. However, we can gain even more power by learning the parameters of the feature extractor $\boldsymbol{\phi}(\boldsymbol{x})$ in addition to linear weights $\boldsymbol{w}$; we discuss how to do this in Part III.

In Figure 10.3, we used a quadratic expansion of the features. We can also use a higher order polynomial, as in Section 1.2.2.2. In Figure 1.7, we show the effects of using polynomial expansion up to degree K on a 2d logistic regression problem. As in Figure 1.7, we see that the model becomes more complex as the number of parameters increases, and eventually results in overfitting. We discuss ways to reduce overfitting in Section 10.2.7.

10.2.3   Maximum likelihood estimation

In this section, we discuss how to estimate the parameters of a logistic regression model using maximum likelihood estimation.

10.2.3.1   Objective function

The negative log likelihood (scaled by the dataset size N) is given by the following (we assume the bias term b is absorbed into the weight vector $\boldsymbol{w}$):

$$\text{NLL}(\boldsymbol{w}) = -\frac{1}{N} \log p(\mathcal{D}|\boldsymbol{w}) = -\frac{1}{N} \log \prod_{n=1}^{N} \text{Ber}(y_n|\mu_n) \tag{10.6}$$

$$= -\frac{1}{N} \sum_{n=1}^{N} \log[\mu_n^{y_n} \times (1 - \mu_n)^{1-y_n}] \tag{10.7}$$

$$= -\frac{1}{N} \sum_{n=1}^{N} [y_n \log \mu_n + (1 - y_n) \log(1 - \mu_n)] \tag{10.8}$$

$$= \frac{1}{N} \sum_{n=1}^{N} \mathbb{H}_{ce}(y_n, \mu_n) \tag{10.9}$$

where $\mu_n = \sigma(a_n)$ is the probability of class 1, $a_n = \boldsymbol{w}^\mathsf{T}\boldsymbol{x}_n$ is the **logit**, and $\mathbb{H}_{ce}(y_n, \mu_n)$ is the **binary cross entropy** defined by

$$\mathbb{H}_{ce}(p, q) = -[p \log q + (1 - p) \log(1 - q)] \tag{10.10}$$

If we use $\tilde{y}_n \in \{-1, +1\}$ instead of $y_n \in \{0, 1\}$, then we can rewrite this as follows:

$$\text{NLL}(\boldsymbol{w}) = -\frac{1}{N} \sum_{n=1}^{N} [\mathbb{I}(\tilde{y}_n = 1) \log(\sigma(a_n)) + \mathbb{I}(\tilde{y}_n = -1) \log(\sigma(-a_n))] \tag{10.11}$$

$$= -\frac{1}{N} \sum_{n=1}^{N} \log(\sigma(\tilde{y}_n a_n)) \tag{10.12}$$

$$= \frac{1}{N} \sum_{n=1}^{N} \log(1 + \exp(-\tilde{y}_n a_n)) \tag{10.13}$$

However, in this book, we will mostly use the $y_n \in \{0, 1\}$ notation, since it is easier to generalize to the multiclass case (Section 10.3), and makes the connection with cross-entropy easier to see.

10.2.3.2   Optimizing the objective

To find the MLE, we must solve

$$\nabla_{\boldsymbol{w}} \text{NLL}(\boldsymbol{w}) = \boldsymbol{g}(\boldsymbol{w}) = \boldsymbol{0} \tag{10.14}$$

We can use any gradient-based optimization algorithm to solve this, such as those we discuss in Chapter 8. We give a specific example in Section 10.2.4. But first we must derive the gradient, as we explain below.

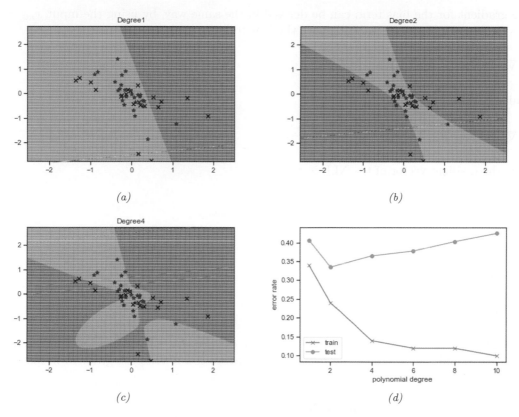

Figure 10.4: *Polynomial feature expansion applied to a two-class, two-dimensional logistic regression problem. (a) Degree $K = 1$. (b) Degree $K = 2$. (c) Degree $K = 4$. (d) Train and test error vs degree. Generated by logreg_poly_demo.ipynb.*

10.2.3.3 Deriving the gradient

Although we can use automatic differentiation methods (Section 13.3) to compute the gradient of the NLL, it is also easy to do explicitly, as we show below. Fortunately the resulting equations will turn out to have a simple and intuitive interpretation, which can be used to derive other methods, as we will see.

To start, note that

$$\frac{d\mu_n}{da_n} = \sigma(a_n)(1 - \sigma(a_n)) \tag{10.15}$$

where $a_n = \boldsymbol{w}^\mathsf{T}\boldsymbol{x}_n$ and $\mu_n = \sigma(a_n)$. Hence by the chain rule (and the rules of vector calculus, discussed in Section 7.8) we have

$$\frac{\partial}{\partial w_d}\mu_n = \frac{\partial}{\partial w_d}\sigma(\boldsymbol{w}^\mathsf{T}\boldsymbol{x}_n) = \frac{\partial}{\partial a_n}\sigma(a_n)\frac{\partial a_n}{\partial w_d} = \mu_n(1 - \mu_n)x_{nd} \tag{10.16}$$

The gradient for the bias term can be derived in the same way, by using the input $x_{n0} = 1$ in the above equation. However, we will ignore the bias term for simplicity. Hence

$$\nabla_{\boldsymbol{w}} \log(\mu_n) = \frac{1}{\mu_n} \nabla_{\boldsymbol{w}} \mu_n = (1 - \mu_n)\boldsymbol{x}_n \tag{10.17}$$

Similarly,

$$\nabla_{\boldsymbol{w}} \log(1 - \mu_n) = \frac{-\mu_n(1 - \mu_n)\boldsymbol{x}_n}{1 - \mu_n} = -\mu_n \boldsymbol{x}_n \tag{10.18}$$

Thus the gradient vector of the NLL is given by

$$\nabla_{\boldsymbol{w}} \text{NLL}(\boldsymbol{w}) = -\frac{1}{N} \sum_{n=1}^{N} [y_n(1 - \mu_n)\boldsymbol{x}_n - (1 - y_n)\mu_n \boldsymbol{x}_n] \tag{10.19}$$

$$= -\frac{1}{N} \sum_{n=1}^{N} [y_n \boldsymbol{x}_n - y_n \boldsymbol{x}_n \mu_n - \boldsymbol{x}_n \mu_n + y_n \boldsymbol{x}_n \mu_n)] \tag{10.20}$$

$$= \frac{1}{N} \sum_{n=1}^{N} (\mu_n - y_n)\boldsymbol{x}_n \tag{10.21}$$

If we interpret $e_n = \mu_n - y_n$ as an error signal, we can see that the gradient weights each input $\boldsymbol{x}_n$ by its error, and then averages the result. Note that we can rewrite the gradient in matrix form as follows:

$$\nabla_{\boldsymbol{w}} \text{NLL}(\boldsymbol{w}) = \frac{1}{N} (\mathbf{1}_N^{\mathsf{T}} (\text{diag}(\boldsymbol{\mu} - \boldsymbol{y})\mathbf{X}))^{\mathsf{T}} \tag{10.22}$$

where $\mathbf{X}$ is the $N \times D$ design matrix containing the examples $\boldsymbol{x}_n$ in each row.

10.2.3.4 Deriving the Hessian

Gradient-based optimizers will find a stationary point where $\boldsymbol{g}(\boldsymbol{w}) = \mathbf{0}$. This could either be a global optimum or a local optimum. To be sure the stationary point is the global optimum, we must show that the objective is **convex**, for reasons we explain in Section 8.1.1.1. Intuitvely this means that the NLL has a **bowl shape**, with a unique lowest point, which is indeed the case, as illustrated in Figure 10.5b.

More formally, we must prove that the Hessian is positive semi-definite, which we now do. (See Chapter 7 for relevant background information on linear algebra.) One can show that the Hessian is given by

$$\mathbf{H}(\boldsymbol{w}) = \nabla_{\boldsymbol{w}} \nabla_{\boldsymbol{w}}^{\mathsf{T}} \text{NLL}(\boldsymbol{w}) = \frac{1}{N} \sum_{n=1}^{N} (\mu_n(1 - \mu_n)\boldsymbol{x}_n)\boldsymbol{x}_n^{\mathsf{T}} = \frac{1}{N} \mathbf{X}^{\mathsf{T}} \mathbf{S} \mathbf{X} \tag{10.23}$$

where

$$\mathbf{S} \triangleq \text{diag}(\mu_1(1 - \mu_1), \dots, \mu_N(1 - \mu_N)) \tag{10.24}$$

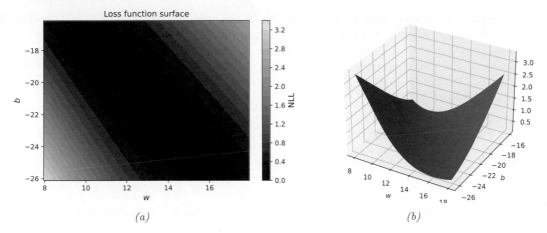

Figure 10.5: *NLL loss surface for binary logistic regression applied to Iris dataset with 1 feature and 1 bias term. The goal is to minimize the function. The global MLE is at the center of the plot. Generated by iris_logreg_loss_surface.ipynb.*

We see that $\mathbf{H}$ is positive definite, since for any nonzero vector $\boldsymbol{v}$, we have

$$\boldsymbol{v}^\mathsf{T}\mathbf{X}^\mathsf{T}\mathbf{S}\mathbf{X}\boldsymbol{v} = (\boldsymbol{v}^\mathsf{T}\mathbf{X}^\mathsf{T}\mathbf{S}^{\frac{1}{2}})(\mathbf{S}^{\frac{1}{2}}\mathbf{X}\boldsymbol{v}) = ||\boldsymbol{v}^\mathsf{T}\mathbf{X}^\mathsf{T}\mathbf{S}^{\frac{1}{2}}||_2^2 > 0 \tag{10.25}$$

This follows since $\mu_n > 0$ for all n, because of the use of the sigmoid function. Consequently the NLL is strictly convex. However, in practice, values of μ_n which are close to 0 or 1 might cause the Hessian to be close to singular. We can avoid this by using ℓ_2 regularization, as we discuss in Section 10.2.7.

10.2.4 Stochastic gradient descent

Our goal is to solve the following optimization problem

$$\hat{\boldsymbol{w}} \triangleq \operatorname*{argmin}_{\boldsymbol{w}} \mathcal{L}(\boldsymbol{w}) \tag{10.26}$$

where $\mathcal{L}(\boldsymbol{w})$ is the loss function, in this case the negative log likelihood:

$$\mathrm{NLL}(\boldsymbol{w}) = -\frac{1}{N}\sum_{n=1}^{N}[y_n \log \mu_n + (1-y_n)\log(1-\mu_n)] \tag{10.27}$$

where $\mu_n = \sigma(a_n)$ is the probability of class 1, and $a_n = \boldsymbol{w}^\mathsf{T}\boldsymbol{x}_n$ is the log odds.

There are many algorithms we could use to solve Equation (10.26), as we discuss in Chapter 8. Perhaps the simplest is to use stochastic gradient descent (Section 8.4). If we use a minibatch of size 1, then we get the following simple update equation:

$$\boldsymbol{w}_{t+1} = \boldsymbol{w}_t - \eta_t \nabla_{\boldsymbol{w}}\mathrm{NLL}(\boldsymbol{w}_t) = \boldsymbol{w}_t - \eta_t(\mu_n - y_n)\boldsymbol{x}_n \tag{10.28}$$

where we replaced the average over all N examples in the gradient of Equation (10.21) with a single stochastically chosen sample n. (The index n changes with t.)

Since we know the objective is convex (see Section 10.2.3.4), then one can show that this procedure will converge to the global optimum, provided we decay the learning rate at the appropriate rate (see Section 8.4.3). We can improve the convergence speed using variance reduction techniques such as SAGA (Section 8.4.5.2).

10.2.5   Perceptron algorithm

A **perceptron**, first introduced in [Ros58], is a deterministic binary classifier of the following form:

$$f(\boldsymbol{x}_n; \boldsymbol{\theta}) = \mathbb{I}\left(\boldsymbol{w}^\mathsf{T}\boldsymbol{x}_n + b > 0\right) \tag{10.29}$$

This can be seen to be a limiting case of a binary logistic regression classifier, in which the sigmoid function $\sigma(a)$ is replaced by the Heaviside step function $H(a) \triangleq \mathbb{I}(a > 0)$. See Figure 2.10 for a comparison of these two functions.

Since the Heaviside function is not differentiable, we cannot use gradient-based optimization methods to fit this model. However, Rosenblatt proposed the **perceptron learning algorithm** instead. The basic idea is to start with random weights, and then iteratively update them whenever the model makes a prediction mistake. More precisely, we update the weights using

$$\boldsymbol{w}_{t+1} = \boldsymbol{w}_t - \eta_t(\hat{y}_n - y_n)\boldsymbol{x}_n \tag{10.30}$$

where $(\boldsymbol{x}_n, y_n)$ is the labeled example sampled at iteration t, and η_t is the learning rate or step size. (We can set the step size to 1, since the magnitude of the weights does not affect the decision boundary.) See perceptron_demo_2d.ipynb for a simple implementation of this algorithm.

The perceptron update rule in Equation (10.30) has an intuitive interpretation: if the prediction is correct, no change is made, otherwise we move the weights in a direction so as to make the correct answer more likely. More precisely, if $y_n = 1$ and $\hat{y}_n = 0$, we have $\boldsymbol{w}_{t+1} = \boldsymbol{w}_t + \boldsymbol{x}_n$, and if $y_n = 0$ and $\hat{y}_n = 1$, we have $\boldsymbol{w}_{t+1} = \boldsymbol{w}_t - \boldsymbol{x}_n$.

By comparing Equation (10.30) to Equation (10.28), we see that the perceptron update rule is equivalent to the SGD update rule for binary logistic regression using the approximation where we replace the soft probabilities $\mu_n = p(y_n = 1|\boldsymbol{x}_n)$ with hard labels $\hat{y}_n = f(\boldsymbol{x}_n)$. The advantage of the perceptron method is that we don't need to compute probabilities, which can be useful when the label space is very large. The disadvantage is that the method will only converge when the data is linearly separable [Nov62], whereas SGD for minimizing the NLL for logistic regression will always converge to the globally optimal MLE, even if the data is not linearly separable.

In Section 13.2, we will generalize perceptrons to nonlinear functions, thus significantly enhancing their usefulness.

10.2.6   Iteratively reweighted least squares

Gradient descent is a **first order** optimization method, which means it only uses first order gradients to navigate through the loss landscape. This can be slow, especially when some directions of space point steeply downhill, whereas other have a shallower gradient, as is the case in Figure 10.5a. In such problems, it can be much faster to use a **second order** optimization method, that takes the curvature of the space into account.

We discuss such methods in more detail in Section 8.3. Here we just consider a simple second order method that works well for logistic regression. We focus on the full batch setting (so we assume N is small), since it is harder to make second order methods work in the stochastic setting (see e.g., [Byr+16; Liu+18b] for some methods).

The classic second-order method is **Newton's method**. This consists of updates of the form

$$\boldsymbol{w}_{t+1} = \boldsymbol{w}_t - \eta_t \mathbf{H}_t^{-1} \boldsymbol{g}_t \tag{10.31}$$

where

$$\mathbf{H}_t \triangleq \nabla^2 \mathcal{L}(\boldsymbol{w})|_{\boldsymbol{w}_t} = \nabla^2 \mathcal{L}(\boldsymbol{w}_t) = \mathbf{H}(\boldsymbol{w}_t) \tag{10.32}$$

is assumed to be positive-definite to ensure the update is well-defined. If the Hessian is exact, we can set the step size to $\eta_t = 1$.

We now apply this method to logistic regression. Recall from Section 10.2.3.3 that the gradient and Hessian are given by

$$\nabla_{\boldsymbol{w}} \text{NLL}(\boldsymbol{w}) = \frac{1}{N} \sum_{n=1}^{N} (\mu_n - y_n) \boldsymbol{x}_n \tag{10.33}$$

$$\mathbf{H} = \frac{1}{N} \mathbf{X}^\mathsf{T} \mathbf{S} \mathbf{X} \tag{10.34}$$

$$\mathbf{S} \triangleq \text{diag}(\mu_1 (1 - \mu_1), \dots, \mu_N (1 - \mu_N)) \tag{10.35}$$

Hence the Newton update has the form

$$\boldsymbol{w}_{t+1} = \boldsymbol{w}_t - \mathbf{H}^{-1} \boldsymbol{g}_t \tag{10.36}$$

$$= \boldsymbol{w}_t + (\mathbf{X}^\mathsf{T} \mathbf{S}_t \mathbf{X})^{-1} \mathbf{X}^\mathsf{T} (\boldsymbol{y} - \boldsymbol{\mu}_t) \tag{10.37}$$

$$= (\mathbf{X}^\mathsf{T} \mathbf{S}_t \mathbf{X})^{-1} \left[(\mathbf{X}^\mathsf{T} \mathbf{S}_t \mathbf{X}) \boldsymbol{w}_t + \mathbf{X}^\mathsf{T} (\boldsymbol{y} - \boldsymbol{\mu}_t) \right] \tag{10.38}$$

$$= (\mathbf{X}^\mathsf{T} \mathbf{S}_t \mathbf{X})^{-1} \mathbf{X}^\mathsf{T} \left[\mathbf{S}_t \mathbf{X} \boldsymbol{w}_t + \boldsymbol{y} - \boldsymbol{\mu}_t \right] \tag{10.39}$$

$$= (\mathbf{X}^\mathsf{T} \mathbf{S}_t \mathbf{X})^{-1} \mathbf{X}^\mathsf{T} \mathbf{S}_t \boldsymbol{z}_t \tag{10.40}$$

where we have defined the **working response** as

$$\boldsymbol{z}_t \triangleq \mathbf{X} \boldsymbol{w}_t + \mathbf{S}_t^{-1} (\boldsymbol{y} - \boldsymbol{\mu}_t) \tag{10.41}$$

and $\mathbf{S}_t = \text{diag}(\mu_{t,n}(1 - \mu_{t,n}))$. Since $\mathbf{S}_t$ is a diagonal matrix, we can rewrite the targets in component form as follows:

$$z_{t,n} = \boldsymbol{w}_t^\mathsf{T} \boldsymbol{x}_n + \frac{y_n - \mu_{t,n}}{\mu_{t,n}(1 - \mu_{t,n})} \tag{10.42}$$

Equation (10.40) is an example of a weighted least squares problem (Section 11.2.2.4), which is a minimizer of

$$\sum_{n=1}^{N} S_{t,n} (z_{t,n} - \boldsymbol{w}_t^\mathsf{T} \boldsymbol{x}_n)^2 \tag{10.43}$$

Algorithm 10.1: Iteratively reweighted least squares (IRLS)

---

1 $\boldsymbol{w} = \boldsymbol{0}$
2 **repeat**
3   **for** $n = 1 : N$ **do**
4         $a_n = \boldsymbol{w}^\mathsf{T}\boldsymbol{x}_n$
5         $\mu_n = \sigma(a_n)$
6         $s_n = \mu_n(1 - \mu_n)$
7         $z_n = a_n + \frac{y_n - \mu_n}{s_n}$
8     $\mathbf{S} = \mathrm{diag}(s_{1:N})$
9     $\boldsymbol{w} = (\mathbf{X}^\mathsf{T}\mathbf{S}\mathbf{X})^{-1}\mathbf{X}^\mathsf{T}\mathbf{S}\boldsymbol{z}$
10 **until** *converged*

The overall method is therefore known as the **iteratively reweighted least squares (IRLS)** algorithm, since at each iteration we solve a weighted least squares problem, where the weight matrix $\mathbf{S}_t$ changes at each iteration. See Algorithm 10.1 for some pseudocode.

Note that **Fisher scoring** is the same as IRLS except we replace the Hessian of the actual log-likelihood with its expectation, i.e., we use the Fisher information matrix (Section 4.7.2) instead of $\mathbf{H}$. Since the Fisher information matrix is independent of the data, it can be precomputed, unlike the Hessian, which must be reevaluated at every iteration. This can be faster for problems with many parameters.

10.2.7 MAP estimation

In Figure 10.4, we saw how logistic regression can overfit when there are too many parameters compared to training examples. This is a consequence of the ability of maximum likelihood to find weights that force the decision boundary to "wiggle" in just the right way so as to curve around the examples. To get this behavior, the weights often need to be set to large values. For example, in Figure 10.4, when we use degree $K = 1$, we find that the MLE for the two input weights (ignoring the bias) is

$$\hat{\boldsymbol{w}} = [0.51291712, 0.11866937] \tag{10.44}$$

When we use degree $K = 2$, we get

$$\hat{\boldsymbol{w}} = [2.27510513, 0.05970325, 11.84198867, 15.40355969, 2.51242311] \tag{10.45}$$

And when $K = 4$, we get

$$\hat{\boldsymbol{w}} = [-3.07813766, \cdots, -59.03196044, 51.77152431, 10.25054164] \tag{10.46}$$

One way to reduce such overfitting is to prevent the weights from becoming so large. We can do this by using a zero-mean Gaussian prior, $p(\boldsymbol{w}) = \mathcal{N}(\boldsymbol{w}|\boldsymbol{0}, C\mathbf{I})$, and then using MAP estimation, as we discussed in Section 4.5.3. The new training objective becomes

$$\mathcal{L}(\boldsymbol{w}) = \mathrm{NLL}(\boldsymbol{w}) + \lambda||\boldsymbol{w}||_2^2 \tag{10.47}$$

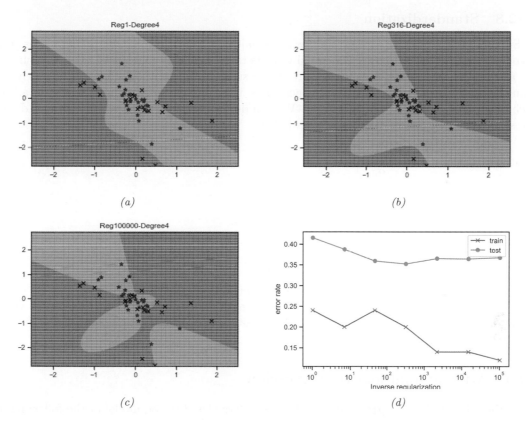

Figure 10.6: Weight decay with variance C applied to two-class, two-dimensional logistic regression problem with a degree 4 polynomial. (a) $C = 1$. (b) $C = 316$. (c) $C = 100,000$. (d) Train and test error vs C. Generated by logreg_poly_demo.ipynb.

where $||\boldsymbol{w}||_2^2 = \sum_{d=1}^{D} w_d^2$ and $\lambda = 1/C$. This is called ℓ_2 **regularization** or **weight decay**. The larger the value of λ, the more the parameters are penalized for being "large" (deviating from the zero-mean prior), and thus the less flexible the model. See Figure 10.6 for an illustration.

We can compute the MAP estimate by slightly modifying the input to the above gradient-based optimization algorithms. The gradient and Hessian of the penalized negative log likelihood have the following forms:

$$\text{PNLL}(\boldsymbol{w}) = \text{NLL}(\boldsymbol{w}) + \lambda \boldsymbol{w}^{\mathsf{T}} \boldsymbol{w} \tag{10.48}$$

$$\nabla_{\boldsymbol{w}} \text{PNLL}(\boldsymbol{w}) = \boldsymbol{g}(\boldsymbol{w}) + 2\lambda \boldsymbol{w} \tag{10.49}$$

$$\nabla_{\boldsymbol{w}}^2 \text{PNLL}(\boldsymbol{w}) = \mathbf{H}(\boldsymbol{w}) + 2\lambda \mathbf{I} \tag{10.50}$$

where $\boldsymbol{g}(\boldsymbol{w})$ is the gradient and $\mathbf{H}(\boldsymbol{w})$ is the Hessian of the unpenalized NLL.

For an interesting exercise related to ℓ_2 regularized logistic regression, see Exercise 10.2.

10.2.8   Standardization

In Section 10.2.7, we use an isotropic prior $\mathcal{N}(\boldsymbol{w}|\boldsymbol{0}, \lambda^{-1}\mathbf{I})$ to prevent overfitting. This implicitly encodes the assumption that we expect all weights to be similar in magnitude, which in turn encodes the assumption we expect all input features to be similar in magnitude. However, in many datasets, input features are on different scales. In such cases, it is common to **standardize** the data, to ensure each feature has mean 0 and variance 1. We can do this by subtracting the mean and dividing by the standard deviation of each feature, as follows:

$$\text{standardize}(x_{nd}) = \frac{x_{nd} - \hat{\mu}_d}{\hat{\sigma}_d} \tag{10.51}$$

$$\hat{\mu}_d = \frac{1}{N} \sum_{n=1}^{N} x_{nd} \tag{10.52}$$

$$\hat{\sigma}_d^2 = \frac{1}{N} \sum_{n=1}^{N} (x_{nd} - \hat{\mu}_d)^2 \tag{10.53}$$

An alternative is to use **min-max scaling**, in which we rescale the inputs so they lie in the interval $[0, 1]$. Both methods ensure the features are comparable in magnitude, which can help with model fitting and inference, even if we don't use MAP estimation. (See Section 11.7.5 for a discussion of this point.)

10.3   Multinomial logistic regression

Multinomial logistic regression is a discriminative classification model of the following form:

$$p(y|\boldsymbol{x}, \boldsymbol{\theta}) = \text{Cat}(y|\text{softmax}(\mathbf{W}\boldsymbol{x} + \boldsymbol{b})) \tag{10.54}$$

where $\boldsymbol{x} \in \mathbb{R}^D$ is the input vector, $y \in \{1, \ldots, C\}$ is the class label, softmax() is the softmax function (Section 2.5.2), $\mathbf{W}$ is a $C \times D$ weight matrix, $\boldsymbol{b}$ is C-dimensional bias vector, $\boldsymbol{\theta} = (\mathbf{W}, \boldsymbol{b})$ are all the parameters. (We will henceforth assume we have prepended each $\boldsymbol{x}$ with a 1, and added $\boldsymbol{b}$ to the first column of $\mathbf{W}$, so this simplifies to $\boldsymbol{\theta} = \mathbf{W}$.)

If we let $\boldsymbol{a} = \mathbf{W}\boldsymbol{x}$ be the C-dimensional vector of **logits**, then we can rewrite the above as follows:

$$p(y = c|\boldsymbol{x}, \boldsymbol{\theta}) = \frac{e^{a_c}}{\sum_{c'=1}^{C} e^{a_{c'}}} \tag{10.55}$$

Because of the normalization condition $\sum_{c=1}^{C} p(y_n = c|\boldsymbol{x}_n, \boldsymbol{\theta}) = 1$, we can set $\boldsymbol{w}_C = \boldsymbol{0}$. (For example, in binary logistic regression, where $C = 2$, we only learn a single weight vector.) Therefore the parameters $\boldsymbol{\theta}$ correspond to a weight matrix $\mathbf{W}$ of size $(C - 1) \times D$, where $\boldsymbol{x}_n \in \mathbb{R}^D$.

Note that this model assumes the labels are mutually exclusive, i.e., there is only one true label. For some applications (e.g., **image tagging**), we want to predict one or more labels for an input; in this case, the output space is the set of subsets of $\{1, \ldots, C\}$. This is called **multi-label classification**, as opposed to **multi-class classification**. This can be viewed as a bit vector, $\mathcal{Y} = \{0, 1\}^C$, where the c'th output is set to 1 if the c'th tag is present. We can tackle this using a modified version of

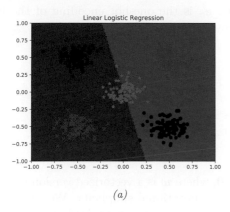
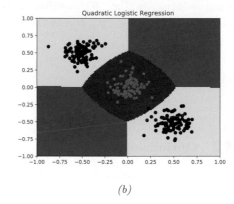

(a)   (b)

Figure 10.7: Example of 3-class logistic regression with 2d inputs. (a) Original features. (b) Quadratic features. Generated by logreg_multiclass_demo.ipynb.

binary logistic regression with multiple outputs:

$$p(\boldsymbol{y}|\boldsymbol{x},\boldsymbol{\theta}) = \prod_{c=1}^{C} \mathrm{Ber}(y_c|\sigma(\boldsymbol{w}_c^\mathsf{T}\boldsymbol{x})) \tag{10.56}$$

10.3.1 Linear and nonlinear classifiers

Logistic regression computes linear decision boundaries in the input space, as shown in Figure 10.7(a) for the case where $\boldsymbol{x} \in \mathbb{R}^2$ and we have $C = 3$ classes. However, we can always transform the inputs in some way to create nonlinear boundaries. For example, suppose we replace $\boldsymbol{x} = (x_1, x_2)$ by

$$\boldsymbol{\phi}(\boldsymbol{x}) = [1, x_1, x_2, x_1^2, x_2^2, x_1 x_2] \tag{10.57}$$

This lets us create quadratic decision boundaries, as illustrated in Figure 10.7(b).

10.3.2 Maximum likelihood estimation

In this section, we discuss how to compute the maximum likelihood estimate (MLE) by minimizing the negative log likelihood (NLL).

10.3.2.1 Objective

The NLL is given by

$$\mathrm{NLL}(\boldsymbol{\theta}) = -\frac{1}{N}\log\prod_{n=1}^{N}\prod_{c=1}^{C}\mu_{nc}^{y_{nc}} = -\frac{1}{N}\sum_{n=1}^{N}\sum_{c=1}^{C}y_{nc}\log\mu_{nc} = \frac{1}{N}\sum_{n=1}^{N}\mathbb{H}_{ce}(\boldsymbol{y}_n,\boldsymbol{\mu}_n) \tag{10.58}$$

where $\mu_{nc} = p(y_{nc} = 1|\boldsymbol{x}_n, \boldsymbol{\theta}) = \text{softmax}(f(\boldsymbol{x}_n, \boldsymbol{\theta}))_c$, $\boldsymbol{y}_n$ is the one-hot encoding of the label (so $y_{nc} = \mathbb{I}(y_n = c)$), and $\mathbb{H}_{ce}(\boldsymbol{y}_n, \boldsymbol{\mu}_n)$ is the cross-entropy:

$$\mathbb{H}_{ce}(\boldsymbol{p}, \boldsymbol{q}) = -\sum_{c=1}^{C} p_c \log q_c \tag{10.59}$$

10.3.2.2   Optimizing the objective

To find the optimum, we need to solve $\nabla_{\boldsymbol{w}}\text{NLL}(\boldsymbol{w}) = \boldsymbol{0}$, where $\boldsymbol{w}$ is a vectorized version of the weight matrix $\mathbf{W}$, and where we are ignoring the bias term for notational simplicity. We can find such a stationary point using any gradient-based optimizer; we give some examples below. But first we derive the gradient and Hessian, and then prove that the objective is convex.

10.3.2.3   Deriving the gradient

To derive the gradient of the NLL, we need to use the Jacobian of the softmax function, which is as follows (see Exercise 10.1 for the proof):

$$\frac{\partial \mu_c}{\partial a_j} = \mu_c(\delta_{cj} - \mu_j) \tag{10.60}$$

where $\delta_{cj} = \mathbb{I}(c = j)$. For example, if we have 3 classes, the Jacobian matrix is given by

$$\left[\frac{\partial \mu_c}{\partial a_j}\right]_{cj} = \begin{pmatrix} \mu_1(1 - \mu_1) & -\mu_1\mu_2 & -\mu_1\mu_3 \\ -\mu_2\mu_1 & \mu_2(1 - \mu_2) & -\mu_2\mu_3 \\ -\mu_3\mu_1 & -\mu_3\mu_2 & \mu_3(1 - \mu_3) \end{pmatrix} \tag{10.61}$$

In matrix form, this can be written as

$$\frac{\partial \boldsymbol{\mu}}{\partial \boldsymbol{a}} = (\boldsymbol{\mu}\boldsymbol{1}^{\mathsf{T}}) \odot (\mathbf{I} - \boldsymbol{1}\boldsymbol{\mu}^{\mathsf{T}}) \tag{10.62}$$

where $\odot$ is elementwise product, $\boldsymbol{\mu}\boldsymbol{1}^{\mathsf{T}}$ copies $\boldsymbol{\mu}$ across each column, and $\boldsymbol{1}\boldsymbol{\mu}^{\mathsf{T}}$ copies $\boldsymbol{\mu}$ across each row.

We now derive the gradient of the NLL for a single example, indexed by n. To do this, we flatten the $D \times C$ weight matrix into a vector $\boldsymbol{w}$ of size CD (or $(C - 1)D$ if we freeze one of the classes to have zero weight) by concatenating the rows, and then transposing into a column vector. We use $\boldsymbol{w}_j$ to denote the vector of weights associated with class j. The gradient wrt this vector is giving by the following (where we use the Kronecker delta notation, δ_{jc}, which equals 1 if $j = c$ and 0 otherwise):

$$\nabla_{\boldsymbol{w}_j} \text{NLL}_n = \sum_c \frac{\partial \text{NLL}_n}{\partial \mu_{nc}} \frac{\partial \mu_{nc}}{\partial a_{nj}} \frac{\partial a_{nj}}{\partial \boldsymbol{w}_j} \tag{10.63}$$

$$= -\sum_c \frac{y_{nc}}{\mu_{nc}} \mu_{nc}(\delta_{jc} - \mu_{nj})\boldsymbol{x}_n \tag{10.64}$$

$$= \sum_c y_{nc}(\mu_{nj} - \delta_{jc})\boldsymbol{x}_n \tag{10.65}$$

$$= (\sum_c y_{nc})\mu_{nj}\boldsymbol{x}_n - \sum_c \delta_{jc} y_{nj}\boldsymbol{x}_n \tag{10.66}$$

$$= (\mu_{nj} - y_{nj})\boldsymbol{x}_n \tag{10.67}$$

We can repeat this computation for each class, to get the full gradient vector. The gradient of the overall NLL is obtained by summing over examples, to give the $D \times C$ matrix

$$\boldsymbol{g}(\boldsymbol{w}) = \frac{1}{N} \sum_{n=1}^{N} \boldsymbol{x}_n (\boldsymbol{\mu}_n - \boldsymbol{y}_n)^\mathsf{T} \tag{10.68}$$

This has the same form as in the binary logistic regression case, namely an error term times the input.

10.3.2.4   Deriving the Hessian

Exercise 10.1 asks you to show that the Hessian of the NLL for multinomial logistic regression is given by

$$\mathbf{H}(\boldsymbol{w}) = \frac{1}{N} \sum_{n=1}^{N} (\text{diag}(\boldsymbol{\mu}_n) - \boldsymbol{\mu}_n \boldsymbol{\mu}_n^\mathsf{T}) \otimes (\boldsymbol{x}_n \boldsymbol{x}_n^\mathsf{T}) \tag{10.69}$$

where $\mathbf{A} \otimes \mathbf{B}$ is the Kronecker product (Section 7.2.5). In other words, the block c, c' submatrix is given by

$$\mathbf{H}_{c,c'}(\boldsymbol{w}) = \frac{1}{N} \sum_n \mu_{nc}(\delta_{c,c'} - \mu_{n,c'})\boldsymbol{x}_n \boldsymbol{x}_n^\mathsf{T} \tag{10.70}$$

For example, if we have 3 features and 2 classes, this becomes

$$\mathbf{H}(\boldsymbol{w}) = \frac{1}{N} \sum_n \begin{pmatrix} \mu_{n1} - \mu_{n1}^2 & -\mu_{n1}\mu_{n2} \\ -\mu_{n1}\mu_{n2} & \mu_{n2} - \mu_{n2}^2 \end{pmatrix} \otimes \begin{pmatrix} x_{n1}x_{n1} & x_{n1}x_{n2} & x_{n1}x_{n3} \\ x_{n2}x_{n1} & x_{n2}x_{n2} & x_{n2}x_{n3} \\ x_{n3}x_{n1} & x_{n3}x_{n2} & x_{n3}x_{n3} \end{pmatrix} \tag{10.71}$$

$$= \frac{1}{N} \sum_n \begin{pmatrix} (\mu_{n1} - \mu_{n1}^2)\mathbf{X}_n & -\mu_{n1}\mu_{n2}\mathbf{X}_n \\ -\mu_{n1}\mu_{n2}\mathbf{X}_n & (\mu_{n2} - \mu_{n2}^2)\mathbf{X}_n \end{pmatrix} \tag{10.72}$$

where $\mathbf{X}_n = \boldsymbol{x}_n \boldsymbol{x}_n^\mathsf{T}$. Exercise 10.1 also asks you to show that this is a positive definite matrix, so the objective is convex.

10.3.3   Gradient-based optimization

It is straightforward to use the gradient in Section 10.3.2.3 to derive the SGD algorithm. Similarly, we can use the Hessian in Section 10.3.2.4 to derive a second-order optimization method. However, computing the Hessian can be expensive, so it is common to approximate it using quasi-Newton methods, such as limited memory BFGS. (BFGS stands for Broyden, Fletcher, Goldfarb and Shanno.) See Section 8.3.2 for details. Another approach, which is similar to IRLS, is described in Section 10.3.4.

All of these methods rely on computing the gradient of the log-likelihood, which in turn requires computing normalized probabilities, which can be computed from the logits vector $\boldsymbol{a} = \mathbf{W}\boldsymbol{x}$ using

$$p(y = c|\boldsymbol{x}) = \exp(a_c - \mathrm{lse}(\boldsymbol{a})) \tag{10.73}$$

where lse is the log-sum-exp function defined in Section 2.5.4. For this reason, many software libraries define a version of the cross-entropy loss that takes unnormalized logits as input.

10.3.4   Bound optimization

In this section, we consider an approach for fitting logistic regression using a class of algorithms known as bound optimization, which we describe in Section 8.7. The basic idea is to iteratively construct a lower bound on the function you want to maximize, and then to update the bound, so it "pushes up" on the true function. Optimizing the bound is often easier than updating the function directly.

If $\ell(\boldsymbol{\theta})$ is a concave function we want to maximize, then one way to obtain a valid lower bound is to use a bound on its Hessian, i.e., to find a negative definite matrix $\mathbf{B}$ such that $\mathbf{H}(\boldsymbol{\theta}) \succ \mathbf{B}$. In this case, one can show that

$$\ell(\boldsymbol{\theta}) \geq \ell(\boldsymbol{\theta}^t) + (\boldsymbol{\theta} - \boldsymbol{\theta}^t)^{\mathsf{T}} \boldsymbol{g}(\boldsymbol{\theta}^t) + \frac{1}{2}(\boldsymbol{\theta} - \boldsymbol{\theta}^t)^{\mathsf{T}} \mathbf{B}(\boldsymbol{\theta} - \boldsymbol{\theta}^t) \tag{10.74}$$

where $\boldsymbol{g}(\boldsymbol{\theta}^t) = \nabla\ell(\boldsymbol{\theta}^t)$. Defining $Q(\boldsymbol{\theta}, \boldsymbol{\theta}^t)$ as the right-hand-side of Equation (10.74), the update becomes

$$\boldsymbol{\theta}^{t+1} = \boldsymbol{\theta}^t - \mathbf{B}^{-1}\boldsymbol{g}(\boldsymbol{\theta}^t) \tag{10.75}$$

This is similar to a Newton update, except we use $\mathbf{B}$, which is a fixed matrix, rather than $\mathbf{H}(\boldsymbol{\theta}^t)$, which changes at each iteration. This can give us some of the advantages of second order methods at lower computational cost.

Let us now apply this to logistic regression, following [Kri+05], Let $\boldsymbol{\mu}_n(\boldsymbol{w}) = [p(y_n = 1|\boldsymbol{x}_n, \boldsymbol{w}), \ldots, p(y_n = C|\boldsymbol{x}_n, \boldsymbol{w})]$ and $\boldsymbol{y}_n = [\mathbb{I}\,(y_n = 1), \ldots, \mathbb{I}\,(y_n = C)]$. We want to *maximize* the log-likelihood, which is as follows:

$$\ell(\boldsymbol{w}) = \sum_{n=1}^{N} \left[\sum_{c=1}^{C} y_{nc}\boldsymbol{w}_c^{\mathsf{T}}\boldsymbol{x}_n - \log\sum_{c=1}^{C} \exp(\boldsymbol{w}_c^{\mathsf{T}}\boldsymbol{x}_n) \right] \tag{10.76}$$

The gradient is given by the following (see Section 10.3.2.3 for details of the derivation):

$$\boldsymbol{g}(\boldsymbol{w}) = \sum_{n=1}^{N} (\boldsymbol{y}_n - \boldsymbol{\mu}_n(\boldsymbol{w})) \otimes \boldsymbol{x}_n \tag{10.77}$$

where $\otimes$ denotes Kronecker product (which, in this case, is just outer product of the two vectors). The Hessian is given by the following (see Section 10.3.2.4 for details of the derivation):

$$\mathbf{H}(\boldsymbol{w}) = -\sum_{n=1}^{N} (\mathrm{diag}(\boldsymbol{\mu}_n(\boldsymbol{w})) - \boldsymbol{\mu}_n(\boldsymbol{w})\boldsymbol{\mu}_n(\boldsymbol{w})^{\mathsf{T}}) \otimes (\boldsymbol{x}_n \boldsymbol{x}_n^{\mathsf{T}}) \tag{10.78}$$

We can construct a lower bound on the Hessian, as shown in [Boh92]:

$$\mathbf{H}(\boldsymbol{w}) \succ -\frac{1}{2}[\mathbf{I} - \mathbf{11}^{\mathsf{T}}/C] \otimes \left(\sum_{n=1}^{N} \boldsymbol{x}_n \boldsymbol{x}_n^{\mathsf{T}} \right) \triangleq \mathbf{B} \tag{10.79}$$

where $\mathbf{I}$ is a C-dimensional identity matrix, and $\mathbf{1}$ is a C-dimensional vector of all 1s.[1] In the binary case, this becomes

$$\mathbf{H}(\boldsymbol{w}) \succ -\frac{1}{2}\left(1 - \frac{1}{2}\right)\left(\sum_{n=1}^{N} \boldsymbol{x}_n \boldsymbol{x}_n^{\mathsf{T}} \right) = -\frac{1}{4}\mathbf{X}^{\mathsf{T}}\mathbf{X} \tag{10.80}$$

This follows since $\mu_n \leq 0.5$ so $-(\mu_n - \mu_n^2) \geq -0.25$.

We can use this lower bound to construct an MM algorithm to find the MLE. The update becomes

$$\boldsymbol{w}^{t+1} = \boldsymbol{w}^t - \mathbf{B}^{-1}\boldsymbol{g}(\boldsymbol{w}^t) \tag{10.81}$$

This iteration can be faster than IRLS (Section 10.2.6) since we can precompute $\mathbf{B}^{-1}$ in time independent of N, rather than having to invert the Hessian at each iteration. For example, let us consider the binary case, so $\boldsymbol{g}^t = \nabla\ell(\boldsymbol{w}^t) = \mathbf{X}^{\mathsf{T}}(\boldsymbol{y} - \boldsymbol{\mu}^t)$, where $\boldsymbol{\mu}^t = [p_n(\boldsymbol{w}^t), (1 - p_n(\boldsymbol{w}^t))]_{n=1}^N$. The update becomes

$$\boldsymbol{w}^{t+1} = \boldsymbol{w}^t - 4(\mathbf{X}^{\mathsf{T}}\mathbf{X})^{-1}\boldsymbol{g}^t \tag{10.82}$$

Compare this to Equation (10.37), which has the following form:

$$\boldsymbol{w}^{t+1} = \boldsymbol{w}^t - \mathbf{H}^{-1}\boldsymbol{g}(\boldsymbol{w}^t) = \boldsymbol{w}^t - (\mathbf{X}^{\mathsf{T}}\mathbf{S}^t\mathbf{X})^{-1}\boldsymbol{g}^t \tag{10.83}$$

where $\mathbf{S}^t = \mathrm{diag}(\boldsymbol{\mu}^t \odot (1 - \boldsymbol{\mu}^t))$. We see that Equation (10.82) is faster to compute, since we can precompute the constant matrix $(\mathbf{X}^{\mathsf{T}}\mathbf{X})^{-1}$.

10.3.5   MAP estimation

In Section 10.2.7 we discussed the benefits of ℓ_2 regularization for binary logistic regression. These benefits hold also in the multi-class case. However, there is also an additional, and surprising, benefit to do with **identifiability** of the parameters, as pointed out in [HTF09, Ex.18.3]. (We say that the parameters are identifiable if there is a unique value that maximizes the likelihood; equivalently, we require that the NLL be *strictly* convex.)

---

1. If we enforce that $\boldsymbol{w}_C = \mathbf{0}$, we can use $C - 1$ dimensions for these vectors / matrices.

To see why identifiability is an issue, recall that multiclass logistic regression has the form

$$p(y = c|\boldsymbol{x}, \mathbf{W}) = \frac{\exp(\boldsymbol{w}_c^T \boldsymbol{x})}{\sum_{k=1}^{C} \exp(\boldsymbol{w}_k^T \boldsymbol{x})} \tag{10.84}$$

where $\mathbf{W}$ is a $C \times D$ weight matrix. We can arbitrarily define $\boldsymbol{w}_c = \mathbf{0}$ for one of the classes, say $c = C$, since $p(y = C|\boldsymbol{x}, \mathbf{W}) = 1 - \sum_{c=1}^{C-1} p(y = c|\boldsymbol{x}, \boldsymbol{w})$. In this case, the model has the form

$$p(y = c|\boldsymbol{x}, \mathbf{W}) = \frac{\exp(\boldsymbol{w}_c^T \boldsymbol{x})}{1 + \sum_{k=1}^{C-1} \exp(\boldsymbol{w}_k^T \boldsymbol{x})} \tag{10.85}$$

If we don't "clamp" one of the vectors to some constant value, the parameters will be unidentifiable. However, suppose we don't clamp $\boldsymbol{w}_c = \mathbf{0}$, so we are using Equation 10.84, but we add ℓ_2 regularization by optimizing

$$\text{PNLL}(\mathbf{W}) = -\sum_{n=1}^{N} \log p(y_n|\boldsymbol{x}_n, \mathbf{W}) + \lambda \sum_{c=1}^{C} ||\boldsymbol{w}_c||_2^2 \tag{10.86}$$

where we have absorbed the $1/N$ term into λ. At the optimum we have $\sum_{c=1}^{C} \hat{w}_{cj} = 0$ for $j = 1 : D$, so the weights automatically satisfy a sum-to-zero constraint, thus making them uniquely identifiable. To see why, note that at the optimum we have

$$\nabla \text{NLL}(\boldsymbol{w}) + 2\lambda \boldsymbol{w} = \mathbf{0} \tag{10.87}$$

$$\sum_n (\boldsymbol{y}_n - \boldsymbol{\mu}_n) \otimes \boldsymbol{x}_n = \lambda \boldsymbol{w} \tag{10.88}$$

Hence for any feature dimension j we have

$$\lambda \sum_c w_{cj} = \sum_n \sum_c (y_{nc} - \mu_{nc})x_{nj} = \sum_n (\sum_c y_{nc} - \sum_c \mu_{nc})x_{nj} = \sum_n (1-1)x_{nj} = 0 \tag{10.89}$$

Thus if $\lambda > 0$ we have $\sum_c \hat{w}_{cj} = 0$, so the weights will sum to zero across classes for each feature dimension.

10.3.6   Maximum entropy classifiers

Recall that the multinomial logistic regression model can be written as

$$p(y = c|\boldsymbol{x}, \mathbf{W}) = \frac{\exp(\boldsymbol{w}_c^\mathsf{T} \boldsymbol{x})}{Z(\boldsymbol{w}, \boldsymbol{x})} = \frac{\exp(\boldsymbol{w}_c^\mathsf{T} \boldsymbol{x})}{\sum_{c'=1}^{C} \exp(\boldsymbol{w}_{c'}^\mathsf{T} \boldsymbol{x})} \tag{10.90}$$

where $Z(\boldsymbol{w}, \boldsymbol{x}) = \sum_c \exp(\boldsymbol{w}_c^\mathsf{T} \boldsymbol{x})$ is the partition function (normalization constant). This uses the same features, but a different weight vector, for every class. There is a slight extension of this model that allows us to use features that are class-dependent. This model can be written as

$$p(y = c|\boldsymbol{x}, \boldsymbol{w}) = \frac{1}{Z(\boldsymbol{w}, \boldsymbol{x})} \exp(\boldsymbol{w}^\mathsf{T} \boldsymbol{\phi}(\boldsymbol{x}, c)) \tag{10.91}$$

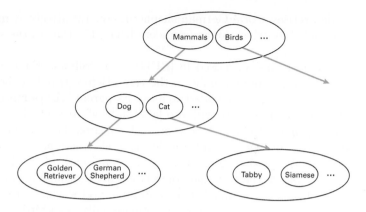

Figure 10.8: A simple example of a label hierarchy. Nodes within the same ellipse have a mutual exclusion relationship between them.

where $\phi(\boldsymbol{x}, c)$ is the feature vector for class c. This is called a **maximum entropy classifer**, or **maxent classifier** for short. (The origin of this term is explained in Section 3.4.4.)

Maxent classifiers include multinomial logistic regression as a special case. To see this let $\boldsymbol{w} = [\boldsymbol{w}_1, \ldots, \boldsymbol{w}_C]$, and define the feature vector as follows:

$$\phi(\boldsymbol{x}, c) = [\boldsymbol{0}, \ldots, \boldsymbol{x}, \ldots, \boldsymbol{0}] \tag{10.92}$$

where $\boldsymbol{x}$ is embedded in the c'th block, and the remaining blocks are zero. In this case, $\boldsymbol{w}^\mathsf{T}\phi(\boldsymbol{x}, c) = \boldsymbol{w}_c^\mathsf{T}\boldsymbol{x}$, so we recover multinomial logistic regression.

Maxent classifiers are very widely used in the field of natural language processing. For example, consider the problem of **semantic role labeling**, where we classify a word $\boldsymbol{x}$ into a semantic role y, such as person, place or thing. We might define (binary) features such as the following:

$$\phi_1(\boldsymbol{x}, y) = \mathbb{I}(y = \text{person} \land \boldsymbol{x} \text{ occurs after "Mr." or "Mrs"}) \tag{10.93}$$
$$\phi_2(\boldsymbol{x}, y) = \mathbb{I}(y = \text{person} \land \boldsymbol{x} \text{ is in whitelist of common names}) \tag{10.94}$$
$$\phi_3(\boldsymbol{x}, y) = \mathbb{I}(y = \text{place} \land \boldsymbol{x} \text{ is in Google maps}) \tag{10.95}$$
$$\vdots$$

We see that the features we use depend on the label.

There are two main ways of creating these features. The first is to manually specify many possibly useful features using various templates, and then use a feature selection algorithm, such as the group lasso method of Section 11.4.7. The second is to incrementally add features to the model, using a heuristic feature generation method.

10.3.7 Hierarchical classification

Sometimes the set of possible labels can be structured into a **hierarchy** or **taxonomy**. For example, we might want to predict what kind of an animal is in an image: it could be a dog or a cat; if it is a dog, it could be a golden retriever or a German shepherd, etc. Intuitively, it makes sense to try to predict the most precise label for which we are confident [Den+12], that is, the system should "hedge its bets".

One simple way to achieve this, proposed in [RF17], is as follows. First, create a model with a binary output label for every possible node in the tree. Before training the model, we will use **label smearing**, so that a label is propagated to all of its parents (**hypernyms**). For example, if an image is labeled "golden retriever", we will also label it "dog". If we train a multi-label classifier (which produces a vector $p(\boldsymbol{y}|\boldsymbol{x})$ of binary labels) on such smeared data, it will perform hierarchical classification, predicting a set of labels at different levels of abstraction.

However, this method could predict "golden retriever", "cat" and "bird" all with probability 1.0, since the model does not capture the fact that some labels are mutually exclusive. To prevent this, we can add a mutual exclusion constraint between all label nodes which are siblings, as shown in Figure 10.8. For example, this model enforces that $p(\text{mammal}|\boldsymbol{x}) + p(\text{bird}|\boldsymbol{x}) = 1$, since these two labels are children of the root node. We can further partition the mammal probability into dogs and cats, so we have $p(\text{dog}|\boldsymbol{x}) + p(\text{cat}|\boldsymbol{x}) = p(\text{mammal}|\boldsymbol{x})$.

[Den+14; Din+15] generalize the above method by using a conditional graphical model where the graph structure can be more complex than a tree. In addition, they allow for soft constraints between labels, in addition to hard constraints.

10.3.8 Handling large numbers of classes

In this section, we discuss some issues that arise when there are a large number of potential labels, e.g., if the labels correspond to words from a language.

10.3.8.1 Hierarchical softmax

In regular softmax classifiers, computing the normalization constant, which is needed to compute the gradient of the log likelihood, takes $O(C)$ time, which can become the bottleneck if C is large. However, if we structure the labels as a tree, we can compute the probability of any label in $O(\log C)$ time, by multiplying the probabilities of each edge on the path from the root to the leaf. For example, consider the tree in Figure 10.9. We have

$$p(y = \text{I'm}|C) = 0.57 \times 0.68 \times 0.72 = 0.28 \tag{10.96}$$

Thus we replace the "flat" output softmax with a tree-structured sequence of binary classifiers. This is called **hierarchical softmax** [Goo01; MB05].

A good way to structure such a tree is to use Huffman encoding, where the most frequent labels are placed near the top of the tree, as suggested in [Mik+13a]. (For a different appproach, based on clustering the most common labels together, see [Gra+17]. And for yet another approach, based on sampling labels, see [Tit16].)

10.3.8.2 Class imbalance and the long tail

Another issue that often arises when there are a large number of classes is that for most classes, we may have very few examples. More precisely, if N_c is the number of examples of class c, then the empirical distribution $p(N_1, \ldots, N_C)$ may have a **long tail**. The result is an extreme form of **class**

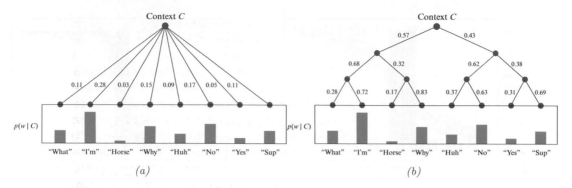

Figure 10.9: *A flat and hierarchical softmax model $p(w|C)$, where C are the input features (context) and w is the output label (word). Adapted from https://www.quora.com/What-is-hierarchical-softmax.*

imbalance (see e.g., [ASR15]). Since the rare classes will have a smaller effect on the overall loss than the common classes, the model may "focus its attention" on the common classes.

One method that can help is to set the bias terms $\boldsymbol{b}$ such that $\text{softmax}(\boldsymbol{b})_c = N_c/N$; such a model will match the empirical label prior even when using weights of $\boldsymbol{w} = \boldsymbol{0}$. We can then "subtract off" the prior term by using **logit adjustment** [Men+21], which ensures good performance across all groups.

Another common approach is to resample the data to make it more balanced, before (or during) training. In particular, suppose we sample a datapoint from class c with probability

$$p_c = \frac{N_c^q}{\sum_i^C N_i^q} \tag{10.97}$$

If we set $q = 1$, we recover standard **instance-balanced sampling**, where $p_c \propto N_c$; the common classes will be sampled more than rare classes. If we set $q = 0$, we recover **class-balanced sampling**, where $p_c = 1/C$; this can be thought of as first sampling a class uniformly at random, and then sampling an instance of this class. Finally, we can consider other options, such as $q = 0.5$, which is known as **square-root sampling** [Mah+18].

Yet another method that is simple and can easily handle the long tail is to use the **nearest class mean classifier**. This has the form

$$f(\boldsymbol{x}) = \underset{c}{\text{argmin}} \, ||\boldsymbol{x} - \boldsymbol{\mu}_c||_2^2 \tag{10.98}$$

where $\boldsymbol{\mu}_c = \frac{1}{N_c} \sum_{n:y_n=c} \boldsymbol{x}_n$ is the mean of the features belonging to class c. This induces a softmax posterior, as we discussed in Section 9.2.5. We can get much better results if we first use a neural network (see Part III) to learn good features, by training a DNN classifier with cross-entropy loss on the original unbalanced data. We then replace $\boldsymbol{x}$ with $\phi(\boldsymbol{x})$ in Equation (10.98). This simple approach can give very good performance on long-tailed distributions [Kan+20].

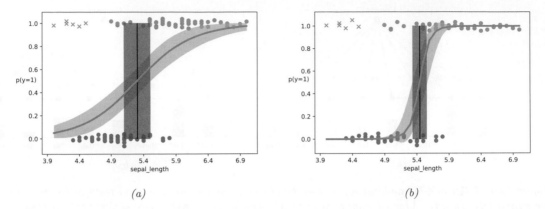

(a)   (b)

Figure 10.10: (a) Logistic regression on some data with outliers (denoted by x). Training points have been (vertically) jittered to avoid overlapping too much. Vertical line is the decision boundary, and its posterior credible interval. (b) Same as (a) but using robust model, with a mixture likelihood. Adapted from Figure 4.13 of [Mar18]. Generated by logreg_iris_bayes_robust_1d_pymc3.ipynb.

10.4   Robust logistic regression *

Sometimes we have **outliers** in our data, which are often due to labeling errors, also called **label noise**. To prevent the model from being adversely affected by such contamination, we will use **robust logistic regression**. In this section, we discuss some approaches to this problem. (Note that the methods can also be applied to DNNs. For a more thorough survey of label noise, and how it impacts deep learning, see [Han+20].)

10.4.1   Mixture model for the likelihood

One of the simplest ways to define a robust logistic regression model is to modify the likelihood so that it predicts that each output label y is generated uniformly at random with probability π, and otherwise is generated using the usual conditional model. In the binary case, this becomes

$$p(y|\boldsymbol{x}) = \pi \mathrm{Ber}(y|0.5) + (1 - \pi)\mathrm{Ber}(y|\sigma(\boldsymbol{w}^\mathsf{T}\boldsymbol{x})) \tag{10.99}$$

This approach, of using a mixture model for the observation model to make it robust, can be applied to many different models (e.g., DNNs).

We can fit this model using standard methods, such as SGD or Bayesian inference methods such as MCMC. For example, let us create a "contaminated" version of the 1d, two-class Iris dataset that we discussed in Section 4.6.7.2. We will add 6 examples of class 1 (Versicolor) with abnormally low sepal length. In Figure 10.10a, we show the results of fitting a standard (Bayesian) logistic regression model to this dataset. In Figure 10.10b, we show the results of fitting the above robust model. In the latter case, we see that the decision boundary is similar to the one we inferred from non-contaminated data, as shown in Figure 4.20b. We also see that the posterior uncertainty about the decision boundary's location is smaller than when using a non-robust model.

10.4.2   Bi-tempered loss

In this section, we present an approach to robust logistic regression proposed in [Ami+19].

The first observation is that examples that are far from the decision boundary, but mislabeled, will have undue adverse affect on the model if the loss function is convex [LS10]. This can be overcome by replacing the usual cross entropy loss with a "tempered" version, that uses a temperature parameter $0 \le t_1 < 1$ to ensure the loss from outliers is bounded. In particular, consider the standard relative entropy loss function:

$$\mathcal{L}(\boldsymbol{y}, \hat{\boldsymbol{y}}) = \mathbb{H}_{ce}(\boldsymbol{y}, \hat{\boldsymbol{y}}) = \sum_c y_c \log \hat{y}_c \tag{10.100}$$

where $\boldsymbol{y}$ is the true label distribution (often one-hot) and $\hat{\boldsymbol{y}}$ is the predicted distribution. We define the **tempered cross entropy** loss as follows:

$$\mathcal{L}(\boldsymbol{y}, \hat{\boldsymbol{y}}) = \sum_c \left[y_c(\log_{t_1} y_c - \log_{t_1} \hat{y}_c) - \frac{1}{2 - t_1}(y_c^{2-t_1} - \hat{y}_c^{2-t_1}) \right] \tag{10.101}$$

which simplifes to the following when the true distribution $\boldsymbol{y}$ is one-hot, with all its mass on class c:

$$\mathcal{L}(c, \hat{\boldsymbol{y}}) = -\log_{t_1} \hat{y}_c - \frac{1}{2 - t_1}\left(1 - \sum_{c'=1}^{C} \hat{y}_{c'}^{2-t_1} \right) \tag{10.102}$$

Here $\log_t$ is tempered version of the log function:

$$\log_t(x) \triangleq \frac{1}{1 - t}(x^{1-t} - 1) \tag{10.103}$$

This is mononotically increasing and concave, and reduces to the standard (natural) logarithm when $t = 1$. (Similarly, tempered cross entropy reduces to standard cross entropy when $t = 1$.) However, the tempered log function is bounded from below by $-1/(1 - t)$ for $0 \le t < 1$, and hence the cross entropy loss is bounded from above (see Figure 10.11).

The second observation is that examples that are near the decision boundary, but mislabeled, need to use a transfer function (that maps from activations $\mathbb{R}^C$ to probabilities $[0, 1]^C$) that has heavier tails than the softmax, which is based on the exponential, so it can "look past" the neighborhood of the immediate examples. In particular, the standard softmax is defined by

$$\hat{y}_c = \frac{a_c}{\sum_{c'=1}^{C} \exp(a_{c'})} = \exp\left[a_c - \log \sum_{c'=1}^{C} \exp(a_{c'}) \right] \tag{10.104}$$

where $\boldsymbol{a}$ is the logits vector. We can make a heavy tailed version by using the **tempered softmax**, which uses a temperature parameter $t_2 > 1 > t_1$ as follows:

$$\hat{y}_c = \exp_{t_2}(a_c - \lambda_{t_2}(\boldsymbol{a})) \tag{10.105}$$

where

$$\exp_t(x) \triangleq [1 + (1 - t)x]_+^{1/(1-t)} \tag{10.106}$$

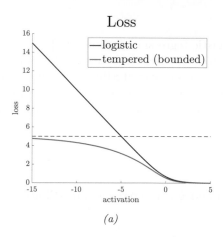
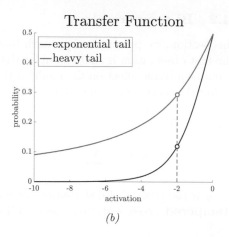

(a)   (b)

Figure 10.11: (a) Illustration of logistic and tempered logistic loss with $t_1 = 0.8$. (b) Illustration of sigmoid and tempered sigmoid transfer function with $t_2 = 2.0$. From `https://ai.googleblog.com/2019/08/bi-tempered-logistic-loss-for-training.html`. Used with kind permission of Ehsan Amid.

is a tempered version of the exponential function. (This reduces to the standard exponental function as $t \to 1$.) In Figure 10.11(right), we show that the tempered softmax (in the two-class case) has heavier tails, as desired.

All that remains is a way to compute $\lambda_{t_2}(\boldsymbol{a})$. This must satisfy the following fixed point equation:

$$\sum_{c=1}^{C} \exp_{t_2}(a_c - \lambda(\boldsymbol{a})) = 1 \tag{10.107}$$

We can solve for λ using binary search, or by using the iterative procedure in Algorithm 10.2.

Algorithm 10.2: Iterative algorithm for computing $\lambda(\boldsymbol{a})$ in Equation (10.107). From [AWS19].

---
1 Input: logits $\boldsymbol{a}$, temperature $t > 1$
2 $\mu := \max(\boldsymbol{a})$
3 $\boldsymbol{a} := \boldsymbol{a} - \mu$
4 **while** $\boldsymbol{a}$ *not converged* **do**
5 $\quad$ $Z(\boldsymbol{a}) := \sum_{c=1}^{C} \exp_t(a_c)$
6 $\quad$ $\boldsymbol{a} := Z(\boldsymbol{a})^{1-t}(\boldsymbol{a} - \mu\mathbf{1})$
7 Return $-\log_t \frac{1}{Z(\boldsymbol{a})} + \mu$

Combining the tempered softmax with the tempered cross entropy results in a method called **bi-tempered logistic regression**. In Figure 10.12, we show an example of this in 2d. The top row is standard logistic regression, the bottom row is bi-tempered. The first column is clean data. The second column has label noise near the boundary. The robust version uses $t_1 = 1$ (standard cross entropy) but $t_2 = 4$ (tempered softmax with heavy tails). The third column has label noise far

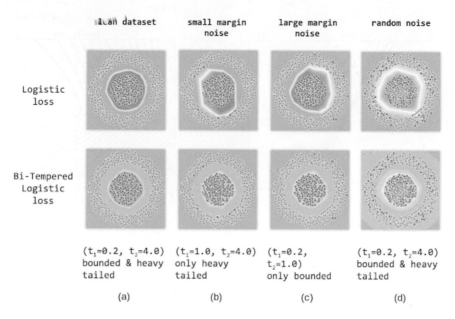

clean dataset   small margin   large margin   random noise
noise   noise

Logistic loss

Bi-Tempered Logistic loss

(t_1=0.2, t_2=4.0)   (t_1=1.0, t_2=4.0)   (t_1=0.2,   (t_1=0.2, t_2=4.0)
bounded & heavy   only heavy t_2=1.0)   bounded & heavy
tailed   tailed   only bounded   tailed

(a)   (b)   (c)   (d)

Figure 10.12: *Illustration of standard and bi-tempered logistic regression on data with label noise. From* https://ai.googleblog.com/2019/08/bi-tempered-logistic-loss-for-training.html. *Used with kind permission of Ehsan Amid.*

from the boundary. The robust version uses $t_1 = 0.2$ (tempered cross entropy with bounded loss) but $t_2 = 1$ (standard softmax). The fourth column has both kinds of noise; in this case, the robust version uses $t_1 = 0.2$ and $t_2 = 4$.

10.5 Bayesian logistic regression *

So far we have focused on point estimates of the parameters, either the MLE or the MAP estimate. However, in some cases we want to compute the posterior, $p(\boldsymbol{w}|\mathcal{D})$, in order to capture our uncertainty. This can be particularly useful in settings where we have little data, and where choosing the wrong decision may be costly.

Unlike with linear regression, it is not possible to compute the posterior exactly for a logistic regression model. A wide range of approximate algorithms can be used,. In this section, we use one of the simplest, known as the Laplace approximation (Section 4.6.8.2). See the sequel to this book, [Mur23] for more advanced approximations.

10.5.1 Laplace approximation

As we discuss in Section 4.6.8.2, the Laplace approximation approximates the posterior using a Gaussian. The mean of the Gaussian is equal to the MAP estimate $\hat{\boldsymbol{w}}$, and the covariance is equal to the inverse Hessian $\mathbf{H}$ computed at the MAP estimate, i.e., $p(\boldsymbol{w}|\mathcal{D}) \approx \mathcal{N}(\boldsymbol{w}|\hat{\boldsymbol{w}}, \mathbf{H}^{-1})$, We can find the mode using a standard optimization method (see Section 10.2.7), and then we can use the results

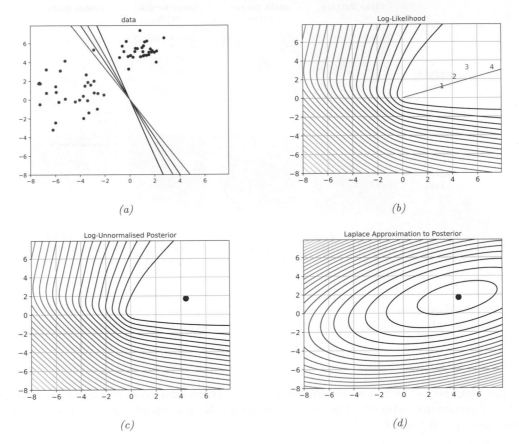

Figure 10.13: (a) Illustration of the data. (b) Log-likelihood for a logistic regression model. The line is drawn from the origin in the direction of the MLE (which is at infinity). The numbers correspond to 4 points in parameter space, corresponding to the lines in (a). (c) Unnormalized log posterior (assuming vague spherical prior). (d) Laplace approximation to posterior. Adapted from a figure by Mark Girolami. Generated by logreg_laplace_demo.ipynb.

from Section 10.2.3.4 to compute the Hessian at the mode.

As an example, consider the data illustrated in Figure 10.13(a). There are many parameter settings that correspond to lines that perfectly separate the training data; we show 4 example lines. The likelihood surface is shown in Figure 10.13(b). The diagonal line connects the origin to the point in the grid with maximum likelihood, $\hat{\boldsymbol{w}}_{\mathrm{mle}} = (8.0, 3.4)$. (The unconstrained MLE has $||\boldsymbol{w}|| = \infty$, as we discussed in Section 10.2.7; this point can be obtained by following the diagonal line infinitely far to the right.)

For each decision boundary in Figure 10.13(a), we plot the corresponding parameter vector in Figure 10.13(b). These parameters values are $\boldsymbol{w}_1 = (3, 1)$, $\boldsymbol{w}_2 = (4, 2)$, $\boldsymbol{w}_3 = (5, 3)$, and $\boldsymbol{w}_4 = (7, 3)$. These points all approximately satisfy $\boldsymbol{w}_i(1)/\boldsymbol{w}_i(2) \approx \hat{\boldsymbol{w}}_{\mathrm{mle}}(1)/\hat{\boldsymbol{w}}_{\mathrm{mle}}(2)$, and hence are close to the

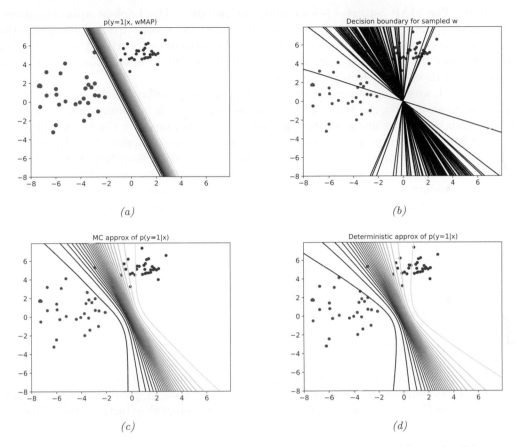

Figure 10.14: *Posterior predictive distribution for a logistic regression model in 2d. (a): contours of $p(y = 1|\boldsymbol{x}, \hat{\boldsymbol{w}}_{map})$. (b): samples from the posterior predictive distribution. (c): Averaging over these samples. (d): moderated output (probit approximation). Adapted from a figure by Mark Girolami. Generated by logreg_laplace_demo.ipynb.*

orientation of the maximum likelihood decision boundary. The points are ordered by increasing weight norm (3.16, 4.47, 5.83, and 7.62).

To ensure a unique solution, we use a (spherical) Gaussian prior centered at the origin, $\mathcal{N}(\boldsymbol{w}|\mathbf{0}, \sigma^2\mathbf{I})$. The value of σ^2 controls the strength of the prior. If we set $\sigma^2 = 0$, we force the MAP estimate to be $\boldsymbol{w} = \mathbf{0}$; this will result in maximally uncertain predictions, since all points $\boldsymbol{x}$ will produce a predictive distribution of the form $p(y = 1|\boldsymbol{x}) = 0.5$. If we set $\sigma^2 = \infty$, the prior becomes uninformative, and MAP estimate becomes the MLE, resulting in minimally uncertain predictions. (In particular, all positively labeled points will have $p(y = 1|\boldsymbol{x}) = 1.0$, and all negatively labeled points will have $p(y = 1|\boldsymbol{x}) = 0.0$, since the data is separable.) As a compromise (to make a nice illustration), we pick the value $\sigma^2 = 100$.

Multiplying this prior by the likelihood results in the unnormalized posterior shown in Figure 10.13(c). The MAP estimate is shown by the red dot. The Laplace approximation to this posterior is shown in Figure 10.13(d). We see that it gets the mode correct (by construction), but the shape of the posterior is somewhat distorted. (The southwest-northeast orientation captures uncertainty about the magnitude of w, and the southeast-northwest orientation captures uncertainty about the orientation of the decision boundary.)

In Figure 10.14, we show contours of the posterior predictive distribution. Figure 10.14(a) shows the plugin approximation using the MAP estimate. We see that there is no uncertainty about the decision boundary, even though we are generating probabilistic predictions over the labels. Figure 10.14(b) shows what happens when we plug in samples from the Gaussian posterior. Now we see that there is considerable uncertainty about the orientation of the "best" decision boundary. Figure 10.14(c) shows the average of these samples. By averaging over multiple predictions, we see that the uncertainty in the decision boundary "splays out" as we move further from the training data. Figure 10.14(d) shows that the probit approximation gives very similar results to the Monte Carlo approximation.

10.5.2   Approximating the posterior predictive

The posterior $p(w|\mathcal{D})$ tells us everything we know about the parameters of the model given the data. However, in machine learning applications, the main task of interest is usually to predict an output y given an input x, rather than to try to understand the parameters of our model. Thus we need to compute the **posterior predictive distribution**

$$p(y|x, \mathcal{D}) = \int p(y|x, w)p(w|\mathcal{D})dw \tag{10.108}$$

As we discussed in Section 4.6.7.1, a simple approach to this is to first compute a point estimate $\hat{w}$ of the parameters, such as the MLE or MAP estimate, and then to ignore all posterior uncertainty, by assuming $p(w|\mathcal{D}) = \delta(w - \hat{w})$. In this case, the above integral reduces to the following plugin approximation:

$$p(y|x, \mathcal{D}) \approx \int p(y|x, w)\delta(w - \hat{w})dw = p(y|x, \hat{w}) \tag{10.109}$$

However, if we want to compute uncertainty in our predictions, we should use a non-degenerate posterior. It is common to use a Gaussian posterior, as we will see. But we still need to approximate the integral in Equation (10.108). We discuss some approaches to this below.

10.5.2.1   Monte Carlo approximation

The simplest approach is to use a **Monte Carlo approximation** to the integral. This means we draw S samples from the posterior, $w_s \sim p(w|\mathcal{D})$. and then compute

$$p(y = 1|x, \mathcal{D}) \approx \frac{1}{S}\sum_{s=1}^{S} \sigma(w_s^\mathsf{T} x) \tag{10.110}$$

10.5.2.2   Probit approximation

Although the Monte Carlo approximation is simple, it can be slow, since we need to draw S samples *at test time* for each input x. Fortunately, if $p(w|\mathcal{D}) = \mathcal{N}(w|\mu, \Sigma)$, there is a simple yet accurate deterministic approximation, first suggested in [SL90]. To explain this approximation, we follow the presentation of [Bis06, p219]. The key observation is that the sigmoid function $\sigma(a)$ is similar in shape to the Gaussian cdf (see Section 2.6.1) $\Phi(a)$. In particular we have $\sigma(a) \approx \Phi(\lambda a)$, where $\lambda^2 = \pi/8$ ensures the two functions have the same slope at the origin. This is useful since we can integrate a Gaussian cdf wrt a Gaussian pdf exactly:

$$\int \Phi(\lambda a) \mathcal{N}(a|m, v) da = \Phi\left(\frac{m}{(\lambda^{-2} + v)^{\frac{1}{2}}}\right) = \Phi\left(\frac{\lambda m}{(1 + \lambda^2 v)^{\frac{1}{2}}}\right) \approx \sigma(\kappa(v)m) \tag{10.111}$$

where we have defined

$$\kappa(v) \triangleq (1 + \pi v/8)^{-\frac{1}{2}} \tag{10.112}$$

Thus if we define $a = \boldsymbol{x}^\mathsf{T}\boldsymbol{w}$, we have

$$p(y = 1|\boldsymbol{x}, \mathcal{D}) \approx \sigma(\kappa(v)m) \tag{10.113}$$

$$m = \mathbb{E}[a] = \boldsymbol{x}^\mathsf{T}\boldsymbol{\mu} \tag{10.114}$$

$$v = \mathbb{V}[a] = \mathbb{V}\left[\boldsymbol{x}^\mathsf{T}\boldsymbol{w}\right] = \boldsymbol{x}^\mathsf{T}\boldsymbol{\Sigma}\boldsymbol{x} \tag{10.115}$$

where we used Equation (2.165) in the last line. Since Φ is the inverse of the probit function, we will call this the **probit approximation**.

Using Equation (10.113) results in predictions that are less extreme (in terms of their confidence) than the plug-in estimate. To see this, note that $0 < \kappa(v) < 1$ and hence $\kappa(v)m < m$, so $\sigma(\kappa(v)m)$ is closer to 0.5 than $\sigma(m)$ is. However, the decision boundary itself will not be affected. To see this, note that the decision boundary is the set of points $\boldsymbol{x}$ for which $p(y = 1|\boldsymbol{x}, \mathcal{D}) = 0.5$. This implies $\kappa(v)m = 0$, which implies $m = \overline{\boldsymbol{w}}^\mathsf{T}\boldsymbol{x} = 0$; but this is the same as the decision boundary from the plugin estimate. Thus "being Bayesian" doesn't change the misclassification rate (in this case), but it does change the confidence estimates of the model, which can be important, as we illustrate in Section 10.5.1.

In the multiclass case we can use the **generalized probit approximation** [Gib97]:

$$p(y = c|\boldsymbol{x}, \mathcal{D}) \approx \frac{\exp(\kappa(v_c)m_c)}{\sum_{c'} \exp(\kappa(v_{c'})m_{c'})} \tag{10.116}$$

$$m_c = \overline{\boldsymbol{m}}_c^\mathsf{T}\boldsymbol{x} \tag{10.117}$$

$$v_c = \boldsymbol{x}^\mathsf{T}\mathbf{V}_{c,c}\boldsymbol{x} \tag{10.118}$$

where κ is defined in Equation (10.112). Unlike the binary case, taking into account posterior covariance gives different predictions than the plug-in approach (see Exercise 3.10.3 of [RW06]).

For further approximations of Gaussian integrals combined with sigmoid and softmax functions, see [Dau17].

10.6 Exercises

Exercise 10.1 [Gradient and Hessian of log-likelihood for multinomial logistic regression]

a. Let $\mu_{ik} = \mathrm{softmax}(\boldsymbol{\eta}_i)_k$, where $\boldsymbol{\eta}_i = \boldsymbol{w}^T\boldsymbol{x}_i$. Show that the Jacobian of the softmax is

$$\frac{\partial \mu_{ik}}{\partial \eta_{ij}} = \mu_{ik}(\delta_{kj} - \mu_{ij}) \tag{10.119}$$

where $\delta_{kj} = I(k = j)$.

b. Hence show that the gradient of the NLL is given by

$$\nabla_{\boldsymbol{w}_c} \ell = \sum_i (y_{ic} - \mu_{ic}) \boldsymbol{x}_i \qquad (10.120)$$

Hint: use the chain rule and the fact that $\sum_c y_{ic} = 1$.

c. Show that the block submatrix of the Hessian for classes c and c' is given by

$$\mathbf{H}_{c,c'} = -\sum_i \mu_{ic} (\delta_{c,c'} - \mu_{i,c'}) \boldsymbol{x}_i \boldsymbol{x}_i^T \qquad (10.121)$$

Hence show that the Hessian of the NLL is positive definite.

Exercise 10.2 [Regularizing separate terms in 2d logistic regression *]
(Source: Jaakkola.)

a. Consider the data in Figure 10.15a, where we fit the model $p(y = 1|\boldsymbol{x}, \boldsymbol{w}) = \sigma(w_0 + w_1 x_1 + w_2 x_2)$. Suppose we fit the model by maximum likelihood, i.e., we minimize

$$J(\boldsymbol{w}) = -\ell(\boldsymbol{w}, \mathcal{D}_{\text{train}}) \qquad (10.122)$$

where $\ell(\boldsymbol{w}, \mathcal{D}_{\text{train}})$ is the log likelihood on the training set. Sketch a possible decision boundary corresponding to $\hat{\boldsymbol{w}}$. (Copy the figure first (a rough sketch is enough), and then superimpose your answer on your copy, since you will need multiple versions of this figure). Is your answer (decision boundary) unique? How many classification errors does your method make on the training set?

b. Now suppose we regularize only the w_0 parameter, i.e., we minimize

$$J_0(\boldsymbol{w}) = -\ell(\boldsymbol{w}, \mathcal{D}_{\text{train}}) + \lambda w_0^2 \qquad (10.123)$$

Suppose λ is a very large number, so we regularize w_0 all the way to 0, but all other parameters are unregularized. Sketch a possible decision boundary. How many classification errors does your method make on the training set? Hint: consider the behavior of simple linear regression, $w_0 + w_1 x_1 + w_2 x_2$ when $x_1 = x_2 = 0$.

c. Now suppose we heavily regularize only the w_1 parameter, i.e., we minimize

$$J_1(\boldsymbol{w}) = -\ell(\boldsymbol{w}, \mathcal{D}_{\text{train}}) + \lambda w_1^2 \qquad (10.124)$$

Sketch a possible decision boundary. How many classification errors does your method make on the training set?

d. Now suppose we heavily regularize only the w_2 parameter. Sketch a possible decision boundary. How many classification errors does your method make on the training set?

Exercise 10.3 [Logistic regression vs LDA/QDA *]
(Source: Jaakkola.) Suppose we train the following binary classifiers via maximum likelihood.

a. GaussI: A generative classifier, where the class-conditional densities are Gaussian, with both covariance matrices set to $\mathbf{I}$ (identity matrix), i.e., $p(\boldsymbol{x}|y = c) = \mathcal{N}(\boldsymbol{x}|\boldsymbol{\mu}_c, \mathbf{I})$. We assume $p(y)$ is uniform.

b. GaussX: as for GaussI, but the covariance matrices are unconstrained, i.e., $p(\boldsymbol{x}|y = c) = \mathcal{N}(\boldsymbol{x}|\boldsymbol{\mu}_c, \boldsymbol{\Sigma}_c)$.

c. LinLog: A logistic regression model with linear features.

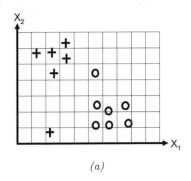

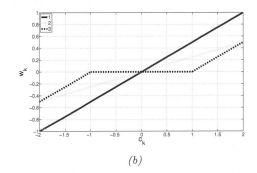

(a)   *(b)*

Figure 10.15: (a) Data for logistic regression question. (b) Plot of $\hat{w}_k$ vs amount of correlation c_k for three different estimators.

d. QuadLog: A logistic regression model, using linear and quadratic features (i.e., polynomial basis function expansion of degree 2).

After training we compute the performance of each model M on the training set as follows:

$$L(M) = \frac{1}{n} \sum_{i=1}^{n} \log p(y_i | \boldsymbol{x}_i, \hat{\boldsymbol{\theta}}, M) \tag{10.125}$$

(Note that this is the *conditional* log-likelihood $p(y|\boldsymbol{x}, \hat{\boldsymbol{\theta}})$ and not the joint log-likelihood $p(y, \boldsymbol{x}|\hat{\boldsymbol{\theta}})$.) We now want to compare the performance of each model. We will write $L(M) \leq L(M')$ if model M *must* have lower (or equal) log likelihood (on the training set) than M', for any training set (in other words, M is worse than M', at least as far as training set logprob is concerned). For each of the following model pairs, state whether $L(M) \leq L(M')$, $L(M) \geq L(M')$, or whether no such statement can be made (i.e., M might sometimes be better than M' and sometimes worse); also, for each question, briefly (1-2 sentences) explain why.

a. GaussI, LinLog.

b. GaussX, QuadLog.

c. LinLog, QuadLog.

d. GaussI, QuadLog.

e. Now suppose we measure performance in terms of the average misclassification rate on the training set:

$$R(M) = \frac{1}{n} \sum_{i=1}^{n} I(y_i \neq \hat{y}(\boldsymbol{x}_i)) \tag{10.126}$$

Is it true in general that $L(M) > L(M')$ implies that $R(M) < R(M')$? Explain why or why not.

11 Linear Regression

11.1 Introduction

In this chapter, we discuss **linear regression**, which is a very widely used method for predicting a real-valued output (also called the **dependent variable** or **target**) $y \in \mathbb{R}$, given a vector of real-valued inputs (also called **independent variables**, **explanatory variables**, or **covariates**) $\boldsymbol{x} \in \mathbb{R}^D$. The key property of the model is that the expected value of the output is assumed to be a linear function of the input, $\mathbb{E}[y|\boldsymbol{x}] = \boldsymbol{w}^\mathsf{T}\boldsymbol{x}$, which makes the model easy to interpret, and easy to fit to data. We discuss nonlinear extensions later in this book.

11.2 Least squares linear regression

In this section, we discuss the most common form of linear regression model.

11.2.1 Terminology

The term "linear regression" usually refers to a model of the following form:

$$p(y|\boldsymbol{x},\boldsymbol{\theta}) = \mathcal{N}(y|w_0 + \boldsymbol{w}^\mathsf{T}\boldsymbol{x}, \sigma^2) \tag{11.1}$$

where $\boldsymbol{\theta} = (w_0, \boldsymbol{w}, \sigma^2)$ are all the parameters of the model. (In statistics, the parameters w_0 and $\boldsymbol{w}$ are usually denoted by β_0 and $\boldsymbol{\beta}$.)

The vector of parameters $\boldsymbol{w}_{1:D}$ are known as the **weights** or **regression coefficients**. Each coefficient w_d specifies the change in the output we expect if we change the corresponding input feature x_d by one unit. For example, suppose x_1 is the age of a person, x_2 is their education level (represented as a continuous number), and y is their income. Thus w_1 corresponds to the increase in income we expect as someone becomes one year older (and hence get more experience), and w_2 corresponds to the increase in income we expect as someone's education level increases by one level. The term w_0 is the **offset** or **bias** term, and specifies the output value if all the inputs are 0. This captures the unconditional mean of the response, $w_0 = \mathbb{E}[y]$, and acts as a baseline. We will usually assume that $\boldsymbol{x}$ is written as $[1, x_1, \ldots, x_D]$, so we can absorb the offset term w_0 into the weight vector $\boldsymbol{w}$.

If the input is one-dimensional (so $D = 1$), the model has the form $f(\boldsymbol{x}; \boldsymbol{w}) = ax + b$, where $b = w_0$ is the intercept, and $a = w_1$ is the slope. This is called **simple linear regression**. If the input is multi-dimensional, $\boldsymbol{x} \in \mathbb{R}^D$ where $D > 1$, the method is called **multiple linear regression**. If the

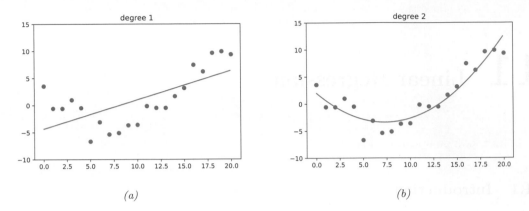

Figure 11.1: Polynomial of degrees 1 and 2 fit to 21 datapoints. Generated by linreg_poly_vs_degree.ipynb.

output is also multi-dimensional, $\boldsymbol{y} \in \mathbb{R}^J$, where $J > 1$, it is called **multivariate linear regression**,

$$p(\boldsymbol{y}|\boldsymbol{x}, \mathbf{W}) = \prod_{j=1}^{J} \mathcal{N}(y_j | \boldsymbol{w}_j^\mathsf{T} \boldsymbol{x}, \sigma_j^2) \tag{11.2}$$

See Exercise 11.1 for a simple numerical example.

In general, a straight line will not provide a good fit to most data sets. However, we can always apply a nonlinear transformation to the input features, by replacing $\boldsymbol{x}$ with $\boldsymbol{\phi}(\boldsymbol{x})$ to get

$$p(y|\boldsymbol{x}, \boldsymbol{\theta}) = \mathcal{N}(y | \boldsymbol{w}^\mathsf{T} \boldsymbol{\phi}(\boldsymbol{x}), \sigma^2) \tag{11.3}$$

As long as the parameters of the **feature extractor** $\boldsymbol{\phi}$ are fixed, the model remains *linear in the parameters*, even if it is not linear in the inputs. (We discuss ways to learn the feature extractor, and the final linear mapping, in Part III.)

As a simple example of a nonlinear transformation, consider the case of **polynomial regression**, which we introduced in Section 1.2.2.2. If the input is 1d, and we use a polynomial expansion of degree d, we get $\boldsymbol{\phi}(x) = [1, x, x^2, \ldots, x^d]$. See Figure 11.1 for an example. (See also Section 11.5 where we discuss splines.)

11.2.2   Least squares estimation

To fit a linear regression model to data, we will minimize the negative log likelihood on the training set. The objective function is given by

$$\mathrm{NLL}(\boldsymbol{w}, \sigma^2) = -\sum_{n=1}^{N} \log\left[\left(\frac{1}{2\pi\sigma^2}\right)^{\frac{1}{2}} \exp\left(-\frac{1}{2\sigma^2}(y_n - \boldsymbol{w}^\mathsf{T}\boldsymbol{x}_n)^2\right) \right] \tag{11.4}$$

$$= \frac{1}{2\sigma^2}\sum_{n=1}^{N}(y_n - \hat{y}_n)^2 + \frac{N}{2}\log(2\pi\sigma^2) \tag{11.5}$$

where we have defined the predicted response $\hat{y}_n \triangleq \boldsymbol{w}^\mathsf{T}\boldsymbol{x}_n$. The MLE is the point where $\nabla_{\boldsymbol{w},\sigma}\mathrm{NLL}(\boldsymbol{w},\sigma^2) = \boldsymbol{0}$. We can first optimize wrt $\boldsymbol{w}$, and then solve for the optimal σ.

In this section, we just focus on estimating the weights $\boldsymbol{w}$. In this case, the NLL is equal (up to irrelevant constants) to the **residual sum of squares**, which is given by

$$\mathrm{RSS}(\boldsymbol{w}) = \frac{1}{2}\sum_{n=1}^{N}(y_n - \boldsymbol{w}^\mathsf{T}\boldsymbol{x}_n)^2 = \frac{1}{2}||\mathbf{X}\boldsymbol{w} - \boldsymbol{y}||_2^2 = \frac{1}{2}(\mathbf{X}\boldsymbol{w} - \boldsymbol{y})^\mathsf{T}(\mathbf{X}\boldsymbol{w} - \boldsymbol{y}) \tag{11.6}$$

We discuss how to optimize this below.

11.2.2.1 Ordinary least squares

From Equation (7.264) we can show that the gradient is given by

$$\nabla_{\boldsymbol{w}}\mathrm{RSS}(\boldsymbol{w}) = \mathbf{X}^\mathsf{T}\mathbf{X}\boldsymbol{w} - \mathbf{X}^\mathsf{T}\boldsymbol{y} \tag{11.7}$$

Setting the gradient to zero and solving gives

$$\mathbf{X}^\mathsf{T}\mathbf{X}\boldsymbol{w} = \mathbf{X}^\mathsf{T}\boldsymbol{y} \tag{11.8}$$

These are known as the **normal equations**, since, at the optimal solution, $\boldsymbol{y} - \mathbf{X}\boldsymbol{w}$ is normal (orthogonal) to the range of $\mathbf{X}$, as we explain in Section 11.2.2.2. The corresponding solution $\hat{\boldsymbol{w}}$ is the **ordinary least squares (OLS)** solution, which is given by

$$\hat{\boldsymbol{w}} = (\mathbf{X}^\mathsf{T}\mathbf{X})^{-1}\mathbf{X}^\mathsf{T}\boldsymbol{y} \tag{11.9}$$

The quantity $\mathbf{X}^\dagger = (\mathbf{X}^\mathsf{T}\mathbf{X})^{-1}\mathbf{X}^\mathsf{T}$ is the (left) pseudo inverse of the (non-square) matrix $\mathbf{X}$ (see Section 7.5.3 for more details).

We can check that the solution is unique by showing that the Hessian is positive definite. In this case, the Hessian is given by

$$\mathbf{H}(\boldsymbol{w}) = \frac{\partial^2}{\partial \boldsymbol{w}^2}\mathrm{RSS}(\boldsymbol{w}) = \mathbf{X}^\mathsf{T}\mathbf{X} \tag{11.10}$$

If $\mathbf{X}$ is full rank (so the columns of $\mathbf{X}$ are linearly independent), then $\mathbf{H}$ is positive definite, since for any $\boldsymbol{v} > \boldsymbol{0}$, we have

$$\boldsymbol{v}^\mathsf{T}(\mathbf{X}^\mathsf{T}\mathbf{X})\boldsymbol{v} = (\mathbf{X}\boldsymbol{v})^\mathsf{T}(\mathbf{X}\boldsymbol{v}) = ||\mathbf{X}\boldsymbol{v}||^2 > 0 \tag{11.11}$$

Hence in the full rank case, the least squares objective has a unique global minimum. See Figure 11.2 for an illustration.

11.2.2.2 Geometric interpretation of least squares

The normal equations have an elegant geometrical interpretation, deriving from Section 7.7, as we now explain. We will assume $N > D$, so there are more observations than unknowns. (This is known

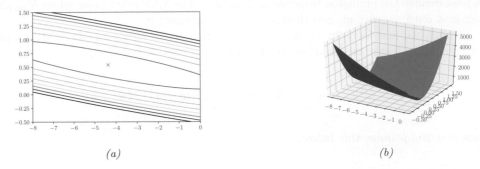

(a)   (b)

Figure 11.2: (a) Contours of the RSS error surface for the example in Figure 11.1a. The blue cross represents the MLE. (b) Corresponding surface plot. Generated by linreg_contours_sse_plot.ipynb.

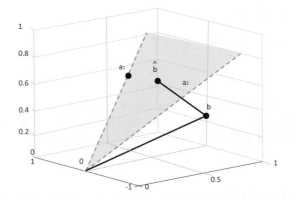

Figure 11.3: Graphical interpretation of least squares for $m = 3$ equations and $n = 2$ unknowns when solving the system $\mathbf{A}x = b$. a_1 and a_2 are the columns of $\mathbf{A}$, which define a 2d linear subspace embedded in $\mathbb{R}^3$. The target vector b is a vector in $\mathbb{R}^3$; its orthogonal projection onto the linear subspace is denoted $\hat{b}$. The line from b to $\hat{b}$ is the vector of residual errors, whose norm we want to minimize.

as an **overdetermined system**.) We seek a vector $\hat{y} \in \mathbb{R}^N$ that lies in the linear subspace spanned by $\mathbf{X}$ and is as close as possible to y, i.e., we want to find

$$\underset{\hat{y} \in \text{span}(\{x_{:,1}, \dots, x_{:,d}\})}{\text{argmin}} \|y - \hat{y}\|_2. \tag{11.12}$$

where $x_{:,d}$ is the d'th column of $\mathbf{X}$. Since $\hat{y} \in \text{span}(\mathbf{X})$, there exists some weight vector w such that

$$\hat{y} = w_1 x_{:,1} + \dots + w_D x_{:,D} = \mathbf{X}w \tag{11.13}$$

To minimize the norm of the residual, $y - \hat{y}$, we want the residual vector to be orthogonal to every column of $\mathbf{X}$. Hence

$$x_{:,d}^\mathsf{T}(y - \hat{y}) = 0 \Rightarrow \mathbf{X}^\mathsf{T}(y - \mathbf{X}w) = 0 \Rightarrow w = (\mathbf{X}^\mathsf{T}\mathbf{X})^{-1}\mathbf{X}^\mathsf{T}y \tag{11.14}$$

Hence our projected value of $\boldsymbol{y}$ is given by

$$\hat{\boldsymbol{y}} = \mathbf{X}\boldsymbol{w} = \mathbf{X}(\mathbf{X}^\mathsf{T}\mathbf{X})^{-1}\mathbf{X}^\mathsf{T}\boldsymbol{y} \tag{11.15}$$

This corresponds to an **orthogonal projection** of $\boldsymbol{y}$ onto the column space of $\mathbf{X}$. For example, consider the case where we have $N = 3$ training examples, each of dimensionality $D = 2$. The training data defines a 2d linear subspace, defined by the 2 columns of $\mathbf{X}$, each of which is a point in 3d. We project $\boldsymbol{y}$, which is also a point in 3d, onto this 2d subspace, as shown in Figure 11.3.

The **projection matrix**

$$\mathrm{Proj}(\mathbf{X}) \triangleq \mathbf{X}(\mathbf{X}^\mathsf{T}\mathbf{X})^{-1}\mathbf{X}^\mathsf{T} \tag{11.16}$$

is sometimes called the **hat matrix**, since $\hat{\boldsymbol{y}} = \mathrm{Proj}(\mathbf{X})\boldsymbol{y}$. In the special case that $\mathbf{X} = \boldsymbol{x}$ is a column vector, the orthogonal projection of $\boldsymbol{y}$ onto the line $\boldsymbol{x}$ becomes

$$\mathrm{Proj}(\boldsymbol{x})\boldsymbol{y} = \boldsymbol{x}\,\frac{\boldsymbol{x}^\mathsf{T}\boldsymbol{y}}{\boldsymbol{x}^\mathsf{T}\boldsymbol{x}} \tag{11.17}$$

11.2.2.3 Algorithmic issues

Recall that the OLS solution is

$$\hat{\boldsymbol{w}} = \mathbf{X}^\dagger \boldsymbol{y} = (\mathbf{X}^\mathsf{T}\mathbf{X})^{-1}\mathbf{X}^\mathsf{T}\boldsymbol{y} \tag{11.18}$$

However, even if it is theoretically possible to compute the pseudo-inverse by inverting $\mathbf{X}^\mathsf{T}\mathbf{X}$, we should not do so for numerical reasons, since $\mathbf{X}^\mathsf{T}\mathbf{X}$ may be ill conditioned or singular.

A better (and more general) approach is to compute the pseudo-inverse using the SVD. Indeed, if you look at the source code for the function sklearn.linear_model.fit, you will see that it uses the scipy.linalg.lstsq function, which in turns calls DGELSD, which is an SVD-based solver implemented by the LAPACK library, written in Fortran.[1]

However, if $\mathbf{X}$ is tall and skinny (i.e., $N \gg D$), it can be quicker to use QR decomposition (Section 7.6.2). To do this, let $\mathbf{X} = \mathbf{QR}$, where $\mathbf{Q}^\mathsf{T}\mathbf{Q} = \mathbf{I}$. In Section 7.7, we show that OLS is equivalent to solving the system of linear equations $\mathbf{X}\boldsymbol{w} = \boldsymbol{y}$ in a way that minimizes $||\mathbf{X}\boldsymbol{w} - \boldsymbol{y}||_2^2$. (If $N = D$ and $\mathbf{X}$ is full rank, the equations have a unique solution, and the error will be 0.) Using QR decomposition, we can rewrite this system of equations as follows:

$$(\mathbf{QR})\boldsymbol{w} = \boldsymbol{y} \tag{11.19}$$

$$\mathbf{Q}^\mathsf{T}\mathbf{QR}\boldsymbol{w} = \mathbf{Q}^\mathsf{T}\boldsymbol{y} \tag{11.20}$$

$$\boldsymbol{w} = \mathbf{R}^{-1}(\mathbf{Q}^\mathsf{T}\boldsymbol{y}) \tag{11.21}$$

Since $\mathbf{R}$ is upper triangular, we can solve this last set of equations using backsubstitution, thus avoiding matrix inversion. See linsys_solve_demo.ipynb for a demo.

An alternative to the use of direct methods based on matrix decomposition (such as SVD and QR) is to use iterative solvers, such as the **conjugate gradient** method (which assumes $\mathbf{X}$ is symmetric

---

1. Note that a lot of the "Python" scientific computing stack sits on top of source code that is written in Fortran or C++, for reasons of speed. This makes it hard to change the underlying algorithms. By contrast, the scientific computing libraries in the Julia language are written in Julia itself, aiding clarity without sacrificing speed.

positive definite), and the **GMRES** (generalized minimal residual method), that works for general **X**. (In SciPy, this is implemented by `sparse.linalg.gmres`.) These methods just require the ability to perform matrix-vector multiplications (i.e., an implementation of a **linear operator**), and thus are well-suited to problems where **X** is sparse or structured. For details, see e.g., [TB97].

A final important issue is that it is usually essential to **standardize** the input features before fitting the model, to ensure that they are zero mean and unit variance. We can do this using Equation (10.51).

11.2.2.4   Weighted least squares

In some cases, we want to associate a weight with each example. For example, in **heteroskedastic regression**, the variance depends on the input, so the model has the form

$$p(y|\boldsymbol{x};\boldsymbol{\theta}) = \mathcal{N}(y|\boldsymbol{w}^\mathsf{T}\boldsymbol{x}, \sigma^2(\boldsymbol{x})) = \frac{1}{\sqrt{2\pi\sigma^2(\boldsymbol{x})}} \exp\left(-\frac{1}{2\sigma^2(\boldsymbol{x})}(y - \boldsymbol{w}^\mathsf{T}\boldsymbol{x})^2\right) \tag{11.22}$$

Thus

$$p(\boldsymbol{y}|\boldsymbol{x};\boldsymbol{\theta}) = \mathcal{N}(\boldsymbol{y}|\mathbf{X}\boldsymbol{w}, \boldsymbol{\Lambda}^{-1}) \tag{11.23}$$

where $\boldsymbol{\Lambda} = \operatorname{diag}(1/\sigma^2(\boldsymbol{x}_n))$. This is known as **weighted linear regression**. One can show that the MLE is given by

$$\hat{\boldsymbol{w}} = (\mathbf{X}^\mathsf{T}\boldsymbol{\Lambda}\mathbf{X})^{-1}\mathbf{X}^\mathsf{T}\boldsymbol{\Lambda}\boldsymbol{y} \tag{11.24}$$

This is known as the **weighted least squares** estimate.

11.2.3   Other approaches to computing the MLE

In this section, we discuss other approaches for computing the MLE.

11.2.3.1   Solving for offset and slope separately

Typically we use a model of the form $p(y|\boldsymbol{x},\boldsymbol{\theta}) = \mathcal{N}(y|w_0 + \boldsymbol{w}^\mathsf{T}\boldsymbol{x}, \sigma^2)$, where w_0 is an offset or "bias" term. We can compute $(w_0, \boldsymbol{w})$ at the same time by adding a column of 1s to **X**, and the computing the MLE as above. Alternatively, we can solve for $\boldsymbol{w}$ and w_0 separately. (This will be useful later.) In particular, one can show that

$$\hat{\boldsymbol{w}} = (\mathbf{X}_c^\mathsf{T}\mathbf{X}_c)^{-1}\mathbf{X}_c^\mathsf{T}\boldsymbol{y}_c = \left[\sum_{i=1}^N (\boldsymbol{x}_n - \overline{\boldsymbol{x}})(\boldsymbol{x}_n - \overline{\boldsymbol{x}})^\mathsf{T}\right]^{-1}\left[\sum_{i=1}^N (y_n - \overline{y})(\boldsymbol{x}_n - \overline{\boldsymbol{x}})\right] \tag{11.25}$$

$$\hat{w}_0 = \frac{1}{N}\sum_n y_n - \frac{1}{N}\sum_n \boldsymbol{x}_n^\mathsf{T}\hat{\boldsymbol{w}} = \overline{y} - \overline{\boldsymbol{x}}^\mathsf{T}\hat{\boldsymbol{w}} \tag{11.26}$$

where $\mathbf{X}_c$ is the centered input matrix containing $\boldsymbol{x}_n^c = \boldsymbol{x}_n - \overline{\boldsymbol{x}}$ along its rows, and $\boldsymbol{y}_c = \boldsymbol{y} - \overline{y}$ is the centered output vector. Thus we can first compute $\hat{\boldsymbol{w}}$ on centered data, and then estimate w_0 using $\overline{y} - \overline{\boldsymbol{x}}^\mathsf{T}\hat{\boldsymbol{w}}$.

11.2.3.2 Simple linear regression (1d inputs)

In the case of 1d (scalar) inputs, the results from Section 11.2.3.1 reduce to the following simple form, which may be familiar from basic statistics classes:

$$\hat{w}_1 = \frac{\sum_n (x_n - \bar{x})(y_n - \bar{y})}{\sum_n (x_n - \bar{x})^2} = \frac{C_{xy}}{C_{xx}} \tag{11.27}$$

$$\hat{w}_0 = s\mathbb{E}[y] - w_1\mathbb{E}[x] \approx \bar{y} - \hat{w}_1\bar{x} \tag{11.28}$$

where $C_{xy} = \text{Cov}[X,Y]$ and $C_{xx} = \text{Cov}[X,X] = \mathbb{V}[X]$. We will use this result below.

11.2.3.3 Partial regression

From Equation (11.27), we can compute the **regression coefficient** of Y on X as follows:

$$R_{YX} \triangleq \frac{\partial}{\partial x}\mathbb{E}[Y|X=x] = w_1 = \frac{C_{xy}}{C_{xx}} \tag{11.29}$$

This is the slope of the linear prediction for Y given X.

Now consider the case where we have 2 inputs, so $Y = w_0 + w_1 X_1 + w_2 X_2 + \epsilon$, where $\mathbb{E}[\epsilon] = 0$. One can show that the optimal regression coefficient for w_1 is given by $R_{YX_1 \cdot X_2}$, which is the **partial regression coefficient** of Y on X_1, keeping X_2 constant:

$$w_1 = R_{YX_1 \cdot X_2} = \frac{\partial}{\partial x}\mathbb{E}[Y|X_1=x, X_2] \tag{11.30}$$

Note that this quantity is invariant to the specific value of X_2 we condition on.

We can derive w_2 in a similar manner. Indeed, we can extend this to multiple input variables. In each case, we find the optimal coefficients are equal to the partial regression coefficients. This means that we can interpret the j'th coefficient $\hat{w}_j$ as the change in output y we expect per unit change in input x_j, keeping all the other inputs constant.

11.2.3.4 Recursively computing the MLE

OLS is a batch method for computing the MLE. In some applications, the data arrives in a continual stream, so we want to compute the estimate online, or **recursively**, as we discussed in Section 4.4.2. In this section, we show how to do this for the case of simple (1d) linear regession.

Recall from Section 11.2.3.2 that the batch MLE for simple linear regression is given by

$$\hat{w}_1 = \frac{\sum_n (x_n - \bar{x})(y_n - \bar{y})}{\sum_n (x_n - \bar{x})^2} = \frac{C_{xy}}{C_{xx}} \tag{11.31}$$

$$\hat{w}_0 = \bar{y} - \hat{w}_1\bar{x} \tag{11.32}$$

where $C_{xy} = \text{Cov}[X,Y]$ and $C_{xx} = \text{Cov}[X,X] = \mathbb{V}[X]$.

We now discuss how to compute these results in a recursive fashion. To do this, let us define the following sufficient statistics:

$$\overline{x}^{(n)} = \frac{1}{n}\sum_{i=1}^{n}x_i, \quad \overline{y}^{(n)} = \frac{1}{n}\sum_{i=1}^{n}y_i \tag{11.33}$$

$$C_{xx}^{(n)} = \frac{1}{n}\sum_{i=1}^{n}(x_i - \overline{x})^2, \quad C_{xy}^{(n)} = \frac{1}{n}\sum_{i=1}^{n}(x_i - \overline{x})(y_i - \overline{y}), \quad C_{yy}^{(n)} = \frac{1}{n}\sum_{i=1}^{n}(y_i - \overline{y})^2 \tag{11.34}$$

We can update the means online using

$$\overline{x}^{(n+1)} = \overline{x}^{(n)} + \frac{1}{n+1}(x_{n+1} - \overline{x}^{(n)}), \quad \overline{y}^{(n+1)} = \overline{y}^{(n)} + \frac{1}{n+1}(y_{n+1} - \overline{y}^{(n)}) \tag{11.35}$$

To update the covariance terms, let us first rewrite $C_{xy}^{(n)}$ as follows:

$$C_{xy}^{(n)} = \frac{1}{n}\left[(\sum_{i=1}^{n}x_iy_i) + (\sum_{i=1}^{n}\overline{x}^{(n)}\overline{y}^{(n)}) - \overline{x}^{(n)}(\sum_{i=1}^{n}y_i) - \overline{y}^{(n)}(\sum_{i=1}^{n}x_i)\right] \tag{11.36}$$

$$= \frac{1}{n}\left[(\sum_{i=1}^{n}x_iy_i) + n\overline{x}^{(n)}\overline{y}^{(n)} - \overline{x}^{(n)}n\overline{y}^{(n)} - \overline{y}^{(n)}n\overline{x}^{(n)}\right] \tag{11.37}$$

$$= \frac{1}{n}\left[(\sum_{i=1}^{n}x_iy_i) - n\overline{x}^{(n)}\overline{y}^{(n)}\right] \tag{11.38}$$

Hence

$$\sum_{i=1}^{n}x_iy_i = nC_{xy}^{(n)} + n\overline{x}^{(n)}\overline{y}^{(n)} \tag{11.39}$$

and so

$$C_{xy}^{(n+1)} = \frac{1}{n+1}\left[x_{n+1}y_{n+1} + nC_{xy}^{(n)} + n\overline{x}^{(n)}\overline{y}^{(n)} - (n+1)\overline{x}^{(n+1)}\overline{y}^{(n+1)}\right] \tag{11.40}$$

We can derive the update for $C_{xx}^{(n+1)}$ in a similar manner.

See Figure 11.4 for a simple illustration of these equations in action for a 1d regression model.

To extend the above analysis to D-dimensional inputs, the easiest approach is to use SGD. The resulting algorithm is called the **least mean squares** algorithm; see Section 8.4.2 for details.

11.2.3.5   Deriving the MLE from a generative perspective

Linear regression is a discriminative model of the form $p(y|\boldsymbol{x})$. However, we can also use generative models for regression, by analogy to how we use generative models for classification in Chapter 9, The goal is to compute the conditional expectation

$$f(\boldsymbol{x}) = \mathbb{E}\left[y|\boldsymbol{x}\right] = \int y\, p(y|\boldsymbol{x})dy = \frac{\int y\, p(\boldsymbol{x},y)dy}{\int p(\boldsymbol{x},y)dy} \tag{11.41}$$

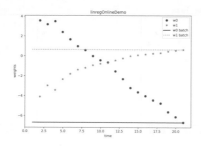

Figure 11.4: Regression coefficients over time for the 1d model in Figure 1.7a(a). Generated by linregOnlineDemo.ipynb.

Suppose we fit $p(\boldsymbol{x}, y)$ using an MVN. The MLEs for the parameters of the joint distribution are the empiricial means and covariances (see Section 4.2.6 for a proof of this result):

$$\boldsymbol{\mu}_x = \frac{1}{N} \sum_n \boldsymbol{x}_n \tag{11.42}$$

$$\mu_y = \frac{1}{N} \sum_n y_n \tag{11.43}$$

$$\boldsymbol{\Sigma}_{xx} = \frac{1}{N} \sum_n (\boldsymbol{x}_n - \overline{\boldsymbol{x}})(\boldsymbol{x}_n - \overline{\boldsymbol{x}})^\mathsf{T} = \frac{1}{N} \mathbf{X}_c^\mathsf{T} \mathbf{X}_c \tag{11.44}$$

$$\boldsymbol{\Sigma}_{xy} = \frac{1}{N} \sum_n (\boldsymbol{x}_n - \overline{\boldsymbol{x}})(y_n - \overline{y}) = \frac{1}{N} \mathbf{X}_c^\mathsf{T} \boldsymbol{y}_c \tag{11.45}$$

Hence from Equation (3.28), we have

$$\mathbb{E}\left[y|\boldsymbol{x}\right] = \mu_y + \boldsymbol{\Sigma}_{xy}^\mathsf{T} \boldsymbol{\Sigma}_{xx}^{-1} (\boldsymbol{x} - \boldsymbol{\mu}_x) \tag{11.46}$$

We can rewrite this as $\mathbb{E}\left[y|\boldsymbol{x}\right] = w_0 + \boldsymbol{w}^\mathsf{T} \boldsymbol{x}$ by defining

$$w_0 = \mu_y - \boldsymbol{w}^\mathsf{T} \boldsymbol{\mu}_x = \overline{y} - \boldsymbol{w}^\mathsf{T} \overline{\boldsymbol{x}} \tag{11.47}$$

$$\boldsymbol{w} = \boldsymbol{\Sigma}_{xx}^{-1} \boldsymbol{\Sigma}_{xy} = \left(\mathbf{X}_c^\mathsf{T} \mathbf{X}_c\right)^{-1} \mathbf{X}_c^\mathsf{T} \boldsymbol{y}_c \tag{11.48}$$

This matches the MLEs for the discriminative model as we showed in Section 11.2.3.1. Thus we see that fitting the joint model, and then conditioning it, yields the same result as fitting the conditional model. However, this is only true for Gaussian models (see Section 9.4 for further discussion of this point).

11.2.3.6 Deriving the MLE for σ^2

After estimating $\hat{\boldsymbol{w}}_{\text{mle}}$ using one of the above methods, we can estimate the noise variance. It is easy to show that the MLE is given by

$$\hat{\sigma}_{\text{mle}}^2 = \underset{\sigma^2}{\operatorname{argmin}} \operatorname{NLL}(\hat{\boldsymbol{w}}, \sigma^2) = \frac{1}{N} \sum_{n=1}^{N} (y_n - \boldsymbol{x}_n^\mathsf{T} \hat{\boldsymbol{w}})^2 \tag{11.49}$$

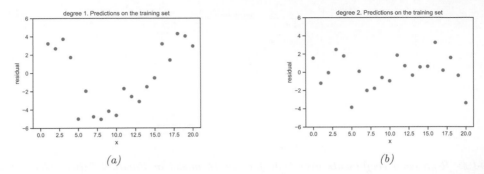

Figure 11.5: *Residual plot for polynomial regression of degree 1 and 2 for the functions in Figure 1.7a(a-b). Generated by* linreg_poly_vs_degree.ipynb.

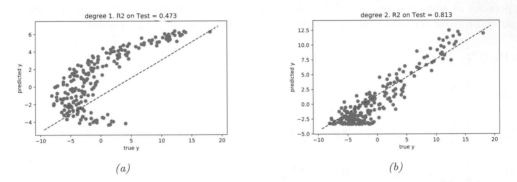

Figure 11.6: *Fit vs actual plots for polynomial regression of degree 1 and 2 for the functions in Figure 1.7a(a-b). Generated by* linreg_poly_vs_degree.ipynb.

This is just the MSE of the residuals, which is an intuitive result.

11.2.4   Measuring goodness of fit

In this section, we discuss some simple ways to assess how well a regression model fits the data (which is known as **goodness of fit**).

11.2.4.1   Residual plots

For 1d inputs, we can check the reasonableness of the model by plotting the residuals, $r_n = y_n - \hat{y}_n$, vs the input x_n. This is called a **residual plot**. The model assumes that the residuals have a $\mathcal{N}(0, \sigma^2)$ distribution, so the residual plot should be a cloud of points more or less equally above and below the horizontal line at 0, without any obvious trends.

As an example, in Figure 11.5(a), we plot the residuals for the linear model in Figure 1.7a(a). We see that there is some curved structure to the residuals, indicating a lack of fit. In Figure 11.5(b), we plot the residuals for the quadratic model in Figure 1.7a(b). We see a much better fit.

To extend this approach to multi-dimensional inputs, we can plot predictions $\hat{y}_n$ vs the true output y_n, rather than plotting vs x_n. A good model will have points that lie on a diagonal line. See Figure 11.6 for some examples.

11.2.4.2 Prediction accuracy and R^2

We can assess the fit quantitatively by computing the RSS (residual sum of squares) on the dataset: $\text{RSS}(\boldsymbol{w}) = \sum_{n=1}^{N}(y_n - \boldsymbol{w}^\mathsf{T}\boldsymbol{x}_n)^2$. A model with lower RSS fits the data better. Another measure that is used is **root mean squared error** or **RMSE**:

$$\text{RMSE}(\boldsymbol{w}) \triangleq \sqrt{\frac{1}{N}\text{RSS}(\boldsymbol{w})} \tag{11.50}$$

A more interpretable measure can be computed using the **coefficient of determination**, denoted by R^2:

$$R^2 \triangleq 1 - \frac{\sum_{n=1}^{N}(\hat{y}_n - y_n)^2}{\sum_{n=1}^{N}(\bar{y} - y_n)^2} = 1 - \frac{\text{RSS}}{\text{TSS}} \tag{11.51}$$

where $\bar{y} = \frac{1}{N}\sum_{n=1}^{N}y_n$ is the empirical mean of the response, $\text{RSS} = \sum_{n=1}^{N}(y_n - \hat{y}_n)^2$ is the residual sum of squares, and $\text{TSS} = \sum_{n=1}^{N}(y_n - \bar{y})^2$ is the total sum of squares. Thus we see that R^2 measures the variance in the predictions relative to a simple constant prediction of $\hat{y}_n = \bar{y}$. One can show that $0 \leq R^2 \leq 1$, where larger values imply a greater reduction in variance (better fit). This is illustrated in Figure 11.6.

11.3 Ridge regression

Maximum likelihood estimation can result in overfitting, as we discussed in Section 1.2.2.2. A simple solution to this is to use MAP estimation with a zero-mean Gaussian prior on the weights, $p(\boldsymbol{w}) = \mathcal{N}(\boldsymbol{w}|\boldsymbol{0}, \lambda^{-1}\mathbf{I})$, as we discused in Section 4.5.3. This is called **ridge regression**.

In more detail, we compute the MAP estimate as follows:

$$\hat{\boldsymbol{w}}_{\text{map}} = \text{argmin}\, \frac{1}{2\sigma^2}(\boldsymbol{y} - \mathbf{X}\boldsymbol{w})^\mathsf{T}(\boldsymbol{y} - \mathbf{X}\boldsymbol{w}) + \frac{1}{2\tau^2}\boldsymbol{w}^\mathsf{T}\boldsymbol{w} \tag{11.52}$$

$$= \text{argmin}\, \text{RSS}(\boldsymbol{w}) + \lambda||\boldsymbol{w}||_2^2 \tag{11.53}$$

where $\lambda \triangleq \frac{\sigma^2}{\tau^2}$ is proportional to the strength of the prior, and

$$||\boldsymbol{w}||_2 \triangleq \sqrt{\sum_{d=1}^{D}|w_d|^2} = \sqrt{\boldsymbol{w}^\mathsf{T}\boldsymbol{w}} \tag{11.54}$$

is the ℓ_2 norm of the vector $\boldsymbol{w}$. Thus we are penalizing weights that become too large in magnitude. In general, this technique is called ℓ_2 **regularization** or **weight decay**, and is very widely used. See Figure 4.5 for an illustration.

Note that we do not penalize the offset term w_0, since that only affects the global mean of the output, and does not contribute to overfitting. See Exercise 11.2.

11.3.1 Computing the MAP estimate

In this section, we discuss algorithms for computing the MAP estimate.

The MAP estimate corresponds to minimizing the following penalized objective:

$$J(\boldsymbol{w}) = (\boldsymbol{y} - \mathbf{X}\boldsymbol{w})^{\mathsf{T}}(\boldsymbol{y} - \mathbf{X}\boldsymbol{w}) + \lambda\|\boldsymbol{w}\|_2^2 \tag{11.55}$$

where $\lambda = \sigma^2/\tau^2$ is the strength of the regularizer. The derivative is given by

$$\nabla_{\boldsymbol{w}} J(\boldsymbol{w}) = 2\left(\mathbf{X}^{\mathsf{T}}\mathbf{X}\boldsymbol{w} - \mathbf{X}^{\mathsf{T}}\boldsymbol{y} + \lambda\boldsymbol{w}\right) \tag{11.56}$$

and hence

$$\hat{\boldsymbol{w}}_{\text{map}} = (\mathbf{X}^{\mathsf{T}}\mathbf{X} + \lambda\mathbf{I}_D)^{-1}\mathbf{X}^{\mathsf{T}}\boldsymbol{y} = \left(\sum_n \boldsymbol{x}_n\boldsymbol{x}_n^{\mathsf{T}} + \lambda\mathbf{I}_D\right)^{-1}\left(\sum_n y_n\boldsymbol{x}_n\right) \tag{11.57}$$

11.3.1.1 Solving using QR

Naively computing the primal estimate $\boldsymbol{w} = (\mathbf{X}^{\mathsf{T}}\mathbf{X} + \lambda\mathbf{I})^{-1}\mathbf{X}^{\mathsf{T}}\boldsymbol{y}$ using matrix inversion is a bad idea, since it can be slow and numerically unstable. In this section, we describe a way to convert the problem to a standard least squares problem, to which we can apply QR decomposition, as discussed in Section 11.2.2.3.

We assume the prior has the form $p(\boldsymbol{w}) = \mathcal{N}(\mathbf{0}, \boldsymbol{\Lambda}^{-1})$, where $\boldsymbol{\Lambda}$ is the precision matrix. In the case of ridge regression, $\boldsymbol{\Lambda} = (1/\tau^2)\mathbf{I}$. We can emulate this prior by adding "virtual data" to the training set to get

$$\tilde{\mathbf{X}} = \begin{pmatrix} \mathbf{X}/\sigma \\ \sqrt{\boldsymbol{\Lambda}} \end{pmatrix}, \quad \tilde{\boldsymbol{y}} = \begin{pmatrix} \boldsymbol{y}/\sigma \\ \mathbf{0}_{D\times 1} \end{pmatrix} \tag{11.58}$$

where $\boldsymbol{\Lambda} = \sqrt{\boldsymbol{\Lambda}}\sqrt{\boldsymbol{\Lambda}}^{\mathsf{T}}$ is a Cholesky decomposition of $\boldsymbol{\Lambda}$. We see that $\tilde{\mathbf{X}}$ is $(N+D) \times D$, where the extra rows represent pseudo-data from the prior.

We now show that the RSS on this expanded data is equivalent to penalized RSS on the original data:

$$f(\boldsymbol{w}) = (\tilde{\boldsymbol{y}} - \tilde{\mathbf{X}}\boldsymbol{w})^{\mathsf{T}}(\tilde{\boldsymbol{y}} - \tilde{\mathbf{X}}\boldsymbol{w}) \tag{11.59}$$

$$= \left(\begin{pmatrix} \boldsymbol{y}/\sigma \\ \mathbf{0} \end{pmatrix} - \begin{pmatrix} \mathbf{X}/\sigma \\ \sqrt{\boldsymbol{\Lambda}} \end{pmatrix}\boldsymbol{w}\right)^{\mathsf{T}}\left(\begin{pmatrix} \boldsymbol{y}/\sigma \\ \mathbf{0} \end{pmatrix} - \begin{pmatrix} \mathbf{X}/\sigma \\ \sqrt{\boldsymbol{\Lambda}} \end{pmatrix}\boldsymbol{w}\right) \tag{11.60}$$

$$= \begin{pmatrix} \frac{1}{\sigma}(\boldsymbol{y} - \mathbf{X}\boldsymbol{w}) \\ -\sqrt{\boldsymbol{\Lambda}}\boldsymbol{w} \end{pmatrix}^{\mathsf{T}}\begin{pmatrix} \frac{1}{\sigma}(\boldsymbol{y} - \mathbf{X}\boldsymbol{w}) \\ -\sqrt{\boldsymbol{\Lambda}}\boldsymbol{w} \end{pmatrix} \tag{11.61}$$

$$= \frac{1}{\sigma^2}(\boldsymbol{y} - \mathbf{X}\boldsymbol{w})^{\mathsf{T}}(\boldsymbol{y} - \mathbf{X}\boldsymbol{w}) + (\sqrt{\boldsymbol{\Lambda}}\boldsymbol{w})^{\mathsf{T}}(\sqrt{\boldsymbol{\Lambda}}\boldsymbol{w}) \tag{11.62}$$

$$= \frac{1}{\sigma^2}(\boldsymbol{y} - \mathbf{X}\boldsymbol{w})^{\mathsf{T}}(\boldsymbol{y} - \mathbf{X}\boldsymbol{w}) + \boldsymbol{w}^{\mathsf{T}}\boldsymbol{\Lambda}\boldsymbol{w} \tag{11.63}$$

Hence the MAP estimate is given by

$$\hat{\boldsymbol{w}}_{\text{map}} = (\tilde{\mathbf{X}}^{\mathsf{T}}\tilde{\mathbf{X}})^{-1}\tilde{\mathbf{X}}^{\mathsf{T}}\tilde{\boldsymbol{y}} \tag{11.64}$$

which can be solved using standard OLS methods. In particular, we can compute the QR decomposition of $\tilde{\mathbf{X}}$, and then proceed as in Section 11.2.2.3. This takes $O((N+D)D^2)$ time.

11.3.1.2 Solving using SVD

In this section, we assume $D > N$, which is the usual case when using ridge regression. In this case, it is faster to use SVD than QR. To see how this works, let $\mathbf{X} = \mathbf{U}\mathbf{S}\mathbf{V}^\mathsf{T}$ be the SVD of $\mathbf{X}$, where $\mathbf{V}^\mathsf{T}\mathbf{V} = \mathbf{I}_N$, $\mathbf{U}\mathbf{U}^\mathsf{T} = \mathbf{U}^\mathsf{T}\mathbf{U} = \mathbf{I}_N$, and $\mathbf{S}$ is a diagonal $N \times N$ matrix. Now let $\mathbf{R} = \mathbf{U}\mathbf{S}$ be an $N \times N$ matrix. One can show (see Exercise 18.4 of [HTF09]) that

$$\hat{\boldsymbol{w}}_{\text{map}} = \mathbf{V}(\mathbf{R}^\mathsf{T}\mathbf{R} + \lambda\mathbf{I}_N)^{-1}\mathbf{R}^\mathsf{T}\boldsymbol{y} \tag{11.65}$$

In other words, we can replace the D-dimensional vectors $\boldsymbol{x}_i$ with the N-dimensional vectors $\boldsymbol{r}_i$ and perform our penalized fit as before. The overall time is now $O(DN^2)$ operations, which is less than $O(D^3)$ if $D > N$.

11.3.2 Connection between ridge regression and PCA

In this section, we discuss an interesting connection between ridge regression and PCA (which we describe in Section 20.1), in order to gain further insight into why ridge regression works well. Our discussion is based on [HTF09, p66].

Let $\mathbf{X} = \mathbf{U}\mathbf{S}\mathbf{V}^\mathsf{T}$ be the SVD of $\mathbf{X}$, where $\mathbf{V}^\mathsf{T}\mathbf{V} = \mathbf{I}_N$, $\mathbf{U}\mathbf{U}^\mathsf{T} = \mathbf{U}^\mathsf{T}\mathbf{U} = \mathbf{I}_N$, and $\mathbf{S}$ is a diagonal $N \times N$ matrix. Using Equation (11.65) we can see that the ridge predictions on the training set are given by

$$\hat{\boldsymbol{y}} = \mathbf{X}\hat{\boldsymbol{w}}_{\text{map}} = \mathbf{U}\mathbf{S}\mathbf{V}^\mathsf{T}\mathbf{V}(\mathbf{S}^2 + \lambda\mathbf{I})^{-1}\mathbf{S}\mathbf{U}^\mathsf{T}\boldsymbol{y} \tag{11.66}$$

$$= \mathbf{U}\tilde{\mathbf{S}}\mathbf{U}^\mathsf{T}\boldsymbol{y} = \sum_{j=1}^{D} \boldsymbol{u}_j \tilde{S}_{jj} \boldsymbol{u}_j^\mathsf{T}\boldsymbol{y} \tag{11.67}$$

where

$$\tilde{S}_{jj} \triangleq [\mathbf{S}(\mathbf{S}^2 + \lambda I)^{-1}\mathbf{S}]_{jj} = \frac{\sigma_j^2}{\sigma_j^2 + \lambda} \tag{11.68}$$

and σ_j are the singular values of $\mathbf{X}$. Hence

$$\hat{\boldsymbol{y}} = \mathbf{X}\hat{\boldsymbol{w}}_{\text{map}} = \sum_{j=1}^{D} \boldsymbol{u}_j \frac{\sigma_j^2}{\sigma_j^2 + \lambda} \boldsymbol{u}_j^\mathsf{T}\boldsymbol{y} \tag{11.69}$$

In contrast, the least squares prediction is

$$\hat{\boldsymbol{y}} = \mathbf{X}\hat{\boldsymbol{w}}_{\text{mle}} = (\mathbf{U}\mathbf{S}\mathbf{V}^\mathsf{T})(\mathbf{V}\mathbf{S}^{-1}\mathbf{U}^\mathsf{T}\boldsymbol{y}) = \mathbf{U}\mathbf{U}^\mathsf{T}\boldsymbol{y} = \sum_{j=1}^{D} \boldsymbol{u}_j \boldsymbol{u}_j^\mathsf{T}\boldsymbol{y} \tag{11.70}$$

If σ_j^2 is large compared to λ, then $\sigma_j^2/(\sigma_j^2 + \lambda) \approx \sigma_j^2/\sigma_j^2 = 1$, so direction $\boldsymbol{u}_j$ is not affected, but if σ_j^2 is small compared to λ, and if λ is large, then $\sigma_j^2/(\sigma_j^2 + \lambda) \approx 1/\lambda \approx 0$, so direction $\boldsymbol{u}_j$ will be downweighted. In view of this, we define the effective number of **degrees of freedom** of the model as follows:

$$\text{dof}(\lambda) = \sum_{j=1}^{D} \frac{\sigma_j^2}{\sigma_j^2 + \lambda} \tag{11.71}$$

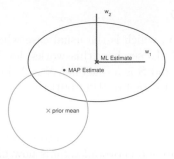

Figure 11.7: Geometry of ridge regression. The likelihood is shown as an ellipse, and the prior is shown as a circle centered on the origin. Adapted from Figure 3.15 of [Bis06]. Generated by geom_ridge.ipynb.

When $\lambda = 0$, $\mathrm{dof}(\lambda) = D$, and as $\lambda \to \infty$, $\mathrm{dof}(\lambda) \to 0$.

Let us try to understand why this behavior is desirable. In Section 11.7, we show that $\mathrm{Cov}\left[\boldsymbol{w}|\mathcal{D}\right] \propto (\mathbf{X}^\mathsf{T}\mathbf{X})^{-1}$, if we use a uniform prior for $\boldsymbol{w}$. Thus the directions in which we are most uncertain about $\boldsymbol{w}$ are determined by the eigenvectors of $(\mathbf{X}^\mathsf{T}\mathbf{X})^{-1}$ with the largest eigenvalues, as shown in Figure 7.6. These directions correspond to the eigenvectors of $\mathbf{X}^\mathsf{T}\mathbf{X}$ with the smallest eigenvalues, and hence (from Section 7.5.2) the smallest singular values. So if σ_j^2 is small relative to λ, ridge regression will downweight direction $\boldsymbol{u}_j$.

This process is illustrated in Figure 11.7. The horizontal w_1 parameter is not-well determined by the data (has high posterior variance), but the vertical w_2 parameter is well-determined. Hence $w_{\mathrm{map}}(2)$ is close to $w_{\mathrm{mle}}(2)$, but $w_{\mathrm{map}}(1)$ is shifted strongly towards the prior mean, which is 0. In this way, ill-determined parameters are reduced in size towards 0. This is called **shrinkage**.

There is a related, but different, technique called **principal components regression**, which is a supervised version of PCA, which we explain in Section 20.1. The idea is this: first use PCA to reduce the dimensionality to K dimensions, and then use these low dimensional features as input to regression. However, this technique does not work as well as ridge regression in terms of predictive accuracy [HTF01, p70]. The reason is that in PC regression, only the first K (derived) dimensions are retained, and the remaining $D - K$ dimensions are entirely ignored. By contrast, ridge regression uses a "soft" weighting of all the dimensions.

11.3.3   Choosing the strength of the regularizer

To find the optimal value of λ, we can try a finite number of distinct values, and use cross validation to estimate their expected loss, as discussed in Section 4.5.5.2. See Figure 4.5d for an example.

This approach can be quite expensive if we have many values to choose from. Fortunately, we can often **warm start** the optimization procedure, using the value of $\hat{\boldsymbol{w}}(\lambda_k)$ as an initializer for $\hat{\boldsymbol{w}}(\lambda_{k+1})$, where $\lambda_{k+1} < \lambda_k$; in other words, we start with a highly constrained model (strong regularizer), and then gradually relax the constraints (decrease the amount of regularization). The set of parameters $\hat{\boldsymbol{w}}_k$ that we sweep out in this way is known as the **regularization path**. See Figure 11.10(a) for an example.

We can also use an empirical Bayes approach to choose λ. In particular, we choose the hyperparameter by computing $\hat{\lambda} = \mathrm{argmax}_\lambda \log p(\mathcal{D}|\lambda)$, where $p(\mathcal{D}|\lambda)$ is the marginal likelihood or evidence.

Figure 4.7b shows that this gives essentially the same result as the CV estimate. However, the Bayesian approach has several advantages: computing $p(\mathcal{D}|\lambda)$ can be done by fitting a single model, whereas CV has to fit the same model K times; and $p(\mathcal{D}|\lambda)$ is a smooth function of λ, so we can use gradient-based optimization instead of discrete search.

11.4 Lasso regression

In Section 11.3, we assumed a Gaussian prior for the regression coefficients when fitting linear regression models. This is often a good choice, since it encourages the parameters to be small, and hence prevents overfitting. However, sometimes we want the parameters to not just be small, but to be exactly zero, i.e., we want $\hat{\boldsymbol{w}}$ to be **sparse**, so that we minimize the **L0-norm**:

$$||\boldsymbol{w}||_0 = \sum_{d=1}^{D} \mathbb{I}\left(|w_d| > 0\right) \tag{11.72}$$

This is useful because it can be used to perform **feature selection**. To see this, note that the prediction has the form $f(\boldsymbol{x}; \boldsymbol{w}) = \sum_{d=1}^{D} w_d x_d$, so if any $w_d = 0$, we ignore the corresponding feature x_d. (The same idea can be applied to nonlinear models, such as DNNs, by encouraging the first layer weights to be sparse.)

11.4.1 MAP estimation with a Laplace prior (ℓ_1 regularization)

There are many ways to compute such sparse estimates (see e.g., [Bha+19]). In this section we focus on MAP estimation using the Laplace distribution (which we discussed in Section 11.6.1) as the prior:

$$p(\boldsymbol{w}|\lambda) = \prod_{d=1}^{D} \text{Laplace}(w_d|0, 1/\lambda) \propto \prod_{d=1}^{D} e^{-\lambda|w_d|} \tag{11.73}$$

where λ is the sparsity parameter, and

$$\text{Laplace}(w|\mu, b) \triangleq \frac{1}{2b} \exp\left(-\frac{|w - \mu|}{b}\right) \tag{11.74}$$

Here μ is a location parameter and $b > 0$ is a scale parameter. Figure 2.15 shows that $\text{Laplace}(w|0, b)$ puts more density on 0 than $\mathcal{N}(w|0, \sigma^2)$, even when we fix the variance to be the same.

To perform MAP estimation of a linear regression model with this prior, we just have to minimize the following objective:

$$\text{PNLL}(\boldsymbol{w}) = -\log p(\mathcal{D}|\boldsymbol{w}) - \log p(\boldsymbol{w}|\lambda) = ||\mathbf{X}\boldsymbol{w} - \boldsymbol{y}||_2^2 + \lambda||\boldsymbol{w}||_1 \tag{11.75}$$

where $||\boldsymbol{w}||_1 \triangleq \sum_{d=1}^{D} |w_d|$ is the ℓ_1 norm of $\boldsymbol{w}$. This method is called **lasso**, which stands for "least absolute shrinkage and selection operator" [Tib96]. (We explain the reason for this name below.) More generally, MAP estimation with a Laplace prior is called ℓ_1-**regularization**.

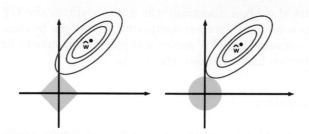

Figure 11.8: Illustration of ℓ_1 (left) vs ℓ_2 (right) regularization of a least squares problem. Adapted from Figure 3.12 of [HTF01].

Note also that we could use other norms for the weight vector. In general, the q-norm is defined as follows:

$$\|\boldsymbol{w}\|_q = \left(\sum_{d=1}^{D} |w_d|^q\right)^{1/q} \tag{11.76}$$

For $q < 1$, we can get even sparser solutions. In the limit where $q = 0$, we get the ℓ_0-**norm**:

$$\|\boldsymbol{w}\|_0 = \sum_{d=1}^{D} \mathbb{I}\left(|w_d| > 0\right) \tag{11.77}$$

However, one can show that for any $q < 1$, the problem becomes non-convex (see e.g., [HTW15]). Thus ℓ_1-norm is the tightest **convex relaxation** of the ℓ_0-norm.

11.4.2   Why does ℓ_1 regularization yield sparse solutions?

We now explain why ℓ_1 regularization results in sparse solutions, whereas ℓ_2 regularization does not. We focus on the case of linear regression, although similar arguments hold for other models.

The lasso objective is the following non-smooth objective (see Section 8.1.4 for a discussion of smoothness):

$$\min_{\boldsymbol{w}} \text{NLL}(\boldsymbol{w}) + \lambda\|\boldsymbol{w}\|_1 \tag{11.78}$$

This is the Lagrangian for the following quadratic program (see Section 8.5.4):

$$\min_{\boldsymbol{w}} \text{NLL}(\boldsymbol{w}) \quad \text{s.t.} \quad \|\boldsymbol{w}\|_1 \leq B \tag{11.79}$$

where B is an upper bound on the ℓ_1-norm of the weights: a small (tight) bound B corresponds to a large penalty λ, and vice versa.

Similarly, we can write the ridge regression objective $\min_{\boldsymbol{w}} \text{NLL}(\boldsymbol{w}) + \lambda\|\boldsymbol{w}\|_2^2$ in bound constrained form:

$$\min_{\boldsymbol{w}} \text{NLL}(\boldsymbol{w}) \quad \text{s.t.} \quad \|\boldsymbol{w}\|_2^2 \leq B \tag{11.80}$$

In Figure 11.8, we plot the contours of the NLL objective function, as well as the contours of the ℓ_2 and ℓ_1 constraint surfaces. From the theory of constrained optimization (Section 8.5) we know that the optimal solution occurs at the point where the lowest level set of the objective function intersects the constraint surface (assuming the constraint is active). It should be geometrically clear that as we relax the constraint B, we "grow" the ℓ_1 "ball" until it meets the objective; the corners of the ball are more likely to intersect the ellipse than one of the sides, especially in high dimensions, because the corners "stick out" more. The corners correspond to sparse solutions, which lie on the coordinate axes. By contrast, when we grow the ℓ_2 ball, it can intersect the objective at any point; there are no "corners", so there is no preference for sparsity.

11.4.3 Hard vs soft thresholding

The lasso objective has the form $\mathcal{L}(\boldsymbol{w}) = \text{NLL}(\boldsymbol{w}) + \lambda||\boldsymbol{w}||_1$. One can show (Exercise 11.3) that the gradient for the smooth NLL part is given by

$$\frac{\partial}{\partial w_d}\text{NLL}(\boldsymbol{w}) = a_d w_d - c_d \tag{11.81}$$

$$a_d = \sum_{n=1}^{N} x_{nd}^2 \tag{11.82}$$

$$c_d = \sum_{n=1}^{N} x_{nd}(y_n - \boldsymbol{w}_{-d}^\mathsf{T}\boldsymbol{x}_{n,-d}) \tag{11.83}$$

where $\boldsymbol{w}_{-d}$ is $\boldsymbol{w}$ without component d, and similarly $\boldsymbol{x}_{n,-d}$ is feature vector $\boldsymbol{x}_n$ without component d. We see that c_d is proportional to the correlation between d'th column of features, $\boldsymbol{x}_{:,d}$, and the residual error obtained by predicting using all the other features, $\boldsymbol{r}_{-d} = \boldsymbol{y} - \mathbf{X}_{:,-d}\boldsymbol{w}_{-d}$. Hence the magnitude of c_d is an indication of how relevant feature d is for predicting $\boldsymbol{y}$, relative to the other features and the current parameters. Setting the gradient to 0 gives the optimal update for w_d, keeping all other weights fixed:

$$w_d = c_d/a_d = \frac{\boldsymbol{x}_{:,d}^\mathsf{T}\boldsymbol{r}_{-d}}{||\boldsymbol{x}_{:,d}||_2^2} \tag{11.84}$$

The corresponding new prediction for $\boldsymbol{r}_{-d}$ becomes $\hat{\boldsymbol{r}}_{-d} = w_d\boldsymbol{x}_{:,d}$, which is the orthogonal projection of the residual onto the column vector $\boldsymbol{x}_{:,d}$, consistent with Equation (11.15).

Now we add in the ℓ_1 term. Unfortunately, the $||\boldsymbol{w}||_1$ term is not differentiable whenever $w_d = 0$. Fortunately, we can still compute a subgradient at this point. Using Equation (8.14) we find that

$$\partial_{w_d}\mathcal{L}(\boldsymbol{w}) = (a_d w_d - c_d) + \lambda\partial_{w_d}||\boldsymbol{w}||_1 \tag{11.85}$$

$$= \begin{cases} \{a_d w_d - c_d - \lambda\} & \text{if } w_d < 0 \\ [-c_d - \lambda, -c_d + \lambda] & \text{if } w_d = 0 \\ \{a_d w_d - c_d + \lambda\} & \text{if } w_d > 0 \end{cases} \tag{11.86}$$

Depending on the value of c_d, the solution to $\partial_{w_d}\mathcal{L}(\boldsymbol{w}) = 0$ can occur at 3 different values of w_d, as follows:

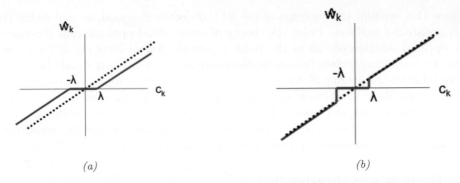

(a)   (b)

Figure 11.9: Left: soft thresholding. Right: hard thresholding. In both cases, the horizontal axis is the residual error incurred by making predictions using all the coefficients except for w_k, and the vertical axis is the estimated coefficient $\hat{w}_k$ that minimizes this penalized residual. The flat region in the middle is the interval $[-\lambda, +\lambda]$.

1. If $c_d < -\lambda$, so the feature is strongly negatively correlated with the residual, then the subgradient is zero at $\hat{w}_d = \frac{c_d + \lambda}{a_d} < 0$.

2. If $c_d \in [-\lambda, \lambda]$, so the feature is only weakly correlated with the residual, then the subgradient is zero at $\hat{w}_d = 0$.

3. If $c_d > \lambda$, so the feature is strongly positively correlated with the residual, then the subgradient is zero at $\hat{w}_d = \frac{c_d - \lambda}{a_d} > 0$.

In summary, we have

$$\hat{w}_d(c_d) = \begin{cases} (c_d + \lambda)/a_d & \text{if } c_d < -\lambda \\ 0 & \text{if } c_d \in [-\lambda, \lambda] \\ (c_d - \lambda)/a_d & \text{if } c_d > \lambda \end{cases} \tag{11.87}$$

We can write this as follows:

$$\hat{w}_d = \text{SoftThreshold}(\frac{c_d}{a_d}, \lambda/a_d) \tag{11.88}$$

where

$$\text{SoftThreshold}(x, \delta) \triangleq \text{sign}(x)\,(|x| - \delta)_+ \tag{11.89}$$

and $x_+ = \max(x, 0)$ is the positive part of x. This is called **soft thresholding** (see also Section 8.6.2). This is illustrated in Figure 11.9(a), where we plot $\hat{w}_d$ vs c_d. The dotted black line is the line $w_d = c_d/a_d$ corresponding to the least squares fit. The solid red line, which represents the regularized estimate $\hat{w}_d$, shifts the dotted line down (or up) by λ, except when $-\lambda \leq c_d \leq \lambda$, in which case it sets $w_d = 0$.

By contrast, in Figure 11.9(b), we illustrate **hard thresholding**. This sets values of w_d to 0 if $-\lambda \leq c_d \leq \lambda$, but it does not shrink the values of w_d outside of this interval. The slope of the soft

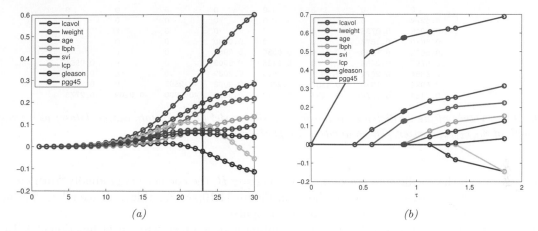

Figure 11.10: (a) Profiles of ridge coefficients for the prostate cancer example vs bound B on ℓ_2 norm of $\boldsymbol{w}$, so small B (large λ) is on the left. The vertical line is the value chosen by 5-fold CV using the 1 standard error rule. Adapted from Figure 3.8 of [HTF09]. Generated by ridgePathProstate.ipynb. (b) Same as (a) but using ℓ_1 norm of $\boldsymbol{w}$. The x-axis shows the critical values of $\lambda = 1/B$, where the regularization path is discontinuous. Adapted from Figure 3.10 of [HTF09]. Generated by lassoPathProstate.ipynb.

thresholding line does not coincide with the diagonal, which means that even large coefficients are shrunk towards zero. This is why lasso stands for "least absolute selection *and shrinkage* operator". Consequently, lasso is a biased estimator (see Section 4.7.6.1).

A simple solution to the biased estimate problem, known as **debiasing**, is to use a two-stage estimation process: we first estimate the support of the weight vector (i.e., identify which elements are non-zero) using lasso; we then re-estimate the chosen coefficients using least squares. For an example of this in action, see Figure 11.13.

11.4.4 Regularization path

If $\lambda = 0$, we get the OLS solution. which will be dense. As we increase λ, the solution vector $\hat{\boldsymbol{w}}(\lambda)$ will tend to get sparser. If λ is bigger than some critical value, we get $\hat{\boldsymbol{w}} = \boldsymbol{0}$. This critical value is obtained when the gradient of the NLL cancels out with the gradient of the penalty:

$$\lambda_{\max} = \max_d |\nabla_{w_d} \text{NLL}(\boldsymbol{0})| = \max_d c_d(\boldsymbol{w} = 0) = \max_d |\boldsymbol{y}^\mathsf{T} \boldsymbol{x}_{:,d}| = ||\mathbf{X}^\mathsf{T} \boldsymbol{y}||_\infty \tag{11.90}$$

Alternatively, we can work with the bound B on the ℓ_1 norm. When $B = 0$, we get $\hat{\boldsymbol{w}} = \boldsymbol{0}$. As we increase B, the solution becomes denser. The largest value of B for which any component is zero is given by $B_{\max} = ||\hat{\boldsymbol{w}}_{\text{mle}}||_1$.

As we increase λ, the solution vector $\hat{\boldsymbol{w}}$ gets sparser, although not necessarily monotonically. We can plot the values $\hat{w}_d$ vs λ (or vs the bound B) for each feature d; this is known as the **regularization path**. This is illustrated in Figure 11.10(b), where we apply lasso to the prostate cancer regression dataset from [HTF09]. (We treat features `gleason` and `svi` as numeric, not categorical.) On the left,

0	0	0	0	0	0	0	0
0.4279	0	0	0	0	0	0	0
0.5015	0.0735	0	0	0	0	0	0
0.5610	0.1878	0	0	0.0930	0	0	0
0.5622	0.1890	0	0.0036	0.0963	0	0	0
0.5797	0.2456	0	0.1435	0.2003	0	0	0.0901
0.5864	0.2572	-0.0321	0.1639	0.2082	0	0	0.1066
0.6994	0.2910	-0.1337	0.2062	0.3003	-0.2565	0	0.2452
0.7164	0.2926	-0.1425	0.2120	0.3096	-0.2890	-0.0209	0.2773

Table 11.1: *Values of the coefficients for linear regression model fit to prostate cancer dataset as we vary the strength of the ℓ_1 regularizer. These numbers are plotted in Figure 11.10(b).*

when $B = 0$, all the coefficients are zero. As we increase B, the coefficients gradually "turn on".[2] The analogous result for ridge regression is shown in Figure 11.10(a). For ridge, we see all coefficients are non-zero (assuming $\lambda > 0$), so the solution is not sparse.

Remarkably, it can be shown that the lasso solution path is a piecewise linear function of λ [Efr+04; GL15]. That is, there are a set of critical values of λ where the active set of non-zero coefficients changes. For values of λ between these critical values, each non-zero coefficient increases or decreases in a linear fashion. This is illustrated in Figure 11.10(b). Furthermore, one can solve for these critical values analytically [Efr+04]. In Table 11.1. we display the actual coefficient values at each of these critical steps along the regularization path (the last line is the least squares solution).

By changing λ from $\lambda_{\max}$ to 0, we can go from a solution in which all the weights are zero to a solution in which all weights are non-zero. Unfortunately, not all subset sizes are achievable using lasso. In particular, one can show that, if $D > N$, the optimal solution can have at most N variables in it, before reaching the complete set corresponding to the OLS solution of minimal ℓ_1 norm. In Section 11.4.8, we will see that by using an ℓ_2 regularizer as well as an ℓ_1 regularizer (a method known as the elastic net), we can achieve sparse solutions which contain more variables than training cases. This lets us explore model sizes between N and D.

11.4.5   Comparison of least squares, lasso, ridge and subset selection

In this section, we compare least squares, lasso, ridge and subset selection. For simplicity, we assume all the features of $\mathbf{X}$ are orthonormal, so $\mathbf{X}^\mathsf{T}\mathbf{X} = \mathbf{I}$. In this case, the NLL is given by

$$\text{NLL}(\boldsymbol{w}) = ||\boldsymbol{y} - \mathbf{X}\boldsymbol{w}||^2 = \boldsymbol{y}^\mathsf{T}\boldsymbol{y} + \boldsymbol{w}^\mathsf{T}\mathbf{X}^\mathsf{T}\mathbf{X}\boldsymbol{w} - 2\boldsymbol{w}^\mathsf{T}\mathbf{X}^\mathsf{T}\boldsymbol{y} \tag{11.91}$$

$$= \text{const} + \sum_d w_d^2 - 2\sum_d \sum_n w_d x_{nd} y_n \tag{11.92}$$

so we see this factorizes into a sum of terms, one per dimension. Hence we can write down the MAP and ML estimates analytically for each w_d separately, as given below.

- **MLE** From Equation (11.85), the OLS solution is given by

$$\hat{w}_d^{\text{mle}} = c_d/a_d = \boldsymbol{x}_{:d}^\mathsf{T}\boldsymbol{y} \tag{11.93}$$

where $\boldsymbol{x}_{:d}$ is the d'th column of $\mathbf{X}$.

---

2. It is common to plot the solution versus the **shrinkage factor**, defined as $s(B) = B/B_{\max}$, rather than against B. This merely affects the scale of the horizontal axis, not the shape of the curves.

Term	OLS	Best Subset	Ridge	Lasso
intercept	2.465	2.477	2.467	2.465
lcavol	0.676	0.736	0.522	0.548
lweight	0.262	0.315	0.255	0.224
age	-0.141	0.000	-0.089	0.000
lbph	0.209	0.000	0.186	0.129
svi	0.304	0.000	0.259	0.186
lcp	-0.287	0.000	-0.095	0.000
gleason	-0.021	0.000	0.025	0.000
pgg45	0.266	0.000	0.169	0.083
Test error	0.521	0.492	0.487	0.457
Std error	0.176	0.141	0.157	0.146

Figure 11.11: *Results of different methods on the prostate cancer data, which has 8 features and 67 training cases. Methods are: OLS = ordinary least squares, Subset = best subset regression, Ridge, Lasso. Rows represent the coefficients; we see that subset regression and lasso give sparse solutions. Bottom row is the mean squared error on the test set (30 cases). Adapted from Table 3.3. of [HTF09]. Generated by* prostate_comparison.ipynb.

- **Ridge** One can show that the ridge estimate is given by

$$\hat{w}_d^{\text{ridge}} = \frac{\hat{w}_d^{\text{mle}}}{1 + \lambda} \quad (11.94)$$

- **Lasso** From Equation (11.88), and using the fact that $\hat{w}_d^{\text{mle}} = c_d/a_d$, we have

$$\hat{w}_d^{\text{lasso}} = \text{sign}(\hat{w}_d^{\text{mle}}) \left(|\hat{w}_d^{\text{mle}}| - \lambda\right)_+ \quad (11.95)$$

This corresponds to soft thresholding, shown in Figure 11.9(a).

- **Subset selection** If we pick the best K features using subset selection, the parameter estimate is as follows

$$\hat{w}_d^{\text{ss}} = \begin{cases} \hat{w}_d^{\text{mle}} & \text{if rank}(|\hat{w}_d^{\text{mle}}|) \leq K \\ 0 & \text{otherwise} \end{cases} \quad (11.96)$$

where rank refers to the location in the sorted list of weight magnitudes. This corresponds to hard thresholding, shown in Figure 11.9(b).

We now experimentally compare the prediction performance of these methods on the prostate cancer regression dataset from [HTF09]. (We treat features `gleason` and `svi` as numeric, not categorical.) Figure 11.11 shows the estimated coefficients at the value of λ (or K) chosen by cross-validation; we see that the subset method is the sparsest, then lasso. In terms of predictive performance, all methods are very similar, as can be seen from Figure 11.12.

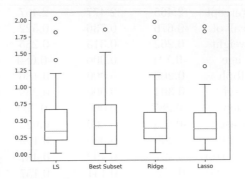

Figure 11.12: *Boxplot displaying (absolute value of) prediction errors on the prostate cancer test set for different regression methods. Generated by prostate_comparison.ipynb.*

11.4.6   Variable selection consistency

It is common to use ℓ_1 regularization to estimate the set of relevant variables, a process known as **variable selection**. A method that can recover the true set of relevant variables (i.e., the support of $\boldsymbol{w}^*$) in the $N \to \infty$ limit is called **model selection consistent**. (This is a theoretical notion that assumes the data comes from the model.)

Let us give an example. We first generate a sparse signal $\boldsymbol{w}^*$ of size $D = 4096$, consisting of 160 randomly placed ± 1 spikes. Next we generate a random design matrix $\mathbf{X}$ of size $N \times D$, where $N = 1024$. Finally we generate a noisy observation $\boldsymbol{y} = \mathbf{X}\boldsymbol{w}^* + \boldsymbol{\epsilon}$, where $\epsilon_n \sim \mathcal{N}(0, 0.01^2)$. We then estimate $\boldsymbol{w}$ from $\boldsymbol{y}$ and $\mathbf{X}$. The original $\boldsymbol{w}^*$ is shown in the first row of Figure 11.13. The second row is the ℓ_1 estimate $\hat{\boldsymbol{w}}_{L1}$ using $\lambda = 0.1\lambda_{\max}$. We see that this has "spikes" in the right places, so it has correctly identified the relevant variables. However, although we see that $\hat{\boldsymbol{w}}_{L1}$ has correctly identified the non-zero components, but they are too small, due to shrinkage. In the third row, we show the results of using the debiasing technique discussed in Section 11.4.3. This shows that we can recover the original weight vector. By contrast, the final row shows the OLS estimate, which is dense. Furthermore, it is visually clear that there is no single threshold value we can apply to $\hat{\boldsymbol{w}}_{\mathrm{mle}}$ to recover the correct sparse weight vector.

To use lasso to perform variable selection, we have to pick λ. It is common to use cross validation to pick the optimal value on the regularization path. However, it is important to note that cross validation is picking a value of λ that results in good predictive accuracy. This is not usually the same value as the one that is likely to recover the "true" model. To see why, recall that ℓ_1 regularization performs selection *and* shrinkage, that is, the chosen coefficients are brought closer to 0. In order to prevent relevant coefficients from being shrunk in this way, cross validation will tend to pick a value of λ that is not too large. Of course, this will result in a less sparse model which contains irrelevant variables (false positives). Indeed, it was proved in [MB06] that the prediction-optimal value of λ does not result in model selection consistency. However, various extensions to the basic method have been devised that are model selection consistent (see e.g., [BG11; HTW15]).

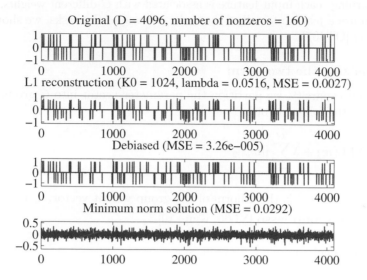

Figure 11.13: *Example of recovering a sparse signal using lasso. See text for details. Adapted from Figure 1 of [FNW07]. Generated by sparse_sensing_demo.ipynb.*

11.4.7 Group lasso

In standard ℓ_1 regularization, we assume that there is a 1:1 correspondence between parameters and variables, so that if $\hat{w}_d = 0$, we interpret this to mean that variable d is excluded. But in more complex models, there may be many parameters associated with a given variable. In particular, each variable d may have a vector of weights $\boldsymbol{w}_d$ associated with it, so the overall weight vector has block structure, $\boldsymbol{w} = [\boldsymbol{w}_1, \boldsymbol{w}_2, \ldots, \boldsymbol{w}_D]$. If we want to exclude variable d, we have to force the whole subvector $\boldsymbol{w}_d$ to go to zero. This is called **group sparsity**.

11.4.7.1 Applications

Here are some examples where group sparsity is useful:

- Linear regression with categorical inputs: If the d'th variable is categorical with K possible levels, then it will be represented as a one-hot vector of length K (Section 1.5.3.1), so to exclude variable d, we have to set the whole vector of incoming weights to 0.

- Multinomial logistic regression: The d'th variable will be associated with C different weights, one per class (Section 10.3), so to exclude variable d, we have to set the whole vector of outgoing weights to 0.

- Neural networks: the k'th neuron will have multiple inputs, so if we want to "turn the neuron off", we have to set all the incoming weights to zero. This allows us to use group sparsity to learn neural network structure (for details, see e.g., [GEH19]).

- Multi-task learning: each input feature is associated with C different weights, one per output task. If we want to use a feature for all of the tasks or none of the tasks, we should select weights at the group level [OTJ07].

11.4.7.2   Penalizing the two-norm

To encourage group sparsity, we partition the parameter vector into G groups, $\boldsymbol{w} = [\boldsymbol{w}_1, \ldots, \boldsymbol{w}_G]$. Then we minimize the following objective

$$\text{PNLL}(\boldsymbol{w}) = \text{NLL}(\boldsymbol{w}) + \lambda \sum_{g=1}^{G} ||\boldsymbol{w}_g||_2 \tag{11.97}$$

where $||\boldsymbol{w}_g||_2 = \sqrt{\sum_{d \in g} w_d^2}$ is the 2-norm of the group weight vector. If the NLL is least squares, this method is called **group lasso** [YL06; Kyu+10].

Note that if we had used the sum of the squared 2-norms in Equation (11.97), then the model would become equivalent to ridge regression, since

$$\sum_{g=1}^{G} ||\boldsymbol{w}_g||_2^2 = \sum_{g} \sum_{d \in g} w_d^2 = ||\boldsymbol{w}||_2^2 \tag{11.98}$$

By using the square root, we are penalizing the radius of a ball containing the group's weight vector: the only way for the radius to be small is if all elements are small.

Another way to see why the square root version enforces sparsity at the group level is to consider the gradient of the objective. Suppose there is only one group of two variables, so the penalty has the form $\sqrt{w_1^2 + w_2^2}$. The derivative wrt w_1 is

$$\frac{\partial}{\partial w_1} (w_1^2 + w_2^2)^{\frac{1}{2}} = \frac{w_1}{\sqrt{w_1^2 + w_2^2}} \tag{11.99}$$

If w_2 is close to zero, then the derivative approaches 1, and w_1 is driven to zero as well, with force proportional to λ. If, however, w_2 is large, the derivative approaches 0, and w_1 is free to stay large as well. So all the coefficients in the group will have similar size.

11.4.7.3   Penalizing the infinity norm

A variant of this technique replaces the 2-norm with the infinity-norm [TVW05; ZRY05]:

$$||\boldsymbol{w}_g||_\infty = \max_{d \in g} |w_d| \tag{11.100}$$

It is clear that this will also result in group sparsity, since if the largest element in the group is forced to zero, all the smaller ones will be as well.

11.4.7.4   Example

An illustration of these techniques is shown in Figure 11.14 and Figure 11.15. We have a true signal $\boldsymbol{w}$ of size $D = 2^{12} = 4096$, divided into 64 groups each of size 64. We randomly choose 8 groups

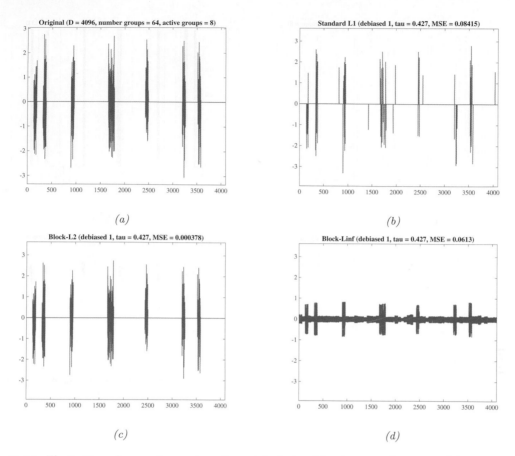

Figure 11.14: *Illustration of group lasso where the original signal is piecewise Gaussian. (a) Original signal. (b) Vanilla lasso estimate. (c) Group lasso estimate using an ℓ_2 norm on the blocks. (d) Group lasso estimate using an ℓ_∞ norm on the blocks. Adapted from Figures 3-4 of [WNF09]. Generated by groupLassoDemo.ipynb.*

of $\boldsymbol{w}$ and assign them non-zero values. In Figure 11.14 the values are drawn from a $\mathcal{N}(0,1)$; in Figure 11.15, the values are all set to 1. We then sample a random design matrix $\mathbf{X}$ of size $N \times D$, where $N = 2^{10} = 1024$. Finally, we generate $\boldsymbol{y} = \mathbf{X}\boldsymbol{w} + \boldsymbol{\epsilon}$, where $\boldsymbol{\epsilon} \sim \mathcal{N}(\mathbf{0}, 10^{-4}\mathbf{I}_N)$. Given this data, we estimate the support of $\boldsymbol{w}$ using ℓ_1 or group ℓ_1, and then estimate the non-zero values using least squares (debiased estimate).

We see from the figures that group lasso does a much better job than vanilla lasso, since it respects the known group structure. We also see that the ℓ_∞ norm has a tendency to make all the elements within a block to have similar magnitude. This is appropriate in the second example, but not the first. (The value of λ was the same in all examples, and was chosen by hand.)

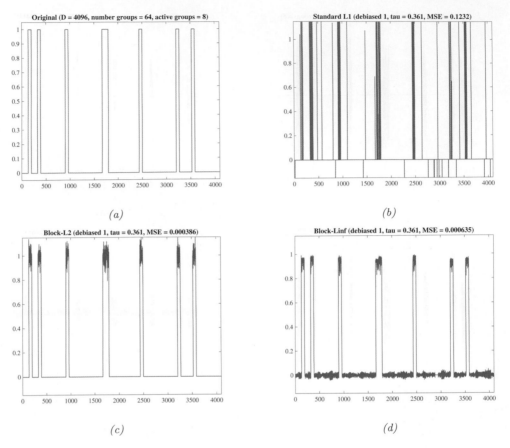

Figure 11.15: Same as Figure 11.14, except the original signal is piecewise constant. Generated by groupLas-soDemo.ipynb.

11.4.8   Elastic net (ridge and lasso combined)

In group lasso, we need to specify the group structure ahead of time. For some problems, we don't know the group structure, and yet we would still like highly correlated coefficients to be treated as an implicit group. One way to achieve this effect, proposed in [ZH05], is to use the **elastic net**, which is a hybrid between lasso and ridge regression.[3] This corresponds to minimizing the following objective:

$$\mathcal{L}(\boldsymbol{w}, \lambda_1, \lambda_2) = ||\boldsymbol{y} - \mathbf{X}\boldsymbol{w}||^2 + \lambda_2||\boldsymbol{w}||_2^2 + \lambda_1||\boldsymbol{w}||_1 \tag{11.101}$$

This penalty function is *strictly convex* (assuming $\lambda_2 > 0$) so there is a unique global minimum, even if $\mathbf{X}$ is not full rank. It can be shown [ZH05] that any strictly convex penalty on $\boldsymbol{w}$ will exhibit a **grouping effect**, which means that the regression coefficients of highly correlated variables tend to

---

3. It is apparently called the "elastic net" because it is "like a stretchable fishing net that retains all the big fish" [ZH05].

be equal. In particular, if two features are identically equal, so $\mathbf{X}_{:j} = \mathbf{X}_{:k}$, one can show that their estimates are also equal, $\hat{w}_j = \hat{w}_k$. By contrast, with lasso, we may have that $\hat{w}_j = 0$ and $\hat{w}_k \neq 0$ or vice versa, resulting in less stable estimates.

In addition to its soft grouping behavior, elastic net has other advantages. In particular, if $D > N$, the maximum number of non-zero elements that can be selected (excluding the MLE, which has D non-zero elements) is N. By contrast, elastic net can select more than N non-zero variables on its path to the dense estimate, thus exploring more possible subsets of variables.

11.4.9   Optimization algorithms

A large variety of algorithms have been proposed to solve the lasso problem, and other ℓ_1-regularized convex objectives. In this section, we briefly mention some of the most popular methods.

11.4.9.1   Coordinate descent

Sometimes it is hard to optimize all the variables simultaneously, but it easy to optimize them one by one. In particular, we can solve for the j'th coefficient with all the others held fixed as follows:

$$w_j^* = \operatorname*{argmin}_{\eta} \mathcal{L}(\boldsymbol{w} + \eta \boldsymbol{e}_j) \tag{11.102}$$

where $\boldsymbol{e}_j$ is the j'th unit vector. This is called **coordinate descent**. We can either cycle through the coordinates in a deterministic fashion, or we can sample them at random, or we can choose to update the coordinate for which the gradient is steepest.

This method is particularly appealing if each one-dimensional optimization problem can be solved analytically, as is the case for lasso (see Equation (11.87)). This is known as the **shooting** algorithm [Fu98; WL08]. (The term "shooting" is a reference to cowboy theme inspired by the term "lasso".) See Algorithm 11.1 for details.

This coordinate descent method has been generalized to the GLM case in [FHT10], and is the basis of the popular **glmnet** software library.

Algorithm 11.1: Coordinate descent for lasso (aka shooting algorithm)

---

1 Initialize $\boldsymbol{w} = (\mathbf{X}^\mathsf{T}\mathbf{X} + \lambda \mathbf{I})^{-1}\mathbf{X}^\mathsf{T}\boldsymbol{y}$
2 **repeat**
3 $\quad$ **for** $d = 1, \ldots, D$ **do**
4 $\quad\quad a_d = \sum_{n=1}^N x_{nd}^2$
5 $\quad\quad c_d = \sum_{n=1}^N x_{nd}(y_n - \boldsymbol{w}^\mathsf{T}\boldsymbol{x}_n + w_d x_{nd})$
6 $\quad\quad w_d = \text{SoftThreshold}(\frac{c_d}{a_d}, \lambda/a_d)$
7 **until** *converged*

11.4.9.2   Projected gradient descent

In this section, we convert the non-differentiable ℓ_1 penalty into a smooth regularizer. To do this, we first use the **split variable trick** to define $\boldsymbol{w} = \boldsymbol{w}^+ - \boldsymbol{w}^-$, where $\boldsymbol{w}^+ = \max\{\boldsymbol{w}, 0\}$ and

$\boldsymbol{w}^- = -\min\{\boldsymbol{w}, 0\}$. Now we can replace $||\boldsymbol{w}||_1$ with $\sum_d (w_d^+ + w_d^-)$. We also have to replace $\text{NLL}(\boldsymbol{w})$ with $\text{NLL}(\boldsymbol{w}^+ + \boldsymbol{w}^-)$. Thus we get the following smooth, but constrained, optimization problem:

$$\min_{\boldsymbol{w}^+ \geq 0, \boldsymbol{w}^- \geq 0} \text{NLL}(\boldsymbol{w}^+ - \boldsymbol{w}^-) + \lambda \sum_{d=1}^{D} (w_d^+ + w_d^-) \tag{11.103}$$

In this case of a Gaussian likelihood, the NLL becomes a least squares loss, and the objective becomes a quadratic program (Section 8.5.4). One way to solve such problems is to use projected gradient descent (Section 8.6.1). Specifically, we can enforce the constraint by projecting onto the positive orthant, which we can do using $w_d := \max(w_d, 0)$; this operation is denoted by P_+. Thus the projected gradient update takes the following form:

$$\begin{pmatrix} \boldsymbol{w}_{t+1}^+ \\ \boldsymbol{w}_{t+1}^- \end{pmatrix} = P_+ \left(\begin{bmatrix} \boldsymbol{w}_t^+ - \eta_t \nabla \text{NLL}(\boldsymbol{w}_t^+ - \boldsymbol{w}_t^-) - \eta_t \lambda \boldsymbol{e} \\ \boldsymbol{w}_t^- + \eta_t \nabla \text{NLL}(\boldsymbol{w}_t^+ - \boldsymbol{w}_t^-) - \eta_t \lambda \boldsymbol{e} \end{bmatrix} \right) \tag{11.104}$$

where $\boldsymbol{e}$ is the unit vector of all ones.

11.4.9.3 Proximal gradient descent

In Section 8.6, we introduced proximal gradient descent, which can be used to optimize smooth functions with non-smooth penalties, such as ℓ_1. In Section 8.6.2, we showed that the proximal operator for the ℓ_1 penalty corresponds to soft thresholding. Thus the proximal gradient descent update can be written as

$$\boldsymbol{w}_{t+1} = \text{SoftThreshold}(\boldsymbol{w}_t - \eta_t \nabla \text{NLL}(\boldsymbol{w}_t), \eta_t \lambda) \tag{11.105}$$

where the soft thresholding operator (Equation (8.134)) is applied elementwise. This is called the **iterative soft thresholding algorithm** or **ISTA** [DDDM04; Don95]. If we combine this with Nesterov acceleration, we get the method known as "fast ISTA" or **FISTA** [BT09], which is widely used to fit sparse linear models.

11.4.9.4 LARS

In this section, we discuss methods that can generate a set of solutions for different values of λ, starting with the empty set, i.e., they compute the full regularization path (Section 11.4.4). These algorithms exploit the fact that one can quickly compute $\hat{\boldsymbol{w}}(\lambda_k)$ from $\hat{\boldsymbol{w}}(\lambda_{k-1})$ if $\lambda_k \approx \lambda_{k-1}$; this is known as **warm starting**. In fact, even if we only want the solution for a single value of λ, call it λ_*, it can sometimes be computationally more efficient to compute a set of solutions, from $\lambda_{\max}$ down to λ_*, using warm-starting; this is called a **continuation method** or **homotopy** method. This is often much faster than directly "cold-starting" at λ_*; this is particularly true if λ_* is small.

The **LARS** algorithm [Efr+04], which stands for "least angle regression and shrinkage", is an example of a homotopy method for the lasso problem. This can compute $\hat{\boldsymbol{w}}(\lambda)$ for all possible values of λ in an efficient manner. (A similar algorithm was independently invented in [OPT00b; OPT00a]).

LARS works as follows. It starts with a large value of λ, such that only the variable that is most correlated with the response vector $\boldsymbol{y}$ is chosen. Then λ is decreased until a second variable is found which has the same correlation (in terms of magnitude) with the current residual as the first variable, where the residual at step k on the path is defined as $r_k = y - \mathbf{X}_{:,F_k} w_k$, where F_k is the current **active set** (cf., Equation (11.83)). Remarkably, one can solve for this new value of λ analytically, by using a geometric argument (hence the term "least angle"). This allows the algorithm to quickly "jump" to the next point on the regularization path where the active set changes. This repeats until all the variables are added.

It is necessary to allow variables to be removed from the current active set, even as we increase λ, if we want the sequence of solutions to correspond to the regularization path of lasso. If we disallow variable removal, we get a slightly different algorithm called **least angle regression** or **LAR**. LAR is very similar to **greedy forward selection**, and a method known as **least squares boosting** (see e.g., [HTW15]).

11.5 Regression splines *

We have seen how we can use polynomial basis functions to create nonlinear mappings from input to output, even though the model remains linear in the parameters. One problem with polynomials is that they are a global approximation to the function. We can achieve more flexibility by using a series of local approximations. To do this, we just need to define a set of basis functions that have local support. The notion of "locality" is hard to define in high-dimensional input spaces, so in this section, we restrict ourselves to 1d inputs. We can then approximate the function using

$$f(x; \boldsymbol{\theta}) = \sum_{i=1}^{m} w_i B_i(x) \tag{11.106}$$

where B_i is the i'th basis function.

A common way to define such basis functions is to use **B-splines**. ("B" stands for "basis", and the term "spline" refers to a flexible piece of material used by artists to draw curves.) We discuss this in more detail in Section 11.5.1.

11.5.1 B-spline basis functions

A spline is a piecewise polynomial of degree D, where the locations of the pieces are defined by a set of **knots**, $t_1 < \cdots < t_m$. More precisely, the polynomial is defined on each of the intervals $(-\infty, t_1)$, $[t_1, t_2], \cdots, [t_m, \infty)$. The function is continuous and has continuous derivatives of orders $1, \ldots, D-1$ at its knot points. It is common to use **cubic splines**, in which $D = 3$. This ensures the function is continuous, and has continuous first and second derivatives at each knot.

We will skip the details on how B-splines are computed, since it is not relevant to our purposes. Suffice it to say that we can call the patsy.bs function to convert the $N \times 1$ data matrix $\mathbf{X}$ into an $N \times (K+D+1)$ design matrix $\mathbf{B}$, where K is the number of knots and D is the degree. (Alternatively, you can specify the desired number of basis functions, and let patsy work out the number and locations of the knots.)

Figure 11.16 illustrates this approach, where we use B-splines of degree 0, 1 and 3, with 3 knots. By taking a weighted combination of these basis functions, we can get increasingly smooth functions, as shown in the bottom row.

We see from Figure 11.16 that each individual basis function has local support. At any given input point x, only $D + 1$ basis functions will be "active". This is more obvious if we plot the design matrix

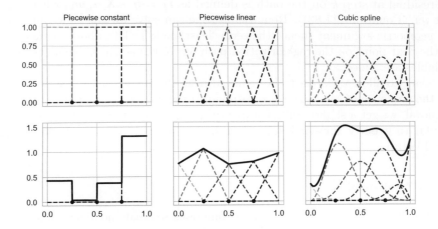

Figure 11.16: *Illustration of B-splines of degree 0, 1 and 3. Top row: unweighted basis functions. Dots mark the locations of the 3 internal knots at* [0.25, 0.5, 0.75]. *Bottom row: weighted combination of basis functions using random weights. Generated by* splines_basis_weighted.ipynb. *Adapted from Figure 5.4 of [MKL11]. Used with kind permission of Osvaldo Martin.*

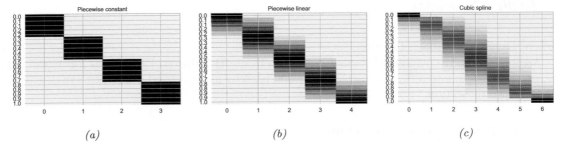

Figure 11.17: *Design matrix for B-splines of degree (a) 0, (b) 1 and (c) 3. We evaluate the splines on 20 inputs ranging from 0 to 1. Generated by* splines_basis_heatmap.ipynb. *Adapted from Figure 5.6 of [MKL11]. Used with kind permission of Osvaldo Martin.*

B itself. Let us first consider the piecewise constant spline, shown in Figure 11.17(a). The first B-spline (column 1) is 1 for the first 5 observations, and otherwise 0. The second B-spline (column 0) is 0 for the first 5 observations, 1 for the second 5, and then 0 again. And so on. Now consider the linear spline, shown in Figure 11.17(b). The first B-spline (column 0) goes from 1 to 0, the next three splines go from 0 to 1 and back to 0; and the last spline (column 4) goes from 0 to 1; this reflects the triangular shapes shown in the top middle panel of Figure 11.16. Finally consider the cubic spline, shown in Figure 11.17(c). Here the pattern of activations is smoother, and the resulting model fits will be smoother too.

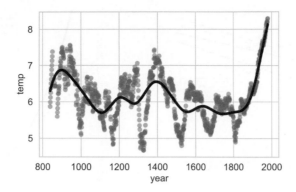

Figure 11.18: Fitting a cubic spline regression model with 15 knots to a 1d dataset. Generated by splines_cherry_blossoms.ipynb. Adapted from Figure 5.3 of [McE20].

11.5.2   Fitting a linear model using a spline basis

Once we have computed the design matrix $\mathbf{B}$, we can use it to fit a linear model using least squares or ridge regression. (It is usually best to use some regularization.) As an example, we consider a dataset from [McE20, Sec 4.5], which records the the first day of the year, and the corresponding temperature, that marks the start of the cherry blossom season in Japan. (We use this dataset since it has interesting semi-periodic structure.) We fit the data using a cubic spline. We pick 15 knots, spaced according to quantiles of the data. The results are shown in Figure 11.18. We see that the fit is reasonable. Using more knots would improve the quality of the fit, but would eventually result in overfitting. We can select the number of knots using a model selection method, such as grid search plus cross validation.

11.5.3   Smoothing splines

Smoothing splines are related to regression splines, but use N knots, where N is the number of datapoints. That is, they are non-parametric models, since the number of parameters grows with the size of the data, rather than being fixed a priori. To avoid overfitting, smoothing splines rely on ℓ_2 regularization. This technique is closely related to Gaussian process regression, which we discuss in Section 17.2.

11.5.4   Generalized additive models

A **generalized additive model** or **GAM** extends spline regression to the case of multidimensional inputs [HT90]. It does this by ignoring interactions between the inputs, and assuming the function has the following additive form:

$$f(\boldsymbol{x}; \boldsymbol{\theta}) = \alpha + \sum_{d=1}^{D} f_d(x_d) \tag{11.107}$$

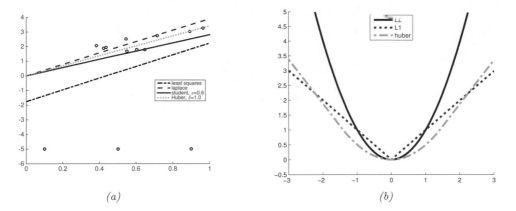

Figure 11.19: (a) Illustration of robust linear regression. Generated by linregRobustDemoCombined.ipynb. (b) Illustration of ℓ_2, ℓ_1, and Huber loss functions with $\delta = 1.5$. Generated by huberLossPlot.ipynb.

where each f_d is a regression or smoothing spline. This model can be fit using **backfitting**, which iteratively fits each f_d to the partial residuals generated by the other terms. We can extend GAMs beyond the regression case (e.g., to classification) by using a link function, as in generalized linear models (Chapter 12).

11.6   Robust linear regression *

It is very common to model the noise in regression models using a Gaussian distribution with zero mean and constant variance, $r_n \sim \mathcal{N}(0, \sigma^2)$, where $r_n = y_n - \boldsymbol{w}^\mathsf{T}\boldsymbol{x}_n$. In this case, maximizing likelihood is equivalent to minimizing the sum of squared residuals, as we have seen. However, if we have **outliers** in our data, this can result in a poor fit, as illustrated in Figure 11.19(a). (The outliers are the points on the bottom of the figure.) This is because squared error penalizes deviations quadratically, so points far from the line have more effect on the fit than points near to the line.

One way to achieve **robustness** to outliers is to replace the Gaussian distribution for the response variable with a distribution that has **heavy tails**. Such a distribution will assign higher likelihood to outliers, without having to perturb the straight line to "explain" them. We discuss several possible alternative probability distributions for the response variable below; see Table 11.2 for a summary.

11.6.1   Laplace likelihood

In Section 2.7.3, we noted that the Laplace distribution is also robust to outliers. If we use this as our observation model for regression, we get the following likelihood:

$$p(y|\boldsymbol{x}, \boldsymbol{w}, b) = \text{Laplace}(y|\boldsymbol{w}^\mathsf{T}\boldsymbol{x}, b) \propto \exp(-\frac{1}{b}|y - \boldsymbol{w}^\mathsf{T}\boldsymbol{x}|) \tag{11.108}$$

The robustness arises from the use of $|y - \boldsymbol{w}^\mathsf{T}\boldsymbol{x}|$ instead of $(y - \boldsymbol{w}^\mathsf{T}\boldsymbol{x})^2$. Figure 11.19(a) gives an example of the method in action.

Likelihood	Prior	Posterior	Name	Section
Gaussian	Uniform	Point	Least squares	11.2.2
Student	Uniform	Point	Robust regression	11.6.2
Laplace	Uniform	Point	Robust regression	11.6.1
Gaussian	Gaussian	Point	Ridge	11.3
Gaussian	Laplace	Point	Lasso	11.4
Gaussian	Gauss-Gamma	Gauss-Gamma	Bayesian lin. reg	11.7

Table 11.2: *Summary of various likelihoods, priors and posteriors used for linear regression. The likelihood refers to the distributional form of $p(y|\boldsymbol{x}, \boldsymbol{w}, \sigma^2)$, and the prior refers to the distributional form of $p(\boldsymbol{w})$. The posterior refers to the distributional form of $p(\boldsymbol{w}|\mathcal{D})$. "Point" stands for the degenerate distribution $\delta(\boldsymbol{w} - \hat{\boldsymbol{w}})$, where $\hat{\boldsymbol{w}}$ is the MAP estimate. MLE is equivalent to using a point posterior and a uniform prior.*

11.6.1.1   Computing the MLE using linear programming

We can compute the MLE for this model using linear programming. As we explain in Section 8.5.3, this is a way to solve a constrained optimization problems of the form

$$\underset{\boldsymbol{v}}{\operatorname{argmin}} \, \boldsymbol{c}^\mathsf{T}\boldsymbol{v} \quad \text{s.t.} \quad \mathbf{A}\boldsymbol{v} \leq \boldsymbol{b} \tag{11.109}$$

where $\boldsymbol{v} \in \mathbb{R}^n$ is the set of n unknown parameters, $\boldsymbol{c}^\mathsf{T}\boldsymbol{v}$ is the linear objective function we want to minimize, and $\boldsymbol{a}_i^\mathsf{T}\boldsymbol{v} \leq b_i$ is a set of m linear constraints we must satisfy. To apply this to our problem, let us define $\boldsymbol{v} = (w_1, \ldots, w_D, e_1, \ldots, e_N) \in \mathbb{R}^{D+N}$, where $e_i = |y_i - \hat{y}_i|$ is the residual error for example i. We want to minimize the sum of the residuals, so we define $\boldsymbol{c} = (0, \cdots, 0, 1, \cdots, 1) \in \mathbb{R}^{D+N}$, where the first D elements are 0, and the last N elements are 1.

We need to enforce the constraint that $e_i = |\hat{y}_i - y_i|$. In fact it is sufficient to enforce the constraint that $|\boldsymbol{w}^\mathsf{T}\boldsymbol{x}_i - y_i| \leq e_i$, since minimizing the sum of the e_i's will "push down" on this constraint and make it tight. Since $|a| \leq b \implies -b \leq a \leq b$, we can encode $|\boldsymbol{w}^\mathsf{T}\boldsymbol{x}_i - y_i| \leq e_i$ as two linear constraints:

$$e_i \geq \boldsymbol{w}^\mathsf{T}\boldsymbol{x}_i - y_i \tag{11.110}$$

$$e_i \geq -(\boldsymbol{w}^\mathsf{T}\boldsymbol{x}_i - y_i) \tag{11.111}$$

We can write Equation (11.110) as

$$\left(\boldsymbol{x}_i, 0, \cdots, 0, -1, 0, \cdots, 0\right)^\mathsf{T} \boldsymbol{v} \leq y_i \tag{11.112}$$

where the first D entries are filled with $\boldsymbol{x}_i$, and the -1 is in the $(D + i)$'th entry of the vector. Similarly we can write Equation (11.111) as

$$\left(-\boldsymbol{x}_i, 0, \cdots, 0, -1, 0, \cdots, 0\right)^\mathsf{T} \boldsymbol{v} \leq -y_i \tag{11.113}$$

We can write these constraints in the form $\mathbf{A}\boldsymbol{v} \leq \boldsymbol{b}$ by defining $\mathbf{A} \in \mathbb{R}^{2N \times (N+D)}$ as follows:

$$
\mathbf{A} = \begin{pmatrix}
\boldsymbol{x}_1 & -1 & 0 & 0 \cdots & 0 \\
-\boldsymbol{x}_1 & -1 & 0 & 0 \cdots & 0 \\
\boldsymbol{x}_2 & 0 & -1 & 0 \cdots & 0 \\
-\boldsymbol{x}_2 & 0 & -1 & 0 \cdots & 0 \\
& & \vdots & &
\end{pmatrix}
\tag{11.114}
$$

and defining $\boldsymbol{b} \in \mathbb{R}^{2N}$ as

$$
\boldsymbol{b} = \left(y_1, -y_1, y_2, -y_2, \cdots, y_N, -y_N \right)
\tag{11.115}
$$

11.6.2   Student-t likelihood

In Section 2.7.1, we discussed the robustness properties of the Student distribution. To use this in a regression context, we can just make the mean be a linear function of the inputs, as proposed in [Zel76]:

$$
p(y|\boldsymbol{x}, \boldsymbol{w}, \sigma^2, \nu) = \mathcal{T}(y|\boldsymbol{w}^\mathsf{T}\boldsymbol{x}, \sigma^2, \nu)
\tag{11.116}
$$

We can fit this model using SGD or EM (see [Mur23] for details).

11.6.3   Huber loss

An alternative to minimizing the NLL using a Laplace or Student likelihood is to use the **Huber loss**, which is defined as follows:

$$
\ell_{\text{huber}}(r, \delta) = \begin{cases} r^2/2 & \text{if } |r| \leq \delta \\ \delta|r| - \delta^2/2 & \text{if } |r| > \delta \end{cases}
\tag{11.117}
$$

This is equivalent to ℓ_2 for errors that are smaller than δ, and is equivalent to ℓ_1 for larger errors. See Figure 5.3 for a plot.

The advantage of this loss function is that it is everywhere differentiable. Consequently optimizing the Huber loss is much faster than using the Laplace likelihood, since we can use standard smooth optimization methods (such as SGD) instead of linear programming. Figure 11.19 gives an illustration of the Huber loss function in action. The results are qualitatively similiar to the Laplace and Student methods.

The parameter δ, which controls the degree of robustness, is usually set by hand, or by cross-validation. However, [Bar19] shows how to approximate the Huber loss such that we can optimize δ by gradient methods.

11.6.4   RANSAC

In the computer vision community, a common approach to robust regression is to use **RANSAC**, which stands for "random sample consensus" [FB81]. This works as follows: we sample a small initial set of points, fit the model to them, identify outliers wrt this model (based on large residuals), remove the outliers, and then refit the model to the inliers. We repeat this for many random initial sets and pick the best model.

A deterministic alternative to RANSAC is the following iterative scheme: intially we assume that all datapoints are inliers, and we fit the model to compute $\hat{w}_0$; then, for each iteration t, we identify the outlier points as those with large residual under the model $\hat{w}_t$, remove them, and refit the model to the remaining points to get $\hat{w}_{t+1}$. Even though this hard thresholding scheme makes the problem nonconvex, this simple scheme can be proved to rapidly converge to the optimal estimate under some reasonable assumptions [Muk+19; Sug+19].

11.7 Bayesian linear regression *

We have seen how to compute the MLE and MAP estimate for linear regression models under various priors. In this section, we discuss how to compute the posterior over the parameters, $p(\boldsymbol{\theta}|\mathcal{D})$. For simplicity, we assume the variance is known, so we just want to compute $p(\boldsymbol{w}|\mathcal{D}, \sigma^2)$. See the sequel to this book, [Mur23], for the general case.

11.7.1 Priors

For simplicity, we will use a Gaussian prior:

$$p(\boldsymbol{w}) = \mathcal{N}(\boldsymbol{w}|\,\breve{\boldsymbol{w}}, \breve{\boldsymbol{\Sigma}}) \tag{11.118}$$

This is a small generalization of the prior that we use in ridge regression (Section 11.3). See the sequel to this book, [Mur23], for a discussion of other priors.

11.7.2 Posteriors

We can rewrite the likelihood in terms of an MVN as follows:

$$p(\mathcal{D}|\boldsymbol{w}, \sigma^2) = \prod_{n=1}^{N} p(y_n|\boldsymbol{w}^\mathsf{T}\boldsymbol{x}, \sigma^2) = \mathcal{N}(\boldsymbol{y}|\mathbf{X}\boldsymbol{w}, \sigma^2\mathbf{I}_N) \tag{11.119}$$

where $\mathbf{I}_N$ is the $N \times N$ identity matrix. We can then use Bayes rule for Gaussians (Equation (3.37)) to derive the posterior, which is as follows:

$$p(\boldsymbol{w}|\mathbf{X}, \boldsymbol{y}, \sigma^2) \propto \mathcal{N}(\boldsymbol{w}|\,\breve{\boldsymbol{w}}, \breve{\boldsymbol{\Sigma}})\mathcal{N}(\boldsymbol{y}|\mathbf{X}\boldsymbol{w}, \sigma^2\mathbf{I}_N) = \mathcal{N}(\boldsymbol{w}|\,\hat{\boldsymbol{w}}, \hat{\boldsymbol{\Sigma}}) \tag{11.120}$$

$$\hat{\boldsymbol{w}} \triangleq \hat{\boldsymbol{\Sigma}}\,(\breve{\boldsymbol{\Sigma}}^{-1}\breve{\boldsymbol{w}} + \frac{1}{\sigma^2}\mathbf{X}^\mathsf{T}\boldsymbol{y}) \tag{11.121}$$

$$\hat{\boldsymbol{\Sigma}} \triangleq (\breve{\boldsymbol{\Sigma}}^{-1} + \frac{1}{\sigma^2}\mathbf{X}^\mathsf{T}\mathbf{X})^{-1} \tag{11.122}$$

where $\hat{\boldsymbol{w}}$ is the posterior mean, and $\hat{\boldsymbol{\Sigma}}$ is the posterior covariance.

If $\breve{\boldsymbol{w}} = \mathbf{0}$ and $\breve{\boldsymbol{\Sigma}} = \tau^2\mathbf{I}$, then the posterior mean becomes $\hat{\boldsymbol{w}} = \frac{1}{\sigma^2}\hat{\boldsymbol{\Sigma}}\mathbf{X}^\mathsf{T}\boldsymbol{y}$. If we define $\lambda = \frac{\sigma^2}{\tau^2}$, we recover the ridge regression estimate, $\hat{\boldsymbol{w}} = (\lambda\mathbf{I} + \mathbf{X}^\mathsf{T}\mathbf{X})^{-1}\mathbf{X}^\mathsf{T}\boldsymbol{y}$, which matches Equation (11.57).

11.7.3 Example

Suppose we have a 1d regression model of the form $f(x; \boldsymbol{w}) = w_0 + w_1 x_1$, where the true parameters are $w_0 = -0.3$ and $w_1 = 0.5$. We now perform inference $p(\boldsymbol{w}|\mathcal{D})$ and visualize the 2d prior and posterior as the size of the training set N increases.

In particular, in Figure 11.20 (which inspired the front cover of this book), we plot the likelihood, the posterior, and an approximation to the posterior predictive distribution.[4] Each row plots these distributions as we increase the amount of training data, N. We now explain each row:

- In the first row, $N = 0$, so the posterior is the same as the prior. In this case, our predictions are "all over the place", since our prior is essentially uniform.

- In the second row, $N = 1$, so we have seen one data point (the blue circle in the plot in the third column). Our posterior becomes constrained by the corresponding likelihood, and our predictions pass close to the observed data. However, we see that the posterior has a ridge-like shape, reflecting the fact that there are many possible solutions, with different slopes/intercepts. This makes sense since we cannot uniquely infer two parameters (w_0 and w_1) from one observation.

- In the third row, $N = 2$. In this case, the posterior becomes much narrower since we have two constraints from the likelihood. Our predictions about the future are all now closer to the training data.

- In the fourth (last) row, $N = 100$. Now the posterior is essentially a delta function, centered on the true value of $\boldsymbol{w}_* = (-0.3, 0.5)$, indicated by a white cross in the plots in the first and second columns. The variation in our predictions is due to the inherent Gaussian noise with magnitude σ^2.

This example illustrates that, as the amount of data increases, the posterior mean estimate, $\hat{\boldsymbol{\mu}} = \mathbb{E}[\boldsymbol{w}|\mathcal{D}]$, converges to the true value $\boldsymbol{w}_*$ that generated the data. We thus say that the Bayesian estimate is a consistent estimator (see Section 5.3.2 for more details). We also see that our posterior uncertainty decreases over time. This is what we mean when we say we are "learning" about the parameters as we see more data.

11.7.4 Computing the posterior predictive

We have discussed how to compute our uncertainty about the parameters of the model, $p(\boldsymbol{w}|\mathcal{D})$. But what about the uncertainty associated with our predictions about future outputs? Using Equation (3.38), we can show that the posterior predictive distribution at a test point $\boldsymbol{x}$ is also Gaussian:

$$p(y|\boldsymbol{x}, \mathcal{D}, \sigma^2) = \int \mathcal{N}(y|\boldsymbol{x}^\mathsf{T}\boldsymbol{w}, \sigma^2) \mathcal{N}(\boldsymbol{w}|\hat{\boldsymbol{\mu}}, \hat{\boldsymbol{\Sigma}}) d\boldsymbol{w} \tag{11.123}$$

$$= \mathcal{N}(y|\hat{\boldsymbol{\mu}}^\mathsf{T}\boldsymbol{x}, \hat{\sigma}^2(\boldsymbol{x})) \tag{11.124}$$

---

4. To approximate this, we draw some samples from the posterior, $\boldsymbol{w}_s \sim \mathcal{N}(\boldsymbol{\mu}, \boldsymbol{\Sigma})$, and then plot the line $\mathbb{E}[y|x, \boldsymbol{w}_s]$, where x ranges over $[-1, 1]$, for each sampled parameter value.

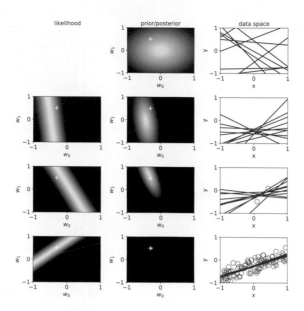

Figure 11.20: Sequential Bayesian inference of the parameters of a linear regression model $p(y|\boldsymbol{x}) = \mathcal{N}(y|w_0 + w_1 x_1, \sigma^2)$. Left column: likelihood function for current data point. Middle column: posterior given first N data points, $p(w_0, w_1|\boldsymbol{x}_{1:N}, y_{1:N}, \sigma^2)$. Right column: samples from the current posterior predictive distribution. Row 1: prior distribution ($N = 0$). Row 2: after 1 data point. Row 3: after 2 data points. Row 4: after 100 data points. The white cross in columns 1 and 2 represents the true parameter value; we see that the mode of the posterior rapidly converges to this point. The blue circles in column 3 are the observed data points. Adapted from Figure 3.7 of [Bis06]. Generated by linreg_2d_bayes_demo.ipynb.

where $\widehat{\sigma}^2(\boldsymbol{x}) \triangleq \sigma^2 + \boldsymbol{x}^\mathsf{T} \widehat{\boldsymbol{\Sigma}} \, \boldsymbol{x}$ is the variance of the posterior predictive distribution at point $\boldsymbol{x}$ after seeing the N training examples. The predicted variance depends on two terms: the variance of the observation noise, σ^2, and the variance in the parameters, $\widehat{\boldsymbol{\Sigma}}$. The latter translates into variance about observations in a way which depends on how close $\boldsymbol{x}$ is to the training data $\mathcal{D}$. This is illustrated in Figure 11.21(b), where we see that the error bars get larger as we move away from the training points, representing increased uncertainty. This can be important for certain applications, such as active learning, where we choose where to collect training data (see Section 19.4).

In some cases, it is computationally intractable to compute the parameter posterior, $p(\boldsymbol{w}|\mathcal{D})$. In such cases, we may choose to use a point estimate, $\hat{\boldsymbol{w}}$, and then to use the plugin approximation. This gives

$$p(y|\boldsymbol{x}, \mathcal{D}, \sigma^2) = \int \mathcal{N}(y|\boldsymbol{x}^\mathsf{T}\boldsymbol{w}, \sigma^2)\delta(\boldsymbol{w} - \hat{\boldsymbol{w}})d\boldsymbol{w} = p(y|\boldsymbol{x}^\mathsf{T}\hat{\boldsymbol{w}}, \sigma^2). \tag{11.125}$$

We see that the posterior predictive variance is constant, and independent of the data, as illustrated in Figure 11.21(a). If we sample a parameter from this posterior, we will always recover a single function, as shown in Figure 11.21(c). By contrast, if we sample from the true posterior, $\boldsymbol{w}_s \sim p(\boldsymbol{w}|\mathcal{D}, \sigma^2)$, we will get a range of different functions, as shown in Figure 11.21(d), which more accurately reflects our uncertainty.

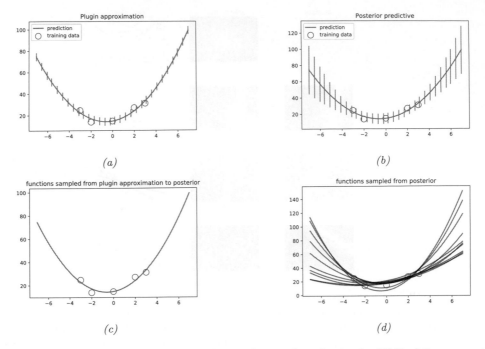

Figure 11.21: (a) Plugin approximation to predictive density (we plug in the MLE of the parameters) when fitting a second degree polynomial to some 1d data. (b) Posterior predictive density, obtained by integrating out the parameters. Black curve is posterior mean, error bars are 2 standard deviations of the posterior predictive density. (c) 10 samples from the plugin approximation to posterior predictive distribution. (d) 10 samples from the true posterior predictive distribution. Generated by linreg_post_pred_plot.ipynb.

11.7.5   The advantage of centering

The astute reader might notice that the shape of the 2d posterior in Figure 11.20 is an elongated ellipse (which eventually collapses to a point as $N \to \infty$). This implies that there is a lot of posterior correlation between the two parameters, which can cause computational difficulties.

To understand why this happens, note that each data point induces a likelihood function corresponding to a line which goes through that data point. When we look at all the data together, we see that predictions with maximum likelihood must correspond to lines that go through the mean of the data, $(\overline{x}, \overline{y})$. There are many such lines, but if we increase the slope, we must decrease the intercept. Thus we can think of the set of high probability lines as spinning around the data mean, like a wheel of fortune.[5] This correlation between w_0 and w_1 is why the posterior has the form of a diagonal line. (The Gaussian prior converts this into an elongated ellipse, but the posterior correlation still persists until the sample size causes the posterior to shrink to a point.)

It can be hard to compute such elongated posteriors. One simple solution is to center the input data, i.e., by using $x'_n = x_n - \overline{x}$. Now the lines can pivot around the origin, reducing the posterior

---

5. This analogy is from [Mar18, p96].

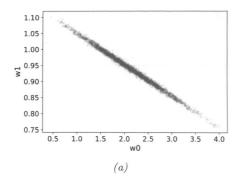
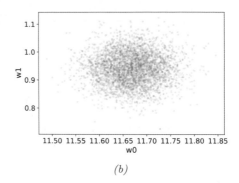

(a)   (b)

Figure 11.22: *Posterior samples of $p(w_0, w_1|\mathcal{D})$ for 1d linear regression model $p(y|x, \boldsymbol{\theta}) = \mathcal{N}(y|w_0 + w_1 x, \sigma^2)$ with a Gaussian prior. (a) Original data. (b) Centered data. Generated by lin-reg_2d_bayes_centering_pymc3.ipynb.*

correlation between w_0 and w_1. See Figure 11.22 for an illustration. (We may also choose to divide each x_n by the standard deviation of that feature, as discussed in Section 10.2.8.)

Note that we can convert the posterior derived from fitting to the centered data back to the original coordinates by noting that

$$y' = w_0' + w_1' x' = w_0' + w_1'(x - \overline{x}) = (w_0' - w_1'\overline{x}) + w_1' x \tag{11.126}$$

Thus the parameters on the uncentered data are $w_0 = w_0' - w_1'\overline{x}$ and $w_1 = w_1'$.

11.7.6   Dealing with multicollinearity

In many datasets, the input variables can be highly correlated with each other. Including all of them does not generally harm predictive accuracy (provided you use a suitable prior or regularizer to prevent overfitting). However, it can make interpretation of the coefficients more difficult.

To illustrate this, we use a toy example from [McE20, Sec 6.1]. Suppose we have a dataset of N people in which we record their heights h_i, as well as the length of their left legs l_i and right legs r_i. Suppose $h_i \sim \mathcal{N}(10, 2)$, so the average height is $\overline{h} = 10$ (in unspecified units). Suppose the length of the legs is some fraction $\rho_i \sim \text{Unif}(0.4, 0.5)$ of the height, plus a bit of Gaussian noise, specifically $l_i \sim \mathcal{N}(\rho_i h_i, 0.02)$ and $r_i \sim \mathcal{N}(\rho_i h_i, 0.02)$.

Now suppose we want to predict the height of a person given measurement of their leg lengths. (I did mention this is a toy example!) Since both left and right legs are noisy measurements of the unknown quantity, it is useful to use both of them. So we use linear regression to fit $p(h|l, r) = \mathcal{N}(h|\alpha + \beta_l l + \beta_r r, \sigma^2)$. We use vague priors, $\alpha, \beta_l, \beta_r \sim \mathcal{N}(0, 100)$, and $\sigma \sim \text{Expon}(1)$.

Since the average leg length is $\overline{l} = 0.45\overline{h} = 4.5$, we might expect each β coefficient to be around $\overline{h}/\overline{l} = 10/4.5 = 2.2$. However, the posterior marginals shown in Figure 11.23 tell a different story: we see that the posterior mean of β_l is near 2.6, but β_r is near -0.6. Thus it seems like the right leg feature is not needed. This is because the regression coefficient for feature j encodes the value of knowing x_j given that all the other features $\boldsymbol{x}_{-j}$ are already known, as we discussed in Section 11.2.2.1. If we already know the left leg, the marginal value of also knowing the right leg is small. However, if we

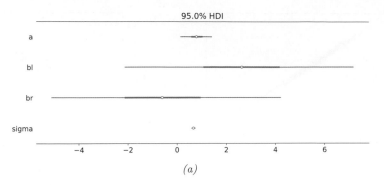

(a)

Figure 11.23: Posterior marginals for the parameters in the multi-leg example.   Generated by multi_collinear_legs_numpyro.ipynb.

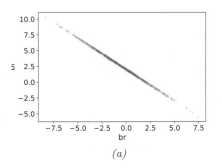

(a)

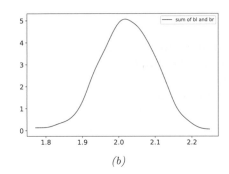

(b)

Figure 11.24: Posteriors for the multi-leg example. (a) Joint posterior $p(\beta_l, \beta_r | \mathcal{D})$ (b) Posterior of $p(\beta_l + \beta_r | data)$. Generated by multi_collinear_legs_numpyro.ipynb.

rerun this example with slightly different data, we may reach the opposite conclusion, and favor the right leg over the left.

We can gain more insight by looking at the joint distribution $p(\beta_l, \beta_r | \mathcal{D})$, shown in Figure 11.24a. We see that the parameters are very highly correlated, so if β_r is large, then β_l is small, and vice versa. The marginal distribution for each parameter does not capture this. However, it does show that there is a lot of uncertainty about each parameter, showing that they are **non-identifiable**. However, their *sum* is well-determined, as can be seen from Figure 11.24b, where we plot $p(\beta_l + \beta_r | \mathcal{D})$; this is centered on 2.2, as we might expect.

This example goes to show that we must be careful trying to interpret the significance of individual coefficient estimates in a model, since they do not mean much in isolation.

11.7.7   Automatic relevancy determination (ARD) *

Consider a linear regression model with known observation noise but unknown regression weights, $\mathcal{N}(\boldsymbol{y} | \mathbf{X}\boldsymbol{w}, \sigma^2 \mathbf{I})$. Suppose we use a Gaussian prior for the weights, $w_j \sim \mathcal{N}(0, 1/\alpha_j)$, where α_j is the precision of the j'th parameter. Now suppose we estimate the prior precisions as follows:

$$\hat{\boldsymbol{\alpha}} = \underset{\boldsymbol{\alpha}}{\operatorname{argmax}}\, p(\boldsymbol{y}|\mathbf{X}, \boldsymbol{\alpha}) \tag{11.127}$$

where

$$p(\boldsymbol{y}|\mathbf{X}, \boldsymbol{\alpha}) = \int p(\boldsymbol{y}|\mathbf{X}\boldsymbol{w}, \sigma^2) p(\boldsymbol{w}|\mathbf{0}, \operatorname{diag}(\boldsymbol{\alpha})^{-1}) d\boldsymbol{w} \tag{11.128}$$

is the marginal likelihood. This is an example of empirical Bayes, since we are estimating the prior from data. We can view this as a computational shortcut to a fully Bayesian approach. However, there are additional advantages. In particular, suppose, after estimating $\boldsymbol{\alpha}$, we compute the MAP estimate

$$\hat{\boldsymbol{w}} = \underset{\boldsymbol{w}}{\operatorname{argmax}}\, \mathcal{N}(\boldsymbol{w}|\mathbf{0}, \hat{\boldsymbol{\alpha}}^{-1}) \tag{11.129}$$

This results in a sparse estimate for $\hat{\boldsymbol{w}}$, which is perhaps surprising given that the Gaussian prior for $\boldsymbol{w}$ is not sparsity promoting. The reasons for this are explained in the sequel to this book.

This technique is known as **sparse Bayesian learning** [Tip01] or **automatic relevancy determination** (**ARD**) [Mac95; Nea96]. It was originally developed for neural networks (where sparsity is applied to the first layer weights), but here we apply it to linear models. See also Section 17.4.1, where we apply it kernelized linear models.

11.8 Exercises

Exercise 11.1 [Multi-output linear regression *]
(Source: Jaakkola.)

Consider a linear regression model with a 2 dimensional response vector $\boldsymbol{y}_i \in \mathbb{R}^2$. Suppose we have some binary input data, $x_i \in \{0, 1\}$. The training data is as follows:

x	y
0	$(-1, -1)^T$
0	$(-1, -2)^T$
0	$(-2, -1)^T$
1	$(1, 1)^T$
1	$(1, 2)^T$
1	$(2, 1)^T$

Let us embed each x_i into 2d using the following basis function:

$$\boldsymbol{\phi}(0) = (1, 0)^T, \quad \boldsymbol{\phi}(1) = (0, 1)^T \tag{11.130}$$

The model becomes

$$\hat{\boldsymbol{y}} = \mathbf{W}^T \boldsymbol{\phi}(x) \tag{11.131}$$

where $\mathbf{W}$ is a 2×2 matrix. Compute the MLE for $\mathbf{W}$ from the above data.

Exercise 11.2 [Centering and ridge regression]
Assume that $\bar{\boldsymbol{x}} = 0$, so the input data has been centered. Show that the optimizer of

$$J(\boldsymbol{w}, w_0) = (\boldsymbol{y} - \mathbf{X}\boldsymbol{w} - w_0 \mathbf{1})^T (\boldsymbol{y} - \mathbf{X}\boldsymbol{w} - w_0 \mathbf{1}) + \lambda \boldsymbol{w}^T \boldsymbol{w} \tag{11.132}$$

is

$$\hat{w}_0 = \bar{y} \tag{11.133}$$

$$\boldsymbol{w} = (\mathbf{X}^T\mathbf{X} + \lambda\mathbf{I})^{-1}\mathbf{X}^T\boldsymbol{y} \tag{11.134}$$

Exercise 11.3 [Partial derivative of the RSS *]

Let $RSS(\boldsymbol{w}) = ||\mathbf{X}\boldsymbol{w} - \boldsymbol{y}||_2^2$ be the residual sum of squares.

a. Show that

$$\frac{\partial}{\partial w_k} RSS(\boldsymbol{w}) = a_k w_k - c_k \tag{11.135}$$

$$a_k = 2\sum_{i=1}^{n} x_{ik}^2 = 2||\boldsymbol{x}_{:,k}||^2 \tag{11.136}$$

$$c_k = 2\sum_{i=1}^{n} x_{ik}(y_i - \boldsymbol{w}_{-k}^T\boldsymbol{x}_{i,-k}) = 2\boldsymbol{x}_{:,k}^T\boldsymbol{r}_k \tag{11.137}$$

where $\boldsymbol{w}_{-k} = \boldsymbol{w}$ without component k, $\boldsymbol{x}_{i,-k}$ is $\boldsymbol{x}_i$ without component k, and $\boldsymbol{r}_k = \boldsymbol{y} - \boldsymbol{w}_{-k}^T\boldsymbol{x}_{:,-k}$ is the residual due to using all the features except feature k. Hint: Partition the weights into those involving k and those not involving k.

b. Show that if $\frac{\partial}{\partial w_k} RSS(\boldsymbol{w}) = 0$, then

$$\hat{w}_k = \frac{\boldsymbol{x}_{:,k}^T\boldsymbol{r}_k}{||\boldsymbol{x}_{:,k}||^2} \tag{11.138}$$

Hence when we sequentially add features, the optimal weight for feature k is computed by computing orthogonally projecting $\boldsymbol{x}_{:,k}$ onto the current residual.

Exercise 11.4 [Reducing elastic net to lasso]

Define

$$J_1(\boldsymbol{w}) = ||\boldsymbol{y} - \mathbf{X}\boldsymbol{w}||^2 + \lambda_2||\boldsymbol{w}||_2^2 + \lambda_1||\boldsymbol{w}||_1 \tag{11.139}$$

and

$$J_2(\boldsymbol{w}) = ||\tilde{\boldsymbol{y}} - \tilde{\mathbf{X}}\boldsymbol{w}||^2 + c\lambda_1||\boldsymbol{w}||_1 \tag{11.140}$$

where $||\boldsymbol{w}||^2 = ||\boldsymbol{w}||_2^2 = \sum_i w_i^2$ is the squared 2-norm, $||\boldsymbol{w}||_1 = \sum_i |w_i|$ is the 1-norm, $c = (1 + \lambda_2)^{-\frac{1}{2}}$, and

$$\tilde{\mathbf{X}} = c\begin{pmatrix} \mathbf{X} \\ \sqrt{\lambda_2}\mathbf{I}_d \end{pmatrix}, \quad \tilde{\boldsymbol{y}} = \begin{pmatrix} \boldsymbol{y} \\ \mathbf{0}_{d \times 1} \end{pmatrix} \tag{11.141}$$

Show

$$\operatorname{argmin} J_1(\boldsymbol{w}) = c(\operatorname{argmin} J_2(\boldsymbol{w})) \tag{11.142}$$

i.e.

$$J_1(c\boldsymbol{w}) = J_2(\boldsymbol{w}) \tag{11.143}$$

and hence that one can solve an elastic net problem using a lasso solver on modified data.

Exercise 11.5 [Shrinkage in linear regression *]

(Source: Jaakkola.) Consider performing linear regression with an orthonormal design matrix, so $||\boldsymbol{x}_{:,k}||_2^2 = 1$ for each column (feature) k, and $\boldsymbol{x}_{:,k}^T \boldsymbol{x}_{:,j} = 0$, so we can estimate each parameter w_k separately.

Figure 10.15b plots $\hat{w}_k$ vs $c_k = 2\boldsymbol{y}^T \boldsymbol{x}_{:,k}$, the correlation of feature k with the response, for 3 different estimation methods: ordinary least squares (OLS), ridge regression with parameter λ_2, and lasso with parameter λ_1.

a. Unfortunately we forgot to label the plots. Which method does the solid (1), dotted (2) and dashed (3) line correspond to?

b. What is the value of λ_1?

c. What is the value of λ_2?

Exercise 11.6 [EM for mixture of linear regression experts]

Derive the EM equations for fitting a mixture of linear regression experts.

12 Generalized Linear Models *

12.1 Introduction

In Chapter 10, we discussed logistic regression, which, in the binary case, corresponds to the model $p(y|\boldsymbol{x}, \boldsymbol{w}) = \text{Ber}(y|\sigma(\boldsymbol{w}^\mathsf{T}\boldsymbol{x}))$. In Chapter 11, we discussed linear regression, which corresponds to the model $p(y|\boldsymbol{x}, \boldsymbol{w}) = \mathcal{N}(y|\boldsymbol{w}^\mathsf{T}\boldsymbol{x}, \sigma^2)$. These are obviously very similar to each other. In particular, the mean of the output, $\mathbb{E}[y|\boldsymbol{x}, \boldsymbol{w}]$, is a linear function of the inputs $\boldsymbol{x}$ in both cases.

It turns out that there is a broad family of models with this property, known as **generalized linear models** or **GLMs** [MN89].

A GLM is a conditional version of an exponential family distribution (Section 3.4), in which the natural parameters are a linear function of the input. More precisely, the model has the following form:

$$p(y_n|\boldsymbol{x}_n, \boldsymbol{w}, \sigma^2) = \exp\left[\frac{y_n \eta_n - A(\eta_n)}{\sigma^2} + \log h(y_n, \sigma^2)\right] \tag{12.1}$$

where $\eta_n \triangleq \boldsymbol{w}^\mathsf{T}\boldsymbol{x}_n$ is the (input dependent) natural parameter, $A(\eta_n)$ is the log normalizer, $\mathcal{T}(y) = y$ is the sufficient statistic, and σ^2 is the dispersion term.[1]

We will denote the mapping from the linear inputs to the mean of the output using $\mu_n = \ell^{-1}(\eta_n)$, where the function ℓ is known as the **link function**, and ℓ^{-1} is known as the **mean function**.

Based on the results in Section 3.4.3, we can show that the mean and variance of the response variable are as follows:

$$\mathbb{E}[y_n|\boldsymbol{x}_n, \boldsymbol{w}, \sigma^2] = A'(\eta_n) \triangleq \ell^{-1}(\eta_n) \tag{12.2}$$
$$\mathbb{V}[y_n|\boldsymbol{x}_n, \boldsymbol{w}, \sigma^2] = A''(\eta_n)\sigma^2 \tag{12.3}$$

12.2 Examples

In this section, we give some examples of widely used GLMs.

---

1. Technically speaking, GLMs use a slight extension of the natural exponential family known as the **exponential dispersion family**. For a scalar variable, this has the form $p(y|\eta, \sigma^2) = h(y, \sigma^2) \exp\left[\frac{\eta y - A(\eta)}{\sigma^2}\right]$. Here σ^2 is called the **dispersion parameter**. For fixed σ^2, this is a natural exponential family.

12.2.1   Linear regression

Recall that linear regression has the form

$$p(y_n|\boldsymbol{x}_n,\boldsymbol{w},\sigma^2) = \frac{1}{\sqrt{2\pi\sigma^2}}\exp(-\frac{1}{2\sigma^2}(y_n-\boldsymbol{w}^\mathsf{T}\boldsymbol{x}_n)^2) \tag{12.4}$$

Hence

$$\log p(y_n|\boldsymbol{x}_n,\boldsymbol{w},\sigma^2) = -\frac{1}{2\sigma^2}(y_n-\eta_n)^2 - \frac{1}{2}\log(2\pi\sigma^2) \tag{12.5}$$

where $\eta_n = \boldsymbol{w}^\mathsf{T}\boldsymbol{x}_n$. We can write this in GLM form as follows:

$$\log p(y_n|\boldsymbol{x}_n,\boldsymbol{w},\sigma^2) = \frac{y_n\eta_n - \frac{\eta_n^2}{2}}{\sigma^2} - \frac{1}{2}\left(\frac{y_n^2}{\sigma^2}+\log(2\pi\sigma^2)\right) \tag{12.6}$$

We see that $A(\eta_n) = \eta_n^2/2$ and hence

$$\mathbb{E}[y_n] = \eta_n = \boldsymbol{w}^\mathsf{T}\boldsymbol{x}_n \tag{12.7}$$
$$\mathbb{V}[y_n] = \sigma^2 \tag{12.8}$$

12.2.2   Binomial regression

If the response variable is the number of successes in N_n trials, $y_n \in \{0,\dots,N_n\}$, we can use **binomial regression**, which is defined by

$$p(y_n|\boldsymbol{x}_n,N_n,\boldsymbol{w}) = \mathrm{Bin}(y_n|\sigma(\boldsymbol{w}^\mathsf{T}\boldsymbol{x}_n),N_n) \tag{12.9}$$

We see that binary logistic regression is the special case when $N_n = 1$.

The log pdf is given by

$$\log p(y_n|\boldsymbol{x}_n,N_n,\boldsymbol{w}) = y_n\log\mu_n + (N_n-y_n)\log(1-\mu_n) + \log\binom{N_n}{y_n} \tag{12.10}$$

$$= y_n\log(\frac{\mu_n}{1-\mu_n}) + N_n\log(1-\mu_n) + \log\binom{N_n}{y_n} \tag{12.11}$$

where $\mu_n = \sigma(\eta_n)$. To rewrite this in GLM form, let us define

$$\eta_n \triangleq \log\left[\frac{\mu_n}{(1-\mu_n)}\right] = \log\left[\frac{1}{1+e^{-\boldsymbol{w}^\mathsf{T}\boldsymbol{x}_n}}\frac{1+e^{-\boldsymbol{w}^\mathsf{T}\boldsymbol{x}_n}}{e^{-\boldsymbol{w}^\mathsf{T}\boldsymbol{x}_n}}\right] = \log\frac{1}{e^{-\boldsymbol{w}^\mathsf{T}\boldsymbol{x}_n}} = \boldsymbol{w}^\mathsf{T}\boldsymbol{x}_n \tag{12.12}$$

Hence we can write binomial regression in GLM form as follows

$$\log p(y_n|\boldsymbol{x}_n,N_n,\boldsymbol{w}) = y_n\eta_n - A(\eta_n) + h(y_n) \tag{12.13}$$

where $h(y_n) = \log\binom{N_n}{y_n}$ and

$$A(\eta_n) = -N_n\log(1-\mu_n) = N_n\log(1+e^{\eta_n}) \tag{12.14}$$

Hence

$$\mathbb{E}\left[y_n\right] = \frac{dA}{d\eta_n} = \frac{N_n e^{\eta_n}}{1 + e^{\eta_n}} = \frac{N_n}{1 + e^{-\eta_n}} = N_n \mu_n \tag{12.15}$$

and

$$\mathbb{V}\left[y_n\right] = \frac{d^2 A}{d\eta_n^2} = N_n \mu_n (1 - \mu_n) \tag{12.16}$$

12.2.3 Poisson regression

If the response variable is an integer count, $y_n \in \{0, 1, \ldots\}$, we can use **Poisson regression**, which is defined by

$$p(y_n | \boldsymbol{x}_n, \boldsymbol{w}) = \text{Poi}(y_n | \exp(\boldsymbol{w}^\mathsf{T} \boldsymbol{x}_n)) \tag{12.17}$$

where

$$\text{Poi}(y | \mu) = e^{-\mu} \frac{\mu^y}{y!} \tag{12.18}$$

is the Poisson distribution. Poisson regression is widely used in bio-statistical applications, where y_n might represent the number of diseases of a given person or place, or the number of reads at a genomic location in a high-throughput sequencing context (see e.g., [Kua+09]).

The log pdf is given by

$$\log p(y_n | \boldsymbol{x}_n, \boldsymbol{w}) = y_n \log \mu_n - \mu_n - \log(y_n!) \tag{12.19}$$

where $\mu_n = \exp(\boldsymbol{w}^\mathsf{T} \boldsymbol{x}_n)$. Hence in GLM form we have

$$\log p(y_n | \boldsymbol{x}_n, \boldsymbol{w}) = y_n \eta_n - A(\eta_n) + h(y_n) \tag{12.20}$$

where $\eta_n = \log(\mu_n) = \boldsymbol{w}^\mathsf{T} \boldsymbol{x}_n$, $A(\eta_n) = \mu_n = e^{\eta_n}$, and $h(y_n) = -\log(y_n!)$. Hence

$$\mathbb{E}\left[y_n\right] = \frac{dA}{d\eta_n} = e^{\eta_n} = \mu_n \tag{12.21}$$

and

$$\mathbb{V}\left[y_n\right] = \frac{d^2 A}{d\eta_n^2} = e^{\eta_n} = \mu_n \tag{12.22}$$

12.3 GLMs with non-canonical link functions

We have seen how the mean parameters of the output distribution are given by $\mu = \ell^{-1}(\eta)$, where the function ℓ is the link function. There are several choices for this function, as we now discuss.

The **canonical link function** ℓ satisfies the property that $\theta = \ell(\mu)$, where θ are the canonical (natural) parameters. Hence

$$\theta = \ell(\mu) = \ell(\ell^{-1}(\eta)) = \eta \tag{12.23}$$

This is what we have assumed so far. For example, for the Bernoulli distribution, the canonical parameter is the log-odds $\theta = \log(\mu/(1-\mu))$, which is given by the logit transform

$$\theta = \ell(\mu) = \text{logit}(\mu) = \log\left(\frac{\mu}{1-\mu}\right) \tag{12.24}$$

The inverse of this is the sigmoid or logistic function $\mu = \sigma(\theta) = 1/(1+e^{-\theta})$.

However, we are free to use other kinds of link function. For example, the **probit link function** has the form

$$\eta = \ell(\mu) = \Phi^{-1}(\mu) \tag{12.25}$$

Another link function that is sometimes used for binary responses is the **complementary log-log function**

$$\eta = \ell(\mu) = \log(-\log(1-\mu)) \tag{12.26}$$

This is used in applications where we either observe 0 events (denoted by $y = 0$) or one or more (denoted by $y = 1$), where events are assumed to be governed by a Poisson distribution with rate λ. Let E be the number of events. The Poisson assumption means $p(E = 0) = \exp(-\lambda)$ and hence

$$p(y = 0) = (1 - \mu) = p(E = 0) = \exp(-\lambda) \tag{12.27}$$

Thus $\lambda = -\log(1-\mu)$. When λ is a function of covariates, we need to ensure it is positive, so we use $\lambda = e^{\eta}$, and hence

$$\eta = \log(\lambda) = \log(-\log(1-\mu)) \tag{12.28}$$

12.4   Maximum likelihood estimation

GLMs can be fit using similar methods to those that we used to fit logistic regression. In particular, the negative log-likelihood has the following form (ignoring constant terms):

$$\text{NLL}(\boldsymbol{w}) = -\log p(\mathcal{D}|\boldsymbol{w}) = -\frac{1}{\sigma^2}\sum_{n=1}^{N}\ell_n \tag{12.29}$$

where

$$\ell_n \triangleq \eta_n y_n - A(\eta_n) \tag{12.30}$$

where $\eta_n = \boldsymbol{w}^\mathsf{T}\boldsymbol{x}_n$. For notational simplicity, we will assume $\sigma^2 = 1$.

We can compute the gradient for a single term as follows:

$$\boldsymbol{g}_n \triangleq \frac{\partial \ell_n}{\partial \boldsymbol{w}} = \frac{\partial \ell_n}{\partial \eta_n}\frac{\partial \eta_n}{\partial \boldsymbol{w}} = (y_n - A'(\eta_n))\boldsymbol{x}_n = (y_n - \mu_n)\boldsymbol{x}_n \tag{12.31}$$

where $\mu_n = f(\boldsymbol{w}^\mathsf{T}\boldsymbol{x})$, and f is the inverse link function that maps from canonical parameters to mean parameters. For example, in the case of logistic regression, $f(\eta_n) = \sigma(\eta_n)$, so we recover

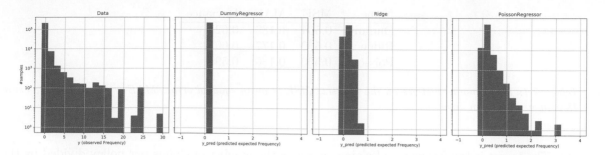

Figure 12.1: *Predictions of insurance claim rates on the test set. (a) Data. (b) Constant predictor. (c) Linear regression. (d) Poisson regression. Generated by poisson_regression_insurance.ipynb.*

Equation (10.21). This gradient expression can be used inside SGD, or some other gradient method, in the obvious way.

The Hessian is given by

$$\mathbf{H} = \frac{\partial^2}{\partial \boldsymbol{w} \partial \boldsymbol{w}^{\mathsf{T}}} \mathrm{NLL}(\boldsymbol{w}) = -\sum_{n=1}^{N} \frac{\partial \boldsymbol{g}_n}{\partial \boldsymbol{w}^{\mathsf{T}}} \tag{12.32}$$

where

$$\frac{\partial \boldsymbol{g}_n}{\partial \boldsymbol{w}^{\mathsf{T}}} = \frac{\partial \boldsymbol{g}_n}{\partial \mu_n} \frac{\partial \mu_n}{\partial \boldsymbol{w}^{\mathsf{T}}} = -\boldsymbol{x}_n f'(\boldsymbol{w}^{\mathsf{T}} \boldsymbol{x}_n) \boldsymbol{x}_n^{\mathsf{T}} \tag{12.33}$$

Hence

$$\mathbf{H} = \sum_{n=1}^{N} f'(\eta_n) \boldsymbol{x}_n \boldsymbol{x}_n^{\mathsf{T}} \tag{12.34}$$

For example, in the case of logistic regression, $f(\eta_n) = \sigma(\eta_n)$, and $f'(\eta_n) = \sigma(\eta_n)(1 - \sigma(\eta_n))$, so we recover Equation (10.23). In general, we see that the Hessian is positive definite, since $f'(\eta_n) > 0$; hence the negative log likelihood is convex, so the MLE for a GLM is unique (assuming $f(\eta_n) > 0$ for all n).

Based on the above results, we can fit GLMs using gradient based solvers in a manner that is very similar to how we fit logistic regression models.

12.5 Worked example: predicting insurance claims

In this section, we give an example of predicting insurance claims using linear and Poisson regression.[2]. The goal is to predict the expected number of insurance claims per year following car accidents. The dataset consists of 678k examples with 9 features, such as driver age, vehicle age, vehicle power,

---

2. This example is from https://scikit-learn.org/stable/auto_examples/linear_model/plot_poisson_regression_non_normal_loss.html

Name	MSE	MAE	Deviance
Dummy	0.564	0.189	0.625
Ridge	0.560	0.177	0.601
Poisson	0.560	0.186	0.594

Table 12.1: Performance metrics on the test set. MSE = mean squared error. MAE = mean absolute error. Deviance = Poisson deviance.

etc. The target is the frequency of claims, which is the number of claims per policy divided by the exposure (i.e., the duration of the policy in years).

We plot the test set in Figure 12.1(a). We see that for 94% of the policies, no claims are made, so the data has lots of 0s, as is typical for count and rate data. The average frequency of claims is 10%. This can be converted into a dummy model, which always predicts this constant. This results in the predictions shown in Figure 12.1(b). The goal is to do better than this.

A simple approach is to use linear regression, combined with some simple feature engineering (binning the continuous values, and one-hot encoding the categoricals). (We use a small amount of ℓ_2 regularization, so technically this is ridge regression.) This gives the results shown in Figure 12.1(c). This is better than the baseline, but still not very good. In particular, it can predict negative outcomes, and fails to capture the long tail.

We can do better using Poisson regression, using the same features but a log link function. The results are shown in Figure 12.1(d). We see that predictions are much better.

An interesting question is how to quantify performance in this kind of problem. If we use mean squared error, or mean absolute error, we may conclude from Table 12.1 that ridge regression is better than Poisson regression, but this is clearly not true, as shown in Figure 12.1. Instead it is more common to measure performance using the **deviance**, which is defined as

$$D(\boldsymbol{y}, \hat{\boldsymbol{\mu}}) = 2 \sum_i \left(\log p(y_i|\mu_i^*) - \log p(y_i|\mu_i) \right) \tag{12.35}$$

where μ_i is the predicted parameters for the i'th example (based on the input features $\boldsymbol{x}_i$ and the training set $\mathcal{D}$), and μ_i^* is the optimal parameter estimated by fitting the model just to the true output y_i. (This is the so-called saturated model, that perfectly fits the test set.) In the case of Poisson regression, we have $\mu_i^* = y_i$. Hence

$$D(\boldsymbol{y}, \boldsymbol{\mu}) = 2 \sum_i \left[(y_i \log y_i - y_i - \log(y_i!)) - (y_i \log \hat{\mu}_i - \hat{\mu}_i - \log(y_i!)) \right] \tag{12.36}$$

$$= 2 \sum_i \left[\left(y_i \log \frac{y_i}{\hat{\mu}_i} + \hat{\mu}_i - y_i \right) \right] \tag{12.37}$$

By this metric, the Poisson model is clearly better (see last column of Table 12.1).

We can also compute a **calibration plot**, which plots the actual frequency vs the predicted frequency. To compute this, we bin the predictions into intervals, and then count the empirical frequency of claims for all examples whose predicted frequency falls into that bin. The results are shown in Figure 12.2. We see that the constant baseline is well calibrated, but of course it is not very accurate. The ridge model is miscalibrated in the low frequency regime. In particular, it

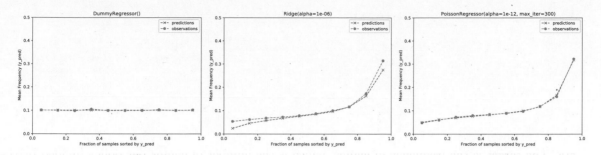

Figure 12.2: Calibration plot for insurance claims prediction. Generated by poisson_regression_insurance.ipynb.

underestimates the total number of claims in the test set to be 10,693, whereas the truth is 11,935. The Poisson model is better calibrated (i.e., when it predicts examples will have a high claim rate, they do in fact have a high claim rate), and it predicts the total number of claims to be 11,930.

Figure 12.X.X Calibration plot for insurance churn prediction. Generated by ... insurance_churn.ipynb.

underestimates the total number of claims in the test set to be 10,605, whereas the truth is 11,015. The Poisson model is better calibrated (i.e., when it predicts examples will have a high claim rate, they do in fact have a high claim rate), and it predicts the total number of claims to be 11,039.

PART III

Deep Neural Networks

13 Neural Networks for Tabular Data

13.1 Introduction

In Part II, we discussed linear models for regression and classification. In particular, in Chapter 10, we discussed logistic regression, which, in the binary case, corresponds to the model $p(y|\boldsymbol{x}, \boldsymbol{w}) = \text{Ber}(y|\sigma(\boldsymbol{w}^\mathsf{T}\boldsymbol{x}))$, and in the multiclass case corresponds to the model $p(y|\boldsymbol{x}, \mathbf{W}) = \text{Cat}(y|\text{softmax}(\mathbf{W}\boldsymbol{x}))$. In Chapter 11, we discussed linear regression, which corresponds to the model $p(y|\boldsymbol{x}, \boldsymbol{w}) = \mathcal{N}(y|\boldsymbol{w}^\mathsf{T}\boldsymbol{x}, \sigma^2)$. And in Chapter 12, we discussed generalized linear models, which generalizes these models to other kinds of output distributions, such as Poisson. However, all these models make the strong assumption that the input-output mapping is linear.

A simple way of increasing the flexibility of such models is to perform a feature transformation, by replacing $\boldsymbol{x}$ with $\boldsymbol{\phi}(\boldsymbol{x})$. For example, we can use a polynomial transform, which in 1d is given by $\boldsymbol{\phi}(x) = [1, x, x^2, x^3, \ldots]$, as we discussed in Section 1.2.2.2. This is sometimes called **basis function expansion**. The model now becomes

$$f(\boldsymbol{x}; \boldsymbol{\theta}) = \mathbf{W}\boldsymbol{\phi}(\boldsymbol{x}) + \boldsymbol{b} \tag{13.1}$$

This is still linear in the parameters $\boldsymbol{\theta} = (\mathbf{W}, \boldsymbol{b})$, which makes model fitting easy (since the negative log-likelihood is convex). However, having to specify the feature transformation by hand is very limiting.

A natural extension is to endow the feature extractor with its own parameters, $\boldsymbol{\theta}_2$, to get

$$f(\boldsymbol{x}; \boldsymbol{\theta}) = \mathbf{W}\boldsymbol{\phi}(\boldsymbol{x}; \boldsymbol{\theta}_2) + \boldsymbol{b} \tag{13.2}$$

where $\boldsymbol{\theta} = (\boldsymbol{\theta}_1, \boldsymbol{\theta}_2)$ and $\boldsymbol{\theta}_1 = (\mathbf{W}, \boldsymbol{b})$. We can obviously repeat this process recursively, to create more and more complex functions. If we compose L functions, we get

$$f(\boldsymbol{x}; \boldsymbol{\theta}) = f_L(f_{L-1}(\cdots(f_1(\boldsymbol{x}))\cdots)) \tag{13.3}$$

where $f_\ell(\boldsymbol{x}) = f(\boldsymbol{x}; \boldsymbol{\theta}_\ell)$ is the function at layer ℓ. This is the key idea behind **deep neural networks** or **DNNs**.

The term "DNN" actually encompasses a larger family of models, in which we compose differentiable functions into any kind of DAG (directed acyclic graph), mapping input to output. Equation (13.3) is the simplest example where the DAG is a chain. This is known as a **feedforward neural network** (**FFNN**) or **multilayer perceptron** (**MLP**).

An MLP assumes that the input is a fixed-dimensional vector, say $\boldsymbol{x} \in \mathbb{R}^D$. It is common to call such data "**structured data**" or "**tabular data**", since the data is often stored in an $N \times D$

x_1	x_2	y
0	0	0
0	1	1
1	0	1
1	1	0

Table 13.1: Truth table for the XOR (exclusive OR) function, $y = x_1 \veebar x_2$.

design matrix, where each column (feature) has a specific meaning, such as height, weight, age, etc. In later chapters, we discuss other kinds of DNNs that are more suited to "**unstructured data**" such as images and text, where the input data is variable sized, and each individual element (e.g., pixel or word) is often meaningless on its own.[1] In particular, in Chapter 14, we discuss **convolutional neural networks** (**CNN**), which are designed to work with images; in Chapter 15, we discuss **recurrent neural networks** (**RNN**) and **transformers**, which are designed to work with sequences; and in Chapter 23, we discuss **graph neural networks** (**GNN**), which are designed to work with graphs.

Although DNNs can work well, there are often a lot of engineering details that need to be addressed to get good performance. Some of these details are discussed in the supplementary material to this book, available at probml.ai. There are also various other books that cover this topic in more depth (e.g., [Zha+20; Cho21; Gér19; GBC16; Raf22]), as well as a multitude of online courses. For a more theoretical treatment, see e.g., [Ber+21; Cal20; Aro+21; RY21].

13.2   Multilayer perceptrons (MLPs)

In Section 10.2.5, we explained that a **perceptron** is a deterministic version of logistic regression. Specifically, it is a mapping of the following form:

$$f(\boldsymbol{x};\boldsymbol{\theta}) = \mathbb{I}\left(\boldsymbol{w}^\mathsf{T}\boldsymbol{x} + b \geq 0\right) = H(\boldsymbol{w}^\mathsf{T}\boldsymbol{x} + b) \tag{13.4}$$

where $H(a)$ is the **heaviside step function**, also known as a **linear threshold function**. Since the decision boundaries represented by perceptrons are linear, they are very limited in what they can represent. In 1969, Marvin Minsky and Seymour Papert published a famous book called *Perceptrons* [MP69] in which they gave numerous examples of pattern recognition problems which perceptrons cannot solve. We give a specific example below, before discussing how to solve the problem.

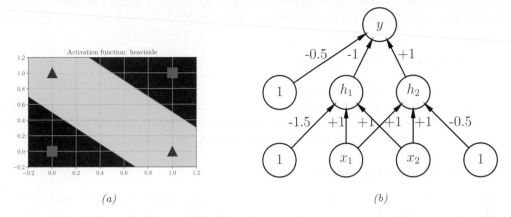

$$(a) \qquad\qquad\qquad\qquad (b)$$

Figure 13.1: (a) Illustration of the fact that the XOR function is not linearly separable, but can be separated by the two layer model using Heaviside activation functions. Adapted from Figure 10.6 of [Gér19]. Generated by xor_heaviside.ipynb. (b) A neural net with one hidden layer, whose weights have been manually constructed to implement the XOR function. h_1 is the AND function and h_2 is the OR function. The bias terms are implemented using weights from constant nodes with the value 1.

13.2.1 The XOR problem

One of the most famous examples from the *Perceptrons* book is the **XOR problem**. Here the goal is to learn a function that computes the exclusive OR of its two binary inputs. The truth table for this function is given in Table 13.1. We visualize this function in Figure 13.1a. It is clear that the data is not linearly separable, so a perceptron cannot represent this mapping.

However, we can overcome this problem by stacking multiple perceptrons on top of each other. This is called a **multilayer perceptron (MLP)**. For example, to solve the XOR problem, we can use the MLP shown in Figure 13.1b. This consists of 3 perceptrons, denoted h_1, h_2 and y. The nodes marked x are inputs, and the nodes marked 1 are constant terms. The nodes h_1 and h_2 are called **hidden units**, since their values are not observed in the training data.

The first hidden unit computes $h_1 = x_1 \wedge x_2$ by using appropriately set weights. (Here $\wedge$ is the AND operation.) In particular, it has inputs from x_1 and x_2, both weighted by 1.0, but has a bias term of -1.5 (this is implemented by a "wire" with weight -1.5 coming from a dummy node whose value is fixed to 1). Thus h_1 will fire iff x_1 and x_2 are both on, since then

$$w_1^\mathsf{T} x - b_1 = [1.0, 1.0]^\mathsf{T}[1, 1] - 1.5 = 0.5 > 0 \qquad\qquad (13.5)$$

---

1. The term "unstructured data" is a bit misleading, since images and text *do* have structure. For example, neighboring pixels in an image are highly correlated, as are neighboring words in a sentence. Indeed, it is precisely this structure that is exploited (assumed) by CNNs and RNNs. By contrast, MLPs make no assumptions about their inputs. This is useful for applications such as tabular data, where the structure (dependencies between the columns) is usually not obvious, and thus needs to be learned. We can also apply MLPs to images and text, as we will see, but performance will usually be worse compared to specialized models, such as as CNNs and RNNs. (There are some exceptions, such as the **MLP-mixer** model of [Tol+21], which is an unstructured model that can learn to perform well on image and text data, but such models need massive datasets to overcome their lack of inductive bias.)

Similarly, the second hidden unit computes $h_2 = x_1 \vee x_2$, where $\vee$ is the OR operation, and the third computes the output $y = \overline{h_1} \wedge h_2$, where $\overline{h} = \neg h$ is the NOT (logical negation) operation. Thus y computes

$$y = f(x_1, x_2) = \overline{(x_1 \wedge x_2)} \wedge (x_1 \vee x_2) \tag{13.6}$$

This is equivalent to the XOR function.

By generalizing this example, we can show that an MLP can represent any logical function. However, we obviously want to avoid having to specify the weights and biases by hand. In the rest of this chapter, we discuss ways to learn these parameters from data.

13.2.2   Differentiable MLPs

The MLP we discussed in Section 13.2.1 was defined as a stack of perceptrons, each of which involved the non-differentiable Heaviside function. This makes such models difficult to train, which is why they were never widely used. However, suppose we replace the Heaviside function $H : \mathbb{R} \to \{0, 1\}$ with a differentiable **activation function** $\varphi : \mathbb{R} \to \mathbb{R}$. More precisely, we define the hidden units z_l at each layer l to be a linear transformation of the hidden units at the previous layer passed elementwise through this activation function:

$$z_l = f_l(z_{l-1}) = \varphi_l \left(b_l + \mathbf{W}_l z_{l-1} \right) \tag{13.7}$$

or, in scalar form,

$$z_{kl} = \varphi_l \left(b_{kl} + \sum_{j=1}^{K_{l-1}} w_{lkj} z_{jl-1} \right) \tag{13.8}$$

The quantity that is passed to the activation function is called the **pre-activations**:

$$a_l = b_l + \mathbf{W}_l z_{l-1} \tag{13.9}$$

so $z_l = \varphi_l(a_l)$.

If we now compose L of these functions together, as in Equation (13.3), then we can compute the gradient of the output wrt the parameters in each layer using the chain rule, also known as **backpropagation**, as we explain in Section 13.3. (This is true for any kind of differentiable activation function, although some kinds work better than others, as we discuss in Section 13.2.3.) We can then pass the gradient to an optimizer, and thus minimize some training objective, as we discuss in Section 13.4. For this reason, the term "MLP" almost always refers to this differentiable form of the model, rather than the historical version with non-differentiable linear threshold units.

13.2.3   Activation functions

We are free to use any kind of differentiable activation function we like at each layer. However, if we use a *linear* activation function, $\varphi_\ell(a) = c_\ell a$, then the whole model reduces to a regular linear model. To see this, note that Equation (13.3) becomes

$$f(\boldsymbol{x}; \boldsymbol{\theta}) = \mathbf{W}_L c_L (\mathbf{W}_{L-1} c_{L-1} (\cdots (\mathbf{W}_1 \boldsymbol{x}) \cdots)) \propto \mathbf{W}_L \mathbf{W}_{L-1} \cdots \mathbf{W}_1 \boldsymbol{x} = \mathbf{W}' \boldsymbol{x} \tag{13.10}$$

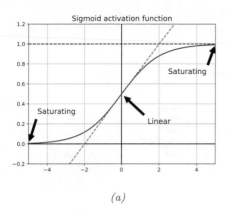

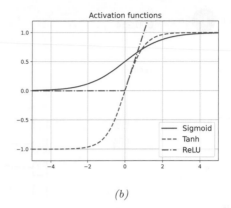

(a)   (b)

Figure 13.2: *(a) Illustration of how the sigmoid function is linear for inputs near 0, but saturates for large positive and negative inputs. Adapted from 11.1 of [Gér19]. (b) Plots of some neural network activation functions. Generated by* activation_fun_plot.ipynb.

where we dropped the bias terms for notational simplicity. For this reason, it is important to use nonlinear activation functions.

In the early days of neural networks, a common choice was to use a sigmoid (logistic) function, which can be seen as a smooth approximation to the Heaviside function used in a perceptron:

$$\sigma(a) = \frac{1}{1 + e^{-a}} \tag{13.11}$$

However, as shown in Figure 13.2a, the sigmoid function **saturates** at 1 for large positive inputs, and at 0 for large negative inputs. Another common choice is the tanh function, which has a similar shape, but saturates at -1 and +1. See Figure 13.2b.

In the saturated regimes, the gradient of the output wrt the input will be close to zero, so any gradient signal from higher layers will not be able to propagate back to earlier layers. This is called the **vanishing gradient problem**, and it makes it hard to train the model using gradient descent (see Section 13.4.2 for details). One of the keys to being able to train very deep models is to use non-saturating activation functions. Several different functions have been proposed. The most common is **rectified linear unit** or **ReLU**, proposed in [GBB11; KSH12]. This is defined as

$$\text{ReLU}(a) = \max(a, 0) = a\mathbb{I}(a > 0) \tag{13.12}$$

The ReLU function simply "turns off" negative inputs, and passes positive inputs unchanged: see Figure 13.2b for a plot, and Section 13.4.3 for more details.

When neural networks are used to represent functions defined on a continuous input space — such as points in time, $f(t)$, or in 3d space, $f(x, y, z)$ — they are often called **neural implicit representations** or **coordinated based representations** of the underlying signal. In such cases, it is often important to capture high frequencies to represent the signal faithfully. Unfortunately MLPs have an intrinsic bias to low frequency functions [Tan+20; RML22]. One simple solution is to use a sine function, $\sin(a)$, as the nonlinearity, instead of ReLU, as explained in [Sit+20].

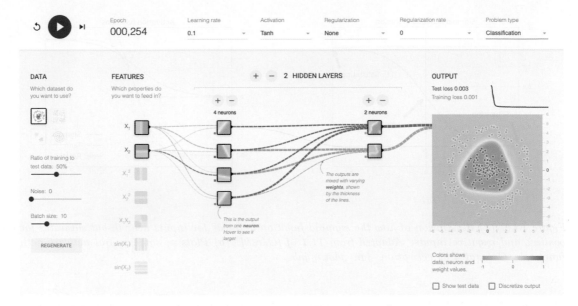

Figure 13.3: An MLP with 2 hidden layers applied to a set of 2d points from 2 classes, shown in the top left corner. The visualizations associated with each hidden unit show the decision boundary at that part of the network. The final output is shown on the right. The input is $\boldsymbol{x} \in \mathbb{R}^2$, the first layer activations are $\boldsymbol{z}_1 \in \mathbb{R}^4$, the second layer activations are $\boldsymbol{z}_2 \in \mathbb{R}^2$, and the final logit is $a_3 \in \mathbb{R}$, which is converted to a probability using the sigmoid function. This is a screenshot from the interactive demo at $http://playground.tensorflow.org$.

13.2.4   Example models

MLPs can be used to perform classification and regression for many kinds of data. We give some examples below.

13.2.4.1   MLP for classifying 2d data into 2 categories

Figure 13.3 gives an illustration of an MLP with two hidden layers applied to a 2d input vector, corresponding to points in the plane, coming from two concentric circles. This model has the following form:

$$p(y|\boldsymbol{x};\boldsymbol{\theta}) = \mathrm{Ber}(y|\sigma(a_3)) \tag{13.13}$$

$$a_3 = \boldsymbol{w}_3^\mathsf{T}\boldsymbol{z}_2 + b_3 \tag{13.14}$$

$$\boldsymbol{z}_2 = \varphi(\mathbf{W}_2\boldsymbol{z}_1 + \boldsymbol{b}_2) \tag{13.15}$$

$$\boldsymbol{z}_1 = \varphi(\mathbf{W}_1\boldsymbol{x} + \boldsymbol{b}_1) \tag{13.16}$$

Here a_3 is the final logit score, which is converted to a probability via the sigmoid (logistic) function. The value a_3 is computed by taking a linear combination of the 2 hidden units in layer 2, using $a_3 = \boldsymbol{w}_3^\mathsf{T}\boldsymbol{z}_2 + b_3$. In turn, layer 2 is computed by taking a nonlinear combination of the 4 hidden units in layer 1, using $\boldsymbol{z}_2 = \varphi(\mathbf{W}_2\boldsymbol{z}_1 + \boldsymbol{b}_2)$. Finally, layer 1 is computed by taking a nonlinear combination of

```
Model: "sequential"
_____
Layer (type)                 Output Shape              Param #
=================================================================
flatten (Flatten)            (None, 784)               0
_____
dense (Dense)                (None, 128)               100480
_____
dense_1 (Dense)              (None, 128)               16512
_____
dense_2 (Dense)              (None, 10)                1290
=================================================================
Total params: 118,282
Trainable params: 118,282
Non-trainable params: 0
```

Table 13.2: *Structure of the MLP used for MNIST classification. Note that* $100,480 = (784 + 1) \times 128$, *and* $16,512 = (128 + 1) \times 128$. *mlp_mnist_tf.ipynb.*

the 2 input units, using $z_1 = \varphi(\mathbf{W}_1 x + b_1)$. By adjusting the parameters, $\boldsymbol{\theta} = (\mathbf{W}_1, b_1, \mathbf{W}_2, b_2, w_3, b_3)$, to minimize the negative log likelihood, we can fit the training data very well, despite the highly nonlinear nature of the decision boundary. (You can find an interactive version of this figure at http://playground.tensorflow.org.)

13.2.4.2   MLP for image classification

To apply an MLP to image classification, we need to "**flatten**" the 2d input into 1d vector. We can then use a feedforward architecture similar to the one described in Section 13.2.4.1. For example, consider building an MLP to classifiy MNIST digits (Section 3.5.2). These are $28 \times 28 = 784$-dimensional. If we use 2 hidden layers with 128 units each, followed by a final 10 way softmax layer, we get the model shown in Table 13.2.

We show some predictions from this model in Figure 13.4. We train it for just two "epochs" (passes over the dataset), but already the model is doing quite well, with a test set accuracy of 97.1%. Furthermore, the errors seem sensible, e.g., 9 is mistaken as a 3. Training for more epochs can further improve test accuracy.

In Chapter 14 we discuss a different kind of model, called a convolutional neural network, which is better suited to images. This gets even better performance and uses fewer parameters, by exploiting prior knowledge about the spatial structure of images. By contrast, with an MLP, we can randomly shuffle (permute) the pixels without affecting the output (assuming we use the same random permutation for all inputs).

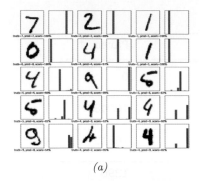   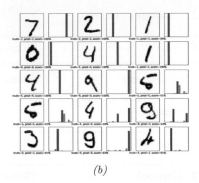

(a)   (b)

Figure 13.4: Results of applying an MLP (with 2 hidden layers with 128 units and 1 output layer with 10 units) to some MNIST images (cherry picked to include some errors). Red is incorrect, blue is correct. (a) After 1 epoch of training. (b) After 2 epochs. Generated by mlp_mnist_tf.ipynb.

13.2.4.3   MLP for text classification

To apply MLPs to text classification, we need to convert the variable-length sequence of words $v_1, \ldots, v_T$ (where each v_t is a one-hot vector of length V, where V is the vocabulary size) into a fixed dimensional vector x. The easiest way to do this is as follows. First we treat the input as an unordered bag of words (Section 1.5.4.1), $\{v_t\}$. The first layer of the model is a $E \times V$ embedding matrix $\mathbf{W}_1$, which converts each sparse V-dimensional vector to a dense E-dimensional embedding, $e_t = \mathbf{W}_1 v_t$ (see Section 20.5 for more details on word embeddings). Next we convert this set of T E-dimensional embeddings into a fixed-sized vector using **global average pooling**, $\bar{e} = \frac{1}{T}\sum_{t=1}^{T} e_t$. This can then be passed as input to an MLP. For example, if we use a single hidden layer, and a logistic output (for binary classification), we get

$$p(y|x;\theta) = \text{Ber}(y|\sigma(w_3^\mathsf{T} h + b_3)) \tag{13.17}$$

$$h = \varphi(\mathbf{W}_2 \bar{e} + b_2) \tag{13.18}$$

$$\bar{e} = \frac{1}{T}\sum_{t=1}^{T} e_t \tag{13.19}$$

$$e_t = \mathbf{W}_1 v_t \tag{13.20}$$

If we use a vocabulary size of $V = 10,000$, an embedding size of $E = 16$, and a hidden layer of size 16, we get the model shown in Table 13.3. If we apply this to the IMDB movie review sentiment classification dataset discussed in Section 1.5.2.1, we get 86% on the validation set.

We see from Table 13.3 that the model has a lot of parameters, which can result in overfitting, since the IMDB training set only has 25k examples. However, we also see that most of the parameters are in the embedding matrix, so instead of learning these in a supervised way, we can perform unsupervised pre-training of word embedding models, as we discuss in Section 20.5. If the embedding matrix $\mathbf{W}_1$ is fixed, we just have to fine-tune the parameters in layers 2 and 3 for this specific labeled task, which requires much less data. (See also Chapter 19, where we discuss general techniques for training with limited labeled data.)

```
Model: "sequential"
_____
Layer (type)                 Output Shape              Param #
=================================================================
embedding (Embedding)        (None, None, 16)          160000
_____
global_average_pooling1d (Gl (None, 16)                0
_____
dense (Dense)                (None, 16)                272
_____
dense_1 (Dense)              (None, 1)                 17
=================================================================
Total params: 160,289
Trainable params: 160,289
Non-trainable params: 0
```

Table 13.3: *Structure of the MLP used for IMDB review classification. We use a vocabulary size of $V = 10,000$, an embedding size of $E = 16$, and a hidden layer of size 16. The embedding matrix $\mathbf{W}_1$ has size $10,000 \times 16$, the hidden layer (labeled "dense") has a weight matrix $\mathbf{W}_2$ of size 16×16 and bias $\boldsymbol{b}_2$ of size 16 (note that $16 \times 16 + 16 = 272$), and the final layer (labeled "dense_1") has a weight vector $\boldsymbol{w}_3$ of size 16 and a bias b_3 of size 1. The global average pooling layer has no free parameters.* mlp_imdb_tf.ipynb.

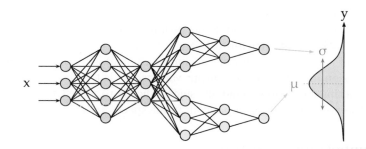

Figure 13.5: *Illustration of an MLP with a shared "backbone" and two output "heads", one for predicting the mean and one for predicting the variance. From* https://brendanhasz.github.io/2019/07/23/bayesian-density-net.html. *Used with kind permission of Brendan Hasz.*

13.2.4.4   MLP for heteroskedastic regression

We can also use MLPs for regression. Figure 13.5 shows how we can make a model for heteroskedastic nonlinear regression. (The term "heteroskedastic" just means that the predicted output variance is input-dependent, as discussed in Section 2.6.3.) This function has two outputs which compute $f_\mu(\boldsymbol{x}) = \mathbb{E}[y|\boldsymbol{x}, \boldsymbol{\theta}]$ and $f_\sigma(\boldsymbol{x}) = \sqrt{\mathbb{V}[y|\boldsymbol{x}, \boldsymbol{\theta}]}$. We can share most of the layers (and hence parameters) between these two functions by using a common "**backbone**" and two output "**heads**", as shown in Figure 13.5. For the μ head, we use a linear activation, $\varphi(a) = a$. For the σ head, we use a softplus

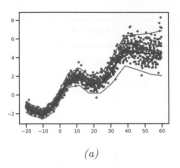
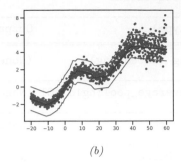

(a)   (b)

Figure 13.6: Illustration of predictions from an MLP fit using MLE to a 1d regression dataset with growing noise. (a) Output variance is input-dependent, as in Figure 13.5. (b) Mean is computed using same model as in (a), but output variance is treated as a fixed parameter σ^2, which is estimated by MLE after training, as in Section 11.2.3.6. Generated by mlp_1d_regression_hetero_tfp.ipynb.

activation, $\varphi(a) = \sigma_+(a) = \log(1 + e^a)$. If we use linear heads and a nonlinear backbone, the overall model is given by

$$p(y|\boldsymbol{x}, \boldsymbol{\theta}) = \mathcal{N}\left(y|\boldsymbol{w}_{\boldsymbol{\mu}}^{\mathsf{T}} f(\boldsymbol{x}; \boldsymbol{w}_{\text{shared}}), \sigma_+(\boldsymbol{w}_{\boldsymbol{\sigma}}^{\mathsf{T}} f(\boldsymbol{x}; \boldsymbol{w}_{\text{shared}}))\right) \tag{13.21}$$

Figure 13.6 shows the advantage of this kind of model on a dataset where the mean grows linearly over time, with seasonal oscillations, and the variance increases quadratically. (This is a simple example of a **stochastic volatility model**; it can be used to model financial data, as well as the global temperature of the earth, which (due to climate change) is increasing in mean *and* in variance.) We see that a regression model where the output variance σ^2 is treated as a fixed (input-independent) parameter will sometimes be underconfident, since it needs to adjust to the overall noise level, and cannot adapt to the noise level at each point in input space.

13.2.5   The importance of depth

One can show that an MLP *with one hidden layer* is a **universal function approximator**, meaning it can model any suitably smooth function, given enough hidden units, to any desired level of accuracy [HSW89; Cyb89; Hor91]. Intuitively, the reason for this is that each hidden unit can specify a half plane, and a sufficiently large combination of these can "carve up" any region of space, to which we can associate any response (this is easiest to see when using piecewise linear activation functions, as shown in Figure 13.7).

However, various arguments, both experimental and theoretical (e.g., [Has87; Mon+14; Rag+17; Pog+17]), have shown that deep networks work better than shallow ones. The reason is that later layers can leverage the features that are learned by earlier layers; that is, the function is defined in a **compositional** or **hierarchical** way. For example, suppose we want to classify DNA strings, and the positive class is associated with the regular expression *AA??CGCG??AA*. Although we could fit this with a single hidden layer model, intuitively it will be easier to learn if the model first learns to detect the AA and CG "motifs" using the hidden units in layer 1, and then uses these features

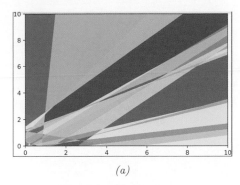
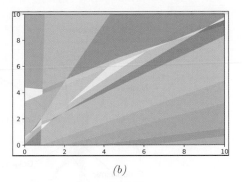

(a)   (b)

Figure 13.7: A decomposition of $\mathbb{R}^2$ into a finite set of linear decision regions produced by an MLP with ReLU activations with (a) one hidden layer of 25 hidden units and (b) two hidden layers. From Figure 1 of [HAB19]. Used with kind permission of Maksym Andriuschenko.

to define a simple linear classifier in layer 2, analogously to how we solved the XOR problem in Section 13.2.1.

13.2.6 The "deep learning revolution"

Although the ideas behind DNNs date back several decades, it was not until the 2010s that they started to become very widely used. The first area to adopt these methods was the field of automatic speech recognition (ASR), based on breakthrough results in [Dah+11]. This approach rapidly became the standard paradigm, and was widely adopted in academia and industry [Hin+12].

However, the moment that got the most attention was when [KSH12] showed that deep CNNs could significantly improve performance on the challenging ImageNet image classification benchmark, reducing the error rate from 26% to 16% in a single year (see Figure 1.14b); this was a huge jump compared to the previous rate of progress of about 2% reduction per year.

The "explosion" in the usage of DNNs has several contributing factors. One is the availability of cheap **GPUs** (graphics processing units); these were originally developed to speed up image rendering for video games, but they can also massively reduce the time it takes to fit large CNNs, which involve similar kinds of matrix-vector computations. Another is the growth in large labeled datasets, which enables us to fit complex function approximators with many parameters without overfitting. (For example, ImageNet has 1.3M labeled images, and is used to fit models that have millions of parameters.) Indeed, if deep learning systems are viewed as "rockets", then large datasets have been called the fuel.[2]

Motivated by the outstanding empirical success of DNNs, various companies started to become interested in this technology. This had led to the development of high quality open-source software libraries, such as Tensorflow (made by Google), PyTorch (made by Facebook), and MXNet (made by Amazon). These libraries support automatic differentiation (see Section 13.3) and scalable gradient-based optimization (see Section 8.4) of complex differentiable functions. We will use some

---

2. This popular analogy is due to Andrew Ng, who mentioned it in a keynote talk at the GPU Technology Conference (GTC) in 2015. His slides are available at https://bit.ly/38RTxzH.

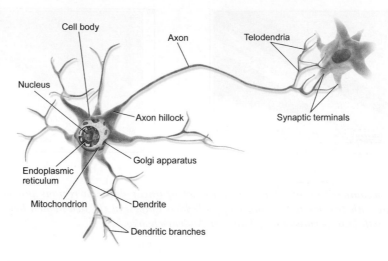

Figure 13.8: Illustration of two neurons connected together in a "circuit". The output axon of the left neuron makes a synaptic connection with the dendrites of the cell on the right. Electrical charges, in the form of ion flows, allow the cells to communicate. From $\mathtt{https://en.wikipedia.org/wiki/Neuron}$. Used with kind permission of Wikipedia author BruceBlaus.

of these libraries in various places throughout the book to implement a variety of models, not just DNNs.[3]

More details on the history of the "deep learning revolution" can be found in e.g., [Sej18; Met21].

13.2.7   Connections with biology

In this section, we discuss the connections between the kinds of neural networks we have discussed above, known as **artificial neural networks** or **ANN**s, and real neural networks. The details on how real biological brains work are quite complex (see e.g., [Kan+12]), but we can give a simple "cartoon".

We start by considering a model of a single neuron. To a first approximation, we can say that whether neuron k fires, denoted by $h_k \in \{0, 1\}$, depends on the activity of its inputs, denoted by $\boldsymbol{x} \in \mathbb{R}^D$, as well as the strength of the incoming connections, which we denote by $\boldsymbol{w}_k \in \mathbb{R}^D$. We can compute a weighted sum of the inputs using $a_k = \boldsymbol{w}_k^\mathsf{T} \boldsymbol{x}$. These weights can be viewed as "wires" connecting the inputs x_d to neuron h_k; these are analogous to **dendrites** in a real neuron (see Figure 13.8). This weighted sum is then compared to a threshold, b_k, and if the activation exceeds the threshold, the neuron fires; this is analogous to the neuron emitting an electrical output or **action potential**. Thus we can model the behavior of the neuron using $h_k(\boldsymbol{x}) = H(\boldsymbol{w}_k^\mathsf{T} \boldsymbol{x} - b_k)$, where $H(a) = \mathbb{I}(a > 0)$ is the Heaviside function. This is called the **McCulloch-Pitts model** of the neuron, and was proposed in 1943 [MP43].

We can combine multiple such neurons together to make an ANN. The result has sometimes been

---

3. Note, however, that some have argued (see e.g., [BI19]) that current libraries are too inflexible, and put too much emphasis on methods based on dense matrix-vector multiplication, as opposed to more general algorithmic primitives.

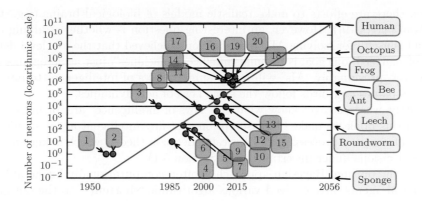

Figure 13.9: *Plot of neural network sizes over time. Models 1, 2, 3 and 4 correspond to the perceptron [Ros58], the adaptive linear unit [WH60] the neocognitron [Fuk80], and the first MLP trained by backprop [RHW86]. Approximate number of neurons for some living organisms are shown on the right scale (the sponge has 0 neurons), based on* https://en.wikipedia.org/wiki/List_of_animals_by_number_of_neurons. *From Figure 1.11 of [GBC16]. Used with kind permission of Ian Goodfellow.*

viewed as a model of the brain. However, ANNs differs from biological brains in many ways, including the following:

- Most ANNs use backpropagation to modify the strength of their connections (see Section 13.3). However, real brains do not use backprop, since there is no way to send information backwards along an axon [Ben+15b; BS16; KH19]. Instead, they use local update rules for adjusting synaptic strengths.

- Most ANNs are strictly feedforward, but real brains have many feedback connections. It is believed that this feedback acts like a prior, which can be combined with bottom up likelihoods from the sensory system to compute a posterior over hidden states of the world, which can then be used for optimal decision making (see e.g., [Doy+07]).

- Most ANNs use simplified neurons consisting of a weighted sum passed through a nonlinearity, but real biological neurons have complex dendritic tree structures (see Figure 13.8), with complex spatio-temporal dynamics.

- Most ANNs are smaller in size and number of connections than biological brains (see Figure 13.9). Of course, ANNs are getting larger every week, fueled by various new **hardware accelerators**, such as GPUs and **TPUs** (**tensor processing units**), etc. However, even if ANNs match biological brains in terms of number of units, the comparison is misleading since the processing capability of a biological neuron is much higher than an artificial neuron (see point above).

- Most ANNs are designed to model a single function, such as mapping an image to a label, or a sequence of words to another sequence of words. By contrast, biological brains are very complex systems, composed of multiple specialized interacting modules, which implement different kinds of functions or behaviors such as perception, control, memory, language, etc (see e.g., [Sha88; Kan+12]).

Of course, there are efforts to make realistic models of biological brains (e.g., the **Blue Brain Project** [Mar06; Yon19]). However, an interesting question is whether studying the brain at this level of detail is useful for "solving AI". It is commonly believed that the low level details of biological brains do not matter if our goal is to build "intelligent machines", just as aeroplanes do not flap their wings. However, presumably "AIs" will follow similar "laws of intelligence" to intelligent biological agents, just as planes and birds follow the same laws of aerodynamics.

Unfortunately, we do not yet know what the "laws of intelligence" are, or indeed if there even are such laws. In this book we make the assumption that any intelligent agent should follow the basic principles of information processing and Bayesian decision theory, which is known to be the optimal way to make decisions under uncertainty (see Section 5.1).

In practice, the optimal Bayesian approach is often computationally intractable. In the natural world, biological agents have evolved various algorithmic "shortcuts" to the optimal solution; this can explain many of the **heuristics** that people use in everyday reasoning [KST82; GTA00; Gri20]. As the tasks we want our machines to solve become harder, we may be able to gain insights from neuroscience and cognitive science for how to solve such tasks in an approximate way (see e.g., [MWK16; Has+17; Lak+17; HG21]). However, we should also bear in mind that AI/ML systems are increasingly used for safety-critical applications, in which we might want and expect the machine to do better than a human. In such cases, we may want more than just heuristic solutions that often work; instead we may want provably reliable methods, similar to other engineering fields (see Section 1.6.3 for further discussion).

13.3   Backpropagation

This section is coauthored with Mathieu Blondel.

In this section, we describe the famous **backpropagation algorithm**, which can be used to compute the gradient of a loss function applied to the output of the network wrt the parameters in each layer. This gradient can then be passed to a gradient-based optimization algorithm, as we discuss in Section 13.4.

The backpropagation algorithm was originally discovered in [BH69], and independently in [Wer74]. However, it was [RHW86] that brought the algorithm to the attention of the "mainstream" ML community. See the wikipedia page[4] for more historical details.

We initially assume the computation graph is a simple linear chain of stacked layers, as in an MLP. In this case, backprop is equivalent to repeated applications of the chain rule of calculus (see Equation (7.261)). However, the method can be generalized to arbitrary directed acyclic graphs (DAGs), as we discuss in Section 13.3.4. This general procedure is often called **automatic differentiation** or **autodiff**.

13.3.1   Forward vs reverse mode differentiation

Consider a mapping of the form $o = f(x)$, where $x \in \mathbb{R}^n$ and $o \in \mathbb{R}^m$. We assume that f is defined as a composition of functions:

$$f = f_4 \circ f_3 \circ f_2 \circ f_1 \tag{13.22}$$

---

4. https://en.wikipedia.org/wiki/Backpropagation#History

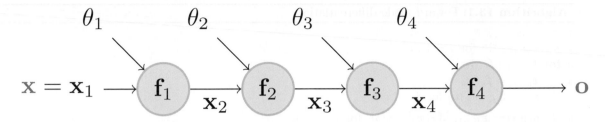

Figure 13.10: A simple linear-chain feedforward model with 4 layers. Here $\boldsymbol{x}$ is the input and $\boldsymbol{o}$ is the output. From [Blo20].

where $\boldsymbol{f}_1 : \mathbb{R}^n \to \mathbb{R}^{m_1}$, $\boldsymbol{f}_2 : \mathbb{R}^{m_1} \to \mathbb{R}^{m_2}$, $\boldsymbol{f}_3 : \mathbb{R}^{m_2} \to \mathbb{R}^{m_3}$, and $\boldsymbol{f}_4 : \mathbb{R}^{m_3} \to \mathbb{R}^m$. The intermediate steps needed to compute $\boldsymbol{o} = \boldsymbol{f}(\boldsymbol{x})$ are $\boldsymbol{x}_2 = \boldsymbol{f}_1(\boldsymbol{x})$, $\boldsymbol{x}_3 = \boldsymbol{f}_2(\boldsymbol{x}_2)$, $\boldsymbol{x}_4 = \boldsymbol{f}_3(\boldsymbol{x}_3)$, and $\boldsymbol{o} = \boldsymbol{f}_4(\boldsymbol{x}_4)$.

We can compute the Jacobian $\mathbf{J}_{\boldsymbol{f}}(\boldsymbol{x}) = \frac{\partial \boldsymbol{o}}{\partial \boldsymbol{x}} \in \mathbb{R}^{m \times n}$ using the chain rule:

$$\frac{\partial \boldsymbol{o}}{\partial \boldsymbol{x}} = \frac{\partial \boldsymbol{o}}{\partial \boldsymbol{x}_4} \frac{\partial \boldsymbol{x}_4}{\partial \boldsymbol{x}_3} \frac{\partial \boldsymbol{x}_3}{\partial \boldsymbol{x}_2} \frac{\partial \boldsymbol{x}_2}{\partial \boldsymbol{x}} = \frac{\partial \boldsymbol{f}_4(\boldsymbol{x}_4)}{\partial \boldsymbol{x}_4} \frac{\partial \boldsymbol{f}_3(\boldsymbol{x}_3)}{\partial \boldsymbol{x}_3} \frac{\partial \boldsymbol{f}_2(\boldsymbol{x}_2)}{\partial \boldsymbol{x}_2} \frac{\partial \boldsymbol{f}_1(\boldsymbol{x})}{\partial \boldsymbol{x}} \tag{13.23}$$

$$= \mathbf{J}_{\boldsymbol{f}_4}(\boldsymbol{x}_4)\mathbf{J}_{\boldsymbol{f}_3}(\boldsymbol{x}_3)\mathbf{J}_{\boldsymbol{f}_2}(\boldsymbol{x}_2)\mathbf{J}_{\boldsymbol{f}_1}(\boldsymbol{x}) \tag{13.24}$$

We now discuss how to compute the Jacobian $\mathbf{J}_{\boldsymbol{f}}(\boldsymbol{x})$ efficiently. Recall that

$$\mathbf{J}_{\boldsymbol{f}}(\boldsymbol{x}) = \frac{\partial \boldsymbol{f}(\boldsymbol{x})}{\partial \boldsymbol{x}} = \begin{pmatrix} \frac{\partial f_1}{\partial x_1} & \cdots & \frac{\partial f_1}{\partial x_n} \\ \vdots & \ddots & \vdots \\ \frac{\partial f_m}{\partial x_1} & \cdots & \frac{\partial f_m}{\partial x_n} \end{pmatrix} = \begin{pmatrix} \nabla f_1(\boldsymbol{x})^{\mathsf{T}} \\ \vdots \\ \nabla f_m(\boldsymbol{x})^{\mathsf{T}} \end{pmatrix} = \left(\frac{\partial \boldsymbol{f}}{\partial x_1}, \cdots, \frac{\partial \boldsymbol{f}}{\partial x_n} \right) \in \mathbb{R}^{m \times n} \tag{13.25}$$

where $\nabla f_i(\boldsymbol{x})^{\mathsf{T}} \in \mathbb{R}^{1 \times n}$ is the i'th row (for $i = 1 : m$) and $\frac{\partial \boldsymbol{f}}{\partial x_j} \in \mathbb{R}^m$ is the j'th column (for $j = 1 : n$). Note that, in our notation, when $m = 1$, the gradient, denoted $\nabla \boldsymbol{f}(\boldsymbol{x})$, has the same shape as $\boldsymbol{x}$. It is therefore a column vector, while $\mathbf{J}_{\boldsymbol{f}}(\boldsymbol{x})$ is a row vector. In this case, we therefore technically have $\nabla \boldsymbol{f}(\boldsymbol{x}) = \mathbf{J}_{\boldsymbol{f}}(\boldsymbol{x})^{\mathsf{T}}$.

We can extract the i'th row from $\mathbf{J}_{\boldsymbol{f}}(\boldsymbol{x})$ by using a vector Jacobian product (VJP) of the form $\boldsymbol{e}_i^{\mathsf{T}} \mathbf{J}_{\boldsymbol{f}}(\boldsymbol{x})$, where $\boldsymbol{e}_i \in \mathbb{R}^m$ is the unit basis vector. Similarly, we can extract the j'th column from $\mathbf{J}_{\boldsymbol{f}}(\boldsymbol{x})$ by using a Jacobian vector product (JVP) of the form $\mathbf{J}_{\boldsymbol{f}}(\boldsymbol{x})\boldsymbol{e}_j$, where $\boldsymbol{e}_j \in \mathbb{R}^n$. This shows that the computation of $\mathbf{J}_{\boldsymbol{f}}(\boldsymbol{x})$ reduces to either n JVPs or m VJPs.

If $n < m$, it is more efficient to compute $\mathbf{J}_{\boldsymbol{f}}(\boldsymbol{x})$ for each column $j = 1 : n$ by using JVPs in a right-to-left manner. The right multiplication with a column vector $\boldsymbol{v}$ is

$$\mathbf{J}_{\boldsymbol{f}}(\boldsymbol{x})\boldsymbol{v} = \underbrace{\mathbf{J}_{\boldsymbol{f}_4}(\boldsymbol{x}_4)}_{m \times m_3} \underbrace{\mathbf{J}_{\boldsymbol{f}_3}(\boldsymbol{x}_3)}_{m_3 \times m_2} \underbrace{\mathbf{J}_{\boldsymbol{f}_2}(\boldsymbol{x}_2)}_{m_2 \times m_1} \underbrace{\mathbf{J}_{\boldsymbol{f}_1}(\boldsymbol{x}_1)}_{m_1 \times n} \underbrace{\boldsymbol{v}}_{n \times 1} \tag{13.26}$$

This can be computed using **forward mode differentiation**; see Algorithm 13.1 for the pseudocode. Assuming $m = 1$ and $n = m_1 = m_2 = m_3$, the cost of computing $\mathbf{J}_{\boldsymbol{f}}(\boldsymbol{x})$ is $O(n^3)$.

If $n > m$ (e.g., if the output is a scalar), it is more efficient to compute $\mathbf{J}_{\boldsymbol{f}}(\boldsymbol{x})$ for each row $i = 1 : m$ by using VJPs in a left-to-right manner. The left multiplication with a row vector $\boldsymbol{u}^{\mathsf{T}}$ is

$$\boldsymbol{u}^{\mathsf{T}}\mathbf{J}_{\boldsymbol{f}}(\boldsymbol{x}) = \underbrace{\boldsymbol{u}^{\mathsf{T}}}_{1 \times m} \underbrace{\mathbf{J}_{\boldsymbol{f}_4}(\boldsymbol{x}_4)}_{m \times m_3} \underbrace{\mathbf{J}_{\boldsymbol{f}_3}(\boldsymbol{x}_3)}_{m_3 \times m_2} \underbrace{\mathbf{J}_{\boldsymbol{f}_2}(\boldsymbol{x}_2)}_{m_2 \times m_1} \underbrace{\mathbf{J}_{\boldsymbol{f}_1}(\boldsymbol{x}_1)}_{m_1 \times n} \tag{13.27}$$

Algorithm 13.1: Foward mode differentiation

---
1 $\boldsymbol{x}_1 := \boldsymbol{x}$
2 $\boldsymbol{v}_j := \boldsymbol{e}_j \in \mathbb{R}^n$ for $j = 1:n$
3 for $k = 1:K$ do
4     $\boldsymbol{x}_{k+1} = \boldsymbol{f}_k(\boldsymbol{x}_k)$
5     $\boldsymbol{v}_j := \mathbf{J}_{\boldsymbol{f}_k}(\boldsymbol{x}_k)\boldsymbol{v}_j$ for $j = 1:n$
6 Return $\boldsymbol{o} = \boldsymbol{x}_{K+1}$, $[\mathbf{J}_{\boldsymbol{f}}(\boldsymbol{x})]_{:,j} = \boldsymbol{v}_j$ for $j = 1:n$

This can be done using **reverse mode differentiation**; see Algorithm 13.2 for the pseudocode. Assuming $m = 1$ and $n = m_1 = m_2 = m_3$, the cost of computing $\mathbf{J}_{\boldsymbol{f}}(\boldsymbol{x})$ is $O(n^2)$.

Algorithm 13.2: Reverse mode differentiation

---
1 $\boldsymbol{x}_1 := \boldsymbol{x}$
2 for $k = 1:K$ do
3     $\boldsymbol{x}_{k+1} = \boldsymbol{f}_k(\boldsymbol{x}_k)$
4 $\boldsymbol{u}_i := \boldsymbol{e}_i \in \mathbb{R}^m$ for $i = 1:m$
5 for $k = K:1$ do
6     $\boldsymbol{u}_i^{\mathsf{T}} := \boldsymbol{u}_i^{\mathsf{T}}\mathbf{J}_{\boldsymbol{f}_k}(\boldsymbol{x}_k)$ for $i = 1:m$
7 Return $\boldsymbol{o} = \boldsymbol{x}_{K+1}$, $[\mathbf{J}_{\boldsymbol{f}}(\boldsymbol{x})]_{i,:} = \boldsymbol{u}_i^{\mathsf{T}}$ for $i = 1:m$

Both Algorithms 13.1 and 13.2 can be adapted to compute JVPs and VJPs against *any* collection of input vectors, by accepting $\{\boldsymbol{v}_j\}_{j=1,\ldots,n}$ and $\{\boldsymbol{u}_i\}_{i=1,\ldots,m}$ as respective inputs. Initializing these vectors to the standard basis is useful specifically for producing the complete Jacobian as output.

13.3.2   Reverse mode differentiation for multilayer perceptrons

In the previous section, we considered a simple linear-chain feedforward model where each layer does not have any learnable parameters. In this section, each layer can now have (optional) parameters $\boldsymbol{\theta}_1, \ldots, \boldsymbol{\theta}_4$. See Figure 13.10 for an illustration. We focus on the case where the mapping has the form $\mathcal{L}: \mathbb{R}^n \to \mathbb{R}$, so the output is a scalar. For example, consider ℓ_2 loss for a MLP with one hidden layer:

$$\mathcal{L}((\boldsymbol{x}, \boldsymbol{y}), \boldsymbol{\theta}) = \frac{1}{2}||\boldsymbol{y} - \mathbf{W}_2\varphi(\mathbf{W}_1\boldsymbol{x})||_2^2 \tag{13.28}$$

we can represent this as the following feedforward model:

$$\mathcal{L} = \boldsymbol{f}_4 \circ \boldsymbol{f}_3 \circ \boldsymbol{f}_2 \circ \boldsymbol{f}_1 \tag{13.29}$$

$$\boldsymbol{x}_2 = \boldsymbol{f}_1(\boldsymbol{x}, \boldsymbol{\theta}_1) = \mathbf{W}_1 \boldsymbol{x} \tag{13.30}$$

$$\boldsymbol{x}_3 = \boldsymbol{f}_2(\boldsymbol{x}_2, \emptyset) = \varphi(\boldsymbol{x}_2) \tag{13.31}$$

$$\boldsymbol{x}_4 = \boldsymbol{f}_3(\boldsymbol{x}_3, \boldsymbol{\theta}_3) = \mathbf{W}_2 \boldsymbol{x}_3 \tag{13.32}$$

$$\mathcal{L} = \boldsymbol{f}_4(\boldsymbol{x}_4, \boldsymbol{y}) = \frac{1}{2} ||\boldsymbol{x}_4 - \boldsymbol{y}||^2 \tag{13.33}$$

We use the notation $\boldsymbol{f}_k(\boldsymbol{x}_k, \boldsymbol{\theta}_k)$ to denote the function at layer k, where $\boldsymbol{x}_k$ is the previous output and $\boldsymbol{\theta}_k$ are the optional parameters for this layer.

In this example, the final layer returns a scalar, since it corresponds to a loss function $\mathcal{L} \in \mathbb{R}$. Therefore it is more efficient to use reverse mode differentation to compute the gradient vectors.

We first discuss how to compute the gradient of the scalar output wrt the parameters in each layer. We can easily compute the gradient wrt the predictions in the final layer $\frac{\partial \mathcal{L}}{\partial \boldsymbol{x}_4}$. For the gradient wrt the parameters in the earlier layers, we can use the chain rule to get

$$\frac{\partial \mathcal{L}}{\partial \boldsymbol{\theta}_3} = \frac{\partial \mathcal{L}}{\partial \boldsymbol{x}_4} \frac{\partial \boldsymbol{x}_4}{\partial \boldsymbol{\theta}_3} \tag{13.34}$$

$$\frac{\partial \mathcal{L}}{\partial \boldsymbol{\theta}_2} = \frac{\partial \mathcal{L}}{\partial \boldsymbol{x}_4} \frac{\partial \boldsymbol{x}_4}{\partial \boldsymbol{x}_3} \frac{\partial \boldsymbol{x}_3}{\partial \boldsymbol{\theta}_2} \tag{13.35}$$

$$\frac{\partial \mathcal{L}}{\partial \boldsymbol{\theta}_1} = \frac{\partial \mathcal{L}}{\partial \boldsymbol{x}_4} \frac{\partial \boldsymbol{x}_4}{\partial \boldsymbol{x}_3} \frac{\partial \boldsymbol{x}_3}{\partial \boldsymbol{x}_2} \frac{\partial \boldsymbol{x}_2}{\partial \boldsymbol{\theta}_1} \tag{13.36}$$

where each $\frac{\partial \mathcal{L}}{\partial \boldsymbol{\theta}_k} = (\nabla_{\boldsymbol{\theta}_k} \mathcal{L})^\mathsf{T}$ is a d_k-dimensional gradient row vector, where d_k is the number of parameters in layer k. We see that these can be computed recursively, by multiplying the gradient row vector at layer k by the Jacobian $\frac{\partial \boldsymbol{x}_k}{\partial \boldsymbol{x}_{k-1}}$ which is an $n_k \times n_{k-1}$ matrix, where n_k is the number of hidden units in layer k. See Algorithm 13.3 for the pseudocode.

This algorithm computes the gradient of the loss wrt the parameters at each layer. It also computes the gradient of the loss wrt the input, $\nabla_{\boldsymbol{x}} \mathcal{L} \in \mathbb{R}^n$, where n is the dimensionality of the input. This latter quantity is not needed for parameter learning, but can be useful for generating inputs to a model (see Section 14.6 for some applications).

All that remains is to specify how to compute the vector Jacobian product (VJP) of all supported layers. The details of this depend on the form of the function at each layer. We discuss some examples below.

13.3.3 Vector-Jacobian product for common layers

Recall that the Jacobian for a layer of the form $\boldsymbol{f} : \mathbb{R}^n \to \mathbb{R}^m$. is defined by

$$\mathbf{J}_{\boldsymbol{f}}(\boldsymbol{x}) = \frac{\partial \boldsymbol{f}(\boldsymbol{x})}{\partial \boldsymbol{x}} = \begin{pmatrix} \frac{\partial f_1}{\partial x_1} & \cdots & \frac{\partial f_1}{\partial x_n} \\ \vdots & \ddots & \vdots \\ \frac{\partial f_m}{\partial x_1} & \cdots & \frac{\partial f_m}{\partial x_n} \end{pmatrix} = \begin{pmatrix} \nabla f_1(\boldsymbol{x})^\mathsf{T} \\ \vdots \\ \nabla f_m(\boldsymbol{x})^\mathsf{T} \end{pmatrix} = \left(\frac{\partial \boldsymbol{f}}{\partial x_1}, \cdots, \frac{\partial \boldsymbol{f}}{\partial x_n} \right) \in \mathbb{R}^{m \times n} \tag{13.37}$$

where $\nabla f_i(\boldsymbol{x})^\mathsf{T} \in \mathbb{R}^n$ is the i'th row (for $i = 1 : m$) and $\frac{\partial \boldsymbol{f}}{\partial x_j} \in \mathbb{R}^m$ is the j'th column (for $j = 1 : n$). In this section, we describe how to compute the VJP $\boldsymbol{u}^\mathsf{T} \mathbf{J}_{\boldsymbol{f}}(\boldsymbol{x})$ for common layers.

Algorithm 13.3: Backpropagation for an MLP with K layers

---

1 // Forward pass
2 $\boldsymbol{x}_1 := \boldsymbol{x}$
3 **for** $k = 1 : K$ **do**
4 $\quad\lfloor\quad \boldsymbol{x}_{k+1} = \boldsymbol{f}_k(\boldsymbol{x}_k, \boldsymbol{\theta}_k)$
5 // Backward pass
6 $\boldsymbol{u}_{K+1} := 1$
7 **for** $k = K : 1$ **do**
8 $\quad\big|\quad \boldsymbol{g}_k := \boldsymbol{u}_{k+1}^\mathsf{T} \frac{\partial \boldsymbol{f}_k(\boldsymbol{x}_k, \boldsymbol{\theta}_k)}{\partial \boldsymbol{\theta}_k}$
9 $\quad\lfloor\quad \boldsymbol{u}_k^\mathsf{T} := \boldsymbol{u}_{k+1}^\mathsf{T} \frac{\partial \boldsymbol{f}_k(\boldsymbol{x}_k, \boldsymbol{\theta}_k)}{\partial \boldsymbol{x}_k}$
10 // Output
11 Return $\mathcal{L} = \boldsymbol{x}_{K+1}$, $\nabla_{\boldsymbol{x}} \mathcal{L} = \boldsymbol{u}_1$, $\{\nabla_{\boldsymbol{\theta}_k} \mathcal{L} = \boldsymbol{g}_k : k = 1 : K\}$

13.3.3.1 Cross entropy layer

Consider a cross-entropy loss layer taking logits $\boldsymbol{x}$ and target labels $\boldsymbol{y}$ as input, and returning a scalar:

$$z = f(\boldsymbol{x}) = \text{CrossEntropyWithLogits}(\boldsymbol{y}, \boldsymbol{x}) = -\sum_c y_c \log(\text{softmax}(\boldsymbol{x})_c) = -\sum_c y_c \log p_c \quad (13.38)$$

where $\boldsymbol{p} = \text{softmax}(\boldsymbol{x}) = \frac{e^{x_c}}{\sum_{c'=1}^{C} e^{x_{c'}}}$ are the predicted class probabilites, and $\boldsymbol{y}$ is the true distribution over labels (often a one-hot vector). The Jacobian wrt the input is

$$\mathbf{J} = \frac{\partial z}{\partial \boldsymbol{x}} = (\boldsymbol{p} - \boldsymbol{y})^\mathsf{T} \in \mathbb{R}^{1 \times C} \quad (13.39)$$

To see this, assume the target label is class c. We have

$$z = f(\boldsymbol{x}) = -\log(p_c) = -\log\left(\frac{e^{x_c}}{\sum_j e^{x_j}}\right) = \log\left(\sum_j e^{x_j}\right) - x_c \quad (13.40)$$

Hence

$$\frac{\partial z}{\partial x_i} = \frac{\partial}{\partial x_i} \log \sum_j e^{x_j} - \frac{\partial}{\partial x_i} x_c = \frac{e^{x_i}}{\sum_j e^{x_j}} - \frac{\partial}{\partial x_i} x_c = p_i - \mathbb{I}(i = c) \quad (13.41)$$

If we define $\boldsymbol{y} = [\mathbb{I}(i = c)]$, we recover Equation (13.39). Note that the Jacobian of this layer is a row vector, since the output is a scalar.

13.3.3.2 Elementwise nonlinearity

Consider a layer that applies an elementwise nonlinearity, $z = f(x) = \varphi(x)$, so $z_i = \varphi(x_i)$. The (i, j) element of the Jacobian is given by

$$\frac{\partial z_i}{\partial x_j} = \begin{cases} \varphi'(x_i) & \text{if } i = j \\ 0 & \text{otherwise} \end{cases} \tag{13.42}$$

where $\varphi'(a) = \frac{d}{da}\varphi(a)$. In other words, the Jacobian wrt the input is

$$\mathbf{J} = \frac{\partial f}{\partial x} = \text{diag}(\varphi'(x)) \tag{13.43}$$

For an arbitrary vector u, we can compute $u^\mathsf{T}\mathbf{J}$ by elementwise multiplication of the diagonal elements of $\mathbf{J}$ with u. For example, if

$$\varphi(a) = \text{ReLU}(a) = \max(a, 0) \tag{13.44}$$

we have

$$\varphi'(a) = \begin{cases} 0 & a < 0 \\ 1 & a > 0 \end{cases} \tag{13.45}$$

The subderivative (Section 8.1.4.1) at $a = 0$ is any value in $[0, 1]$. It is often taken to be 0. Hence

$$\text{ReLU}'(a) = H(a) \tag{13.46}$$

where H is the Heaviside step function.

13.3.3.3 Linear layer

Now consider a linear layer, $z = f(x, \mathbf{W}) = \mathbf{W}x$, where $\mathbf{W} \in \mathbb{R}^{m \times n}$, so $x \in \mathbb{R}^n$ and $z \in \mathbb{R}^m$. We can compute the Jacobian wrt the input vector, $\mathbf{J} = \frac{\partial z}{\partial x} \in \mathbb{R}^{m \times n}$, as follows. Note that

$$z_i = \sum_{k=1}^{n} W_{ik} x_k \tag{13.47}$$

So the (i, j) entry of the Jacobian will be

$$\frac{\partial z_i}{\partial x_j} = \frac{\partial}{\partial x_j} \sum_{k=1}^{n} W_{ik} x_k = \sum_{k=1}^{n} W_{ik} \frac{\partial}{\partial x_j} x_k = W_{ij} \tag{13.48}$$

since $\frac{\partial}{\partial x_j} x_k = \mathbb{I}(k = j)$. Hence the Jacobian wrt the input is

$$\mathbf{J} = \frac{\partial z}{\partial x} = \mathbf{W} \tag{13.49}$$

The VJP between $\boldsymbol{u}^{\mathsf{T}} \in \mathbb{R}^{1 \times m}$ and $\mathbf{J} \in \mathbb{R}^{m \times n}$ is

$$\boldsymbol{u}^{\mathsf{T}} \frac{\partial \boldsymbol{z}}{\partial \boldsymbol{x}} = \boldsymbol{u}^{\mathsf{T}} \mathbf{W} \in \mathbb{R}^{1 \times n} \tag{13.50}$$

Now consider the Jacobian wrt the weight matrix, $\mathbf{J} = \frac{\partial \boldsymbol{z}}{\partial \mathbf{W}}$. This can be represented as a $m \times (m \times n)$ matrix, which is complex to deal with. So instead, let us focus on taking the gradient wrt a single weight, W_{ij}. This is easier to compute, since $\frac{\partial \boldsymbol{z}}{\partial W_{ij}}$ is a vector. To compute this, note that

$$z_k = \sum_{l=1}^{n} W_{kl} x_l \tag{13.51}$$

$$\frac{\partial z_k}{\partial W_{ij}} = \sum_{l=1}^{n} x_l \frac{\partial}{\partial W_{ij}} W_{kl} = \sum_{l=1}^{n} x_l \mathbb{I} \left(i = k \text{ and } j = l \right) \tag{13.52}$$

Hence

$$\frac{\partial \boldsymbol{z}}{\partial W_{ij}} = \begin{pmatrix} 0 & \cdots & 0 & x_j & 0 & \cdots & 0 \end{pmatrix}^{\mathsf{T}} \tag{13.53}$$

where the non-zero entry occurs in location i. The VJP between $\boldsymbol{u}^{\mathsf{T}} \in \mathbb{R}^{1 \times m}$ and $\frac{\partial \boldsymbol{z}}{\partial \mathbf{W}} \in \mathbb{R}^{m \times (m \times n)}$ can be represented as a matrix of shape $1 \times (m \times n)$. Note that

$$\boldsymbol{u}^{\mathsf{T}} \frac{\partial \boldsymbol{z}}{\partial W_{ij}} = \sum_{k=1}^{m} u_k \frac{\partial z_k}{\partial W_{ij}} = u_i x_j \tag{13.54}$$

Therefore

$$\left[\boldsymbol{u}^{\mathsf{T}} \frac{\partial \boldsymbol{z}}{\partial \mathbf{W}} \right]_{1,:} = \boldsymbol{u} \boldsymbol{x}^{\mathsf{T}} \in \mathbb{R}^{m \times n} \tag{13.55}$$

13.3.3.4 Putting it all together

For an exercise that puts this all together, see Exercise 13.1.

13.3.4 Computation graphs

MLPs are a simple kind of DNN in which each layer feeds directly into the next, forming a chain structure, as shown in Figure 13.10. However, modern DNNs can combine differentiable components in much more complex ways, to create a **computation graph**, analogous to how programmers combine elementary functions to make more complex ones. (Indeed, some have suggested that "deep learning" be called "**differentiable programming**".) The only restriction is that the resulting computation graph corresponds to a **directed acyclic graph** (**DAG**), where each node is a differentiable function of all its inputs.

For example, consider the function

$$f(x_1, x_2) = x_2 e^{x_1} \sqrt{x_1 + x_2 e^{x_1}} \tag{13.56}$$

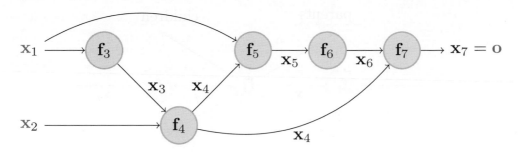

Figure 13.11: An example of a computation graph with 2 (scalar) inputs and 1 (scalar) output. From [Blo20].

We can compute this using the DAG in Figure 13.11, with the following intermediate functions:

$$x_3 = f_3(x_1) = e^{x_1} \tag{13.57}$$
$$x_4 = f_4(x_2, x_3) = x_2 x_3 \tag{13.58}$$
$$x_5 = f_5(x_1, x_4) = x_1 + x_4 \tag{13.59}$$
$$x_6 = f_6(x_5) = \sqrt{x_5} \tag{13.60}$$
$$x_7 = f_7(x_4, x_6) = x_4 x_6 \tag{13.61}$$

Note that we have numbered the nodes in topological order (parents before children). During the backward pass, since the graph is no longer a chain, we may need to sum gradients along multiple paths. For example, since x_4 influences x_5 and x_7, we have

$$\frac{\partial o}{\partial x_4} = \frac{\partial o}{\partial x_5}\frac{\partial x_5}{\partial x_4} + \frac{\partial o}{\partial x_7}\frac{\partial x_7}{\partial x_4} \tag{13.62}$$

We can avoid repeated computation by working in reverse topological order. For example,

$$\frac{\partial o}{\partial x_7} = \frac{\partial x_7}{\partial x_7} = \mathbf{I}_m \tag{13.63}$$

$$\frac{\partial o}{\partial x_6} = \frac{\partial o}{\partial x_7}\frac{\partial x_7}{\partial x_6} \tag{13.64}$$

$$\frac{\partial o}{\partial x_5} = \frac{\partial o}{\partial x_6}\frac{\partial x_6}{\partial x_5} \tag{13.65}$$

$$\frac{\partial o}{\partial x_4} = \frac{\partial o}{\partial x_5}\frac{\partial x_5}{\partial x_4} + \frac{\partial o}{\partial x_7}\frac{\partial x_7}{\partial x_4} \tag{13.66}$$

In general, we use

$$\frac{\partial o}{\partial x_j} = \sum_{k \in \mathrm{Ch}(j)} \frac{\partial o}{\partial x_k}\frac{\partial x_k}{\partial x_j} \tag{13.67}$$

where the sum is over all children k of node j, as shown in Figure 13.12. The $\frac{\partial o}{\partial x_k}$ gradient vector has already been computed for each child k; this quantity is called the **adjoint**. This gets multiplied by the Jacobian $\frac{\partial x_k}{\partial x_j}$ of each child.

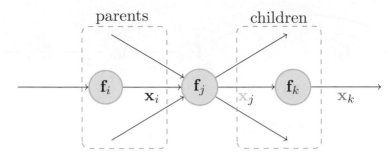

Figure 13.12: Notation for automatic differentiation at node j in a computation graph. From [Blo20].

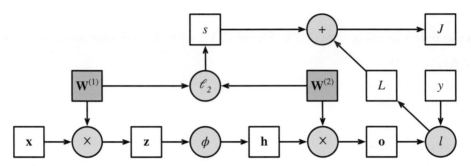

Figure 13.13: Computation graph for an MLP with input $\boldsymbol{x}$, hidden layer $\boldsymbol{h}$, output $\boldsymbol{o}$, loss function $L = \ell(\boldsymbol{o}, y)$, an ℓ_2 regularizer s on the weights, and total loss $J = L + s$. From Figure 4.7.1 of [Zha+20]. Used with kind permission of Aston Zhang.

The computation graph can be computed ahead of time, by using an API to define a **static graph**. (This is how Tensorflow 1 worked.) Alternatively, the graph can be computed "**just in time**", by **tracing** the execution of the function on an input argument. (This is how Tensorflow eager mode works, as well as JAX and PyTorch.) The latter approach makes it easier to work with a **dynamic graph**, whose shape can change depending on the values computed by the function.

Figure 13.13 shows a computation graph corresponding to an MLP with one hidden layer with weight decay. More precisely, the model computes the linear pre-activations $\boldsymbol{z} = \mathbf{W}^{(1)}\boldsymbol{x}$, the hidden activations $\boldsymbol{h} = \phi(\boldsymbol{z})$, the linear outputs $\boldsymbol{o} = \mathbf{W}^{(2)}\boldsymbol{h}$, the loss $L = \ell(\boldsymbol{o}, y)$, the regularizer $s = \frac{\lambda}{2}(||\mathbf{W}^{(1)}||_F^2 + ||\mathbf{W}^{(2)}||_F^2)$, and the total loss $J = L + s$.

13.4   Training neural networks

In this section, we discuss how to fit DNNs to data. The standard approach is to use maximum likelihood estimation, by minimizing the NLL:

$$\mathcal{L}(\boldsymbol{\theta}) = -\log p(\mathcal{D}|\boldsymbol{\theta}) = -\sum_{n=1}^{N} \log p(\boldsymbol{y}_n|\boldsymbol{x}_n; \boldsymbol{\theta}) \tag{13.68}$$

It is also common to add a regularizer (such as the negative log prior), as we discuss in Section 13.5.

In principle we can just use the backprop algorithm (Section 13.3) to compute the gradient of this loss and pass it to an off-the-shelf optimizer, such as those discussed in Chapter 8. (The Adam optimizer of Section 8.4.6.3 is a popular choice, due to its ability to scale to large datasets (by virtue of being an SGD-type algorithm), and to converge fairly quickly (by virtue of using diagonal preconditioning and momentum).) However, in practice this may not work well. In this section, we discuss various problems that may arise, as well as some solutions. For more details on the practicalities of training DNNs, see various other books, such as [HG20; Zha+20; Gér19].

In addition to practical issues, there are important theoretical issues. In particular, we note that the DNN loss is not a convex objective, so in general we will not be able to find the global optimum. Nevertheless, SGD can often find suprisingly good solutions. The research into why this is the case is still being conducted; see [Bah+20] for a recent review of some of this work.

13.4.1 Tuning the learning rate

It is important to tune the learning rate (step size), to ensure convergence to a good solution. We discuss this issue in Section 8.4.3.

13.4.2 Vanishing and exploding gradients

When training very deep models, the gradient tends to become either very small (this is called the **vanishing gradient problem**) or very large (this is called the **exploding gradient problem**), because the error signal is being passed through a series of layers which either amplify or diminish it [Hoc+01]. (Similar problems arise in RNNs on long sequences, as we explain in Section 15.2.6.)

To explain the problem in more detail, consider the gradient of the loss wrt a node at layer l:

$$\frac{\partial \mathcal{L}}{\partial z_l} = \frac{\partial \mathcal{L}}{\partial z_{l+1}} \frac{\partial z_{l+1}}{\partial z_l} = \mathbf{J}_l g_{l+1} \tag{13.69}$$

where $\mathbf{J}_l = \frac{\partial z_{l+1}}{\partial z_l}$ is the Jacobian matrix, and $g_{l+1} = \frac{\partial \mathcal{L}}{\partial z_{l+1}}$ is the gradient at the next layer. If $\mathbf{J}_l$ is constant across layers, it is clear that the contribution of the gradient from the final layer, g_L, to layer l will be $\mathbf{J}^{L-l} g_L$. Thus the behavior of the system depends on the eigenvectors of $\mathbf{J}$.

Although $\mathbf{J}$ is a real-valued matrix, it is not (in general) symmetric, so its eigenvalues and eigenvectors can be complex-valued, with the imaginary components corresponding to oscillatory behavior. Let λ be the **spectral radius** of $\mathbf{J}$, which is the maximum of the absolute values of the eigenvalues. If this is greater than 1, the gradient can explode; if this is less than 1, the gradient can vanish. (Similarly, the spectral radius of $\mathbf{W}$, connecting z_l to z_{l+1}, determines the stability of the dynamical system when run in forwards mode.)

The exploding gradient problem can be ameliorated by **gradient clipping**, in which we cap the magnitude of the gradient if it becomes too large, i.e., we use

$$g' = \min(1, \frac{c}{||g||}) g \tag{13.70}$$

This way, the norm of g' can never exceed c, but the vector is always in the same direction as g.

However, the vanishing gradient problem is more difficult to solve. There are various solutions, such as the following:

Name	Definition	Range	Reference
Sigmoid	$\sigma(a) = \frac{1}{1+e^{-a}}$	$[0,1]$	
Hyperbolic tangent	$\tanh(a) = 2\sigma(2a) - 1$	$[-1,1]$	
Softplus	$\sigma_+(a) = \log(1 + e^a)$	$[0,\infty]$	[GBB11]
Rectified linear unit	$\mathrm{ReLU}(a) = \max(a,0)$	$[0,\infty]$	[GBB11; KSH12]
Leaky ReLU	$\max(a,0) + \alpha\min(a,0)$	$[-\infty,\infty]$	[MHN13]
Exponential linear unit	$\max(a,0) + \min(\alpha(e^a - 1),0)$	$[-\infty,\infty]$	[CUH16]
Swish	$a\sigma(a)$	$[-\infty,\infty]$	[RZL17]
GELU	$a\Phi(a)$	$[-\infty,\infty]$	[HG16]

Table 13.4: List of some popular activation functions for neural networks.

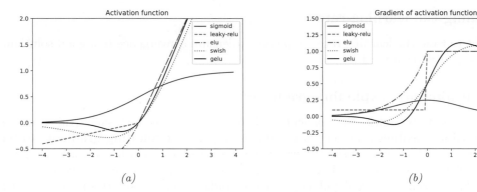

Figure 13.14: (a) Some popular activation functions. (b) Plot of their gradients. Generated by activation_fun_deriv_jax.ipynb.

- Modify the the activation functions at each layer to prevent the gradient from becoming too large or too small; see Section 13.4.3.

- Modify the architecture so that the updates are additive rather than multiplicative; see Section 13.4.4.

- Modify the architecture to standardize the activations at each layer, so that the distribution of activations over the dataset remains constant during training; see Section 14.2.4.1.

- Carefully choose the initial values of the parameters; see Section 13.4.5.

13.4.3   Non-saturating activation functions

In Section 13.2.3, we mentioned that the sigmoid activation function saturates at 0 for large negative inputs, and at 1 for large positive inputs. It turns out that the gradient signal in these regimes is 0, preventing backpropagation from working.

To see why the gradient vanishes, consider a layer which computes $\boldsymbol{z} = \sigma(\mathbf{W}\boldsymbol{x})$, where

$$\varphi(a) = \sigma(a) = \frac{1}{1 + \exp(-a)} \tag{13.71}$$

If the weights are initialized to be large (positive or negative), then it becomes very easy for $\boldsymbol{a} = \mathbf{W}\boldsymbol{x}$ to take on large values, and hence for $\boldsymbol{z}$ to saturate near $\mathbf{0}$ or $\mathbf{1}$, since the sigmoid saturates, as shown in Figure 13.14a. Now let us consider the gradient of the loss wrt the inputs $\boldsymbol{x}$ (from an earlier layer) and the parameters $\mathbf{W}$. The derivative of the activation function is given by

$$\varphi'(a) = \sigma(a)(1 - \sigma(a)) \tag{13.72}$$

See Figure 13.14b for a plot. In Section 13.3.3, we show that the gradient of the loss wrt the inputs is

$$\frac{\partial \mathcal{L}}{\partial \boldsymbol{x}} = \mathbf{W}^\mathsf{T} \boldsymbol{\delta} = \mathbf{W}^\mathsf{T} \boldsymbol{z}(1 - \boldsymbol{z}) \tag{13.73}$$

and the gradient of the loss wrt the parameters is

$$\frac{\partial \mathcal{L}}{\partial \mathbf{W}} = \boldsymbol{\delta}\boldsymbol{x}^\mathsf{T} = \boldsymbol{z}(1 - \boldsymbol{z})\boldsymbol{x}^\mathsf{T} \tag{13.74}$$

Hence, if $\boldsymbol{z}$ is near 0 or 1, the gradients will go to 0.

One of the keys to being able to train very deep models is to use **non-saturating activation functions**. Several different functions have been proposed: see Table 13.4 for a summary, and `https://mlfromscratch.com/activation-functions-explained` for more details.

13.4.3.1   ReLU

The most common is **rectified linear unit** or **ReLU**, proposed in [GBB11; KSH12]. This is defined as

$$\text{ReLU}(a) = \max(a, 0) = a\mathbb{I}(a > 0) \tag{13.75}$$

The ReLU function simply "turns off" negative inputs, and passes positive inputs unchanged. The gradient has the following form:

$$\text{ReLU}'(a) = \mathbb{I}(a > 0) \tag{13.76}$$

Now suppose we use this in a layer to compute $\boldsymbol{z} = \text{ReLU}(\mathbf{W}\boldsymbol{x})$. In Section 13.3.3, we show that the gradient wrt the inputs has the form

$$\frac{\partial \mathcal{L}}{\partial \boldsymbol{x}} = \mathbf{W}^\mathsf{T}\mathbb{I}(\boldsymbol{z} > \mathbf{0}) \tag{13.77}$$

and wrt the parameters has the form

$$\frac{\partial \mathcal{L}}{\partial \mathbf{W}} = \mathbb{I}(\boldsymbol{z} > \mathbf{0})\,\boldsymbol{x}^\mathsf{T} \tag{13.78}$$

Hence the gradient will not vanish, as long a z is positive.

Unfortunately, if the weights are initialized to be large and negative, then it becomes very easy for (some components of) $a = \mathbf{W}x$ to take on large negative values, and hence for z to go to 0. This will cause the gradient for the weights to go to 0. The algorithm will never be able to escape this situation, so the hidden units (components of z) will stay permanently off. This is called the "**dead ReLU**" problem [Lu+19].

13.4.3.2   Non-saturating ReLU

The problem of dead ReLU's can be solved by using non-saturating variants of ReLU. One alternate is the **leaky ReLU**, proposed in [MHN13]. This is defined as

$$\text{LReLU}(a; \alpha) = \max(\alpha a, a) \tag{13.79}$$

where $0 < \alpha < 1$. The slope of this function is 1 for positive inputs, and α for negative inputs, thus ensuring there is some signal passed back to earlier layers, even when the input is negative. See Figure 13.14b for a plot. If we allow the parameter α to be learned, rather than fixed, the leaky ReLU is called **parametric ReLU** [He+15].

Another popular choice is the **ELU**, proposed in [CUH16]. This is defined by

$$\text{ELU}(a; \alpha) = \begin{cases} \alpha(e^a - 1) & \text{if } a \leq 0 \\ a & \text{if } a > 0 \end{cases} \tag{13.80}$$

This has the advantage over leaky ReLU of being a smooth function.[5] See Figure 13.14 for plot.

A slight variant of ELU, known as **SELU** (self-normalizing ELU), was proposed in [Kla+17]. This has the form

$$\text{SELU}(a; \alpha, \lambda) = \lambda \text{ELU}(a; \alpha) \tag{13.81}$$

Surprisingly, they prove that by setting α and λ to carefully chosen values, this activation function is guaranteed to ensure that the output of each layer is standardized (provided the input is also standardized), even without the use of techniques such as batchnorm (Section 14.2.4.1). This can help with model fitting.

13.4.3.3   Other choices

As an alternative to manually discovering good activation functions, we can use blackbox optimization methods to search over the space of functional forms. Such an approach was used in [RZL17], where they discovered a function they call **swish** that seems to do well on some image classification benchmarks. It is defined by

$$\text{swish}(a; \beta) = a\sigma(\beta a) \tag{13.82}$$

(The same function, under the name **SiLU** (for Sigmoid Linear Unit), was independently proposed in [HG16].) See Figure 13.14 for plot.

---

5. ELU only has a continuous first derivative if $\alpha = 1$.

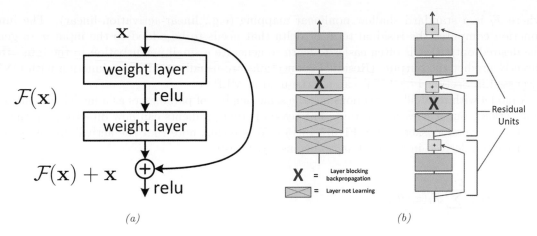

Figure 13.15: (a) Illustration of a residual block. (b) Illustration of why adding residual connections can help when training a very deep model. Adapted from Figure 14.16 of [Gér19].

Another popular activation function is **GELU**, which stands for "Gaussian Error Linear Unit" [HG16]. This is defined as follows:

$$\text{GELU}(a) = a\Phi(a) \tag{13.83}$$

where $\Phi(a)$ is the cdf of a standard normal:

$$\Phi(a) = \text{Pr}(\mathcal{N}(0,1) \le a) = \frac{1}{2}\left(1 + \text{erf}(a/\sqrt{2})\right) \tag{13.84}$$

We see from Figure 13.14 that this is not a convex or monontonic function, unlike most other activation functions.

We can think of GELU as a "soft" version of ReLU, since it replaces the step function $\mathbb{I}(a > 0)$ with the Gaussian cdf, $\Phi(a)$. Alternatively, the GELU can be motivated as an adaptive version of dropout (Section 13.5.4), where we multiply the input by a binary scalar mask, $m \sim \text{Ber}(\Phi(a))$, where the probability of being dropped is given by $1 - \Phi(a)$. Thus the expected output is

$$\mathbb{E}[a] = \Phi(a) \times a + (1 - \Phi(a)) \times 0 = a\Phi(a) \tag{13.85}$$

We can approximate GELU using swish with a particular parameter setting, namely

$$\text{GELU}(a) \approx a\sigma(1.702a) \tag{13.86}$$

13.4.4 Residual connections

One solution to the vanishing gradient problem for DNNs is to use a **residual network** or **ResNet** [He+16a]. This is a feedforward model in which each layer has the form of a **residual block**, defined by

$$\mathcal{F}'_l(\boldsymbol{x}) = \mathcal{F}_l(\boldsymbol{x}) + \boldsymbol{x} \tag{13.87}$$

where $\mathcal{F}_l$ is a standard shallow nonlinear mapping (e.g., linear-activation-linear). The inner $\mathcal{F}_l$ function computes the residual term or delta that needs to be added to the input $\boldsymbol{x}$ to generate the desired output; it is often easier to learn to generate a small perturbation to the input than to directly predict the output. (Residual connections are usually used in conjunction with CNNs, as discussed in Section 14.3.4, but can also be used in MLPs.)

A model with residual connections has the same number of parameters as a model without residual connections, but it is easier to train. The reason is that gradients can flow directly from the output to earlier layers, as sketched in Figure 13.15b. To see this, note that the activations at the output layer can be derived in terms of any previous layer l using

$$z_L = z_l + \sum_{i=l}^{L-1} \mathcal{F}_i(z_i; \boldsymbol{\theta}_i). \tag{13.88}$$

We can therefore compute the gradient of the loss wrt the parameters of the l'th layer as follows:

$$\frac{\partial \mathcal{L}}{\partial \boldsymbol{\theta}_l} = \frac{\partial z_l}{\partial \boldsymbol{\theta}_l} \frac{\partial \mathcal{L}}{\partial z_l} \tag{13.89}$$

$$= \frac{\partial z_l}{\partial \boldsymbol{\theta}_l} \frac{\partial \mathcal{L}}{\partial z_L} \frac{\partial z_L}{\partial z_l} \tag{13.90}$$

$$= \frac{\partial z_l}{\partial \boldsymbol{\theta}_l} \frac{\partial \mathcal{L}}{\partial z_L} \left(1 + \sum_{i=l}^{L-1} \frac{\partial \mathcal{F}_i(z_i; \boldsymbol{\theta}_i)}{\partial z_l}\right) \tag{13.91}$$

$$= \frac{\partial z_l}{\partial \boldsymbol{\theta}_l} \frac{\partial \mathcal{L}}{\partial z_L} + \text{other terms} \tag{13.92}$$

Thus we see that the gradient at layer l depends directly on the gradient at layer L in a way that is independent of the depth of the network.

13.4.5 Parameter initialization

Since the objective function for DNN training is non-convex, the way that we initialize the parameters of a DNN can play a big role on what kind of solution we end up with, as well as how easy the function is to train (i.e., how well information can flow forwards and backwards through the model). In the rest of this section, we present some common heuristic methods that are used for initializing parameters.

13.4.5.1 Heuristic initialization schemes

In [GB10], they show that sampling parameters from a standard normal with fixed variance can result in exploding activations or gradients. To see why, consider a linear unit with no activation function given by $o_i = \sum_{j=1}^{n_{\text{in}}} w_{ij} x_j$; suppose $w_{ij} \sim \mathcal{N}(0, \sigma^2)$, and $\mathbb{E}[x_j] = 0$ and $\mathbb{V}[x_j] = \gamma^2$, where we assume x_j are independent of w_{ij}. The mean and variance of the output is given by

$$\mathbb{E}\left[o_i\right] = \sum_{j=1}^{n_{\text{in}}} \mathbb{E}\left[w_{ij}x_j\right] = \sum_{j=1}^{n_{\text{in}}} \mathbb{E}\left[w_{ij}\right]\mathbb{E}\left[x_j\right] = 0 \tag{13.93}$$

$$\mathbb{V}\left[o_i\right] = \mathbb{E}\left[o_i^2\right] - (\mathbb{E}\left[o_i\right])^2 = \sum_{j=1}^{n_{\text{in}}} \mathbb{E}\left[w_{ij}^2 x_j^2\right] - 0 = \sum_{j=1}^{n_{\text{in}}} \mathbb{E}\left[w_{ij}^2\right]\mathbb{E}\left[x_j^2\right] = n_{\text{in}}\sigma^2\gamma^2 \tag{13.94}$$

To keep the output variance from blowing up, we need to ensure $n_{\text{in}}\sigma^2 = 1$ (or some other constant), where n_{in} is the **fan-in** of a unit (number of incoming connections).

Now consider the backwards pass. By analogous reasoning, we see that the variance of the gradients can blow up unless $n_{\text{out}}\sigma^2 = 1$, where n_{out} is the **fan-out** of a unit (number of outgoing connections). To satisfy both requirements at once, we set $\frac{1}{2}(n_{\text{in}} + n_{\text{out}})\sigma^2 = 1$, or equivalently

$$\sigma^2 = \frac{2}{n_{\text{in}} + n_{\text{out}}} \tag{13.95}$$

This is known as **Xavier initialization** or **Glorot initialization**, named after the first author of [GB10].

A special case arises if we use $\sigma^2 = 1/n_{\text{in}}$; this is known as **LeCun initialization**, named after Yann LeCun, who proposed it in the 1990s. This is equivalent to Glorot initialization when $n_{\text{in}} = n_{\text{out}}$. If we use $\sigma^2 = 2/n_{\text{in}}$, the method is called **He initialization**, named after Kaiming He, who proposed it in [He+15].

Note that it is not necessary to use a Gaussian distribution. Indeed, the above derivation just worked in terms of the first two moments (mean and variance), and made no assumptions about Gaussianity. For example, suppose we sample weights from a uniform distribution, $w_{ij} \sim \text{Unif}(-a, a)$. The mean is 0, and the variance is $\sigma^2 = a^2/3$. Hence we should set $a = \sqrt{\frac{6}{n_{\text{in}}+n_{\text{out}}}}$.

Although the above derivation assumes a linear output unit, the technique works well empirically even for nonlinear units. The best choice of initialization method depends on which activation function you use. For linear, tanh, logistic, and softmax, Glorot is recommended. For ReLU and variants, He is recommended. For SELU, LeCun is recommended. See e.g., [Gér19] for more heuristics, and e.g., [HDR19] for some theory.

13.4.5.2   Data-driven initializations

We can also adopt a data-driven approach to parameter initialization. For example, [MM16] proposed a simple but effective scheme known as **layer-sequential unit-variance** (LSUV) initialization, which works as follows. First we initialize the weights of each (fully connected or convolutional) layer with orthonormal matrices, as proposed in [SMG14]. (This can be achieved by drawing from $w \sim \mathcal{N}(\mathbf{0}, \mathbf{I})$, reshaping to w to a matrix $\mathbf{W}$, and then computing an orthonormal basis using QR or SVD decomposition.) Then, for each layer l, we compute the variance v_l of the activations across a minibatch; we then rescale using $\mathbf{W}_l := \mathbf{W}_l/\sqrt{v_l}$. This scheme can be viewed as an orthonormal initialization combined with batch normalization performed only on the first mini-batch. This is faster than full batch normalization, but can sometimes work just as well.

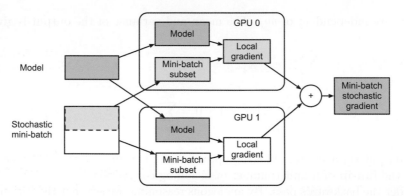

Figure 13.16: Calculation of minibatch stochastic gradient using data parallelism and two GPUs. From Figure 12.5.2 of [Zha+20]. Used with kind permission of Aston Zhang.

13.4.6 Parallel training

It can be quite slow to train large models on large datasets. One way to speed this process up is to use specialized hardware, such as **graphics processing units** (**GPUs**) and **tensor processing units** (**TPUs**), which are very efficient at performing matrix-matrix multiplication. If we have multiple GPUs, we can sometimes further speed things up. There are two main approaches: **model parallelism**, in which we partition the model between machines, and **data parallelism**, in which each machine has its own copy of the model, and applies it to a different set of data.

Model parallelism can be quite complicated, since it requires tight communication between machines to ensure they compute the correct answer. We will not discuss this further. Data parallelism is generally much simpler, since it is **embarassingly parallel**. To use this to speed up training, at each training step t, we do the following: 1) we partition the minibatch across the K machines to get $\mathcal{D}_t^k$; 2) each machine k computes its own gradient, $\boldsymbol{g}_t^k = \nabla_{\boldsymbol{\theta}} \mathcal{L}(\boldsymbol{\theta}; \mathcal{D}_t^k)$; 3) we collect all the local gradients on a central machine (e.g., device 0) and sum them using $\boldsymbol{g}_t = \sum_{k=1}^{K} \boldsymbol{g}_t^k$; 4) we broadcast the summed gradient back to all devices, so $\tilde{\boldsymbol{g}}_t^k = \boldsymbol{g}_t$; 5) each machine updates its own copy of the parameters using $\boldsymbol{\theta}_t^k := \boldsymbol{\theta}_t^k - \eta_t \tilde{\boldsymbol{g}}_t^k$. See Figure 13.16 for an illustration and multi_gpu_training_jax.ipynb for some sample code.

Note that steps 3 and 4 are usually combined into one atomic step; this is known as an **all-reduce** operation (where we use sum to reduce the set of (gradient) vectors into one). If each machine blocks until receiving the centrally aggregated gradient, $\boldsymbol{g}_t$, the method is known as **synchronous training**. This will give the same results as training with one machine (with a larger batchsize), only faster (assuming we ignore any batch normalization layers). If we let each machine update its parameters using its own local gradient estimate, and not wait for the broadcast to/from the other machines, the method is called **asynchronous training**. This is not guaranteed to work, since the different machines may get out of step, and hence will be updating different versions of the parameters; this approach has therefore been called **hogwild training** [Niu+11]. However, if the updates are sparse, so each machine "touches" a different part of the parameter vector, one can prove that hogwild training behaves like standard synchronous SGD.

13.5 Regularization

In Section 13.4 we discussed computational issues associated with training (large) neural networks. In this section, we discuss statistical issues. In particular, we focus on ways to avoid overfitting. This is crucial, since large neural networks can easily have millions of parameters.

13.5.1 Early stopping

Perhaps the simplest way to prevent overfitting is called **early stopping**, which refers to the heuristic of stopping the training procedure when the error on the validation set starts to increase (see Figure 4.8 for an example). This method works because we are restricting the ability of the optimization algorithm to transfer information from the training examples to the parameters, as explained in [AS19].

13.5.2 Weight decay

A common approach to reduce overfitting is to impose a prior on the parameters, and then use MAP estimation. It is standard to use a Gaussian prior for the weights $\mathcal{N}(\boldsymbol{w}|\mathbf{0}, \alpha^2\mathbf{I})$ and biases, $\mathcal{N}(\boldsymbol{b}|\mathbf{0}, \beta^2\mathbf{I})$. This is equivalent to ℓ_2 regularization of the objective. In the neural networks literature, this is called **weight decay**, since it encourages small weights, and hence simpler models, as in ridge regression (Section 11.3).

13.5.3 Sparse DNNs

Since there are many weights in a neural network, it is often helpful to encourage sparsity. This allows us to perform **model compression**, which can save memory and time. To do this, we can use ℓ_1 regularization (as in Section 11.4), or ARD (as in Section 11.7.7), or several other methods (see e.g., [Hoe+21; Bha+20] for recent reviews). As a simple example, Figure 13.17 shows a 5 layer MLP which has been fit to some 1d regression data using an ℓ_1 regularizer on the weights. We see that the resulting graph topology is sparse.

Despite the intuitive appeal of sparse topology, in practice these methods are not widely used, since modern GPUs are optimized for *dense* matrix multiplication, and there are few computational benefits to sparse weight matrices. However, if we use methods that encourage *group* sparsity, we can prune out whole layers of the model. This results in *block sparse* weight matrices, which can result in speedups and memory savings (see e.g., [Sca+17; Wen+16; MAV17; LUW17]).

13.5.4 Dropout

Suppose that we randomly (on a per-example basis) turn off all the outgoing connections from each neuron with probability p, as illustrated in Figure 13.18. This technique is known as **dropout** [Sri+14].

Dropout can dramatically reduce overfitting and is very widely used. Intuitively, the reason dropout works well is that it prevents complex co-adaptation of the hidden units. In other words, each unit must learn to perform well even if some of the other units are missing at random. This prevents the

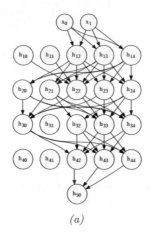
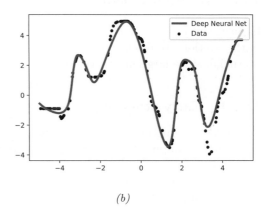

(a)   (b)

Figure 13.17: (a) A deep but sparse neural network. The connections are pruned using ℓ_1 regularization. At each level, nodes numbered 0 are clamped to 1, so their outgoing weights correspond to the offset/bias terms. (b) Predictions made by the model on the training set. Generated by sparse_mlp.ipynb.

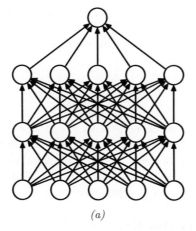
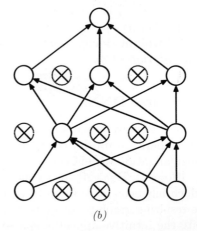

(a)   (b)

Figure 13.18: Illustration of dropout. (a) A standard neural net with 2 hidden layers. (b) An example of a thinned net produced by applying dropout with $p_0 = 0.5$. Units that have been dropped out are marked with an x. From Figure 1 of [Sri+14]. Used with kind permission of Geoff Hinton.

units from learning complex, but fragile, dependencies on each other.[6] A more formal explanation, in terms of Gaussian scale mixture priors, can be found in [NHLS19].

We can view dropout as estimating a noisy version of the weights, $\theta_{lji} = w_{lji}\epsilon_{li}$, where $\epsilon_{li} \sim$ Ber$(1-p)$ is a Bernoulli noise term. (So if we sample $\epsilon_{li} = 0$, then all of the weights going out of unit i in layer $l-1$ into any j in layer l will be set to 0.) At test time, we usually turn the noise off.

---

6. Geoff Hinton, who invented dropout, said he was inspired by a talk on sexual reproduction, which encourages genes to be individually useful (or at most depend on a small number of other genes), even when combined with random other genes.

To ensure the weights have the same expectation at test time as they did during training (so the input activation to the neurons is the same, on average), at test time we should use $w_{lij} = \theta_{lji}\mathbb{E}\left[\epsilon_{li}\right]$. For Bernoulli noise, we have $\mathbb{E}\left[\epsilon\right] = 1 - p$, so we should multiply the weights by the keep probability, $1 - p$, before making predictions.

We can, however, use dropout at test time if we wish. The result is an **ensemble** of networks, each with slightly different sparse graph structures. This is called **Monte Carlo dropout** [GG16; KG17], and has the form

$$p(\boldsymbol{y}|\boldsymbol{x}, \mathcal{D}) \approx \frac{1}{S}\sum_{s=1}^{S} p(\boldsymbol{y}|\boldsymbol{x}, \hat{\mathbf{W}}\epsilon^s + \hat{\boldsymbol{b}}) \tag{13.96}$$

where S is the number of samples, and we write $\hat{\mathbf{W}}\epsilon^s$ to indicate that we are multiplying all the estimated weight matrices by a sampled noise vector. This can sometimes provide a good approximation to the Bayesian posterior predictive distribution $p(\boldsymbol{y}|\boldsymbol{x}, \mathcal{D})$, especially if the noise rate is optimized [GHK17].

13.5.5 Bayesian neural networks

Modern DNNs are usually trained using a (penalized) maximum likelihood objective to find a single setting of parameters. However, with large models, there are often many more parameters than data points, so there may be multiple possible models which fit the training data equally well, yet which generalize in different ways. It is often useful to capture the induced uncertainty in the posterior predictive distribution. This can be done by *marginalizing out* the parameters by computing

$$p(\boldsymbol{y}|\boldsymbol{x}, \mathcal{D}) = \int p(\boldsymbol{y}|\boldsymbol{x}, \boldsymbol{\theta})p(\boldsymbol{\theta}|\mathcal{D})d\boldsymbol{\theta} \tag{13.97}$$

The result is known as a **Bayesian neural network** or **BNN**. It can be thought of as an infinite ensemble of differently weight neural networks. By marginalizing out the parameters, we can avoid overfitting [Mac95]. Bayesian marginalization is challenging for large neural networks, but also can lead to significant performance gains [WI20]. For more details on the topic of **Bayesian deep learning**, see the sequel to this book, [Mur23].

13.5.6 Regularization effects of (stochastic) gradient descent *

Some optimization methods (in particular, second-order batch methods) are able to find "needles in haystacks", corresponding to narrow but deep "holes" in the loss landscape, corresponding to parameter settings with very low loss. These are known as **sharp minima**, see Figure 13.19(right). From the point of view of minimizing the empirical loss, the optimizer has done a good job. However, such solutions generally correspond to a model that has overfit the data. It is better to find points that correspond to **flat minima**, as shown in Figure 13.19(left); such solutions are more robust and generalize better. To see why, note that flat minima correspond to regions in parameter space where there is a lot of posterior uncertainty, and hence samples from this region are less able to precisely memorize irrelevant details about the training set [AS17]. SGD often finds such flat minima by virtue of the addition of noise, which prevents it from "entering" narrow regions of the loss landscape (see e.g., [SL18]). This is called **implicit regularization**. It is also possible to explicitly encourage

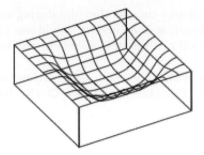 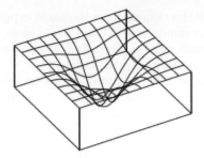

Figure 13.19: Flat vs sharp minima. From Figures 1 and 2 of [HS97a]. Used with kind permission of Jürgen Schmidhuber.

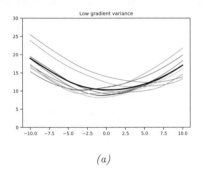 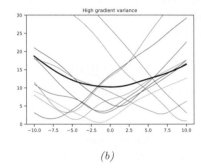

(a)   (b)

Figure 13.20: Each curve shows how the loss varies across parameter values for a given minibatch. (a) A stable local minimum. (b) An unstable local minimum. Generated by sgd_minima_variance.ipynb. Adapted from https://bit.ly/3wTc1L6.

SGD to find such flat minima, using **entropy SGD** [Cha+17], **sharpness aware minimization** [For+21], **stochastic weight averaging** (SWA) [Izm+18], and other related techniques.

Of course, the loss landscape depends not just on the parameter values, but also on the data. Since we usually cannot afford to do full-batch gradient descent, we will get a set of loss curves, one per minibatch. If each one of these curves corresponds to a wide basin, as shown in Figure 13.20a, we are at a point in parameter space that is robust to perturbations, and will likely generalize well. However, if the overall wide basin is the result of averaging over many different narrow basins, as shown in Figure 13.20b, the resulting estimate will likely generalize less well.

This can be formalized using the analysis in [Smi+21; BD21]. Specifically, they consider continuous time gradient flow which approximates the behavior of (S)GD. In [BD21], they consider full-batch GD, and show that the flow has the form $\dot{\boldsymbol{w}} = -\nabla_{\boldsymbol{w}}\tilde{\mathcal{L}}_{GD}(\boldsymbol{w})$, where

$$\tilde{\mathcal{L}}_{GD}(\boldsymbol{w}) = \mathcal{L}(\boldsymbol{w}) + \frac{\epsilon}{4}||\nabla\mathcal{L}(\boldsymbol{w})||^2 \tag{13.98}$$

where $\mathcal{L}(\boldsymbol{w})$ is the original loss, ϵ is the learning rate, and the second term is an implicit regularization term that penalizes solutions with large gradients (high curvature).

In [Smi+21], they extend this analysis to the SGD case. They show that the flow has the form $\dot{\boldsymbol{w}} = -\nabla_{\boldsymbol{w}} \tilde{\mathcal{L}}_{SGD}(\boldsymbol{w})$, where

$$\tilde{\mathcal{L}}_{SGD}(\boldsymbol{w}) = \mathcal{L}(\boldsymbol{w}) + \frac{\epsilon}{4m} \sum_{k=1}^{m} ||\nabla \mathcal{L}_k(\boldsymbol{w})||^2 \tag{13.99}$$

where m is the number of minibatches, and $\mathcal{L}_k(\boldsymbol{w})$ is the loss on the k'th such minibatch. Comparing this to the full-batch GD loss, we see

$$\tilde{\mathcal{L}}_{SGD}(\boldsymbol{w}) = \tilde{\mathcal{L}}_{GD}(\boldsymbol{w}) + \frac{\epsilon}{4m} \sum_{k=1}^{m} ||\nabla \mathcal{L}_k(\boldsymbol{w}) - \nabla \mathcal{L}(\boldsymbol{w})||^2 \tag{13.100}$$

The second term estimates the variance of the minibatch gradients, which is a measure of stability, and hence of generalization ability.

The above analysis shows that SGD not only has computational advantages (since it is faster than full-batch GD or second-order methods), but also statistical advantages.

13.6   Other kinds of feedforward networks *

13.6.1   Radial basis function networks

Consider a 1 layer neural net where the hidden layer is given by the feature vector

$$\boldsymbol{\phi}(\boldsymbol{x}) = [\mathcal{K}(\boldsymbol{x}, \boldsymbol{\mu}_1), \ldots, \mathcal{K}(\boldsymbol{x}, \boldsymbol{\mu}_K)] \tag{13.101}$$

where $\boldsymbol{\mu}_k \in \mathcal{X}$ are a set of K **centroids** or **exemplars**, and $\mathcal{K}(\boldsymbol{x}, \boldsymbol{\mu}) \geq 0$ is a **kernel function**. We describe kernel functions in detail in Section 17.1. Here we just give an example, namely the **Gaussian kernel**

$$\mathcal{K}_{\text{gauss}}(\boldsymbol{x}, \boldsymbol{c}) \triangleq \exp\left(-\frac{1}{2\sigma^2} ||\boldsymbol{c} - \boldsymbol{x}||_2^2\right) \tag{13.102}$$

The parameter σ is known as the **bandwidth** of the kernel. Note that this kernel is shift invariant, meaning it is only a function of the distance $r = ||\boldsymbol{x} - \boldsymbol{c}||_2$, so we can equivalently write this as

$$\mathcal{K}_{\text{gauss}}(r) \triangleq \exp\left(-\frac{1}{2\sigma^2} r^2\right) \tag{13.103}$$

This is therefore called a **radial basis function kernel** or **RBF kernel**.

A 1 layer neural net in which we use Equation (13.101) as the hidden layer, with RBF kernels, is called an **RBF network** [BL88]. This has the form

$$p(y|\boldsymbol{x}; \boldsymbol{\theta}) = p(y|\boldsymbol{w}^\mathsf{T} \boldsymbol{\phi}(\boldsymbol{x})) \tag{13.104}$$

where $\boldsymbol{\theta} = (\boldsymbol{\mu}, \boldsymbol{w})$. If the centroids $\boldsymbol{\mu}$ are fixed, we can solve for the optimal weights $\boldsymbol{w}$ using (regularized) least squares, as discussed in Chapter 11. If the centroids are unknown, we can estimate them by using an unsupervised clustering method, such as K-means (Section 21.3). Alternatively, we

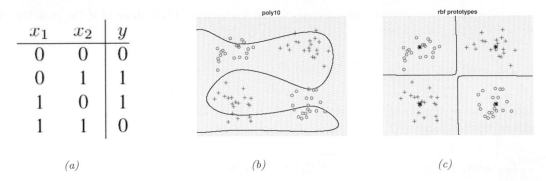

x_1	x_2	y
0	0	0
0	1	1
1	0	1
1	1	0

(a)   (b)   (c)

Figure 13.21: (a) xor truth table. (b) Fitting a linear logistic regression classifier using degree 10 polynomial expansion. (c) Same model, but using an RBF kernel with centroids specified by the 4 black crosses. Generated by logregXorDemo.ipynb.

can associate one centroid per data point in the training set, to get $\boldsymbol{\mu}_n = \boldsymbol{x}_n$, where now $K = N$. This is an example of a **non-parametric model**, since the number of parameters grows (in this case linearly) with the amount of data, and is not independent of N. If $K = N$, the model can perfectly interpolate the data, and hence may overfit. However, by ensuring that the output weight vector $\boldsymbol{w}$ is sparse, the model will only use a finite subset of the input examples; this is called a **sparse kernel machine**, and will be discussed in more detail in Section 17.4.1 and Section 17.3. Another way to avoid overfitting is to adopt a Bayesian approach, by integrating out the weights $\boldsymbol{w}$; this gives rise to a model called a **Gaussian process**, which will be discussed in more detail in Section 17.2.

13.6.1.1 RBF network for regression

We can use RBF networks for regression by defining $p(y|\boldsymbol{x}, \boldsymbol{\theta}) = \mathcal{N}(\boldsymbol{w}^T \boldsymbol{\phi}(\boldsymbol{x}), \sigma^2)$. For example, Figure 13.22 shows a 1d data set fit with $K = 10$ uniformly spaced RBF prototypes, but with the bandwidth ranging from small to large. Small values lead to very wiggly functions, since the predicted function value will only be non-zero for points $\boldsymbol{x}$ that are close to one of the prototypes $\boldsymbol{\mu}_k$. If the bandwidth is very large, the design matrix reduces to a constant matrix of 1's, since each point is equally close to every prototype; hence the corresponding function is just a straight line.

13.6.1.2 RBF network for classification

We can use RBF networks for binary classification by defining $p(y|\boldsymbol{x}, \boldsymbol{\theta}) = \mathrm{Ber}(\sigma(\boldsymbol{w}^T \boldsymbol{\phi}(\boldsymbol{x})))$. As an example, consider the data coming from the exclusive or function. This is a binary-valued function of two binary inputs. Its truth table is shown in Figure 13.21(a). In Figure 13.21(b), we have shown some data labeled by the xor function, but we have **jittered** the points to make the picture clearer.[7] We see we cannot separate the data even using a degree 10 polynomial. However, using an RBF kernel and just 4 prototypes easily solves the problem as shown in Figure 13.21(c).

---

7. Jittering is a common visualization trick in statistics, wherein points in a plot/display that would otherwise land on top of each other are dispersed with uniform additive noise.

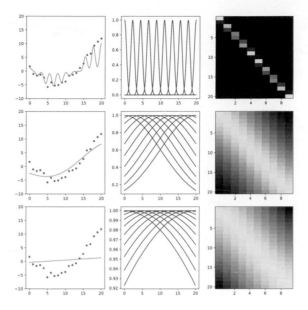

Figure 13.22: *Linear regression using 10 equally spaced RBF basis functions in 1d. Left column: fitted function. Middle column: basis functions evaluated on a grid. Right column: design matrix. Top to bottom we show different bandwidths for the kernel function: $\sigma = 0.5, 10, 50$. Generated by linregRbfDemo.ipynb.*

13.6.2 Mixtures of experts

When considering regression problems, it is common to assume a unimodal output distribution, such as a Gaussian or Student distribution, where the mean and variance is some function of the input, i.e.,

$$p(\boldsymbol{y}|\boldsymbol{x}) = \mathcal{N}(\boldsymbol{y}|f_\mu(\boldsymbol{x}), \mathrm{diag}(\sigma_+(f_\sigma(\boldsymbol{x})))) \tag{13.105}$$

where the f functions may be MLPs (possibly with some shared hidden units, as in Figure 13.5). However, this will not work well for **one-to-many functions**, in which each input can have multiple possible outputs.

Figure 13.23a gives a simple example of such a function. We see that in the middle of the plot there are certain x values for which there are two equally probable y values. There are many real world problems of this form, e.g., 3d pose prediction of a person from a single image [Bo+08], colorization of a black and white image [Gua+17], predicting future frames of a video sequence [VT17], etc. Any model which is trained to maximize likelihood using a unimodal output density — even if the model is a flexible nonlinear model, such as neural network — will work poorly on one-to-many functions such as these, since it will just produce a blurry average output.

To prevent this problem of regression to the mean, we can use a **conditional mixture model**. That is, we assume the output is a weighted mixture of K different outputs, corresponding to different

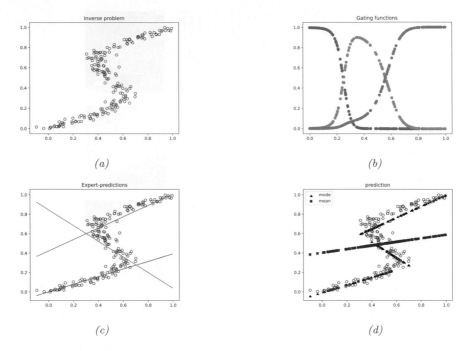

Figure 13.23: (a) Some data from a one-to-many function. Horizontal axis is the input x, vertical axis is the target y = f(x). (b) The responsibilities of each expert for the input domain. (c) Prediction of each expert (colored lines) superimposed on the training data. (d) Overall prediction. Mean is red cross, mode is black square. Adapted from Figures 5.20 and 5.21 of [Bis06]. Generated by mixexpDemoOneToMany.ipynb.

modes of the output distribution for each input $\boldsymbol{x}$. In the Gaussian case, this becomes

$$p(\boldsymbol{y}|\boldsymbol{x}) = \sum_{k=1}^{K} p(\boldsymbol{y}|\boldsymbol{x}, z = k)p(z = k|\boldsymbol{x}) \tag{13.106}$$

$$p(\boldsymbol{y}|\boldsymbol{x}, z = k) = \mathcal{N}(\boldsymbol{y}|f_{\mu,k}(\boldsymbol{x}), \text{diag}(f_{\sigma,k}(\boldsymbol{x}))) \tag{13.107}$$

$$p(z = k|\boldsymbol{x}) = \text{Cat}(z|\text{softmax}(f_z(\boldsymbol{x}))) \tag{13.108}$$

Here $f_{\mu,k}$ predicts the mean of the k'th Gaussian, $f_{\sigma,k}$ predicts its variance terms, and f_z predicts which mixture component to use. This model is called a **mixture of experts** (**MoE**) [Jac+91; JJ94; YWG12; ME14]. The idea is that the k'th submodel $p(\boldsymbol{y}|\boldsymbol{x}, z = k)$ is considered to be an "expert" in a certain region of input space. The function $p(z = k|\boldsymbol{x})$ is called a **gating function**, and decides which expert to use, depending on the input values. By picking the most likely expert for a given input $\boldsymbol{x}$, we can "activate" just a subset of the model. This is an example of **conditional computation**, since we decide what expert to run based on the results of earlier computations from the gating network [Sha+17].

We can train this model using SGD, or using the EM algorithm (see Section 8.7.3 for details on the latter method).

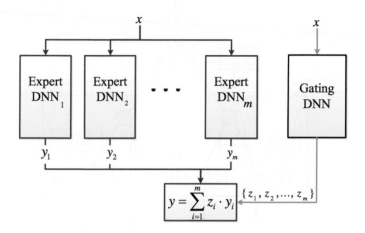

Figure 13.24: Deep MOE with m experts, represented as a neural network. From Figure 1 of [CGG17]. Used with kind permission of Jacob Goldberger.

13.6.2.1 Mixture of linear experts

In this section, we consider a simple example in which we use linear regression experts and a linear classification gating function, i.e., the model has the form:

$$p(y|\boldsymbol{x}, z = k, \boldsymbol{\theta}) = \mathcal{N}(y|\boldsymbol{w}_k^\mathsf{T}\boldsymbol{x}, \sigma_k^2) \tag{13.109}$$

$$p(z = k|\boldsymbol{x}, \boldsymbol{\theta}) = \text{Cat}(z|\text{softmax}_k(\mathbf{V}\boldsymbol{x})) \tag{13.110}$$

where softmax_k is the k'th output from the softmax function. The individual weighting term $p(z = k|\boldsymbol{x})$ is called the **responsibility** for expert k for input $\boldsymbol{x}$. In Figure 13.23b, we see how the gating networks softly partitions the input space amongst the $K = 3$ experts.

Each expert $p(y|\boldsymbol{x}, z = k)$ corresponds to a linear regression model with different parameters. These are shown in Figure 13.23c.

If we take a weighted combination of the experts as our output, we get the red curve in Figure 13.23d, which is clearly is a bad predictor. If instead we only predict using the most active expert (i.e., the one with the highest responsibility), we get the discontinuous black curve, which is a much better predictor.

13.6.2.2 Mixture density networks

The gating function and experts can be any kind of conditional probabilistic model, not just a linear model. If we make them both DNNs, then resulting model is called a **mixture density network** (**MDN**) [Bis94; ZS14] or a **deep mixture of experts** [CGG17]. See Figure 13.24 for a sketch of the model.

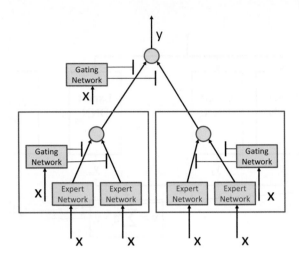

Figure 13.25: A 2-level hierarchical mixture of experts as a neural network. The top gating network chooses between the left and right expert, shown by the large boxes; the left and right experts themselves choose between their left and right sub-experts.

13.6.2.3 Hierarchical MOEs

If each expert is itself an MoE model, the resulting model is called a **hierarchical mixture of experts** [JJ94]. See Figure 13.25 for an illustration of such a model with a two level hierarchy.

An HME with L levels can be thought of as a "soft" decision tree of depth L, where each example is passed through every branch of the tree, and the final prediction is a weighted average. (We discuss decision trees in Section 18.1.)

13.7   Exercises

Exercise 13.1 [Backpropagation for a MLP]

(Based on an exercise by Kevin Clark.)

Consider the following classification MLP with one hidden layer:

$$\boldsymbol{x} = \text{input} \in \mathbb{R}^D \tag{13.111}$$

$$\boldsymbol{z} = \mathbf{W}\boldsymbol{x} + \boldsymbol{b}_1 \in \mathbb{R}^K \tag{13.112}$$

$$\boldsymbol{h} = \text{ReLU}(\boldsymbol{z}) \in \mathbb{R}^K \tag{13.113}$$

$$\boldsymbol{a} = \mathbf{V}\boldsymbol{h} + \boldsymbol{b}_2 \in \mathbb{R}^C \tag{13.114}$$

$$\mathcal{L} = \text{CrossEntropy}(\boldsymbol{y}, \text{softmax}(\boldsymbol{a})) \in \mathbb{R} \tag{13.115}$$

where $\boldsymbol{x} \in \mathbb{R}^D$, $\boldsymbol{b}_1 \in \mathbb{R}^K$, $\mathbf{W} \in \mathbb{R}^{K \times D}$, $\boldsymbol{b}_2 \in \mathbb{R}^C$, $\mathbf{V} \in \mathbb{R}^{C \times K}$, where D is the size of the input, K is the number of hidden units, and C is the number of classes. Show that the gradients for the parameters and input are as follows:

$$\nabla_{\mathbf{V}} \mathcal{L} = \left[\frac{\partial \mathcal{L}}{\partial \mathbf{V}} \right]_{1,:} = \boldsymbol{u}_2 \boldsymbol{h}^{\mathsf{T}} \in \mathbb{R}^{C \times K} \tag{13.116}$$

$$\nabla_{b_2} \mathcal{L} = \left(\frac{\partial \mathcal{L}}{\partial \boldsymbol{b}_2} \right)^{\mathsf{T}} = \boldsymbol{u}_2 \in \mathbb{R}^{C} \tag{13.117}$$

$$\nabla_{\mathbf{W}} \mathcal{L} = \left[\frac{\partial \mathcal{L}}{\partial \mathbf{W}} \right]_{1,:} = \boldsymbol{u}_1 \boldsymbol{x}^{\mathsf{T}} \in \mathbb{R}^{K \times D} \tag{13.118}$$

$$\nabla_{b_1} \mathcal{L} = \left(\frac{\partial \mathcal{L}}{\partial \boldsymbol{b}_1} \right)^{\mathsf{T}} = \boldsymbol{u}_1 \in \mathbb{R}^{K} \tag{13.119}$$

$$\nabla_{x} \mathcal{L} = \left(\frac{\partial \mathcal{L}}{\partial \boldsymbol{x}} \right)^{\mathsf{T}} = \mathbf{W}^{\mathsf{T}} \boldsymbol{u}_1 \in \mathbb{R}^{D} \tag{13.120}$$

where the gradients of the loss wrt the two layers (logit and hidden) are given by the following:

$$\boldsymbol{u}_2 = \nabla_{a} \mathcal{L} = \left(\frac{\partial \mathcal{L}}{\partial \boldsymbol{a}} \right)^{\mathsf{T}} = (\boldsymbol{p} - \boldsymbol{y}) \in \mathbb{R}^{C} \tag{13.121}$$

$$\boldsymbol{u}_1 = \nabla_{z} \mathcal{L} = \left(\frac{\partial \mathcal{L}}{\partial \boldsymbol{z}} \right)^{\mathsf{T}} = (\mathbf{V}^{\mathsf{T}} \boldsymbol{u}_2) \odot H(\boldsymbol{z}) \in \mathbb{R}^{K} \tag{13.122}$$

with H is the Heaviside function. Note that, in our notation, the gradient (which has the same shape as the variable with respect to which we differentiate) is equal to the Jacobian's transpose when the variable is a vector and to the first slice of the Jacobian when the variable is a matrix.

14 Neural Networks for Images

14.1 Introduction

In Chapter 13, we discussed multilayered perceptrons (MLPs) as a way to learn functions mapping "unstructured" input vectors $\boldsymbol{x} \in \mathbb{R}^D$ to outputs. In this chapter, we extend this to the case where the input $\boldsymbol{x}$ has 2d spatial structure. (Similar ideas apply to 1d temporal structure, or 3d spatio-temporal structure.)

To see why it is not a good idea to apply MLPs directly to image data, recall that the core operation in an MLP at each hidden layer is computing the activations $\boldsymbol{z} = \varphi(\mathbf{W}\boldsymbol{x})$, where $\boldsymbol{x}$ is the input to a layer, $\mathbf{W}$ are the weights, and $\varphi()$ is the nonlinear activation function. Thus the j'th element of the hidden layer has value $z_j = \varphi(\boldsymbol{w}_j^\mathsf{T} \boldsymbol{x})$. We can think of this inner product operation as comparing the input $\boldsymbol{x}$ to a learned template or pattern $\boldsymbol{w}_j$; if the match is good (large positive inner product), the activation of that unit will be large (assuming a ReLU nonlinearity), signalling that the j'th pattern is present in the input.

However, this does not work well if the input is a variable-sized image, $\boldsymbol{x} \in \mathbb{R}^{WHC}$, where W is the width, H is the height, and C is the number of input **channels** (e.g., $C = 3$ for RGB color). The problem is that we would need to learn a different-sized weight matrix $\mathbf{W}$ for every size of input image. In addition, even if the input was fixed size, the number of parameters needed would be prohibitive for reasonably sized images, since the weight matrix would have size $(W \times H \times C) \times D$, where D is the number of outputs (hidden units). The final problem is that a pattern that occurs in one location may not be recognized when it occurs in a different location — that is, the model may not exhibit **translation invariance** — because the weights are not shared across locations (see Figure 14.1).

To solve these problems, we will use **convolutional neural networks** (**CNN**s), in which we replace matrix multiplication with a convolution operation. We explain this in detail in Section 14.2, but the basic idea is to divide the input into overlapping 2d **image patches**, and to compare each patch with a set of small weight matrices, or **filters**, which represent parts of an object; this is illustrated in Figure 14.2. We can think of this as a form of **template matching**. We will learn these templates from data, as we explain below. Because the templates are small (often just 3x3 or 5x5), the number of parameters is significantly reduced. And because we use convolution to do the template matching, instead of matrix multiplication, the model will be translationally invariant. This is useful for tasks such as image classification, where the goal is to classify if an object is present, regardless of its location.

CNNs have many other applications besides image classification, as we will discuss later in this chapter. They can also be applied to 1d inputs (see Section 15.3) and 3d inputs; however, we mostly

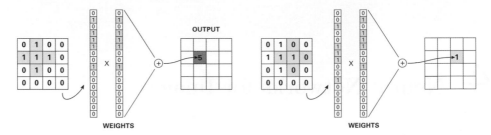

Figure 14.1: Detecting patterns in 2d images using unstructured MLPs does not work well, because the method is not translation invariant. We can design a weight vector to act as a **matched filter** *for detecting the desired cross-shape. This will give a strong response of 5 if the object is on the left, but a weak response of 1 if the object is shifted over to the right. Adapted from Figure 7.16 of [SAV20].*

Figure 14.2: We can classify a digit by looking for certain discriminative features (image templates) occuring in the correct (relative) locations. From Figure 5.1 of [Cho17]. Used with kind permission of Francois Chollet.

focus on the 2d case in this chapter.

14.2   Common layers

In this section, we discuss the basics of CNNs.

14.2.1   Convolutional layers

We start by describing the basics of convolution in 1d, and then in 2d, and then describe how they are used as a key component of CNNs.

14.2.1.1   Convolution in 1d

The **convolution** between two functions, say $f, g : \mathbb{R}^D \to \mathbb{R}$, is defined as

$$[f \circledast g](\boldsymbol{z}) = \int_{\mathbb{R}^D} f(\boldsymbol{u}) g(\boldsymbol{z} - \boldsymbol{u}) d\boldsymbol{u} \tag{14.1}$$

Now suppose we replace the functions with finite-length vectors, which we can think of as functions defined on a finite set of points. For example, suppose f is evaluated at the points $\{-L, -L +$

		1	2	3	4	-	-	
7	6	5	-	-	-	-	-	$z_0 = x_0 w_0 = 5$
-	7	6	5	-	-	-	-	$z_1 = x_0 w_1 + x_1 w_0 = 16$
-	-	7	6	5	-	-	-	$z_2 = x_0 w_2 + x_1 w_1 + x_2 w_0 = 34$
-	-	-	7	6	5	-	-	$z_3 = x_1 w_2 + x_2 w_1 + x_3 w_0 = 52$
-	-	-	-	7	6	5	-	$z_4 = x_2 w_2 + x_3 w_1 = 45$
-	-	-	-	-	7	6	5	$z_5 = x_3 w_2 = 28$

Figure 14.3: Discrete convolution of $\boldsymbol{x} = [1, 2, 3, 4]$ with $\boldsymbol{w} = [5, 6, 7]$ to yield $\boldsymbol{z} = [5, 16, 34, 52, 45, 28]$. We see that this operation consists of "flipping" $\boldsymbol{w}$ and then "dragging" it over $\boldsymbol{x}$, multiplying elementwise, and adding up the results.

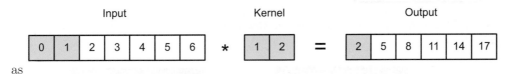

Figure 14.4: 1d cross correlation. From Figure 15.3.2 of [Zha+20]. Used with kind permission of Aston Zhang.

$1, \ldots, 0, 1, \ldots, L\}$ to yield the weight vector (also called a **filter** or **kernel**) $w_{-L} = f(-L)$ up to $w_L = f(L)$. Now let g be evaluated at points $\{-N, \ldots, N\}$ to yield the feature vector $x_{-N} = g(-N)$ up to $x_N = g(N)$. Then the above equation becomes

$$[\boldsymbol{w} \circledast \boldsymbol{x}](i) = w_{-L} x_{i+L} + \cdots + w_{-1} x_{i+1} + w_0 x_i + w_1 x_{i-1} + \cdots + w_L x_{i-L} \quad (14.2)$$

(We discuss boundary conditions (edge effects) later on.) We see that we "flip" the weight vector $\boldsymbol{w}$ (since indices of $\boldsymbol{w}$ are reversed), and then "drag" it over the $\boldsymbol{x}$ vector, summing up the local windows at each point, as illustrated in Figure 14.3.

There is a very closely related operation, in which we do not flip $\boldsymbol{w}$ first:

$$[\boldsymbol{w} * \boldsymbol{x}](i) = w_{-L} x_{i-L} + \cdots + w_{-1} x_{i-1} + w_0 x_i + w_1 x_{i+1} + \cdots + w_L x_{i+L} \quad (14.3)$$

This is called **cross correlation**; If the weight vector is symmetric, as is often the case, then cross correlation and convolution are the same. In the deep learning literature, the term "convolution" is usually used to mean cross correlation; we will follow this convention.

We can also evaluate the weights $\boldsymbol{w}$ on domain $\{0, 1, \ldots, L - 1\}$ and the features $\boldsymbol{x}$ on domain $\{0, 1, \ldots, N - 1\}$, to eliminate negative indices. Then the above equation becomes

$$[\boldsymbol{w} \circledast \boldsymbol{x}](i) = \sum_{u=0}^{L-1} w_u x_{i+u} \quad (14.4)$$

See Figure 14.4 for an example.

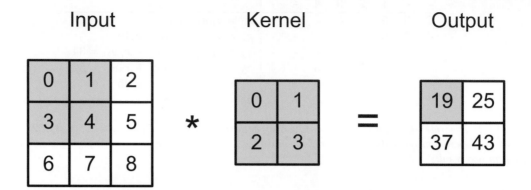

Figure 14.5: *Illustration of 2d cross correlation. Generated by conv2d_jax.ipynb. Adapted from Figure 6.2.1 of [Zha+20].*

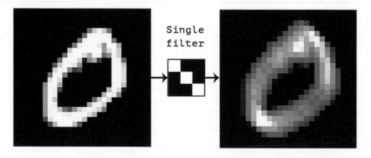

Figure 14.6: *Convolving a 2d image (left) with a 3×3 filter (middle) produces a 2d response map (right). The bright spots of the response map correspond to locations in the image which contain diagonal lines sloping down and to the right. From Figure 5.3 of [Cho17]. Used with kind permission of Francois Chollet.*

14.2.1.2   Convolution in 2d

In 2d, Equation (14.4) becomes

$$[\mathbf{W} \circledast \mathbf{X}](i,j) = \sum_{u=0}^{H-1} \sum_{v=0}^{W-1} w_{u,v} x_{i+u,j+v} \tag{14.5}$$

where the 2d filter $\mathbf{W}$ has size $H \times W$. For example, consider convolving a 3×3 input $\mathbf{X}$ with a 2×2 kernel $\mathbf{W}$ to compute a 2×2 output $\mathbf{Y}$:

$$\mathbf{Y} = \begin{pmatrix} w_1 & w_2 \\ w_3 & w_4 \end{pmatrix} \circledast \begin{pmatrix} x_1 & x_2 & x_3 \\ x_4 & x_5 & x_6 \\ x_7 & x_8 & x_9 \end{pmatrix} \tag{14.6}$$

$$= \begin{pmatrix} (w_1 x_1 + w_2 x_2 + w_3 x_4 + w_4 x_5) & (w_1 x_2 + w_2 x_3 + w_3 x_5 + w_4 x_6) \\ (w_1 x_4 + w_2 x_5 + w_3 x_7 + w_4 x_8) & (w_1 x_5 + w_2 x_6 + w_3 x_8 + w_4 x_9) \end{pmatrix} \tag{14.7}$$

See Figure 14.5 for a visualization of this process.

We can think of 2d convolution as **template matching**, since the output at a point (i, j) will be large if the corresponding image patch centered on (i, j) is similar to $\mathbf{W}$. If the template $\mathbf{W}$ corresponds to an oriented edge, then convolving with it will cause the output **heat map** to "light up" in regions that contain edges that match that orientation, as shown in Figure 14.6. More generally, we can think of convolution as a form of **feature detection**. The resulting output $\mathbf{Y} = \mathbf{W} \circledast \mathbf{X}$ is therefore called a **feature map**.

14.2.1.3 Convolution as matrix-vector multiplication

Since convolution is a linear operator, we can represent it by matrix multiplication. For example, consider Equation (14.7). We can rewrite this as matrix-vector mutiplication by flattening the 2d matrix $\mathbf{X}$ into a 1d vector $\boldsymbol{x}$, and multiplying by a Toeplitz-like matrix $\mathbf{C}$ derived from the kernel $\mathbf{W}$, as follows:

$$\boldsymbol{y} = \mathbf{C}\boldsymbol{x} = \left(\begin{array}{ccc|ccc|ccc} w_1 & w_2 & 0 & w_3 & w_4 & 0 & 0 & 0 & 0 \\ 0 & w_1 & w_2 & 0 & w_3 & w_4 & 0 & 0 & 0 \\ 0 & 0 & 0 & w_1 & w_2 & 0 & w_3 & w_4 & 0 \\ 0 & 0 & 0 & 0 & w_1 & w_2 & 0 & w_3 & w_4 \end{array} \right) \begin{pmatrix} x_1 \\ x_2 \\ x_3 \\ x_4 \\ x_5 \\ x_6 \\ x_7 \\ x_8 \\ x_9 \end{pmatrix} \quad (14.8)$$

$$= \begin{pmatrix} w_1 x_1 + w_2 x_2 + w_3 x_4 + w_4 x_5 \\ w_1 x_2 + w_2 x_3 + w_3 x_5 + w_4 x_6 \\ w_1 x_4 + w_2 x_5 + w_3 x_7 + w_4 x_8 \\ w_1 x_5 + w_2 x_6 + w_3 x_8 + w_4 x_9 \end{pmatrix} \quad (14.9)$$

We can recover the 2×2 output by reshaping the 4×1 vector $\boldsymbol{y}$ back to $\mathbf{Y}$.[1]

Thus we see that CNNs are like MLPs where the weight matrices have a special sparse structure, and the elements are tied across spatial locations. This implements the idea of translation invariance, and massively reduces the number of parameters compared to a weight matrix in a standard fully connected or dense layer, as used in MLPs.

14.2.1.4 Boundary conditions and padding

In Equation (14.7), we saw that convolving a 3×3 image with a 2×2 filter resulted in a 2×2 output. In general, convolving a $f_h \times f_w$ filter over an image of size $x_h \times x_w$ produces an output of size $(x_h - f_h + 1) \times (x_w - f_w + 1)$; this is called **valid convolution**, since we only apply the filter to "valid" parts of the input, i.e., we don't let it "slide off the ends". If we want the output to have the same size as the input, we can use **zero-padding**, which means we add a border of 0s to the image, as illustrated in Figure 14.7. This is called **same convolution**.

---

1. See conv2d_jax.ipynb for a demo.

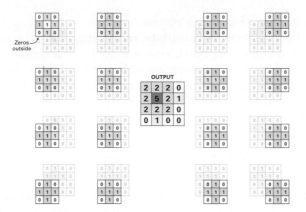

Figure 14.7: Same-convolution (using zero-padding) ensures the output is the same size as the input. Adapted from Figure 8.3 of [SAV20].

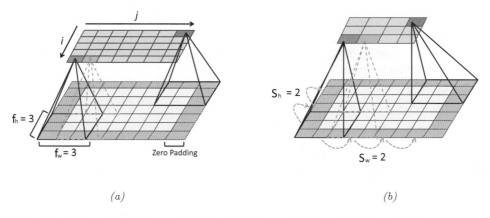

$$(a) \qquad\qquad\qquad\qquad\qquad (b)$$

Figure 14.8: Illustration of padding and strides in 2d convolution. (a) We apply "same convolution" to a 5×7 input (with zero padding) using a 3×3 filter to create a 5×7 output. (b) Now we use a stride of 2, so the output has size 3×4. Adapted from Figures 14.3–14.4 of [Gér19].

In general, if the input has size $x_h \times x_w$, we use a kernel of size $f_h \times f_w$, we use zero padding on each side of size p_h and p_w, then the output has the following size [DV16]:

$$(x_h + 2p_h - f_h + 1) \times (x_w + 2p_w - f_w + 1) \tag{14.10}$$

For example, consider Figure 14.8a. We have $p = 1$, $f = 3$, $x_h = 5$ and $x_w = 7$, so the output has size

$$(5 + 2 - 3 + 1) \times (7 + 2 - 3 + 1) = 5 \times 7 \tag{14.11}$$

If we set $2p = f - 1$, then the output will have the same size as the input.

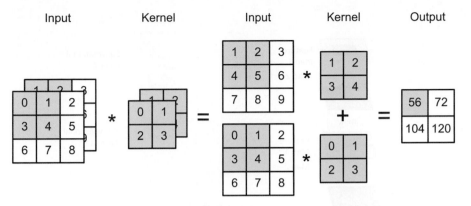

Figure 14.9: *Illustration of 2d convolution applied to an input with 2 channels. Generated by conv2d_jax.ipynb. Adapted from Figure 6.4.1 of [Zha+20].*

14.2.1.5 Strided convolution

Since each output pixel is generated by a weighted combination of inputs in its **receptive field** (based on the size of the filter), neighboring outputs will be very similar in value, since their inputs are overlapping. We can reduce this redundancy (and speedup computation) by skipping every s'th input. This is called **strided convolution**. This is illustrated in Figure 14.8b, where we convolve a 5×7 image with a 3×3 filter with stride 2 to get a 3×4 output.

In general, if the input has size $x_h \times x_w$, we use a kernel of size $f_h \times f_w$, we use zero padding on each side of size p_h and p_w, and we use strides of size s_h and s_w, then the output has the following size [DV16]:

$$\left\lfloor \frac{x_h + 2p_h - f_h + s_h}{s_h} \right\rfloor \times \left\lfloor \frac{x_w + 2p_w - f_w + s_w}{s_w} \right\rfloor \tag{14.12}$$

For example, consider Figure 14.8b, where we set the stride to $s = 2$. Now the output is smaller than the input, and has size

$$\left\lfloor \frac{5 + 2 - 3 + 2}{2} \right\rfloor \times \left\lfloor \frac{7 + 2 - 3 + 2}{2} \right\rfloor = \left\lfloor \frac{6}{2} \right\rfloor \times \left\lfloor \frac{4}{1} \right\rfloor = 3 \times 4 \tag{14.13}$$

14.2.1.6 Multiple input and output channels

In Figure 14.6, the input was a gray-scale image. In general, the input will have multiple **channels** (e.g., RGB, or hyper-spectral bands for satellite images). We can extend the definition of convolution to this case by defining a kernel for each input channel; thus now $\mathbf{W}$ is a 3d weight matrix or **tensor**. We compute the output by convolving channel c of the input with kernel $\mathbf{W}_{:,:,c}$, and then summing over channels:

$$z_{i,j} = b + \sum_{u=0}^{H-1} \sum_{v=0}^{W-1} \sum_{c=0}^{C-1} x_{si+u,sj+v,c} w_{u,v,c} \tag{14.14}$$

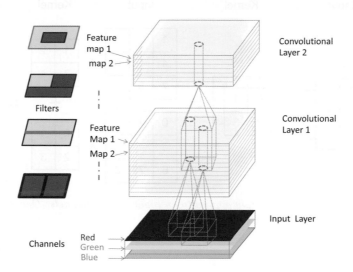

Figure 14.10: Illustration of a CNN with 2 convolutional layers. The input has 3 color channels. The feature maps at internal layers have multiple channels. The cylinders correspond to hypercolumns, which are feature vectors at a certain location. Adapted from Figure 14.6 of [Gér19].

where s is the stride (which we assume is the same for both height and width, for simplicity), and b is the bias term. This is illustrated in Figure 14.9.

Each weight matrix can detect a single kind of feature. We typically want to detect multiple kinds of features, as illustrated in Figure 14.2. We can do this by making $\mathbf{W}$ into a 4d weight matrix. The filter to detect feature type d in input channel c is stored in $\mathbf{W}_{:,:,c,d}$. We extend the definition of convolution to this case as follows:

$$z_{i,j,d} = b_d + \sum_{u=0}^{H-1} \sum_{v=0}^{W-1} \sum_{c=0}^{C-1} x_{si+u,sj+v,c} w_{u,v,c,d} \qquad (14.15)$$

This is illustrated in Figure 14.10. Each vertical cylindrical column denotes the set of output features at a given location, $\mathbf{z}_{i,j,1:D}$; this is sometimes called a **hypercolumn**. Each element is a different weighted combination of the C features in the receptive field of each of the feature maps in the layer below.[2]

14.2.1.7 1×1 (pointwise) convolution

Sometimes we just want to take a weighted combination of the features at a given location, rather than across locations. This can be done using **1x1 convolution**, also called **pointwise convolution**.

---

2. In Tensorflow, a filter for 2d CNNs has shape (H, W, C, D), and a minibatch of feature maps has shape (batch-size, image-height, image-width, image-channels); this is called **NHWC** format. Other systems use different data layouts.

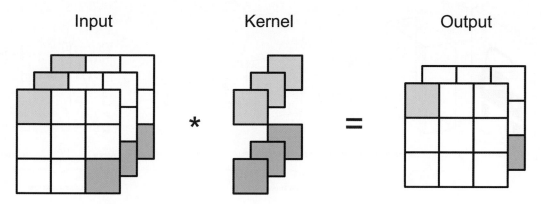

Figure 14.11: *Mapping 3 channels to 2 using convolution with a filter of size* $1 \times 1 \times 3 \times 2$. *Adapted from Figure 6.4.2 of [Zha+20].*

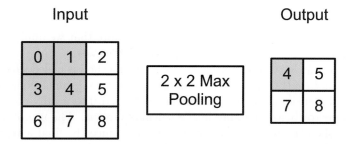

Figure 14.12: *Illustration of maxpooling with a 2x2 filter and a stride of 1. Adapted from Figure 6.5.1 of [Zha+20].*

This changes the number of channels from C to D, without changing the spatial dimensionality:

$$z_{i,j,d} = b_d + \sum_{c=0}^{C-1} x_{i,j,c} w_{0,0,c,d} \qquad (14.16)$$

This can be thought of as a single layer MLP applied to each feature column in parallel.

14.2.2 Pooling layers

Convolution will preserve information about the location of input features (modulo reduced resolution), a property known as **equivariance**. In some case we want to be invariant to the location. For example, when performing image classification, we may just want to know if an object of interest (e.g., a face) is present anywhere in the image.

One simple way to achieve this is called **max pooling**, which just computes the maximum over its incoming values, as illustrated in Figure 14.12. An alternative is to use **average pooling**, which replaces the max by the mean. In either case, the output neuron has the same response no matter

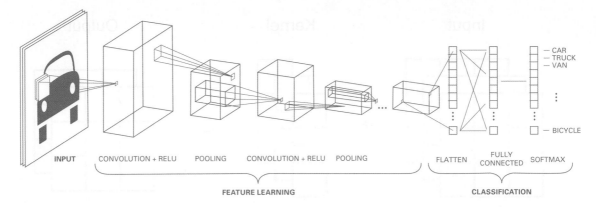

Figure 14.13: A simple CNN for classifying images. Adapted from `https://blog.floydhub.com/building-your-first-convnet/`.

where the input pattern occurs within its receptive field. (Note that we apply pooling to each feature channel independently.)

If we average over all the locations in a feature map, the method is called **global average pooling**. Thus we can convert a $H \times W \times D$ feature map into a $1 \times 1 \times D$ dimensional feature map; this can be reshaped to a D-dimensional vector, which can be passed into a fully connected layer to map it to a C-dimensional vector before passing into a softmax output. The use of global average pooling means we can apply the classifier to an image of any size, since the final feature map will always be converted to a fixed D-dimensional vector before being mapped to a distribution over the C classes.

14.2.3 Putting it all together

A common design pattern is to create a CNN by alternating convolutional layers with max pooling layers, followed by a final linear classification layer at the end. This is illustrated in Figure 14.13. (We omit normalization layers in this example, since the model is quite shallow.) This design pattern first appeared in Fukushima's **neocognitron** [Fuk75], and was inspired by Hubel and Wiesel's model of simple and complex cells in the human visual cortex [HW62]. In 1998 Yann LeCun used a similar design in his eponymous **LeNet** model [LeC+98], which used backpropagation and SGD to estimate the parameters. This design pattern continues to be popular in neurally-inspired models of visual object recognition [RP99], as well as various practical applications (see Section 14.3 and Section 14.5).

14.2.4 Normalization layers

The basic design in Figure 14.13 works well for shallow CNNs, but it can be difficult to scale it to deeper models, due to problems with vanishing or exploding gradients, as explained in Section 13.4.2. A common solution to this problem is to add extra layers to the model, to standardize the statistics of the hidden units (i.e., to ensure they are zero mean and unit variance), just like we do to the inputs of many models. We discuss various kinds of **normalization layers** below.

14.2.4.1 Batch normalization

The most popular normalization layer is called **batch normalization (BN)** [IS15]. This ensures the distribution of the activations within a layer has zero mean and unit variance, when averaged across the samples in a minibatch. More precisely, we replace the activation vector z_n (or sometimes the pre-activation vector a_n) for example n (in some layer) with $\tilde{z}_n$, which is computed as follows:

$$\tilde{z}_n = \gamma \odot \hat{z}_n + \beta \tag{14.17}$$

$$\hat{z}_n = \frac{z_n - \mu_{\mathcal{B}}}{\sqrt{\sigma_{\mathcal{B}}^2 + \epsilon}} \tag{14.18}$$

$$\mu_{\mathcal{B}} = \frac{1}{|\mathcal{B}|} \sum_{z \in \mathcal{B}} z \tag{14.19}$$

$$\sigma_{\mathcal{B}}^2 = \frac{1}{|\mathcal{B}|} \sum_{z \in \mathcal{B}} (z - \mu_{\mathcal{B}})^2 \tag{14.20}$$

where $\mathcal{B}$ is the minibatch containing example n, $\mu_{\mathcal{B}}$ is the mean of the activations for this batch[3], $\sigma_{\mathcal{B}}^2$ is the corresponding variance, $\hat{z}_n$ is the standardized activation vector, $\tilde{z}_n$ is the shifted and scaled version (the output of the BN layer), β and γ are learnable parameters for this layer, and $\epsilon > 0$ is a small constant. Since this transformation is differentiable, we can easily pass gradients back to the input of the layer and to the BN parameters β and γ.

When applied to the input layer, batch normalization is equivalent to the usual standardization procedure we discussed in Section 10.2.8. Note that the mean and variance for the input layer can be computed once, since the data is static. However, the empirical means and variances of the internal layers keep changing, as the parameters adapt. (This is sometimes called "**internal covariate shift**".) This is why we need to recompute μ and σ^2 on each minibatch.

At test time, we may have a single input, so we cannot compute batch statistics. The standard solution to this is as follows: after training, compute μ_l and σ_l^2 for layer l across all the examples in the training set (i.e. using the full batch), and then "freeze" these parameters, and add them to the list of other parameters for the layer, namely β_l and γ_l. At test time, we then use these frozen training values for μ_l and σ_l^2, rather than computing statistics from the test batch. Thus when using a model with BN, we need to specify if we are using it for inference or training. (See batchnorm_jax.ipynb for some sample code.)

For speed, we can combine a frozen batch norm layer with the previous layer. In particular suppose the previous layer computes $\mathbf{XW} + b$; combining this with BN gives $\gamma \odot (\mathbf{XW} + b - \mu)/\sigma + \beta$. If we define $\mathbf{W}' = \gamma \odot \mathbf{W}/\sigma$ and $b' = \gamma \odot (b - \mu)/\sigma + \beta$, then we can write the combined layers as $\mathbf{XW}' + b'$. This is called **fused batchnorm**. Similar tricks can be developed to speed up BN during training [Jun+19].

The benefits of batch normalization (in terms of training speed and stability) can be quite dramatic, especially for deep CNNs. The exact reasons for this are still unclear, but BN seems to make the optimization landscape significantly smoother [San+18b]. It also reduces the sensitivity to the learning rate [ALL18]. In addition to computational advantages, it has statistical advantages. In

---

3. When applied to a convolutional layer, we average across spatial locations and across examples, but not across channels (so the length of μ is the number of channels). When applied to a fully connected layer, we just average across examples (so the length of μ is the width of the layer).

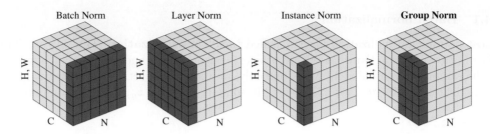

Figure 14.14: Illustration of different activation normalization methods for a CNN. Each subplot shows a feature map tensor, with N as the batch axis, C as the channel axis, and (H, W) as the spatial axes. The pixels in blue are normalized by the same mean and variance, computed by aggregating the values of these pixels. Left to right: batch norm, layer norm, instance norm, and group norm (with 2 groups of 3 channels). From Figure 2 of [WH18]. Used with kind permission of Kaiming He.

particular, BN acts like a regularizer; indeed it can be shown to be equivalent to a form of approximate Bayesian inference [TAS18; Luo+19].

However, the reliance on a minibatch of data causes several problems. In particular, it can result in unstable estimates of the parameters when training with small batch sizes, although a more recent version of the method, known as **batch renormalization** [Iof17], partially addresses this. We discuss some other alternatives to batch norm below.

14.2.4.2   Other kinds of normalization layer

In Section 14.2.4.1 we discussed **batch normalization**, which standardizes all the activations within a given feature channel to be zero mean and unit variance. This can significantly help with training, and allow for a larger learning rate. (See batchnorm_jax.ipynb for some sample code.)

Although batch normalization works well, it struggles when the batch size is small, since the estimated mean and variance parameters can be unreliable. One solution is to compute the mean and variance by pooling statistics across other dimensions of the tensor, but not across examples in the batch. More precisely, let z_i refer to the i'th element of a tensor; in the case of 2d images, the index i has 4 components, indicating batch, height, width and channel, $i = (i_N, i_H, i_W, i_C)$. We compute the mean and standard deviation for each index z_i as follows:

$$\mu_i = \frac{1}{|\mathcal{S}_i|} \sum_{k \in \mathcal{S}_i} z_k, \ \sigma_i = \sqrt{\frac{1}{|\mathcal{S}_i|} \sum_{k \in \mathcal{S}_i} (z_k - \mu_i)^2 + \epsilon} \tag{14.21}$$

where $\mathcal{S}_i$ is the set of elements we average over. We then compute $\hat{z}_i = (z_i - \mu_i)/\sigma_i$ and $\tilde{z}_i = \gamma_c \hat{z}_i + \beta_c$, where c is the channel corresponding to index i.

In batch norm, we pool over batch, height, width, so $\mathcal{S}_i$ is the set of all location in the tensor that match the channel index of i. To avoid problems with small batches, we can instead pool over channel, height and width, but match on the batch index. This is known as **layer normalization** [BKH16]. (See layer_norm_jax.ipynb for some sample code.) Alternatively, we can have separate normalization parameters for each example in the batch and for each channel. This is known as **instance normalization** [UVL16].

A natural generalization of the above methods is known as **group normalization** [WH18], where we pool over all locations whose channel is in the same group as i's. This is illustrated in Figure 14.14. Layer normalization is a special case in which there is a single group, containing all the channels. Instance normalization is a special case in which there are C groups, one per channel. In [WH18], they show experimentally that it can be better (in terms of training speed, as well as training and test accuracies) to use groups that are larger than individual channels, but smaller than all the channels.

More recently, [SK20] proposed **filter response normalization** which is an alternative to batch norm that works well even with a minibatch size of 1. The idea is to define each group as all locations with a single channel and batch sample (as in instance normalization), but then to just divide by the mean squared norm instead of standardizing. That is, if the input (for a given channel and batch entry) is $z = \mathbf{Z}_{b,:,:,c} \in \mathbb{R}^N$, we compute $\hat{z} = z/\sqrt{\nu^2 + \epsilon}$, where $\nu^2 = \sum_{ij} z_{bijc}^2/N$, and then $\tilde{z} = \gamma_c \hat{z} + \beta_c$. Since there is no mean centering, the activations can drift away from 0, which can have detrimental effects, especially with ReLU activations. To compensate for this, the authors propose to add a **thresholded linear unit** at the output. This has the form $y = \max(x, \tau)$, where τ is a learnable offset. The combination of FRN and TLU results in good performance on image classification and object detection even with a batch size of 1.

14.2.4.3 Normalizer-free networks

Recently, [Bro+21] have proposed a method called **normalizer-free networks**, which is a way to train deep residual networks without using batchnorm or any other form of normalization layer. The key is to replace it with adaptive gradient clipping, as an alternative way to avoid training instabilities. That is, we use Equation (13.70), but adapt the clipping strength dynamically. The resulting model is faster to train, and more accurate, than other competitive models trained with batchnorm.

14.3 Common architectures for image classification

It is common to use CNNs to perform image classification, which is the task of estimating the function $f : \mathbb{R}^{H \times W \times K} \to \{0, 1\}^C$, where K is the number of input channels (e.g., $K = 3$ for RGB images), and C is the number of class labels.

In this section, we briefly review various CNNs that have been developed over the years to solve image classification tasks. See e.g., [Kha+20] for a more extensive review of CNNs, and e.g., `https://github.com/rwightman/pytorch-image-models` for an up-to-date repository of code and models (in PyTorch).

14.3.1 LeNet

One of the earliest CNNs, created in 1998, is known as **LeNet** [LeC+98], named after its creator, Yann LeCun. It was designed to classify images of handwritten digits, and was trained on the MNIST dataset introduced in Section 3.5.2. The model is shown in Figure 14.15. (See also Figure 14.16a for a more compact representation of the model.) Some predictions of this model are shown in Figure 14.17. After just 1 epoch, the test accuracy is already 98.8%. By contrast, the MLP in Section 13.2.4.2 had an accuracy of 95.9% after 1 epoch. More rounds of training can further increase accuracy to a point where performance is indistinguishable from label noise. (See lenet_jax.ipynb for some sample code.)

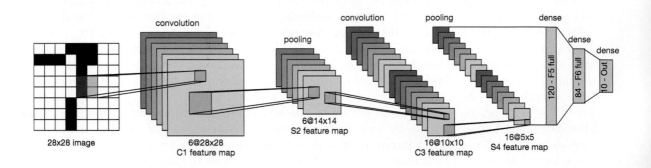

Figure 14.15: *LeNet5, a convolutional neural net for classifying handwritten digits. From Figure 6.6.1 of [Zha+20]. Used with kind permission of Aston Zhang.*

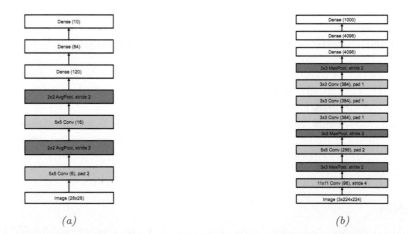

Figure 14.16: *(a) LeNet5. We assume the input has size $1 \times 28 \times 28$, as is the case for MNIST. From Figure 6.6.2 of [Zha+20]. Used with kind permission of Aston Zhang. (b) AlexNet. We assume the input has size $3 \times 224 \times 224$, as is the case for (cropped and rescaled) images from ImageNet. From Figure 7.1.2 of [Zha+20]. Used with kind permission of Aston Zhang.*

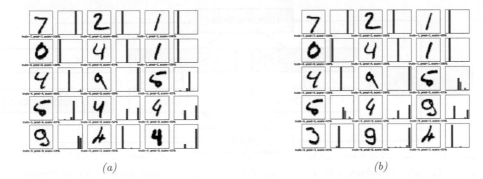

(a)   (b)

Figure 14.17: Results of applying a CNN to some MNIST images (cherry picked to include some errors). Red is incorrect, blue is correct. (a) After 1 epoch of training. (b) After 2 epochs. Generated by cnn_mnist_tf.ipynb.

Of course, classifying isolated digits is of limited applicability: in the real world, people usually write strings of digits or other letters. This requires both segmentation and classification. LeCun and colleagues devised a way to combine convolutional neural networks with a model similar to a conditional random field to solve this problem. The system was deployed by the US postal service. See [LeC+98] for a more detailed account of the system.

14.3.2 AlexNet

Although CNNs have been around for many years, it was not until the paper of [KSH12] in 2012 that mainstream computer vision researchers paid attention to them. In that paper, the authors showed how to reduce the (top 5) error rate on the ImageNet challenge (Section 1.5.1.2) from the previous best of 26% to 15%, which was a dramatic improvement. This model became known as **AlexNet** model, named after its creator, Alex Krizhevsky.

Figure 14.16b(b) shows the architecture. It is very similar to LeNet, shown in Figure 14.16a, with the following differences: it is deeper (8 layers of adjustable parameters (i.e., excluding the pooling layers) instead of 5); it uses ReLU nonlinearities instead of tanh (see Section 13.2.3 for why this is important); it uses dropout (Section 13.5.4) for regularization instead of weight decay; and it stacks several convolutional layers on top of each other, rather than strictly alternating between convolution and pooling. Stacking multiple convolutional layers together has the advantage that the receptive fields become larger as the output of one layer is fed into another (for example, three 3×3 filters in a row will have a receptive field size of 7×7). This is better than using a single layer with a larger receptive field, since the multiple layers also have nonlinearities in between. Also, three 3×3 filters have fewer parameters than one 7×7.

Note that AlexNet has 60M free parameters (which is much more than the 1M labeled examples), mostly due to the three fully connected layers at the output. Fitting this model relied on using two GPUs (due to limited memory of GPUs at that time), and is widely considered an engineering *tour de force*.[4] Figure 1.14a shows some predictions made by the model on some images from ImageNet.

---

4. The 3 authors of the paper (Alex Krizhevsky, Ilya Sutskever and Geoff Hinton) were subsequently hired by Google, although Ilya left in 2015, and Alex left in 2017. For more historical details, see https://en.wikipedia.org/wiki/AlexNet. Note that AlexNet was not the first CNN implemented on a GPU; that honor goes to a group at Microsoft

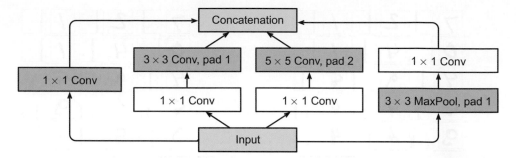

Figure 14.18: Inception module. The 1×1 convolutional layers reduce the number of channels, keeping the spatial dimensions the same. The parallel pathways through convolutions of different sizes allows the model to learn which filter size to use for each layer. The final depth concatenation block combines the outputs of all the different pathways (which all have the same spatial size). From Figure 7.4.1 of [Zha+20]. Used with kind permission of Aston Zhang.

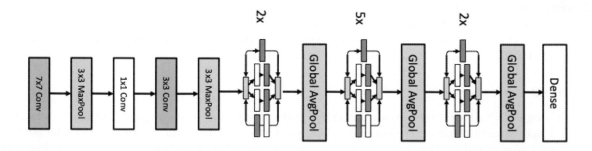

Figure 14.19: GoogLeNet (slightly simplified from the original). Input is on the left. From Figure 7.4.2 of [Zha+20]. Used with kind permission of Aston Zhang.

14.3.3   GoogLeNet (Inception)

Google who developed a model known as **GoogLeNet** [Sze+15a]. (The name is a pun on Google and LeNet.) The main difference from earlier models is that GoogLeNet used a new kind of block, known as an **inception block**[5], that employs multiple parallel pathways, each of which has a convolutional filter of a different size. See Figure 14.18 for an illustration. This lets the model learn what the optimal filter size should be at each level. The overall model consists of 9 inception blocks followed by global average pooling. See Figure 14.19 for an illustration. Since this model first came out, various extensions were proposed; details can be found in [IS15; Sze+15b; SIV17].

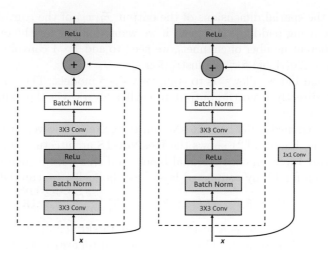

Figure 14.20: A residual block for a CNN. Left: standard version. Right: version with 1x1 convolution, to allow a change in the number of channels between the input to the block and the output. From Figure 7.6.3 of [Zha+20]. Used with kind permission of Aston Zhang.

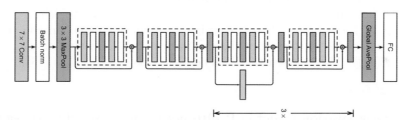

Figure 14.21: The ResNet-18 architecture. Each dotted module is a residual block shown in Figure 14.20. From Figure 7.6.4 of [Zha+20]. Used with kind permission of Aston Zhang.

14.3.4 ResNet

The winner of the 2015 ImageNet classification challenge was a team at Microsoft, who proposed a model known as **ResNet** [He+16a]. The key idea is to replace $\boldsymbol{x}_{l+1} = \mathcal{F}_l(\boldsymbol{x}_l)$ with

$$\boldsymbol{x}_{l+1} = \varphi(\boldsymbol{x}_l + \mathcal{F}_l(\boldsymbol{x}_l)) \tag{14.22}$$

This is known as a **residual block**, since $\mathcal{F}_l$ only needs to learn the residual, or difference, between input and output of this layer, which is a simpler task. In [He+16a], $\mathcal{F}$ has the form conv-BN-relu-conv-BN, where conv is a convolutional layer, and BN is a batch norm layer (Section 14.2.4.1). See Figure 14.20(left) for an illustration.

[CPS06], who got a 4x speedup over CPUs, and then [Cir+11], who got a 60x speedup.
5. This term comes from the movie *Inception*, in which the phrase "We need to go deeper" was uttered. This became a popular meme in 2014.

We can ensure the spatial dimensions of the output $\mathcal{F}_l(\boldsymbol{x}_l)$ of the convolutional layer match those of the input $\boldsymbol{x}_l$ by using padding. However, if we want to allow for the output of the convolutional layer to have a different number of channels, we need to add 1×1 convolution to the skip connection on $\boldsymbol{x}_l$. See Figure 14.20(right) for an illustration.

The use of residual blocks allows us to train very deep models. The reason this is possible is that gradient can flow directly from the output to earlier layers, via the skip connections, for reasons explained in Section 13.4.4.

In [He+16a] they trained a 152 layer ResNet on ImageNet. However, it is common to use shallower models. For example, Figure 14.21 shows the **ResNet-18** architecture, which has 18 trainable layers: there are 2 3x3 conv layers in each residual block, and there are 8 such blocks, with an initial 7x7 conv (stride 2) and a final fully connected layer. Symbolically, we can define the model as follows:

```
(Conv : BN : Max) : (R : R) : (R'  : R)  : (R'  : R)  : (R'  : R) : Avg : FC
```

where R is a residual block, R' is a residual block with skip connection (due to the change in the number of channels) with stride 2, FC is fully connected (dense) layer, and : denotes concatenation. Note that the input size gets reduced spatially by a factor of $2^5 = 32$ (factor of 2 for each R' block, plus the initial Conv-7x7(2) and Max-pool), so a 224x224 images becomes a 7x7 image before going into the global average pooling layer.

Some code to fit these models can be found online.[6]

In [He+16b], they showed how a small modification of the above scheme allows us to train models with up to 1001 layers. The key insight is that the signal on the skip connections is still being attenuated due to the use of the nonlinear activation function after the addition step, $\boldsymbol{x}_{l+1} = \varphi(\boldsymbol{x}_l + \mathcal{F}(\boldsymbol{x}_l))$. They showed that it is better to use

$$\boldsymbol{x}_{l+1} = \boldsymbol{x}_l + \varphi(\mathcal{F}_l(\boldsymbol{x}_l)) \tag{14.23}$$

This is called a **preactivation resnet** or **PreResnet** for short. Now it is very easy for the network to learn the identity function at a given layer: if we use ReLU activations, we just need to ensure that $\mathcal{F}_l(\boldsymbol{x}_l) = \boldsymbol{0}$, which we can do by setting the weights and biases to 0.

An alternative to using a very deep model is to use a very "wide" model, with lots of feature channels per layer. This is the idea behind the **wide resnet** model [ZK16], which is quite popular.

14.3.5   DenseNet

In a residual net, we add the output of each function to its input. An alternative approach would be to concatenate the output with the input, as illustrated in Figure 14.22a. If we stack a series of such blocks, we can get an architecture similar to Figure 14.22b. This is known as a **DenseNets** [Hua+17a], since each layer densely depends on all previous layers. Thus the overall model is computing a function of the form

$$\boldsymbol{x} \rightarrow [\boldsymbol{x}, f_1(\boldsymbol{x}), f_2(\boldsymbol{x}, f_1(\boldsymbol{x})), f_3(\boldsymbol{x}, f_1(\boldsymbol{x}), f_2(\boldsymbol{x}, f_1(\boldsymbol{x}))), \ldots] \tag{14.24}$$

---

6. The notebook resnet_jax.ipynb fits this model on FashionMNIST. The notebook cifar10_cnn_lightning.ipynb fits it on the more challenging CIFAR-10 dataset. The latter code uses various tricks to achieve 89% top-1 accuracy on the CIFAR test set after 20 training epochs. The tricks are data augmentation (Section 19.1), consisting of random crops and horizontal flips, and to use one-cycle learning rate schedule (Section 8.4.3). If you use 50 epochs, and stochastic weight averaging (Section 8.4.4), you can get to $\sim 94\%$ accuracy.

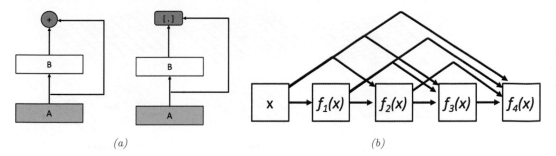

Figure 14.22: (a) Left: a residual block adds the output to the input. Right: a densenet block concatenates the output with the input. (b) Illustration of a densenet. From Figures 7.7.1–7.7.2 of [Zha+20]. Used with kind permission of Aston Zhang.

The dense connectivity increases the number of parameters, since the channels get stacked depthwise. We can compensate for this by adding 1×1 convolution layers in between. We can also add pooling layers with a stride of 2 to reduce the spatial resolution. (See densenet_jax.ipynb for some sample code.)

DenseNets can perform better than ResNets, since all previously computed features are directly accessible to the output layer. However, they can be more computationally expensive.

14.3.6 Neural architecture search

We have seen how many CNNs are fairly similar in their design, and simply rearrange various building blocks (such as convolutional or pooling layers) in different topologies, and adjust various parameter settings (e.g., stride, number of channels, or learning rate). Indeed, the recent **ConvNeXt** model of [Liu+22] — which, at the time of writing (April 2022) is considered the state of the art CNN architecture for a wide variety of vision tasks — was created by combining multiple such small improvements on top of a standard ResNet architecture.

We can automate this design process using blackbox (derivative free) optimization methods to find architectures that minimize the validation loss. This is called **AutoML** (see e.g., [HKV19]). In the context of neural nets, it is called **neural architecture search** or **NAS** [EMH19].

When performing NAS, we can optimize for multiple objectives at the same time, such as accuracy, model size, training or inference speed, etc (this is how **EfficientNetv2** is created [TL21]). The main challenge arises due to the expense of computing the objective (since it requires training each candidate point in model space). One way to reduce the number of calls to the objective function is to use Bayesian optimization (see e.g., [WNS19]). Another approach is to create differentiable approximations to the loss (see e.g., [LSY19; Wan+21]), or to convert the architecture into a kernel function (using the neural tangent kernel method, Section 17.2.8), and then to analyze properties of its eigenvalues, which can predict performance without actually training the model [CGW21]. The field of NAS is very large and still growing. See [EMH19] for a more thorough review.

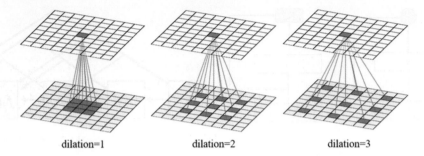

Figure 14.23: *Dilated convolution with a 3x3 filter using rate 1, 2 and 3. From Figure 1 of [Cui+19]. Used with kind permission of Ximin Cui.*

14.4   Other forms of convolution *

We discussed the basics of convolution in Section 14.2. In this section, we discuss some extensions, which are needed for applications such as image segmentation and image generation.

14.4.1   Dilated convolution

Convolution is an operation that combines the pixel values in a local neighborhood. By using striding, and stacking many layers of convolution together, we can enlarge the receptive field of each neuron, which is the region of input space that each neuron responds to. However, we would need many layers to give each neuron enough context to cover the entire image (unless we used very large filters, which would be slow and require too many parameters).

As an alternative, we can use **convolution with holes** [Mal99], sometimes known by the French term **à trous algorithm**, and recently renamed **dilated convolution** [YK16]. This method simply takes every r'th input element when performing convolution, where r is known as the **rate** or **dilation factor**. For example, in 1d, convolving with filter $\boldsymbol{w}$ using rate $r = 2$ is equivalent to regular convolution using the filter $\tilde{\boldsymbol{w}} = [w_1, 0, w_2, 0, w_3]$, where we have inserted 0s to expand the receptive field (hence the term "convolution with holes"). This allows us to get the benefit of increased receptive fields without increasing the number of parameters or the amount of compute. See Figure 14.23 for an illustration.

More precisely, dilated convolution in 2d is defined as follows:

$$z_{i,j,d} = b_d + \sum_{u=0}^{H-1} \sum_{v=0}^{W-1} \sum_{c=0}^{C-1} x_{i+ru,j+rv,c} w_{u,v,c,d} \tag{14.25}$$

where we assume the same rate r for both height and width, for simplicity. Compare this to Equation (14.15), where the stride parameter uses $x_{si+u,sj+v,c}$.

14.4.2   Transposed convolution

In convolution, we reduce from a large input $\mathbf{X}$ to a small output $\mathbf{Y}$ by taking a weighted combination of the input pixels and the convolutional kernel $\mathbf{K}$. This is easiest to explain in code:

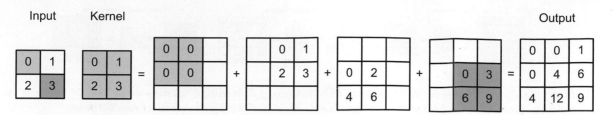

Figure 14.24: Transposed convolution with 2x2 kernel. From Figure 13.10.1 of [Zha+20]. Used with kind permission of Aston Zhang.

```
def conv(X, K):
    h, w = K.shape
    Y = zeros((X.shape[0] - h + 1, X.shape[1] - w + 1))
    for i in range(Y.shape[0]):
        for j in range(Y.shape[1]):
            Y[i, j] = (X[i:i + h, j:j + w] * K).sum()
    return Y
```

In **transposed convolution**, we do the opposite, in order to produce a larger output from a smaller input:

```
def trans_conv(X, K):
    h, w = K.shape
    Y = zeros((X.shape[0] + h - 1, X.shape[1] + w - 1))
    for i in range(X.shape[0]):
        for j in range(X.shape[1]):
            Y[i:i + h, j:j + w] += X[i, j] * K
    return Y
```

This is equivalent to padding the input image with $(h - 1, w - 1)$ 0s (on the bottom right), where (h, w) is the kernel size, then placing a weighted copy of the kernel on each one of the input locations, where the weight is the corresponding pixel value, and then adding up. This process is illustrated in Figure 14.24. We can think of the kernel as a "stencil" that is used to generate the output, modulated by the weights in the input.

The term "transposed convolution" comes from the interpretation of convolution as matrix multiplication, which we discussed in Section 14.2.1.3. If $\mathbf{W}$ is the matrix derived from kernel $\mathbf{K}$ using the process illustrated in Equation (14.9), then one can show that $\mathbf{Y} = \text{transposed-conv}(\mathbf{X}, \mathbf{K})$ is equivalent to $\mathbf{Y} = \text{reshape}(\mathbf{W}^{\mathsf{T}}\text{vec}(\mathbf{X}))$. See transposed_conv_jax.ipynb for a demo.

Note that transposed convolution is also sometimes called **deconvolution**, but this is an incorrect usage of the term: deconvolution is the process of "undoing" the effect of convolution with a known filter, such as a blur filter, to recover the original input, as illustrated in Figure 14.25.

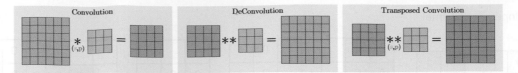

Figure 14.25: *Convolution, deconvolution and transposed convolution. Here s is the stride and p is the padding. From* `https://tinyurl.com/ynxcxsut`. *Used with kind permission of Aqeel Anwar.*

14.4.3 Depthwise separable convolution

Standard convolution uses a filter of size $H \times W \times C \times D$, which requires a lot of data to learn and a lot of time to compute with. A simplification, known as **depthwise separable convolution**, first convolves each input channel by a corresponding 2d filter $\boldsymbol{w}$, and then maps these C channels to D channels using 1×1 convolution $\boldsymbol{w}'$:

$$z_{i,j,d} = b_d + w'_{c,d} \sum_{c=0}^{C-1} \left(\sum_{u=0}^{H-1} \sum_{v=0}^{W-1} x_{i+u,j+v,c} w_{u,v} \right) \tag{14.26}$$

See Figure 14.26 for an illustration.

To see the advantage of this, let us consider a simple numerical example.[7] Regular convolution of a $12 \times 12 \times 3$ input with a $5 \times 5 \times 3 \times 256$ filter gives a $8 \times 8 \times 256$ output (assuming valid convolution: 12-5+1=8), as illustrated in Figure 14.13. With separable convolution, we start with $12 \times 12 \times 3$ input, convolve with a $5 \times 5 \times 1 \times 1$ filter (across space but not channels) to get $8 \times 8 \times 3$, then pointwise convolve (across channels but not space) with a $1 \times 1 \times 3 \times 256$ filter to get a $8 \times 8 \times 256$ output. So the output has the same size as before, but we used many fewer parameters to define the layer, and used much less compute. For this reason, separable convolution is often used in lightweight CNN models, such as the **MobileNet** model [How+17; San+18a] and other **edge devices**.

14.5 Solving other discriminative vision tasks with CNNs *

In this section, we briefly discuss how to tackle various other vision tasks using CNNs. Each task also introduces a new architectural innovation to the library of basic building blocks we have already seen. More details on CNNs for computer vision can be found in e.g., [Bro19].

14.5.1 Image tagging

Image classification associates a single label with the whole image, i.e., the outputs are assumed to be mutually exclusive. In many problems, there may be multiple objects present, and we want to label all of them. This is known as **image tagging**, and is an application of multi-label prediction. In this case, we define the output space as $\mathcal{Y} = \{0, 1\}^C$, where C is the number of tag types. Since the output bits are independent (given the image), we should replace the final softmax with a set of C logistic units.

---

7. This example is from `https://bit.ly/2Uj64Vo` by Chi-Feng Wang.

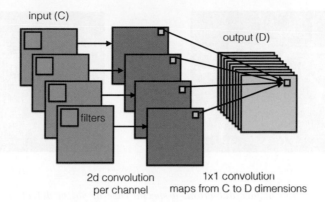

input (C)

output (D)

filters

2d convolution
per channel

1x1 convolution
maps from C to D dimensions

Figure 14.26: Depthwise separable convolutions: each of the C input channels undergoes a 2d convolution to produce C output channels, which get combined pointwise (via 1x1 convolution) to produce D output channels. From `https://bit.ly/2L9fm2o`. *Used with kind permission of Eugenio Culurciello.*

Users of social media sites like **Instagram** often create hashtags for their images; this therefore provides a "free" way of creating large supervised datasets. Of course, many tags may be quite sparsely used, and their meaning may not be well-defined visually. (For example, someone may take a photo of themselves after they get a COVID test and tag the image "#covid"; however, visually it just looks like any other image of a person.) Thus this kind of user-generated labeling is usually considered quite noisy. However, it can be useful for "pre-training", as discussed in [Mah+18].

Finally, it is worth noting that image tagging is often a much more sensible objective than image classification, since many images have multiple objects in them, and it can be hard to know which one we should be labeling. Indeed, Andrej Karpathy, who created the "human performance benchmark" on ImageNet, noted the following:[8]

> Both [CNNs] and humans struggle with images that contain multiple ImageNet classes (usually many more than five), with little indication of which object is the focus of the image. This error is only present in the classification setting, since every image is constrained to have exactly one correct label. In total, we attribute *16% of human errors* to this category.

14.5.2 Object detection

In some cases, we want to produce a variable number of outputs, corresponding to a variable number of objects of interest that may be present in the image. (This is an example of an **open world** problem, with an unknown number of objects.)

A canonical example of this is **object detection**, in which we must return a set of **bounding boxes** representing the locations of objects of interest, together with their class labels. A special case of this is **face detection**, where there is only one class of interest. This is illustrated in Figure 14.27a.[9]

---

8. Source: `https://bit.ly/3cFbALk`

9. Note that face detection is different from **face recognition**, which is a classification task that tries to predict the

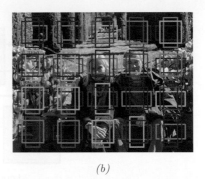

(a)   *(b)*

Figure 14.27: (a) Illustration of face detection, a special case of object detection. (Photo of author and his wife Margaret, taken at Filoli in California in Feburary, 2018. Image processed by Jonathan Huang using SSD face model.) (b) Illustration of anchor boxes. Adapted from [Zha+20, Sec 12.5].

The simplest way to tackle such detection problems is to convert it into a closed world problem, in which there is a finite number of possible locations (and orientations) any object can be in. These candidate locations are known as **anchor boxes**. We can create boxes at multiple locations, scales and aspect ratios, as illustrated in Figure 14.27b. For each box, we train the system to predict what category of object it contains (if any); we can also perform regression to predict the offset of the object location from the center of the anchor. (These residual regression terms allow sub-grid spatial localization.)

Abstractly, we are learning a function of the form

$$f_{\boldsymbol{\theta}} : \mathbb{R}^{H \times W \times K} \to [0,1]^{A \times A} \times \{1, \ldots, C\}^{A \times A} \times (\mathbb{R}^4)^{A \times A} \tag{14.27}$$

where K is the number of input channels, A is the number of anchor boxes in each dimension, and C is the number of object types (class labels). For each box location (i,j), we predict three outputs: an object presence probability, $p_{ij} \in [0,1]$, an object category, $y_{ij} \in \{1, \ldots, C\}$, and two 2d offset vectors, $\boldsymbol{\delta}_{ij} \in \mathbb{R}^4$, which can be added to the centroid of the box to get the top left and bottom right corners.

Several models of this type have been proposed, including the **single shot detector** model of [Liu+16], and the **YOLO** (you only look once) model of [Red+16]. Many other methods for object detection have been proposed over the years. These models make different tradeoffs between speed, accuracy, simplicity, etc. See [Hua+17b] for an empirical comparison, and [Zha+18] for a more recent review.

14.5.3   Instance segmentation

In object detection, we predict a label and bounding box for each object. In **instance segmentation**, the goal is to predict the label and 2d shape mask of each object instance in the image, as illustrated in Figure 14.28. This can be done by applying a semantic segmentation model to each detected box,

identity of a person from a set or "**gallery**" of possible people. Face recognition is usually solved by applying the classifier to all the patches that are detected as containing faces.

Figure 14.28: Illustration of object detection and instance segmentation using Mask R-CNN. From https://github.com/matterport/Mask_RCNN. Used with kind permission of Waleed Abdulla.

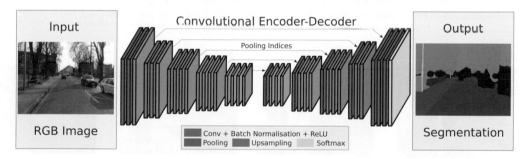

Figure 14.29: Illustration of an **encoder-decoder** (aka **U-net**) CNN for semantic segmentation. The encoder uses convolution (which downsamples), and the decoder uses transposed convolution (which upsamples). From Figure 1 of [BKC17]. Used with kind permission of Alex Kendall.

which has to label each pixel as foreground or background. (See Section 14.5.4 for more details on semantic segmentation.)

14.5.4 Semantic segmentation

In **semantic segmentation**, we have to predict a class label $y_i \in \{1, \ldots, C\}$ for each pixel, where the classes may represent things like sky, road, car, etc. In contrast to instance segmentation, which we discussed in Section 14.5.3, all car pixels get the same label, so semantic segmentation does not differentiate between objects. We can combine semantic segmentation of "stuff" (like sky, road) and instance segmentation of "things" (like car, person) into a coherent framework called "**panoptic segmentation**" [Kir+19].

A common way to tackle semantic segmentation is to use an **encoder-decoder** architecture, as illustrated in Figure 14.29. The encoder uses standard convolution to map the input into a small 2d bottleneck, which captures high level properties of the input at a coarse spatial resolution. (This typically uses a technique called dilated convolution that we explain in Section 14.4.1, to capture a

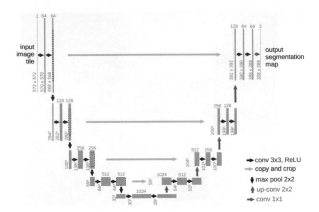

Figure 14.30: Illustration of the U-Net model for semantic segmentation. Each blue box corresponds to a multi-channel feature map. The number of channels is shown on the top of the box, and the height/width is shown in the bottom left. White boxes denote copied feature maps. The different colored arrows correspond to different operations. From Figure 1 from [RFB15]. Used with kind permission of Olaf Ronenberg.

Figure 14.31: Illustration of a multi-task dense prediction problem. From Figure 1 of [EF15]. Used with kind permission of Rob Fergus.

large field of view, i.e., more context.) The decoder maps the small 2d bottleneck back to a full-sized output image using a technique called transposed convolution that we explain in Section 14.4.2. Since the bottleneck loses information, we can also add skip connections from input layers to output layers. We can redraw this model as shown in Figure 14.30. Since the overall structure resembles the letter U, this is also known as a **U-net** [RFB15].

A similar encoder-decoder architecture can be used for other **dense prediction** or **image-to-image** tasks, such as **depth prediction** (predict the distance from the camera, $z_i \in \mathbb{R}$, for each pixel i), **surface normal prediction** (predict the orientation of the surface, $z_i \in \mathbb{R}^3$, at each image patch), etc. We can of course train one model to solve all of these tasks simultaneously, using multiple output heads, as illustrated in Figure 14.31. (See e.g., [Kok17] for details.)

14.5.5   Human pose estimation

We can train an object detector to detect people, and to predict their 2d shape, as represented by a mask. However, we can also train the model to predict the location of a fixed set of skeletal keypoints,

Figure 14.32: *Illustration of keypoint detection for body, hands and face using the OpenPose system. From Figure 8 of [Cao+18]. Used with kind permission of Yaser Sheikh.*

e.g., the location of the head or hands. This is called **human pose estimation**. See Figure 14.32 for an example. There are several techniques for this, e.g., **PersonLab** [Pap+18] and **OpenPose** [Cao+18]. See [Bab19] for a recent review.

We can also predict 3d properties of each detected object. The main limitation is the ability to collect enough labeled training data, since it is difficult for human annotators to label things in 3d. However, we can use **computer graphics** engines to create simulated images with infinite ground truth 3d annotations (see e.g., [GNK18]).

14.6   Generating images by inverting CNNs *

A CNN trained for image classification is a discriminative model of the form $p(y|\boldsymbol{x})$, which takes as input an image, and returns as output a probability distribution over C class labels. In this section we discuss how to "invert" this model, by converting it into a (conditional) **generative image model** of the form $p(\boldsymbol{x}|y)$. This will allow us to generate images that belong to a specific class. (We discuss more principled approaches to creating generative models for images in the sequel to this book, [Mur23].)

14.6.1   Converting a trained classifier into a generative model

We can define a joint distribution over images and labels using $p(\boldsymbol{x}, y) = p(\boldsymbol{x})p(y|\boldsymbol{x})$, where $p(y|\boldsymbol{x})$ is the CNN classifier, and $p(\boldsymbol{x})$ is some prior over images. If we then clamp the class label to a specific value, we can create a conditional generative model using $p(\boldsymbol{x}|y) \propto p(\boldsymbol{x})p(y|\boldsymbol{x})$. Note that the discriminative classifier $p(y|\boldsymbol{x})$ was trained to "throw away" information, so $p(y|\boldsymbol{x})$ is not an invertible function. Thus the prior term $p(\boldsymbol{x})$ will play an important role in regularizing this process, as we see in Section 14.6.2.

One way to sample from this model is to use the Metropolis Hastings algorithm (Section 4.6.8.4), treating $\mathcal{E}_c(\boldsymbol{x}) = \log p(y = c|\boldsymbol{x}) + \log p(\boldsymbol{x})$ as the energy function. Since gradient information is available, we can use a proposal of the form $q(\boldsymbol{x}'|\boldsymbol{x}) = \mathcal{N}(\boldsymbol{\mu}(\boldsymbol{x}), \epsilon\mathbf{I})$, where $\boldsymbol{\mu}(\boldsymbol{x}) = \boldsymbol{x} + \frac{\epsilon}{2}\nabla \log \mathcal{E}_c(\boldsymbol{x})$. This is called the **Metropolis-adjusted Langevin algorithm** (MALA). As an approximation, we can ignore the rejection step, and accept every proposal. This is called the **unadjusted Langevin algorithm**, and was used in [Ngu+17] for conditional image generation. In addition, we can scale the gradient of the log prior and log likelihood independently. Thus we get an update over the space of images that looks like a noisy version of SGD, except we take derivatives wrt the input pixels (using Equation (13.50)), instead of the parameters:

$$\boldsymbol{x}_{t+1} = \boldsymbol{x}_t + \epsilon_1 \frac{\partial \log p(\boldsymbol{x}_t)}{\partial \boldsymbol{x}_t} + \epsilon_2 \frac{\partial \log p(y = c|\boldsymbol{x}_t)}{\partial \boldsymbol{x}_t} + \mathcal{N}(\boldsymbol{0}, \epsilon_3^2 \mathbf{I}) \tag{14.28}$$

We can interpret each term in this equation as follows: the ϵ_1 term ensures the image is plausible under the prior, the ϵ_2 term ensures the image is plausible under the likelihood, and the ϵ_3 term is a noise term, in order to generate diverse samples. If we set $\epsilon_3 = 0$, the method becomes a deterministic algorithm to (approximately) generate the "most likely image" for this class.

14.6.2   Image priors

In this section, we discuss various kinds of image priors that we can use to regularize the ill-posed problem of inverting a classifier. These priors, together with the image that we start the optimization from, will determine the kinds of outputs that we generate.

14.6.2.1   Gaussian prior

Just specifying the class label is not enough information to specify the kind of images we want. We also need a prior $p(\boldsymbol{x})$ over what constitutes a "plausible" image. The prior can have a large effect on the quality of the resulting image, as we show below.

Arguably the simplest prior is $p(\boldsymbol{x}) = \mathcal{N}(\boldsymbol{x}|\boldsymbol{0}, \mathbf{I})$, as suggested in [SVZ14]. (This assumes the image pixels have been centered.) This can prevent pixels from taking on extreme values. In this case, the update due to the prior term has the form

$$\nabla_{\boldsymbol{x}} \log p(\boldsymbol{x}_t) = \nabla_{\boldsymbol{x}} \left[-\frac{1}{2} ||\boldsymbol{x}_t - \boldsymbol{0}||_2^2 \right] = -\boldsymbol{x}_t \tag{14.29}$$

Thus the overall update (assuming $\epsilon_2 = 1$ and $\epsilon_3 = 0$) has the form

$$\boldsymbol{x}_{t+1} = (1 - \epsilon_1)\boldsymbol{x}_t + \frac{\partial \log p(y = c|\boldsymbol{x}_t)}{\partial \boldsymbol{x}_t} \tag{14.30}$$

See Figure 14.33 for some samples generated by this method.

14.6.2.2   Total variation (TV) prior

We can generate slightly more realistic looking images if we use additional regularizers. [MV15; MV16] suggested computing the **total variation** or **TV** norm of the image. This is equal to the integral of the per-pixel gradients, which can be approximated as follows:

$$\text{TV}(\boldsymbol{x}) = \sum_{ijk} (x_{ijk} - x_{i+1,j,k})^2 + (x_{ijk} - x_{i,j+1,k})^2 \tag{14.31}$$

where x_{ijk} is the pixel value in row i, column j and channel k (for RGB images). We can rewrite this in terms of the horizontal and vertical **Sobel edge detector** applied to each channel:

$$\text{TV}(\boldsymbol{x}) = \sum_{k} ||\mathbf{H}(\boldsymbol{x}_{:,:,k})||_F^2 + ||\mathbf{V}(\boldsymbol{x}_{:,:,k})||_F^2 \tag{14.32}$$

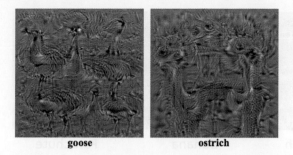

Figure 14.33: *Images that maximize the probability of ImageNet classes "goose" and "ostrich" under a simple Gaussian prior. From* http://yosinski.com/deepvis. *Used with kind permission of Jeff Clune.*

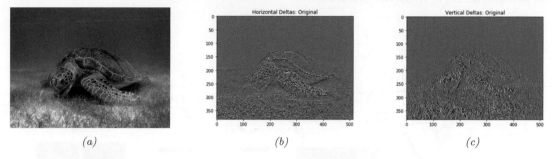

Figure 14.34: *Illustration of total variation norm. (a) Input image: a green sea turtle (Used with kind permission of Wikimedia author P. Lindgren). (b) Horizontal deltas. (c) Vertical deltas. Adapted from* https://www.tensorflow.org/tutorials/generative/style_transfer.

See Figure 14.34 for an illustration of these edge detectors. Using $p(\boldsymbol{x}) \propto \exp(-\mathrm{TV}(\boldsymbol{x}))$ discourages images from having high frequency artefacts. In [Yos+15], they use Gaussian blur instead of TV norm, but this has a similar effect.

In Figure 14.35 we show some results of optimizing $\log p(y = c, \boldsymbol{x})$ using a TV prior and a CNN likelihood for different class labels c starting from random noise.

14.6.3 Visualizing the features learned by a CNN

It is interesting to ask what the "neurons" in a CNN are learning. One way to do this is to start with a random image, and then to optimize the input pixels so as to maximize the average activation of a particular neuron. This is called **activation maximization** (AM), and uses the same technique as in Section 14.6.1 but fixes an internal node to a specific value, rather than clamping the output class label.

Figure 14.36 illustrates the output of this method (with the TV prior) when applied to the AlexNet CNN trained on Imagenet classification. We see that, as the depth increases, neurons are learning to recognize simple edges/blobs, then texture patterns, then object parts, and finally whole objects. This is believed to be roughly similar to the hierarchical structure of the visual cortex (see e.g., [Kan+12]).

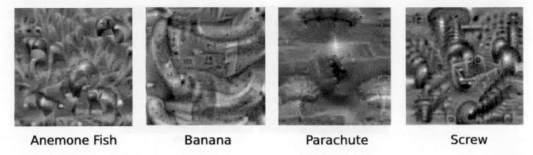

Anemone Fish   **Banana**   **Parachute**   **Screw**

Figure 14.35: Images that maximize the probability of certain ImageNet classes under a TV prior. From https://research.googleblog.com/2015/06/inceptionism-going-deeper-into-neural.html. Used with kind permission of Alexander Mordvintsev.

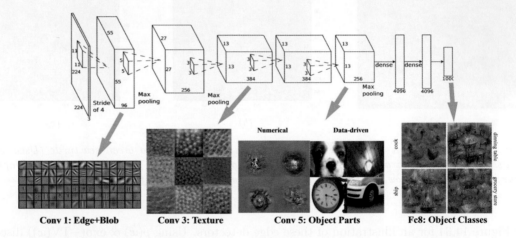

Figure 14.36: We visualize "optimal stimuli" for neurons in layers Conv 1, 3, 5 and fc8 in the AlexNet architecture, trained on the ImageNet dataset. For Conv5, we also show retrieved real images (under the column "data driven") that produce similar activations. Based on the method in [MV16]. Used with kind permission of Donglai Wei.

An alternative to optimizing in pixel space is to search the training set for images that maximally activate a given neuron. This is illustrated in Figure 14.36 for the Conv5 layer.

For more information on feature visualization see e.g., [OMS17].

14.6.4   Deep Dream

So far we have focused on generating images which maximize the class label or some other neuron of interest. In this section we tackle a more artistic application, in which we want to generate versions of an input image that emphasize certain features.

To do this, we view our pre-trained image classifier as a feature extractor. Based on the results in Section 14.6.3, we know the activity of neurons in different layers correspond to different kinds

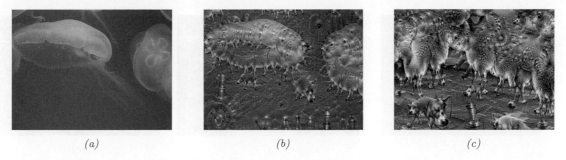

(a)   (b)   (c)

Figure 14.37: Illustration of DeepDream. The CNN is an Inception classifier trained on ImageNet. (a) Starting image of an Aurelia aurita (also called moon jelly). (b) Image generated after 10 iterations. (c) Image generated after 50 iterations. From https://en.wikipedia.org/wiki/DeepDream. Used with kind permission of Wikipedia author Martin Thoma.

of features in the image. Suppose we are interested in "amplifying" features from layers $l \in \mathcal{L}$. We can do this by defining an energy or loss function of the form $\mathcal{L}(\boldsymbol{x}) = \sum_{l \in \mathcal{L}} \overline{\phi}_l(\boldsymbol{x})$, where $\overline{\phi}_l = \frac{1}{HWC} \sum_{hwc} \phi_{lhwc}(\boldsymbol{x})$ is the feature vector for layer l. We can now use gradient descent to optimize this energy. The resulting process is called **DeepDream** [MOT15], since the model amplifies features that were only hinted at in the original image and then creates images with more and more of them.[10]

Figure 14.37 shows an example. We start with an image of a jellyfish, which we pass into a CNN that was trained to classify ImageNet images. After several iterations, we generate some image which is a hybrid of the input and the kinds of "hallucinations" we saw in Figure 14.33; these hallucinations involve dog parts, since ImageNet has so many kinds of dogs in its label set. See [Tho16] for details, and https://deepdreamgenerator.com for a fun web-based demo.

14.6.5   Neural style transfer

The DeepDream system in Figure 14.37 shows one way that CNNs can be used to create "art". However, it is rather creepy. In this section, we discuss a related approach that gives the user more control. In particular, the user has to specify a reference "style image" $\boldsymbol{x}_s$ and "content image" $\boldsymbol{x}_c$. The system will then try to generate a new image $\boldsymbol{x}$ that "re-renders" $\boldsymbol{x}_c$ in the style of $\boldsymbol{x}_s$. This is called **neural style transfer**, and is illustrated in Figure 14.38 and Figure 14.39. This technique was first proposed in [GEB16], and there are now many papers on this topic; see [Jin+17] for a recent review.

14.6.5.1   How it works

Style transfer works by optimizing the following energy function:

$$\mathcal{L}(\boldsymbol{x}|\boldsymbol{x}_s, \boldsymbol{x}_c) = \lambda_{TV}\mathcal{L}_{\text{TV}}(\boldsymbol{x}) + \lambda_c\mathcal{L}_{\text{content}}(\boldsymbol{x}, \boldsymbol{x}_c) + \lambda_s\mathcal{L}_{\text{style}}(\boldsymbol{x}, \boldsymbol{x}_s) \tag{14.33}$$

See Figure 14.40 for a high level illustration.

---

10. The method was originally called **Inceptionism**, since it uses the inception CNN (Section 14.3.3).

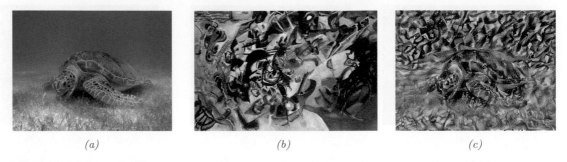

(a)   (b)   (c)

Figure 14.38: *Example output from a neural style transfer system. (a) Content image: a green sea turtle (Used with kind permission of Wikimedia author P. Lindgren). (b) Style image: a painting by Wassily Kandinsky called "Composition 7". (c) Output of neural style generation. Adapted from* `https://www.tensorflow.org/tutorials/generative/style_transfer`.

Figure 14.39: *Neural style transfer applied to photos of the "production team", who helped create code and demos for this book and its sequel. From top to bottom, left to right: Kevin Murphy (the author), Mahmoud Soliman, Aleyna Kara, Srikar Jilugu, Drishti Patel, Ming Liang Ang, Gerardo Durán-Martín, Coco (the team dog). Each content photo used a different artistic style. Adapted from* `https://www.tensorflow.org/tutorials/generative/style_transfer`.

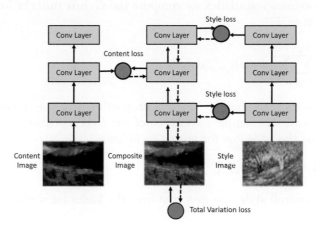

Figure 14.40: Illustration of how neural style transfer works. Adapted from Figure 12.12.2 of [Zha+20].

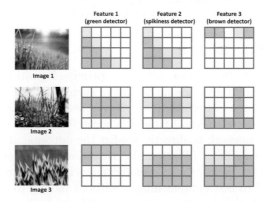

Figure 14.41: Schematic representation of 3 kinds of feature maps for 3 different input images. Adapted from Figure 5.16 of [Fos19].

The first term in Equation (14.33) is the total variation prior discussed in Section 14.6.2.2. The second term measures how similar $\boldsymbol{x}$ is to $\boldsymbol{x}_c$ by comparing feature maps of a pre-trained CNN $\boldsymbol{\phi}(\boldsymbol{x})$ in the relevant "content layer" l:

$$\mathcal{L}_{\text{content}}(\boldsymbol{x}, \boldsymbol{x}_c) = \frac{1}{C_\ell H_\ell W_\ell} ||\boldsymbol{\phi}_\ell(\boldsymbol{x}) - \boldsymbol{\phi}_\ell(\boldsymbol{x}_c)||_2^2 \tag{14.34}$$

Finally we have to define the style term. We can interpret visual style as the statistical distribution of certain kinds of image features. The location of these features in the image may not matter, but their co-occurence does. This is illustrated in Figure 14.41. It is clear (to a human) that image 1 is more similar in style to image 2 than to image 3. Intuitively this is because both image 1 and image 2 have spiky green patches in them, whereas image 3 has spiky things that are not green.

To capture the co-occurence statistics we compute the **Gram matrix** for an image using feature maps from a specific layer ℓ:

$$G_\ell(\boldsymbol{x})_{c,d} = \frac{1}{H_\ell W_\ell} \sum_{h=1}^{H_\ell} \sum_{w=1}^{W_\ell} \phi_\ell(\boldsymbol{x})_{h,w,c} \, \phi_\ell(\boldsymbol{x})_{h,w,d} \tag{14.35}$$

The Gram matrix is a $C_\ell \times C_\ell$ matrix which is proportional to the uncentered covariance of the C_ℓ-dimensional feature vectors sampled over each of the $H_\ell W_\ell$ locations.

Given this, we define the style loss for layer ℓ as follows:

$$\mathcal{L}_{\text{style}}^\ell(\boldsymbol{x}, \boldsymbol{x}_s) = ||\mathbf{G}_\ell(\boldsymbol{x}) - \mathbf{G}_\ell(\boldsymbol{x}_s)||_F^2 \tag{14.36}$$

Finally, we define the overall style loss as a sum over the losses for a set $\mathcal{S}$ of layers:

$$\mathcal{L}_{\text{style}}(\boldsymbol{x}, \boldsymbol{x}_s) = \sum_{\ell \in \mathcal{S}} \mathcal{L}_{\text{style}}^\ell(\boldsymbol{x}, \boldsymbol{x}_s) \tag{14.37}$$

For example, in Figure 14.40, we compute the style loss at layers 1 and 3. (Lower layers will capture visual texture, and higher layers will capture object layout.)

14.6.5.2 Speeding up the method

In [GEB16], they used L-BFGS (Section 8.3.2) to optimize Equation (14.33), starting from white noise. We can get faster results if we use an optimizer such as Adam instead of BFGS, and initialize from the content image instead of white noise. Nevertheless, running an optimizer for every new style and content image is slow. Several papers (see e.g., [JAFF16; Uly+16; UVL16; LW16]) have proposed to train a neural network to directly predict the outcome of this optimization, rather than solving it for each new image pair. (This can be viewed as a form of amortized optimization.) In particular, for every style image $\boldsymbol{x}_s$, we fit a model f_s such that $f_s(\boldsymbol{x}_c) = \text{argmin}_{\boldsymbol{x}} \mathcal{L}(\boldsymbol{x}|\boldsymbol{x}_s, \boldsymbol{x}_c)$. We can then apply this model to new content images without having to reoptimize.

More recently, [DSK16] has shown how it is possible to train a single network that takes as input both the content and a discrete representation s of the style, and then produces $f(\boldsymbol{x}_c, s) = \text{argmin}_{\boldsymbol{x}} \mathcal{L}(\boldsymbol{x}|s, \boldsymbol{x}_c)$ as the output. This avoids the need to train a separate network for every style image. The key idea is to standardize the features at a given layer using scale and shift parameters that are style specific. In particular, we use the following **conditional instance normalization** transformation:

$$\text{CIN}(\phi(\boldsymbol{x}_c), s) = \gamma_s \left(\frac{\phi(\boldsymbol{x}_c) - \mu(\phi(\boldsymbol{x}_c))}{\sigma(\phi(\boldsymbol{x}_c))} \right) + \beta_s \tag{14.38}$$

where $\mu(\phi(\boldsymbol{x}_c))$ is the mean of the features in a given layer, $\sigma(\phi(\boldsymbol{x}_c))$ is the standard deviation, and β_s and γ_s are parameters for style type s. (See Section 14.2.4.2 for more details on instance normalization.) Surprisingly, this simple trick is enough to capture many kinds of styles.

The drawback of the above technique is that it only works for a fixed number of discrete styles. [HB17] proposed to generalize this by replacing the constants β_s and γ_s by the output of another CNN, which takes an arbitrary style image $\boldsymbol{x}_s$ as input. That is, in Equation (14.38), we set $\beta_s = f_{\boldsymbol{\beta}}(\phi(\boldsymbol{x}_s))$

and $\gamma_s = f_{\boldsymbol{\gamma}}(\phi(\boldsymbol{x}_s))$, and we learn the parameters $\boldsymbol{\beta}$ and $\boldsymbol{\gamma}$ along with all the other parameters. The model becomes

$$\mathrm{AIN}(\phi(\boldsymbol{x}_c), \phi(\boldsymbol{x}_s)) = f_{\boldsymbol{\gamma}}(\phi(\boldsymbol{x}_s)) \left(\frac{\phi(\boldsymbol{x}_c) - \mu(\phi(\boldsymbol{x}_c))}{\sigma(\phi(\boldsymbol{x}_c))} \right) + f_{\boldsymbol{\beta}}(\phi(\boldsymbol{x}_s)) \tag{14.39}$$

They call their method **adaptive instance normalization**.

15 Neural Networks for Sequences

15.1 Introduction

In this chapter, we discuss various kinds of neural networks for sequences. We will consider the case where the input is a sequence, the output is a sequence, or both are sequences. Such models have many applications, such as machine translation, speech recognition, text classification, image captioning, etc. Our presentation borrows from parts of [Zha+20], which should be consulted for more details.

15.2 Recurrent neural networks (RNNs)

A **recurrent neural network** or **RNN** is a neural network which maps from an input space of sequences to an output space of sequences in a stateful way. That is, the prediction of output y_t depends not only on the input x_t, but also on the hidden state of the system, h_t, which gets updated over time, as the sequence is processed. Such models can be used for sequence generation, sequence classification, and sequence translation, as we explain below.[1]

15.2.1 Vec2Seq (sequence generation)

In this section, we discuss how to learn functions of the form $f_{\boldsymbol{\theta}} : \mathbb{R}^D \to \mathbb{R}^{N_\infty C}$, where D is the size of the input vector, and the output is an arbitrary-length sequence of vectors, each of size C. (Note that words are discrete tokens, but can be converted to real-valued vectors as we discuss in Section 1.5.4.) We call these **vec2seq** models, since they map a vector to a sequence.

The output sequence $y_{1:T}$ is generated one token at a time. At each step we sample $\tilde{y}_t$ from the hidden state h_t of the model, and then "feed it back in" to the model to get the new state h_{t+1} (which also depends on the input x). See Figure 15.1 for an illustration. In this way the model defines a conditional generative model of the form $p(y_{1:T}|x)$, which captures dependencies between the output tokens. We explain this in more detail below.

---

1. For a more detailed introduction, see `http://karpathy.github.io/2015/05/21/rnn-effectiveness/`.

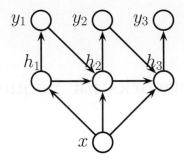

Figure 15.1: Recurrent neural network (RNN) for generating a variable length output sequence $\boldsymbol{y}_{1:T}$ given an optional fixed length input vector $\boldsymbol{x}$.

15.2.1.1 Models

For notational simplicity, let T be the length of the output (with the understanding that this is chosen dynamically). The RNN then corresponds to the following conditional generative model:

$$p(\boldsymbol{y}_{1:T}|\boldsymbol{x}) = \sum_{\boldsymbol{h}_{1:T}} p(\boldsymbol{y}_{1:T}, \boldsymbol{h}_{1:T}|\boldsymbol{x}) = \sum_{\boldsymbol{h}_{1:T}} \prod_{t=1}^{T} p(\boldsymbol{y}_t|\boldsymbol{h}_t) p(\boldsymbol{h}_t|\boldsymbol{h}_{t-1}, \boldsymbol{y}_{t-1}, \boldsymbol{x}) \tag{15.1}$$

where $\boldsymbol{h}_t$ is the hidden state, and where we define $p(\boldsymbol{h}_1|\boldsymbol{h}_0, \boldsymbol{y}_0, \boldsymbol{x}) = p(\boldsymbol{h}_1|\boldsymbol{x})$ as the initial hidden state distribution (often deterministic).

The output distribution is usually given by

$$p(\boldsymbol{y}_t|\boldsymbol{h}_t) = \mathrm{Cat}(\boldsymbol{y}_t|\mathrm{softmax}(\mathbf{W}_{hy}\boldsymbol{h}_t + \boldsymbol{b}_y)) \tag{15.2}$$

where $\mathbf{W}_{hy}$ are the hidden-to-output weights, and $\boldsymbol{b}_y$ is the bias term. However, for real-valued outputs, we can use

$$p(\boldsymbol{y}_t|\boldsymbol{h}_t) = \mathcal{N}(\boldsymbol{y}_t|\mathbf{W}_{hy}\boldsymbol{h}_t + \boldsymbol{b}_y, \sigma^2\mathbf{I}) \tag{15.3}$$

We assume the hidden state is computed deterministically as follows:

$$p(\boldsymbol{h}_t|\boldsymbol{h}_{t-1}, \boldsymbol{y}_{t-1}, \boldsymbol{x}) = \mathbb{I}\left(\boldsymbol{h}_t = f(\boldsymbol{h}_{t-1}, \boldsymbol{y}_{t-1}, \boldsymbol{x})\right) \tag{15.4}$$

for some deterministic function f. The update function f is usually given by

$$\boldsymbol{h}_t = \varphi(\mathbf{W}_{xh}[\boldsymbol{x}; \boldsymbol{y}_{t-1}] + \mathbf{W}_{hh}\boldsymbol{h}_{t-1} + \boldsymbol{b}_h) \tag{15.5}$$

where $\mathbf{W}_{hh}$ are the hidden-to-hidden weights, $\mathbf{W}_{xh}$ are the input-to-hidden weights, and $\boldsymbol{b}_h$ are the bias terms. See Figure 15.1 for an illustration, and rnn_jax.ipynb for some code.

Note that $\boldsymbol{y}_t$ depends on $\boldsymbol{h}_t$, which depends on $\boldsymbol{y}_{t-1}$, which depends on $\boldsymbol{h}_{t-1}$, and so on. Thus $\boldsymbol{y}_t$ implicitly depends on all past observations (as well as the optional fixed input $\boldsymbol{x}$). Thus an RNN overcomes the limitations of standard Markov models, in that they can have unbounded memory. This makes RNNs theoretically as powerful as a **Turing machine** [SS95; PMB19]. In practice,

the githa some thong the time traveller held in his hand was a glitteringmetallic framework scarcely larger than a small clock and verydelicately made there was ivory in it and the latter than s bettyre tat howhong s ie time thave ler simk you a dimensions le ghat dionthat shall travel indifferently in any direction of space and timeas the driver determinesfilby contented himself with laughterbut i have experimental verification said the time travellerit would be remarkably convenient for the histo

Figure 15.2: *Example output of length 500 generated from a character level RNN when given the prefix "the". We use greedy decoding, in which the most likely character at each step is computed, and then fed back into the model. The model is trained on the book* The Time Machine *by H. G. Wells. Generated by rnn_jax.ipynb.*

however, the memory length is determined by the size of the latent state and the strength of the parameters; see Section 15.2.7 for further discussion of this point.

When we generate from an RNN, we sample from $\tilde{\boldsymbol{y}}_t \sim p(\boldsymbol{y}_t|\boldsymbol{h}_t)$, and then "feed in" the sampled value into the hidden state, to deterministically compute $\boldsymbol{h}_{t+1} = f(\boldsymbol{h}_t, \tilde{\boldsymbol{y}}_t, \boldsymbol{x})$, from which we sample $\tilde{\boldsymbol{y}}_{t+1} \sim p(\boldsymbol{y}_{t+1}|\boldsymbol{h}_{t+1})$, etc. Thus the only stochasticity in the system comes from the noise in the observation (output) model, which is fed back to the system in each step. (However, there is a variant, known as a **variational RNN** [Chu+15], that adds stochasticity to the dynamics of $\boldsymbol{h}_t$ independent of the observation noise.)

15.2.1.2   Applications

RNNs can be used to generate sequences unconditionally (by setting $\boldsymbol{x} = \emptyset$) or conditionally on $\boldsymbol{x}$. Unconditional sequence generation is often called **language modeling**; this refers to learning joint probability distributions over sequences of discrete tokens, i.e., models of the form $p(y_1, \ldots, y_T)$. (See also Section 3.6.1.2, where we discuss using Markov chains for language modeling.)

Figure 15.2 shows a sequence generated from a simple RNN trained on the book *The Time Machine* by H. G. Wells. (This is a short science fiction book, with just 32,000 words and 170k characters.) We see that the generated sequence looks plausible, even though it is not very meaningful. By using more sophisticated RNN models (such as those that we discuss in Section 15.2.7.1 and Section 15.2.7.2), and by training on more data, we can create RNNs that give state-of-the-art performance on the language modeling task [CNB17]. (In the language modeling community, performance is usually measured by perplexity, which is just the exponential of the average per-token negative log likelihood; see Section 6.1.5 for more information.)

We can also make the generated sequence depend on some kind of input vector $\boldsymbol{x}$. For example, consider the task of **image captioning**: in this case, $\boldsymbol{x}$ is some embedding of the image computed by a CNN, as illustrated in Figure 15.3. See e.g., [Hos+19; LXW19] for a review of image captioning methods, and `https://bit.ly/2Wvs1GK` for a tutorial with code.

It is also possible to use RNNs to generate sequences of real-valued feature vectors, such as pen strokes for hand-written characters [Gra13] and hand-drawn shapes [HE18]. This can also be useful for time series forecasting real-value sequences.

15.2.2   Seq2Vec (sequence classification)

In this section, we assume we have a single fixed-length output vector $\boldsymbol{y}$ we want to predict, given a variable length sequence as input. Thus we want to learn a function of the form $f_{\boldsymbol{\theta}} : \mathbb{R}^{TD} \to \mathbb{R}^C$. We

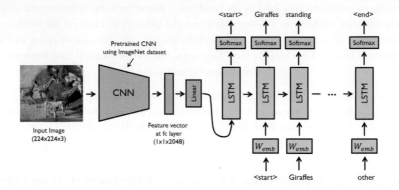

Figure 15.3: Illustration of a CNN-RNN model for image captioning. The pink boxes labeled "LSTM" refer to a specific kind of RNN that we discuss in Section 15.2.7.2. The pink boxes labeled W_{emb} refer to embedding matrices for the (sampled) one-hot tokens, so that the input to the model is a real-valued vector. From https://bit.ly/2FKnqHm. *Used with kind permission of Yunjey Choi.*

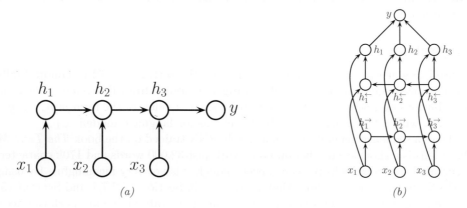

Figure 15.4: (a) RNN for sequence classification. (b) Bi-directional RNN for sequence classification.

call this a **seq2vec** model. We will focus on the case where the output is a class label, $y \in \{1, \ldots, C\}$, for notational simplicity.

The simplest approach is to use the final state of the RNN as input to the classifier:

$$p(y|\boldsymbol{x}_{1:T}) = \text{Cat}(y|\text{softmax}(\mathbf{W}\boldsymbol{h}_T)) \qquad (15.6)$$

See Figure 15.4a for an illustration.

We can often get better results if we let the hidden states of the RNN depend on the past and future context. To do this, we create two RNNs, one which recursively computes hidden states in the forwards direction, and one which recursively computes hidden states in the backwards direction. This is called a **bidirectional RNN** [SP97].

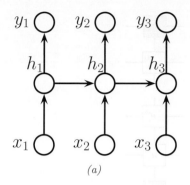 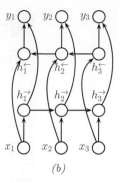

(a)   (b)

Figure 15.5: (a) RNN for transforming a sequence to another, aligned sequence. (b) Bi-directional RNN for the same task.

More precisely, the model is defined as follows:

$$\boldsymbol{h}_t^{\rightarrow} = \varphi(\mathbf{W}_{xh}^{\rightarrow}\boldsymbol{x}_t + \mathbf{W}_{hh}^{\rightarrow}\boldsymbol{h}_{t-1}^{\rightarrow} + \boldsymbol{b}_h{}') \tag{15.7}$$
$$\boldsymbol{h}_t^{\leftarrow} = \varphi(\mathbf{W}_{xh}^{\leftarrow}\boldsymbol{x}_t + \mathbf{W}_{hh}^{\leftarrow}\boldsymbol{h}_{t+1}^{\leftarrow} + \boldsymbol{b}_h^{\leftarrow}) \tag{15.8}$$

We can then define $\boldsymbol{h}_t = [\boldsymbol{h}_t^{\rightarrow}, \boldsymbol{h}_t^{\leftarrow}]$ to be the representation of the state at time t, taking into account past and future information. Finally we average pool over these hidden states to get the final classifier:

$$p(y|\boldsymbol{x}_{1:T}) = \text{Cat}(y|\mathbf{W}\text{softmax}(\overline{\boldsymbol{h}})) \tag{15.9}$$

$$\overline{\boldsymbol{h}} = \frac{1}{T}\sum_{t=1}^{T}\boldsymbol{h}_t \tag{15.10}$$

See Figure 15.4b for an illustration, and rnn_sentiment_jax.ipynb for some code. (This is similar to the 1d CNN text classifier1 in Section 15.3.1.)

15.2.3   Seq2Seq (sequence translation)

In this section, we consider learning functions of the form $f_{\boldsymbol{\theta}} : \mathbb{R}^{TD} \to \mathbb{R}^{T'C}$. We consider two cases: one in which $T' = T$, so the input and output sequences have the same length (and hence are aligned), and one in which $T' \neq T$, so the input and output sequences have different lengths. This is called a **seq2seq** problem.

15.2.3.1   Aligned case

In this section, we consider the case where the input and output sequences are aligned. We can also think of it as **dense sequence labeling**, since we predict one label per location. It is straightforward to modify an RNN to solve this task, as shown in Figure 15.5a. This corresponds to

$$p(\boldsymbol{y}_{1:T}|\boldsymbol{x}_{1:T}) = \sum_{\boldsymbol{h}_{1:T}}\prod_{t=1}^{T}p(\boldsymbol{y}_t|\boldsymbol{h}_t)\mathbb{I}\left(\boldsymbol{h}_t = f(\boldsymbol{h}_{t-1}, \boldsymbol{x}_t)\right) \tag{15.11}$$

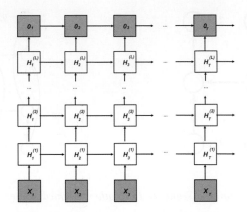

Figure 15.6: Illustration of a deep RNN. Adapted from Figure 9.3.1 of [Zha+20].

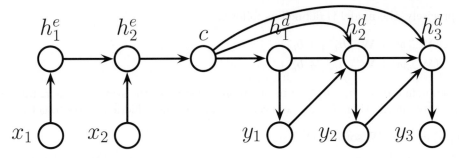

Figure 15.7: Encoder-decoder RNN architecture for mapping sequence $\boldsymbol{x}_{1:T}$ to sequence $\boldsymbol{y}_{1:T'}$.

where we define $\boldsymbol{h}_1 = f(\boldsymbol{h}_0, \boldsymbol{x}_1) = f_0(\boldsymbol{x}_1)$ to be the initial state.

Note that $\boldsymbol{y}_t$ depends on $\boldsymbol{h}_t$ which only depends on the past inputs, $\boldsymbol{x}_{1:t}$. We can get better results if we let the decoder look into the "future" of $\boldsymbol{x}$ as well as the past, by using a bidirectional RNN, as shown in Figure 15.5b.

We can create more expressive models by stacking multiple hidden chains on top of each other, as shown in Figure 15.6. The hidden units for layer l at time t are computed using

$$\boldsymbol{h}_t^l = \varphi_l(\mathbf{W}_{xh}^l \boldsymbol{h}_t^{l-1} + \mathbf{W}_{hh}^l \boldsymbol{h}_{t-1}^l + \boldsymbol{b}_h^l) \tag{15.12}$$

The output is given by

$$\boldsymbol{o}_t = \mathbf{W}_{ho} \boldsymbol{h}_t^L + \boldsymbol{b}_o \tag{15.13}$$

15.2.3.2   Unaligned case

In this section, we discuss how to learn a mapping from one sequence of length T to another of length T'. We first encode the input sequence to get the context vector $\boldsymbol{c} = f_e(\boldsymbol{x}_{1:T})$, using the last state of an RNN (or average pooling over a biRNN). We then generate the output sequence using an RNN

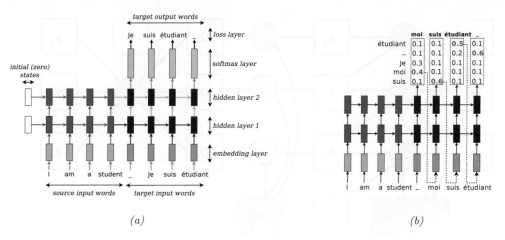

Figure 15.8: (a) Illustration of a seq2seq model for translating English to French. The - character represents the end of a sentence. From Figure 2.4 of [Luo16]. Used with kind permission of Minh-Thang Luong. (b) Illustration of greedy decoding. The most likely French word at each step is highlighted in green, and then fed in as input to the next step of the decoder. From Figure 2.5 of [Luo16]. Used with kind permission of Minh-Thang Luong.

decoder $\boldsymbol{y}_{1:T'} = f_d(\boldsymbol{c})$. This is called an **encoder-decoder architecture** [SVL14; Cho+14a]. See Figure 15.7 for an illustration.

An important application of this is **machine translation**. When this is tackled using RNNs, it is called **neural machine translation** (as opposed to the older approach called **statistical machine translation**, that did not use neural networks). See Figure 15.8a for the basic idea, and nmt_jax.ipynb for some code which has more details. For a review of the NMT literature, see [Luo16; Neu17].

15.2.4 Teacher forcing

When training a language model, the likelihood of a sequence of words $w_1, w_2, \ldots, w_T$, is given by

$$p(\boldsymbol{w}_{1:T}) = \prod_{t=1}^{T} p(w_t | \boldsymbol{w}_{1:t-1}) \tag{15.14}$$

In an RNN, we therefore set the input to $x_t = w_{t-1}$ and the output to $y_t = w_t$. Note that we condition on the *ground truth* labels from the past, $\boldsymbol{w}_{1:t-1}$, not labels generated from the model. This is called **teacher forcing**, since the teacher's values are "force fed" into the model as input at each step (i.e., x_t is set to w_{t-1}).

Unfortunately, teacher forcing can sometimes result in models that perform poorly at test time. The reason is that the model has only ever been trained on inputs that are "correct", so it may not know what to do if, at test time, it encounters an input sequence $\boldsymbol{w}_{1:t-1}$ generated from the previous step that deviates from what it saw in training.

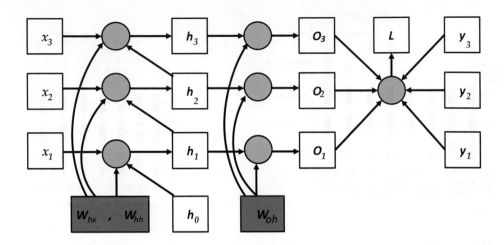

Figure 15.9: An RNN unrolled (vertically) for 3 time steps, with the target output sequence and loss node shown explicitly. From Figure 8.7.2 of [Zha+20]. Used with kind permission of Aston Zhang.

A common solution to this is known as **scheduled sampling** [Ben+15a]. This starts off using teacher forcing, but at random time steps, feeds in samples from the model instead; the fraction of time this happens is gradually increased.

An alternative solution is to use other kinds of models where MLE training works better, such as 1d CNNs (Section 15.3) and transformers (Section 15.5).

15.2.5   Backpropagation through time

We can compute the maximum likelihood estimate of the parameters for an RNN by solving $\boldsymbol{\theta}^* = \operatorname{argmax}_{\boldsymbol{\theta}} p(\boldsymbol{y}_{1:T}|\boldsymbol{x}_{1:T}, \boldsymbol{\theta})$, where we have assumed a single training sequence for notational simplicity. To compute the MLE, we have to compute gradients of the loss wrt the parameters. To do this, we can unroll the computation graph, as shown in Figure 15.9, and then apply the backpropagation algorithm. This is called **backpropagation through time** (BPTT) [Wer90].

More precisely, consider the following model:

$$\boldsymbol{h}_t = \mathbf{W}_{hx}\boldsymbol{x}_t + \mathbf{W}_{hh}\boldsymbol{h}_{t-1} \tag{15.15}$$

$$\boldsymbol{o}_t = \mathbf{W}_{ho}\boldsymbol{h}_t \tag{15.16}$$

where $\boldsymbol{o}_t$ are the output logits, and where we drop the bias terms for notational simplicity. We assume y_y are the true target labels for each time step, so we define the loss to be

$$L = \frac{1}{T}\sum_{t=1}^{T}\ell(y_t, \boldsymbol{o}_t) \tag{15.17}$$

We need to compute the derivatives $\frac{\partial L}{\partial \mathbf{W}_{hx}}$, $\frac{\partial L}{\partial \mathbf{W}_{hh}}$, and $\frac{\partial L}{\partial \mathbf{W}_{ho}}$. The latter term is easy, since it is local to each time step. However, the first two terms depend on the hidden state, and thus require working backwards in time.

We simplify the notation by defining

$$\boldsymbol{h}_t = f(\boldsymbol{x}_t, \boldsymbol{h}_{t-1}, \boldsymbol{w}_h) \tag{15.18}$$

$$\boldsymbol{o}_t = g(\boldsymbol{h}_t, \boldsymbol{w}_o) \tag{15.19}$$

where $\boldsymbol{w}_h$ is the flattened version of $\mathbf{W}_{hh}$ and $\mathbf{W}_{hx}$ stacked together. We focus on computing $\frac{\partial L}{\partial \boldsymbol{w}_h}$. By the chain rule, we have

$$\frac{\partial L}{\partial \boldsymbol{w}_h} = \frac{1}{T} \sum_{t=1}^{T} \frac{\partial \ell(y_t, \boldsymbol{o}_t)}{\partial \boldsymbol{w}_h} = \frac{1}{T} \sum_{t=1}^{T} \frac{\partial \ell(y_t, \boldsymbol{o}_t)}{\partial \boldsymbol{o}_t} \frac{\partial g(\boldsymbol{h}_t, \boldsymbol{w}_o)}{\partial \boldsymbol{h}_t} \frac{\partial \boldsymbol{h}_t}{\partial \boldsymbol{w}_h} \tag{15.20}$$

We can expand the last term as follows:

$$\frac{\partial \boldsymbol{h}_t}{\partial \boldsymbol{w}_h} = \frac{\partial f(\boldsymbol{x}_t, \boldsymbol{h}_{t-1}, \boldsymbol{w}_h)}{\partial \boldsymbol{w}_h} + \frac{\partial f(\boldsymbol{x}_t, \boldsymbol{h}_{t-1}, \boldsymbol{w}_h)}{\partial \boldsymbol{h}_{t-1}} \frac{\partial \boldsymbol{h}_{t-1}}{\partial \boldsymbol{w}_h} \tag{15.21}$$

If we expand this recursively, we find the following result (see the derivation in [Zha+20, Sec 8.7]):

$$\frac{\partial \boldsymbol{h}_t}{\partial \boldsymbol{w}_h} = \frac{\partial f(\boldsymbol{x}_t, \boldsymbol{h}_{t-1}, \boldsymbol{w}_h)}{\partial \boldsymbol{w}_h} + \sum_{i=1}^{t-1} \left(\prod_{j=i+1}^{t} \frac{\partial f(\boldsymbol{x}_j, \boldsymbol{h}_{j-1}, \boldsymbol{w}_h)}{\partial \boldsymbol{h}_{j-1}} \right) \frac{\partial f(\boldsymbol{x}_i, \boldsymbol{h}_{i-1}, \boldsymbol{w}_h)}{\partial \boldsymbol{w}_h} \tag{15.22}$$

Unfortunately, this takes $O(T)$ time to compute per time step, for a total of $O(T^2)$ overall. It is therefore standard to truncate the sum to the most recent K terms. It is possible to adaptively pick a suitable truncation parameter K [AFF19]; however, it is usually set equal to the length of the subsequence in the current minibatch.

When using truncated BPTT, we can train the model with batches of short sequences, usually created by extracting non-overlapping subsequences (windows) from the original sequence. If the previous subsequence ends at time $t-1$, and the current subsequence starts at time t, we can "carry over" the hidden state of the RNN across batch updates during training. However, if the subsequences are not ordered, we need to reset the hidden state. See rnn_jax.ipynb for some sample code that illustrates these details.

15.2.6 Vanishing and exploding gradients

Unfortunately, the activations in an RNN can decay or explode as we go forwards in time, since we multiply by the weight matrix $\mathbf{W}_{hh}$ at each time step. Similarly, the gradients in an RNN can decay or explode as we go backwards in time, since we multiply the Jacobians at each time step (see Section 13.4.2 for details). A simple heuristic is to use gradient clipping (Equation (13.70)). More sophisticated methods attempt to control the spectral radius λ of the forward mapping, $\mathbf{W}_{hh}$, as well as the backwards mapping, given by the Jacobian $\mathbf{J}_{hh}$.

The simplest way to control the spectral radius is to randomly initialize $\mathbf{W}_{hh}$ in such a way as to ensure $\lambda \approx 1$, and then keep it fixed (i.e., we do not learn $\mathbf{W}_{hh}$). In this case, only the output matrix $\mathbf{W}_{ho}$ needs to be learned, resulting in a convex optimization problem. This is called an **echo state network** [JH04]. A closely related approach, known as a **liquid state machine** [MNM02], uses binary-valued (spiking) neurons instead of real-valued neurons. A generic term for both ESNs

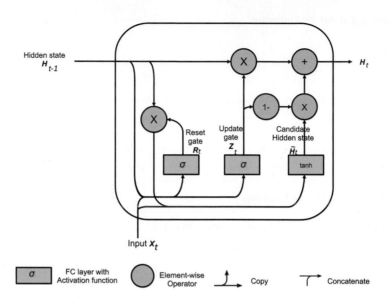

Figure 15.10: Illustration of a GRU. Adapted from Figure 9.1.3 of [Zha+20].

and LSMs is **reservoir computing** [LJ09]. Another approach to this problem is use constrained optimization to ensure the $\mathbf{W}_{hh}$ matrix remains orthogonal [Vor+17].

An alternative to explicitly controlling the spectral radius is to modify the RNN architecture itself, to use additive rather than multiplicative updates to the hidden states, as we discuss in Section 15.2.7. This significantly improves training stability.

15.2.7   Gating and long term memory

RNNs with enough hidden units can in principle remember inputs from long in the past. However, in practice "vanilla" RNNs fail to do this because of the vanishing gradient problem (Section 13.4.2). In this section we give a solution to this in which we update the hidden state in an additive way, similar to a residual net (Section 14.3.4).

15.2.7.1   Gated recurrent units (GRU)

In this section, we discuss models which use **gated recurrent units** (**GRU**), as proposed in [Cho+14a]. The key idea is to learn when to update the hidden state, by using a gating unit. This can be used to selectively "remember" important pieces of information when they are first seen. The model can also learn when to reset the hidden state, and thus forget things that are no longer useful.

To explain the model in more detail, we present it in two steps, following the presentation of [Zha+20, Sec 8.8]. We assume $\mathbf{X}_t$ is a $N \times D$ matrix, where N is the batch size, and D is the vocabulary size. Similarly, $\mathbf{H}_t$ is a $N \times H$ matrix, where H is the number of hidden units at time t.

The **reset gate** $\mathbf{R}_t \in \mathbb{R}^{N \times H}$ and **update gate** $\mathbf{Z}_t \in \mathbb{R}^{N \times H}$ are computed using

$$\mathbf{R}_t = \sigma(\mathbf{X}_t \mathbf{W}_{xr} + \mathbf{H}_{t-1} \mathbf{W}_{hr} + \boldsymbol{b}_r) \tag{15.23}$$

$$\mathbf{Z}_t = \sigma(\mathbf{X}_t \mathbf{W}_{xz} + \mathbf{H}_{t-1} \mathbf{W}_{hz} + \boldsymbol{b}_z) \tag{15.24}$$

Note that each element of $\mathbf{R}_t$ and $\mathbf{Z}_t$ is in $[0, 1]$, because of the sigmoid function.

Given this, we define a "candidate" next state vector using

$$\tilde{\mathbf{H}}_t = \tanh(\mathbf{X}_t \mathbf{W}_{xh} + (\mathbf{R}_t \odot \mathbf{H}_{t-1}) \mathbf{W}_{hh} + \boldsymbol{b}_h) \tag{15.25}$$

This combines the old memories that are not reset (computed using $\mathbf{R}_t \odot \mathbf{H}_{t-1}$) with the new inputs $\mathbf{X}_t$. We pass the resulting linear combination through a tanh function to ensure the hidden units remain in the interval $(-1, 1)$. If the entries of the reset gate $\mathbf{R}_t$ are close to 1, we recover the standard RNN update rule. If the entries are close to 0, the model acts more like an MLP applied to $\mathbf{X}_t$. Thus the reset gate can capture new, short-term information.

Once we have computed the candidate new state, the model computes the actual new state by using the dimensions from the candidate state $\tilde{\mathbf{H}}_t$ chosen by the update gate, $1 - \mathbf{Z}_t$, and keeping the remaining dimensions at their old values of $\mathbf{H}_{t-1}$:

$$\mathbf{H}_t = \mathbf{Z}_t \odot \mathbf{H}_{t-1} + (1 - \mathbf{Z}_t) \odot \tilde{\mathbf{H}}_t \tag{15.26}$$

When $Z_{td} = 1$, we pass $H_{t-1,d}$ through unchanged, and ignore $\mathbf{X}_t$. Thus the update gate can capture long-term dependencies.

See Figure 15.10 for an illustration of the overall architecture, and gru_jax.ipynb for some sample code.

15.2.7.2 Long short term memory (LSTM)

In this section, we discuss the **long short term memory** (**LSTM**) model of [HS97b], which is a more sophisticated version of the GRU (and pre-dates it by almost 20 years). For a more detailed introduction, see `https://colah.github.io/posts/2015-08-Understanding-LSTMs`.

The basic idea is to augment the hidden state $\boldsymbol{h}_t$ with a **memory cell** $\boldsymbol{c}_t$. We need three gates to control this cell: the **output gate** $\mathbf{O}_t$ determines what gets read out; the **input gate** $\mathbf{I}_t$ determines what gets read in; and the **forget gate** $\mathbf{F}_t$ determines when we should reset the cell. These gates are computed as follows:

$$\mathbf{O}_t = \sigma(\mathbf{X}_t \mathbf{W}_{xo} + \mathbf{H}_{t-1} \mathbf{W}_{ho} + \boldsymbol{b}_o) \tag{15.27}$$

$$\mathbf{I}_t = \sigma(\mathbf{X}_t \mathbf{W}_{xi} + \mathbf{H}_{t-1} \mathbf{W}_{hi} + \boldsymbol{b}_i) \tag{15.28}$$

$$\mathbf{F}_t = \sigma(\mathbf{X}_t \mathbf{W}_{xf} + \mathbf{H}_{t-1} \mathbf{W}_{hf} + \boldsymbol{b}_f) \tag{15.29}$$

We then compute a candidate cell state:

$$\tilde{\mathbf{C}}_t = \tanh(\mathbf{X}_t \mathbf{W}_{xc} + \mathbf{H}_{t-1} \mathbf{W}_{hc} + \boldsymbol{b}_c) \tag{15.30}$$

The actual update to the cell is either the candidate cell (if the input gate is on) or the old cell (if the not-forget gate is on):

$$\mathbf{C}_t = \mathbf{F}_t \odot \mathbf{C}_{t-1} + \mathbf{I}_t \odot \tilde{\mathbf{C}}_t \tag{15.31}$$

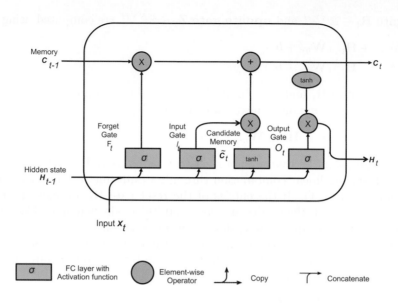

Figure 15.11: Illustration of an LSTM. Adapted from Figure 9.2.4 of [Zha+20].

If $\mathbf{F}_t = 1$ and $\mathbf{I}_t = 0$, this can remember long term memories.[2]

Finally, we compute the hidden state to be a transformed version of the cell, provided the output gate is on:

$$\mathbf{H}_t = \mathbf{O}_t \odot \tanh(\mathbf{C}_t) \tag{15.32}$$

Note that $\mathbf{H}_t$ is used as the output of the unit as well as the hidden state for the next time step. This lets the model remember what it has just output (short-term memory), whereas the cell $\mathbf{C}_t$ acts as a long-term memory. See Figure 15.11 for an illustration of the overall model, and lstm_jax.ipynb for some sample code.

Sometimes we add **peephole connections**, where we pass the cell state as an additional input to the gates. Many other variants have been proposed. In fact, [JZS15] used genetic algorithms to test over 10,000 different architectures. Some of these worked better than LSTMs or GRUs, but in general, LSTMs seemed to do consistently well across most tasks. Similar conclusions were reached in [Gre+17]. More recently, [ZL17] used an RNN controller to generate strings which specify RNN architectures, and then trained the controller using reinforcement learning. This resulted in a novel cell structure that outperformed LSTM. However, it is rather complex and has not been adopted by the community.

---

2. One important detail pointed out in [JZS15] is that we need to initialize the bias term for the forget gate $\boldsymbol{b}_f$ to be large, so the sigmoid is close to 1. This ensures that information can easily pass through the $\mathbf{C}$ chain over time. Without this trick, performance is often much worse.

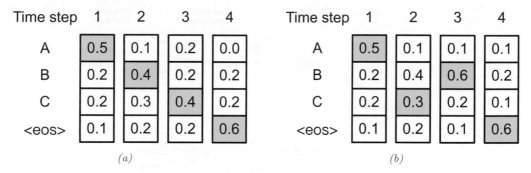

Figure 15.12: *Conditional probabilities of generating each token at each step for two different sequences. From Figures 9.8.1–9.8.2 of [Zha+20]. Used with kind permission of Aston Zhang.*

15.2.8 Beam search

The simplest way to generate from an RNN is to use **greedy decoding**, in which we compute $\hat{y}_t = \text{argmax}_y \, p(y_t = y | \hat{\boldsymbol{y}}_{1:t}, \boldsymbol{x})$ at each step. We can repeat this process until we generate the end-of-sentence token. See Figure 15.8b for an illustration of this method applied to NMT.

Unfortunately greedy decoding will not generate the MAP sequence, which is defined by $\boldsymbol{y}_{1:T}^* = \text{argmax}_{\boldsymbol{y}_{1:T}} \, p(\boldsymbol{y}_{1:T} | \boldsymbol{x})$. The reason is that the locally optimal symbol at step t might not be on the globally optimal path.

As an example, consider Figure 15.12a. We greedily pick the MAP symbol at step 1, which is A. Conditional on this, suppose we have $p(y_2 | y_1 = A) = [0.1, 0.4, 0.3, 0.2]$, as shown. We greedily pick the MAP symbol from this, which is B. Conditional on this, suppose we have $p(y_3 | y_1 = A, y_2 = B) = [0.2, 0.2, 0.4, 0.2]$, as shown. We greedily pick the MAP symbol from this, which is C. Conditional on this, suppose we have $p(y_4 | y_1 = A, y_2 = B, y_3 = C) = [0.0, 0.2, 0.2, 0.6]$, as shown. We greedily pick the MAP symbol from this, which is eos (end of sentence), so we stop generating. The overall probability of the generated sequence is $0.5 \times 0.4 \times 0.4 \times 0.6 = 0.048$.

Now consider Figure 15.12b. At step 2, suppose we pick the second most probable token, namely C. Conditional on this, suppose we have $p(y_3 | y_1 = A, y_2 = C) = [0.1, 0.6, 0.2, 0.1]$, as shown. We greedily pick the MAP symbol from this, which is B. Conditional on this, suppose we have $p(y_4 | y_1 = A, y_2 = C, y_3 = B) = [0.1, 0.2, 0.1, 0.6]$, as shown. We greedily pick the MAP symbol from this, which is eos (end of sentence), so we stop generating. The overall probability of the generated sequence is $0.5 \times 0.3 \times 0.6 \times 0.6 = 0.054$. So by being less greedy, we found a sequence with overall higher likelihood.

For hidden Markov models, we can use an algorithm called **Viterbi decoding** (which is an example of **dynamic programming**) to compute the globally optimal sequence in $O(TV^2)$ time, where V is the number of words in the vocabulary. (See [Mur23] for details.) But for RNNs, computing the global optimum takes $O(V^T)$, since the hidden state is not a sufficient statistic for the data.

Beam search is a much faster heuristic method. In this approach, we compute the top K candidate outputs at each step; we then expand each one in all V possible ways, to generate VK candidates, from which we pick the top K again. This process is illustrated in Figure 15.13.

It is also possible to extend the algorithm to sample the top K sequences without replacement

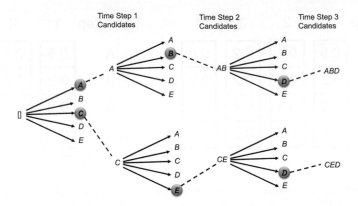

Figure 15.13: Illustration of beam search using a beam of size $K = 2$. The vocabulary is $\mathcal{Y} = \{A, B, C, D, E\}$, with size $V = 5$. We assume the top 2 symbols at step 1 are A,C. At step 2, we evaluate $p(y_1 = A, y_2 = y)$ and $p(y_1 = C, y_2 = y)$ for each $y \in \mathcal{Y}$. This takes $O(KV)$ time. We then pick the top 2 partial paths, which are $(y_1 = A, y_2 = B)$ and $(y_1 = C, y_2 = E)$, and continue in the obvious way. Adapted from Figure 9.8.3 of [Zha+20].

(i.e., pick the top one, renormalize, pick the new top one, etc.), using a method called **stochastic beam search**. This perturbs the model's partial probabilities at each step with Gumbel noise. See [KHW19] for details. and [SBS20] for a sequential alternative. These sampling methods can improve diversity of the outputs. (See also the deterministic **diverse beam search** method of [Vij+18].)

15.3   1d CNNs

Convolutional neural networks (Chapter 14) compute a function of some local neighborhood for each input using tied weights, and return an output. They are usually used for 2d inputs, but can also be applied in the 1d case, as we discuss below. They are an interesting alternative to RNNs that are much easier to train, because they don't have to maintain long term hidden state.

15.3.1   1d CNNs for sequence classification

In this section, we discuss the use of 1d CNNs for learning a mapping from variable-length sequences to a fixed length output, i.e., a function of the form $f_{\boldsymbol{\theta}} : \mathbb{R}^{DT} \to \mathbb{R}^C$, where T is the length of the input, D is the number of features per input, and C is the size of the output vector (e.g., class logits).

A basic 1d convolution operation applied to a 1d sequence is shown in Figure 14.4. Typically the input sequence will have $D > 1$ input channels (feature dimensions). In this case, we can convolve each channel separately and add up the result, using a different 1d filter (kernel) for each input channel to get $z_i = \sum_d \boldsymbol{x}_{i-k:i+k,d}^{\mathsf{T}} \boldsymbol{w}_d$, where k is size of the 1d receptive field, and $\boldsymbol{w}_d$ is the filter for input channel d. This produces a 1d vector $\boldsymbol{z} \in \mathbb{R}^T$ encoding the input (ignoring boundary effects). We can create a vector representation for each location using a different weight vector for each output channel c to get $z_{ic} = \sum_d \boldsymbol{x}_{i-k:i+k,d}^{\mathsf{T}} \boldsymbol{w}_{d,c}$. This implements a mapping from TD to TC. To reduce this to a fixed sized vector, $\boldsymbol{z} \in \mathbb{R}^C$, we can use max-pooling over time to get $z_c = \max_i z_{ic}$. We can

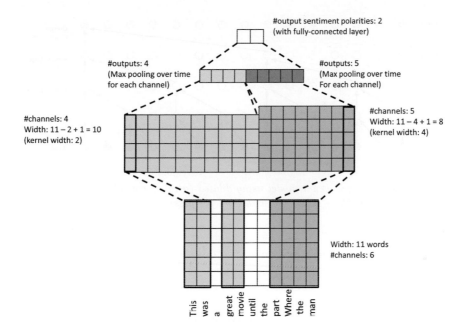

Figure 15.14: Illustration of the TextCNN model for binary sentiment classification. Adapted from Figure 15.3.5 of [Zha+20].

then pass this into a softmax layer.

In [Kim14], they applied this model to sequence classification. The idea is to embed each word using an embedding layer, and then to compute various features using 1d kernels of different widths, to capture patterns of different length scales. We then apply max pooling over time, and concatenate the results, and pass to a fully connected layer. See Figure 15.14 for an illustration, and cnn1d_sentiment_jax.ipynb for some code.

15.3.2 Causal 1d CNNs for sequence generation

To use 1d CNNs in a generative setting, we must convert them to a **causal CNN**, in which each output variable only depends on previously generated variables. (This is also called a **convolutional Markov model**.) In particular, we define the model as follows:

$$p(\boldsymbol{y}) = \prod_{t=1}^{T} p(y_t | \boldsymbol{y}_{1:t-1}) = \prod_{t=1}^{T} \mathrm{Cat}(y_t | \mathrm{softmax}(\varphi(\sum_{\tau=1}^{t-k} \boldsymbol{w}^\mathsf{T} \boldsymbol{y}_{\tau:\tau+k}))) \tag{15.33}$$

where $\boldsymbol{w}$ is the convolutional filter of size k, and we have assumed a single nonlinearity φ and categorical output, for notational simplicity. This is like regular 1d convolution except we "mask out" future inputs, so that y_t only depends on the past values, rather than past and future values. This is

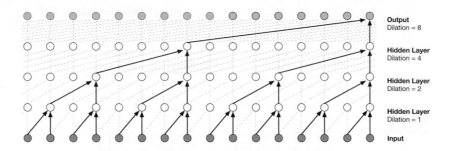

Figure 15.15: *Illustration of the wavenet model using dilated (atrous) convolutions, with dilation factors of 1, 2, 4 and 8. From Figure 3 of [Oor+16]. Used with kind permission of Aaron van den Oord.*

called **causal convolution**. We can of course use deeper models, and we can condition on input features x.

In order to capture long-range dependencies, we can use dilated convolution (Section 14.4.1), as illustrated in Figure 15.15. This model has been successfully used to create a state of the art **text to speech** (TTS) synthesis system known as **wavenet** [Oor+16]. In particular, they stack 10 causal 1d convolutional layers with dilation rates $1, 2, 4, \ldots, 256, 512$ to get a convolutional block with an effective receptive field of 1024. (They left-padded the input sequences with a number of zeros equal to the dilation rate before every layer, so that every layer has the same length.) They then repeat this block 3 times to compute deeper features.

In wavenet, the conditioning information x is a set of linguistic features derived from an input sequence of words; the model then generates raw audio using the above model. It is also possible to create a fully end-to-end approach, which starts with raw words rather than linguistic features (see [Wan+17]).

Although wavenet produces high quality speech, it is too slow for use in production systems. However, it can be "distilled" into a parallel generative model [Oor+18]. We discuss these kinds of parallel generative models in the sequel to this book, [Mur23].

15.4 Attention

In all of the neural networks we have considered so far, the hidden activations are a linear combination of the input activations, followed by a nonlinearity: $\mathbf{Z} = \varphi(\mathbf{X}\mathbf{W})$, where $\mathbf{X} \in \mathbb{R}^{m \times v}$ are the hidden feature vectors, and $\mathbf{W} \in \mathbb{R}^{v \times v'}$ are a fixed set of weights that are learned on a training set to produce $\mathbf{Z} \in \mathbb{R}^{m \times v'}$ outputs.

However, we can imagine a more flexible model in which the weights depend on the inputs, i.e., $\mathbf{Z} = \varphi(\mathbf{X}\mathbf{W}(\mathbf{X}))$. This kind of **multiplicative interaction** is called **attention**. More generally, we can write $\mathbf{Z} = \varphi(\mathbf{V}\mathbf{W}(\mathbf{Q}, \mathbf{K}))$, where $\mathbf{Q} \in \mathbb{R}^{m \times q}$ are a set of **queries** (derived from $\mathbf{X}$) used to describe what each input is "looking for", $\mathbf{K} \in \mathbb{R}^{m \times q}$ are a set of **keys** (derived from $\mathbf{X}$) used to describe what each input vector contains, and $\mathbf{V} \in \mathbb{R}^{m \times v}$ are a set of **values** $\mathbf{V} \in \mathbb{R}^{m \times v}$ (derived from $\mathbf{X}$) used to describe how each input should be transmitted to the output. (We usually compute these quantities using linear projections of the input, $\mathbf{Q} = \mathbf{W}_q\mathbf{X}$, $\mathbf{K} = \mathbf{W}_k\mathbf{X}$, and $\mathbf{V} = \mathbf{W}_v\mathbf{X}$.)

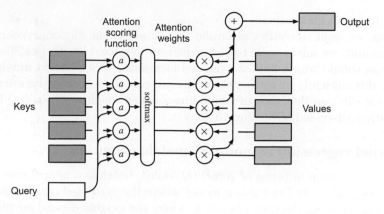

Figure 15.16: *Attention computes a weighted average of a set of values, where the weights are derived by comparing the query vector to a set of keys. From Figure 10.3.1 of [Zha+20]. Used with kind permission of Aston Zhang.*

When using atttention to compute output z_j, we use its corresponding query q_j and compare it to each key k_i to get a similarity score, $0 \leq \alpha_{ij} \leq 1$, where $\sum_i \alpha_{ij} = 1$; we then set $z_j = \sum_i \alpha_{ij} v_i$. (We assume $\varphi(u) = u$ is the identity function.) For example, suppose $\mathbf{V} = \mathbf{X}$, and query q_j equally matches keys 1 and 2, so $\alpha_{1j} = \alpha_{2j} = 0.5$; then we have $z_j = 0.5 x_1 + 0.5 x_2$. Thus the outputs become a dynamic weighted combination of the inputs, rather than a fixed weighted combination. And rather than learning the weight matrix, we learn the projection matrices $\mathbf{W}_q$, $\mathbf{W}_k$ and $\mathbf{W}_v$. We explain this in more detail below.

Note that attention was originally developed for natural language sequence models. However, nowadays it is applied to a variety of models, including vision models. Our presentation in the following sections is based on [Zha+20, Chap 10.].

15.4.1   Attention as soft dictionary lookup

We will focus on a single output vector, with corresponding query vector q. We can think of attention as a dictionary lookup, in which we compare the query q to each key k_i, and then retrieve the corresponding value v_i. To make this lookup operation differentiable, instead of retrieving a single value v_i, we compute a convex combination of the values, as follows:

$$\text{Attn}(q, (k_1, v_1), \ldots, (k_m, v_m)) = \text{Attn}(q, (k_{1:m}, v_{1:m})) = \sum_{i=1}^{m} \alpha_i(q, k_{1:m}) v_i \in \mathbb{R}^v \tag{15.34}$$

where $\alpha_i(q, k_{1:m})$ is the i'th **attention weight**; these weights satisfy $0 \leq \alpha_i(q, k_{1:m}) \leq 1$ for each i and $\sum_i \alpha_i(q, k_{1:m}) = 1$.

The attention weights can be computed from an **attention score** function $a(q, k_i) \in \mathbb{R}$, that computes the similarity of query q to key k_i. We will discuss several such score function below. Given the scores, we can compute the attention weights using the softmax function:

$$\alpha_i(q, k_{1:m}) = \text{softmax}_i([a(q, k_1), \ldots, a(q, k_m)]) = \frac{\exp(a(q, k_i))}{\sum_{j=1}^{m} \exp(a(q, k_j))} \tag{15.35}$$

See Figure 15.16 for an illustration.

In some cases, we want to restrict attention to a subset of the dictionary, corresponding to valid entries. For example, we might want to pad sequences to a fixed length (for efficient minibatching), in which case we should "mask out" the padded locations. This is called **masked attention**. We can implement this efficiently by setting the attention score for the masked entries to a large negative number, such as -10^6, so that the corresponding softmax weights will be 0. (This is analogous to causal convolution, discussed in Section 15.3.2.)

15.4.2   Kernel regression as non-parametric attention

We can interpret attention in terms of kernel regression, which is a nonparametric model which we discuss in Section 16.3.5. In brief this a model where the predicted output at query point x is a weighted combination of all the target labels y_i, where the weights depend on the similarity of query point x to each training point x_i:

$$f(\boldsymbol{x}) = \sum_{i=1}^{n} \alpha_i(\boldsymbol{x}, \boldsymbol{x}_{1:n}) y_i \tag{15.36}$$

where $\alpha_i(\boldsymbol{x}, \boldsymbol{x}_{1:n}) \geq 0$ measures the normalized similarity of test input x to training input x_i. This similarity measure is usually computed by defining the attention score in terms of a density kernel, such as the Gaussian:

$$\mathcal{K}_\sigma(u) = \frac{1}{\sqrt{2\pi\sigma^2}} e^{-\frac{1}{2\sigma^2}u^2} \tag{15.37}$$

where σ is called the bandwidth. We then define $a(x, x_i) = \mathcal{K}_\sigma(x - x_i)$.

Because the scores are normalized, we can drop the $\frac{1}{\sqrt{2\pi\sigma^2}}$ term. In addition, we rewrite the kernel in terms of $\beta^2 = 1/\sigma^2$ to get

$$\mathcal{K}(u; \beta) = \exp(-\frac{\beta^2}{2}u^2) \tag{15.38}$$

Plugging this in to Equation (15.36), we get

$$f(\boldsymbol{x}) = \sum_{i=1}^{n} \alpha_i(\boldsymbol{x}, \boldsymbol{x}_{1:n}) y_i \tag{15.39}$$

$$= \sum_{i=1}^{n} \frac{\exp[-\frac{1}{2}((\boldsymbol{x} - \boldsymbol{x}_i)\beta)^2]}{\sum_{j=1}^{n} \exp[-\frac{1}{2}((\boldsymbol{x} - \boldsymbol{x}_j)\beta)^2]} y_i \tag{15.40}$$

$$= \sum_{i=1}^{n} \text{softmax}_i \left[-\frac{1}{2}((\boldsymbol{x} - \boldsymbol{x}_1)\beta)^2, \cdots, -\frac{1}{2}((\boldsymbol{x} - \boldsymbol{x}_n)\beta)^2 \right] y_i \tag{15.41}$$

We can interpret this as a form of nonparametric attention, where the queries are the test points x, the keys are the training inputs x_i, and the values are the training labels y_i. If we set $\beta = 1$, the resulting attention matrix $A_{ji} = \alpha_i(\boldsymbol{x}_j, \boldsymbol{x}_{1:n})$ for test input j is shown in Figure 15.17a. The resulting predicted curve is shown in Figure 15.17b.

The size of the diagonal band in Figure 15.17a, and hence the sparsity of the attention mechanism, depends on the parameter β. If we increase β, corresponding to reducing the kernel bandwidth, the band will get narrower, but the model will start to overfit.

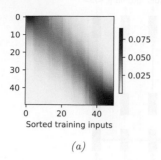
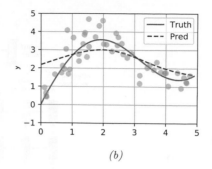

(a)   (b)

Figure 15.17: Kernel regression in 1d. (a) Kernel weight matrix. (b) Resulting predictions on a dense grid of test points. Generated by kernel_regression_attention.ipynb.

15.4.3 Parametric attention

In Section 15.4.2, we defined the attention score in terms of the Gaussian kernel, comparing a query (test point) to each of the values in the training set. However, non-parametric methods do not scale well to large training sets, or high-dimensional inputs. We will therefore turn our attention (no pun intended) to parametric models, where we have a fixed set of keys and values, and where we compare queries and keys in a learned embedding space.

There are several ways to do this. In the general case, the query $q \in \mathbb{R}^q$ and the key $k \in \mathbb{R}^k$ may have different sizes. To compare them, we can map them to a common embedding space of size h by computing $\mathbf{W}_q q$ and $\mathbf{W}_k k$, where $\mathbf{W}_q \in \mathbb{R}^{h \times q}$ and $\mathbf{W}_k \in \mathbb{R}^{h \times k}$. We can then pass these into an MLP to get the following **additive attention** scoring function:

$$a(q, k) = w_v^\mathsf{T} \tanh(\mathbf{W}_q q + \mathbf{W}_k k) \in \mathbb{R} \tag{15.42}$$

A more computationally efficient approach is to assume the queries and keys both have length d, so we can compute $q^\mathsf{T} k$ directly. If we assume these are independent random variables with 0 mean and unit variance, the mean of their inner product is 0, and the variance is d. (This follows from Equation (2.34) and Equation (2.39).) To ensure the variance of the inner product remains 1 regardless of the size of the inputs, it is standard to divide by $\sqrt{d}$. This gives rise to the **scaled dot-product attention**:

$$a(q, k) = q^\mathsf{T} k / \sqrt{d} \in \mathbb{R} \tag{15.43}$$

In practice, we usually deal with minibatches of n vectors at a time. Let the corresponding matrices of queries, keys and values be denoted by $\mathbf{Q} \in \mathbb{R}^{n \times d}$, $\mathbf{K} \in \mathbb{R}^{m \times d}$, $\mathbf{V} \in \mathbb{R}^{m \times v}$. Then we can compute the attention-weighted outputs as follows:

$$\text{Attn}(\mathbf{Q}, \mathbf{K}, \mathbf{V}) = \text{softmax}\left(\frac{\mathbf{Q}\mathbf{K}^\mathsf{T}}{\sqrt{d}}\right)\mathbf{V} \in \mathbb{R}^{n \times v} \tag{15.44}$$

where the softmax function softmax is applied row-wise. See attention_jax.ipynb for some sample code.

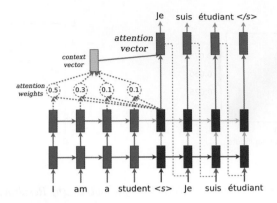

Figure 15.18: Illustration of seq2seq with attention for English to French translation. Used with kind permission of Minh-Thang Luong.

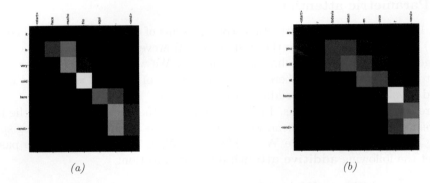

Figure 15.19: Illustration of the attention heatmaps generated while translating two sentences from Spanish to English. (a) Input is "hace mucho frio aqui.", output is "it is very cold here.". (b) Input is "¿todavia estan en casa?", output is "are you still at home?". Note that when generating the output token "home", the model should attend to the input token "casa", but in fact it seems to attend to the input token "?". Adapted from https://www.tensorflow.org/tutorials/text/nmt_with_attention.

15.4.4   Seq2Seq with attention

Recall the seq2seq model from Section 15.2.3. This uses an RNN decoder of the form $h_t^d = f_d(h_{t-1}^d, y_{t-1}, c)$, where c is a fixed-length context vector, representing the encoding of the input $x_{1:T}$. Usually we set $c = h_T^e$, which is the final state of the encoder RNN (or we use a bidirectional RNN with average pooling). However, for tasks such as machine translation, this can result in poor performance, since the output does not have access to the input words themselves. We can avoid this bottleneck by allowing the output words to directly "look at" the input words. But which inputs should it look at? After all, word order is not always preserved across languages (e.g., German often puts verbs at the end of a sentence), so we need to infer the **alignment** between source and target.

We can solve this problem (in a differentiable way) by using (soft) **attention**, as first proposed in [BCB15; LPM15]. In particular, we can replace the fixed context vector c in the decoder with a dynamic context vector $\boldsymbol{c}_t$ computed as follows:

$$\boldsymbol{c}_t = \sum_{i=1}^{T} \alpha_i(\boldsymbol{h}_{t-1}^d, \boldsymbol{h}_{1:T}^e)\boldsymbol{h}_i^e \tag{15.45}$$

This uses attention where the query is the hidden state of the decoder at the previous step, $\boldsymbol{h}_{t-1}^d$, the keys are all the hidden states from the encoder, and the values are also the hidden states from the encoder. (When the RNN has multiple hidden layers, we usually take the top layer from the encoder, as the keys and values, and the top layer of the decoder as the query.) This context vector is concatenated with the input vector of the decoder, $\boldsymbol{y}_{t-1}$, and fed into the decoder, along with the previous hidden state $\boldsymbol{h}_{t-1}^d$, to create $\boldsymbol{h}_t^d$. See Figure 15.18 for an illustration of the overall model.

We can train this model in the usual way on sentence pairs, and then use it to perform machine translation. (See nmt_attention_jax.ipynb for some sample code.) We can also visualize the attention weights computed at each step of decoding, to get an idea of which parts of the input the model thinks are most relevant for generating the corresponding output. Some examples are shown in Figure 15.19.

15.4.5 Seq2vec with attention (text classification)

We can also use attention with sequence classifiers. For example [Raj+18] apply an RNN classifier to the problem of predicting if a patient will die or not. The input is a set of **electronic health records**, which is a time series containing structured data, as well as unstructured text (clinical notes). Attention is useful for identifying "relevant" parts of the input, as illustrated in Figure 15.20.

15.4.6 Seq+Seq2Vec with attention (text pair classification)

Suppose we see the sentence "A person on a horse jumps over a log" (call this the **premise**) and then we later read "A person is outdoors on a horse" (call this the **hypothesis**). We may reasonably say that the premise **entails** the hypothesis, meaning that the hypothesis is more likely given the premise.[3] Now suppose the hypothesis is "A person is at a diner ordering an omelette". In this case, we would say that the premise **contradicts** the hypothesis, since the hypothesis is less likely given the premise. Finally, suppose the hypothesis is "A person is training his horse for a competition". In this case, we see that the relationship between premise and hypothesis is **neutral**, since the hypothesis may or may not follow from the premise. The task of classifying a sentence pair into these three categories is known as **textual entailment** or "**natural language inference**". A standard benchmark in this area is the **Stanford Natural Language Inference** or **SNLI** corpus [Bow+15]. This consists of 550,000 labeled sentence pairs.

An interesting solution to this classification problem was presented in [Par+16a]; at the time, it was the state of the art on the SNLI dataset. The overall approach is sketched in Figure 15.21. Let $\mathbf{A} = (\boldsymbol{a}_1, \ldots, \boldsymbol{a}_m)$ be the premise and $\mathbf{B} = (\boldsymbol{b}_1, \ldots, \boldsymbol{b}_n)$ be the hypothesis, where $\boldsymbol{a}_i, \boldsymbol{b}_j \in \mathbb{R}^E$ are embedding vectors for the words. The model has 3 steps. First, each word in the premise, $\boldsymbol{a}_i$, attends

---

3. Note that the premise does not logically imply the hypothesis, since the person could be horse-back riding indoors, but generally people ride horses outdoors. Also, we are assuming the phrase "a person" refers to the same person in the two sentences.

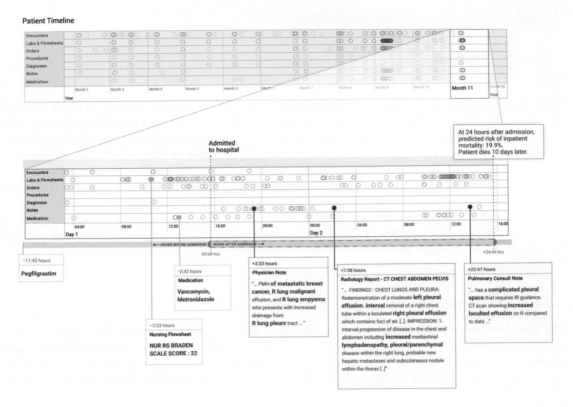

Figure 15.20: *Example of an electronic health record. In this example, 24h after admission to the hospital, the RNN classifier predicts the risk of death as 19.9%; the patient ultimately died 10 days after admission. The "relevant" keywords from the input clinical notes are shown in red, as identified by an attention mechanism. From Figure 3 of [Raj+18]. Used with kind permission of Alvin Rajkomar.*

to each word in the hypothesis, $\boldsymbol{b}_j$, to compute an attention weight

$$e_{ij} = f(\boldsymbol{a}_i)^{\mathsf{T}} f(\boldsymbol{b}_j) \tag{15.46}$$

where $f : \mathbb{R}^E \to \mathbb{R}^D$ is an MLP; we then compute a weighted average of the matching words in the hypothesis,

$$\boldsymbol{\beta}_i = \sum_{j=1}^{n} \frac{\exp(e_{ij})}{\sum_{k=1}^{n} \exp(e_{ik})} \boldsymbol{b}_j \tag{15.47}$$

Next, we compare $\boldsymbol{a}_i$ with $\boldsymbol{\beta}_i$ by mapping their concatenation to a hidden space using an MLP $g : \mathbb{R}^{2E} \to \mathbb{R}^H$:

$$\boldsymbol{v}_{A,i} = g([\boldsymbol{a}_i, \boldsymbol{\beta}_i]), \ i = 1, \dots, m \tag{15.48}$$

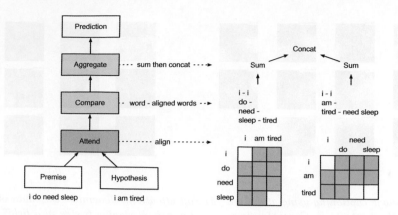

Figure 15.21: Illustration of sentence pair entailment classification using an MLP with attention to align the premise ("I do need sleep") with the hypothesis ("I am tired"). White squares denote active attention weights, blue squares are inactive. (We are assuming hard 0/1 attention for simplicity.) From Figure 15.5.2 of [Zha+20]. Used with kind permission of Aston Zhang.

Finally, we aggregate over the comparisons to get an overall similarity of premise to hypothesis:

$$\boldsymbol{v}_A = \sum_{i=1}^{m} \boldsymbol{v}_{A,i} \tag{15.49}$$

We can similarly compare the hypothesis to the premise using

$$\boldsymbol{\alpha}_j = \sum_{i=1}^{m} \frac{\exp(e_{ij})}{\sum_{k=1}^{m} \exp(e_{ki})} \boldsymbol{a}_i \tag{15.50}$$

$$\boldsymbol{v}_{B,j} = g([\boldsymbol{b}_j, \boldsymbol{\alpha}_j]), \; j = 1, \ldots, n \tag{15.51}$$

$$\boldsymbol{v}_B = \sum_{j=1}^{n} \boldsymbol{v}_{B,j} \tag{15.52}$$

At the end, we classify the output using another MLP $h : \mathbb{R}^{2H} \to \mathbb{R}^3$:

$$\hat{y} = h([\boldsymbol{v}_A, \boldsymbol{v}_B]) \tag{15.53}$$

See entailment_attention_mlp_jax.ipynb for some sample code.

We can modify this model to learn other kinds of mappings from sentence pairs to output labels. For example, in the **semantic textual similarity** task, the goal is to predict how semantically related two input sentences are. A standard dataset for this is the **STS Benchmark** [Cer+17], where relatedness ranges from 0 (meaning unrelated) to 5 (meaning maximally related).

15.4.7   Soft vs hard attention

If we force the attention heatmap to be sparse, so that each output can only attend to one input location instead of a weighted combination of all of them, the method is called **hard attention**. We

Figure 15.22: *Image captioning using attention. (a) Soft attention. Generates "a woman is throwing a frisbee in a park". (b) Hard attention. Generates "a man and a woman playing frisbee in a field". From Figure 6 of [Xu+15]. Used with kind permission of Kelvin Xu.*

compare these two approaches for an image captioning problem in Figure 15.22. Unfortunately, hard attention results in a nondifferentiable training objective, and requires methods such as reinforcement learning to fit the model. See [Xu+15] for the details.

It seems from the above examples that these attention heatmaps can "explain" why the model generates a given output. However, the interpretability of attention is controversial (see e.g., [JW19; WP19; SS19; Bru+19] for discussion).

15.5   Transformers

The **transformer** model [Vas+17] is a seq2seq model which uses attention in the encoder as well as the decoder, thus eliminating the need for RNNs, as we explain below. Transformers have been used for many (conditional) sequence generation tasks, such as machine translation [Vas+17], constituency parsing [Vas+17], music generation [Hua+18], protein sequence generation [Mad+20; Cho+20b], abstractive text summarization [Zha+19a], image generation [Par+18] (treating the image as a rasterized 1d sequence), etc.

The transformer is a rather complex model that uses several new kinds of building blocks or layers. We introduce these new blocks below, and then discuss how to put them all together.[4]

15.5.1   Self-attention

In Section 15.4.4 we showed how the decoder of an RNN could use attention to the input sequence in order to capture contexual embeddings of each input. However, rather than the decoder attending to the encoder, we can modify the model so the encoder attends to itself. This is called **self attention** [CDL16; Par+16b].

In more detail, given a sequence of input tokens $x_1, \ldots, x_n$, where $x_i \in \mathbb{R}^d$, self-attention can generate a sequence of outputs of the same size using

$$y_i = \text{Attn}(x_i, (x_1, x_1), \ldots, (x_n, x_n)) \tag{15.54}$$

---

4. For a more detailed introduction, see `https://huggingface.co/course/chapter1`.

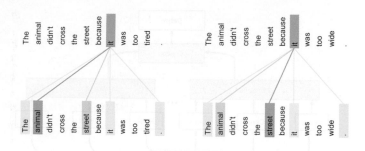

Figure 15.23: *Illustration of how encoder self-attention for the word "it" differs depending on the input context. From* https://ai.googleblog.com/2017/08/transformer-novel-neural-network.html. *Used with kind permission of Jakob Uszkoreit.*

where the query is x_i, and the keys and values are all the (valid) inputs $x_1, \ldots, x_n$.

To use this in a decoder, we can set $x_i = y_{i-1}$, and $n = i - 1$, so all the previously generated outputs are available. At training time, all the outputs are already known, so we can evaluate the above function in parallel, overcoming the sequential bottleneck of using RNNs.

In addition to improved speed, self-attention can give improved representations of context. As an example, consider translating the English sentences "The animal didn't cross the street because it was too *tired*" and "The animal didn't cross the street because it was too *wide*" into French. To generate a pronoun of the correct gender in French, we need to know what "it" refers to (this is called **coreference resolution**). In the first case, the word "it" refers to the animal. In the second case, the word "it" now refers to the street.

Figure 15.23 illustrates how self attention applied to the English sentence is able to resolve this ambiguity. In the first sentence, the representation for "it" depends on the earlier representations of "animal", whereas in the latter, it depends on the earlier representations of "street".

15.5.2 Multi-headed attention

If we think of an attention matrix as like a kernel matrix (as discussed in Section 15.4.2), it is natural to want to use multiple attention matrices, to capture different notions of similarity. This is the basic idea behind **multi-headed attention** (MHA). In more detail, given a query $q \in \mathbb{R}^{d_q}$, keys $k_j \in \mathbb{R}^{d_k}$, and values $v_j \in \mathbb{R}^{d_v}$, we define the i'th attention head to be

$$h_i = \text{Attn}(\mathbf{W}_i^{(q)} q, \{\mathbf{W}_i^{(k)} k_j, \mathbf{W}_i^{(v)} v_j\}) \in \mathbb{R}^{p_v} \tag{15.55}$$

where $\mathbf{W}_i^{(q)} \in \mathbb{R}^{p_q \times d_q}$, $\mathbf{W}_i^{(k)} \in \mathbb{R}^{p_k \times d_k}$, and $\mathbf{W}_i^{(v)} \in \mathbb{R}^{p_v \times d_v}$ are projection matrices. We then stack the h heads together, and project to $\mathbb{R}^{p_o}$ using

$$h = \text{MHA}(q, \{k_j, v_j\}) = \mathbf{W}_o \begin{pmatrix} h_1 \\ \vdots \\ h_h \end{pmatrix} \in \mathbb{R}^{p_o} \tag{15.56}$$

where h_i is defined in Equation (15.55), and $\mathbf{W}_o \in \mathbb{R}^{p_o \times h p_v}$. If we set $p_q h = p_k h = p_v h = p_o$, we can compute all the output heads in parallel. See multi_head_attention_jax.ipynb for some sample

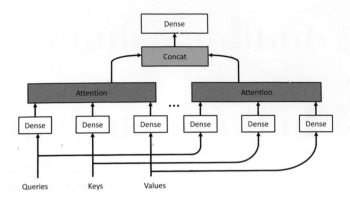

Figure 15.24: Multi-head attention. Adapted from Figure 9.3.3 of [Zha+20].

code.

15.5.3   Positional encoding

The performance of "vanilla" self-attention can be low, since attention is permutation invariant, and hence ignores the input word ordering. To overcome this, we can concatenate the word embeddings with a **positional embedding**, so that the model knows what order the words occur in.

One way to do this is to represent each position by an integer. However, neural networks cannot natively handle integers. To overcome this, we can encode the integer in binary form. For example, if we assume the sequence length is $n = 3$, we get the following sequence of $d = 3$-dimensional bit vectors for each location: 000, 001, 010, 011, 100, 101, 110, 111. We see that the right most index toggles the fastest (has highest frequency), whereas the left most index (most significant bit) toggles the slowest. (We could of course change this, so that the left most bit toggles fastest.) We can represent this as a position matrix $\mathbf{P} \in \mathbb{R}^{n \times d}$.

We can think of the above representation as using a set of basis functions (corresponding to powers of 2), where the coefficients are 0 or 1. We can obtain a more compact code by using a different set of basis functions, and real-valued weights. [Vas+17] propose to use a sinusoidal basis, as follows:

$$p_{i,2j} = \sin\left(\frac{i}{C^{2j/d}}\right), \; p_{i,2j+1} = \cos\left(\frac{i}{C^{2j/d}}\right), \tag{15.57}$$

where $C = 10,000$ corresponds to some maximum sequence length. For example, if $d = 4$, the i'th row is

$$\boldsymbol{p}_i = [\sin(\frac{i}{C^{0/4}}), \cos(\frac{i}{C^{0/4}}), \sin(\frac{i}{C^{2/4}}), \cos(\frac{i}{C^{2/4}})] \tag{15.58}$$

Figure 15.25a shows the corresponding position matrix for $n = 60$ and $d = 32$. In this case, the left-most columns toggle fastest. We see that each row has a real-valued "fingerprint" representing its location in the sequence. Figure 15.25b shows some of the basis functions (column vectors) for dimensions 6 to 9.

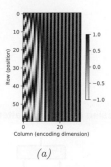

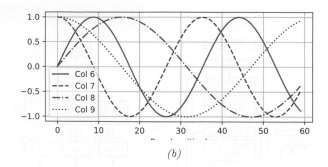

(a)   (b)

Figure 15.25: (a) Positional encoding matrix for a sequence of length $n = 60$ and an embedding dimension of size $d = 32$. (b) Basis functions for columns 6 to 9. Generated by positional_encoding_jax.ipynb.

The advantage of this representation is two-fold. First, it can be computed for arbitrary length inputs (up to $T \leq C$), unlike a learned mapping from integers to vectors. Second, the representation of one location is linearly predictable from any other, given knowledge of their relative distance. In particular, we have $\boldsymbol{p}_{t+\phi} = f(\boldsymbol{p}_t)$, where f is a linear transformation. To see this, note that

$$\begin{pmatrix} \sin(\omega_k(t+\phi)) \\ \cos(\omega_k(t+\phi)) \end{pmatrix} = \begin{pmatrix} \sin(\omega_k t)\cos(\omega_k\phi) + \cos(\omega_k t)\sin(\omega_k\phi) \\ \cos(\omega_k t)\cos(\omega_k\phi) - \sin(\omega t)\sin(\omega_k\phi) \end{pmatrix} \tag{15.59}$$

$$= \begin{pmatrix} \cos(\omega_k\phi) & \sin(\omega_k\phi) \\ -\sin(\omega_k\phi) & \cos(\omega_k\phi) \end{pmatrix} \begin{pmatrix} \sin(\omega_k t) \\ \cos(\omega_k t) \end{pmatrix} \tag{15.60}$$

So if ϕ is small, then $\boldsymbol{p}_{t+\phi} \approx \boldsymbol{p}_t$. This provides a useful form of inductive bias.

Once we have computed the positional embeddings $\mathbf{P}$, we need to combine them with the original word embeddings $\mathbf{X}$ using the following:[5]

$$\text{POS}(\text{Embed}(\mathbf{X})) = \mathbf{X} + \mathbf{P}. \tag{15.61}$$

15.5.4 Putting it all together

A transformer is a seq2seq model that uses self-attention for the encoder and decoder rather than an RNN. The encoder uses a series of encoder blocks, each of which uses multi-headed attention (Section 15.5.2), residual connections (Section 13.4.4), feedforward layers (Section 13.2), and layer normalization (Section 14.2.4.2). More precisely, the encoder block can be defined as follows:

```
def EncoderBlock(X):
    Z = LayerNorm(MultiHeadAttn(Q=X, K=X, V=X) + X)
    E = LayerNorm(FeedForward(Z) + Z)
    return E
```

---

5. A more obvious combination scheme would be to concatenate, $\mathbf{X}$ and $\mathbf{P}$, but adding takes less space. Furthermore, since the $\mathbf{X}$ embeddings are learned, the model could emulate concatentation by setting the first K dimensions of $\mathbf{X}$, and the last $D - K$ dimensions of $\mathbf{P}$, to 0, where K is defined implicitly by the sparsity pattern. For more discussion, see https://bit.ly/3rMG1at.

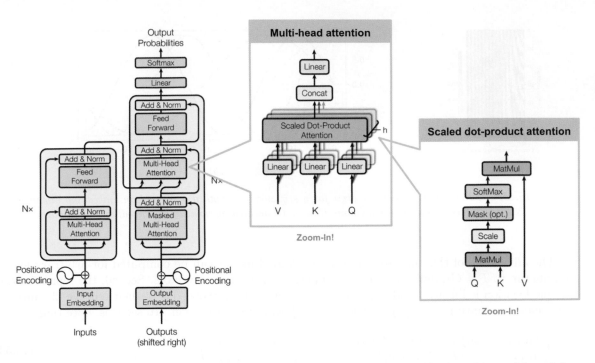

Figure 15.26: The transformer. From [Wen18]. Used with kind permission of Lilian Weng. Adapted from Figures 1–2 of [Vas+17].

Note that the MHA layer combines information across the sequence, and the feedforward layer combines information across the dimensions at each location in parallel. (Most of the parameters of large transformer models are stored inside these MLPs, and it has been conjectured that this is where most of the "world knowledge" lives [Men+22].) The layer norm can either be applied after the module (i.e., $z = \text{LN}(\text{module}(x) + x)$) or before (i.e., $z = \text{module}(\text{LN}(x) + x)$); these are known as **post-norm** and **pre-norm**.

The overall encoder is defined by applying positional encoding to the embedding of the input sequence, following by N copies of the encoder block, where N controls the depth of the block:

```
def Encoder(X, N):
  E = POS(Embed(X))
  for n in range(N):
    E = EncoderBlock(E)
  return E
```

See the LHS of Figure 15.26 for an illustration.

The decoder has a somewhat more complex structure. It is given access to the encoder via another multi-head attention block. But it is also given access to previously generated outputs: these are shifted, and then combined with a positional embedding, and then fed into a masked (causal) multi-head attention model. Finally the output distribution over tokens at each location is computed

Layer type	Complexity	Sequential ops.	Max. path length
Self-attention	$O(n^2d)$	$O(1)$	$O(1)$
Recurrent	$O(nd^2)$	$O(n)$	$O(n)$
Convolutional	$O(knd^2)$	$O(1)$	$O(\log_k n)$

Table 15.1: *Comparison of the transformer with other neural sequential generative models. n is the sequence length, d is the dimensionality of the input features, and k is the kernel size for convolution. Based on Table 1 of [Vas+17].*

in parallel.

In more detail, the decoder block is defined as follows:

```
def DecoderBlock(Y, E):
  Z = LayerNorm(MultiHeadAttn(Q=Y, K=Y, V=Y) + Y)
  Z' = LayerNorm(MultiHeadAttn(Q=Z, K=E, V=E) + Z)
  D = LayerNorm(FeedForward(Z') + Z')
  return D
```

The overall decoder is defined by N copies of the decoder block:

```
def Decoder(Y, E, N):
  D = POS(Embed(Y))
  for n in range(N):
     D = DecoderBlock(D,E)
  return D
```

See the RHS of Figure 15.26 for an illustration.

During training time, all the inputs $\mathbf{Y}$ to the decoder are known in advance, since they are derived from embedding the lagged target output sequence. During inference (test) time, we need to decode sequentially, and use masked attention, where we feed the generated output into the embedding layer, and add it to the set of keys/values that can be attended to. (We initialize by feeding in the start-of-sequence token.) See transformers_jax.ipynb for some sample code, and [Rus18; Ala18] for a detailed tutorial on this model.

15.5.5 Comparing transformers, CNNs and RNNs

In Figure 15.27, we visually compare three different architectures for mapping a sequence $x_{1:n}$ to another sequence $y_{1:n}$: a 1d CNN, an RNN, and an attention-based model. Each model makes different tradeoffs in terms of speed and expressive power, where the latter can be quantified in terms of the maximum path length between any two inputs. See Table 15.1 for a summary.

For a 1d CNN with kernel size k and d feature channels, the time to compute the output is $O(knd^2)$, which can be done in parallel. We need a stack of n/k layers, or $\log_k(n)$ if we use dilated convolution, to ensure all pairs can communicate. For example, in Figure 15.27, we see that x_1 and x_5 are initially 5 apart, and then 3 apart in layer 1, and then connected in layer 2.

For an RNN, the computational complexity is $O(nd^2)$, for a hidden state of size d, since we have to perform matrix-vector multiplication at each step. This is an inherently sequential operation. The maximum path length is $O(n)$.

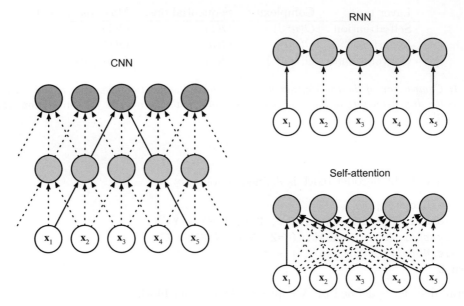

Figure 15.27: Comparison of (1d) CNNs, RNNs and self-attention models. From Figure 10.6.1 of [Zha+20]. Used with kind permission of Aston Zhang.

Finally, for self-attention models, every output is directly connected to every input, so the maximum path length is $O(1)$. However, the computational cost is $O(n^2 d)$. For short sequences, we typically have $n \ll d$, so this is fine. For longer sequences, we discuss various fast versions of attention in Section 15.6.

15.5.6   Transformers for images *

CNNs (Chapter 14) are the most common model type for processing image data, since they have useful built-in inductive bias, such as locality (due to small kernels), equivariance (due to weight tying), and invariance (due to pooling). Suprisingly, it has been found that transformers can also do well at image classification [Rag+21], at least if trained on enough data. (They need a lot of data to overcome their lack of relevant inductive bias.)

The first model of this kind, known as **ViT** (vision transformer) [Dos+21], chops the input up into 16x16 patches, projects each patch into an embedding space, and then passes this set of embeddings $\boldsymbol{x}_{1:T}$ to a transformer, analogous to the way word embeddings are passed to a transformer. The input is also prepended with a special [CLASS] embedding, $\boldsymbol{x}_0$. The output of the transformer is a set of encodings $\boldsymbol{e}_{0:T}$; the model maps $\boldsymbol{e}_0$ to the target class label y, and is trained in a supervised way. See Figure 15.28 for an illustration.

After supervised pretraining, the model is fine-tuned on various downstream classification tasks, an approach known as transfer learning (see Section 19.2 for more details). When trained on "small" datasets such as ImageNet (which has 1k classes and 1.3M images), they find that they cannot outperform a pretrained CNN ResNet model (Section 14.3.4) known as **BiT** (big transfer) [Kol+20].

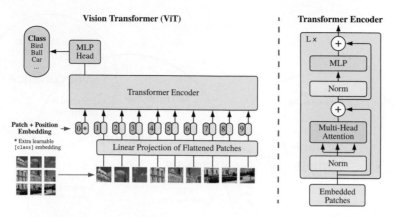

Figure 15.28: The Vision Transformer (ViT) model. This treats an image as a set of input patches. The input is prepended with the special CLASS embedding vector (denoted by *) in location 0. The class label for the image is derived by applying softmax to the final output encoding at location 0. From Figure 1 of [Dos+21]. Used with kind permission of Alexey Dosovitskiy

However, when trained on larger datasets, such as ImageNet-21k (with 21k classes and 14M images), or the Google-internal JFT dataset (with 18k classes and 303M images), they find that ViT does better than BiT at transfer learning.[6] ViT is also cheaper to train than ResNet at this scale. (However, training is still expensive: the large ViT model on ImageNet-21k takes 30 days on a Google Cloud TPUv3 with 8 cores!)

15.5.7 Other transformer variants *

Many extensions of transformers have been published in the last few years. For example, the **Gshard** paper [Lep+21] shows how to scale up transformers to even more parameters by replacing some of the feed forward dense layers with a mixture of experts (Section 13.6.2) regression module. This allows for sparse conditional computation, in which only a subset of the model capacity (chosen by the gating network) is used for any given input.

As another example, the **conformer** paper [Gul+20] showed how to add convolutional layers inside the transformer architecture, which was shown to be helpful for various speech recognition tasks.

15.6 Efficient transformers *

This section is written by Krzysztof Choromanski.

Regular transformers take $O(N^2)$ time and space complexity, for a sequence of length N, which makes them impractical to apply to long sequences. In the past few years, researchers have proposed several more efficient variants of transformers to bypass this difficulty. In this section, we give a

---

6. More recent work, specifically the ConvNeXt model of [Liu+22], has shown that CNNs can be made be to outperform ViT.

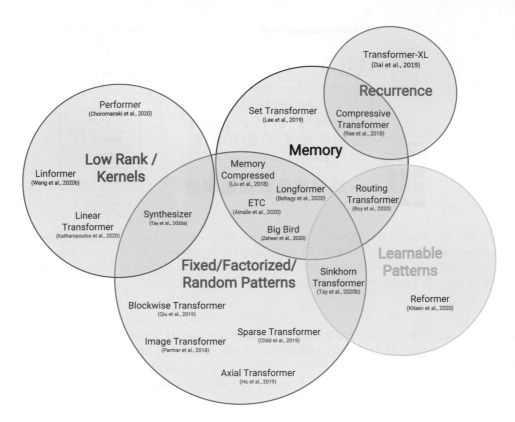

Figure 15.29: Venn diagram presenting the taxonomy of different efficient transformer architectures. From [Tay+20b]. Used with kind permission of Yi Tay.

brief survey of some of these methods (see Figure 15.29 for a summary). For more details, see e.g., [Tay+20b; Tay+20a; Lin+21].

15.6.1   Fixed non-learnable localized attention patterns

The simplest modification of the attention mechanism is to constrain it to a fixed non-learnable localized window, in other words restrict each token to attend only to a pre-selected set of other tokens. If for instance, each sequence is chunked into K blocks, each of length $\frac{N}{K}$, and attention is conducted only within a block, then space/time complexity is reduced from $O(N^2)$ to $\frac{N^2}{K}$. For $K \gg 1$ this constitutes substantial overall computational improvements. Such an approach is applied in particular in [Qiu+19b; Par+18]. The attention patterns do not need to be in the form of blocks. Other approaches involve strided / dilated windows, or hybrid patterns, where several fixed attention patterns are combined together [Chi+19b; BPC20].

15.6.2   Learnable sparse attention patterns

A natural extension of the above approach is to allow the above compact patterns to be learned. The attention is still restricted to pairs of tokens within a single partition of some partitioning of the set of all the tokens, but now those partitionings are trained. In this class of methods we can distinguish two main approaches: based on hashing and clustering. In the hashing scenario all tokens are hashed and thus different partitions correspond to different hashing-buckets. This is the case for instance for the **Reformer** architecture [KKL20], where locality sensitive hashing (LSH) is applied. That leads to time complexity $O(NM^2 \log(M))$ of the attention module, where M stands for the dimenionsality of tokens' embeddings.

Hashing approaches require the set of queries to be identical to the set of keys. Furthermore, the number of hashes needed for precise partitioning (which in the above expression is treated as a constant) can be a large constant. In the clustering approach, tokens are clustered using standard clustering algorithms such as K-means (Section 21.3); this is known as the "clustering transformer" [Roy+20]. As in the block-case, if K equal-size clusters are used then space complexity of the attention module is reduced to $O(\frac{N^2}{K})$. In practice K is often taken to be of order $K = \Theta(\sqrt{N})$, yet imposing that the clusters be similar in size is in practice difficult.

15.6.3   Memory and recurrence methods

In some approaches, a side memory module can access several tokens simultaneously. This method is often instantiated in the form of a *global memory* algorithm as used in [Lee+19; Zah+20].

Another approach is to connect different local blocks via recurrence. A flagship example of this approach is the class of Transformer-XL methods [Dai+19].

15.6.4   Low-rank and kernel methods

In this section, we discuss methods that approximate attention using low rank matrices. In [She+18; Kat+20] they approximate the attention matrix $\mathbf{A}$ directly by a low rank matrix, so that

$$A_{ij} = \phi(\boldsymbol{q}_i)^\mathsf{T} \phi(\boldsymbol{k}_j) \tag{15.62}$$

where $\phi(\boldsymbol{x}) \in \mathbb{R}^M$ is some finite-dimensional vector with $M < D$. One can leverage this structure to compute $\mathbf{AV}$ in $O(N)$ time. Unfortunately, for softmax attention, the $\mathbf{A}$ is not low rank.

In **Linformer** [Wan+20a], they instead transform the keys and values via random Gaussian projections. They then apply the theory of the Johnson-Lindenstrauss Transform [AL13] to approximate softmax attention in this lower dimensional space.

In **Performer** [Cho+20a; Cho+20b], they show that the attention matrix can be computed using a (positive definite) kernel function. We define kernel functions in Section 17.1, but the basic idea is that $\mathcal{K}(\boldsymbol{q}, \boldsymbol{k}) \geq 0$ is some measure of similarity between $\boldsymbol{q} \in \mathbb{R}^D$ and $\boldsymbol{k} \in \mathbb{R}^D$. For example, the Gaussian kernel, also called the radial basis function kernel, has the form

$$\mathcal{K}_{\text{gauss}}(\boldsymbol{q}, \boldsymbol{k}) = \exp\left(-\frac{1}{2\sigma^2}||\boldsymbol{q} - \boldsymbol{k}||_2^2\right) \tag{15.63}$$

To see how this can be used to compute an attention matrix, note that [Cho+20a] show the following:

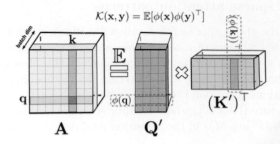

$$\mathcal{K}(\mathbf{x}, \mathbf{y}) = \mathbb{E}[\phi(\mathbf{x})\phi(\mathbf{y})^\top]$$

Figure 15.30: Attention matrix $\mathbf{A}$ rewritten as a product of two lower rank matrices $\mathbf{Q}'$ and $(\mathbf{K}')^\top$ with random feature maps $\phi(\boldsymbol{q}_i) \in \mathbb{R}^M$ and $\phi(\boldsymbol{v}_k) \in \mathbb{R}^M$ for the corresponding queries/keys stored in the rows/columns. Used with kind permission of Krzysztof Choromanski.

$$A_{i,j} = \exp(\frac{\boldsymbol{q}_i^\top \boldsymbol{k}_j}{\sqrt{D}}) = \exp(\frac{-\|\boldsymbol{q}_i - \boldsymbol{k}_j\|_2^2}{2\sqrt{D}}) \times \exp(\frac{\|\boldsymbol{q}_i\|_2^2}{2\sqrt{D}}) \times \exp(\frac{\|\boldsymbol{k}_j\|_2^2}{2\sqrt{D}}). \tag{15.64}$$

The first term in the above expression is equal to $\mathcal{K}_{\text{gauss}}(\boldsymbol{q}_i D^{-1/4}, \boldsymbol{k}_j D^{-1/4})$ with $\sigma = 1$, and the other two terms are just independent scaling factors.

So far we have not gained anything computationally. However, we will show in Section 17.2.9.3 that the Gaussian kernel can be written as the expectation of a set of random features:

$$\mathcal{K}_{\text{gauss}}(\boldsymbol{x}, \boldsymbol{y}) = \mathbb{E}\left[\boldsymbol{\eta}(\boldsymbol{x})^\top \boldsymbol{\eta}(\boldsymbol{y})\right] \tag{15.65}$$

where $\boldsymbol{\eta}(\boldsymbol{x}) \in \mathbb{R}^M$ is a random feature vector derived from $\boldsymbol{x}$, either based on trigonometric functions Equation (17.60) or exponential functions Equation (17.61). (The latter has the advantage that all the features are positive, which gives much better results [Cho+20b].) Therefore for the regular softmax attention, $A_{i,j}$ can be rewritten as

$$A_{i,j} = \mathbb{E}[\phi(\boldsymbol{q}_i)^\top \phi(\boldsymbol{k}_j)] \tag{15.66}$$

where ϕ is defined as:

$$\phi(\boldsymbol{x}) \triangleq \exp\left(\frac{\|\boldsymbol{x}\|_2^2}{2\sqrt{D}}\right) \boldsymbol{\eta}\left(\frac{\boldsymbol{x}}{D^{\frac{1}{4}}}\right). \tag{15.67}$$

We can write the full attention matrix as follows

$$\mathbf{A} = \mathbb{E}[\mathbf{Q}'(\mathbf{K}')^\top] \tag{15.68}$$

where $\mathbf{Q}', \mathbf{K}' \in \mathbb{R}^{N \times M}$ have rows encoding random feature maps corresponding to the queries and keys. (Note that we can get better performance if we ensure these random features are orthogonal, see [Cho+20a] for the details.) See Figure 15.30 for an illustration.

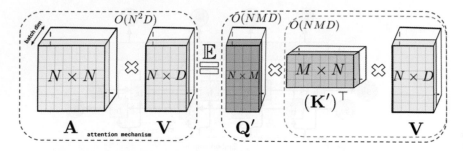

Figure 15.31: *Decomposition of the attention matrix* **A** *can be leveraged to improve attention computations via matrix associativity property. To compute* **AV**, *we first calculate* $\mathbf{G} = (\boldsymbol{k}')^{\mathsf{T}}\mathbf{V}$ *and then* $\boldsymbol{q}'\mathbf{G}$, *resulting in linear in* N *space and time complexity. Used with kind permission of Krzysztof Choromanski.*

We can create an approximation to **A** by using a single sample of the random features $\phi(\boldsymbol{q}_i)$ and $\phi(\boldsymbol{k}_j)$, and using a small value of M, say $M = O(D\log(D))$. We can then approximate the entire attention operator in $O(N)$ time using

$$\widehat{\text{attention}}(\mathbf{Q}, \mathbf{K}, \mathbf{V}) = \text{diag}^{-1}(\mathbf{Q}'((\mathbf{K}')^{\mathsf{T}}\mathbf{1}_N))(\mathbf{Q}'((\mathbf{K}')^{\mathsf{T}}\mathbf{V})) \tag{15.69}$$

This can be shown to be an unbiased approximation to the exact softmax attention operator. See Figure 15.31 for an illustration. (For details on how to generalize this to masked (causal) attention, see [Cho+20a].)

15.7 Language models and unsupervised representation learning

We have discussed how RNNs and autoregressive (decoder-only) transformers can be used as **language models**, which are generative sequence models of the form $p(x_1, \ldots, x_T) = \prod_{t=1}^{T} p(x_t | \boldsymbol{x}_{1:t-1})$, where each x_t is a discrete token, such as a word or wordpiece. (See Section 1.5.4 for a discussion of text preprocessing methods.) The latent state of these models can then be used as a continuous vector representation of the text. That is, instead of using the one-hot vector $\boldsymbol{x}_t$, or a learned embedding of it (such as those discussed in Section 20.5), we use the hidden state $\boldsymbol{h}_t$, which depends on all the previous words in the sentence. These vectors can then be used as **contextual word embeddings**, for purposes such as text classification or seq2seq tasks (see e.g. [LKB20] for a review). The advantage of this approach is that we can **pre-train** the language model in an unsupervised way, on a large corpus of text, and then we can **fine-tune** the model in a supervised way on a small labeled task-specific dataset. (This general approach is called **transfer learning**, see Section 19.2 for details.)

If our primary goal is to compute useful representations for transfer learning, as opposed to generating text, we can replace the generative sequence model with non-causal models that can compute a representation of a sentence, but cannot generate it. These models have the advantage that now the hidden state $\boldsymbol{h}_t$ can depend on the past, $\boldsymbol{y}_{1:t-1}$, present $\boldsymbol{y}_t$, and future, $\boldsymbol{y}_{t+1:T}$. This can sometimes result in better representations, since it takes into account more context.

In the sections below, we briefly discuss some unsupervised models for representation learning on text, using both causal and non-causal models.

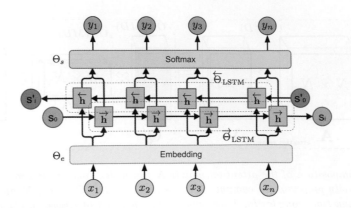

Figure 15.32: Illustration of ELMo bidirectional language model. Here $y_t = x_{t+1}$ when acting as the target for the forwards LSTM, and $y_t = x_{t-1}$ for the backwards LSTM. (We add bos *and* eos *sentinels to handle the edge cases.) From [Wen19]. Used with kind permission of Lilian Weng.*

15.7.1   ELMo

In [Pet+18], they present a method called **ELMo**, which is short for "Embeddings from Language Model". The basic idea is to fit two RNN language models, one left-to-right, and one right-to-left, and then to combine their hidden state representations to come up with an embedding for each word. Unlike a biRNN (Section 15.2.2), which needs an input-output pair, ELMo is trained in an unsupervised way, to minimize the negative log likelihood of the input sentence $\boldsymbol{x}_{1:T}$:

$$\mathcal{L}(\boldsymbol{\theta}) = -\sum_{t=1}^{T} \left[\log p(x_t | \boldsymbol{x}_{1:t-1}; \boldsymbol{\theta}_e, \boldsymbol{\theta}^{\rightarrow}, \boldsymbol{\theta}_s) + \log p(x_t | \boldsymbol{x}_{t+1:T}; \boldsymbol{\theta}_e, \boldsymbol{\theta}^{\leftarrow}, \boldsymbol{\theta}_s) \right] \tag{15.70}$$

where $\boldsymbol{\theta}_e$ are the shared parameters of the embedding layer, $\boldsymbol{\theta}_s$ are the shared parameters of the softmax output layer, and $\boldsymbol{\theta}^{\rightarrow}$ and $\boldsymbol{\theta}^{\leftarrow}$ are the parameters of the two RNN models. (They use LSTM RNNs, described in Section 15.2.7.2.) See Figure 15.32 for an illustration.

After training, we define the contextual representation $\boldsymbol{r}_t = [\boldsymbol{e}_t, \boldsymbol{h}_{t,1:L}^{\rightarrow}, \boldsymbol{h}_{t,1:L}^{\leftarrow}]$, where L is the number of layers in the LSTM. We then learn a task-specific set of linear weights to map this to the final context-specific embedding of each token: $\boldsymbol{r}_t^j = \boldsymbol{r}_t^{\mathsf{T}} \boldsymbol{w}^j$, where j is the task id. If we are performing a syntactic task like **part-of-speech** (**POS**) tagging (i.e., labeling each word as a noun, verb, adjective, etc), then the task will learn to put more weight on lower layers. If we are performing a semantic task like **word sense disambiguation** (**WSD**), then the task will learn to put more weight on higher layers. In both cases, we only need a small amount of task-specific labeled data, since we are just learning a single weight vector, to map from $\boldsymbol{r}_{1:T}$ to the target labels $\boldsymbol{y}_{1:T}$.

15.7.2   BERT

In this section, we describe the **BERT** model (Bidirectional Encoder Representations from Transformers) of [Dev+19]. Like ELMo, this is a non-causal model, that can be used to create representations of text, but not to generate text. In particular, it uses a transformer model to map a modified version

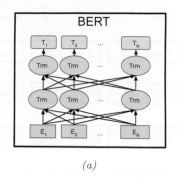 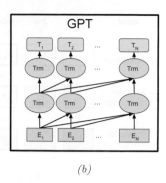

(a)   (b)

Figure 15.33: Illustration of (a) BERT and (b) GPT. E_t is the embedding vector for the input token at location t, and T_t is the output target to be predicted. From Figure 3 of [Dev+19]. Used with kind permission of Ming-Wei Chang.

of a sequence back to the unmodified form. The modified input at location t omits all words except for the t'th, and the task is to predict the missing word. This is called the **fill-in-the-blank** or **cloze** task.

15.7.2.1 Masked language model task

More precisely, the model is trained to minimize the negative log **pseudo-likelihood**:

$$\mathcal{L} = \mathbb{E}_{\boldsymbol{x} \sim \mathcal{D}} \mathbb{E}_{\boldsymbol{m}} \sum_{i \in \boldsymbol{m}} -\log p(x_i | \boldsymbol{x}_{-\boldsymbol{m}}) \tag{15.71}$$

where $\boldsymbol{m}$ is a random binary mask. For example, if we train the model on transcripts from cooking videos, we might create a training sentence of the form

```
Let's make [MASK] chicken! [SEP] It [MASK] great with orange sauce.
```

where [SEP] is a separator token inserted between two sentences. The desired target labels for the masked words are "some" and "tastes". (This example is from [Sun+19a].)

The conditional probability is given by applying a softmax to the final layer hidden vector at location i:

$$p(x_i | \hat{\boldsymbol{x}}) = \frac{\exp(\boldsymbol{h}(\hat{\boldsymbol{x}})_i^\mathsf{T} \boldsymbol{e}(x_i))}{\sum_{x'} \exp(\boldsymbol{h}(\hat{\boldsymbol{x}})_i^\mathsf{T} \boldsymbol{e}(x'))} \tag{15.72}$$

where $\hat{\boldsymbol{x}} = \boldsymbol{x}_{-\boldsymbol{m}}$ is the masked input sentence, and $\boldsymbol{e}(x)$ is the embedding for token x. This is used to compute the loss at the masked locations; this is therefore called a **masked language model**. (This is similar to a denoising autoencoder, Section 20.3.2). See Figure 15.33a for an illustration of the model.

15.7.2.2 Next sentence prediction task

In addition to the masked language model objective, the original BERT paper added an additional objective, in which the model is trained to classify if one sentence follows another. More precisely,

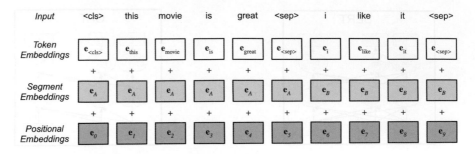

Figure 15.34: Illustration of how a pair of input sequences, denoted A and B, are encoded before feeding to BERT. From Figure 14.8.2 of [Zha+20]. Used with kind permission of Aston Zhang.

the model is fed as input

$$\text{CLS } A_1 \ A_2; \dots \ A_m; \ \text{SEP } B_1 \ B_2; \dots; B_n \ \text{SEP} \tag{15.73}$$

where SEP is a special separator token, and CLS is a special token marking the class. If sentence B follows A in the original text, we set the target label to $y = 1$, but if B is a randomly chosen sentence, we set the target label to $y = 0$. This is called the **next sentence prediction** task. This kind of pre-training can be useful for sentence-pair classification tasks, such as textual entailment or textual similarity, which we discussed in Section 15.4.6. (Note that this kind of pre-training is considered unsupervised, or self-supervised, since the target labels are automatically generated.)

When performing next sentence prediction, the input to the model is specified using 3 different embeddings: one per token, one for each segment label (sentence A or B), and one per location (using a learned positional embedding). These are then added. See Figure 15.34 for an illustration. BERT then uses a transformer encoder to learn a mapping from this input embedding sequence to an output embedding sequence, which gets decoded into word labels (for the masked locations) or a class label (for the CLS location).

15.7.2.3   Fine-tuning BERT for NLP applications

After pre-training BERT in an unsupervised way, we can use it for various downtream tasks by performing supervised fine-tuning. (See Section 19.2 for more background on such transfer learning methods.) Figure 15.35 illustrates how we can modify a BERT model to perform different tasks, by simply adding one or more new output heads to the final hidden layer. See bert_jax.ipynb for some sample code.

In Figure 15.35(a), we show how we can tackle single sentence classification (e.g., sentiment analysis): we simply take the feature vector associated with the dummy CLS token and feed it into an MLP. Since each output attends to all inputs, this hidden vector will summarize the entire sentence. The MLP then learns to map this to the desired label space.

In Figure 15.35(b), we show how we can tackle sentence-pair classification (e.g., textual entailment, as discussed in Section 15.4.6): we just feed in the two input sentences, formatted as in Equation (15.73), and then classify the CLS token.

In Figure 15.35(c), we show how we can tackle single sentence tagging, in which we associate a

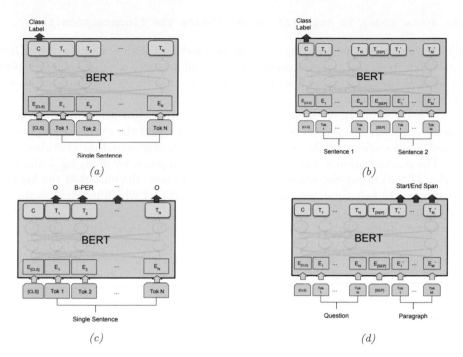

Figure 15.35: Illustration of how BERT can be used for different kinds of supervised NLP tasks. (a) Single sentence classification (e.g., sentiment analysis); (b) Sentence-pair classification (e.g., textual entailment); (c) Single sentence tagging (e.g., shallow parsing); (d) Question answering. From Figure 4 of [Dev+19]. Used with kind permission of Ming-Wei Chang.

label or tag with each word, instead of just the entire sentence. A common application of this is part of speech tagging, in which we annotate each words a noun, verb, adjective, etc. Another application of this is **noun phrase chunking**, also called **shallow parsing**, in which we must annotate the span of each noun phrase. The span is encoded using the **BIO** notation, in which B is the beginning of an entity, I-x is for inside, and O is for outside any entity. For example, consider the following sentence:

```
B       I       O     O     O         B    I         O   B    I    I
British Airways rose after announcing its withdrawl from the UAI deal
```

We see that there are 3 noun phrases, "British Airways", "its withdrawl" and "the UAI deal". (We require that the B, I and O labels occur in order, so this a prior constraint that can be included in the model.)

We can also associate types with each noun phrase, for example distinguishing person, location, organization, and other. Thus the label space becomes {B-Per, I-Per, B-Loc, I-Loc, B-Org, I-Org, Outside }. This is called **named entity recognition**, and is a key step in **information extraction**. For example, consider the following sentence:

```
BP  IP    O   O     O  BL  IL   BP   O    O    O        O
```

```
Mrs Green spoke today in New York. Green chairs the finance committee.
```

From this, we infer that the first sentence has two named entities, namely "Mrs Green" (of type Person) and "New York" (of type Location). The second sentence mentions another person, "Green", that most likely is the same as the first person, although this across-sentence entity resolution is not part of the basic NER task.

Finally, in Figure 15.35(d), we show how we can tackle **question answering**. Here the first input sentence is the question, the second is the background text, and the output is required to specifying the start and end locations of the relevant part of the background that contains the answer (see Table 1.4). The start location s and end location e are computed by applying 2 different MLPs to a pooled version of the output encodings for the background text; the output of the MLPs is a softmax over all locations. At test time, we can extract the span (i, j) which maximizes the sum of scores $s_i + e_j$ for $i \leq j$.

BERT achieves state-of-the-art performance on many NLP tasks. Interestingly, [TDP19] shows that BERT implicitly rediscovers the standard NLP pipeline, in which different layers perform tasks such as part of speech (POS) tagging, parsing, named entity relationship (NER) detection, semantic role labeling (SRL), coreference resolution, etc. More details on NLP can be found in [JM20].

15.7.3   GPT

In [Rad+18], they propose a model called **GPT**, which is short for "Generative Pre-training Transformer". This is a causal (generative) model, that uses a masked transformer as the decoder. See Figure 15.33b for an illustration.

In the original GPT paper, they jointly optimize on a large unlabeled dataset, and a small labeled dataset. In the classification setting, the loss is given by $\mathcal{L} = \mathcal{L}_{\text{cls}} + \lambda \mathcal{L}_{\text{LM}}$, where $\mathcal{L}_{\text{cls}} = -\sum_{(\boldsymbol{x},y) \in \mathcal{D}_L} \log p(y|\boldsymbol{x})$ is the classification loss on the labeled data, and $\mathcal{L}_{\text{LM}} = -\sum_{\boldsymbol{x} \in \mathcal{D}_U} \sum_t p(x_t | \boldsymbol{x}_{1:t-1})$ is the language modeling loss on the unlabeled data.

In [Rad+19], they propose **GPT-2**, which is a larger version of GPT, trained on a large web corpus called **WebText**. They also eliminate any task-specific training, and instead just train it as a language model. More recently, OpenAI released **GPT-3** [Bro+20], which is an even larger version of GPT-2, but based on the same principles. An open-source version of the model is available at https://huggingface.co/EleutherAI, which was trained on an 800GB English-language web corpus called "**The Pile**" [Gao+20].

15.7.3.1   Applications of GPT

GPT can generate text given an initial input **prompt**. The prompt can specify a task; if the generated response fulfills the task "out of the box", we say the model is performing **zero-shot task transfer** (see Section 19.6 for details).

For example, to perform **abstractive summarization** of some input text $\boldsymbol{x}_{1:T}$ (as opposed to **extractive summarization**, which just selects a subset of the input words), we sample from $p(\boldsymbol{x}_{T+1:T+100} | [\boldsymbol{x}_{1:T}; \text{TL;DR}])$, where **TL;DR** is a special token added to the end of the input text, which tells the system the user wants a summary. TL;DR stands for "too long; didn't read" and frequently occurs in webtext followed by a human-created summary. By adding this token to the input, the user hopes to "trigger" the transformer decoder into a state in which it enters summarization

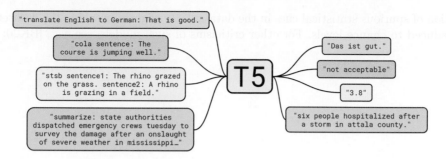

Figure 15.36: Illustration of how the T5 model ("Text-to-text Transfer Transformer") can be used to perform multiple NLP tasks, such as translating English to German; determining if a sentence is linguistic valid or not (**CoLA** stands for "Corpus of Linguistic Acceptability"); determining the degree of semantic similarity (**STSB** stands for "Semantic Textual Similarity Benchmark"); and abstractive summarization. From Figure 1 of [Raf+20]. Used with kind permission of Colin Raffel.

mode. (A better way to tell the model what task to perform is to train it on input-output pairs, as discussed in Section 15.7.4.)

15.7.4 T5

Many models are trained in an unsupervised way, and then fine-tuned on specific tasks. It is also possible to train a single model to perform multiple tasks, by telling the system what task to perform as part of the input sentence, and then training it as a seq2seq model, as illustrated in Figure 15.36. This is the approach used in **T5** [Raf+20], which stands for "Text-to-text Transfer Transformer". The model is a standard seq2seq transformer, that is pretrained on unsupervised (x', x'') pairs, where x' is a masked version of x and x'' are the missing tokens that need to be predicted, and then fine-tuned on multiple supervised (x, y) pairs.

The unsupervised data comes from **C4**, or the "Colossal Clean Crawled Corpus", a 750GB corpus of web text. This is used for pretraining using a BERT-like denoising objective. For example, the sentence $x =$"Thank you for inviting me to your party last week" may get converted to the input $x' =$ "Thank you <X> me to your party <Y> week" and the output (target) $x'' =$ "<X> for inviting <Y> last <EOS>", where $< X >$ and $< Y >$ are tokens that are unique to this example. The supervised datasets are manually created, and are taken from the literature. This approach is currently the state-of-the-art on many NLP tasks.

15.7.5 Discussion

Giant language models, such as BERT and GPT-3, have recently generated a lot of interest, and have even made their way into the mainstream media.[7] However, there is some doubt about whether such systems "understand" language in any meaningful way, beyond just rearranging word patterns seen in their massive training sets. For example, [NK19] show that the ability of BERT to perform almost as well as humans on the Argument Reasoning Comprehension Task is "entirely accounted for by

---

7. See e.g., https://www.nytimes.com/2020/11/24/science/artificial-intelligence-ai-gpt3.html.

exploitation of spurious statistical cues in the dataset". By slightly tweaking the dataset, performance can be reduced to chance levels. For other criticisms of such models, see e.g., [BK20; Mar20].

PART IV

Nonparametric Models

16 Exemplar-based Methods

So far in this book, we have mostly focused on **parametric models**, either unconditional $p(\boldsymbol{y}|\boldsymbol{\theta})$ or conditional $p(\boldsymbol{y}|\boldsymbol{x}, \boldsymbol{\theta})$, where $\boldsymbol{\theta}$ is a fixed-dimensional vector of parameters. The parameters are estimated from a variable-sized dataset, $\mathcal{D} = \{(\boldsymbol{x}_n, \boldsymbol{y}_n) : n = 1 : N\}$, but after model fitting, the data is thrown away.

In this section we consider various kinds of **nonparametric models**, that keep the training data around. Thus the effective number of parameters of the model can grow with $|\mathcal{D}|$. We focus on models that can be defined in terms of the **similarity** between a test input, $\boldsymbol{x}$, and each of the training inputs, $\boldsymbol{x}_n$. Alternatively, we can define the models in terms of a dissimilarity or distance function $d(\boldsymbol{x}, \boldsymbol{x}_n)$. Since the models keep the training examples around at test time, we call them **exemplar-based models**. (This approach is also called **instance-based learning** [AKA91], or **memory-based learning**.)

16.1 K nearest neighbor (KNN) classification

In this section, we discuss one of the simplest kind of classifier, known as the **K nearest neighbor (KNN)** classifier. The idea is as follows: to classify a new input $\boldsymbol{x}$, we find the K closest examples to $\boldsymbol{x}$ in the training set, denoted $N_K(\boldsymbol{x}, \mathcal{D})$, and then look at their labels, to derive a distribution over the outputs for the local region around $\boldsymbol{x}$. More precisely, we compute

$$p(y = c | \boldsymbol{x}, \mathcal{D}) = \frac{1}{K} \sum_{n \in N_K(\boldsymbol{x}, \mathcal{D})} \mathbb{I}(y_n = c) \tag{16.1}$$

We can then return this distribution, or the majority label.

The two main parameters in the model are the size of the neighborhood, K, and the distance metric $d(\boldsymbol{x}, \boldsymbol{x}')$. For the latter, it is common to use the **Mahalanobis distance**

$$d_{\mathbf{M}}(\boldsymbol{x}, \boldsymbol{\mu}) = \sqrt{(\boldsymbol{x} - \boldsymbol{\mu})^{\mathsf{T}} \mathbf{M} (\boldsymbol{x} - \boldsymbol{\mu})} \tag{16.2}$$

where $\mathbf{M}$ is a positive definite matrix. If $\mathbf{M} = \mathbf{I}$, this reduces to Euclidean distance. We discuss how to learn the distance metric in Section 16.2.

Despite the simplicity of KNN classifiers, it can be shown that this approach becomes within a factor of 2 of the Bayes error (which measures the performance of the best possible classifier) if $N \to \infty$ [CH67; CD14]. (Of course the convergence rate to this optimal performance may be poor in practice, for reasons we discuss in Section 16.1.2.)

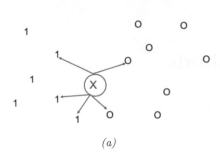
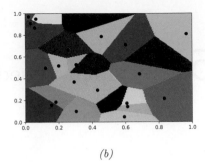

(a)   (b)

Figure 16.1: (a) Illustration of a K-nearest neighbors classifier in 2d for $K = 5$. The nearest neighbors of test point $\boldsymbol{x}$ have labels $\{1, 1, 1, 0, 0\}$, so we predict $p(y = 1|\boldsymbol{x}, \mathcal{D}) = 3/5$. (b) Illustration of the Voronoi tessellation induced by 1-NN. Adapted from Figure 4.13 of [DHS01]. Generated by knn_voronoi_plot.ipynb.

16.1.1   Example

We illustrate the KNN classifier in 2d in Figure 16.1(a) for $K = 5$. The test point is marked as an "x". 3 of the 5 nearest neighbors have label 1, and 2 of the 5 have label 0. Hence we predict $p(y = 1|\boldsymbol{x}, \mathcal{D}) = 3/5 = 0.6$.

If we use $K = 1$, we just return the label of the nearest neighbor, so the predictive distribution becomes a delta function. A KNN classifier with $K = 1$ induces a **Voronoi tessellation** of the points (see Figure 16.1(b)). This is a partition of space which associates a region $V(\boldsymbol{x}_n)$ with each point $\boldsymbol{x}_n$ in such a way that all points in $V(\boldsymbol{x}_n)$ are closer to $\boldsymbol{x}_n$ than to any other point. Within each cell, the predicted label is the label of the corresponding training point. Thus the training error will be 0 when $K = 1$. However, such a model is usually overfitting the training set, as we show below.

Figure 16.2 gives an example of KNN applied to a 2d dataset, in which we have three classes. We see how, with $K = 1$, the method makes zero errors on the training set. As K increases, the decision boundaries become smoother (since we are averaging over larger neighborhoods), so the training error increases, as we start to underfit. This is shown in Figure 16.2(d). The test error shows the usual U-shaped curve.

16.1.2   The curse of dimensionality

The main statistical problem with KNN classifiers is that they do not work well with high dimensional inputs, due to the **curse of dimensionality**.

The basic problem is that the volume of space grows exponentially fast with dimension, so you might have to look quite far away in space to find your nearest neighbor. To make this more precise, consider this example from [HTF09, p22]. Suppose we apply a KNN classifier to data where the inputs are uniformly distributed in the D-dimensional unit cube. Suppose we estimate the density of class labels around a test point $\boldsymbol{x}$ by "growing" a hyper-cube around $\boldsymbol{x}$ until it contains a desired fraction p of the data points. The expected edge length of this cube will be $e_D(s) \triangleq p^{1/D}$; this function is plotted in Figure 16.3(b). If $D = 10$, and we want to base our estimate on 10% of the

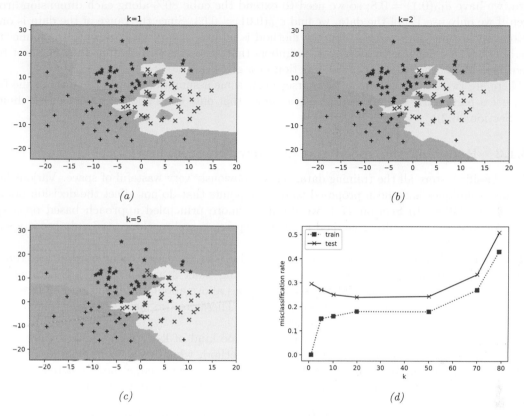

Figure 16.2: *Decision boundaries induced by a KNN classifier.* (a) $K = 1$. (b) $K = 2$. (c) $K = 5$. (d) *Train and test error vs* K. *Generated by* knn_classify_demo.ipynb.

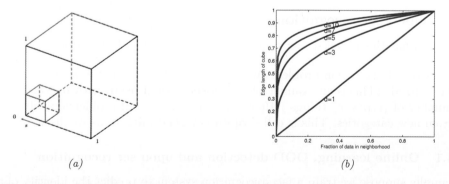

Figure 16.3: *Illustration of the curse of dimensionality.* (a) *We embed a small cube of side* s *inside a larger unit cube.* (b) *We plot the edge length of a cube needed to cover a given volume of the unit cube as a function of the number of dimensions. Adapted from Figure 2.6 from [HTF09]. Generated by* curse_dimensionality_plot.ipynb.

data, we have $e_{10}(0.1) = 0.8$, so we need to extend the cube 80% along each dimension around $\boldsymbol{x}$. Even if we only use 1% of the data, we find $e_{10}(0.01) = 0.63$. Since the range of the data is only 0 to 1 along each dimension, we see that the method is no longer very local, despite the name "nearest neighbor". The trouble with looking at neighbors that are so far away is that they may not be good predictors about the behavior of the function at a given point.

There are two main solutions to the curse: make some assumptions about the form of the function (i.e., use a parametric model), and/or use a metric that only cares about a subset of the dimensions (see Section 16.2).

16.1.3 Reducing the speed and memory requirements

KNN classifiers store all the training data. This is obviously very wasteful of space. Various heuristic pruning techniques have been proposed to remove points that do not affect the decision boundaries, see e.g., [WM00]. In Section 17.4, we discuss a more principled approach based on a sparsity promoting prior; the resulting method is called a sparse kernel machine, and only keeps a subset of the most useful exemplars.

In terms of running time, the challenge is to find the K nearest neighbors in less than $O(N)$ time, where N is the size of the training set. Finding exact nearest neighbors is computationally intractable when the dimensionality of the space goes above about 10 dimensions, so most methods focus on finding the approximate nearest neighbors. There are two main classes of techniques, based on partitioning space into regions, or using hashing.

For partitioning methods, one can either use some kind of **k-d tree**, which divides space into axis-parallel regions, or some kind of clustering method, which uses anchor points. For hashing methods, **locality sensitive hashing** (**LSH**) [GIM99] is widely used, although more recent methods learn the hashing function from data (see e.g., [Wan+15]). See [LRU14] for a good introduction to hashing methods.

An open-source library called **FAISS**, for efficient exact and approximate nearest neighbor search (and K-means clustering) of dense vectors, is available at `https://github.com/facebookresearch/faiss`, and described in [JDJ17].

16.1.4 Open set recognition

> Ask not what this is called, ask what this is like. — Moshe Bar.[Bar09]

In all of the classification problems we have considered so far, we have assumed that the set of classes $\mathcal{C}$ is fixed. (This is an example of the **closed world assumption**, which assumes there is a fixed number of (types of) things.) However, many real world problems involve test samples that come from new categories. This is called **open set recognition**, as we discuss below.

16.1.4.1 Online learning, OOD detection and open set recognition

For example, suppose we train a face recognition system to predict the identity of a person from a fixed set or **gallery** of face images. Let $\mathcal{D}_t = \{(\boldsymbol{x}_n, y_n) : \boldsymbol{x}_n \in \mathcal{X}, y_n \in \mathcal{C}_t, n = 1 : N_t\}$ be the labeled dataset at time t, where $\mathcal{X}$ is the set of (face) images, and $\mathcal{C}_t = \{1, \dots, C_t\}$ is the set of people known to the system at time t (where $C_t \leq t$). At test time, the system may encounter a new person that it has not seen before. Let $\boldsymbol{x}_{t+1}$ be this new image, and $y_{t+1} = C_{t+1}$ be its new label. The system needs to recognize that the input is from a new category, and not accidentally classify it with a label from $\mathcal{C}_t$. This is called **novelty detection**. In this case, the input is being generated from the distribution $p(\boldsymbol{x}|y = C_{t+1})$, where $C_{t+1} \notin \mathcal{C}_t$ is the new "class label". Detecting that $\boldsymbol{x}_{t+1}$ is from a novel class may be hard if the appearance of this new image is similar to the appearance of any of the existing images in $\mathcal{D}_t$.

If the system is successful at detecting that $\boldsymbol{x}_{t+1}$ is novel, then it may ask for the id of this new instance, call it C_{t+1}. It can then add the labeled pair $(\boldsymbol{x}_{t+1}, C_{t+1})$ to the dataset to create $\mathcal{D}_{t+1}$, and can grow the set of unique classes by adding C_{t+1} to $\mathcal{C}_t$ (c.f., [JK13]). This is called **incremental learning**, **online learning**, **life-long learning**, or **continual learning**. At future time points, the system may encounter an image sampled from $p(\boldsymbol{x}|y = c)$, where c is an existing class, or where c is a new class, or the image may be sampled from some entirely different kind of distribution $p'(\boldsymbol{x})$ unrelated to faces (e.g., someone uploads a photo of their dog). (Detecting this latter kind of event is called **out-of-distribution** or **OOD** detection.)

In this online setting, we often only get a few (sometimes just one) example of each class. Prediction in this setting is known as **few-shot classification**, and is discussed in more detail in Section 19.6. KNN classifiers are well-suited to this task. For example, we can just store all the instances of each class in a gallery of examples, as we explained above. At time $t + 1$, when we get input $\boldsymbol{x}_{t+1}$, rather than predicting a label for $\boldsymbol{x}_{t+1}$ by comparing it to some parametric model for each class, we just find the example in the gallery that is nearest (most similar) to $\boldsymbol{x}_{t+1}$, call it $\boldsymbol{x}'$. We then need to determine if $\boldsymbol{x}'$ and $\boldsymbol{x}_{t+1}$ are sufficiently similar to constitute a match. (In the context of person classification, this is known as **person re-identification** or **face verification**, see e.g., [WSH16]).) If there is no match, we can declare the input to be novel or OOD.

The key ingredient for all of the above problems is the (dis)similarity metric between inputs. We discuss ways to learn this in Section 16.2.

16.1.4.2 Other open world problems

The problem of open-set recognition, and incremental learning, are just examples of problems that require the **open world assumption** c.f., [Rus15]. There are many other examples of such problems.

For example, consider the problem of **entity resolution**, called **entity linking**. In this problem, we need to determine if different strings (e.g., "John Smith" and "Jon Smith") refer to the same entity or not. See e.g. [SHF15] for details.

Another important application is in **multi-object tracking**. For example, when a radar system detects a new "blip", is it due to an existing missile that is being tracked, or is it a new objective that has entered the airspace? An elegant mathematical framework for dealing with such problems, known as **random finite sets**, is described in [Mah07; Mah13; Vo+15].

16.2 Learning distance metrics

Being able to compute the "semantic distance" between a pair of points, $d(\boldsymbol{x}, \boldsymbol{x}') \in \mathbb{R}^+$ for $\boldsymbol{x}, \boldsymbol{x}' \in \mathcal{X}$, or equivalently their similarity $s(\boldsymbol{x}, \boldsymbol{x}') \in \mathbb{R}^+$, is of crucial importance to tasks such as nearest neighbor classification (Section 16.1), self-supervised learning (Section 19.2.4.4), similarity-based clustering (Section 21.5), content-based retrieval, visual tracking, etc.

When the input space is $\mathcal{X} = \mathbb{R}^D$, the most common distance metric is the Mahalanobis distance

$$d_{\mathbf{M}}(\boldsymbol{x}, \boldsymbol{x}') = \sqrt{(\boldsymbol{x} - \boldsymbol{x}')^{\mathsf{T}} \mathbf{M} (\boldsymbol{x} - \boldsymbol{x}')} \tag{16.3}$$

We discuss some methods to learn the matrix $\mathbf{M}$ in Section 16.2.1. For high dimensional inputs, or structured inputs, it is better to first learn an embedding $\boldsymbol{e} = f(\boldsymbol{x})$, and then to compute distances in embedding space. When f is a DNN, this is called **deep metric learning**; we discuss this in Section 16.2.2.

16.2.1   Linear and convex methods

In this section, we discuss some methods that try to learn the Mahalanobis distance matrix $\mathbf{M}$, either directly (as a convex problem), or indirectly via a linear projection. For other approaches to metric learning, see e.g., [Kul13; Kim19] for more details.

16.2.1.1   Large margin nearest neighbors

In [WS09], they propose to learn the Mahalanobis matrix $\mathbf{M}$ so that the resulting distance metric works well when used by a nearest neighbor classifier. The resulting method is called **large margin nearest neighbor** or **LMNN**.

This works as follows. For each example data point i, let N_i be a set of **target neighbors**; these are usually chosen to be the set of K points with the same class label that are closest in Euclidean distance. We now optimize $\mathbf{M}$ so that we minimize the distance between each point i and all of its target neighbors $j \in N_i$:

$$\mathcal{L}_{\text{pull}}(\mathbf{M}) = \sum_{i=1}^{N} \sum_{j \in N_i} d_{\mathbf{M}}(\boldsymbol{x}_i, \boldsymbol{x}_j)^2 \tag{16.4}$$

We also want to ensure that examples with incorrect labels are far away. To do this, we ensure that each example i is closer (by some margin $m \geq 0$) to its target neighbors j than to other points l with different labels (so-called **impostors**). We can do this by minimizing

$$\mathcal{L}_{\text{push}}(\mathbf{M}) = \sum_{i=1}^{N} \sum_{j \in N_i} \sum_{l=1}^{N} \mathbb{I}(y_i \neq y_l) \left[m + d_{\mathbf{M}}(\boldsymbol{x}_i, \boldsymbol{x}_j)^2 - d_{\mathbf{M}}(\boldsymbol{x}_i, \boldsymbol{x}_l)^2 \right]_+ \tag{16.5}$$

where $[z]_+ = \max(z, 0)$ is the hinge loss function (Section 4.3.2). The overall objective is $\mathcal{L}(\mathbf{M}) = (1 - \lambda) \mathcal{L}_{\text{pull}}(\mathbf{M}) + \lambda \mathcal{L}_{\text{push}}(\mathbf{M})$, where $0 < \lambda < 1$. This is a convex function defined over a convex set, which can be minimized using **semidefinite programming**. Alternatively, we can parameterize the problem using $\mathbf{M} = \mathbf{W}^{\mathsf{T}} \mathbf{W}$, and then minimize wrt $\mathbf{W}$ using unconstrained gradient methods. This is no longer convex, but allows us to use a low-dimensional mapping $\mathbf{W}$.

For large datasets, we need to tackle the $O(N^3)$ cost of computing Equation (16.5). We discuss some speedup tricks in Section 16.2.5.

16.2.1.2   Neighborhood components analysis

Another way to learn a linear mapping $\mathbf{W}$ such that $\mathbf{M} = \mathbf{W}^{\mathsf{T}} \mathbf{W}$ is known as **neighborhood components analysis** or **NCA** [Gol+05]. This defines the probability that sample $\boldsymbol{x}_i$ has $\boldsymbol{x}_j$ as its

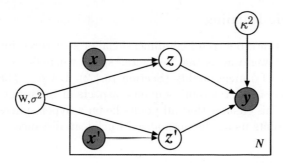

Figure 16.4: Illustration of latent coincidence analysis (LCA) as a directed graphical model. The inputs $\boldsymbol{x}, \boldsymbol{x}' \in \mathbb{R}^D$ are mapped into Gaussian latent variables $\boldsymbol{z}, \boldsymbol{z}' \in \mathbb{R}^L$ via a linear mapping $\mathbf{W}$. If the two latent points coincide (within length scale κ) then we set the similarity label to $y = 1$, otherwise we set it to $y = 0$. From Figure 1 of [DS12]. Used with kind permission of Lawrence Saul.

nearest neighbor using the linear softmax function

$$p_{ij}^{\mathbf{W}} = \frac{\exp(-||\mathbf{W}\boldsymbol{x}_i - \mathbf{W}\boldsymbol{x}_j||_2^2)}{\sum_{l \neq i} \exp(-||\mathbf{W}\boldsymbol{x}_i - \mathbf{W}\boldsymbol{x}_l||_2^2)} \tag{16.6}$$

(This is a supervised version of stochastic neighborhood embeddings discussed in Section 20.4.10.1.) The expected number of correctly classified examples according for a 1NN classifier using distance $\mathbf{W}$ is given by $J(\mathbf{W}) = \sum_{i=1}^{N} \sum_{j \neq i: y_j = y_i} p_{ij}^{\mathbf{W}}$. Let $\mathcal{L}(\mathbf{W}) = 1 - J(\mathbf{W})/N$ be the leave one out error. We can minimize $\mathcal{L}$ wrt $\mathbf{W}$ using gradient methods.

16.2.1.3   Latent coincidence analysis

Yet another way to learn a linear mapping $\mathbf{W}$ such that $\mathbf{M} = \mathbf{W}^\mathsf{T}\mathbf{W}$ is known as **latent coincidence analysis** or **LCA** [DS12]. This defines a conditional latent variable model for mapping a pair of inputs, $\boldsymbol{x}$ and $\boldsymbol{x}'$, to a label $y \in \{0, 1\}$, which specifies if the inputs are similar (e.g., have same class label) or dissimilar. Each input $\boldsymbol{x} \in \mathbb{R}^D$ is mapped to a low dimensional latent point $\boldsymbol{z} \in \mathbb{R}^L$ using a stochastic mapping $p(\boldsymbol{z}|\boldsymbol{x}) = \mathcal{N}(\boldsymbol{z}|\mathbf{W}\boldsymbol{x}, \sigma^2\mathbf{I})$, and $p(\boldsymbol{z}'|\boldsymbol{x}') = \mathcal{N}(\boldsymbol{z}'|\mathbf{W}\boldsymbol{x}', \sigma^2\mathbf{I})$. (Compare this to factor analysis, discussed in Section 20.2.) We then define the probability that the two inputs are similar using $p(y = 1|\boldsymbol{z}, \boldsymbol{z}') = \exp(-\frac{1}{2\kappa^2}||\boldsymbol{z} - \boldsymbol{z}'||)$. See Figure 16.4 for an illustration of the modeling assumptions.

We can maximize the log marginal likelihood $\ell(\mathbf{W}, \sigma^2, \kappa^2) = \sum_n \log p(y_n|\boldsymbol{x}_n, \boldsymbol{x}'_n)$ using the EM algorithm (Section 8.7.2). (We can set $\kappa = 1$ WLOG, since it just changes the scale of $\mathbf{W}$.) More precisely, in the E step, we compute the posterior $p(\boldsymbol{z}, \boldsymbol{z}'|\boldsymbol{x}, \boldsymbol{x}', y)$ (which can be done in closed form), and in the M step, we solve a weighted least squares problem (c.f., Section 13.6.2). EM will monotonically increase the objective, and does not need step size adjustment, unlike the gradient based methods used in NCA (Section 16.2.1.2). (It is also possible to use variational Bayes (Section 4.6.8.3) to fit this model, as well as various sparse and nonlinear extensions, as discussed in [ZMY19].)

16.2.2   Deep metric learning

When measuring the distance between high-dimensional or structured inputs, it is very useful to first learn an embedding to a lower dimensional "semantic" space, where distances are more meaningful, and less subject to the curse of dimensionality (Section 16.1.2). Let $\boldsymbol{e} = f(\boldsymbol{x}; \boldsymbol{\theta}) \in \mathbb{R}^L$ be an embedding of the input that preserves the "relevant" semantic aspects of the input, and let $\hat{\boldsymbol{e}} = \boldsymbol{e}/\|\boldsymbol{e}\|_2$ be the ℓ_2-normalized version. This ensures that all points lie on a hyper-sphere. We can then measure the distance between two points using the normalized Euclidean distance

$$d(\boldsymbol{x}_i, \boldsymbol{x}_j; \boldsymbol{\theta}) = \|\hat{\boldsymbol{e}}_i - \hat{\boldsymbol{e}}_j\|_2^2 \tag{16.7}$$

where smaller values means more similar, or the cosine similarity

$$d(\boldsymbol{x}_i, \boldsymbol{x}_j; \boldsymbol{\theta}) = \hat{\boldsymbol{e}}_i^{\mathsf{T}} \hat{\boldsymbol{e}}_j \tag{16.8}$$

where larger values means more similar. (Cosine similarity measures the angle between the two vectors, as illustrated in Figure 20.43.) These quantities are related via

$$\|\hat{\boldsymbol{e}}_i - \hat{\boldsymbol{e}}_j\|_2^2 = (\hat{\boldsymbol{e}}_i - \hat{\boldsymbol{e}}_j)^{\mathsf{T}} (\hat{\boldsymbol{e}}_i - \hat{\boldsymbol{e}}_j) = 2 - 2\hat{\boldsymbol{e}}_i^{\mathsf{T}} \hat{\boldsymbol{e}}_j \tag{16.9}$$

This overall approach is called **deep metric learning** or DML.

The basic idea in DML is to learn the embedding function such that similar examples are closer than dissimilar examples. More precisely, we assume we have a labeled dataset, $\mathcal{D} = \{(\boldsymbol{x}_i, y_i) : i = 1 : N\}$, from which we can derive a set of similar pairs, $\mathcal{S} = \{(i, j) : y_i = y_j\}$. If $(i, j) \in \mathcal{S}$ but $(i, k) \notin S$, then we assume that $\boldsymbol{x}_i$ and $\boldsymbol{x}_j$ should be close in embedding space, whereas $\boldsymbol{x}_i$ and $\boldsymbol{x}_k$ should be far. We discuss various ways to enforce this property below. Note that these methods also work when we do not have class labels, provided we have some other way of defining similar pairs. For example, in Section 19.2.4.3, we discuss self-supervised approaches to representation learning, that automatically create semantically similar pairs, and learn embeddings to force these pairs to be closer than unrelated pairs.

Before discussing DML in more detail, it is worth mentioning that many recent approaches to DML are not as good as they claim to be, as pointed out in [MBL20; Rot+20]. (The claims in some of these papers are often invalid due to improper experimental comparisons, a common flaw in contemporary ML research, as discussed in e.g., [BLV19; LS19b].) We therefore focus on (slightly) older and simpler methods, that tend to be more robust.

16.2.3   Classification losses

Suppose we have labeled data with C classes. Then we can fit a classification model in $O(NC)$ time, and then reuse the hidden features as an embedding function. (It is common to use the second-to-last layer, since it generalizes better to new classes than the final layer.) This approach is simple and scalable. However, it only learns to embed examples on the correct side of a decision boundary, which does not necessarily result in similar examples being placed close together and dissimilar examples being placed far apart. In addition, this method cannot be used if we do not have labeled training data.

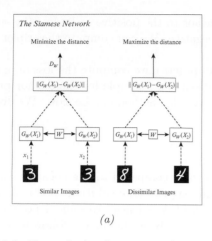

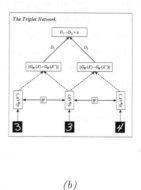

(a)   *(b)*

Figure 16.5: *Networks for deep metric learning. (a) Siamese network. (b) Triplet network. Adapted from Figure 5 of [KB19].*

16.2.4 Ranking losses

In this section, we consider minimizing **ranking loss**, to ensure that similar examples are closer than dissimilar examples. Most of these methods do not need class labels (although we sometimes assume that labels exist as a notationally simple way to define similarity).

16.2.4.1 Pairwise (contrastive) loss and Siamese networks

One of the earliest approaches to representation learning from similar/dissimilar pairs was based on minimizing the following **contrastive loss** [CHL05]:

$$\mathcal{L}(\boldsymbol{\theta}; \boldsymbol{x}_i, \boldsymbol{x}_j) = \mathbb{I}(y_i = y_j) \, d(\boldsymbol{x}_i, \boldsymbol{x}_j)^2 + \mathbb{I}(y_i \neq y_j) \, [m - d(\boldsymbol{x}_i, \boldsymbol{x}_j)]_+^2 \tag{16.10}$$

where $[z]_+ = \max(0, z)$ is the hinge loss and $m > 0$ is a margin parameter. Intuitively, we want to force positive pairs (with the same label) to be close, and negative pairs (with different labels) to be further apart than some minimal safety margin. We minimize this loss over all pairs of data. Naively this takes $O(N^2)$ time; see Section 16.2.5 for some speedups.

Note that we use the same feature extractor $\boldsymbol{f}(\cdot; \boldsymbol{\theta})$ for both inputs, $\boldsymbol{x}_i$ and $\boldsymbol{x}_j$. when computing the distance, as illustrated in Figure 16.5a. The resulting network is therefore called a **Siamese network** (named after Siamese twins).

16.2.4.2 Triplet loss

One disadvantage of pairwise losses is that the optimization of the positive pairs is independent of the negative pairs, which can make their magnitudes incomparable. A solution to this is to use the **triplet loss** [SKP15]. This is defined as follows. For each example i (known as an **anchor**), we find a similar (positive) example $\boldsymbol{x}_i^+$ and a dissimilar (negative) example $\boldsymbol{x}_i^-$. We then minimize the following loss, averaged overall all triples:

$$\mathcal{L}(\boldsymbol{\theta}; \boldsymbol{x}_i, \boldsymbol{x}_i^+, \boldsymbol{x}_i^-) = [d_{\boldsymbol{\theta}}(\boldsymbol{x}_i, \boldsymbol{x}_i^+)^2 - d_{\boldsymbol{\theta}}(\boldsymbol{x}_i, \boldsymbol{x}_i^-)^2 + m]_+ \tag{16.11}$$

Intuitively this says we want the distance from the anchor to the positive to be less (by some safety margin m) than the distance from the anchor to the negative. We can compute the triplet loss using a triplet network as shown in Figure 16.5b.

Naively minimizing triplet loss takes $O(N^3)$ time. In practice we compute the loss on a minibatch (chosen so that there is at least one similar and one dissimilar example for the anchor point, often taken to be the first entry in the minibatch). Nevertheless the method can be slow. We discuss some speedups in Section 16.2.5.

16.2.4.3   N-pairs loss

One problem with the triplet loss is that each anchor is only compared to one negative example at a time. This might not provide a strong enough learning signal. One solution to this is to create a multi-class classification problem in which we create a set of $N - 1$ negatives and 1 positive for every anchor. This is called the **N-pairs loss** [Soh16]. More precisely, we define the following loss for each set:

$$\mathcal{L}(\boldsymbol{\theta}; \boldsymbol{x}, \boldsymbol{x}^+, \{\boldsymbol{x}_k^-\}_{k=1}^{N-1}) = \log\left(1 + \left[\sum_{k=1}^{N-1} \exp(\hat{\boldsymbol{e}}_{\boldsymbol{\theta}}(\boldsymbol{x})^\mathsf{T}\hat{\boldsymbol{e}}_{\boldsymbol{\theta}}(\boldsymbol{x}_k^-))\right] - \hat{\boldsymbol{e}}_{\boldsymbol{\theta}}(\boldsymbol{x})^\mathsf{T}\hat{\boldsymbol{e}}_{\boldsymbol{\theta}}(\boldsymbol{x}^+)\right) \tag{16.12}$$

$$= -\log \frac{\exp(\hat{\boldsymbol{e}}_{\boldsymbol{\theta}}(\boldsymbol{x})^\mathsf{T}\hat{\boldsymbol{e}}_{\boldsymbol{\theta}}(\boldsymbol{x}^+))}{\exp(\hat{\boldsymbol{e}}_{\boldsymbol{\theta}}(\boldsymbol{x})^\mathsf{T}\hat{\boldsymbol{e}}_{\boldsymbol{\theta}}(\boldsymbol{x}^+)) + \sum_{k=1}^{N-1}\exp(\hat{\boldsymbol{e}}_{\boldsymbol{\theta}}(\boldsymbol{x})^\mathsf{T}\hat{\boldsymbol{e}}_{\boldsymbol{\theta}}(\boldsymbol{x}_k^-))} \tag{16.13}$$

Note that the N-pairs loss is the same as the **InfoNCE** loss used in the CPC paper [OLV18]. In [Che+20a], they propose a version where they scale the similarities by a temperature term; they call this the **NT-Xent** (normalized temperature-scaled cross-entropy) loss. We can view the temperature parameter as scaling the radius of the hypersphere on which the data lives.

When $N = 2$, the loss reduces to the logistic loss

$$\mathcal{L}(\boldsymbol{\theta}; \boldsymbol{x}, \boldsymbol{x}^+, \boldsymbol{x}^-) = \log\left(1 + \exp(\hat{\boldsymbol{e}}_{\boldsymbol{\theta}}(\boldsymbol{x})^\mathsf{T}\hat{\boldsymbol{e}}_{\boldsymbol{\theta}}(\boldsymbol{x}^-) - \hat{\boldsymbol{e}}_{\boldsymbol{\theta}}(\boldsymbol{x})^\mathsf{T}\hat{\boldsymbol{e}}_{\boldsymbol{\theta}}(\boldsymbol{x}^+))\right) \tag{16.14}$$

Compare this to the margin loss used by triplet learning (when $m = 1$):

$$\mathcal{L}(\boldsymbol{\theta}; \boldsymbol{x}, \boldsymbol{x}^+, \boldsymbol{x}^-) = \max\left(0, \hat{\boldsymbol{e}}(\boldsymbol{x})^\mathsf{T}\hat{\boldsymbol{e}}(\boldsymbol{x}^-) - \hat{\boldsymbol{e}}(\boldsymbol{x})^\mathsf{T}\hat{\boldsymbol{e}}(\boldsymbol{x}^+) + 1\right) \tag{16.15}$$

See Figure 4.2 for a comparison of these two functions.

16.2.5   Speeding up ranking loss optimization

The main disadvantage of ranking loss is the $O(N^2)$ or $O(N^3)$ cost of computing the loss function, due to the need to compare all pairs or triples of examples. In this section, we discuss various speedup tricks.

16.2.5.1   Mining techniques

A key insight is that we don't need to consider all negative examples for each anchor, since most will be uninformative (i.e., will incur zero loss). Instead we can focus attention on negative examples which are closer to the anchor than its nearest positive example. These are called **hard negatives**, and are particularly useful for speeding up triplet loss.

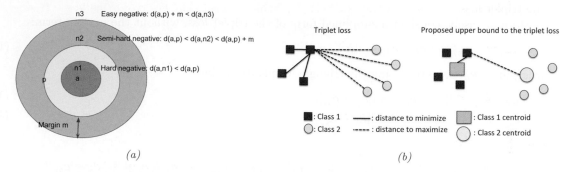

Figure 16.6: *Speeding up triplet loss minimization. (a) Illustration of hard vs easy negatives. Here a is the anchor point, p is a positive point, and n_i are negative points. Adapted from Figure 4 of [KB19]. (b) Standard triplet loss would take $8 \times 3 \times 4 = 96$ calculations, whereas using a proxy loss (with one proxy per class) takes $8 \times 2 = 16$ calculations. From Figure 1 of [Do+19]. Used with kind permission of Gustavo Cerneiro.*

More precisely, if a is an anchor and p is its nearest positive example, we say that n is a hard negative (for a) if $d(\boldsymbol{x}_a, \boldsymbol{x}_n) < d(\boldsymbol{x}_a, \boldsymbol{x}_p)$ and $y_n \neq y_a$. Sometimes an anchor may not have any hard negatives. We can therefore increase the pool of candidates by considering **semi-hard negatives**, for which

$$d(\boldsymbol{x}_a, \boldsymbol{x}_p) < d(\boldsymbol{x}_a, \boldsymbol{x}_n) < d(\boldsymbol{x}_a, \boldsymbol{x}_p) + m \tag{16.16}$$

where $m > 0$ is a margin parameter. See Figure 16.6a for an illustration. This is the technique used by Google's **FaceNet** model [SKP15], which learns an embedding function for faces, so it can cluster similar looking faces together, to which the user can attach a name.

In practice, the hard negatives are usually chosen from within the minibatch. This therefore requires large batch sizes to ensure sufficient diversity. Alternatively, we can have a separate process that continually updates the set of candidate hard negatives, as the distance measure evolves during training.

16.2.5.2 Proxy methods

Triplet loss minimization is expensive even with hard negative mining (Section 16.2.5.1). Ideally we can find a method that is $O(N)$ time, just like classification loss.

One such method, proposed in [MA+17], measures the distance between each anchor and a set of P **proxies** that represent each class, rather than directly measuring distance between examples. These proxies need to be updated online as the distance metric evolves during learning. The overall procedure takes $O(NP^2)$ time, where $P \sim C$.

More recently, [Qia+19] proposed to represent each class with multiple prototypes, while still achieving linear time complexity, using a **soft triple** loss.

16.2.5.3 Optimizing an upper bound

[Do+19] proposed a simple and fast method for optimizing the triplet loss. The key idea is to define one *fixed* proxy or centroid per class, and then to use distance to the proxy as an upper bound on the triplet loss.

More precisely, consider a simplified form of the triplet loss, without the margin term:

$$\ell_t(\boldsymbol{x}_i, \boldsymbol{x}_j, \boldsymbol{x}_k) = ||\hat{\boldsymbol{e}}_i - \hat{\boldsymbol{e}}_j|| - ||\hat{\boldsymbol{e}}_i - \hat{\boldsymbol{e}}_k|| \qquad (16.17)$$

where $\hat{\boldsymbol{e}}_i = \hat{\boldsymbol{e}}_{\boldsymbol{\theta}}(\boldsymbol{x}_i)$, etc. Using the triangle inequality we have

$$||\hat{\boldsymbol{e}}_i - \hat{\boldsymbol{e}}_j|| \le ||\hat{\boldsymbol{e}}_i - \boldsymbol{c}_{y_i}|| + ||\hat{\boldsymbol{e}}_j - \boldsymbol{c}_{y_i}|| \qquad (16.18)$$

$$||\hat{\boldsymbol{e}}_i - \hat{\boldsymbol{e}}_k|| \ge ||\hat{\boldsymbol{e}}_i - \boldsymbol{c}_{y_k}|| - ||\hat{\boldsymbol{e}}_k - \boldsymbol{c}_{y_k}|| \qquad (16.19)$$

Hence

$$\ell_t(\boldsymbol{x}_i, \boldsymbol{x}_j, \boldsymbol{x}_k) \le \ell_u(\boldsymbol{x}_i, \boldsymbol{x}_j, \boldsymbol{x}_k) \triangleq ||\hat{\boldsymbol{e}}_i - \boldsymbol{c}_{y_i}|| - ||\hat{\boldsymbol{e}}_i - \boldsymbol{c}_{y_k}|| + ||\hat{\boldsymbol{e}}_j - \boldsymbol{c}_{y_i}|| + ||\hat{\boldsymbol{e}}_k - \boldsymbol{c}_{y_k}|| \qquad (16.20)$$

We can use this to derive a tractable upper bound on the triplet loss as follows:

$$\mathcal{L}_t(\mathcal{D}, \mathcal{S}) = \sum_{(i,j) \in \mathcal{S}, (i,k) \notin \mathcal{S}, i,j,k \in \{1,\dots,N\}} \ell_t(\boldsymbol{x}_i, \boldsymbol{x}_j, \boldsymbol{x}_k) \le \sum_{(i,j) \in \mathcal{S}, (i,k) \notin \mathcal{S}, i,j,k \in \{1,\dots,N\}} \ell_u(\boldsymbol{x}_i, \boldsymbol{x}_j, \boldsymbol{x}_k)$$

$$(16.21)$$

$$= C' \sum_{i=1}^{N} \left(||\boldsymbol{x}_i - \boldsymbol{c}_{y_i}|| - \frac{1}{3(C-1)} \sum_{m=1, m \neq y_i}^{C} ||\boldsymbol{x}_i - \boldsymbol{c}_m|| \right) \triangleq \mathcal{L}_u(\mathcal{D}, \mathcal{S}) \qquad (16.22)$$

where $C' = 3(C-1)(\frac{N}{C}-1)\frac{N}{C}$ is a constant. It is clear that $\mathcal{L}_u$ can be computed in $O(NC)$ time. See Figure 16.6b for an illustration.

In [Do+19], they show that $0 \le \mathcal{L}_t - \mathcal{L}_u \le \frac{N^3}{C^2} K$, where K is some constant that depends on the spread of the centroids. To ensure the bound is tight, the centroids should be as far from each other as possible, and the distances between them should be as similar as possible. An easy way to ensure is to define the $\boldsymbol{c}_m$ vectors to be one-hot vectors, one per class. These vectors already have unit norm, and are orthogonal to each other. The distance between each pair of centroids is $\sqrt{2}$, which ensures the upper bound is fairly tight.

The downside of this approach is that it assumes the embedding layer is $L = C$ dimensional. There are two solutions to this. First, after training, we can add a linear projection layer to map from C to $L \neq C$, or we can take the second-to-last layer of the embedding network. The second approach is to sample a large number of points on the L-dimensional unit hyper-sphere (which we can do by sampling from the standard normal, and then normalizing [Mar72]), and then running K-means clustering (Section 21.3) with $K = C$. In the experiments reported in [Do+19], these two approaches give similar results.

Interestingly, in [Rot+20], they show that increasing $\pi_{\text{intra}}/\pi_{\text{inter}}$ results in improved downstream performance on various retrieval tasks, where

$$\pi_{\text{intra}} = \frac{1}{Z_{\text{intra}}} \sum_{c=1}^{C} \sum_{i \neq j: y_i = y_j = c} d(\boldsymbol{x}_i, \boldsymbol{x}_j) \qquad (16.23)$$

is the average intra-class distance, and

$$\pi_{\text{inter}} = \frac{1}{Z_{\text{inter}}} \sum_{c=1}^{C} \sum_{c'=1}^{C} d(\boldsymbol{\mu}_c, \boldsymbol{\mu}_{c'}) \qquad (16.24)$$

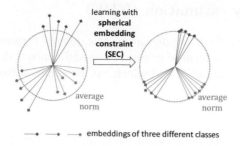

Figure 16.7: Adding spherical embedding constraint to a deep metric learning method. Used with kind permission of Dingyi Zhang.

is the average inter-class distance, where $\boldsymbol{\mu}_c = \frac{1}{Z_c} \sum_{i:y_i=c} \hat{\boldsymbol{e}}_i$ is the mean embedding for examples from class c. This suggests that we should not only keep the centroids far apart (in order to maximize the numerator), but we should also prevent examples from getting too close to their centroids (in order to minimize the denominator); this latter term is not captured in the method of [Do+19].

16.2.6 Other training tricks for DML

Besides the speedup tricks in Section 16.2.5, there are a lot of other details that are important to get right in order to ensure good DML performance. Many of these details are discussed in [MBL20; Rot+20]. Here we just briefly mention a few.

One important issue is how the minibatches are created. In classification problems (at least with balanced classes), selecting examples at random from the training set is usually sufficient. However, for DML, we need to ensure that each example has some other examples in the minibatch that are similar to it, as well as some others that are dissimilar to it. One approach is to use hard mining techniques (Section 16.2.5.1). Another idea is to use coreset methods applied to previously learned embeddings to select a diverse minibatch at each step [Sin+20]. However, [Rot+20] show that the following simple strategy also works well for creating each batch: pick B/n classes, and then pick N_c examples randomly from each class, where B is the batch size, and $N_c = 2$ is a tuning parameter.

Another important issue is avoiding overfitting. Since most datasets used in the DML literature are small, it is standard to use an image classifier, such as GoogLeNet (Section 14.3.3) or ResNet (Section 14.3.4), which has been pre-trained on ImageNet, and then to fine-tune the model using the DML loss. (See Section 19.2 for more details on this kind of transfer learning.) In addition, it is standard to use data augmentation (see Section 19.1). (Indeed, with some self-supervised learning methods, data aug is the only way to create similar pairs.)

In [ZLZ20], they propose to add a **spherical embedding constraint** (SEC), which is an additional batchwise regularization term, which encourages all the examples to have the same norm. That is, the regularizer is just the empirical variance of the norms of the (unnormalized) embeddings in that batch. See Figure 16.7 for an illustration. This regularizer can be added to any of the existing DML losses to modestly improve training speed and stability, as well as final performance, analogously to how batchnorm (Section 14.2.4.1) is used.

16.3 Kernel density estimation (KDE)

In this section, we consider a form of non-parametric density estimation known as **kernel density estimation** or **KDE**. This is a form of generative model, since it defines a probability distribution $p(\boldsymbol{x})$ that can be evaluated pointwise, and which can be sampled from to generate new data.

16.3.1 Density kernels

Before explaining KDE, we must define what we mean by a "kernel". This term has several different meanings in machine learning and statistics.[1] In this section, we use a specific kind of kernel which we refer to as a **density kernel**. This is a function $\mathcal{K} : \mathbb{R} \to \mathbb{R}_+$ such that $\int \mathcal{K}(x)dx = 1$ and $\mathcal{K}(-x) = \mathcal{K}(x)$. This latter symmetry property implies the $\int x\mathcal{K}(x)dx = 0$, and hence

$$\int x\mathcal{K}(x - x_n)dx = x_n \tag{16.25}$$

A simple example of such a kernel is the **boxcar kernel**, which is the uniform distribution within the unit interval around the origin:

$$\mathcal{K}(x) \triangleq 0.5\mathbb{I}\left(|x| \leq 1\right) \tag{16.26}$$

Another example is the **Gaussian kernel**:

$$\mathcal{K}(x) = \frac{1}{(2\pi)^{\frac{1}{2}}}e^{-x^2/2} \tag{16.27}$$

We can control the width of the kernel by introducing a **bandwidth** parameter h:

$$\mathcal{K}_h(x) \triangleq \frac{1}{h}\mathcal{K}(\frac{x}{h}) \tag{16.28}$$

We can generalize to vector valued inputs by defining a **radial basis function** or **RBF** kernel:

$$\mathcal{K}_h(\boldsymbol{x}) \propto \mathcal{K}_h(||\boldsymbol{x}||) \tag{16.29}$$

In the case of the Gaussian kernel, this becomes

$$\mathcal{K}_h(\boldsymbol{x}) = \frac{1}{h^D(2\pi)^{D/2}} \prod_{d=1}^{D} \exp(-\frac{1}{2h^2}x_d^2) \tag{16.30}$$

Although Gaussian kernels are popular, they have unbounded support. Some alternative kernels, which have compact support (which can be computationally faster), are listed in Table 16.1. See Figure 16.8 for a plot of these kernel functions.

---

1. For a good blog post on this, see `https://francisbach.com/cursed-kernels/`.

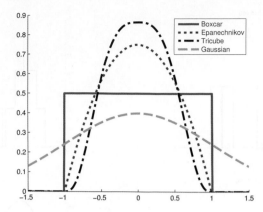

Figure 16.8: *A comparison of some popular normalized kernels. Generated by smoothingKernelPlot.ipynb.*

Name	Definition	Compact	Smooth	Boundaries
Gaussian	$\mathcal{K}(x) = (2\pi)^{-\frac{1}{2}} e^{-x^2/2}$	0	1	1
Boxcar	$\mathcal{K}(x) = \frac{1}{2}\mathbb{I}\left(\lvert x \rvert \leq 1\right)$	1	0	0
Epanechnikov kernel	$\mathcal{K}(x) = \frac{3}{4}(1 - x^2)\mathbb{I}\left(\lvert x \rvert \leq 1\right)$	1	1	0
Tri-cube kernel	$\mathcal{K}(x) = \frac{70}{81}(1 - \lvert x \rvert^3)^3\mathbb{I}\left(\lvert x \rvert \leq 1\right)$	1	1	1

Table 16.1: *List of some popular normalized kernels in 1d. Compact=1 means the function is non-zero for a finite range of inputs. Smooth=1 means the function is differentiable over the range of its support. Boundaries=1 means the function is also differentiable at the boundaries of its support.*

16.3.2 Parzen window density estimator

To explain how to use kernels to define a nonparametric density estimate, recall the form of the Gaussian mixture model from Section 3.5.1. If we assume a fixed spherical Gaussian covariance and uniform mixture weights, we get

$$p(\boldsymbol{x}|\boldsymbol{\theta}) = \frac{1}{K} \sum_{k=1}^{K} \mathcal{N}(\boldsymbol{x}|\boldsymbol{\mu}_k, \sigma^2 \mathbf{I}) \tag{16.31}$$

One problem with this model is that it requires specifying the number K of clusters, as well as their locations $\boldsymbol{\mu}_k$. An alternative to estimating these parameters is to allocate one cluster center per data point. In this case, the model becomes

$$p(\boldsymbol{x}|\boldsymbol{\theta}) = \frac{1}{N} \sum_{n=1}^{N} \mathcal{N}(\boldsymbol{x}|\boldsymbol{x}_n, \sigma^2 \mathbf{I}) \tag{16.32}$$

We can generalize Equation (16.32) by writing

$$p(\boldsymbol{x}|\mathcal{D}) = \frac{1}{N} \sum_{n=1}^{N} \mathcal{K}_h\left(\boldsymbol{x} - \boldsymbol{x}_n\right) \tag{16.33}$$

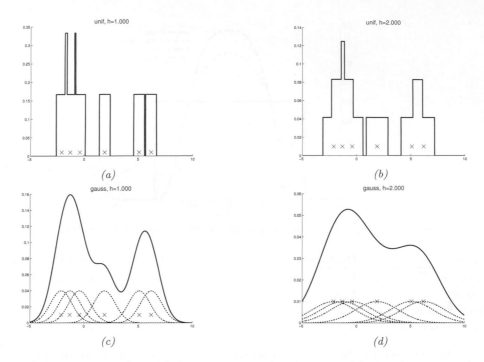

Figure 16.9: A nonparametric (Parzen) density estimator in 1d estimated from 6 data points, denoted by x. Top row: uniform kernel. Bottom row: Gaussian kernel. Left column: bandwidth parameter $h = 1$. Right column: bandwidth parameter $h = 2$. Adapted from http: // en. wikipedia. org/ wiki/ Kernel_ density_ estimation. Generated by parzen_window_demo2.ipynb.

where $\mathcal{K}_h$ is a density kernel. This is called a **Parzen window density estimator**, or **kernel density estimator (KDE)**.

The advantage over a parametric model is that no model fitting is required (except for choosing h, discussed in Section 16.3.3), and there is no need to pick the number of cluster centers. The disadvantage is that the model takes a lot of memory (you need to store all the data) and a lot of time to evaluate.

Figure 16.9 illustrates KDE in 1d for two kinds of kernel. On the top, we use a boxcar kernel; the resulting model just counts how many data points land within an interval of size h around each x_n to get a piecewise constant density. On the bottom, we use a Gaussian kernel, which results in a smoother density.

16.3.3   How to choose the bandwidth parameter

We see from Figure 16.9 that the bandwidth parameter h has a large effect on the learned distribution. We can view this as controlling the complexity of the model.

In the case of 1d data, where the "true" data generating distribution is assumed to be a Gaussian, one can show [BA97a] that the optimal bandwidth for a Gaussian kernel (from the point of view of minimizing frequentist risk) is given by $h = \sigma \left(\frac{4}{3N}\right)^{1/5}$. We can compute a robust approximation to the standard deviation by first computing the **median absolute deviation**, $\text{median}(|\boldsymbol{x} - \text{median}(\boldsymbol{x})|)$, and then using $\hat{\sigma} = 1.4826 \text{ MAD}$. If we have D dimensions, we can estimate h_d separately for each dimension, and then set $h = (\prod_{d=1}^{D} h_d)^{1/D}$.

16.3.4 From KDE to KNN classification

In Section 16.1, we discussed the K nearest neighbor classifier as a heuristic approach to classification. Interestingly, we can derive it as a generative classifier in which the class conditional densities $p(\boldsymbol{x}|y = c)$ are modeled using KDE. Rather than using a fixed bandwidth and counting how many data points fall within the hyper-cube centered on a datapoint, we will allow the bandwidth or volume to be different for each data point. Specifically, we will "grow" a volume around $\boldsymbol{x}$ until we encounter K data points, regardless of their class label. This is called a **balloon kernel density estimator** [TS92]. Let the resulting volume have size $V(\boldsymbol{x})$ (this was previously h^D), and let there be $N_c(\boldsymbol{x})$ examples from class c in this volume. Then we can estimate the class conditional density as follows:

$$p(\boldsymbol{x}|y = c, \mathcal{D}) = \frac{N_c(\boldsymbol{x})}{N_c V(\boldsymbol{x})} \tag{16.34}$$

where N_c is the total number of examples in class c in the whole data set. If we take the class prior to be $p(y = c) = N_c/N$, then the class posterior is given by

$$p(y = c|\boldsymbol{x}, \mathcal{D}) = \frac{\frac{N_c(\boldsymbol{x})}{N_c V(\boldsymbol{x})} \frac{N_c}{N}}{\sum_{c'} \frac{N_{c'}(\boldsymbol{x})}{N_{c'} V(\boldsymbol{x})} \frac{N_{c'}}{N}} = \frac{N_c(\boldsymbol{x})}{\sum_{c'} N_{c'}(\boldsymbol{x})} = \frac{N_c(\boldsymbol{x})}{K} = \frac{1}{K} \sum_{n \in N_K(\boldsymbol{x}, \mathcal{D})} \mathbb{I}(y_n = c) \tag{16.35}$$

where we used the fact that $\sum_c N_c(\boldsymbol{x}) = K$, since we choose a total of K points (regardless of class) around every point. This matches Equation (16.1).

16.3.5 Kernel regression

Just as KDE can be used for generative classifiers (see Section 16.1), it can also be used for generative models for regression, as we discuss below.

16.3.5.1 Nadaraya-Watson estimator for the mean

In regression, our goal is to compute the conditional expectation

$$\mathbb{E}[y|\boldsymbol{x}, \mathcal{D}] = \int y \, p(y|\boldsymbol{x}, \mathcal{D}) dy = \frac{\int y \, p(\boldsymbol{x}, y|\mathcal{D}) dy}{\int p(\boldsymbol{x}, y|\mathcal{D}) dy} \tag{16.36}$$

If we use an MVN for $p(y, \boldsymbol{x}|\mathcal{D})$, we derive a result which is equivalent to linear regression, as we showed in Section 11.2.3.5. However, the assumption that $p(y, \boldsymbol{x}|\mathcal{D})$ is Gaussian is rather limiting. We can use KDE to more accurately approximate the joint density $p(\boldsymbol{x}, y|\mathcal{D})$ as follows:

$$p(y, \boldsymbol{x}|\mathcal{D}) \approx \frac{1}{N} \sum_{n=1}^{N} \mathcal{K}_h(\boldsymbol{x} - \boldsymbol{x}_n) \mathcal{K}_h(y - y_n) \tag{16.37}$$

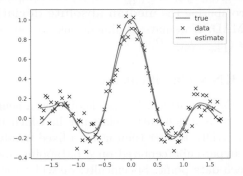

Figure 16.10: *An example of kernel regression in 1d using a Gaussian kernel. Generated by kernelRegression-Demo.ipynb.*

Hence

$$\mathbb{E}\left[y|\boldsymbol{x}, \mathcal{D}\right] = \frac{\frac{1}{N} \sum_{n=1}^{N} \mathcal{K}_h(\boldsymbol{x} - \boldsymbol{x}_n) \int y \mathcal{K}_h(y - y_n) dy}{\frac{1}{N} \sum_{n'=1}^{N} \mathcal{K}_h(\boldsymbol{x} - \boldsymbol{x}_{n'}) \int \mathcal{K}_h(y - y_{n'}) dy} \tag{16.38}$$

We can simplify the numerator using the fact that $\int y \mathcal{K}_h(y - y_n) dy = y_n$ (from Equation (16.25)). We can simplify the denominator using the fact that density kernels integrate to one, i.e., $\int \mathcal{K}_h(y - y_n) dy = 1$. Thus

$$\mathbb{E}\left[y|\boldsymbol{x}, \mathcal{D}\right] = \frac{\sum_{n=1}^{N} \mathcal{K}_h(\boldsymbol{x} - \boldsymbol{x}_n) y_n}{\sum_{n'=1}^{N} \mathcal{K}_h(\boldsymbol{x} - \boldsymbol{x}_{n'})} = \sum_{n=1}^{N} y_n w_n(\boldsymbol{x}) \tag{16.39}$$

$$w_n(\boldsymbol{x}) \triangleq \frac{\mathcal{K}_h(\boldsymbol{x} - \boldsymbol{x}_n)}{\sum_{n'=1}^{N} \mathcal{K}_h(\boldsymbol{x} - \boldsymbol{x}_{n'})} \tag{16.40}$$

We see that the prediction is just a weighted sum of the outputs at the training points, where the weights depend on how similar $\boldsymbol{x}$ is to the stored training points. This method is called **kernel regression**, **kernel smoothing**, or the **Nadaraya-Watson** (N-W) model. See Figure 16.10 for an example, where we use a Gaussian kernel.

In Section 17.2.3, we discuss the connection between kernel regression and Gaussian process regression.

16.3.5.2   Estimator for the variance

Sometimes it is useful to compute the predictive variance, as well as the predictive mean. We can do this by noting that

$$\mathbb{V}\left[y|\boldsymbol{x}, \mathcal{D}\right] = \mathbb{E}\left[y^2|\boldsymbol{x}, \mathcal{D}\right] - \mu(\boldsymbol{x})^2 \tag{16.41}$$

where $\mu(\boldsymbol{x}) = \mathbb{E}[y|\boldsymbol{x}, \mathcal{D}]$ is the N-W estimate. If we use a Gaussian kernel with variance σ^2, we can compute $\mathbb{E}[y^2|\boldsymbol{x}, \mathcal{D}]$ as follows:

$$\mathbb{E}[y^2|\boldsymbol{x}, \mathcal{D}] = \frac{\sum_{n=1}^{N} \mathcal{K}_h(\boldsymbol{x} - \boldsymbol{x}_n) \int y^2 \mathcal{K}_h(y - y_n) dy}{\sum_{n'=1}^{N} \mathcal{K}_h(\boldsymbol{x} - \boldsymbol{x}_{n'}) \int \mathcal{K}_h(y - y_{n'}) dy} \tag{16.42}$$

$$= \frac{\sum_{n=1}^{N} \mathcal{K}_h(\boldsymbol{x} - \boldsymbol{x}_n)(\sigma^2 + y_n^2)}{\sum_{n'=1}^{N} \mathcal{K}_h(\boldsymbol{x} - \boldsymbol{x}_{n'})} \tag{16.43}$$

where we used the fact that

$$\int y^2 \mathcal{N}(y|y_n, \sigma^2) dy = \sigma^2 + y_n^2 \tag{16.44}$$

Combining Equation (16.43) with Equation (16.41) gives

$$\mathbb{V}[y|\boldsymbol{x}, \mathcal{D}] = \sigma^2 + \sum_{n=1}^{N} w_n(\boldsymbol{x}) y_n^2 - \mu(\boldsymbol{x})^2 \tag{16.45}$$

This matches Eqn. 8 of [BA10] (modulo the initial σ^2 term).

16.3.5.3   Locally weighted regression

We can drop the normalization term from Equation (16.39) to get

$$\mu(\boldsymbol{x}) = \sum_{n=1}^{N} y_n \mathcal{K}_h(\boldsymbol{x} - \boldsymbol{x}_n) \tag{16.46}$$

This is just a weighted sum of the observed responses, where the weights depend on how similar the test input $\boldsymbol{x}$ is to the training points $\boldsymbol{x}_n$.

Rather than just interpolating the stored responses y_n, we can fit a locally linear model around each training point:

$$\mu(\boldsymbol{x}) = \min_{\boldsymbol{\beta}} \sum_{n=1}^{N} [y_n - \boldsymbol{\beta}^\mathsf{T} \boldsymbol{\phi}(\boldsymbol{x}_n)]^2 \, \mathcal{K}_h(\boldsymbol{x} - \boldsymbol{x}_n) \tag{16.47}$$

where $\boldsymbol{\phi}(\boldsymbol{x}) = [1, \boldsymbol{x}]$. This is called **locally linear regression (LRR)** or **locally-weighted scatterplot smoothing**, and is commonly known by the acronym **LOWESS** or **LOESS** [CD88]. This is often used when annotating scatter plots with local trend lines.

17 Kernel Methods *

In this chapter, we consider **nonparametric methods** for regression and classification. Such methods do not assume a fixed parametric form for the prediction function, but instead try to estimate the function itself (rather than the parameters) directly from data. The key idea is that we observe the function value at a fixed set of N points, namely $y_n = f(\boldsymbol{x}_n)$ for $n = 1 : N$, where f is the unknown function, so to predict the function value at a new point, say $\boldsymbol{x}_*$, we just have to compare how "similar" $\boldsymbol{x}_*$ is to each of the N training points, $\{\boldsymbol{x}_n\}$, and then we can predict that $f(\boldsymbol{x}_*)$ is some weighted combination of the $\{f(\boldsymbol{x}_n)\}$ values. Thus we may need to "remember" the entire training set, $\mathcal{D} = \{(\boldsymbol{x}_n, y_n)\}$, in order to make predictions at test time — we cannot "compress" $\mathcal{D}$ into a fixed-sized parameter vector.

The weights that are used for prediction are determined by the similarity between $\boldsymbol{x}_*$ and each $\boldsymbol{x}_n$, which is computed using a special kind of function known as kernel function, $\mathcal{K}(\boldsymbol{x}_n, \boldsymbol{x}_*) \geq 0$, which we explain in Section 17.1. This approach is similar to RBF networks (Section 13.6.1), except we use the datapoints $\{\boldsymbol{x}_n\}$ themselves as the "anchors", rather than learning the RBF centroids $\{\boldsymbol{\mu}_k\}$.

In Section 17.2, we discuss an approach called Gaussian processes, which allows us to use the kernel to define a *prior over functions*, which we can update given data to get a *posterior over functions*. Alternatively we can use the same kernel with a method called Support Vector Machines to compute a MAP estimate of the function, as we explain in Section 17.3.

17.1 Mercer kernels

The key to nonparametric methods is that we need a way to encode prior knowledge about the similarity of two input vectors. If we know that $\boldsymbol{x}_i$ is similar to $\boldsymbol{x}_j$, then we can encourage the model to make the predicted output at both locations (i.e., $f(\boldsymbol{x}_i)$ and $f(\boldsymbol{x}_j)$) to be similar.

To define similarity, we introduce the notion of a **kernel function**. The word "kernel" has many different meanings in mathematics, including density kernels (Section 16.3.1), transition kernels of a Markov chain (Section 3.6.1.2), and convolutional kernels (Section 14.1). Here we consider a **Mercer kernel**, also called a **positive definite kernel**. This is any symmetric function $\mathcal{K} : \mathcal{X} \times \mathcal{X} \to \mathbb{R}^+$ such that

$$\sum_{i=1}^{N} \sum_{j=1}^{N} \mathcal{K}(\boldsymbol{x}_i, \boldsymbol{x}_j) c_i c_j \geq 0 \tag{17.1}$$

for any set of N (unique) points $\boldsymbol{x}_i \in \mathcal{X}$, and any choice of numbers $c_i \in \mathbb{R}$. (We assume $\mathcal{K}(\boldsymbol{x}_i, \boldsymbol{x}_j) > 0$, so that we can only achieve equality in the above equation if $c_i = 0$ for all i.)

Another way to understand this condition is the following. Given a set of N datapoints, let us define the **Gram matrix** as the following $N \times N$ similarity matrix:

$$\mathbf{K} = \begin{pmatrix} \mathcal{K}(\boldsymbol{x}_1, \boldsymbol{x}_1) & \cdots & \mathcal{K}(\boldsymbol{x}_1, \boldsymbol{x}_N) \\ & \vdots & \\ \mathcal{K}(\boldsymbol{x}_N, \boldsymbol{x}_1) & \cdots & \mathcal{K}(\boldsymbol{x}_N, \boldsymbol{x}_N) \end{pmatrix} \tag{17.2}$$

We say that $\mathcal{K}$ is a Mercer kernel iff the Gram matrix is positive definite for any set of (distinct) inputs $\{\boldsymbol{x}_i\}_{i=1}^N$.

The most widely used kernel for real-valued inputs is the **squared exponential kernel** (SE), also called the **exponentiated quadratic kernel** (EQ), **Gaussian kernel**, or **RBF kernel**. It is defined by

$$\mathcal{K}(\boldsymbol{x}, \boldsymbol{x}') = \exp\left(-\frac{||\boldsymbol{x} - \boldsymbol{x}'||^2}{2\ell^2}\right) \tag{17.3}$$

Here ℓ corresponds to the length scale of the kernel, i.e., the distance over which we expect differences to matter. This is known as the **bandwidth** parameter. The RBF kernel measures similarity between two vectors in $\mathbb{R}^D$ using (scaled) Euclidean distance. In Section 17.1.2, we will discuss several other kinds of kernel.

In Section 17.2, we show how to use kernels to define priors and posteriors over functions. The basic idea is this: if $\mathcal{K}(\boldsymbol{x}, \boldsymbol{x}')$ is large, meaning the inputs are similar, then we expect the output of the function to be similar as well, so $f(\boldsymbol{x}) \approx f(\boldsymbol{x}')$. More precisely, information we learn about $f(\boldsymbol{x})$ will help us predict $f(\boldsymbol{x}')$ for all $\boldsymbol{x}'$ which are correlated with $\boldsymbol{x}$, and hence for which $\mathcal{K}(\boldsymbol{x}, \boldsymbol{x}')$ is large.

In Section 17.3, we show how to use kernels to generalize from Euclidean distance to a more general notion of distance, so that we can use geometric methods such as linear discriminant analysis in an implicit feature space instead of input space.

17.1.1 Mercer's theorem

Recall from Section 7.4 that any positive definite matrix $\mathbf{K}$ can be represented using an eigendecomposition of the form $\mathbf{K} = \mathbf{U}^\mathsf{T} \boldsymbol{\Lambda} \mathbf{U}$, where $\boldsymbol{\Lambda}$ is a diagonal matrix of eigenvalues $\lambda_i > 0$, and $\mathbf{U}$ is a matrix containing the eigenvectors. Now consider element (i, j) of $\mathbf{K}$:

$$k_{ij} = (\boldsymbol{\Lambda}^{\frac{1}{2}} \mathbf{U}_{:i})^\mathsf{T} (\boldsymbol{\Lambda}^{\frac{1}{2}} \mathbf{U}_{:j}) \tag{17.4}$$

where $\mathbf{U}_{:i}$ is the i'th column of $\mathbf{U}$. If we define $\boldsymbol{\phi}(\boldsymbol{x}_i) = \boldsymbol{\Lambda}^{\frac{1}{2}} \mathbf{U}_{:i}$, then we can write

$$k_{ij} = \boldsymbol{\phi}(\boldsymbol{x}_i)^\mathsf{T} \boldsymbol{\phi}(\boldsymbol{x}_j) = \sum_m \phi_m(\boldsymbol{x}_i) \phi_m(\boldsymbol{x}_j) \tag{17.5}$$

Thus we see that the entries in the kernel matrix can be computed by performing an inner product of some feature vectors that are implicitly defined by the eigenvectors of the kernel matrix. This idea can be generalized to apply to kernel functions, not just kernel matrices; this result is known as **Mercer's theorem**.

For example, consider the **quadratic kernel** $\mathcal{K}(\boldsymbol{x}, \boldsymbol{x}') = \langle \boldsymbol{x}, \boldsymbol{x}' \rangle^2$. In 2d, we have

$$\mathcal{K}(\boldsymbol{x}, \boldsymbol{x}') = (x_1 x_1' + x_2 x_2')^2 = x_1^2 (x_1')^2 + 2x_1 x_2 x_1' x_2' + x_2^2 (x_2')^2 \tag{17.6}$$

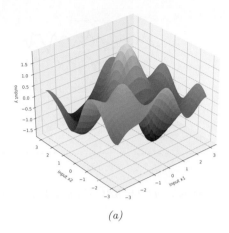 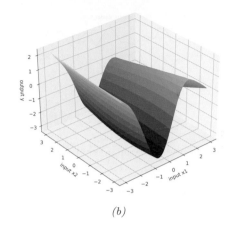

(a)   (b)

Figure 17.1: Function samples from a GP with an ARD kernel. (a) $\ell_1 = \ell_2 = 1$. Both dimensions contribute to the response. (b) $\ell_1 = 1$, $\ell_2 = 5$. The second dimension is essentially ignored. Adapted from Figure 5.1 of [RW06]. Generated by gprDemoArd.ipynb.

We can write this as $\mathcal{K}(\boldsymbol{x}, \boldsymbol{x}') = \boldsymbol{\phi}(\boldsymbol{x})^{\mathsf{T}} \boldsymbol{\phi}(\boldsymbol{x})$ if we define $\boldsymbol{\phi}(x_1, x_2) = [x_1^2, \sqrt{2}x_1 x_2, x_2^2] \in \mathbb{R}^3$. So we embed the 2d inputs $\boldsymbol{x}$ into a 3d feature space $\boldsymbol{\phi}(\boldsymbol{x})$.

Now consider the RBF kernel. In this case, the corresponding feature representation is infinite dimensional (see Section 17.2.9.3 for details). However, by working with kernel functions, we can avoid having to deal with infinite dimensional vectors.

17.1.2   Some popular Mercer kernels

In the sections below, we describe some popular Mercer kernels. More details can be found at [Wil14] and https://www.cs.toronto.edu/~duvenaud/cookbook/.

17.1.2.1   Stationary kernels for real-valued vectors

For real-valued inputs, $\mathcal{X} = \mathbb{R}^D$, it is common to use **stationary kernels**, which are functions of the form $\mathcal{K}(\boldsymbol{x}, \boldsymbol{x}') = \mathcal{K}(||\boldsymbol{x} - \boldsymbol{x}'||)$; thus the value only depends on the elementwise difference between the inputs. The RBF kernel is a stationary kernel. We give some other examples below.

ARD kernel

We can generalize the RBF kernel by replacing Euclidean distance with Mahalanobis distance, as follows:

$$\mathcal{K}(\boldsymbol{r}) = \sigma^2 \exp\left(-\frac{1}{2}\boldsymbol{r}^{\mathsf{T}}\boldsymbol{\Sigma}^{-1}\boldsymbol{r}\right) \qquad (17.7)$$

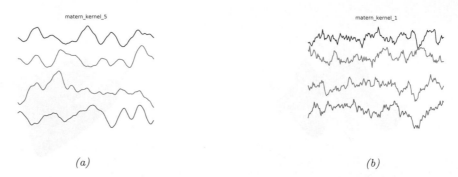

(a)   (b)

Figure 17.2: Functions sampled from a GP with a Matern kernel. (a) $\nu = 5/2$. (b) $\nu = 1/2$. Generated by gpKernelPlot.ipynb.

where $r = x - x'$. If $\boldsymbol{\Sigma}$ is diagonal, this can be written as

$$\mathcal{K}(r; \ell, \sigma^2) = \sigma^2 \exp\left(-\frac{1}{2}\sum_{d=1}^{D}\frac{1}{\ell_d^2}r_d^2\right) = \prod_{d=1}^{D}\mathcal{K}(r_d; \ell_d, \sigma^{2/d}) \qquad (17.8)$$

where

$$\mathcal{K}(r; \ell, \tau^2) = \tau^2 \exp\left(-\frac{1}{2}\frac{1}{\ell^2}r^2\right) \qquad (17.9)$$

We can interpret σ^2 as the overall variance, and ℓ_d as defining the **characteristic length scale** of dimension d. If d is an irrelevant input dimension, we can set $\ell_d = \infty$, so the corresponding dimension will be ignored. This is known as **automatic relevancy determination** or **ARD** (Section 11.7.7). Hence the corresponding kernel is called the **ARD kernel**. See Figure 17.1 for an illustration of some 2d functions sampled from a GP using this prior.

Matern kernels

The SE kernel gives rise to functions that are infinitely differentiable, and therefore are very smooth. For many applications, it is better to use the **Matern kernel**, which gives rise to "rougher" functions, which can better model local "wiggles" without having to make the overall length scale very small.

The Matern kernel has the following form:

$$\mathcal{K}(r; \nu, \ell) = \frac{2^{1-\nu}}{\Gamma(\nu)}\left(\frac{\sqrt{2\nu}r}{\ell}\right)^{\nu} K_\nu\left(\frac{\sqrt{2\nu}r}{\ell}\right) \qquad (17.10)$$

where K_ν is a modified Bessel function and ℓ is the length scale. Functions sampled from this GP are k-times differentiable iff $\nu > k$. As $\nu \to \infty$, this approaches the SE kernel.

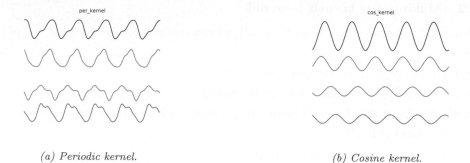

(a) Periodic kernel.   (b) Cosine kernel.

Figure 17.3: Functions sampled from a GP using various stationary periodic kernels. Generated by gpKernelPlot.ipynb.

For values $\nu \in \{\frac{1}{2}, \frac{3}{2}, \frac{5}{2}\}$, the function simplifies as follows:

$$\mathcal{K}(r; \frac{1}{2}, \ell) = \exp(-\frac{r}{\ell}) \tag{17.11}$$

$$\mathcal{K}(r; \frac{3}{2}, \ell) = \left(1 + \frac{\sqrt{3}r}{\ell}\right) \exp\left(-\frac{\sqrt{3}r}{\ell}\right) \tag{17.12}$$

$$\mathcal{K}(r; \frac{5}{2}, \ell) = \left(1 + \frac{\sqrt{5}r}{\ell} + \frac{5r^2}{3\ell^2}\right) \exp\left(-\frac{\sqrt{5}r}{\ell}\right) \tag{17.13}$$

The value $\nu = \frac{1}{2}$ corresponds to the **Ornstein-Uhlenbeck process**, which describes the velocity of a particle undergoing Brownian motion. The corresponding function is continuous but not differentiable, and hence is very "jagged". See Figure 17.2b for an illustration.

Periodic kernels

The **periodic kernel** captures repeating structure, and has the form

$$\mathcal{K}_{\text{per}}(r; \ell, p) = \exp\left(-\frac{2}{\ell^2} \sin^2(\pi \frac{r}{p})\right) \tag{17.14}$$

where p is the period. See Figure 17.3a for an illustration.
A related kernel is the **cosine kernel**:

$$\mathcal{K}(r; p) = \cos\left(2\pi \frac{r}{p}\right) \tag{17.15}$$

See Figure 17.3b for an illustration.

17.1.2.2　Making new kernels from old

Given two valid kernels $\mathcal{K}_1(\boldsymbol{x}, \boldsymbol{x}')$ and $\mathcal{K}_2(\boldsymbol{x}, \boldsymbol{x}')$, we can create a new kernel using any of the following methods:

$$\mathcal{K}(\boldsymbol{x}, \boldsymbol{x}') = c\mathcal{K}_1(\boldsymbol{x}, \boldsymbol{x}'), \text{ for any constant } c > 0 \tag{17.16}$$

$$\mathcal{K}(\boldsymbol{x}, \boldsymbol{x}') = f(\boldsymbol{x})\mathcal{K}_1(\boldsymbol{x}, \boldsymbol{x}')f(\boldsymbol{x}'), \text{ for any function } f \tag{17.17}$$

$$\mathcal{K}(\boldsymbol{x}, \boldsymbol{x}') = q(\mathcal{K}_1(\boldsymbol{x}, \boldsymbol{x}')) \text{ for any function polynomial } q \text{ with nonneg. coef.} \tag{17.18}$$

$$\mathcal{K}(\boldsymbol{x}, \boldsymbol{x}') = \exp(\mathcal{K}_1(\boldsymbol{x}, \boldsymbol{x}')) \tag{17.19}$$

$$\mathcal{K}(\boldsymbol{x}, \boldsymbol{x}') = \boldsymbol{x}^\mathsf{T}\mathbf{A}\boldsymbol{x}', \text{ for any psd matrix } \mathbf{A} \tag{17.20}$$

For example, suppose we start with the linear kernel $\mathcal{K}(\boldsymbol{x}, \boldsymbol{x}') = \boldsymbol{x}^\mathsf{T}\boldsymbol{x}'$. We know this is a valid Mercer kernel, since the corresponding Gram matrix is just the (scaled) covariance matrix of the data. From the above rules, we can see that the polynomial kernel $\mathcal{K}(\boldsymbol{x}, \boldsymbol{x}') = (\boldsymbol{x}^\mathsf{T}\boldsymbol{x}')^M$ is a valid Mercer kernel. This contains all monomials of order M. For example, if $M = 2$ and the inputs are 2d, we have

$$(\boldsymbol{x}^\mathsf{T}\boldsymbol{x}')^2 = (x_1 x_1' + x_2 x_2')^2 = (x_1 x_1')^2 + (x_2 x_2)^2 + 2(x_1 x_1')(x_2 x_2') \tag{17.21}$$

We can generalize this to contain all terms up to degree M by using the kernel $\mathcal{K}(\boldsymbol{x}, \boldsymbol{x}') = (\boldsymbol{x}^\mathsf{T}\boldsymbol{x}' + c)^M$. For example, if $M = 2$ and the inputs are 2d, we have

$$\begin{aligned}(\boldsymbol{x}^\mathsf{T}\boldsymbol{x}' + 1)^2 &= (x_1 x_1')^2 + (x_1 x_1')(x_2 x_2') + (x_1 x_1') \\ &\quad + (x_2 x_2)(x_1 x_1') + (x_2 x_2')^2 + (x_2 x_2') \\ &\quad + (x_1 x_1') + (x_2 x_2') + 1\end{aligned} \tag{17.22}$$

We can also use the above rules to establish that the Gaussian kernel is a valid kernel. To see this, note that

$$||\boldsymbol{x} - \boldsymbol{x}'||^2 = \boldsymbol{x}^\mathsf{T}\boldsymbol{x} + (\boldsymbol{x}')^\mathsf{T}\boldsymbol{x}' - 2\boldsymbol{x}^\mathsf{T}\boldsymbol{x}' \tag{17.23}$$

and hence

$$\mathcal{K}(\boldsymbol{x}, \boldsymbol{x}') = \exp(-||\boldsymbol{x} - \boldsymbol{x}'||^2/2\sigma^2) = \exp(-\boldsymbol{x}^\mathsf{T}\boldsymbol{x}/2\sigma^2)\exp(\boldsymbol{x}^\mathsf{T}\boldsymbol{x}'/\sigma^2)\exp(-(\boldsymbol{x}')^\mathsf{T}\boldsymbol{x}'/2\sigma^2) \tag{17.24}$$

is a valid kernel.

17.1.2.3　Combining kernels by addition and multiplication

We can also combine kernels using addition or multiplication:

$$\mathcal{K}(\boldsymbol{x}, \boldsymbol{x}') = \mathcal{K}_1(\boldsymbol{x}, \boldsymbol{x}') + \mathcal{K}_2(\boldsymbol{x}, \boldsymbol{x}') \tag{17.25}$$

$$\mathcal{K}(\boldsymbol{x}, \boldsymbol{x}') = \mathcal{K}_1(\boldsymbol{x}, \boldsymbol{x}') \times \mathcal{K}_2(\boldsymbol{x}, \boldsymbol{x}') \tag{17.26}$$

Multiplying two positive-definite kernels together always results in another positive definite kernel. This is a way to get a conjunction of the individual properties of each kernel, as illustrated in Figure 17.4.

In addition, adding two positive-definite kernels together always results in another positive definite kernel. This is a way to get a disjunction of the individual properties of each kernel, as illustrated in Figure 17.5.

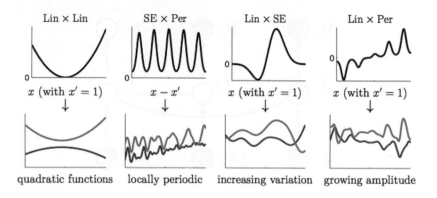

Figure 17.4: *Examples of 1d structures obtained by multiplying elementary kernels. Top row shows* $\mathcal{K}(x, x' = 1)$. *Bottom row shows some functions sampled from* $GP(f|0, \mathcal{K})$. *From Figure 2.2 of [Duv14]. Used with kind permission of David Duvenaud.*

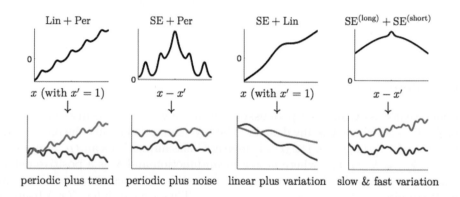

Figure 17.5: *Examples of 1d structures obtained by adding elementary kernels. Here* $\mathrm{SE}^{(\mathrm{short})}$ *and* $\mathrm{SE}^{(\mathrm{long})}$ *are two SE kernels with different length scales. From Figure 2.4 of [Duv14]. Used with kind permission of David Duvenaud.*

17.1.2.4 Kernels for structured inputs

Kernels are particularly useful when the inputs are structured objects, such as strings and graphs, since it is often hard to "featurize" variable-sized inputs. For example, we can define a **string kernel** which compares strings in terms of the number of n-grams they have in common [Lod+02; BC17].

We can also define kernels on graphs [KJM19]. For example, the **random walk kernel** conceptually performs random walks on two graphs simultaneously, and then counts the number of paths that were produced by both walks. This can be computed efficiently as discussed in [Vis+10]. For more details on graph kernels, see [KJM19].

For a review of kernels on structured objects, see e.g., [Gär03].

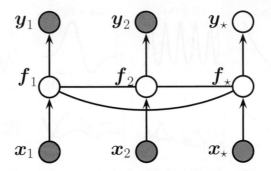

Figure 17.6: A Gaussian process for 2 training points, $\boldsymbol{x}_1$ and $\boldsymbol{x}_2$, and 1 testing point, $\boldsymbol{x}_*$, represented as a graphical model representing $p(\boldsymbol{y}, \boldsymbol{f}_X | \mathbf{X}) = \mathcal{N}(\boldsymbol{f}_X | m(\mathbf{X}), \mathcal{K}(\mathbf{X})) \prod_i p(y_i | f_i)$. The hidden nodes $f_i = f(\boldsymbol{x}_i)$ represent the value of the function at each of the data points. These hidden nodes are fully interconnected by undirected edges, forming a Gaussian graphical model; the edge strengths represent the covariance terms $\Sigma_{ij} = \mathcal{K}(\boldsymbol{x}_i, \boldsymbol{x}_j)$. If the test point $\boldsymbol{x}_*$ is similar to the training points $\boldsymbol{x}_1$ and $\boldsymbol{x}_2$, then the value of the hidden function f_* will be similar to f_1 and f_2, and hence the predicted output y_* will be similar to the training values y_1 and y_2.

17.2   Gaussian processes

In this section, we discuss **Gaussian processes**, which is a way to define distributions over functions of the form $f : \mathcal{X} \to \mathbb{R}$, where $\mathcal{X}$ is any domain. The key assumption is that the function values at a set of $M > 0$ inputs, $\boldsymbol{f} = [f(\boldsymbol{x}_1), \ldots, f(\boldsymbol{x}_M)]$, is jointly Gaussian, with mean $(\boldsymbol{\mu} = m(\boldsymbol{x}_1), \ldots, m(\boldsymbol{x}_M))$ and covariance $\boldsymbol{\Sigma}_{ij} = \mathcal{K}(\boldsymbol{x}_i, \boldsymbol{x}_j)$, where m is a mean function and $\mathcal{K}$ is a positive definite (Mercer) kernel. Since we assume this holds for any $M > 0$, this includes the case where $M = N + 1$, containing N training points $\boldsymbol{x}_n$ and 1 test point $\boldsymbol{x}_*$. Thus we can infer $f(\boldsymbol{x}_*)$ from knowledge of $f(\boldsymbol{x}_1), \ldots, f(\boldsymbol{x}_n)$ by manipulating the joint Gaussian distribution $p(f(\boldsymbol{x}_1), \ldots, f(\boldsymbol{x}_N), f(\boldsymbol{x}_*))$, as we explain below. We can also extend this to work with the case where we observe noisy functions of $f(\boldsymbol{x}_n)$, such as in regression or classification problems.

17.2.1   Noise-free observations

Suppose we observe a training set $\mathcal{D} = \{(\boldsymbol{x}_n, y_n) : n = 1 : N\}$, where $y_n = f(\boldsymbol{x}_n)$ is the noise-free observation of the function evaluated at $\boldsymbol{x}_n$. If we ask the GP to predict $f(\boldsymbol{x})$ for a value of $\boldsymbol{x}$ that it has already seen, we want the GP to return the answer $f(\boldsymbol{x})$ with no uncertainty. In other words, it should act as an **interpolator** of the training data.

Now we consider the case of predicting the outputs for new inputs that may not be in $\mathcal{D}$. Specifically, given a test set $\mathbf{X}_*$ of size $N_* \times D$, we want to predict the function outputs $\boldsymbol{f}_* = [f(\boldsymbol{x}_{*1}), \ldots, f(\boldsymbol{x}_{*,N_*})]$. By definition of the GP, the joint distribution $p(\boldsymbol{f}_X, \boldsymbol{f}_* | \mathbf{X}, \mathbf{X}_*)$ has the following form

$$\begin{pmatrix} \boldsymbol{f}_X \\ \boldsymbol{f}_* \end{pmatrix} \sim \mathcal{N}\left(\begin{pmatrix} \boldsymbol{\mu}_X \\ \boldsymbol{\mu}_* \end{pmatrix}, \begin{pmatrix} \mathbf{K}_{X,X} & \mathbf{K}_{X,*} \\ \mathbf{K}_{X,*}^{\mathsf{T}} & \mathbf{K}_{*,*} \end{pmatrix} \right) \tag{17.27}$$

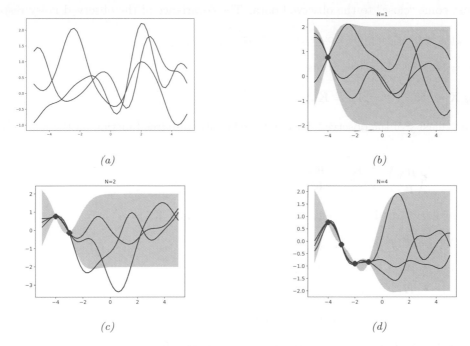

Figure 17.7: (a) some functions sampled from a GP prior with squared exponential kernel. (b-d) : some samples from a GP posterior, after conditioning on 1,2, and 4 noise-free observations. The shaded area represents $\mathbb{E}\left[f(\boldsymbol{x})\right] \pm 2\text{std}\left[f(\boldsymbol{x})\right]$. Adapted from Figure 2.2 of [RW06]. Generated by gprDemoNoiseFree.ipynb.

where $\boldsymbol{\mu}_X = [m(\boldsymbol{x}_1), \ldots, m(\boldsymbol{x}_N)]$, $\boldsymbol{\mu}_* = [m(\boldsymbol{x}_1^*), \ldots, m(\boldsymbol{x}_{N_*}^*)]$, $\mathbf{K}_{X,X} = \mathcal{K}(\mathbf{X}, \mathbf{X})$ is $N \times N$, $\mathbf{K}_{X,*} = \mathcal{K}(\mathbf{X}, \mathbf{X}_*)$ is $N \times N_*$, and $\mathbf{K}_{*,*} = \mathcal{K}(\mathbf{X}_*, \mathbf{X}_*)$ is $N_* \times N_*$. See Figure 17.6 for an illustration. By the standard rules for conditioning Gaussians (Section 3.2.3), the posterior has the following form

$$p(\boldsymbol{f}_*|\mathbf{X}_*, \mathcal{D}) = \mathcal{N}(\boldsymbol{f}_*|\boldsymbol{\mu}_*, \boldsymbol{\Sigma}_*) \tag{17.28}$$

$$\boldsymbol{\mu}_* = m(\mathbf{X}_*) + \mathbf{K}_{X,*}^{\mathsf{T}} \mathbf{K}_{X,X}^{-1} (\boldsymbol{f}_X - m(\mathbf{X})) \tag{17.29}$$

$$\boldsymbol{\Sigma}_* = \mathbf{K}_{*,*} - \mathbf{K}_{X,*}^{\mathsf{T}} \mathbf{K}_{X,X}^{-1} \mathbf{K}_{X,*} \tag{17.30}$$

This process is illustrated in Figure 17.7. On the left we show some samples from the prior, $p(f)$, where we use an RBF kernel (Section 17.1) and a zero mean function. On the right, we show samples from the posterior, $p(f|\mathcal{D})$. We see that the model perfectly interpolates the training data, and that the predictive uncertainty increases as we move further away from the observed data.

17.2.2 Noisy observations

Now let us consider the case where what we observe is a noisy version of the underlying function, $y_n = f(\boldsymbol{x}_n) + \epsilon_n$, where $\epsilon_n \sim \mathcal{N}(0, \sigma_y^2)$. In this case, the model is not required to interpolate the data, but it must come "close" to the observed data. The covariance of the observed noisy responses is

$$\text{Cov}\left[y_i, y_j\right] = \text{Cov}\left[f_i, f_j\right] + \text{Cov}\left[\epsilon_i, \epsilon_j\right] = \mathcal{K}(\boldsymbol{x}_i, \boldsymbol{x}_j) + \sigma_y^2 \delta_{ij} \tag{17.31}$$

where $\delta_{ij} = \mathbb{I}\left(i = j\right)$. In other words

$$\text{Cov}\left[\boldsymbol{y}|\mathbf{X}\right] = \mathbf{K}_{X,X} + \sigma_y^2 \mathbf{I}_N \triangleq \mathbf{K}_\sigma \tag{17.32}$$

The joint density of the observed data and the latent, noise-free function on the test points is given by

$$\begin{pmatrix} \boldsymbol{y} \\ \boldsymbol{f}_* \end{pmatrix} \sim \mathcal{N}\left(\begin{pmatrix} \boldsymbol{\mu}_X \\ \boldsymbol{\mu}_* \end{pmatrix}, \begin{pmatrix} \mathbf{K}_\sigma & \mathbf{K}_{X,*} \\ \mathbf{K}_{X,*}^\mathsf{T} & \mathbf{K}_{*,*} \end{pmatrix}\right) \tag{17.33}$$

Hence the posterior predictive density at a set of test points $\mathbf{X}_*$ is

$$p(\boldsymbol{f}_*|\mathcal{D}, \mathbf{X}_*) = \mathcal{N}(\boldsymbol{f}_*|\boldsymbol{\mu}_{*|X}, \boldsymbol{\Sigma}_{*|X}) \tag{17.34}$$
$$\boldsymbol{\mu}_{*|X} = \boldsymbol{\mu}_* + \mathbf{K}_{X,*}^\mathsf{T}\mathbf{K}_\sigma^{-1}(\boldsymbol{y} - \boldsymbol{\mu}_X) \tag{17.35}$$
$$\boldsymbol{\Sigma}_{*|X} = \mathbf{K}_{*,*} - \mathbf{K}_{X,*}^\mathsf{T}\mathbf{K}_\sigma^{-1}\mathbf{K}_{X,*} \tag{17.36}$$

In the case of a single test input, this simplifies as follows

$$p(f_*|\mathcal{D}, \boldsymbol{x}_*) = \mathcal{N}(f_*|m_* + \boldsymbol{k}_*^\mathsf{T}\mathbf{K}_\sigma^{-1}(\boldsymbol{y} - \boldsymbol{\mu}_X), \ k_{**} - \boldsymbol{k}_*^\mathsf{T}\mathbf{K}_\sigma^{-1}\boldsymbol{k}_*) \tag{17.37}$$

where $\boldsymbol{k}_* = [\mathcal{K}(\boldsymbol{x}_*, \boldsymbol{x}_1), \dots, \mathcal{K}(\boldsymbol{x}_*, \boldsymbol{x}_N)]$ and $k_{**} = \mathcal{K}(\boldsymbol{x}_*, \boldsymbol{x}_*)$. If the mean function is zero, we can write the posterior mean as follows

$$\mu_{*|X} = \boldsymbol{k}_*^\mathsf{T}(\mathbf{K}_\sigma^{-1}\boldsymbol{y}) \triangleq \boldsymbol{k}_*^\mathsf{T}\boldsymbol{\alpha} = \sum_{n=1}^N \mathcal{K}(\boldsymbol{x}_*, \boldsymbol{x}_n)\alpha_n \tag{17.38}$$

This is identical to the predictions from kernel ridge regression in Equation (17.108).

17.2.3 Comparison to kernel regression

In Section 16.3.5, we discussed kernel regression, which is a generative approach to regression in which we approximate $p(y, \boldsymbol{x})$ using kernel density estimation. In particular, Equation (16.39) gives us

$$\mathbb{E}\left[y|\boldsymbol{x}, \mathcal{D}\right] = \frac{\sum_{n=1}^N \mathcal{K}_h(\boldsymbol{x} - \boldsymbol{x}_n)y_n}{\sum_{n'=1}^N \mathcal{K}_h(\boldsymbol{x} - \boldsymbol{x}_{n'})} = \sum_{n=1}^N y_n w_n(\boldsymbol{x}) \tag{17.39}$$
$$w_n(\boldsymbol{x}) \triangleq \frac{\mathcal{K}_h(\boldsymbol{x} - \boldsymbol{x}_n)}{\sum_{n'=1}^N \mathcal{K}_h(\boldsymbol{x} - \boldsymbol{x}_{n'})} \tag{17.40}$$

This is very similar to Equation (17.38). However, there are a few important differences. Firstly, in a GP, we use a positive definite (Mercer) kernel instead of a density kernel; Mercer kernels can be defined on structured objects, such as strings and graphs, which is harder to do for density kernels.

Second, a GP is an interpolator (at least when $\sigma^2 = 0$), so $\mathbb{E}[y|\boldsymbol{x}_n, \mathcal{D}] = y_n$. By contrast, kernel regression is not an interpolator (although it can be made into one by iteratively fitting the residuals, as in [KJ16]). Third, a GP is a Bayesian method, which means we can estimate hyperparameters (of the kernel) by maximizing the marginal likelihood; by contrast, in kernel regression we must use cross-validation to estimate the kernel parameters, such as the bandwidth. Fourth, computing the weights w_n for kernel regression takes $O(N)$ time, where $N = |\mathcal{D}|$, whereas computing the weights α_n for GP regression takes $O(N^3)$ time (although there are approximation methods that can reduce this to $O(NM^2)$, as we discuss in Section 17.2.9).

17.2.4 Weight space vs function space

In this section, we show how Bayesian linear regression is a special case of a GP.

Consider the linear regression model $y = f(\boldsymbol{x}) + \epsilon$, where $f(\boldsymbol{x}) = \boldsymbol{w}^\mathsf{T} \boldsymbol{\phi}(\boldsymbol{x})$ and $\epsilon \sim \mathcal{N}(0, \sigma_y^2)$. If we use a Gaussian prior $p(\boldsymbol{w}) = \mathcal{N}(\boldsymbol{w}|\boldsymbol{0}, \boldsymbol{\Sigma}_w)$, then the posterior is as follows (see Section 11.7.2 for the derivation):

$$p(\boldsymbol{w}|\mathcal{D}) = \mathcal{N}(\boldsymbol{w}|\frac{1}{\sigma_y^2}\mathbf{A}^{-1}\boldsymbol{\Phi}^T \boldsymbol{y}, \mathbf{A}^{-1}) \tag{17.41}$$

where $\boldsymbol{\Phi}$ is the $N \times D$ design matrix, and

$$\mathbf{A} = \sigma_y^{-2}\boldsymbol{\Phi}^\mathsf{T}\boldsymbol{\Phi} + \boldsymbol{\Sigma}_w^{-1} \tag{17.42}$$

The posterior predictive distribution for $f_* = f(\boldsymbol{x}_*)$ is therefore

$$p(f_*|\mathcal{D}, \boldsymbol{x}_*) = \mathcal{N}(f_*|\frac{1}{\sigma_y^2}\boldsymbol{\phi}_*^\mathsf{T}\mathbf{A}^{-1}\boldsymbol{\Phi}^\mathsf{T}\boldsymbol{y}, \ \boldsymbol{\phi}_*^\mathsf{T}\mathbf{A}^{-1}\boldsymbol{\phi}_*) \tag{17.43}$$

where $\boldsymbol{\phi}_* = \boldsymbol{\phi}(\boldsymbol{x}_*)$. This views the problem of inference and prediction in **weight space**.

We now show that this is equivalent to the predictions made by a GP using a kernel of the form $\mathcal{K}(\boldsymbol{x}, \boldsymbol{x}') = \boldsymbol{\phi}(\boldsymbol{x})^\mathsf{T}\boldsymbol{\Sigma}_w\boldsymbol{\phi}(\boldsymbol{x}')$. To see this, let $\mathbf{K} = \boldsymbol{\Phi}\boldsymbol{\Sigma}_w\boldsymbol{\Phi}^\mathsf{T}$, $\boldsymbol{k}_* = \boldsymbol{\Phi}\boldsymbol{\Sigma}_w\boldsymbol{\phi}_*$, and $k_{**} = \boldsymbol{\phi}_*^\mathsf{T}\boldsymbol{\Sigma}_w\boldsymbol{\phi}_*$. Using this notation, and the matrix inversion lemma, we can rewrite Equation (17.43) as follows

$$p(f_*|\mathcal{D}, \boldsymbol{x}_*) = \mathcal{N}(f_*|\boldsymbol{\mu}_{*|X}, \boldsymbol{\Sigma}_{*|X}) \tag{17.44}$$

$$\boldsymbol{\mu}_{*|X} = \boldsymbol{\phi}_*^\mathsf{T}\boldsymbol{\Sigma}_w\boldsymbol{\Phi}^\mathsf{T}(\mathbf{K} + \sigma_y^2\mathbf{I})^{-1}\boldsymbol{y} = \boldsymbol{k}_*^\mathsf{T}\mathbf{K}_\sigma^{-1}\boldsymbol{y} \tag{17.45}$$

$$\boldsymbol{\Sigma}_{*|X} = \boldsymbol{\phi}_*^\mathsf{T}\boldsymbol{\Sigma}_w\boldsymbol{\phi}_* - \boldsymbol{\phi}_*^\mathsf{T}\boldsymbol{\Sigma}_w\boldsymbol{\Phi}^\mathsf{T}(\mathbf{K} + \sigma_y^2\mathbf{I})^{-1}\boldsymbol{\Phi}\boldsymbol{\Sigma}_w\boldsymbol{\phi}_* = k_{**} - \boldsymbol{k}_*^\mathsf{T}\mathbf{K}_\sigma^{-1}\boldsymbol{k}_* \tag{17.46}$$

which matches the results in Equation (17.37), assuming $m(\boldsymbol{x}) = 0$. (Non-zero mean can be captured by adding a constant feature with value 1 to $\boldsymbol{\phi}(\boldsymbol{x})$.)

Thus we can derive a GP from Bayesian linear regression. Note, however, that linear regression assumes $\boldsymbol{\phi}(\boldsymbol{x})$ is a finite length vector, whereas a GP allows us to work directly in terms of kernels, which may correspond to infinite length feature vectors (see Section 17.1.1). That is, a GP works in **function space**.

17.2.5 Numerical issues

In this section, we discuss computational and numerical issues which arise when implementing the above equations. For notational simplicity, we assume the prior mean is zero, $m(\boldsymbol{x}) = 0$.

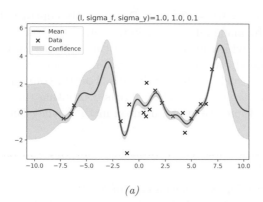
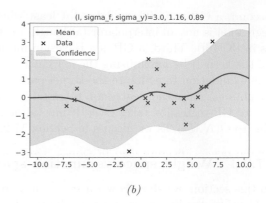

Figure 17.8: Some 1d GPs with SE kernels but different hyper-parameters fit to 20 noisy observations. The hyper-parameters $(\ell, \sigma_f, \sigma_y)$ are as follows: (a) (1,1,0.1) (b) (3.0, 1.16, 0.89). Adapted from Figure 2.5 of [RW06]. Generated by gprDemoChangeHparams.ipynb.

The posterior predictive mean is given by $\mu_* = \boldsymbol{k}_*^{\mathsf{T}}\mathbf{K}_\sigma^{-1}\boldsymbol{y}$. For reasons of numerical stability, it is unwise to directly invert $\mathbf{K}_\sigma$. A more robust alternative is to compute a Cholesky decomposition, $\mathbf{K}_\sigma = \mathbf{L}\mathbf{L}^{\mathsf{T}}$, which takes $O(N^3)$ time. Then we compute $\boldsymbol{\alpha} = \mathbf{L}^{\mathsf{T}} \setminus (\mathbf{L} \setminus \boldsymbol{y})$, where we have used the backslash operator to represent backsubstitution (Section 7.7.1). Given this, we can compute the posterior mean for each test case in $O(N)$ time using

$$\mu_* = \boldsymbol{k}_*^{\mathsf{T}}\mathbf{K}_\sigma^{-1}\boldsymbol{y} = \boldsymbol{k}_*^{\mathsf{T}}\mathbf{L}^{-\mathsf{T}}(\mathbf{L}^{-1}\boldsymbol{y}) = \boldsymbol{k}_*^{\mathsf{T}}\boldsymbol{\alpha} \tag{17.47}$$

We can compute the variance in $O(N^2)$ time for each test case using

$$\sigma_*^2 = k_{**} - \boldsymbol{k}_*^{\mathsf{T}}\mathbf{L}^{-T}\mathbf{L}^{-1}\boldsymbol{k}_* = k_{**} - \boldsymbol{v}^{\mathsf{T}}\boldsymbol{v} \tag{17.48}$$

where $\boldsymbol{v} = \mathbf{L} \setminus \boldsymbol{k}_*$.

Finally, the log marginal likelihood (needed for kernel learning, Section 17.2.6) can be computed using

$$\log p(\boldsymbol{y}|\mathbf{X}) = -\frac{1}{2}\boldsymbol{y}^{\mathsf{T}}\boldsymbol{\alpha} - \sum_{n=1}^{N}\log L_{nn} - \frac{N}{2}\log(2\pi) \tag{17.49}$$

17.2.6   Estimating the kernel

Most kernels have some free parameters, which can have a large effect on the predictions from the model. For example, suppose we are performing 1d regression using a GP with an RBF kernel of the form

$$\mathcal{K}(x_p, x_q) = \sigma_f^2 \exp(-\frac{1}{2\ell^2}(x_p - x_q)^2) \tag{17.50}$$

Here ℓ is the horizontal scale over which the function changes, σ_f^2 controls the vertical scale of the function. We assume observation noise with variance σ_y^2.

We sampled 20 observations from an MVN with a covariance given by $\boldsymbol{\Sigma} = \mathcal{K}(x_i, x_j)$ for a grid of points $\{x_i\}$, and added observation noise of value σ_y. We then fit this data using a GP with the same kernel, but with a range of hyperparmameters. Figure 17.8 illustrates the effects of changing these parameters. In Figure 17.8(a), we use $(\ell, \sigma_f, \sigma_y) = (1, 1, 0.1)$, and the result is a good fit. In Figure 17.8(b), we increase the length scale to $\ell = 3$; now the function looks overly smooth.

17.2.6.1 Empirical Bayes

To estimate the kernel parameters $\boldsymbol{\theta}$ (sometimes called hyperparameters), we could use exhaustive search over a discrete grid of values, with validation loss as an objective, but this can be quite slow. (This is the approach used by nonprobabilistic methods, such as SVMs (Section 17.3) to tune kernels.) Here we consider an empirical Bayes approach (Section 4.6.5.3), which will allow us to use gradient-based optimization methods, which are much faster. In particular, we will maximize the marginal likelihood

$$p(\boldsymbol{y}|\mathbf{X}, \boldsymbol{\theta}) = \int p(\boldsymbol{y}|\boldsymbol{f}, \mathbf{X}) p(\boldsymbol{f}|\mathbf{X}, \boldsymbol{\theta}) d\boldsymbol{f} \tag{17.51}$$

(The reason it is called the marginal likelihood, rather than just likelihood, is because we have marginalized out the latent Gaussian vector $\boldsymbol{f}$.)

For notational simplicity, we assume the mean function is 0. Since $p(\boldsymbol{f}|\mathbf{X}) = \mathcal{N}(\boldsymbol{f}|\boldsymbol{0}, \mathbf{K})$, and $p(\boldsymbol{y}|\boldsymbol{f}) = \prod_{n=1}^{N} \mathcal{N}(y_n|f_n, \sigma_y^2)$, the marginal likelihood is given by

$$\log p(\boldsymbol{y}|\mathbf{X}, \boldsymbol{\theta}) = \log \mathcal{N}(\boldsymbol{y}|\boldsymbol{0}, \mathbf{K}_\sigma) = -\frac{1}{2}\boldsymbol{y}^\mathsf{T}\mathbf{K}_\sigma^{-1}\boldsymbol{y} - \frac{1}{2}\log|\mathbf{K}_\sigma| - \frac{N}{2}\log(2\pi) \tag{17.52}$$

where the dependence of $\mathbf{K}_\sigma = \mathbf{K}_{X,X} + \sigma_2^2 \mathbf{I}_N$ on $\boldsymbol{\theta}$ is implicit. The first term is a data fit term, the second term is a model complexity term, and the third term is just a constant. To understand the tradeoff between the first two terms, consider a SE kernel in 1D, as we vary the length scale ℓ and hold σ_y^2 fixed. For short length scales, the fit will be good, so $\boldsymbol{y}^\mathsf{T}\mathbf{K}_\sigma^{-1}\boldsymbol{y}$ will be small. However, the model complexity will be high: $\mathbf{K}$ will be almost diagonal, (as in Figure 13.22, top right), since most points will not be considered "near" any others, so the $\log|\mathbf{K}_\sigma|$ term will be large. For long length scales, the fit will be poor but the model complexity will be low: $\mathbf{K}$ will be almost all 1's, (as in Figure 13.22, bottom right), so $\log|\mathbf{K}_\sigma|$ will be small.

We now discuss how to maximize the marginal likelihood. One can show that

$$\frac{\partial}{\partial \theta_j} \log p(\boldsymbol{y}|\mathbf{X}, \boldsymbol{\theta}) = \frac{1}{2}\boldsymbol{y}^\mathsf{T}\mathbf{K}_\sigma^{-1}\frac{\partial \mathbf{K}_\sigma}{\partial \theta_j}\mathbf{K}_\sigma^{-1}\boldsymbol{y} - \frac{1}{2}\mathrm{tr}(\mathbf{K}_\sigma^{-1}\frac{\partial \mathbf{K}_\sigma}{\partial \theta_j}) \tag{17.53}$$

$$= \frac{1}{2}\mathrm{tr}\left((\boldsymbol{\alpha}\boldsymbol{\alpha}^\mathsf{T} - \mathbf{K}_\sigma^{-1})\frac{\partial \mathbf{K}_\sigma}{\partial \theta_j}\right) \tag{17.54}$$

where $\boldsymbol{\alpha} = \mathbf{K}_\sigma^{-1}\boldsymbol{y}$. It takes $O(N^3)$ time to compute $\mathbf{K}_\sigma^{-1}$, and then $O(N^2)$ time per hyper-parameter to compute the gradient.

The form of $\frac{\partial \mathbf{K}_\sigma}{\partial \theta_j}$ depends on the form of the kernel, and which parameter we are taking derivatives with respect to. Often we have constraints on the hyper-parameters, such as $\sigma_y^2 \geq 0$. In this case, we can define $\theta = \log(\sigma_y^2)$, and then use the chain rule.

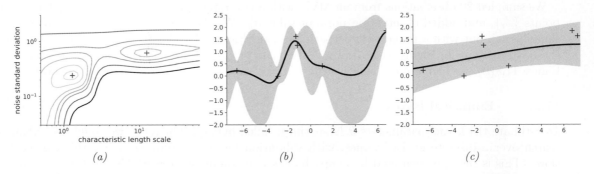

Figure 17.9: Illustration of local minima in the marginal likelihood surface. (a) We plot the log marginal likelihood vs kernel length scale ℓ and observation noise σ_y, for fixed signal level $\sigma_f = 1$, using the 7 data points shown in panels b and c. (b) The function corresponding to the lower left local minimum, $(\ell, \sigma_y) \approx (1, 0.2)$. This is quite "wiggly" and has low noise. (c) The function corresponding to the top right local minimum, $(\ell, \sigma_y) \approx (10, 0.8)$. This is quite smooth and has high noise. The data was generated using $(\ell, \sigma_f, \sigma_y) = (1, 1, 0.1)$. Adapted from Figure 5.5 of [RW06]. Generated by gpr_demo_marglik.ipynb.

Given an expression for the log marginal likelihood and its derivative, we can estimate the kernel parameters using any standard gradient-based optimizer. However, since the objective is not convex, local minima can be a problem, as we illustrate below, so we may need to use multiple restarts.

As an example, consider the RBF in Equation (17.50) with $\sigma_f^2 = 1$. In Figure 17.9(a), we plot $\log p(\boldsymbol{y}|\mathbf{X}, \ell, \sigma_y^2)$ (where $\mathbf{X}$ and $\boldsymbol{y}$ are the 7 data points shown in panels b and c) as we vary ℓ and σ_y^2. The two local optima are indicated by +. The bottom left optimum corresponds to a low-noise, short-length scale solution (shown in panel b). The top right optimum corresponds to a high-noise, long-length scale solution (shown in panel c). With only 7 data points, there is not enough evidence to confidently decide which is more reasonable, although the more complex model (panel b) has a marginal likelihood that is about 60% higher than the simpler model (panel c). With more data, the more complex model would become even more preferred.

Figure 17.9 illustrates some other interesting (and typical) features. The region where $\sigma_y^2 \approx 1$ (top of panel a) corresponds to the case where the noise is very high; in this regime, the marginal likelihood is insensitive to the length scale (indicated by the horizontal contours), since all the data is explained as noise. The region where $\ell \approx 0.5$ (left hand side of panel a) corresponds to the case where the length scale is very short; in this regime, the marginal likelihood is insensitive to the noise level (indicated by the vertical contours), since the data is perfectly interpolated. Neither of these regions would be chosen by a good optimizer.

17.2.6.2 Bayesian inference

When we have a small number of datapoints (e.g., when using GPs for Bayesian optimization), using a point estimate of the kernel parameters can give poor results [Bul11; WF14]. In such cases, we may wish to approximate the posterior over the kernel parameters. Several methods can be used. For example, [MA10] shows how to use slice sampling, [Hen+15] shows how to use Hamiltonian Monte Carlo, and [BBV11] shows how to use sequential Monte Carlo.

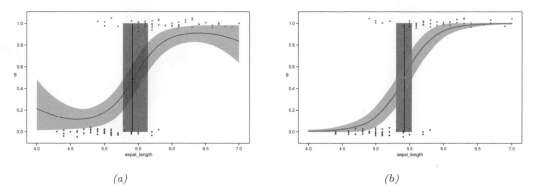

Figure 17.10: *GP classifier for a binary classification problem on Iris flowers (Setosa vs Versicolor) using a single input feature (sepal length). The fat vertical line is the credible interval for the decision boundary. (a) SE kernel. (b) SE plus linear kernel. Adapted from Figures 7.11–7.12 of [Mar18]. Generated by gp_classify_iris_1d_pymc3.ipynb.*

17.2.7 GPs for classification

So far, we have focused on GPs for regression using Gaussian likelihoods. In this case, the posterior is also a GP, and all computation can be performed analytically. However, if the likelihood is non-Gaussian, such as the Bernoulli likelihood for binary classification, we can no longer compute the posterior exactly.

There are various approximations we can make, some of which we discuss in the sequel to this book, [Mur23]. In this section, we use the Hamiltonian Monte Carlo method (Section 4.6.8.4), both for the latent Gaussian function $\boldsymbol{f}$ as well as the kernel hyperparameters $\boldsymbol{\theta}$. The basic idea is to specify the negative log joint

$$-\mathcal{E}(\boldsymbol{f}, \boldsymbol{\theta}) = \log p(\boldsymbol{f}, \boldsymbol{\theta}|\mathbf{X}, \boldsymbol{y}) = \log \mathcal{N}(\boldsymbol{f}|\mathbf{0}, \mathbf{K}(\mathbf{X}, \mathbf{X})) + \sum_{n=1}^{N} \log \text{Ber}(y_n|f_n(\boldsymbol{x}_n)) + \log p(\boldsymbol{\theta}) \quad (17.55)$$

We then use autograd to compute $\nabla_{\boldsymbol{f}}\mathcal{E}(\boldsymbol{f}, \boldsymbol{\theta})$ and $\nabla_{\boldsymbol{\theta}}\mathcal{E}(\boldsymbol{f}, \boldsymbol{\theta})$, and use these gradients as inputs to a Gaussian proposal distribution.

Let us consider a 1d example from [Mar18]. This is similar to the Bayesian logistic regression example from Figure 4.20, where the goal is to classify iris flowers as being Setosa or Versicolor, $y_n \in \{0, 1\}$, given information about the sepal length, x_n. We will use an SE kernel with length scale ℓ. We put a Ga(2, 0.5) prior on ℓ.

Figure 17.10a shows the results using the SE kernel. This is similar to the results of linear logistic regression (see Figure 4.20), except that at the edges (away from the data), the probability curves towards 0.5. This is because the prior mean function is $m(x) = 0$, and $\sigma(0) = 0.5$. We can eliminate this artefact by using a more flexible kernel, which encodes the prior knowledge that we expect the output to be monotonically increasing or decreasing in the input. We can do this using a **linear kernel**,

$$\mathcal{K}(x, x') = (x - c)(x' - c) \quad (17.56)$$

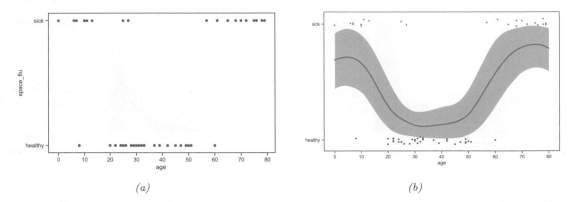

Figure 17.11: (a) Fictitious "space flu" binary classification problem. (b) Fit from a GP with SE kernel. Adapted from Figures 7.13–7.14 of [Mar18]. Generated by gp_classify_spaceflu_1d_pymc3.ipynb.

We can scale and add this to the SE kernel to get

$$\mathcal{K}(x, x') = \tau(x - c)(x' - c) + \exp\left[-\frac{(x - x')^2}{2\ell^2}\right] \tag{17.57}$$

The results are shown in Figure 17.10b, and look more reasonable.

One might wonder why we bothered to use a GP, when the results are no better than a simple linear logistic regression model. The reason is that the GP is much more flexible, and makes fewer a priori assumptions, beyond smoothness. For example, suppose the data looked like Figure 17.11a. In this case, a linear logistic regression model could not fit the data. We could in principle use a neural network, but it may not work well since we only have 60 data points. However, GPs are well designed to handle the small sample setting. In Figure 17.11b, we show the results of fitting a GP with an SE kernel to this data. The results look reasonable.

17.2.8   Connections with deep learning

It turns out that there are many interesting connections and similarities between GPs and deep neural networks. For example, one can show that a neural network with a single, **infinitely wide** layer of RBF units is equivalent to a GP with an RBF kernel. (This follows from the fact that the RBF kernel can be expressed as the inner product of an infinite number of features.) In fact, many kinds of DNNs (in the infinite limit) can be converted to an equivalent GP using a specific kind of kernel known as the **neural tangent kernel** [JGH18]. See the sequel to this book, [Mur23], for details.

17.2.9   Scaling GPs to large datasets

The main disadvantage of GPs (and other kernel methods, such as SVMs, which we discuss in Section 17.3) is that inverting the $N \times N$ kernel matrix takes $O(N^3)$ time, making the method too slow for big datasets. Many different approximate schemes have been proposed to speedup GPs (see e.g., [Liu+18a] for a review). In this section, we briefly mention some of them. For more details, see the sequel to this book, [Mur23].

17.2.9.1 Sparse (inducing-point) approximations

A simple approach to speeding up GP inference is to use less data. A better approach is to try to "summarize" the N training points $\mathbf{X}$ into $M \ll N$ **inducing points** or **pseudo inputs Z**. This lets us replace $p(\boldsymbol{f}|\boldsymbol{f}_X)$ with $p(\boldsymbol{f}|\boldsymbol{f}_Z)$, where $\boldsymbol{f}_X = \{f(\boldsymbol{x}) : \boldsymbol{x} \in \mathbf{Z}\}$ is the vector of observed function values at the training points, and $\boldsymbol{f}_Z = \{f(\boldsymbol{x}) : \boldsymbol{x} \in \mathbf{Z}\}$ is the vector of estimated function values at the inducing points. By optimizing $(\mathbf{Z}, \boldsymbol{f}_Z)$ we can learn to "compress" the training data $(\mathbf{X}, \boldsymbol{f}_X)$ into a "bottleneck" $(\mathbf{Z}, \boldsymbol{f}_Z)$, thus speeding up computation from $O(N^3)$ to $O(M^3)$. This is called a **sparse GP**. This whole process can be made rigorous using the framework of variational inference. For details, see the sequel to this book, [Mur23].

17.2.9.2 Exploiting parallelization and kernel matrix structure

It takes $O(N^3)$ time to compute the Cholesky decomposition of $\mathbf{K}_{X,X}$, which is needed to solve the linear system $\mathbf{K}_\sigma \boldsymbol{\alpha} = \boldsymbol{y}$ and to compute $|\mathbf{K}_{X,X}|$, where $\mathbf{K}_\sigma = \mathbf{K}_{X,X} + \sigma^2 \mathbf{I}_N$. An alternative to Cholesky decomposition is to use linear algebra methods, often called **Krylov subspace methods**, which are based just on **matrix vector multiplication** or **MVM**. These approaches are often much faster, since they can naturally exploit structure in the kernel matrix. Moreover, even if the kernel matrix does not have special structure, matrix multiplies are trivial to parallelize, and can thus be greatly accelerated by GPUs, unlike Cholesky based methods which are largely sequential. This is the basis of the popular **GPyTorch** package [Gar+18]. For more details, see the sequel to this book, [Mur23].

17.2.9.3 Random feature approximation

Although the power of kernels resides in the ability to avoid working with featurized representations of the inputs, such kernelized methods take $O(N^3)$ time, in order to invert the Gram matrix $\mathbf{K}$. This can make it difficult to use such methods on large scale data. Fortunately, we can approximate the feature map for many (shift invariant) kernels using a randomly chosen finite set of M basis functions, thus reducing the cost to $O(NM + M^3)$. We briefly discuss this idea below. For more details, see e.g., [Liu+20].

Random features for RBF kernel

We will focus on the case of the Gaussian RBF kernel. One can show that

$$\mathcal{K}(\boldsymbol{x}, \boldsymbol{x}') \approx \boldsymbol{\phi}(\boldsymbol{x})^{\mathsf{T}} \boldsymbol{\phi}(\boldsymbol{x}') \tag{17.58}$$

where the (real-valued) feature vector is given by

$$\boldsymbol{\phi}(\boldsymbol{x}) \triangleq \frac{1}{\sqrt{T}}[(\sin(\boldsymbol{\omega}_1^{\mathsf{T}}\boldsymbol{x}), ..., \sin(\boldsymbol{\omega}_T^{\mathsf{T}}\boldsymbol{x}), \cos(\boldsymbol{\omega}_1^{\mathsf{T}}\boldsymbol{x}), ..., \cos(\boldsymbol{\omega}_T^{\mathsf{T}}\boldsymbol{x}))] \tag{17.59}$$

$$= \frac{1}{\sqrt{T}}[\sin(\boldsymbol{\Omega}\boldsymbol{x}), \cos(\boldsymbol{\Omega}\boldsymbol{x})] \tag{17.60}$$

where $T = M/2$, and $\mathbf{\Omega} \in \mathbb{R}^{T \times D}$ is a random Gaussian matrix, where the entries are sampled iid from $\mathcal{N}(0, 1/\sigma^2)$, where σ is the kernel bandwidth. The bias of the approximation decreases as we increase M. In practice, we use a finite M, and compute a single sample Monte Carlo approximation to the expectation by drawing a single random matrix. The features in Equation (17.60) are called **random Fourier features (RFF)** [RR08] or "weighted sums of random kitchen sinks" [RR09].

We can also use positive random features, rather than trigonometric random features, which can be preferable in some applications, such as models which use attention (see Section 15.6.4). In particular, we can use

$$\phi(\boldsymbol{x}) \triangleq e^{-||\boldsymbol{x}||^2/2} \frac{1}{\sqrt{M}} \left[(\exp(\boldsymbol{\omega}_1^\mathsf{T} \boldsymbol{x}), \cdots, (\exp(\boldsymbol{\omega}_M^\mathsf{T} \boldsymbol{x})) \right] \tag{17.61}$$

where $\boldsymbol{\omega}_m$ are sampled as before. For details, see [Cho+20b].

Regardless of whether we use trigonometric or positive features, we can obtain a lower variance estimate by ensuring that the rows of $\mathbf{Z}$ are random but orthogonal; these are called **orthogonal random features**. Such sampling can be conducted efficiently via Gram-Schmidt orthogonalization of the unstructured Gaussian matrices [Yu+16], or several approximations that are even faster (see [CRW17; Cho+19]).

Fastfood approximation

Unfortunately, storing the random matrix $\mathbf{\Omega}$ takes $O(DM)$ space, and computing $\mathbf{\Omega}\boldsymbol{x}$ takes $O(DM)$ time, where D is the input dimensionality, and M is the number of random features. This can be prohibitive if $M \gg D$, which it may need to be in order to get any benefits over using the original set of features. Fortunately, we can use the **fast Hadamard transform** to reduce the memory from $O(MD)$ to $O(M)$, and reduce the time from $O(MD)$ to $O(M \log D)$. This approach has been called **fastfood** [LSS13], a reference to the original term "kitchen sinks".

Extreme learning machines

We can use the random features approximation to the kernel to convert a GP into a linear model of the form

$$f(\boldsymbol{x}; \boldsymbol{\theta}) = \mathbf{W}\phi(\boldsymbol{x}) = \mathbf{W}h(\mathbf{Z}\boldsymbol{x}) \tag{17.62}$$

where $h(a) = \sqrt{1/M}[\sin(a), \cos(a)]$ for RBF kernels. This is equivalent to a one-layer MLP with random (and fixed) input-to-hidden weights. When $M > N$, this corresponds to an over-parameterized model, which can perfectly interpolate the training data.

In [Cur+17], they apply this method to fit a logistic regression model of the form $f(\boldsymbol{x}; \boldsymbol{\theta}) = \mathbf{W}^\mathsf{T} h(\hat{\mathbf{Z}}\boldsymbol{x}) + \boldsymbol{b}$ using SGD; they call the resulting method "**McKernel**". We can also optimize $\mathbf{Z}$ as well as $\mathbf{W}$, as discussed in [Alb+17], although now the problem is no longer convex.

Alternatively, we can use $M < N$, but stack many such random nonlinear layers together, and just optimize the output weights. This has been called an **extreme learning machine** or **ELM** (see e.g., [Hua14]), although this work is controversial.[1]

---

1. The controversy has arisen because the inventor Guang-Bin Huang has been accused of not citing related prior work, such as the equivalent approach based on random feature approximations to kernels. For details, see https://en.wikipedia.org/wiki/Extreme_learning_machine#Controversy.

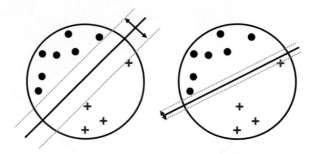

Figure 17.12: Illustration of the large margin principle. Left: a separating hyper-plane with large margin. Right: a separating hyper-plane with small margin.

17.3 Support vector machines (SVMs)

In this section, we discuss a form of (non-probabilistic) predictors for classification and regression problems which have the form

$$f(\boldsymbol{x}) = \sum_{i=1}^{N} \alpha_i \mathcal{K}(\boldsymbol{x}, \boldsymbol{x}_i) \tag{17.63}$$

By adding suitable constraints, we can ensure that many of the α_i coefficients are 0, so that predictions at test time only depend on a subset of the training points, known as "**support vectors**". Hence the resulting model is called a **support vector machine** or **SVM**. We give a brief summary below. More details, can be found in e.g., [VGS97; SS01].

17.3.1 Large margin classifiers

Consider a binary classifier of the form $h(\boldsymbol{x}) = \mathrm{sign}(f(\boldsymbol{x}))$, where the decision boundary is given by the following linear function:

$$f(\boldsymbol{x}) = \boldsymbol{w}^{\mathsf{T}} \boldsymbol{x} + w_0 \tag{17.64}$$

(In the SVM literature, it is common to assume the class labels are -1 and $+1$, rather than 0 and 1. To avoid confusion, we denote such target labels by $\tilde{y}$ rather than y.) There may be many lines that separate the data. However, intuitively we would like to pick the one that has maximum **margin**, which is the distance of the closest point to the decision boundary, since this will give us the most robust solution. This idea is illustrated in Figure 17.12: the solution on the left has larger margin than the one on the right, so it will be less sensitive to perturbations of the data.

How can we compute such a **large margin classifier**? First we need to derive an expression for the distance of a point to the decision boundary. Referring to Figure 17.13(a), we see that

$$\boldsymbol{x} = \boldsymbol{x}_{\perp} + r \frac{\boldsymbol{w}}{||\boldsymbol{w}||} \tag{17.65}$$

where r is the distance of $\boldsymbol{x}$ from the decision boundary whose normal vector is $\boldsymbol{w}$, and $\boldsymbol{x}_{\perp}$ is the orthogonal projection of $\boldsymbol{x}$ onto this boundary.

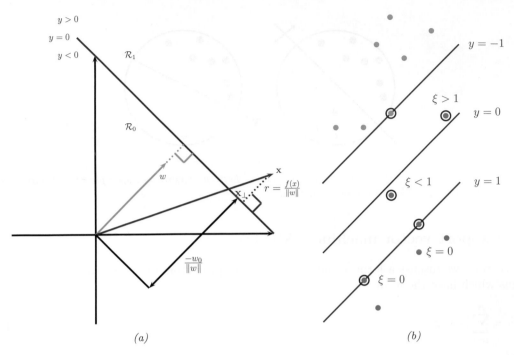

Figure 17.13: (a) Illustration of the geometry of a linear decision boundary in 2d. A point $\boldsymbol{x}$ is classified as belonging in decision region $\mathcal{R}_1$ if $f(\boldsymbol{x}) > 0$, otherwise it belongs in decision region $\mathcal{R}_0$; $\boldsymbol{w}$ is a vector which is perpendicular to the decision boundary. The term w_0 controls the distance of the decision boundary from the origin. $\boldsymbol{x}_\perp$ is the orthogonal projection of $\boldsymbol{x}$ onto the boundary. The signed distance of $\boldsymbol{x}$ from the boundary is given by $f(\boldsymbol{x})/||\boldsymbol{w}||$. Adapted from Figure 4.1 of [Bis06]. (b) Points with circles around them are support vectors, and have dual variables $\alpha_n > 0$. In the soft margin case, we associate a slack variable ξ_n with each example. If $0 < \xi_n < 1$, the point is inside the margin, but on the correct side of the decision boundary. If $\xi_n > 1$, the point is on the wrong side of the boundary. Adapted from Figure 7.3 of [Bis06].

We would like to maximize r, so we need to express it as a function of $\boldsymbol{w}$. First, note that

$$f(\boldsymbol{x}) = \boldsymbol{w}^\mathsf{T}\boldsymbol{x} + w_0 = (\boldsymbol{w}^\mathsf{T}\boldsymbol{x}_\perp + w_0) + r\frac{\boldsymbol{w}^\mathsf{T}\boldsymbol{w}}{||\boldsymbol{w}||} = (\boldsymbol{w}^\mathsf{T}\boldsymbol{x}_\perp + w_0) + r||\boldsymbol{w}|| \tag{17.66}$$

Since $0 = f(\boldsymbol{x}_\perp) = \boldsymbol{w}^\mathsf{T}\boldsymbol{x}_\perp + w_0$, we have $f(\boldsymbol{x}) = r||\boldsymbol{w}||$ and hence $r = \frac{f(\boldsymbol{x})}{||\boldsymbol{w}||}$.

Since we want to ensure each point is on the correct side of the boundary, we also require $f(\boldsymbol{x}_n)\tilde{y}_n > 0$. We want to maximize the distance of the closest point, so our final objective becomes

$$\max_{\boldsymbol{w},w_0} \frac{1}{||\boldsymbol{w}||} \min_{n=1}^{N} \left[\tilde{y}_n(\boldsymbol{w}^\mathsf{T}\boldsymbol{x}_n + w_0)\right] \tag{17.67}$$

Note that by rescaling the parameters using $\boldsymbol{w} \to k\boldsymbol{w}$ and $w_0 \to kw_0$, we do not change the distance of any point to the boundary, since the k factor cancels out when we divide by $||\boldsymbol{w}||$. Therefore let us define the scale factor such that $\tilde{y}_n f_n = 1$ for the point that is closest to the decision boundary.

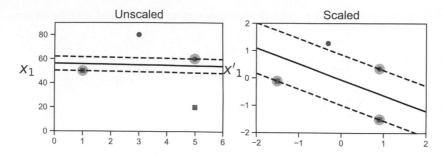

Figure 17.14: Illustration of the benefits of scaling the input features before computing a max margin classifier. Adapted from Figure 5.2 of [Gér19]. Generated by svm_classifier_feature_scaling.ipynb.

Hence we require $\tilde{y}_n f_n \geq 1$ for all n. Finally, note that maximizing $1/||\boldsymbol{w}||$ is equivalent to minimizing $||\boldsymbol{w}||^2$. Thus we get the new objective

$$\min_{\boldsymbol{w}, w_0} \frac{1}{2} ||\boldsymbol{w}||^2 \quad \text{s.t.} \quad \tilde{y}_n(\boldsymbol{w}^\mathsf{T} \boldsymbol{x}_n + w_0) \geq 1, n = 1 : N \tag{17.68}$$

(The factor of $\frac{1}{2}$ is added for convenience and doesn't affect the optimal parameters.) The constraint says that we want all points to be on the correct side of the decision boundary with a margin of at least 1.

Note that it is important to scale the input variables before using an SVM, otherwise the margin measures distance of a point to the boundary using all input dimensions equally. See Figure 17.14 for an illustration.

17.3.2 The dual problem

The objective in Equation (17.68) is a standard quadratic programming problem (Section 8.5.4), since we have a quadratic objective subject to linear constraints. This has $N + D + 1$ variables subject to N constraints, and is known as a **primal problem**.

In convex optimization, for every primal problem we can derive a **dual problem**. Let $\boldsymbol{\alpha} \in \mathbb{R}^N$ be the dual variables, corresponding to Lagrange multipliers that enforce the N inequality constraints. The generalized Lagrangian is given below (see Section 8.5.2 for relevant background information on constrained optimization):

$$\mathcal{L}(\boldsymbol{w}, w_0, \boldsymbol{\alpha}) = \frac{1}{2} \boldsymbol{w}^\mathsf{T} \boldsymbol{w} - \sum_{n=1}^{N} \alpha_n(\tilde{y}_n(\boldsymbol{w}^\mathsf{T} \boldsymbol{x}_n + w_0) - 1) \tag{17.69}$$

To optimize this, we must find a stationary point that satisfies

$$(\hat{\boldsymbol{w}}, \hat{w}_0, \hat{\boldsymbol{\alpha}}) = \min_{\boldsymbol{w}, w_0} \max_{\boldsymbol{\alpha}} \mathcal{L}(\boldsymbol{w}, w_0, \boldsymbol{\alpha}) \tag{17.70}$$

We can do this by computing the partial derivatives wrt $\boldsymbol{w}$ and w_0 and setting to zero. We have

$$\nabla_{\boldsymbol{w}}\mathcal{L}(\boldsymbol{w}, w_0, \boldsymbol{\alpha}) = \boldsymbol{w} - \sum_{n=1}^{N} \alpha_n \tilde{y}_n \boldsymbol{x}_n \tag{17.71}$$

$$\frac{\partial}{\partial w_0}\mathcal{L}(\boldsymbol{w}, w_0, \boldsymbol{\alpha}) = -\sum_{n=1}^{N} \alpha_n \tilde{y}_n \tag{17.72}$$

and hence

$$\hat{\boldsymbol{w}} = \sum_{n=1}^{N} \hat{\alpha}_n \tilde{y}_n \boldsymbol{x}_n \tag{17.73}$$

$$0 = \sum_{n=1}^{N} \hat{\alpha}_n \tilde{y}_n \tag{17.74}$$

Plugging these into the Lagrangian yields the following

$$\mathcal{L}(\hat{\boldsymbol{w}}, \hat{w}_0, \boldsymbol{\alpha}) = \frac{1}{2}\hat{\boldsymbol{w}}^{\mathsf{T}}\hat{\boldsymbol{w}} - \sum_{n=1}^{N} \alpha_n \tilde{y}_n \hat{\boldsymbol{w}}^{\mathsf{T}} \boldsymbol{x}_n - \sum_{n=1}^{N} \alpha_n \tilde{y}_n w_0 + \sum_{n=1}^{N} \alpha_n \tag{17.75}$$

$$= \frac{1}{2}\hat{\boldsymbol{w}}^{\mathsf{T}}\hat{\boldsymbol{w}} - \hat{\boldsymbol{w}}^{\mathsf{T}}\hat{\boldsymbol{w}} - 0 + \sum_{n=1}^{N} \alpha_n \tag{17.76}$$

$$= -\frac{1}{2}\sum_{i=1}^{N}\sum_{j=1}^{N} \alpha_i \alpha_j \tilde{y}_i \tilde{y}_j \boldsymbol{x}_i^{\mathsf{T}} \boldsymbol{x}_j + \sum_{n=1}^{N} \alpha_n \tag{17.77}$$

This is called the **dual form** of the objective. We want to maximize this wrt $\boldsymbol{\alpha}$ subject to the constraints that $\sum_{n=1}^{N} \alpha_n \tilde{y}_n = 0$ and $0 \leq \alpha_n$ for $n = 1:N$.

The above objective is a quadratic problem in N variables. Standard QP solvers take $O(N^3)$ time. However, specialized algorithms, which avoid the use of generic QP solvers, have been developed for this problem, such as the **sequential minimal optimization** or **SMO** algorithm [Pla98], which takes $O(N)$ to $O(N^2)$ time.

Since this is a convex objective, the solution must satisfy the KKT conditions (Section 8.5.2), which tell us that the following properties hold:

$$\alpha_n \geq 0 \tag{17.78}$$
$$\tilde{y}_n f(\boldsymbol{x}_n) - 1 \geq 0 \tag{17.79}$$
$$\alpha_n(\tilde{y}_n f(\boldsymbol{x}_n) - 1) = 0 \tag{17.80}$$

Hence either $\alpha_n = 0$ (in which case example n is ignored when computing $\hat{\boldsymbol{w}}$) or the constraint $\tilde{y}_n(\hat{\boldsymbol{w}}^{\mathsf{T}}\boldsymbol{x}_n + \hat{w}_0) = 1$ is active. This latter condition means that example n lies on the decision boundary; these points are known as the **support vectors**, as shown in Figure 17.13(b). We denote the set of support vectors by $\mathcal{S}$.

To perform prediction, we use

$$f(\boldsymbol{x}; \hat{\boldsymbol{w}}, \hat{w}_0) = \hat{\boldsymbol{w}}^\mathsf{T} \boldsymbol{x} + \hat{w}_0 = \sum_{n \in \mathcal{S}} \alpha_n \tilde{y}_n \boldsymbol{x}_n^\mathsf{T} \boldsymbol{x} + \hat{w}_0 \tag{17.81}$$

To solve for $\hat{w}_0$ we can use the fact that for any support vector, we have $\tilde{y}_n f(\boldsymbol{x}; \hat{\boldsymbol{w}}, \hat{w}_0) = 1$. Multiplying both sides by $\tilde{y}_n$, and exploiting the fact that $\tilde{y}_n^2 = 1$, we get $\hat{w}_0 = \tilde{y}_n - \hat{\boldsymbol{w}}^\mathsf{T} \boldsymbol{x}_n$. In practice we get better results by averaging over all the support vectors to get

$$\hat{w}_0 = \frac{1}{|\mathcal{S}|} \sum_{n \in \mathcal{S}} (\tilde{y}_n - \hat{\boldsymbol{w}}^\mathsf{T} \boldsymbol{x}_n) = \frac{1}{|\mathcal{S}|} \sum_{n \in \mathcal{S}} (\tilde{y}_n - \sum_{m \in \mathcal{S}} \alpha_m \tilde{y}_m \boldsymbol{x}_m^\mathsf{T} \boldsymbol{x}_n) \tag{17.82}$$

17.3.3 Soft margin classifiers

If the data is not linearly separable, there will be no feasible solution in which $\tilde{y}_n f_n \geq 1$ for all n. We therefore introduce **slack variables** $\xi_n \geq 0$ and replace the hard constraints that $\tilde{y}_n f_n \geq 0$ with the **soft margin constraints** that $\tilde{y}_n f_n \geq 1 - \xi_n$. The new objective becomes

$$\min_{\boldsymbol{w}, w_0, \boldsymbol{\xi}} \frac{1}{2} ||\boldsymbol{w}||^2 + C \sum_{n=1}^{N} \xi_n \quad \text{s.t.} \quad \xi_n \geq 0, \quad \tilde{y}_n(\boldsymbol{x}_n^\mathsf{T} \boldsymbol{w} + w_0) \geq 1 - \xi_n \tag{17.83}$$

where $C \geq 0$ is a hyper parameter controlling how many points we allow to violate the margin constraint. (If $C = \infty$, we recover the unregularized, hard-margin classifier.)

The corresponding Lagrangian for the soft margin classifier becomes

$$\mathcal{L}(\boldsymbol{w}, w_0, \boldsymbol{\alpha}, \boldsymbol{\xi}, \boldsymbol{\mu}) = \frac{1}{2} \boldsymbol{w}^\mathsf{T} \boldsymbol{w} + C \sum_{n=1}^{N} \xi_n - \sum_{n=1}^{N} \alpha_n(\tilde{y}_n(\boldsymbol{w}^\mathsf{T} \boldsymbol{x}_n + w_0) - 1 + \xi_n) - \sum_{n=1}^{N} \mu_n \xi_n \tag{17.84}$$

where $\alpha_n \geq 0$ and $\mu_n \geq 0$ are the Lagrange multipliers. Optimizing out $\boldsymbol{w}$, w_0 and $\boldsymbol{\xi}$ gives the dual form

$$\mathcal{L}(\boldsymbol{\alpha}) = \sum_{i=1}^{N} \alpha_i - \frac{1}{2} \sum_{i=1}^{N} \sum_{j=1}^{N} \alpha_i \alpha_j \tilde{y}_i \tilde{y}_j \boldsymbol{x}_i^\mathsf{T} \boldsymbol{x}_j \tag{17.85}$$

This is identical to the hard margin case; however, the constraints are different. In particular, the KKT conditions imply

$$0 \leq \alpha_n \leq C \tag{17.86}$$

$$\sum_{n=1}^{N} \alpha_n \tilde{y}_n = 0 \tag{17.87}$$

If $\alpha_n = 0$, the point is ignored. If $0 < \alpha_n < C$ then $\xi_n = 0$, so the point lies on the margin. If $\alpha_n = C$, the point can lie inside the margin, and can either be correctly classified if $\xi_n \leq 1$, or misclassified if $\xi_n > 1$. See Figure 17.13(b) for an illustration. Hence $\sum_n \xi_n$ is an upper bound on the number of misclassified points.

As before, the bias term can be computed using

$$\hat{w}_0 = \frac{1}{|\mathcal{M}|} \sum_{n \in \mathcal{M}} (\tilde{y}_n - \sum_{m \in \mathcal{S}} \alpha_m \tilde{y}_m \boldsymbol{x}_m^\mathsf{T} \boldsymbol{x}_n) \tag{17.88}$$

where $\mathcal{M}$ is the set of points having $0 < \alpha_n < C$.

There is an alternative formulation of the soft margin SVM known as the ν-**SVM classifier** [Sch+00]. This involves maximizing

$$\mathcal{L}(\boldsymbol{\alpha}) = -\frac{1}{2} \sum_{i=1}^{N} \sum_{j=1}^{N} \alpha_i \alpha_j \tilde{y}_i \tilde{y}_j \boldsymbol{x}_i^\mathsf{T} \boldsymbol{x}_j \tag{17.89}$$

subject to the constraints that

$$0 \le \alpha_n \le 1/N \tag{17.90}$$

$$\sum_{n=1}^{N} \alpha_n \tilde{y}_n = 0 \tag{17.91}$$

$$\sum_{n=1}^{M} \alpha_n \ge \nu \tag{17.92}$$

This has the advantage that the parameter ν, which replaces C, can be interpreted as an upper bound on the fraction of **margin errors** (points for which $\xi_n > 0$), as well as a lower bound on the number of support vectors.

17.3.4   The kernel trick

So far we have converted the large margin binary classification problem into a dual problem in N unknowns ($\boldsymbol{\alpha}$) which (in general) takes $O(N^3)$ time to solve, which can be slow. However, the principal benefit of the dual problem is that we can replace all inner product operations $\boldsymbol{x}^\mathsf{T} \boldsymbol{x}'$ with a call to a positive definite (Mercer) kernel function, $\mathcal{K}(\boldsymbol{x}, \boldsymbol{x}')$. This is called the **kernel trick**.

In particular, we can rewrite the prediction function in Equation (17.81) as follows:

$$f(\boldsymbol{x}) = \hat{\boldsymbol{w}}^\mathsf{T} \boldsymbol{x} + \hat{w}_0 = \sum_{n \in \mathcal{S}} \alpha_n \tilde{y}_n \boldsymbol{x}_n^\mathsf{T} \boldsymbol{x} + \hat{w}_0 = \sum_{n \in \mathcal{S}} \alpha_n \tilde{y}_n \mathcal{K}(\boldsymbol{x}_n, \boldsymbol{x}) + \hat{w}_0 \tag{17.93}$$

We also need to kernelize the bias term. This can be done by kernelizing Equation (17.82) as follows:

$$\hat{w}_0 = \frac{1}{|\mathcal{S}|} \sum_{i \in \mathcal{S}} \left(\tilde{y}_i - (\sum_{j \in \mathcal{S}} \hat{\alpha}_j \tilde{y}_j \boldsymbol{x}_j)^\mathsf{T} \boldsymbol{x}_i \right) = \frac{1}{|\mathcal{S}|} \sum_{i \in \mathcal{S}} \left(\tilde{y}_i - \sum_{j \in \mathcal{S}} \hat{\alpha}_j \tilde{y}_j \mathcal{K}(\boldsymbol{x}_j, \boldsymbol{x}_i) \right) \tag{17.94}$$

The kernel trick allows us to avoid having to deal with an explicit feature representation of our data, and allows us to easily apply classifiers to structured objects, such as strings and graphs.

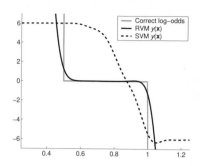

Figure 17.15: *Log-odds vs x for 3 different methods. Adapted from Figure 10 of [Tip01]. Used with kind permission of Mike Tipping.*

17.3.5   Converting SVM outputs into probabilities

An SVM classifier produces a hard-labeling, $\hat{y}(\boldsymbol{x}) = \text{sign}(f(\boldsymbol{x}))$. However, we often want a measure of confidence in our prediction. One heuristic approach is to interpret $f(\boldsymbol{x})$ as the log-odds ratio, $\log \frac{p(y=1|\boldsymbol{x})}{p(y=0|\boldsymbol{x})}$. We can then convert the output of an SVM to a probability using

$$p(y = 1|\boldsymbol{x}, \boldsymbol{\theta}) = \sigma(af(\boldsymbol{x}) + b) \tag{17.95}$$

where a, b can be estimated by maximum likelihood on a separate validation set. (Using the training set to estimate a and b leads to severe overfitting.) This technique was first proposed in [Pla00], and is known as **Platt scaling**.

However, the resulting probabilities are not particularly well calibrated, since there is nothing in the SVM training procedure that justifies interpreting $f(\boldsymbol{x})$ as a log-odds ratio. To illustrate this, consider an example from [Tip01]. Suppose we have 1d data where $p(x|y = 0) = \text{Unif}(0, 1)$ and $p(x|y = 1) = \text{Unif}(0.5, 1.5)$. Since the class-conditional distributions overlap in the $[0.5, 1]$ range, the log-odds of class 1 over class 0 should be zero in this region, and infinite outside this region. We sampled 1000 points from the model, and then fit a probabilistic kernel classifier (an RVM, described in Section 17.4.1) and an SVM with a Gaussian kernel of width 0.1. Both models can perfectly capture the decision boundary, and achieve a generalization error of 25%, which is Bayes optimal in this problem. The probabilistic output from the RVM is a good approximation to the true log-odds, but this is not the case for the SVM, as shown in Figure 17.15.

17.3.6   Connection with logistic regression

We have seen that data points that are on the correct side of the decision boundary have $\xi_n = 0$; for the others, we have $\xi_n = 1 - \tilde{y}_n f(\boldsymbol{x}_n)$. Therefore we can rewrite the objective in Equation (17.83) as follows:

$$\mathcal{L}(\boldsymbol{w}) = \sum_{n=1}^{N} \ell_{\text{hinge}}(\tilde{y}_n, f(\boldsymbol{x}_n))) + \lambda \|\boldsymbol{w}\|^2 \tag{17.96}$$

where $\lambda = (2C)^{-1}$ and $\ell_{\text{hinge}}(y, \eta)$ is the **hinge loss** function defined by

$$\ell_{\text{hinge}}(\tilde{y}, \eta) = \max(0, 1 - \tilde{y}\eta) \tag{17.97}$$

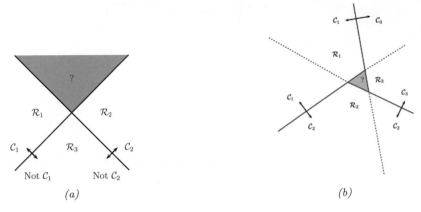

Figure 17.16: (a) The one-versus-rest approach. The green region is predicted to be both class 1 and class 2. (b) The one-versus-one approach. The label of the green region is ambiguous. Adapted from Figure 4.2 of [Bis06].

As we see from Figure 4.2, this is a convex, piecewise differentiable upper bound to the 0-1 loss, that has the shape of a partially open door hinge.

By contrast, (penalized) logistic regression optimizes

$$\mathcal{L}(\boldsymbol{w}) = \sum_{n=1}^{N} \ell_{ll}(\tilde{y}_n, f(\boldsymbol{x}_n))) + \lambda \|\boldsymbol{w}\|^2 \tag{17.98}$$

where the **log loss** is given by

$$\ell_{ll}(\tilde{y}, \eta) = -\log p(y|\eta) = \log(1 + e^{-\tilde{y}\eta}) \tag{17.99}$$

This is also plotted in Figure 4.2. We see that it is similar to the hinge loss, but with two important differences. First the hinge loss is piecewise linear, so we cannot use regular gradient methods to optimize it. (We can, however, compute the subgradient at $\tilde{y}\eta = 1$.) Second, the hinge loss has a region where it is strictly 0; this results in sparse estimates.

We see that both functions are convex upper bounds on the 0-1 loss, which is given by

$$\ell_{01}(\tilde{y}, \hat{y}) = \mathbb{I}(\tilde{y} \neq \hat{y}) = \mathbb{I}(\tilde{y}\,\hat{y} < 0) \tag{17.100}$$

These upper bounds are easier to optimize and can be viewed as surrogates for the 0-1 loss. See Section 4.3.2 for details.

17.3.7   Multi-class classification with SVMs

SVMs are inherently a binary classifier. One way to convert them to a multi-class classification model is to train C binary classifiers, where the data from class c is treated as positive, and the data from all the other classes is treated as negative. We then use the rule $\hat{y}(\boldsymbol{x}) = \arg\max_c f_c(\boldsymbol{x})$ to

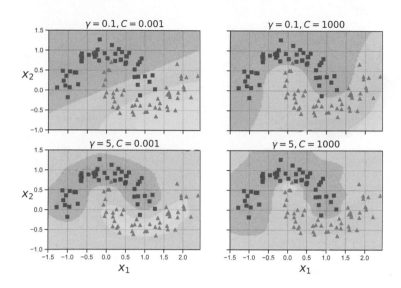

Figure 17.17: *SVM classifier with RBF kernel with precision γ and regularizer C applied to two moons data. Adapted from Figure 5.9 of [Gér19]. Generated by svm_classifier_2d.ipynb.*

predict the final label, where $f_c(\boldsymbol{x}) = \log \frac{p(c=1|\boldsymbol{x})}{p(c=0|\boldsymbol{x})}$ is the score given by classifier c. This is known as the **one-versus-the-rest** approach (also called **one-vs-all**).

Unfortunately, this approach has several problems. First, it can result in regions of input space which are ambiguously labeled. For example, the green region at the top of Figure 17.16(a) is predicted to be both class 2 and class 1. A second problem is that the magnitude of the f_c's scores are not calibrated with each other, so it is hard to compare them. Finally, each binary subproblem is likely to suffer from the class imbalance problem (Section 10.3.8.2). For example, suppose we have 10 equally represented classes. When training f_1, we will have 10% positive examples and 90% negative examples, which can hurt performance.

Another approach is to use the **one-versus-one** or OVO approach, also called **all pairs**, in which we train $C(C-1)/2$ classifiers to discriminate all pairs $f_{c,c'}$. We then classify a point into the class which has the highest number of votes. However, this can also result in ambiguities, as shown in Figure 17.16(b). Also, this requires fitting $O(C^2)$ models.

17.3.8 How to choose the regularizer C

SVMs require that you specify the kernel function and the parameter C. Typically C is chosen by cross-validation. Note, however, that C interacts quite strongly with the kernel parameters. For example, suppose we are using an RBF kernel with precision $\gamma = \frac{1}{2\sigma^2}$. If γ is large, corresponding to narrow kernels, we may need heavy regularization, and hence small C. If γ is small, a larger value of C should be used. So we see that γ and C are tightly coupled, as illustrated in Figure 17.17.

The authors of libsvm [HCL03] recommend using CV over a 2d grid with values $C \in \{2^{-5}, 2^{-3}, \dots, 2^{15}\}$

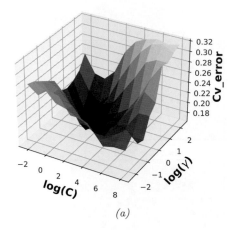 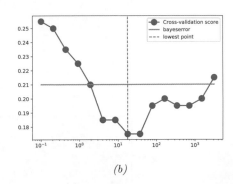

(a) (b)

Figure 17.18: (a) A cross validation estimate of the 0-1 error for an SVM classifier with RBF kernel with different precisions $\gamma = 1/(2\sigma^2)$ and different regularizer $\lambda = 1/C$, applied to a synthetic data set drawn from a mixture of 2 Gaussians. (b) A slice through this surface for $\gamma = 5$ The red dotted line is the Bayes optimal error, computed using Bayes rule applied to the model used to generate the data. Adapted from Figure 12.6 of [HTF09]. Generated by svmCgammaDemo.ipynb.

and $\gamma \in \{2^{-15}, 2^{-13}, \ldots, 2^3\}$. See Figure 17.18 which shows the CV estimate of the 0-1 risk as a function of C and γ.

To choose C efficiently, one can develop a path following algorithm in the spirit of lars (Section 11.4.4). The basic idea is to start with C small, so that the margin is wide, and hence all points are inside of it and have $\alpha_i = 1$. By slowly increasing C, a small set of points will move from inside the margin to outside, and their α_i values will change from 1 to 0, as they cease to be support vectors. When C is maximal, the margin becomes empty, and no support vectors remain. See [Has+04] for the details.

17.3.9   Kernel ridge regression

Recall the equation for ridge regression from Equation (11.55):

$$\hat{\boldsymbol{w}}_{\mathrm{map}} = (\mathbf{X}^\mathsf{T}\mathbf{X} + \lambda \mathbf{I}_D)^{-1}\mathbf{X}^\mathsf{T}\boldsymbol{y} = (\sum_n \boldsymbol{x}_n \boldsymbol{x}_n^\mathsf{T} + \lambda \mathbf{I}_D)^{-1}(\sum_n \tilde{y}_n \boldsymbol{x}_n) \qquad (17.101)$$

Using the matrix inversion lemma (Section 7.3.3), we can rewrite the ridge estimate as follows

$$\boldsymbol{w} = \mathbf{X}^\mathsf{T}(\mathbf{X}\mathbf{X}^\mathsf{T} + \lambda \mathbf{I}_N)^{-1}\boldsymbol{y} = \sum_n \boldsymbol{x}_n ((\sum_n \boldsymbol{x}_n^\mathsf{T}\boldsymbol{x}_n + \lambda \mathbf{I}_N)^{-1}\boldsymbol{y})_n \qquad (17.102)$$

Let us define the following **dual variables**:

$$\boldsymbol{\alpha} \triangleq (\mathbf{X}\mathbf{X}^\mathsf{T} + \lambda \mathbf{I}_N)^{-1}\boldsymbol{y} = (\sum_n \boldsymbol{x}_n^\mathsf{T}\boldsymbol{x}_n + \lambda \mathbf{I}_N)^{-1}\boldsymbol{y} \qquad (17.103)$$

Then we can rewrite the **primal variables** as follows

$$\boldsymbol{w} = \mathbf{X}^\mathsf{T}\boldsymbol{\alpha} = \sum_{n=1}^{N} \alpha_n \boldsymbol{x}_n \tag{17.104}$$

This tells us that the solution vector is just a linear sum of the N training vectors. When we plug this in at test time to compute the predictive mean, we get

$$f(\boldsymbol{x};\boldsymbol{w}) = \boldsymbol{w}^\mathsf{T}\boldsymbol{x} = \sum_{n=1}^{N} \alpha_n \boldsymbol{x}_n^\mathsf{T}\boldsymbol{x} \tag{17.105}$$

We can then use the kernel trick to rewrite this as

$$f(\boldsymbol{x};\boldsymbol{w}) = \sum_{n=1}^{N} \alpha_n \mathcal{K}(\boldsymbol{x}_n, \boldsymbol{x}) \tag{17.106}$$

where

$$\boldsymbol{\alpha} = (\mathbf{K} + \lambda \mathbf{I}_N)^{-1}\boldsymbol{y} \tag{17.107}$$

In other words,

$$f(\boldsymbol{x};\boldsymbol{w}) = \boldsymbol{k}^\mathsf{T}(\mathbf{K} + \lambda \mathbf{I}_N)^{-1}\boldsymbol{y} \tag{17.108}$$

where $\boldsymbol{k} = [\mathcal{K}(\boldsymbol{x}, \boldsymbol{x}_1), \ldots, \mathcal{K}(\boldsymbol{x}, \boldsymbol{x}_N)]$. This is called **kernel ridge regression**.

The trouble with the above approach is that the solution vector $\boldsymbol{\alpha}$ is not sparse, so predictions at test time will take $O(N)$ time. We discuss a solution to this in Section 17.3.10.

17.3.10 SVMs for regression

Consider the following ℓ_2-regularized ERM problem:

$$J(\boldsymbol{w}, \lambda) = \lambda||\boldsymbol{w}||^2 + \sum_{n=1}^{N} \ell(\tilde{y}_n, \hat{y}_n) \tag{17.109}$$

where $\hat{y}_n = \boldsymbol{w}^\mathsf{T}\boldsymbol{x}_n + w_0$. If we use the quadratic loss, $\ell(y, \hat{y}) = (y - \hat{y})^2$, where $y, \hat{y} \in \mathbb{R}$, we recover ridge regression (Section 11.3). If we then apply the kernel trick, we recover kernel ridge regression (Section 17.3.9).

The problem with kernel ridge regression is that the solution depends on all N training points, which makes it computationally intractable. However, by changing the loss function, we can make the optimal set of basis function coefficients, $\boldsymbol{\alpha}^*$, be sparse, as we show below.

In particular, consider the following variant of the Huber loss function (Section 5.1.5.3) called the **epsilon insensitive loss function**:

$$L_\epsilon(y, \hat{y}) \triangleq \begin{cases} 0 & \text{if } |y - \hat{y}| < \epsilon \\ |y - \hat{y}| - \epsilon & \text{otherwise} \end{cases} \tag{17.110}$$

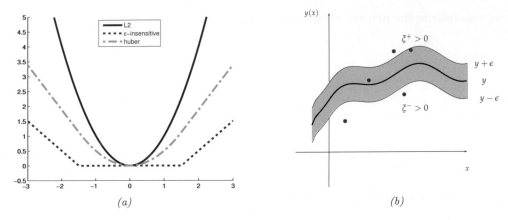

Figure 17.19: (a) Illustration of ℓ_2, Huber and ϵ-insensitive loss functions, where $\epsilon = 1.5$. Generated by huberLossPlot.ipynb. (b) Illustration of the ϵ-tube used in SVM regression. Points above the tube have $\xi_i^+ > 0$ and $\xi_i^- = 0$. Points below the tube have $\xi_i^+ = 0$ and $\xi_i^- > 0$. Points inside the tube have $\xi_i^+ = \xi_i^- = 0$. Adapted from Figure 7.7 of [Bis06].

This means that any point lying inside an ϵ-**tube** around the prediction is not penalized, as in Figure 17.19.

The corresponding objective function is usually written in the following form

$$J = \frac{1}{2}||\boldsymbol{w}||^2 + C \sum_{n=1}^{N} L_\epsilon(\tilde{y}_n, \hat{y}_n) \tag{17.111}$$

where $\hat{y}_n = f(\boldsymbol{x}_n) = \boldsymbol{w}^\mathsf{T}\boldsymbol{x}_n + w_0$ and $C = 1/\lambda$ is a regularization constant. This objective is convex and unconstrained, but not differentiable, because of the absolute value function in the loss term. As in Section 11.4.9, where we discussed the lasso problem, there are several possible algorithms we could use. One popular approach is to formulate the problem as a constrained optimization problem. In particular, we introduce **slack variables** to represent the degree to which each point lies outside the tube:

$$\tilde{y}_n \le f(\boldsymbol{x}_n) + \epsilon + \xi_n^+ \tag{17.112}$$
$$\tilde{y}_n \ge f(\boldsymbol{x}_n) - \epsilon - \xi_n^- \tag{17.113}$$

Given this, we can rewrite the objective as follows:

$$J = \frac{1}{2}||\boldsymbol{w}||^2 + C \sum_{n=1}^{N} (\xi_n^+ + \xi_n^-) \tag{17.114}$$

This is a quadratic function of $\boldsymbol{w}$, and must be minimized subject to the linear constraints in Equations 17.112-17.113, as well as the positivity constraints $\xi_n^+ \ge 0$ and $\xi_n^- \ge 0$. This is a standard quadratic program in $2N + D + 1$ variables.

By forming the Lagrangian and optimizing, as we did above, one can show that the optimal solution has the following form

$$\hat{\boldsymbol{w}} = \sum_n \alpha_n \boldsymbol{x}_n \tag{17.115}$$

where $\alpha_n \geq 0$ are the dual variables. (See e.g., [SS02] for details.) Fortunately, the $\boldsymbol{\alpha}$ vector is sparse, meaning that many of its entries are equal to 0. This is because the loss doesn't care about errors which are smaller than ϵ. The degree of sparsity is controlled by C and ϵ.

The $\boldsymbol{x}_n$ for which $\alpha_n > 0$ are called the **support vectors**; these are points for which the errors lie on or outside the ϵ tube. These are the only training examples we need to keep for prediction at test time, since

$$f(\boldsymbol{x}) = \hat{w}_0 + \hat{\boldsymbol{w}}^\mathsf{T} \boldsymbol{x} = \hat{w}_0 + \sum_{n:\alpha_n > 0} \alpha_n \boldsymbol{x}_n^\mathsf{T} \boldsymbol{x} \tag{17.116}$$

Finally, we can use the kernel trick to get

$$f(\boldsymbol{x}) = \hat{w}_0 + \sum_{n:\alpha_n > 0} \alpha_n \mathcal{K}(\boldsymbol{x}_n, \boldsymbol{x}) \tag{17.117}$$

This overall technique is called **support vector machine regression** or **SVM regression** for short, and was first proposed in [VGS97].

In Figure 17.20, we give an example where we use an RBF kernel with $\gamma = 1$. When C is small, the model is heavily regularized; when C is large, the model is less regularized and can fit the data better. We also see that when ϵ is small, the tube is smaller, so there are more support vectors.

17.4 Sparse vector machines

GPs are very flexible models, but incur an $O(N)$ time cost at prediction time, which can be prohibitive. SVMs solve that problem by estimating a sparse weight vector. However, SVMs do not give calibrated probabilistic outputs.

We can get the best of both worlds by using parametric models, where the feature vector is defined using basis functions centered on each of the training points, as follows:

$$\boldsymbol{\phi}(\boldsymbol{x}) = [\mathcal{K}(\boldsymbol{x}, \boldsymbol{x}_1), \ldots, \mathcal{K}(\boldsymbol{x}, \boldsymbol{x}_N)] \tag{17.118}$$

where $\mathcal{K}$ is any similarity kernel, not necessarily a Mercer kernel. Equation (17.118) maps $\boldsymbol{x} \in \mathcal{X}$ into $\boldsymbol{\phi}(\boldsymbol{x}) \in \mathbb{R}^N$. We can plug this new feature vector into any discriminative model, such as logistic regression. Since we have $D = N$ parameters, we need to use some kind of regularization, to prevent overfitting. If we fit such a model using ℓ_2 regularization (which we will call **L2VM**, for ℓ_2-vector machine), the result often has good predictive performance, but the weight vector $\boldsymbol{w}$ will be dense, and will depend on all N training points. A natural solution is to impose a sparsity-promoting prior on $\boldsymbol{w}$, so that not all the exemplars need to be kept. We call such methods **sparse vector machines**.

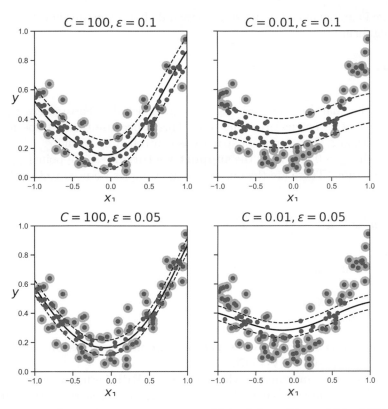

Figure 17.20: Illustration of support vector regression. Adapted from Figure 5.11 of [Gér19]. Generated by svm_regression_1d.ipynb.

17.4.1   Relevance vector machines (RVMs)

The simplest way to ensure w is sparse is to use ℓ_1 regularization, as in Section 11.4. We call this **L1VM** or **Laplace vector machine**, since this approach is equivalent to using MAP estimation with a Laplace prior for w.

However, sometimes ℓ_1 regularization does not result in a sufficient level of sparsity for a given level of accuracy. An alternative approach is based on the use of **ARD** or **automatic relevancy determination**, which uses type II maximum likelihood (aka empirical Bayes) to estimate a sparse weight vector [Mac95; Nea96]. If we apply this technique to a feature vector defined in terms of kernels, as in Equation (17.118), we get a method called the **relevance vector machine** or **RVM** [Tip01; TF03].

17.4.2   Comparison of sparse and dense kernel methods

In Figure 17.21, we compare L2VM, L1VM, RVM and an SVM using an RBF kernel on a binary classification problem in 2d. We use cross validation to pick $C = 1/\lambda$ for the SVM (see Section 17.3.8),

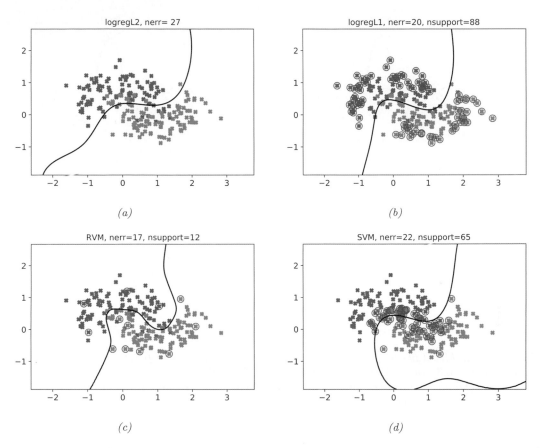

Figure 17.21: *Example of non-linear binary classification using an RBF kernel with bandwidth $\sigma = 0.3$. (a) L2VM. (b) L1VM. (c) RVM. (d) SVM. Green circles denote the support vectors. Generated by kernelBinaryClassifDemo.ipynb.*

and then use the same value of the regularizer for L2VM and L1VM. We see that all the methods give similar predictive performance. However, we see that the RVM is the sparsest model, so it will be the fastest at run time.

In Figure 17.22, we compare L2VM, L1VM, RVM and an SVM using an RBF kernel on a 1d regression problem. Again, we see that predictions are quite similar, but RVM is the sparsest, then L1VM, then SVM. This is further illustrated in Figure 17.23.

Beyond these small empirical examples, we provide a more general summary of the different methods in Table 17.1. The columns of this table have the following meaning:

- Optimize $\boldsymbol{w}$: a key question is whether the objective $\mathcal{L}(\boldsymbol{w}) = -\log p(\mathcal{D}|\boldsymbol{w}) - \log p(\boldsymbol{w})$ is convex or not. L2VM, L1VM and SVMs have convex objectives. RVMs do not. GPs are Bayesian methods that integrate out the weights $\boldsymbol{w}$.

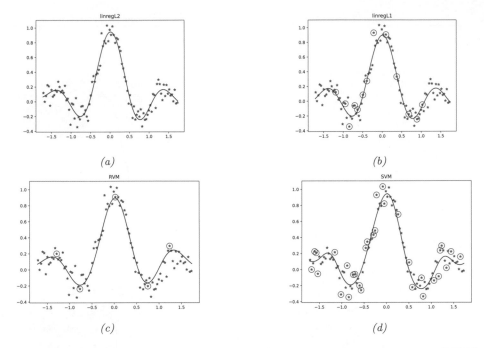

Figure 17.22: *Model fits for kernel based regression on the noisy sinc function using an RBF kernel with bandwidth $\sigma = 0.3$. (a) L2VM with $\lambda = 0.5$. (b) L1VM with $\lambda = 0.5$. (c) RVM. (d) SVM regression with $C = 1/\lambda$. chosen by cross validation. Red circles denote the retained training exemplars. Generated by rvm_regression_1d.ipynb.*

- Optimize kernel: all the methods require that we "tune" the kernel parameters, such as the bandwidth of the RBF kernel, as well as the level of regularization. For methods based on Gaussian priors, including L2VM, RVMs and GPs, we can use efficient gradient based optimizers to maximize the marginal likelihood. For SVMs and L1VMs, we must use cross validation, which is slower (see Section 17.3.8).

- Sparse: L1VM, RVMs and SVMs are sparse kernel methods, in that they only use a subset of the training examples. GPs and L2VM are not sparse: they use all the training examples. The principle advantage of sparsity is that prediction at test time is usually faster. However, this usually results in overconfidence in the predictions.

- Probabilistic: All the methods except for SVMs produce probabilistic output of the form $p(y|\boldsymbol{x})$. SVMs produce a "confidence" value that can be converted to a probability, but such probabilities are usually very poorly calibrated (see Section 17.3.5).

- Multiclass: All the methods except for SVMs naturally work in the multiclass setting, by using a categorical distribution instead of a Bernoulli. The SVM can be made into a multiclass classifier, but there are various difficulties with this approach, as discussed in Section 17.3.7.

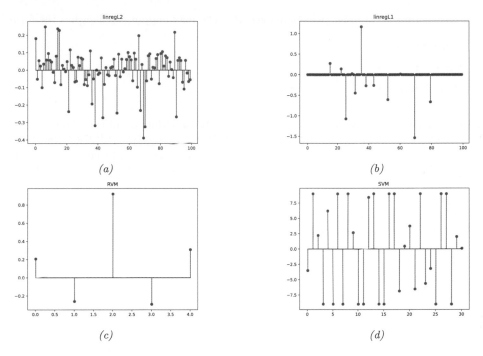

Figure 17.23: Estimated coefficients for the models in Figure 17.22. Generated by rvm_regression_1d.ipynb.

Method	Opt. w	Opt. kernel	Sparse	Prob.	Multiclass	Non-Mercer	Section
SVM	Convex	CV	Yes	No	Indirectly	No	17.3
L2VM	Convex	EB	No	Yes	Yes	Yes	17.4.1
L1VM	Convex	CV	Yes	Yes	Yes	Yes	17.4.1
RVM	Not convex	EB	Yes	Yes	Yes	Yes	17.4.1
GP	N/A	EB	No	Yes	Yes	No	17.2.7

Table 17.1: Comparison of various kernel based classifiers. EB = empirical Bayes, CV = cross validation. See text for details.

- Mercer kernel: SVMs and GPs require that the kernel is positive definite; the other techniques do not, since the kernel function in Equation (17.118) can be an arbitrary function of two inputs.

17.5 Exercises

Exercise 17.1 [Fitting an SVM classifier by hand *]

(Source: Jaakkola.) Consider a dataset with 2 points in 1d: $x_1 = 0$ with label $y_1 = -1$ and $x_2 = \sqrt{2}$ with label $y_2 = 1$. Consider mapping each point to 3d using the feature vector $\phi(x) = [1, \sqrt{2}x, x^2]^T$. (This is equivalent to using a second order polynomial kernel.) The max margin classifier has the form

$$\min ||\boldsymbol{w}||^2 \quad \text{s.t.} \tag{17.119}$$

$$y_1(\boldsymbol{w}^T \phi(\boldsymbol{x}_1) + w_0) \geq 1 \tag{17.120}$$

$$y_2(\boldsymbol{w}^T \phi(\boldsymbol{x}_2) + w_0) \geq 1 \tag{17.121}$$

a. Write down a vector that is parallel to the optimal vector $\boldsymbol{w}$. Hint: recall from Figure 17.12(a) that $\boldsymbol{w}$ is perpendicular to the decision boundary between the two points in the 3d feature space.

b. What is the value of the margin that is achieved by this $\boldsymbol{w}$? Hint: recall that the margin is the distance from each support vector to the decision boundary. Hint 2: think about the geometry of 2 points in space, with a line separating one from the other.

c. Solve for $\boldsymbol{w}$, using the fact that the margin is equal to $1/||\boldsymbol{w}||$.

d. Solve for w_0 using your value for $\boldsymbol{w}$ and Equations 17.119 to 17.121. Hint: the points will be on the decision boundary, so the inequalities will be tight.

e. Write down the form of the discriminant function $f(x) = w_0 + \boldsymbol{w}^T \phi(x)$ as an explicit function of x.

18 Trees, Forests, Bagging, and Boosting

18.1 Classification and regression trees (CART)

Classification and regression trees or **CART** models [BFO84], also called **decision trees** [Qui86; Qui93], are defined by recursively partitioning the input space, and defining a local model in each resulting region of input space. The overall model can be represented by a tree, with one leaf per region, as we explain below.

18.1.1 Model definition

We start by considering regression trees, where all inputs are real-valued. The tree consists of a set of nested decision rules. At each node i, the feature dimension d_i of the input vector $\boldsymbol{x}$ is compared to a threshold value t_i, and the input is then passed down to the left or right branch, depending on whether it is above or below threshold. At the leaves of the tree, the model specifies the predicted output for any input that falls into that part of the input space.

For example, consider the regression tree in Figure 18.1(a). The first node asks if x_1 is less than some threshold t_1. If yes, we then ask if x_2 is less than some other threshold t_2. If yes, we enter the bottom left leaf node. This corresponds to the region of space defined by

$$R_1 = \{\boldsymbol{x} : x_1 \le t_1, x_2 \le t_2\} \tag{18.1}$$

We can associate this region with the predicted output, say $y = 2$. In a similar way, we can partition the entire input space into 5 regions using **axis parallel splits**, as shown in Figure 18.1(b).[1]

Formally, a regression tree can be defined by

$$f(\boldsymbol{x}; \boldsymbol{\theta}) = \sum_{j=1}^{J} w_j \mathbb{I}(\boldsymbol{x} \in R_j) \tag{18.2}$$

where R_j is the region specified by the j'th leaf node, w_j is the predicted output for that node,

$$w_j = \frac{\sum_{n=1}^{N} y_n \mathbb{I}(\boldsymbol{x}_n \in R_j)}{\sum_{n=1}^{N} \mathbb{I}(\boldsymbol{x}_n \in R_j)} \tag{18.3}$$

---

1. By using enough splits (i.e., deep enough trees), we can make a piecewise linear approximation to decision boundaries with more complex shapes, but it may require a lot of data to fit such a model.

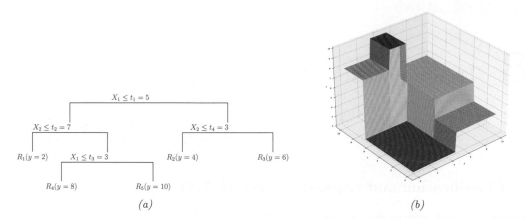

Figure 18.1: (a) A regression tree on two inputs. (b) Corresponding piecewise constant surface, where the regions have heights 2, 4, 6, 8 and 10. Adapted from Figure 9.2 of [HTF09]. Generated by regtreeSurfaceDemo.ipynb.

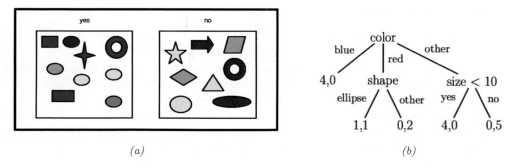

Figure 18.2: (a) A set of shapes with corresponding binary labels. The features are: color (values "blue", "red", "other"), shape (values "ellipse", "other"), and size (real-valued). (b) A hypothetical classification tree fitted to this data. A leaf labeled as (n_1, n_0) means that there are n_1 positive examples that fall into this partition, and n_0 negative examples.

and $\boldsymbol{\theta} = \{(R_j, w_j) : j = 1 : J\}$, where J is the number of nodes. The regions themselves are defined by the feature dimensions that are used in each split, and the corresponding thresholds, on the path from the root to the leaf. For example, in Figure 18.1(a), we have $R_1 = [(x_1 \leq t_1), (x_2 \leq t_2)]$, $R_4 = [(x_1 \leq t_1), (x_2 > t_2), (x_3 \leq t_3)]$, etc. (For categorical inputs, we can define the splits based on comparing feature x_i to each of the possible values for that feature, rather than comparing to a numeric threshold.) We discuss how to learn these regions in Section 18.1.2.

For classification problems, the leaves contain a distribution over the class labels, rather than just the mean response. See Figure 18.2 for an example of a classification tree.

18.1.2 Model fitting

To fit the model, we need to minimize the following loss:

$$\mathcal{L}(\boldsymbol{\theta}) = \sum_{n=1}^{N} \ell(y_n, f(\boldsymbol{x}_n; \boldsymbol{\theta})) = \sum_{j=1}^{J} \sum_{\boldsymbol{x}_n \in R_j} \ell(y_n, w_j) \tag{18.4}$$

Unfortunately, this is not differentiable, because of the need to learn the discrete tree structure. Indeed, finding the optimal partitioning of the data is NP-complete [HR76]. The standard practice is to use a greedy procedure, in which we iteratively grow the tree one node at a time. This approach is used by CART [BFO84], **C4.5** [Qui93], and **ID3** [Qui86], which are three popular implementations of the method.

The idea is as follows. Suppose we are at node i; let $\mathcal{D}_i = \{(\boldsymbol{x}_n, y_n) \in N_i\}$ be the set of examples that reach this node. We will consider how to split this node into a left branch and right branch so as to minimize the error in each child subtree.

If the j'the feature is a real-valued scalar, we can partition the data at node i by comparing to a threshold t. The set of possible thresholds $\mathcal{T}_j$ for feature j can be obtained by sorting the unique values of $\{x_{nj}\}$. For example, if feature 1 has the values $\{4.5, -12, 72, -12\}$, then we set $\mathcal{T}_1 = \{-12, 4.5, 72\}$. For each possible threshold, we define the left and right splits, $\mathcal{D}_i^L(j, t) = \{(\boldsymbol{x}_n, y_n) \in N_i : x_{n,j} \leq t\}$ and $\mathcal{D}_i^R(j, t) = \{(\boldsymbol{x}_n, y_n) \in N_i : x_{n,j} > t\}$.

If the j'th feature is categorical, with K_j possible values, then we check if the feature is equal to each of those values or not. This defines a set of K_j possible binary splits: $\mathcal{D}_i^L(j, t) = \{(\boldsymbol{x}_n, y_n) \in N_i : x_{n,j} = t\}$ and $\mathcal{D}_i^R(j, t) = \{(\boldsymbol{x}_n, y_n) \in N_i : x_{n,j} \neq t\}$.) (Alternatively, we could allow for a multi-way split, as in Figure 18.2(b). However, this may cause **data fragmentation**, in which too little data might "fall" into each subtree, resulting in overfitting. Therefore it is more common to use binary splits.)

Once we have computed $\mathcal{D}_i^L(j, t)$ and $\mathcal{D}_i^R(j, t)$ for each j and t at node i, we choose the best feature j_i to split on, and the best value for that feature, t_i, as follows:

$$(j_i, t_i) = \arg \min_{j \in \{1, \dots, D\}} \min_{t \in \mathcal{T}_j} \frac{|\mathcal{D}_i^L(j, t)|}{|\mathcal{D}_i|} c(\mathcal{D}_i^L(j, t)) + \frac{|\mathcal{D}_i^R(j, t)|}{|\mathcal{D}_i|} c(\mathcal{D}_i^R(j, t)) \tag{18.5}$$

We now discuss the cost function $c(\mathcal{D}_i)$ which is used to evaluate the cost of node i. For regression, we can use the mean squared error

$$\text{cost}(\mathcal{D}_i) = \frac{1}{|\mathcal{D}|} \sum_{n \in \mathcal{D}_i} (y_n - \overline{y})^2 \tag{18.6}$$

where $\overline{y} = \frac{1}{|\mathcal{D}|} \sum_{n \in \mathcal{D}_i} y_n$ is the mean of the response variable for examples reaching node i.

For classification, we first compute the empirical distribution over class labels for this node:

$$\hat{\pi}_{ic} = \frac{1}{|\mathcal{D}_i|} \sum_{n \in \mathcal{D}_i} \mathbb{I}(y_n = c) \tag{18.7}$$

Given this, we can then compute the **Gini index**

$$G_i = \sum_{c=1}^{C} \hat{\pi}_{ic}(1 - \hat{\pi}_{ic}) = \sum_c \hat{\pi}_{ic} - \sum_c \hat{\pi}_{ic}^2 = 1 - \sum_c \hat{\pi}_{ic}^2 \tag{18.8}$$

This is the expected error rate. To see this, note that $\hat{\pi}_{ic}$ is the probability a random entry in the leaf belongs to class c, and $1 - \hat{\pi}_{ic}$ is the probability it would be misclassified.

Alternatively we can define cost as the entropy or **deviance** of the node:

$$H_i = \mathbb{H}(\hat{\boldsymbol{\pi}}_i) = -\sum_{c=1}^{C} \hat{\pi}_{ic} \log \hat{\pi}_{ic} \tag{18.9}$$

A node that is **pure** (i.e., only has examples of one class) will have 0 entropy.

Given one of the above cost functions, we can use Equation (18.5) to pick the best feature, and best threshold at each node. We then partition the data, and call the fitting algorithm recursively on each subset of the data.

18.1.3 Regularization

If we let the tree become deep enough, it can achieve 0 error on the training set (assuming no label noise), by partioning the input space into sufficiently small regions where the output is constant. However, this will typically result in overfitting. To prevent this, there are two main approaches. The first is to stop the tree growing process according to some heuristic, such as having too few examples at a node, or reaching a maximum depth. The second approach is to grow the tree to its maximum depth, where no more splits are possible, and then to **prune** it back, by merging split subtrees back into their parent (see e.g., [BA97b]). This can partially overcome the greedy nature of top-down tree growing. (For example, consider applying the top-down approach to the xor data in Figure 13.1: the algorithm would never make any splits, since each feature on its own has no predictive power.) However, forward growing and backward pruning is slower than the greedy top-down approach.

18.1.4 Handling missing input features

In general, it is hard for discriminative models, such as neural networks, to handle missing input features, as we discussed in Section 1.5.5. However, for trees, there are some simple heuristics that can work well.

The standard heuristic for handling missing inputs in decision trees is to look for a series of "backup" variables, which can induce a similar partition to the chosen variable at any given split; these can be used in case the chosen variable is unobserved at test time. These are called **surrogate splits**. This method finds highly correlated features, and can be thought of as learning a local joint model of the input. This has the advantage over a generative model of not modeling the entire joint distribution of inputs, but it has the disadvantage of being entirely ad hoc. A simpler approach, applicable to categorical variables, is to code "missing" as a new value, and then to treat the data as fully observed.

18.1.5 Pros and cons

Tree models are popular for several reasons:

- They are easy to interpret.

- They can easily handle mixed discrete and continuous inputs.

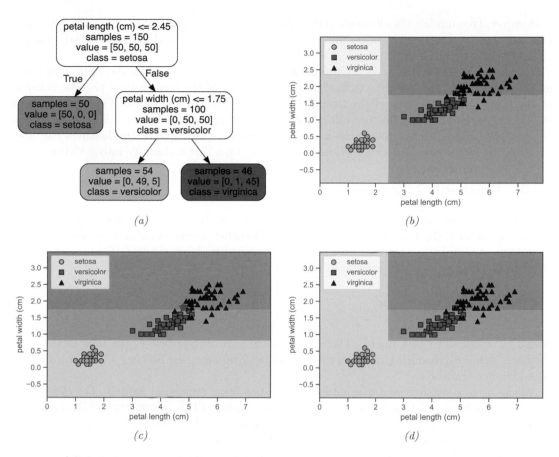

Figure 18.3: *(a) A decision tree of depth 2 fit to the iris data, using just the petal length and petal width features. Leaf nodes are color coded according to the majority class. The number of training samples that pass from the root to each node is shown inside each box, as well as how many of these values fall into each class. This can be normalized to get a distribution over class labels for each node. (b) Decision surface induced by (a). (c) Fit to data where we omit a single data point (shown by red star). (d) Ensemble of the two models in (b) and (c). Generated by* dtree_sensitivity.ipynb.

- They are insensitive to monotone transformations of the inputs (because the split points are based on ranking the data points), so there is no need to standardize the data.

- They perform automatic variable selection.

- They are relatively robust to outliers.

- They are fast to fit, and scale well to large data sets.

- They can handle missing input features.

However, tree models also have some disadvantages. The primary one is that they do not predict very accurately compared to other kinds of model. This is in part due to the greedy nature of the tree construction algorithm.

A related problem is that trees are **unstable**: small changes to the input data can have large effects on the structure of the tree, due to the hierarchical nature of the tree-growing process, causing errors at the top to affect the rest of the tree. For example, consider the tree in Figure 18.3b. Omitting even a single data point from the training set can result in a dramatically different decision surface, as shown in Figure 18.3c, due to the use of axis parallel splits. (Omitting features can also cause instability.) In Section 18.3 and Section 18.4, we will turn this instability into a virtue.

18.2   Ensemble learning

In Section 18.1, we saw that decision trees can be quite unstable, in the sense that their predictions might vary a lot if the training data is perturbed. In other words, decision trees are a high variance estimator. A simple way to reduce variance is to average multiple models. This is called **ensemble learning**. The result model has the form

$$f(y|\boldsymbol{x}) = \frac{1}{|\mathcal{M}|} \sum_{m \in \mathcal{M}} f_m(y|\boldsymbol{x}) \tag{18.10}$$

where f_m is the m'th base model. The ensemble will have similar bias to the base models, but lower variance, generally resulting in improved overall performance (see Section 4.7.6.3 for details on the bias-variance tradeoff).

Averaging is a sensible way to combine predictions from regression models. For classifiers, it can sometimes be better to take a majority vote of the outputs. (This is sometimes called a **committee method**.) To see why this can help, suppose each base model is a binary classifier with an accuracy of θ, and suppose class 1 is the correct class. Let $Y_m \in \{0, 1\}$ be the prediction for the m'th model, and let $S = \sum_{m=1}^{M} Y_m$ be the number of votes for class 1. We define the final predictor to be the majority vote, i.e., class 1 if $S > M/2$ and class 0 otherwise. The probability that the ensemble will pick class 1 is

$$p = \Pr(S > M/2) = 1 - B(M/2, M, \theta) \tag{18.11}$$

where $B(x, M, \theta)$ is the cdf of the binomial distribution with parameters M and θ evaluated at x. For $\theta = 0.51$ and $M = 1000$, we get $p = 0.73$ and with $M = 10,000$ we get $p = 0.97$.

The performance of the voting approach is dramatically improved, because we assumed each predictor made independent errors. In practice, their mistakes may be correlated, but as long as we ensemble sufficiently diverse models, we can still come out ahead.

18.2.1   Stacking

An alternative to using an unweighted average or majority vote is to learn how to combine the base models, by using

$$f(y|\boldsymbol{x}) = \sum_{m \in \mathcal{M}} w_m f_m(y|\boldsymbol{x}) \tag{18.12}$$

This is called **stacking**, which stands for "stacked generalization" [Wol92]. Note that the combination weights used by stacking need to be trained on a separate dataset, otherwise they would put all their mass on the best performing base model.

18.2.2 Ensembling is not Bayes model averaging

It is worth noting that an ensemble of models is not the same as using Bayes model averaging over models (Section 4.6), as pointed out in [Min00]. An ensemble considers a larger hypothesis class of the form

$$p(y|\boldsymbol{x}, \boldsymbol{w}, \boldsymbol{\theta}) = \sum_{m \in \mathcal{M}} w_m p(y|\boldsymbol{x}, \boldsymbol{\theta}_m) \tag{18.13}$$

whereas BMA uses

$$p(y|\boldsymbol{x}, \mathcal{D}) = \sum_{m \in \mathcal{M}} p(m|\mathcal{D}) p(y|\boldsymbol{x}, m, \mathcal{D}) \tag{18.14}$$

The key difference is that in the case of BMA, the weights $p(m|\mathcal{D})$ sum to one, and in the limit of infinite data, only a single model will be chosen (namely the MAP model). By contrast, the ensemble weights w_m are arbitrary, and don't collapse in this way to a single model.

18.3 Bagging

In this section, we discuss **bagging** [Bre96], which stands for "bootstrap aggregating". This is a simple form of ensemble learning in which we fit M different base models to different randomly sampled versions of the data; this encourages the different models to make diverse predictions. The datasets are sampled with replacement (a technique known as bootstrap sampling, Section 4.7.3), so a given example may appear multiple times, until we have a total of N examples per model (where N is the number of original data points).

The disadvantage of bootstrap is that each base model only sees, on average, 63% of the unique input examples. To see why, note that the chance that a single item will not be selected from a set of size N in any of N draws is $(1 - 1/N)^N$. In the limit of large N, this becomes $e^{-1} \approx 0.37$, which means only $1 - 0.37 = 0.63$ of the data points will be selected.

The 37% of the training instances that are not used by a given base model are called **out-of-bag instances** (oob). We can use the predicted performance of the base model on these oob instances as an estimate of test set performance. This provides a useful alternative to cross validation.

The main advantage of bootstrap is that it prevents the ensemble from relying too much on any individual training example, which enhances robustness and generalization [Gra04]. For example, comparing Figure 18.3b and Figure 18.3c, we see that omitting a single example from the training set can have a large impact on the decision tree that we learn (even though the tree growing algorithm is otherwise deterministic). By averaging the predictions from both of these models, we get the more reasonable prediction model in Figure 18.3d. This advantage generally increases with the size of the ensemble, as shown in Figure 18.4. (Of course, larger ensembles take more memory and more time.)

Bagging does not always improve performance. In particular, it relies on the base models being unstable estimators, so that omitting some of the data significantly changes the resulting model fit.

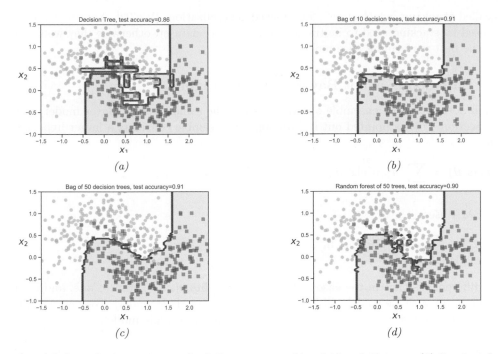

Figure 18.4: (a) A single decision tree. (b-c) Bagging ensemble of 10 and 50 trees. (d) Random forest of 50 trees. Adapted from Figure 7.5 of [Gér19]. Generated by bagging_trees.ipynb and rf_demo_2d.ipynb.

This is the case for decision trees, but not for other models, such as nearest neighbor classifiers. For neural networks, the story is more mixed. They can be unstable wrt their training set. On the other hand, deep networks will underperform if they only see 63% of the data, so bagged DNNs do not usually work well [NTL20].

18.4   Random forests

Bagging relies on the assumption that re-running the same learning algorithm on different subsets of the data will result in sufficiently diverse base models. The technique known as **random forests** [Bre01] tries to decorrelate the base learners even further by learning trees based on a randomly chosen subset of input variables (at each node of the tree), as well as a randomly chosen subset of data cases. It does this by modifying Equation (18.5) so the the feature split dimension j is optimized over a random subset of the features, $S_i \subset \{1, \ldots, D\}$.

For example, consider the email spam dataset [HTF09, p301]. This dataset contains 4601 email messages, each of which is classified as spam (1) or non-spam (0). The data was open sourced by George Forman from Hewlett-Packard (HP) Labs.

There are 57 quantitative (real-valued) features, as follows:

- 48 features corresponding to the percentage of words in the email that match a given word, such as "remove" or "labs".

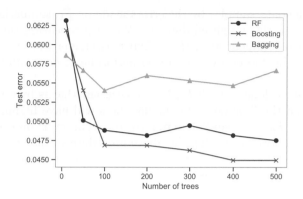

Figure 18.5: Preditive accuracy vs size of tree ensemble for bagging, random forests and gradient boosting with log loss. Adapted from Figure 15.1 of [HTF09]. Generated by spam_tree_ensemble_compare.ipynb.

- 6 features corresponding to the percentage of characters in the email that match a given character, namely ; . [! $ #

- 3 features corresponding to the average length, max length, and sum of lengths of uninterrupted sequences of capital letters. (These features are called CAPAVE, CAPMAX and CAPTOT.)

Figure 18.5 shows that random forests work much better than bagged decision trees, because many input features are irrelevant. (We also see that a method called "boosting", discussed in Section 18.5, works even better; however, this requires sequentially fitting trees, whereas random forests can be fit in parallel.)

18.5   Boosting

Ensembles of trees, whether fit by bagging or the random forest algorithm, corresponding to a model of the form

$$f(\boldsymbol{x};\boldsymbol{\theta}) = \sum_{m=1}^{M} \beta_m F_m(\boldsymbol{x};\boldsymbol{\theta}_m) \qquad (18.15)$$

where F_m is the m'th tree, and β_m is the corresponding weight, often set to $\beta_m = 1/M$. We can generalize this by allowing the F_m functions to be general function approximators, such as neural networks, not just trees. The result is called an **additive model** [HTF09]. We can think of this as a linear model with **adaptive basis functions**. The goal, as usual, is to minimize the empirical loss (with an optional regularizer):

$$\mathcal{L}(f) = \sum_{i=1}^{N} \ell(y_i, f(\boldsymbol{x}_i)) \qquad (18.16)$$

Boosting [Sch90; FS96] is an algorithm for sequentially fitting additive models where each F_m is a binary classifier that returns $F_m \in \{-1, +1\}$. In particular, we first fit F_1 on the original data, and then we weight the data samples by the errors made by F_1, so misclassified examples get more weight. Next we fit F_2 to this weighted data set. We keep repeating this process until we have fit the desired number M of components. (M is a hyper-parameter that controls the complexity of the overall model, and can be chosen by monitoring performance on a validation set, and using early stopping.)

It can be shown that, as long as each F_m has an accuracy that is better than chance (even on the weighted dataset), then the final ensemble of classifiers will have higher accuracy than any given component. That is, if F_m is a **weak learner** (so its accuracy is only slightly better than 50%), then we can boost its performance using the above procedure so that the final f becomes a **strong learner**. (See e.g., [SF12] for more details on the learning theory approach to boosting.)

Note that boosting reduces the bias of the strong learner, by fitting trees that depend on each other, whereas bagging and RF reduce the variance by fitting independent trees. In many cases, boosting can work better. See Figure 18.5 for an example.

The original boosting algorithm focused on binary classification with a particular loss function that we will explain in Section 18.5.3, and was derived from the PAC learning theory framework (see Section 5.4.4). In the rest of this section, we focus on a more statistical version of boosting, due to [FHT00; Fri01], which works with arbitrary loss functions, making the method suitable for regression, multi-class classification, ranking, etc. Our presentation is based on [HTF09, ch10] and [BH07], which should be consulted for further details.

18.5.1   Forward stagewise additive modeling

In this section, we discuss **forward stagewise additive modeling**, in which we sequentially optimize the objective in Equation (18.16) for general (differentiable) loss functions, where f is an additive model as in Equation 18.15. That is, at iteration m, we compute

$$(\beta_m, \boldsymbol{\theta}_m) = \underset{\beta, \boldsymbol{\theta}}{\operatorname{argmin}} \sum_{i=1}^{N} \ell(y_i, f_{m-1}(\boldsymbol{x}_i) + \beta F(\boldsymbol{x}_i; \boldsymbol{\theta})) \tag{18.17}$$

We then set

$$f_m(\boldsymbol{x}) = f_{m-1}(\boldsymbol{x}) + \beta_m F(\boldsymbol{x}; \boldsymbol{\theta}_m) = f_{m-1}(\boldsymbol{x}) + \beta_m F_m(\boldsymbol{x}) \tag{18.18}$$

(Note that we do not adjust the parameters of previously added models.) The details on how to perform this optimization step depend on the loss function that we choose, and (in some cases) on the form of the weak learner F, as we discuss below.

18.5.2   Quadratic loss and least squares boosting

Suppose we use squared error loss, $\ell(y, \hat{y}) = (y - \hat{y})^2$. In this case, the i'th term in the objective at step m becomes

$$\ell(y_i, f_{m-1}(\boldsymbol{x}_i) + \beta F(\boldsymbol{x}_i; \boldsymbol{\theta})) = (y_i - f_{m-1}(\boldsymbol{x}_i) - \beta F(\boldsymbol{x}_i; \boldsymbol{\theta}))^2 = (r_{im} - \beta F(\boldsymbol{x}_i; \boldsymbol{\theta}))^2 \tag{18.19}$$

where $r_{im} = y_i - f_{m-1}(\boldsymbol{x}_i)$ is the residual of the current model on the i'th observation. We can minimize the above objective by simply setting $\beta = 1$, and fitting F to the residual errors. This is called **least squares boosting** [BY03].

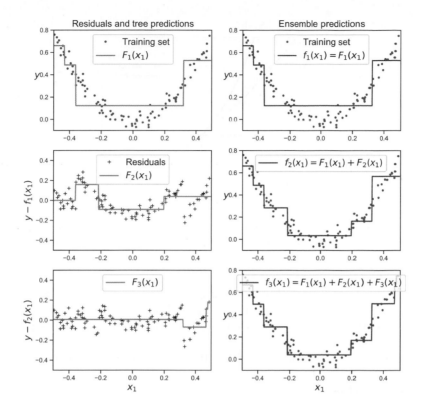

Figure 18.6: *Illustration of boosting using a regression tree of depth 2 applied to a 1d dataset. Adapted from Figure 7.9 of [Gér19]. Generated by boosted_regr_trees.ipynb.*

We give an example of this process in Figure 18.6, where we use a regression tree of depth 2 as the weak learner. On the left, we show the result of fitting the weak learner to the residuals, and on the right, we show the current strong learner. We see how each new weak learner that is added to the ensemble corrects the errors made by earlier versions of the model.

18.5.3   Exponential loss and AdaBoost

Suppose we are interested in binary classification, i.e., predicting $\tilde{y}_i \in \{-1, +1\}$. Let us assume the weak learner computes

$$p(y = 1|\boldsymbol{x}) = \frac{e^{F(\boldsymbol{x})}}{e^{-F(\boldsymbol{x})} + e^{F(\boldsymbol{x})}} = \frac{1}{1 + e^{-2F(\boldsymbol{x})}} \tag{18.20}$$

so $F(\boldsymbol{x})$ returns half the log odds. We know from Equation (10.13) that the negative log likelihood is given by

$$\ell(\tilde{y}, F(\boldsymbol{x})) = \log(1 + e^{-2\tilde{y}F(\boldsymbol{x})}) \tag{18.21}$$

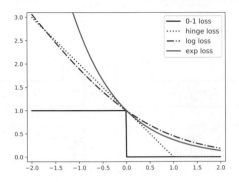

Figure 18.7: Illustration of various loss functions for binary classification. The horizontal axis is the margin $m(\boldsymbol{x}) = \tilde{y}F(\boldsymbol{x})$, the vertical axis is the loss. The log loss uses log base 2. Generated by hinge_loss_plot.ipynb.

We can minimize this by ensuring that the **margin** $m(\boldsymbol{x}) = \tilde{y}F(\boldsymbol{x})$ is as large as possible. We see from Figure 18.7 that the log loss is a smooth upper bound on the 0-1 loss. We also see that it penalizes negative margins more heavily than positive ones, as desired (since positive margins are already correctly classified).

However, we can also use other loss functions. In this section, we consider the **exponential loss**

$$\ell(\tilde{y}, F(\boldsymbol{x})) = \exp(-\tilde{y}F(\boldsymbol{x})) \tag{18.22}$$

We see from Figure 18.7 that this is also a smooth upper bound on the 0-1 loss. In the population setting (with infinite sample size), the optimal solution to the exponential loss is the same as for log loss. To see this, we can just set the derivative of the expected loss (for each $\boldsymbol{x}$) to zero:

$$\frac{\partial}{\partial F(\boldsymbol{x})} \mathbb{E}\left[e^{-\tilde{y}f(\boldsymbol{x})}|\boldsymbol{x}\right] = \frac{\partial}{\partial F(\boldsymbol{x})}[p(\tilde{y}=1|\boldsymbol{x})e^{-F(\boldsymbol{x})} + p(\tilde{y}=-1|\boldsymbol{x})e^{F(\boldsymbol{x})}] \tag{18.23}$$

$$= -p(\tilde{y}=1|\boldsymbol{x})e^{-F(\boldsymbol{x})} + p(\tilde{y}=-1|\boldsymbol{x})e^{F(\boldsymbol{x})} \tag{18.24}$$

$$= 0 \Rightarrow \frac{p(\tilde{y}=1|\boldsymbol{x})}{p(\tilde{y}=-1|\boldsymbol{x})} = e^{2F(\boldsymbol{x})} \tag{18.25}$$

However, it turns out that the exponential loss is easier to optimize in the boosting setting, as we show below. (We consider the log loss case in Section 18.5.4.)

We now discuss how to solve for the m'th weak learner, F_m, when we use exponential loss. We will assume that the base classifier F_m returns a binary class label; the resulting algorithm is called **discrete AdaBoost** [FHT00]. If F_m returns a probability instead, a modified algorithm, known as **real AdaBoost**, can be used [FHT00].

At step m we have to minimize

$$L_m(F) = \sum_{i=1}^{N} \exp[-\tilde{y}_i(f_{m-1}(\boldsymbol{x}_i) + \beta F(\boldsymbol{x}_i))] = \sum_{i=1}^{N} \omega_{i,m} \exp(-\beta\tilde{y}_i F(\boldsymbol{x}_i)) \tag{18.26}$$

where $\omega_{i,m} \triangleq \exp(-\tilde{y}_i f_{m-1}(\boldsymbol{x}_i))$ is a weight applied to datacase i, and $\tilde{y}_i \in \{-1, +1\}$. We can rewrite this objective as follows:

$$L_m = e^{-\beta} \sum_{\tilde{y}_i = F(\boldsymbol{x}_i)} \omega_{i,m} + e^{\beta} \sum_{\tilde{y}_i \neq F(\boldsymbol{x}_i)} \omega_{i,m} \tag{18.27}$$

$$= (e^{\beta} - e^{-\beta}) \sum_{i=1}^{N} \omega_{i,m} \mathbb{I}\left(\tilde{y}_i \neq F(\boldsymbol{x}_i)\right) + e^{-\beta} \sum_{i=1}^{N} \omega_{i,m} \tag{18.28}$$

Consequently the optimal function to add is

$$F_m = \operatorname*{argmin}_{F} \sum_{i=1}^{N} \omega_{i,m} \mathbb{I}\left(\tilde{y}_i \neq F(\boldsymbol{x}_i)\right) \tag{18.29}$$

This can be found by applying the weak learner to a weighted version of the dataset, with weights $\omega_{i,m}$.

All that remains is to solve for the size of the update, β. Subsituting F_m into L_m and solving for β we find

$$\beta_m = \frac{1}{2} \log \frac{1 - \mathrm{err}_m}{\mathrm{err}_m} \tag{18.30}$$

where

$$\mathrm{err}_m = \frac{\sum_{i=1}^{N} \omega_{i,m} \mathbb{I}\left(\tilde{y}_i \neq F_m(\boldsymbol{x}_i)\right)}{\sum_{i=1}^{N} \omega_{i,m}} \tag{18.31}$$

Therefore overall update becomes

$$f_m(\boldsymbol{x}) = f_{m-1}(\boldsymbol{x}) + \beta_m F_m(\boldsymbol{x}) \tag{18.32}$$

After updating the strong learner, we need to recompute the weights for the next iteration, as follows:

$$\omega_{i,m+1} = e^{-\tilde{y}_i f_m(\boldsymbol{x}_i)} = e^{-\tilde{y}_i f_{m-1}(\boldsymbol{x}_i) - \tilde{y}_i \beta_m F_m(\boldsymbol{x}_i)} = \omega_{i,m} e^{-\tilde{y}_i \beta_m F_m(\boldsymbol{x}_i)} \tag{18.33}$$

If $\tilde{y}_i = F_m(\boldsymbol{x}_i)$, then $\tilde{y}_i F_m(\boldsymbol{x}_i) = 1$, and if $\tilde{y}_i \neq F_m(\boldsymbol{x}_i)$, then $\tilde{y}_i F_m(\boldsymbol{x}_i) = -1$. Hence $-\tilde{y}_i F_m(\boldsymbol{x}_i) = 2\mathbb{I}\left(\tilde{y}_i \neq F_m(\boldsymbol{x}_o)\right) - 1$, so the update becomes

$$\omega_{i,m+1} = \omega_{i,m} e^{\beta_m (2\mathbb{I}(\tilde{y}_i \neq F_m(\boldsymbol{x}_i)) - 1)} = \omega_{i,m} e^{2\beta_m \mathbb{I}(\tilde{y}_i \neq F_m(\boldsymbol{x}_i))} e^{-\beta_m} \tag{18.34}$$

Since the $e^{-\beta_m}$ is constant across all examples, it can be dropped. If we then define $\alpha_m = 2\beta_m$, the update becomes

$$\omega_{i,m+1} = \begin{cases} \omega_{i,m} e^{\alpha_m} & \text{if } \tilde{y}_i \neq F_m(\boldsymbol{x}_i) \\ \omega_{i,m} & \text{otherwise} \end{cases} \tag{18.35}$$

Thus we see that we exponentially increase weights of misclassified examples. The resulting algorithm shown in Algorithm 18.1, and is known as **Adaboost.M1** [FS96].

A multiclass generalization of exponential loss, and an adaboost-like algorithm to minimize it, known as **SAMME** (stagewise additive modeling using a multiclass exponential loss function), is described in [Has+09]. This is implemented in scikit learn (the AdaBoostClassifier class).

Algorithm 18.1: Adaboost.M1, for binary classification with exponential loss

---

1 $\omega_i = 1/N$
2 **for** $m = 1 : M$ **do**
3   Fit a classifier $F_m(\boldsymbol{x})$ to the training set using weights $\boldsymbol{w}$
4   Compute $\mathrm{err}_m = \frac{\sum_{i=1}^{N} \omega_{i,m} \mathbb{I}(\tilde{y}_i \neq F_m(\boldsymbol{x}_i))}{\sum_{i=1}^{N} \omega_{i,m}}$
5   Compute $\alpha_m = \log[(1 - \mathrm{err}_m)/\mathrm{err}_m]$
6   Set $\omega_i \leftarrow \omega_i \exp[\alpha_m \mathbb{I}(\tilde{y}_i \neq F_m(\boldsymbol{x}_i))]$

7 Return $f(\boldsymbol{x}) = \mathrm{sgn}\left[\sum_{m=1}^{M} \alpha_m F_m(\boldsymbol{x})\right]$

18.5.4   LogitBoost

The trouble with exponential loss is that it puts a lot of weight on misclassified examples, as is apparent from the exponential blowup on the left hand side of Figure 18.7. This makes the method very sensitive to outliers (mislabeled examples). In addition, $e^{-\tilde{y}f}$ is not the logarithm of any pmf for binary variables $\tilde{y} \in \{-1, +1\}$; consequently we cannot recover probability estimates from $f(\boldsymbol{x})$.

A natural alternative is to use log loss, as we discussed in Section 18.5.3. This only punishes mistakes linearly, as is clear from Figure 18.7. Furthermore, it means that we will be able to extract probabilities from the final learned function, using

$$p(y = 1|\boldsymbol{x}) = \frac{e^{f(\boldsymbol{x})}}{e^{-f(\boldsymbol{x})} + e^{f(\boldsymbol{x})}} = \frac{1}{1 + e^{-2f(\boldsymbol{x})}} \tag{18.36}$$

The goal is to minimze the expected log-loss, given by

$$L_m(F) = \sum_{i=1}^{N} \log\left[1 + \exp\left(-2\tilde{y}_i(f_{m-1}(\boldsymbol{x}) + F(\boldsymbol{x}_i))\right)\right] \tag{18.37}$$

By performing a Newton update on this objective (similar to IRLS), one can derive the algorithm shown in Algorithm 18.2. This is known as **logitBoost** [FHT00]. The key subroutine is the ability of the weak learner F to solve a weighted least squares problem. This method can be generalized to the multi-class setting, as explained in [FHT00].

18.5.5   Gradient boosting

Rather than deriving new versions of boosting for every different loss function, it is possible to derive a generic version, known as **gradient boosting** [Fri01; Mas+00]. To explain this, imagine solving $\hat{\boldsymbol{f}} = \mathrm{argmin}_{\boldsymbol{f}} \mathcal{L}(\boldsymbol{f})$ by performing gradient descent in the space of functions. Since functions are infinite dimensional objects, we will represent them by their values on the training set, $\boldsymbol{f} = (f(\boldsymbol{x}_1), \ldots, f(\boldsymbol{x}_N))$. At step m, let $\boldsymbol{g}_m$ be the gradient of $\mathcal{L}(\boldsymbol{f})$ evaluated at $\boldsymbol{f} = \boldsymbol{f}_{m-1}$:

$$g_{im} = \left[\frac{\partial \ell(y_i, f(\boldsymbol{x}_i))}{\partial f(\boldsymbol{x}_i)}\right]_{f=f_{m-1}} \tag{18.38}$$

Algorithm 18.2: LogitBoost, for binary classification with log-loss

1   $\omega_i = 1/N$, $\pi_i = 1/2$
2   **for** $m = 1 : M$ **do**
3   Compute the working response $z_i = \frac{y_i^* - \pi_i}{\pi_i(1-\pi_i)}$
4   Compute the weights $\omega_i = \pi_i(1 - \pi_i)$
5      $F_m = \mathrm{argmin}_F \sum_{i=1}^{N} \omega_i (z_i - F(\boldsymbol{x}_i))^2$
6   Update $f(\boldsymbol{x}) \leftarrow f(\boldsymbol{x}) + \frac{1}{2} F_m(\boldsymbol{x})$
7   Compute $\pi_i = 1/(1 + \exp(-2f(\boldsymbol{x}_i)))$;
8   Return $f(\boldsymbol{x}) = \mathrm{sgn}\left[\sum_{m=1}^{M} F_m(\boldsymbol{x})\right]$

Name	Loss	$-\partial \ell(y_i, f(\boldsymbol{x}_i))/\partial f(\boldsymbol{x}_i)$
Squared error	$\frac{1}{2}(y_i - f(\boldsymbol{x}_i))^2$	$y_i - f(\boldsymbol{x}_i)$
Absolute error	$\lvert y_i - f(\boldsymbol{x}_i) \rvert$	$\mathrm{sgn}(y_i - f(\boldsymbol{x}_i))$
Exponential loss	$\exp(-\tilde{y}_i f(\boldsymbol{x}_i))$	$-\tilde{y}_i \exp(-\tilde{y}_i f(\boldsymbol{x}_i))$
Binary Logloss	$\log(1 + e^{-\tilde{y}_i f_i})$	$y_i - \pi_i$
Multiclass logloss	$-\sum_c y_{ic} \log \pi_{ic}$	$y_{ic} - \pi_{ic}$

Table 18.1: *Some commonly used loss functions, their gradients, and their population minimizers F^*. For binary classification problems, we assume $\tilde{y}_i \in \{-1, +1\}$, and $\pi_i = \sigma(2f(\boldsymbol{x}_i))$. For regression problems, we assume $y_i \in \mathbb{R}$. Adapted from [HTF09, p360] and [BH07, p483].*

Gradients of some common loss functions are given in Table 18.1. We then make the update

$$\boldsymbol{f}_m = \boldsymbol{f}_{m-1} - \beta_m \boldsymbol{g}_m \tag{18.39}$$

where β_m is the step length, chosen by

$$\beta_m = \mathrm{argmin}_{\beta} \mathcal{L}(\boldsymbol{f}_{m-1} - \beta \boldsymbol{g}_m) \tag{18.40}$$

In its current form, this is not much use, since it only optimizes f at a fixed set of N points, so we do not learn a function that can generalize. However, we can modify the algorithm by fitting a weak learner to approximate the negative gradient signal. That is, we use this update

$$F_m = \mathrm{argmin}_{F} \sum_{i=1}^{N} (-g_{im} - F(\boldsymbol{x}_i))^2 \tag{18.41}$$

The overall algorithm is summarized in Algorithm 18.3. We have omitted the line search step for β_m, which is not strictly necessary, as argued in [BH07]. However, we have introduced a learning rate or **shrinkage factor** $0 < \nu \leq 1$, to control the size of the updates, for regularization purposes.

If we apply this algorithm using squared loss, we recover L2Boosting, since $-g_{im} = y_i - f_{m-1}(\boldsymbol{x}_i)$ is just the residual error. We can also apply this algorithm to other loss functions, such as absolute loss or Huber loss (Section 5.1.5.3), which is useful for robust regression problems.

Algorithm 18.3: Gradient boosting

---

1 Initialize $f_0(\boldsymbol{x}) = \operatorname{argmin}_F \sum_{i=1}^N L(y_i, F(\boldsymbol{x}_i))$

2 for $m = 1 : M$ **do**

3 $\quad\Big|\quad$ Compute the gradient residual using $r_{im} = -\left[\frac{\partial L(y_i, f(\boldsymbol{x}_i))}{\partial f(\boldsymbol{x}_i)}\right]_{f(\boldsymbol{x}_i) = f_{m-1}(\boldsymbol{x}_i)}$

4 $\quad\Big|\quad$ Use the weak learner to compute $F_m = \operatorname{argmin}_F \sum_{i=1}^N (r_{im} - F(\boldsymbol{x}_i))^2$

5 $\quad\Big|\quad$ Update $f_m(\boldsymbol{x}) = f_{m-1}(\boldsymbol{x}) + \nu F_m(\boldsymbol{x})$

6 Return $f(\boldsymbol{x}) = f_M(\boldsymbol{x})$

For classification, we can use log-loss. In this case, we get an algorithm known as **BinomialBoost** [BH07]. The advantage of this over LogitBoost is that it does not need to be able to do weighted fitting: it just applies any black-box regression model to the gradient vector. To apply this to multi-class classification, we can fit C separate regression trees, using the pseudo residual of the form

$$-g_{icm} = \frac{\partial \ell(y_i, f_{1m}(\boldsymbol{x}_i), \dots, f_{Cm}(\boldsymbol{x}_i))}{\partial f_{cm}(\boldsymbol{x}_i)} = \mathbb{I}(y_i = c) - \pi_{ic} \tag{18.42}$$

Although the trees are fit separately, their predictions are combined via a softmax transform

$$p(y = c|\boldsymbol{x}) = \frac{e^{f_c(\boldsymbol{x})}}{\sum_{c'=1}^C e^{f_{c'}(\boldsymbol{x})}} \tag{18.43}$$

When we have large datasets, we can use a stochastic variant in which we subsample (without replacement) a random fraction of the data to pass to the regression tree at each iteration. This is called **stochastic gradient boosting** [Fri99]. Not only is it faster, but it can also generalize better, because subsampling the data is a form of regularization.

18.5.5.1 Gradient tree boosting

In practice, gradient boosting nearly always assumes that the weak learner is a regression tree, which is a model of the form

$$F_m(\boldsymbol{x}) = \sum_{j=1}^{J_m} w_{jm} \mathbb{I}(\boldsymbol{x} \in R_{jm}) \tag{18.44}$$

where w_{jm} is the predicted output for region R_{jm}. (In general, w_{jm} could be a vector.) This combination is called **gradient boosted regression trees**, or **gradient tree boosting**. (A related version is known as **MART**, which stands for "multivariate additive regression trees" [FM03].)

To use this in gradient boosting, we first find good regions R_{jm} for tree m using standard regression tree learning (see Section 18.1) on the residuals; we then (re)solve for the weights of each leaf by solving

$$\hat{w}_{jm} = \operatorname*{argmin}_w \sum_{\boldsymbol{x}_i \in R_{jm}} \ell(y_i, f_{m-1}(\boldsymbol{x}_i) + w) \tag{18.45}$$

For squared error (as used by gradient boosting), the optimal weight $\hat{w}_{jm}$ is the just the mean of the residuals in that leaf.

18.5.5.2 XGBoost

XGBoost (https://github.com/dmlc/xgboost), which stands for "extreme gradient boosting", is a very efficient and widely used implementation of gradient boosted trees, that adds a few more improvements beyond the description in Section 18.5.5.1. The details can be found in [CG16], but in brief, the extensions are as follows: it adds a regularizer on the tree complexity, it uses a second order approximation of the loss (from [FHT00]) instead of just a linear approximation, it samples features at internal nodes (as in random forests), and it uses various computer science methods (such as handling out-of-core computation for large datasets) to ensure scalability.[2]

In more detail, XGBoost optimizes the following regularized objective

$$\mathcal{L}(f) = \sum_{i=1}^{N} \ell(y_i, f(\boldsymbol{x}_i)) + \Omega(f) \tag{18.46}$$

where

$$\Omega(f) = \gamma J + \frac{1}{2}\lambda \sum_{j=1}^{J} w_j^2 \tag{18.47}$$

is the regularizer, where J is the number of leaves, and $\gamma \geq 0$ and $\lambda \geq 0$ are regularization coefficients. At the m'th step, the loss is given by

$$\mathcal{L}_m(F_m) = \sum_{i=1}^{N} \ell(y_i, f_{m-1}(\boldsymbol{x}_i) + F_m(\boldsymbol{x}_i)) + \Omega(F_m) + \text{const} \tag{18.48}$$

We can compute a second order Taylor expansion of this as follows:

$$\mathcal{L}_m(F_m) \approx \sum_{i=1}^{N} \left[\ell(y_i, f_{m-1}(\boldsymbol{x}_i)) + g_{im} F_m(\boldsymbol{x}_i) + \frac{1}{2} h_{im} F_m^2(\boldsymbol{x}_i) \right] + \Omega(F_m) + \text{const} \tag{18.49}$$

where h_{im} is the Hessian

$$h_{im} = \left[\frac{\partial^2 \ell(y_i, f(\boldsymbol{x}_i))}{\partial f(\boldsymbol{x}_i)^2} \right]_{f=f_{m-1}} \tag{18.50}$$

In the case of regression trees, we have $F(\boldsymbol{x}) = w_{q(\boldsymbol{x})}$, where $q : \mathbb{R}^D \to \{1, \ldots, J\}$ specifies which leaf node $\boldsymbol{x}$ belongs to, and $\boldsymbol{w} \in \mathbb{R}^J$ are the leaf weights. Hence we can rewrite Equation (18.49) as

---

2. Some other popular gradient boosted trees packages are **CatBoost** (https://catboost.ai/) and **LightGBM** (https://github.com/Microsoft/LightGBM).

follows, dropping terms that are independent of F_m:

$$\mathcal{L}_m(q, \boldsymbol{w}) \approx \sum_{i=1}^{N} \left[g_{im} F_m(\boldsymbol{x}_i) + \frac{1}{2} h_{im} F_m^2(\boldsymbol{x}_i) \right] + \gamma J + \frac{1}{2} \lambda \sum_{j=1}^{J} w_j^2 \qquad (18.51)$$

$$= \sum_{j=1}^{J} \left[(\sum_{i \in I_j} g_{im}) w_j + \frac{1}{2} (\sum_{i \in I_j} h_i + \lambda) w_j^2 \right] + \gamma J \qquad (18.52)$$

$_j = \{i : q(\boldsymbol{x}_i) = j\}$ is the set of indices of data points assigned to the j'th leaf. Let us define $G_{jm} = \sum_{i \in I_j} g_{im}$ and $H_{jm} = \sum_{i \in I_j} h_{im}$. Then the above simplifies to

$$\mathcal{L}_m(q, \boldsymbol{w}) = \sum_{j=1}^{J} \left[G_{jm} w_j + \frac{1}{2} (H_{jm} + \lambda) w_j^2 \right] + \gamma J \qquad (18.53)$$

This is a quadratic in each w_jm so the optimal weights are given by

$$w_j^* = -\frac{G_{jm}}{H_{jm} + \lambda} \qquad (18.54)$$

The loss for evaluating different tree structures q then becomes

$$\mathcal{L}_m(q, \boldsymbol{w}^*) = -\frac{1}{2} \sum_{j=1}^{J} \frac{G_{jm}^2}{H_{jm} + \lambda} + \gamma J \qquad (18.55)$$

We can greedily optimize this using a recursive node splitting procedure, as in Section 18.1. Specifically, for a given leaf j, we consider splitting it into a left and right half, $I = I_L \cup I_R$. We can compute the gain (reduction in loss) of such a split as follows:

$$\text{gain} = \frac{1}{2} \left[\frac{G_L^2}{H_L + \lambda} + \frac{G_R^2}{H_R + \lambda} - \frac{(G_L + G_R)^2}{(H_L + H_R) + \lambda} \right] - \gamma \qquad (18.56)$$

where $G_L = \sum_{i \in I_L} g_{im}$, $G_R = \sum_{i \in I_R} g_{im}$, $H_L = \sum_{i \in I_L} h_{im}$, and $H_R = \sum_{i \in I_R} h_{im}$. Thus we see that it is not worth splitting a node if the gain is negative (i.e., the first term is less than γ).

A fast approximation for evaluating this objective, that does not require sorting the features (for choosing the optimal threshold to split on), is described in [CG16].

18.6   Interpreting tree ensembles

Trees are popular because they are interpretable. Unfortunately, ensembles of trees (whether in the form of bagging, random forests, or boosting) lose that property. Fortunately, there are some simple methods we can use to interpret what function has been learned.

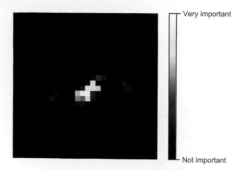

Figure 18.8: Feature importance of a random forest classifier trained to distinguish MNIST digits from classes 0 and 8. Adapted from Figure 7.6 of [Gér19]. Generated by rf_feature_importance_mnist.ipynb.

18.6.1   Feature importance

For a single decision tree T, [BFO84] proposed the following measure for **feature importance** of feature k:

$$R_k(T) = \sum_{j=1}^{J-1} G_j \mathbb{I}(v_j = k)$$

(18.57)

where the sum is over all non-leaf (internal) nodes, G_j is the gain in accuracy (reduction in cost) at node j, and $v_j = k$ if node j uses feature k. We can get a more reliable estimate by averaging over all trees in the ensemble:

$$R_k = \frac{1}{M} \sum_{m=1}^{M} R_k(T_m)$$

(18.58)

After computing these scores, we can normalize them so the largest value is 100%. We give some examples below.

Figure 18.8 gives an example of estimating feature importance for a classifier trained to distinguish MNIST digits from classes 0 and 8. We see that it focuses on the parts of the image that differ between these classes.

In Figure 18.9, we plot the relative importance of each of the features for the spam dataset (Section 18.4). Not surprisingly, we find that the most important features are the words "george" (the name of the recipient) and "hp" (the company he worked for), as well as the characters ! and $. (Note it can be the presence or absence of these features that is informative.)

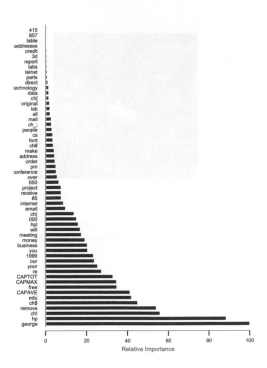

Figure 18.9: *Feature importance of a gradient boosted classifier trained to distinguish spam from non-spam email. The dataset has X training examples with Y features, corresponding to token frequency. Adapted from Figure 10.6 of [HTF09]. Generated by spam_tree_ensemble_interpret.ipynb.*

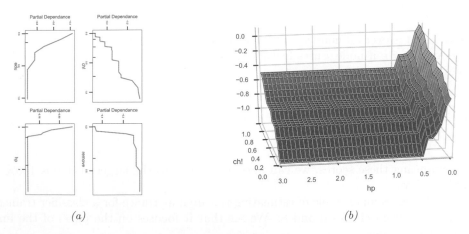

Figure 18.10: *(a) Partial dependence of log-odds of the spam class for 4 important predictors. The red ticks at the base of the plot are deciles of the empirical distribution for this feature. (b) Joint partial dependence of log-odds on the features hp and !. Adapted from Figure 10.6–10.8 of [HTF09]. Generated by spam_tree_ensemble_interpret.ipynb.*

18.6.2 Partial dependency plots

After we have identified the most relevant input features, we can try to assess the impact they have on the output. A **partial dependency plot** for feature k is a plot of

$$\overline{f}_k(x_k) = \frac{1}{N} \sum_{n=1}^{N} f(\boldsymbol{x}_{n,-k}, x_k) \tag{18.59}$$

vs x_k. Thus we marginalize out all features except k. In the case of a binary classifier, we can convert this to log odds, $\log p(y=1|x_k)/p(y=0|x_k)$, before plotting. We illustrate this for our spam example in Figure 18.10a for 4 different features. We see that as the frequency of ! and "remove" increases, so does the probability of spam. Conversely, as the frequency of "edu" or "hp" increases, the probability of spam decreases.

We can also try to capture interaction effects between features j and k by computing

$$\overline{f}_{jk}(x_j, x_k) = \frac{1}{N} \sum_{n=1}^{N} f(\boldsymbol{x}_{n,-jk}, x_j, x_k) \tag{18.60}$$

We illustrate this for our spam example in Figure 18.10b for hp and !. We see that higher frequency of ! makes it more likely to be spam, but much more so if the word "hp" is missing.

PART V

Beyond Supervised Learning

19 Learning with Fewer Labeled Examples

Many ML models, especially neural networks, often have many more parameters than we have labeled training examples. For example, a ResNet CNN (Section 14.3.4) with 50 layers has 23 million parameters. Transformer models (Section 15.5) can be even bigger. Of course these parameters are highly correlated, so they are not independent "degrees of freedom". Nevertheless, such big models are slow to train and, more importantly, they may easily overfit. This is particularly a problem when you do not have a large labeled training set. In this chapter, we discuss some ways to tackle this issue, beyond the generic regularization techniques we discussed in Section 13.5 such as early stopping, weight decay and dropout.

19.1 Data augmentation

Suppose we just have a single small labeled dataset. In some cases, we may be able to create artificially modified versions of the input vectors, which capture the kinds of variations we expect to see at test time, while keeping the original labels unchanged. This is called **data augmentation**.[1] We give some examples below, and then discuss why this approach works.

19.1.1 Examples

For image classification tasks, standard data augmentation methods include random crops, zooms, and mirror image flips, as illustrated in Figure 19.1. [GVZ16] gives a more sophisticated example, where they render text characters onto an image in a realistic way, thereby creating a very large dataset of text "in the wild". They used this to train a state of the art visual text localization and reading system. Other examples of data augmentation include artifically adding background noise to clean speech signals, and artificially replacing characters or words at random in text documents.

If we afford to train and test the model many times using different versions of the data, we can learn which augmentations work best, using blackbox optimization methods such as RL (see e.g., [Cub+19]) or Bayesian optimization (see e.g., [Lim+19]); this is called **AutoAugment**. We can also learn to combine multiple augmentations together; this is called **AutoAugment** [Cub+19].

For some examples of augmentation in NLP, see e.g., [Fen+21].

---

1. The term "data augmentation" is also used in statistics to mean the addition of auxiliary latent variables to a model in order to speed up convergence of posterior inference algorithms [DM01].

Figure 19.1: Illustration of random crops and zooms of a image images. Generated by image_augmentation_jax.ipynb.

19.1.2 Theoretical justification

Data augmentation often significantly improves performance (predictive accuracy, robustness, etc). At first this might seem like we are getting something for nothing, since we have not provided additional data. However, the data augmentation mechanism can be viewed as a way to algorithmically inject prior knowledge.

To see this, recall that in standard ERM training, we minimize the empirical risk

$$R(f) = \int \ell(f(\boldsymbol{x}), \boldsymbol{y}) p^*(\boldsymbol{x}, \boldsymbol{y}) d\boldsymbol{x} d\boldsymbol{y} \tag{19.1}$$

where we approximate $p^*(\boldsymbol{x}, \boldsymbol{y})$ by the empirical distribution

$$p_{\mathcal{D}}(\boldsymbol{x}, \boldsymbol{y}) = \frac{1}{N} \sum_{n=1}^{N} \delta(\boldsymbol{x} - \boldsymbol{x}_n) \delta(\boldsymbol{y} - \boldsymbol{y}_n) \tag{19.2}$$

We can think of data augmentation as replacing the empirical distribution with the following algorithmically smoothed distribution

$$p_{\mathcal{D}}(\boldsymbol{x}, \boldsymbol{y} | A) = \frac{1}{N} \sum_{n=1}^{N} p(\boldsymbol{x} | \boldsymbol{x}_n, A) \delta(\boldsymbol{y} - \boldsymbol{y}_n) \tag{19.3}$$

where A is the data augmentation algorithm, which generates a sample $\boldsymbol{x}$ from a training point $\boldsymbol{x}_n$, such that the label ("semantics") is not changed. (A very simple example would be a Gaussian kernel, $p(\boldsymbol{x} | \boldsymbol{x}_n, A) = \mathcal{N}(\boldsymbol{x} | \boldsymbol{x}_n, \sigma^2 \mathbf{I})$.) This has been called **vicinal risk minimization** [Cha+01], since we are minimizing the risk in the vicinity of each training point $\boldsymbol{x}$. For more details on this perspective, see [Zha+17b; CDL19; Dao+19].

19.2 Transfer learning

This section is coauthored with Colin Raffel.

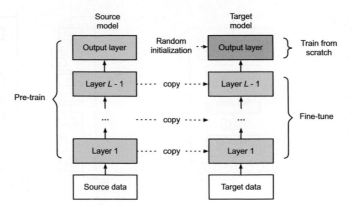

Figure 19.2: Illustration of fine-tuning a model on a new dataset. The final output layer is trained from scratch, since it might correspond to a different label set. The other layers are initialized at their previous parameters, and then optionally updated using a small learning rate. From Figure 13.2.1 of [Zha+20]. Used with kind permission of Aston Zhang.

Many data-poor tasks have some high-level structural similarity to other data-rich tasks. For example, consider the task of **fine-grained visual classification** of endangered bird species. Given that endangered birds are by definition rare, it is unlikely that a large quantity of diverse labeled images of these birds exist. However, birds bear many structural similarities across species - for example, most birds have wings, feathers, beaks, claws, etc. We therefore might expect that first training a model on a large dataset of non-endangered bird species and then continuing to train it on a small dataset of endangered species could produce better performance than training on the small dataset alone.

This is called **transfer learning**, since we are transferring information from one dataset to another, via a shared set of parameters. More precisely, we first perform a **pre-training phase**, in which we train a model with parameters $\boldsymbol{\theta}$ on a large **source dataset** $\mathcal{D}_p$; this may be labeled or unlabeled. We then perform a second **fine-tuning phase** on the small labeled **target dataset** $\mathcal{D}_q$ of interest. We discuss these two phases in more detail below, but for more information, see e.g., [Tan+18; Zhu+21] for recent surveys.

19.2.1 Fine-tuning

Suppose, for now, that we already have a pretrained classifier, $p(y|\boldsymbol{x}, \boldsymbol{\theta}_p)$, such as a CNN, that works well for inputs $\boldsymbol{x} \in \mathcal{X}_p$ (e.g. natural images) and outputs $y \in \mathcal{Y}_p$ (e.g., ImageNet labels), where the data comes from a distribution $p(\boldsymbol{x}, y)$ similar to the one used in training. Now we want to create a new model $q(y|\boldsymbol{x}, \boldsymbol{\theta}_q)$ that works well for inputs $\boldsymbol{x} \in \mathcal{X}_q$ (e.g. bird images) and outputs $y \in \mathcal{Y}_q$ (e.g., fine-grained bird labels), where the data comes from a distribution $q(\boldsymbol{x}, y)$ which may be different from p.

We will assume that the set of possible inputs is the same, so $\mathcal{X}_q \approx \mathcal{X}_p$ (e.g., both are RGB images), or that we can easily transform inputs from domain p to domain q (e.g., we can convert an RGB image to grayscale by dropping the chrominance channels and just keeping luminance). (If this is not

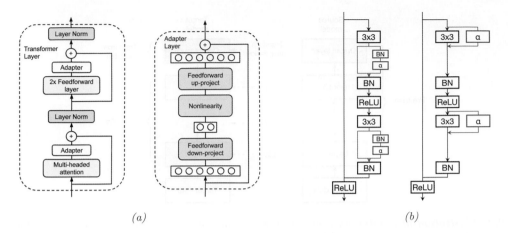

$$(a) \qquad\qquad\qquad\qquad\qquad\qquad (b)$$

Figure 19.3: (a) Adding adapter layers to a transformer. From Figure 2 of [Hou+19]. Used with kind permission of Neil Houlsby. (b) Adding adapter layers to a resnet. From Figure 2 of [RBV18]. Used with kind permission of Sylvestre-Alvise Rebuffi.

the case, then we may need to use a method called domain adaptation, that modifies models to map between modalities, as discussed in Section 19.2.5.)

However, the output domains are usually different, i.e., $\mathcal{Y}_q \neq \mathcal{Y}_p$. For example, $\mathcal{Y}_p$ might be Imagenet labels and $\mathcal{Y}_q$ might be medical labels (e.g., types of diabetic retinopathy [Arc+19]). In this case, we need to "translate" the output of the pre-trained model to the new domain. This is easy to do with neural networks: we simply "chop off" the final layer of the original model, and add a new "head" to model the new class labels, as illustrated in Figure 19.2. For example, suppose $p(y|\boldsymbol{x}, \boldsymbol{\theta}_p) = \mathrm{softmax}(y|\mathbf{W}_2 \boldsymbol{h}(\boldsymbol{x}; \boldsymbol{\theta}_1) + \boldsymbol{b}_2)$, where $\boldsymbol{\theta}_p = (\mathbf{W}_2, \boldsymbol{b}_2, \boldsymbol{\theta}_1)$. Then we can construct $q(y|\boldsymbol{\theta}_q) = \mathrm{softmax}(y|\mathbf{W}_3 \boldsymbol{h}(\boldsymbol{x}; \boldsymbol{\theta}_1) + \boldsymbol{b}_3)$, where $\boldsymbol{\theta}_q = (\mathbf{W}_3, \boldsymbol{b}_3, \boldsymbol{\theta}_1)$ and $\boldsymbol{h}(\boldsymbol{x}; \boldsymbol{\theta}_1)$ is the shared nonlinear feature extractor.

After performing this "model surgery", we can fine-tune the new model with parameters $\boldsymbol{\theta}_q = (\boldsymbol{\theta}_1, \boldsymbol{\theta}_3)$, where $\boldsymbol{\theta}_1$ parameterizes the feature extractor, and $\boldsymbol{\theta}_3$ parameterizes the final linear layer that maps features to the new set of labels. If we treat $\boldsymbol{\theta}_1$ as "**frozen parameters**", then the resulting model $q(y|\boldsymbol{x}, \boldsymbol{\theta}_q)$ is linear in its parameters, so we have a convex optimization problem for which many simple and efficient fitting methods exist (see Part II). This is particularly helpful in the long-tail setting, where some classes are very rare [Kan+20]. However, a linear "decoder" may be too limiting, so we can also allow $\boldsymbol{\theta}_1$ to be fine-tuned as well, but using a lower learning rate, to prevent the values moving too far from the values estimated on $\mathcal{D}_p$.

19.2.2   Adapters

One disadvantage of fine-tuning all the model parameters of a pre-trained model is that it can be slow, since there are often many parameters, and we may need to use a small learning rate to prevent the low-level feature extractors from diverging too far from their prior values. In addition, every new task requires a new model to be trained, making task sharing hard. An alternative approach is to keep the pre-trained model untouched, but to add new parameters to modify its internal behavior to customize the feature extraction process for each task. This idea is called **adapters**, and has been explored in several papers (e.g., [RBV17; RBV18; Hou+19]).

Figure 19.3a illustrates adapters for transformer networks (Section 15.5), as proposed in [Hou+19]. The basic idea is to insert two shallow bottleneck MLPs inside each transformer layer, one after the multi-head attention and once after the feed-forward layers. Note that these MLPs have skip connections, so that they can be initialized to implement the identity mapping. If the transformer layer has features of dimensionality D, and the adapter uses a bottleneck of size M, this introduces $O(DM)$ new parameters per layer. These adapter MLPs, as well as the layer norm parameters and final output head, are trained for each new task, but the all remaining parameters are frozen. Empirically on several NLP benchmarks, this is found to give better performance than fine tuning, while only needing about 1-10% of the original parameters.

Figure 19.3b illustrates adapters for residual networks (Section 14.3.4), as proposed in [RBV17; RBV18]. The basic idea is to add a 1x1 convolution layer $\boldsymbol{\alpha}$, which is analogous to the MLP adapter in the transformer case, to the internal layers of the CNN. This can be added in series or in parallel, as shown in the diagram. If we denote the adapter layer by $\rho(\boldsymbol{x})$, we can define the series adapter to be

$$\rho(\boldsymbol{x}) = \boldsymbol{x} + \mathrm{diag}_1(\boldsymbol{\alpha}) \circledast \boldsymbol{x} = \mathrm{diag}_1(\mathbf{I} + \boldsymbol{\alpha}) \circledast \boldsymbol{x} \tag{19.4}$$

where $\mathrm{diag}_1(\boldsymbol{\alpha}) \in \mathbb{R}^{1 \times 1 \times C \times D}$ reshapes a matrix $\boldsymbol{\alpha} \in \mathbb{R}^{C \times D}$ into a matrix that can be applied to each spatial location in parallel. (We have omitted batch normalization for simplicity.) If we insert this after a regular convolution layer $\boldsymbol{f} \circledast \boldsymbol{x}$ we get

$$\boldsymbol{y} = \rho(\boldsymbol{f} \circledast \boldsymbol{x}) = (\mathrm{diag}_1(\mathbf{I} + \boldsymbol{\alpha}) \circledast \boldsymbol{f}) \circledast \boldsymbol{x} \tag{19.5}$$

This can be interpreted as a low-rank multiplicative perturbation to the original filter $\boldsymbol{f}$. The parallel adapter can be defined by

$$\boldsymbol{y} = \boldsymbol{f} \circledast \boldsymbol{x} + \mathrm{diag}_1(\boldsymbol{\alpha}) \circledast \boldsymbol{x} = (\boldsymbol{f} + \mathrm{diag}_L(\boldsymbol{\alpha})) \circledast \boldsymbol{x} \tag{19.6}$$

This can be interpreted as a low-rank additive perturbation to the original filter $\boldsymbol{f}$. In both cases, setting $\boldsymbol{\alpha} = \boldsymbol{0}$ ensures the adapter layers can be initialized to the identity transformation. In addition, both methods required $O(C^2)$ parameters per layer.

19.2.3   Supervised pre-training

The pre-training task may be supervised or unsupervised; the main requirements are that it can teach the model basic structure about the problem domain and that it is sufficiently similar to the downstream fine-tuning task. The notion of task similarity is not rigorously defined, but in practice the domain of the pre-training task is often more broad than that of the fine-tuning task (e.g., pre-train on all bird species and fine-tune on endangered ones).

The most straightforward form of transfer learning is the case where a large labeled dataset is suitable for pre-training. For example, it is very common to use the ImageNet dataset (Section 1.5.1.2) to pretrain CNNs, which can then be used for an a variety of downstream tasks and datasets (see e.g., [Kol+19]). Imagenet has 1.28 million natural images, each associated with a label from one of 1,000 classes. The classes constitute a wide variety of different concepts, including animals, foods, buildings, musical instruments, clothing, and so on. The images themselves are diverse in the sense that they contain objects from many angles and in many sizes with a wide variety of backgrounds. This diversity and scale may partially explain why it has become a de-facto pre-training task for transfer learning in computer vision. (See finetune_cnn_jax.ipynb for some example code.)

However, Imagenet pre-training has been shown to be less helpful when the domain of the fine-tuning task is quite different from natural images (e.g. medical images [Rag+19]). And in some cases where it is helpful (e.g., training object detection systems), it seems to be more of a speedup trick (by warm-starting optimization at a good point) rather than something that is essential, in the sense that one can achieve comparable performance on the downstream task when training from scratch, if done for long enough [HGD19].

Supervised pre-training is somewhat less common in non-vision applications. One notable exception is to pre-train on natural language inference data (i.e. whether a sentence implies or contradicts another) to learn vector representations of sentences [Con+17], though this approach has largely been supplanted by unsupervised methods (Section 19.2.4). Another non-vision application of transfer learning is to pre-train a speech recognition on a large English-labeled corpus before fine-tuning on low-resource languages [Ard+20].

19.2.4   Unsupervised pre-training (self-supervised learning)

It is increasingly common to use **unsupervised pre-training**, because unlabeled data is often easy to acquire, e.g., unlabeled images or text documents from the web.

For a short period of time it was common to pre-train deep neural networks using an unsupervised objective (e.g., reconstruction error, as discussed in Section 20.3) over the labeled dataset (i.e. ignoring the labels) before proceeding with standard supervised training [HOT06; Vin+10b; Erh+10]. While this technique is also called unsupervised pre-training, it differs from the form of pre-training for transfer learning we discuss in this section, which uses a (large) unlabeled dataset for pre-training before fine-tuning on a different (smaller) labeled dataset.

Pre-training tasks that use unlabeled data are often called **self-supervised** rather than unsupervised. This term is used because the labels are created by the algorithm, rather than being provided externally by a human, as in standard supervised learning. Both supervised and self-supervised learning are discriminative tasks, since they require predicting outputs given inputs. By contrast, other unsupervised approaches, such as some of those discussed in Chapter 20, are generative, since they predict outputs unconditionally.

There are many different self-supervised learning heuristics that have been tried (see e.g., [GR18; JT19; Ren19] for a review, and https://github.com/jason718/awesome-self-supervised-learning for an extensive list of papers). We can identify at least three main broad groups, which we discuss below.

19.2.4.1   Imputation tasks

One approach to self-supervised learning is to solve **imputation tasks**. In this approach, we partition the input vector x into two parts, $x = (x_h, x_v)$, and then try to predict the hidden part x_h given the remaining visible part, x_v, using a model of the form $\hat{x}_h = f(x_v, x_h = 0)$. We can think of this as a "**fill-in-the-blank**" task; in the NLP community, this is called a **cloze task**. See Figure 19.4 for some visual examples, and Section 15.7.2 for some NLP examples.

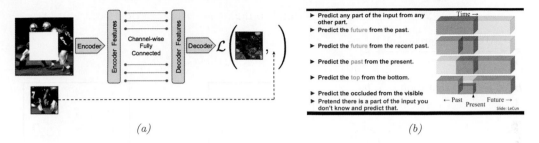

(a)   (b)

Figure 19.4: (a) Context encoder for self-supervised learning. From [Pat+16]. Used with kind permission of Deepak Pathak. (b) Some other proxy tasks for self-supervised learning. From [LeC18]. Used with kind permission of Yann LeCun.

19.2.4.2 Proxy tasks

Another approach to SSL is to solve **proxy tasks**, also called **pretext tasks**. In this setup, we create pairs of inputs, (x_1, x_2), and then train a Siamese network classifier (Figure 16.5a) of the form $p(y|x_1, x_2) = p(y|r[f(x_1), f(x_2)])$, where $f(x)$ is some function that performs "**representation learning**" [BCV13], and y is some label that captures the relationship between x_1 and x_2, which is predicted by $r(f_1, f_2)$. For example, suppose x_1 is an image patch, and $x_2 = t(x_1)$ is some transformation of x_1 that we control, such as a random rotation; then we define y to be the rotation angle that we used [GSK18].

19.2.4.3 Contrastive tasks

The currently most popular approach to self-supervised learning is to use various kinds of **contrastive tasks**. The basic idea is to create pairs of examples that are semantically similar to each other, using data augmentation methods (Section 19.1), and then to ensure that the distance between their representations is closer (in embedding space) than the distance between two unrelated examples. This is exactly the same idea that is used in deep metric learning (Section 16.2.2) — the only difference is that the algorithm creates its own similar pairs, rather than relying on an externally provided measure of similarity, such as labels. We give some examples of this in Section 19.2.4.4 and Section 19.2.4.5.

19.2.4.4 SimCLR

In this section, we discuss **SimCLR**, which stands for "Simple contrastive learning of visual representations" [Che+20b; Che+20c]. This has shown state of the art performance on transfer learning and semi-supervised learning. The basic idea is as follows. Each input $x \in \mathbb{R}^D$ is converted to two augmented "views' $x_1 = t_1(x)$, $x_2 = t_2(x)$, which are "semantically equivalent" versions of the input generated by some transformations t_1, t_2. For example, if x is an image, these could be small perturbations to the image, such as random crops, as discussed in Section 19.1. In addition, we sample "negative" examples $x_1^-, \ldots, x_n^- \in N(x)$ from the dataset which represent "semantically different" images (in practice, these are the other examples in the minibatch). Next we define some feature mapping $F : \mathbb{R}^D \to \mathbb{R}^E$, where D is the size of the input, and E is the size of the embedding.

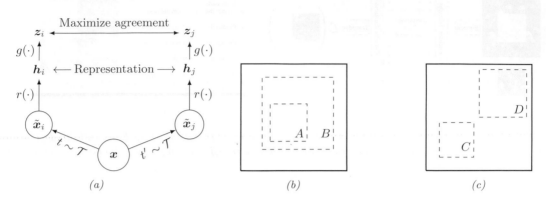

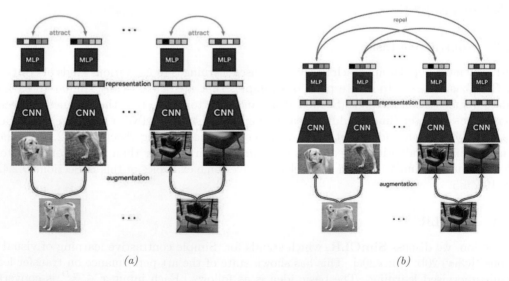

Figure 19.5: (a) Illustration of SimCLR training. $\mathcal{T}$ is a set of stochastic semantics-preserving transformations (data augmentations). (b-c) Illustration of the benefit of random crops. Solid rectangles represent the original image, dashed rectangles are random crops. In (b), the model is forced to predict the local view A from the global view B (and vice versa). In (c), the model is forced to predict the appearance of adjacent views (C,D). From Figures 2–3 of [Che+20b]. Used with kind permission of Ting Chen.

Figure 19.6: Visualization of SimCLR training. Each input image in the minibatch is randomly modified in two different ways (using cropping (followed by resize), flipping, and color distortion), and then fed into a Siamese network. The embeddings (final layer) for each pair derived from the same image is forced to be close, whereas the embeddings for all other pairs are forced to be far. From https://ai.googleblog.com/ 2020/04/advancing-self-supervised-and-semi.html. Used with kind permission of Ting Chen.

We then try to maximize the similarity of the similar views, while minimizing the similarity of the different views, for each input $\boldsymbol{x}$:

$$J = F(t_1(\boldsymbol{x}))^\mathsf{T} F(t_2(\boldsymbol{x})) - \log \sum_{\boldsymbol{x}_i^- \in N(\boldsymbol{x})} \exp\left[F(\boldsymbol{x}_i^-)^\mathsf{T} F(t_1(\boldsymbol{x})) \right] \tag{19.7}$$

In practice, we use cosine similarity, so we ℓ_2-normalize the representations produced by F before taking inner products, but this is omitted in the above equation. See Figure 19.5a for an illustration. (In this figure, we assume $F(\boldsymbol{x}) = g(r(\boldsymbol{x}))$, where the intermediate representation $\boldsymbol{h} = r(\boldsymbol{x})$ is the one that will be later used for fine-tuning, and g is an additional transformation applied during training.)

Interestingly, we can interpret this as a form of conditional **energy based model** of the form

$$p(\boldsymbol{x}_2|\boldsymbol{x}_1) = \frac{\exp[-\mathcal{E}(\boldsymbol{x}_2|\boldsymbol{x}_1)]}{Z(\boldsymbol{x}_1)} \tag{19.8}$$

where $\mathcal{E}(\boldsymbol{x}_2|\boldsymbol{x}_1) = -F(\boldsymbol{x}_2)^\mathsf{T} F(\boldsymbol{x}_1)$ is the energy, and

$$Z(\boldsymbol{x}) = \int \exp[-\mathcal{E}(\boldsymbol{x}^-|\boldsymbol{x})]d\boldsymbol{x}^- = \int \exp[F(\boldsymbol{x}^-)^\mathsf{T} F(\boldsymbol{x})]d\boldsymbol{x}^- \tag{19.9}$$

is the normalization constant, known as the **partition function**. The conditional log likelihood under this model has the form

$$\log p(\boldsymbol{x}_2|\boldsymbol{x}_1) = F(\boldsymbol{x}_2)^\mathsf{T} F(\boldsymbol{x}_1) - \log \int \exp[F(\boldsymbol{x}^-)^\mathsf{T} F(\boldsymbol{x}_1)]d\boldsymbol{x}^- \tag{19.10}$$

The only difference from Equation (19.7) is that we replace the integral with a Monte Carlo upper bound derived from the negative samples. Thus we can think of contrastive learning as approximate maximum likelihood estimation of a conditional energy based generative model [Gra+20]. More details on such models can be found in the sequel to this book, [Mur23].

A critical ingredient to the success of SimCLR is the choice of data augmentation methods. By using random cropping, they can force the model to predict local views from global views, as well as to predict adjacent views of the same image (see Figure 19.5). After cropping, all images are resized back to the same size. In addition, they randomly flip the image some fraction of the time.[2]

SimCLR relies on large batch training, in order to ensure a sufficiently diverse set of negatives. When this is not possible, we can use a memory bank of past (negative) embeddings, which can be updated using exponential moving averaging (Section 4.4.2.2). This is known as **momentum contrastive learning** or **MoCo** [He+20].

19.2.4.5 CLIP

In this section, we describe **CLIP**, which stands for "Contrastive Language-Image Pre-training" [Rad+]. This is a contrastive approach to representation learning which uses a massive corpus of

---

2. It turns out that distinguishing positive crops (from the same image) from negative crops (from different images) is often easy to do just based on color histograms. To prevent this kind of "cheating", they also apply a random color distortion, thus cutting off this "short circuit". The combination of random cropping and color distortion is found to work better than either method alone.

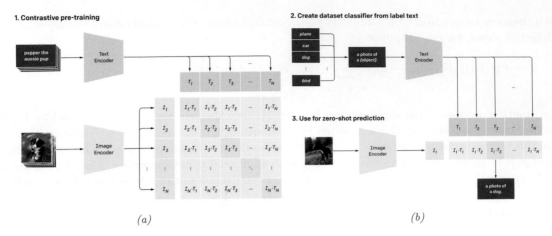

Figure 19.7: Illustration of the CLIP model. From Figure 1 of [Rad+]. Used with kind permission of Alec Radford.

400M (image, text) pairs extracted from the web. Let $\boldsymbol{x}_i$ be the i'th image and $\boldsymbol{y}_i$ be its matching text. Rather than trying to predict the exact words associated with the image, it is simpler to just determine if $\boldsymbol{y}_i$ is more likely to be the correct text compared to $\boldsymbol{y}_j$, for some other text string j in the minibatch. Similarly, the model can try to determine if image $\boldsymbol{x}_i$ is more likely to be matched than $\boldsymbol{x}_j$ to a given text $\boldsymbol{y}_i$.

More precisely, let $\boldsymbol{f}_I(\boldsymbol{x}_i)$ be the embedding of the image, $\boldsymbol{f}_T(\boldsymbol{y}_j)$ be the embedding of the text, $\mathbf{I}_i = \boldsymbol{f}_I(\boldsymbol{x}_i)/\|\boldsymbol{f}_I(\boldsymbol{x}_i)\|_2$ be the unit-norm version of the image embedding, and $\mathbf{T}_j = \boldsymbol{f}_T(\boldsymbol{y}_j)/\|\boldsymbol{f}_T(\boldsymbol{y}_j)\|_2$ be the unit-norm version of the text embedding. Define the vector of pairwise logits (similarity scores) to be

$$L_{ij} = \mathbf{I}_i^\mathsf{T} \mathbf{T}_j \tag{19.11}$$

We now train the parameters of the two embedding functions $\boldsymbol{f}_I$ and $\boldsymbol{f}_T$ to minimize the following loss, averaged over minibatches of size N:

$$J = \frac{1}{2}\left[\sum_{i=1}^{N} \mathrm{CE}(\mathbf{L}_{i,:}, \mathbf{1}_i) + \sum_{j=1}^{N} \mathrm{CE}(\mathbf{L}_{:,j}, \mathbf{1}_j)\right] \tag{19.12}$$

where CE is the cross entropy loss

$$\mathrm{CE}(\boldsymbol{p}, \boldsymbol{q}) = -\sum_{k=1}^{K} p_k \log q_k \tag{19.13}$$

and $\mathbf{1}_i$ is a one-hot encoding of label i. See Figure 19.7a for an illustration. (In practice, the normalized embeddings are scaled by a temperature parameter which is also learned; this controls the sharpness of the softmax.)

In their paper, they considered using a ResNet (Section 14.3.4) and a vision transformer (Section 15.5.6) for the function $\boldsymbol{f}_I$, and a text transformer (Section 15.5) for $\boldsymbol{f}_T$. They used a very large minibatch of $N \sim 32k$, and trained for many days on 100s of GPUs.

After the model is trained, it can be used for **zero-shot classification** of an image $\boldsymbol{x}$ as follows. First each of the K possible class labels for a given dataset is converted into a text string $\boldsymbol{y}_k$ that might occur on the web. For example, "dog" becomes "a photo of a dog". Second, we compute the normalized embeddings $\mathbf{I} \propto \boldsymbol{f}_I(\boldsymbol{x})$ and $\mathbf{T}_k \propto \boldsymbol{f}_T(\boldsymbol{y}_k)$. Third, we compute the softmax probabilites

$$p(y = k|\boldsymbol{x}) = \mathrm{softmax}([\mathbf{I}^\mathsf{T}\mathbf{T}_1, \ldots, \mathbf{I}^\mathsf{T}\mathbf{T}_k])_k \tag{19.14}$$

See Figure 19.7b for an illustration. (A similar approach was adopted in the visual n-grams paper [Li+17].)

Remarkably, this approach can perform as well as standard supervised learning on tasks such as ImageNet classification, without ever being explicitly trained on specific labeled datasets. Of course, the images in ImageNet come from the web, and were found using text-based web-search, so the model has seen similar data before. Nevertheless, its generalization to new tasks, and robustness to distribution shift, are quite impressive (see the paper for examples).

One drawback of the approach, however, is that it is sensitive to how class labels are converted to textual form. For example, to make the model work on food classification, it is necessary to use text strings of the form "a photo of guacamole, a type of food", "a photo of ceviche, a type of food", etc. Disambiguating phrases such as "a type of food" are currently added by hand, on a per-dataset basis. This is called **prompt engineering**, and is needed since the raw class names can be ambiguous across (and sometimes within) a dataset.

19.2.5   Domain adaptation

Consider a problem in which we have inputs from different domains, such as a **source domain** $\mathcal{X}_s$ and **target domain** $\mathcal{X}_t$, but a common set of output labels, $\mathcal{Y}$. (This is the "dual" of transfer learning, since the input domains are different, but the output domains the same.) For example, the domains might be images from a computer graphics system and real images, or product reviews and movie reviews. We assume we do not have labeled examples from the target domain. Our goal is to fit the model on the source domain, and then modify its parameters so it works on the target domain. This is called (unsupervised) **domain adaptation** (see e.g., [KL21] for a review).

A common approach to this problem is to train the source classifier in such a way that it cannot distinguish whether the input is coming from the source or target distribution; in this case, it will only be able to use features that are common to both domains. This is called **domain adversarial learning** [Gan+16]. More formally, let $d_n \in \{s, t\}$ be a label that specifies if the data example n comes from domain s or t. We want to optimize

$$\min_{\boldsymbol{\phi}} \max_{\boldsymbol{\theta}} \frac{1}{N_s + N_t} \sum_{n \in \mathcal{D}_s, \mathcal{D}_t} \ell(d_n, f_{\boldsymbol{\theta}}(\boldsymbol{x}_n)) + \frac{1}{N_s} \sum_{m \in \mathcal{D}_s} \ell(y_m, g_{\boldsymbol{\phi}}(f_{\boldsymbol{\theta}}(\boldsymbol{x}_m))) \tag{19.15}$$

where $N_s = |\mathcal{D}_s|$, $N_t = |\mathcal{D}_t|$, f maps $\mathcal{X}_s \cup \mathcal{X}_t \to \mathcal{H}$, and g maps $\mathcal{H} \to \mathcal{Y}_t$. The objective in Equation (19.15) minimizes the loss on the desired task of classifying y, but *maximizes* the loss on the auxiliary task of classifying the source domain d. This can be implemented by the **gradient sign reversal** trick, and is related to GANs (generative adversarial networks). See e.g., [Csu17; Wu+19] for some other approaches to domain adaptation.

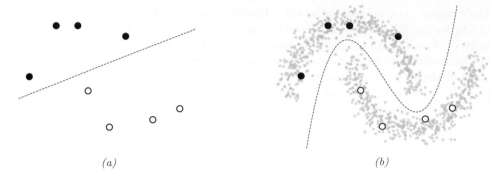

(a)   *(b)*

Figure 19.8: Illustration of the benefits of semi-supervised learning for a binary classification problem. Labeled points from each class are shown as black and white circles respectively. (a) Decision boundary we might learn given only labeled data. (b) Decision boundary we might learn if we also had a lot of unlabeled data points, shown as smaller grey circles.

19.3   Semi-supervised learning

This section is co-authored with Colin Raffel.

Many recent successful applications of machine learning are in the supervised learning setting, where a large dataset of labeled examples are available for training a model. However, in many practical applications it is expensive to obtain this labeled data. Consider the case of automatic speech recognition: Modern datasets contain thousands of hours of audio recordings [Pan+15; Ard+20]. The process of annotating the words spoken in a recording is many times slower than realtime, potentially resulting in a long (and costly) annotation process. To make matters worse, in some applications data must be labeled by an expert (such as a doctor in medical applications) which can further increase costs.

Semi-supervised learning can alleviate the need for labeled data by taking advantage of unlabeled data. The general goal of semi-supervised learning is to allow the model to learn the high-level structure of the data distribution from unlabeled data and only rely on the labeled data for learning the fine-grained details of a given task. Whereas in standard supervised learning we assume that we have access to samples from the joint distribution of data and labels $\boldsymbol{x}, y \sim p(\boldsymbol{x}, y)$, semi-supervised learning assumes that we additionally have access to samples from the marginal distribution of $\boldsymbol{x}$, namely $\boldsymbol{x} \sim p(\boldsymbol{x})$, as illustrated in Figure 19.8. Further, it is generally assumed that we have many more of these unlabeled samples since they are typically cheaper to obtain. Continuing the example of automatic speech recognition, it is often much cheaper to simply record people talking (which would produce unlabeled data) than it is to transcribe recorded speech. Semi-supervised learning is a good fit for the scenario where a large amount of unlabeled data has been collected and the practitioner would like to avoid having to label all of it.

19.3.1   Self-training and pseudo-labeling

An early and straightforward approach to semi-supervised learning is **self-training** [Scu65; Agr70; McL75]. The basic idea behind self-training is to use the model itself to infer predictions on unlabeled data, and then treat these predictions as labels for subsequent training. Self-training has endured as a semi-supervised learning method because of its simplicity and general applicability; i.e. it is applicable to any model that can generate predictions for the unlabeled data. Recently, it has become common to refer to this approach as "**pseudo-labeling**" [Lee13] because the inferred labels for unlabeled data are only "pseudo-correct" in comparison with the true, ground-truth targets used in supervised learning.

Algorithmically, self-training typically follows one of the following two procedures. In the first approach, pseudo-labels are first predicted for the entire collection of unlabeled data and the model is re-trained (possibly from scratch) to convergence on the combination of the labeled and (pseudo-labeled) unlabeled data. Then, the unlabeled data is re-labeled by the model and the process repeats itself until a suitable solution is found. The second approach instead continually generates predictions on randomly-chosen batches of unlabeled data and immediately trains the model against these pseudo-labels. Both approaches are currently common in practice; the first "offline" variant has been shown to be particularly successful when leveraging giant collections of unlabeled data [Yal+19; Xie+20] whereas the "online" approach is often used as one component of more sophisticated semi-supervised learning methods [Soh+20]. Neither variant is fundamentally better than the other. Offline self-training can result in training the model on "stale" pseudo-labels, since they are only updated each time the model converges. However, online pseudo-labeling can incur larger computational costs since it involves constantly "re-labeling" unlabeled data.

Self-training can suffer from an obvious problem: If the model generates incorrect predictions for unlabeled data and then is re-trained on these incorrect predictions, it can become progressively worse and worse at the intended classification task until it eventually learns a totally invalid solution. This issue has been dubbed **confirmation bias** [TV17] because the model is continually confirming its own (incorrect) bias about the decision rule.

A common way to mitigate confirmation bias is to use a "selection metric" [RHS05] which heuristically tries to only retain pseudo-labels that are correct. For example, assuming that a model outputs probabilities for each possible class, a frequently-used selection metric is to only retain pseudo-labels whose largest class probability is above a threshold [Yar95; RHS05]. If the model's class probability estimates are well-calibrated, then this selection metric will only retain labels that are highly likely to be correct (according to the model, at least). More sophisticated selection metrics can be designed according to the problem domain.

19.3.2 Entropy minimization

Self-training has the implicit effect of encouraging the model to output low-entropy (i.e. high-confidence) predictions. This effect is most apparent in the online setting with a cross-entropy loss, where the model minimizes the following loss function $\mathcal{L}$ on unlabeled data:

$$\mathcal{L} = -\max_c \log p_\theta(y = c | \boldsymbol{x}) \tag{19.16}$$

where $p_\theta(y|\boldsymbol{x})$ is the model's class probability distribution given input $\boldsymbol{x}$. This function is minimized when the model assigns all of its class probability to a single class c^*, i.e. $p(y = c^*|\boldsymbol{x}) = 1$ and $p(y \neq c^*|\boldsymbol{x}) = 0$.

A closely-related semi-supervised learning method is **entropy minimization** [GB05], which

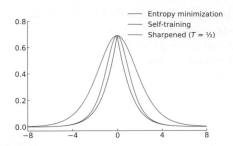

Figure 19.9: Comparison of the entropy minimization, self-training, and "sharpened" entropy minimization loss functions for a binary classification problem.

minimizes the following loss function:

$$\mathcal{L} = -\sum_{c=1}^{C} p_\theta(y = c|\boldsymbol{x}) \log p_\theta(y = c|\boldsymbol{x}) \tag{19.17}$$

Note that this function is also minimized when the model assigns all of its class probability to a single class. We can make the entropy-minimization loss in Equation (19.17) equivalent to the online self-training loss in Equation (19.16) by replacing the first $p_\theta(y = c|\boldsymbol{x})$ term with a "one-hot" vector that assigns a probability of 1 for the class that was assigned the highest probability. In other words, online self-training minimizes the cross-entropy between the model's output and the "hard" target $\arg\max p_\theta(y|\boldsymbol{x})$, whereas entropy minimization uses the the "soft" target $p_\theta(y|\boldsymbol{x})$. One way to trade off between these two extremes is to adjust the "temperature" of the target distribution by raising each probability to the power of $1/T$ and renormalizing; this is the basis of the **mixmatch** method of [Ber+19b; Ber+19a; Xie+19]. At $T = 1$, this is equivalent to entropy minimization; as $T \to 0$, it becomes hard online self-training. A comparison of these loss functions is shown in Figure 19.9.

19.3.2.1   The cluster assumption

Why is entropy minimization a good idea? A basic assumption of many semi-supervised learning methods is that the decision boundary between classes should fall in a low-density region of the data manifold. This effectively assumes that the data corresponding to different classes are clustered together. A good decision boundary, therefore, should not pass through clusters; it should simply separate them. Semi-supervised learning methods that make the "**cluster assumption**" can be thought of as using unlabeled data to estimate the shape of the data manifold and moving the decision boundary away from it.

Entropy minimization is one such method. To see why, first assume that the decision boundary between two classes is "smooth", i.e. the model does not abruptly change its class prediction anywhere in its domain. This is true in practice for simple and/or regularized models. In this case, if the decision boundary passes through a high-density region of data, it will by necessity produce high-entropy predictions for some samples from the data distribution. Entropy minimization will therefore encourage the model to place its decision boundary in low-density regions of the input space to

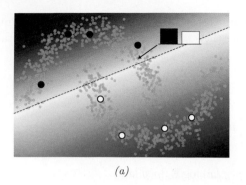
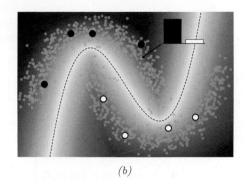

(a)   (b)

Figure 19.10: Visualization demonstrating how entropy minimization enforces the cluster assumption. The classifier assigns a higher probability to class 1 (black dots) or 2 (white dots) in red or blue regions respectively. The predicted class probabilities for one particular unlabeled datapoint is shown in the bar plot. In (a), the decision boundary passes through high-density regions of data, so the classifier is forced to output high-entropy predictions. In (b), the classifier avoids high-density regions and is able to assign low-entropy predictions to most of the unlabeled data.

avoid transitioning from one class to another in a region of space where data may be sampled. A visualization of this behavior is shown in Figure 19.10.

19.3.2.2 Input-output mutual information

An alternative justification for the entropy minimization objective was proposed by Bridle, Heading, and MacKay [BHM92], where it was shown that it naturally arises from maximizing the mutual information (Section 6.3) between the data and the label (i.e. the input and output of a model). Denoting $\boldsymbol{x}$ as the input and y as the target, the input-output mutual information can be written as

$$\mathcal{I}(y; \boldsymbol{x}) = \iint p(y, \boldsymbol{x}) \log \frac{p(y, \boldsymbol{x})}{p(y)p(\boldsymbol{x})} dy d\boldsymbol{x} \tag{19.18}$$

$$= \iint p(y|\boldsymbol{x})p(\boldsymbol{x}) \log \frac{p(y, \boldsymbol{x})}{p(y)p(\boldsymbol{x})} dy d\boldsymbol{x} \tag{19.19}$$

$$= \int p(\boldsymbol{x}) d\boldsymbol{x} \int p(y|\boldsymbol{x}) \log \frac{p(y|\boldsymbol{x})}{p(y)} dy \tag{19.20}$$

$$= \int p(\boldsymbol{x}) d\boldsymbol{x} \int p(y|\boldsymbol{x}) \log \frac{p(y|\boldsymbol{x})}{\int p(\boldsymbol{x})p(y|\boldsymbol{x}) d\boldsymbol{x}} dy \tag{19.21}$$

Note that the first integral is equivalent to taking an expectation over $\boldsymbol{x}$, and the second integral is equivalent to summing over all possible values of the class y. Using these relations, we obtain

$$\mathcal{I}(y;\boldsymbol{x}) = \mathbb{E}_{\boldsymbol{x}}\left[\sum_{i=1}^{L} p(y_i|\boldsymbol{x}) \log \frac{p(y_i|\boldsymbol{x})}{\mathbb{E}_{\boldsymbol{x}}[p(y_i|\boldsymbol{x})]}\right] \tag{19.22}$$

$$= \mathbb{E}_{\boldsymbol{x}}\left[\sum_{i=1}^{L} p(y_i|\boldsymbol{x}) \log p(y_i|\boldsymbol{x})\right] - \mathbb{E}_{\boldsymbol{x}}\left[\sum_{i=1}^{L} p(y_i|\boldsymbol{x}) \log \mathbb{E}_{\boldsymbol{x}}[p(y_i|\boldsymbol{x})]\right] \tag{19.23}$$

$$= \mathbb{E}_{\boldsymbol{x}}\left[\sum_{i=1}^{L} p(y_i|\boldsymbol{x}) \log p(y_i|\boldsymbol{x})\right] - \sum_{i=1}^{L} \mathbb{E}_{\boldsymbol{x}}[p(y_i|\boldsymbol{x}) \log \mathbb{E}_{\boldsymbol{x}}[p(y_i|\boldsymbol{x})]] \tag{19.24}$$

Since we had initially sought to *maximize* the mutual information, and we typically *minimize* loss functions, we can convert this to a suitable loss function by negating it:

$$\mathcal{I}(y;\boldsymbol{x}) = -\mathbb{E}_{\boldsymbol{x}}\left[\sum_{i=1}^{L} p(y_i|\boldsymbol{x}) \log p(y_i|\boldsymbol{x})\right] + \sum_{i=1}^{L} \mathbb{E}_{\boldsymbol{x}}[p(y_i|\boldsymbol{x}) \log \mathbb{E}_{\boldsymbol{x}}[p(y_i|\boldsymbol{x})]] \tag{19.25}$$

The first term is exactly the entropy minimization objective in expectation. The second term specifies that we should maximize the entropy of the expected class prediction, i.e. the average class prediction over our training set. This encourages the model to predict each possible class with equal probability, which is only appropriate when we know a priori that all classes are equally likely.

19.3.3 Co-training

Co-training [BM98] is also similar to self-training, but makes an additional assumption that there are two complementary "views" (i.e. independent sets of features) of the data, both of which can be used separately to train a reasonable model. After training two models separately on each view, unlabeled data is classified by each model to obtain candidate pseudo-labels. If a particular pseudo-label receives a low-entropy prediction (indicating high confidence) from one model and a high-entropy prediction (indicating low confidence) from the other, then that pseudo-labeled datapoint is added to the training set for the low-confidence model. Then, the process is repeated with the new, larger training datasets. The procedure of only retaining pseudo-labels when one of the models is confident ideally builds up the training sets with correctly-labeled data.

Co-training makes the strong assumption that there are two informative-but-independent views of the data, which may not be true for many problems. The **Tri-Training** algorithm [ZL05] circumvents this issue by instead using *three* models that are first trained on independently-sampled (with replacement) subsets of the labeled data. Ideally, initially training on different collections of labeled data results in models that do not always agree on their predictions. Then, pseudo-labels are generated for the unlabeled data independently by each of the three models. For a given unlabeled datapoint, if two of the models agree on the pseudo-label, it is added to the training set for the third model. This can be seen as a selection metric, because it only retains pseudo-labels where two (differently initialized) models agree on the correct label. The models are then re-trained on the combination of the labeled data and the new pseudo-labels, and the whole process is repeated iteratively.

19.3.4 Label propagation on graphs

If two datapoints are "similar" in some meaningful way, we might expect that they share a label. This idea has been referred to as the **manifold assumption**. **Label propagation** is a semi-supervised learning technique that leverages the manifold assumption to assign labels to unlabeled data. Label propagation first constructs a graph where the nodes are the data examples and the edge weights represent the degree of similarity. The node labels are known for nodes corresponding to labeled data but are unknown for unlabeled data. Label propagation then propagates the known labels across edges of the graph in such a way that there is minimal disagreement in the labels of a given node's neighbors. This provides label guesses for the unlabeled data, which can then be used in the usual way for supervised training of a model.

More specifically, the basic label propagation algorithm [ZG02] proceeds as follows: First, let $w_{i,j}$ denote a non-negative edge weight between $\boldsymbol{x}_i$ and $\boldsymbol{x}_j$ that provides a measure of similarity for the two (labeled or unlabeled) datapoints. Assuming that we have M labeled datapoints and N unlabeled datapoints, define the $(M + N) \times (M + N)$ transition matrix $\mathbf{T}$ as having entries

$$\mathbf{T}_{i,j} = \frac{w_{i,j}}{\sum_k w_{k,j}} \tag{19.26}$$

$\mathbf{T}_{i,j}$ represents the probability of propagating the label for node j to node i. Further, define the $(M + N) \times C$ label matrix $\mathbf{Y}$, where C is the number of possible classes. The ith row of $\mathbf{Y}$ represents the class probability distribution of datapoint i. Then, repeat the following steps until the values in $\mathbf{Y}$ do not change significantly: First, use the transition matrix $\mathbf{T}$ to propagate labels in $\mathbf{Y}$ by setting $\mathbf{Y} \leftarrow \mathbf{TY}$. Then, re-normalize the rows of Y by setting $\mathbf{Y}_{i,c} \leftarrow \mathbf{Y}_{i,c}/\sum_k \mathbf{Y}_{i,k}$. Finally, replace the rows of $\mathbf{Y}$ corresponding to labeled datapoints with their one-hot representation (i.e. $\mathbf{Y}_{i,c} = 1$ if datapoint i has ground-truth label c and 0 otherwise). After convergence, guessed labels are chosen based on the highest class probability for each datapoint in $\mathbf{Y}$.

This algorithm iteratively uses the similarity of datapoints (encoded in the weights used to construct the transition matrix) to propagate information from the (fixed) labels onto the unlabeled data. At each iteration, the label distribution for a given datapoint is computed as the weighted average of the label distributions for all of its connected datapoints, where the weighting corresponds to the edge weights in $\mathbf{T}$. It can be shown that this procedure converges to a single fixed point, whose computational cost mainly involves the inversion of the matrix of unlabled-to-unlabled transition probabilities [ZG02].

The overall approach can be seen as a form of **transductive learning**, since it is learning to predict labels for a fixed unlabeled dataset, rather than learning a model that generalizes. However, given the induced labeling. we can perform **inductive learning** in the usual way.

The success of label propagation depends heavily on the notion of similarity used to construct the weights between different nodes (datapoints). For simple data, measuring the Euclidean distance between datapoints can be sufficient. However, for complex and high-dimensional data the Euclidean distance might not meaningfully reflect the likelihood that two datapoints share the same class. The similarity weights can also be set arbitrarily according to problem-specific knowledge. For a few examples of different ways of constructing the similarity graph, see Zhu [Zhu05, chapter 3]. For some recent papers that use this approach in conjunction with deep learning, see e.g., [BRR18; Isc+19].

19.3.5   Consistency regularization

Consistency regularization leverages the simple idea that perturbing a given datapoint (or the model itself) should not cause the model's output to change dramatically. Since measuring consistency in this way only makes use of the model's outputs (and not ground-truth labels), it is readily applicable to unlabeled data and therefore can be used to create appropriate loss functions for semi-supervised learning. This idea was first proposed under the framework of "learning with pseudo-ensembles" [BAP14], with similar variants following soon thereafter [LA16; SJT16].

In its most general form, both the model $p_\theta(y|\boldsymbol{x})$ and the transformations applied to the input can be stochastic. For example, in computer vision problems we may transform the input by using data augmentation like randomly rotating or adding noise the input image, and the network may include stochastic components like dropout (Section 13.5.4) or weight noise [Gra11]. A common and simple form of consistency regularization first samples $\boldsymbol{x}' \sim q(\boldsymbol{x}'|\boldsymbol{x})$ (where $q(\boldsymbol{x}'|\boldsymbol{x})$ is the distribution induced by the stochastic input transformations) and then minimizes the loss $\|p_\theta(y|\boldsymbol{x}) - p_\theta(y|\boldsymbol{x}')\|^2$. In practice, the first term $p_\theta(y|\boldsymbol{x})$ is typically treated as fixed (i.e. gradients are not propagated through it). In the semi-supervised setting, the combined loss function over a batch of labeled data $(\boldsymbol{x}_1, y_1), (\boldsymbol{x}_2, y_2), \ldots, (\boldsymbol{x}_M, y_M)$ and unlabeled data $\boldsymbol{x}_1, \boldsymbol{x}_2, \ldots, \boldsymbol{x}_N$ is

$$\mathcal{L}(\boldsymbol{\theta}) = -\sum_{i=1}^{M} \log p_\theta(y = y_i|\boldsymbol{x}_i) + \lambda \sum_{j=1}^{N} \|p_\theta(y|\boldsymbol{x}_j) - p_\theta(y|\boldsymbol{x}_j')\|^2 \tag{19.27}$$

where λ is a scalar hyperparameter that balances the importance of the loss on unlabeled data and, for simplicity, we write $\boldsymbol{x}_j'$ to denote a sample drawn from $q(\boldsymbol{x}'|\boldsymbol{x}_j)$.

The basic form of consistency regularization in Equation (19.27) reveals many design choices that impact the success of this semi-supervised learning approach. First, the value chosen for the λ hyperparameter is important. If it is too large, then the model may not give enough weight to learning the supervised task and will instead start to reinforce its own bad predictions (as with confirmation bias in self-training). Since the model is often poor at the start of training before it has been trained on much labeled data, it is common in practice to initialize set λ to zero and increase its value over the course of training.

A second important consideration are the random transformations applied to the input, i.e., $q(\boldsymbol{x}'|\boldsymbol{x})$. Generally speaking, these transformations should be designed so that they do not change the label of $\boldsymbol{x}$. As mentioned above, a common choice is to use domain-specific data augmentations. It has recently been shown that using strong data augmentations that heavily corrupt the input (but, arguably, still do not change the label) can produce particularly strong results [Xie+19; Ber+19a; Soh+20].

The use of data augmentation requires expert knowledge to determine what kinds of transformations are label-preserving and appropriate for a given problem. An alternative technique, called **virtual adversarial training** (VAT), instead transforms the input using an analytically-found perturbation designed to maximally change the model's output. Specifically, VAT computes a perturbation $\boldsymbol{\delta}$ that approximates $\boldsymbol{\delta} = \mathrm{argmax}_{\boldsymbol{\delta}} D_{\mathrm{KL}} (p_\theta(y|\boldsymbol{x}) \| p_\theta(y|\boldsymbol{x} + \boldsymbol{\delta}))$. The approximation is done by sampling $\boldsymbol{d}$ from a multivariate Gaussian distribution, initializing $\boldsymbol{\delta} = \boldsymbol{d}$, and then setting

$$\boldsymbol{\delta} \leftarrow \nabla_{\boldsymbol{\delta}} D_{\mathrm{KL}} (p_\theta(y|\boldsymbol{x}) \| p_\theta(y|\boldsymbol{x} + \boldsymbol{\delta}))|_{\boldsymbol{\delta} = \xi \boldsymbol{d}} \tag{19.28}$$

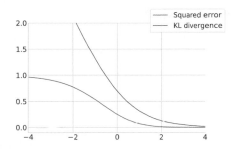

Figure 19.11: Comparison of the squared error and KL divergence lossses for a consistency regularization. This visualization is for a binary classification problem where it is assumed that the model's output for the unperturbed input is 1. The figure plots the loss incurred for a particular value of the logit (i.e. the pre-activation fed into the output sigmoid nonlinearity) for the perturbed input. As the logit grows towards infinity, the model predicts a class label of 1 (in agreement with the prediction for the unperturbed input); as it grows towards negative infinity, the model predictions class 0. The squared error loss saturates (and has zero gradients) when the model predicts one class or the other with high probability, but the KL divergence grows without bound as the model predicts class 0 with more and more confidence.

where ξ is a small constant, typically 10^{-6}. VAT then sets

$$x' = x + \epsilon \frac{\delta}{\|\delta\|_2} \tag{19.29}$$

and proceeds as usual with consistency regularization (as in Equation (19.27)), where ϵ is a scalar hyperparameter that sets the L2-norm of the perturbation applied to x.

Consistency regularization can also profoundly affect the geometry properties of the training objective, and the trajectory of SGD, such that performance can particularly benefit from non-standard training procedures. For example, the Euclidean distances between weights at different training epochs is significantly larger for objectives that use consistency regularization. Athiwaratkun et al. [Ath+19] show that a variant of **stochastic weight averaging** (SWA) [Izm+18] can achieve state-of-the-art performance on semi-supervised learning tasks by exploiting the geometric properties of consistency regularization.

A final consideration when using consistency regularization is the function used to measure the difference between the network's output with and without perturbations. Equation (19.27) uses the squared L2 distance (also referred to as the Brier score), which is a common choice [SJT16; TV17; LA16; Ber+19b]. It is also common to use the KL divergence $D_{KL}(p_\theta(y|x) \| p_\theta(y|x'))$ in analogy with the cross-entropy loss (i.e. KL divergence between ground-truth label and prediction) used for labeled examples [Miy+18; Ber+19a; Xie+19]. The gradient of the squared-error loss approaches zero as the model's predictions on the perturbed and unperturbed input differ more and more, assuming the model uses a softmax nonlinearity on its output. Using the squared-error loss therefore has a possible advantage that the model is not updated when its predictions are very unstable. However, the KL divergence has the same scale as the cross-entropy loss used for labeled data, which makes for more intuitive tuning of the unlabeled loss hyperparameter λ. A comparison of the two loss functions is shown in Figure 19.11.

19.3.6   Deep generative models *

Generative models provide a natural way of making use of unlabeled data through learning a model of the marginal distribution by minimizing $\mathcal{L}_U = -\sum_n \log p_{\boldsymbol{\theta}}(\boldsymbol{x}_n)$. Various approaches have leveraged generative models for semi-supervised by developing ways to use the model of $p_{\boldsymbol{\theta}}(\boldsymbol{x}_n)$ to help produce a better supervised model.

19.3.6.1   Variational autoencoders

In Section 20.3.5, we describe the variational autoencoder (VAE), which defines a probabilistic model of the joint distribution of data $\boldsymbol{x}$ and latent variables $\boldsymbol{z}$. Data is assumed to be generated by first sampling $\boldsymbol{z} \sim p(\boldsymbol{z})$ and then sampling $\boldsymbol{x} \sim p(\boldsymbol{x}|\boldsymbol{z})$. For learning, the VAE uses an encoder $\boldsymbol{q}_{\lambda}(\boldsymbol{z}|\boldsymbol{x})$ to approximate the posterior and a decoder $p_{\boldsymbol{\theta}}(\boldsymbol{x}|\boldsymbol{z})$ to approximate the likelihood. The encoder and decoder are typically deep neural networks. The parameters of the encoder and decoder can be jointly trained by maximizing the evidence lower bound (ELBO) of data.

The marginal distribution of latent variables $p(\boldsymbol{z})$ is often chosen to be a simple distribution like a diagonal-covariance Gaussian. In practice, this can make the latent variables $\boldsymbol{z}$ more amenable to downstream classification thanks to the facts that $\boldsymbol{z}$ is typically lower-dimensional than $\boldsymbol{x}$, that $\boldsymbol{z}$ is constructed via cascaded nonlinear transformations, and that the dimensions of the latent variables are designed to be independent. In other words, the latent variables can provide a (learned) representation where data may be more easily separable. In [Kin+14], this approach is called **M1** and it is indeed shown that the latent variables can be used to train stronger models when labels are scarce. (The general idea of unsupervised learning of representations to help with downstream classification tasks is described further in Section 19.2.4.)

An alternative approach to leveraging VAEs, also proposed in [Kin+14] and called **M2**, has the form

$$p_{\boldsymbol{\theta}}(\boldsymbol{x}, y) = p_{\boldsymbol{\theta}}(y)p_{\boldsymbol{\theta}}(\boldsymbol{x}|y) = p_{\boldsymbol{\theta}}(y) \int p_{\boldsymbol{\theta}}(\boldsymbol{x}|y, \boldsymbol{z})p_{\boldsymbol{\theta}}(\boldsymbol{z})d\boldsymbol{z} \tag{19.30}$$

where $\boldsymbol{z}$ is a latent variable, $p_{\boldsymbol{\theta}}(\boldsymbol{z}) = \mathcal{N}(\boldsymbol{z}|\boldsymbol{\mu}_{\boldsymbol{\theta}}, \boldsymbol{\Sigma}_{\boldsymbol{\theta}})$ is the latent prior (typically we fix $\boldsymbol{\mu}_{\boldsymbol{\theta}} = \boldsymbol{0}$ and $\boldsymbol{\Sigma}_{\boldsymbol{\theta}} = \mathbf{I}$), $p_{\boldsymbol{\theta}}(y) = \mathrm{Cat}(y|\boldsymbol{\pi}_{\boldsymbol{\theta}})$ the label prior, and $p_{\boldsymbol{\theta}}(\boldsymbol{x}|y, \boldsymbol{z}) = p(\boldsymbol{x}|f_{\boldsymbol{\theta}}(y, \boldsymbol{z}))$ is the likelihood, such as a Gaussian, with parameters computed by f (a deep neural network). The main innovation of this approach is to assume that data is generated according to both a latent class variable y as well as the continuous latent variable $\boldsymbol{z}$. The class variable y is observed for labeled data and unobserved for unlabled data.

To compute the likelihood for the *labeled data*, $p_{\boldsymbol{\theta}}(\boldsymbol{x}, y)$, we need to marginalize over $\boldsymbol{z}$, which we can do by using an inference network of the form

$$q_{\boldsymbol{\phi}}(\boldsymbol{z}|y, \boldsymbol{x}) = \mathcal{N}(\boldsymbol{z}|\boldsymbol{\mu}_{\boldsymbol{\phi}}(y, \boldsymbol{x}), \mathrm{diag}(\sigma_{\boldsymbol{\phi}}^2(\boldsymbol{x})) \tag{19.31}$$

We then use the following variational lower bound

$$\log p_{\boldsymbol{\theta}}(\boldsymbol{x}, y) \geq \mathbb{E}_{q_{\boldsymbol{\phi}}(\boldsymbol{z}|\boldsymbol{x}, y)} \left[\log p_{\boldsymbol{\theta}}(\boldsymbol{x}|y, \boldsymbol{z}) + \log p_{\boldsymbol{\theta}}(y) + \log p_{\boldsymbol{\theta}}(\boldsymbol{z}) - \log q_{\boldsymbol{\phi}}(\boldsymbol{z}|\boldsymbol{x}, y) \right] = -\mathcal{L}(\boldsymbol{x}, y) \tag{19.32}$$

as is standard for VAEs (see Section 20.3.5). The only difference is that we observe two kinds of data: $\boldsymbol{x}$ and y.

To compute the likelihood for the *unlabeled* data, $p_{\boldsymbol{\theta}}(\boldsymbol{x})$, we need to marginalize over $\boldsymbol{z}$ *and* y, which we can do by using an inference network of the form

$$q_{\boldsymbol{\phi}}(\boldsymbol{z}, y | \boldsymbol{x}) = q_{\boldsymbol{\phi}}(\boldsymbol{z} | \boldsymbol{x}) q_{\boldsymbol{\phi}}(y | \boldsymbol{x}) \tag{19.33}$$

$$q_{\boldsymbol{\phi}}(\boldsymbol{z} | \boldsymbol{x}) = \mathcal{N}(\boldsymbol{z} | \boldsymbol{\mu}_{\boldsymbol{\phi}}(\boldsymbol{x}), \mathrm{diag}(\sigma_{\boldsymbol{\phi}}^2(\boldsymbol{x})) \tag{19.34}$$

$$q_{\boldsymbol{\phi}}(y | \boldsymbol{x}) = \mathrm{Cat}(y | \boldsymbol{\pi}_{\boldsymbol{\phi}}(\boldsymbol{x})) \tag{19.35}$$

Note that $q_{\boldsymbol{\phi}}(y | \boldsymbol{x})$ acts like a discriminative classifier, that imputes the missing labels. We then use the following variational lower bound:

$$\log p_{\boldsymbol{\theta}}(\boldsymbol{x}) \geq \mathbb{E}_{q_{\boldsymbol{\phi}}(\boldsymbol{z}, y | \boldsymbol{x})} \left[\log p_{\boldsymbol{\theta}}(\boldsymbol{x} | y, \boldsymbol{z}) + \log p_{\boldsymbol{\theta}}(y) + \log p_{\boldsymbol{\theta}}(\boldsymbol{z}) - \log q_{\boldsymbol{\phi}}(\boldsymbol{z}, y | \boldsymbol{x}) \right] \tag{19.36}$$

$$= -\sum_y q_{\boldsymbol{\phi}}(y | \boldsymbol{x}) \mathcal{L}(\boldsymbol{x}, y) + \mathbb{H}\left(q_{\boldsymbol{\phi}}(y | \boldsymbol{x})\right) = -\mathcal{U}(\boldsymbol{x}) \tag{19.37}$$

Note that the discriminative classifier $q_{\boldsymbol{\phi}}(y | \boldsymbol{x})$ is only used to compute the log-likelihood of the unlabeled data, which is undesirable. We can therefore add an extra classification loss on the supervised data, to get the following overall objective function:

$$\mathcal{L}(\boldsymbol{\theta}) = \mathbb{E}_{(\boldsymbol{x}, y) \sim \mathcal{D}_L} \left[\mathcal{L}(\boldsymbol{x}, y) \right] + \mathbb{E}_{\boldsymbol{x} \sim \mathcal{D}_U} \left[\mathcal{U}(\boldsymbol{x}) \right] + \alpha \mathbb{E}_{(\boldsymbol{x}, y) \sim \mathcal{D}_L} \left[-\log q_{\boldsymbol{\phi}}(y | \boldsymbol{x}) \right] \tag{19.38}$$

where α is a hyperparameter that controls the relative weight of generative and discriminative learning.

Of course, the probablistic model used in M2 is just one of many ways to decompose the dependencies between the observed data, the class labels, and the continuous latent variables. There are also many ways other than variational inference to perform approximate inference. The best technique will be problem dependent, but overall the main advantage of the generative approach is that we can incorporate domain knowledge. For example, we can model the missing data mechanism, since the absence of a label may be informative about the underlying data (e.g., people may be reluctant to answer a survey question about their health if they are unwell).

19.3.6.2 Generative adversarial networks

Generative adversarial networks (GANs) (described in more detail in the sequel to this book, [Mur23]) are a popular class of generative models that learn an implicit model of the data distribution. They consist of a generator network, which maps samples from a simple latent distribution to the data space, and a critic network, which attempts to distinguish between the outputs of the generator and samples from the true data distribution. The generator is trained to generate samples that the critic classifies as "real".

Since standard GANs do not produce a learned latent representation of a given datapoint and do not learn an explicit model of the data distribution, we cannot use the same approaches as were used for VAEs. Instead, semi-supervised learning with GANs is typically done by modifying the critic so that it outputs either a class label or "fake" instead of simply classifying real vs. fake [Sal+16; Ode16]. For labeled real data, the critic is trained to output the appropriate class label, and for unlabeled real data, it is trained to raise the probability of any of the class labels. As with standard GAN training, the critic is trained to classify outputs from the generator as fake and the generator is trained to fool the critic.

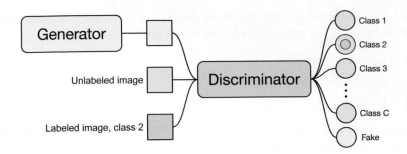

Figure 19.12: Diagram of the semi-supervised GAN framework. The discriminator is trained to output the class of labeled datapoints (red), a "fake" label for outputs from the generator (yellow), and any label for unlabeled data (green).

In more detail, let $p_\theta(y|\boldsymbol{x})$ denote the critic with $C+1$ outputs corresponding to C classes plus a "fake" class, and let $G(\boldsymbol{z})$ denote the generator which takes as input samples from the prior distribution $p(\boldsymbol{z})$. Let us assume that we are using the standard cross-entropy GAN loss as originally proposed in [Goo+14]. Then the critic's loss is

$$-\mathbb{E}_{\boldsymbol{x},y\sim p(\boldsymbol{x},y)}\log p_\theta(y|\boldsymbol{x}) - \mathbb{E}_{\boldsymbol{x}\sim p(\boldsymbol{x})}\log[1-p_\theta(y=C+1|\boldsymbol{x})] - \mathbb{E}_{\boldsymbol{z}\sim p(\boldsymbol{z})}\log p_\theta(y=C+1|G(\boldsymbol{z})) \quad (19.39)$$

This tries to maximize the probability of the correct class for the labeled examples, to minimize the probability of the fake class for real unlabeled examples, and to maximize the probability of the fake class for generated examples. The generator's loss is simpler, namely

$$\mathbb{E}_{z\sim p(\boldsymbol{z})}\log p_\theta(y=C+1|G(\boldsymbol{z})) \quad (19.40)$$

A diagram visualizing the semi-supervised GAN framework is shown in Figure 19.12.

19.3.6.3 Normalizing flows

Normalizing flows (described in more detail in the sequel to this book, [Mur23]) are a tractable way to define deep generative models. More precisely, they define an invertible mapping $f_\theta : \mathcal{X} \to \mathcal{Z}$, with parameters θ, from the data space $\mathcal{X}$ to the latent space $\mathcal{Z}$. The density in data space can be written starting from the density in the latent space using the change of variables formula:

$$p(x) = p(f(x)) \cdot \left| \det\left(\frac{\partial f}{\partial x}\right) \right|. \quad (19.41)$$

We can extend this to semi-supervised learning, as proposed in [Izm+20]. For class labels $y \in \{1 \dots \mathcal{C}\}$, we can specify the latent distribution, conditioned on a label k, as Gaussian with mean μ_k and covariance Σ_k: $p(z|y=k) = \mathcal{N}(z|\mu_k,\Sigma_k)$. The marginal distribution of z is then a Gaussian mixture. The likelihood for labeled data is then

$$p_\mathcal{X}(x|y=k) = \mathcal{N}\left(f(x)|\mu_k,\Sigma_k\right) \cdot \left| \det\left(\frac{\partial f}{\partial x}\right) \right|, \quad (19.42)$$

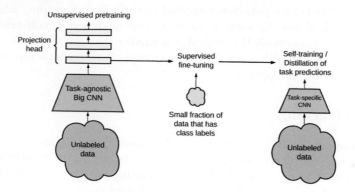

Figure 19.13: Combining self-supervised learning on unlabeled data (left), supervised fine-tuning (middle), and self-training on pseudo-labeled data (right). From Figure 3 of [Che+20c]. Used with kind permission of Ting Chen.

and the likelihood for data with unknown label is $p(x) = \sum_k p(x|y = k)p(y = k)$.

For semi-supervised learning we can then maximize the joint likelihood of the labeled $\mathcal{D}_\ell$ and unlabeled data $\mathcal{D}_u$:

$$p(\mathcal{D}_\ell, \mathcal{D}_u | \theta) = \prod_{(x_i, y_i) \in \mathcal{D}_\ell} p(x_i, y_i) \prod_{x_j \in \mathcal{D}_u} p(x_j), \tag{19.43}$$

over the parameters θ of the bijective function f, which learns a density model for a Bayes classifier.

Given a test point x, the model predictive distribution is given by

$$p_\mathcal{X}(y = c|x) = \frac{p(x|y = c)p(y = c)}{p(x)} = \frac{p(x|y = c)p(y = c)}{\sum_{k=1}^{C} p(x|y = k)p(y = k)} = \frac{\mathcal{N}(f(x)|\mu_c, \Sigma_c)}{\sum_{k=1}^{C} \mathcal{N}(f(x)|\mu_k, \Sigma_k)}, \tag{19.44}$$

where we have assumed $p(y = c) = 1/C$. We can make predictions for a test point x with the Bayes decision rule $y = \arg\max_{c \in \{1,...,C\}} p(y = c|x)$.

19.3.7 Combining self-supervised and semi-supervised learning

It is possible to combine self-supervised and semi-supervised learning. For example, [Che+20c] use SimCLR (Section 19.2.4.4) to perform self-supervised representation learning on the unlabeled data, they then fine-tune this representation on a small labeled dataset (as in transfer learning, Section 19.2), and finally, they apply the trained model back to the original unlabeled dataset, and distill the predictions from this teacher model T into a student model S. (**Knowledge distillation** is the name given to the approach of training one model on the predictions of another, as originally proposed in [HVD14].) That is, after fine-tuning T, they train S by minimizing

$$\mathcal{L}(T) = -\sum_{\boldsymbol{x}_i \in \mathcal{D}} \left[\sum_y p^T(y|\boldsymbol{x}_i; \tau) \log p^S(y|\boldsymbol{x}_i; \tau) \right] \tag{19.45}$$

where $\tau > 0$ is a temperature parameter applied to the softmax output, which is used to perform **label smoothing**. If S has the same form as T, this is known as **self-training**, as discussed in Section 19.3.1. However, normally the student S is smaller than the teacher T. (For example, T might be a high capacity model, and S is a lightweight version that runs on a phone.) See Figure 19.13 for an illustration of the overall approach.

19.4   Active learning

In **active learning**, the goal is to identify the true predictive mapping $y = f(\boldsymbol{x})$ by querying as few $(\boldsymbol{x}, y)$ points as possible. There are three main variants. In **query synthesis**, the algorithm gets to choose any input $\boldsymbol{x}$, and can ask for its corresponding output $y = f(\boldsymbol{x})$. In **pool-based active learning**, there is a large, but fixed, set of unlabeled data points, and the algorithm gets to ask for a label for one or more of these points. Finally, in **stream-based active learning**, the incoming data is arriving continuously, and the algorithm must choose whether it wants to request a label for the current input or not.

There are various closely related problems. In **Bayesian optimization** the goal is to estimate the location of the global optimum $\boldsymbol{x}^* = \operatorname{argmin}_{\boldsymbol{x}} f(\boldsymbol{x})$ in as few queries as possible; typically we fit a surrogate (response surface) model to the intermediate $(\boldsymbol{x}, y)$ queries, to decide which question to ask next. In **experiment design**, the goal is to infer a parameter vector of some model, using carefully chosen data samples $\mathcal{D} = \{\boldsymbol{x}_1, \ldots, \boldsymbol{x}_N\}$, i.e. we want to estimate $p(\boldsymbol{\theta}|\mathcal{D})$ using as little data as possible. (This can be thought of as an unsupervised, or generalized, form of active learning.)

In this section, we give a brief review of the pool based approach to active learning. For more details, see e.g., [Set12] for a review.

19.4.1   Decision-theoretic approach

In the decision theoretic approach to active learning, proposed in [KHB07; RM01], we define the utility of querying $\boldsymbol{x}$ in terms of the **value of information**. In particular, we define the utility of issuing query $\boldsymbol{x}$ as

$$U(\boldsymbol{x}) \triangleq \mathbb{E}_{p(y|\boldsymbol{x},\mathcal{D})} \left[\min_a \left(\rho(a|\mathcal{D}) - \rho(a|\mathcal{D}, (\boldsymbol{x}, y)) \right) \right] \tag{19.46}$$

where $\rho(a|\mathcal{D}) = \mathbb{E}_{p(\theta|\mathcal{D})} [\ell(\theta, a)]$ is the posterior expected loss of taking some future action a given the data $\mathcal{D}$ observed so far. Unfortunately, evaluating $U(\boldsymbol{x})$ for each $\boldsymbol{x}$ is quite expensive, since for each possible response y we might observe, we have to update our beliefs given $(\boldsymbol{x}, y)$ to see what effect it might have on our future decisions (similar to look ahead search technique applied to belief states).

19.4.2   Information-theoretic approach

In the information theoretic approach to active supervised learning, we avoid using task-specific loss functions, and instead focus on learning our model as well as we can. In particular, [Lin56] proposed to define the utility of querying $\boldsymbol{x}$ in terms of **information gain** about the parameters $\boldsymbol{\theta}$, i.e., the reduction in entropy:

$$U(\boldsymbol{x}) \triangleq \mathbb{H}\left(p(\boldsymbol{\theta}|\mathcal{D})\right) - \mathbb{E}_{p(y|\boldsymbol{x},\mathcal{D})}\left[\mathbb{H}\left(p(\boldsymbol{\theta}|\mathcal{D}, \boldsymbol{x}, y)\right)\right] \tag{19.47}$$

(Note that the first term is a constant wrt $\boldsymbol{x}$, but we include it for later convenience.) Exercise 19.1 asks you to show that this objective is identical to the expected change in the posterior over the parameters which is given by

$$U'(\boldsymbol{x}) \triangleq \mathbb{E}_{p(y|\boldsymbol{x},\mathcal{D})} \left[D_{\mathbb{KL}} \left(p(\boldsymbol{\theta}|\mathcal{D}, \boldsymbol{x}, y) \parallel p(\boldsymbol{\theta}|\mathcal{D}) \right) \right] \tag{19.48}$$

Using symmetry of the mutual information, we can rewrite Equation (19.47) as follows:

$$U(\boldsymbol{x}) = \mathbb{H}\left(p(\boldsymbol{\theta}|\mathcal{D})\right) - \mathbb{E}_{p(y|\boldsymbol{x},\mathcal{D})} \left[\mathbb{H}\left(p(\boldsymbol{\theta}|\mathcal{D}, \boldsymbol{x}, y)\right) \right] \tag{19.49}$$

$$= \mathbb{I}(\boldsymbol{\theta}, y|\mathcal{D}, \boldsymbol{x}) \tag{19.50}$$

$$= \mathbb{H}\left(p(y|\boldsymbol{x}, \mathcal{D})\right) - \mathbb{E}_{p(\boldsymbol{\theta}|\mathcal{D})} \left[\mathbb{H}\left(p(y|\boldsymbol{x}, \boldsymbol{\theta})\right) \right] \tag{19.51}$$

The advantage of this approach is that we now only have to reason about the uncertainty of the predictive distribution over outputs y, not over the parameters $\boldsymbol{\theta}$.

Equation (19.51) has an interesting interpretation. The first term prefers examples $\boldsymbol{x}$ for which there is uncertainty in the predicted label. Just using this as a selection criterion is called **maximum entropy sampling** [SW87]. However, this can have problems with examples which are inherently ambiguous or mislabeled. The second term in Equation (19.51) will discourage such behavior, since it prefers examples $\boldsymbol{x}$ for which the predicted label is fairly certain once we know $\boldsymbol{\theta}$; this will avoid picking inherently hard-to-predict examples. In other words, Equation (19.51) will select examples $\boldsymbol{x}$ for which the model makes confident predictions which are highly diverse. This approach has therefore been called **Bayesian active learning by disagreement** or **BALD** [Hou+12].

This method can be used to train classifiers for other domains where expert labels are hard to acquire, such as medical images or astronomical images [Wal+20].

19.4.3 Batch active learning

So far, we have assumed a greedy or **myopic** strategy, in which we select a single example $\boldsymbol{x}$, as if it were the last datapoint to be selected. But sometimes we have a budget to collect a set of B samples, call them $(\mathbf{X}, \mathbf{Y})$. In this case, the information gain criterion becomes $U(\boldsymbol{x}) = \mathbb{H}\left(p(\boldsymbol{\theta}|\mathcal{D})\right) - \mathbb{E}_{p(\mathbf{Y}|\boldsymbol{x},\mathcal{D})} \left[\mathbb{H}\left(p(\boldsymbol{\theta}|\mathbf{Y}, \boldsymbol{x}, \mathcal{D})\right) \right]$. Unfortunately, optimizing this is NP-hard in the horizon length B [KLQ95; KG05].

Fortunately, under certain conditions, the greedy strategy is near-optimal, as we now explain. Let us fix query $\boldsymbol{x}$ and define $f(\boldsymbol{y}) \triangleq \mathbb{H}\left(p(\boldsymbol{\theta}|\mathcal{D})\right) - \mathbb{H}\left(p(\boldsymbol{\theta}|\mathbf{Y}, \boldsymbol{x}, \mathcal{D})\right)$ as the information gain function, so $U(\boldsymbol{x}) = \mathbb{E}_{\boldsymbol{y}} \left[f(\boldsymbol{y}, \boldsymbol{x}) \right]$. It is clear that $f(\emptyset) = 0$, and that f is non-decreasing, meaning $f(Y^{\text{large}}) \geq f(Y^{\text{small}})$, due to the "more information never hurts" principle. Furthermore, [KG05] proved that f is **submodular**. As a consequence, a sequential greedy approach is within a constant factor of optimal. If we combine this greedy technique with the BALD objective, we get a method called **BatchBALD** [KAG19].

19.5 Meta-learning

We can think of a learning algorithm as a function A that maps data to a parameter estimate, $\theta = A(\mathcal{D})$. The function A usually has its own parameter — call them ϕ — such as the initial values for θ, or the learning rate, etc. We denote this by $\theta = A(\mathcal{D}; \phi)$. We can imagine learning ϕ itself,

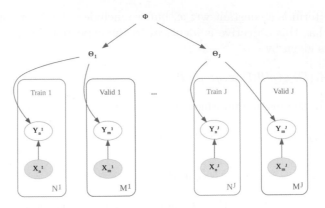

Figure 19.14: Illustration of a hierarchical Bayesian model for meta-learning. Generated by hbayes_maml.ipynb.

given a collection of datasets $\mathcal{D}_{1:J}$ and some **meta-learning** algorithm M, i.e., $\phi = M(\mathcal{D}_{1:J})$. We can then apply $A(\cdot; \phi)$ to learn the parameters θ_{J+1} on some new dataset $\mathcal{D}_{J+1}$. There are many techniques for meta-learning — see e.g., [Van18; HRP21] for recent reviews. Below we discuss one particularly popular method. (Note that meta-learning is also called **learning to learn** [TP97].)

19.5.1   Model-agnostic meta-learning (MAML)

A natural approach to meta learning is to use a hierarchical Bayesian model, as illustrated in Figure 19.14. The parameters for each task $\boldsymbol{\theta}_j$ are assumed to come from a common prior, $p(\boldsymbol{\theta}_j|\boldsymbol{\xi})$, which can be used to help pool statistical strength from multiple data-poor problems. Meta-learning becomes equivalent to learning the prior ϕ. Rather than performing full Bayesian inference in this model, a more efficient approach is to use the following empirical Bayes (Section 4.6.5.3) approximation:

$$\boldsymbol{\xi}^* = \operatorname*{argmax}_{\boldsymbol{\xi}} \frac{1}{J} \sum_{j=1}^{J} \log p(\mathcal{D}_{\text{valid}}^j | \hat{\boldsymbol{\theta}}_j(\boldsymbol{\xi}, \mathcal{D}_{\text{train}}^j)) \tag{19.52}$$

where $\hat{\boldsymbol{\theta}}_j = \hat{\boldsymbol{\theta}}(\boldsymbol{\xi}, \mathcal{D}_{\text{train}}^j)$ is a point estimate of the parameters for task j based on $\mathcal{D}_{\text{train}}^j$ and prior $\boldsymbol{\xi}$, and where we use a cross-validation approximation to the marginal likelihood (Section 5.2.4).

To compute the point estimate of the parameters for the target task $\hat{\boldsymbol{\theta}}_{J+1}$, we use K steps of a gradient ascent procedure starting at $\boldsymbol{\xi}$ with a learning rate of η. This is known as **model-agnostic meta-learning** or **MAML** [FAL17]. This can be shown to be equivalent to an approximate MAP estimate using a Gaussian prior centered at $\boldsymbol{\xi}$, where the strength of the prior is controlled by the number of gradient steps [San96; Gra+18]. (This is an example of **fast adapation** of the task specific weights starting from the shared prior $\boldsymbol{\xi}$.)

Training task 1   **Training task 2** · · ·   **Test task 1** · · ·

Figure 19.15: Illustration of meta-learning for few-shot learning. Here, each task is a 3-way-2-shot classification problem because each training task contains a support set with three classes, each with two examples. From `https://bit.ly/3rruSjw`. *Copyright (2019) Borealis AI. Used with kind permission of Simon Prince and April Cooper.*

19.6   Few-shot learning

People can learn to predict from very few labeled examples. This is called **few-shot learning**. In the extreme in which the person or system learns from a single example of each class, this is called **one-shot learning**, and if no labeled examples are given, it is called **zero-shot learning**.

A common way to evaluate methods for FSL is to use **C-way N-shot classification**, in which the system is expected to learn to classify C classes using just N training examples of each class. Typically N and C are very small, e.g., Figure 19.15 illustrates the case where we have $C = 3$ classes, each with $N = 2$ examples. Since the amount of data from the new domain (here, ducks, dolphins and hens) is so small, we cannot expect to learn from scratch. Therefore we turn to meta-learning.

During training, the meta-algorithm M trains on a labeled support set from group j, returns a predictor f^j, which is then evaluated on a disjoint query set also from group j. We optimize M over all J groups. Finally we can apply M to our new labeled support set to get f^{test}, which is applied to the query set from the test domain. This is illustrated in Figure 19.15. We see that there is no overlap between the classes in the two training tasks ({cat, lamb, pig} and {dog, shark, lion}) and those in the test task ({duck, dolphin, hen}). Thus the algorithm M must learn to predict image classes in general rather than any particular set of labels.

There are many approaches to few-shot learning. We discuss one such method in Section 19.6.1. For more methods, see e.g., [Wan+20b].

19.6.1   Matching networks

One approach to few shot learning is to learn a distance metric on some other dataset, and then to use $d_{\boldsymbol{\theta}}(\boldsymbol{x}, \boldsymbol{x}')$ inside of a nearest neighbor classifier. Essentially this defines a semi-parametric model of the form $p_{\boldsymbol{\theta}}(y|\boldsymbol{x}, \mathcal{S})$, where $\mathcal{S}$ is the small labeled dataset (known as the support set), and $\boldsymbol{\theta}$ are the parameters of the distance function. This approach is widely used for **fine-grained classification**

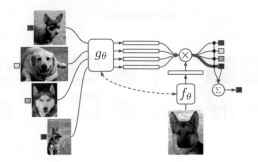

Figure 19.16: Illustration of a matching network for one-shot learning. From Figure 1 of [Vin+16]. Used with kind permission of Oriol Vinyals.

tasks, where there are many different visually similar categories, such as face images from a gallery, or product images from a catalog.

An extension of this approach is to learn a function of the form

$$p_{\boldsymbol{\theta}}(y|\boldsymbol{x}, \mathcal{S}) = \mathbb{I}\left(y = \sum_{n \in \mathcal{S}} a_{\boldsymbol{\theta}}(\boldsymbol{x}, \boldsymbol{x}_n; \mathcal{S}) y_n\right) \tag{19.53}$$

where $a_{\boldsymbol{\theta}}(\boldsymbol{x}, \boldsymbol{x}_n; \mathcal{S}) \in \mathbb{R}^+$ is some kind of adaptive similarity kernel. For example, we can use an **attention kernel** of the form

$$a(\boldsymbol{x}, \boldsymbol{x}_n; \mathcal{S}) = \frac{\exp(c(f(\boldsymbol{x}), g(\boldsymbol{x}_n)))}{\sum_{n'=1}^{N} \exp(c(f(\boldsymbol{x}), g(\boldsymbol{x}_{n'})))} \tag{19.54}$$

where $c(\boldsymbol{u}, \boldsymbol{v})$ is the cosine distance. (We can make f and g be the same function if we want.) Intuitively, the attention kernel will compare $\boldsymbol{x}$ to $\boldsymbol{x}_n$ in the context of all the labeled examples, which provides an implicit signal about which feature dimensions are relevant. (We discuss attention mechanisms in more detail in Section 15.4.) This is called a **matching network** [Vin+16]. See Figure 19.16 for an illustration.

We can train the f and g functions using multiple small datasets, as in meta-learning (Section 19.5). More precisely, let $\mathcal{D}$ be a large labeled dataset (e.g., ImageNet), and let $p(\mathcal{L})$ be a distribution over its labels. We create a task by sampling a small set of labels (say 25), $\mathcal{L} \sim p(\mathcal{L})$, and then sampling a small support set of examples from $\mathcal{D}$ with those labels, $\mathcal{S} \sim \mathcal{L}$, and finally sampling a small test set with those same labels, $\mathcal{T} \sim \mathcal{L}$. We then train the model to predict the test labels given the support set, i.e., we optimize the following objective:

$$\mathcal{L}(\boldsymbol{\theta}; \mathcal{D}) = \mathbb{E}_{\mathcal{L} \sim p(\mathcal{L})}\left[\mathbb{E}_{\mathcal{S} \sim \mathcal{L}, \mathcal{T} \sim \mathcal{L}}\left[\sum_{(\boldsymbol{x}, y) \in \mathcal{T}} \log p_{\boldsymbol{\theta}}(y|\boldsymbol{x}, \mathcal{S})\right]\right] \tag{19.55}$$

After training, we freeze $\boldsymbol{\theta}$, and apply Equation (19.53) to a test support set $\mathcal{S}$.

19.7 Weakly supervised learning

The term **weakly supervised learning** refers to scenarios where we do not have an exact label associated with every feature vector in the training set.

One scenario is when we have a *distribution* over labels for each case, rather than a single label. Fortunately, we can still do maximum likelihood training: we just have to minimize the cross entropy,

$$\mathcal{L}(\boldsymbol{\theta}) = -\sum_n \sum_y p(y|\boldsymbol{x}_n) \log q_{\boldsymbol{\theta}}(y|\boldsymbol{x}_n) \tag{19.56}$$

where $p(y|\boldsymbol{x}_n)$ is the label distribution for case n, and $q_{\boldsymbol{\theta}}(y|\boldsymbol{x}_n)$ is the predicted distribution. Indeed, it is often useful to artificially replace exact labels with a "soft" version, in which we replace the delta function with a distribution that puts, say, 90% of its mass on the observed label, and spreads the remaining mass uniformly over the other choices. This is called **label smoothing**, and is a useful form of regularization (see e.g., [MKH19]).

Another scenario is when we have a set, or **bag**, of instances, $\boldsymbol{x}_n = \{\boldsymbol{x}_{n,1}, \dots, \boldsymbol{x}_{n,B}\}$, but we only have a label for the entire bag, y_n, not for the members of the bag, y_{nb}. We often assume that if any member of the bag is positive, the whole bag is labeled positive, so $y_n = \vee_{b=1}^{B} y_{nb}$, but we do not know which member "caused" the positive outcome. However, if all the members are negative, the entire bag is negative. This is known as **multi-instance learning** [DLLP97]. (For a recent example of this in the context of COVID-19 risk score learning, see [MKS21].) Various algortims can be used to solve the MIL problem, depending on what assumptions we make about the correlation between the labels in each bag, and the fraction of positive members we expect to see (see e.g., [KF05]).

Yet another scenario is known as **distant supervision** [Min+09], which is often used to train information extraction systems. The idea is that we have some fact, such as "Married(B,M)", that we know to be true (since it is stored in a database). We use this to label every sentence (in our unlabeled training corpus) in which the entities B and M are mentioned as being a positive example of the "Married" relation. For example, the sentence "B and M invited 100 people to their wedding" will be labeled positive. But this heuristic may include false positives, for example "B and M went out to dinner" will also be labeled positive. Thus the resulting labels will be noisy. We discuss some ways to handle label noise in Section 10.4.

19.8 Exercises

Exercise 19.1 [Information gain equations]

Consider the following two objectives for evaluating the utility of querying a datapoint $\boldsymbol{x}$ in an active learning setting:

$$U(\boldsymbol{x}) \triangleq \mathbb{H}\left(p(\boldsymbol{\theta}|\mathcal{D})\right) - \mathbb{E}_{p(y|\boldsymbol{x},\mathcal{D})}\left[\mathbb{H}\left(p(\boldsymbol{\theta}|\mathcal{D}, \boldsymbol{x}, y)\right)\right] \tag{19.57}$$

$$U'(\boldsymbol{x}) \triangleq \mathbb{E}_{p(y|\boldsymbol{x},\mathcal{D})}\left[D_{\mathrm{KL}}\left(p(\boldsymbol{\theta}|\mathcal{D}, \boldsymbol{x}, y) \parallel p(\boldsymbol{\theta}|\mathcal{D})\right)\right] \tag{19.58}$$

Prove that these are equal.

20 Dimensionality Reduction

A common form of unsupervised learning is **dimensionality reduction**, in which we learn a mapping from the high-dimensional visible space, $\boldsymbol{x} \in \mathbb{R}^D$, to a low-dimensional latent space, $\boldsymbol{z} \in \mathbb{R}^L$. This mapping can either be a parametric model $\boldsymbol{z} = f(\boldsymbol{x}; \boldsymbol{\theta})$ which can be applied to any input, or it can be a nonparametric mapping where we compute an **embedding** $\boldsymbol{z}_n$ for each input $\boldsymbol{x}_n$ in the data set, but not for any other points. This latter approach is mostly used for data visualization, whereas the former approach can also be used as a preprocessing step for other kinds of learning algorithms. For example, we might first reduce the dimensionality by learning a mapping from $\boldsymbol{x}$ to $\boldsymbol{z}$, and then learn a simple linear classifier on this embedding, by mapping $\boldsymbol{z}$ to y.

20.1 Principal components analysis (PCA)

The simplest and most widely used form of dimensionality reduction is **principal components analysis** or **PCA**. The basic idea is to find a linear and orthogonal projection of the high dimensional data $\boldsymbol{x} \in \mathbb{R}^D$ to a low dimensional subspace $\boldsymbol{z} \in \mathbb{R}^L$, such that the low dimensional representation is a "good approximation" to the original data, in the following sense: if we project or **encode** $\boldsymbol{x}$ to get $\boldsymbol{z} = \mathbf{W}^\mathsf{T} \boldsymbol{x}$, and then unproject or **decode** $\boldsymbol{z}$ to get $\hat{\boldsymbol{x}} = \mathbf{W} \boldsymbol{z}$, then we want $\hat{\boldsymbol{x}}$ to be close to $\boldsymbol{x}$ in ℓ_2 distance. In particular, we can define the following **reconstruction error** or **distortion**:

$$\mathcal{L}(\mathbf{W}) \triangleq \frac{1}{N} \sum_{n=1}^{N} ||\boldsymbol{x}_n - \text{decode}(\text{encode}(\boldsymbol{x}_n; \mathbf{W}); \mathbf{W})||_2^2 \tag{20.1}$$

where the encode and decoding stages are both linear maps, as we explain below.

In Section 20.1.2, we show that we can minimize this objective by setting $\hat{\mathbf{W}} = \mathbf{U}_L$, where $\mathbf{U}_L$ contains the L eigenvectors with largest eigenvalues of the empirical covariance matrix

$$\hat{\boldsymbol{\Sigma}} = \frac{1}{N} \sum_{n=1}^{N} (\boldsymbol{x}_n - \overline{\boldsymbol{x}})(\boldsymbol{x}_n - \overline{\boldsymbol{x}})^\mathsf{T} = \frac{1}{N} \mathbf{X}_c^\mathsf{T} \mathbf{X}_c \tag{20.2}$$

where $\mathbf{X}_c$ is a centered version of the $N \times D$ design matrix. In Section 20.2.2, we show that this is equivalent to maximizing the likelihood of a latent linear Gaussian model known as probabilistic PCA.

20.1.1 Examples

Before giving the details, we start by showing some examples.

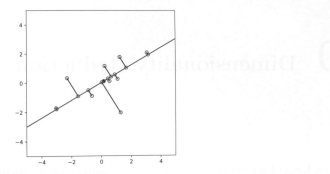

Figure 20.1: *An illustration of PCA where we project from 2d to 1d. Red circles are the original data points, blue circles are the reconstructions. The red dot is the data mean. Generated by pcaDemo2d.ipynb.*

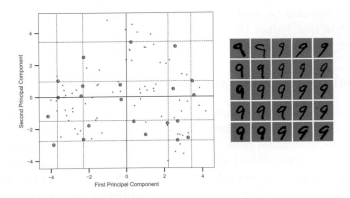

Figure 20.2: *An illustration of PCA applied to MNIST digits from class 9. Grid points are at the 5, 25, 50, 75, 95 % quantiles of the data distribution along each dimension. The circled points are the closest projected images to the vertices of the grid. Adapted from Figure 14.23 of [HTF09]. Generated by pca_digits.ipynb.*

Figure 20.1 shows a very simple example, where we project 2d data to a 1d line. This direction captures most of the variation in the data.

In Figure 20.2, we show what happens when we project some MNIST images of the digit 9 down to 2d. Although the inputs are high dimensional (specifically $28 \times 28 = 784$ dimensional), the number of "effective degrees of freedom" is much less, since the pixels are correlated, and many digits look similar. Therefore we can represent each image as a point in a low dimensional linear space.

In general, it can be hard to interpret the latent dimensions to which the data is projected. However, by looking at several projected points along a given direction, and the examples from which they are derived, we see that the first principal component (horizontal direction) seems to capture the orientation of the digit, and the second component (vertical direction) seems to capture line thickness.

In Figure 20.3, we show PCA applied to another image dataset, known as the Olivetti face dataset,

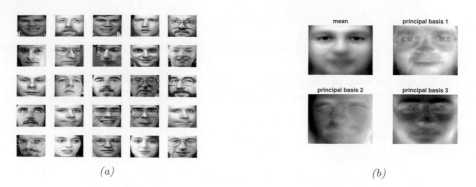

Figure 20.3: a) Some randomly chosen 64×64 pixel images from the Olivetti face database. (b) The mean and the first three PCA components represented as images. Generated by pcaImageDemo.ipynb.

which is a set of 64×64 grayscale images. We project these to a 3d subspace. The resulting basis vectors (columns of the projection matrix $\mathbf{W}$) are shown as images in in Figure 20.3b; these are known as **eigenfaces** [Tur13], for reasons that will be explained in Section 20.1.2. We see that the main modes of variation in the data are related to overall lighting, and then differences in the eyebrow region of the face. If we use enough dimensions (but fewer than the 4096 we started with), we can use the representation $\boldsymbol{z} = \mathbf{W}^\mathsf{T}\boldsymbol{x}$ as input to a nearest-neighbor classifier to perform face recognition; this is faster and more reliable than working in pixel space [MWP98].

20.1.2 Derivation of the algorithm

Suppose we have an (unlabeled) dataset $\mathcal{D} = \{\boldsymbol{x}_n : n = 1 : N\}$, where $\boldsymbol{x}_n \in \mathbb{R}^D$. We can represent this as an $N \times D$ data matrix $\mathbf{X}$. We will assume $\overline{\boldsymbol{x}} = \frac{1}{N}\sum_{n=1}^{N} \boldsymbol{x}_n = \mathbf{0}$, which we can ensure by centering the data.

We would like to approximate each $\boldsymbol{x}_n$ by a low dimensional representation, $\boldsymbol{z}_n \in \mathbb{R}^L$. We assume that each $\boldsymbol{x}_n$ can be "explained" in terms of a weighted combination of basis functions $\boldsymbol{w}_1, \ldots, \boldsymbol{w}_L$, where each $\boldsymbol{w}_k \in \mathbb{R}^D$, and where the weights are given by $\boldsymbol{z}_n \in \mathbb{R}^L$, i.e., we assume $\boldsymbol{x}_n \approx \sum_{k=1}^{L} z_{nk}\boldsymbol{w}_k$. The vector $\boldsymbol{z}_n$ is the low dimensional representation of $\boldsymbol{x}_n$, and is known as the **latent vector**, since it consists of latent or "hidden" values that are not observed in the data. The collection of these latent variables are called the **latent factors**.

We can measure the error produced by this approximation as follows:

$$\mathcal{L}(\mathbf{W}, \mathbf{Z}) = \frac{1}{N}||\mathbf{X} - \mathbf{Z}\mathbf{W}^\mathsf{T}||_F^2 = \frac{1}{N}||\mathbf{X}^\mathsf{T} - \mathbf{W}\mathbf{Z}^\mathsf{T}||_F^2 = \frac{1}{N}\sum_{n=1}^{N}||\boldsymbol{x}_n - \mathbf{W}\boldsymbol{z}_n||^2 \tag{20.3}$$

where the rows of $\mathbf{Z}$ contain the low dimension versions of the rows of $\mathbf{X}$. This is known as the (average) **reconstruction error**, since we are approximating each $\boldsymbol{x}_n$ by $\hat{\boldsymbol{x}}_n = \mathbf{W}\boldsymbol{z}_n$.

We want to minimize this subject to the constraint that $\mathbf{W}$ is an orthogonal matrix. Below we show that the optimal solution is obtained by setting $\hat{\mathbf{W}} = \mathbf{U}_L$, where $\mathbf{U}_L$ contains the L eigenvectors with largest eigenvalues of the empirical covariance matrix.

20.1.2.1   Base case

Let us start by estimating the best 1d solution, $\boldsymbol{w}_1 \in \mathbb{R}^D$. We will find the remaining basis vectors $\boldsymbol{w}_2$, $\boldsymbol{w}_3$, etc. later.

Let the coefficients for each of the data points associated with the first basis vector be denoted by $\tilde{\mathbf{z}}_1 = [z_{11}, \ldots, z_{N1}] \in \mathbb{R}^N$. The reconstruction error is given by

$$\mathcal{L}(\boldsymbol{w}_1, \tilde{\mathbf{z}}_1) = \frac{1}{N} \sum_{n=1}^{N} ||\boldsymbol{x}_n - z_{n1}\boldsymbol{w}_1||^2 = \frac{1}{N} \sum_{n=1}^{N} (\boldsymbol{x}_n - z_{n1}\boldsymbol{w}_1)^{\mathsf{T}} (\boldsymbol{x}_n - z_{n1}\boldsymbol{w}_1) \tag{20.4}$$

$$= \frac{1}{N} \sum_{n=1}^{N} [\boldsymbol{x}_n^{\mathsf{T}}\boldsymbol{x}_n - 2z_{n1}\boldsymbol{w}_1^{\mathsf{T}}\boldsymbol{x}_n + z_{n1}^2 \boldsymbol{w}_1^{\mathsf{T}}\boldsymbol{w}_1] \tag{20.5}$$

$$= \frac{1}{N} \sum_{n=1}^{N} [\boldsymbol{x}_n^{\mathsf{T}}\boldsymbol{x}_n - 2z_{n1}\boldsymbol{w}_1^{\mathsf{T}}\boldsymbol{x}_n + z_{n1}^2] \tag{20.6}$$

since $\boldsymbol{w}_1^{\mathsf{T}}\boldsymbol{w}_1 = 1$ (by the orthonormality assumption). Taking derivatives wrt z_{n1} and equating to zero gives

$$\frac{\partial}{\partial z_{n1}} \mathcal{L}(\boldsymbol{w}_1, \tilde{\mathbf{z}}_1) = \frac{1}{N} [-2\boldsymbol{w}_1^{\mathsf{T}}\boldsymbol{x}_n + 2z_{n1}] = 0 \Rightarrow z_{n1} = \boldsymbol{w}_1^{\mathsf{T}}\boldsymbol{x}_n \tag{20.7}$$

So the optimal embedding is obtained by orthogonally projecting the data onto $\boldsymbol{w}_1$ (see Figure 20.1). Plugging this back in gives the loss for the weights:

$$\mathcal{L}(\boldsymbol{w}_1) = \mathcal{L}(\boldsymbol{w}_1, \tilde{\mathbf{z}}_1^*(\boldsymbol{w}_1)) = \frac{1}{N} \sum_{n=1}^{N} [\boldsymbol{x}_n^{\mathsf{T}}\boldsymbol{x}_n - z_{n1}^2] = \text{const} - \frac{1}{N} \sum_{n=1}^{N} z_{n1}^2 \tag{20.8}$$

To solve for $\boldsymbol{w}_1$, note that

$$\mathcal{L}(\boldsymbol{w}_1) = -\frac{1}{N} \sum_{n=1}^{N} z_{n1}^2 = -\frac{1}{N} \sum_{n=1}^{N} \boldsymbol{w}_1^{\mathsf{T}}\boldsymbol{x}_n \boldsymbol{x}_n^{\mathsf{T}}\boldsymbol{w}_1 = -\boldsymbol{w}_1^{\mathsf{T}}\hat{\boldsymbol{\Sigma}}\boldsymbol{w}_1 \tag{20.9}$$

where $\boldsymbol{\Sigma}$ is the empirical covariance matrix (since we assumed the data is centered). We can trivially optimize this by letting $||\boldsymbol{w}_1|| \to \infty$, so we impose the constraint $||\boldsymbol{w}_1|| = 1$ and instead optimize

$$\tilde{\mathcal{L}}(\boldsymbol{w}_1) = \boldsymbol{w}_1^{\mathsf{T}}\hat{\boldsymbol{\Sigma}}\boldsymbol{w}_1 - \lambda_1(\boldsymbol{w}_1^{\mathsf{T}}\boldsymbol{w}_1 - 1) \tag{20.10}$$

where λ_1 is a Lagrange multiplier (see Section 8.5.1). Taking derivatives and equating to zero we have

$$\frac{\partial}{\partial \boldsymbol{w}_1} \tilde{\mathcal{L}}(\boldsymbol{w}_1) = 2\hat{\boldsymbol{\Sigma}}\boldsymbol{w}_1 - 2\lambda_1\boldsymbol{w}_1 = 0 \tag{20.11}$$

$$\hat{\boldsymbol{\Sigma}}\boldsymbol{w}_1 = \lambda_1\boldsymbol{w}_1 \tag{20.12}$$

Hence the optimal direction onto which we should project the data is an eigenvector of the covariance matrix. Left multiplying by $\boldsymbol{w}_1^{\mathsf{T}}$ (and using $\boldsymbol{w}_1^{\mathsf{T}}\boldsymbol{w}_1 = 1$) we find

$$\boldsymbol{w}_1^{\mathsf{T}}\hat{\boldsymbol{\Sigma}}\boldsymbol{w}_1 = \lambda_1 \tag{20.13}$$

Since we want to maximize this quantity (minimize the loss), we pick the eigenvector which corresponds to the largest eigenvalue.

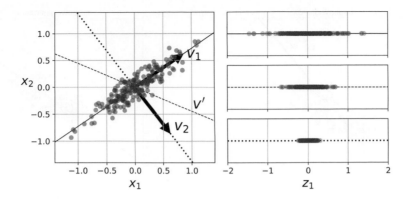

Figure 20.4: *Illustration of the variance of the points projected onto different 1d vectors.* v_1 *is the first principal component, which maximizes the variance of the projection.* v_2 *is the second principal component which is direction orthogonal to* v_1. *Finally* v' *is some other vector in between* v_1 *and* v_2. *Adapted from Figure 8.7 of [Gér19]. Generated by pca_projected_variance.ipynb*

20.1.2.2   Optimal weight vector maximizes the variance of the projected data

Before continuing, we make an interesting observation. Since the data has been centered, we have

$$\mathbb{E}\left[z_{n1}\right] = \mathbb{E}\left[\boldsymbol{x}_n^\mathsf{T}\boldsymbol{w}_1\right] = \mathbb{E}\left[\boldsymbol{x}_n\right]^\mathsf{T}\boldsymbol{w}_1 = 0 \tag{20.14}$$

Hence variance of the projected data is given by

$$\mathbb{V}\left[\tilde{\mathbf{z}}_1\right] = \mathbb{E}\left[\tilde{\mathbf{z}}_1^2\right] - (\mathbb{E}\left[\tilde{\mathbf{z}}_1\right])^2 = \frac{1}{N}\sum_{n=1}^{N} z_{n1}^2 - 0 = -\mathcal{L}(\boldsymbol{w}_1) + \text{const} \tag{20.15}$$

From this, we see that *minimizing* the reconstruction error is equivalent to *maximizing* the variance of the projected data:

$$\arg\min_{\boldsymbol{w}_1} \mathcal{L}(\boldsymbol{w}_1) = \arg\max_{\boldsymbol{w}_1} \mathbb{V}\left[\tilde{\mathbf{z}}_1(\boldsymbol{w}_1)\right] \tag{20.16}$$

This is why it is often said that PCA finds the directions of maximal variance. (See Figure 20.4 for an illustration.) However, the minimum error formulation is easier to understand and is more general.

20.1.2.3   Induction step

Now let us find another direction $\boldsymbol{w}_2$ to further minimize the reconstruction error, subject to $\boldsymbol{w}_1^\mathsf{T}\boldsymbol{w}_2 = 0$ and $\boldsymbol{w}_2^\mathsf{T}\boldsymbol{w}_2 = 1$. The error is

$$\mathcal{L}(\boldsymbol{w}_1, \tilde{\mathbf{z}}_1, \boldsymbol{w}_2, \tilde{\mathbf{z}}_2) = \frac{1}{N}\sum_{n=1}^{N} ||\boldsymbol{x}_n - z_{n1}\boldsymbol{w}_1 - z_{n2}\boldsymbol{w}_2||^2 \tag{20.17}$$

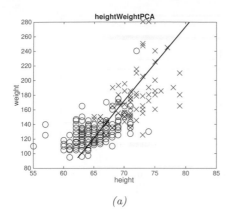
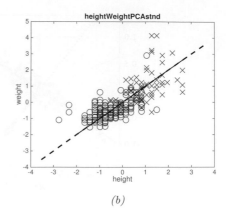

(a)   (b)

Figure 20.5: Effect of standardization on PCA applied to the height/weight dataset. (Red=female, blue=male.) Left: PCA of raw data. Right: PCA of standardized data. Generated by pcaStandardization.ipynb.

Optimizing wrt $\boldsymbol{w}_1$ and $\boldsymbol{z}_1$ gives the same solution as before. Exercise 20.3 asks you to show that $\frac{\partial \mathcal{L}}{\partial \boldsymbol{z}_2} = 0$ yields $z_{n2} = \boldsymbol{w}_2^\mathsf{T} \boldsymbol{x}_n$. Substituting in yields

$$\mathcal{L}(\boldsymbol{w}_2) = \frac{1}{N} \sum_{n=1}^{N} [\boldsymbol{x}_n^\mathsf{T} \boldsymbol{x}_n - \boldsymbol{w}_1^\mathsf{T} \boldsymbol{x}_n \boldsymbol{x}_n^\mathsf{T} \boldsymbol{w}_1 - \boldsymbol{w}_2^\mathsf{T} \boldsymbol{x}_n \boldsymbol{x}_n^\mathsf{T} \boldsymbol{w}_2] = \text{const} - \boldsymbol{w}_2^\mathsf{T} \hat{\boldsymbol{\Sigma}} \boldsymbol{w}_2 \qquad (20.18)$$

Dropping the constant term, plugging in the optimal $\boldsymbol{w}_1$ and adding the constraints yields

$$\tilde{\mathcal{L}}(\boldsymbol{w}_2) = -\boldsymbol{w}_2^\mathsf{T} \hat{\boldsymbol{\Sigma}} \boldsymbol{w}_2 + \lambda_2(\boldsymbol{w}_2^\mathsf{T} \boldsymbol{w}_2 - 1) + \lambda_{12}(\boldsymbol{w}_2^\mathsf{T} \boldsymbol{w}_1 - 0) \qquad (20.19)$$

Exercise 20.3 asks you to show that the solution is given by the eigenvector with the second largest eigenvalue:

$$\hat{\boldsymbol{\Sigma}} \boldsymbol{w}_2 = \lambda_2 \boldsymbol{w}_2 \qquad (20.20)$$

The proof continues in this way to show that $\hat{\mathbf{W}} = \mathbf{U}_L$.

20.1.3   Computational issues

In this section, we discuss various practical issues related to using PCA.

20.1.3.1   Covariance matrix vs correlation matrix

We have been working with the eigendecomposition of the covariance matrix. However, it is better to use the correlation matrix instead. The reason is that otherwise PCA can be "misled" by directions in which the variance is high merely because of the measurement scale. Figure 20.5 shows an example of this. On the left, we see that the vertical axis uses a larger range than the horizontal axis. This results in a first principal component that looks somewhat "unnatural". On the right, we show the results of PCA after standardizing the data (which is equivalent to using the correlation matrix instead of the covariance matrix); the results look much better.

20.1.3.2   Dealing with high-dimensional data

We have presented PCA as the problem of finding the eigenvectors of the $D \times D$ covariance matrix $\mathbf{X}^\mathsf{T}\mathbf{X}$. If $D > N$, it is faster to work with the $N \times N$ Gram matrix $\mathbf{X}\mathbf{X}^\mathsf{T}$. We now show how to do this.

First, let $\mathbf{U}$ be an orthogonal matrix containing the eigenvectors of $\mathbf{X}\mathbf{X}^\mathsf{T}$ with corresponding eigenvalues in $\mathbf{\Lambda}$. By definition we have $(\mathbf{X}\mathbf{X}^\mathsf{T})\mathbf{U} = \mathbf{U}\mathbf{\Lambda}$. Pre-multiplying by $\mathbf{X}^\mathsf{T}$ gives

$$(\mathbf{X}^\mathsf{T}\mathbf{X})(\mathbf{X}^\mathsf{T}\mathbf{U}) = (\mathbf{X}^\mathsf{T}\mathbf{U})\mathbf{\Lambda} \tag{20.21}$$

from which we see that the eigenvectors of $\mathbf{X}^\mathsf{T}\mathbf{X}$ are $\mathbf{V} = \mathbf{X}^\mathsf{T}\mathbf{U}$, with eigenvalues given by $\mathbf{\Lambda}$ as before. However, these eigenvectors are not normalized, since $||\boldsymbol{v}_j||^2 = \boldsymbol{u}_j^\mathsf{T}\mathbf{X}\mathbf{X}^\mathsf{T}\boldsymbol{u}_j = \lambda_j \boldsymbol{u}_j^\mathsf{T}\boldsymbol{u}_j = \lambda_j$. The normalized eigenvectors are given by

$$\mathbf{V} = \mathbf{X}^\mathsf{T}\mathbf{U}\mathbf{\Lambda}^{-\frac{1}{2}} \tag{20.22}$$

This provides an alternative way to compute the PCA basis. It also allows us to use the kernel trick, as we discuss in Section 20.4.6.

20.1.3.3   Computing PCA using SVD

In this section, we show the equivalence between PCA as computed using eigenvector methods (Section 20.1) and the truncated SVD.[1]

Let $\mathbf{U}_\Sigma \mathbf{\Lambda}_\Sigma \mathbf{U}_\Sigma^\mathsf{T}$ be the top L eigendecomposition of the covariance matrix $\mathbf{\Sigma} \propto \mathbf{X}^\mathsf{T}\mathbf{X}$ (we assume $\mathbf{X}$ is centered). Recall from Section 20.1.2 that the optimal estimate of the projection weights $\mathbf{W}$ is given by the top L eigenvalues, so $\mathbf{W} = \mathbf{U}_\Sigma$.

Now let $\mathbf{U}_X \mathbf{S}_X \mathbf{V}_X^\mathsf{T} \approx \mathbf{X}$ be the L-truncated SVD approximation to the data matrix $\mathbf{X}$. From Equation (7.184), we know that the right singular vectors of $\mathbf{X}$ are the eigenvectors of $\mathbf{X}^\mathsf{T}\mathbf{X}$, so $\mathbf{V}_X = \mathbf{U}_\Sigma = \mathbf{W}$. (In addition, the eigenvalues of the covariance matrix are related to the singular values of the data matrix via $\lambda_k = s_k^2/N$.)

Now suppose we are interested in the projected points (also called the principal components or PC scores), rather than the projection matrix. We have

$$\mathbf{Z} = \mathbf{X}\mathbf{W} = \mathbf{U}_X \mathbf{S}_X \mathbf{V}_X^\mathsf{T} \mathbf{V}_X = \mathbf{U}_X \mathbf{S}_X \tag{20.23}$$

Finally, if we want to approximately reconstruct the data, we have

$$\hat{\mathbf{X}} = \mathbf{Z}\mathbf{W}^\mathsf{T} = \mathbf{U}_X \mathbf{S}_X \mathbf{V}_X^\mathsf{T} \tag{20.24}$$

This is precisely the same as a truncated SVD approximation (Section 7.5.5).

Thus we see that we can perform PCA either using an eigendecomposition of $\mathbf{\Sigma}$ or an SVD decomposition of $\mathbf{X}$. The latter is often preferable, for computational reasons. For very high dimensional problems, we can use a randomized SVD algorithm, see e.g., [HMT11; SKT14; DM16]. For example, the randomized solver used by sklearn takes $O(NL^2) + O(L^3)$ time for N examples and L principal components, whereas exact SVD takes $O(ND^2) + O(D^3)$ time.

---

1. A more detailed explanation can be found at `https://bit.ly/2I5660K`.

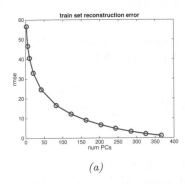
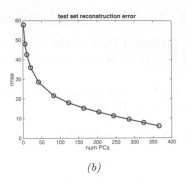

(a)   *(b)*

Figure 20.6: Reconstruction error on MNIST vs number of latent dimensions used by PCA. (a) Training set. (b) Test set. Generated by pcaOverfitDemo.ipynb.

20.1.4   Choosing the number of latent dimensions

In this section, we discuss how to choose the number of latent dimensions L for PCA.

20.1.4.1   Reconstruction error

Let us define the reconstruction error on some dataset $\mathcal{D}$ incurred by the model when using L dimensions:

$$\mathcal{L}_L = \frac{1}{|\mathcal{D}|} \sum_{n \in \mathcal{D}} ||\boldsymbol{x}_n - \hat{\boldsymbol{x}}_n||^2 \tag{20.25}$$

where the reconstruction is given by $\hat{\boldsymbol{x}}_n = \mathbf{W}\boldsymbol{z}_n + \boldsymbol{\mu}$, where $\boldsymbol{z}_n = \mathbf{W}^\mathsf{T}(\boldsymbol{x}_n - \boldsymbol{\mu})$ and $\boldsymbol{\mu}$ is the empirical mean, and $\mathbf{W}$ is estimated as above. Figure 20.6(a) plots $\mathcal{L}_L$ vs L on the MNIST training data. We see that it drops off quite quickly, indicating that we can capture most of the empirical correlation of the pixels with a small number of factors.

Of course, if we use $L = \text{rank}(\mathbf{X})$, we get zero reconstruction error on the training set. To avoid overfitting, it is natural to plot reconstruction error on the test set. This is shown in Figure 20.6(b). Here we see that the error continues to go down even as the model becomes more complex! Thus we do not get the usual U-shaped curve that we typically expect to see in supervised learning. The problem is that PCA is not a proper generative model of the data: If you give it more latent dimensions, it will be able to approximate the test data more accurately. (A similar problem arises if we plot reconstruction error on the test set using K-means clustering, as discussed in Section 21.3.7.) We discuss some solutions to this below.

20.1.4.2   Scree plots

A common alternative to plotting reconstruction error vs L is to use something called a **scree plot**, which is a plot of the eigenvalues λ_j vs j in order of decreasing magnitude. One can show

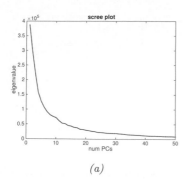 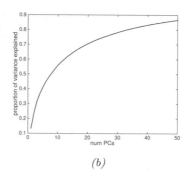

(a) (b)

Figure 20.7: (a) Scree plot for training set, corresponding to Figure 20.6(a). (b) Fraction of variance explained. Generated by pcaOverfitDemo.ipynb.

(Exercise 20.4) that

$$\mathcal{L}_L = \sum_{j=L+1}^{D} \lambda_j \tag{20.26}$$

Thus as the number of dimensions increases, the eigenvalues get smaller, and so does the reconstruction error, as shown in Figure 20.7a.[2] A related quantity is the **fraction of variance explained**, defined as

$$F_L = \frac{\sum_{j=1}^{L} \lambda_j}{\sum_{j'=1}^{L^{\max}} \lambda_{j'}} \tag{20.27}$$

This captures the same information as the scree plot, but goes up with L (see Figure 20.7b).

20.1.4.3 Profile likelihood

Although there is no U-shape in the reconstruction error plot, there is sometimes a "knee" or "elbow" in the curve, where the error suddenly changes from relatively large errors to relatively small. The idea is that for $L < L^*$, where L^* is the "true" latent dimensionality (or number of clusters), the rate of decrease in the error function will be high, whereas for $L > L^*$, the gains will be smaller, since the model is already sufficiently complex to capture the true distribution.

One way to automate the detection of this change in the gradient of the curve is to compute the **profile likelihood**, as proposed in [ZG06]. The idea is this. Let λ_L be some measure of the error incurred by a model of size L, such that $\lambda_1 \geq \lambda_2 \geq \cdots \geq \lambda_{L^{\max}}$. In PCA, these are the eigenvalues, but the method can also be applied to the reconstruction error from K-means clustering (see Section 21.3.7). Now consider partitioning these values into two groups, depending on whether $k < L$ or $k > L$, where L is some threshold which we will determine. To measure the quality of L,

---

2. The reason for the term "scree plot" is that "the plot looks like the side of a mountain, and 'scree' refers to the debris fallen from a mountain and lying at its base". (Quotation from Kenneth Janda, https://bit.ly/2kqG1yW.)

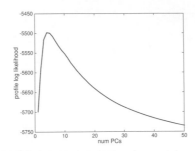

Figure 20.8: Profile likelihood corresponding to PCA model in Figure 20.6(a). Generated by pcaOverfit-Demo.ipynb.

we will use a simple change-point model, where $\lambda_k \sim \mathcal{N}(\mu_1, \sigma^2)$ if $k \leq L$, and $\lambda_k \sim \mathcal{N}(\mu_2, \sigma^2)$ if $k > L$. (It is important that σ^2 be the same in both models, to prevent overfitting in the case where one regime has less data than the other.) Within each of the two regimes, we assume the λ_k are iid, which is obviously incorrect, but is adequate for our present purposes. We can fit this model for each $L = 1 : L^{\max}$ by partitioning the data and computing the MLEs, using a pooled estimate of the variance:

$$\mu_1(L) = \frac{\sum_{k \leq L} \lambda_k}{L} \tag{20.28}$$

$$\mu_2(L) = \frac{\sum_{k > L} \lambda_k}{L^{\max} - L} \tag{20.29}$$

$$\sigma^2(L) = \frac{\sum_{k \leq L}(\lambda_k - \mu_1(L))^2 + \sum_{k > L}(\lambda_k - \mu_2(L))^2}{L^{\max}} \tag{20.30}$$

We can then evaluate the profile log likelihood

$$\ell(L) = \sum_{k=1}^{L} \log \mathcal{N}(\lambda_k | \mu_1(L), \sigma^2(L)) + \sum_{k=L+1}^{L^{\max}} \log \mathcal{N}(\lambda_k | \mu_2(L), \sigma^2(L)) \tag{20.31}$$

This is illustrated in Figure 20.8. We see that the peak $L^* = \operatorname{argmax} \ell(L)$ is well determined.

20.2   Factor analysis *

PCA is a simple method for computing a linear low-dimensional representation of data. In this section, we present a generalization of PCA known as **factor analysis**. This is based on a probabilistic model, which means we can treat it as a building block for more complex models, such as the mixture of FA models in Section 20.2.6, or the nonlinear FA model in Section 20.3.5. We can recover PCA as a special limiting case of FA, as we discuss in Section 20.2.2.

20.2.1   Generative model

Factor analysis corresponds to the following linear-Gaussian latent variable generative model:

$$p(\boldsymbol{z}) = \mathcal{N}(\boldsymbol{z}|\boldsymbol{\mu}_0, \boldsymbol{\Sigma}_0) \tag{20.32}$$

$$p(\boldsymbol{x}|\boldsymbol{z}, \boldsymbol{\theta}) = \mathcal{N}(\boldsymbol{x}|\mathbf{W}\boldsymbol{z} + \boldsymbol{\mu}, \boldsymbol{\Psi}) \tag{20.33}$$

where $\mathbf{W}$ is a $D \times L$ matrix, known as the **factor loading matrix**, and $\boldsymbol{\Psi}$ is a diagonal $D \times D$ covariance matrix.

FA can be thought of as a low-rank version of a Gaussian distribution. To see this, note that the induced marginal distribution $p(\boldsymbol{x}|\boldsymbol{\theta})$ is a Gaussian (see Equation (3.38) for the derivation):

$$p(\boldsymbol{x}|\boldsymbol{\theta}) = \int \mathcal{N}(\boldsymbol{x}|\mathbf{W}\boldsymbol{z} + \boldsymbol{\mu}, \boldsymbol{\Psi})\mathcal{N}(\boldsymbol{z}|\boldsymbol{\mu}_0, \boldsymbol{\Sigma}_0)d\boldsymbol{z} \tag{20.34}$$

$$= \mathcal{N}(\boldsymbol{x}|\mathbf{W}\boldsymbol{\mu}_0 + \boldsymbol{\mu}, \boldsymbol{\Psi} + \mathbf{W}\boldsymbol{\Sigma}_0\mathbf{W}^{\mathsf{T}}) \tag{20.35}$$

Hence $\mathbb{E}[\boldsymbol{x}] = \mathbf{W}\boldsymbol{\mu}_0 + \boldsymbol{\mu}$ and $\text{Cov}[\boldsymbol{x}] = \mathbf{W}\text{Cov}[\boldsymbol{z}]\mathbf{W}^{\mathsf{T}} + \boldsymbol{\Psi} = \mathbf{W}\boldsymbol{\Sigma}_0\mathbf{W}^{\mathsf{T}} + \boldsymbol{\Psi}$. From this, we see that we can set $\boldsymbol{\mu}_0 = \mathbf{0}$ without loss of generality, since we can always absorb $\mathbf{W}\boldsymbol{\mu}_0$ into $\boldsymbol{\mu}$. Similarly, we can set $\boldsymbol{\Sigma}_0 = \mathbf{I}$ without loss of generality, since we can always absorb a correlated prior by using a new weight matrix, $\tilde{\mathbf{W}} = \mathbf{W}\boldsymbol{\Sigma}_0^{-\frac{1}{2}}$. After these simplifications we have

$$p(\boldsymbol{z}) = \mathcal{N}(\boldsymbol{z}|\mathbf{0}, \mathbf{I}) \tag{20.36}$$

$$p(\boldsymbol{x}|\boldsymbol{z}) = \mathcal{N}(\boldsymbol{x}|\mathbf{W}\boldsymbol{z} + \boldsymbol{\mu}, \boldsymbol{\Psi}) \tag{20.37}$$

$$p(\boldsymbol{x}) = \mathcal{N}(\boldsymbol{x}|\boldsymbol{\mu}, \mathbf{W}\mathbf{W}^{\mathsf{T}} + \boldsymbol{\Psi}) \tag{20.38}$$

For example, suppose where $L = 1$, $D = 2$ and $\boldsymbol{\Psi} = \sigma^2\mathbf{I}$. We illustrate the generative process in this case in Figure 20.9. We can think of this as taking an isotropic Gaussian "spray can", representing the likelihood $p(\boldsymbol{x}|\boldsymbol{z})$, and "sliding it along" the 1d line defined by $\boldsymbol{w}z + \boldsymbol{\mu}$ as we vary the 1d latent prior z. This induces an elongated (and hence correlated) Gaussian in 2d. That is, the induced distribution has the form $p(\boldsymbol{x}) = \mathcal{N}(\boldsymbol{x}|\boldsymbol{\mu}, \boldsymbol{w}\boldsymbol{w}^{\mathsf{T}} + \sigma^2\mathbf{I})$.

In general, FA approximates the covariance matrix of the visible vector using a low-rank decomposition:

$$\mathbf{C} = \text{Cov}[\boldsymbol{x}] = \mathbf{W}\mathbf{W}^{\mathsf{T}} + \boldsymbol{\Psi} \tag{20.39}$$

This only uses $O(LD)$ parameters, which allows a flexible compromise between a full covariance Gaussian, with $O(D^2)$ parameters, and a diagonal covariance, with $O(D)$ parameters.

From Equation (20.39), we see that we should restrict $\boldsymbol{\Psi}$ to be diagonal, otherwise we could set $\mathbf{W} = \mathbf{0}$, thus ignoring the latent factors, while still being able to model any covariance. The marginal variance of each visible variable is given by $\mathbb{V}[x_d] = \sum_{k=1}^{L} w_{dk}^2 + \psi_d$, where the first term is the variance due to the common factors, and the second ψ_d term is called the **uniqueness**, and is the variance term that is specific to that dimension.

We can estimate the parameters of an FA model using EM (see Section 20.2.3). Once we have fit the model, we can compute probabilistic latent embeddings using $p(\boldsymbol{z}|\boldsymbol{x})$. Using Bayes rule for Gaussians we have

$$p(\boldsymbol{z}|\boldsymbol{x}) = \mathcal{N}(\boldsymbol{z}|\mathbf{W}^{\mathsf{T}}\mathbf{C}^{-1}(\boldsymbol{x} - \boldsymbol{\mu}), \mathbf{I} - \mathbf{W}^{\mathsf{T}}\mathbf{C}^{-1}\mathbf{W}) \tag{20.40}$$

where $\mathbf{C}$ is defined in Equation (20.39).

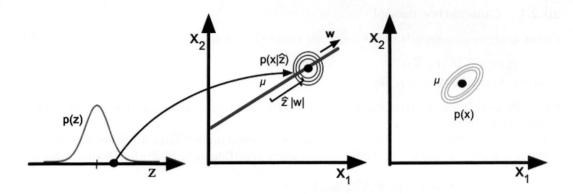

Figure 20.9: *Illustration of the FA generative process, where we have $L = 1$ latent dimension generating $D = 2$ observed dimensions; we assume $\boldsymbol{\Psi} = \sigma^2 \mathbf{I}$. The latent factor has value $z \in \mathbb{R}$, sampled from $p(z)$; this gets mapped to a 2d offset $\boldsymbol{\delta} = z\boldsymbol{w}$, where $\boldsymbol{w} \in \mathbb{R}^2$, which gets added to $\boldsymbol{\mu}$ to define a Gaussian $p(\boldsymbol{x}|z) = \mathcal{N}(\boldsymbol{x}|\boldsymbol{\mu} + \boldsymbol{\delta}, \sigma^2 \mathbf{I})$. By integrating over z, we "slide" this circular Gaussian "spray can" along the principal component axis $\boldsymbol{w}$, which induces elliptical Gaussian contours in $\boldsymbol{x}$ space centered on $\boldsymbol{\mu}$. Adapted from Figure 12.9 of [Bis06].*

20.2.2   Probabilistic PCA

In this section, we consider a special case of the factor analysis model in which $\mathbf{W}$ has orthonormal columns, and $\boldsymbol{\Psi} = \sigma^2 \mathbf{I}$. This model is called **probabilistic principal components analysis** (**PPCA**) [TB99], or **sensible PCA** [Row97]. The marginal distribution on the visible variables has the form

$$p(\boldsymbol{x}|\boldsymbol{\theta}) = \int \mathcal{N}(\boldsymbol{x}|\mathbf{W}\boldsymbol{z}, \sigma^2 \mathbf{I})\mathcal{N}(\boldsymbol{z}|\mathbf{0}, \mathbf{I})d\boldsymbol{z} = \mathcal{N}(\boldsymbol{x}|\boldsymbol{\mu}, \mathbf{C}) \tag{20.41}$$

where

$$\mathbf{C} = \mathbf{W}\mathbf{W}^\mathsf{T} + \sigma^2 \mathbf{I} \tag{20.42}$$

The log likelihood for PPCA is given by

$$\log p(\mathbf{X}|\boldsymbol{\mu}, \mathbf{W}, \sigma^2) = -\frac{ND}{2}\log(2\pi) - \frac{N}{2}\log|\mathbf{C}| - \frac{1}{2}\sum_{n=1}^{N}(\boldsymbol{x}_n - \boldsymbol{\mu})^\mathsf{T}\mathbf{C}^{-1}(\boldsymbol{x}_n - \boldsymbol{\mu}) \tag{20.43}$$

The MLE for $\boldsymbol{\mu}$ is $\overline{\boldsymbol{x}}$. Plugging in gives

$$\log p(\mathbf{X}|\boldsymbol{\mu}, \mathbf{W}, \sigma^2) = -\frac{N}{2}\left[D\log(2\pi) + \log|\mathbf{C}| + \mathrm{tr}(\mathbf{C}^{-1}\mathbf{S})\right] \tag{20.44}$$

where $\mathbf{S} = \frac{1}{N}\sum_{n=1}^{N}(\boldsymbol{x}_n - \overline{\boldsymbol{x}})(\boldsymbol{x}_n - \overline{\boldsymbol{x}})^\mathsf{T}$ is the empirical covariance matrix.

In [TB99; Row97] they show that the maximum of this objective must satisfy

$$\mathbf{W} = \mathbf{U}_L(\mathbf{L}_L - \sigma^2 \mathbf{I})^{\frac{1}{2}}\mathbf{R} \tag{20.45}$$

where $\mathbf{U}_L$ is a $D \times L$ matrix whose columns are given by the L eigenvectors of $\mathbf{S}$ with largest eigenvalues, $\mathbf{L}_L$ is the $L \times L$ diagonal matrix of eigenvalues, and $\mathbf{R}$ is an arbitrary $L \times L$ orthogonal matrix, which (WLOG) we can take to be $\mathbf{R} = \mathbf{I}$. In the noise-free limit, where $\sigma^2 = 0$, we see that $\mathbf{W}_{\mathrm{mle}} = \mathbf{U}_L \mathbf{L}_L^{\frac{1}{2}}$, which is proportional to the PCA solution.

The MLE for the observation variance is

$$\sigma^2 = \frac{1}{D - L} \sum_{i=L+1}^{D} \lambda_i \tag{20.46}$$

which is the average distortion associated with the discarded dimensions. If $L = D$, then the estimated noise is 0, since the model collapses to $\mathbf{z} = \mathbf{x}$.

To compute the likelihood $p(\mathbf{X}|\boldsymbol{\mu}, \mathbf{W}, \sigma^2)$, we need to evaluate $\mathbf{C}^{-1}$ and $\log |\mathbf{C}|$, where $\mathbf{C}$ is a $D \times D$ matrix. To do this efficiently, we can use the matrix inversion lemma to write

$$\mathbf{C}^{-1} = \sigma^{-2} \left[\mathbf{I} - \mathbf{W} \mathbf{M}^{-1} \mathbf{W}^{\mathsf{T}} \right] \tag{20.47}$$

where the $L \times L$ dimensional matrix $\mathbf{M}$ is given by

$$\mathbf{M} = \mathbf{W}^{\mathsf{T}} \mathbf{W} + \sigma^2 \mathbf{I} \tag{20.48}$$

When we plug in the MLE for $\mathbf{W}$ from Equation (20.45) (using $\mathbf{R} = \mathbf{I}$) we find

$$\mathbf{M} = \mathbf{U}_L (\mathbf{L}_L - \sigma^2 \mathbf{I}) \mathbf{U}_L^{\mathsf{T}} + \sigma^2 \mathbf{I} \tag{20.49}$$

and hence

$$\mathbf{C}^{-1} = \sigma^{-2} \left[\mathbf{I} - \mathbf{U}_L (\mathbf{L}_L - \sigma^2 \mathbf{I}) \boldsymbol{\Lambda}_L^{-1} \mathbf{U}_L^{\mathsf{T}} \right] \tag{20.50}$$

$$\log |\mathbf{C}| = (D - L) \log \sigma^2 + \sum_{j=1}^{L} \log \lambda_j \tag{20.51}$$

Thus we can avoid all matrix inversions (since $\boldsymbol{\Lambda}_L^{-1} = \mathrm{diag}(1/\lambda_j)$).

To use PPCA as an alternative to PCA, we need to compute the posterior mean $\mathbb{E}\left[\mathbf{z}|\mathbf{x}\right]$, which is the equivalent of the encoder model. Using Bayes rule for Gaussians we have

$$p(\mathbf{z}|\mathbf{x}) = \mathcal{N}(\mathbf{z}|\mathbf{M}^{-1} \mathbf{W}^{\mathsf{T}} (\mathbf{x} - \boldsymbol{\mu}), \sigma^2 \mathbf{M}^{-1}) \tag{20.52}$$

where $\mathbf{M}$ is defined in Equation (20.48). In the $\sigma^2 = 0$ limit, the posterior mean using the MLE parameters becomes

$$\mathbb{E}\left[\mathbf{z}|\mathbf{x}\right] = (\mathbf{W}^{\mathsf{T}} \mathbf{W})^{-1} \mathbf{W}^{\mathsf{T}} (\mathbf{x} - \overline{\mathbf{x}}) \tag{20.53}$$

which is the orthogonal projection of the data into the latent space, as in standard PCA.

20.2.3 EM algorithm for FA/PPCA

In this section, we describe one method for computing the MLE for the FA model using the EM algorithm, based on [RT82; GH96].

20.2.3.1   EM for FA

In the E step, we compute the posterior embeddings

$$p(\boldsymbol{z}_i|\boldsymbol{x}_i,\boldsymbol{\theta}) = \mathcal{N}(\boldsymbol{z}_i|\boldsymbol{m}_i,\boldsymbol{\Sigma}_i) \tag{20.54}$$

$$\boldsymbol{\Sigma}_i \triangleq (\mathbf{I}_L + \mathbf{W}^\mathsf{T}\boldsymbol{\Psi}^{-1}\mathbf{W})^{-1} \tag{20.55}$$

$$\boldsymbol{m}_i \triangleq \boldsymbol{\Sigma}_i(\mathbf{W}^\mathsf{T}\boldsymbol{\Psi}^{-1}(\boldsymbol{x}_i - \boldsymbol{\mu})) \tag{20.56}$$

In the M step, it is easiest to estimate $\boldsymbol{\mu}$ and $\mathbf{W}$ at the same time, by defining $\tilde{\mathbf{W}} = (\mathbf{W}, \boldsymbol{\mu})$, $\tilde{\boldsymbol{z}} = (\boldsymbol{z}, 1)$, Also, define

$$\boldsymbol{b}_i \triangleq \mathbb{E}\left[\tilde{\mathbf{z}}|\boldsymbol{x}_i\right] = [\boldsymbol{m}_i; 1] \tag{20.57}$$

$$\mathbf{C}_i \triangleq \mathbb{E}\left[\tilde{\mathbf{z}}\tilde{\mathbf{z}}^T|\boldsymbol{x}_i,\right] = \begin{pmatrix} \mathbb{E}\left[\boldsymbol{z}\boldsymbol{z}^T|\boldsymbol{x}_i\right] & \mathbb{E}\left[\boldsymbol{z}|\boldsymbol{x}_i\right] \\ \mathbb{E}\left[\boldsymbol{z}|\boldsymbol{x}_i\right]^T & 1 \end{pmatrix} \tag{20.58}$$

Then the M step is as follows:

$$\hat{\tilde{\mathbf{W}}} = \left[\sum_i \boldsymbol{x}_i \boldsymbol{b}_i^\mathsf{T}\right]\left[\sum_i \mathbf{C}_i\right]^{-1} \tag{20.59}$$

$$\hat{\boldsymbol{\Psi}} = \frac{1}{N}\mathrm{diag}\left\{\sum_i \left(\boldsymbol{x}_i - \hat{\tilde{\mathbf{W}}}\boldsymbol{b}_i\right)\boldsymbol{x}_i^T\right\} \tag{20.60}$$

Note that these updates are for "vanilla" EM. A much faster version of this algorithm, based on ECM, is described in [ZY08].

20.2.3.2   EM for (P)PCA

We can also use EM to fit the PPCA model, which provides a useful alternative to eigenvector methods. This relies on the probabilistic formulation of PCA. However the algorithm continues to work in the zero noise limit, $\sigma^2 = 0$, as shown by [Row97].

In particular, let $\tilde{\mathbf{Z}} = \mathbf{Z}^\mathsf{T}$ be a $L \times N$ matrix storing the posterior means (low-dimensional representations) along its columns. Similarly, let $\tilde{\mathbf{X}} = \mathbf{X}^\mathsf{T}$ store the original data along its columns. From Equation (20.52), when $\sigma^2 = 0$, we have

$$\tilde{\mathbf{Z}} = (\mathbf{W}^T\mathbf{W})^{-1}\mathbf{W}^T\tilde{\mathbf{X}} \tag{20.61}$$

This constitutes the E step. Notice that this is just an orthogonal projection of the data.

From Equation 20.59, the M step is given by

$$\hat{\mathbf{W}} = \left[\sum_i \boldsymbol{x}_i \mathbb{E}\left[\boldsymbol{z}_i\right]^T\right]\left[\sum_i \mathbb{E}\left[\boldsymbol{z}_i\right]\mathbb{E}\left[\boldsymbol{z}_i\right]^T\right]^{-1} \tag{20.62}$$

where we exploited the fact that $\boldsymbol{\Sigma} = \mathrm{Cov}\left[\boldsymbol{z}_i|\boldsymbol{x}_i,\boldsymbol{\theta}\right] = \mathbf{0}\mathbf{I}$ when $\sigma^2 = 0$.

It is worth comparing this expression to the MLE for multi-output linear regression (Equation 11.2), which has the form $\mathbf{W} = (\sum_i \boldsymbol{y}_i\boldsymbol{x}_i^T)(\sum_i \boldsymbol{x}_i\boldsymbol{x}_i^T)^{-1}$. Thus we see that the M step is like linear regression where we replace the observed inputs by the expected values of the latent variables.

In summary, here is the entire algorithm:

$$\tilde{\mathbf{Z}} = (\mathbf{W}^T\mathbf{W})^{-1}\mathbf{W}^T\tilde{\mathbf{X}} \text{ (E step)} \tag{20.63}$$

$$\mathbf{W} = \tilde{\mathbf{X}}\tilde{\mathbf{Z}}^T(\tilde{\mathbf{Z}}\tilde{\mathbf{Z}}^T)^{-1} \text{ (M step)} \tag{20.64}$$

[TB99] showed that the only stable fixed point of the EM algorithm is the globally optimal solution. That is, the EM algorithm converges to a solution where $\mathbf{W}$ spans the same linear subspace as that defined by the first L eigenvectors. However, if we want $\mathbf{W}$ to be orthogonal, and to contain the eigenvectors in descending order of eigenvalue, we have to orthogonalize the resulting matrix (which can be done quite cheaply). Alternatively, we can modify EM to give the principal basis directly [AO03].

This algorithm has a simple physical analogy in the case $D = 2$ and $L = 1$ [Row97]. Consider some points in $\mathbb{R}^2$ attached by springs to a rigid rod, whose orientation is defined by a vector $\boldsymbol{w}$. Let z_i be the location where the i'th spring attaches to the rod. In the E step, we hold the rod fixed, and let the attachment points slide around so as to minimize the spring energy (which is proportional to the sum of squared residuals). In the M step, we hold the attachment points fixed and let the rod rotate so as to minimize the spring energy. See Figure 20.10 for an illustration.

20.2.3.3 Advantages

EM for PCA has the following advantages over eigenvector methods:

- EM can be faster. In particular, assuming $N, D \gg L$, the dominant cost of EM is the projection operation in the E step, so the overall time is $O(TLND)$, where T is the number of iterations. [Row97] showed experimentally that the number of iterations is usually very small (the mean was 3.6), regardless of N or D. (This result depends on the ratio of eigenvalues of the empirical covariance matrix.) This is much faster than the $O(\min(ND^2, DN^2))$ time required by straightforward eigenvector methods, although more sophisticated eigenvector methods, such as the Lanczos algorithm, have running times comparable to EM.

- EM can be implemented in an online fashion, i.e., we can update our estimate of $\mathbf{W}$ as the data streams in.

- EM can handle missing data in a simple way (see e.g., [IR10; DJ15]).

- EM can be extended to handle mixtures of PPCA/ FA models (see Section 20.2.6).

- EM can be modified to variational EM or to variational Bayes EM to fit more complex models (see e.g., Section 20.2.7).

20.2.4 Unidentifiability of the parameters

The parameters of a FA model are unidentifiable. To see this, consider a model with weights $\mathbf{W}$ and observation covariance $\boldsymbol{\Psi}$. We have

$$\text{Cov}\left[\boldsymbol{x}\right] = \mathbf{W}\mathbb{E}\left[\boldsymbol{z}\boldsymbol{z}^\mathsf{T}\right]\mathbf{W}^\mathsf{T} + \mathbb{E}\left[\boldsymbol{\epsilon}\boldsymbol{\epsilon}^\mathsf{T}\right] = \mathbf{W}\mathbf{W}^\mathsf{T} + \boldsymbol{\Psi} \tag{20.65}$$

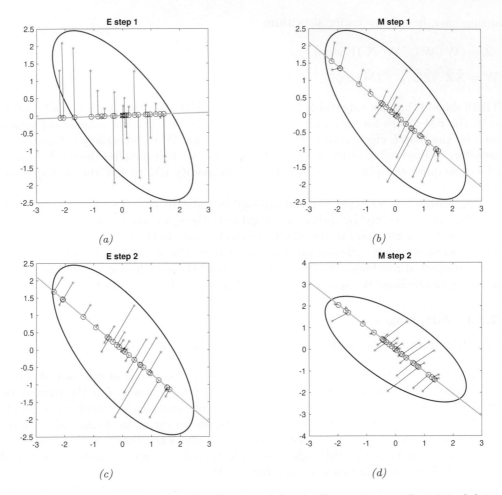

Figure 20.10: *Illustration of EM for PCA when $D = 2$ and $L = 1$. Green stars are the original data points, black circles are their reconstructions. The weight vector $\boldsymbol{w}$ is represented by blue line. (a) We start with a random initial guess of $\boldsymbol{w}$. The E step is represented by the orthogonal projections. (b) We update the rod $\boldsymbol{w}$ in the M step, keeping the projections onto the rod (black circles) fixed. (c) Another E step. The black circles can 'slide' along the rod, but the rod stays fixed. (d) Another M step. Adapted from Figure 12.12 of [Bis06]. Generated by pcaEmStepByStep.ipynb.*

Now consider a different model with weights $\tilde{\mathbf{W}} = \mathbf{W}\mathbf{R}$, where $\mathbf{R}$ is an arbitrary orthogonal rotation matrix, satisfying $\mathbf{R}\mathbf{R}^\mathsf{T} = \mathbf{I}$. This has the same likelihood, since

$$\text{Cov}\left[\boldsymbol{x}\right] = \tilde{\mathbf{W}}\mathbb{E}\left[\boldsymbol{z}\boldsymbol{z}^\mathsf{T}\right]\tilde{\mathbf{W}}^\mathsf{T} + \mathbb{E}\left[\boldsymbol{\epsilon}\boldsymbol{\epsilon}^\mathsf{T}\right] = \mathbf{W}\mathbf{R}\mathbf{R}^\mathsf{T}\mathbf{W}^\mathsf{T} + \boldsymbol{\Psi} = \mathbf{W}\mathbf{W}^\mathsf{T} + \boldsymbol{\Psi} \tag{20.66}$$

Geometrically, multiplying $\mathbf{W}$ by an orthogonal matrix is like rotating $\boldsymbol{z}$ before generating $\boldsymbol{x}$; but since $\boldsymbol{z}$ is drawn from an isotropic Gaussian, this makes no difference to the likelihood. Consequently, we cannot uniquely identify $\mathbf{W}$, and therefore cannot uniquely identify the latent factors, either.

To break this symmetry, several solutions can be used, as we discuss below.

- **Forcing W to have orthonormal columns**. Perhaps the simplest solution to the identifiability problem is to force $\mathbf{W}$ to have orthonormal columns. This is the approach adopted by PCA. The resulting posterior estimate will then be unique, up to permutation of the latent dimensions. (In PCA, this ordering ambiguity is resolved by sorting the dimensions in order of decreasing eigenvalues of $\mathbf{W}$.)

- **Forcing W to be lower triangular**. One way to resolve permutation unidentifiability, which is popular in the Bayesian community (e.g., [LW04c]), is to ensure that the first visible feature is only generated by the first latent factor, the second visible feature is only generated by the first two latent factors, and so on. For example, if $L = 3$ and $D = 4$, the corresponding factor loading matrix is given by

$$\mathbf{W} = \begin{pmatrix} w_{11} & 0 & 0 \\ w_{21} & w_{22} & 0 \\ w_{31} & w_{32} & w_{33} \\ w_{41} & w_{42} & w_{43} \end{pmatrix} \tag{20.67}$$

We also require that $w_{kk} > 0$ for $k = 1 : L$. The total number of parameters in this constrained matrix is $D + DL - L(L-1)/2$, which is equal to the number of uniquely identifiable parameters in FA.[3] The disadvantage of this method is that the first L visible variables, known as the **founder variables**, affect the interpretation of the latent factors, and so must be chosen carefully.

- **Sparsity promoting priors on the weights**. Instead of pre-specifying which entries in $\mathbf{W}$ are zero, we can encourage the entries to be zero, using ℓ_1 regularization [ZHT06], ARD [Bis99; AB08], or spike-and-slab priors [Rat+09]. This is called sparse factor analysis. This does not necessarily ensure a unique MAP estimate, but it does encourage interpretable solutions.

- **Choosing an informative rotation matrix**. There are a variety of heuristic methods that try to find rotation matrices $\mathbf{R}$ which can be used to modify $\mathbf{W}$ (and hence the latent factors) so as to try to increase the interpretability, typically by encouraging them to be (approximately) sparse. One popular method is known as **varimax** [Kai58].

- **Use of non-Gaussian priors for the latent factors**. If we replace the prior on the latent variables, $p(\mathbf{z})$, with a non-Gaussian distribution, we can sometimes uniquely identify $\mathbf{W}$, as well as the latent factors. See e.g., [KKH20] for details.

20.2.5 Nonlinear factor analysis

The FA model assumes the observed data can be modeled as arising from a linear mapping from a low-dimensional set of Gaussian factors. One way to relax this assumption is to let the mapping from $\mathbf{z}$ to $\mathbf{x}$ be a nonlinear model, such as a neural network. That is, the model becomes

$$p(\mathbf{x}) = \int \mathcal{N}(\mathbf{x}|f(\mathbf{z};\boldsymbol{\theta}), \boldsymbol{\Psi})\mathcal{N}(\mathbf{z}|\mathbf{0},\mathbf{I})d\mathbf{z} \tag{20.68}$$

---

3. We get D parameters for $\boldsymbol{\Psi}$ and DL for $\mathbf{W}$, but we need to remove $L(L-1)/2$ degrees of freedom coming from $\mathbf{R}$, since that is the dimensionality of the space of orthogonal matrices of size $L \times L$. To see this, note that there are $L-1$ free parameters in $\mathbf{R}$ in the first column (since the column vector must be normalized to unit length), there are $L-2$ free parameters in the second column (which must be orthogonal to the first), and so on.

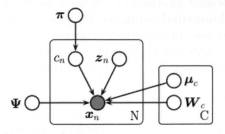

Figure 20.11: Mixture of factor analyzers as a PGM.

This is called **nonlinear factor analysis**. Unfortunately we can no longer compute the posterior or the MLE exactly, so we need to use approximate methods. In Section 20.3.5, we discuss variational autoencoders, which is the most common way to approximate a nonlinear FA model.

20.2.6   Mixtures of factor analysers

The factor analysis model (Section 20.2) assumes the observed data can be modeled as arising from a linear mapping from a low-dimensional set of Gaussian factors. One way to relax this assumption is to assume the model is only locally linear, so the overall model becomes a (weighted) combination of FA models; this is called a **mixture of factor analysers**. The overall model for the data is a mixture of linear manifolds, which can be used to approximate an overall curved manifold.

More precisely, let latent indicator $m_n \in \{1, \ldots, K\}$, specifying which subspace (cluster) we should use to generate the data. If $m_n = k$, we sample z_n from a Gaussian prior and pass it through the $\mathbf{W}_k$ matrix and add noise, where $\mathbf{W}_k$ maps from the L-dimensional subspace to the D-dimensional visible space.[4] More precisely, the model is as follows:

$$p(x_n | z_n, m_n = k, \boldsymbol{\theta}) = \mathcal{N}(x_n | \boldsymbol{\mu}_k + \mathbf{W}_k z_n, \boldsymbol{\Psi}_k) \tag{20.69}$$

$$p(z_n | \boldsymbol{\theta}) = \mathcal{N}(z_n | \mathbf{0}, \mathbf{I}) \tag{20.70}$$

$$p(m_n | \boldsymbol{\theta}) = \text{Cat}(m_n | \boldsymbol{\pi}) \tag{20.71}$$

This is called a **mixture of factor analysers** (MFA) [GH96]. The corresponding distribution in the visible space is given by

$$p(\boldsymbol{x} | \boldsymbol{\theta}) = \sum_k p(c = k) \int d\boldsymbol{z} \, p(\boldsymbol{z} | c) p(\boldsymbol{x} | \boldsymbol{z}, c) = \sum_k \pi_k \int d\boldsymbol{z} \, \mathcal{N}(\boldsymbol{z} | \boldsymbol{\mu}_k, \mathbf{I}) \mathcal{N}(\boldsymbol{x} | \mathbf{W}\boldsymbol{z}, \sigma^2 \mathbf{I}) \tag{20.72}$$

In the special case that $\boldsymbol{\Psi}_k = \sigma^2 \mathbf{I}$, we get a mixture of PPCA models (although it is difficult to ensure orthogonality of the $\mathbf{W}_k$ in this case). See Figure 20.12 for an example of the method applied to some 2d data.

We can think of this as a low-rank version of a mixture of Gaussians. In particular, this model needs $O(KLD)$ parameters instead of the $O(KD^2)$ parameters needed for a mixture of full covariance Gaussians. This can reduce overfitting.

---

4. If we allow z_n to depend on m_n, we can let each subspace have a different dimensionality, as suggested in [KS15].

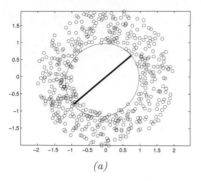 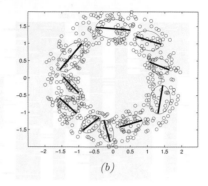

(a)   *(b)*

Figure 20.12: *Mixture of PPCA models fit to a 2d dataset, using $L = 1$ latent dimensions. (a) $K = 1$ mixture components. (b) $K = 10$ mixture components. Generated by* mixPpcaDemo.ipynb.

20.2.7 Exponential family factor analysis

So far we have assumed the observed data is real-valued, so $\boldsymbol{x}_n \in \mathbb{R}^D$. If we want to model other kinds of data (e.g., binary or categorical), we can simply replace the Gaussian output distribution with a suitable member of the exponential family, where the natural parameters are given by a linear function of $\boldsymbol{z}_n$. That is, we use

$$p(\boldsymbol{x}_n | \boldsymbol{z}_n) = \exp(\mathcal{T}(\boldsymbol{x})^\mathsf{T} \boldsymbol{\theta} + h(\boldsymbol{x}) - g(\boldsymbol{\theta})) \tag{20.73}$$

where the $N \times D$ matrix of natural parameters is assumed to be given by the low rank decomposition $\boldsymbol{\Theta} = \mathbf{ZW}$, where $\mathbf{Z}$ is $N \times L$ and $\mathbf{W}$ is $L \times D$. The resulting model is called **exponential family factor analysis**.

Unlike the linear-Gaussian FA, we cannot compute the exact posterior $p(\boldsymbol{z}_n | \boldsymbol{x}_n, \mathbf{W})$ due to the lack of conjugacy between the expfam likelihood and the Gaussian prior. Furthermore, we cannot compute the exact marginal likelihood either, which prevents us from finding the optimal MLE.

[CDS02] proposed a coordinate ascent method for a deterministic variant of this model, known as **exponential family PCA**. This alternates between computing a point estimate of $\boldsymbol{z}_n$ and $\mathbf{W}$. This can be regarded as a degenerate version of variational EM, where the E step uses a delta function posterior for $\boldsymbol{z}_n$. [GS08] present an improved algorithm that finds the global optimum, and [Ude+16] presents an extension called **generalized low rank models**, that covers many different kinds of loss function.

However, it is often preferable to use a probabilistic version of the model, rather than computing point estimates of the latent factors. In this case, we must represent the posterior using a non-degenerate distribution to avoid overfitting, since the number of latent variables is proportional to the number of datacases [WCS08]. Fortunately, we can use a non-degenerate posterior, such as a Gaussian, by optimizing the variational lower bound. We give some examples of this below.

20.2.7.1 Example: binary PCA

Consider a factored Bernoulli likelihood:

$$p(\boldsymbol{x} | \boldsymbol{z}) = \prod_d \mathrm{Ber}(x_d | \sigma(\boldsymbol{w}_d^\mathsf{T} \boldsymbol{z})) \tag{20.74}$$

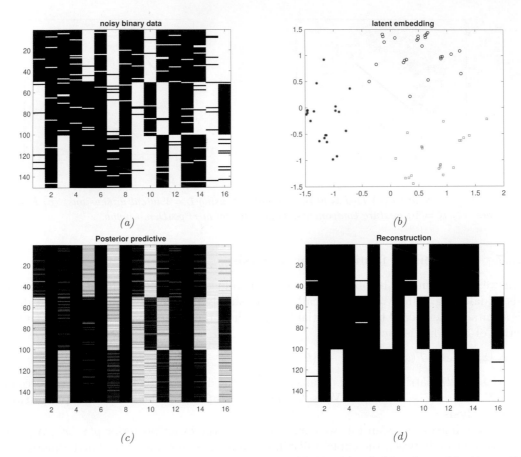

Figure 20.13: (a) 150 synthetic 16 dimensional bit vectors. (b) The 2d embedding learned by binary PCA, fit using variational EM. We have color coded points by the identity of the true "prototype" that generated them. (c) Predicted probability of being on. (d) Thresholded predictions. Generated by binary_fa_ demo.ipynb.

Suppose we observe $N = 150$ bit vectors of length $D = 16$. Each example is generated by choosing one of three binary prototype vectors, and then by flipping bits at random. See Figure 20.13(a) for the data. We can fit this using the variational EM algorithm (see [Tip98] for details). We use $L = 2$ latent dimensions to allow us to visualize the latent space. In Figure 20.13(b), we plot $\mathbb{E}\left[\boldsymbol{z}_n | \boldsymbol{x}_n, \hat{\mathbf{W}}\right]$. We see that the projected points group into three distinct clusters, as is to be expected. In Figure 20.13(c), we plot the reconstructed version of the data, which is computed as follows:

$$p(\hat{x}_{nd} = 1 | \boldsymbol{x}_n) = \int d\boldsymbol{z}_n \, p(\boldsymbol{z}_n | \boldsymbol{x}_n) p(\hat{x}_{nd} | \boldsymbol{z}_n) \qquad (20.75)$$

If we threshold these probabilities at 0.5 (corresponding to a MAP estimate), we get the "denoised" version of the data in Figure 20.13(d).

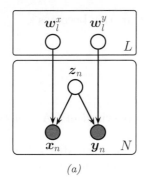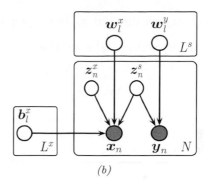

(a)   (b)

Figure 20.14: *Gaussian latent factor models for paired data. (a) Supervised PCA. (b) Partial least squares.*

20.2.7.2   Example: categorical PCA

We can generalize the model in Section 20.2.7.1 to handle categorical data by using the following likelihood:

$$p(\boldsymbol{x}|\boldsymbol{z}) = \prod_d \mathrm{Cat}(x_d|\mathrm{softmax}(\mathbf{W}_d \boldsymbol{z})) \tag{20.76}$$

We call this **categorical PCA (CatPCA)**. A variational EM algorithm for fitting this is described in [Kha+10].

20.2.8   Factor analysis models for paired data

In this section, we discuss linear-Gaussian factor analysis models when we have two kinds of observed variables, $\boldsymbol{x} \in \mathbb{R}^{D_x}$ and $\boldsymbol{y} \in \mathbb{R}^{D_y}$, which are paired. These often correspond to different sensors or modalities (e.g., images and sound). We follow the presentation of [Vir10].

20.2.8.1   Supervised PCA

In **supervised PCA** [Yu+06], we model the joint $p(\boldsymbol{x}, \boldsymbol{y})$ using a shared low-dimensional representation using the following linear Gaussian model:

$$p(\boldsymbol{z}_n) = \mathcal{N}(\boldsymbol{z}_n|\boldsymbol{0}, \mathbf{I}_L) \tag{20.77}$$

$$p(\boldsymbol{x}_n|\boldsymbol{z}_n, \boldsymbol{\theta}) = \mathcal{N}(\boldsymbol{x}_n|\mathbf{W}_x \boldsymbol{z}_n, \sigma_x^2 \mathbf{I}_{D_x}) \tag{20.78}$$

$$p(\boldsymbol{y}_n|\boldsymbol{z}_n, \boldsymbol{\theta}) = \mathcal{N}(\boldsymbol{y}_n|\mathbf{W}_y \boldsymbol{z}_n, \sigma_y^2 \mathbf{I}_{D_y}) \tag{20.79}$$

This is illustrated as a graphical model in Figure 20.14a. The intuition is that $\boldsymbol{z}_n$ is a shared latent subspace, that captures features that $\boldsymbol{x}_n$ and $\boldsymbol{y}_n$ have in common. The variance terms σ_x and σ_y control how much emphasis the model puts on the two different signals. If we put a prior on the parameters $\boldsymbol{\theta} = (\mathbf{W}_x, \mathbf{W}_y, \sigma_x, \sigma_y)$, we recover the **Bayesian factor regression** model of [Wes03].

We can marginalize out $\boldsymbol{z}_n$ to get $p(\boldsymbol{y}_n|\boldsymbol{x}_n)$. If $\boldsymbol{y}_n$ is a scalar, this becomes

$$p(y_n|\boldsymbol{x}_n, \boldsymbol{\theta}) = \mathcal{N}(y_n|\boldsymbol{x}_n^{\mathsf{T}}\boldsymbol{v}, \boldsymbol{w}_y^{\mathsf{T}}\mathbf{C}\boldsymbol{w}_y + \sigma_y^2) \tag{20.80}$$

$$\mathbf{C} = (\mathbf{I} + \sigma_x^{-2}\mathbf{W}_x^{\mathsf{T}}\mathbf{W}_x)^{-1} \tag{20.81}$$

$$\boldsymbol{v} = \sigma_x^{-2}\mathbf{W}_x\mathbf{C}\boldsymbol{w}_y \tag{20.82}$$

To apply this to the classification setting, we can use supervised ePCA [Guo09], in which we replace the Gaussian $p(\boldsymbol{y}|\boldsymbol{z})$ with a logistic regression model.

This model is completely symmetric in $\boldsymbol{x}$ and $\boldsymbol{y}$. If our goal is to predict $\boldsymbol{y}$ from $\boldsymbol{x}$ via the latent bottleneck $\boldsymbol{z}$, then we might want to upweight the likelihood term for $\boldsymbol{y}$, as proposed in [Ris+08]. This gives

$$p(\mathbf{X}, \mathbf{Y}, \mathbf{Z}|\boldsymbol{\theta}) = p(\mathbf{Y}|\mathbf{Z}, \mathbf{W}_y)p(\mathbf{X}|\mathbf{Z}, \mathbf{W}_x)^{\alpha}p(\mathbf{Z}) \tag{20.83}$$

where $\alpha \leq 1$ controls the relative importance of modeling the two sources. The value of α can be chosen by cross-validation.

20.2.8.2   Partial least squares

Another way to improve the predictive performance in supervised tasks is to allow the inputs $\boldsymbol{x}$ to have their own "private" noise source that is independent on the target variable, since not all variation in $\boldsymbol{x}$ is relevant for predictive purposes. We can do this by introducing an extra latent variable $\boldsymbol{z}_n^x$ just for the inputs, that is different from $\boldsymbol{z}_n^s$ that is the shared bottleneck between $\boldsymbol{x}_n$ and $\boldsymbol{y}_n$. In the Gaussian case, the overall model has the form

$$p(\boldsymbol{z}_n) = \mathcal{N}(\boldsymbol{z}_n^s|\boldsymbol{0}, \mathbf{I})\mathcal{N}(\boldsymbol{z}_n^x|\boldsymbol{0}, \mathbf{I}) \tag{20.84}$$

$$p(\boldsymbol{x}_n|\boldsymbol{z}_n, \boldsymbol{\theta}) = \mathcal{N}(\boldsymbol{x}_n|\mathbf{W}_x\boldsymbol{z}_n^s + \mathbf{B}_x\boldsymbol{z}_n^x, \sigma_x^2\mathbf{I}) \tag{20.85}$$

$$p(\boldsymbol{y}_n|\boldsymbol{z}_n, \boldsymbol{\theta}) = \mathcal{N}(\boldsymbol{y}_n|\mathbf{W}_y\boldsymbol{z}_n^s, \sigma_y^2\mathbf{I}) \tag{20.86}$$

See Figure 20.14b. MLE for $\boldsymbol{\theta}$ in this model is equivalent to the technique of **partial least squares** (**PLS**) [Gus01; Nou+02; Sun+09].

20.2.8.3   Canonical correlation analysis

In some cases, we want to use a fully symmetric model, so we can capture the dependence between $\boldsymbol{x}$ and $\boldsymbol{y}$, while allowing for domain-specific or "private" noise sources. We can do this by introducing a latent variable $\boldsymbol{z}_n^x$ just for $\boldsymbol{x}_n$, a latent variable $\boldsymbol{z}_n^y$ just for $\boldsymbol{y}_n$, and a shared latent variable $\boldsymbol{z}_n^s$. In the Gaussian case, the overall model has the form

$$p(\boldsymbol{z}_n) = \mathcal{N}(\boldsymbol{z}_n^s|\boldsymbol{0}, \mathbf{I})\mathcal{N}(\boldsymbol{z}_n^x|\boldsymbol{0}, \mathbf{I})\mathcal{N}(\boldsymbol{z}_n^y|\boldsymbol{0}, \mathbf{I}) \tag{20.87}$$

$$\tag{20.88}$$

$$p(\boldsymbol{x}_n|\boldsymbol{z}_n, \boldsymbol{\theta}) = \mathcal{N}(\boldsymbol{x}_n|\mathbf{W}_x\boldsymbol{z}_n^s + \mathbf{B}_x\boldsymbol{z}_n^x, \sigma_x^2\mathbf{I}) \tag{20.89}$$

$$p(\boldsymbol{y}_n|\boldsymbol{z}_n, \boldsymbol{\theta}) = \mathcal{N}(\boldsymbol{y}_n|\mathbf{W}_y\boldsymbol{z}_n^s + \mathbf{B}_y\boldsymbol{z}_n^y, \sigma_y^2\mathbf{I}) \tag{20.90}$$

where $\mathbf{W}_x$ and $\mathbf{W}_y$ are $L^s \times D$ dimensional, $\mathbf{V}_x$ is $L^x \times D$ dimensional, and $\mathbf{V}_y$ is $L^y \times D$ dimensional. See Figure 20.15 for the PGM.

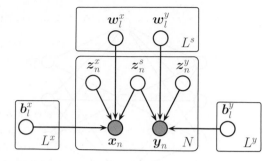

Figure 20.15: Canonical correlation analysis as a PGM.

If we marginalize out all the latent variables, we get the following distribution on the visibles (where we assume $\sigma_x = \sigma_y = \sigma$):

$$p(\boldsymbol{x}_n, \boldsymbol{y}_n) = \int d\boldsymbol{z}_n p(\boldsymbol{z}_n) p(\boldsymbol{x}_n, \boldsymbol{y}_n | \boldsymbol{z}_n) = \mathcal{N}(\boldsymbol{x}_n, \boldsymbol{y}_n | \boldsymbol{\mu}, \mathbf{W}\mathbf{W}^\mathsf{T} + \sigma^2 \mathbf{I}) \tag{20.91}$$

where $\boldsymbol{\mu} = (\boldsymbol{\mu}_x; \boldsymbol{\mu}_y)$, and $\mathbf{W} = [\mathbf{W}_x; \mathbf{W}_y]$. Thus the induced covariance is the following low rank matrix:

$$\mathbf{W}\mathbf{W}^\mathsf{T} = \begin{pmatrix} \mathbf{W}_x \mathbf{W}_x^\mathsf{T} & \mathbf{W}_x \mathbf{W}_y^\mathsf{T} \\ \mathbf{W}_y \mathbf{W}_x^\mathsf{T} & \mathbf{W}_y \mathbf{W}_y^\mathsf{T} \end{pmatrix} \tag{20.92}$$

[BJ05] showed that MLE for this model is equivalent to a classical statistical method known as **canonical correlation analysis** or **CCA** [Hot36]. However, the PGM perspective allows us to easily generalize to multiple kinds of observations (this is known as **generalized CCA** [Hor61]) or to nonlinear models (this is known as **deep CCA** [WLL16; SNM16]), or exponential family CCA [KVK10]. See [Uur+17] for further discussion of CCA and its extensions.

20.3 Autoencoders

We can think of PCA (Section 20.1) and factor analysis (Section 20.2) as learning a (linear) mapping from $\boldsymbol{x} \to \boldsymbol{z}$, called the **encoder**, f_e, and learning another (linear) mapping $\boldsymbol{z} \to \boldsymbol{x}$, called the **decoder**, f_d. The overall reconstruction function has the form $r(\boldsymbol{x}) = f_d(f_e(\boldsymbol{x}))$. The model is trained to minimize $\mathcal{L}(\boldsymbol{\theta}) = ||r(\boldsymbol{x}) - \boldsymbol{x}||_2^2$. More generally, we can use $\mathcal{L}(\boldsymbol{\theta}) = -\log p(\boldsymbol{x}|r(\boldsymbol{x}))$.

In this section, we consider the case where the encoder and decoder are nonlinear mappings implemented by neural networks. This is called an **autoencoder**. If we use an MLP with one hidden layer, we get the model shown Figure 20.16. We can think of the hidden units in the middle as a low-dimensional **bottleneck** between the input and its reconstruction.

Of course, if the hidden layer is wide enough, there is nothing to stop this model from learning the identity function. To prevent this degenerate solution, we have to restrict the model in some way. The simplest approach is to use a narrow bottleneck layer, with $L \ll D$; this is called an **undercomplete representation**. The other approach is to use $L \gg D$, known as an **overcomplete representation**, but to impose some other kind of regularization, such as adding noise to the inputs, forcing the

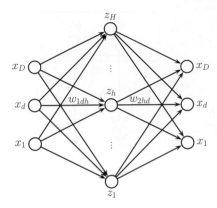

Figure 20.16: An autoencoder with one hidden layer.

activations of the hidden units to be sparse, or imposing a penalty on the derivatives of the hidden units. We discuss these options in more detail below.

20.3.1 Bottleneck autoencoders

We start by considering the special case of a **linear autoencoder**, in which there is one hidden layer, the hidden units are computed using $z = \mathbf{W}_1 x$, and the output is reconstructed using $\hat{x} = \mathbf{W}_2 z$, where $\mathbf{W}_1$ is a $L \times D$ matrix, $\mathbf{W}_2$ is a $D \times L$ matrix, and $L < D$. Hence $\hat{x} = \mathbf{W}_2 \mathbf{W}_1 x = \mathbf{W} x$ is the output of the model. If we train this model to minimize the squared reconstruction error, $\mathcal{L}(\mathbf{W}) = \sum_{n=1}^{N} ||x_n - \mathbf{W} x_n||_2^2$, one can show [BH89; KJ95] that $\hat{\mathbf{W}}$ is an orthogonal projection onto the first L eigenvectors of the empirical covariance matrix of the data. This is therefore equivalent to PCA.

If we introduce nonlinearities into the autoencoder, we get a model that is strictly more powerful than PCA, as proved in [JHG00]. Such methods can learn very useful low dimensional representations of data.

Consider fitting an autoencoder to the Fashion MNIST dataset. We consider both an MLP architecture (with 2 layers and a bottleneck of size 30), and a CNN based architecture (with 3 layers and a 3d bottleneck with 64 channels). We use a Bernoulli likelihood model and binary cross entropy as the loss. Figure 20.17 shows some test images and their reconstructions. We see that the CNN model reconstructs the images more accurately than the MLP model. However, both models are small, and were only trained for 5 epochs; results can be improved by using larger models, and training for longer.

Figure 20.18 visualizes the first 2 (of 30) latent dimensions produced by the MLP-AE. More precisely, we plot the tSNE embeddings (see Section 20.4.10), color coded by class label. We also show some corresponding images from the dataset, from which the embeddings were derived. We see that the method has done a good job of separating the classes in a fully unsupervised way. We also see that the latent space of the MLP and CNN models is very similar (at least when viewed through this 2d projection).

(a) (b)

Figure 20.17: *Results of applying an autoencoder to the Fashion MNIST data. Top row are first 5 images from validation set. Bottom row are reconstructions. (a) MLP model (trained for 20 epochs). The encoder is an MLP with architecture 784-100-30. The decoder is the mirror image of this. (b) CNN model (trained for 5 epochs). The encoder is a CNN model with architecture Conv2D(16, 3 × 3, same, selu), MaxPool2D(2x2), Conv2D(32, 3 × 3, same, selu), MaxPool2D(2 × 2), Conv2D(64, 3 × 3, same, selu), MaxPool2D(2 × 2). The decoder is the mirror image of this, using transposed convolution and without the max pooling layers. Adapted from Figure 17.4 of [Gér19]. Generated by ae_mnist_tf.ipynb.*

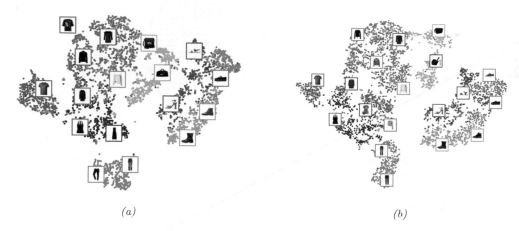

(a) (b)

Figure 20.18: *tSNE plot of the first 2 latent dimensions of the Fashion MNIST validation set using an autoencoder. (a) MLP. (b) CNN. Adapted from Figure 17.5 of [Gér19]. Generated by ae_mnist_tf.ipynb.*

20.3.2 Denoising autoencoders

One useful way to control the capacity of an autoencoder is to add noise to its input, and then train the model to reconstruct a clean (uncorrupted) version of the original input. This is called a **denoising autoencoder** [Vin+10a].

We can implement this by adding Gaussian noise, or using Bernoulli dropout. Figure 20.19 shows some reconstructions of corrupted images computed using a DAE. We see that the model is able to "hallucinate" details that are missing in the input, since it has seen similar images before, and can store this information in the parameters of the model.

Suppose we train a DAE using Gaussian corruption and squared error reconstruction, i.e., we use $p_c(\tilde{\boldsymbol{x}}|\boldsymbol{x}) = \mathcal{N}(\tilde{\boldsymbol{x}}|\boldsymbol{x}, \sigma^2 \mathbf{I})$ and $\ell(\boldsymbol{x}, r(\tilde{\boldsymbol{x}})) = ||\boldsymbol{e}||_2^2$, where $\boldsymbol{e}(\boldsymbol{x}) = r(\tilde{\boldsymbol{x}}) - \boldsymbol{x}$ is the residual error for example

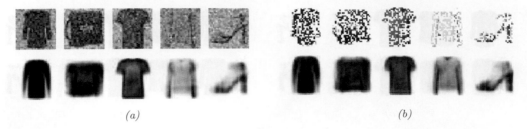

(a)   (b)

Figure 20.19: Denoising autoencoder (MLP architecture) applied to some noisy Fashion MNIST images from the validation set. (a) Gaussian noise. (b) Bernoulli dropout noise. Top row: input. Bottom row: output. Adapted from Figure 17.9 of [Gér19]. Generated by ae_mnist_tf.ipynb.

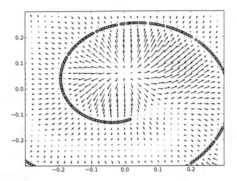

Figure 20.20: The residual error from a DAE, $e(x) = r(\tilde{x}) - x$, can learn a vector field corresponding to the score function. Arrows point towards higher probability regions. The length of the arrow is proportional to $||e(x)||$, so points near the 1d data manifold (represented by the curved line) have smaller arrows. From Figure 5 of [AB14]. Used with kind permission of Guillaume Alain.

x. Then one can show [AB14] the remarkable result that, as $\sigma \to 0$ (and with a sufficiently powerful model and enough data), the residuals approximate the **score function**, which is the log probability of the data, i.e., $e(x) \approx \nabla_x \log p(x)$. That is, the DAE learns a **vector field**, corresponding to the gradient of the log data density. Thus points that are close to the data manifold will be projected onto it via the sampling process. See Figure 20.20 for an illustration.

20.3.3   Contractive autoencoders

A different way to regularize autoencoders is by adding the penalty term

$$\Omega(z, x) = \lambda ||\frac{\partial f_e(x)}{\partial x}||_F^2 = \lambda \sum_k ||\nabla_x\, h_k(x)||_2^2 \qquad (20.93)$$

to the reconstruction loss, where h_k is the value of the k'th hidden embedding unit. That is, we penalize the Frobenius norm of the encoder's Jacobian. This is called a **contractive autoencoder**

[Rif+11]. (A linear operator with Jacobian $\mathbf{J}$ is called a **contraction** if $||\mathbf{J}\boldsymbol{x}|| \leq 1$ for all unit-norm inputs $\boldsymbol{x}$.)

To understand why this is useful, consider Figure 20.20. We can approximate the curved low-dimensional manifold by a series of locally linear manifolds. These linear approximations can be computed using the Jacobian of the encoder at each point. By encouraging these to be contractive, we ensure the model "pushes" inputs that are off the manifold to move back towards it.

Another way to think about CAEs is as follows. To minimize the penalty term, the model would like to ensure the encoder is a constant function. However, if it was completely constant, it would ignore its input, and hence incur high reconstruction cost. Thus the two terms together encourage the model to learn a representation where only a few units change in response to the most significant variations in the input.

One possible degenerate solution is that the encoder simply learns to multiply the input by a small constant ϵ (which scales down the Jacobian), followed by a decoder that divides by ϵ (which reconstructs perfectly). To avoid this, we can tie the weights of the encoder and decoder, by setting the weight matrix for layer ℓ of f_d to be the transpose of the weight matrix for layer ℓ of f_e, but using untied bias terms. Unfortunately CAEs are slow to train, because of the expense of computing the Jacobian.

20.3.4 Sparse autoencoders

Yet another way to regularize autoencoders is to add a sparsity penalty to the latent activations of the form $\Omega(\boldsymbol{z}) = \lambda ||\boldsymbol{z}||_1$. (This is called **activity regularization**.)

An alternative way to implement sparsity, that often gives better results, is to use logistic units, and then to compute the expected fraction of time each unit k is on within a minibatch (call this q_k), and ensure that this is close to a desired target value p, as proposed in [GBB11]. In particular, we use the regularizer $\Omega(\boldsymbol{z}_{1:L,1:N}) = \lambda \sum_k D_{\mathrm{KL}}(\boldsymbol{p} \parallel \boldsymbol{q}_k)$ for latent dimensions $1:L$ and examples $1:N$, where $\boldsymbol{p} = (p, 1-p)$ is the desired target distribution, and $\boldsymbol{q}_k = (q_k, 1-q_k)$ is the empirical distribution for unit k, computed using $q_k = \frac{1}{N} \sum_{n=1}^{N} \mathbb{I}(z_{n,k} = 1)$.

Figure 20.21 shows the results when fitting an AE-MLP (with 300 hidden units) to Fashion MNIST. If we set $\lambda = 0$ (i.e., if we don't impose a sparsity penalty), we see that the average activation value is about 0.4, with most neurons being partially activated most of the time. With the ℓ_1 penalty, we see that most units are off all the time, which means they are not being used at all. With the KL penalty, we see that about 70% of neurons are off on average, but unlike the ℓ_1 case, we don't see units being permanently turned off (the average activation level is 0.1). This latter kind of sparse firing pattern is similar to that observed in biological brains (see e.g., [Bey+19]).

20.3.5 Variational autoencoders

In this section, we discuss the **variational autoencoder** or **VAE** [KW14; RMW14; KW19a], which can be thought of as a probabilistic version of a deterministic autoencoder (Section 20.3) The principal advantage is that a VAE is a generative model that can create new samples, whereas an autoencoder just computes embeddings of input vectors.

We discuss VAEs in detail in the sequel to this book, [Mur23]. However, in brief, the VAE combines two key ideas. First we create a non-linear extension of the factor analysis generative model, i.e., we

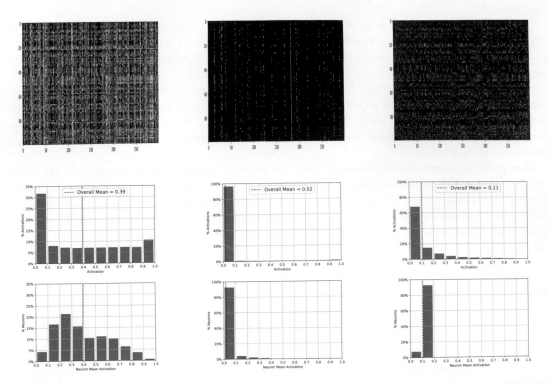

Figure 20.21: Neuron activity (in the bottleneck layer) for an autoencoder applied to Fashion MNIST. We show results for three models, with different kinds of sparsity penalty: no penalty (left column), ℓ_1 penalty (middle column), KL penalty (right column). Top row: Heatmap of 300 neuron activations (columns) across 100 examples (rows). Middle row: Histogram of activation levels derived from this heatmap. Bottom row: Histogram of the mean activation per neuron, averaged over all examples in the validation set. Adapted from Figure 17.11 of [Gér19]. Generated by ae_mnist_tf.ipynb.

replace $p(\boldsymbol{x}|\boldsymbol{z}) = \mathcal{N}(\boldsymbol{x}|\mathbf{W}\boldsymbol{z}, \sigma^2\mathbf{I})$ with

$$p_{\boldsymbol{\theta}}(\boldsymbol{x}|\boldsymbol{z}) = \mathcal{N}(\boldsymbol{x}|f_d(\boldsymbol{z};\boldsymbol{\theta}), \sigma^2\mathbf{I}) \tag{20.94}$$

where f_d is the decoder. For binary observations we should use a Bernoulli likelihood:

$$p(\boldsymbol{x}|\boldsymbol{z}, \boldsymbol{\theta}) = \prod_{i=1}^{D} \text{Ber}(x_i|f_d(\boldsymbol{z};\boldsymbol{\theta}), \sigma^2\mathbf{I}) \tag{20.95}$$

Second, we create another model, $q(\boldsymbol{z}|\boldsymbol{x})$, called the **recognition network** or **inference network**, that is trained simultaneously with the generative model to do approximate posterior inference. If we assume the posterior is Gaussian, with diagonal covariance, we get

$$q_{\boldsymbol{\phi}}(\boldsymbol{z}|\boldsymbol{x}) = \mathcal{N}(\boldsymbol{z}|f_{e,\mu}(\boldsymbol{x};\boldsymbol{\phi}), \text{diag}(f_{e,\sigma}(\boldsymbol{x};\boldsymbol{\phi}))) \tag{20.96}$$

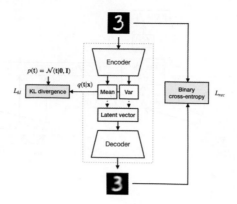

Figure 20.22: Schematic illustration of a VAE. From a figure from http://krasserm.github.io/2018/07/27/dfc-vae/. *Used with kind permission of Martin Krasser.*

where f_e is the encoder. See Figure 20.22 for a sketch.

The idea of training an inference network to "invert" a generative network, rather than running an optimization algorithm to infer the latent code, is called **amortized inference**. This idea was first proposed in the **Helmholtz machine** [Day+95]. However, that paper did not present a single unified objective function for inference and generation, but instead used the wake sleep method for training, which alternates between optimizing the generative model and inference model. By contrast, the VAE optimizes a variational lower bound on the log-likelihood, which is more principled, since it is a single unified objective.

20.3.5.1 Training VAEs

We cannot compute the exact marginal likelihood $p(\boldsymbol{x}|\boldsymbol{\theta})$ needed for MLE training, because posterior inference in a nonlinear FA model is intractable. However, we can use the inference network to compute an approximate posterior, $q(\boldsymbol{z}|\boldsymbol{x})$. We can then use this to compute the **evidence lower bound** or **ELBO**. For a single example $\boldsymbol{x}$, this is given by

$$\textit{Ł}(\boldsymbol{\theta}, \boldsymbol{\phi}|\boldsymbol{x}) = \mathbb{E}_{q_{\boldsymbol{\phi}}(\boldsymbol{z}|\boldsymbol{x})}\left[\log p_{\boldsymbol{\theta}}(\boldsymbol{x}, \boldsymbol{z}) - \log q_{\boldsymbol{\phi}}(\boldsymbol{z}|\boldsymbol{x})\right] \tag{20.97}$$

$$= \mathbb{E}_{q(\boldsymbol{z}|\boldsymbol{x}, \boldsymbol{\phi})}\left[\log p(\boldsymbol{x}|\boldsymbol{z}, \boldsymbol{\theta})\right] - D_{\mathrm{KL}}\left(q(\boldsymbol{z}|\boldsymbol{x}, \boldsymbol{\phi}) \parallel p(\boldsymbol{z})\right) \tag{20.98}$$

This can be interpreted as the expected log likelihood, plus a regularizer, that penalizes the posterior from deviating too much from the prior. (This is different than the approach in Section 20.3.4, where we applied the KL penalty to the aggregate posterior in each minibatch.)

The ELBO is a lower bound of the log marginal likelihood (aka evidence), as can be seen from Jensen's inequality:

$$\textit{Ł}(\boldsymbol{\theta}, \boldsymbol{\phi}|\boldsymbol{x}) = \int q_{\boldsymbol{\phi}}(\boldsymbol{z}|\boldsymbol{x}) \log \frac{p_{\boldsymbol{\theta}}(\boldsymbol{x}, \boldsymbol{z})}{q_{\boldsymbol{\phi}}(\boldsymbol{z}|\boldsymbol{x})} d\boldsymbol{z} \tag{20.99}$$

$$\leq \log \int q_{\boldsymbol{\phi}}(\boldsymbol{z}|\boldsymbol{x}) \frac{p_{\boldsymbol{\theta}}(\boldsymbol{x}, \boldsymbol{z})}{q_{\boldsymbol{\phi}}(\boldsymbol{z}|\boldsymbol{x})} d\boldsymbol{z} = \log p_{\boldsymbol{\theta}}(\boldsymbol{x}) \tag{20.100}$$

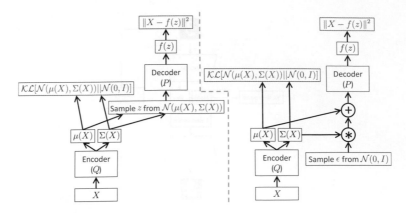

Figure 20.23: *Computation graph for VAEs. where* $p(\boldsymbol{z}) = \mathcal{N}(\boldsymbol{z}|\boldsymbol{0}, \mathbf{I})$, $p(\boldsymbol{x}|\boldsymbol{z}, \boldsymbol{\theta}) = \mathcal{N}(\boldsymbol{x}|f(\boldsymbol{z}), \sigma^2 \mathbf{I})$, *and* $q(\boldsymbol{z}|\boldsymbol{x}, \boldsymbol{\phi}) = \mathcal{N}(\boldsymbol{z}|\mu(\boldsymbol{x}), \Sigma(\boldsymbol{x}))$. *Red boxes show sampling operations which are not differentiable. Blue boxes show loss layers (we assume Gaussian likelihoods and priors). (Left) Without the reparameterization trick. (Right) With the reparameterization trick. Gradients can flow from the output loss, back through the decoder and into the encoder. From Figure 4 of [Doe16]. Used with kind permission of Carl Doersch.*

Thus for fixed inference network parameters $\boldsymbol{\phi}$, increasing the ELBO should increase the log likelihood of the data, similar to EM Section 8.7.2.

20.3.5.2   The reparameterization trick

In this section, we discuss how to compute the ELBO and its gradient. For simplicity, let us suppose that the inference network estimates the parameters of a Gaussian posterior. Since $q_{\boldsymbol{\phi}}(\boldsymbol{z}|\boldsymbol{x})$ is Gaussian, we can write

$$\boldsymbol{z} = f_{e,\mu}(\boldsymbol{x}; \boldsymbol{\phi}) + f_{e,\sigma}(\boldsymbol{x}; \boldsymbol{\phi}) \odot \boldsymbol{\epsilon} \qquad (20.101)$$

where $\boldsymbol{\epsilon} \sim \mathcal{N}(\boldsymbol{0}, \mathbf{I})$. Hence

$$Ł(\boldsymbol{\theta}, \boldsymbol{\phi}|\boldsymbol{x}) = \mathbb{E}_{\boldsymbol{\epsilon} \sim \mathcal{N}(\boldsymbol{0},\mathbf{I})} \left[\log p_{\boldsymbol{\theta}}(\boldsymbol{x}|\boldsymbol{z} = \mu_{\boldsymbol{\phi}}(\boldsymbol{x}) + \sigma_{\boldsymbol{\phi}}(\boldsymbol{x}) \odot \boldsymbol{\epsilon}) \right] - D_{\mathrm{KL}}\left(q_{\boldsymbol{\phi}}(\boldsymbol{z}|\boldsymbol{x}) \,\|\, p(\boldsymbol{z})\right) \qquad (20.102)$$

Now the expectation is independent of the parameters of the model, so we can safely push gradients inside and use backpropagation for training in the usual way, by minimizing $-\mathbb{E}_{\boldsymbol{x} \sim \mathcal{D}}\left[Ł(\boldsymbol{\theta}, \boldsymbol{\phi}|\boldsymbol{x})\right]$ wrt $\boldsymbol{\theta}$ and $\boldsymbol{\phi}$. This is known as the **reparameterization trick**. See Figure 20.23 for an illustration.

The first term in the ELBO can be approximated by sampling $\boldsymbol{\epsilon}$, scaling it by the output of the inference network to get $\boldsymbol{z}$, and then evaluating $\log p(\boldsymbol{x}|\boldsymbol{z})$ using the decoder network.

The second term in the ELBO is the KL of two Gaussians, which has a closed form solution. In particular, inserting $p(\boldsymbol{z}) = \mathcal{N}(\boldsymbol{z}|\boldsymbol{0}, \mathbf{I})$ and $q(\boldsymbol{z}) = \mathcal{N}(\boldsymbol{z}|\boldsymbol{\mu}, \mathrm{diag}(\boldsymbol{\sigma}))$ into Equation (6.33), we get

$$D_{\mathrm{KL}}\left(q \,\|\, p\right) = \sum_{k=1}^{K} \left[\log(\frac{1}{\sigma_k}) + \frac{\sigma_k^2 + (\mu_k - 0)^2}{2 \cdot 1} - \frac{1}{2} \right] = -\frac{1}{2} \sum_{k=1}^{K} \left[\log \sigma_k^2 - \sigma_k^2 - \mu_k^2 + 1 \right] \qquad (20.103)$$

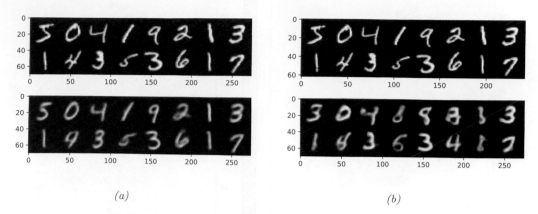

(a)   (b)

Figure 20.24: *Reconstructing MNIST digits using a 20 dimensional latent space. Top row: input images. Bottom row: reconstructions. (a) VAE. Generated by vae_mnist_conv_lightning.ipynb. (b) Deterministic AE. Generated by ae_mnist_conv.ipynb.*

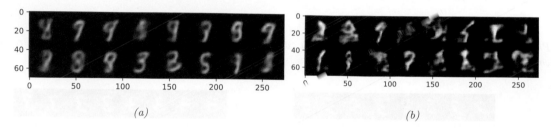

(a)   (b)

Figure 20.25: *Sampling MNIST digits using a 20 dimensional latent space. (a) VAE. Generated by vae_mnist_conv_lightning.ipynb. (b) Deterministic AE. Generated by ae_mnist_conv.ipynb.*

20.3.5.3 Comparison of VAEs and autoencoders

VAEs are very similar to autoencoders. In particular, the generative model, $p_\theta(x|z)$, acts like the decoder, and the inference network, $q_\phi(z|x)$, acts like the encoder. The reconstruction abilities of both models are similar, as can be seen by comparing Figure 20.24a with Figure 20.24b.

The primary advantage of the VAE is that it can be used to generate new data from random noise. In particular, we sample z from the Gaussian prior $\mathcal{N}(z|0, I)$, and then pass this through the decoder to get $\mathbb{E}[x|z] = f(z; \theta)$. The VAE's decoder is trained to convert random points in the embedding space (generated by perturbing the input encodings) to sensible outputs. By contrast, the decoder for the deterministic autoencoder only ever gets as inputs the exact encodings of the training set, so it does not know what to do with random inputs that are outside what it was trained on. So a standard autoencoder cannot create new samples. This difference can be seen by comparing Figure 20.25a with Figure 20.25b.

The reason the VAE is better at sample is that it it embeds images into Gaussians in latent space, whereas the AE embeds images into points, which are like delta functions. The advantage of using a

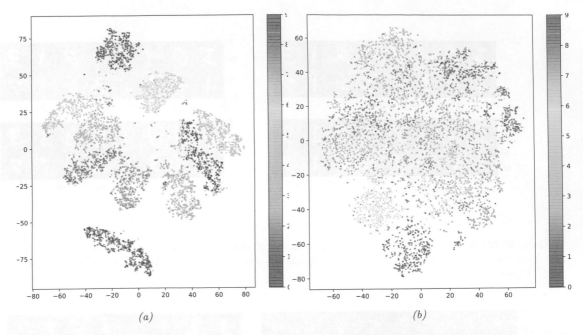

Figure 20.26: tSNE projection of a 20 dimensional latent space. (a) VAE. Generated by vae_mnist_conv_lightning.ipynb. (b) Deterministic AE. Generated by ae_mnist_conv.ipynb.

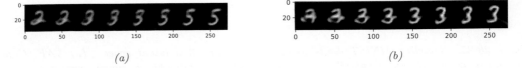

Figure 20.27: Linear interpolation between the left and right images in a 20 dimensional latent space. (a) VAE. (b) Deterministic AE. Generated by vae_mnist_conv_lightning.ipynb.

latent *distribution* is that it encourages local smoothness, since a given image may map to multiple nearby places, depending on the stochastic sampling. By contrast, in an AE, the latent space is typically not smooth, so images from different classes often end up next to each other. This difference can be seen by comparing Figure 20.26a with Figure 20.26b.

We can leverage the smoothness of the latent space to perform **image interpolation**. Rather than working in pixel space, we can work in the latent space of the model. Specifically, let x_1 and x_2 be two images, and let $z_1 = \mathbb{E}_{q(z|x_1)}[z]$ and $z_2 = \mathbb{E}_{q(z|x_2)}[z]$ be their encodings. We can now generate new images that interpolate between these two anchors by computing $z = \lambda z_1 + (1 - \lambda)z_2$, where $0 \leq \lambda \leq 1$, and then decoding by computing $\mathbb{E}[x|z]$. This is called **latent space interpolation**. (The justification for taking a linear interpolation is that the learned manifold has approximately zero curvature, as shown in [SKTF18].) A VAE is more useful for latent space interpolation than an AE because its latent space is smoother, and because the model can generate from almost any point in latent space. This difference can be seen by comparing Figure 20.27a with Figure 20.27b.

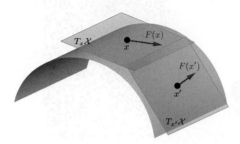

Figure 20.28: Illustration of the tangent space and tangent vectors at two different points on a 2d curved manifold. From Figure 1 of [Bro+17a]. Used with kind permission of Michael Bronstein.

20.4 Manifold learning *

In this section, we discuss the problem of recovering the underlying low-dimensional structure in a high-dimensional dataset. This structure is often assumed to be a curved manifold (explained in Section 20.4.1), so this problem is called **manifold learning** or **nonlinear dimensionality reduction**. The key difference from methods such as autoencoders (Section 20.3) is that we will focus on non-parametric methods, in which we compute an embedding for each point in the training set, as opposed to learning a generic model that can embed any input vector. That is, the methods we discuss do not (easily) support **out-of-sample generalization**. However, they can be easier to fit, and are quite flexible. Such methods can be a useful for unsupervised learning (knowledge discovery), data visualization, and as a preprocessing step for supervised learning. See [AAB21] for a recent review of this field.

20.4.1 What are manifolds?

Roughly speaking, a **manifold** is a topological space which is locally Euclidean. One of the simplest examples is the surface of the earth, which is a curved 2d surface embedded in a 3d space. At each local point on the surface, the earth seems flat.

More formally, a d-dimensional manifold $\mathcal{X}$ is a space in which each point $x \in \mathcal{X}$ has a neighborhood which is topologically equivalent to a d-dimensional Euclidean space, called the **tangent space**, denoted $\mathcal{T}_x = T_x\mathcal{X}$. This is illustrated in Figure 20.28.

A **Riemannian manifold** is a differentiable manifold that associates an inner product operator at each point x in tangent space; this is assumed to depend smoothly on the position x. The inner product induces a notion of distance, angles, and volume. The collection of these inner products is called a **Riemannian metric**. It can be shown that any sufficiently smooth Riemannian manifold can be embedded into a Euclidean space of potentially higher dimension; the Riemannian inner product at a point then becomes Euclidean inner product in that tangent space.

20.4.2 The manifold hypothesis

Most "naturally occuring" high dimensional dataset lie a low dimensional manifold. This is called the **manifold hypothesis** [FMN16]. For example, consider the case of an image. Figure 20.29a shows a

 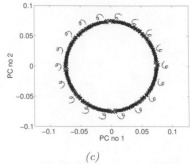

(a)   (b)   (c)

Figure 20.29: Illustration of the image manifold. (a) An image of the digit 6 from the USPS dataset, of size $64 \times 57 = 3,648$. (b) A random sample from the space $\{0,1\}^{3648}$ reshaped as an image. (c) A dataset created by rotating the original image by one degree 360 times. We project this data onto its first two principal components, to reveal the underlying 2d circular manifold. From Figure 1 of [Law12]. Used with kind permission of Neil Lawrence.

single image of size 64×57. This is a vector in a 3,648-dimensional space, where each dimension corresponds to a pixel intensity. Suppose we try to generate an image by drawing a random point in this space; it is unlikely to look like the image of a digit, as shown in Figure 20.29b. However, the pixels are not independent of each other, since they are generated by some lower dimensional structure, namely the shape of the digit 6.

As we vary the shape, we will generate different images. We can often characterize the space of shape variations using a low-dimensional manifold. This is illustrated in Figure 20.29c, where we apply PCA (Section 20.1) to project a dataset of 360 images, each one a slightly rotated version of the digit 6, into a 2d space. We see that most of the variation in the data is captured by an underlying curved 2d manifold. We say that the **intrinsic dimensionality** d of the data is 2, even though the **ambient dimensionality** D is 3,648.

20.4.3   Approaches to manifold learning

In the rest of this section, we discuss ways to learn manifolds from data. There are many different algorithms that have been proposed, which make different assumptions about the nature of the manifold, and which have different computational properties. We discuss a few of these methods in the following sections. For more details, see e.g., [Bur10].

The methods can be categorized as shown in Table 20.1. The term "nonparametric" refers to methods that learn a low dimensional embedding z_i for each datapoint x_i, but do not learn a mapping function which can be applied to an out-of-sample datapoint. (However, [Ben+04b] discusses how to extend many of these methods beyond the training set by learning a kernel.)

In the sections below, we compare some of these methods using 2 different datasets: a set of 1000 3d-points sampled from the 2d "**Swiss roll**" manifold, and a set of 1797 64-dimensional points sampled from the UCI digits dataset. See Figure 20.30 for an illustration of the data. We will learn a 2d manifold, so we can visualize the data.

Method	Parametric	Convex	Section
PCA / classical MDS	N	Y (Dense)	Section 20.1
Kernel PCA	N	Y (Dense)	Section 20.4.6
Isomap	N	Y (Dense)	Section 20.4.5
LLE	N	Y (Sparse)	Section 20.4.8
Laplacian Eigenmaps	N	Y (Sparse)	Section 20.4.9
tSNE	N	N	Section 20.4.10
Autoencoder	Y	N	Section 20.3

Table 20.1: *A list of some approaches to dimensionality reduction. If a method is convex, we specify in parentheses whether it requires solving a sparse or dense eigenvalue problem.*

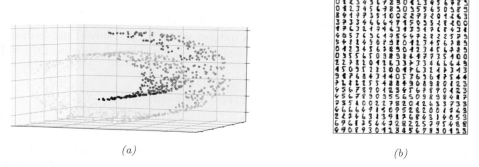

(a)   (b)

Figure 20.30: *Illustration of some data generated from low-dimensional manifolds. (a) The 2d Swiss-roll manifold embedded into 3d. Generated by manifold_swiss_sklearn.ipynb. (b) Sample of some UCI digits, which have size $8 \times 8 = 64$. Generated by manifold_digits_sklearn.ipynb.*

20.4.4   Multi-dimensional scaling (MDS)

The simplest approach to manifold learning is **multidimensional scaling** (**MDS**). This tries to find a set of low dimensional vectors $\{z_i \in \mathbb{R}^L : i = 1 : N\}$ such that the pairwise distances between these vectors is as similar as possible to a set of pairwise dissimilarities $\mathbf{D} = \{d_{ij}\}$ provided by the user. There are several variants of MDS, one of which turns out to be equivalent to PCA, as we discuss below.

20.4.4.1   Classical MDS

Suppose we start an $N \times D$ data matrix $\mathbf{X}$ with rows x_i. Let us define the centered Gram (similarity) matrix as follows:

$$\tilde{K}_{ij} = \langle x_i - \overline{x}, x_j - \overline{x} \rangle \tag{20.104}$$

In matrix notation, we have $\tilde{\mathbf{K}} = \tilde{\mathbf{X}}\tilde{\mathbf{X}}^\mathsf{T}$, where $\tilde{\mathbf{X}} = \mathbf{C}_N \mathbf{X}$ and $\mathbf{C}_N = \mathbf{I}_N - \frac{1}{N}\mathbf{1}_N \mathbf{1}_N^\mathsf{T}$ is the centering matrix.

Now define the **strain** of a set of embeddings as follows:

$$\mathcal{L}_{\text{strain}}(\mathbf{Z}) = \sum_{i,j} (\tilde{K}_{ij} - \langle \tilde{z}_i, \tilde{z}_j \rangle)^2 = ||\tilde{\mathbf{K}} - \tilde{\mathbf{Z}}\tilde{\mathbf{Z}}^\mathsf{T}||_F^2 \tag{20.105}$$

where $\tilde{z}_i = z_i - \overline{z}$ is the centered embedding vector. Intuitively this measures how well similarities in the high-dimensional data space, $\tilde{K}_{ij}$, are matched by similarities in the low-dimensional embedding space, $\langle \tilde{z}_i, \tilde{z}_j \rangle$. Minimizing this loss is called **classical MDS**.

We know from Section 7.5 that the best rank L approximation to a matrix is its truncated SVD representation, $\tilde{\mathbf{K}} = \mathbf{U}\mathbf{S}\mathbf{V}^\mathsf{T}$. Since $\tilde{\mathbf{K}}$ is positive semi definite, we have that $\mathbf{V} = \mathbf{U}$. Hence the optimal embedding satisfies

$$\tilde{\mathbf{Z}}\tilde{\mathbf{Z}}^\mathsf{T} = \mathbf{U}\mathbf{S}\mathbf{U}^\mathsf{T} = (\mathbf{U}\mathbf{S}^{\frac{1}{2}})(\mathbf{S}^{\frac{1}{2}}\mathbf{U}^\mathsf{T}) \tag{20.106}$$

Thus we can set the embedding vectors to be the rows of $\tilde{\mathbf{Z}} = \mathbf{U}\mathbf{S}^{\frac{1}{2}}$.

Now we describe how to apply classical MDS to a dataset where we just have Euclidean distances, rather than raw features. First we compute a matrix of squared Euclidean distances, $\mathbf{D}^{(2)} = \mathbf{D} \odot \mathbf{D}$, which has the following entries:

$$D_{ij}^{(2)} = ||\boldsymbol{x}_i - \boldsymbol{x}_j||^2 = ||\boldsymbol{x}_i - \overline{\boldsymbol{x}}||^2 + ||\boldsymbol{x}_j - \overline{\boldsymbol{x}}||^2 - 2\langle \boldsymbol{x}_i - \overline{\boldsymbol{x}}, \boldsymbol{x}_j - \overline{\boldsymbol{x}} \rangle \tag{20.107}$$

$$= ||\boldsymbol{x}_i - \overline{\boldsymbol{x}}||^2 + ||\boldsymbol{x}_j - \overline{\boldsymbol{x}}||^2 - 2\tilde{K}_{ij} \tag{20.108}$$

We see that $\mathbf{D}^{(2)}$ only differs from $\tilde{\mathbf{K}}$ by some row and column constants (and a factor of -2). Hence we can compute $\tilde{\mathbf{K}}$ by double centering $\mathbf{D}^{(2)}$ using Equation (7.89) to get $\tilde{\mathbf{K}} = -\frac{1}{2}\mathbf{C}_N \mathbf{D}^{(2)} \mathbf{C}_N$. In other words,

$$\tilde{K}_{ij} = -\frac{1}{2} \left(d_{ij}^2 - \frac{1}{N}\sum_{l=1}^{N} d_{il}^2 - \frac{1}{N}\sum_{l=1}^{N} d_{jl}^2 + \frac{1}{N^2}\sum_{l=1}^{N}\sum_{m=1}^{N} d_{lm}^2 \right) \tag{20.109}$$

We can then compute the embeddings as before.

It turns out that classical MDS is equivalent to PCA (Section 20.1). To see this, let $\tilde{\mathbf{K}} = \mathbf{U}_L \mathbf{S}_L \mathbf{U}_L^\mathsf{T}$ be the rank L truncated SVD of the centered kernel matrix. The MDS embedding is given by $\mathbf{Z}_{\text{MDS}} = \mathbf{U}_L \mathbf{S}_L^{\frac{1}{2}}$. Now consider the rank L SVD of the centered data matrix, $\tilde{\mathbf{X}} = \mathbf{U}_X \mathbf{S}_X \mathbf{V}_X^\mathsf{T}$. The PCA embedding is $\mathbf{Z}_{\text{PCA}} = \mathbf{U}_X \mathbf{S}_X$. Now

$$\tilde{\mathbf{K}} = \tilde{\mathbf{X}}\tilde{\mathbf{X}}^\mathsf{T} = \mathbf{U}_X \mathbf{S}_X \mathbf{V}_X^\mathsf{T} \mathbf{V}_X \mathbf{S}_X \mathbf{U}_X^\mathsf{T} = \mathbf{U}_X \mathbf{S}_X^2 \mathbf{U}_X^\mathsf{T} = \mathbf{U}_L \mathbf{S}_L \mathbf{U}_L^\mathsf{T} \tag{20.110}$$

Hence $\mathbf{U}_X = \mathbf{U}_L$ and $\mathbf{S}_X = \mathbf{S}_L^2$, and so $\mathbf{Z}_{\text{PCA}} = \mathbf{Z}_{\text{MDS}}$.

20.4.4.2 Metric MDS

Classical MDS assumes Euclidean distances. We can generalize it to allow for any dissimilarity measure by defining the **stress function**

$$\mathcal{L}_{\text{stress}}(\mathbf{Z}) = \sqrt{\frac{\sum_{i<j}(d_{i,j} - \hat{d}_{ij})^2}{\sum_{ij} d_{ij}^2}} \tag{20.111}$$

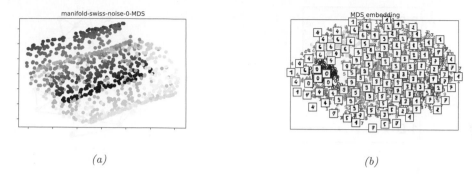

(a)   (b)

Figure 20.31: Metric MDS applied to (a) Swiss roll. Generated by manifold_swiss_sklearn.ipynb. (b) UCI digits. Generated by manifold_digits_sklearn.ipynb.

where $\hat{d}_{ij} = ||z_i - z_j||$. This is called **metric MDS**. Note that this is a different objective than the one used by classical MDS, so even if d_{ij} are Euclidean distances, the results will be different.

We can use gradient descent to solve the optimization problem. However, it is better to use a bound optimization algorithm (Section 8.7) called **SMACOF** [Lee77], which stands for "Scaling by MAjorizing a COmplication Function". (This is the method implemented in scikit-learn.) See Figure 20.31 for the results of applying this to our running example.

20.4.4.3 Non-metric MDS

Instead of trying to match the distance between points, we can instead just try to match the ranking of how similar points are. To do this, let $f(d)$ be a monotonic transformation from distances to ranks. Now define the loss

$$\mathcal{L}_{\mathrm{NM}}(\mathbf{Z}) = \sqrt{\frac{\sum_{i<j}(f(d_{i,j}) - \hat{d}_{ij})^2}{\sum_{ij} \hat{d}_{ij}^2}} \tag{20.112}$$

where $\hat{d}_{ij} = ||z_i - z_j||$. Minimizing this is known as **non-metric MDS**.

This objective can be optimized iteratively. First the function f is optimized, for a given $\mathbf{Z}$, using isotonic regression; this finds the optimal monotonic transformation of the input distances to match the current embedding distances. Then the embeddings $\mathbf{Z}$ are optimized, for a given f, using gradient descent, and the process repeats.

20.4.4.4 Sammon mapping

Metric MDS tries to minimize the sum of squared distances, so it puts the most emphasis on large distances. However, for many embedding methods, small distances matter more, since they capture local structure. One way to capture this is to divide each term of the loss by d_{ij}, so small distances get upweighted:

$$\mathcal{L}_{\mathrm{sammon}}(\mathbf{Z}) = \left(\frac{1}{\sum_{i<j} d_{ij}}\right) \sum_{i \neq j} \frac{(\hat{d}_{ij} - d_{ij})^2}{d_{ij}} \tag{20.113}$$

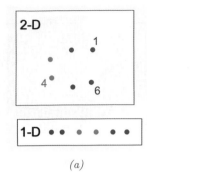
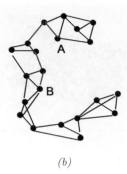

(a)   (b)

Figure 20.32: (a) If we measure distances along the manifold, we find $d(1,6) > d(1,4)$, whereas if we measure in ambient space, we find $d(1,6) < d(1,4)$. The plot at the bottom shows the underlying 1d manifold. (b) The K-nearest neighbors graph for some datapoints; the red path is the shortest distance between A and B on this graph. From [Hin13]. Used with kind permission of Geoff Hinton.

Minimizing this results in a **Sammon mapping**. (The coefficient in front of the sum is just to simplify the gradient of the loss.) Unfortunately this is a non-convex objective, and it arguably puts too much emphasis on getting very small distances exactly right. We will discuss better methods for capturing local structure later on.

20.4.5   Isomap

If the high-dimensional data lies on or near a curved manifold, such as the Swiss roll example, then MDS might consider two points to be close even if their distance along the manifold is large. This is illustrated in Figure 20.32a.

One way to capture this is to create the K-nearest neighbor graph between datapoints[5], and then approximate the manifold distance between a pair of points by the shortest distance along this graph; this can be computed efficiently using Dijkstra's shortest path algorithm. See Figure 20.32b for an illustration. Once we have computed this new distance metric, we can apply classical MDS (i.e., PCA). This is a way to capture local structure while avoiding local optima. The overall method is called **isomap** [TSL00].

See Figure 20.33 for the results of this method on our running example. We see that they are quite reasonable. However, if the data is noisy, there can be "false" edges in the nearest neighbor graph, which can result in "short circuits" which significantly distort the embedding, as shown in Figure 20.34. This problem is known as "**topological instability**" [BS02]. Choosing a very small neighborhood does not solve this problem, since this can fragment the manifold into a large number of disconnected regions. Various other solutions have been proposed, e.g., [CC07].

20.4.6   Kernel PCA

PCA (and classical MDS) finds the best linear projection of the data, so as to preserve pairwise similarities between all the points. In this section, we consider nonlinear projections. The key idea

---

5. In scikit-learn, you can use the function `sklearn.neighbors.kneighbors_graph`.

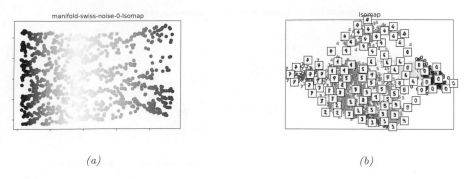

(a)   (b)

Figure 20.33: Isomap applied to (a) Swiss roll. Generated by manifold_swiss_sklearn.ipynb. (b) UCI digits. Generated by manifold_digits_sklearn.ipynb.

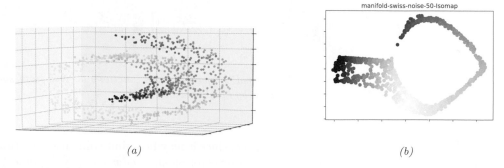

(a)   (b)

Figure 20.34: (a) Noisy version of Swiss roll data. We perturb each point by adding $\mathcal{N}(0, 0.5^2)$ noise. (b) Results of Isomap applied to this data. Generated by manifold_swiss_sklearn.ipynb.

is to solve PCA by finding the eigenvectors of the inner product (Gram) matrix $\mathbf{K} = \mathbf{X}\mathbf{X}^\mathsf{T}$, as in Section 20.1.3.2, and then to use the kernel trick (Section 17.3.4), which lets us replace inner products such as $\boldsymbol{x}_i^\mathsf{T}\boldsymbol{x}_j$ with a kernel function, $K_{ij} = \mathcal{K}(\boldsymbol{x}_i, \boldsymbol{x}_k)$. This is known as **kernel PCA** [SSM98].

Recall from Mercer's theorem that the use of a kernel implies some underlying feature space, so we are implicitly replacing $\boldsymbol{x}_i$ with $\boldsymbol{\phi}(\boldsymbol{x}_i) = \boldsymbol{\phi}_i$. Let $\boldsymbol{\Phi}$ be the corresponding (notional) design matrix, and $\mathbf{K} = \mathbf{X}\mathbf{X}^\mathsf{T}$ be the Gram matrix. Finally, let $\mathbf{S}_\phi = \frac{1}{N}\sum_i \boldsymbol{\phi}_i\boldsymbol{\phi}_i^\mathsf{T}$ be the covariance matrix in feature space. (We are assuming for now the features are centered.) From Equation (20.22), the normalized eigenvectors of $\mathbf{S}$ are given by $\mathbf{V}_{\mathrm{kPCA}} = \boldsymbol{\Phi}^\mathsf{T}\mathbf{U}\boldsymbol{\Lambda}^{-\frac{1}{2}}$, where $\mathbf{U}$ and $\boldsymbol{\Lambda}$ contain the eigenvectors and eigenvalues of $\mathbf{K}$. Of course, we can't actually compute $\mathbf{V}_{\mathrm{kPCA}}$, since $\boldsymbol{\phi}_i$ is potentially infinite dimensional. However, we can compute the projection of a test vector $\boldsymbol{x}_*$ onto the feature space as follows:

$$\boldsymbol{\phi}_*^\mathsf{T}\mathbf{V}_{\mathrm{kPCA}} = \boldsymbol{\phi}_*^\mathsf{T}\boldsymbol{\Phi}^\mathsf{T}\mathbf{U}\boldsymbol{\Lambda}^{-\frac{1}{2}} = \boldsymbol{k}_*^\mathsf{T}\mathbf{U}\boldsymbol{\Lambda}^{-\frac{1}{2}} \tag{20.114}$$

where $\boldsymbol{k}_* = [\mathcal{K}(\boldsymbol{x}_*, \boldsymbol{x}_1), \dots, \mathcal{K}(\boldsymbol{x}_*, \boldsymbol{x}_N)]$.

There is one final detail to worry about. The covariance matrix is only given by $\mathbf{S} = \boldsymbol{\Phi}^\mathsf{T}\boldsymbol{\Phi}$ if the features is zero-mean. Thus we can only use the Gram matrix $\mathbf{K} = \boldsymbol{\Phi}\boldsymbol{\Phi}^\mathsf{T}$ if $\mathbb{E}[\boldsymbol{\phi}_i] = \mathbf{0}$. Unfortunately,

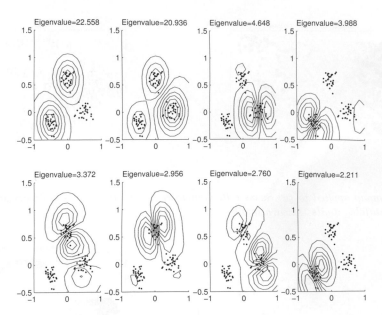

Figure 20.35: Visualization of the first 8 kernel principal component basis functions derived from some 2d data. We use an RBF kernel with $\sigma^2 = 0.1$. Generated by kpcaScholkopf.ipynb.

we cannot simply subtract off the mean in feature space, since it may be infinite dimensional. However, there is a trick we can use. Define the centered feature vector as $\tilde{\phi}_i = \phi(\boldsymbol{x}_i) - \frac{1}{N} \sum_{j=1}^{N} \phi(\boldsymbol{x}_j)$. The Gram matrix of the centered feature vectors is given by $\tilde{K}_{ij} = \tilde{\phi}_i^\mathsf{T} \tilde{\phi}_j$. Using the double centering trick from Equation (7.89), we can write this in matrix form as $\tilde{\mathbf{K}} = \mathbf{C}_N \mathbf{K} \mathbf{C}_N$, where $\mathbf{C}_N \triangleq \mathbf{I}_N - \frac{1}{N} \mathbf{1}_N \mathbf{1}_N^\mathsf{T}$ is the centering matrix.

If we apply kPCA with a linear kernel, we recover regular PCA (classical MDS). This is limited to using $L \leq D$ embedding dimensions. If we use a non-degenerate kernel, we can use up to N components, since the size of $\boldsymbol{\Phi}$ is $N \times D^*$, where D^* is the (potentially infinite) dimensionality of embedded feature vectors. Figure 20.35 gives an example of the method applied to some $D = 2$ dimensional data using an RBF kernel. We project points in the unit grid onto the first 8 components and visualize the corresponding surfaces using a contour plot. We see that the first two components separate the three clusters, and the following components split the clusters.

See Figure 20.36 for some the results on kPCA (with an RBF kernel) on our running example. In this case, the results are arguably not very useful. In fact, it can be shown that kPCA with an RBF kernel expands the feature space instead of reducing it [WSS04], as we saw in Figure 20.35, which makes it not very useful as a method for dimensionality reduction. We discuss a solution to this in Section 20.4.7.

20.4.7   Maximum variance unfolding (MVU)

kPCA with certain kernels, such as RBF, might not result in a low dimensional embedding, as discussed in Section 20.4.6. This observation led to the development of the **semidefinite embedding**

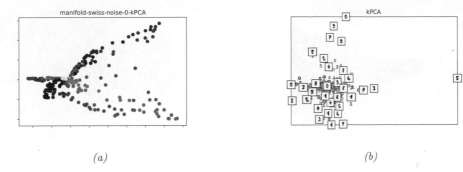

Figure 20.36: Kernel PCA applied to (a) Swiss roll. Generated by manifold_swiss_sklearn.ipynb. *(b) UCI digits. Generated by* manifold_digits_sklearn.ipynb.

algorithm [WSS04], also called **maximum variance unfolding**, which tries to learn an embedding $\{z_i\}$ such that

$$\max \sum_{ij} ||z_i - z_j||_2^2 \quad \text{s.t.} \quad ||z_i - z_j||_2^2 = ||x_i - x_j||_2^2 \text{ for all } (i,j) \in G \tag{20.115}$$

where G is the nearest neighbor graph (as in Isomap). This approach explicitly tries to 'unfold' the data manifold while respecting the nearest neighbor constraints.

This can be reformulated as a **semidefinite programming** (SDP) problem by defining the kernel matrix $\mathbf{K} = \mathbf{ZZ}^\mathsf{T}$ and then optimizing

$$\max \operatorname{tr}(\mathbf{K}) \quad \text{s.t.} \quad ||z_i - z_j||_2^2 = ||x_i - x_j||_2^2, \ \sum_{ij} K_{ij} = 0, \ \mathbf{K} \succ 0 \tag{20.116}$$

The resulting kernel is then passed to kPCA, and the resulting eigenvectors give the low dimensional embedding.

20.4.8 Local linear embedding (LLE)

The techniques we have discussed so far all rely on an eigendecomposition of a full matrix of pairwise similarities, either in the ambient space (PCA), in feature space (kPCA), or along the KNN graph (Isomap). In this section, we discuss **local linear embedding** (LLE) [RS00], a technique that solves a sparse eigenproblem, thus focusing more on local structure in the data.

LLE assumes the data manifold around each point x_i is locally linear. The best linear approximation can be found by predicting x_i as a linear combination of its K nearest neighbors using reconstruction weights w_i. This can be found by solving

$$\hat{\mathbf{W}} = \min_{\mathbf{W}} \sum_{i=1}^{N} (x_i - \sum_{j=1}^{N} w_{ij} x_j)^2 \tag{20.117}$$

$$\text{subject to} \begin{cases} w_{ij} = 0 & \text{if } x_j \notin \operatorname{nbr}(x_i, K) \\ \sum_{j=1}^{N} w_{ij} = 1 & \text{for } i = 1 : N \end{cases} \tag{20.118}$$

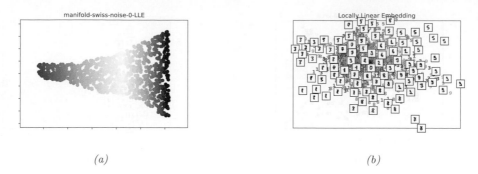

Figure 20.37: LLE applied to (a) Swiss roll. Generated by manifold_ swiss_ sklearn.ipynb. (b) UCI digits. Generated by manifold_ digits_ sklearn.ipynb.

Note that we need the sum-to-one constraint on the weights to prevent the trivial solution $\mathbf{W} = \mathbf{0}$. The resulting vector of weights $\boldsymbol{w}_{i,:}$ constitute the **barycentric coordinates** of $\boldsymbol{x}_i$.

Any linear mapping of this hyperplane to a lower dimensional space preserves the reconstruction weights, and thus the local geometry. Thus we can solve for the low-dimensional embeddings for each point by solving

$$\hat{\mathbf{Z}} = \underset{\mathbf{Z}}{\operatorname{argmin}} \sum_i ||\boldsymbol{z}_i - \sum_{j=1}^N \hat{w}_{ij}\boldsymbol{z}_j||_2^2 \tag{20.119}$$

where $\hat{w}_{ij} = 0$ if j is not one of the K nearest neighbors of i. We can rewrite this loss as

$$\mathcal{L}(\mathbf{Z}) = ||\mathbf{Z} - \mathbf{W}\mathbf{Z}||^2 = \mathbf{Z}^{\mathsf{T}}(\mathbf{I} - \mathbf{W})^{\mathsf{T}}(\mathbf{I} - \mathbf{W})\mathbf{Z} \tag{20.120}$$

Thus the solution is given by the eigenvectors of $(\mathbf{I} - \mathbf{W})^{\mathsf{T}}(\mathbf{I} - \mathbf{W})$ corresponding to the smallest nonzero eigenvalues, as shown in Section 7.4.8.

See Figure 20.37 for some the results on LLE on our running example. In this case, the results do not seem as good as those produced by Isomap. However, the method tends to be somewhat less sensitive to short-circuiting (noise).

20.4.9   Laplacian eigenmaps

In this section, we describe **Laplacian eigenmaps** or **spectral embedding** [BN01]. The idea is to compute a low-dimensional representation of the data in which the weighted distances between a datapoint and its K nearest neighbors are minimized. We put more weight on the first nearest neighbor than the second, etc. We give the details below.

20.4.9.1   Using eigenvectors of the graph Laplacian to compute embeddings

We want to find embeddings which minimize

$$\mathcal{L}(\mathbf{Z}) = \sum_{(i,j) \in E} W_{i,j} ||\boldsymbol{z}_i - \boldsymbol{z}_j||_2^2 \tag{20.121}$$

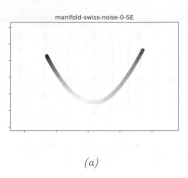

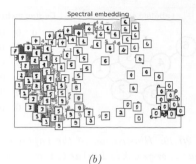

(a)   *(b)*

Figure 20.38: Laplacian eigenmaps applied to (a) Swiss roll. Generated by manifold_swiss_sklearn.ipynb. (b) UCI digits. Generated by manifold_digits_sklearn.ipynb.

where $W_{ij} = \exp(-\frac{1}{2\sigma^2}||\boldsymbol{x}_i - \boldsymbol{x}_j||_2^2)$ if $i - j$ are neighbors in the KNN graph and 0 otherwise. We add the constraint $\mathbf{Z}^\mathsf{T}\mathbf{D}\mathbf{Z} = \mathbf{I}$ to avoid the degenerate solution where $\mathbf{Z} = \mathbf{0}$, where $\mathbf{D}$ is the diagonal weight matrix storing the degree of each node, $D_{ii} = \sum_j W_{i,j}$.

We can rewrite the above objective as follows:

$$\mathcal{L}(\mathbf{Z}) = \sum_{ij} W_{ij}(||\boldsymbol{z}_i||^2 + ||\boldsymbol{z}_j||^2 - 2\boldsymbol{z}_i^\mathsf{T}\boldsymbol{z}_j) \tag{20.122}$$

$$= \sum_i D_{ii}||\boldsymbol{z}_i||^2 + \sum_j D_{jj}||\boldsymbol{z}_j||^2 - 2\sum_{ij} W_{ij}\boldsymbol{z}_i\boldsymbol{z}_j^\mathsf{T} \tag{20.123}$$

$$= 2\mathrm{tr}(\mathbf{Z}^\mathsf{T}\mathbf{D}\mathbf{Z}) - 2\mathrm{tr}(\mathbf{Z}^\mathsf{T}\mathbf{W}\mathbf{Z}) = 2\mathrm{tr}(\mathbf{Z}^\mathsf{T}\mathbf{L}\mathbf{Z}) \tag{20.124}$$

where $\mathbf{L} = \mathbf{D} - \mathbf{W}$ is the graph Laplacian (see Section 20.4.9.2). One can show that minimizing this is equivalent to solving the (generalized) eigenvalue problem $\mathbf{L}\boldsymbol{z}_i = \lambda_i\mathbf{D}\boldsymbol{z}_i$ for the L smallest nonzero eigenvalues.

See Figure 20.38 for the results of applying this method (with an RBF kernel) to our running example.

20.4.9.2 What is the graph Laplacian?

We saw above that we can compute the eigenvectors of the graph Laplacian in order to learn a good embedding of the high dimensional points. In this section, we give some intuition as to why this works.

Let $\mathbf{W}$ be a symmetric weight matrix for a graph, where $W_{ij} = W_{ji} \geq 0$. Let $\mathbf{D} = \mathrm{diag}(d_i)$ be a diagonal matrix containing the weighted degree of each node, $d_i = \sum_j w_{ij}$. We define the **graph Laplacian** as follows:

$$\mathbf{L} \triangleq \mathbf{D} - \mathbf{W} \tag{20.125}$$

Labelled graph	Degree matrix	Adjacency matrix	Laplacian matrix
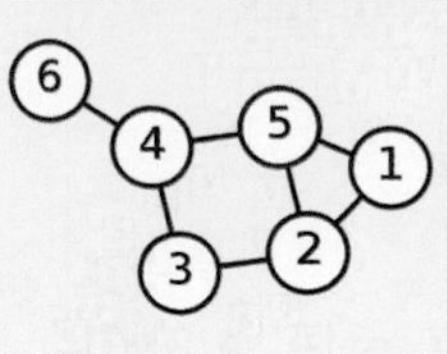 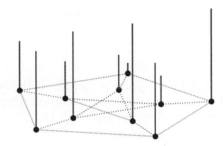	$\begin{pmatrix} 2 & 0 & 0 & 0 & 0 & 0 \\ 0 & 3 & 0 & 0 & 0 & 0 \\ 0 & 0 & 2 & 0 & 0 & 0 \\ 0 & 0 & 0 & 3 & 0 & 0 \\ 0 & 0 & 0 & 0 & 3 & 0 \\ 0 & 0 & 0 & 0 & 0 & 1 \end{pmatrix}$	$\begin{pmatrix} 0 & 1 & 0 & 0 & 1 & 0 \\ 1 & 0 & 1 & 0 & 1 & 0 \\ 0 & 1 & 0 & 1 & 0 & 0 \\ 0 & 0 & 1 & 0 & 1 & 1 \\ 1 & 1 & 0 & 1 & 0 & 0 \\ 0 & 0 & 0 & 1 & 0 & 0 \end{pmatrix}$	$\begin{pmatrix} 2 & -1 & 0 & 0 & -1 & 0 \\ -1 & 3 & -1 & 0 & -1 & 0 \\ 0 & -1 & 2 & -1 & 0 & 0 \\ 0 & 0 & -1 & 3 & -1 & -1 \\ -1 & -1 & 0 & -1 & 3 & 0 \\ 0 & 0 & 0 & -1 & 0 & 1 \end{pmatrix}$

Figure 20.39: Illustration of the Laplacian matrix derived from an undirected graph. From `https://en.`
`wikipedia.org/wiki/Laplacian_matrix`. *Used with kind permission of Wikipedia author AzaToth.*

*Figure 20.40: Illustration of a (positive) function defined on a graph. From Figure 1 of [Shu+13]. Used with
kind permission of Pascal Frossard.*

Thus the elements of $\mathbf{L}$ are given by

$$L_{ij} = \begin{cases} d_i & \text{if } i = j \\ -w_{ij} & \text{if } i \neq j \text{ and } w_{ij} \neq 0 \\ 0 & \text{otherwise} \end{cases} \tag{20.126}$$

See Figure 20.39 for an example of how to compute this.

Suppose we associate a value $f_i \in \mathbb{R}$ with each node i in the graph (see Figure 20.40 for example).
Then we can use the graph Laplacian as a difference operator, to compute a discrete derivative of
the function at a point:

$$(\mathbf{L}\boldsymbol{f})(i) = \sum_{j \in \text{nbr}_i} W_{ij}[f(i) - f(j)] \tag{20.127}$$

where nbr_i is the set of neighbors of node i. We can also compute an overall measure of "smoothness" of the function f by computing its **Dirichlet energy** as follows:

$$\boldsymbol{f}^T \mathbf{L} \boldsymbol{f} = \boldsymbol{f}^T \mathbf{D} \boldsymbol{f} - \boldsymbol{f}^T \mathbf{W} \boldsymbol{f} = \sum_i d_i f_i^2 - \sum_{i,j} f_i f_j w_{ij} \tag{20.128}$$

$$= \frac{1}{2} \left(\sum_i d_i f_i^2 - 2 \sum_{i,j} f_i f_j w_{ij} + \sum_j d_j f_j^2 \right) = \frac{1}{2} \sum_{i,j} w_{ij} (f_i - f_j)^2 \tag{20.129}$$

By studying the eigenvalues and eigenvectors of the Laplacian matrix, we can determine various useful properties of the function. (Applying linear algebra to study the adjacency matrix of a graph, or related matrices, is called **spectral graph theory** [Chu97].) For example, we see that $\mathbf{L}$ is symmetric and positive semi-definite, since we have $\boldsymbol{f}^T \mathbf{L} \boldsymbol{f} \geq 0$ for all $\boldsymbol{f} \in \mathbb{R}^N$, which follows from Equation (20.129) due to the assumption that $w_{ij} \geq 0$. Consequently $\mathbf{L}$ has N non-negative, real-valued eigenvalues, $0 \leq \lambda_1 \leq \lambda_2 \leq \ldots \leq \lambda_N$. The corresponding eigenvectors form an orthogonal basis for the function f defined on the graph, in order of decreasing smoothness.

In Section 20.4.9.1, we discuss Laplacian eigenmaps, which is a way to learn low dimensional embeddings for high dimensional data vectors. The approach is to let $z_{id} = f_i^d$ be the d'th embedding dimension for input i, and then to find a basis for these functions (i.e., embedding of the points) that varies smoothly over the graph, thus respecting distance of the points in ambient space.

There are many other applications of the graph Laplacian in ML. For example, in Section 21.5.1, we discuss normalized cuts, which is a way to learn a clustering of high dimensional data vectors based on pairwise similarity; and [WTN19] discusses how to use the eigenvectors of the state transition matrix to learn representations for RL.

20.4.10   t-SNE

In this section, we describe a very popular nonconvex technique for learning low dimensional embeddings called **t-SNE** [MH08]. This extends the earlier **stochastic neighbor embedding** method of [HR03], so we first describe SNE, before describing the t-SNE extension.

20.4.10.1   Stochastic neighborhood embedding (SNE)

The basic idea in SNE is to convert high-dimensional Euclidean distances into conditional probabilities that represent similarities. More precisely, we define $p_{j|i}$ to be the probability that point i would pick point j as its neighbor if neighbors were picked in proportion to their probability under a Gaussian centered at $\boldsymbol{x}_i$:

$$p_{j|i} = \frac{\exp(-\frac{1}{2\sigma_i^2} ||\boldsymbol{x}_i - \boldsymbol{x}_j||^2)}{\sum_{k \neq i} \exp(-\frac{1}{2\sigma_i^2} ||\boldsymbol{x}_i - \boldsymbol{x}_k||^2)} \tag{20.130}$$

Here σ_i^2 is the variance for data point i, which can be used to "magnify" the scale of points in dense regions of input space, and diminish the scale in sparser regions. (We discuss how to estimate the length scales σ_i^2 shortly).

Let $\boldsymbol{z}_i$ be the low dimensional embedding representing $\boldsymbol{x}_i$. We define similarities in the low dimensional space in an analogous way:

$$q_{j|i} = \frac{\exp(-||\boldsymbol{z}_i - \boldsymbol{z}_j||^2)}{\sum_{k \neq i} \exp(-||\boldsymbol{z}_i - \boldsymbol{z}_k||^2)} \tag{20.131}$$

In this case, the variance is fixed to a constant; changing it would just rescale the learned map, and not change its topology.

If the embedding is a good one, then $q_{j|i}$ should match $p_{j|i}$. Therefore, SNE defines the objective to be

$$\mathcal{L} = \sum_i D_{\mathbb{KL}}\left(P_i \parallel Q_i\right) = \sum_i \sum_j p_{j|i} \log \frac{p_{j|i}}{q_{j|i}} \tag{20.132}$$

where P_i is the conditional distribution over all other data points given $\boldsymbol{x}_i$, Q_i is the conditional distribution over all other latent points given $\boldsymbol{z}_i$, and $D_{\mathbb{KL}}\left(P_i \parallel Q_i\right)$ is the KL divergence (Section 6.2) between the distributions.

Note that this is an asymmetric objective. In particular, there is a large cost if a small $q_{j|i}$ is used to model a large $p_{j|i}$. This objective will prefer to pull distant points together rather than push nearby points apart. We can get a better idea of the geometry by looking at the gradient for each embedding vector, which is given by

$$\nabla_{\boldsymbol{z}_i} \mathcal{L}(\mathbf{Z}) = 2 \sum_j (\boldsymbol{z}_j - \boldsymbol{z}_i)(p_{j|i} - q_{j|i} + p_{i|j} - q_{i|j}) \tag{20.133}$$

Thus points are pulled towards each other if the p's are bigger than the q's, and repelled if the q's are bigger than the p's.

Although this is an intuitively sensible objective, it is not convex. Nevertheless it can be minimized using SGD. In practice, it helps to add Gaussian noise to the embedding points, and to gradually anneal the amount of noise. [Hin13] recommends to "spend a long time at the noise level at which the global structure starts to form from the hot plasma of map points" before reducing it.[6]

20.4.10.2 Symmetric SNE

There is a slightly simpler version of SNE that minimizes a single KL between the joint distribution P in high dimensional space and Q in low dimensional space:

$$\mathcal{L} = D_{\mathbb{KL}}\left(P \parallel Q\right) = \sum_{i<j} p_{ij} \log \frac{p_{ij}}{q_{ij}} \tag{20.134}$$

This is called **symmetric SNE**.

The obvious way to define p_{ij} is to use

$$p_{ij} = \frac{\exp(-\frac{1}{2\sigma^2}||\boldsymbol{x}_i - \boldsymbol{x}_j||^2)}{\sum_{k<l} \exp(-\frac{1}{2\sigma^2}||\boldsymbol{x}_k - \boldsymbol{x}_l||^2)} \tag{20.135}$$

---

6. See [Ros98; WF20] for a discussion of annealing and phase transitions in unsupervised learning. See also [CP10] for a discussion of the **elastic embedding** algorithm, which uses a homotopy method to more efficiently optimize a model that is related to both SNE and Laplacian eigenmaps.

We can define q_{ij} similarily.

The corresponding gradient becomes

$$\nabla_{z_i}\mathcal{L}(\mathbf{Z}) = 2\sum_j (z_j - z_i)(p_{ij} - q_{ij}) \tag{20.136}$$

As before, points are pulled towards each other if the p's are bigger than the q's, and repelled if the q's are bigger than the p's.

Although symmetric SNE is slightly easier to implement, it loses the nice property of regular SNE that the data is its own optimal embedding if the embedding dimension L is set equal to the ambient dimension D. Nevertheless, the methods seems to give similar results in practice on real datasets where $L \ll D$.

20.4.10.3   t-distributed SNE

A fundamental problem with SNE and many other embedding techniques is that they tend to squeeze points that are relatively far away in the high dimensional space close together in the low dimensional (usually 2d) embedding space; this is called the **crowding problem**, and arises due to the use of squared errors (or Gaussian probabilities).

One solution to this is to use a probability distribution in latent space that has heavier tails, which eliminates the unwanted attractive forces between points that are relatively far in the high dimensional space. An obvious choice is the Student-t distribution (Section 2.7.1). In t-SNE, they set the degree of freedom parameter to $\nu = 1$, so the distribution becomes equivalent to a Cauchy:

$$q_{ij} = \frac{(1 + ||z_i - z_j||^2)^{-1}}{\sum_{k<l}(1 + ||z_k - z_l||^2)^{-1}} \tag{20.137}$$

We can use the same global KL objective as in Equation (20.134). For t-SNE, the gradient turns out to be

$$\nabla_{z_i}\mathcal{L} = 4\sum_j (p_{ij} - q_{ij})(z_i - z_j)(1 + ||z_i - z_j||^2)^{-1} \tag{20.138}$$

The gradient for symmetric (Gaussian) SNE is the same, but lacks the $(1 + ||z_i - z_j||^2)^{-1}$ term. This term is useful because $(1 + ||z_i - z_j||^2)^{-1}$ acts like an inverse square law. This means that points in embedding space act like stars and galaxies, forming many well-separated clusters (galaxies) each of which has many stars tightly packed inside. This can be useful for separating different classes of data in an unsupervised way (see Figure 20.41 for an example).

20.4.10.4   Choosing the length scale

An important parameter in t-SNE is the local bandwidth σ_i^2. This is usually chosen so that P_i has a perplexity chosen by the user.[7] This can be interpreted as a smooth measure of the effective number of neighbors.

_____

[7] The perplexity is defined to be $2^{\mathbb{H}(P_i)}$, where $\mathbb{H}(P_i) = -\sum_j p_{j|i} \log_2 p_{j|i}$ is the entropy; see Section 6.1.5 for details. radius around each point (large value of σ_i) will result in a high entropy, and thus high perplexity.

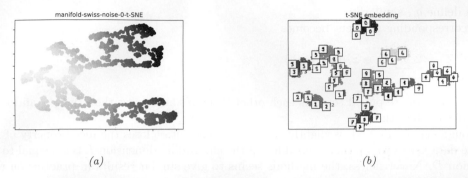

(a)   (b)

Figure 20.41: *tSNE applied to (a) Swiss roll. Generated by manifold_swiss_sklearn.ipynb. (b) UCI digits. Generated by manifold_digits_sklearn.ipynb.*

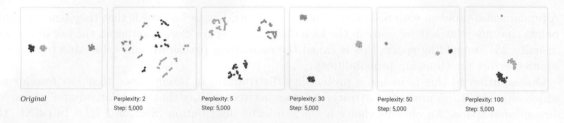

Figure 20.42: *Illustration of the effect of changing the perplexity parameter when t-SNE is applied to some 2d data. From [WVJ16]. See* `http://distill.pub/2016/misread-tsne` *for an animated version of these figures. Used with kind permission of Martin Wattenberg.*

Unfortunately, the results of t-SNE can be quite sensitive to the perplexity parameter, so it is wise to run the algorithm with many different values. This is illustrated in Figure 20.42. The input data is 2d, so there is no distortion generating by mapping to a 2d latent space. If the perplexity is too small, the method tends to find structure within each cluster which is not truly present. At perplexity 30 (the default for scikit-learn), the clusters seem equi-distant in embedding space, even though some are closer than others in the data space. Many other caveats in interpreting t-SNE plots can be found in [WVJ16].

20.4.10.5   Computational issues

The naive implementation of t-SNE takes $O(N^2)$ time, as can be seen from the gradient term in Equation (20.138). A faster version can be created by leveraging an analogy to N-body simulation in physics. In particular, the gradient requires computing the force of N points on each of N points. However, points that are far away can be grouped into clusters (computationally speaking), their effective force can be approximated by a few representative points per cluster. We can approximate the forces using the **Barnes-Hut algorithm** [BH86], which takes $O(N \log N)$ ti proposed in [Maa14]. Unfortunately, this only works well for low dimensional embeddings, s $L = 2$.

20.4.10.6 UMAP

Various extensions of tSNE have been proposed, that try to improve its speed, the quality of the embedding space, or the ability to embed into more than 2 dimensions.

One popular recent extension is called **UMAP** (which stands for "Uniform Manifold Approximation and Projection"), was proposed in [MHM18]. At a high level, this is similar to tSNE, but it tends to preserve global structure better, and it is much faster. This makes it easier to try multiple values of the hyperparameters. For an interactive tutorial on UMAP, and a comparison to tSNE, see [CP19].

20.5 Word embeddings

Words are categorical random variables, so their corresponding one-hot vector representations are sparse. The problem with this binary representation is that semantically similar words may have very different vector representations. For example, the pair of related words "man" and "woman" will be Hamming distance 1 apart, as will the pair of unrelated words "man" and "banana".

The standard way to solve this problem is to use **word embeddings**, in which we map each sparse one-hot vector, $s_{n,t} \in \{0,1\}^M$, representing the t'th word in document n, to a lower-dimensional dense vector, $z_{n,t} \in \mathbb{R}^D$, such that semantically similar words are placed close by. This can significantly help with data sparsity. There are many ways to learn such embeddings, as we discuss below.

Before discussing methods, we have to define what we mean by "semantically similar" words. We will assume that two words are semantically similar if they occur in similar contexts. This is known as the **distributional hypothesis** [Har54], which is often summarized by the phrase (originally from [Fir57]) "a word is characterized by the company it keeps". Thus the methods we discuss will all learn a mapping from a word's context to an embedding vector for that word.

20.5.1 Latent semantic analysis / indexing

In this section, we discuss a simple way to learn word embeddings based on singular value decomposition (Section 7.5) of a term-frequency count matrix.

20.5.1.1 Latent semantic indexing (LSI)

Let C_{ij} be the number of times "term" i occurs in "context" j. The definition of what we mean by "term" is application-specific. In English, we often take it to be the set of unique tokens that are separated by punctuation or whitespace; for simplicity, we will call these "words". However, we may preprocess the text data to remove very frequent or infrequent words, or perform other kinds of preprocessing. as we discuss in Section 1.5.4.1.

The definition of what we mean by "context" is also application-specific. In this section, we count how many times word i occurs in each document $j \in \{1, \dots, N\}$ from a set or **corpus** of documents; the resulting matrx $\mathbf{C}$ is called a **term-document frequency matrix**, as in Figure 1.15. (Sometimes we apply the TF-IDF transformation to the counts, as discussed in Section 1.5.4.2.)

Let $\mathbf{C} \in \mathbb{R}^{M \times N}$ be the count matrix, and let $\hat{\mathbf{C}}$ be the rank K approximation that minimizes the following loss:

$$\mathcal{L}(\hat{\mathbf{C}}) = ||\mathbf{C} - \hat{\mathbf{C}}||_F = \sum_{ij}(C_{ij} - \hat{C}_{ij})^2 \tag{20.139}$$

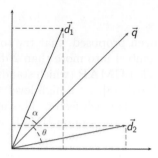

Figure 20.43: Illustration of the cosine similarity between a query vector $\boldsymbol{q}$ and two document vectors $\boldsymbol{d}_1$ and $\boldsymbol{d}_2$. Since angle α is less than angle θ, we see that the query is more similar to document 1. From `https://en.wikipedia.org/wiki/Vector_space_model`*. Used with kind permission of Wikipedia author Riclas.*

One can show that the minimizer of this is given by the rank K truncated SVD approximation, $\hat{\mathbf{C}} = \mathbf{USV}$. This means we can represent each c_{ij} as a bilinear product:

$$c_{ij} \approx \sum_{k=1}^{K} u_{ik} s_k v_{jk} \qquad (20.140)$$

We define $\boldsymbol{u}_i$ to be the embedding for word i, and $\boldsymbol{s} \odot \boldsymbol{v}_j$ to be the embedding for context j.

We can use these embeddings for **document retrieval**. The idea is to compute an embedding for the query words using $\boldsymbol{u}_i$, and to compare this to the embedding of all the documents or contexts $\boldsymbol{v}_j$. This is known as **latent semantic indexing** or **LSI** [Dee+90].

In more detail, suppose the query is a bag of words $w_1, \ldots, w_B$; we represent this by the vector $\boldsymbol{q} = \frac{1}{B} \sum_{b=1}^{B} \boldsymbol{u}_{w_b}$, where $\boldsymbol{u}_{w_b}$ is the embedding for word w_b. Let document j be represented by $\boldsymbol{v}_j$. We then rank documents by the **cosine similarity** between the query vector and document, defined by

$$\text{sim}(\boldsymbol{q}, \boldsymbol{d}) = \frac{\boldsymbol{q}^\mathsf{T} \boldsymbol{d}}{||\boldsymbol{q}|| \, ||\boldsymbol{d}||} \qquad (20.141)$$

where $||\boldsymbol{q}|| = \sqrt{\sum_i q_i^2}$ is the ℓ_2-norm of $\boldsymbol{q}$. This measures the angles between the two vectors, as shown in Figure 20.43. Note that if the vectors are unit norm, cosine similarity is the same as inner product; it is also equal to the squared Euclidean distance, up to a change of sign and an irrelevant additive constant:

$$||\boldsymbol{q} - \boldsymbol{d}||^2 = (\boldsymbol{q} - \boldsymbol{d})^\mathsf{T}(\boldsymbol{q} - \boldsymbol{d}) = \boldsymbol{q}^\mathsf{T}\boldsymbol{q} + \boldsymbol{d}^\mathsf{T}\boldsymbol{d} - 2\boldsymbol{q}^\mathsf{T}\boldsymbol{d} = 2(1 - \text{sim}(\boldsymbol{q}, \boldsymbol{d})) \qquad (20.142)$$

20.5.1.2   Latent semantic analysis (LSA)

Now suppose we define context more generally to be some local neighborhood of words $j \in \{1, \ldots, M^h\}$, where h is the window size. Thus C_{ij} is how many times word i occurs in a neighborhood of type j. We can compute the SVD of this matrix as before, to get $c_{ij} \approx \sum_{k=1}^{K} u_{ik} s_k v_{jk}$. We define $\boldsymbol{u}_i$ to be the embedding for word i, and $\boldsymbol{s} \odot \boldsymbol{v}_j$ to be the embedding for context j. This is known as **latent semantic analysis** or **LSA** [Dee+90].

For example, suppose we compute $\mathbf{C}$ on the British National Corpus.[8] For each word, let us retrieve the K nearest neighbors in embedding space ranked by cosine similarity (i.e., normalized inner product). If the query word is "dog", and we use $h = 2$ or $h = 30$, the nearest neighbors are as follows:

```
h=2: cat, horse, fox, pet, rabbit, pig, animal, mongrel, sheep, pigeon
h=30: kennel, puppy, pet, bitch, terrier, rottweiler, canine, cat, to bark
```

The 2-word context window is more sensitive to syntax, while the 30-word window is more sensitive to semantics. The "optimal" value of context size h depends on the application.

20.5.1.3 PMI

In practice LSA (and other similar methods) give much better results if we replace the raw counts C_{ij} with **pointwise mutual information** (**PMI**) [CH90], defined as

$$\mathbb{PMI}(i, j) = \log \frac{p(i, j)}{p(i)p(j)} \tag{20.143}$$

If word i is strongly associated with context j, we will have $\mathbb{PMI}(i, j) > 0$. If the PMI is negative, it means i and j co-occur less often that if they were independent; however, such negative correlations can be unreliable, so it is common to use the **positive PMI**: $\mathbb{PPMI}(i, j) = \max(\mathbb{PMI}(i, j), 0)$. In [BL07b], they show that SVD applied to the PPMI matrix results in word embeddings that perform well on a many tasks related to word meaning. See Section 20.5.5 for a theoretical model that explains this empirical performance.

20.5.2 Word2vec

In this section, we discuss the popular **word2vec** model from [Mik+13a; Mik+13b], which are "shallow" neural nets for predicting a word given its context. In Section 20.5.5, we will discuss the connections with SVD of the PMI matrix.

There are two versions of the word2vec model. The first is called CBOW, which stands for "continuous bag of words". The second is called skipgram. We discuss both of these below.

20.5.2.1 Word2vec CBOW model

In the continuous bag of words (**CBOW**) model (see Figure 20.44(a)), the log likelihood of a sequence of words is computed using the following model:

$$\log p(\boldsymbol{w}) = \sum_{t=1}^{T} \log p(w_t | \boldsymbol{w}_{t-m:t+m}) = \sum_{t=1}^{T} \log \frac{\exp(\boldsymbol{v}_{w_t}^{\mathsf{T}} \overline{\boldsymbol{v}}_t)}{\sum_{w'} \exp(\boldsymbol{v}_{w'}^{\mathsf{T}} \overline{\boldsymbol{v}}_t)} \tag{20.144}$$

$$= \sum_{t=1}^{T} \boldsymbol{v}_{w_t}^{\mathsf{T}} \overline{\boldsymbol{v}}_t - \log \sum_{i \in \mathcal{V}} \exp(\boldsymbol{v}_i^{\mathsf{T}} \overline{\boldsymbol{v}}_t) \tag{20.145}$$

---

8. This example is taken from [Eis19, p312].

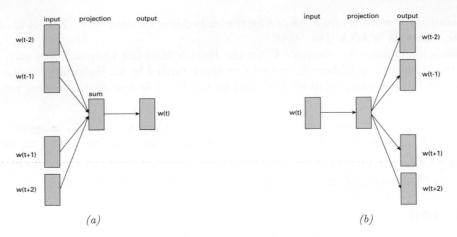

Figure 20.44: Illustration of word2vec model with window size of 2. (a) CBOW version. (b) Skip-gram version.

where $\boldsymbol{v}_{w_t}$ is the vector for the word at location w_t, $\mathcal{V}$ is the set of all words, m is the context size, and

$$\bar{\boldsymbol{v}}_t = \frac{1}{2m} \sum_{h=1}^{m} (\boldsymbol{v}_{w_{t+h}} + \boldsymbol{v}_{w_{t-h}}) \qquad (20.146)$$

is the average of the word vectors in the window around word w_t. Thus we try to predict each word given its context. The model is called CBOW because it uses a bag of words assumption for the context, and represents each word by a continuous embedding.

20.5.2.2 Word2vec Skip-gram model

In CBOW, each word is predicted from its context. A variant of this is to predict the context (surrounding words) given each word. This yields the following objective:

$$-\log p(\boldsymbol{w}) = -\sum_{t=1}^{T} \left[\sum_{j=1}^{m} \log p(w_{t-j}|w_t) + \log p(w_{t+j}|w_t) \right] \qquad (20.147)$$

$$= -\sum_{t=1}^{T} \sum_{-m \leq j \leq m, j \neq 0} \log p(w_{t+j}|w_t) \qquad (20.148)$$

where m is the context window length. We define the log probability of some other context word w_o given the central word w_c to be

$$\log p(w_o|w_c) = \boldsymbol{u}_o^\mathsf{T} \boldsymbol{v}_c - \log \left(\sum_{i \in \mathcal{V}} \exp(\boldsymbol{u}_i^\mathsf{T} \boldsymbol{v}_c) \right) \qquad (20.149)$$

where $\mathcal{V}$ is the vocabulary. Here $\boldsymbol{u}_i$ is the embedding of a word if used as context, and $\boldsymbol{v}_i$ is the embedding of a word if used as a central (target) word to be predicted. This model is known as the **skipgram model**. See Figure 20.44(b) for an illustration.

20.5.2.3 Negative sampling

Computing the conditional probability of each word using Equation (20.149) is expensive, due to the need to normalize over all possible words in the vocabulary. This makes it slow to compute the log likelihood and its gradient, for both the CBOW and skip-gram models.

In [Mik+13b], they propose a fast approximation, called **skip-gram with negative sampling** (**SGNS**). The basic idea is to create a set of $K + 1$ context words for each central word w_t, and to label the one that actually occurs as positive, and the rest as negative. The negative words are called noise words, and can be sampled from a reweighted unigram distribution, $p(w) \propto \text{freq}(w)^{3/4}$, which has the effect of redistributing probability mass from common to rare words. The conditional probability is now approximated by

$$p(w_{t+j}|w_t) = p(D = 1|w_t, w_{t+j}) \prod_{k=1}^{K} p(D = 0|w_t, w_k) \tag{20.150}$$

where $w_k \sim p(w)$ are noise words, and $D = 1$ is the event that the word pair actually occurs in the data, and $D = 0$ is the event that the word pair does not occur. The binary probabilities are given by

$$p(D = 1|w_t, w_{t+j}) = \sigma(\boldsymbol{u}_{w_{t+j}}^{\mathsf{T}} \boldsymbol{v}_{w_t}) \tag{20.151}$$

$$p(D = 0|w_t, w_k) = 1 - \sigma(\boldsymbol{u}_{w_k}^{\mathsf{T}} \boldsymbol{v}_{w_t}) \tag{20.152}$$

To train this model, we just need to compute the contexts for each central word, and a set of negative noise words. We associate a label of 1 with the context words, and a label of 0 with the noise words. We can then compute the log probability of the data, and optimize the embedding vectors $\boldsymbol{u}_i$ and $\boldsymbol{v}_i$ for each word using SGD. See skipgram_jax.ipynb for some sample code.

20.5.3 GloVE

A popular alternative to Skipgram is the **GloVe** model of [PSM14a]. (GloVe stands for "global vectors for word representation".) This method uses a simpler objective, which is much faster to optimize.

To explain the method, recall that in the skipgram model, the predicted conditional probability of word j occuring in the context window of central word i as

$$q_{ij} = \frac{\exp(\boldsymbol{u}_j^{\mathsf{T}} \boldsymbol{v}_i)}{\sum_{k \in \mathcal{V}} \exp(\boldsymbol{u}_k^{\mathsf{T}} \boldsymbol{v}_i)} \tag{20.153}$$

Let x_{ij} be the number of times word j occurs in any context window of i. (Note that if word i occurs in the window of j, then j will occur in the window of i, so we have $x_{ij} = x_{ji}$.) Then we can rewrite Equation (20.148) as follows:

$$\mathcal{L} = -\sum_{i \in \mathcal{V}} \sum_{j \in \mathcal{V}} x_{ij} \log q_{ij} \tag{20.154}$$

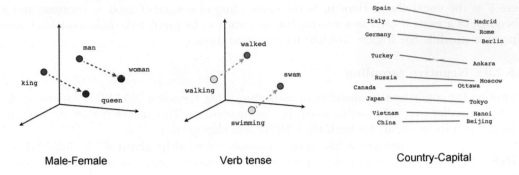

Figure 20.45: Visualization of arithmetic operations in word2vec embedding space. From `https://www.`
`tensorflow.org/tutorials/representation/word2vec.`

If we define $p_{ij} = x_{ij}/x_i$ to be the empirical probability of word j occuring in the context window of central word i, we can rewrite the skipgram loss as a cross entropy loss:

$$\mathcal{L} = -\sum_{i\in\mathcal{V}} x_i \sum_{j\in\mathcal{V}} p_{ij} \log q_{ij} \tag{20.155}$$

The problem with this objective is that computing q_{ij} is expensive, due to the need to normalize over all words. In GloVe, we work with unnormalized probabilities, $p'_{ij} = x_{ij}$ and $q'_{ij} = \exp(\boldsymbol{u}_j^\mathsf{T}\boldsymbol{v}_i + b_i + c_j)$, where b_i and c_j are bias terms to capture marginal probabilities. In addition, we minimize the squared loss, $(\log p'_{ij} - \log q'_{ij})^2$, which is more robust to errors in estimating small probablities than log loss. Finally, we upweight rare words for which $x_{ij} < c$, where $c = 100$, by weighting the squared errors by $h(x_{ij})$, where $h(x) = (x/c)^{0.75}$ if $x < c$, and $h(x) = 1$ otherwise. This gives the final GloVe objective:

$$\mathcal{L} = -\sum_{i\in\mathcal{V}}\sum_{j\in\mathcal{V}} h(x_{ij})(\boldsymbol{u}_j^\mathsf{T}\boldsymbol{v}_i + b_i + c_j - \log x_{ij})^2 \tag{20.156}$$

We can precompute x_{ij} offline, and then optimize the above objective using SGD. After training, we define the embedding of word i to be the average of $\boldsymbol{v}_i$ and $\boldsymbol{u}_i$.

Empirically GloVe gives similar results to skigram, but it is faster to train. See Section 20.5.5 for a theoretical model that explains why these methods work.

20.5.4   Word analogies

One of the most remarkable properties of word embeddings produced by word2vec, GloVe, and other similar methods is that the learned vector space seems to capture relational semantics in terms of simple vector addition. For example, consider the **word analogy problem** "man is to woman as king is to queen", often written as man:woman::king:queen. Suppose we are given the words a=man, b=woman, c=king; how do we find d=queen? Let $\boldsymbol{\delta} = \boldsymbol{v}_b - \boldsymbol{v}_a$ be the vector representing the concept of "converting the gender from male to female". Intuitively we can find word d by computing

$v_d = c + \delta$, and then finding the closest word in the vocabulary to v_d. See Figure 20.45 for an illustration of this process, and word_analogies_jax.ipynb for some code.

In [PSM14a], they conjecture that $a : b :: c : d$ holds iff for every word w in the vocabulary, we have

$$\frac{p(w|a)}{p(w|b)} \approx \frac{p(w|c)}{p(w|d)} \tag{20.157}$$

In [Aro+16], they show that this follows from the RAND-WALK modeling assumptions in Section 20.5.5. See also [AH19; EDH19] for other explanations of why word analogies work, based on different modeling assumptions.

20.5.5 RAND-WALK model of word embeddings

Word embeddings significantly improve the performance of various kinds of NLP models compared to using one-hot encodings for words. It is natural to wonder why the above word embeddings work so well. In this section, we give a simple generative model for text documents that explains this phenomenon, based on [Aro+16].

Consider a sequence of words $w_1, \ldots, w_T$. We assume each word is generated by a latent context or discourse vector $z_t \in \mathbb{R}^D$ using the following **log bilinear language model**, similar to [MH07]:

$$p(w_t = w|z_t) = \frac{\exp(z_t^\mathsf{T} v_w)}{\sum_{w'} \exp(z_t^\mathsf{T} v_{w'})} = \frac{\exp(z_t^\mathsf{T} v_w)}{Z(z_t)} \tag{20.158}$$

where $v_w \in \mathbb{R}^D$ is the embedding for word w, and $Z(z_t)$ is the partition function. We assume $D < M$, the number of words in the vocabulary.

Let us further assume the prior for the word embeddings v_w is an isotropic Gaussian, and that the latent topic z_t undergoes a slow Gaussian random walk. (This is therefore called the **RAND-WALK** model.) Under this model, one can show that $Z(z_t)$ is approximately equal to a fixed constant, Z, independent of the context. This is known as the **self-normalization property** of log-linear models [AK15]. Furthermore, one can show that the pointwise mutual information of predictions from the model is given by

$$\mathbb{PMI}(w, w') = \frac{p(w, w')}{p(w)p(w')} \approx \frac{v_w^\mathsf{T} v_{w'}}{D} \tag{20.159}$$

We can therefore fit the RAND-WALK model by matching the model's predicted values for PMI with the empirical values, i.e., we minimize

$$\mathcal{L} = \sum_{w,w'} X_{w,w'} (\mathbb{PMI}(w, w') - v_w^\mathsf{T} v_{w'})^2 \tag{20.160}$$

where $X_{w,w'}$ is the number of times w and w' occur next to each other. This objective can be seen as a frequency-weighted version of the SVD loss in Equation (20.139). (See [LG14] for more connections between word embeddings and SVD.)

Furthermore, some additional approximations can be used to show that the NLL for the RAND-WALK model is equivalent to the CBOW and SGNS word2vec objectives. We can also derive the objective for GloVE from this approach.

20.5.6   Contextual word embeddings

Consider the sentences "I was eating an apple" and "I bought a new phone from Apple". The meaning of the word "apple" is different in both cases, but a fixed word embedding, of the type discussed in Section 20.5, would not be able to capture this. In Section 15.7, we discuss **contextual word embeddings**, where the embedding of a word is a function of all the words in its context (usually a sentence). This can give much improved results, and is currently the standard approach to representing natural language data, as a pre-processing step before doing transfer learning (see Section 19.2).

20.6   Exercises

Exercise 20.1 [EM for FA]

Derive the EM updates for the factor analysis model. For simplicity, you can optionally assume $\boldsymbol{\mu} = \mathbf{0}$ is fixed.

Exercise 20.2 [EM for mixFA *]

Derive the EM updates for a mixture of factor analysers.

Exercise 20.3 [Deriving the second principal component]

a. Let

$$J(\boldsymbol{v}_2, \boldsymbol{z}_2) = \frac{1}{n} \sum_{i=1}^{n} (\boldsymbol{x}_i - z_{i1}\boldsymbol{v}_1 - z_{i2}\boldsymbol{v}_2)^T (\boldsymbol{x}_i - z_{i1}\boldsymbol{v}_1 - z_{i2}\boldsymbol{v}_2) \tag{20.161}$$

Show that $\frac{\partial J}{\partial \boldsymbol{z}_2} = 0$ yields $z_{i2} = \boldsymbol{v}_2^T \boldsymbol{x}_i$.

b. Show that the value of $\boldsymbol{v}_2$ that minimizes

$$\tilde{J}(\boldsymbol{v}_2) = -\boldsymbol{v}_2^T \mathbf{C} \boldsymbol{v}_2 + \lambda_2 (\boldsymbol{v}_2^T \boldsymbol{v}_2 - 1) + \lambda_{12} (\boldsymbol{v}_2^T \boldsymbol{v}_1 - 0) \tag{20.162}$$

is given by the eigenvector of $\mathbf{C}$ with the second largest eigenvalue. Hint: recall that $\mathbf{C}\boldsymbol{v}_1 = \lambda_1 \boldsymbol{v}_1$ and $\frac{\partial \boldsymbol{x}^T \mathbf{A} \boldsymbol{x}}{\partial \boldsymbol{x}} = (\mathbf{A} + \mathbf{A}^T)\boldsymbol{x}$.

Exercise 20.4 [Deriving the residual error for PCA *]

a. Prove that

$$\left\| \boldsymbol{x}_i - \sum_{j=1}^{K} z_{ij}\boldsymbol{v}_j \right\|^2 = \boldsymbol{x}_i^T \boldsymbol{x}_i - \sum_{j=1}^{K} \boldsymbol{v}_j^T \boldsymbol{x}_i \boldsymbol{x}_i^T \boldsymbol{v}_j \tag{20.163}$$

Hint: first consider the case $K = 2$. Use the fact that $\boldsymbol{v}_j^T \boldsymbol{v}_j = 1$ and $\boldsymbol{v}_j^T \boldsymbol{v}_k = 0$ for $k \neq j$. Also, recall $z_{ij} = \boldsymbol{x}_i^T \boldsymbol{v}_j$.

b. Now show that

$$J_K \triangleq \frac{1}{n} \sum_{i=1}^{n} \left(\boldsymbol{x}_i^T \boldsymbol{x}_i - \sum_{j=1}^{K} \boldsymbol{v}_j^T \boldsymbol{x}_i \boldsymbol{x}_i^T \boldsymbol{v}_j \right) = \frac{1}{n} \sum_{i=1}^{n} \boldsymbol{x}_i^T \boldsymbol{x}_i - \sum_{j=1}^{K} \lambda_j \tag{20.164}$$

Hint: recall $\boldsymbol{v}_j^T \mathbf{C} \boldsymbol{v}_j = \lambda_j \boldsymbol{v}_j^T \boldsymbol{v}_j = \lambda_j$.

c. If $K = d$ there is no truncation, so $J_d = 0$. Use this to show that the error from only using $K < d$ terms is given by

$$J_K = \sum_{j=K+1}^{d} \lambda_j \tag{20.165}$$

Hint: partition the sum $\sum_{j=1}^{d} \lambda_j$ into $\sum_{j=1}^{K} \lambda_j$ and $\sum_{j=K+1}^{d} \lambda_j$.

Exercise 20.5 [PCA via successive deflation]

Let $v_1, v_2, \ldots, v_k$ be the first k eigenvectors with largest eigenvalues of $\mathbf{C} = \frac{1}{n}\mathbf{X}^T\mathbf{X}$, where $\mathbf{X}$ is the centered $N \times D$ design matrix; these are known as the principal basis vectors. These satisfy

$$v_j^T v_k = \begin{cases} 0 & \text{if } j \neq k \\ 1 & \text{if } j = k \end{cases} \tag{20.166}$$

We will construct a method for finding the v_j sequentially.

As we showed in class, v_1 is the first principal eigenvector of $\mathbf{C}$, and satisfies $\mathbf{C}v_1 = \lambda_1 v_1$. Now define $\tilde{x}_i$ as the orthogonal projection of x_i onto the space orthogonal to v_1:

$$\tilde{x}_i = \mathbf{P}_{\perp v_1}\, x_i = (\mathbf{I} - v_1 v_1^T)x_i \tag{20.167}$$

Define $\tilde{\mathbf{X}} = [\tilde{x}_1; \ldots; \tilde{x}_n]$ as the **deflated matrix** of rank $d - 1$, which is obtained by removing from the d dimensional data the component that lies in the direction of the first principal direction:

$$\tilde{\mathbf{X}} = (\mathbf{I} - v_1 v_1^T)^T \mathbf{X} = (\mathbf{I} - v_1 v_1^T)\mathbf{X} \tag{20.168}$$

a. Using the facts that $\mathbf{X}^T\mathbf{X}v_1 = n\lambda_1 v_1$ (and hence $v_1^T\mathbf{X}^T\mathbf{X} = n\lambda_1 v_1^T$) and $v_1^T v_1 = 1$, show that the covariance of the deflated matrix is given by

$$\tilde{\mathbf{C}} \triangleq \frac{1}{n}\tilde{\mathbf{X}}^T\tilde{\mathbf{X}} = \frac{1}{n}\mathbf{X}^T\mathbf{X} - \lambda_1 v_1 v_1^T \tag{20.169}$$

b. Let u be the principal eigenvector of $\tilde{\mathbf{C}}$. Explain why $u = v_2$. (You may assume u is unit norm.)

c. Suppose we have a simple method for finding the leading eigenvector and eigenvalue of a pd matrix, denoted by $[\lambda, u] = f(\mathbf{C})$. Write some pseudo code for finding the first K principal basis vectors of $\mathbf{X}$ that only uses the special f function and simple vector arithmetic, i.e., your code should not use SVD or the `eig` function. Hint: this should be a simple iterative routine that takes 2–3 lines to write. The input is $\mathbf{C}$, K and the function f, the output should be v_j and λ_j for $j = 1 : K$.

Exercise 20.6 [PPCA variance terms]

Recall that in the PPCA model, $\mathbf{C} = \mathbf{W}\mathbf{W}^T + \sigma^2\mathbf{I}$. We will show that this model correctly captures the variance of the data along the principal axes, and approximates the variance in all the remaining directions with a single average value σ^2.

Consider the variance of the predictive distribution $p(x)$ along some direction specified by the unit vector v, where $v^T v = 1$, which is given by $v^T \mathbf{C}v$.

a. First suppose v is orthogonal to the principal subspace. and hence $v^T\mathbf{U} = 0$. Show that $v^T\mathbf{C}v = \sigma^2$.

b. Now suppose v is parallel to the principal subspace. and hence $v = u_i$ for some eigenvector u_i. Show that $v^T\mathbf{C}v = (\lambda_i - \sigma^2) + \sigma^2 = \lambda_i$.

Exercise 20.7 [Posterior inference in PPCA *]

Derive $p(\boldsymbol{z}_n|\boldsymbol{x}_n)$ for the PPCA model.

Exercise 20.8 [Imputation in a FA model *]

Derive an expression for $p(\boldsymbol{x}_h|\boldsymbol{x}_v, \boldsymbol{\theta})$ for a FA model, where $\boldsymbol{x} = (\boldsymbol{x}_h, \boldsymbol{x}_v)$ is a partition of the data vector.

Exercise 20.9 [Efficiently evaluating the PPCA density]

Derive an expression for $p(\boldsymbol{x}|\hat{\mathbf{W}}, \hat{\sigma}^2)$ for the PPCA model based on plugging in the MLEs and using the matrix inversion lemma.

21 Clustering

21.1 Introduction

Clustering is a very common form of unsupervised learning. There are two main kinds of methods. In the first approach, the input is a set of data samples $\mathcal{D} = \{\boldsymbol{x}_n : n = 1 : N\}$, where $\boldsymbol{x}_n \in \mathcal{X}$, where typically $\mathcal{X} = \mathbb{R}^D$. In the second approach, the input is an $N \times N$ pairwise dissimilarity metric $D_{ij} \geq 0$. In both cases, the goal is to assign similar data points to the same cluster.

As is often the case with unsupervised learning, it is hard to evaluate the quality of a clustering algorithm. If we have labeled data for some of the data, we can use the similarity (or equality) between the labels of two data points as a metric for determining if the two inputs "should" be assigned to the same cluster or not. If we don't have labels, but the method is based on a generative model of the data, we can use log likelihood as a metric. We will see examples of both approaches below.

21.1.1 Evaluating the output of clustering methods

> The validation of clustering structures is the most difficult and frustrating part of cluster analysis. Without a strong effort in this direction, cluster analysis will remain a black art accessible only to those true believers who have experience and great courage. — Jain and Dubes [JD88]

Clustering is an unsupervised learning technique, so it is hard to evaluate the quality of the output of any given method [Kle02; LWG12]. If we use probabilistic models, we can always evaluate the likelihood of the data, but this has two drawbacks: first, it does not directly assess any clustering that is discovered by the model; and second, it does not apply to non-probabilistic methods. So now we discuss some performance measures not based on likelihood.

Intuitively, the goal of clustering is to assign points that are similar to the same cluster, and to ensure that points that are dissimilar are in different clusters. There are several ways of measuring these quantities e.g., see [JD88; KR90]. However, these internal criteria may be of limited use. An alternative is to rely on some external form of data with which to validate the method. For example, if we have labels for each object, then we can assume that objects with the same label are similar. We can then use the metrics we discuss below to quantify the quality of the clusters. (If we do not have labels, but we have a reference clustering, we can derive labels from that clustering.)

Figure 21.1: Three clusters with labeled objects inside.

21.1.1.1   Purity

Let N_{ij} be the number of objects in cluster i that belong to class j, and let $N_i = \sum_{j=1}^{C} N_{ij}$ be the total number of objects in cluster i. Define $p_{ij} = N_{ij}/N_i$; this is the empirical distribution over class labels for cluster i. We define the **purity** of a cluster as $p_i \triangleq \max_j p_{ij}$, and the overall purity of a clustering as

$$\text{purity} \triangleq \sum_i \frac{N_i}{N} p_i \tag{21.1}$$

For example, in Figure 21.1, we have that the purity is

$$\frac{6}{17}\frac{5}{6} + \frac{6}{17}\frac{4}{6} + \frac{5}{17}\frac{3}{5} = \frac{5+4+3}{17} = 0.71 \tag{21.2}$$

The purity ranges between 0 (bad) and 1 (good). However, we can trivially achieve a purity of 1 by putting each object into its own cluster, so this measure does not penalize for the number of clusters.

21.1.1.2   Rand index

Let $U = \{u_1, \ldots, u_R\}$ and $V = \{v_1, \ldots, v_C\}$ be two different partitions of the N data points. For example, U might be the estimated clustering and V is reference clustering derived from the class labels. Now define a 2×2 contingency table, containing the following numbers: TP is the number of pairs that are in the same cluster in both U and V (true positives); TN is the number of pairs that are in the different clusters in both U and V (true negatives); FN is the number of pairs that are in the different clusters in U but the same cluster in V (false negatives); and FP is the number of pairs that are in the same cluster in U but different clusters in V (false positives). A common summary statistic is the **Rand index**:

$$R \triangleq \frac{TP + TN}{TP + FP + FN + TN} \tag{21.3}$$

This can be interpreted as the fraction of clustering decisions that are correct. Clearly $0 \le R \le 1$.

For example, consider Figure 21.1, The three clusters contain 6, 6 and 5 points, so the number of "positives" (i.e., pairs of objects put in the same cluster, regardless of label) is

$$TP + FP = \binom{6}{2} + \binom{6}{2} + \binom{5}{2} = 40 \tag{21.4}$$

Of these, the number of true positives is given by

$$TP = \binom{5}{2} + \binom{4}{2} + \binom{3}{2} + \binom{2}{2} = 20 \tag{21.5}$$

where the last two terms come from cluster 3: there are $\binom{3}{2}$ pairs labeled C and $\binom{2}{2}$ pairs labeled A. So $FP = 40 - 20 = 20$. Similarly, one can show $FN = 24$ and $TN = 72$. So the Rand index is $(20 + 72)/(20 + 20 + 24 + 72) = 0.68$.

The Rand index only achieves its lower bound of 0 if $TP = TN = 0$, which is a rare event. One can define an **adjusted Rand index** [HA85] as follows:

$$ AR \triangleq \frac{\text{index} - \text{expected index}}{\text{max index} - \text{expected index}} \tag{21.6} $$

Here the model of randomness is based on using the generalized hyper-geometric distribution, i.e., the two partitions are picked at random subject to having the original number of classes and objects in each, and then the expected value of $TP + TN$ is computed. This model can be used to compute the statistical significance of the Rand index.

The Rand index weights false positives and false negatives equally. Various other summary statistics for binary decision problems, such as the F-score (Section 5.1.4), can also be used.

21.1.1.3 Mutual information

Another way to measure cluster quality is to compute the mutual information between two candidate partitions U and V, as proposed in [VD99]. To do this, let $p_{UV}(i, j) = \frac{|u_i \cap v_j|}{N}$ be the probability that a randomly chosen object belongs to cluster u_i in U and v_j in V. Also, let $p_U(i) = |u_i|/N$ be the be the probability that a randomly chosen object belongs to cluster u_i in U; define $p_V(j) = |v_j|/N$ similarly. Then we have

$$ \mathbb{I}(U, V) = \sum_{i=1}^{R} \sum_{j=1}^{C} p_{UV}(i, j) \log \frac{p_{UV}(i, j)}{p_U(i)p_V(j)} \tag{21.7} $$

This lies between 0 and $\min\{\mathbb{H}(U), \mathbb{H}(V)\}$. Unfortunately, the maximum value can be achieved by using lots of small clusters, which have low entropy. To compensate for this, we can use the **normalized mutual information**,

$$ NMI(U, V) \triangleq \frac{\mathbb{I}(U, V)}{(\mathbb{H}(U) + \mathbb{H}(V))/2} \tag{21.8} $$

This lies between 0 and 1. A version of this that is adjusted for chance (under a particular random data model) is described in [VEB09]. Another variant, called **variation of information**, is described in [Mei05].

21.2 Hierarchical agglomerative clustering

A common form of clustering is known as **hierarchical agglomerative clustering** or **HAC**. The input to the algorithm is an $N \times N$ dissimilarity matrix $D_{ij} \geq 0$, and the output is a tree structure in which groups i and j with small disimilarity are grouped together in a hierarchical fashion.

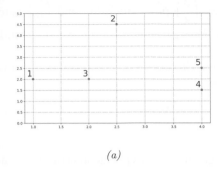 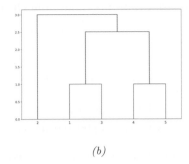

(a)   (b)

Figure 21.2: (a) An example of single link clustering using city block distance. Pairs (1,3) and (4,5) are both distance 1 apart, so get merged first. (b) The resulting dendrogram. Adapted from Figure 7.5 of [Alp04]. Generated by agglomDemo.ipynb.

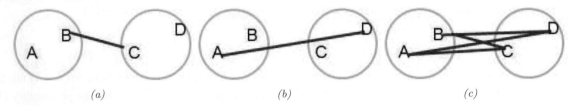

(a)   (b)   (c)

Figure 21.3: Illustration of (a) Single linkage. (b) Complete linkage. (c) Average linkage.

For example, consider the set of 5 inputs points in Figure 21.2(a), $\boldsymbol{x}_n \in \mathbb{R}^2$. We will use **city block distance** between the points to define the dissimilarity, i.e.,

$$d_{ij} = \sum_{k=1}^{2} |x_{ik} - x_{jk}| \tag{21.9}$$

We start with a tree with N leaves, each corresponding to a cluster with a single data point. Next we compute the pair of points that are closest, and merge them. We see that (1,3) and (4,5) are both distance 1 apart, so they get merged first. We then measure the dissimilarity between the sets $\{1, 3\}$, $\{4, 5\}$ and $\{2\}$ using some measure (details below), and group them, and repeat. The result is a binary tree known as a **dendrogram**, as shown in Figure 21.2(b). By cutting this tree at different heights, we can induce a different number of (nested) clusters. We give more details below.

21.2.1   The algorithm

Agglomerative clustering starts with N groups, each initially containing one object, and then at each step it merges the two most similar groups until there is a single group, containing all the data. See Algorithm 21.1 for the pseudocode. Since picking the two most similar clusters to merge takes $O(N^2)$ time, and there are $O(N)$ steps in the algorithm, the total running time is $O(N^3)$. However, by using a priority queue, this can be reduced to $O(N^2 \log N)$ (see e.g., [MRS08, ch. 17] for details).

Algorithm 21.1: Agglomerative clustering

---

1 Initialize clusters as singletons: **for** $i \leftarrow 1$ **to** n **do** $C_i \leftarrow \{i\}$

2

3 Initialize set of clusters available for merging: $S \leftarrow \{1, \dots, n\}$; **repeat**

4   Pick 2 most similar clusters to merge: $(j, k) \leftarrow \arg\min_{j,k \in S} d_{j,k}$

5   Create new cluster $C_\ell \leftarrow C_j \cup C_k$

6   Mark j and k as unavailable: $S \leftarrow S \setminus \{j, k\}$

7   **if** $C_\ell \neq \{1, \dots, n\}$ **then**

8   Mark ℓ as available, $S \leftarrow S \cup \{\ell\}$

9   **foreach** $i \in S$ **do**

10   Update dissimilarity matrix $d(i, \ell)$

11 **until** *no more clusters are available for merging*

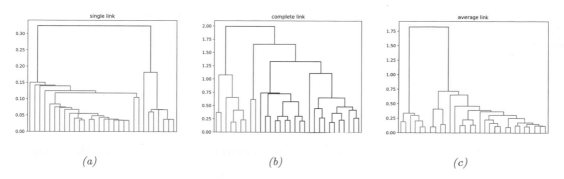

Figure 21.4: *Hierarchical clustering of yeast gene expression data. (a) Single linkage. (b) Complete linkage. (c) Average linkage. Generated by hclust_yeast_demo.ipynb.*

There are actually three variants of agglomerative clustering, depending on how we define the dissimilarity between groups of objects. We give the details below.

21.2.1.1 Single link

In **single link clustering**, also called **nearest neighbor clustering**, the distance between two groups G and H is defined as the distance between the two closest members of each group:

$$d_{SL}(G, H) = \min_{i \in G, i' \in H} d_{i,i'} \tag{21.10}$$

See Figure 21.3(a).

The tree built using single link clustering is a minimum spanning tree of the data, which is a tree that connects all the objects in a way that minimizes the sum of the edge weights (distances). To see this, note that when we merge two clusters, we connect together the two closest members of the clusters; this adds an edge between the corresponding nodes, and this is guaranteed to be the "lightest weight" edge joining these two clusters. And once two clusters have been merged, they will never be considered again, so we cannot create cycles. As a consequence of this, we can actually implement single link clustering in $O(N^2)$ time, whereas the other variants take $O(N^3)$ time.

21.2.1.2 Complete link

In **complete link clustering**, also called **furthest neighbor clustering**, the distance between two groups is defined as the distance between the two most distant pairs:

$$d_{CL}(G, H) = \max_{i \in G, i' \in H} d_{i,i'} \tag{21.11}$$

See Figure 21.3(b).

Single linkage only requires that a single pair of objects be close for the two groups to be considered close together, regardless of the similarity of the other members of the group. Thus clusters can be formed that violate the **compactness** property, which says that all the observations within a group should be similar to each other. In particular if we define the **diameter** of a group as the largest dissimilarity of its members, $d_G = \max_{i \in G, i' \in G} d_{i,i'}$, then we can see that single linkage can produce clusters with large diameters. Complete linkage represents the opposite extreme: two groups are considered close only if all of the observations in their union are relatively similar. This will tend to produce clusterings with small diameter, i.e., compact clusters. (Compare Figure 21.4(a) with Figure 21.4(b).)

21.2.1.3 Average link

In practice, the preferred method is **average link clustering**, which measures the average distance between all pairs:

$$d_{avg}(G, H) = \frac{1}{n_G n_H} \sum_{i \in G} \sum_{i' \in H} d_{i,i'} \tag{21.12}$$

where n_G and n_H are the number of elements in groups G and H. See Figure 21.3(c).

Average link clustering represents a compromise between single and complete link clustering. It tends to produce relatively compact clusters that are relatively far apart. (See Figure 21.4(c).) However, since it involves averaging of the $d_{i,i'}$'s, any change to the measurement scale can change the result. In contrast, single linkage and complete linkage are invariant to monotonic transformations of $d_{i,i'}$, since they leave the relative ordering the same.

21.2.2 Example

Suppose we have a set of time series measurements of the expression levels for $N = 300$ genes at $T = 7$ points. Thus each data sample is a vector $\boldsymbol{x}_n \in \mathbb{R}^7$. See Figure 21.5 for a visualization of the data. We see that there are several kinds of genes, such as those whose expression level goes up monotonically over time (in response to a given stimulus), those whose expression level goes down monotonically, and those with more complex response patterns.

Suppose we use Euclidean distance to compute a pairwise dissimilarity matrix, $\mathbf{D} \in \mathbb{R}^{300 \times 300}$, and apply HAC using average linkage. We get the dendrogram in Figure 21.6(a). If we cut the tree at

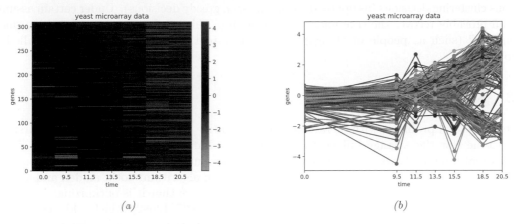

(a)   (b)

Figure 21.5: (a) Some yeast gene expression data plotted as a heat map. (b) Same data plotted as a time series. Generated by yeast_data_viz.ipynb.

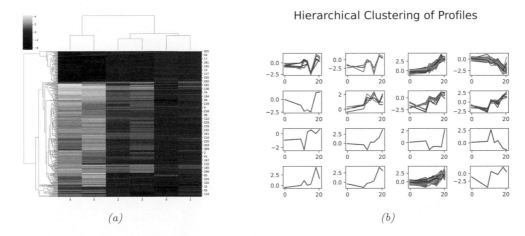

(a)   (b)

Figure 21.6: Hierarchical clustering applied to the yeast gene expression data. (a) The rows are permuted according to a hierarchical clustering scheme (average link agglomerative clustering), in order to bring similar rows close together. (b) 16 clusters induced by cutting the average linkage tree at a certain height. Generated by hclust_yeast_demo.ipynb.

a certain height, we get the 16 clusters shown in Figure 21.6(b). The time series assigned to each cluster do indeed "look like" each other.

21.2.3 Extensions

There are many extensions to the basic HAC algorithm. For example, [Mon+21] present a more scalable version of the bottom up algorithm that builds sub-clusters in parallel. And g [Mon+19] discusses an online version of the algorithm, that can cluster data as it arrives, while reconsidering previous clustering decisions (as opposed to only making greedy decisions). Under certain assumptions, this can provably recover the true underlying structure. This can be useful for clustering "mentions" of "entities" (such as people or things) in streaming text data. (This problem is called **entity discovery**.)

21.3   K means clustering

There are several problems with hierarchical agglomerative clustering (Section 21.2). First, it takes $O(N^3)$ time (for the average link method), making it hard to apply to big datasets. Second, it assumes that a dissimilarity matrix has already been computed, whereas the notion of "similarity" is often unclear and needs to be learned. Third, it is just an algorithm, not a model, and so it is hard to evaluate how good it is. That is, there is no clear objective that it is optimizing.

In this section, we discuss the **K-means algorithm** [Mac67; Llo82], which addresses these issues. First, it runs in $O(NKT)$ time, where T is the number of iterations. Second, it computes similarity in terms of Euclidean distance to learned cluster centers $\boldsymbol{\mu}_k \in \mathbb{R}^D$, rather than requiring a dissimilarity matrix. Third, it optimizes a well-defined cost function, as we will see.

21.3.1   The algorithm

We assume there are K cluster centers $\boldsymbol{\mu}_k \in \mathbb{R}^D$, so we can cluster the data by assigning each data point $\boldsymbol{x}_n \in \mathbb{R}^D$ to it closest center:

$$z_n^* = \arg\min_k ||\boldsymbol{x}_n - \boldsymbol{\mu}_k||_2^2 \tag{21.13}$$

Of course, we don't know the cluster centers, but we can estimate them by computing the average value of all points assigned to them:

$$\boldsymbol{\mu}_k = \frac{1}{N_k} \sum_{n:z_n=k} \boldsymbol{x}_n \tag{21.14}$$

We can then iterate these steps to convergence.

More formally, we can view this as finding a local minimum of the following cost function, known as the **distortion**:

$$J(\mathbf{M}, \mathbf{Z}) = \sum_{n=1}^{N} ||\boldsymbol{x}_n - \boldsymbol{\mu}_{z_n}||^2 = ||\mathbf{X} - \mathbf{Z}\mathbf{M}^\mathsf{T}||_F^2 \tag{21.15}$$

where $\mathbf{X} \in \mathbb{R}^{N \times D}$, $\mathbf{Z} \in [0,1]^{N \times K}$, and $\mathbf{M} \in \mathbb{R}^{D \times K}$ contains the cluster centers $\boldsymbol{\mu}_k$ in its columns. K-means optimizes this using alternating minimization. (This is closely related to the EM algorithm for GMMs, as we discuss in Section 21.4.1.1.)

21.3.2   Examples

In this section, we give some examples of K-means clustering.

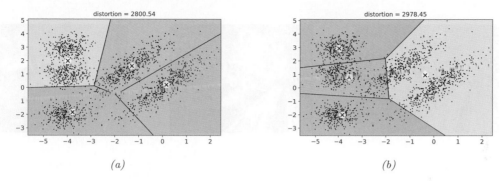

(a) *(b)*

Figure 21.7: Illustration of K-means clustering in 2d. We show the result of using two different random seeds. Adapted from Figure 9.5 of [Gér19]. Generated by kmeans_voronoi.ipynb.

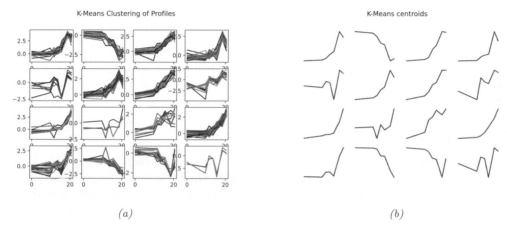

(a) *(b)*

Figure 21.8: Clustering the yeast data from Figure 21.5 using K-means clustering with $K = 16$. (a) Visualizing all the time series assigned to each cluster. (b) Visualizing the 16 cluster centers as prototypical time series. Generated by kmeans_yeast_demo.ipynb.

21.3.2.1 Clustering points in the 2d plane

Figure 21.7 gives an illustration of K-means clustering applied to some points in the 2d plane. We see that the method induces a **Voronoi tessellation** of the points. The resulting clustering is sensitive to the initialization. Indeed, we see that the lower quality clustering on the right has higher distortion. By default, sklearn uses 10 random restarts (combined with the K-means++ initialization described in Section 21.3.4) and returns the clustering with lowest distortion. (In sklearn, the distortion is called the "inertia".)

21.3.2.2 Clustering gene expression time series data from yeast cells

In Figure 21.8, we show the result of applying K-means clustering with $K = 16$ to the 300×7 yeast time series matrix shown in Figure 21.5. We see that time series that "look similar" to each other are

(a)   (b)   (c)

Figure 21.9: An image compressed using vector quantization with a codebook of size K. (a) $K = 2$. (b) $K = 4$. (c) Original uncompressed image. Generated by vqDemo.ipynb.

assigned to the same cluster. We also see that the centroid of each cluster is a reasonabe summary all the data points assigned to that cluster. Finally we notice that group 6 was not used, since no points were assigned to it. However, this is just an accident of the initialization process, and we are not guaranteed to get the same clustering, or number of clusters, if we repeat the algorithm. (We discuss good ways to initialize the method in Section 21.3.4, and ways to choose K in Section 21.3.7.)

21.3.3   Vector quantization

Suppose we want to perform lossy compression of some real-valued vectors, $\boldsymbol{x}_n \in \mathbb{R}^D$. A very simple approach to this is to use **vector quantization** or **VQ**. The basic idea is to replace each real-valued vector $\boldsymbol{x}_n \in \mathbb{R}^D$ with a discrete symbol $z_n \in \{1, \ldots, K\}$, which is an index into a **codebook** of K prototypes, $\boldsymbol{\mu}_k \in \mathbb{R}^D$. Each data vector is encoded by using the index of the most similar prototype, where similarity is measured in terms of Euclidean distance:

$$\text{encode}(\boldsymbol{x}_n) = \arg \min_k ||\boldsymbol{x}_n - \boldsymbol{\mu}_k||^2 \tag{21.16}$$

We can define a cost function that measures the quality of a codebook by computing the **reconstruction error** or **distortion** it induces:

$$J \triangleq \frac{1}{N} \sum_{n=1}^{N} ||\boldsymbol{x}_n - \text{decode}(\text{encode}(\boldsymbol{x}_n))||^2 = \frac{1}{N} \sum_{n=1}^{N} ||\boldsymbol{x}_n - \boldsymbol{\mu}_{z_n}||^2 \tag{21.17}$$

where $\text{decode}(k) = \boldsymbol{\mu}_k$. This is exactly the cost function that is minimized by the K-means algorithm.

Of course, we can achieve zero distortion if we assign one prototype to every data vector, by using $K = N$ and assigning $\boldsymbol{\mu}_n = \boldsymbol{x}_n$. However, this does not compress the data at all. In particular, it takes $O(NDB)$ bits, where N is the number of real-valued data vectors, each of length D, and B is the number of bits needed to represent a real-valued scalar (the quantization accuracy to represent each $\boldsymbol{x}_n$).

We can do better by detecting similar vectors in the data, creating prototypes or centroids for them, and then representing the data as deviations from these prototypes. This reduces the space requirement to $O(N \log_2 K + KDB)$ bits. The $O(N \log_2 K)$ term arises because each of the N data vectors needs to specify which of the K codewords it is using; and the $O(KDB)$ term arises because we have to store each codebook entry, each of which is a D-dimensional vector. When N is large, the first term dominates the second, so we can approximate the **rate** of the encoding scheme (number of bits needed per object) as $O(\log_2 K)$, which is typically much less than $O(DB)$.

One application of VQ is to image compression. Consider the 200×320 pixel image in Figure 21.9; we will treat this as a set of $N = 64,000$ scalars. If we use one byte to represent each pixel (a gray-scale intensity of 0 to 255), then $B = 8$, so we need $NB = 512,000$ bits to represent the image in uncompressed form. For the compressed image, we need $O(N \log_2 K)$ bits. For $K = 4$, this is about 128kb, a factor of 4 compression, yet it results in negligible perceptual loss (see Figure 21.9(b)).

Greater compression could be achieved if we modeled spatial correlation between the pixels, e.g., if we encoded 5x5 blocks (as used by JPEG). This is because the residual errors (differences from the model's predictions) would be smaller, and would take fewer bits to encode. This shows the deep connection between data compression and density estimation. See the sequel to this book, [Mur23], for more information.

21.3.4   The K-means++ algorithm

K-means is optimizing a non-convex objective, and hence needs to be initialized carefully. A simple approach is to pick K data points at random, and to use these as the initial values for $\boldsymbol{\mu}_k$. We can improve on this by using **multiple restarts**, i.e., we run the algorithm multiple times from different random starting points, and then pick the best solution. However, this can be slow.

A better approach is to pick the centers sequentially so as to try to "cover" the data. That is, we pick the initial point uniformly at random, and then each subsequent point is picked from the remaining points, with probability proportional to its squared distance to the point's closest cluster center. That is, at iteration t, we pick the next cluster center to be $\boldsymbol{x}_n$ with probability

$$p(\boldsymbol{\mu}_t = \boldsymbol{x}_n) = \frac{D_{t-1}(\boldsymbol{x}_n)}{\sum_{n'=1}^{N} D_{t-1}(\boldsymbol{x}_{n'})} \tag{21.18}$$

where

$$D_t(\boldsymbol{x}) = \min_{k=1}^{t-1} ||\boldsymbol{x} - \boldsymbol{\mu}_k||_2^2 \tag{21.19}$$

is the squared distance of $\boldsymbol{x}$ to the closest existing centroid. Thus points that are far away from a centroid are more likely to be picked, thus reducing the distortion. This is known as **farthest point clustering** [Gon85], or **K-means++** [AV07; Bah+12; Bac+16; BLK17; LS19a]. Surprisingly, this simple trick can be shown to guarantee that the recontruction error is never more than $O(\log K)$ worse than optimal [AV07].

21.3.5   The K-medoids algorithm

There is a variant of K-means called **K-medoids** algorithm, in which we estimate each cluster center $\boldsymbol{\mu}_k$ by choosing the data example $\boldsymbol{x}_n \in \mathcal{X}$ whose average dissimilarity to all other points in that cluster is minimal; such a point is known as a **medoid**. By contrast, in K-means, we take averages over points $\boldsymbol{x}_n \in \mathbb{R}^D$ assigned to the cluster to compute the center. K-medoids can be more robust to outliers (although that issue can also be tackled by using mixtures of Student distributions, instead of mixtures of Gaussians). More importantly, K-medoids can be applied to data that does not live in $\mathbb{R}^D$, where averaging may not be well defined. In K-medoids, the input to the algorithm is $N \times N$ pairwise distance matrix, $D(n, n')$, not an $N \times D$ feature matrix.

The classic algorithm for solving the K-medoids is the **partitioning around medoids** or **PAM** method [KR87]. In this approach, at each iteration, we loop over all K medoids. For each medoid m, we consider each non-medoid point o, swap m and o, and recompute the cost (sum of all the distances of points to their medoid). If the cost has decreased, we keep this swap. The running time of this algorithm is $O(N^2 KT)$, where T is the number of iterations.

There is also a simpler and faster method, known as the **Voronoi iteration** method due to [PJ09]. In this approach, at each iteration, we have two steps, similar to K-means. First, for each cluster k, look at all the points currently assigned to that cluster, $S_k = \{n : z_n = k\}$, and then set m_k to be the index of the medoid of that set. (To find the medoid requires examining all $|S_k|$ candidate points, and choosing the one that has the smallest sum of distances to all the other points in S_k.) Second, for each point n, assign it to its closest medoid, $z_n = \mathrm{argmin}_k D(n, k)$. The pseudo-code is given in Algorithm 21.2.

Algorithm 21.2: K-medoids algorithm

---

1 Initialize $m_{1:K}$ as a random subset of size K from $\{1, \dots, N\}$
2 **repeat**
3 $\quad$ $z_n = \mathrm{argmin}_k d(n, m_k)$ for $n = 1 : N$
4 $\quad$ $m_k = \mathrm{argmin}_{n:z_n=k} \sum_{n':z_{n'}=k} d(n, n')$ for $k = 1 : K$
5 **until** *converged*

21.3.6   Speedup tricks

K-means clustering takes $O(NKI)$ time, where I is the number of iterations, but we can reduce the constant factors using various tricks. For example, [Elk03] shows how to use the triangle inequality to keep track of lower and upper bounds for the distances between inputs and the centroids; this can be used to eliminate some redundant computations. Another approach is to use a minibatch approximation, as proposed in [Scu10]. This can be significantly faster, although can result in slightly worse loss (see Figure 21.10).

21.3.7   Choosing the number of clusters K

In this section, we discuss how to choose the number of clusters K in the K-means algorithm and other related methods.

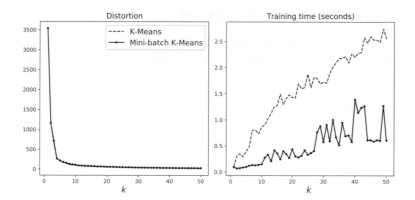

Figure 21.10: Illustration of batch vs mini-batch K-means clustering on the 2d data from Figure 21.7. Left: distortion vs K. Right: Training time vs K. Adapted from Figure 9.6 of [Gér19]. Generated by kmeans_minibatch.ipynb.

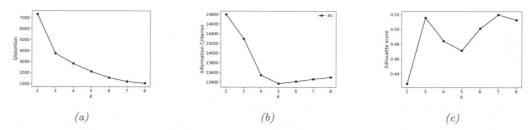

Figure 21.11: Performance of K-means and GMM vs K on the 2d dataset from Figure 21.7. (a) Distortion on validation set vs K. Generated by kmeans_silhouette.ipynb. (b) BIC vs K. Generated by gmm_2d.ipynb. (c) Silhouette score vs K. Generated by kmeans_silhouette.ipynb.

21.3.7.1 Minimizing the distortion

Based on our experience with supervised learning, a natural choice for picking K is to pick the value that minimizes the reconstruction error on a validation set, defined as follows:

$$\text{err}(\mathcal{D}_{\text{valid}}, K) = \frac{1}{|\mathcal{D}_{\text{valid}}|} \sum_{n \in \mathcal{D}_{\text{valid}}} ||\boldsymbol{x}_n - \hat{\boldsymbol{x}}_n||_2^2 \qquad (21.20)$$

where $\hat{\boldsymbol{x}}_n = \text{decode}(\text{encode}(\boldsymbol{x}_n))$ is the reconstruction of $\boldsymbol{x}_n$.

Unfortunately, this technique will not work. Indeed, as we see in Figure 21.11a, the distortion monotonically decreases with K. To see why, note that the K-means model is a degenerate density model which consists of K "spikes" at the $\boldsymbol{\mu}_k$ centers. As we increase K, we "cover" more of the input space. Hence any given input point is more likely to find a close prototype to accurately represent it as K increases, thus decreasing reconstruction error. Thus unlike with supervised learning, *we cannot use reconstruction error on a validation set as a way to select the best unsupervised model.* (This comment also applies to picking the dimensionality for PCA, see Section 20.1.4.)

21.3.7.2 Maximizing the marginal likelihood

A method that does work is to use a proper probabilistic model, such as a GMM, as we describe in Section 21.4.1. We can then use the log marginal likelihood (LML) of the data to perform model selection.

We can approximate the LML using the BIC score as we discussed in Section 5.2.5.1. From Equation (5.59), we have

$$\text{BIC}(K) = \log p(\mathcal{D}|\hat{\boldsymbol{\theta}}_k) - \frac{D_K}{2}\log(N) \tag{21.21}$$

where D_K is the number of parameters in a model with K clusters, and $\hat{\boldsymbol{\theta}}_K$ is the MLE. We see from Figure 21.11b that this exhibits the typical U-shaped curve, where the penalty decreases and then increases.

The reason this works is that each cluster is associated with a Gaussian distribution that fills a volume of the input space, rather than being a degenerate spike. Once we have enough clusters to cover the true modes of the distribution, the Bayesian Occam's razor (Section 5.2.3) kicks in, and starts penalizing the model for being unncessarily complex.

See Section 21.4.1.3 for more discussion of Bayesian model selection for mixture models.

21.3.7.3 Silhouette coefficient

In this section, we describe a common heuristic method for picking the number of clusters in a K-means clustering model. This is designed to work for spherical (not elongated) clusters. First we define the **silhouette coefficient** of an instance i to be $sc(i) = (b_i - a_i)/\max(a_i, b_i)$, where a_i is the mean distance to the other instances in cluster $k_i = \text{argmin}_k \|\boldsymbol{\mu}_k - \boldsymbol{x}_i\|$, and b_i is the mean distance to the other instances in the next closest cluster, $k'_i = \text{argmin}_{k\neq k_i} \|\boldsymbol{\mu}_k - \boldsymbol{x}_i\|$. Thus a_i is a measure of compactness of i's cluster, and b_i is a measure of distance between the clusters. The silhouette coefficient varies from -1 to +1. A value of +1 means the instance is close to all the members of its cluster, and far from other clusters; a value of 0 means it is close to a cluster boundary; and a value of -1 means it may be in the wrong cluster. We define the **silhouette score** of a clustering K to be the mean silhouette coefficient over all instances.

In Figure 21.11a, we plot the distortion vs K for the data in Figure 21.7. As we explained above, it goes down monotonically with K. There is a slight "**kink**" or "**elbow**" in the curve at $K = 3$, but this is hard to detect. In Figure 21.11c, we plot the silhouette score vs K. Now we see a more prominent peak at $K = 3$, although it seems $K = 7$ is almost as good. See Figure 21.12 for a comparison of some of these clusterings.

It can be informative to look at the individual silhouette coefficients, and not just the mean score. We can plot these in a **silhouette diagram**, as shown in Figure 21.13, where each colored region corresponds to a different cluster. The dotted vertical line is the average coefficient. Clusters with many points to the left of this line are likely to be of low quality. We can also use the silhouette diagram to look at the size of each cluster, even if the data is not 2d.

21.3.7.4 Incrementally growing the number of mixture components

An alternative to searching for the best value of K is to incrementally "grow" GMMs. We can start with a small value of K, and after each round of training, we consider splitting the cluster with the

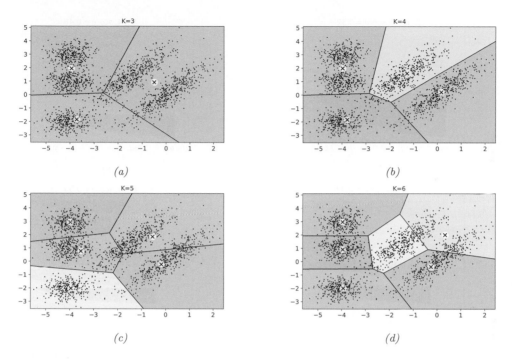

Figure 21.12: *Voronoi diagrams for K-means for different K on the 2d dataset from Figure 21.7. Generated by kmeans_silhouette.ipynb.*

highest mixing weight into two, with the new centroids being random perturbations of the original centroid, and the new scores being half of the old scores. If a new cluster has too small a score, or too narrow a variance, it is removed. We continue in this way until the desired number of clusters is reached. See [FJ02] for details.

21.3.7.5 Sparse estimation methods

Another approach is to pick a large value of K, and then to use some kind of sparsity-promoting prior or inference method to "kill off" unneeded mixture components, such as variational Bayes. See the sequel to this book, [Mur23], for details.

21.4 Clustering using mixture models

We have seen how the K-means algorithm can be used to cluster data vectors in $\mathbb{R}^D$. However, this method assumes that all clusters have the same spherical shape, which is a very restrictive assumption. In addition, K-means assumes that all clusters can be described by Gaussians in the input space, so it cannot be applied to discrete data. By using mixture models (Section 3.5), we can overcome both of these problems, as we illustrate below.

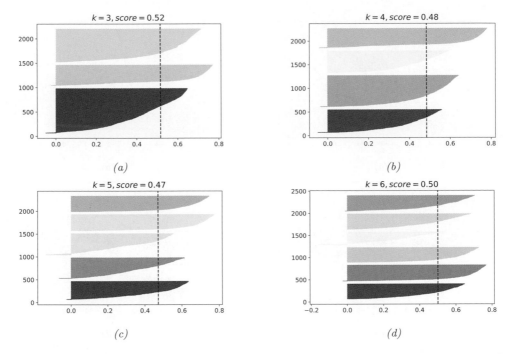

Figure 21.13: Silhouette diagrams for K-means for different K on the 2d dataset from Figure 21.7. Generated by kmeans_silhouette.ipynb.

21.4.1   Mixtures of Gaussians

Recall from Section 3.5.1 that a Gaussian mixture model (GMM) is a model of the form

$$p(\boldsymbol{x}|\boldsymbol{\theta}) = \sum_{k=1}^{K} \pi_k \mathcal{N}(\boldsymbol{x}|\boldsymbol{\mu}_k, \boldsymbol{\Sigma}_k) \tag{21.22}$$

If we know the model parameters $\boldsymbol{\theta} = (\boldsymbol{\pi}, \{\boldsymbol{\mu}_k, \boldsymbol{\Sigma}_k\})$, we can use Bayes rule to compute the responsibility (posterior membership probability) of cluster k for data point $\boldsymbol{x}_n$:

$$r_{nk} \triangleq p(z_n = k|\boldsymbol{x}_n, \boldsymbol{\theta}) = \frac{p(z_n = k|\boldsymbol{\theta})p(\boldsymbol{x}_n|z_n = k, \boldsymbol{\theta})}{\sum_{k'=1}^{K} p(z_n = k'|\boldsymbol{\theta})p(\boldsymbol{x}_n|z_n = k', \boldsymbol{\theta})} \tag{21.23}$$

Given the responsibilities, we can compute the most probable cluster assignment as follows:

$$\hat{z}_n = \arg\max_k r_{nk} = \arg\max_k \left[\log p(\boldsymbol{x}_n|z_n = k, \boldsymbol{\theta}) + \log p(z_n = k|\boldsymbol{\theta})\right] \tag{21.24}$$

This is known as **hard clustering**.

21.4.1.1   K-means is a special case of EM

We can estimate the parameters of a GMM using the EM algorithm (Section 8.7.3). It turns out that the K-means algorithm is a special case of this algorithm, in which we make two approximations:

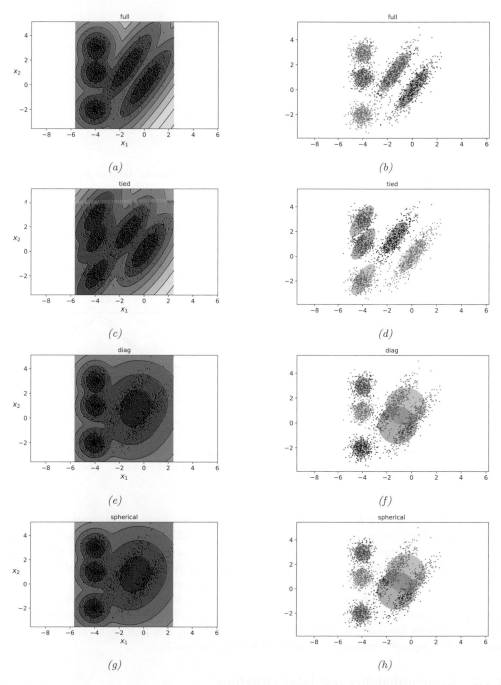

Figure 21.14: *Some data in 2d fit using a GMM with K = 5 components. Left column: marginal distribution p($\boldsymbol{x}$). Right column: visualization of each mixture distribution, and the hard assignment of points to their most likely cluster. (a-b) Full covariance. (c-d) Tied full covariance. (e-f) Diagonal covairance, (g-h) Spherical covariance. Color coding is arbitrary. Generated by gmm_2d.ipynb.*

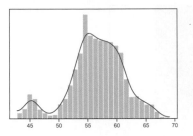

Figure 21.15: Some 1d data, with a kernel density estimate superimposed. Adapted from Figure 6.2 of [Mar18]. Generated by gmm_identifiability_pymc3.ipynb.

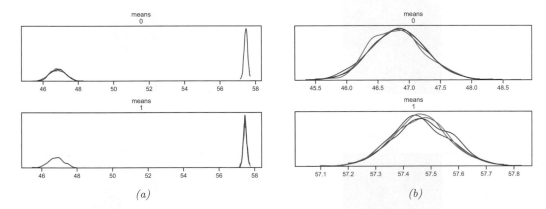

Figure 21.16: Illustration of the label switching problem when performing posterior inference for the parameters of a GMM. We show a KDE estimate of the posterior marginals derived from 1000 samples from 4 HMC chains. (a) Unconstrained model. Posterior is symmetric. (b) Constrained model, where we add a penalty to ensure $\mu_0 < \mu_1$. Adapted from Figure 6.6-6.7 of [Mar18]. Generated by gmm_identifiability_pymc3.ipynb.

we fix $\boldsymbol{\Sigma}_k = \mathbf{I}$ and $\pi_k = 1/K$ for all the clusters (so we just have to estimate the means $\boldsymbol{\mu}_k$), and we approximate the E step, by replacing the soft responsibilities with hard cluster assignments, i.e., we compute $z_n^* = \operatorname{argmax}_k r_{nk}$, and set $r_{nk} \approx \mathbb{I}(k = z_n^*)$ instead of using the soft responsibilities, $r_{nk} = p(z_n = k|\boldsymbol{x}_n, \boldsymbol{\theta})$. With this approximation, the weighted MLE problem in Equation (8.165) of the M step reduces to Equation (21.14), so we recover K-means.

However, the assumption that all the clusters have the same spherical shape is very restrictive. For example, Figure 21.14 shows the marginal density and clustering induced using different shaped covariance matrices for some 2d data. We see that modeling this particular dataset needs the ability to capture off-diagonal covariance for some clusters (top row).

21.4.1.2   Unidentifiability and label switching

Note that we are free to permute the labels in a mixture model without changing the likelihood. This is called the **label switching problem**, and is an example of **non-identifiability** of the parameters.

This can cause problems if we wish to perform posterior inference over the parameters (as opposed to just computing the MLE or a MAP estimate). For example, suppose we fit a GMM with $K = 2$ components to the data in Figure 21.15 using HMC. The posterior over the means, $p(\mu_1, \mu_2 | \mathcal{D})$, is shown in Figure 21.16a. We see that the marginal posterior for each component, $p(\mu_k | \mathcal{D})$, is bimodal. This reflects the fact that there are two equally good explanations of the data: either $\mu_1 \approx 47$ and $\mu_2 \approx 57$, or vice versa.

To break symmetry, we can add an **ordering constraint** on the centers, so that $\mu_1 < \mu_2$. We can do this by adding a penalty or potential function to the objective if the constraint is violated. More precisely, the penalized log joint becomes

$$\ell'(\boldsymbol{\theta}) = \log p(\mathcal{D}|\boldsymbol{\theta}) + \log p(\boldsymbol{\theta}) + \phi(\boldsymbol{\mu}) \tag{21.25}$$

where

$$\phi(\boldsymbol{\mu}) = \begin{cases} -\infty & \text{if } \mu_1 < \mu_0 \\ 0 & \text{otherwise} \end{cases} \tag{21.26}$$

This has the desired effect, as shown in Figure 21.16b.

A more general approach is to apply a transformation to the parameters, to ensure identifiability. That is, we sample the parameters $\boldsymbol{\theta}$ from a proposal, and then apply an invertible transformation $\boldsymbol{\theta}' = f(\boldsymbol{\theta})$ to them before computing the log joint, $\log p(\mathcal{D}, \boldsymbol{\theta}')$. To account for the change of variables (Section 2.8.3), we add the log of the determinant of the Jacobian. In the case of a 1d ordering transformation, which just sorts its inputs, the determinant of the Jacobian is 1, so the log-det-Jacobian term vanishes.

Unfortunately, this approach does not scale to more than 1 dimensional problems, because there is no obvious way to enforce an ordering constraint on the centers $\boldsymbol{\mu}_k$.

21.4.1.3 Bayesian model selection

Once we have a reliable way to ensure identifiability, we can use Bayesian model selection techniques from Section 5.2.2 to select the number of clusters K. In Figure 21.17, we illustrate the results of fitting a GMM with $K = 3 - 6$ components to the data in Figure 21.15. We use the ordering transform on the means, and perform inference using HMC. We compare the resulting GMM model fits to the fit of a kernel density estimate (Section 16.3), which often over-smooths the data. We see fairly strong evidence for two bumps, corresponding to different subpopulations.

We can compare these models more quantitatively by computing their WAIC scores (widely applicable information criterion) which is an approximation to the log marginal likelihood (see [Wat10; Wat13; VGG17] for details). The results are shown in Figure 21.18. (This kind of visualization was proposed in [McE20, p228].) We see that the model with $K = 6$ scores significantly higher than for the other models, although $K = 5$ is a close second. This is consistent with the plot in Figure 21.17.

21.4.2 Mixtures of Bernoullis

As we discussed in Section 3.5.2, we can use a mixtures of Bernoullis to cluster binary data. The model has the form

$$p(\boldsymbol{y}|z = k, \boldsymbol{\theta}) = \prod_{d=1}^{D} \text{Ber}(y_d|\mu_{dk}) = \prod_{d=1}^{D} \mu_{dk}^{y_d}(1 - \mu_{dk})^{1-y_d} \tag{21.27}$$

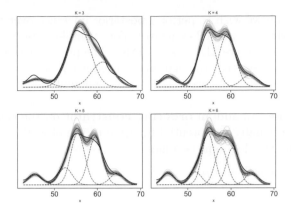

Figure 21.17: Fitting GMMs with different numbers of clusters K to the data in Figure 21.15. Black solid line is KDE fit. Solid blue line is posterior mean; feint blue lines are posterior samples. Dotted lines show the individual Gaussian mixture components, evaluated by plugging in their posterior mean parameters. Adapted from Figure 6.8 of [Mar18]. Generated by gmm_chooseK_pymc3.ipynb.

Here μ_{dk} is the probability that bit d turns on in cluster k. We can fit this model with EM, SGD, MCMC, etc. See Figure 3.13 for an example, where we cluster some binarized MNIST digits.

21.5   Spectral clustering *

In this section, we discuss an approach to clustering based on eigenvalue analysis of a pairwise similarity matrix. It uses the eigenvectors to derive feature vectors for each datapoint, which are then clustered using a feature-based clustering method, such as K-means (Section 21.3). This is known as **spectral clustering** [SM00; Lux07].

21.5.1   Normalized cuts

We start by creating a weighted undirected graph $\mathbf{W}$, where each data vector is a node, and the strength of the $i - j$ edge is a measure of similarity. Typically we only connected a node to its most similar neighbors, to ensure the graph is sparse, which speeds computation.

Our goal is to find K clusters of similar points. That is, we want to find a **graph partition** into $S_1, \ldots, S_K$ disjoint sets of nodes so as to minimize some kind of cost.

Our first attempt at a cost function is to compute the weight of connections between nodes in each cluster to nodes outside each cluster:

$$\text{cut}(S_1, \ldots, S_K) \triangleq \frac{1}{2} \sum_{k=1}^{K} W(S_k, \overline{S}_k) \tag{21.28}$$

where $W(A, B) \triangleq \sum_{i \in A, j \in B} w_{ij}$ and $\overline{S}_k = V \setminus S_k$ is the complement of S_k, where $V = \{1, \ldots, N\}$.

Unfortunately the optimal solution to this often just partitions off a single node from the rest, since that minimizes the weight of the cut. To prevent this, we can divide by the size of each set, to

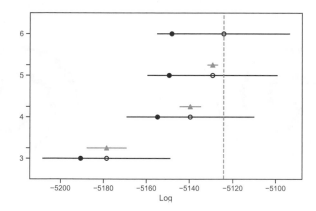

Figure 21.18: WAIC scores for the different GMMs. The empty circle is the posterior mean WAIC score for each model, and the black lines represent the standard error of the mean. The solid circle is the in-sample deviance of each model, i.e., the unpenalized log-likelihood. The dashed vertical line corresponds to the maximum WAIC value. The gray triangle is the difference in WAIC score for that model compared to the best model. Adapted from Figure 6.10 of [Mar18]. Generated by gmm_chooseK_pymc3.ipynb.

get the following objective, known as the **normalized cut**:

$$\text{Ncut}(S_1, \dots, S_K) \triangleq \frac{1}{2} \sum_{k=1}^{K} \frac{\text{cut}(S_k, \overline{S}_k)}{\text{vol}(S_k)} \tag{21.29}$$

where $\text{vol}(A) \triangleq \sum_{i \in A} d_i$ is the total weight of set A and $d_i = \sum_{j=1}^{N} w_{ij}$ is the weighted degree of node i. This splits the graph into K clusters such that nodes within each cluster are similar to each other, but are different to nodes in other clusters.

We can formulate the Ncut problem in terms of searching for binary vectors $c_i \in \{0, 1\}^N$ that minimizes the above objective, where $c_{ik} = 1$ iff point i belongs to cluster k. Unfortunately this is NP-hard [WW93]. Below we discuss a continuous relaxation of the problem based on eigenvector methods that is easier to solve.

21.5.2 Eigenvectors of the graph Laplacian encode the clustering

In Section 20.4.9.2, we discussed the graph Laplacian, which is defined as $\mathbf{L} \triangleq \mathbf{D} - \mathbf{W}$, where $\mathbf{W}$ is a symmetric weight matrix for the graph, and $\mathbf{D} = \text{diag}(d_i)$ is a diagonal matrix containing the weighted degree of each node, $d_i = \sum_j w_{ij}$. To get some intuition as to why $\mathbf{L}$ might be useful for graph-based clustering, we note the following result.

Theorem 21.5.1. *The set of eigenvectors of $\mathbf{L}$ with eigenvalue 0 is spanned by the indicator vectors $\mathbf{1}_{S_1}, \dots, \mathbf{1}_{S_K}$, where S_k are the K connected components of the graph.*

Proof. Let us start with the case $K = 1$. If $\boldsymbol{f}$ is an eigenvector with eigenvalue 0, then $0 = \sum_{ij} w_{ij}(f_i - f_j)^2$. If two nodes are connected, so $w_{ij} > 0$, we must have that $f_i = f_j$. Hence $\boldsymbol{f}$ is constant for all vertices which are connected by a path in the graph. Now suppose $K > 1$. In this

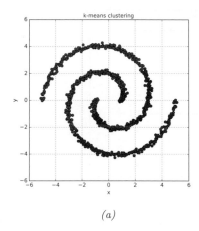
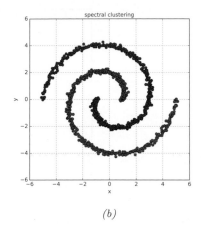

(a)   (b)

Figure 21.19: Results of clustering some data. (a) K-means. (b) Spectral clustering. Generated by spectral_clustering_demo.ipynb.

case, $\mathbf{L}$ will be block diagonal. A similar argument to the above shows that we will have K indicator functions, which "select out" the connected components.   □

This suggests the following clustering algorithm. Compute the eigenvectors and values of $\mathbf{L}$, and let $\mathbf{U}$ be an $N \times K$ matrix with the K eigenvectors with smallest eigenvalue in its columns. (Fast methods for computing such "bottom" eigenvectors are discussed in [YHJ09]). Let $\boldsymbol{u}_i \in \mathbb{R}^K$ be the i'th *row* of $\mathbf{U}$. Since these $\boldsymbol{u}_i$ will be piecewise constant, we can apply K-means clustering (Section 21.3) to them to recover the connected components. (Note that the vectors $\boldsymbol{u}_i$ are the same as those computed by Laplacian eigenmaps discussed in Section 20.4.9.)

Real data may not exhibit such clean block structure, but one can show, using results from perturbation theory, that the eigenvectors of a "perturbed" Laplacian will be close to these ideal indicator functions [NJW01].

In practice, it is important to normalize the graph Laplacian, to account for the fact that some nodes are more highly connected than others. One way to do this (proposed in [NJW01]) is to create a symmetric matrix

$$\mathbf{L}_{sym} \triangleq \mathbf{D}^{-\frac{1}{2}} \mathbf{L} \mathbf{D}^{-\frac{1}{2}} = \mathbf{I} - \mathbf{D}^{-\frac{1}{2}} \mathbf{W} \mathbf{D}^{-\frac{1}{2}} \tag{21.30}$$

This time the eigenspace of 0 is spanned by $\mathbf{D}^{\frac{1}{2}} \mathbf{1}_{S_k}$. This suggests the following algorithm: find the smallest K eigenvectors of $\mathbf{L}_{sym}$, stack them into the matrix $\mathbf{U}$, normalize each *row* to unit norm by creating $t_{ij} = u_{ij} / \sqrt{(\sum_k u_{ik}^2)}$ to make the matrix $\mathbf{T}$, cluster the rows of $\mathbf{T}$ using K-means, then infer the partitioning of the original points.

21.5.3   Example

Figure 21.19 illustrates the method in action. In Figure 21.19(a), we see that K-means does a poor job of clustering, since it implicitly assumes each cluster corresponds to a spherical Gaussian. Next we try spectral clustering. We compute a dense similarity matrix $\mathbf{W}$ using a Gaussian kernel,

$W_{ij} = \exp(-\frac{1}{2\sigma^2}||\boldsymbol{x}_i - \boldsymbol{x}_j||_2^2)$. We then compute the first two eigenvectors of the normalized Laplacian L_{sym}. From this we infer the clustering using K-means, with $K = 2$; the results are shown in Figure 21.19(b).

21.5.4　Connection with other methods

Spectral clustering is closely related to several other methods for unsupervised learning, some of which we discuss below.

21.5.4.1　Connection with kPCA

Spectral clustering is closely related to kernel PCA (Section 20.4.6). In particular, kPCA uses the largest eigenvectors of $\mathbf{W}$; these are equivalent to the smallest eigenvectors of $\mathbf{I} - \mathbf{W}$. This is similar to the above method, which computes the smallest eigenvectors of $\mathbf{L} = \mathbf{D} - \mathbf{W}$. See [Ben+04a] for details. In practice, spectral clustering tends to give better results than kPCA.

21.5.4.2　Connection with random walk analysis

In practice we get better results by computing the eigenvectors of the normalized graph Laplacian. One way to normalize the graph Laplacian, which is used in [SM00; Mei01], is to define

$$\mathbf{L}_{rw} \triangleq \mathbf{D}^{-1}\mathbf{L} = \mathbf{I} - \mathbf{D}^{-1}\mathbf{W} \tag{21.31}$$

One can show that for $\mathbf{L}_{rw}$, the eigenspace of 0 is again spanned by the indicator vectors $\mathbf{1}_{S_k}$ [Lux07], so we can perform clustering directly on the K smallest eigenvectors $\mathbf{U}$.

There is an interesting connection between this approach and random walks on a graph. First note that $\mathbf{P} = \mathbf{D}^{-1}\mathbf{W} = \mathbf{I} - \mathbf{L}_{rw}$ is a stochastic matrix, where $p_{ij} = w_{ij}/d_i$ can be interpreted as the probability of going from i to j. If the graph is connected and non-bipartite, it possesses a unique stationary distribution $\boldsymbol{\pi} = (\boldsymbol{\pi}_1, \ldots, \boldsymbol{\pi}_N)$, where $\pi_i = d_i/\text{vol}(V)$, and $\text{vol}(V) = \sum_i d_i$ is the sum of all the node degrees. Furthermore, one can show that for a partition of size 2,

$$\text{Ncut}(S, \overline{S}) = p(\overline{S}|S) + p(S|\overline{S}) \tag{21.32}$$

This means that we are looking for a cut such that a random walk spends more time transitioning to similar points, and rarely makes transitions from S to $\overline{S}$ or vice versa. This analysis can be extended to $K > 2$; for details, see [Mei01].

21.6　Biclustering *

In some cases, we have a data matrix $\mathbf{X} \in \mathbb{R}^{N_r \times N_c}$ and we want to cluster the rows *and* the columns; this is known as **biclustering** or **coclustering**. This is widely used in bioinformatics, where the rows often represent genes and the columns represent conditions. It can also be used for collaborative filtering, where the rows represent users and the columns represent movies.

A variety of ad hoc methods for biclustering have been proposed; see [MO04] for a review. In Section 21.6.1, we present a simple probabilistic generative model in which we assign a latent cluster id to each row, and a differnet latent cluster id to each column. In Section 21.6.2, we extend this to the case where each row can belong to multiple clusters, depending on which groups of features (columns) we choose to use to define the different groups of objects (rows).

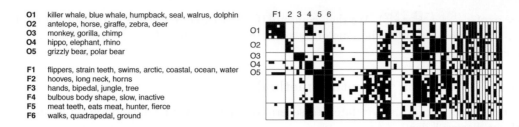

Figure 21.20: Illustration of biclustering. We show 5 of the 12 organism clusters, and 6 of the 33 feature clusters. The original data matrix is shown, partitioned according to the discovered clusters. From Figure 3 of [Kem+06]. Used with kind permission of Charles Kemp.

21.6.1 Basic biclustering

Here we present a simple probabilistic generative model for biclustering based on [Kem+06] (see also [SMM03] for a related approach). The idea is to associate each row and each column with a latent indicator, $u_i \in \{1, \ldots, N_u\}$, $v_j \in \{1, \ldots, N_v\}$, where N_u is the number of row clusters, and N_v is the number of column clusters. We then use the following generative model:

$$p(\mathbf{U}) = \prod_{i=1}^{N_r} \text{Unif}(u_i | \{1, \ldots, N_u\}) \tag{21.33}$$

$$p(\mathbf{V}) = \prod_{j=1}^{N_c} \text{Cat}(v_j | \{1, \ldots, N_v\}) \tag{21.34}$$

$$p(\mathbf{X} | \mathbf{U}, \mathbf{V}, \boldsymbol{\theta}) = \prod_{i=1}^{N_r} \prod_{j=1}^{N_c} p(X_{ij} | \boldsymbol{\theta}_{u_i, v_j}) \tag{21.35}$$

where $\boldsymbol{\theta}_{a,b}$ are the parameters for row cluster a and column cluster b.

Figure 21.20 shows a simple example. The data has the form $X_{ij} = 1$ iff animal i has feature j, where $i = 1 : 50$ and $j = 1 : 85$. The animals represent whales, bears, horses, etc. The features represent properties of the habitat (jungle, tree, coastal), or anatomical properties (has teeth, quadripedal), or behavioral properties (swims, eats meat), etc. The method discovered 12 animal clusters and 33 feature clusters. ([Kem+06] use a Bayesian nonparametric method to infer the number of clusters.) For example, the O2 cluster is { antelope, horse, giraffe, zebra, deer }, which is characterized by feature clusters F2 = { hooves, long neck, horns} and F6 = { walks, quadripedal, ground }, whereas the O4 cluster is { hippo, elephant, rhino }, which is characterized by feature clusters F4 = { bulbous body shape, slow, inactive } and F6.

21.6.2 Nested partition models (Crosscat)

The problem with basic biclustering (Section 21.6.1) is that each object (row) can only belong to one cluster. Intuitively, an object can have multiple roles, and can be assigned to different clusters depending on which subset of features you use. For example, in the animal dataset, we may want to group the animals on the basis of anatomical features (e.g., mammals are warm blooded, reptiles are

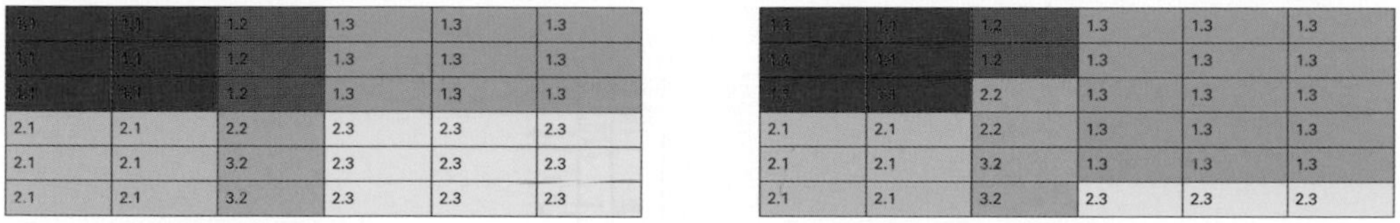

		1.2	1.3	1.3	1.3
		1.2	1.3	1.3	1.3
		1.2	1.3	1.3	1.3
2.1	2.1	2.2	2.3	2.3	2.3
2.1	2.1	3.2	2.3	2.3	2.3
2.1	2.1	3.2	2.3	2.3	2.3

(a)

		1.2	1.3	1.3	1.3
		1.2	1.3	1.3	1.3
		2.2	1.3	1.3	1.3
2.1	2.1	2.2	1.3	1.3	1.3
2.1	2.1	3.2	1.3	1.3	1.3
2.1	2.1	3.2	2.3	2.3	2.3

(b)

Figure 21.21: *(a) Example of biclustering. Each row is assigned to a unique cluster, and each column is assigned to a unique cluster. (b) Example of multi-clustering using a nested partition model. The rows can belong to different clusters depending on which subset of column features we are looking at.*

not), or on the basis of behavioral features (e.g., predators vs prey).

We now present a model that can capture this phenomenon. We illustrate the method with an example. Suppose we have a 6×6 matrix, with $N_u = 2$ row clusters and $N_v = 3$ column clusters. Furthermore, suppose the latent column assignments are as follows: $\boldsymbol{v} = [1, 1, 2, 3, 3, 3]$. This means we put columns 1 and 2 into group 1, column 3 into group 2, and columns 4 to 6 into group 3. For the columns that get clustered into group 1, we cluster the rows as follows: $\boldsymbol{u}_{:,1} = [1, 1, 1, 2, 2, 2]$; For the columns that get clustered into group 2, we cluster the rows as follows: $\boldsymbol{u}_{:,2} = [1, 1, 2, 2, 2, 2]$; and for the columns that get clustered into group 3, we cluster the rows as follows: $\boldsymbol{u}_{:,3} = [1, 1, 1, 1, 1, 2]$. The resulting partition is shown in Figure 21.21(b). We see that the clustering of the rows depends on which group of columns we choose to focus on.

Formally, we can define the model as follows:

$$p(\mathbf{U}) = \prod_{i=1}^{N_r} \prod_{l=1}^{N_v} \mathrm{Unif}(u_{il}|\{1, \ldots, N_u\}) \tag{21.36}$$

$$p(\mathbf{V}) = \prod_{j=1}^{N_c} \mathrm{Unif}(v_j|\{1, \ldots, N_v\}) \tag{21.37}$$

$$p(\mathbf{Z}|\mathbf{U}, \mathbf{V}) = \prod_{i=1}^{N_r} \prod_{j=1}^{N_c} \mathbb{I}\left(Z_{ij} = (u_{i,v_j}, v_j)\right) \tag{21.38}$$

$$p(\mathbf{X}|\mathbf{Z}, \boldsymbol{\theta}) = \prod_{i=1}^{N_r} \prod_{j=1}^{N_c} p(X_{ij}|\boldsymbol{\theta}_{z_{ij}}) \tag{21.39}$$

where $\boldsymbol{\theta}_{k,l}$ are the parameters for cocluster $k \in \{1, \ldots, N_u\}$ and $l \in \{1, \ldots, N_v\}$.

This model was independently proposed in [Sha+06; Man+16] who call it **crosscat** (for cross-categorization), in [Gua+10; CFD10], who call it **multi-clust**, and in [RG11], who call it **nested partitioning**. In all of these papers, the authors propose to use Dirichlet processes, to avoid the problem of estimating the number of clusters. Here we assume the number of clusters is known, and show the parameters explicitly, for notational simplicity.

Figure 21.22 illustrates the model applied to some binary data containing 22 animals and 106 features. The figure shows the (approximate) MAP partition. The first partition of the columns contains taxonomic features, such as "has bones", "is warm-blooded", "lays eggs", etc. This divides the

Figure 21.22: MAP estimate produced by the crosscat system when applied to a binary data matrix of animals (rows) by features (columns). See text for details. From Figure 7 of [Sha+06]. Used with kind permission of Vikash Mansingkha.

animals into birds, reptiles/ amphibians, mammals, and invertebrates. The second partition of the columns contains features that are treated as noise, with no apparent structure (except for the single row labeled "frog"). The third partition of the columns contains ecological features like "dangerous", "carnivorous", "lives in water", etc. This divides the animals into prey, land predators, sea predators and air predators. Thus each animal (row) can belong to a different cluster depending on what set of features are considered.

22 Recommender Systems

Recommender systems are systems which recommend **items** (such as movies, books, ads) to **users** based on various information, such as their past viewing/ purchasing behavior (e.g., which movies they rated high or low, which ads they clicked on), as well as optional "side information" such as demographics about the user, or information about the content of the item (e.g., its title, genre or price). Such systems are widely used by various internet companies, such as Facebook, Amazon, Netflix, Google, etc. In this chapter, we give a brief introduction to the topic. More details can be found in e.g., [DKK12; Pat12; Yan+14; AC16; Agg16; Zha+19b]..

22.1 Explicit feedback

In this section, we consider the simplest setting in which the user gives **explicit feedback** to the system in terms of a **rating**, such as +1 or -1 (for like/dislike) or a score from 1 to 5. Let $Y_{ui} \in \mathbb{R}$ be the rating that user u gives to item i. We can represent this as an $M \times N$ matrix, where M is the number of users, and N is the number of items. Typically this matrix will be very large but very sparse, since most users will not provide any feedback on most items. See Figure 22.1(a) for an example. We can also view this sparse matrix as a bipartite graph, where the weight of the $u - i$ edge is Y_{ui}. This reflects the fact that we are dealing with **relational data**, i.e., the values of u and i have no intrinsic meaning (they are just arbitrary indices), it is the fact that u and i are connected that matters.

If Y_{ui} is missing, it could be because user u has not interacted with item i, or it could be that they knew they wouldn't like it and so they chose not to engage with it. In the former case, some of the data is **missing at random**; in the latter case, the missingness is informative about the true value of Y_{ui}. (See e.g., [Mar+11] for further discussion of this point.) We will assume the data is missing at random, for simplicity.

22.1.1 Datasets

A famous example of an explicit ratings matrix was made available by the movie streaming company Netflix. In 2006, they released a large dataset of 100,480,507 movie ratings (on a scale of 1 to 5) from 480,189 users of 17,770 movies. Despite the large size of the training set, the ratings matrix is still 99% sparse (unknown). Along with the data, they offered a prize of $1M, known as the **Netflix Prize**, to any team that could predict the true ratings of a set of test (user, item) pairs more accurately than their incumbent system. The prize was claimed on September 21, 2009 by a team known as "BellKor's Pragmatic Chaos". They used an ensemble of different methods, as

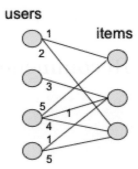

Figure 22.1: Example of a relational dataset represented as a sparse matrix (left) or a sparse bipartite graph (right). Values corresponding to empty cells (missing edges) are unknown. Rows 3 and 4 are similar to each other, indicating that users 3 and 4 might have similar preferences, so we can use the data from user 3 to predict user 4's preferences. However, user 1 seems quite different in their preferences, and seems to give low ratings to all items. For user 2, we have very little observed data, so it is hard to make reliable predictions.

described in [Kor09; BK07; FHK12]. However, a key component in their ensemble was the method described in Section 22.1.3.

Unfortunately the Netflix data is no longer available due to privacy concerns. Fortunately the **MovieLens** group at the University of Minnesota have released an anonymized public dataset of movie ratings, on a scale of 1-5, that can be used for research [HK15]. There are also various other public explicit ratings datasets, such as the **Jester** jokes dataset from [Gol+01] and the **BookCrossing** dataset from [Zie+05].

22.1.2   Collaborative filtering

The original approach to the recommendation problem is called **collaborative filtering** [Gol+92]. The idea is that users collaborate on recommending items by sharing their ratings with other users; then if u wants to know if they interact with i, they can see what ratings other users u' have given to i, and take a weighted average:

$$\hat{Y}_{ui} = \sum_{u':Y_{u',i}\neq?} \text{sim}(u,u')\, Y_{u',i} \tag{22.1}$$

where we assume $Y_{u',i} =?$ if the entry is unknown. The traditional approach measured the similarity of two users by comparing the sets $S_u = \{Y_{u,i} \neq ? : i \in \mathcal{I}\}$ and $S_{u'} = \{Y_{u',i} \neq ? : i \in \mathcal{I}\}$, where $\mathcal{I}$ is the set of items. However, this can suffer from data sparsity. In Section 22.1.3 we discuss an approach based on learning dense embedding vectors for each item and each user, so we can compute similarity in a low dimensional feature space.

22.1.3 Matrix factorization

We can view the recommender problem as one of **matrix completion**, in which we wish to predict all the missing entries of $\mathbf{Y}$. We can formulate this as the following optimization problem:

$$\mathcal{L}(\mathbf{Z}) = \sum_{ij:Y_{ij}\neq?} (Z_{ij} - Y_{ij})^2 = ||\mathbf{Z} - \mathbf{Y}||_F^2 \tag{22.2}$$

However, this is an under-specified problem, since there are an infinite number of ways of filling in the missing entries of $\mathbf{Z}$.

We need to add some constraints. Suppose we assume that $\mathbf{Y}$ is low rank. Then we can write it in the form $\mathbf{Z} = \mathbf{U}\mathbf{V}^\mathsf{T} \approx \mathbf{Y}$, where $\mathbf{U}$ is an $M \times K$ matrix, $\mathbf{V}$ is a $N \times K$ matrix, K is the rank of the matrix, M is the number of users, and N is the number of items. This corresponds to a prediction of the form by writing

$$\hat{y}_{ui} = \boldsymbol{u}_u^\mathsf{T} \boldsymbol{v}_i \tag{22.3}$$

This is called **matrix factorization**.

If we observe all the Y_{ij} entries, we can find the optimal $\mathbf{Z}$ using SVD (Section 7.5). However, when $\mathbf{Y}$ has missing entries, the corresponding objective is no longer convex, and does not have a unique optimum [SJ03]. We can fit this using **alternating least squares** (**ALS**), where we estimate $\mathbf{U}$ given $\mathbf{V}$ and then estimate $\mathbf{V}$ given $\mathbf{U}$ (for details, see e.g., [KBV09]). Alternatively we can just use SGD.

In practice, it is important to also allow for user-specific and item-specific baselines, by writing

$$\hat{y}_{ui} = \mu + b_u + c_i + \boldsymbol{u}_u^\mathsf{T} \boldsymbol{v}_i \tag{22.4}$$

This can capture the fact that some users might always tend to give low ratings and others may give high ratings; in addition, some items (e.g., very popular movies) might have unusually high ratings.

In addition, we can add some ℓ_2 regularization to the parameters to get the objective

$$\mathcal{L}(\boldsymbol{\theta}) = \sum_{ij:Y_{ij}\neq?} (y_{ij} - \hat{y}_{ij})^2 + \lambda(b_u^2 + c_i^2 + ||\boldsymbol{u}_u||^2 + ||\boldsymbol{v}_i||^2) \tag{22.5}$$

We can optimize this using SGD by sampling a random (u, i) entry from the set of observed values, and performing the following updates:

$$b_u = b_u + \eta(e_{ui} - \lambda b_u) \tag{22.6}$$
$$c_i = c_i + \eta(e_{ui} - \lambda c_i) \tag{22.7}$$
$$\boldsymbol{u}_u = \boldsymbol{u}_u + \eta(e_{ui}\boldsymbol{v}_i - \lambda\boldsymbol{u}_u) \tag{22.8}$$
$$\boldsymbol{v}_i = \boldsymbol{v}_i + \eta(e_{ui}\boldsymbol{u}_u - \lambda\boldsymbol{v}_i) \tag{22.9}$$

where $e_{ui} = y_{ui} - \hat{y}_{ui}$ is the error term, and $\eta \geq 0$ is the learning rate. This approach was first proposed by Simon Funk, who was one of the first to do well in the early days of the Netflix competition.[1]

---

1. https://sifter.org/~simon/journal/20061211.html.

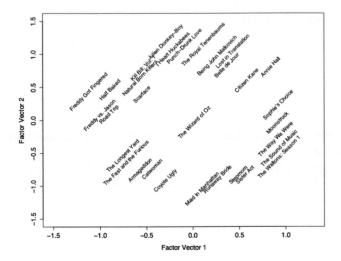

Figure 22.2: Visualization of the first two latent movie factors estimated from the Netflix challenge data. Each movie j is plotted at the location specified by $\boldsymbol{v}_j$. See text for details. From Figure 3 of [KBV09]. Used with kind permission of Yehuda Koren.

22.1.3.1   Probabilistic matrix factorization (PMF)

We can convert matrix factorization into a probabilistic model by defining

$$p(y_{ui} = y) = \mathcal{N}(y|\mu + b_u + c_i + \boldsymbol{u}_u^{\mathsf{T}}\boldsymbol{v}_i, \sigma^2) \tag{22.10}$$

This is known as **probabilistic matrix factorization** (**PMF**) [SM08]. The NLL of this model is equivalent to the matrix factorization objective in Equation (22.2). However, the probabilistic perspective allows us to generalize the model more easily. For example, we can capture the fact that the ratings are integers (often mostly 0s), and not reals, using a Poisson or negative Binomial likelihood (see e.g., [GOF18]). This is similar to exponential family PCA (Section 20.2.7), except that we view rows and columns symmetrically.

22.1.3.2   Example: Netflix

Suppose we apply PMF to the Netflix dataset using $K = 2$ latent factors. Figure 22.2 visualizes the learned embedding vectors $\boldsymbol{u}_i$ for a few movies. On the left of the plot we have low-brow humor and horror movies (*Half Baked, Freddy vs Jason*), and on the right we have more serious dramas (*Sophie's Choice, Moonstruck*). On the top we have critically acclaimed independent movies (*Punch-Drunk Love, I Heart Huckabees*), and on the bottom we have mainstream Hollywood blockbusters (*Armageddon, Runway Bride*). The *Wizard of Oz* is right in the middle of these axes, since it is in some senses an "average movie".

Users are embedded into the same spaces as movies. We can then predict the rating for any user-video pair using proximity in the latent embedding space.

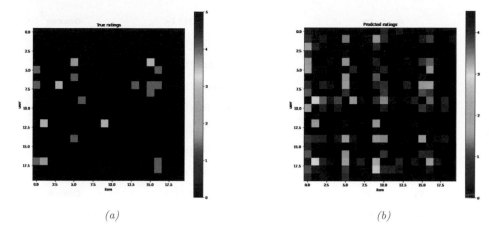

(a)   *(b)*

Figure 22.3: (a) A fragment of the observed ratings matrix from the MovieLens-1M dataset. (b) Predictions using SVD with 50 latent components. Generated by matrix_factorization_recommender.ipynb.

22.1.3.3   Example: MovieLens

Now suppose we apply PMF to the MovieLens-1M dataset with 6040 users, 3706 movies, and 1,000,209 ratings. We will use $K = 50$ factors. For simplicity, we fit this using SVD applied to the dense ratings matrix, where we replace missing values with 0. (This is just a simple approximation to keep the demo code simple.) In Figure 22.3 we show a snippet of the true and predicted ratings matrix. (We truncate the predictions to lie in the range [1,5].) We see that the model is not particularly accurate, but does capture some structure in the data.

Furthermore, it seems to behave in a qualitatively sensible way. For example, in Figure 22.4 we show the top 10 movies rated by a given user as well as the top 10 predictions for movies they had not seen. The model seems to have "picked up" on the underlying preferences of the user. For example, we see that many of the predicted movies are action or film-noir, and both of these genres feature in the user's own top-10 list, even though explicit genre information is not used during model training.

22.1.4   Autoencoders

Matrix factorization is a (bi)linear model. We can make a nonlinear version using autoencoders. Let $\boldsymbol{y}_{:,i} \in \mathbb{R}^M$ be the i'th column of the ratings matrix, where unknown ratings are set to 0. We can predict this ratings vector using an autoencoder of the form

$$f(\boldsymbol{y}_{:,i}; \boldsymbol{\theta}) = \mathbf{W}^{\mathsf{T}}\varphi(\mathbf{V}\boldsymbol{y}_{:,i} + \boldsymbol{\mu}) + \boldsymbol{b} \tag{22.11}$$

where $\mathbf{V} \in \mathbb{R}^{KM}$ maps the ratings to an embedding space, $\mathbf{W} \in \mathbb{R}^{KM}$ maps the embedding space to a distribution over ratings, $\boldsymbol{\mu} \in \mathbb{R}^K$ are the biases of the hidden units, and $\boldsymbol{b} \in \mathbb{R}^M$ are the biases of the output units. This is called the (item-based) version of the **AutoRec** model [Sed+15]. This has $2MK + M + K$ parameters. There is also a user-based version, that can be derived in a similar manner, which has $2NK + N + K$ parameters. (On MovieLens and Netflix, the authors find that the item-based method works better.)

	MovieID	Title	Genres
36	858	Godfather, The (1972)	Action|Crime|Drama
35	1387	Jaws (1975)	Action|Horror
65	2028	Saving Private Ryan (1998)	Action|Drama|War
63	1221	Godfather: Part II, The (1974)	Action|Crime|Drama
11	913	Maltese Falcon, The (1941)	Film-Noir|Mystery
20	3417	Crimson Pirate, The (1952)	Adventure|Comedy|Sci-Fi
34	2186	Strangers on a Train (1951)	Film-Noir|Thriller
55	2791	Airplane! (1980)	Comedy
31	1188	Strictly Ballroom (1992)	Comedy|Romance
28	1304	Butch Cassidy and the Sundance Kid (1969)	Action|Comedy|Western

(a)

	MovieID	Title	Genres
516	527	Schindler's List (1993)	Drama|War
1848	1953	French Connection, The (1971)	Action|Crime|Drama|Thriller
596	608	Fargo (1996)	Crime|Drama|Thriller
1235	1284	Big Sleep, The (1946)	Film-Noir|Mystery
2085	2194	Untouchables, The (1987)	Action|Crime|Drama
1188	1230	Annie Hall (1977)	Comedy|Romance
1198	1242	Glory (1989)	Action|Drama|War
897	922	Sunset Blvd. (a.k.a. Sunset Boulevard) (1950)	Film-Noir
1849	1954	Rocky (1976)	Action|Drama
581	593	Silence of the Lambs, The (1991)	Drama|Thriller

(b)

Figure 22.4: (a) Top 10 movies (from a list of 69) that user "837" has already highly rated. (b) Top 10 predictions (from a list of 3637) from the algorithm. Generated by matrix_factorization_recommender.ipynb.

We can fit this by only updating parameters that are associated with the observed entries of $\boldsymbol{y}_{:,i}$. Furthermore, we can add an ℓ_2 regularizer to the weight matrices to get the objective

$$\mathcal{L}(\boldsymbol{\theta}) = \sum_{i=1}^{N} \sum_{u:y_{ui} \neq ?} (y_{u,i} - f(\boldsymbol{y}_{:,i};\boldsymbol{\theta})_u)^2 + \frac{\lambda}{2}(||\mathbf{W}||_F^2 + ||\mathbf{V}||_F^2) \tag{22.12}$$

Despite the simplicity of this method, the authors find that this does better than more complex methods such as restricted Boltzmann machines (RBMs, [SMH07]) and local low-rank matrix approximation (LLORMA, [Lee+13]).

22.2 Implicit feedback

So far, we have assumed that the user gives explicit ratings for each item that they interact with. This is a very restrictive assumption. More generally, we would like to learn from the **implicit feedback** that users give just by interacting with a system. For example, we can treat the list of movies that user u watches as positives, and regard all the other movies as negatives. Thus we get a sparse, positive-only ratings matrix.

Alternatively, we can view the fact that they watched movie i but did not watch movie j as an implicit signal that they prefer i to j. The resulting data can be represented as a set of tuples of the form $y_n = (u, i, j)$, where (u, i) is a positive pair, and (u, j) is a negative (or unlabeled) pair.

22.2.1 Bayesian personalized ranking

To fit a model to data of the form (u, i, j), we need to use a **ranking loss**, so that the model ranks i ahead of j for user u. A simple way to do this is to use a Bernoulli model of the form

$$p(y_n = (u, i, j)|\boldsymbol{\theta}) = \sigma(f(u, i; \boldsymbol{\theta}) - f(u, j; \boldsymbol{\theta})) \tag{22.13}$$

If we combine this with a Gaussian prior for $\boldsymbol{\theta}$, we get the following MAP estimation problem:

$$\mathcal{L}(\boldsymbol{\theta}) = \sum_{(u,i,j) \in \mathcal{D}} \log \sigma(f(u, i; \boldsymbol{\theta}) - f(u, j; \boldsymbol{\theta})) - \lambda ||\boldsymbol{\theta}||^2 \tag{22.14}$$

where $\mathcal{D} = \{(u, i, j) : i \in \mathcal{I}_u^+, j \in \mathcal{I} \setminus \mathcal{I}_u^+\}$, where $\mathcal{I}_u^+$ are the set of all items that user u selected, and $\mathcal{I} \setminus \mathcal{I}_u^+$ are all the other items (which they may dislike, or simply may not have seen). This is known as **Bayesian personalized ranking** or BPR [Ren+09].

Let us consider this example from [Zha+20, Sec 16.5]. There are 4 items in total, $\mathcal{I} = \{i_1, i_2, i_3, i_4\}$, and user u chose to interact with $\mathcal{I}_u^+ = \{i_2, i_3\}$. In this case, the implicit item-item preference matrix for user u has the form

$$\mathbf{Y}_u = \begin{pmatrix} . & + & + & ? \\ - & . & ? & - \\ - & ? & . & - \\ ? & + & + & . \end{pmatrix} \tag{22.15}$$

where $Y_{u,i,i'} = +$ means user u prefers i' to i, $Y_{u,i,i'} = -$ means user u prefers i to i', and $Y_{u,i,i'} = ?$ means we cannot tell what the user's preference is. For example, focusing on the second column, we see that this user rates i_2 higher than i_1 and i_4, since they selected i_2 but not i_1 or i_4; however, we cannot tell if they prefer i_2 over i_3 or vice versa.

When the set of posssible items is large, the number of negatives in $\mathcal{I} \setminus \mathcal{I}_u^+$ can be very large. Fortunately we can approximate the loss by subsampling negatives.

Note that an alternative to the log-loss above is to use a hinge loss, similar to the approach used in SVMs (Section 17.3). This has the form

$$\mathcal{L}(y_n = (u, i, j), f) = \max(m - (f(u, i) - f(u, j)), 0) = \max(m - f(u, i) + f(u, j), 0) \tag{22.16}$$

where $m \geq 0$ is the safety margin. This tries to ensure the negative items j never score more than m higher than the positive items i.

22.2.2   Factorization machines

The AutoRec approach of Section 22.1.4 is nonlinear, but treats users and items asymmetrically. In this section, we discuss a more symmetric discriminative modeling approach. We start with a linear version. The basic idea is to predict the output (such as a rating) for any given user-item pair, $\boldsymbol{x} = [\text{one-hot}(u), \text{one-hot}(i)]$, using

$$f(\boldsymbol{x}) = \mu + \sum_{i=1}^{D} w_i x_i + \sum_{i=1}^{D} \sum_{j=i+1}^{D} (\boldsymbol{v}_i^\mathsf{T} \boldsymbol{v}_j) x_i x_j \tag{22.17}$$

where $\boldsymbol{x} \in \mathbb{R}^D$ where $D = (M + N)$ is the number of inputs, $\mathbf{V} \in \mathbb{R}^{D \times K}$ is a weight matrix, $\boldsymbol{w} \in \mathbb{R}^D$ is a weight vector, and $\mu \in \mathbb{R}$ is a global offset. This is known as a **factorization machine** (FM) [Ren12].

The term $(\boldsymbol{v}_i^\mathsf{T} \boldsymbol{v}_j) x_i x_j$ measures the interaction between feature i and j in the input. This generalizes the matrix factorization model of Equation (22.4), since it can handle other kinds of information in the input $\boldsymbol{x}$, beyond just user and item, as we discuss in Section 22.3.

Computing Equation (22.17) takes $O(KD^2)$ time, since it considers all possible pairwise interactions between every user and every item. Fortunately we can rewrite this so that we can compute it in $O(KD)$ time as follows:

$$\sum_{i=1}^{D} \sum_{j=i+1}^{D} (\boldsymbol{v}_i^\mathsf{T} \boldsymbol{v}_j) x_i x_j = \frac{1}{2} \sum_{i=1}^{D} \sum_{j=1}^{D} (\boldsymbol{v}_i^\mathsf{T} \boldsymbol{v}_j) x_i x_j - \frac{1}{2} \sum_{i=1}^{D} (\boldsymbol{v}_i^\mathsf{T} \boldsymbol{v}_i) x_i x_i \tag{22.18}$$

$$= -\frac{1}{2} \left(\sum_{i=1}^{D} \sum_{j=1}^{D} \sum_{k=1}^{K} v_{ik} v_{jk} x_i x_j - \sum_{i=1}^{D} \sum_{k=1}^{K} v_{ik} v_{ik} x_i x_i \right) \tag{22.19}$$

$$= -\frac{1}{2} \sum_{k=1}^{K} \left((\sum_{i=1}^{D} v_{ik} x_i)^2 - \sum_{i=1}^{D} v_{ik}^2 x_i^2 \right) \tag{22.20}$$

For sparse vectors, the overall complexity is linear in the number of non-zero components. So if we use one-hot encodings of the user and item id, the complexity is just $O(K)$, analogous to the original matrix factorization objective of Equation (22.4).

We can fit this model to minimize any loss we want. For example, if we have explicit feedback, we may choose MSE loss, and if we have implicit feedback, we may choosing ranking loss.

In [Guo+17], they propose a model called **deep factorization machines**, which combines the above method with an MLP applied to a concatenation of the embedding vectors, instead of the inner product. More precisely, it is a model of the form

$$f(\boldsymbol{x}; \boldsymbol{\theta}) = \sigma(\text{FM}(\boldsymbol{x}) + \text{MLP}(\boldsymbol{x})) \tag{22.21}$$

This is closely related to the **wide and deep** model proposed in [Che+16]. The idea is that the bilinear FM model captures explicit interactions between specific users and items (a form of memorization), whereas the MLP captures implicit interactions between user features and item features, which allows the model to generalize.

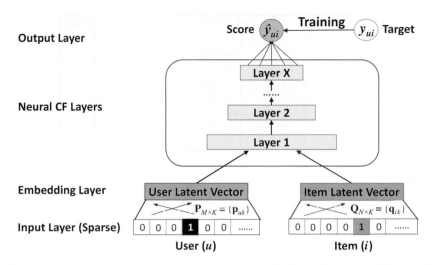

Figure 22.5: Illustration of the neural matrix factorization model. From Figure 2 of [He+17]. Used with kind permission of Xiangnan He.

22.2.3 Neural matrix factorization

In this section, we describe the **neural matrix factorization** model of [He+17]. This is another way to combine bilinear models with deep neural networks. The bilinear part is used to define the following generalized matrix factorization (GMF) pathway, which computes the following feature vector for user u and item i:

$$z_{ui}^1 = \mathbf{P}_{u,:} \odot \mathbf{Q}_{i,:} \tag{22.22}$$

where $\mathbf{P} \in \mathbb{R}^{MK}$ is a user embedding matrix, and $\mathbf{Q} \in \mathbb{R}^{NK}$ is an item embedding matrix. The DNN part is just an MLP applied to a concatenation of the embedding vectors (using different embedding matrices):

$$z_{ui}^2 = \mathrm{MLP}([\tilde{\mathbf{U}}_{u,:}, \tilde{\mathbf{V}}_{i,:}]) \tag{22.23}$$

Finally, the model combines these to get

$$f(u, i; \boldsymbol{\theta}) = \sigma(\boldsymbol{w}^\mathsf{T}[z_{ui}^1, z_{ui}^2]) \tag{22.24}$$

See Figure 22.5 for an illustration.

In [He+17], the model is trained on implicit feedback, where $y_{ui} = 1$ if the interaction of user u with item i is observed, and $y_{ui} = 0$ otherwise. However, it could be trained to minimize BPR loss.

22.3 Leveraging side information

So far, we have assumed that the only information available to the predictor are the integer id of the user and the integer id of the item. This is an extremely impoverished representation, and will fail to

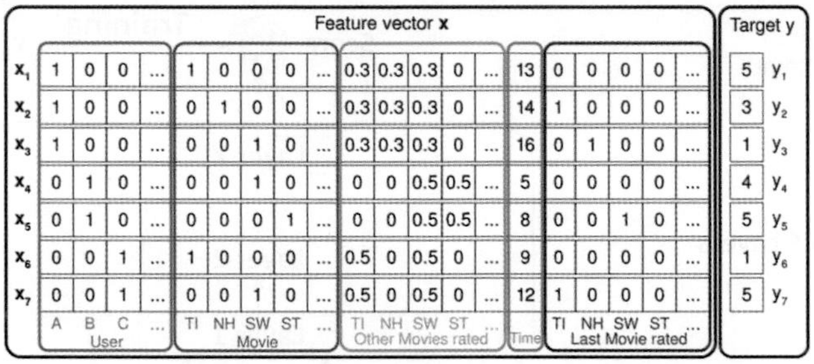

	Feature vector **x**						Target y
	User (A B C ...)	**Movie** (TI NH SW ST ...)	**Other Movies rated** (TI NH SW ST ...)	**Time**	**Last Movie rated** (TI NH SW ST ...)		
x_1	1 0 0 ...	1 0 0 0 ...	0.3 0.3 0.3 0 ...	13	0 0 0 0 ...	5	y_1
x_2	1 0 0 ...	0 1 0 0 ...	0.3 0.3 0.3 0 ...	14	1 0 0 0 ...	3	y_2
x_3	1 0 0 ...	0 0 1 0 ...	0.3 0.3 0.3 0 ...	16	0 1 0 0 ...	1	y_3
x_4	0 1 0 ...	0 0 1 0 ...	0 0 0.5 0.5 ...	5	0 0 0 0 ...	4	y_4
x_5	0 1 0 ...	0 0 0 1 ...	0 0 0.5 0.5 ...	8	0 0 1 0 ...	5	y_5
x_6	0 0 1 ...	1 0 0 0 ...	0.5 0 0.5 0 ...	9	0 0 0 0 ...	1	y_6
x_7	0 0 1 ...	0 0 1 0 ...	0.5 0 0.5 0 ...	12	1 0 0 0 ...	5	y_7

Figure 22.6: *Illustration of a design matrix for a movie recommender system, where we show the id of the user and movie, as well as other side information. From Figure 1 of [Ren12]. Used with kind permission of Stefen Rendle.*

work if we encounter a new user or new item (the so-called **cold start** problem). To overcome this, we need to leverage "**side information**", beyond just the id of the user/item.

There are many forms of side information we can use. For items, we often have rich meta-data, such text (e.g., title), images (e.g., cover), high-dimensional categorical variables (e.g., location), or just scalars (eg., price). For users, the side information available depends on the specific form of the interactive system. For search engines, it is the list of queries the user has issued, and (if they are logged in), information derived from websites they have visited (which is tracked via cookies). For online shopping sites, it is the list of searches plus past viewing and purchasing behavior. For social networking sites, there is information about the friendship graph of each user.

It is very easy to capture this side information in the factorization machines framework, by expanding our definition of x beyond the two one-hot vectors, as illustrated in Figure 22.6. The same input encoding can of course be fed into other kinds of models, such as deepFM or neuralMF.

In addition to features about the user and item, there may be other contextual features, such as the time of the interaction (e.g., the day or evening). The order (sequence) of the most recently viewed items is often also a useful signal. The "Convolutional Sequence Embedding Recommendation" or **Caser** model proposed in [TW18] captures this by embedding the last M items, and then treating the $M \times K$ input as an image, by using a convolutional layer as part of the model.

Many other kinds of neural models can be designed for the recommender task. See e.g., [Zha+19b] for a review.

22.4 Exploration-exploitation tradeoff

An interesting "twist" to recommender systems that does not arise in other kinds of prediction problems is the fact that the data that the system is trained on is a consequence of recommendations made by earlier versions of the system. Thus there is a feedback loop [Bot+13]. For example, consider the YouTube video recommendation system [CAS16]. There are millions of videos on the site, so the system must come up with a shortlist, or "**slate**", of videos to show the user, to help them find what they want (see e.g., [Ie+19]). If the user watches one of these videos, the system can consider this positive feedback that it made a good recommendation, and it can update the model parameters accordingly. However, maybe there was some other video that the user would have liked even more?

It is impossible to answer this counterfactual unless the system takes a chance and shows some items for which the user response is uncertain. This is an example of the **exploration-exploitation tradeoff**.

In addition to needing to explore, the system may have to wait for a long time until it can detect if a change it made its recommendation policies was beneficial. It is common to use **reinforcement learning** to learn policies which optimize long-term reward. See the sequel to this book, [Mur23], for details.

23 Graph Embeddings *

This chapter is coauthored with Bryan Perozzi, Sami Abu-El-Haija and Ines Chami, and is based on [Cha+21].

23.1 Introduction

We now turn our focus to data which has semantic relationships between training samples $\{\mathbf{x}_n\}_{n=1}^N$. The relationships (known as edges) connect training samples (nodes) with an application specific meaning (commonly similarity). Graphs provide the mathematical foundations for reasoning about these kind of relationships

Graphs are universal data structures that can represent complex relational data (composed of nodes and edges), and appear in multiple domains such as social networks, computational chemistry [Gil+17], biology [Sta+06], recommendation systems [KSJ09], semi-supervised learning [GB18], and others.

Let $\mathbf{A} \in \{0,1\}^{N \times N}$ be the adjacency matrix, where N is the number of nodes, and let $\mathbf{W} \in \mathbb{R}^{N \times N}$ be a weighted version. In the methods we discuss below, some set $\mathbf{W} = \mathbf{A}$ while others set $\mathbf{W}$ to a transformation of $\mathbf{A}$, such as row-wise normalization. Finally, let $\mathbf{X} \in \mathbb{R}^{N \times D}$ be a matrix of node features.

When designing and training a neural network model over graph data, we desire the designed method be applicable to nodes which participate in different graph settings (e.g. have differing connections and community structure). Contrast this with a neural network model designed for images, where each pixel (node) has the same neighborhood structure. By contrast, an arbitrary graph has no specified alignment of nodes, and further, each node might have a different neighborhood structure. See Figure 23.1 for a comparison. Consequently, operations like Euclidean spatial convolution cannot be directly applied on irregular graphs: Euclidean convolutions strongly rely on geometric priors (such as shift invariance), which don't generalize to non-Euclidean domains.

These challenges led to the development of **Geometric Deep Learning** (GDL) research [Bro+17b], which aims at applying deep learning techniques to non-Euclidean data. In particular, given the widespread prevalence of graphs in real-world applications, there has been a surge of interest in applying machine learning methods to graph-structured data. Among these, **Graph Representation Learning** (GRL) [Cha+21] methods aim at learning low-dimensional continuous vector representations for graph-structured data, also called embeddings.

We divide GRL here into two classes of problems: **unsupervised** and **supervised** (or semi-supervised) GRL. The first class aims at learning low-dimensional Euclidean representations optimizing

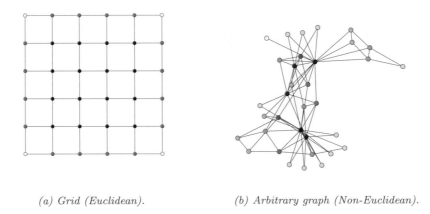

(a) Grid (Euclidean).   (b) Arbitrary graph (Non-Euclidean).

Figure 23.1: *An illustration of Euclidean vs. non-Euclidean graphs. Used with permission from [Cha+21].*

an objective, e.g. one that preserve the structure of an input graph. The second class also learns low-dimensional Euclidean representations but for a specific downstream prediction task such as node or graph classification. Further, the graph structure can be fixed throughout training and testing, which is known as the **transductive** learning setting (e.g. predicting user properties in a large social network), or alternatively the model is expected to answer questions about graphs not seen during training, known as the **inductive** learning setting (e.g. classifying molecular structures). Finally, while most supervised and unsupervised methods learn representations in Euclidean vector spaces, there recently has been interest for **non-Euclidean representation learning**, which aims at learning non-Euclidean embedding spaces such as hyperbolic or spherical spaces. The main motivations for this body of work is to use a continuous embedding space that resembles the underlying discrete structure of the input data it tries to embed (e.g. the hyperbolic space is a continuous version of trees [Sar11]).

23.2   Graph Embedding as an Encoder/Decoder Problem

While there are many approaches to GRL, many methods follow a similar pattern. First, the network input (node features $\mathbf{X} \in \mathbb{R}^{N \times D}$ and graph edges in $\mathbf{A}$ or $\mathbf{W} \in \mathbb{R}^{N \times N}$) is encoded from the discrete domain of the graph into a continuous representation (embedding), $\mathbf{Z} \in \mathbb{R}^{N \times L}$. Next, the learned representation $\mathbf{Z}$ is used to optimize a particular objective (such as reconstructing the links of the graph). In this section we will use the graph encoder-decoder model (GRAPHEDM) proposed by Chami et al. [Cha+21] to analyze popular families of GRL methods.

The GRAPHEDM framework (Figure 23.2, [Cha+21]) provides a general framework that encapsulates a wide variety of supervised and unsupervised graph embedding methods: including ones utilizing the graph as a regularizer (e.g. [ZG02]), positional embeddings(e.g. [PARS14]), and graph neural networks such as ones based on message passing [Gil+17; Sca+09] or graph convolutions

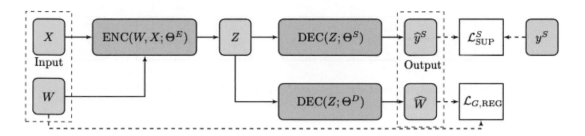

Figure 23.2: Illustration of the GRAPHEDM *framework from Chami et al. [Cha+21]. Based on the supervision available, methods will use some or all of the branches. In particular, unsupervised methods do not leverage label decoding for training and only optimize the similarity decoder (lower branch). On the other hand, semi-supervised and supervised methods leverage the additional supervision to learn models' parameters (upper branch). Reprinted with permission from [Cha+21].*

[Bru+14; KW16a]).

The GRAPHEDM framework takes as input a weighted graph $\mathbf{W} \in \mathbb{R}^{N \times N}$, and optional node features $\mathbf{X} \in \mathbb{R}^{N \times D}$. In (semi-)supervised settings, we assume that we are given training target labels for nodes (denoted N), edges (denoted E), and/or for the entire graph (denoted G). We denote the supervision signal as $S \in \{N, E, G\}$, as presented below.

The GRAPHEDM model itself can be decomposed into the following components:

- **Graph encoder network** $\mathrm{ENC}_{\Theta^E} : \mathbb{R}^{N \times N} \times \mathbb{R}^{N \times D} \to \mathbb{R}^{N \times L}$, parameterized by Θ^E, which combines the graph structure with optional node features to produce a node embedding matrix $\mathbf{Z} \in \mathbb{R}^{N \times L}$ as follows:

$$\mathbf{Z} = \mathrm{ENC}(\mathbf{W}, \mathbf{X}; \Theta^E).\tag{23.1}$$

As we shall see next, this node embedding matrix might capture different graph properties depending on the supervision used for training.

- **Graph decoder network** $\mathrm{DEC}_{\Theta^D} : \mathbb{R}^{N \times L} \to \mathbb{R}^{N \times N}$, parameterized by Θ^D, which uses the node embeddings Z to compute similarity scores for all node pairs in matrix $\widehat{\mathbf{W}} \in \mathbb{R}^{N \times N}$ as follows:

$$\widehat{\mathbf{W}} = \mathrm{DEC}(\mathbf{Z}; \Theta^D).\tag{23.2}$$

- **Classification network** $\mathrm{DEC}_{\Theta^S} : \mathbb{R}^{N \times L} \to \mathbb{R}^{N \times |\mathcal{Y}|}$, where $\mathcal{Y}$ is the label space. This network is used in (semi-)supervised settings and parameterized by Θ^S. The output is a distribution over the labels $\hat{y}^S$, using node embeddings, as follows:

$$\hat{y}^S = \mathrm{DEC}(\mathbf{Z}; \Theta^S).\tag{23.3}$$

Specific choices of the aforementioned (encoder and decoder) networks allows GRAPHEDM to realize specific graph embedding methods, as we explain in the next subsections.

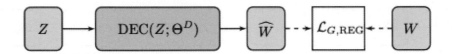

Figure 23.3: Shallow embedding methods. The encoder is a simple embedding look-up and the graph structure is only used in the loss function. Reprinted with permission from [Cha+21].

The output of a model, as described by GraphEDM framework, is a reconstructed graph similarity matrix $\widehat{W}$ (often used to train *unsupervised* embedding algorithms), and/or labels $\widehat{y}^S$ for *supervised* applications. The label output space $\mathcal{Y}$ is application dependent. For instance, in node-level classification, $\widehat{y}^N \in \mathcal{Y}^N$, with $\mathcal{Y}$ representing the node label space. Alternately, for edge-level labeling, $\widehat{y}^E \in \mathcal{Y}^{N \times N}$, with $\mathcal{Y}$ representing the edge label space. Finally, we note that other kinds of labeling are possible, such as graph-level labeling (where we would say $\widehat{y}^G \in \mathcal{Y}$, with $\mathcal{Y}$ representing the graph label space).

Finally, a loss must be specified. This can be used to optimize the parameters $\Theta = \{\Theta^E, \Theta^D, \Theta^S\}$. GraphEDM models can be optimized using a combination of three different terms. First, a supervised loss term, $\mathcal{L}_{\text{SUP}}^S$, compares the predicted labels $\hat{y}^S$ to the ground truth labels y^S. Next, a graph reconstruction loss term, $\mathcal{L}_{G,\text{RECON}}$, may leverage the graph structure to impose regularization constraints on the model parameters. Finally, a weight regularization loss term, $\mathcal{L}_{\text{REG}}$, allows representing priors on trainable model parameters for reducing overfitting. Models realizable by GraphEDM framework are trained by minimizing the total loss $\mathcal{L}$ defined as:

$$\mathcal{L} = \alpha \mathcal{L}_{\text{SUP}}^S(y^S, \hat{y}^S; \Theta) + \beta \mathcal{L}_{G,\text{RECON}}(\mathbf{W}, \widehat{\mathbf{W}}; \Theta) + \gamma \mathcal{L}_{\text{REG}}(\Theta), \tag{23.4}$$

where α, β and γ are hyper-parameters, that can be tuned or set to zero. Note that graph embedding methods can be trained in a *supervised* ($\alpha \neq 0$) or *unsupervised* ($\alpha = 0$) fashion. Supervised graph embedding approaches leverage an additional source of information to learn embeddings such as node or graph labels. On the other hand, unsupervised network embedding approaches rely on the graph structure only to learn node embeddings.

23.3   Shallow graph embeddings

Shallow embedding methods are transductive graph embedding methods, where the encoder function maps categorical node IDs onto a Euclidean space through an embedding matrix. Each node $v_i \in V$ has a corresponding low-dimensional learnable embedding vector $\mathbf{Z}_i \in \mathbb{R}^L$ and the shallow encoder function is

$$\mathbf{Z} = \text{ENC}(\Theta^E) \triangleq \Theta^E \quad \text{where} \quad \Theta^E \in \mathbb{R}^{N \times L}. \tag{23.5}$$

Crucially, the embedding dictionary $\mathbf{Z}$ is directly learned as model parameters. In the unsupervised case, embeddings $\mathbf{Z}$ are optimized to recover some information about the input graph (e.g., the adjacency matrix $\mathbf{W}$, or some transformation of it). This is somewhat similar to dimensionality reduction methods, such as PCA (Section 20.1), but for graph data structures. In the supervised case, the embeddings are optimized to predict some labels, for nodes, edges and/or the whole graph.

23.3.1 Unsupervised embeddings

In the unsupervised case, we will consider two main types of shallow graph embedding methods: distance-based and outer product-based. Distance-based methods optimize the embedding dictionary $\mathbf{Z} = \Theta^E \in \mathbb{R}^{N \times L}$ such that nodes i and j which are close in the graph (as measured by some graph distance function) are embedded in $\mathbf{Z}$ such that $d_2(\mathbf{Z}_i, \mathbf{Z}_j)$ is small, where $d_2(.,.)$ is a pairwise distance function between embedding vectors. The distance function $d_2(\cdot, \cdot)$ can be customized, which can lead to Euclidean (Section 23.3.2) or non-Euclidean (Section 23.3.3) embeddings. The decoder outputs a node-to-node matrix $\widehat{\mathbf{W}} = \mathrm{DEC}(\mathbf{Z}; \Theta^D)$, with $\widehat{W}_{ij} = d_2(\mathbf{Z}_i, \mathbf{Z}_j)$.

Alternatively, some methods rely on pairwise dot-products to compute node similarities. The decoder network can be written as: $\widehat{W} = \mathrm{DEC}(\mathbf{Z}; \Theta^D) = \mathbf{Z}\mathbf{Z}^\top$.

In both cases, unsupervised embeddings for distance- and product-based methods are learned by minimizing the graph regularization loss:

$$\mathcal{L}_{G,\mathrm{RECON}}(\mathbf{W}, \widehat{\mathbf{W}}; \Theta) = d_1(s(\mathbf{W}), \widehat{\mathbf{W}}), \tag{23.6}$$

where $s(\mathbf{W})$ is an optional transformation of the adjacency matrix $\mathbf{W}$, and d_1 is pairwise distance function between matrices, which does not need to be of the same form as d_2. As we shall see, there are many plausible choices for s, d_1, d_2. For instance, we can let s be the adjacency matrix itself, $s(\mathbf{W}) = \mathbf{W}$ or a power of it e.g. $s(\mathbf{W}) = \mathbf{W}^2$. If the input is a weighted binary matrix $\mathbf{W} = \mathbf{A}$, we can set $s(\mathbf{W}) = 1 - \mathbf{W}$, so that connected nodes with $A_{ij} = 1$ get a weight (distance) of 0.

23.3.2 Distance-based: Euclidean methods

Distance-based methods minimize Euclidean distances between similar (connected) nodes. We give some examples below.

Multi-dimensional scaling (MDS, Section 20.4.4) is equivalent to setting $s(\mathbf{W})$ to some distance matrix measuring the dissimilarity between nodes (e.g. proportional to pairwise shortest distance) and then defining

$$d_1(s(W), \widehat{W}) = \sum_{i,j} (s(W)_{ij} - \widehat{W}_{ij})^2 = ||s(\mathbf{W}) - \widehat{\mathbf{W}}||_F^2 \tag{23.7}$$

where $\widehat{W}_{ij} = d_2(\mathbf{Z}_i, \mathbf{Z}_j) = ||\mathbf{Z}_i - \mathbf{Z}_j||$ (although other distance metrics are plausible).

Laplacian eigenmaps (Section 20.4.9) learn embeddings by solving the generalized eigenvector problem

$$\min_{\mathbf{Z} \in \mathbb{R}^{|V| \times d}} \mathrm{tr}(\mathbf{Z}^\mathsf{T} \mathbf{L} \, \mathbf{Z}) \text{ s.t. } \mathbf{Z}^\mathsf{T} \mathbf{D} \mathbf{Z} = \mathbf{I} \text{ and } \mathbf{Z}^\mathsf{T} \mathbf{D} \mathbf{1} = 0 \tag{23.8}$$

where $\mathbf{L} = \mathbf{D} - \mathbf{W}$ is the graph Laplacian (Section 20.4.9.2), and $\mathbf{D}$ is a diagonal matrix containing the sum across columns for each row. The first constraint removes an arbitrary scaling factor in the embedding and the second one removes trivial solutions corresponding to the constant eigenvector (with eigenvalue zero for connected graphs). Further, note that $\mathrm{tr}(\mathbf{Z}^\mathsf{T} \mathbf{L} \mathbf{Z}) = \frac{1}{2} \sum_{i,j} W_{ij} ||\mathbf{Z}_i - \mathbf{Z}_j||_2^2$, where $\mathbf{Z}_i$ is the i'th row of $\mathbf{Z}$; therefore the minimization objective can be equivalently written as a graph reconstruction term, as follows:

$$d_1(s(\mathbf{W}), \widehat{\mathbf{W}}) = \sum_{i,j} \mathbf{W}_{ij} \times \widehat{\mathbf{W}}_{ij} \qquad (23.9)$$

$$\widehat{\mathbf{W}}_{ij} = d_2(\mathbf{Z}_i, \mathbf{Z}_j) = ||\mathbf{Z}_i - \mathbf{Z}_j||_2^2 \qquad (23.10)$$

where $s(\mathbf{W}) = \mathbf{W}$.

23.3.3   Distance-based: non-Euclidean methods

So far, we have discussed methods which assume that embeddings lie in an Euclidean Space. However, recent work has considered hyperbolic geometry for graph embedding. In particular, hyperbolic embeddings are ideal for embedding trees and offer an exciting alternative to Euclidean geometry for graphs that exhibit hierarchical structures. We give some examples below.

Nickel and Kiela [NK17] learn embeddings of hierarchical graphs using the **Poincaré model** of hyperbolic space. This is simple to represent in our notation as we only need to change $d_2(\mathbf{Z}_i, \mathbf{Z}_j)$ to the Poincaré distance function:

$$d_2(\mathbf{Z}_i, \mathbf{Z}_j) = d_{\text{Poincaré}}(\mathbf{Z}_i, \mathbf{Z}_j) = \text{arcosh}\left(1 + 2\frac{||\mathbf{Z}_i - \mathbf{Z}_j||_2^2}{(1 - ||\mathbf{Z}_i||_2^2)(1 - ||\mathbf{Z}_j||_2^2)}\right). \qquad (23.11)$$

The optimization then learns embeddings which minimize distances between connected nodes while maximizing distances between disconnected nodes:

$$d_1(\mathbf{W}, \widehat{\mathbf{W}}) = \sum_{i,j} \mathbf{W}_{ij} \log \frac{e^{-\widehat{\mathbf{W}}_{ij}}}{\sum_{k|\mathbf{W}_{ik}=0} e^{-\widehat{\mathbf{W}}_{ik}}} \qquad (23.12)$$

where the denominator is approximated using negative sampling. Note that since the hyperbolic space has a manifold structure, care needs to be taken to ensure that the embeddings remain on the manifold (using Riemannian optimization techniques [Bon13]).

Other variants of these methods have been proposed. Nickel and Kiela [NK18] explore the **Lorentz model** of hyperbolic space , and show that it provides better numerical stability than the Poincaré model. Another line of work extends non-Euclidean embeddings to mixed-curvature product spaces [Gu+18], which provide more flexibility for other types of graphs (e.g. ring of trees). Finally, work by Chamberlain, Clough, and Deisenroth [CCD17] extends Poincaré embeddings using skip-gram losses with hyperbolic inner products.

23.3.4   Outer product-based: Matrix factorization methods

Matrix factorization approaches learn embeddings that lead to a low rank representation of some similarity matrix $s(\mathbf{W})$, with $s : \mathbb{R}^{N \times N} \to \mathbb{R}^{N \times N}$. The following are frequent choices: $s(\mathbf{W}) = \mathbf{W}$, $s(\mathbf{W}) = L$ (Graph Laplacian), or other proximity measure such as the Katz centrality index, Common Neighbors or Adamic/Adar index.

The decoder function in matrix factorization methods is just a dot product:

$$\widehat{\mathbf{W}} = \text{DEC}(\mathbf{Z}; \Theta^D) = \mathbf{Z}\mathbf{Z}^{\mathsf{T}} \qquad (23.13)$$

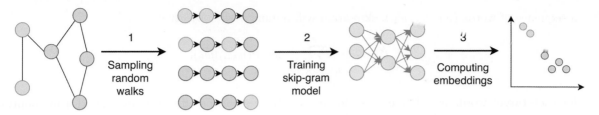

Figure 23.4: An overview of the pipeline for random-walk graph embedding methods. Reprinted with permission from [God18].

Matrix factorization methods learn $\mathbf{Z}$ by minimizing a regularization loss $\mathcal{L}_{G,\text{RECON}}(\mathbf{W}, \widehat{\mathbf{W}}; \Theta) = ||s(\mathbf{W}) - \widehat{\mathbf{W}}||_F^2$.

The **graph factorization** method of [Ahm+13] learns a low-rank factorization of a graph by minimizing the graph regularization loss $\mathcal{L}_{G,\text{RECON}}(\mathbf{W}, \widehat{\mathbf{W}}; \Theta) = \sum_{(v_i, v_j) \in E} (\mathbf{W}_{ij} - \widehat{\mathbf{W}}_{ij})^2$.

Note that if $\mathbf{A}$ is the binary adjacency matrix, ($\mathbf{A}_{ij} = 1$ iff $(v_i, v_j) \in E$ and $\mathbf{A}_{ij} = 0$ otherwise), the graph regularization loss can be expressed in terms of the Frobenius norm:

$$\mathcal{L}_{G,\text{RECON}}(\mathbf{W}, \widehat{\mathbf{W}}; \Theta) = ||\mathbf{A} \odot (\mathbf{W} - \widehat{\mathbf{W}})||_F^2, \tag{23.14}$$

where $\odot$ is the element-wise matrix multiplication operator. Therefore, GF also learns a low-rank factorization of the adjacency matrix W measured in Frobenuis norm. We note that this is a sparse operation (summing only over edges which exist in the graph), and so the method has computational complexity $O(M)$.

The methods described so far are all symmetric, that is, they assume that $\mathbf{W}_{ij} = \mathbf{W}_{ji}$. This is a limiting assumption when working with directed graphs as some relationships are not reciprocal. The **GraRep** method of [CLX15] overcomes this limitation by learning two embeddings per node, a source embedding $\mathbf{Z}^s$ and a target embedding $\mathbf{Z}^t$, which capture asymmetric proximity in directed networks. In addition to asymmetry, GraRep learns embeddings that preserve k-hop neighborhoods via powers of the adjacency matrix and minimizes a graph reconstruction loss with:

$$\widehat{\mathbf{W}}^{(k)} = \mathbf{Z}^{(k),s} \mathbf{Z}^{(k),t^\mathsf{T}} \tag{23.15}$$

$$\mathcal{L}_{G,\text{RECON}}(\mathbf{W}, \widehat{\mathbf{W}}^{(k)}; \Theta) = ||\mathbf{D}^{-k} \mathbf{W}^k - \widehat{\mathbf{W}}^{(k)}||_F^2, \tag{23.16}$$

for each $1 \leq k \leq K$. GraRep concatenates all representations to get source embeddings $\mathbf{Z}^s = [\mathbf{Z}^{(1),s} | \ldots | \mathbf{Z}^{(K),s}]$ and target embeddings $\mathbf{Z}^t = [\mathbf{Z}^{(1),t} | \ldots | \mathbf{Z}^{(K),t}]$. Unfortunately, GraRep is not very scalable, since it uses a matrix power, $\mathbf{D}^{-1}\mathbf{W}$, making it increasingly more dense. This limitation can be circumvented by using implicit matrix factorization [Per+17] as discussed below.

23.3.5 Outer product-based: Skip-gram methods

Skip-gram graph embedding models were inspired by research in natural language processing to model the distributional behavior of words [Mik+13c; PSM14b]. Skip-gram word embeddings are optimized to predict words in their context (the surrounding words) for each target word in a sentence. Given a sequence of words $(w_1, \ldots, w_T)$, skip-gram will minimize the objective:

$$\mathcal{L} = - \sum_{-K \leq i \leq K, i \neq 0} \log \mathbb{P}(w_{k-i} | w_k),$$

for each target words w_k. These conditional probabilities can be efficiently estimated using neural networks. See Section 20.5.2.2 for details.

This idea has been leveraged for graph embeddings in the **DeepWalk** framework of [PARS14]. They justified this by showing empirically how the frequency statistics induced by random walks in real graphs follow a distribution similar to that of words used in natural language. In terms of GraphEDM, skip-gram graph embedding methods use an outer product (Equation 23.13) as their decoder function and a graph reconstruction term computed over random walks on the graph.

In more detail, DeepWalk trains node embeddings to maximize the probability of predicting *context nodes* for each *center node*. The context nodes are nodes appearing adjacent to the center node, in simulated random walks on $\mathbf{A}$. To train embeddings, DeepWalk generates sequences of nodes using truncated unbiased random walks on the graph—which can be compared to sentences in natural language models—and then maximize their log-likelihood. Each random walk starts with a node $v_{i_1} \in V$ and repeatedly samples the next node uniformly at random: $v_{i_{j+1}} \in \{v \in V \mid (v_{i_j}, v) \in E\}$. The walk length is a hyperparameter. All generated random-walks can then be encoded by a sequence model. This two-step paradigm introduced by [PARS14] has been followed by many subsequent works, such as **node2vec** [GL16].

We note that it is common for underlying implementations to use two distinct representations for each node, one for when a node is center of a truncated random walk, and one when it is in the context. The implications of this modeling choice is studied further in [AEHPAR17].

To present DeepWalk in the GraphEDM framework, we can set:

$$s(\mathbf{W}) = \mathbb{E}_q \left[\left(\mathbf{D}^{-1} \mathbf{W} \right)^q \right] \text{ with } q \sim P(Q) = \text{Categorical}([1, 2, \ldots, T_{\max}]) \tag{23.17}$$

where $P(Q = q) = \frac{T_{\max} - 1 + q}{T_{\max}}$ (see [AEH+18] for the derivation).

Training DeepWalk is equivalent to minimizing:

$$\mathcal{L}_{G,\text{RECON}}(W, \widehat{W}; \Theta) = \log Z(\mathbf{Z}) - \sum_{v_i \in V, v_j \in V} s(\mathbf{W})_{ij} \widehat{\mathbf{W}}_{ij}, \tag{23.18}$$

where $\widehat{\mathbf{W}} = \mathbf{Z}\mathbf{Z}^\mathsf{T}$, and the partition function is given by $Z(\mathbf{Z}) = \prod_i \sum_j \exp(\widehat{\mathbf{W}}_{ij})$ can be approximated in $O(N)$ time via hierarchical softmax (see Section 20.5.2). (It is also common to model $\widehat{\mathbf{W}} = \mathbf{Z}_{\text{out}} \mathbf{Z}_{\text{in}}^\mathsf{T}$ for directed graphs using embedding dictionaries $\mathbf{Z}_{\text{out}}, \mathbf{Z}_{\text{in}} \in \mathbb{R}^{N \times L}$.)

As noted by [LG14], Skip-gram methods can be viewed as implicit matrix factorization, and the methods discussed here are related to those of Matrix Factorization (see Section 23.3.4). This relationship is discussed in depth by [Qiu+18], who propose a general matrix factorization framework, **NetMF**, which uses the same underlying graph proximity information as DeepWalk, LINE [Tan+15], and node2vec [GL16]. Casting the node embedding problem as matrix factorization can inherit benefits of efficient sparse matrix operations [Qiu+19a].

23.3.6   Supervised embeddings

In many applications, we have labeled data in addition to node features and graph structure. While it is possible to tackle a supervised task by first learning unsupervised representations and then using them as features in a secondary model, this is not the ideal workflow. Unsupervised node embeddings might not preserve important properties of graphs (e.g., node neighborhoods or attributes), that are most useful for a downstream supervised task.

In light of this limitation, a number of methods combining these two steps, namely learning embeddings and predicting node or graph labels, have been proposed. Here, we focus on simple shallow methods. We discuss deep, nonlinear embeddings later on.

23.3.6.1   Label propagation

Label propagation (LP) [ZG02] is a very popular algorithm for graph-based semi-supervised node classification. The encoder is a shallow model represented by a lookup table $\mathbf{Z}$. LP uses the label space to represent the node embeddings directly (i.e. the decoder in LP is simply the identity function):

$$\hat{y}^N = \text{DEC}(\mathbf{Z}; \Theta^C) = \mathbf{Z}.$$

In particular, LP uses the graph structure to smooth the label distribution over the graph by adding a regularization term to the loss function, using the underlying assumption that neighbor nodes should have similar labels (i.e. there exist some label consistency between connected nodes). Laplacian eigenmaps are utilized in the regularization to enforce this smoothness:

$$\mathcal{L}_{G,\text{RECON}}(\mathbf{W}, \widehat{\mathbf{W}}; \Theta) = \sum_{i,j} \mathbf{W}_{ij} ||y_i^N - \hat{y}_j^N||_2^2 \tag{23.19}$$

LP minimizes this energy function over the space of functions that take fixed values on labeled nodes (i.e. $\hat{y}_i^N = y_i^N \ \forall i | v_i \in V_L$) using an iterative algorithm that updates an unlabeled node's label distribution via the weighted average of its neighbors' labels.

Label spreading (LS) [Zho+04] is a variant of label propagation which minimizes the following energy function:

$$\mathcal{L}_{G,\text{RECON}}(\mathbf{W}, \widehat{\mathbf{W}}; \Theta) = \sum_{i,j} \mathbf{W}_{ij} \left|\left| \frac{\hat{y}_i^N}{\sqrt{D_i}} - \frac{\hat{y}_j^N}{\sqrt{D_j}} \right|\right|_2^2, \tag{23.20}$$

where $D_i = \sum_j W_{ij}$ is the degree of node v_i.

In both methods, the supervised loss is simply the sum of distances between predicted labels and ground truth labels (one-hot vectors):

$$\mathcal{L}_{\text{SUP}}^N(y^N, \hat{y}^N; \Theta) = \sum_{i|v_i \in V_L} ||y_i^N - \hat{y}_i^N||_2^2. \tag{23.21}$$

Note that while the regularization term is computed over all nodes in the graph, the supervised loss is computed over labeled nodes only. These methods are expected to work well with *consistent* graphs, that is graphs where node proximity in the graph is positively correlated with label similarity.

23.4   Graph Neural Networks

An extensive area of research focuses on defining convolutions over graph data. In the notation of Chami et al. [Cha+21], these (semi-)supervised neighborhood aggregation methods can be represented by an encoder of the form $\mathbf{Z} = \text{ENC}(\mathbf{X}, \mathbf{W}; \Theta^E)$, and decoders of the form $\widehat{\mathbf{W}} = \text{DEC}(\mathbf{Z}; \Theta^D)$ and/or $\hat{y}^S = \text{DEC}(\mathbf{Z}; \Theta^S)$. There are many models in this family; we review some of them below.

23.4.1   Message passing GNNs

The original **graph neural network** (**GNN**) model of [GMS05; Sca+09] was the first formulation of deep learning methods for graph-structured data. It views the supervised graph embedding problem as an information diffusion mechanism, where nodes send information to their neighbors until some stable equilibrium state is reached. More concretely, given randomly initialized node embeddings $\mathbf{Z}^0$, it applies the following recursion:

$$\mathbf{Z}^{t+1} = \text{ENC}(\mathbf{X}, \mathbf{W}, \mathbf{Z}^t; \Theta^E), \tag{23.22}$$

where parameters Θ^E are reused at every iteration. After convergence ($t = T$), the node embeddings $\mathbf{Z}^T$ are used to predict the final output such as node or graph labels:

$$\hat{y}^S = \text{DEC}(\mathbf{X}, \mathbf{Z}^T; \Theta^S). \tag{23.23}$$

This process is repeated several times and the GNN parameters Θ^E and Θ^D are learned with backpropagation via the Almeda-Pineda algorithm [Alm87; Pin88]. By Banach's fixed point theorem, this process is guaranteed to converge to a unique solution when the recursion provides a contraction mapping. In light of this, Scarselli et al. [Sca+09] explore maps that can be expressed using message passing networks:

$$\mathbf{Z}_i^{t+1} = \sum_{j|(v_i,v_j)\in E} f(\mathbf{X}_i, \mathbf{X}_j, \mathbf{Z}_j^t; \Theta^E), \tag{23.24}$$

where $f(\cdot)$ is a multi-layer perception (MLP) constrained to be a contraction mapping. The decoder function, however, has no constraints and can be any MLP.

Li et al. [Li+15] propose **Gated Graph Sequence Neural Networks** (GGSNNs), which remove the contraction mapping requirement from GNNs. In GGSNNs, the recursive algorithm in Equation 23.22 is relaxed by applying mapping functions for a fixed number of steps, where each mapping function is a gated recurrent unit [Cho+14b] with parameters shared for every iteration. The GGSNN model outputs predictions at every step, and so is particularly useful for tasks which have sequential structure (such as temporal graphs).

Gilmer et al. [Gil+17] provide a framework for graph neural networks called **message passing neural networks** (MPNNs), which encapsulates many recent models. In contrast with the GNN model which runs for an indefinite number of iterations, MPNNs provide an abstraction for modern approaches, which consist of multi-layer neural networks with a *fixed* number of layers. At every layer ℓ, message functions $f^\ell(.)$ receive messages from neighbors (based on neighbor's hidden state), which are then passed to aggregation functions $h^{\ell}(.)$:

$$\mathbf{m}_i^{\ell+1} = \sum_{j|(v_i,v_j)\in E} f^{\ell}(\mathbf{H}_i^{\ell}, \mathbf{H}_j^{\ell}) \tag{23.25}$$

$$\mathbf{H}_i^{\ell+1} = h^{\ell}(\mathbf{H}_i^{\ell}, \mathbf{m}_i^{\ell+1}), \tag{23.26}$$

where $\mathbf{H}^0 = \mathbf{X}$. After ℓ layers of message passing, nodes' hidden representations encode information within ℓ-hop neighborhoods

Battaglia et al. [Bat+18] propose **GraphNet**, which further extends the MPNN framework to learn representations for edges, nodes and the entire graph using message passing functions. The explicit addition of edge and graph representations adds additional expressivity to the MPNN model, and allows the application of graph models to additional domains.

23.4.2 Spectral Graph Convolutions

Spectral methods define graph convolutions using the spectral domain of the graph Laplacian matrix. These methods broadly fall into two categories: *spectrum-based methods*, which explicitly compute an eigendecomposition of the Laplacian (e.g., **spectral CNNs** [Bru+14]) and *spectrum-free* methods, which are motivated by spectral graph theory but do not actually perform a spectral decomposition (e.g., **Graph convolutional networks** or **GCN** [KW16a]).

A major disadvantage of spectrum-based methods is that they rely on the spectrum of the graph Laplacian and are therefore domain-dependent (i.e. cannot generalize to new graphs). Moreover, computing the Laplacian's spectral decomposition is computationally expensive. Spectrum-free methods overcome these limitations by utilizing approximations of these spectral filters. However, spectrum-free methods require using the whole graph $\mathbf{W}$, and so do not scale well.

For more details on spectral approaches, see e.g., [Bro+17b; Cha+21].

23.4.3 Spatial Graph Convolutions

Spectrum-based methods have an inherent domain dependency which limits the application of a model trained on one graph to a new dataset. Additionally, *spectrum-free* methods (e.g. GCNs) require using the entire graph $\mathbf{A}$, which can quickly become unfeasible as the size of the graph grows.

To overcome these limitations, another branch of graph convolutions (*spatial* methods) borrow ideas from standard CNNs – applying convolutions in the spatial domain as defined by the graph topology. For instance, in computer vision, convolutional filters are spatially localized by using fixed rectangular patches around each pixel. Combined with the natural ordering of pixels in images (top, left, bottom, right), it is possible to reuse filters' weights at every location. This process significantly reduces the total number of parameters needed for a model. While such spatial convolutions cannot directly be applied in graph domains, spatial graph convolutions take inspiration from them. The core idea is to use *neighborhood sampling* and *attention mechanisms* to create fixed-size graph patches, overcoming the irregularity of graphs.

23.4.3.1 Sampling-based spatial methods

To overcome the domain dependency and storage limitations of GCNs, Hamilton, Ying, and Leskovec [HYL17] propose **GraphSAGE**, a framework to learn inductive node embeddings. Instead of

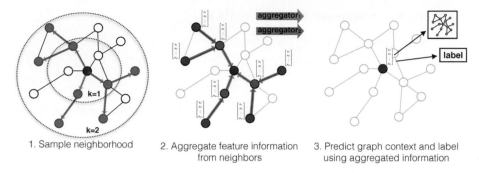

1. Sample neighborhood   2. Aggregate feature information   3. Predict graph context and label
                                    from neighbors   using aggregated information

Figure 23.5: Illustration of the GraphSAGE model. Reprinted with permission from [HYL17].

averaging signals from all one-hop neighbors (via multiplications with the Laplacian matrix), SAGE
samples fixed neighborhoods (of size q) for each node. This removes the strong dependency on fixed
graph structure and allows generalization to new graphs. At every SAGE layer, nodes aggregate
information from nodes sampled from their neighborhood (see Figure 23.5). In the GRAPHEDM
notation, the propagation rule can be written as:

$$\mathbf{H}_{:,i}^{\ell+1} = \sigma(\Theta_1^\ell \mathbf{H}_{:,i}^\ell + \Theta_2^\ell \mathrm{AGG}(\{\mathbf{H}_{:,j}^\ell \mid v_j \in \mathrm{Sample}(\mathrm{nbr}(v_i), q)\})), \tag{23.27}$$

where $\mathrm{AGG}(\cdot)$ is an aggregation function. This aggregation function can be any permutation invariant
operator such as averaging (SAGE-mean) or max-pooling (SAGE-pool). As SAGE works with fixed
size neighborhoods (and not the entire adjacency matrix), it also reduces the computational complexity
of training GCNs.

23.4.3.2   Attention-based spatial methods

Attention mechanisms (Section 15.4) have been successfully used in language models where they, for
example, allow models to identify relevant parts of long sequence inputs. Inspired by their success
in language, similar ideas have been proposed for graph convolution networks. Such graph-based
attention models learn to focus their attention on important neighbors during the message passing
step via parametric patches which are learned on top of node features. This provides more flexibility
in inductive settings, compared to methods that rely on fixed weights such as GCNs.

The **Graph attention network** (GAT) model of [Vel+18] is an attention-based version of GCNs.
At every GAT layer, it attends over the neighborhood of each node and learns to selectively pick
nodes which lead to the best performance for some downstream task. The intuition behind this is
similar to SAGE [HYL17] and makes GAT suitable for inductive and transductive problems. However
unlike SAGE, which limits the convolution step to fixed size-neighborhoods, GAT allows each node
to attend over the entirety of its neighbors – assigning each of them different weights. The attention
parameters are trained through backpropagation, and the attention scores are then row-normalized
with a softmax activation.

23.4.3.3 Geometric spatial methods

Monti et al. [Mon+17] propose **MoNet**, a general framework that works particularly well when the node features lie in a geometric space, such as 3D point clouds or meshes. MoNet learns attention patches using parametric functions in a pre-defined spatial domain (e.g. spatial coordinates), and then applies convolution filters in the resulting graph domain.

MoNet generalizes spatial approaches which introduce constructions for convolutions on manifolds, such as the Geodesic CNN (GCNN) [Mas+15] and the Anisotropic CNN (ACNN) [Bos+16]. Both GCNN and ACNN use fixed patches that are defined on a specific coordinate system and therefore cannot generalize to graph-structured data. However, the MoNet framework is more general; any pseudo-coordinates (i.e. node features) can be used to induce the patches. More formally, if $\mathbf{U}^s$ are pseudo-coordinates and $\mathbf{H}^\ell$ are features from another domain, the MoNet layer can be expressed in our notation as:

$$\mathbf{H}^{\ell+1} = \sigma\left(\sum_{k=1}^{K}(\mathbf{W} \odot g_k(\mathbf{U}^s))\mathbf{H}^\ell\Theta_k^\ell\right), \tag{23.28}$$

where $g_k(U^s)$ are the learned parametric patches, which are $N \times N$ matrices. In practice, MoNet uses Gaussian kernels to learn patches, such that:

$$g_k(\mathbf{U}^s) = \exp\left(-\frac{1}{2}(\mathbf{U}^s - \boldsymbol{\mu}_k)^\mathsf{T}\boldsymbol{\Sigma}_k^{-1}(\mathbf{U}^s - \boldsymbol{\mu}_k)\right), \tag{23.29}$$

where $\boldsymbol{\mu}_k$ and $\boldsymbol{\Sigma}_k$ are learned parameters, and $\boldsymbol{\Sigma}_k$ is restricted to be diagonal.

23.4.4 Non-Euclidean Graph Convolutions

As we discussed in Section 23.3.3, hyperbolic geometry enables learning of shallow embeddings of hierarchical graphs which have smaller distortion than Euclidean embeddings. However, one major downside of shallow embeddings is that they do not generalize well (if at all) across graphs. On the other hand, Graph Neural Networks, which leverage node features, have achieved good results on many inductive graph embedding tasks.

It is natural then, that there has been recent interest in extending Graph Neural Networks to learn non-Euclidean embeddings. One major challenge in doing so again revolves around the nature of convolution itself. How should we perform convolutions in a non-Euclidean space, where standard operations such as inner products and matrix multiplications are not defined?

Hyperbolic Graph Convolution Networks (HGCN) [Cha+19a] and Hyperbolic Graph Neural Networks (HGNN) [LNK19] apply graph convolutions in hyperbolic space by leveraging the Euclidean tangent space, which provides a first-order approximation of the hyperbolic manifold at a point. For every graph convolution step, node embeddings are mapped to the Euclidean tangent space at the origin, where convolutions are applied, and then mapped back to the hyperbolic space. These approaches yield significant improvements on graphs that exhibit hierarchical structure (Figure 23.6).

23.5 Deep graph embeddings

In this section, we use graph neural networks to devise graph embeddings in the unsupervised and semi-supervised cases.

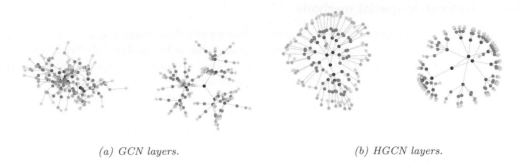

(a) GCN layers.   (b) HGCN layers.

Figure 23.6: Euclidean (left) and hyperbolic (right) embeddings of a tree graph. Hyperbolic embeddings learn natural hierarchies in the embedding space (depth indicated by color). Reprinted with permission from [Cha+19a].

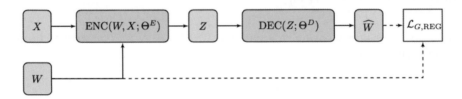

Figure 23.7: Unsupervised graph neural networks. Graph structure and input features are mapped to low-dimensional embeddings using a graph neural network encoder. Embeddings are then decoded to compute a graph regularization loss (unsupervised). Reprinted with permission from [Cha+21].

23.5.1   Unsupervised embeddings

In this section, we discuss unsupervised losses for GNNs, as illustrated in Figure 23.7.

23.5.1.1   Structural deep network embedding

The **structural deep network embedding** (SDNE) method of [WCZ16] uses auto-encoders which preserve first and second-order node proximity. The SDNE encoder takes a row of the adjacency matrix as input (setting $s(\mathbf{W}) = \mathbf{W}$) and produces node embeddings $\mathbf{Z} = \mathrm{ENC}(\mathbf{W}; \theta^E)$. (Note that this ignores any node features.) The SDNE decoder returns $\widehat{\mathbf{W}} = \mathrm{DEC}(\mathbf{Z}; \Theta^D)$, a reconstruction trained to recover the original graph adjacency matrix. SDNE preserves second order node proximity by minimizing the following loss:

$$||(s(\mathbf{W}) - \widehat{\mathbf{W}}) \cdot \mathbb{I}\,(s(\mathbf{W}) > 0)\,||_F^2 + \alpha_{\mathrm{SDNE}} \sum_{ij} s(\mathbf{W})_{ij}||\mathbf{Z}_i - \mathbf{Z}_j||_2^2 \tag{23.30}$$

The first term is similar to the matrix factorization regularization objective, except that $\widehat{\mathbf{W}}$ is not computed using outer products. The second term is used by distance-based shallow embedding methods.

23.5.1.2 (Variational) graph auto-encoders

Kipf and Welling [KW16b] use graph convolutions (Section 23.4.2) to learn node embeddings $\mathbf{Z} = \text{GCN}(\mathbf{W}, \mathbf{X}; \Theta^E)$. The decoder is an outer product: $\text{DEC}(\mathbf{Z}; \Theta^D) = \mathbf{Z}\mathbf{Z}^\mathsf{T}$. The graph reconstruction term is the sigmoid cross entropy between the true adjacency and the predicted edge similarity scores:

$$\mathcal{L}_{G,\text{RECON}}(\mathbf{W}, \widehat{\mathbf{W}}; \Theta) = -\left(\sum_{i,j} (1 - \mathbf{W}_{ij})\log(1 - \sigma(\widehat{\mathbf{W}}_{ij})) + \mathbf{W}_{ij}\log\sigma(\widehat{\mathbf{W}}_{ij}) \right). \tag{23.31}$$

Computing the regularization term over all possible nodes pairs is computationally challenging in practice, so the Graph Auto Encoders (GAE) model uses negative sampling to overcome this challenge.

Whereas GAE is a deterministic model, the authors also introduce variational graph auto-encoders (VGAE), which relies on variational auto-encoders (as in Section 20.3.5) to encode and decode the graph structure. In VGAE, the embedding $\mathbf{Z}$ is modeled as a latent variable with a standard multivariate normal prior $p(\mathbf{Z}) = \mathcal{N}(\mathbf{Z}|\mathbf{0}, \mathbf{I})$ and a graph convolution is used as the amortized inference network, $q_\Phi(\mathbf{Z}|\mathbf{W}, \mathbf{X})$. The model is trained by minimizing the corresponding negative evidence lower bound:

$$\text{NELBO}(\mathbf{W}, \mathbf{X}; \Theta) = -\mathbb{E}_{q_\Phi(\mathbf{Z}|\mathbf{W},\mathbf{X})}[\log p(\mathbf{W}|\mathbf{Z})] + \text{KL}(q_\Phi(\mathbf{Z}|\mathbf{W}, \mathbf{X})||p(\mathbf{Z})) \tag{23.32}$$

$$= \mathcal{L}_{G,\text{RECON}}(\mathbf{W}, \widehat{\mathbf{W}}; \Theta) + \text{KL}(q_\Phi(\mathbf{Z}|\mathbf{W}, \mathbf{X})||p(\mathbf{Z})). \tag{23.33}$$

23.5.1.3 Iterative generative modelling of graphs (Graphite)

The **graphite** model of [GZE19] extends GAE and VGAE by introducing a more complex decoder. This decoder iterates between pairwise decoding functions and graph convolutions, as follows:

$$\widehat{\mathbf{W}}^{(k)} = \frac{\mathbf{Z}^{(k)}\mathbf{Z}^{(k)\mathsf{T}}}{||\mathbf{Z}^{(k)}||_2^2} + \frac{\mathbf{1}\mathbf{1}^\mathsf{T}}{N}$$
$$\mathbf{Z}^{(k+1)} = \text{GCN}(\widehat{\mathbf{W}}^{(k)}, \mathbf{Z}^{(k)})$$

where $\mathbf{Z}^{(0)}$ is initialized using the output of the encoder network. This process allows Graphite to learn more expressive decoders. Finally, similar to GAE, Graphite can be deterministic or variational.

23.5.1.4 Methods based on contrastive losses

The **deep graph infomax** method of [Vel+19] is a GAN-like method for creating graph-level embeddings. Given one or more *real* (positive) graphs, each with its adjacency matrix $\mathbf{W} \in \mathbb{R}^{N \times N}$ and node features $\mathbf{X} \in \mathbb{R}^{N \times D}$, this method creates *fake* (negative) adjacency matrices $\mathbf{W}^- \in \mathbb{R}^{N^- \times N^-}$ and their features $X^- \in \mathbb{R}^{N^- \times D}$. It trains (i) an encoder that processes both real and fake samples, respectively giving $Z = \text{ENC}(\mathbf{X}, \mathbf{W}; \Theta^E) \in \mathbb{R}^{N \times L}$ and $\mathbf{Z}^- = \text{ENC}(\mathbf{X}^-, \mathbf{W}^-; \Theta^E) \in \mathbb{R}^{N^- \times L}$, (ii) a (readout) graph pooling function $\mathcal{R} : \mathbb{R}^{N \times L} \to \mathbb{R}^L$, and (iii) a descriminator function $\mathcal{D} : \mathbb{R}^L \times \mathbb{R}^L \to [0, 1]$ which is trained to output $\mathcal{D}(\mathbf{Z}_i, \mathcal{R}(\mathbf{Z})) \approx 1$ and $\mathcal{D}(\mathbf{Z}_j^-, \mathcal{R}(\mathbf{Z}^-)) \approx 0$, respectively, for nodes corresponding to given graph $i \in V$ and fake graph $j \in V^-$. Specifically, DGI optimizes:

$$\min_{\Theta} - \mathop{\mathbb{E}}_{\mathbf{X},\mathbf{W}} \sum_{i=1}^{N} \log \mathcal{D}(\mathbf{Z}_i, \mathcal{R}(\mathbf{Z})) - \mathop{\mathbb{E}}_{\mathbf{X}^-,\mathbf{W}^-} \sum_{j=1}^{N^-} \log \left(1 - \mathcal{D}(\mathbf{Z}_j^-, \mathcal{R}(\mathbf{Z}^-))\right), \qquad (23.34)$$

where Θ contains Θ^E and the parameters of $\mathcal{R}, \mathcal{D}$. In the first expectation, DGI samples from the real (positive) graphs. If only one graph is given, it could sample some subgraphs from it (e.g. connected components). The second expectation samples fake (negative) graphs. In DGI, fake samples use the real adjacency $W^- := W$ but fake features X^- are a row-wise random permutation of real X. The ENC used in DGI is a graph convolutional network, though any GNN can be used. The readout $\mathcal{R}$ summarizes an entire (variable-size) graph to a single (fixed-dimension) vector. Veličković et al. [Vel+19] use $\mathcal{R}$ as a row-wise mean, though other graph pooling might be used e.g. ones aware of the adjacency.

The optimization of Equation (23.34) is shown by [Vel+19] to maximize a lower-bound on the mutual information between the outputs of the encoder and the graph pooling function, i.e., between individual node representations and the graph representation.

In [Pen+20] they present a variant called **Graphical Mutual Information**. Rather than maximizing MI of node information and an entire graph, GMI maximizes the MI between the representation of a node and its neighbors.

23.5.2 Semi-supervised embeddings

In this section, we discuss semi-supervised losses for GNNs. We consider the simple special case in which we use a nonlinear encoder of the node features, but ignore the graph structure, i.e., we use $\mathbf{Z} = \text{ENC}(\mathbf{X}; \Theta^E)$.

23.5.2.1 SemiEmb

[WRC08] propose an approach called **semi-supervised embeddings** (SemiEmb) They use an MLP for the encoder of $\mathbf{X}$. For the decoder, we can use a distance-based graph decoder: $\widehat{\mathbf{W}}_{ij} = \text{DEC}(\mathbf{Z}; \Theta^D)_{ij} = ||\mathbf{Z}_i - \mathbf{Z}_j||^2$, where $|| \cdot ||$ can be the L2 or L1 norm.

SemiEmb regularizes intermediate or auxiliary layers in the network using the same regularizer as the label propagation loss in Equation (23.19). SemiEmb uses a feed forward network to predict labels from intermediate embeddings, which are then compared to ground truth labels using the Hinge loss.

23.5.2.2 Planetoid

Unsupervised skip-gram methods like DeepWalk and node2vec learn embeddings in a multi-step pipeline, where random walks are first generated from the graph and then used to learn embeddings. These embeddings are likely not optimal for downstream classification tasks. The **Planetoid** method of [YCS16] extends such random walk methods to leverage node label information during the embedding algorithm.

Planetoid first maps nodes to embeddings $\mathbf{Z} = [\mathbf{Z}^c || \mathbf{Z}^F] = \text{ENC}(\mathbf{X}; \Theta^E)$ using a neural network (again ignoring graph structure). The node embeddings $\mathbf{Z}^c$ capture structural information while the node embeddings $\mathbf{Z}^F$ capture feature information. There are two variants, a transductive version that directly learns $\mathbf{Z}^c$ (as an embedding lookup), and an inductive model where $\mathbf{Z}^c$ is computed with parametric mappings that act on input features $\mathbf{X}$. The Planetoid objective contains both a supervised loss and a graph regularization loss. The graph regularization loss measures the ability to predict context using nodes embeddings:

$$\mathcal{L}_{\text{G,RECON}}(\mathbf{W}, \widehat{\mathbf{W}}; \Theta) = -\mathbb{E}_{(i,j,\gamma)} \log \sigma \left(\gamma \widehat{\mathbf{W}}_{ij} \right), \tag{23.35}$$

with $\widehat{\mathbf{W}}_{ij} = \mathbf{Z}_i^\mathsf{T} \mathbf{Z}_j$ and $\gamma \in \{-1, 1\}$ with $\gamma = 1$ if $(v_i, v_j) \in E$ is a positive pair and $\gamma = -1$ if (v_i, v_j) is a negative pair. The distribution under the expectation is directly defined through a sampling process

The supervised loss in Planetoid is the negative log-likelihood of predicting the correct labels:

$$\mathcal{L}_{\text{SUP}}^N(y^N, \widehat{y}^N; \Theta) = -\frac{1}{|V_L|} \sum_{i|v_i \in V_L} \sum_{1 \leq k \leq C} y_{ik}^N \log \widehat{y}_{ik}^N, \tag{23.36}$$

where i is a node's index while k indicates label classes, and $\widehat{y}_i^N$ are computed using a neural network followed by a softmax activation, mapping $\mathbf{Z}_i$ to predicted labels.

23.6 Applications

There are many applications of graph embeddings, both unsupervised and supervised. We give some examples in the sections below.

23.6.1 Unsupervised applications

In this section, we discuss common unsupervised applications.

23.6.1.1 Graph reconstruction

A popular unsupervised graph application is graph reconstruction. In this setting, the goal is to learn mapping functions (which can be parametric or not) that map nodes onto a manifold which can reconstruct the graph. This is regarded as *unsupervised* in the sense that there is no supervision beyond the graph structure. Models can be trained by minimizing a reconstruction error, which is the error in recovering the original graph from learned embeddings. Several algorithms were designed specifically for this task, and we refer to Section 23.3.1 and Section 23.5.1 for some examples of reconstruction objectives. At a high level, graph reconstruction is similar to dimensionality reduction in the sense that the main goal is to summarize some input data into a low-dimensional embedding. Instead of compressing high dimensional vectors into low-dimensional ones as standard dimensionality reduction methods (e.g. PCA) do, the goal of graph reconstruction models is to compress data defined on graphs into low-dimensional vectors.

23.6.1.2 Link prediction

The goal in **link prediction** is to predict missing or unobserved links (e.g., links that may appear in the future for dynamic and temporal networks). Link prediction can also help identify spurious

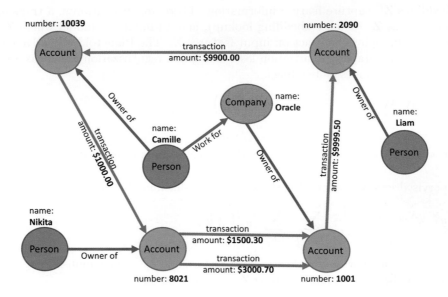

Figure 23.8: *A graph representation of some financial transactions. Adapted from* `http://pgql-lang.org/spec/1.2/`.

links and remove them. It is a major application of graph learning models in industry, and common example of applications include predicting friendships in **social networks** predicting user-product interactions in **recommendation systems**, predicting suspicious links in a **fraud detection system** (see Figure 23.8), or predicting missing relationships between entities in a **knowledge graph** (see e.g., [Nic+15]).

A common approach for training link prediction models is to mask some edges in the graph (positive and negative edges), train a model with the remaining edges and then test it on the masked set of edges. Note that link prediction is different from graph reconstruction. In link prediction, we aim at predicting links that are not observed in the original graph while in graph reconstruction, we only want to compute embeddings that preserve the graph structure through reconstruction error minimization.

Finally, while link prediction has similarities with supervised tasks in the sense that we have labels for edges (positive, negative, unobserved), we group it under the unsupervised class of applications since edge labels are usually not used during training, but only used to measure the predictive quality of embeddings.

23.6.1.3   Clustering

Clustering is particularly useful for discovering communities and has many real-world applications. For instance, clusters exist in biological networks (e.g. as groups of proteins with similar properties), or in social networks (e.g. as groups of people with similar interests).

The unsupervised methods introduced in this chapter can be used to solve clustering problems by applying the clustering algorithm (e.g. k-means) to embeddings that are output by an encoder. Further, clustering can be joined with the learning algorithm while learning a shallow [Roz+19] or Graph Convolution [Chi+19a; CEL19] embedding model.

23.6.1.4 Visualization

There are many off-the-shelf tools for mapping graph nodes onto two-dimensional manifolds for the purpose of visualization. Visualizations allow network scientists to qualitatively understand graph properties, understand relationships between nodes or visualize node clusters. Among the popular tools are methods based on *Force-Directed Layouts*, with various web-app Javascript implementations.

Unsupervised graph embedding methods are also used for visualization purposes: by first training an encoder-decoder model (corresponding to a shallow embedding or graph convolution network), and then mapping every node representation onto a two-dimensional space using t-SNE (Section 20.4.10) or PCA (Section 20.1). Such a process (embedding → dimensionality reduction) is commonly used to qualitatively evaluate the performance of graph learning algorithms. If nodes have attributes, one can use these attributes to color the nodes on 2D visualization plots. Good embedding algorithms embed nodes that have similar attributes nearby in the embedding space, as demonstrated in visualizations of various methods [PARS14; KW16a; AEH+18]. Finally, beyond mapping every node to a 2D coordinate, methods which map every graph to a representation [ARZP19] can similarly be projected into two dimensions to visualize and qualitatively analyze graph-level properties.

23.6.2 Supervised applications

In this section, we discuss common supervised applications.

23.6.2.1 Node classification

Node classification is an important supervised graph application, where the goal is to learn node representations that can accurately predict node labels. (This is sometimes called **statistical relational learning** [GT07].) For instance, node labels could be scientific topics in citation networks, or gender and other attributes in social networks.

Since labeling large graphs can be time-consuming and expensive, semi-supervised node classification is a particularly common application. In semi-supervised settings, only a fraction of nodes are labeled and the goal is to leverage links between nodes to predict attributes of unlabeled nodes. This setting is transductive since there is only one partially labeled fixed graph. It is also possible to do inductive node classification, which corresponds to the task of classifying nodes in multiple graphs.

Note that node features can significantly boost the performance on node classification tasks if these are descriptive for the target label. Indeed, recent methods such as GCN (Section 23.4.2) GraphSAGE (Section 23.4.3.1) have achieved state-of-the-art performance on multiple node classification benchmarks due to their ability to combine structural information and semantics coming from features. On the other hand, other methods such as random walks on graphs fail to leverage feature information and therefore achieve lower performance on these tasks.

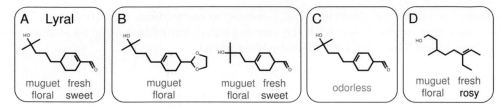

Figure 23.9: Structurally similar molecules do not necessarily have similar odor descriptors. (A) Lyral, the reference molecule. (B) Molecules with similar structure can share similar odor descriptors. (C) However, a small structural change can render the molecule odorless. (D) Further, large structural changes can leave the odor of the molecule largely unchanged. From Figure 1 of [SL+19], originally from [OPK12]. Used with kind permission of Benjamin Sanchez-Lengeling.

23.6.2.2 Graph classification

Graph classification is a supervised application where the goal is to predict graph labels. Graph classification problems are inductive and a common example is classifying chemical compounds (e.g. predicting toxicity or odor from a molecule, as shown in Figure 23.9).

Graph classification requires some notion of pooling, in order to aggregate node-level information into graph-level information. As discussed earlier, generalizing this notion of pooling to arbitrary graphs is non trivial because of the lack of regularity in the graph structure making graph pooling an active research area. In addition to the supervised methods discussed above, a number of unsupervised methods for learning graph-level representations have been proposed [Tsi+18; ARZP19; TMP20].

A Notation

A.1 Introduction

It is very difficult to come up with a single, consistent notation to cover the wide variety of data, models and algorithms that we discuss in this book. Furthermore, conventions differ between different fields (such as machine learning, statistics and optimization), and between different books and papers within the same field. Nevertheless, we have tried to be as consistent as possible. Below we summarize most of the notation used in this book, although individual sections may introduce new notation. Note also that the same symbol may have different meanings depending on the context, although we try to avoid this where possible.

A.2 Common mathematical symbols

We list some common symbols below.

Symbol	Meaning
∞	Infinity
$\rightarrow$	Tends towards, e.g., $n \rightarrow \infty$
$\propto$	Proportional to, so $y = ax$ can be written as $y \propto x$
$\triangleq$	Defined as
$O(\cdot)$	Big-O: roughly means order of magnitude
$\mathbb{Z}_+$	The positive integers
$\mathbb{R}$	The real numbers
$\mathbb{R}_+$	The positive reals
$\mathcal{S}_K$	The K-dimensional probability simplex
$\mathcal{S}_{++}^D$	Cone of positive definite $D \times D$ matrices
$\approx$	Approximately equal to
$\{1, \ldots, N\}$	The finite set $\{1, 2, \ldots, N\}$
$1 : N$	The finite set $\{1, 2, \ldots, N\}$
$[\ell, u]$	The continuous interval $\{\ell \leq x \leq u\}$.

A.3   Functions

Generic functions will be denoted by f (and sometimes g or h). We will encounter many named functions, such as $\tanh(x)$ or $\sigma(x)$. A scalar function applied to a vector is assumed to be applied elementwise, e.g., $\boldsymbol{x}^2 = [x_1^2, \ldots, x_D^2]$. Functionals (functions of a function) are written using "blackboard" font, e.g., $\mathbb{H}(p)$ for the entropy of a distribution p. A function parameterized by fixed parameters $\boldsymbol{\theta}$ will be denoted by $f(\boldsymbol{x}; \boldsymbol{\theta})$ or sometimes $f_{\boldsymbol{\theta}}(\boldsymbol{x})$. We list some common functions (with no free parameters) below.

A.3.1   Common functions of one argument

Symbol	Meaning
$\lfloor x \rfloor$	Floor of x, i.e., round down to nearest integer
$\lceil x \rceil$	Ceiling of x, i.e., round up to nearest integer
$\neg a$	logical NOT
$\mathbb{I}(x)$	Indicator function, $\mathbb{I}(x) = 1$ if x is true, else $\mathbb{I}(x) = 0$
$\delta(x)$	Dirac delta function, $\delta(x) = \infty$ if $x = 0$, else $\delta(x) = 0$
$|x|$	Absolute value
$|\mathcal{S}|$	Size (cardinality) of a set
$n!$	Factorial function
$\log(x)$	Natural logarithm of x
$\exp(x)$	Exponential function e^x
$\Gamma(x)$	Gamma function, $\Gamma(x) = \int_0^\infty u^{x-1}e^{-u}du$
$\Psi(x)$	Digamma function, $\Psi(x) = \frac{d}{dx}\log\Gamma(x)$
$\sigma(x)$	Sigmoid (logistic) function, $\frac{1}{1+e^{-x}}$

A.3.2   Common functions of two arguments

Symbol	Meaning
$a \wedge b$	logical AND
$a \vee b$	logical OR
$B(a,b)$	Beta function, $B(a,b) = \frac{\Gamma(a)\Gamma(b)}{\Gamma(a+b)}$
$\binom{n}{k}$	n choose k, equal to $n!/(k!(n-k)!)$
δ_{ij}	Kronecker delta, equals $\mathbb{I}(i = j)$
$\boldsymbol{u} \odot \boldsymbol{v}$	Elementwise product of two vectors
$\boldsymbol{u} \circledast \boldsymbol{v}$	Convolution of two vectors

A.3.3   Common functions of > 2 arguments

Symbol	Meaning
$B(\boldsymbol{x})$	Multivariate beta function, $\frac{\prod_k \Gamma(x_k)}{\Gamma(\sum_k x_k)}$
$\Gamma(\boldsymbol{x})$	Multi. gamma function, $\pi^{D(D-1)/4}\prod_{d=1}^{D}\Gamma(x + (1-d)/2)$

$$\text{softmax}(\boldsymbol{x}) \quad \text{Softmax function, } \left[\frac{e^{x_c}}{\sum_{c'=1}^{C} e^{x_{c'}}}\right]_{c=1}^{C}$$

A.4   Linear algebra

In this section, we summarize the notation we use for linear algebra (see Chapter 7 for details).

A.4.1   General notation

Vectors are bold lower case letters such as $\boldsymbol{x}$, $\boldsymbol{w}$. Matrices are bold upper case letters, such as $\mathbf{X}$, $\mathbf{W}$. Scalars are non-bold lower case. When creating a vector from a list of N scalars, we write $\boldsymbol{x} = [x_1, \ldots, x_N]$; this may be a column vector or a row vector, depending on the context. (Vectors are assumed to be column vectors, unless noted otherwise.) When creating an $M \times N$ matrix from a list of vectors, we write $\mathbf{X} = [\boldsymbol{x}_1, \ldots, \boldsymbol{x}_N]$ if we stack along the columns, or $\mathbf{X} = [\boldsymbol{x}_1; , \ldots; \boldsymbol{x}_M]$ if we stack along the rows.

A.4.2   Vectors

Here is some standard notation for vectors. (We assume $\boldsymbol{u}$ and $\boldsymbol{v}$ are both N-dimensional vectors.)

Symbol	Meaning
$\boldsymbol{u}^\top \boldsymbol{v}$	Inner (scalar) product, $\sum_{i=1}^{N} u_i v_i$
$\boldsymbol{u}\boldsymbol{v}^\top$	Outer product ($N \times N$ matrix)
$\boldsymbol{u} \odot \boldsymbol{v}$	Elementwise product, $[u_1 v_1, \ldots, u_N v_N]$
$\boldsymbol{v}^\top$	Transpose of $\boldsymbol{v}$
$\dim(\boldsymbol{v})$	Dimensionality of $\boldsymbol{v}$ (namely N)
$\text{diag}(\boldsymbol{v})$	Diagonal $N \times N$ matrix made from vector $\boldsymbol{v}$
$\mathbf{1}$ or $\mathbf{1}_N$	Vector of ones (of length N)
$\mathbf{0}$ or $\mathbf{0}_N$	Vector of zeros (of length N)
$\lVert\boldsymbol{v}\rVert = \lVert\boldsymbol{v}\rVert_2$	Euclidean or ℓ_2 norm $\sqrt{\sum_{i=1}^{N} v_i^2}$
$\lVert\boldsymbol{v}\rVert_1$	ℓ_1 norm $\sum_{i=1}^{N} |v_i|$

A.4.3   Matrices

Here is some standard notation for matrices. (We assume $\mathbf{S}$ is a square $N \times N$ matrix, $\mathbf{X}$ and $\mathbf{Y}$ are of size $M \times N$, and $\mathbf{Z}$ is of size $M' \times N'$.)

Symbol	Meaning
$\mathbf{X}_{:,j}$	j'th column of matrix
$\mathbf{X}_{i,:}$	i'th row of matrix (treated as a column vector)
X_{ij}	Element (i, j) of matrix
$\mathbf{S} \succ 0$	True iff $\mathbf{S}$ is a positive definite matrix
$\text{tr}(\mathbf{S})$	Trace of a square matrix
$\det(\mathbf{S})$	Determinant of a square matrix
$|\mathbf{S}|$	Determinant of a square matrix

$$
\begin{array}{ll}
\mathbf{S}^{-1} & \text{Inverse of a square matrix} \\
\mathbf{X}^{\dagger} & \text{Pseudo-inverse of a matrix} \\
\mathbf{X}^{\mathsf{T}} & \text{Transpose of a matrix} \\
\text{diag}(\mathbf{S}) & \text{Diagonal vector extracted from square matrix} \\
\mathbf{I} \text{ or } \mathbf{I}_N & \text{Identity matrix of size } N \times N \\
\mathbf{X} \odot \mathbf{Y} & \text{Elementwise product} \\
\mathbf{X} \otimes \mathbf{Z} & \text{Kronecker product (see Section 7.2.5)}
\end{array}
$$

A.4.4 Matrix calculus

In this section, we summarize the notation we use for matrix calculus (see Section 7.8 for details).

Let $\boldsymbol{\theta} \in \mathbb{R}^N$ be a vector and $f : \mathbb{R}^N \to \mathbb{R}$ be a scalar valued function. The derivative of f wrt its argument is denoted by the following:

$$
\nabla_{\boldsymbol{\theta}} f(\boldsymbol{\theta}) \triangleq \nabla f(\boldsymbol{\theta}) \triangleq \nabla f \triangleq \left(\frac{\partial f}{\partial \theta_1} \quad \cdots \quad \frac{\partial f}{\partial \theta_N} \right) \tag{A.1}
$$

The gradient is a vector that must be evaluated at a point in space. To emphasize this, we will sometimes write

$$
\boldsymbol{g}_t \triangleq \boldsymbol{g}(\boldsymbol{\theta}_t) \triangleq \nabla f(\boldsymbol{\theta}) \Big|_{\boldsymbol{\theta}_t} \tag{A.2}
$$

We can also compute the (symmetric) $N \times N$ matrix of second partial derivatives, known as the **Hessian**:

$$
\nabla^2 f \triangleq \begin{pmatrix} \frac{\partial^2 f}{\partial \theta_1^2} & \cdots & \frac{\partial^2 f}{\partial \theta_1 \partial \theta_N} \\ & \vdots & \\ \frac{\partial^2 f}{\partial \theta_N \theta_1} & \cdots & \frac{\partial^2 f}{\partial \theta_N^2} \end{pmatrix} \tag{A.3}
$$

The Hessian is a matrix that must be evaluated at a point in space. To emphasize this, we will sometimes write

$$
\mathbf{H}_t \triangleq \mathbf{H}(\boldsymbol{\theta}_t) \triangleq \nabla^2 f(\boldsymbol{\theta}) \Big|_{\boldsymbol{\theta}_t} \tag{A.4}
$$

A.5 Optimization

In this section, we summarize the notation we use for optimization (see Chapter 8 for details).

We will often write an objective or cost function that we wish to minimize as $\mathcal{L}(\boldsymbol{\theta})$, where $\boldsymbol{\theta}$ are the variables to be optimized (often thought of as parameters of a statistical model). We denote the parameter value that achieves the minimum as $\boldsymbol{\theta}_* = \operatorname{argmin}_{\boldsymbol{\theta} \in \Theta} \mathcal{L}(\boldsymbol{\theta})$, where Θ is the set we are optimizing over. (Note that there may be more than one such optimal value, so we should really write $\boldsymbol{\theta}_* \in \operatorname{argmin}_{\boldsymbol{\theta} \in \Theta} \mathcal{L}(\boldsymbol{\theta})$.)

When performing iterative optimization, we use t to index the iteration number. We use η as a step size (learning rate) parameter. Thus we can write the gradient descent algorithm (explained in Section 8.4) as follows: $\boldsymbol{\theta}_{t+1} = \boldsymbol{\theta}_t - \eta_t \boldsymbol{g}_t$.

We often use a hat symbol to denote an estimate or prediction (e.g., $\hat{\boldsymbol{\theta}}$, $\hat{y}$), a star subscript or superscript to denote a true (but usually unknown) value (e.g., $\boldsymbol{\theta}_*$ or $\boldsymbol{\theta}^*$), an overline to denote a mean value (e.g., $\overline{\boldsymbol{\theta}}$).

A.6 Probability

In this section, we summarize the notation we use for probability theory (see Chapter 2 for details).

We denote a probability density function (pdf) or probability mass function (pmf) by p, a cumulative distribution function (cdf) by P, and the probability of a binary event by Pr. We write $p(X)$ for the distribution for random variable X, and $p(Y)$ for the distribution for random variable Y — these refer to different distributions, even though we use the same p symbol in both cases. (In cases where confusion may arise, we write $p_X(\cdot)$ and $p_Y(\cdot)$.) Approximations to a distribution p will often be represented by q, or sometimes $\hat{p}$.

In some cases, we distinguish between a random variable (rv) and the values it can take on. In this case, we denote the variable in upper case (e.g., X), and its value in lower case (e.g., x). However, we often ignore this distinction between variables and values. For example, we sometimes write $p(x)$ to denote either the scalar value (the distribution evaluated at a point) or the distribution itself, depending on whether X is observed or not.

We write $X \sim p$ to denote that X is distributed according to distribution p. We write $X \perp Y \mid Z$ to denote that X is conditionally independent of Y given Z. If $X \sim p$, we denote the expected value of $f(X)$ using

$$\mathbb{E}\left[f(X)\right] = \mathbb{E}_{p(X)}\left[f(X)\right] = \mathbb{E}_X\left[f(X)\right] = \int_x f(x)p(x)dx \tag{A.5}$$

If f is the identity function, we write $\overline{X} \triangleq \mathbb{E}[X]$. Similarly, the variance is denoted by

$$\mathbb{V}\left[f(X)\right] = \mathbb{V}_{p(X)}\left[f(X)\right] = \mathbb{V}_X\left[f(X)\right] = \int_x (f(x) - \mathbb{E}\left[f(X)\right])^2 p(x)dx \tag{A.6}$$

If $\boldsymbol{x}$ is a random vector, the covariance matrix is denoted

$$\text{Cov}\left[\boldsymbol{x}\right] = \mathbb{E}\left[(\boldsymbol{x} - \overline{\boldsymbol{x}})(\boldsymbol{x} - \overline{\boldsymbol{x}})^\mathsf{T}\right] \tag{A.7}$$

If $X \sim p$, the mode of a distribution is denoted by

$$\hat{x} = \text{mode}\left[p\right] = \underset{x}{\text{argmax}}\, p(x) \tag{A.8}$$

We denote parametric distributions using $p(\boldsymbol{x}|\boldsymbol{\theta})$, where $\boldsymbol{x}$ are the random variables, $\boldsymbol{\theta}$ are the parameters and p is a pdf or pmf. For example, $\mathcal{N}(x|\mu, \sigma^2)$ is a Gaussian (normal) distribution with mean μ and standard deviation σ.

A.7 Information theory

In this section, we summarize the notation we use for information theory (see Chapter 6 for details).

If $X \sim p$, we denote the (differential) entropy of the distribution by $\mathbb{H}(X)$ or $\mathbb{H}(p)$. If $Y \sim q$, we denote the KL divergence from distribution p to q by $D_{\mathbb{KL}}(p \parallel q)$. If $(X, Y) \sim p$, we denote the mutual information between X and Y by $\mathbb{I}(X; Y)$.

A.8 Statistics and machine learning

We briefly summarize the notation we use for statistical learning.

A.8.1 Supervised learning

For supervised learning, we denote the observed features (also called inputs or **covariates**) by $\boldsymbol{x} \in \mathcal{X}$. Often $\mathcal{X} = \mathbb{R}^D$, meaning the features are real-valued. (Note that this includes the case of discrete-valued inputs, which can be represented as one-hot vectors.) Sometimes we compute manually-specified features of the input; we denote these by $\boldsymbol{\phi}(\boldsymbol{x})$. We also have outputs (also called **targets** or **response variables**) $\boldsymbol{y} \in \mathcal{Y}$ that we wish to predict. Our task is to learn a conditional probability distribution $p(\boldsymbol{y}|\boldsymbol{x}, \boldsymbol{\theta})$, where $\boldsymbol{\theta}$ are the parameters of the model. If $\mathcal{Y} = \{1, \ldots, C\}$, we call this **classification**. If $\mathcal{Y} = \mathbb{R}^C$, we call this **regression** (often $C = 1$, so we are just predicting a scalar response).

The parameters $\boldsymbol{\theta}$ are estimated from **training data**, denoted by $\mathcal{D} = \{(\boldsymbol{x}_n, \boldsymbol{y}_n) : n \in \{1, \ldots, N\}\}$ (so N is the number of training cases). If $\mathcal{X} = \mathbb{R}^D$, we can store the training inputs in an $N \times D$ **design matrix** denoted by $\mathbf{X}$. If $\mathcal{Y} = \mathbb{R}^C$, we can store the training outputs in an $N \times C$ matrix $\mathbf{Y}$. If $\mathcal{Y} = \{1, \ldots, C\}$, we can represent each class label as a C-dimensional bit vector, with one element turned on (this is known as a **one-hot encoding**), so we can store the training outputs in an $N \times C$ binary matrix $\mathbf{Y}$.

A.8.2 Unsupervised learning and generative models

Unsupervised learning is usually formalized as the task of unconditional density estimation, namely modeling $p(\boldsymbol{x}|\boldsymbol{\theta})$. In some cases, we want to perform conditional density estimation; we denote the values we are conditioning on by $\boldsymbol{u}$, so the model becomes $p(\boldsymbol{x}|\boldsymbol{u}, \boldsymbol{\theta})$. This is similar to supervised learning, except that $\boldsymbol{x}$ is usually high dimensional (e.g., an image) and $\boldsymbol{u}$ is usually low dimensional (e.g., a class label or a text description).

In some models, we have **latent variables**, also called **hidden variables**, which are never observed in the training data. We call such models **latent variable models** (LVM). We denote the latent variables for data case n by $\boldsymbol{z}_n \in \mathcal{Z}$. Sometimes latent variables are known as **hidden variables**, and are denoted by $\boldsymbol{h}_n$. By contrast, the **visible variables** will be denoted by $\boldsymbol{v}_n$. Typically the latent variables are continuous or discrete, i.e., $\mathcal{Z} = \mathbb{R}^L$ or $\mathcal{Z} = \{1, \ldots, K\}$.

Most LVMs have the form $p(\boldsymbol{x}_n, \boldsymbol{z}_n|\boldsymbol{\theta})$; such models can be used for unsupervised learning. However, LVMs can also be used for supervised learning. In particular, we can either create a generative (unconditional) model of the form $p(\boldsymbol{x}_n, \boldsymbol{y}_n, \boldsymbol{z}_n|\boldsymbol{\theta})$, or a discriminative (conditional) model of the form $p(\boldsymbol{y}_n, \boldsymbol{z}_n|\boldsymbol{x}_n, \boldsymbol{\theta})$.

A.8.3 Bayesian inference

When working with Bayesian inference, we write the prior over the parameters as $p(\boldsymbol{\theta}|\boldsymbol{\xi})$, where $\boldsymbol{\xi}$ are the hyperparameters. For conjugate models, the posterior has the same form as the prior (by definition). We can therefore just update the hyperparameters from their prior value, $\breve{\boldsymbol{\xi}}$, to their posterior value, $\widehat{\boldsymbol{\xi}}$.

In variational inference (Section 4.6.8.3), we use $\boldsymbol{\psi}$ to represent the parameters of the variational posterior, i.e., $p(\boldsymbol{\theta}|\mathcal{D}) \approx q(\boldsymbol{\theta}|\boldsymbol{\psi})$. We optimize the ELBO wrt $\boldsymbol{\psi}$ to make this a good approximation.

When performing Monte Carlo sampling, we use a s subscript or superscript to denote a sample (e.g., $\boldsymbol{\theta}_s$ or $\boldsymbol{\theta}^s$).

A.9   Abbreviations

Here are some of the abbreviations used in the book.

Abbreviation	Meaning
cdf	Cumulative distribution function
CNN	Convolutional neural network
DAG	Directed acyclic graph
DML	Deep metric learning
DNN	Deep neural network
dof	Degrees of freedom
EB	Empirical Bayes
EM	Expectation maximization algorithm
GLM	Generalized linear model
GMM	Gaussian mixture model
HMC	Hamiltonian Monte Carlo
HMM	Hidden Markov model
iid	Independent and identically distributed
iff	If and only if
KDE	Kernel density estimation
KL	Kullback Leibler divergence
KNN	K nearest neighbor
LHS	Left hand side (of an equation)
LSTM	Long short term memory (a kind of RNN)
LVM	Latent variable model
MAP	Maximum A Posterior estimate
MCMC	Markov chain Monte Carlo
MLE	Maximum likelihood estimate
MLP	Multilayer perceptron
MSE	Mean squared error
NLL	Negative log likelihood
OLS	Ordinary least squares
psd	Positive definite (matrix)
pdf	Probability density function
pmf	Probability mass function
PNLL	Penalized NLL
PGM	Probabilistic graphical model
RNN	Recurrent neural network
RHS	Right hand side (of an equation)
RSS	Residual sum of squares
rv	Random variable
RVM	Relevance vector machine

SGD	Stochastic gradient descent
SSE	Sum of squared errors
SVI	Stochastic variational inference
SVM	Support vector machine
VB	Variational Bayes
wrt	With respect to

Index

Bibliography

[AAB21]   A. Agrawal, A. Ali, and S. Boyd. "Minimum-distortion embedding". en. In: *Foundations and Trends in Machine Learning* 14.3 (2021), pp. 211–378.

[AB08]   C. Archambeau and F. Bach. "Sparse probabilistic projections". In: *NIPS*. 2008.

[AB14]   G. Alain and Y. Bengio. "What Regularized Auto-Encoders Learn from the Data-Generating Distribution". In: *JMLR* (2014).

[AC16]   D. K. Agarwal and B.-C. Chen. *Statistical Methods for Recommender Systems*. en. 1st edition. Cambridge University Press, 2016.

[Ace]   "The Turing Test is Bad for Business". In: (2021).

[AEH+18]   S. Abu-El-Haija, B. Perozzi, R. Al-Rfou, and A. A. Alemi. "Watch your step: Learning node embeddings via graph attention". In: *Advances in Neural Information Processing Systems*. 2018, pp. 9180–9190.

[AEHPAR17]   S. Abu-El-Haija, B. Perozzi, and R. Al-Rfou. "Learning Edge Representations via Low-Rank Asymmetric Projections". In: *Proceedings of the 2017 ACM on Conference on Information and Knowledge Management*. CIKM '17. 2017, 1787–1796.

[AEM18]   Ö. D. Akyildiz, V. Elvira, and J. Miguez. "The Incremental Proximal Method: A Probabilistic Perspective". In: *ICASSP*, 2018.

[AFF19]   C. Aicher, N. J. Foti, and E. B. Fox. "Adaptively Truncating Backpropagation Through Time to Control Gradient Bias". In: (2019). arXiv: 1905.07473 [cs.LG].

[Agg16]   C. C. Aggarwal. *Recommender Systems: The Textbook*. en. 1st ed. 2016 edition. Springer, 2016.

[Agg20]   C. C. Aggarwal. *Linear Algebra and Optimization for Machine Learning: A Textbook*. en. 1st ed. 2020 edition. Springer, 2020.

[AGM19]   V. Amrhein, S. Greenland, and B. McShane. "Scientists rise up against statistical significance". In: *Nature* 567.7748 (2019), p. 305.

[Agr70]   A. Agrawala. "Learning with a probabilistic teacher". In: *IEEE Transactions on Information Theory* 16.4 (1970), pp. 373–379.

[AH19]   C. Allen and T. Hospedales. "Analogies Explained: Towards Understanding Word Embeddings". In: *ICML*. 2019.

[AHK12]   A. Anandkumar, D. Hsu, and S. M. Kakade. "A Method of Moments for Mixture Models and Hidden Markov Models". In: *COLT*. Vol. 23. Proceedings of Machine Learning Research. PMLR, 2012, pp. 33.1–33.34.

[Ahm+13]   A. Ahmed, N. Shervashidze, S. Narayanamurthy, V. Josifovski, and A. J. Smola. "Distributed large-scale natural graph factorization". In: *Proceedings of the 22nd international conference on World Wide Web*. ACM. 2013, pp. 37–48.

[AK15]   J. Andreas and D. Klein. "When and why are log-linear models self-normalizing?" In: *Proc. ACL*. Association for Computational Linguistics, 2015, pp. 244–249.

[Aka74]   H. Akaike. "A new look at the statistical model identification". In: *IEEE Trans. on Automatic Control* 19.6 (1974).

[AKA91]   D. W. Aha, D. Kibler, and M. K. Albert. "Instance-based learning algorithms". In: *Mach. Learn.* 6.1 (1991), pp. 37–66.

[Aky+19]   Ö. D. Akyildiz, É. Chouzenoux, V. Elvira, and J. Míguez. "A probabilistic incremental proximal gradient method". In: *IEEE Signal Process. Lett.* 26.8 (2019).

[AL13]   N. Ailon and E. Liberty. "An Almost Optimal Unrestricted Fast Johnson-Lindenstrauss Transform". In: *ACM Trans. Algorithms* 9.3 (2013), 21:1–21:12.

[Ala18]   J. Alammar. *Illustrated Transformer*. Tech. rep. 2018.

[Alb+17]   M. Alber, P.-J. Kindermans, K. Schütt, K.-R. Müller, and F. Sha. "An Empirical Study on The Properties of Random Bases for Kernel Methods". In: *NIPS*. Curran Associates, Inc., 2017, pp. 2763–2774.

[Alb+18]   D. Albanese, S. Riccadonna, C. Donati, and P. Franceschi. "A practical tool for maximal information coefficient analysis". en. In: *Gigascience* 7.4 (2018), pp. 1–8.

[ALL18]   S. Arora, Z. Li, and K. Lyu. "Theoretical Analysis of Auto Rate-Tuning by Batch Normalization". In: (2018). arXiv: 1812.03981 [cs.LG].

[Alm87]   L. B. Almeida. "A learning rule for asynchronous perceptrons with feedback in a combinatorial environment." In: *Proceedings, 1st First International Conference on Neural Networks*. Vol. 2. IEEE. 1987, pp. 609–618.

[Alo+09]   D. Aloise, A. Deshpande, P. Hansen, and P. Popat. "NP-hardness of Euclidean sum-of-squares clustering". In: *Machine Learning* 75 (2009), pp. 245–249.

[Alp04]   E. Alpaydin. *Introduction to machine learning*. MIT Press, 2004.

[Ami+19]   E. Amid, M. K. Warmuth, R. Anil, and T. Koren. "Robust Bi-Tempered Logistic Loss Based on Bregman Divergences". In: *NIPS*. 2019.

[Amo+16] D. Amodei, C. Olah, J. Steinhardt, P. Christiano, J. Schulman, and D. Mané. "Concrete Problems in AI Safety". In: (2016). arXiv: 1606.06565 [cs.AI].

[Amo17] Amoeba. *What is the difference between ZCA whitening and PCA whitening*. Stackexchange. 2017.

[And01] C. A. Anderson. "Heat and Violence". In: *Current Directions in Psychological Science* 10.1 (2001), pp. 33–38.

[And+18] R. Anderson, J. Huchette, C. Tjandraatmadja, and J. P. Vielma. "Strong convex relaxations and mixed-integer programming formulations for trained neural networks". In: (2018). arXiv: 1811.01988 [math.OC].

[Ani+20] R. Anil, V. Gupta, T. Koren, K. Regan, and Y. Singer. "Scalable Second Order Optimization for Deep Learning". In: (2020). arXiv: 2002.09018 [cs.LG].

[Ans73] F. J. Anscombe. "Graphs in Statistical Analysis". In: *Am. Stat.* 27.1 (1973), pp. 17–21.

[AO03] J.-H. Ahn and J.-H. Oh. "A Constrained EM Algorithm for Principal Component Analysis". In: *Neural Computation* 15 (2003), pp. 57–65.

[Arc+19] F. Arcadu, F. Benmansour, A. Maunz, J. Willis, Z. Haskova, and M. Prunotto. "Deep learning algorithm predicts diabetic retinopathy progression in individual patients". en. In: *NPJ Digit Med* 2 (2019), p. 92.

[Ard+20] R. Ardila, M. Branson, K. Davis, M. Kohler, J. Meyer, M. Henretty, R. Morais, L. Saunders, F. Tyers, and G. Weber. "Common Voice: A Massively-Multilingual Speech Corpus". In: *Proceedings of The 12th Language Resources and Evaluation Conference.* 2020, pp. 4218–4222.

[Arj21] M. Arjovsky. "Out of Distribution Generalization in Machine Learning". In: (2021). arXiv: 2103.02667 [stat.ML].

[Arn+19] S. M. R. Arnold, P.-A. Manzagol, R. Babanezhad, I. Mitliagkas, and N. Le Roux. "Reducing the variance in online optimization by transporting past gradients". In: *NIPS.* 2019.

[Aro+16] S. Arora, Y. Li, Y. Liang, T. Ma, and A. Risteski. "A Latent Variable Model Approach to PMI-based Word Embeddings". In: *TACL* 4 (2016), pp. 385–399.

[Aro+19] L. Aroyo, A. Dumitrache, O. Inel, Z. Szlávik, B. Timmermans, and C. Welty. "Crowdsourcing Inclusivity: Dealing with Diversity of Opinions, Perspectives and Ambiguity in Annotated Data". In: *WWW.* WWW '19. Association for Computing Machinery, 2019, pp. 1294–1295.

[Aro+21] R. Arora et al. *Theory of deep learning.* 2021.

[ARZP19] R. Al-Rfou, D. Zelle, and B. Perozzi. "DDGK: Learning Graph Representations for Deep Divergence Graph Kernels". In: *Proceedings of the 2019 World Wide Web Conference on World Wide Web* (2019).

[AS17] A. Achille and S. Soatto. "On the Emergence of Invariance and Disentangling in Deep Representations". In: (2017). arXiv: 1706.01350 [cs.LG].

[AS19] A. Achille and S. Soatto. "Where is the Information in a Deep Neural Network?" In: (2019). arXiv: 1905.12213 [cs.LG].

[Ash18] J. Asher. "A Rise in Murder? Let's Talk About the Weather". In: *The New York Times* (2018).

[ASR15] A. Ali, S. M. Shamsuddin, and A. L. Ralescu. "Classification with class imbalance problem: A Review". In: *Int. J. Advance Soft Compu. Appl* 7.3 (2015).

[Ath+19] B. Athiwaratkun, M. Finzi, P. Izmailov, and A. G. Wilson. "There Are Many Consistent Explanations of Unlabeled Data: Why You Should Average". In: *ICLR.* 2019.

[AV07] D. Arthur and S. Vassilvitskii. "k-means++: the advantages of careful seeding". In: *Proc. 18th ACM-SIAM symp. on Discrete algorithms.* 2007, 1027–1035.

[AWS19] E. Amid, M. K. Warmuth, and S. Srinivasan. "Two-temperature logistic regression based on the Tsallis divergence". In: *AISTATS.* 2019.

[Axl15] S. Axler. *Linear algebra done right.* 2015.

[BA10] R. Bailey and J. Addison. *A Smoothed-Distribution Form of Nadaraya-Watson Estimation.* Tech. rep. 10-30. Univ. Birmingham, 2010.

[BA97a] A. Bowman and A. Azzalini. *Applied Smoothing Techniques for Data Analysis.* Oxford, 1997.

[BA97b] L. A. Breslow and D. W. Aha. "Simplifying decision trees: A survey". In: *Knowl. Eng. Rev.* 12.1 (1997), pp. 1–40.

[Bab19] S. Babu. *A 2019 guide to Human Pose Estimation with Deep Learning.* 2019.

[Bac+16] O. Bachem, M. Lucic, H. Hassani, and A. Krause. "Fast and Provably Good Seedings for k-Means". In: *NIPS.* 2016, pp. 55–63.

[Bah+12] B. Bahmani, B. Moseley, A. Vattani, R. Kumar, and S. Vassilvitskii. "Scalable k-Means++". In: *VLDB.* 2012.

[Bah+20] Y. Bahri, J. Kadmon, J. Pennington, S. Schoenholz, J. Sohl-Dickstein, and S. Ganguli. "Statistical Mechanics of Deep Learning". In: *Annu. Rev. Condens. Matter Phys.* (2020).

[BAP14] P. Bachman, O. Alsharif, and D. Precup. "Learning with pseudo-ensembles". In: *Advances in neural information processing systems.* 2014, pp. 3365–3373.

[Bar09] M. Bar. "The proactive brain: memory for predictions". en. In: *Philos. Trans. R. Soc. Lond. B Biol. Sci.* 364.1521 (2009), pp. 1235–1243.

[Bar19] J. T. Barron. "A General and Adaptive Robust Loss Function". In: *CVPR.* 2019.

[Bat+18] P. W. Battaglia, J. B. Hamrick, V. Bapst, A. Sanchez-Gonzalez, V. Zambaldi, M. Malinowski, A. Tacchetti, D. Raposo, A. Santoro, R. Faulkner, et al. "Relational inductive biases, deep learning, and graph networks". In: *arXiv preprint arXiv:1806.01261* (2018).

[BB08] O. Bousquet and L. Bottou. "The Tradeoffs of Large Scale Learning". In: *NIPS*. 2008, pp. 161–168.

[BB11] L. Bottou and O. Bousquet. "The Tradeoffs of Large Scale Learning". In: *Optimization for Machine Learning*. Ed. by S. Sra, S. Nowozin, and S. J. Wright. MIT Press, 2011, pp. 351–368.

[BBV11] R. Benassi, J. Bect, and E. Vazquez. "Bayesian optimization using sequential Monte Carlo". In: (2011). arXiv: 1111.4802 [math.OC].

[BC17] D. Beck and T. Cohn. "Learning Kernels over Strings using Gaussian Processes". In: *Proceedings of the Eighth International Joint Conference on Natural Language Processing (Volume 2: Short Papers)*. Vol. 2. 2017, pp. 67–73.

[BCB15] D. Bahdanau, K. Cho, and Y. Bengio. "Neural Machine Translation by Jointly Learning to Align and Translate". In: *ICLR*. 2015.

[BCD01] L. Brown, T. Cai, and A. DasGupta. "Interval Estimation for a Binomial Proportion". In: *Statistical Science* 16.2 (2001), pp. 101–133.

[BCN18] L. Bottou, F. E. Curtis, and J. Nocedal. "Optimization Methods for Large-Scale Machine Learning". In: *SIAM Rev.* 60.2 (2018), pp. 223–311.

[BCV13] Y. Bengio, A. Courville, and P. Vincent. "Representation learning: a review and new perspectives". en. In: *IEEE PAMI* 35.8 (2013), pp. 1798–1828.

[BD20] B. Barz and J. Denzler. "Do We Train on Test Data? Purging CIFAR of Near-Duplicates". In: *J. of Imaging* 6.6 (2020).

[BD21] D. G. T. Barrett and B. Dherin. "Implicit Gradient Regularization". In: *ICLR*. 2021.

[BD87] G. Box and N. Draper. *Empirical Model-Building and Response Surfaces*. Wiley, 1987.

[BDEL03] S. Ben-David, N. Eiron, and P. M. Long. "On the difficulty of approximately maximizing agreements". In: *J. Comput. System Sci.* 66.3 (2003), pp. 496–514.

[Ben+04a] Y. Bengio, O. Delalleau, N. Roux, J. Paiement, P. Vincent, and M. Ouimet. "Learning eigenfunctions links spectral embedding and kernel PCA". In: *Neural Computation* 16 (2004), pp. 2197–2219.

[Ben+04b] Y. Bengio, J.-F. Paiement, P. Vincent, O. Delalleau, N. L. Roux, and M. Ouimet. "Out-of-Sample Extensions for LLE, Isomap, MDS, Eigenmaps, and Spectral Clustering". In: *NIPS*. MIT Press, 2004, pp. 177–184.

[Ben+15a] S. Bengio, O. Vinyals, N. Jaitly, and N. Shazeer. "Scheduled Sampling for Sequence Prediction with Recurrent Neural Networks". In: *NIPS*. 2015.

[Ben+15b] Y. Bengio, D.-H. Lee, J. Bornschein, T. Mesnard, and Z. Lin. "Towards Biologically Plausible Deep Learning". In: (2015). arXiv: 1502.04156 [cs.LG].

[Ben+17] A. Benavoli, G. Corani, J. Demsar, and M. Zaffalon. "Time for a change: a tutorial for comparing multiple classifiers through Bayesian analysis". In: *JMLR* (2017).

[Ber15] D. Bertsekas. *Convex Optimization Algorithms*. Athena Scientific, 2015.

[Ber16] D. Bertsekas. *Nonlinear Programming*. Third. Athena Scientific, 2016.

[Ber+19a] D. Berthelot, N. Carlini, E. D. Cubuk, A. Kurakin, K. Sohn, H. Zhang, and C. Raffel. "Remixmatch: Semi-supervised learning with distribution alignment and augmentation anchoring". In: *arXiv preprint arXiv:1911.09785* (2019).

[Ber+19b] D. Berthelot, N. Carlini, I. Goodfellow, N. Papernot, A. Oliver, and C. Raffel. "Mixmatch: A holistic approach to semi-supervised learning". In: *Advances in Neural Information Processing Systems*. 2019, pp. 5049–5059.

[Ber+21] J. Berner, P. Grohs, G. Kutyniok, and P. Petersen. "The Modern Mathematics of Deep Learning". In: (2021). arXiv: 2105.04026 [cs.LG].

[Ber85] J. Berger. "Bayesian Salesmanship". In: *Bayesian Inference and Decision Techniques with Applications: Essays in Honor of Bruno deFinetti*. Ed. by P. K. Goel and A. Zellner. North-Holland, 1985.

[Ber99] D. Bertsekas. *Nonlinear Programming*. Second. Athena Scientific, 1999.

[Bey+19] M. Beyeler, E. L. Rounds, K. D. Carlson, N. Dutt, and J. L. Krichmar. "Neural correlates of sparse coding and dimensionality reduction". en. In: *PLoS Comput. Biol.* 15.6 (2019), e1006908.

[Bey+20] L. Beyer, O. J. Hénaff, A. Kolesnikov, X. Zhai, and A. van den Oord. "Are we done with ImageNet?" In: (2020). arXiv: 2006.07159 [cs.CV].

[BFO84] L. Breiman, J. Friedman, and R. Olshen. *Classification and regression trees*. Wadsworth, 1984.

[BG11] P. Buhlmann and S. van de Geer. *Statistics for High-Dimensional Data: Methodology, Theory and Applications*. Springer, 2011.

[BH07] P. Buhlmann and T. Hothorn. "Boosting Algorithms: Regularization, Prediction and Model Fitting". In: *Statistical Science* 22.4 (2007), pp. 477–505.

[BH69] A. Bryson and Y.-C. Ho. *Applied optimal control: optimization, estimation, and control*. Blaisdell Publishing Company, 1969.

[BH86] J. Barnes and P. Hut. "A hierarchical O(N log N) force-calculation algorithm". In: *Nature* 324.6096 (1986), pp. 446–449.

[BH89] P. Baldi and K. Hornik. "Neural networks and principal components analysis: Learning from examples without local minima". In: *Neural Networks* 2 (1989), pp. 53–58.

[Bha+19]   A. Bhadra, J. Datta, N. G. Polson, and B. T. Willard. "Lasso Meets Horseshoe: a survey". In: *Bayesian Anal.* 34.3 (2019), pp. 405–427.

[Bha+20]   A. Bhadra, J. Datta, Y. Li, and N. Polson. "Horseshoe regularisation for machine learning in complex and deep models". en. In: *Int. Stat. Rev.* 88.2 (2020), pp. 302–320.

[BHM92]   J. S. Bridle, A. J. Heading, and D. J. MacKay. "Unsupervised Classifiers, Mutual Information and'Phantom Targets". In: *Advances in neural information processing systems.* 1992, pp. 1096–1101.

[BI19]   P. Barham and M. Isard. "Machine Learning Systems are Stuck in a Rut". In: *Proceedings of the Workshop on Hot Topics in Operating Systems.* HotOS '19. Association for Computing Machinery, 2019, pp. 177–183.

[Bis06]   C. Bishop. *Pattern recognition and machine learning.* Springer, 2006.

[Bis94]   C. M. Bishop. *Mixture Density Networks.* Tech. rep. NCRG 4288. Neural Computing Research Group, Department of Computer Science, Aston University, 1994.

[Bis99]   C. Bishop. "Bayesian PCA". In: *NIPS.* 1999.

[BJ05]   F. Bach and M. Jordan. *A probabilistic interpretation of canonical correlation analysis.* Tech. rep. 688. U. C. Berkeley, 2005.

[BJM06]   P. Bartlett, M. Jordan, and J. McAuliffe. "Convexity, Classification, and Risk Bounds". In: *JASA* 101.473 (2006), pp. 138–156.

[BK07]   R. M. Bell and Y. Koren. "Lessons from the Netflix Prize Challenge". In: *SIGKDD Explor. Newsl.* 9.2 (2007), pp. 75–79.

[BK20]   E. M. Bender and A. Koller. "Climbing towards NLU: On Meaning, Form, and Understanding in the Age of Data". In: *Proc. ACL.* 2020, pp. 5185–5198.

[BKC17]   V. Badrinarayanan, A. Kendall, and R. Cipolla. "SegNet: A Deep Convolutional Encoder-Decoder Architecture for Image Segmentation". In: *IEEE PAMI* 39.12 (2017).

[BKH16]   J. L. Ba, J. R. Kiros, and G. E. Hinton. "Layer Normalization". In: (2016). arXiv: 1607.06450 [stat.ML].

[BKL10]   S. Bird, E. Klein, and E. Loper. *Natural Language Processing with Python: Analyzing Text with the Natural Language Toolkit.* 2010.

[BL04]   P. Bickel and E. Levina. "Some theory for Fisher's linear discriminant function, "Naive Bayes", and some alternatives when there are many more variables than observations". In: *Bernoulli* 10 (2004), pp. 989–1010.

[BL07a]   C. M. Bishop and J. Lasserre. "Generative or discriminative? Getting the best of both worlds". In: *Bayesian Statistics 8.* 2007.

[BL07b]   J. A. Bullinaria and J. P. Levy. "Extracting semantic representations from word co-occurrence statistics: a computational study". en. In: *Behav. Res. Methods* 39.3 (2007), pp. 510–526.

[BL12]   J. A. Bullinaria and J. P. Levy. "Extracting semantic representations from word co-occurrence statistics: stop-lists, stemming, and SVD". en. In: *Behav. Res. Methods* 44.3 (2012), pp. 890–907.

[BL88]   D. S. Broomhead and D Lowe. "Multivariable Functional Interpolation and Adaptive Networks". In: *Complex Systems* (1988).

[BLK17]   O. Bachem, M. Lucic, and A. Krause. "Distributed and provably good seedings for k-means in constant rounds". In: *ICML.* 2017, pp. 292–300.

[Blo20]   M. Blondel. *Automatic differentiation.* 2020.

[BLV19]   X. Bouthillier, C. Laurent, and P. Vincent. "Unreproducible Research is Reproducible". In: *ICML.* Vol. 97. Proceedings of Machine Learning Research. PMLR, 2019, pp. 725–734.

[BM98]   A. Blum and T. Mitchell. "Combining labeled and unlabeled data with co-training". In: *Proceedings of the eleventh annual conference on Computational learning theory.* 1998, pp. 92–100.

[BN01]   M. Belkin and P. Niyogi. "Laplacian Eigenmaps and Spectral Techniques for Embedding and Clustering". In: *NIPS.* 2001, pp. 585–591.

[BNJ03]   D. Blei, A. Ng, and M. Jordan. "Latent Dirichlet allocation". In: *JMLR* 3 (2003), pp. 993–1022.

[Bo+08]   L. Bo, C. Sminchisescu, A. Kanaujia, and D. Metaxas. "Fast Algorithms for Large Scale Conditional 3D Prediction". In: *CVPR.* 2008.

[Boh92]   D. Bohning. "Multinomial logistic regression algorithm". In: *Annals of the Inst. of Statistical Math.* 44 (1992), pp. 197–200.

[Bon13]   S. Bonnabel. "Stochastic gradient descent on Riemannian manifolds". In: *IEEE Transactions on Automatic Control* 58.9 (2013), pp. 2217–2229.

[Bos+16]   D. Boscaini, J. Masci, E. Rodolà, and M. Bronstein. "Learning shape correspondence with anisotropic convolutional neural networks". In: *Advances in Neural Information Processing Systems.* 2016, pp. 3189–3197.

[Bot+13]   L. Bottou, J. Peters, J. Quiñonero-Candela, D. X. Charles, D. M. Chickering, E. Portugaly, D. Ray, P. Simard, and E. Snelson. "Counterfactual Reasoning and Learning Systems: The Example of Computational Advertising". In: *JMLR* 14 (2013), pp. 3207–3260.

[Bow+15]   S. R. Bowman, G. Angeli, C. Potts, and C. D. Manning. "A large annotated corpus for learning natural language inference". In: *EMNLP.* Association for Computational Linguistics, 2015, pp. 632–642.

[BPC20]   I. Beltagy, M. E. Peters, and A. Cohan. "Longformer: The Long-Document Transformer". In: *CoRR* abs/2004.05150 (2020). arXiv: 2004.05150.

[Bre01]   L. Breiman. "Random Forests". In: *Machine Learning* 45.1 (2001), pp. 5–32.

[Bre96]   L. Breiman. "Bagging predictors". In: *Machine Learning* 24 (1996), pp. 123–140.

[Bri50]   G. W. Brier. "Verification of forecasts expressed in terms of probability". In: *Monthly Weather Review* 78.1 (1950), pp. 1–3.

[Bri90]   J. Bridle. "Probabilistic Interpretation of Feedforward Classification Network Outputs, with Relationships to Statistical Pattern Recognition". In: *Neurocomputing: Algorithms, Architectures and Applications.* Ed. by F. F. Soulie and J. Herault. Springer Verlag, 1990, pp. 227–236.

[Bro+17a]   M. M. Bronstein, J Bruna, Y LeCun, A Szlam, and P Vandergheynst. "Geometric Deep Learning: Going beyond Euclidean data". In: *IEEE Signal Process. Mag.* 34.4 (2017), pp. 18–42.

[Bro+17b]   M. M. Bronstein, J. Bruna, Y. LeCun, A. Szlam, and P. Vandergheynst. "Geometric deep learning: going beyond euclidean data". In: *IEEE Signal Processing Magazine* 34.4 (2017), pp. 18–42.

[Bro19]   J. Brownlee. *Deep Learning for Computer Vision - Machine Learning Mastery.* Accessed: 2020-6-30. Machine Learning Mastery, 2019.

[Bro+20]   T. B. Brown et al. "Language Models are Few-Shot Learners". In: (2020). arXiv: 2005.14165 [cs.CL].

[Bro+21]   A. Brock, S. De, S. L. Smith, and K. Simonyan. "High-Performance Large-Scale Image Recognition Without Normalization". In: (2021). arXiv: 2102.06171 [cs.CV].

[BRR18]   T. D. Bui, S. Ravi, and V. Ramavajjala. "Neural Graph Machines: Learning Neural Networks Using Graphs". In: *WSDM.* 2018.

[Bru+14]   J. Bruna, W. Zaremba, A. Szlam, and Y. Lecun. "Spectral networks and locally connected networks on graphs International Conference on Learning Representations (ICLR2014)". In: *CBLS, April* (2014).

[Bru+19]   G. Brunner, Y. Liu, D. Pascual, O. Richter, and R. Wattenhofer. "On the Validity of Self-Attention as Explanation in Transformer Models". In: (2019). arXiv: 1908.04211 [cs.CL].

[BS02]   M. Balasubramanian and E. L. Schwartz. "The isomap algorithm and topological stability". en. In: *Science* 295.5552 (2002), p. 7.

[BS16]   P. Baldi and P. Sadowski. "A Theory of Local Learning, the Learning Channel, and the Optimality of Backpropagation". In: *Neural Netw.* 83 (2016), pp. 51–74.

[BS17]   D. M. Blei and P. Smyth. "Science and data science". en. In: *Proc. Natl. Acad. Sci. U. S. A.* (2017).

[BS94]   J. Bernardo and A. Smith. *Bayesian Theory.* John Wiley, 1994.

[BS97]   A. J. Bell and T. J. Sejnowski. "The "independent components" of natural scenes are edge filters". en. In: *Vision Res.* 37.23 (1997), pp. 3327–3338.

[BT04]   G. Bouchard and B. Triggs. "The tradeoff between generative and discriminative classifiers". In: *IASC International Symposium on Computational Statistics (COMPSTAT '04).* 2004.

[BT08]   D. Bertsekas and J. Tsitsiklis. *Introduction to Probability.* 2nd Edition. Athena Scientific, 2008.

[BT09]   A Beck and M Teboulle. "A Fast Iterative Shrinkage-Thresholding Algorithm for Linear Inverse Problems". In: *SIAM J. Imaging Sci.* 2.1 (2009), pp. 183–202.

[BT73]   G. Box and G. Tiao. *Bayesian inference in statistical analysis.* Addison-Wesley, 1973.

[Bul11]   A. D. Bull. "Convergence rates of efficient global optimization algorithms". In: *JMLR* 12 (2011), 2879–2904.

[Bur10]   C. J. C. Burges. "Dimension Reduction: A Guided Tour". en. In: *Foundations and Trends in Machine Learning* (2010).

[BV04]   S. Boyd and L. Vandenberghe. *Convex optimization.* Cambridge, 2004.

[BW08]   P. L. Bartlett and M. H. Wegkamp. "Classification with a Reject Option using a Hinge Loss". In: *JMLR* 9.Aug (2008), pp. 1823–1840.

[BW88]   J. Berger and R. Wolpert. *The Likelihood Principle.* 2nd edition. The Institute of Mathematical Statistics, 1988.

[BWL19]   Y. Bai, Y.-X. Wang, and E. Liberty. "ProxQuant: Quantized Neural Networks via Proximal Operators". In: *ICLR.* 2019.

[BY03]   P. Buhlmann and B. Yu. "Boosting with the L2 loss: Regression and classification". In: *JASA* 98.462 (2003), pp. 324–339.

[Byr+16]   R Byrd, S Hansen, J Nocedal, and Y Singer. "A Stochastic Quasi-Newton Method for Large-Scale Optimization". In: *SIAM J. Optim.* 26.2 (2016), pp. 1008–1031.

[BZ20]   A. Barbu and S.-C. Zhu. *Monte Carlo Methods.* en. Springer, 2020.

[Cal20]   O. Calin. *Deep Learning Architectures: A Mathematical Approach.* en. 1st ed. Springer, 2020.

[Cao+18]   Z. Cao, G. Hidalgo, T. Simon, S.-E. Wei, and Y. Sheikh. "OpenPose: Realtime Multi-Person 2D Pose Estimation using Part Affinity Fields". In: (2018). arXiv: 1812.08008 [cs.CV].

[CAS16]   P. Covington, J. Adams, and E. Sargin. "Deep Neural Networks for YouTube Recommendations". In: *Proceedings of the 10th ACM Conference on Recommender Systems.* RecSys '16. Association for Computing Machinery, 2016, pp. 191–198.

[CB02]   G. Casella and R. Berger. *Statistical inference.* 2nd edition. Duxbury, 2002.

[CBD15]   M. Courbariaux, Y. Bengio, and J.-P. David. "BinaryConnect: Training Deep Neural Networks with binary weights during propagations". In: *NIPS.* 2015.

[CC07]   H. Choi and S. Choi. "Robust kernel Isomap". In: *Pattern Recognit.* 40.3 (2007), pp. 853–862.

[CCD17]   B. P. Chamberlain, J. Clough, and M. P. Deisenroth. "Neural embeddings of graphs in hyperbolic space". In: *arXiv preprint arXiv:1705.10359* (2017).

[CD14]   K. Chaudhuri and S. Dasgupta. "Rates of Convergence for Nearest Neighbor Classification". In: *NIPS*. 2014.

[CD88]   W. Cleveland and S. Devlin. "Locally-Weighted Regression: An Approach to Regression Analysis by Local Fitting". In: *JASA* 83.403 (1988), pp. 596–610.

[CDL16]   J. Cheng, L. Dong, and M. Lapata. "Long Short-Term Memory-Networks for Machine Reading". In: *EMNLP*. Association for Computational Linguistics, 2016, pp. 551–561.

[CDL19]   S. Chen, E. Dobriban, and J. H. Lee. "Invariance reduces Variance: Understanding Data Augmentation in Deep Learning and Beyond". In: (2019). arXiv: 1907.10905 [stat.ML].

[CDS02]   M. Collins, S. Dasgupta, and R. E. Schapire. "A Generalization of Principal Components Analysis to the Exponential Family". In: *NIPS-14*. 2002.

[CEL19]   Z. Chen, J. B. Estrach, and L. Li. "Supervised community detection with line graph neural networks". In: *7th International Conference on Learning Representations, ICLR 2019*. 2019.

[Cer+17]   D. Cer, M. Diab, E. Agirre, I. Lopez-Gazpio, and L. Specia. "SemEval-2017 Task 1: Semantic Textual Similarity Multilingual and Crosslingual Focused Evaluation". In: *Proc. 11th Intl. Workshop on Semantic Evaluation (SemEval-2017)*. Association for Computational Linguistics, 2017, pp. 1–14.

[CFD10]   Y. Cui, X. Z. Fern, and J. G. Dy. "Learning Multiple Nonredundant Clusterings". In: *ACM Transactions on Knowledge Discovery from Data* 4.3 (2010).

[CG16]   T. Chen and C. Guestrin. "XGBoost: A Scalable Tree Boosting System". In: *KDD*. ACM, 2016, pp. 785–794.

[CG18]   J. Chen and Q. Gu. "Closing the Generalization Gap of Adaptive Gradient Methods in Training Deep Neural Networks". In: (2018). arXiv: 1806.06763 [cs.LG].

[CGG17]   S. E. Chazan, J. Goldberger, and S. Gannot. "Speech Enhancement using a Deep Mixture of Experts". In: (2017). arXiv: 1703.09302 [cs.SD].

[CGW21]   W. Chen, X. Gong, and Z. Wang. "Neural Architecture Search on ImageNet in Four GPU Hours: A Theoretically Inspired Perspective". In: *ICLR*. 2021.

[CH67]   T. Cover and P. Hart. " Nearest neighbor pattern classification". In: *IEEE Trans. Inform. Theory* 13.1 (1967), pp. 21–27.

[CH90]   K. W. Church and P. Hanks. "Word Association Norms, Mutual Information, and Lexicography". In: *Computational Linguistics* (1990).

[Cha+01]   O. Chapelle, J. Weston, L. Bottou, and V. Vapnik. "Vicinal Risk Minimization". In: *NIPS*. MIT Press, 2001, pp. 416–422.

[Cha+17]   P. Chaudhari, A. Choromanska, S. Soatto, Y. LeCun, C. Baldassi, C. Borgs, J. Chayes, L. Sagun, and R. Zecchina. "Entropy-SGD: Biasing Gradient Descent Into Wide Valleys". In: *ICLR*. 2017.

[Cha+19a]   I. Chami, Z. Ying, C. Ré, and J. Leskovec. "Hyperbolic graph convolutional neural networks". In: *Advances in Neural Information Processing Systems*. 2019, pp. 4869–4880.

[Cha+19b]   J. J. Chandler, I. Martinez, M. M. Finucane, J. G. Terziev, and A. M. Resch. "Speaking on Data's Behalf: What Researchers Say and How Audiences Choose". en. In: *Eval. Rev.* (2019), p. 193841X19834968.

[Cha+21]   I. Chami, S. Abu-El-Haija, B. Perozzi, C. Ré, and K. Murphy. "Machine Learning on Graphs: A Model and Comprehensive Taxonomy". In: *JMLR* (2021).

[Cha21]   S. H. Chan. *Introduction to Probability for Data Science*. Michigan Publishing, 2021.

[Che+16]   H.-T. Cheng et al. "Wide & Deep Learning for Recommender Systems". In: (2016). arXiv: 1606.07792 [cs.LG].

[Che+20a]   T. Chen, S. Kornblith, M. Norouzi, and G. Hinton. "A Simple Framework for Contrastive Learning of Visual Representations". In: *ICML*. 2020.

[Che+20b]   T. Chen, S. Kornblith, M. Norouzi, and G. Hinton. "A simple framework for contrastive learning of visual representations". In: *ICML*. 2020.

[Che+20c]   T. Chen, S. Kornblith, K. Swersky, M. Norouzi, and G. Hinton. "Big Self-Supervised Models are Strong Semi-Supervised Learners". In: *NIPS*. 2020.

[Chi+19a]   W.-L. Chiang, X. Liu, S. Si, Y. Li, S. Bengio, and C.-J. Hsieh. "Cluster-GCN: An Efficient Algorithm for Training Deep and Large Graph Convolutional Networks". In: *ACM SIGKDD Conference on Knowledge Discovery and Data Mining (KDD)*. 2019.

[Chi+19b]   R. Child, S. Gray, A. Radford, and I. Sutskever. "Generating Long Sequences with Sparse Transformers". In: *CoRR* abs/1904.10509 (2019). arXiv: 1904.10509.

[CHL05]   S. Chopra, R. Hadsell, and Y. LeCun. "Learning a Similarity Metric Discriminatively, with Application to Face Verification". en. In: *CVPR*. 2005.

[Cho+14a]   K. Cho, B. van Merrienboer, C. Gulcehre, D. Bahdanau, F. Bougares, H. Schwenk, and Y. Bengio. "Learning Phrase Representations using RNN Encoder-Decoder for Statistical Machine Translation". In: *EMNLP*. 2014.

[Cho+14b]   K. Cho, B. Van Merriënboer, D. Bahdanau, and Y. Bengio. "On the properties of neural machine translation: Encoder-decoder approaches". In: *arXiv preprint arXiv:1409.1259* (2014).

[Cho+15]   Y. Chow, A. Tamar, S. Mannor, and M. Pavone. "Risk-Sensitive and Robust Decision-Making: a CVaR Optimization Approach". In: *NIPS*. 2015, pp. 1522–1530.

[Cho17]   F. Chollet. *Deep learning with Python*. Manning, 2017.

[Cho+19]   K. Choromanski, M. Rowland, W. Chen, and A. Weller. "Unifying Orthogonal Monte Carlo Methods". In: *Proceedings of the 36th International Conference on Machine Learning, ICML 2019, 9-15 June 2019, Long Beach, California, USA*. Ed. by K. Chaudhuri and R. Salakhutdinov. Vol. 97. Proceedings of Machine Learning Research. PMLR, 2019, pp. 1203–1212.

[Cho+20a]   K. Choromanski et al. "Masked Language Modeling for Proteins via Linearly Scalable Long-Context Transformers". In: (2020). arXiv: 2006.03555 [cs.LG].

[Cho+20b]   K. Choromanski et al. "Rethinking Attention with Performers". In: *CoRR* abs/2009.14794 (2020). arXiv: 2009.14794.

[Cho21]   F. Chollet. *Deep learning with Python (second edition)*. Manning, 2021.

[Chr20]   B. Christian. *The Alignment Problem: Machine Learning and Human Values*. en. 1st ed. W. W. Norton & Company, 2020.

[Chu+15]   J. Chung, K. Kastner, L. Dinh, K. Goel, A. Courville, and Y. Bengio. "A Recurrent Latent Variable Model for Sequential Data". In: *NIPS*. 2015.

[Chu97]   F. Chung. *Spectral Graph Theory*. AMS, 1997.

[Cir+10]   D. C. Ciresan, U. Meier, L. M. Gambardella, and J. Schmidhuber. "Deep Big Simple Neural Nets For Handwritten Digit Recognition". In: *Neural Computation* 22.12 (2010), pp. 3207–3220.

[Cir+11]   D. C. Ciresan, U. Meier, J. Masci, L. M. Gambardella, and J. Schmidhuber. "Flexible, High Performance Convolutional Neural Networks for Image Classification". In: *IJCAI*. 2011.

[CL96]   B. P. Carlin and T. A. Louis. *Bayes and Empirical Bayes Methods for Data Analysis*. Chapman and Hall, 1996.

[Cla21]   A. Clayton. *Bernoulli's Fallacy: Statistical Illogic and the Crisis of Modern Science*. en. Columbia University Press, 2021.

[CLX15]   S. Cao, W. Lu, and Q. Xu. "Grarep: Learning graph representations with global structural information". In: *Proceedings of the 24th ACM International on Conference on Information and Knowledge Management*. ACM. 2015, pp. 891–900.

[CNB17]   C. Chelba, M. Norouzi, and S. Bengio. "N-gram Language Modeling using Recurrent Neural Network Estimation". In: (2017). arXiv: 1703.10724 [cs.CL].

[Coh+17]   G. Cohen, S. Afshar, J. Tapson, and A. van Schaik. "EMNIST: an extension of MNIST to handwritten letters". In: (2017). arXiv: 1702.05373 [cs.CV].

[Coh94]   J. Cohen. "The earth is round (p < .05)". In: *American Psychologist* 49.12 (1994), pp. 997–1003.

[Con+17]   A. Conneau, D. Kiela, H. Schwenk, L. Barrault, and A. Bordes. "Supervised learning of universal sentence representations from natural language inference data". In: *arXiv preprint arXiv:1705.02364* (2017).

[Coo05]   J. Cook. *Exact Calculation of Beta Inequalities*. Tech. rep. M. D. Anderson Cancer Center, Dept. Biostatistics, 2005.

[Cor+16]   C. Cortes, X. Gonzalvo, V. Kuznetsov, M. Mohri, and S. Yang. "AdaNet: Adaptive Structural Learning of Artificial Neural Networks". In: (2016). arXiv: 1607.01097 [cs.LG].

[CP10]   M. A. Carreira-Perpinan. "The Elastic Embedding Algorithm for Dimensionality Reduction". In: *ICML*. 2010.

[CP19]   A. Coenen and A. Pearce. *Understanding UMAP*. 2019.

[CPS06]   K. Chellapilla, S. Puri, and P. Simard. "High Performance Convolutional Neural Networks for Document Processing". In: *10th Intl. Workshop on Frontiers in Handwriting Recognition*. 2006.

[CRW17]   K. Choromanski, M. Rowland, and A. Weller. "The Unreasonable Effectiveness of Structured Random Orthogonal Embeddings". In: *NIPS*. 2017.

[CS20]   F. E. Curtis and K Scheinberg. "Adaptive Stochastic Optimization: A Framework for Analyzing Stochastic Optimization Algorithms". In: *IEEE Signal Process. Mag.* 37.5 (2020), pp. 32–42.

[Csu17]   G. Csurka. "Domain Adaptation for Visual Applications: A Comprehensive Survey". In: *Domain Adaptation in Computer Vision Applications*. Ed. by G. Csurka. 2017.

[CT06]   T. M. Cover and J. A. Thomas. *Elements of Information Theory*. 2nd edition. John Wiley, 2006.

[CT91]   T. M. Cover and J. A. Thomas. *Elements of Information Theory*. John Wiley, 1991.

[Cub+19]   E. D. Cubuk, B. Zoph, D. Mane, V. Vasudevan, and Q. V. Le. "AutoAugment: Learning Augmentation Policies from Data". In: *CVPR*. 2019.

[CUH16]   D.-A. Clevert, T. Unterthiner, and S. Hochreiter. "Fast and Accurate Deep Network Learning by Exponential Linear Units (ELUs)". In: *ICLR*. 2016.

[Cui+19]   X. Cui, K. Zheng, L. Gao, B. Zhang, D. Yang, and J. Ren. "Multiscale Spatial-Spectral Convolutional Network with Image-Based Framework for Hyperspectral Imagery Classification". en. In: *Remote Sensing* 11.19 (2019), p. 2220.

[Cur+17]   J. D. Curtó, I. C. Zarza, F Yang, A Smola, F Torre, C. W. Ngo, and L Gool. "McKernel: A Library for Approximate Kernel Expansions in Log-linear Time". In: (2017). arXiv: 1702.08159v14 [cs.LG].

[Cyb89]   G. Cybenko. "Approximation by superpositions of a sigmoidal function". In: *Mathematics of Control, Signals, and Systems* 2 (1989), 303–331.

[D'A+20]   A. D'Amour et al. "Underspecification Presents Challenges for Credibility in Modern Machine Learning". In: (2020). arXiv: 2011.03395 [cs.LG].

[Dah+11]   G. E. Dahl, D. Yu, L. Deng, and A. Acero. "Large vocabulary continuous speech recognition with context-dependent DBN-HMMS". In: *ICASSP*. IEEE, 2011, pp. 4688–4691.

[Dai+19] Z. Dai, Z. Yang, Y. Yang, J. G. Carbonell, Q. V. Le, and R. Salakhutdinov. "Transformer-XL: Attentive Language Models beyond a Fixed-Length Context". In: *Proc. ACL*. 2019, pp. 2978–2988.

[Dao+19] T. Dao, A. Gu, A. J. Ratner, V. Smith, C. De Sa, and C. Re. "A Kernel Theory of Modern Data Augmentation". In: *ICML*. 2019.

[Dau17] J. Daunizeau. "Semi-analytical approximations to statistical moments of sigmoid and softmax mappings of normal variables". In: (2017). arXiv: 1703.00091 [stat.ML].

[Day+95] P. Dayan, G. Hinton, R. Neal, and R. Zemel. "The Helmholtz machine". In: *Neural Networks* 9.8 (1995).

[DB18] A. Defazio and L. Bottou. "On the Ineffectiveness of Variance Reduced Optimization for Deep Learning". In: (2018). arXiv: 1812.04529 [cs.LG].

[DBLJ14] A. Defazio, F. Bach, and S. Lacoste-Julien. "SAGA: A Fast Incremental Gradient Method With Support for Non-Strongly Convex Composite Objectives". In: *NIPS*. Curran Associates, Inc., 2014, pp. 1646–1654.

[DDDM04] I Daubechies, M Defrise, and C De Mol. "An iterative thresholding algorithm for linear inverse problems with a sparsity constraint". In: *Commun. Pure Appl. Math*. Advances in E 57.11 (2004), pp. 1413–1457.

[Dee+90] S. Deerwester, S. Dumais, G. Furnas, T. Landauer, and R. Harshman. "Indexing by Latent Semantic Analysis". In: *J. of the American Society for Information Science* 41.6 (1990), pp. 391–407.

[DeG70] M. DeGroot. *Optimal Statistical Decisions*. McGraw-Hill, 1970.

[Den+12] J. Deng, J Krause, A. C. Berg, and L. Fei-Fei. "Hedging your bets: Optimizing accuracy-specificity trade-offs in large scale visual recognition". In: *CVPR*. 2012, pp. 3450–3457.

[Den+14] J. Deng, N. Ding, Y. Jia, A. Frome, K. Murphy, S. Bengio, Y. Li, H. Neven, and H. Adam. "Large-Scale Object Classification using Label Relation Graphs". In: *ECCV*. 2014.

[Dev+19] J. Devlin, M.-W. Chang, K. Lee, and K. Toutanova. "BERT: Pre-training of Deep Bidirectional Transformers for Language Understanding". In: *NAACL*. 2019.

[DG06] J. Davis and M. Goadrich. "The Relationship Between Precision-Recall and ROC Curves". In: *ICML*. 2006, pp. 233–240.

[DHM07] P. Diaconis, S. Holmes, and R. Montgomery. "Dynamical Bias in the Coin Toss". In: *SIAM Review* 49.2 (2007), pp. 211–235.

[DHS01] R. O. Duda, P. E. Hart, and D. G. Stork. *Pattern Classification*. 2nd edition. Wiley Interscience, 2001.

[DHS11] J. Duchi, E. Hazan, and Y. Singer. "Adaptive Subgradient Methods for Online Learning and Stochastic Optimization". In: *JMLR* 12 (2011), pp. 2121–2159.

[Die98] T. G. Dietterich. "Approximate Statistical Tests for Comparing Supervised Classification Learning Algorithms". In: *Neural Computation*. 10.7 (1998), pp. 1895–1923.

[Din+15] N. Ding, J. Deng, K. Murphy, and H. Neven. "Probabilistic Label Relation Graphs with Ising Models". In: *ICCV*. 2015.

[DJ15] S. Dray and J. Josse. "Principal component analysis with missing values: a comparative survey of methods". In: *Plant Ecol*. 216.5 (2015), pp. 657–667.

[DKK12] G Dror, N Koenigstein, and Y Koren. "Web-Scale Media Recommendation Systems". In: *Proc. IEEE* 100.9 (2012), pp. 2722–2736.

[DKS95] J. Dougherty, R. Kohavi, and M. Sahami. "Supervised and Unsupervised Discretization of Continuous Features". In: *ICML*. 1995.

[DLLP97] T. Dietterich, R. Lathrop, and T. Lozano-Perez. "Solving the multiple instance problem with axis-parallel rectangles". In: *Artificial Intelligence* 89 (1997), pp. 31–71.

[DLR77] A. P. Dempster, N. M. Laird, and D. B. Rubin. "Maximum likelihood from incomplete data via the EM algorithm". In: *J. of the Royal Statistical Society, Series B* 34 (1977), pp. 1–38.

[DM01] D. van Dyk and X.-L. Meng. "The Art of Data Augmentation". In: *J. Computational and Graphical Statistics* 10.1 (2001), pp. 1–50.

[DM16] P. Drineas and M. W. Mahoney. "RandNLA: Randomized Numerical Linear Algebra". In: *CACM* (2016).

[Do+19] T.-T. Do, T. Tran, I. Reid, V. Kumar, T. Hoang, and G. Carneiro. "A Theoretically Sound Upper Bound on the Triplet Loss for Improving the Efficiency of Deep Distance Metric Learning". In: *CVPR*. 2019, pp. 10404–10413.

[Doe16] C. Doersch. "Tutorial on Variational Autoencoders". In: (2016). arXiv: 1606.05908 [stat.ML].

[Don95] D. L. Donoho. "De-noising by soft-thresholding". In: *IEEE Trans. Inf. Theory* 41.3 (1995), pp. 613–627.

[Dos+21] A. Dosovitskiy et al. "An Image is Worth 16x16 Words: Transformers for Image Recognition at Scale". In: *ICLR*. 2021.

[Doy+07] K. Doya, S. Ishii, A. Pouget, and R. P. N. Rao, eds. *Bayesian Brain: Probabilistic Approaches to Neural Coding*. MIT Press, 2007.

[DP97] P. Domingos and M. Pazzani. "On the Optimality of the Simple Bayesian Classifier under Zero-One Loss". In: *Machine Learning* 29 (1997), pp. 103–130.

[DR21] H. Duanmu and D. M. Roy. "On extended admissibale procedures and their nonstandard Bayes risk". In: *Annals of Statistics* (2021).

[Dri+04] P. Drineas, A. Frieze, R. Kannan, S. Vempala, and V. Vinay. "Clustering Large Graphs via the Singular Value Decomposition". In: *Machine Learning* 56 (2004), pp. 9–33.

[DS12] M. Der and L. K. Saul. "Latent Coincidence Analysis: A Hidden Variable Model for Distance Metric Learning". In: *NIPS*. Curran Associates, Inc., 2012, pp. 3230–3238.

[DSK16] V. Dumoulin, J. Shlens, and M. Kudlur. "A Learned Representation For Artistic Style". In: (2016). arXiv: 1610.07629 [cs.CV].

[Dum+18] A. Dumitrache, O. Inel, B. Timmermans, C. Ortiz, R.-J. Sips, L. Aroyo, and C. Welty. "Empirical Methodology for Crowdsourcing Ground Truth". In: *Semantic Web Journal* (2018).

[Duv14] D. Duvenaud. "Automatic Model Construction with Gaussian Processes". PhD thesis. Computational and Biological Learning Laboratory, University of Cambridge, 2014.

[DV16] V. Dumoulin and F. Visin. "A guide to convolution arithmetic for deep learning". In: (2016). arXiv: 1603.07285 [stat.ML].

[EDH19] K. Ethayarajh, D. Duvenaud, and G. Hirst. "Towards Understanding Linear Word Analogies". In: *Proc. ACL*. Association for Computational Linguistics, 2019, pp. 3253–3262.

[EF15] D. Eigen and R. Fergus. "Predicting Depth, Surface Normals and Semantic Labels with a Common Multi-Scale Convolutional Architecture". In: *ICCV*. 2015.

[Efr+04] B. Efron, I. Johnstone, T. Hastie, and R. Tibshirani. "Least angle regression". In: *Annals of Statistics* 32.2 (2004), pp. 407–499.

[Efr86] B. Efron. "Why Isn't Everyone a Bayesian?" In: *The American Statistician* 40.1 (1986).

[Ein16] A Einstein. "Die Grundlage der allgemeinen Relativitätstheorie". In: *Ann. Phys.* 354.7 (1916), pp. 769–822.

[Eis19] J. Eisenstein. *Introduction to Natural Language Processing*. 2019.

[Elk03] C. Elkan. "Using the triangle inequality to accelerate k-means". In: *ICML*. 2003.

[EMH19] T. Elsken, J. H. Metzen, and F. Hutter. "Neural Architecture Search: A Survey". In: *JMLR* 20 (2019), pp. 1–21.

[Erh+10] D. Erhan, Y. Bengio, A. Courville, P.-A. Manzagol, P. Vincent, and S. Bengio. "Why Does Unsupervised Pre-training Help Deep Learning?" In: *JMLR* 11 (2010), pp. 625–660.

[FAL17] C. Finn, P. Abbeel, and S. Levine. "Model-Agnostic Meta-Learning for Fast Adaptation of Deep Networks". In: *ICML*. 2017.

[FB81] M. A. Fischler and R. Bolles. "Random sample concensus: A paradigm for model fitting with applications to image analysis and automated cartography". In: *Comm. ACM* 24.6 (1981), pp. 381–395.

[Fen+21] S. Y. Feng, V. Gangal, J. Wei, S. Chandar, S. Vosoughi, T. Mitamura, and E. Hovy. "A Survey of Data Augmentation Approaches for NLP". In: (2021). arXiv: 2105.03075 [cs.CL].

[Fer+10] D. Ferrucci et al. "Building Watson: An Overview of the DeepQA Project". In: *AI Magazine* (2010), pp. 59–79.

[FH20] E. Fong and C. Holmes. "On the marginal likelihood and cross-validation". In: *Biometrika* 107.2 (2020).

[FHK12] A. Feuerverger, Y. He, and S. Khatri. "Statistical Significance of the Netflix Challenge". In: *Stat. Sci.* 27.2 (2012), pp. 202–231.

[FHT00] J. Friedman, T. Hastie, and R. Tibshirani. "Additive logistic regression: a statistical view of boosting". In: *Annals of statistics* 28.2 (2000), pp. 337–374.

[FHT10] J. Friedman, T. Hastie, and R. Tibshirani. "Regularization Paths for Generalized Linear Models via Coordinate Descent". In: *J. of Statistical Software* 33.1 (2010).

[Fir57] J. Firth. "A synopsis of linguistic theory 1930-1955". In: *Studies in Linguistic Analysis*. Ed. by F. Palmer. 1957.

[FJ02] M. A. T. Figueiredo and A. K. Jain. "Unsupervised Learning of Finite Mixture Models". In: *IEEE PAMI* 24.3 (2002), pp. 381–396.

[FM03] J. H. Friedman and J. J. Meulman. "Multiple additive regression trees with application in epidemiology". en. In: *Stat. Med.* 22.9 (2003), pp. 1365–1381.

[FMN16] C. Fefferman, S. Mitter, and H. Narayanan. "Testing the manifold hypothesis". In: *J. Amer. Math. Soc.* 29.4 (2016), pp. 983–1049.

[FNW07] M. Figueiredo, R. Nowak, and S. Wright. "Gradient projection for sparse reconstruction: application to compressed sensing and other inverse problems". In: *IEEE. J. on Selected Topics in Signal Processing* (2007).

[For+21] P. Foret, A. Kleiner, H. Mobahi, and B. Neyshabur. "Sharpness-aware Minimization for Efficiently Improving Generalization". In: *ICLR*. 2021.

[Fos19] D. Foster. *Generative Deep Learning: Teaching Machines to Paint, Write, Compose, and Play*. 1 edition. O'Reilly Media, 2019.

[FR07] C. Fraley and A. Raftery. "Bayesian Regularization for Normal Mixture Estimation and Model-Based Clustering". In: *J. of Classification* 24 (2007), pp. 155–181.

[Fra+17] L. Franceschi, M. Donini, P. Frasconi, and M. Pontil. "Forward and Reverse Gradient-Based Hyperparameter Optimization". In: *ICML*. 2017.

[Fre98] B. Frey. *Graphical Models for Machine Learning and Digital Communication*. MIT Press, 1998.

[Fri01] J. Friedman. "Greedy Function Approximation: a Gradient Boosting Machine". In: *Annals of Statistics* 29 (2001), pp. 1189–1232.

[Fri97a] J. Friedman. "On bias, variance, 0-1 loss and the curse of dimensionality". In: *J. Data Mining and Knowledge Discovery* 1 (1997), pp. 55–77.

[Fri97b] J. H. Friedman. "Data mining and statistics: What's the connection". In: *Proceedings of the 29th Symposium on the Interface Between Computer Science and Statistics*. 1997.

[Fri99]   J. Friedman. *Stochastic Gradient Boosting*. Tech. rep. 1999.

[FS96]   Y. Freund and R. R. Schapire. "Experiments with a new boosting algorithm". In: *ICML*. 1996.

[FT05]   M. Fashing and C. Tomasi. "Mean shift is a bound optimization". en. In: *IEEE Trans. Pattern Anal. Mach. Intell.* 27.3 (2005), pp. 471–474.

[Fu98]   W. Fu. "Penalized regressions: the bridge versus the lasso". In: *J. Computational and graphical statistics* 7 (1998), 397– 416.

[Fuk75]   K. Fukushima. "Cognitron: a self-organizing multilayered neural network". In: *Biological Cybernetics* 20.6 (1975), pp. 121–136.

[Fuk80]   K Fukushima. "Neocognitron: a self organizing neural network model for a mechanism of pattern recognition unaffected by shift in position". en. In: *Biol. Cybern.* 36.4 (1980), pp. 193–202.

[Fuk90]   K. Fukunaga. *Introduction to Statistical Pattern Recognition*. 2nd edition. Academic Press, 1990.

[Gag94]   P. Gage. "A New Algorithm for Data Compression". In: *Dr Dobbs Journal* (1994).

[Gan+16]   Y Ganin, E Ustinova, H Ajakan, P Germain, and others. "Domain-adversarial training of neural networks". In: *JMLR* (2016).

[Gao+20]   L. Gao et al. "The Pile: An 800GB Dataset of Diverse Text for Language Modeling". In: (2020). arXiv: 2101.00027 [cs.CL].

[Gär03]   T. Gärtner. "A Survey of Kernels for Structured Data". In: *SIGKDD Explor. Newsl.* 5.1 (2003), pp. 49–58.

[Gar+18]   J. Gardner, G. Pleiss, K. Q. Weinberger, D. Bindel, and A. G. Wilson. "GPyTorch: Blackbox Matrix-Matrix Gaussian Process Inference with GPU Acceleration". In: *NIPS*. Ed. by S Bengio, H Wallach, H Larochelle, K Grauman, N Cesa-Bianchi, and R Garnett. Curran Associates, Inc., 2018, pp. 7576–7586.

[GASG18]   D. G. A. Smith and J. Gray. "opt-einsum - A Python package for optimizing contraction order for einsum-like expressions". In: *JOSS* 3.26 (2018), p. 753.

[GB05]   Y. Grandvalet and Y. Bengio. "Semi-supervised learning by entropy minimization". In: *Advances in neural information processing systems*. 2005, pp. 529–536.

[GB10]   X. Glorot and Y. Bengio. "Understanding the difficulty of training deep feedforward neural networks". In: *AISTATS*. 2010, pp. 249–256.

[GB18]   V. Garcia and J. Bruna. "Few-shot Learning with Graph Neural Networks". In: *International Conference on Learning Representations (ICLR)*. 2018.

[GBB11]   X. Glorot, A. Bordes, and Y. Bengio. "Deep Sparse Rectifer Neural Networks". In: *AISTATS*. 2011.

[GBC16]   I. Goodfellow, Y. Bengio, and A. Courville. *Deep Learning*. http://www.deeplearningbook.org. MIT Press, 2016.

[GBD92]   S. Geman, E. Bienenstock, and R. Doursat. "Neural networks and the bias-variance dilemma". In: *Neural Computing* 4 (1992), pp. 1–58.

[GC20]   A. Gelman and B. Carpenter. "Bayesian analysis of tests with unknown specificity and sensitivity". In: *J. of Royal Stat. Soc. Series C* medrxiv;2020.05.22.20108944v2 (2020).

[GEB16]   L. A. Gatys, A. S. Ecker, and M. Bethge. "Image style transfer using convolutional neural networks". In: *CVPR*. 2016, pp. 2414–2423.

[GEH19]   T. Gale, E. Elsen, and S. Hooker. "The State of Sparsity in Deep Neural Networks". In: (2019). arXiv: 1902.09574 [cs.LG].

[Gel+04]   A. Gelman, J. Carlin, H. Stern, and D. Rubin. *Bayesian data analysis*. 2nd edition. Chapman and Hall, 2004.

[Gel+14]   A. Gelman, J. B. Carlin, H. S. Stern, D. B. Dunson, A. Vehtari, and D. B. Rubin. *Bayesian Data Analysis, Third Edition*. Third edition. Chapman and Hall/CRC, 2014.

[Gel16]   A. Gelman. "The problems with p-values are not just with p-values". In: *American Statistician* (2016).

[Gér17]   A. Géron. *Hands-On Machine Learning with Scikit-Learn and TensorFlow: Concepts, Tools, and Techniques for Building Intelligent Systems*. en. O'Reilly Media, Incorporated, 2017.

[Gér19]   A. Géron. *Hands-On Machine Learning with Scikit-Learn and TensorFlow: Concepts, Tools, and Techniques for Building Intelligent Systems (2nd edition)*. en. O'Reilly Media, Incorporated, 2019.

[GEY19]   Y. Geifman and R. El-Yaniv. "SelectiveNet: A Deep Neural Network with an Integrated Reject Option". In: *ICML*. 2019.

[GG16]   Y. Gal and Z. Ghahramani. "Dropout as a Bayesian Approximation: Representing Model Uncertainty in Deep Learning". In: *ICML*. 2016.

[GH96]   Z. Ghahramani and G. Hinton. *The EM Algorithm for Mixtures of Factor Analyzers*. Tech. rep. Dept. of Comp. Sci., Uni. Toronto, 1996.

[GHK17]   Y. Gal, J. Hron, and A. Kendall. "Concrete Dropout". In: (2017). arXiv: 1705.07832 [stat.ML].

[GHV14]   A. Gelman, J. Hwang, and A. Vehtari. "Understanding predictive information criteria for Bayesian models". In: *Statistics and Computing* 24.6 (2014), pp. 997–1016.

[Gib97]   M. Gibbs. "Bayesian Gaussian Processes for Regression and Classification". PhD thesis. U. Cambridge, 1997.

[Gil+17]   J. Gilmer, S. S. Schoenholz, P. F. Riley, O. Vinyals, and G. E. Dahl. "Neural message passing for quantum chemistry". In: *ICML*. 2017, pp. 1263–1272.

[Gil+21]   J. Gilmer, B. Ghorbani, A. Garg, S. Kudugunta, B. Neyshabur, D. Cardoze, G. Dahl, Z. Nado, and O. Firat. "A Loss Curvature Perspective on Training Instability in

Deep Learning". In: (2021). arXiv: 2110.04369 [cs.LG].

[GIM99] A. Gionis, P. Indyk, and R. Motwani. "Similarity Search in High Dimensions via Hashing". In: *Proc. 25th Intl. Conf. on Very Large Data Bases.* VLDB '99. 1999, pp. 518–529.

[GKS18] V. Gupta, T. Koren, and Y. Singer. "Shampoo: Preconditioned Stochastic Tensor Optimization". In: *ICML.* 2018.

[GL15] B. Gu and C. Ling. "A New Generalized Error Path Algorithm for Model Selection". In: *ICML.* 2015.

[GL16] A. Grover and J. Leskovec. "node2vec: Scalable feature learning for networks". In: *Proceedings of the 22nd ACM SIGKDD international conference on Knowledge discovery and data mining.* ACM. 2016, pp. 855–864.

[GMS05] M. Gori, G. Monfardini, and F. Scarselli. "A new model for learning in graph domains". In: *Proceedings. 2005 IEEE International Joint Conference on Neural Networks, 2005.* Vol. 2. IEEE. 2005, pp. 729–734.

[GNK18] R. A. Güler, N. Neverova, and I. Kokkinos. "Densepose: Dense human pose estimation in the wild". In: *CVPR.* 2018, pp. 7297–7306.

[God18] P. Godec. *Graph Embeddings; The Summary.* https : / / towardsdatascience . com / graph - embeddings-the-summary-cc6075aba007. 2018.

[GOF18] O. Gouvert, T. Oberlin, and C. Févotte. "Negative Binomial Matrix Factorization for Recommender Systems". In: (2018). arXiv: 1801.01708 [cs.LG].

[Gol+01] K. Goldberg, T. Roeder, D. Gupta, and C. Perkins. "Eigentaste: A Constant Time Collaborative Filtering Algorithm". In: *Information Retrieval* 4.2 (2001), pp. 133–151.

[Gol+05] J. Goldberger, S. Roweis, G. Hinton, and R. Salakhutdinov. "Neighbourhood Components Analysis". In: *NIPS.* 2005.

[Gol+92] D. Goldberg, D. Nichols, B. M. Oki, and D. Terry. "Using collaborative filtering to weave an information tapestry". In: *Commun. ACM* 35.12 (1992), pp. 61–70.

[Gon85] T. Gonzales. "Clustering to minimize the maximum intercluster distance". In: *Theor. Comp. Sci.* 38 (1985), pp. 293–306.

[Goo01] N. Goodman. "Classes for fast maximum entropy training". In: *ICASSP.* 2001.

[Goo+14] I. J. Goodfellow, J. Pouget-Abadie, M. Mirza, B. Xu, D. Warde-Farley, S. Ozair, A. Courville, and Y. Bengio. "Generative Adversarial Networks". In: *NIPS.* 2014.

[Gor06] P. F. Gorder. "Neural Networks Show New Promise for Machine Vision". In: *Computing in science & engineering* 8.6 (2006), pp. 4–8.

[Got+19] A. Gotmare, N. S. Keskar, C. Xiong, and R. Socher. "A Closer Look at Deep Learning Heuristics: Learning rate restarts, Warmup and Distillation". In: *ICLR.* 2019.

[GOV18] W Gao, S Oh, and P Viswanath. "Demystifying Fixed k -Nearest Neighbor Information Estimators". In: *IEEE Trans. Inf. Theory* 64.8 (2018), pp. 5629–5661.

[GR07] T. Gneiting and A. E. Raftery. "Strictly Proper Scoring Rules, Prediction, and Estimation". In: *JASA* 102.477 (2007), pp. 359–378.

[GR18] A. Graves and M.-A. Ranzato. "Tutorial on unsupervised deep learning: part 2". In: *NIPS.* 2018.

[Gra04] Y. Grandvalet. "Bagging Equalizes Influence". In: *Mach. Learn.* 55 (2004), pp. 251–270.

[Gra11] A. Graves. "Practical variational inference for neural networks". In: *Advances in neural information processing systems.* 2011, pp. 2348–2356.

[Gra13] A. Graves. "Generating Sequences With Recurrent Neural Networks". In: (2013). arXiv: 1308.0850 [cs.NE].

[Gra+17] E. Grave, A. Joulin, M. Cissé, D. Grangier, and H. Jégou. "Efficient softmax approximation for GPUs". In: *ICML.* 2017.

[Gra+18] E. Grant, C. Finn, S. Levine, T. Darrell, and T. Griffiths. "Recasting Gradient-Based Meta-Learning as Hierarchical Bayes". In: *ICLR.* 2018.

[Gra+20] W. Grathwohl, K.-C. Wang, J.-H. Jacobsen, D. Duvenaud, M. Norouzi, and K. Swersky. "Your classifier is secretly an energy based model and you should treat it like one". In: *ICLR.* 2020.

[Gre+17] K. Greff, R. K. Srivastava, J. Koutník, B. R. Steunebrink, and J. Schmidhuber. "LSTM: A Search Space Odyssey". In: *IEEE Transactions on Neural Networks and Learning Systems* 28.10 (2017).

[Gri20] T. L. Griffiths. "Understanding Human Intelligence through Human Limitations". en. In: *Trends Cogn. Sci.* 24.11 (2020), pp. 873–883.

[GS08] Y Guo and D Schuurmans. "Efficient global optimization for exponential family PCA and low-rank matrix factorization". In: *2008 46th Annual Allerton Conference on Communication, Control, and Computing.* 2008, pp. 1100–1107.

[GS97] C. M. Grinstead and J. L. Snell. *Introduction to probability (2nd edition).* American Mathematical Society, 1997.

[GSK18] S. Gidaris, P. Singh, and N. Komodakis. "Unsupervised Representation Learning by Predicting Image Rotations". In: *ICLR.* 2018.

[GT07] L. Getoor and B. Taskar, eds. *Introduction to Relational Statistical Learning.* MIT Press, 2007.

[GTA00] G. Gigerenzer, P. M. Todd, and ABC Research Group. *Simple Heuristics That Make Us Smart.* en. Illustrated edition. Oxford University Press, 2000.

[Gu+18] A. Gu, F. Sala, B. Gunel, and C. Ré. "Learning Mixed-Curvature Representations in Product Spaces". In: *International Conference on Learning Representations* (2018).

[Gua+10] Y. Guan, J. Dy, D. Niu, and Z. Ghahramani. "Variational Inference for Nonparametric Multiple Clustering". In: *1st Intl. Workshop on Discovering, Summarizing and Using Multiple Clustering (MultiClust).* 2010.

[Gua+17]   S. Guadarrama, R. Dahl, D. Bieber, M. Norouzi, J. Shlens, and K. Murphy. "Pix-Color: Pixel Recursive Colorization". In: *BMVC*. 2017.

[Gul+20]   A. Gulati et al. "Conformer: Convolution-augmented Transformer for Speech Recognition". In: (2020). arXiv: 2005.08100 [eess.AS].

[Guo09]   Y. Guo. "Supervised exponential family principal component analysis via convex optimization". In: *NIPS*. 2009.

[Guo+17]   H. Guo, R. Tang, Y. Ye, Z. Li, and X. He. "DeepFM: a factorization-machine based neural network for CTR prediction". In: *IJCAI*. IJCAI'17. AAAI Press, 2017, pp. 1725–1731.

[Gus01]   M. Gustafsson. "A probabilistic derivation of the partial least-squares algorithm". In: *Journal of Chemical Information and Modeling* 41 (2001), pp. 288–294.

[GVZ16]   A. Gupta, A. Vedaldi, and A. Zisserman. "Synthetic Data for Text Localisation in Natural Images". In: *CVPR*. 2016.

[GZE19]   A. Grover, A. Zweig, and S. Ermon. "Graphite: Iterative Generative Modeling of Graphs". In: *International Conference on Machine Learning*. 2019, pp. 2434–2444.

[HA85]   L. Hubert and P. Arabie. "Comparing Partitions". In: *J. of Classification* 2 (1985), pp. 193–218.

[HAB19]   M. Hein, M. Andriushchenko, and J. Bitterwolf. "Why ReLU networks yield high-confidence predictions far away from the training data and how to mitigate the problem". In: *CVPR*. 2019.

[Hac75]   I. Hacking. *The Emergence of Probability: A Philosophical Study of Early Ideas about Probability, Induction and Statistical Inference*. Cambridge University Press, 1975.

[Háj08]   A. Hájek. "Dutch Book Arguments". In: *The Oxford Handbook of Rational and Social Choice*. Ed. by P. Anand, P. Pattanaik, and C. Puppe. Oxford University Press, 2008.

[Han+20]   B. Han, Q. Yao, T. Liu, G. Niu, I. W. Tsang, J. T. Kwok, and M. Sugiyama. "A Survey of Label-noise Representation Learning: Past, Present and Future". In: (2020). arXiv: 2011.04406 [cs.LG].

[Har54]   Z. Harris. "Distributional structure". In: *Word* 10.23 (1954), pp. 146–162.

[Has+04]   T. Hastie, S. Rosset, R. Tibshirani, and J. Zhu. "The entire regularization path for the support vector machine". In: *JMLR* 5 (2004), pp. 1391–1415.

[Has+09]   T. Hastie, S. Rosset, J. Zhu, and H. Zou. "Multi-class AdaBoost". In: *Statistics and tis Interface* 2.3 (2009), pp. 349–360.

[Has+17]   D. Hassabis, D. Kumaran, C. Summerfield, and M. Botvinick. "Neuroscience-Inspired Artificial Intelligence". en. In: *Neuron* 95.2 (2017), pp. 245–258.

[Has87]   J. Hastad. *Computational limits of small-depth circuits*. MIT Press, 1987.

[HB17]   X. Huang and S. Belongie. "Arbitrary style transfer in real-time with adaptive instance normalization". In: *ICCV*. 2017.

[HCD12]   D. Hoiem, Y. Chodpathumwan, and Q. Dai. "Diagnosing Error in Object Detectors". In: *ECCV*. 2012.

[HCL03]   C.-W. Hsu, C.-C. Chang, and C.-J. Lin. *A Practical Guide to Support Vector Classification*. 2003.

[HDR19]   S. Hayou, A. Doucet, and J. Rousseau. "On the Impact of the Activation Function on Deep Neural Networks Training". In: (2019). arXiv: 1902.06853 [stat.ML].

[He+15]   K. He, X. Zhang, S. Ren, and J. Sun. "Delving Deep into Rectifiers: Surpassing Human-Level Performance on ImageNet Classification". In: *ICCV*. 2015.

[He+16a]   K. He, X. Zhang, S. Ren, and J. Sun. "Deep Residual Learning for Image Recognition". In: *CVPR*. 2016.

[He+16b]   K. He, X. Zhang, S. Ren, and J. Sun. "Identity Mappings in Deep Residual Networks". In: *ECCV*. 2016.

[He+17]   X. He, L. Liao, H. Zhang, L. Nie, X. Hu, and T.-S. Chua. "Neural Collaborative Filtering". In: *WWW*. 2017.

[HE18]   D. Ha and D. Eck. "A Neural Representation of Sketch Drawings". In: *ICLR*. 2018.

[He+20]   K. He, H. Fan, Y. Wu, S. Xie, and R. Girshick. "Momentum contrast for unsupervised visual representation learning". In: *CVPR*. 2020, pp. 9729–9738.

[Hen+15]   J. Hensman, A. Matthews, M. Filippone, and Z. Ghahramani. "MCMC for Variationally Sparse Gaussian Processes". In: *NIPS*. 2015, pp. 1648–1656.

[HG16]   D. Hendrycks and K. Gimpel. "Gaussian Error Linear Units (GELUs)". In: *arXiv [cs.LG]* (2016).

[HG20]   J. Howard and S. Gugger. *Deep Learning for Coders with Fastai and PyTorch: AI Applications Without a PhD*. en. 1st ed. O'Reilly Media, 2020.

[HG21]   M. K. Ho and T. L. Griffiths. "Cognitive science as a source of forward and inverse models of human decisions for robotics and control". In: *Annual Review of Control, Robotics, and Autonomous Systems*. 2021.

[HGD19]   K. He, R. Girshick, and P. Dollár. "Rethinking ImageNet Pre-training". In: *CVPR*. 2019.

[Hin+12]   G. E. Hinton et al. "Deep Neural Networks for Acoustic Modeling in Speech Recognition: The Shared Views of Four Research Groups". In: *IEEE Signal Process. Mag.* 29.6 (2012), pp. 82–97.

[Hin13]   G. Hinton. *CSC 2535 Lecture 11: Non-linear dimensionality reduction*. 2013.

[Hin14]   G. Hinton. *Lecture 6e on neural networks (RMSprop: Divide the gradient by a running average of its recent magnitude)*. 2014.

[HK15] F. M. Harper and J. A. Konstan. "The MovieLens Datasets: History and Context". In: *ACM Trans. Interact. Intell. Syst.* 5.4 (2015), pp. 1–19.

[HKV19] F. Hutter, L. Kotthoff, and J. Vanschoren, eds. *Automated Machine Learning - Methods, Systems, Challenges.* Springer, 2019.

[HL04] D. R. Hunter and K. Lange. "A Tutorial on MM Algorithms". In: *The American Statistician* 58 (2004), pp. 30–37.

[HMT11] N. Halko, P.-G. Martinsson, and J. A. Tropp. "Finding structure with randomness: Probabilistic algorithms for constructing approximate matrix decompositions". In: *SIAM Rev., Survey and Review section* 53.2 (2011), pp. 217–288.

[HN19] C. M. Holmes and I. Nemenman. "Estimation of mutual information for real-valued data with error bars and controlled bias". en. In: *Phys Rev E* 100.2-1 (2019), p. 022404.

[Hoc+01] S. Hochreiter, Y. Bengio, P. Frasconi, and J. Schmidhuber. "Gradient flow in recurrent nets: the difficulty of learning long-term dependencies". In: *A Field Guide to Dynamical Recurrent Neural Networks.* Ed. by S. C. Kremer and J. F. Kolen. 2001.

[Hoe+14] R. Hoekstra, R. D. Morey, J. N. Rouder, and E.-J. Wagenmakers. "Robust misinterpretation of confidence intervals". en. In: *Psychon. Bull. Rev.* 21.5 (2014), pp. 1157–1164.

[Hoe+21] T. Hoefler, D. Alistarh, T. Ben-Nun, N. Dryden, and A. Peste. "Sparsity in Deep Learning: Pruning and growth for efficient inference and training in neural networks". In: (2021). arXiv: 2102.00554 [cs.LG].

[Hof09] P. D. Hoff. *A First Course in Bayesian Statistical Methods.* Springer, 2009.

[Hor61] P Horst. "Generalized canonical correlations and their applications to experimental data". en. In: *J. Clin. Psychol.* 17 (1961), pp. 331–347.

[Hor91] K. Hornik. "Approximation Capabilities of Multilayer Feedforward Networks". In: *Neural Networks* 4.2 (1991), pp. 251–257.

[Hos+19] M. Z. Hossain, F. Sohel, M. F. Shiratuddin, and H. Laga. "A Comprehensive Survey of Deep Learning for Image Captioning". In: *ACM Computing Surveys* (2019).

[HOT06] G. Hinton, S. Osindero, and Y. Teh. "A fast learning algorithm for deep belief nets". In: *Neural Computation* 18 (2006), pp. 1527–1554.

[Hot36] H. Hotelling. "Relations Between Two Sets of Variates". In: *Biometrika* 28.3/4 (1936), pp. 321–377.

[Hou+12] N. Houlsby, F. Huszar, Z. Ghahramani, and J. M. Hernández-lobato. "Collaborative Gaussian Processes for Preference Learning". In: *NIPS.* 2012, pp. 2096–2104.

[Hou+19] N. Houlsby, A. Giurgiu, S. Jastrzebski, B. Morrone, Q. de Laroussilhe, A. Gesmundo, M. Attariyan, and S. Gelly. "Parameter-Efficient Transfer Learning for NLP". In: *ICML.* 2019.

[How+17] A. G. Howard, M. Zhu, B. Chen, D. Kalenichenko, W. Wang, T. Weyand, M. Andreetto, and H. Adam. "MobileNets: Efficient Convolutional Neural Networks for Mobile Vision Applications". In: *CVPR.* 2017.

[HR03] G. E. Hinton and S. T. Roweis. "Stochastic Neighbor Embedding". In: *NIPS.* 2003, pp. 857–864.

[HR76] L. Hyafil and R. Rivest. "Constructing Optimal Binary Decision Trees is NP-complete". In: *Information Processing Letters* 5.1 (1976), pp. 15–17.

[HRP21] M. Huisman, J. N. van Rijn, and A. Plaat. "A Survey of Deep Meta-Learning". In: *AI Review* (2021).

[HS19] J. Haochen and S. Sra. "Random Shuffling Beats SGD after Finite Epochs". In: *ICML.* Vol. 97. Proceedings of Machine Learning Research. PMLR, 2019, pp. 2624–2633.

[HS97a] S Hochreiter and J Schmidhuber. "Flat minima". en. In: *Neural Comput.* 9.1 (1997), pp. 1–42.

[HS97b] S. Hochreiter and J. Schmidhuber. "Long short-term memory". In: *Neural Computation* 9.8 (1997), 1735–1780.

[HSW89] K. Hornik, M. Stinchcombe, and H. White. "Multilayer feedforward networks are universal approximators". In: *Neural Networks* 2.5 (1989), pp. 359–366.

[HT90] T. Hastie and R. Tibshirani. *Generalized additive models.* Chapman and Hall, 1990.

[HTF01] T. Hastie, R. Tibshirani, and J. Friedman. *The Elements of Statistical Learning.* Springer, 2001.

[HTF09] T. Hastie, R. Tibshirani, and J. Friedman. *The Elements of Statistical Learning.* 2nd edition. Springer, 2009.

[HTW15] T. Hastie, R. Tibshirani, and M. Wainwright. *Statistical Learning with Sparsity: The Lasso and Generalizations.* CRC Press, 2015.

[Hua14] G.-B. Huang. "An Insight into Extreme Learning Machines: Random Neurons, Random Features and Kernels". In: *Cognit. Comput.* 6.3 (2014), pp. 376–390.

[Hua+17a] G. Huang, Z. Liu, K. Q. Weinberger, and L. van der Maaten. "Densely Connected Convolutional Networks". In: *CVPR.* 2017.

[Hua+17b] J. Huang et al. "Speed/accuracy trade-offs for modern convolutional object detectors". In: *CVPR.* 2017.

[Hua+18] C.-Z. A. Huang, A. Vaswani, J. Uszkoreit, N. Shazeer, I. Simon, C. Hawthorne, A. M. Dai, M. D. Hoffman, M. Dinculescu, and D. Eck. "Music Transformer". In: (2018). arXiv: 1809.04281 [cs.LG].

[Hub+08] M. F. Huber, T Bailey, H Durrant-Whyte, and U. D. Hanebeck. "On entropy approximation for Gaussian mixture random vectors". In: *2008 IEEE International Conference on Multisensor Fusion and Integration for Intelligent Systems.* 2008, pp. 181–188.

[Hub64] P. Huber. "Robust Estimation of a Location Parameter". In: *Annals of Statistics* 53 (1964), 73–101.

[Hut90] M. F. Hutchinson. "A stochastic estimator of the trace of the influence matrix for laplacian smoothing splines". In: *Communications in Statistics - Simulation and Computation* 19.2 (1990), pp. 433–450.

[HVD14] G. Hinton, O. Vinyals, and J. Dean. "Distilling the Knowledge in a Neural Network". In: *NIPS Deep Learning Workshop*. 2014.

[HW62] D. Hubel and T. Wiesel. "Receptive fields, binocular interaction, and functional architecture in the cat's visual cortex". In: *J. Physiology* 160 (1962), pp. 106–154.

[HY01] M. Hansen and B. Yu. "Model selection and the principle of minimum description length". In: *JASA* (2001).

[HYL17] W. Hamilton, Z. Ying, and J. Leskovec. "Inductive representation learning on large graphs". In: *Advances in Neural Information Processing Systems*. 2017, pp. 1024–1034.

[Idr+17] H. Idrees, A. R. Zamir, Y.-G. Jiang, A. Gorban, I. Laptev, R. Sukthankar, and M. Shah. "The THUMOS challenge on action recognition for videos "in the wild"". In: *Comput. Vis. Image Underst.* 155 (2017), pp. 1–23.

[Ie+19] E. Ie, V. Jain, J. Wang, S. Narvekar, R. Agarwal, R. Wu, H.-T. Cheng, T. Chandra, and C. Boutilier. "SlateQ: A tractable decomposition for reinforcement learning with recommendation sets". In: *IJCAI*. International Joint Conferences on Artificial Intelligence Organization, 2019.

[Iof17] S. Ioffe. "Batch Renormalization: Towards Reducing Minibatch Dependence in Batch-Normalized Models". In: (2017). arXiv: 1702. 03275 [cs.LG].

[Ips09] I. Ipsen. *Numerical matrix analysis: Linear systems and least squares*. SIAM, 2009.

[IR10] A. Ilin and T. Raiko. "Practical Approaches to Principal Component Analysis in the Presence of Missing Values". In: *JMLR* 11 (2010), pp. 1957–2000.

[IS15] S. Ioffe and C. Szegedy. "Batch Normalization: Accelerating Deep Network Training by Reducing Internal Covariate Shift". In: *ICML*. 2015, pp. 448–456.

[Isc+19] A. Iscen, G. Tolias, Y. Avrithis, and O. Chum. "Label Propagation for Deep Semi-supervised Learning". In: *CVPR*. 2019.

[Izm+18] P. Izmailov, D. Podoprikhin, T. Garipov, D. Vetrov, and A. G. Wilson. "Averaging Weights Leads to Wider Optima and Better Generalization". In: *UAI*. 2018.

[Izm+20] P. Izmailov, P. Kirichenko, M. Finzi, and A. G. Wilson. "Semi-supervised learning with normalizing flows". In: *ICML*. 2020, pp. 4615–4630.

[Jac+91] R. Jacobs, M. Jordan, S. Nowlan, and G. Hinton. "Adaptive mixtures of local experts". In: *Neural Computation* (1991).

[JAFF16] J. Johnson, A. Alahi, and L. Fei-Fei. "Perceptual Losses for Real-Time Style Transfer and Super-Resolution". In: *ECCV*. 2016.

[Jan18] E. Jang. *Normalizing Flows Tutorial*. https://blog.evjang.com/2018/01/nf1.html. 2018.

[Jay03] E. T. Jaynes. *Probability theory: the logic of science*. Cambridge university press, 2003.

[Jay76] E. T. Jaynes. "Confidence intervals vs Bayesian intervals". In: *Foundations of Probability Theory, Statistical Inference, and Statistical Theories of Science, vol II*. Ed. by W. L. Harper and C. A. Hooker. Reidel Publishing Co., 1976.

[JD88] A. Jain and R. Dubes. *Algorithms for Clustering Data*. Prentice Hall, 1988.

[JDJ17] J. Johnson, M. Douze, and H. Jégou. "Billion-scale similarity search with GPUs". In: (2017). arXiv: 1702.08734 [cs.CV].

[Jef61] H. Jeffreys. *Theory of Probability*. Oxford, 1961.

[Jef73] H. Jeffreys. *Scientific Inference*. Third edition. Cambridge, 1973.

[JGH18] A. Jacot, F. Gabriel, and C. Hongler. "Neural Tangent Kernel: Convergence and Generalization in Neural Networks". In: *NIPS*. 2018.

[JH04] H. Jaeger and H. Haas. "Harnessing Nonlinearity: Predicting Chaotic Systems and Saving Energy in Wireless Communication". In: *Science* 304.5667 (2004).

[JHG00] N. Japkowicz, S. Hanson, and M. Gluck. "Nonlinear autoassociation is not equivalent to PCA". In: *Neural Computation* 12 (2000), pp. 531–545.

[Jia+20] Y. Jiang, B. Neyshabur, H. Mobahi, D. Krishnan, and S. Bengio. "Fantastic Generalization Measures and Where to Find Them". In: *ICLR*. 2020.

[Jin+17] Y. Jing, Y. Yang, Z. Feng, J. Ye, Y. Yu, and M. Song. "Neural Style Transfer: A Review". In: *arXiv [cs.CV]* (2017).

[JJ94] M. I. Jordan and R. A. Jacobs. "Hierarchical mixtures of experts and the EM algorithm". In: *Neural Computation* 6 (1994), pp. 181–214.

[JK13] A. Jern and C. Kemp. "A probabilistic account of exemplar and category generation". en. In: *Cogn. Psychol.* 66.1 (2013), pp. 85–125.

[JM08] D. Jurafsky and J. H. Martin. *Speech and language processing: An Introduction to Natural Language Processing, Computational Linguistics, and Speech Recognition*. 2nd edition. Prentice-Hall, 2008.

[JM20] D. Jurafsky and J. H. Martin. *Speech and language processing: An Introduction to Natural Language Processing, Computational Linguistics, and Speech Recognition (Third Edition)*. Draft of 3rd edition. 2020.

[Jor19] M. Jordan. "Artificial Intelligence — The Revolution Hasn't Happened Yet". In: *Harvard Data Science Review* 1.1 (2019).

[JT19]   L. Jing and Y. Tian. "Self-supervised Visual Feature Learning with Deep Neural Networks: A Survey". In: (2019). arXiv: 1902 . 06162 [cs.CV].

[Jun+19]   W. Jung, D. Jung, B. Kim, S. Lee, W. Rhee, and J. Anh. "Restructuring Batch Normalization to Accelerate CNN Training". In: *SysML*. 2019.

[JW19]   S. Jain and B. C. Wallace. "Attention is not Explanation". In: *NAACL*. 2019.

[JZ13]   R. Johnson and T. Zhang. "Accelerating Stochastic Gradient Descent using Predictive Variance Reduction". In: *NIPS*. Curran Associates, Inc., 2013, pp. 315–323.

[JZS15]   R. Jozefowicz, W. Zaremba, and I. Sutskever. "An Empirical Exploration of Recurrent Network Architectures". In: *ICML*. 2015, pp. 2342–2350.

[KAG19]   A. Kirsch, J. van Amersfoort, and Y. Gal. "BatchBALD: Efficient and Diverse Batch Acquisition for Deep Bayesian Active Learning". In: *NIPS*. 2019.

[Kai58]   H. Kaiser. "The varimax criterion for analytic rotation in factor analysis". In: *Psychometrika* 23.3 (1958).

[Kan+12]   E. Kandel, J. Schwartz, T. Jessell, S. Siegelbaum, and A. Hudspeth, eds. *Principles of Neural Science*. Fifth Edition. 2012.

[Kan+20]   B. Kang, S. Xie, M. Rohrbach, Z. Yan, A. Gordo, J. Feng, and Y. Kalantidis. "Decoupling Representation and Classifier for Long-Tailed Recognition". In: *ICLR*. 2020.

[Kap16]   J. Kaplan. *Artificial Intelligence: What Everyone Needs to Know*. en. 1st ed. Oxford University Press, 2016.

[Kat+20]   A. Katharopoulos, A. Vyas, N. Pappas, and F. Fleuret. "Transformers are RNNs: Fast Autoregressive Transformers with Linear Attention". In: *ICML*. 2020.

[KB15]   D. Kingma and J. Ba. "Adam: A Method for Stochastic Optimization". In: *ICLR*. 2015.

[KB19]   M. Kaya and H. S. Bilge. "Deep Metric Learning: A Survey". en. In: *Symmetry* 11.9 (2019), p. 1066.

[KBV09]   Y. Koren, R. Bell, and C. Volinsky. "Matrix factorization techniques for recommender systems". In: *IEEE Computer* 42.8 (2009), pp. 30–37.

[KD09]   A. D. Kiureghian and O. Ditlevsen. "Aleatory or epistemic? Does it matter?" In: *Structural Safety* 31.2 (2009), pp. 105–112.

[Kem+06]   C. Kemp, J. Tenenbaum, T. Y. T. Griffiths and, and N. Ueda. "Learning systems of concepts with an infinite relational model". In: *AAAI*. 2006.

[KF05]   H. Kuck and N. de Freitas. "Learning about individuals from group statistics". In: *UAI*. 2005.

[KG05]   A. Krause and C. Guestrin. "Near-optimal value of information in graphical models". In: *UAI*. 2005.

[KG17]   A. Kendall and Y. Gal. "What Uncertainties Do We Need in Bayesian Deep Learning for Computer Vision?" In: *NIPS*. Curran Associates, Inc., 2017, pp. 5574–5584.

[KGS20]   J. von Kügelgen, L. Gresele, and B. Schölkopf. "Simpson's paradox in Covid-19 case fatality rates: a mediation analysis of age-related causal effects". In: (2020). arXiv: 2005.07180 [stat.AP].

[KH09]   A Krizhevsky and G Hinton. *Learning multiple layers of features from tiny images*. Tech. rep. U. Toronto, 2009.

[KH19]   D. Krotov and J. J. Hopfield. "Unsupervised learning by competing hidden units". en. In: *PNAS* 116.16 (2019), pp. 7723–7731.

[Kha+10]   M. E. Khan, B. Marlin, G. Bouchard, and K. P. Murphy. "Variational bounds for mixed-data factor analysis". In: *NIPS*. 2010.

[Kha+20]   A. Khan, A. Sohail, U. Zahoora, and A. S. Qureshi. "A Survey of the Recent Architectures of Deep Convolutional Neural Networks". In: *AI Review* (2020).

[KHB07]   A. Kapoor, E. Horvitz, and S. Basu. "Selective Supervision: Guiding Supervised Learning with Decision-Theoretic Active Learning". In: *IJCAI*. 2007.

[KHW19]   W. Kool, H. van Hoof, and M. Welling. "Stochastic Beams and Where to Find Them: The Gumbel-Top-k Trick for Sampling Sequences Without Replacement". In: *ICML*. 2019.

[Kim14]   Y. Kim. "Convolutional Neural Networks for Sentence Classification". In: *EMNLP*. 2014.

[Kim19]   D. H. Kim. *Survey of Deep Metric Learning*. 2019.

[Kin+14]   D. P. Kingma, D. J. Rezende, S. Mohamed, and M. Welling. "Semi-Supervised Learning with Deep Generative Models". In: *NIPS*. 2014.

[Kir+19]   A. Kirillov, K. He, R. Girshick, C. Rother, and P. Dollár. "Panoptic Segmentation". In: *CVPR*. 2019.

[KJ16]   L Kang and V Joseph. "Kernel Approximation: From Regression to Interpolation". In: *SIAM/ASA J. Uncertainty Quantification* 4.1 (2016), pp. 112–129.

[KJ95]   J. Karhunen and J. Joutsensalo. "Generalizations of principal component analysis, optimization problems, and neural networks". In: *Neural Networks* 8.4 (1995), pp. 549–562.

[KJM19]   N. M. Kriege, F. D. Johansson, and C. Morris. "A Survey on Graph Kernels". In: (2019). arXiv: 1903.11835 [cs.LG].

[KK06]   S. Kotsiantis and D. Kanellopoulos. "Discretization Techniques: A recent survey". In: *GESTS Intl. Trans. on Computer Science and Engineering* 31.1 (2006), pp. 47–58.

[KKH20]   I. Khemakhem, D. P. Kingma, and A. Hyvärinen. "Variational Autoencoders and Nonlinear ICA: A Unifying Framework". In: *AISTATS*. 2020.

[KKL20]   N. Kitaev, L. Kaiser, and A. Levskaya. "Reformer: The Efficient Transformer". In: *8th International Conference on Learning Representations, ICLR 2020, Addis*

Ababa, Ethiopia, April 26-30, 2020. Open-Review.net, 2020.

[KKS20] F. Kunstner, R. Kumar, and M. Schmidt. "Homeomorphic-Invariance of EM: Non-Asymptotic Convergence in KL Divergence for Exponential Families via Mirror Descent". In: (2020). arXiv: 2011.01170 [cs.LG].

[KL17] J. K. Kruschke and T. M. Liddell. "The Bayesian New Statistics: Hypothesis testing, estimation, meta-analysis, and power analysis from a Bayesian perspective". In: *Psychon. Bull. Rev.* (2017).

[KL21] W. M. Kouw and M. Loog. "A review of domain adaptation without target labels". en. In: *IEEE PAMI* (2021).

[Kla+17] G. Klambauer, T. Unterthiner, A. Mayr, and S. Hochreiter. "Self-Normalizing Neural Networks". In: *NIPS*. 2017.

[Kle02] J. Kleinberg. "An Impossibility Theorem for Clustering". In: *NIPS*. 2002.

[Kle+11] A. Kleiner, A. Talwalkar, P. Sarkar, and M. I. Jordan. *A scalable bootstrap for massive data*. Tech. rep. UC Berkeley, 2011.

[Kle13] P. N. Klein. *Coding the Matrix: Linear Algebra through Applications to Computer Science*. en. 1 edition. Newtonian Press, 2013.

[KLQ95] C. Ko, J. Lee, and M. Queyranne. "An exact algorithm for maximum entropy sampling". In: *Operations Research* 43 (1995), 684–691.

[Kok17] I. Kokkinos. "UberNet: Training a Universal Convolutional Neural Network for Low-, Mid-, and High-Level Vision Using Diverse Datasets and Limited Memory". In: *CVPR*. Vol. 2. 2017, p. 8.

[Kol+19] A. Kolesnikov, L. Beyer, X. Zhai, J. Puigcerver, J. Yung, S. Gelly, and N. Houlsby. "Large Scale Learning of General Visual Representations for Transfer". In: (2019). arXiv: 1912.11370 [cs.CV].

[Kol+20] A. Kolesnikov, L. Beyer, X. Zhai, J. Puigcerver, J. Yung, S. Gelly, and N. Houlsby. "Large Scale Learning of General Visual Representations for Transfer". In: *ECCV*. 2020.

[Kon20] M. Konnikova. *The Biggest Bluff: How I Learned to Pay Attention, Master Myself, and Win*. en. Penguin Press, 2020.

[Kor09] Y. Koren. *The BellKor Solution to the Netflix Grand Prize*. Tech. rep. Yahoo! Research, 2009.

[KR19] M. Kearns and A. Roth. *The Ethical Algorithm: The Science of Socially Aware Algorithm Design*. en. Oxford University Press, 2019.

[KR87] L. Kaufman and P. Rousseeuw. "Clustering by means of Medoids". In: *Statistical Data Analysis Based on the L1-norm and Related Methods*. Ed. by Y. Dodge. North-Holland, 1987, 405–416.

[KR90] L. Kaufman and P. Rousseeuw. *Finding Groups in Data: An Introduction to Cluster Analysis*. Wiley, 1990.

[Kri+05] B. Krishnapuram, L. Carin, M. Figueiredo, and A. Hartemink. "Learning sparse Bayesian

classifiers: multi-class formulation, fast algorithms, and generalization bounds". In: *IEEE Transaction on Pattern Analysis and Machine Intelligence* (2005).

[Kru13] J. K. Kruschke. "Bayesian estimation supersedes the t test". In: *J. Experimental Psychology: General* 142.2 (2013), pp. 573–603.

[Kru15] J. Kruschke. *Doing Bayesian Data Analysis: A Tutorial with R, JAGS and STAN*. Second edition. Academic Press, 2015.

[KS15] H. Kaya and A. A. Salah. "Adaptive Mixtures of Factor Analyzers". In: (2015). arXiv: 1507.02801 [stat.ML].

[KSG04] A. Kraskov, H. Stögbauer, and P. Grassberger. "Estimating mutual information". en. In: *Phys. Rev. E Stat. Nonlin. Soft Matter Phys.* 69.6 Pt 2 (2004), p. 066138.

[KSH12] A. Krizhevsky, I. Sutskever, and G. Hinton. "Imagenet classification with deep convolutional neural networks". In: *NIPS*. 2012.

[KSJ09] I. Konstas, V. Stathopoulos, and J. M. Jose. "On social networks and collaborative recommendation". In: *Proceedings of the 32nd international ACM SIGIR conference on Research and development in information retrieval*. 2009, pp. 195–202.

[KST82] D. Kahneman, P. Slovic, and A. Tversky, eds. *Judgment under uncertainty: Heuristics and biases*. Cambridge, 1982.

[KTB11] D. P. Kroese, T. Taimre, and Z. I. Botev. *Handbook of Monte Carlo Methods*. en. 1 edition. Wiley, 2011.

[Kua+09] P. Kuan, G. Pan, J. A. Thomson, R. Stewart, and S. Keles. *A hierarchical semi-Markov model for detecting enrichment with application to ChIP-Seq experiments*. Tech. rep. U. Wisconsin, 2009.

[Kul13] B. Kulis. "Metric Learning: A Survey". In: *Foundations and Trends in Machine Learning* 5.4 (2013), pp. 287–364.

[KV94] M. J. Kearns and U. V. Vazirani. *An Introduction to Computational Learning Theory*. MIT Press, 1994.

[KVK10] A. Klami, S. Virtanen, and S. Kaski. "Bayesian exponential family projections for coupled data sources". In: *UAI*. 2010.

[KW14] D. P. Kingma and M. Welling. "Auto-encoding variational Bayes". In: *ICLR*. 2014.

[KW16a] T. N. Kipf and M. Welling. "Semi-supervised classification with graph convolutional networks". In: *arXiv preprint arXiv:1609.02907* (2016).

[KW16b] T. N. Kipf and M. Welling. "Variational graph auto-encoders". In: *arXiv preprint arXiv:1611.07308* (2016).

[KW19a] D. P. Kingma and M. Welling. "An Introduction to Variational Autoencoders". In: *Foundations and Trends in Machine Learning* 12.4 (2019), pp. 307–392.

[KW19b] M. J. Kochenderfer and T. A. Wheeler. *Algorithms for Optimization*. en. The MIT Press, 2019.

[KWW22]   M. J. Kochenderfer, T. A. Wheeler, and K. Wray. *Algorithms for Decision Making*. The MIT Press, 2022.

[Kyu+10]   M. Kyung, J. Gill, M. Ghosh, and G. Casella. "Penalized Regression, Standard Errors and Bayesian Lassos". In: *Bayesian Analysis* 5.2 (2010), pp. 369–412.

[LA16]   S. Laine and T. Aila. "Temporal ensembling for semi-supervised learning". In: *arXiv preprint arXiv:1610.02242* (2016).

[Lak+17]   B. M. Lake, T. D. Ullman, J. B. Tenenbaum, and S. J. Gershman. "Building Machines That Learn and Think Like People". en. In: *Behav. Brain Sci.* (2017), pp. 1–101.

[Lam18]   B. Lambert. *A Student's Guide to Bayesian Statistics*. en. 1st ed. SAGE Publications Ltd, 2018.

[Law12]   N. D. Lawrence. "A Unifying Probabilistic Perspective for Spectral Dimensionality Reduction: Insights and New Models". In: *JMLR* 13.May (2012), pp. 1609–1638.

[LBM06]   J. A. Lasserre, C. M. Bishop, and T. P. Minka. "Principled Hybrids of Generative and Discriminative Models". In: *CVPR*. Vol. 1. June 2006, pp. 87–94.

[LBS19]   Y. Li, J. Bradshaw, and Y. Sharma. "Are Generative Classifiers More Robust to Adversarial Attacks?" In: *ICML*. Ed. by K. Chaudhuri and R. Salakhutdinov. Vol. 97. Proceedings of Machine Learning Research. PMLR, 2019, pp. 3804–3814.

[LeC18]   Y. LeCun. *Self-supervised learning: could machines learn like humans?* 2018.

[LeC+98]   Y. LeCun, L. Bottou, Y. Bengio, and P. Haffner. "Gradient-Based Learning Applied to Document Recognition". In: *Proceedings of the IEEE* 86.11 (1998), pp. 2278–2324.

[Lee13]   D.-H. Lee. "Pseudo-label: The simple and efficient semi-supervised learning method for deep neural networks". In: *ICML Workshop on Challenges in Representation Learning*. 2013.

[Lee+13]   J. Lee, S. Kim, G. Lebanon, and Y. Singer. "Local Low-Rank Matrix Approximation". In: *ICML*. Vol. 28. Proceedings of Machine Learning Research. PMLR, 2013, pp. 82–90.

[Lee+19]   J. Lee, Y. Lee, J. Kim, A. R. Kosiorek, S. Choi, and Y. W. Teh. "Set Transformer: A Framework for Attention-based Permutation-Invariant Neural Networks". In: *ICML*. 2019.

[Lee77]   J. de Leeuw. "Applications of Convex Analysis to Multidimensional Scaling". In: *Recent Developments in Statistics*. Ed. by J. R. Barra, F Brodeau, G Romier, and B Van Cutsem. 1977.

[Lep+21]   D. Lepikhin, H. Lee, Y. Xu, D. Chen, O. Firat, Y. Huang, M. Krikun, N. Shazeer, and Z. Chen. "GShard: Scaling Giant Models with Conditional Computation and Automatic Sharding". In: *ICLR*. 2021.

[LG14]   O. Levy and Y. Goldberg. "Neural Word Embedding as Implicit Matrix Factorization". In: *NIPS*. 2014.

[LH17]   I. Loshchilov and F. Hutter. "SGDR: Stochastic Gradient Descent with Warm Restarts". In: *ICLR*. 2017.

[Li+15]   Y. Li, D. Tarlow, M. Brockschmidt, and R. Zemel. "Gated graph sequence neural networks". In: *arXiv preprint arXiv:1511.05493* (2015).

[Li+17]   A. Li, A. Jabri, A. Joulin, and L. van der Maaten. "Learning Visual N-Grams from Web Data". In: *ICCV*. 2017.

[Lia20]   S. M. Liao, ed. *Ethics of Artificial Intelligence*. en. 1st ed. Oxford University Press, 2020.

[Lim+19]   S. Lim, I. Kim, T. Kim, C. Kim, and S. Kim. "Fast AutoAugment". In: (2019). arXiv: 1905.00397 [cs.LG].

[Lin06]   D. Lindley. *Understanding Uncertainty*. Wiley, 2006.

[Lin+21]   T. Lin, Y. Wang, X. Liu, and X. Qiu. "A Survey of Transformers". In: (2021). arXiv: 2106.04554 [cs.LG].

[Lin56]   D. Lindley. "On a measure of the information provided by an experiment". In: *The Annals of Math. Stat.* (1956), 986–1005.

[Liu01]   J. Liu. *Monte Carlo Strategies in Scientific Computation*. Springer, 2001.

[Liu+16]   W. Liu, D. Anguelov, D. Erhan, C. Szegedy, and S. Reed. "SSD: Single Shot MultiBox Detector". In: *ECCV*. 2016.

[Liu+18a]   H. Liu, Y.-S. Ong, X. Shen, and J. Cai. "When Gaussian Process Meets Big Data: A Review of Scalable GPs". In: (2018). arXiv: 1807.01065 [stat.ML].

[Liu+18b]   L. Liu, X. Liu, C.-J. Hsieh, and D. Tao. "Stochastic Second-order Methods for Nonconvex Optimization with Inexact Hessian and Gradient". In: (2018). arXiv: 1809.09853 [math.OC].

[Liu+20]   F. Liu, X. Huang, Y. Chen, and J. A. K. Suykens. "Random Features for Kernel Approximation: A Survey on Algorithms, Theory, and Beyond". In: (2020). arXiv: 2004.11154 [stat.ML].

[Liu+22]   Z. Liu, H. Mao, C.-Y. Wu, C. Feichtenhofer, T. Darrell, and S. Xie. "A ConvNet for the 2020s". In: (2022). arXiv: 2201.03545 [cs.CV].

[LJ09]   H. Lukosevicius and H. Jaeger. "Reservoir computing approaches to recurrent neural network training". In: *Computer Science Review* 3.3 (2009), 127–149.

[LKB20]   Q. Liu, M. J. Kusner, and P. Blunsom. "A Survey on Contextual Embeddings". In: (2020). arXiv: 2003.07278 [cs.CL].

[Llo82]   S Lloyd. "Least squares quantization in PCM". In: *IEEE Trans. Inf. Theory* 28.2 (1982), pp. 129–137.

[LLT89]   K. Lange, R. Little, and J. Taylor. "Robust Statistical Modeling Using the T Disribution". In: *JASA* 84.408 (1989), pp. 881–896.

[LM04]   E. Learned-Miller. *Hyperspacings and the estimation of information theoretic quantities.*

Tech. rep. 04-104. U. Mass. Amherst Comp. Sci. Dept, 2004.

[LM86]   R. Larsen and M. Marx. *An introduction to mathematical statistics and its applications*. Prentice Hall, 1986.

[LN81]   D. V. Lindley and M. R. Novick. "The Role of Exchangeability in Inference". cn. In: *Annals of Statistics* 9.1 (1981), pp. 45–58.

[LNK19]   Q. Liu, M. Nickel, and D. Kiela. "Hyperbolic graph neural networks". In: *Advances in Neural Information Processing Systems*. 2019, pp. 8228–8239.

[Loa00]   C. F. V. Loan. "The ubiquitous Kronecker product". In: *J. Comput. Appl. Math.* 123.1 (2000), pp. 85–100.

[Lod+02]   H. Lodhi, C. Saunders, J. Shawe-Taylor, N. Cristianini, and C. Watkins. "Text classification using string kernels". en. In: *J. Mach. Learn. Res.* (2002).

[LPM15]   M.-T. Luong, H. Pham, and C. D. Manning. "Effective Approaches to Attention-based Neural Machine Translation". In: *EMNLP*. 2015.

[LR87]   R. J. Little and D. B. Rubin. *Statistical Analysis with Missing Data*. Wiley and Son, 1987.

[LRU14]   J. Leskovec, A. Rajaraman, and J. Ullman. *Mining of massive datasets*. Cambridge, 2014.

[LS10]   P. Long and R. Servedio. "Random classification noise beats all convex potential boosters". In: *JMLR* 78.3 (2010), pp. 287–304.

[LS19a]   S. Lattanzi and C. Sohler. "A Better k-means++ Algorithm via Local Search". In: *ICML*. Vol. 97. Proceedings of Machine Learning Research. PMLR, 2019, pp. 3662–3671.

[LS19b]   Z. C. Lipton and J. Steinhardt. "Troubling Trends in Machine Learning Scholarship: Some ML papers suffer from flaws that could mislead the public and stymie future research". In: *The Queue* 17.1 (2019), pp. 45–77.

[LSS13]   Q. Le, T. Sarlos, and A. Smola. "Fastfood - Computing Hilbert Space Expansions in loglinear time". In: *ICML*. Vol. 28. Proceedings of Machine Learning Research. PMLR, 2013, pp. 244–252.

[LSY19]   H. Liu, K. Simonyan, and Y. Yang. "DARTS: Differentiable Architecture Search". In: *ICLR*. 2019.

[Lu+19]   L. Lu, Y. Shin, Y. Su, and G. E. Karniadakis. "Dying ReLU and Initialization: Theory and Numerical Examples". In: (2019). arXiv: 1903.06733 [stat.ML].

[Luo16]   M.-T. Luong. "Neural machine translation". PhD thesis. Stanford Dept. Comp. Sci., 2016.

[Luo+19]   P. Luo, X. Wang, W. Shao, and Z. Peng. "Towards Understanding Regularization in Batch Normalization". In: *ICLR*. 2019.

[LUW17]   C. Louizos, K. Ullrich, and M. Welling. "Bayesian Compression for Deep Learning". In: *NIPS*. 2017.

[Lux07]   U. von Luxburg. "A tutorial on spectral clustering". In: *Statistics and Computing* 17.4 (2007), pp. 395–416.

[LW04a]   O. Ledoit and M. Wolf. "A Well-Conditioned Estimator for Large-Dimensional Covariance Matrices". In: *J. of Multivariate Analysis* 88.2 (2004), pp. 365–411.

[LW04b]   O. Ledoit and M. Wolf. "Honey, I Shrunk the Sample Covariance Matrix". In: *J. of Portfolio Management* 31.1 (2004).

[LW04c]   H. Lopes and M. West. "Bayesian model assessment in factor analysis". In: *Statisica Sinica* 14 (2004), pp. 41–67.

[LW16]   C. Li and M. Wand. "Precomputed Real-Time Texture Synthesis with Markovian Generative Adversarial Networks". In: *ECCV*. 2016.

[LWG12]   U. von Luxburg, R. Williamson, and I. Guyon. "Clustering: science or art?" In: *Workshop on Unsupervised and Transfer Learning*. 2012.

[LXW19]   X. Liu, Q. Xu, and N. Wang. "A survey on deep neural network-based image captioning". In: *The Visual Computer* 35.3 (2019), pp. 445–470.

[Lyu+20]   X.-K. Lyu, Y. Xu, X.-F. Zhao, X.-N. Zuo, and C.-P. Hu. "Beyond psychology: prevalence of p value and confidence interval misinterpretation across different fields". In: *Journal of Pacific Rim Psychology* 14 (2020).

[MA10]   I. Murray and R. P. Adams. "Slice sampling covariance hyperparameters of latent Gaussian models". In: *NIPS*. 2010, pp. 1732–1740.

[MA+17]   Y. Movshovitz-Attias, A. Toshev, T. K. Leung, S. Ioffe, and S. Singh. "No Fuss Distance Metric Learning using Proxies". In: *ICCV*. 2017.

[Maa+11]   A. L. Maas, R. E. Daly, P. T. Pham, D. Huang, A. Y. Ng, and C. Potts. "Learning Word Vectors for Sentiment Analysis". In: *Proc. ACL*. 2011, pp. 142–150.

[Maa14]   L. van der Maaten. "Accelerating t-SNE using Tree-Based Algorithms". In: *JMLR* (2014).

[Mac03]   D. MacKay. *Information Theory, Inference, and Learning Algorithms*. Cambridge University Press, 2003.

[Mac09]   L. W. Mackey. "Deflation Methods for Sparse PCA". In: *NIPS*. 2009.

[Mac67]   J MacQueen. "Some methods for classification and analysis of multivariate observations". en. In: *Proceedings of the Fifth Berkeley Symposium on Mathematical Statistics and Probability, Volume 1: Statistics*. The Regents of the University of California, 1967.

[Mac95]   D. MacKay. "Probable networks and plausible predictions — a review of practical Bayesian methods for supervised neural networks". In: *Network: Computation in Neural Systems* 6.3 (1995), pp. 469–505.

[Mad+20]   A. Madani, B. McCann, N. Naik, N. S. Keskar, N. Anand, R. R. Eguchi, P.-S. Huang, and R. Socher. "ProGen: Language Modeling for Protein Generation". en. 2020.

[Mah07] R. P. S. Mahler. *Statistical Multisource-Multitarget Information Fusion*. Artech House, Inc., 2007.

[Mah13] R Mahler. "Statistics 102 for Multisource-Multitarget Detection and Tracking". In: *IEEE J. Sel. Top. Signal Process.* 7.3 (2013), pp. 376–389.

[Mah+18] D. Mahajan, R. Girshick, V. Ramanathan, K. He, M. Paluri, Y. Li, A. Bharambe, and L. van der Maaten. "Exploring the Limits of Weakly Supervised Pretraining". In: (2018). arXiv: 1805.00932 [cs.CV].

[Mai15] J Mairal. "Incremental Majorization-Minimization Optimization with Application to Large-Scale Machine Learning". In: *SIAM J. Optim.* 25.2 (2015), pp. 829–855.

[Mak+19] D. Makowski, M. S. Ben-Shachar, S. H. A. Chen, and D. Lüdecke. "Indices of Effect Existence and Significance in the Bayesian Framework". en. In: *Front. Psychol.* 10 (2019), p. 2767.

[Mal99] S. Mallat. *A Wavelet Tour of Signal Processing*. Academic Press, 1999.

[Man+16] V. Mansinghka, P. Shafto, E. Jonas, C. Petschulat, M. Gasner, and J. Tenenbaum. "Crosscat: A Fully Bayesian, Nonparametric Method For Analyzing Heterogeneous, High-dimensional Data." In: *JMLR* 17 (2016).

[Mar06] H. Markram. "The blue brain project". en. In: *Nat. Rev. Neurosci.* 7.2 (2006), pp. 153–160.

[Mar08] B. Marlin. "Missing Data Problems in Machine Learning". PhD thesis. U. Toronto, 2008.

[Mar+11] B. M. Marlin, R. S. Zemel, S. T. Roweis, and M. Slaney. "Recommender Systems, Missing Data and Statistical Model Estimation". In: *IJCAI*. 2011.

[Mar18] O. Martin. *Bayesian analysis with Python*. Packt, 2018.

[Mar20] G. Marcus. "The Next Decade in AI: Four Steps Towards Robust Artificial Intelligence". In: (2020). arXiv: 2002.06177 [cs.AI].

[Mar72] G. Marsaglia. "Choosing a Point from the Surface of a Sphere". en. In: *Ann. Math. Stat.* 43.2 (1972), pp. 645–646.

[Mas+00] L. Mason, J. Baxter, P. L. Bartlett, and M. R. Frean. "Boosting Algorithms as Gradient Descent". In: *NIPS*. 2000, pp. 512–518.

[Mas+15] J. Masci, D. Boscaini, M. Bronstein, and P. Vandergheynst. "Geodesic convolutional neural networks on riemannian manifolds". In: *Proceedings of the IEEE international conference on computer vision workshops*. 2015, pp. 37–45.

[Mat00] R. Matthews. "Storks Deliver Babies (p = 0.008)". In: *Teach. Stat.* 22.2 (2000), pp. 36–38.

[Mat98] R. Matthews. *Bayesian Critique of Statistics in Health: The Great Health Hoax*. 1998.

[MAV17] D. Molchanov, A. Ashukha, and D. Vetrov. "Variational Dropout Sparsifies Deep Neural Networks". In: *ICML*. 2017.

[MB05] F. Morin and Y. Bengio. "Hierarchical Probabilistic Neural Network Language Model". In: *AISTATS*. 2005.

[MB06] N. Meinshausen and P. Buhlmann. "High dimensional graphs and variable selection with the lasso". In: *The Annals of Statistics* 34 (2006), pp. 1436–1462.

[MBL20] K. Musgrave, S. Belongie, and S.-N. Lim. "A Metric Learning Reality Check". In: *ECCV*. 2020.

[McE20] R. McElreath. *Statistical Rethinking: A Bayesian Course with Examples in R and Stan (2nd edition)*. en. Chapman and Hall/CRC, 2020.

[McL75] G. J. McLachlan. "Iterative reclassification procedure for constructing an asymptotically optimal rule of allocation in discriminant analysis". In: *Journal of the American Statistical Association* 70.350 (1975), pp. 365–369.

[MD97] X. L. Meng and D. van Dyk. "The EM algorithm — an old folk song sung to a fast new tune (with Discussion)". In: *J. Royal Stat. Soc. B* 59 (1997), pp. 511–567.

[ME14] S. Masoudnia and R. Ebrahimpour. "Mixture of experts: a literature survey". In: *Artificial Intelligence Review* 42.2 (2014), pp. 275–293.

[Mei01] M. Meila. "A random walks view of spectral segmentation". In: *AISTATS*. 2001.

[Mci05] M. Meila. "Comparing clusterings: an axiomatic view". In: *ICML*. 2005.

[Men+12] T. Mensink, J. Verbeek, F. Perronnin, and G. Csurka. "Metric Learning for Large Scale Image Classification: Generalizing to New Classes at Near-Zero Cost". In: *ECCV*. Springer Berlin Heidelberg, 2012, pp. 488–501.

[Men+21] A. K. Menon, S. Jayasumana, A. S. Rawat, H. Jain, A. Veit, and S. Kumar. "Long-tail learning via logit adjustment". In: *ICLR*. 2021.

[Men+22] K. Meng, D. Bau, A. Andonian, and Y. Belinkov. "Locating and Editing Factual Associations in GPT". In: (Feb. 2022). arXiv: 2202.05262 [cs.CL].

[Met21] C. Metz. *Genius Mukers: The Mavericks Who Brought AI to Google, Facebook, and the World*. en. Dutton, 2021.

[MF17] J. Matejka and G. Fitzmaurice. "Same Stats, Different Graphs: Generating Datasets with Varied Appearance and Identical Statistics through Simulated Annealing". In: *Proceedings of the 2017 CHI Conference on Human Factors in Computing Systems*. Association for Computing Machinery, 2017, pp. 1290–1294.

[MFR20] G. M. Martin, D. T. Frazier, and C. P. Robert. "Computing Bayes: Bayesian Computation from 1763 to the 21st Century". In: (2020). arXiv: 2004.06425 [stat.CO].

[MG05] I. Murray and Z. Ghahramani. *A note on the evidence and Bayesian Occam's razor*. Tech. rep. Gatsby, 2005.

[MH07]   A. Mnih and G. Hinton. "Three new graphical models for statistical language modelling".
en. In: *ICML*. 2007.

[MH08]   L. v. d. Maaten and G. Hinton. "Visualizing
Data using t-SNE". In: *JMLR* 9.Nov (2008),
pp. 2579–2605.

[MHM18]   L. McInnes, J. Healy, and J. Melville.
"UMAP: Uniform Manifold Approximation
and Projection for Dimension Reduction". In:
(2018). arXiv: 1802.03426 [stat.ML].

[MHN13]   A. L. Maas, A. Y. Hannun, and A. Y. Ng.
"Rectifier Nonlinearities Improve Neural Network Acoustic Models". In: *ICML*. Vol. 28.
2013.

[Mik+13a] T. Mikolov, K. Chen, G. Corrado, and J.
Dean. "Efficient Estimation of Word Representations in Vector Space". In: *ICLR*. 2013.

[Mik+13b] T. Mikolov, I. Sutskever, K. Chen, G. Corrado, and J. Dean. "Distributed Representations of Words and Phrases and their Compo-
sitionality". In: *NIPS*. 2013.

[Mik+13c] T. Mikolov, I. Sutskever, K. Chen, G. S.
Corrado, and J. Dean. "Distributed representations of words and phrases and their compo-
sitionality". In: *NIPS*. 2013, pp. 3111–3119.

[Min00]   T. Minka. *Bayesian model averaging is not
model combination*. Tech. rep. MIT Media
Lab, 2000.

[Min+09]   M. Mintz, S. Bills, R. Snow, and D. Jurafksy.
"Distant supervision for relation extraction
without labeled data". In: *Prof. Conf. Recent
Advances in NLP*. 2009.

[Mit97]   T. Mitchell. *Machine Learning*. McGraw Hill,
1997.

[Miy+18]   T. Miyato, S.-I. Maeda, M. Koyama, and
S. Ishii. "Virtual Adversarial Training: A
Regularization Method for Supervised and
Semi-Supervised Learning". In: *IEEE PAMI*
(2018).

[MK97]   G. J. McLachlan and T. Krishnan. *The EM
Algorithm and Extensions*. Wiley, 1997.

[MKH19]   R. Müller, S. Kornblith, and G. E. Hinton.
"When does label smoothing help?" In: *NIPS*.
2019, pp. 4694–4703.

[MKL11]   O. Martin, R. Kumar, and J. Lao. *Bayesian
Modeling and Computation in Python*. CRC
Press, 2011.

[MKL21]   O. A. Martin, R. Kumar, and J. Lao.
*Bayesian Modeling and Computation in
Python*. CRC Press, 2021.

[MKS21]   K. Murphy, A. Kumar, and S. Serghiou. "Risk
score learning for COVID-19 contact tracing
apps". In: *Machine Learning for Healthcare*.
2021.

[MM16]   D. Mishkin and J. Matas. "All you need is a
good init". In: *ICLR*. 2016.

[MN89]   P. McCullagh and J. Nelder. *Generalized linear models*. 2nd edition. Chapman and Hall,
1989.

[MNM02]   W. Maass, T. Natschlaeger, and H. Markram.
"Real-time computing without stable states:
A new framework for neural computation

based on perturbations". In: *Neural Computation* 14.11 (2002), 2531—2560.

[MO04]   S. C. Madeira and A. L. Oliveira. "Biclustering Algorithms for Biological Data Analysis:
A Survey". In: *IEEE/ACM Transactions on
Computational Biology and Bioinformatics*
1.1 (2004), pp. 24–45.

[Mol04]   C. Moler. *Numerical Computing with MAT-
LAB*. SIAM, 2004.

[Mon+14]   G. F. Montufar, R. Pascanu, K. Cho, and Y.
Bengio. "On the Number of Linear Regions of
Deep Neural Networks". In: *NIPS*. 2014.

[Mon+17]   F. Monti, D. Boscaini, J. Masci, E. Rodola,
J. Svoboda, and M. M. Bronstein. "Geometric
deep learning on graphs and manifolds using
mixture model cnns". In: *Proceedings of the
IEEE Conference on Computer Vision and
Pattern Recognition*. 2017, pp. 5115–5124.

[Mon+19]   N. Monath, A. Kobren, A. Krishnamurthy,
M. R. Glass, and A. McCallum. "Scalable Hi-
erarchical Clustering with Tree Grafting". In:
KDD. KDD '19. Association for Computing
Machinery, 2019, pp. 1438–1448.

[Mon+21]   N. Monath et al. "Scalable Bottom-Up Hierarchical Clustering". In: *KDD*. 2021.

[Mor+16]   R. D. Morey, R. Hoekstra, J. N. Rouder,
M. D. Lee, and E.-J. Wagenmakers. "The fallacy of placing confidence in confidence intervals". en. In: *Psychon. Bull. Rev.* 23.1 (2016),
pp. 103–123.

[MOT15]   A. Mordvintsev, C. Olah, and M. Tyka. *Inceptionism: Going Deeper into Neural Networks*. https://ai.googleblog.com/2015/
06/inceptionism-going-deeper-into-neural.
html. Accessed: NA-NA-NA. 2015.

[MP43]   W. McCulloch and W. Pitts. "A logical calculus of the ideas immanent in nervous activity". In: *Bulletin of Mathematical Biophysics*
5 (1943), pp. 115–137.

[MP69]   M. Minsky and S. Papert. *Perceptrons*. MIT
Press, 1969.

[MRS08]   C. Manning, P. Raghavan, and H. Schuetze.
Introduction to Information Retrieval. Cambridge University Press, 2008.

[MS11]   D. Mayo and A. Spanos. "Error Statistics".
In: *Handbook of Philosophy of Science*. Ed.
by P. S. Bandyopadhyay and M. R. Forster.
2011.

[Muk+19]   B. Mukhoty, G. Gopakumar, P. Jain,
and P. Kar. "Globally-convergent Iteratively
Reweighted Least Squares for Robust Regression Problems". In: *AISTATS*. 2019, pp. 313–
322.

[Mur23]   K. P. Murphy. *Probabilistic Machine Learning: Advanced Topics*. MIT Press, 2023.

[MV15]   A Mahendran and A Vedaldi. "Understanding deep image representations by inverting
them". In: *CVPR*. 2015, pp. 5188–5196.

[MV16]   A. Mahendran and A. Vedaldi. "Visualizing
Deep Convolutional Neural Networks Using
Natural Pre-images". In: *Intl. J. Computer
Vision* (2016), pp. 1–23.

[MWK16]   A. H. Marblestone, G. Wayne, and K. P. Kording. "Toward an Integration of Deep Learning and Neuroscience". en. In: *Front. Comput. Neurosci.* 10 (2016), p. 94.

[MWP98]   B Moghaddam, W Wahid, and A Pentland. "Beyond eigenfaces: probabilistic matching for face recognition". In: *Proceedings Third IEEE International Conference on Automatic Face and Gesture Recognition.* 1998, pp. 30–35.

[Nad+19]   S. Naderi, K. He, R. Aghajani, S. Sclaroff, and P. Felzenszwalb. "Generalized Majorization-Minimization". In: *ICML.* 2019.

[NAM21]   C. G. Northcutt, A. Athalye, and J. Mueller. "Pervasive Label Errors in Test Sets Destabilize Machine Learning Benchmarks". In: *NeurIPS Track on Datasets and Benchmarks.* Mar. 2021.

[Nea96]   R. Neal. *Bayesian learning for neural networks.* Springer, 1996.

[Nes04]   Y. Nesterov. *Introductory Lectures on Convex Optimization. A basic course.* Kluwer, 2004.

[Neu04]   A. Neumaier. "Complete search in continuous global optimization and constraint satisfaction". In: *Acta Numer.* 13 (2004), pp. 271–369.

[Neu17]   G. Neubig. "Neural Machine Translation and Sequence-to-sequence Models: A Tutorial". In: (2017). arXiv: 1703.01619 [cs.CL].

[Ngu+17]   A. Nguyen, J. Yosinski, Y. Bengio, A. Dosovitskiy, and J. Clune. "Plug & Play Generative Networks: Conditional Iterative Generation of Images in Latent Space". In: *CVPR.* 2017.

[NH98]   R. M. Neal and G. E. Hinton. "A View of the EM Algorithm that Justifies Incremental, Sparse, and other Variants". In: *Learning in Graphical Models.* Ed. by M. I. Jordan. Springer Netherlands, 1998, pp. 355–368.

[NHLS19]   E. Nalisnick, J. M. Hernández-Lobato, and P. Smyth. "Dropout as a Structured Shrinkage Prior". In: *ICML.* 2019.

[Nic+15]   M. Nickel, K. Murphy, V. Tresp, and E. Gabrilovich. "A Review of Relational Machine Learning for Knowledge Graphs". In: *Proc. IEEE* (2015).

[Niu+11]   F. Niu, B. Recht, C. Re, and S. J. Wright. "HOGWILD!: A Lock-Free Approach to Parallelizing Stochastic Gradient Descent". In: *NIPS.* 2011.

[NJ02]   A. Y. Ng and M. I. Jordan. "On Discriminative vs. Generative Classifiers: A comparison of logistic regression and Naive Bayes". In: *NIPS-14.* 2002.

[NJW01]   A. Ng, M. Jordan, and Y. Weiss. "On Spectral Clustering: Analysis and an algorithm". In: *NIPS.* 2001.

[NK17]   M. Nickel and D. Kiela. "Poincaré embeddings for learning hierarchical representations". In: *Advances in neural information processing systems.* 2017, pp. 6338–6347.

[NK18]   M. Nickel and D. Kiela. "Learning Continuous Hierarchies in the Lorentz Model of Hyperbolic Geometry". In: *International Confer-*

ence on Machine Learning. 2018, pp. 3779–3788.

[NK19]   T. Niven and H.-Y. Kao. "Probing Neural Network Comprehension of Natural Language Arguments". In: *Proc. ACL.* 2019.

[NMC05]   A. Niculescu-Mizil and R. Caruana. "Predicting Good Probabilities with Supervised Learning". In: *ICML.* 2005.

[Nou+02]   M. N. Nounou, B. R. Bakshi, P. K. Goel, and X. Shen. "Process modeling by Bayesian latent variable regression". In: *Am. Inst. Chemical Engineers Journal* 48.8 (2002), pp. 1775–1793.

[Nov62]   A. Novikoff. "On convergence proofs on perceptrons". In: *Symp. on the Mathematical Theory of Automata* 12 (1962), pp. 615–622.

[NR18]   G. Neu and L. Rosasco. "Iterate Averaging as Regularization for Stochastic Gradient Descent". In: *COLT.* 2018.

[NTL20]   J. Nixon, D. Tran, and B. Lakshminarayanan. "Why aren't bootstrapped neural networks better?" In: *NIPS Workshop on "I can't believe it's not better".* 2020.

[NW06]   J. Nocedal and S. Wright. *Numerical Optimization.* Springer, 2006.

[Ode16]   A. Odena. "Semi-supervised learning with generative adversarial networks". In: *arXiv preprint arXiv:1606.01583* (2016).

[OLV18]   A. van den Oord, Y. Li, and O. Vinyals. "Representation Learning with Contrastive Predictive Coding". In: (2018). arXiv: 1807.03748 [cs.LG].

[OMS17]   C. Olah, A. Mordvintsev, and L. Schubert. "Feature Visualization". In: *Distill* (2017).

[Oor+16]   A. Van den Oord, S. Dieleman, H. Zen, K. Simonyan, O. Vinyals, A. Graves, N. Kalchbrenner, A. Senior, and K. Kavukcuoglu. "WaveNet: A Generative Model for Raw Audio". In: (2016). arXiv: 1609.03499 [cs.SD].

[Oor+18]   A. van den Oord et al. "Parallel WaveNet: Fast High-Fidelity Speech Synthesis". In: *ICML.* Ed. by J. Dy and A. Krause. Vol. 80. Proceedings of Machine Learning Research. PMLR, 2018, pp. 3918–3926.

[OPK12]   G. Ohloff, W. Pickenhagen, and P. Kraft. *Scent and Chemistry.* en. Wiley, 2012.

[OPT00a]   M. R. Osborne, B. Presnell, and B. A. Turlach. "A new approach to variable selection in least squares problems". In: *IMA Journal of Numerical Analysis* 20.3 (2000), pp. 389–403.

[OPT00b]   M. R. Osborne, B. Presnell, and B. A. Turlach. "On the lasso and its dual". In: *J. Computational and graphical statistics* 9 (2000), pp. 319–337.

[Ort+19]   P. A. Ortega et al. "Meta-learning of Sequential Strategies". In: (2019). arXiv: 1905.03030 [cs.LG].

[Osb16]   I. Osband. "Risk versus Uncertainty in Deep Learning: Bayes, Bootstrap and the Dangers of Dropout". In: *NIPS workshop on Bayesian deep learning.* 2016.

[OTJ07]   G. Obozinski, B. Taskar, and M. I. Jordan. *Joint covariate selection for grouped classification*. Tech. rep. UC Berkeley, 2007.

[Pai05]   A. Pais. *Subtle Is the Lord: The Science and the Life of Albert Einstein*. en. Oxford University Press, 2005.

[Pan+15]   V. Panayotov, G. Chen, D. Povey, and S. Khudanpur. "Librispeech: an asr corpus based on public domain audio books". In: *ICASSP*. IEEE. 2015, pp. 5206–5210.

[Pap+18]   G. Papandreou, T. Zhu, L.-C. Chen, S. Gidaris, J. Tompson, and K. Murphy. "Person-Lab: Person Pose Estimation and Instance Segmentation with a Bottom-Up, Part-Based, Geometric Embedding Model". In: *ECCV*. 2018, pp. 269–286.

[Par+16a] A. Parikh, O. Täckström, D. Das, and J. Uszkoreit. "A Decomposable Attention Model for Natural Language Inference". In: *EMNLP*. Association for Computational Linguistics, 2016, pp. 2249–2255.

[Par+16b] A. Parikh, O. Täckström, D. Das, and J. Uszkoreit. "A Decomposable Attention Model for Natural Language Inference". In: *EMNLP*. Association for Computational Linguistics, 2016, pp. 2249–2255.

[Par+18]   N. Parmar, A. Vaswani, J. Uszkoreit, Ł. Kaiser, N. Shazeer, A. Ku, and D. Tran. "Image Transformer". In: *ICLR*. 2018.

[PARS14]   B. Perozzi, R. Al-Rfou, and S. Skiena. "Deepwalk: Online learning of social representations". In: *Proceedings of the 20th ACM SIGKDD international conference on Knowledge discovery and data mining*. ACM. 2014, pp. 701–710.

[Pas14]   R. Pascanu. "On Recurrent and Deep Neural Networks". PhD thesis. U. Montreal, 2014.

[Pat12]   A. Paterek. *Predicting movie ratings and recommender systems*. 2012.

[Pat+16]   D. Pathak, P. Krahenbuhl, J. Donahue, T. Darrell, and A. A. Efros. "Context Encoders: Feature Learning by Inpainting". In: *CVPR*. 2016.

[Pau+20]   A. Paullada, I. D. Raji, E. M. Bender, E. Denton, and A. Hanna. "Data and its (dis)contents: A survey of dataset development and use in machine learning research". In: *NeurIPS 2020 Workshop: ML Retrospectives, Surveys & Meta-analyses (ML-RSA)*. 2020.

[PB+14]   N. Parikh, S. Boyd, et al. "Proximal algorithms". In: *Foundations and Trends in Optimization* 1.3 (2014), pp. 127–239.

[Pea18]   J. Pearl. *Theoretical Impediments to Machine Learning With Seven Sparks from the Causal Revolution*. Tech. rep. UCLA, 2018.

[Pen+20]   Z. Peng, W. Huang, M. Luo, Q. Zheng, Y. Rong, T. Xu, and J. Huang. "Graph Representation Learning via Graphical Mutual Information Maximization". In: *Proceedings of The Web Conference*. 2020.

[Per+17]   B. Perozzi, V. Kulkarni, H. Chen, and S. Skiena. "Don't Walk, Skip! Online Learning of Multi-Scale Network Embeddings". In: *Proceedings of the 2017 IEEE/ACM International Conference on Advances in Social Networks Analysis and Mining 2017*. ASONAM '17. Association for Computing Machinery, 2017, 258–265.

[Pet13]   J. Peters. *When Ice Cream Sales Rise, So Do Homicides. Coincidence, or Will Your Next Cone Murder You?* https://slate.com/ news - and - politics / 2013 / 07 / warm - weather - homicide-rates-when-ice-cream-sales-rise- homicides-rise-coincidence.html. Accessed: 2020-5-20. 2013.

[Pet+18]   M. E. Peters, M. Neumann, M. Iyyer, M. Gardner, C. Clark, K. Lee, and L. Zettlemoyer. "Deep contextualized word representations". In: *NAACL*. 2018.

[Pey20]   G. Peyre. "Course notes on Optimization for Machine Learning". 2020.

[PH18]   T. Parr and J. Howard. "The Matrix Calculus You Need For Deep Learning". In: (2018). arXiv: 1802.01528 [cs.LG].

[Pin88]   F. J. Pineda. "Generalization of back propagation to recurrent and higher order neural networks". In: *Neural information processing systems*. 1988, pp. 602–611.

[Piz01]   Z Pizlo. "Perception viewed as an inverse problem". en. In: *Vision Res.* 41.24 (2001), pp. 3145–3161.

[PJ09]   H.-S. Park and C.-H. Jun. "A simple and fast algorithm for K-medoids clustering". In: *Expert Systems with Applciations* 36.2, Part 2 (2009), pp. 3336–3341.

[PJ92]   B Polyak and A Juditsky. "Acceleration of Stochastic Approximation by Averaging". In: *SIAM J. Control Optim.* 30.4 (1992), pp. 838–855.

[Pla00]   J. Platt. "Probabilities for SV machines". In: *Advances in Large Margin Classifiers*. Ed. by A. Smola, P. Bartlett, B. Schoelkopf, and D. Schuurmans. MIT Press, 2000.

[Pla98]   J. Platt. "Using analytic QP and sparseness to speed training of support vector machines". In: *NIPS*. 1998.

[PM17]   D. L. Poole and A. K. Mackworth. *Artificial intelligenceL foundations computational agents 2nd edition*. Cambridge University Press, 2017.

[PM18]   J. Pearl and D. Mackenzie. *The book of why: the new science of cause and effect*. 2018.

[PMB19]   J. Pérez, J. Marinkovic, and P. Barcelo. "On the Turing Completeness of Modern Neural Network Architectures". In: *ICLR*. 2019.

[Pog+17]   T. Poggio, H. Mhaskar, L. Rosasco, B. Miranda, and Q. Liao. "Why and when can deep-but not shallow-networks avoid the curse of dimensionality: A review". en. In: *Int. J. Autom. Comput.* (2017), pp. 1–17.

[PP+20]   M. Papadatou-Pastou, E. Ntolka, J. Schmitz, M. Martin, M. R. Munafò, S. Ocklenburg, and S. Paracchini. "Human handedness: A meta-analysis". en. In: *Psychol. Bull.* 146.6 (2020), pp. 481–524.

[PPS18]   T. Pierrot, N. Perrin, and O. Sigaud. "First-order and second-order variants of the gradient descent in a unified framework". In: (2018). arXiv: 1810.08102 [cs.LG].

[Pre21]   K. Pretz. "Stop Calling Everything AI, Machine-Learning Pioneer Says". In: *IEEE Spectrum* (2021).

[PSM14a]   J. Pennington, R. Socher, and C. Manning. "GloVe: Global vectors for word representation". In: *EMNLP*. 2014, pp. 1532–1543.

[PSM14b]   J. Pennington, R. Socher, and C. Manning. "Glove: Global vectors for word representation". In: *Proceedings of the 2014 conference on empirical methods in natural language processing (EMNLP)*. 2014, pp. 1532–1543.

[PSW15]   N. G. Polson, J. G. Scott, and B. T. Willard. "Proximal Algorithms in Statistics and Machine Learning". en. In: *Stat. Sci.* 30.4 (2015), pp. 559–581.

[QC+06]   J. Quiñonero-Candela, C. E. Rasmussen, F. Sinz, O. Bousquet, and B. Schölkopf. "Evaluating Predictive Uncertainty Challenge". In: *Machine Learning Challenges. Evaluating Predictive Uncertainty, Visual Object Classification, and Recognising Tectual Entailment*. Lecture Notes in Computer Science. Springer Berlin Heidelberg, 2006, pp. 1–27.

[Qia+19]   Q. Qian, L. Shang, B. Sun, J. Hu, H. Li, and R. Jin. "SoftTriple Loss: Deep Metric Learning Without Triplet Sampling". In: *ICCV*. 2019.

[Qiu+18]   J. Qiu, Y. Dong, H. Ma, J. Li, K. Wang, and J. Tang. "Network embedding as matrix factorization: Unifying deepwalk, line, pte, and node2vec". In: *Proceedings of the Eleventh ACM International Conference on Web Search and Data Mining*. 2018, pp. 459–467.

[Qiu+19a]   J. Qiu, Y. Dong, H. Ma, J. Li, C. Wang, K. Wang, and J. Tang. "NetSMF: Large-Scale Network Embedding as Sparse Matrix Factorization". In: *The World Wide Web Conference*. WWW '19. Association for Computing Machinery, 2019, 1509–1520.

[Qiu+19b]   J. Qiu, H. Ma, O. Levy, S. W. Yih, S. Wang, and J. Tang. "Blockwise Self-Attention for Long Document Understanding". In: *CoRR* abs/1911.02972 (2019). arXiv: 1911.02972.

[Qui86]   J. R. Quinlan. "Induction of decision trees". In: *Machine Learning* 1 (1986), pp. 81–106.

[Qui93]   J. R. Quinlan. *C4.5 Programs for Machine Learning*. Morgan Kauffman, 1993.

[Rad+]   A. Radford et al. *Learning transferable visual models from natural language supervision*. Tech. rep. OpenAI.

[Rad+18]   A. Radford, K. Narasimhan, T. Salimans, and I. Sutskever. *Improving Language Understanding by Generative Pre-Training*. Tech. rep. OpenAI, 2018.

[Rad+19]   A. Radford, J. Wu, R. Child, D. Luan, D. Amodei, and I. Sutskever. *Language Models are Unsupervised Multitask Learners*. Tech. rep. OpenAI, 2019.

[Raf+20]   C. Raffel, N. Shazeer, A. Roberts, K. Lee, S. Narang, M. Matena, Y. Zhou, W. Li, and P. J. Liu. "Exploring the Limits of Transfer Learning with a Unified Text-to-Text Transformer". In: *JMLR* (2020).

[Raf22]   E. Raff. *Inside Deep Learning: Math, Algorithms, Models*. en. Annotated edition. Manning, May 2022.

[Rag+17]   M. Raghu, B. Poole, J. Kleinberg, S. Ganguli, and J. Sohl-Dickstein. "On the Expressive Power of Deep Neural Networks". In: *ICML*. 2017.

[Rag+19]   M. Raghu, C. Zhang, J. Kleinberg, and S. Bengio. "Transfusion: Understanding transfer learning for medical imaging". In: *NIPS*. 2019, pp. 3347–3357.

[Rag+21]   M. Raghu, T. Unterthiner, S. Kornblith, C. Zhang, and A. Dosovitskiy. "Do Vision Transformers See Like Convolutional Neural Networks?" In: *NIPS*. 2021.

[Raj+16]   P. Rajpurkar, J. Zhang, K. Lopyrev, and P. Liang. "SQuAD: 100,000+ Questions for Machine Comprehension of Text". In: *EMNLP*. 2016.

[Raj+18]   A. Rajkomar et al. "Scalable and accurate deep learning with electronic health records". en. In: *NPJ Digit Med* 1 (2018), p. 18.

[Rat+09]   M. Rattray, O. Stegle, K. Sharp, and J. Winn. "Inference algorithms and learning theory for Bayesian sparse factor analysis". In: *Proc. Intl. Workshop on Statistical-Mechanical Informatics*. 2009.

[RB93]   M. Riedmiller and H. Braun. "A direct adaptive method for faster backpropagation learning: The RPROP algorithm". In: *ICNN*. IEEE. 1993, pp. 586–591.

[RBV17]   S.-A. Rebuffi, H. Bilen, and A. Vedaldi. "Learning multiple visual domains with residual adapters". In: *NIPS*. 2017.

[RBV18]   S.-A. Rebuffi, H. Bilen, and A. Vedaldi. "Efficient parametrization of multi-domain deep neural networks". In: *CVPR*. 2018.

[RC04]   C. Robert and G. Casella. *Monte Carlo Statisical Methods*. 2nd edition. Springer, 2004.

[Rec+19]   B. Recht, R. Roelofs, L. Schmidt, and V. Shankar. "Do Image Net Classifiers Generalize to Image Net?" In: *ICML*. 2019.

[Red+16]   J Redmon, S Divvala, R Girshick, and A Farhadi. "You Only Look Once: Unified, Real-Time Object Detection". In: *CVPR*. 2016, pp. 779–788.

[Ren+09]   S. Rendle, C. Freudenthaler, Z. Gantner, and L. Schmidt-Thieme. "BPR: Bayesian Personalized Ranking from Implicit Feedback". In: *UAI*. 2009.

[Ren12]   S. Rendle. "Factorization Machines with libFM". In: *ACM Trans. Intell. Syst. Technol.* 3.3 (2012), pp. 1–22.

[Ren19]   Z. Ren. *List of papers on self-supervised learning*. 2019.

[Res+11]   D. Reshef, Y. Reshef, H. Finucane, S. Grossman, G. McVean, P. Turnbaugh, E. Lander, M. Mitzenmacher, and P. Sabeti. "Detecting Novel Associations in Large Data Sets". In: *Science* 334 (2011), pp. 1518–1524.

[Res+16]   Y. A. Reshef, D. N. Reshef, H. K. Finucane, P. C. Sabeti, and M. Mitzenmacher. "Measuring Dependence Powerfully and Equitably". In: *J. Mach. Learn. Res.* 17.211 (2016), pp. 1–63.

[RF17]   J. Redmon and A. Farhadi. "YOLO9000: Better, Faster, Stronger". In: *CVPR*. 2017.

[RFB15]   O. Ronneberger, P. Fischer, and T. Brox. "U-Net: Convolutional Networks for Biomedical Image Segmentation". In: *MICCAI (Intl. Conf. on Medical Image Computing and Computer Assisted Interventions)*. 2015.

[RG11]   A. Rodriguez and K. Ghosh. *Modeling relational data through nested partition models*. Tech. rep. UC Santa Cruz, 2011.

[RHS05]   C. Rosenberg, M. Hebert, and H. Schneiderman. "Semi-Supervised Self-Training of Object Detection Models". In: *Proceedings of the Seventh IEEE Workshops on Application of Computer Vision (WACV/MOTION'05)-Volume 1-Volume 01*. 2005, pp. 29–36.

[RHW86]   D. Rumelhart, G. Hinton, and R. Williams. "Learning internal representations by error propagation". In: *Parallel Distributed Processing: Explorations in the Microstructure of Cognition*. Ed. by D. Rumelhart, J. McClelland, and the PDD Research Group. MIT Press, 1986.

[Ric95]   J. Rice. *Mathematical statistics and data analysis*. 2nd edition. Duxbury, 1995.

[Rif+11]   S. Rifai, P. Vincent, X. Muller, X. Glorot, and Y. Bengio. "Contractive Auto-Encoders: Explicit Invariance During Feature Extraction". In: *ICML*. 2011.

[Ris+08]   I. Rish, G. Grabarnik, G. Cecchi, F. Pereira, and G. Gordon. "Closed-form supervised dimensionality reduction with generalized linear models". In: *ICML*. 2008.

[RKK18]   S. J. Reddi, S. Kale, and S. Kumar. "On the Convergence of Adam and Beyond". In: *ICLR*. 2018.

[RM01]   N. Roy and A. McCallum. "Toward optimal active learning through Monte Carlo estimation of error reduction". In: *ICML*. 2001.

[RMC09]   H. Rue, S. Martino, and N. Chopin. "Approximate Bayesian Inference for Latent Gaussian Models Using Integrated Nested Laplace Approximations". In: *J. of Royal Stat. Soc. Series B* 71 (2009), pp. 319–392.

[RML22]   S. Ramasinghe, L. Macdonald, and S. Lucey. "On the frequency-bias of coordinate-MLPs". In: *NIPS*. 2022.

[RMW14]   D. J. Rezende, S. Mohamed, and D. Wierstra. "Stochastic Backpropagation and Approximate Inference in Deep Generative Models". In: *ICML*. Ed. by E. P. Xing and T. Jebara. Vol. 32. Proceedings of Machine Learning Research. PMLR, 2014, pp. 1278–1286.

[RN10]   S. Russell and P. Norvig. *Artificial Intelligence: A Modern Approach*. 3rd edition. Prentice Hall, 2010.

[Roo+21]   F. de Roos, C. Jidling, A. Wills, T. Schön, and P. Hennig. "A Probabilistically Motivated Learning Rate Adaptation for Stochastic Optimization". In: (2021). arXiv: 2102 . 10880 [cs.LG].

[Ros58]   F. Rosenblatt. "The Perceptron: A Probabilistic Model for Information Storage and Organization in the Brain". In: *Psychological Review* 65.6 (1958), pp. 386–408.

[Ros98]   K. Rose. "Deterministic Annealing for Clustering, Compression, Classification, Regression, and Related Optimization Problems". In: *Proc. IEEE* 80 (1998), pp. 2210–2239.

[Rot+18]   W. Roth, R. Peharz, S. Tschiatschek, and F. Pernkopf. "Hybrid generative-discriminative training of Gaussian mixture models". In: *Pattern Recognit. Lett.* 112 (Sept. 2018), pp. 131–137.

[Rot+20]   K. Roth, T. Milbich, S. Sinha, P. Gupta, B. Ommer, and J. P. Cohen. "Revisiting Training Strategies and Generalization Performance in Deep Metric Learning". In: *ICML*. 2020.

[Rou+09]   J. Rouder, P. Speckman, D. Sun, and R. Morey. "Bayesian t tests for accepting and rejecting the null hypothesis". In: *Psychonomic Bulletin & Review* 16.2 (2009), pp. 225–237.

[Row97]   S. Roweis. "EM algorithms for PCA and SPCA". In: *NIPS*. 1997.

[Roy+20]   A. Roy, M. Saffar, A. Vaswani, and D. Grangier. "Efficient Content-Based Sparse Attention with Routing Transformers". In: *CoRR* abs/2003.05997 (2020). arXiv: 2003.05997.

[Roz+19]   B. Rozemberczki, R. Davies, R. Sarkar, and C. Sutton. "GEMSEC: Graph Embedding with Self Clustering". In: *Proceedings of the 2019 IEEE/ACM International Conference on Advances in Social Networks Analysis and Mining*. ASONAM '19. Association for Computing Machinery, 2019, 65–72.

[RP99]   M. Riesenhuber and T. Poggio. "Hierarchical Models of Object Recognition in Cortex". In: *Nature Neuroscience* 2 (1999), pp. 1019–1025.

[RR08]   A. Rahimi and B. Recht. "Random Features for Large-Scale Kernel Machines". In: *NIPS*. Curran Associates, Inc., 2008, pp. 1177–1184.

[RR09]   A. Rahimi and B. Recht. "Weighted Sums of Random Kitchen Sinks: Replacing minimization with randomization in learning". In: *NIPS*. Curran Associates, Inc., 2009, pp. 1313–1320.

[RS00]   S. T. Roweis and L. K. Saul. "Nonlinear dimensionality reduction by locally linear embedding". en. In: *Science* 290.5500 (2000), pp. 2323–2326.

[RT82]   D. B. Rubin and D. T. Thayer. "EM algorithms for ML factor analysis". In: *Psychometrika* 47.1 (1982), pp. 69–76.

[Rub84]   D. B. Rubin. "Bayesianly Justifiable and Relevant Frequency Calculations for the Applied Statistician". In: *Ann. Stat.* 12.4 (1984), pp. 1151–1172.

[Rup88]   D Ruppert. *Efficient Estimations from a Slowly Convergent Robbins-Monro Process*. Tech. rep. 1988.

[Rus+15]   O. Russakovsky et al. "ImageNet Large Scale Visual Recognition Challenge". In: *Intl. J. Computer Vision* (2015), pp. 1–42.

[Rus15]   S. Russell. "Unifying Logic and Probability". In: *Commun. ACM* 58.7 (2015), pp. 88–97.

[Rus18]   A. M. Rush. "The Annotated Transformer". In: *Proceedings of ACL Workshop on Open Source Software for NLP.* 2018.

[Rus19]   S. Russell. *Human Compatible: Artificial Intelligence and the Problem of Control.* en. Kindle. Viking, 2019.

[RW06]   C. E. Rasmussen and C. K. I. Williams. *Gaussian Processes for Machine Learning.* MIT Press, 2006.

[RY21]   D. Roberts and S. Yaida. *The Principles of Deep Learning Theory: An Effective Theory Approach to Understanding Neural Network.* 2021.

[RZL17]   P. Ramachandran, B. Zoph, and Q. V. Le. "Searching for Activation Functions". In: (2017). arXiv: 1710.05941 [cs.NE].

[SA93]   P Sinha and E Adelson. "Recovering reflectance and illumination in a world of painted polyhedra". In: *ICCV.* 1993, pp. 156–163.

[Sab21]   W. Saba. "Machine Learning Won't Solve Natural Language Understanding". In: (2021).

[Sal+16]   T. Salimans, I. Goodfellow, W. Zaremba, V. Cheung, A. Radford, and X. Chen. "Improved Techniques for Training GANs". In: (2016). arXiv: 1606.03498 [cs.LG].

[SAM04]   D. J. Spiegelhalter, K. R. Abrams, and J. P. Myles. *Bayesian Approaches to Clinical Trials and Health-Care Evaluation.* Wiley, 2004.

[San+18a] M. Sandler, A. Howard, M. Zhu, A. Zhmoginov, and L.-C. Chen. "Inverted Residuals and Linear Bottlenecks: Mobile Networks for Classification, Detection and Segmentation". In: (2018). arXiv: 1801.04381 [cs.CV].

[San+18b] S. Santurkar, D. Tsipras, A. Ilyas, and A. Madry. "How Does Batch Normalization Help Optimization? (No, It Is Not About Internal Covariate Shift)". In: *NIPS.* 2018.

[San96]   R. Santos. "Equivalence of regularization and truncated iteration for general ill-posed problems". In: *Linear Algebra and its Applications* 236.15 (1996), pp. 25–33.

[Sar11]   R. Sarkar. "Low distortion delaunay embedding of trees in hyperbolic plane". In: *International Symposium on Graph Drawing.* Springer. 2011, pp. 355–366.

[SAV20]   E. Stevens, L. Antiga, and T. Viehmann. *Deep Learning with PyTorch.* Manning, 2020.

[SBB01]   T. Sellke, M. J. Bayarri, and J. Berger. "Calibration of p Values for Testing Precise Null Hypotheses". In: *The American Statistician* 55.1 (2001), pp. 62–71.

[SBP17]   Y Sun, P Babu, and D. P. Palomar. "Majorization-Minimization Algorithms in Signal Processing, Communications, and Machine Learning". In: *IEEE Trans. Signal Process.* 65.3 (2017), pp. 794–816.

[SBS20]   K. Shi, D. Bieber, and C. Sutton. "Incremental sampling without replacement for sequence models". In: *ICML.* 2020.

[Sca+09]   F. Scarselli, M. Gori, A. C. Tsoi, M. Hagenbuchner, and G. Monfardini. "The graph neural network model". In: *IEEE Transactions on Neural Networks* 20.1 (2009), pp. 61–80.

[Sca+17]   S. Scardapane, D. Comminiello, A. Hussain, and A. Uncini. "Group Sparse Regularization for Deep Neural Networks". In: *Neurocomputing* 241 (2017).

[Sch+00]   B Scholkopf, A. J. Smola, R. C. Williamson, and P. L. Bartlett. "New support vector algorithms". en. In: *Neural Comput.* 12.5 (2000), pp. 1207–1245.

[Sch19]   B. Schölkopf. "Causality for Machine Learning". In: (2019). arXiv: 1911.10500 [cs.LG].

[Sch78]   G. Schwarz. "Estimating the dimension of a model". In: *Annals of Statistics* 6.2 (1978), pp. 461–464.

[Sch90]   R. E. Schapire. "The strength of weak learnability". In: *Mach. Learn.* 5.2 (1990), pp. 197–227.

[Sco79]   D. Scott. "On optimal and data-based histograms". In: *Biometrika* 66.3 (1979), pp. 605–610.

[Scu10]   D Sculley. "Web-scale k-means clustering". In: *WWW.* WWW '10. Association for Computing Machinery, 2010, pp. 1177–1178.

[Scu65]   H. Scudder. "Probability of error of some adaptive pattern-recognition machines". In: *IEEE Transactions on Information Theory* 11.3 (1965), pp. 363–371.

[Sed+15]   S. Sedhain, A. K. Menon, S. Sanner, and L. Xie. "AutoRec: Autoencoders Meet Collaborative Filtering". In: *WWW.* WWW '15 Companion. Association for Computing Machinery, 2015, pp. 111–112.

[Sej18]   T. J. Sejnowski. *The Deep Learning Revolution.* en. Kindle. The MIT Press, 2018.

[Set12]   B. Settles. "Active learning". In: *Synthesis Lectures on Artificial Intelligence and Machine Learning* 6 (2012), 1–114.

[SF12]   R. Schapire and Y. Freund. *Boosting: Foundations and Algorithms.* MIT Press, 2012.

[SGJ11]   D. Sontag, A. Globerson, and T. Jaakkola. "Introduction to Dual Decomposition for Inference". In: *Optimization for Machine Learning.* Ed. by S. Sra, S. Nowozin, and S. J. Wright. MIT Press, 2011.

[Sha+06]   P. Shafto, C. Kemp, V. Mansinghka, M. Gordon, and J. B. Tenenbaum. "Learning cross-cutting systems of categories". In: *Cognitive Science Conference.* 2006.

[Sha+17]   N. Shazeer, A. Mirhoseini, K. Maziarz, A. Davis, Q. Le, G. Hinton, and J. Dean. "Outrageously Large Neural Networks: The Sparsely-Gated Mixture-of-Experts Layer". In: *ICLR.* 2017.

[Sha88]   T. Shallice. *From Neuropsychology to Mental Structure.* 1988.

[SHB16]   R. Sennrich, B. Haddow, and A. Birch. "Neural Machine Translation of Rare Words with Subword Units". In: *Proc. ACL*. 2016.

[She+18]   Z. Shen, M. Zhang, S. Yi, J. Yan, and H. Zhao. "Factorized Attention: Self-Attention with Linear Complexities". In: *CoRR* abs/1812.01243 (2018). arXiv: 1812. 01243.

[She94]   J. R. Shewchuk. *An introduction to the conjugate gradient method without the agonizing pain*. Tech. rep. CMU, 1994.

[SHF15]   R. Steorts, R. Hall, and S. Fienberg. "A Bayesian Approach to Graphical Record Linkage and De-duplication". In: *JASA* (2015).

[Shu+13]   D. I. Shuman, S. K. Narang, P Frossard, A Ortega, and P Vandergheynst. "The emerging field of signal processing on graphs: Extending high-dimensional data analysis to networks and other irregular domains". In: *IEEE Signal Process. Mag.* 30.3 (2013), pp. 83–98.

[Sin+20]   S. Sinha, H. Zhang, A. Goyal, Y. Bengio, H. Larochelle, and A. Odena. "Small-GAN: Speeding up GAN Training using Core-Sets". In: *ICML*. Vol. 119. Proceedings of Machine Learning Research. PMLR, 2020, pp. 9005–9015.

[Sit+20]   V. Sitzmann, J. N. P. Martel, A. W. Bergman, D. B. Lindell, and G. Wetzstein. "Implicit Neural Representations with Periodic Activation Functions". In: *NIPS*. https://www.vincentsitzmann.com/siren/. June 2020.

[SIV17]   C. Szegedy, S. Ioffe, and V. Vanhoucke. "Inception-v4, Inception-ResNet and the Impact of Residual Connections on Learning". In: *AAAI*. 2017.

[SJ03]   N. Srebro and T. Jaakkola. "Weighted low-rank approximations". In: *ICML*. 2003.

[SJT16]   M. Sajjadi, M. Javanmardi, and T. Tasdizen. "Regularization with stochastic transformations and perturbations for deep semi-supervised learning". In: *Advances in neural information processing systems*. 2016, pp. 1163–1171.

[SK20]   S. Singh and S. Krishnan. "Filter Response Normalization Layer: Eliminating Batch Dependence in the Training of Deep Neural Networks". In: *CVPR*. 2020.

[SKP15]   F. Schroff, D. Kalenichenko, and J. Philbin. "FaceNet: A Unified Embedding for Face Recognition and Clustering". In: *CVPR*. 2015.

[SKT14]   A. Szlam, Y. Kluger, and M. Tygert. "An implementation of a randomized algorithm for principal component analysis". In: (2014). arXiv: 1412.3510 [stat.CO].

[SKTF18]   H. Shao, A. Kumar, and P Thomas Fletcher. "The Riemannian Geometry of Deep Generative Models". In: *CVPR*. 2018, pp. 315–323.

[SL18]   S. L. Smith and Q. V. Le. "A Bayesian Perspective on Generalization and Stochastic Gradient Descent". In: *ICLR*. 2018.

[SL+19]   B. Sanchez-Lengeling, J. N. Wei, B. K. Lee, R. C. Gerkin, A. Aspuru-Guzik, and A. B. Wiltschko. "Machine Learning for Scent: Learning Generalizable Perceptual Representations of Small Molecules". In: (2019). arXiv: 1910.10685 [stat.ML].

[SL90]   D. J. Spiegelhalter and S. L. Lauritzen. "Sequential updating of conditional probabilities on directed graphical structures". In: *Networks* 20 (1990).

[SLRB17]   M. Schmidt, N. Le Roux, and F. Bach. "Minimizing finite sums with the stochastic average gradient". In: *Mathematical Programming* 162.1-2 (2017), pp. 83–112.

[SM00]   J. Shi and J. Malik. "Normalized Cuts and Image Segmentation". In: *IEEE PAMI* (2000).

[SM08]   R. Salakhutdinov and A. Mnih. "Probabilistic Matrix Factorization". In: *NIPS*. Vol. 20. 2008.

[SMG14]   A. M. Saxe, J. L. McClelland, and S. Ganguli. "Exact solutions to the nonlinear dynamics of learning in deep linear neural networks". In: *ICLR*. 2014.

[SMH07]   R. Salakhutdinov, A. Mnih, and G. Hinton. "Restricted Boltzmann machines for collaborative filtering". In: *ICML*. ICML '07. Association for Computing Machinery, 2007, pp. 791–798.

[Smi18]   L. Smith. "A disciplined approach to neural network hyper-parameters: Part 1 – learning rate, batch size, momentum, and weight decay". In: (2018). arXiv: 1803.09820.

[Smi+21]   S. L. Smith, B. Dherin, D. Barrett, and S. De. "On the Origin of Implicit Regularization in Stochastic Gradient Descent". In: *ICLR*. 2021.

[SMM03]   Q. Sheng, Y. Moreau, and B. D. Moor. "Biclustering Microarray data by Gibbs sampling". In: *Bioinformatics* 19 (2003), pp. ii196–ii205.

[SNM16]   M. Suzuki, K. Nakayama, and Y. Matsuo. "Joint Multimodal Learning with Deep Generative Models". In: (2016). arXiv: 1611.01891 [stat.ML].

[Soh16]   K. Sohn. "Improved Deep Metric Learning with Multi-class N-pair Loss Objective". In: *NIPS*. Curran Associates, Inc., 2016, pp. 1857–1865.

[Soh+20]   K. Sohn, D. Berthelot, C.-L. Li, Z. Zhang, N. Carlini, E. D. Cubuk, A. Kurakin, H. Zhang, and C. Raffel. "FixMatch: Simplifying Semi-Supervised Learning with Consistency and Confidence". In: (2020). arXiv: 2001.07685 [cs.LG].

[SP97]   M Schuster and K. K. Paliwal. "Bidirectional recurrent neural networks". In: *IEEE. Trans on Signal Processing* 45.11 (1997), pp. 2673–2681.

[Spe11]   T. Speed. "A correlation for the 21st century". In: *Science* 334 (2011), pp. 1502–1503.

[Spe+22]   A. Z. Spector, P. Norvig, C. Wiggins, and J. M. Wing. *Data Science in Context: Foundations, Challenges, Opportunities*. en. New edition. Cambridge University Press, Oct. 2022.

[SR15]   T. Saito and M. Rehmsmeier. "The precision-recall plot is more informative than the ROC plot when evaluating binary classifiers on imbalanced datasets". en. In: *PLoS One* 10.3 (2015), e0118432.

[SRG03]   R. Salakhutdinov, S. T. Roweis, and Z. Ghahramani. "Optimization with EM and Expectation-Conjugate-Gradient". In: *ICML*. 2003.

[Sri+14]   N. Srivastava, G. Hinton, A. Krizhevsky, I. Sutskever, and R. Salakhutdinov. "Dropout: A Simple Way to Prevent Neural Networks from Overfitting". In: *JMLR* (2014).

[SS01]   B. Schlkopf and A. J. Smola. *Learning with Kernels: Support Vector Machines, Regularization, Optimization, and Beyond (Adaptive Computation and Machine Learning)*. en. 1st edition. The MIT Press, 2001.

[SS02]   B. Schoelkopf and A. Smola. *Learning with Kernels: Support Vector Machines, Regularization, Optimization, and Beyond*. MIT Press, 2002.

[SS05]   J. Schaefer and K. Strimmer. "A shrinkage approach to large-scale covariance matrix estimation and implications for functional genomics". In: *Statist. Appl. Genet. Mol. Biol* 4.32 (2005).

[SS19]   S. Serrano and N. A. Smith. "Is Attention Interpretable?" In: *Proc. ACL*. 2019.

[SS95]   H. T. Siegelmann and E. D. Sontag. "On the Computational Power of Neural Nets". In: *J. Comput. System Sci.* 50.1 (1995), pp. 132–150.

[SSM98]   B. Schoelkopf, A. Smola, and K.-R. Mueller. "Nonlinear component analysis as a kernel Eigenvalue problem". In: *Neural Computation* 10 (5 1998), pp. 1299 –1319.

[Sta+06]   C. Stark, B.-J. Breitkreutz, T. Reguly, L. Boucher, A. Breitkreutz, and M. Tyers. "BioGRID: a general repository for interaction datasets". In: *Nucleic acids research* 34.suppl_1 (2006), pp. D535–D539.

[Ste56]   C. Stein. "Inadmissibility of the usual estimator for the mean of a multivariate distribution". In: *Proc. 3rd Berkeley Symposium on Mathematical Statistics and Probability* (1956), 197–206.

[Str09]   G. Strang. *Introduction to linear algebra*. 4th edition. SIAM Press, 2009.

[Sug+19]   A. S. Suggala, K. Bhatia, P. Ravikumar, and P. Jain. "Adaptive Hard Thresholding for Near-optimal Consistent Robust Regression". In: *Proceedings of the Annual Conference On Learning Theory (COLT)*. 2019, pp. 2892–2897.

[Sun+09]   L. Sun, S. Ji, S. Yu, and J. Ye. "On the Equivalence Between Canonical Correlation Analysis and Orthonormalized Partial Least Squares". In: *IJCAI*. 2009.

[Sun+19a] C. Sun, A. Myers, C. Vondrick, K. Murphy, and C. Schmid. "VideoBERT: A Joint Model for Video and Language Representation Learning". In: *ICCV*. 2019.

[Sun+19b] S. Sun, Z. Cao, H. Zhu, and J. Zhao. "A Survey of Optimization Methods from a Machine Learning Perspective". In: (2019). arXiv: 1906.06821 [cs.LG].

[SVL14]   I. Sutskever, O. Vinyals, and Q. V. V. Le. "Sequence to Sequence Learning with Neural Networks". In: *NIPS*. 2014.

[SVZ14]   K. Simonyan, A. Vedaldi, and A. Zisserman. "Deep Inside Convolutional Networks: Visualising Image Classification Models and Saliency Maps". In: *ICLR*. 2014.

[SW87]   M. Shewry and H. Wynn. "Maximum entropy sampling". In: *J. Applied Statistics* 14 (1987), 165–170.

[SWY75]   G Salton, A Wong, and C. S. Yang. "A vector space model for automatic indexing". In: *Commun. ACM* 18.11 (1975), pp. 613–620.

[Sze+15a] C. Szegedy, W. Liu, Y. Jia, P. Sermanet, S. Reed, D. Anguelov, D. Erhan, V. Vanhoucke, and A. Rabinovich. "Going Deeper with Convolutions". In: *CVPR*. 2015.

[Sze+15b] C. Szegedy, V. Vanhoucke, S. Ioffe, J. Shlens, and Z. Wojna. "Rethinking the Inception Architecture for Computer Vision". In: (2015). arXiv: 1512.00567 [cs.CV].

[Tal07]   N. Taleb. *The Black Swan: The Impact of the Highly Improbable*. Random House, 2007.

[Tan+15]   J. Tang, M. Qu, M. Wang, M. Zhang, J. Yan, and Q. Mei. "Line: Large-scale information network embedding". In: *Proceedings of the 24th International Conference on World Wide Web*. International World Wide Web Conferences Steering Committee. 2015, pp. 1067–1077.

[Tan+18]   C. Tan, F. Sun, T. Kong, W. Zhang, C. Yang, and C. Liu. "A Survey on Deep Transfer Learning". In: *ICANN*. 2018.

[Tan+20]   M. Tancik, P. P. Srinivasan, B. Mildenhall, S. Fridovich-Keil, N. Raghavan, U. Singhal, R. Ramamoorthi, J. T. Barron, and R. Ng. "Fourier features let networks learn high frequency functions in low dimensional domains". In: *NIPS*. June 2020.

[TAS18]   M. Teye, H. Azizpour, and K. Smith. "Bayesian Uncertainty Estimation for Batch Normalized Deep Networks". In: *ICML*. 2018.

[Tay+20a] Y. Tay, M. Dehghani, S. Abnar, Y. Shen, D. Bahri, P. Pham, J. Rao, L. Yang, S. Ruder, and D. Metzler. "Long Range Arena: A Benchmark for efficient Transformers". In: *CoRR* (2020).

[Tay+20b] Y. Tay, M. Dehghani, D. Bahri, and D. Metzler. "Efficient Transformers: A Survey". In: (2020). arXiv: 2009.06732 [cs.LG].

[TB97]   L. Trefethen and D. Bau. *Numerical Linear Algebra*. SIAM, 1997.

[TB99]   M. Tipping and C. Bishop. "Probabilistic principal component analysis". In: *J. of Royal Stat. Soc. Series B* 21.3 (1999), pp. 611–622.

[TDP19]   I. Tenney, D. Das, and E. Pavlick. "BERT Rediscovers the Classical NLP Pipeline". In: *Proc. ACL*. 2019.

[TF03]   M. Tipping and A. Faul. "Fast marginal likelihood maximisation for sparse Bayesian models". In: *AI/Stats*. 2003.

[Tho16]   M. Thoma. "Creativity in Machine Learning". In: (2016). arXiv: 1601.03642 [cs.CV].

[Tho17]   R. Thomas. *Computational Linear Algebra for Coders*. 2017.

[Tib96]   R. Tibshirani. "Regression shrinkage and selection via the lasso". In: *J. Royal. Statist. Soc B* 58.1 (1996), pp. 267–288.

[Tip01]   M. Tipping. "Sparse Bayesian learning and the relevance vector machine". In: *JMLR* 1 (2001), pp. 211–244.

[Tip98]   M. Tipping. "Probabilistic visualization of high-dimensional binary data". In: *NIPS*. 1998.

[Tit16]   M. Titsias. "One-vs-Each Approximation to Softmax for Scalable Estimation of Probabilities". In: *NIPS*. 2016, pp. 4161–4169.

[TK86]   L. Tierney and J. Kadane. "Accurate approximations for posterior moments and marginal densities". In: *JASA* 81.393 (1986).

[TL21]   M. Tan and Q. V. Le. "EfficientNetV2: Smaller Models and Faster Training". In: (2021). arXiv: 2104.00298 [cs.CV].

[TM15]   D. Trafimow and M. Marks. "Editorial". In: *Basic Appl. Soc. Psych.* 37.1 (2015), pp. 1–2.

[TMP20]   A. Tsitsulin, M. Munkhoeva, and B. Perozzi. "Just SLaQ When You Approximate: Accurate Spectral Distances for Web-Scale Graphs". In: *Proceedings of The Web Conference 2020*. WWW '20. 2020, 2697–2703.

[TOB16]   L. Theis, A. van den Oord, and M. Bethge. "A note on the evaluation of generative models". In: *ICLR*. 2016.

[Tol+21]   I. Tolstikhin et al. "MLP-Mixer: An all-MLP Architecture for Vision". In: (2021). arXiv: 2105.01601 [cs.CV].

[TP10]   P. D. Turney and P. Pantel. "From Frequency to Meaning: Vector Space Models of Semantics". In: *JAIR* 37 (2010), pp. 141–188.

[TP97]   S. Thrun and L. Pratt, eds. *Learning to learn*. Kluwer, 1997.

[TS92]   D. G. Terrell and D. W. Scott. "Variable kernel density estimation". In: *Annals of Statistics* 20.3 (1992), 1236–1265.

[Tsi+18]   A. Tsitsulin, D. Mottin, P. Karras, A. Bronstein, and E. Müller. "NetLSD: Hearing the Shape of a Graph". In: *Proceedings of the 24th ACM SIGKDD International Conference on Knowledge Discovery & Data Mining*. KDD '18. 2018, 2347–2356.

[TSL00]   J. Tenenbaum, V. de Silva, and J. Langford. "A global geometric framework for nonlinear dimensionality reduction". In: *Science* 290.550 (2000), pp. 2319–2323.

[Tur13]   M. Turk. "Over Twenty Years of Eigenfaces". In: *ACM Trans. Multimedia Comput. Commun. Appl.* 9.1s (2013), 45:1–45:5.

[TV17]   A. Tarvainen and H. Valpola. "Mean teachers are better role models: Weight-averaged consistency targets improve semi-supervised deep learning results". In: *Advances in neural information processing systems*. 2017, pp. 1195–1204.

[TVW05]   B. Turlach, W. Venables, and S. Wright. "Simultaneous Variable Selection". In: *Technometrics* 47.3 (2005), pp. 349–363.

[TW18]   J. Tang and K. Wang. "Personalized Top-N Sequential Recommendation via Convolutional Sequence Embedding". In: *WSDM*. WSDM '18. Association for Computing Machinery, 2018, pp. 565–573.

[TXT19]   V. Tjeng, K. Xiao, and R. Tedrake. "Evaluating Robustness of Neural Networks with Mixed Integer Programming". In: *ICLR*. 2019.

[UB05]   I. Ulusoy and C. Bishop. "Generative Versus Discriminative Methods for Object Recognition". In: *CVPR*. 2005.

[Ude+16]   M. Udell, C. Horn, R. Zadeh, and S. Boyd. "Generalized Low Rank Models". In: *Foundations and Trends in Machine Learning* 9.1 (2016), pp. 1–118.

[Uly+16]   D. Ulyanov, V. Lebedev, Andrea, and V. Lempitsky. "Texture Networks: Feed-forward Synthesis of Textures and Stylized Images". In: *ICML*. 2016, pp. 1349–1357.

[Uur+17]   V. Uurtio, J. M. Monteiro, J. Kandola, J. Shawe-Taylor, D. Fernandez-Reyes, and J. Rousu. "A Tutorial on Canonical Correlation Methods". In: *ACM Computing Surveys* (2017).

[UVL16]   D. Ulyanov, A. Vedaldi, and V. Lempitsky. "Instance Normalization: The Missing Ingredient for Fast Stylization". In: (2016). arXiv: 1607.08022 [cs.CV].

[Van06]   L. Vandenberghe. *Applied Numerical Computing: Lecture notes*. 2006.

[Van14]   J. VanderPlas. *Frequentism and Bayesianism III: Confidence, Credibility, and why Frequentism and Science do not Mix*. Blog post. 2014.

[Van18]   J. Vanschoren. "Meta-Learning: A Survey". In: (2018). arXiv: 1810.03548 [cs.LG].

[Vap98]   V. Vapnik. *Statistical Learning Theory*. Wiley, 1998.

[Vas+17]   A. Vaswani, N. Shazeer, N. Parmar, J. Uszkoreit, L. Jones, A. N. Gomez, L. Kaiser, and I. Polosukhin. "Attention Is All You Need". In: *NIPS*. 2017.

[Vas+19]   S. Vaswani, A. Mishkin, I. Laradji, M. Schmidt, G. Gidel, and S. Lacoste-Julien. "Painless Stochastic Gradient: Interpolation, Line-Search, and Convergence Rates". In: *NIPS*. Curran Associates, Inc., 2019, pp. 3727–3740.

[VD99]   S. Vaithyanathan and B. Dom. "Model Selection in Unsupervised Learning With Applications To Document Clustering". In: *ICML*. 1999.

[VEB09]   N. Vinh, J. Epps, and J. Bailey. "Information Theoretic Measures for Clusterings Comparison: Is a Correction for Chance Necessary?" In: *ICML*. 2009.

[Vel+18]   P. Veličković, G. Cucurull, A. Casanova, A. Romero, P. Lio, and Y. Bengio. "Graph attention networks". In: *ICLR*. 2018.

[Vel+19] P. Veličković, W. Fedus, W. L. Hamilton, P. Liò, Y. Bengio, and R. D. Hjelm. "Deep Graph Infomax". In: *International Conference on Learning Representations*. 2019.

[VGG17] A. Vehtari, A. Gelman, and J. Gabry. "Practical Bayesian model evaluation using leave-one-out cross-validation and WAIC". In: *Stat. Comput.* 27.5 (2017), pp. 1413–1432.

[VGS97] V. Vapnik, S. Golowich, and A. Smola. "Support vector method for function approximation, regression estimation, and signal processing". In: *NIPS*. 1997.

[Vig15] T. Vigen. *Spurious Correlations*. en. Gift edition. Hachette Books, 2015.

[Vij+18] A. K. Vijayakumar, M. Cogswell, R. R. Selvaraju, Q. Sun, S. Lee, D. Crandall, and D. Batra. "Diverse Beam Search: Decoding Diverse Solutions from Neural Sequence Models". In: *IJCAI*. 2018.

[Vin+10a] P. Vincent, H. Larochelle, I. Lajoie, Y. Bengio, and P.-A. Manzagol. "Stacked Denoising Autoencoders: Learning Useful Representations in a Deep Network with a Local Denoising Criterion". In: *JMLR* 11 (2010), pp. 3371–3408.

[Vin+10b] P. Vincent, H. Larochelle, I. Lajoie, Y. Bengio, and P.-A. Manzagol. "Stacked denoising autoencoders: Learning useful representations in a deep network with a local denoising criterion". In: *Journal of machine learning research* 11.Dec (2010), pp. 3371–3408.

[Vin+16] O. Vinyals, C. Blundell, T. Lillicrap, K. Kavukcuoglu, and D. Wierstra. "Matching Networks for One Shot Learning". In: *NIPS*. 2016.

[Vir10] S. Virtanen. "Bayesian exponential family projections". MA thesis. Aalto University, 2010.

[Vis+10] S. V. N. Vishwanathan, N. N. Schraudolph, R. Kondor, and K. M. Borgward. "Graph Kernels". In: *JMLR* 11 (2010), pp. 1201–1242.

[Vo+15] B.-N. Vo, M. Mallick, Y. Bar-Shalom, S. Coraluppi, R. Osborne, R. Mahler, B. t Vo, and J. Webster. *Multitarget tracking*. John Wiley and Sons, 2015.

[Vor+17] E. Vorontsov, C. Trabelsi, S. Kadoury, and C. Pal. "On orthogonality and learning recurrent networks with long term dependencies". In: *ICML*. 2017.

[VT17] C. Vondrick and A. Torralba. "Generating the Future with Adversarial Transformers". In: *CVPR*. 2017.

[VV13] G. Valiant and P. Valiant. "Estimating the unseen: improved estimators for entropy and other properties". In: *NIPS*. 2013.

[Wah+22] O. Wahltinez, A. Cheung, R. Alcantara, D. Cheung, M. Daswani, A. Erlinger, M. Lee, P. Yawalkar, M. P. Brenner, and K. Murphy. "COVID-19 Open-Data: a global-scale, spatially granular meta-dataset for SARS-CoV-2". In: (2022). Nature Scientific data.

[Wal+20] M. Walmsley et al. "Galaxy Zoo: probabilistic morphology through Bayesian CNNs and active learning". In: *Monthly Notices Royal Astronomial Society* 491.2 (2020), pp. 1554–1574.

[Wal47] A. Wald. "An Essentially Complete Class of Admissible Decision Functions". en. In: *Ann. Math. Stat.* 18.4 (1947), pp. 549–555.

[Wan+15] J. Wang, W. Liu, S. Kumar, and S.-F. Chang. "Learning to Hash for Indexing Big Data - A Survey". In: *Proc. IEEE* (2015).

[Wan+17] Y. Wang et al. "Tacotron: Towards End-to-End Speech Synthesis". In: *Interspeech*. 2017.

[Wan+20a] S. Wang, B. Z. Li, M. Khabsa, H. Fang, and H. Ma. "Linformer: Self-Attention with Linear Complexity". In: *CoRR* abs/2006.04768 (2020). arXiv: 2006.04768.

[Wan+20b] Y. Wang, Q. Yao, J. Kwok, and L. M. Ni. "Generalizing from a Few Examples: A Survey on Few-Shot Learning". In: *ACM Computing Surveys* 1.1 (2020).

[Wan+21] R. Wang, M. Cheng, X. Chen, X. Tang, and C. J. Hsieh. "Rethinking Architecture Selection in Differentiable NAS". In: *ICLR*. 2021.

[Wat10] S. Watanabe. "Asymptotic Equivalence of Bayes Cross Validation and Widely Applicable Information Criterion in Singular Learning Theory". In: *JMLR* 11 (2010), pp. 3571–3594.

[Wat13] S. Watanabe. "A Widely Applicable Bayesian Information Criterion". In: *JMLR* 14 (2013), pp. 867–897.

[WCS08] M. Welling, C. Chemudugunta, and N. Sutter. "Deterministic Latent Variable Models and their Pitfalls". In: *ICDM*. 2008.

[WCZ16] D. Wang, P. Cui, and W. Zhu. "Structural deep network embedding". In: *Proceedings of the 22nd ACM SIGKDD international conference on Knowledge discovery and data mining*. ACM. 2016, pp. 1225–1234.

[Wei76] J. Weizenbaum. *Computer Power and Human Reason: From Judgment to Calculation*. en. 1st ed. W H Freeman & Co, 1976.

[Wen+16] W. Wen, C. Wu, Y. Wang, Y. Chen, and H. Li. "Learning Structured Sparsity in Deep Neural Networks". In: (2016). arXiv: 1608.03665 [cs.NE].

[Wen18] L. Weng. "Attention? Attention!" In: *lilianweng.github.io/lil-log* (2018).

[Wen19] L. Weng. "Generalized Language Models". In: *lilianweng.github.io/lil-log* (2019).

[Wer74] P. Werbos. "Beyond regression: New Tools for Prediction and Analysis in the Behavioral Sciences". PhD thesis. Harvard, 1974.

[Wer90] P. J. Werbos. "Backpropagation Through Time: What It Does and How to Do It". In: *Proc. IEEE* 78.10 (1990), pp. 1550–1560.

[Wes03] M. West. "Bayesian Factor Regression Models in the "Large p, Small n" Paradigm". In: *Bayesian Statistics* 7 (2003).

[WF14] Z. Wang and N. de Freitas. "Theoretical Analysis of Bayesian Optimisation with Unknown Gaussian Process Hyper-Parameters". In: (2014). arXiv: 1406.7758 [stat.ML].

[WF20]   T. Wu and I. Fischer. "Phase Transitions for the Information Bottleneck in Representation Learning". In: *ICLR*. 2020.

[WH18]   Y. Wu and K. He. "Group Normalization". In: *ECCV*. 2018.

[WH60]   B. Widrow and M. E. Hoff. "Adaptive Switching Circuits". In: *1960 IRE WESCON Convention Record, Part 4*. IRE, 1960, pp. 96–104.

[WI20]   A. G. Wilson and P. Izmailov. "Bayesian Deep Learning and a Probabilistic Perspective of Generalization". In: *NIPS*. 2020.

[Wil14] A. G. Wilson. "Covariance kernels for fast automatic pattern discovery and extrapolation with Gaussian processes". PhD thesis. University of Cambridge, 2014.

[Wil20] C. K. I. Williams. "The Effect of Class Imbalance on Precision-Recall Curves". In: *Neural Comput.* (2020).

[WL08]   T. T. Wu and K. Lange. "Coordinate descent algorithms for lasso penalized regression". In: *Ann. Appl. Stat* 2.1 (2008), pp. 224–244.

[WLL16] W. Wang, H. Lee, and K. Livescu. "Deep Variational Canonical Correlation Analysis". In: *arXiv* (2016).

[WM00]   D. R. Wilson and T. R. Martinez. "Reduction Techniques for Instance-Based Learning Algorithms". In: *Mach. Learn.* 38.3 (2000), pp. 257–286.

[WNF09] S. Wright, R. Nowak, and M. Figueiredo. "Sparse reconstruction by separable approximation". In: *IEEE Trans. on Signal Processing* 57.7 (2009), pp. 2479–2493.

[WNS19] C. White, W. Neiswanger, and Y. Savani. "BANANAS: Bayesian Optimization with Neural Architectures for Neural Architecture Search". In: (2019). arXiv: 1910 . 11858 [cs.LG].

[Wol92] D. Wolpert. "Stacked Generalization". In: *Neural Networks* 5.2 (1992), pp. 241–259.

[Wol96] D. Wolpert. "The lack of a priori distinctions between learning algorithms". In: *Neural Computation* 8.7 (1996), pp. 1341–1390.

[WP19]   S. Wiegreffe and Y. Pinter. "Attention is not not Explanation". In: *EMNLP*. 2019.

[WRC08] J. Weston, F. Ratle, and R. Collobert. "Deep learning via semi-supervised embedding". In: *Proceedings of the 25th international conference on Machine learning*. ACM. 2008, pp. 1168–1175.

[WS09]   K. Weinberger and L. Saul. "Distance Metric Learning for Large Margin Classification". In: *JMLR* 10 (2009), pp. 207–244.

[WSH16] L. Wu, C. Shen, and A. van den Hengel. "PersonNet: Person Re-identification with Deep Convolutional Neural Networks". In: (2016). arXiv: 1601.07255 [cs.CV].

[WSL19] R. L. Wasserstein, A. L. Schirm, and N. A. Lazar. "Moving to a World Beyond "p < 0.05"". In: *The American Statistician* 73.sup1 (2019), pp. 1–19.

[WSS04] K. Q. Weinberger, F. Sha, and L. K. Saul. "Learning a kernel matrix for nonlinear dimensionality reduction". In: *ICML*. 2004.

[WTN19] Y. Wu, G. Tucker, and O. Nachum. "The Laplacian in RL: Learning Representations with Efficient Approximations". In: *ICLR*. 2019.

[Wu+16] Y. Wu et al. "Google's Neural Machine Translation System: Bridging the Gap between Human and Machine Translation". In: (2016). arXiv: 1609.08144 [cs.CL].

[Wu+19] Y. Wu, E. Winston, D. Kaushik, and Z. Lipton. "Domain Adaptation with Asymmetrically-Relaxed Distribution Alignment". In: *ICML*. 2019.

[WVJ16] M. Wattenberg, F. Viégas, and I. Johnson. "How to Use t-SNE Effectively". In: *Distill* 1.10 (2016).

[WW93]   D. Wagner and F. Wagner. "Between min cut and graph bisection". In: *Proc. 18th Intl. Symp. on Math. Found. of Comp. Sci.* 1993, pp. 744–750.

[Xie+19] Q. Xie, Z. Dai, E. Hovy, M.-T. Luong, and Q. V. Le. "Unsupervised data augmentation for consistency training". In: *arXiv preprint arXiv:1904.12848* (2019).

[Xie+20] Q. Xie, M.-T. Luong, E. Hovy, and Q. V. Le. "Self-training with noisy student improves imagenet classification". In: *Proceedings of the IEEE/CVF Conference on Computer Vision and Pattern Recognition*. 2020, pp. 10687–10698.

[XJ96]   L. Xu and M. I. Jordan. "On Convergence Properties of the EM Algorithm for Gaussian Mixtures". In: *Neural Computation* 8 (1996), pp. 129–151.

[XRV17] H. Xiao, K. Rasul, and R. Vollgraf. "Fashion-MNIST: a Novel Image Dataset for Benchmarking Machine Learning Algorithms". In: (2017). arXiv: 1708.07747 [stat.ML].

[Xu+15] K. Xu, J. L. Ba, R. Kiros, K. Cho, A. Courville, R. Salakhutdinov, R. S. Zemel, and Y. Bengio. "Show, Attend and Tell: Neural Image Caption Generation with Visual Attention". In: *ICML*. 2015.

[Yal+19] I. Z. Yalniz, H. Jégou, K. Chen, M. Paluri, and D. Mahajan. "Billion-scale semi-supervised learning for image classification". In: *arXiv preprint arXiv:1905.00546* (2019).

[Yan+14] X. Yang, Y. Guo, Y. Liu, and H. Steck. "A Survey of Collaborative Filtering Based Social Recommender Systems". In: *Comput. Commun.* 41 (2014), pp. 1–10.

[Yar95] D. Yarowsky. "Unsupervised word sense disambiguation rivaling supervised methods". In: *33rd annual meeting of the association for computational linguistics*. 1995, pp. 189–196.

[YB19]   C. Yadav and L. Bottou. "Cold Case: The Lost MNIST Digits". In: *arXiv* (2019).

[YCS16] Z. Yang, W. W. Cohen, and R. Salakhutdinov. "Revisiting semi-supervised learning with graph embeddings". In: *Proceedings of the 33rd International Conference on Inter-*

national Conference on Machine Learning-Volume 48. JMLR. org. 2016, pp. 40–48.

[Yeu91]   R. W. Yeung. "A new outlook on Shannon's information measures". In: *IEEE Trans. Inf. Theory* 37.3 (1991), pp. 466–474.

[YHJ09]   D. Yan, L. Huang, and M. I. Jordan. "Fast approximate spectral clustering". In: *15th ACM Conf. on Knowledge Discovery and Data Mining*. 2009.

[Yin+19] P. Yin, J. Lyu, S. Zhang, S. Osher, Y. Qi, and J. Xin. "Understanding Straight-Through Estimator in Training Activation Quantized Neural Nets". In: *ICLR*. 2019.

[YK16]   F. Yu and V. Koltun. "Multi-Scale Context Aggregation by Dilated Convolutions". In: *ICLR*. 2016.

[YL06]   M. Yuan and Y. Lin. "Model Selection and Estimation in Regression with Grouped Variables". In: *J. Royal Statistical Society, Series B* 68.1 (2006), pp. 49–67.

[YL21]   A. L. Yuille and C. Liu. "Deep Nets: What have they ever done for Vision?" In: *Intl. J. Computer Vision* 129 (2021), pp. 781–802.

[Yon19]   E. Yong. "The Human Brain Project Hasn't Lived Up to Its Promise". In: *The Atlantic* (2019).

[Yos+15] J. Yosinski, J. Clune, A. Nguyen, T. Fuchs, and H. Lipson. "Understanding Neural Networks Through Deep Visualization". In: *ICML Workshop on Deep Learning*. 2015.

[Yu+06]   S. Yu, K. Yu, V. Tresp, K. H-P., and M. Wu. "Supervised probabilistic principal component analysis". In: *KDD*. 2006.

[Yu+16]   F. X. X. Yu, A. T. Suresh, K. M. Choromanski, D. N. Holtmann-Rice, and S. Kumar. "Orthogonal Random Features". In: *NIPS*. Curran Associates, Inc., 2016, pp. 1975–1983.

[YWG12]   S. E. Yuksel, J. N. Wilson, and P. D. Gader. "Twenty Years of Mixture of Experts". In: *IEEE Trans. on neural networks and learning systems* (2012).

[Zah+18] M. Zaheer, S. Reddi, D. Sachan, S. Kale, and S. Kumar. "Adaptive Methods for Nonconvex Optimization". In: *NIPS*. Curran Associates, Inc., 2018, pp. 9815–9825.

[Zah+20] M. Zaheer et al. "Big Bird: Transformers for Longer Sequences". In: *CoRR* abs/2007.14062 (2020). arXiv: 2007.14062.

[Zei12]   M. D. Zeiler. "ADADELTA: An Adaptive Learning Rate Method". In: (2012). arXiv: 1212.5701 [cs.LG].

[Zel76]   A. Zellner. "Bayesian and non-Bayesian analysis of the regression model with multivariate Student-t error terms". In: *JASA* 71.354 (1976), pp. 400–405.

[ZG02]   X. Zhu and Z. Ghahramani. *Learning from labeled and unlabeled data with label propagation*. Tech. rep. CALD tech report CMU-CALD-02-107. CMU, 2002.

[ZG06]   M. Zhu and A. Ghodsi. "Automatic dimensionality selection from the scree plot via the use of profile likelihood". In: *Computa-*

tional Statistics & Data Analysis 51 (2006), pp. 918–930.

[ZH05]   H. Zou and T. Hastie. "Regularization and Variable Selection via the Elastic Net". In: *J. of Royal Stat. Soc. Series B* 67.2 (2005), pp. 301–320.

[Zha+17a] C. Zhang, S. Bengio, M. Hardt, B. Recht, and O. Vinyals. "Understanding deep learning requires rethinking generalization". In: *ICLR*. 2017.

[Zha+17b] H. Zhang, M. Cisse, Y. N. Dauphin, and D. Lopez-Paz. "mixup: Beyond Empirical Risk Minimization". In: *ICLR*. 2017.

[Zha+18] Z.-Q. Zhao, P. Zheng, S.-T. Xu, and X. Wu. "Object Detection with Deep Learning: A Review". In: (2018). arXiv: 1807.05511 [cs.CV].

[Zha+19a] J. Zhang, Y. Zhao, M. Saleh, and P. J. Liu. "PEGASUS: Pre-training with Extracted Gap-sentences for Abstractive Summarization". In: (2019). arXiv: 1912.08777 [cs.CL].

[Zha+19b] S. Zhang, L. Yao, A. Sun, and Y. Tay. "Deep Learning Based Recommender System: A Survey and New Perspectives". In: *ACM Comput. Surv.* 52.1 (2019), pp. 1–38.

[Zha+20] A. Zhang, Z. Lipton, M. Li, and A. Smola. *Dive into deep learning*. 2020.

[Zha+22] Y. Zhang, C. Chen, N. Shi, R. Sun, and Z.-Q. Luo. "Adam Can Converge Without Any Modification On Update Rules". In: (Aug. 2022). arXiv: 2208.09632 [cs.LG].

[Zho+04] D. Zhou, O. Bousquet, T. N. Lal, J. Weston, and B. Schölkopf. "Learning with local and global consistency". In: *Advances in neural information processing systems*. 2004, pp. 321–328.

[Zho+18] D. Zhou, Y. Tang, Z. Yang, Y. Cao, and Q. Gu. "On the Convergence of Adaptive Gradient Methods for Nonconvex Optimization". In: (2018). arXiv: 1808.05671 [cs.LG].

[Zho+21] C. Zhou, X. Ma, P. Michel, and G. Neubig. "Examining and Combating Spurious Features under Distribution Shift". In: *ICML*. 2021.

[ZHT06]   H. Zou, T. Hastie, and R. Tibshirani. "Sparse principal component analysis". In: *JCGS* 15.2 (2006), pp. 202–286.

[Zhu05]   X. Zhu. "Semi-supervised learning with graphs". PhD thesis. Carnegie Mellon University, 2005.

[Zhu+21] F. Zhuang, Z. Qi, K. Duan, D. Xi, Y. Zhu, H. Zhu, H. Xiong, and Q. He. "A Comprehensive Survey on Transfer Learning". In: *Proc. IEEE* 109.1 (2021).

[Zie+05] C.-N. Ziegler, S. M. McNee, J. A. Konstan, and G. Lausen. "Improving recommendation lists through topic diversification". In: *WWW*. WWW '05. Association for Computing Machinery, 2005, pp. 22–32.

[ZK16]   S. Zagoruyko and N. Komodakis. "Wide Residual Networks". In: *BMVC*. 2016.

[ZL05]   Z.-H. Zhou and M. Li. "Tri-training: Exploiting unlabeled data using three classifiers". In:

IEEE Transactions on knowledge and Data Engineering 17.11 (2005), pp. 1529–1541.

[ZL17]   B. Zoph and Q. V. Le. "Neural Architecture Search with Reinforcement Learning". In: *ICLR*. 2017.

[ZLZ20]   D. Zhang, Y. Li, and Z. Zhang. "Deep metric learning with spherical embedding". In: *NIPS*. 2020.

[ZMY19]   D. Zabihzadeh, R. Monsefi, and H. S. Yazdi. "Sparse Bayesian approach for metric learning in latent space". In: *Knowledge-Based Systems* 178 (2019), pp. 11–24.

[ZRY05]   P. Zhao, G. Rocha, and B. Yu. *Grouped and Hierarchical Model Selection through Composite Absolute Penalties*. Tech. rep. UC Berkeley, 2005.

[ZS14]   H. Zen and A Senior. "Deep mixture density networks for acoustic modeling in statistical parametric speech synthesis". In: *ICASSP*. 2014, pp. 3844–3848.

[ZY08]   J.-H. Zhao and P. L. H. Yu. "Fast ML Estimation for the Mixture of Factor Analyzers via an ECM Algorithm". In: *IEEE. Trans. on Neural Networks* 19.11 (2008).